The
Municipal
Year
Book
2009

The authoritative
source book of
local government data
and developments

PRESS

The Municipal Year Book

2009

Washington, DC

ICMA advances professional local government worldwide. Its mission is to create excellence in local governance by developing and advancing professional management of local government. ICMA, the International City/County Management Association, provides member support; publications, data, and information; peer and results-oriented assistance; and training and professional development to more than 9,000 city, town, and county experts and other individuals and organizations throughout the world. The management decisions made by ICMA's members affect 185 million individuals living in thousands of communities, from small villages and towns to large metropolitan areas.

Volume 76, 2009

ISBN: 978-0-87326-185-2
ISSN: 0077-2186
43559

Library of Congress Catalog Card Number: 34-27121

The views expressed in this *Year Book* are those of individual authors and are not necessarily those of ICMA.

Suggested citation for use of material in this *Year Book:* Jane S. Author [and John N. Other], "Title of Article," in *The Municipal Year Book 2009* (Washington, D.C.: ICMA, 2009), 00–000.

Table of Contents

A Management Trends and Issues

B The Intergovernmental Dimension

Acknowledgments

The Municipal Year Book, which provides local government officials with information on local government management, represents an important part of ICMA's extensive research program. Each year, ICMA surveys local officials on a variety of topics, and the data derived from their responses constitute the primary information source for the *Year Book.* Authors from local, state, and federal government agencies; universities; and public interest groups as well as ICMA staff prepare articles that describe the data collected and examine trends and developments affecting local government.

We would like to express our appreciation to the thousands of city and county managers, clerks, finance officers, personnel directors, police chiefs, fire chiefs, and other officials who patiently and conscientiously responded to ICMA questionnaires. It is only because of their time-consuming efforts that we are able to provide the information in this volume.

ICMA also thanks the Alliance for Innovation (transformgov.org), a partnership of ICMA, the Innovation Groups, and Arizona State University, for its article on award-winning innovations in local government. The primary goal of the Alliance is to share best practices, cutting-edge research, and thought-provoking information on topics of interest to local governments. This is the first year the Alliance has contributed to the *Year Book,* and we look forward to the partnership's continued contribution to this publication.

Finally, I would like to thank the ICMA staff who have devoted countless hours to making the *Year Book* so valuable. Ann I. Mahoney is the director of publishing, and Jane C. Cotnoir is the *Year Book* editor. Other ICMA staff members who contributed to this publication are Evelina Moulder, director of survey research and information management; Valerie Hepler, director of publications production; Sebia Clark, program analyst; and Nedra James, editorial assistant. Finally, thanks go to Sandra F. Chizinsky, ICMA consulting editor.

Robert J. O'Neill
Executive Director
ICMA

Inside the *Year Book*

Local government concerns are increasingly complex and sophisticated, and the need for familiarity with a broad range of issues is unsurpassed. Furthering the knowledge base needed to better manage local government is one of ICMA's top goals. Through survey-based research; a summary of selected best practices in local government; a brief review of local-state relations, congressional actions, and Supreme Court decisions in 2008; up-to-date salary and expenditure data; and wide-ranging directories, this edition of *The Municipal Year Book* provides some of the most important and timely information available on issues of importance to local government.

MANAGEMENT TRENDS AND ISSUES

Matching City Power Structures and City Managers' Leadership Styles: A New Model of Fit

The difficult job of the city manager is made even more difficult by the ever-present threat of termination. A high turnover rate can have long-term negative effects on a city as well, as instability in the executive office hampers both effective governance and succession planning. Thus, it is in a jurisdiction's best interests to try to understand and reverse the high turnover trend among managers. Expanding on research that explains turnover rates in terms of the compatibility between a community's political culture—defined as one of seven power structures as reflected in the composition and actions of the city council—and the city manager's preferred leadership and management style, this article (A1) matches the management types with power structures, identifying compatible and incompatible relationships to enable cities to seek out managers with compatible leadership styles and skill sets, and city managers to search for cities with an agreeable political climate.

Cooperative Competition: Alternative Service Delivery, 2002–2007

Since ICMA began tracking local governments' use of alternative service delivery approaches in 1982, survey results have shown that almost all governments use at least one form of alternative service delivery but that the most common approach is public service delivery. Yet data from the most recent survey reveal that use of both direct public delivery and mixed public-private delivery has essentially decreased and use of for-profit privatization and nonprofit contracting has held steady, while use of intergovernmental contracting has grown. This article (A2) reports on this and other trends, as well as on obstacles to private service delivery and on the need to couple contracting with effective monitoring.

County Form of Government: Trends in Structure and Composition

Increasingly over the last century, county governments have been expected to provide not just the traditional services that they have always provided as an arm of the state, but also new public services similar to those provided by cities. To meet these new responsibilities responsively, efficiently, and cost-effectively, counties have had to create new institutional arrangements—reflected, for example, in the growing trend toward the professional administration of services, particularly in urban areas. Presenting the results of ICMA's third *County Form of Government* survey, this article (A3) examines the changing structure and composition of county government. Covering such topics as form of government, selection of department heads, governing bodies and their presiding officers, and provisions for direct democracy, it identifies trends by comparing the 2007 results with results from the 1988 and 2002 surveys.

Cities Leading the Way: The Use of Alternative Work Schedules

As the price of gasoline escalated last summer, local governments and their employees sought ways to cope with rising fuel costs. One strategy that gained attention was alternative work schedules. This article (A4) reports the results of a survey of selected U.S. municipalities to determine the extent to which alternative work schedules are being instituted in local government organizations today. It first identifies and presents data on the prevalence of various types of alternative work schedules in use. Then, after discussing the factors that influence the adoption of such arrangements and the benefits and drawbacks perceived by employees and organizations, it cites research findings and survey results with regard to one type of alternative work schedule in particular: the compressed workweek.

How Will Public Sector Retirement Withstand the Current Recession?

Public employee retirement systems are significant recruitment and retention tools, a key reason that public service is seen as an attractive lifetime career, and an essential element of the implied employment contract. But by the end of 2008, with unemployment up, economic growth down, credit markets nearly dysfunctional, and tax revenues for many state and local governments falling, the continued viability of public retirement plans became a matter of concern. This article (A5) first reviews the collapse of the housing bubble and its impact on individual retirement plans; it then examines the roles of Social Security, Medicare, personal savings, and retiree health care in shaping public sector retirement. By analyzing how the sharp decline in the stock market will affect public employee retirement plans, it provides some insight into the current economic climate and the implications for those in state and local government.

Learning from Award-Winning Innovations in Local Government, 2008

In today's financial crisis, local governments face pressures to adjust their activities and reduce their budgets. To meet these challenges while continuing to provide high-quality services to, and meet the needs of, their constituents, they need to develop new policies, programs, processes, and delivery methods. This article (A6) presents 23 programs recognized by the Alliance for Innovation or ICMA as either exemplary breakthrough innovations or leading examples of ideas that jurisdictions have transplanted, adapted, and recombined to creatively address an urgent need or pursue an opportunity. These programs are in the areas of strengthening communities, remaking the locality, improving health and safety, promoting sustainability, expanding applications of e-government, and improving organizational performance. The article concludes with an assessment of the characteristics common to organizations that succeed at innovation.

THE INTERGOVERNMENTAL DIMENSION

State-Local Relations: Authority and Finances

In recent years, local officials throughout the country have had ongoing concerns about how state mandates, prohibitions, and preemptions affect their authority, and about the lack of state fiscal support for local government. By the end of 2008, these concerns were exacerbated by the nation's economic downturn as officials sought to minimize cuts in aid, stave off increases in unfunded mandates, avoid revenue takeaways, and secure greater flexibility in raising revenues. Of particular concern in 2008 were developments in the area of tax reform: in Florida, for example, voters approved Amendment 1, whose tax-relief measures are expected to cost local governments billions of dollars in lost revenue over the next five years. This article (B1) provides an overview of conditions and developments in the areas of local authority and finance; it also considers significant ballot measures, judicial decisions, and legislation.

Congressional Actions Affecting Local Government: The 110th Congress

With success of the "surge" taking the war in Iraq off center stage, the focus of the American people and their legislators in 2008 shifted to the economy—specifically, the housing and credit crisis and the collapse of the stock market. Responding to the meltdown of the financial market, Congress passed the Emergency Economic Stabilization Act of 2008, authorizing the Treasury secretary to spend up to $700 billion to purchase mortgage-backed securities and bail out financially distressed financial institutions. Other major legislation, as summarized in this article (B2), included the Clean Energy Act, comprehensive legislation intended "to move the United States toward greater energy independence and security"; the Housing and Economic Recovery Act of 2008 to provide short-term relief for the housing market; and the Second Chance Act, authorizing $165 million in federal grants to government agencies and community and faith-based organizations to provide employment assistance, substance abuse treatment, housing, and other services to help reduce repeat offenses and violations of probation and parole.

Recent Supreme Court Actions Affecting Local Government

During its 2007–2008 session, the U.S. Supreme Court dealt with such issues as the regulation of firearms, the right to counsel, search and seizure, the constitutionality of lethal injection, capital punishment, voting rights, elections law, campaign finance, disparate-impact claims, and taxation. This article (B3) reviews the major holdings in these and other cases, each of which has implications for state and local governments. For example, in a significant departure from its earlier Second Amendment jurisprudence, the Court held that the amendment protects an individual's right to possess and carry weapons, and that the District of Columbia's de facto ban on handguns was therefore unconstitutional. For each case the authors provide concise yet comprehensive information about the background, legal precedents, and reasoning behind the Court's decision.

STAFFING AND COMPENSATION

One of the most basic managerial concerns is compensation. This section provides salary data for a variety of positions held by local officials.

The first two articles in this section look at the salaries of 23 municipal positions (C1) and 23 county positions (C2). These articles are based on information obtained between late July and mid December 2008 through SurveyNavigator™ for ICMA, a Web-based interactive version of the annual salary survey that is managed and operated by the Waters Consulting Group, Inc.

The third article, "Police and Fire Personnel, Salaries, and Expenditures for 2008" (C3), presents the following for both police and fire departments in tabular form: total personnel, the number of uniformed personnel, minimum crew per fire apparatus, entrance and maximum salaries, information on longevity pay, and a breakdown of departmental expenditures. Data from the 2008 survey are compared with data from 2007.

DIRECTORIES

The directories section (D1) comprises 10 tables that provide the names of nearly 70,000 contacts in U.S. local government.

A special directory in the Year Book is "Professional, Special Assistance, and Educational Organizations Serving Local and State Governments" (D2). The 81 organizations that are included provide educational and research services to members and others, strengthening professionalism in government administration.

ORGANIZATION OF DATA

Most of the tabular data for The Municipal Year Book 2009 were obtained from public officials through questionnaires developed and administered by ICMA. ICMA maintains databases with the result of these surveys. All survey responses are reviewed for errors. Extreme values are identified and investigated; logic checks are applied in the analysis of the results.

Government Definitions

A municipality, by census definition, is a "political subdivision within which a municipal corporation has been established to provide general local government for a specific population concentration in a defined area." This definition includes all active governmental units officially designated as cities, boroughs (except in Alaska), villages, or towns (except in Minnesota, New York, New England, and Wisconsin), and it generally includes all places incorporated under the procedures established by the several states.

Counties are the primary political administrative divisions of the state. In Louisiana these units are called parishes. Alaska has county-type governments called boroughs. There are certain unorganized areas of some states that are not included in the Year Book database and that have a county

designation from the Census Bureau for strictly administrative purposes. These comprise 12 areas in Alaska, 2 areas in South Dakota, 5 areas in Rhode Island, 8 areas in Connecticut, and 1 area in Montana.[1]

According to the U.S. Bureau of the Census, in January 2002 there were 87,849 governments in the United States (Table 1).

Municipality Classification

Table 2 details the distribution of all municipalities of 2,500 and over in population by population, geographic region and division, metro status, and form of government.

Population This edition of the Year Book generally uses the 2000 Census Bureau figures for placing local governments in the United States into population groups for tabular presentation. The population categories are self-explanatory.

Geographic Classification Nine geographic divisions and four regions are used by the Bureau of the Census (Figure 1). The nine divisions are New England: Connecticut, Maine, Massachusetts, New Hampshire, Rhode Island, and Vermont; *Mid-Atlantic:* New Jersey, New York, and Pennsylvania; *East North-Central:* Illinois, Indiana, Michigan, Ohio, and Wisconsin; *West North-Central:* Iowa, Kansas, Minnesota, Missouri, Nebraska, North Dakota, and South Dakota; *South Atlantic:* Delaware, the District of Columbia, Florida, Georgia, Maryland, North Carolina, South Carolina, Virginia, and West Virginia; *East South-Central:* Alabama, Kentucky, Mississippi, and Tennessee; West South-Central: Arkansas, Louisiana, Oklahoma, and Texas; *Mountain:* Arizona, Colorado, Idaho, Montana, Nevada, New Mexico, Utah, and Wyoming; and *Pacific Coast:* Alaska, California, Hawaii, Oregon, and Washington.

The geographic regions are consolidations of states in divisions: *Northeast:* Connecticut, Maine, Massachusetts, New Hampshire, New Jersey, New York, Pennsylvania, Rhode Island, and Vermont; *North Central:* Illinois, Indiana, Iowa, Kansas, Michigan, Minnesota, Missouri, Nebraska, North Dakota, Ohio, South Dakota, and Wisconsin; *South:* Alabama, Arkansas, Delaware, the District of Columbia, Florida, Georgia, Kentucky, Louisiana, Maryland, Mississippi, North Carolina, Oklahoma, South Carolina, Tennessee, Texas, Virginia, and West Virginia; and *West:* Alaska, Arizona, California, Colorado, Hawaii, Idaho, Montana, Nevada, New Mexico, Oregon, Utah, Washington, and Wyoming.

Metro Status Metro status refers to the status of a municipality within the context of the U.S. Office of Management and Budget (OMB) definition of a metropolitan area. A metropolitan area

Table 1   U.S. LOCAL GOVERNMENTS, 2002

Local governments	87,849
County	3,034
Municipal	19,431
Town or township	16,506
School district	13,522
Special district	35,356

Note: The Census Bureau updates the number of local governments every five years in the years ending in 2 and 7. The vast majority of municipal governments are under 2,500 in population and are not included in the ICMA database.

Table 2 CUMULATIVE DISTRIBUTION OF U.S. MUNICIPALITIES WITH A POPULATION OF 2,500 AND OVER

Classification	Population								
	2,500 and over	5,000 and over	10,000 and over	25,000 and over	50,000 and over	100,000 and over	250,000 and over	500,000 and over	Over 1,000,000
Total, all cities.	7,225	5,177	3,275	1,447	660	247	68	32	9
Population group									
Over 1,000,000	9	9	9	9	9	9	9	9	9
500,000–1,000,000	23	23	23	23	23	23	23	23	. . .[1]
250,000–499,999	36	36	36	36	36	36	36	. . .	. . .
100,000–249,999	179	179	179	179	179	179	. . .	. . .	. . .
50,000–99,999	413	413	413	413	413	. . .	. . .	. . .	. . .
25,000–49,999	787	787	787	787	. . .	. . .	. . .	. . .	. . .
10,000–24,999	1,828	1,828	1,828	. . .	. . .	. . .	. . .	. . .	. . .
5,000–9,000	1,902	1,902	. . .	. . .	. . .	. . .	. . .	. . .	. . .
2,500–4,999	2,048	. . .	. . .	. . .	. . .	. . .	. . .	. . .	. . .
Geographic region									
Northeast	1,972	1,459	889	324	111	33	8	4	2
North-Central	2,108	1,454	916	372	147	44	14	5	1
South	2,065	1,394	845	357	177	77	23	13	3
West	1,080	870	625	394	225	93	23	10	3
Geographic division									
New England	732	555	352	138	46	12	1	1	. . .
Mid-Atlantic	1,240	904	537	186	65	21	7	3	2
East North-Central	1,413	1,026	669	267	103	30	8	5	1
West North-Central	697	429	248	105	44	14	6	. . .	. . .
South Atlantic	882	602	387	170	86	34	9	4	
East South-Central	441	308	169	56	22	12	3	2	
West South-Central	742	483	288	131	69	31	11	7	3
Mountain	388	275	161	94	52	27	8	3	1
Pacific Coast	690	595	464	300	173	66	15	7	2
Metro status									
Central	540	539	539	504	360	175	65	31	9
Suburban	4,286	3,262	2,117	819	293	72	3	1	. . .
Independent	2,399	1,376	619	124	7	. . .	. . .	. . .	. . .
Form of government									
Mayor-council	3,145	2,011	1,178	488	236	98	39	21	6
Council-manager	3,534	2,765	1,873	907	410	144	27	10	3
Commission	143	110	71	25	9	5	2	1	. . .
Town meeting	340	236	107	6	. . .	. . .	. . .	. . .	. . .
Rep. town meeting	63	55	46	21	5	. . .	. . .	. . .	. . .

[1](. . .) indicates data not applicable or not reported.

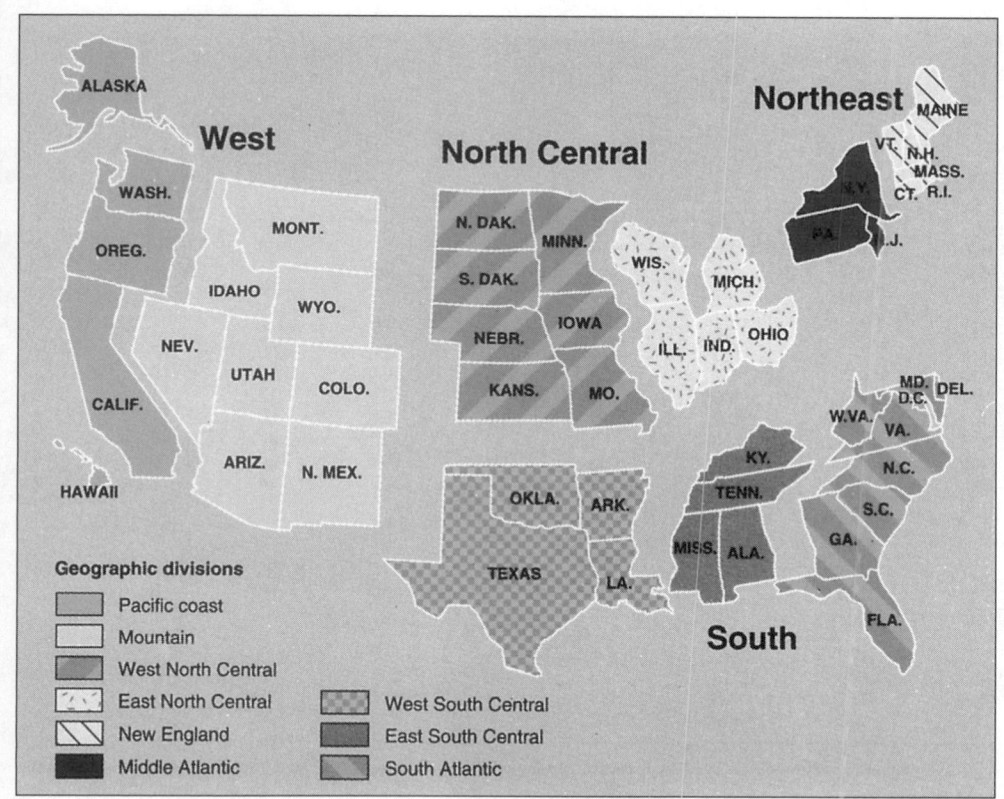

Figure 1 *U.S. Bureau of the Census geographic regions and divisions*

is typically "a core area containing a large population nucleus, together with adjacent communities having a high degree of economic and social integration with that core."2 There are three levels of classification: metropolitan statistical areas, consolidated metropolitan statistical areas, and primary metropolitan statistical areas.

The current standards require that each newly qualifying *metropolitan statistical area* (MSA) must include *either* at least one city with a population of 50,000 or more, *or* a Census Bureau–defined urbanized area of at least 50,000 *and* a total metropolitan population of at least 100,000 (75,000 in New England).[3] The county (or counties) that contains the largest city becomes the central county (counties), along with any adjacent counties that have at least 50% of their population in the urbanized area surrounding the largest city in the MSA. Additional outlying counties are included in the MSA if they meet the specified requirement of commuting to the central counties and other selected requirements of metropolitan character (such as population density and percentage urban). In New England, the MSAs are defined in terms of cities and towns rather than counties.

An area that meets the requirements for an MSA and has a population of 1,000,000 or more may be recognized as a *consolidated metropolitan statistical area* (CMSA) if separate component

areas can be identified within the entire area as meeting statistical criteria specified in the standards and if local opinion indicates support for the component areas. If recognized, the component areas are designated *primary metropolitan statistical areas* (PMSAs). Like the CMSAs that contain them, PMSAs comprise entire counties, except in New England, where they comprise cities and towns. If no PMSAs are recognized, the entire area is designated an MSA.

As of June 30, 1999, there were 258 MSAs and 18 CMSAs, comprising 73 PMSAs in the United States.

The largest city in each MSA/CMSA is designated a *central city*. Additional cities qualify if specified requirements are met for population size and commuting patterns. The title of each MSA consists of the names of up to three of its central cities and the name of each state into which the MSA extends. However, the name of a central city with fewer than 250,000 in population and less than one-third of the population of the area's largest city is not included in the MSA title unless local opinion supports its inclusion. Titles of PMSAs are also typically based on central city names but may consist of county names.

Form of Government Form of government relates primarily to the organization of the leg-

islative and executive branches of municipalities and townships.

In the *mayor-council* form, an elected council or board serves as the legislative body. The head of government is the chief elected official, who is generally elected separately from the council and has significant administrative authority.

Many cities with a mayor-council form of government have a city administrator who is appointed by the elected representatives (council) and/or the chief elected official and is responsible to the elected officials. Appointed city administrators in mayor-council governments have limited administrative authority: they often do not directly appoint department heads or other key city personnel, and their responsibility for budget preparation and administration, although significant, is subordinate to that of the elected officials.

Under the *council-manager* form, the elected council or board and chief elected official (e.g., the mayor) are responsible for making policy. A professional administrator appointed by the council or board has full responsibility for the day-to-day operations of the government.

The *commission* form of government operates with an elected commission performing both legislative and executive functions, generally with

departmental administration divided among the commissioners.

The *town meeting* form of government is a system in which all qualified voters of a municipality meet to make basic policy and elect officials to carry out the policies.

Under the *representative town meeting* form of government, the voters select a large number of citizens to represent them at the town meeting(s). All citizens can participate in the meeting(s), but only the representatives may vote.

County Classification

Counties are the primary political administrative divisions of the states. The county-type governments in Alaska are called boroughs. Table 3 details the distribution of counties throughout the nation, using the same geographic and population categories as Table 2.

Metro Status For counties, metro status refers to the status of a county within the context of the OMB definition of an MSA. "Metro" means that a county is located within an MSA; "nonmetro" indicates that it is located outside the boundaries of an MSA.

Counties that are located in an MSA are classified in a way similar to that for cities. *Central counties* are those in which central cities are lo-

Table 3 CUMULATIVE DISTRIBUTION OF U.S. COUNTIES

Classification	All counties	Population								
		2,500 and over	5,000 and over	10,000 and over	25,000 and over	50,000 and over	100,000 and over	250,000 and over	500,000 and over	Over 1,000,000
Total, all counties	3,039	2,925	2,752	2,366	1,497	859	476	201	91	28
Population group										
Over 1,000,000	28	28	28	28	28	28	28	28	28	28
500,000–1,000,000	63	63	63	63	63	63	63	63	63	. . .[1]
250,000–499,999	110	110	110	110	110	110	110	110	. . .	. . .
100,000–249,999	275	275	275	275	275	275	275	. . .	. . .	. . .
50,000–99,999	383	383	383	383	383	383	. . .	. . .	. . .	. . .
25,000–49,999	638	638	638	638	638	. . .	. . .	. . .	. . .	. . .
10,000–24,999	869	869	869	869	. . .	. . .	. . .	. . .	. . .	. . .
5,000–9,999	386	386	386	. . .	. . .	. . .	. . .	. . .	. . .	. . .
2,500–4,999	173	173	. . .	. . .	. . .	. . .	. . .	. . .	. . .	. . .
Under 2,500.	114	. . .	. . .	. . .	. . .	. . .	. . .	. . .	. . .	. . .
Geographic region										
Northeast.	189	189	188	183	174	129	85	45	19	3
North-Central.	1,054	1,007	914	747	445	229	125	45	19	7
South.	1,372	1,346	1,301	1,152	684	365	178	66	28	7
West	424	383	349	284	194	136	88	45	25	11
Geographic division										
New England.	45	45	45	43	40	24	14	6	2	
Mid-Atlantic	144	144	143	140	134	105	71	39	17	3
East North-Central.	437	436	433	407	298	165	94	33	15	5
West North-Central	617	571	481	340	147	64	31	12	4	2
South Atlantic	545	543	535	482	314	192	101	39	17	3
East South-Central	360	358	356	323	175	73	27	7	2	. . .
West South-Central	467	445	410	347	195	100	50	20	9	4
Mountain	276	245	215	159	93	54	32	14	7	2
Pacific Coast	148	138	134	125	101	82	56	31	18	9
Metro status										
Central.	457	457	457	457	454	439	377	195	89	28
Suburban.	341	339	338	331	283	177	68	6	2	. . .
Independent	2,241	2,129	1,957	1,578	760	243	31	. . .	. . .	. . .
Form of government										
County commission	1,728	1,638	1,500	1,215	665	303	130	46	16	3
Council-manager/administrator	819	806	789	736	546	358	217	87	44	16
Council–elected executive.	491	480	462	414	286	198	129	68	31	9

Note: Form of government change is based on the 2007–2008 *County Form of Government* survey conducted by ICMA. Because of the low number of responses to this survey this year, the form-of-government data presented in this table may not be the most current.
[1](. . .) indicates data not applicable.

cated. *Suburban* counties are the other counties located within an MSA. Counties not located in an MSA are considered *independent*.

Form of Government   For counties, form of government relates to the structural organization of the legislative and executive branches of counties; counties are classified as being with or without an administrator. There are three basic forms of county government: commission, council-administrator, and council–elected executive.

The *commission* form of government is characterized by a governing board that shares the administrative and, to an extent, legislative responsibilities with several independently elected functional officials.

In counties with the *council-administrator* form, an administrator is appointed by, and responsible to, the elected council to carry out directives.

The *council–elected executive* form features two branches of government: the executive and the legislative. The independently elected executive is considered the formal head of the county.

The use of varying types of local government is an institutional response to the needs, requirements, and articulated demands of citizens at the local level. Within each type of local government, structures are developed to provide adequate services. These structural adaptations are a partial result of the geographic location, population, metropolitan status, and form of government of the jurisdiction involved.

Consolidated Governments

The Bureau of the Census defines a consolidated government as a unit of local government in which the functions of a primary incorporated place and

Table 4   LEGALLY DESIGNATED CITY-COUNTY CONSOLIDATED GOVERNMENTS OPERATING AS CITIES

State	Consolidated government
Alaska......	City and Borough of Anchorage
	City and Borough of Juneau
	City and Borough of Sitka
California ...	City and County of San Francisco
Colorado....	City and County of Denver
Hawaii......	City and County of Honolulu
Kansas.....	Kansas City and Wyandotte County
Kentucky....	City of Louisville and Jefferson County
Montana	Anaconda–Deer Lodge
	Butte–Silver Bow

Note: The Census Bureau counts Butte–Silver Bow also as a consolidated city.

Table 5   CONSOLIDATED CITIES

State	Consolidated City
Connecticut.........	City of Milford
Florida.............	City of Jacksonville
Georgia............	Athens–Clarke County
	City of Columbus
	Augusta–Richmond County
Indiana	City of Indianapolis
Tennessee	Nashville–Davidson

Note: The Census Bureau treats these as consolidated cities.

Table 6   COUNTIES THAT MAINTAIN OFFICES AS PART OF ANOTHER GOVERNMENT

State	County	Other government
Florida..................	Duval................................	City of Jacksonville
Georgia.................	Clarke	Athens–Clarke County
	Muscogee	City of Columbus
	Richmond............................	Augusta–Richmond County
Indiana	Marion..............................	City of Indianapolis
Kentucky................	Lexington–Fayette Urban County	Lexington–Fayette
Louisiana...............	Parish of East Baton Rouge.................	City of Baton Rouge
	Parish of Lafayette.....................	City of Lafayette
	Parish of Orleans......................	City of New Orleans
	Terrebonne Parish......................	City of Houma
Massachusetts	County of Nantucket	City of Nantucket
	County of Suffolk	City of Boston
New York................	County of Bronx.......................	New York City
	County of Kings	New York City
	County of New York....................	New York City
	County of Queens	New York City
	County of Richmond	New York City
Pennsylvania.............	County of Philadelphia...................	City of Philadelphia

its county or minor civil division have merged. There are several categories of consolidations: city-county consolidations that operate primarily as cities (Table 4), consolidated cities (Table 5), and counties that maintain certain types of offices but as part of another city or township government (Table 6). One city-county consolidation operates primarily as a county: the City and Borough of Yakutat in Alaska. In addition, the District of Columbia is counted by the Census Bureau as a city, a separate county area, and a separate state area. To avoid double counting in survey results, ICMA counts the District of Columbia only as a city.

Independent Cities

The Census Bureau defines independent cities as those operating outside of a county area and administering functions commonly performed by counties (Table 7). The bureau counts independent cities as counties. For survey research purposes, ICMA counts independent cities as municipal, not county governments.

USES OF STATISTICAL DATA

The Municipal Year Book uses primary and secondary data sources. ICMA collects and publishes the primary source data. Secondary source data are data collected by another organization. Most of the primary source data are collected through survey research. ICMA develops questionnaires on a variety of subjects during a given year and then pretests and refines them to increase the validity of each survey instrument. Once completed, the surveys are sent to officials in all cities above a given population level (e.g., 2,500 and above, 10,000 and above, etc.). For example, the city managers or chief administrative officers receive the *Organizational Structure and Decision Making* survey, and finance officers receive the *Police and Fire Personnel, Salaries, and Expenditures* survey.

ICMA conducts the city, county, and councils of government salary surveys and the *Police and Fire Personnel, Salaries, and Expenditures* survey every year. Other research projects are conducted every five years, and some are one-time efforts to provide information on subjects of current interest.

Table 7   INDEPENDENT CITIES

State	Independent city
Maryland	Baltimore City
Missouri....................	St. Louis
Nevada	Carson City
Virginia....................	Alexandria
Virginia....................	Bristol
Virginia....................	Buena Vista
Virginia....................	Charlottesville
Virginia....................	Chesapeake
Virginia....................	Clifton Forge
Virginia....................	Colonial Heights
Virginia....................	Danville
Virginia....................	Emporia
Virginia....................	Fairfax
Virginia....................	Falls Church
Virginia....................	Franklin
Virginia....................	Fredericksburg
Virginia....................	Galax
Virginia....................	Hampton
Virginia....................	Harrisonburg
Virginia....................	Hopewell
Virginia....................	Lexington
Virginia....................	Lynchburg
Virginia....................	Manassas
Virginia....................	Martinsville
Virginia....................	Newport News
Virginia....................	Norfolk
Virginia....................	Norton
Virginia....................	Petersburg
Virginia....................	Poquoson
Virginia....................	Portsmouth
Virginia....................	Radford
Virginia....................	Richmond
Virginia....................	Roanoke
Virginia....................	Salem
Virginia....................	Staunton
Virginia....................	Suffolk
Virginia....................	Virginia Beach
Virginia....................	Waynesboro
Virginia....................	Williamsburg
Virginia....................	Winchester

LIMITATIONS OF THE DATA

Regardless of the subject or type of data presented, data should be read cautiously. All policy, political, and social data have strengths and limitations. These factors should be considered in any analysis and application. Statistics are no magic guide to perfect understanding and decision making, but they can shed light on particular subjects and questions in lieu of haphazard and subjective information. They can clarify trends in policy

expenditures, processes, and impacts and thus assist in evaluating the equity and efficiency of alternative courses of action. Statistical data are most valuable when one remembers their imperfections, both actual and potential, while drawing conclusions.

For example, readers should examine the response bias for each survey. Surveys may be sent to all municipalities above a certain population threshold, but not all of those surveys are necessarily returned. Jurisdictions that do not respond are rarely mirror images of those that do. ICMA reduces the severity of this problem by maximizing the opportunities to respond through second and (sometimes) third requests. But although this practice mitigates the problem, response bias invariably appears. Consequently, ICMA always includes a "Survey Response" table in each article that analyzes the results of a particular survey. This allows the reader to examine the patterns and degrees of response bias through a variety of demographic and structural variables.

Other possible problems can occur with survey data. Local governments have a variety of record-keeping systems. Therefore, some of the data (particularly those on expenditures) may lack uniformity. In addition, no matter how carefully a questionnaire is refined, problems such as divergent interpretations of directions, definitions, and specific questions invariably arise. However, when inconsistencies or apparently extreme data are reported, every attempt is made to verify these responses through follow-up telephone calls.

TYPES OF STATISTICS

There are basically two types of statistics: descriptive and inferential.

Descriptive

Most of the data presented in this volume are purely descriptive. Descriptive statistics summarize some characteristics of a group of numbers. A few numbers represent many. If someone wants to find out something about the age of a city's workforce, for example, it would be quite cumbersome to read a list of several hundred numbers (each representing the age of individual employees). It would be much easier to have a few summary descriptive statistics, such as the mean (average) or the range (the highest value minus the lowest value). These two "pieces" of information would not convey all the details of the entire data set, but they can help and are much more useful and understandable than complete numerical lists.

There are essentially two types of descriptive statistics: measures of central tendency and measures of dispersion.

Measures of Central Tendency These types of statistics indicate the most common or typical value of a data set. The most popular examples

are the mean and median. The mean is simply the arithmetic average. It is calculated by summing the items in a data set and dividing by the total number of items. For example, given the salaries of \$15,000, \$20,000, \$25,000, \$30,000, and \$35,000, the mean is \$25,000 (\$125,000 divided by 5).

The mean is the most widely used and intuitively obvious measure of central tendency. However, it is sensitive to extreme values. A few large or small numbers in a data set can produce a mean that is not representative of the "typical" value. Consider the example of the five salaries above. Suppose the highest value was not \$35,000 but \$135,000. The mean of the data set would now be \$45,000 (\$225,000 divided by 5). This figure, however, is not representative of this group of numbers because it is substantially greater than four of the five values and is \$90,000 below the high score. A data set such as this is "positively skewed" (i.e., it has one or more extremely high scores). Under these circumstances (or when the data set is "negatively skewed" with extremely low scores), it is more appropriate to use the median as a measure of central tendency.

The median is the middle score of a data set that is arranged in order of increasing magnitude. Theoretically, it represents the point that is equivalent to the 50th percentile. For a data set with an odd number of items, the median has the same number of observations above and below it (e.g., the third value in a data set of 5 or the eighth value in a data set of 15). With an even number of cases, the median is the average of the middle two scores (e.g., the seventh and eighth values in a data set of 14). In the example of the five salaries used above, the median is \$25,000 regardless of whether the largest score is \$35,000 or \$135,000. When the mean exceeds the median, the data set is positively skewed. If the median exceeds the mean, it is negatively skewed.

Measures of Dispersion This form of descriptive statistics indicates how widely scattered or spread out the numbers are in a data set. Some common measures of dispersion are the range and the interquartile range. The range is simply the highest value minus the lowest value. For the numbers 3, 7, 50, 80, and 100, the range is 97 (100 – 3 = 97). For the numbers 3, 7, 50, 80, and 1,000, it is 997 (1,000 – 3 = 997). Quartiles divide a data set into four equal parts similar to the way percentiles divide a data set into 100 equal parts. Consequently, the third quartile is equivalent to the 75th percentile, and the first quartile is equivalent to the 25th percentile. The interquartile range is the value of the third quartile minus the value of the first quartile.

Inferential

Inferential statistics permit the social and policy researcher to make inferences about whether a cor-

relation exists between two (or more) variables in a population based on data from a sample. Specifically, inferential statistics provide the probability that the sample results could have occurred by chance if there were really no relationship between the variables in the population as a whole. If the probability of random occurrence is sufficiently low (below the researcher's preestablished significance level), then the null hypothesis—that there is no association between the variables—is rejected. This lends indirect support to the research hypothesis that a correlation does exist. If they can rule out chance factors (the null hypothesis), researchers conclude that they have found a "statistically significant" relationship between the two variables under examination.

Significance tests are those statistics that permit inferences about whether variables are correlated but provide nothing directly about the strength of such correlations. Measures of association, on the other hand, indicate how strong relationships are between variables. These statistics range from a high of +1.0 (for a perfect positive correlation), to zero (indicating no correlation), to a low of −1.0 (for a perfect negative correlation).

Some common significance tests are the the chi square and difference-of-means tests. Some common measures of association are Yule's Q, Sommer's Gamma, Lambda, Cramer's V, Pearson's C, and the correlation coefficient. Anyone seeking further information on these tests and measures should consult any major statistics textbook.[4]

Inferential statistics are used less frequently in this volume than descriptive statistics. However, whenever possible, the data have been presented so that the user can calculate inferential statistics whenever appropriate.

SUMMARY

All social, political, and economic data are collected with imperfect techniques in an imperfect world. Therefore, users of such data should be continuously cognizant of the strengths and weaknesses of the information from which they are attempting to draw conclusions. Readers should note the limitations of the data published in this volume. Particular attention should be paid to the process of data collection and potential problems such as response bias.

---

[1] The terms *city* and *cities,* as used in this volume, refer to cities, villages, towns, townships, and boroughs.

[2] See census.gov/population/www/estimates/aboutmetro. html.

[3] The vast majority of the text describing metropolitan areas has been taken from the Web site cited in footnote 2.

[4] For additional information on statistics, see Tari Renner's *Statistics Unraveled: A Practical Guide to Using Data in Decision Making* (Washington, D.C.: ICMA, 1988).

A Management Trends and Issues

A 1

Matching City Power Structures and City Managers' Leadership Styles: A New Model of Fit

Siegrun Fox Freyss
California State University, Los Angeles

Selected Findings

Urban politics research has identified seven community power structures, as reflected in the composition and actions of the city council, and each requires a different combination of administrative and leadership skills on the part of city managers.

Machine politics demands the greatest degree of secrecy and behind-the-scenes maneuvering on the part of the city manager; hyperpluralism requires the greatest degree of public engagement and political involvement.

The job of the city manager is a difficult one, made even more difficult by the ever-present threat of termination. Interviews reveal that this threat is a constant subtext in the city manager's daily activities. According to various calculations and definitions, the mean length of service of the appointed chief executive is less than seven years, and the median tenure is five years.[1]

Although council members have had little reason to worry about a high turnover rate among chief administrative officers (CAOs)—the perpetual game of musical chairs has ensured a steady stream of applicants—a high turnover rate can have long-term negative effects on a city. Research indicates that instability in the executive office delays important policy decisions and raises the transaction costs of major contracts with outside providers.[2] Such consequences can be especially detrimental to such critical urban policy areas as emergency preparedness and infrastructure planning. Moreover, as the ranks of city managers, like those of other professions, are graying, succession planning in the crucially important mid- and upper-level management ranks will suffer if there is no chief executive promoting the process in a sustained way.

In addition to the negative impacts of a high turnover rate, it can be assumed that most CAOs favor job security, and that a jurisdiction that can promise stability will have a competitive edge in attracting a strong performer from the next generation.[3] Thus, it is in a jurisdiction's best interest to understand why the turnover rate among CAOs is relatively high and what can be done about it.

The explanations for high turnover, while not mutually exclusive, can be divided into external, political forces and internal, personal reasons. On the one hand, since city managers usually are at-will employees, they can be pushed out when the majority on the city council wishes to exercise this prerogative. On the other hand, city managers can be pulled elsewhere by a job offer that promises personal career advancement and greater job satisfaction. But because managers may be quietly forewarned about a likely termination and encouraged to seek employment elsewhere, the external and internal reasons cannot always be clearly dis-

tinguished: in fact, when responding to surveys, managers may claim personal reasons and downplay the push factor.[4]

Studies analyzing the external, political reasons have identified unstable, fractious political conflicts in the jurisdiction as being inimical to a long tenure for city managers. When no stable voting block controls the city council, and when each election can change the balance of power, appointed executives are in constant danger of removal. However, some managers do survive adversarial politics while others lose their jobs under less trying circumstances. Indeed, analyzing data from ICMA in 1999, Richard Feiock and colleagues found substantial variation in tenure—from less than one year to as many as 39 years; six years later, David Ammons and Matthew Bosse found a similar range in their sample.[5]

The study presented in this article expands on the research that explains turnover rates in terms of the compatibility between the political culture of a community, as reflected in the composition and actions of the city council, and the city manager's preferred leadership and management style. The political cultures in this study are defined as the community power structures, which the rich research in urban politics has uncovered; managerial leadership styles are taken from the literature in public administration and organization theory.

After a brief review of survey findings on CAO retention rates over the past quarter-century, this article summarizes research published since the 1960s analyzing reasons for the variations in tenure. It next distinguishes among the major community power structures discussed in the urban politics literature, and then describes the various executive management styles that have been identified in the business administration and public administration literature. Finally, it matches the management types with power structures, identifying compatible and incompatible relationships. With this knowledge, cities should be able to seek out managers with compatible leadership styles and skill sets, and city managers can search for cities with an agreeable political climate.

To capture the complexity of local politics, community power researchers have relied primarily on the case-study method.[6] Following in

this tradition, this study used the multiple case-study approach to field-test the findings derived from an analysis of the published research.[7] The findings were further refined in interviews with a dozen current and former city managers, as well as in discussions with other observers of local politics, whose insights added substantial nuances to the argument. Since the interviewees were promised confidentiality, their comments are woven into the text without attribution.

CITY MANAGER RETENTION RATES: SURVEY FINDINGS, 1980–2002

Through its periodic surveys of local government managers, ICMA has tracked the turnover rates by asking city managers about their years of service in their current positions. Surveys in 1984 and 1989 found that the average length of service was 5.4 years.[8] A 1994 study revealed that about 25% of city managers had fewer than 3 years of service in their current positions, and that nearly 60% had served for fewer than 7 years in the same positions (see Table 1/1).

The comprehensive 2000 survey of cities and counties revealed an increase in the average length of service in the current position to 6.9 years, but this statistic varied somewhat by the size of the jurisdiction (see Table 1/2). City managers in the smallest communities were found to have the shortest average tenure (4.9 years),

Table 1/1 CITY MANAGERS' LENGTH OF SERVICE IN CURRENT POSITION, 1994

Length of service	No.	Percentage
Total	261	100.0
Less than 3 years	64	24.5
3–6 years	92	35.2
7–10 years	59	22.6
11–15 years	30	11.5
Over 15 years	16	6.1

Note: Percentages do not add to 100% because of rounding.
Source: Victor S. DeSantis and Charldean Newell, "Local Government Managers' Career Paths," in *The Municipal Year Book 1996* (Washington, D.C.: ICMA, 1996), 5

Table 1/2 CITY MANAGERS' LENGTH OF SERVICE IN CURRENT POSITION BY SIZE OF JURISDICTION, 2000

Population	No.	Mean no. of years
Total	3,137	6.9
Over 1,000,000	9	6.1
500,000–1,000,000	20	6.7
250,000–499,999	42	6.8
100,000–249,999	136	7.2
50,000–99,999	241	6.8
25,000–49,999	400	7.4
10,000–24,999	721	7.8
5,000–9,999	617	6.9
2,500–4,999	614	6.6
Under 2,500	337	4.9

Source: Tari Renner, "The Local Government Management Profession at Century's End," in *The Municipal Year Book 2001* (Washington, D.C.: ICMA, 2001), 39

while those in jurisdictions with 10,000–24,999 residents had the longest (7.8 years).[9] In analyzing the staying power of long-serving city managers (those serving 20 years or more), Douglas Watson and Wendy Hassett also found size of jurisdiction (fewer than 30,000 residents) to be an important factor.[10]

However, Ammons and Bosse made an important point concerning the operational definition of *tenure* or *length of service* in these studies. The surveys conducted by Victor DeSantis and Charldean Newell in 1994, and by Tari Renner in 2001, asked sitting city managers for the "length of service in their current position." This approach does not capture information about completed terms, and the phrase should not be taken to mean the "total length of service in the same position." To measure total length, Ammons and Bosse conducted a longitudinal study from 1980 to 2002 and excluded the city managers' current terms in office. Despite the different definitions, the averages ended up to be the same: 6.9 years (see Table 1/3). Ammons and Bosse also showed that to measure the central tendency, the median was the better statistic to use than the arithmetic mean because the average got distorted by a few long-serving managers. The median year was only 5 years, which meant that 50% of the city managers in their study had served for fewer than 5 years in the same position and 50% had served for more than 5 years.[11]

Compared to the turnover rate in the corporate sector, the rate among city managers is not high.

But in the public sector, administrators are expected to serve longer terms in order to provide stability and continuity as a counterbalance to elected officials, whose actions and time horizons tend to be limited by election pressures.

EXPLAINING CITY MANAGERS' RETENTION RATES

The expectation of a long tenure goes back to the founding years of the civil service. The job of the professional city manager emerged in the United States during the Progressive Era with the municipal reform movement, which wanted a public workforce that was competent, stable, and apolitical, providing public service without favoritism. Keeping public administration apart from politics was a way to promote neutral, professional competence.[12] However, following the corporate model of the chief executive officer, the city manager would not be a civil servant and so would not receive job security.[13]

In the 1950s and 1960s, researchers recognized that the politics/administration dichotomy was not reflecting reality, and academics as well as the professional community extensively debated the political and policy-making roles of city managers. The short tenure of CAOs was also noted and researched. According to a 1962 study by Gladys Kammerer and colleagues, in the years after World War II, the average length of service for CAOs in Florida was 3.66 years and in Virginia, 5.49 years.[14] The researchers examined the effects of four variable clusters on manager termination rates in Florida: (1) institutional-structural aspects, such as elections and appointment procedures; (2) personal characteristics, such as the manager's educational background; (3) nonpolitical community factors, such as population growth; and (4) political factors, such as the political stability of the community and political style. The findings related to political factors are of the greatest interest to this study because they reflect an early effort to relate retention rates to political power structures.

On the basis of previous community power studies, Kammerer and her co-investigators developed a tripartite typology. Depending on the "degree of competition between or among leadership cliques," they labeled city politics as monopolistic when one clique was in control of city hall, oligopolistic when a few powerful interests vied for preeminence, or competitive when sev-

eral groups sought influence over local politics. From the totality of Florida cities with the council-manager form of government, they selected ten cities to study the power structure in detail using the case-study method. A not-surprising finding was that in competitive cities, electoral considerations determined most of the involuntary terminations, whereas in monopolistic cities, the power of the mayor had the greatest influence on the likelihood of early termination.[15]

Several years later, John Bollens and John Ries developed a more complex typology of community power structures to examine appropriate leadership styles.[16] The typology included three variables: (1) the distribution of citizen contributions to political decisions, (2) the congruence of the values of political leaders with those of the general citizenry, and (3) the prevailing functions of the city government. It identified various consensual or conflicting situations that required different managerial skills, including expertise in managing growth, ability to provide routine municipal services efficiently, and skills in alliance building and arbitration. As can be expected, Bollens and Ries found that the city manager could expect the greatest job security in cities with a consensual political culture—that is, where major interests value the same policy directions. Such a consensual political culture requires traditional professional and technical skills. Conversely, the tenure was likely to be short when competing elites and shifting alliances dominated local politics.[17]

Over the next two decades, other research teams followed in examining the policy-making and political roles of city managers. One group worked in the San Francisco Bay Area,[18] and another studied city managers in Oklahoma.[19] The general conclusion was that city managers had to be good politicians to stay in office; to lengthen their tenure, however, they should not draw attention to that fact but instead maintain a low public profile.[20]

In the years that followed, researchers lost interest in examining the nexus between city politics and the city manager's roles—possibly because of both the increased specialization of academics and the widespread splitting of the public administration field from political science. But in 1990 James Svara renewed scholarly interest in the politics/administration dichotomy. He clarified the dividing line between the city council's and the manager's proper spheres of influence by expanding the dichotomy to embrace four concepts: mission, policy, administration, and management, and he found substantial agreement between council members and managers over the boundary separating their responsibilities.[21] Nine years later, Svara observed an increased blurring of the lines.[22] He did not address the issue of political climate, however, which would have added even more uncertainty to the manager's expected area of operation.[23]

In researching the variables influencing the relatively short tenure of local government executives, Ruth DeHoog and Gordon Whitaker discovered that political reasons, or push factors, explained about half of the turnover rate, while professional advancement and other pull factors accounted for the other half.[24] However, as has

Table 1/3 CITY MANAGERS' TOTAL LENGTH OF SERVICE IN THE SAME POSITION, 1980–2002

Population	No. of cities	Median	Mean	No. of city managers
Total	120	5.0	6.9	394
More than 200,000	20	5.3	6.2	72
About 200,000	20	6.3	7.8	50
About 100,000	20	5.0	6.9	62
About 75,000	20	5.3	6.4	69
About 50,000	20	5.0	8.0	51
About 25,000	20	4.6	6.3	60

Source: David N. Ammons and Matthew J. Bosse, "Tenure of City Managers: Examining the Dual Meanings of 'Average Tenure,'" *State and Local Government Review* 37, no. 1 (2005): 65.

been noted, the line could not be clearly drawn because of the practice of allowing CAOs to resign rather than be dismissed by the city council. Experienced city managers pass on the advice, "get out before they fire you."[25] The 2000 ICMA survey found that only 10% of the managers who had changed positions in the previous year had left voluntarily; of the 90% who had left involuntarily, 10% had been fired, 20% had been forced to resign, and 70% had been under pressure to resign.[26]

James Kaatz, Edward French, and Hazel Prentiss-Cooper probed the association between political conflicts or policy conflicts on the city council and the city manager's degree of burnout and desire to leave the positions. They found that about 58% of the 168 managers participating in their survey were experiencing a low level of burnout, 14% a transitional form, and 28% a high level. In addition, they discovered that the relationship between political conflicts and high burnout was moderately strong, whereas the association between policy conflicts and high burnout was inconclusive.[27]

Richard Feiock and Christopher Stream used regression analysis to test the possible impact of 12 internal and external factors on the tenure of city managers. Among the professional indicators, they found that an MPA degree lengthened retention by about one year, while community conflict shortened it by about six months.[28] In a subsequent study, Feiock and colleagues found perceived role conflicts between the city manager and mayor, as well as between the city manager and council, to be statistically significant predictors of length of service.[29] And in a third study, Feiock and Stream found that the turnover rate of city council members emerged as the strongest predictor of the city managers' turnover rate.[30] In addition to council member turnover, short-term or long-term economic change can also influence turnover.[31]

George Hanbury, Alka Sapat, and Charles Washington also used regression analysis to examine the impact of several internal and external variables on city managers' length of time in office.[32] The subtitle of their article, "The 'Fit Model' of Leadership," gives the impression of similarity with this current study, but a closer look shows important differences, such as in the definition of leadership style. To define leadership style, the authors used a tool called the Leader Behavior Analysis II–Self Instrument, and they captured the personality dimension by using the Myers-Briggs Type Indicator. To assess the city managers' perception of fit, they asked each respondent to assess how his or her personality type meshed with council expectations. And for each respondent, the perception of the council was obtained from the manager's performance evaluation. Other variables included in the model involved the city manager's personal characteristics, as well as the demographic and economic characteristics of the jurisdiction.

Some of the variables in Hanbury, Sapat, and Washington's study were statistically significant; for instance, the wealth of a jurisdiction was predictive of a manager's longer tenure. However, some of the findings were perplexing. Experience,

calculated as the number of years of previous service, was found to be negatively related to tenure. Homogeneity, in terms of the percentage of the white population, was also negatively related to tenure, but so too was diversity, as determined by the percentage of foreign-born residents.[33]

The contradictory and counterintuitive findings justify an investigation into other factors that may explain a poor or good match between the city council and the city manager. Considering the tenuous political foundation on which city managers build their professional careers, it is appropriate to analyze the political environment in greater detail to find additional indicators for retention and thereby lower the probability of turnover. Whereas researchers in previous studies developed their own typologies of community power to examine appropriate city managers' roles, this study uses types of power structure that have been identified by researchers of urban politics over the last 50 years.

SEVEN COMMUNITY POWER STRUCTURES

According to the urban politics research, control of city hall can range from highly concentrated to highly dispersed. This study focuses on seven major community power structures: (1) the political machine, (2) one elite in power, (3) competing elites, (4) the partnership regime, (5) classical pluralism, (6) hyperpluralism, and (7) network governance.

The Political Machine
The power structure of a jurisdiction can be called a political machine when it exhibits the following characteristics:[34]

- Political power is in the hands of a clique, which controls the majority party and dominates the mayoral election as well as city council races.
- Government jobs and city contracts are used to reward political loyalty.
- Leaders and followers come from a relatively humble background and use political power to enrich themselves and improve their socioeconomic standing.[35]

Political machines gained influence in cities in the later part of the nineteenth century. In subsequent decades, they waxed and waned depending on the strength of countervailing good-government forces. At the present time, investigations by district attorneys' offices and the Federal Bureau of Investigation point us to cities where public corruption has become part of the political culture.

Elite Politics (One Elite in Power)
When an upper class controls a community, the resulting power structure has been identified as elite politics. It has the following properties:[36]

- Political power is dominated by a stratum of like-minded, well-off people who hold influential positions in business, government, and cultural institutions.

- Members of the ruling class hold a stable supermajority on the city council and control the election of the mayor through the nominating process and financial support.
- The policy-making process emphasizes efficiency and effectiveness over democratic inclusiveness.

Evidence in support of the elite theory has been gathered by interviewing knowledgeable individuals in communities, using the so-called reputational method. A second method involves studying the socioeconomic background of persons in positions of power, and a third approach involves analyzing policy outcomes.[37]

Competing Elites
As the analyses by Harvey Molotch in 1976, and by Molotch and John Logan in 1987, have shown, power in local jurisdictions may oscillate between two types of economic interests to produce a situation identified as competing elites, characterized as follows:[38]

- National or international corporate interests are competing with local real estate interests—the so-called growth machine, which includes developers, construction companies, banks, realtors, and unions in the building trades.
- Corporate interests seek jurisdictions with cheap land and low operating costs, while the local growth machine attempts to maximize its financial gain.
- The national and international investment interests seek jurisdictions with low taxes, while the local economic interests accept a certain level of taxation to strengthen the infrastructure and maximize the value of the land.

No representatives of corporate interests may actually sit on the city council. Despite any disagreements, their policy preferences may be promoted by the local growth machine because it seeks to maximize its profits by attracting the investment wealth of large corporations.[39] Depending on historical circumstances, other types of competing interests can dominate the local scene—for example, big-box retailers in the suburbs versus small retailers on Main Street, or environmentalists and smart growth advocates versus pro-growth business interests.[40] Elites can also break up into liberal and conservative camps.

The Partnership Regime
A partnership regime refers to a situation where a relatively stable coalition has been created between a minority-controlled city hall and a white-controlled business sector.[41] In this case,

- Economic power is controlled by whites, while political power and the majority vote are in the hands of African Americans or Latinos.
- There is a balance of power between the two sides, of which both sides are aware. When investor interests are threatened by city hall, finance capital and jobs may leave the city; and when citizen interests are ignored by the economic elite, voters may shift to the opposition or simply not vote.

- Coalition politics is used to accommodate both camps and achieve a balance of power.

In cities like Atlanta, the partnership can be relatively stable and long lasting. However, it may not lead to equal gains for both sides. As planner Larry Keating points out, poverty and segregation have persisted in the black communities of Atlanta's south side.[42]

Classical Pluralism

Classical pluralism describes a condition in which power is dispersed among several major groups in the community. It is associated with the following conditions:[43]

- Mayoral and city council elections are contested among diverse economic, civic, and demographic interests, with no foregone conclusion as to which voting bloc or coalition may win.
- The dispersion of power and the lack of a stable governing coalition can also be observed during the policy-making process. There is not one group or coalition dominating all policy-making activities.
- After due deliberations and under the guidance of elected and appointed government officials, compromises are achieved and policy decisions are made.

The pluralistic sharing of political power is supposed to lead to a somewhat equitable distribution of governmental benefits and burdens.[44]

Hyperpluralism

A community power structure may be identified as hyperpluralistic under the following circumstances:[45]

- Many factions are jostling for political attention and governmental benefits, but no faction or coalition of factions is strong enough to get the city council to agree on important policy decisions.
- The disparate factions create temporary coalitions to block major programmatic decisions, but they cannot agree on an alternative course of action.
- These negative coalitions paralyze the policy-making process, and important city projects remain stalled.

In cities where several demographic groups are at odds with each other, but also with traditional business interests, unions, or environmentalists, the hyperfragmentation of political power can lead to an unending stream of policy demands and few tangible improvements in quality-of-life conditions.

Network Governance

Political scientist Heinz Eulau was an early proponent of empirical research into community power hypothesized as networks.[46] In more recent years, however, network governance has been discussed more in the public administration field than in urban politics.[47] Whereas the traditional community power research analyzes cities as islands or freestanding entities, the focus on networks sees cities as part of an intergovernmental and intersectoral web of policy making and service delivery. The networked governance model has some of the following characteristics:[48]

- A centralized government bureaucracy is replaced or supplemented by a network of partnerships with other jurisdictions, for-profit enterprises, nonprofit organizations, and citizen groups.
- Government agencies may function as facilitators and guarantors of service delivery, but not be the actual providers.
- High-quality outcomes are promoted through intergovernmental and intersectoral networks of professionals who share a common vision of best practices.
- The power of the city council may vary depending on the ability of council members to understand the emerging network structures, provide appropriate policy guidance, and exercise effective oversight.[49]

Network governance is especially appropriate in metropolitan regions, where it can ensure a seamless, areawide infrastructure despite a crazy quilt of jurisdictional boundaries. When functioning well, the networked approach can be low key and noncontroversial, and thus may not be perceived as an exercise in community power. But an analysis of city managers' turnover rates needs to include networks as possible power structures, because a breakdown in intersectoral and interjurisdictional collaboration can lead to governmental paralysis and put the city manager in the hot seat.[50]

The literature indicates that the tenure of city managers is shortest under hyperpluralistic conditions because elected officials use the manager as a scapegoat for their failure to achieve lasting improvements.[51] Although most managers may therefore want to stay away from a highly fragmented jurisdiction, such a situation offers challenges that some executives are willing to confront.

EXECUTIVE MANAGEMENT STYLES IN THE PUBLIC SECTOR

The public administration and business administration literature makes a distinction between management and leadership.[52] Leaders are supposed to generate visions, identify missions, set goals, and provide the resources that will enable the organization to realize its goals. In contrast, managers are expected to use the resources and take the necessary actions to achieve those goals.

City managers are supposed to rely on elected officials to provide the vision, mission, and goals, as well as the needed resources. However, as the community power research indicates, the leadership capacity of the city council varies, so CAOs must be flexible in their responses, able to be low-key or assertive as needed. The following discussion of executive management styles is by no means exhaustive. Emphasis is placed on those executive roles that yield a match with a community power structure.

Our understanding of proper administrative styles was dramatically reversed with the funda-mental shift from the patronage system to the merit system. The former system conjures up the image of a poorly prepared but loyal yea-sayer, caretaker, or conserver.[53] This image stands in stark contrast to the neutral competence of the professional administrator selected under merit system principles.

The political neutrality of the professional administrator is a product of the politics/administration dichotomy, or separation of powers, in which the political side makes public policy while the administration executes it. The first ICMA Code of Ethics, issued in 1924, stated that council members "primarily determine public policy." However, the code did call upon the manager to "exercise *his own judgment* as an executive in accomplishing the policies formulated by the council" (emphasis added). Fourteen years later, a revised code expressed the dichotomy in even stronger terms: the preamble set the guideline that in the council-manager form of government, "policy shall be determined exclusively by the council," and the main part of the code asserted that "the city manager is in no sense a political leader."[54]

When the existence of a politics/administration dichotomy was questioned after World War II, ICMA responded in 1952 by again revising its Code of Ethics and casting the city manager in the role of a community leader; in this capacity, according to Svara, the city manager "submits policy proposals to the council and provides the council with facts and advice on matters of policy to give the council a basis for making decisions on community goals."[55] In their critical analysis of the city manager profession, Bollens and Ries also conclude that the many resources under the control of the city manager give the manager the status of a community leader.[56] Other observers of local government have noted that when the dividing line between politics and administration collapsed conceptually, city managers were told to be politically savvy without revealing this competence.[57]

The image of the city manager that emerged at this time resembled that of an acrobat, able to walk the fine line between inadequate and too much involvement in the political battles of the city. It was a precarious position for the manager to be in, and other styles were recommended. Pluralist democratic theory introduced the image of government as umpire, ensuring fair play as competing political interests bargain and compromise over the distribution of public benefits and burdens.[58] Should the community need more than a referee, government might assume the role of head coach or team builder.[59]

More recently, the concept of power broker has surfaced and been promoted as an appropriate role for managers to play in cities with major factions. Those city managers who are uncomfortable with the notion of brokering political power may instead embrace the role of mediator, which suggests a level-headed person who can listen to and get all sides to agree on a fair allocation of governmental benefits and burdens. *Facilitator* and *negotiator* are other terms used in this context.[60]

Some researchers cast the CAO in the role of a community builder, catalyst, innovator, pioneer, or policy entrepreneur. Such a person can communicate a vision and mobilize needed resources.[61]

However, such a role can also expose appointed executives to unwanted public attention and shorten their tenure. Svara therefore cautions city managers not to exceed the role of a "comprehensive professional leader."[62] Camille Cates Barnett apparently overstepped that line and thus lost her job as city manager of Austin within a relatively short period of time.[63]

Mark Moore, of the Hauser Center for Nonprofit Organizations, expands on this notion of the comprehensive professional leader. He argues that public managers should not only be oriented downward, toward their subordinates and the control of bureaucratic operations, but also upward, toward political superiors and policy making, as well as outward, toward citizens and valued outcomes.[64] This orientation sees the public manager as explorer and as leader of an ongoing discovery process. The notion of a three-dimensional realm of work acknowledges the complexity of the manager's job, and the idea of explorer casts the manager in the role of an inquisitive master student who is a quick study and ahead of the learning curve of elected officials, subordinates, and citizens.[65] The strategic perspective helps the manager to anticipate political conflicts, changing public needs, and internal organizational weaknesses—and to be proactive in addressing them.

But being a quick study may not be the deciding quality that city managers need in order to keep their jobs. This study argues that the seven community power structures, as reflected in the composition and actions of the city council, require different combinations of administrative and leadership skills on the part of city managers if they want to maintain a good rapport with the city council.[66]

MATCHING COMMUNITY POWER STRUCTURES AND EXECUTIVE MANAGEMENT STYLES: THE MODEL AND RELATED CASE STUDIES

This analysis suggests that machine politics demands the greatest degree of secrecy and behind-the-scenes maneuvering on the part of the city manager, while hyperpluralism requires the greatest degree of public engagement and political involvement. Table 1/4 shows the proposed matches in schematic form.

Political Machine and Caretaker CAO

A city dominated by a political machine is likely to have an unreformed city charter and unlikely to have a council-manager form of government. However, if it does have a council-manager form, the manager is not expected to exercise independent professional judgment in administering the city, since personnel decisions, procurement, and other important managerial functions are dictated by the political machine. Accordingly, the best image that comes to mind to identify the appropriate managerial style is that of the caretaker. Such a person will do what he or she has been told to do and will not question the propriety of the directives given by the council and other influential individuals; as caretaker, the city manager will literally protect the interests of the entrenched machine and may thus enjoy job security as long as the machine is in power.

South Gate (population 97,110) and Compton (population 94,425) are two cities near Los Angeles that exemplify this match.[67] In 2003, when indignant voters in South Gate recalled an apparently corrupt faction on the city council as well as the elected city treasurer, the city manager helped the outgoing officials loot the city coffers. As a subsequent investigation revealed, the treasurer and the city manager "spent 90% of the city's $8.9-million emergency reserve, with most of it going to attorneys," in the last seven months in office.[68] In Compton, both the mayor and the city manager were sentenced in 2004 to three years in prison on felony corruption charges.[69]

Elite Politics and Professional CAO

The corrupt or corruptible caretaker style contrasts sharply with the image of the professional chief administrator favored in an elite power structure. The professional CAO is expected to be well educated, holding a professional degree such as an MPA. As manager of a mid-sized city, the professional CAO is also expected to have moved up steadily to increasingly challenging jobs until ready to assume the executive position and lead efficiently, effectively, and quietly—much like a chief executive officer in the business sector. The manager's executive standing can be strengthened through involvement in professional organizations such as ICMA. City politics under elite control is relatively stable, and a competent city manager can remain in office by staying "above politics."[70]

The city of Plano, Texas (population 260,796) provides an example of this power structure–council-manager match. By U.S. and Texas standards, the city is quite homogenous. According to the 2000 census, it is 78.3% white (compared with 73.9% nationwide), and only 4.3% of the population lives below the poverty level (compared with 9.8% nationwide).[71] The current city council appears quite diverse: four women, all white; four men, three white, one black. But their socioeconomic background is quite similar. Most of them have advanced professional degrees and hold important positions in business.[72] Plano's current city manager holds an MPA, has moved up through increasingly challenging positions until he was appointed city manager in 1987, and belongs to several professional organizations—credentials that are apparently well matched with the professionalism on the council.

Competing Elites and Power Broker/Mediator

When the local power structure breaks apart into competing elites, the city manager has to get immersed in politics, and his or her role becomes that of power broker or mediator—the premier problem solver.[73] This requires gaining the trust of both camps, bringing both sides to the table, and getting them both to agree on compromises.[74]

As a review of several case studies from around the country shows, the arrival of a big-box retailer like Wal-Mart can give rise to two opposing political camps. On one side is the local growth machine welcoming the retailer. On the other side is a coalition of small retail businesses, labor interests, and environmentalists that may try to block the development. City managers who are too much identified with one side may fail, as happened in Rosemead, California (population 54,520), in 2006. When a majority on the council, backed by the city manager, voted to bring a Wal-Mart to the city, an energetic and media-savvy opposition, unable to stop the construction, mobilized a recall election and drove the city manager out of office.[75]

A similar situation arose in the city of Vermillion, South Dakota (population 10,251); here, however, compromises were hammered out between competing interests before a Wal-Mart was approved.[76] The community changed city managers during this time, and the new manager was seen as a good fit because of his management style, described by the mayor as a " 'soothing, mediation type of management and personality' " who was able " 'to put both sides at ease and arrive at a solution which would work for everybody.' "[77]

Partnership Regime and Power Broker/Mediator

A partnership regime also requires the skills of a power broker or mediator. However, under the partnership arrangement, one camp consists of powerful minority interests, who can control the majority vote on the council; the other camp consists of investment interests, who may leave the jurisdiction if their economic demands are ignored. The city manager who succeeds under these political conditions must gain the trust of the minority groups while also enjoying the support of corporate interests. A personality type with a knack for brokering or mediating may prevail in such a political culture.[78]

Studies of successful mayors provide examples of masterful brokers and mediators. Political scientist Edward Banfield described Chicago mayor

---

Table 1/4 MATCHING COMMUNITY POWER STRUCTURE WITH APPROPRIATE CAO STYLE: THE MODEL

Community power structure		Chief administrative officer's administrative style
Political machine	→	Caretaker
Elite politics (one elite in power)	→	Professional CAO/chief executive
Competing elites	→	Power broker/mediator
Partnership regime	→	Power broker/mediator
Classical pluralism	→	Umpire/facilitator/coach
Hyperpluralism	→	Community builder/catalyst/change agent/turn-around artist/educator/trustee
Network governance	→	Hub manager/explorer/master student/team leader

Richard J. Daley as a skillful broker in various community conflicts and as a "master broker between Chicago's tradition-minded inner wards and its modern-minded outer wards."[79] More recently, Antonio Villaraigosa, the first Latino mayor of Los Angeles in modern times and a former union official, used his mediating skills to resolve a bargaining impasse between white hotel owners and the minority-controlled hotel workers union. The disruptive forces of a strike and lock-out could have been crippling for the local tourism industry and the local economy in general.[80]

Classical Pluralism and Umpire/Facilitator/Coach

Under classical pluralist conditions, power is dispersed among several political interests. Since the power of individual factions is supposed to be kept in check by competing factions, the city manager is needed less as a power broker or mediator and more as an umpire in the field. In this role, the CAO is expected to ensure that the various political groups play by the rules of the game, which means being willing to communicate with each other as well as to bargain and compromise. The CAO can act as the facilitator by listening to the various grievances, bringing the different interests to the table, and ensuring that all major voices are heard and that compromises are fair. To facilitate cooperation among the various groups, the CAO may also play the role of head coach or team leader.[81]

Keith Mulrooney, past city manager of Claremont (population 35,005), a university town 30 miles east of Los Angeles, described the nature of his work under pluralist conditions as "confronting antiwar demonstrators, holding council meetings in Chicano houses, sitting with hippies in a park discussing last week's narcotics bust, bargaining against a labor pro, or contracting with the Black Student Union. . . ."[82] He survived in the role of a hands-on umpire or coach for eight years. It could be argued that the many factions threatened to sink the city into hyperpluralism, but Mulrooney averted this by gaining the trust of disaffected segments of society and acting as community builder.

The more recent globalization and multicultural trends can also push the city manager into playing the role of umpire, or guardian of written and unwritten rules. Members on the city council may come from different civic traditions and may appreciate the unifying voice and equitable judgment of the city manager.

Hyperpluralism and Community Builder/Catalyst/Educator/Trustee

When political interests break apart into many factions that refuse to compromise, community politics can lead to hyperpluralism and stagnation. City managers who like to get things done quietly and efficiently will be very frustrated in such a tense situation.[83] However, a person who thrives on controversy—a community builder type—may be a better match. The community builder has the charisma to lift the factions above their fragmented demands by sharing a common vision that a majority on the council and in the community can embrace. Such coalition politics

tends to be unstable, but at least it offers temporary solutions to the political paralysis created by hyperpluralism. Sometimes the public leader can also give the appearance of unity and success by effectively manipulating politically charged symbols.[84] Examples of such efforts are planting trees or participating in neighborhood cleanup efforts while the TV cameras are rolling.

Under chaotic or highly complex conditions that defy simple solutions, CAOs can also adopt the role of change agent, turn-around artist, or catalyst.[85] They may be driven, Type-A personalities who like "to tackle the tough stuff,"[86] or they may be empty nesters who are bored with the retirement lifestyle and, with a long and respected career in public service, have the stature to rally a majority on the council behind them.

The role of educator has also been proposed to cope with hyperpluralistic times. Analyzing various failures of American political institutions, including failures in political leadership due to the power of factions and ignorance of voters, Robert Behn, of Harvard's John F. Kennedy School of Government, calls on public managers to lead and to inform: "Educating the public about the broad mission, specific goals, and latest accomplishments can only help to improve governance."[87] The city as a learning community is an extension of Peter Senge's idea of the corporation as a learning organization, which continuously adapts to survive while also expanding its capacity to create its future.[88]

In the face of political gridlock, Northern Kentucky University professor Fred Rhynhart proposes that the city manager assume not only the roles of community builder and educator but also, in light of inadequate council and popular oversight, the classical role of trustee.[89] When democratic controls fail, CAOs should continue the democratic tradition by reminding themselves of their fiduciary responsibilities toward the public. In the end, their decisions should be guided by professional standards, not by concerns for job security. In a similar vein, the late Larry Terry, professor of public administration, argued that top-level administrators should see themselves as conservators of agency mission, values, and resources.[90]

Network Governance and Hub Manager/Explorer/Master Student/ Team Leader

The complexity of network governance calls for a city manager who can assume the lead as a hub manager, the thoughtful role of a master student, the exciting role of an explorer, or the steady role of a team player. As a hub manager and important node in the network, the city manager can promote the strategic and synergistic use of resources in the government bureaucracy, the political structure, corporations, small businesses, or community organizations.[91]

The master student does not claim to know it all but instead invites others to assume the role of educator—a posture that can disarm critics and raise the level of civic discourse. The explorer or pioneer type, rather than being intimidated by complexity and uncertainty, feels challenged and invigorated by the unknown. Seemingly intractable social

and economic problems require a mix of public, business, and nonprofit solutions. A networked approach can make use of the strengths of the different sectoral entities. Network governance also needs reliable team players who show up for meetings, do their homework, pull their weight, and get things done.

However, the myriad interests in a network can also pull the joint projects in different and unforeseen directions, and the CAO, as trustee of the public interest, has to exercise strong oversight "at every stage of the process, from initiation to the ongoing management of the network."[92] The multifaceted role requires strong executive skills—from subject matter competence to personal integrity and interpersonal sensitivity. When the role is performed poorly, the city manager may be quickly out of a job. When it is performed well, however, the effective network leader and hub manager may enjoy job security in his or her current job or advancement to a more desirable position.[93]

Metropolitan regions offer good examples of city managers who practice network management. The city of San Gabriel (population 40,602) east of Los Angeles leverages its resources through collaboration with various community partners. Some of the partners address the needs of youth and families, while others celebrate the cultural contributions of particular immigrant groups. The city manager has been a catalyst in the process, supported by a city council that has kept him in office for 14 years.

In 2005, the city of Durham, North Carolina (population 217,847), undertook a comprehensive, networked effort to combat gangs. To prevent youth from joining gangs, the police department partnered with local community and faith-based organizations, as well as the parks and recreation department and other agencies, in developing after-school activities and employment opportunities. The city also collaborated with universities in researching effective strategies and programs. The city manager of Durham has been in office for only a short period of time, but he was apparently chosen for the job because of his track record: in his previous position as city manager, which he had held for ten years, he encouraged partnerships between city hall and neighborhood associations to make community planning more effective and enhance the quality of life for residents.[94]

CONCLUSIONS

This research adds a piece to the puzzle that seeks to identify the causes of city managers' variable lengths of service. By drawing on the community power literature of the last 50 years to create a community power typology, and by matching the types with appropriate leadership or management styles, this study supplements previous approaches that sought patterns in the external influences on turnover rates and identified regularities between political culture and length of service. Regression analysis is a valuable tool for testing the possible impact of various push and pull factors on turnover rate; however, the need to enter quantifiable vari-

ables into the model limits the nature of the variables tested. This research used the case-study method to add a nuanced and historically grounded understanding of the interaction between city councils and city managers.

The findings have not only theoretical implications but also practical ones. Beyond subject matter competence, urban administrators need proficiency in the analysis of community power structures as well as solid training in interpersonal skills and conflict mediation.[95]

Some academics, consultants, and professional organizations have started the process. ICMA and the National League of Cities have developed a guide to help elected and appointed officials establish effective working relationships.[96] From years of practical experience, William Pammer and colleagues offer a conflict resolution framework that combines features from strategic planning, alternative dispute resolution, nominal group process, and team building to align the perceptions of council members, the city manager, and key administrators.[97] The new model of fit, proposed in this study, offers a conceptual framework that can lead to more effective training outcomes in that leadership advice or conflict resolution strategies can be presented with greater specificity when the council members' power base and the city manager's preferred performance style are known.

Changing jobs has been an easy way for city managers and city councils to resolve their differences in the past. But that practice may no longer be the best one given the increased complexity of urban communities and heightened responsibilities for urban administrators. As research has shown, stability in the executive office improves the capacity of cities to move forward and tackle critical planning issues, such as upgrading the infrastructure, ensuring safety and security, and sustaining succession planning. And while role congruence or incongruence cannot be considered the sole reasons for a city manager's length of service, identifying the optimum match in any given jurisdiction will go a long way toward ensuring that needed stability.

[1]Victor S. DeSantis and Charldean Newell, "Local Government Managers' Career Paths," in *The Municipal Year Book 1996* (Washington, D.C.: ICMA, 1996), 5; Tari Renner, "The Local Government Management Profession at Century's End," in *The Municipal Year Book 2001* (Washington, D.C.: ICMA, 2001), 39; David N. Ammons and Matthew J. Bosse, "Tenure of City Managers: Examining the Dual Meanings of 'Average Tenure,' " *State and Local Government Review* 37, no. 1 (2005): 65.

[2]Richard C. Feiock and Christopher Stream, "Explaining the Tenure of Local Government Managers," *Journal of Public Administration Research and Theory* 8 (January 1998): 118.

[3]Frank Benest, ed., *Preparing the Next Generation* (Washington, D.C.: ICMA, 2003); Ralph Blumenthal, "Unfilled City Manager Posts Hint at Future Gap," *New York Times,* January 11, 2007.

[4]Whether push or pull factors are at work also depends on the city manager's employment contract. The contract may provide for severance pay in the case of a termination, but not in the case of a resignation.

[5]Richard C. Feiock et al., "Politics, Administration, and Manager Turnover" (paper presented at the annual meeting of the American Political Science Association, Atlanta, Georgia, 1999), 9; Ammons and Bosse, "Tenure of City Managers," 66.

[6]Terry Christensen and Tom Hogen-Esch, *Local Politics: A Practical Guide to Governing at the Grassroots,* 2nd ed. (Armonk, N.Y.: M. E. Sharpe, 2006), 263.

[7]Robert K. Yin, *Case Study Research: Design and Methods,* rev. ed. (Newbury Park, Calif.: Sage, 1989).

[8]Mary A. Schellinger, "Local Government Managers: Profile of Professionals in a Maturing Profession," in *The Municipal Year Book 1985* (Washington, D.C.: ICMA, 1985), 181–188; Tari Renner, "Appointed Local Government Managers: Stability and Change," in *The Municipal Year Book 1990* (Washington, D.C.: ICMA, 1990), 41–52.

[9]It needs to be noted that the 2000 ICMA data not only include municipalities, but also counties. The cutoff point for counties was 2,500 residents. In the case of municipalities, the survey included communities with fewer than 2,500 residents that ICMA recognized "as having a professional management position in their jurisdiction" (Renner, "Local Government Management Profession," 36).

[10]Douglas J. Watson and Wendy L. Hassett, "Long-Serving City Managers: Why Do They Stay?" *Public Administration Review* 63, no. 1 (January/February 2003): 71–78.

[11]Ammons and Bosse, "Tenure of City Managers," 61–71.

[12]Woodrow Wilson, "The Study of Administration," *Political Science Quarterly* 2 (1887): 197–222.

[13]Richard J. Stillman, *The Rise of the City Manager: A Public Professional in Local Government* (Albuquerque: University of New Mexico Press, 1974), chap. 1.

[14]Gladys M. Kammerer et al., *City Managers in Politics: An Analysis of Manager Tenure and Termination* (Gainesville: University of Florida Press, 1962), 6.

[15]Ibid., 23.

[16]John C. Bollens and John C. Ries, *The City Manager Profession: Myth and Realities* (Chicago: Public Administration Service, 1969), 21–33.

[17]Ibid., 26–32.

[18]Ronald O. Loveridge, *City Managers in Legislative Politics* (Indianapolis: Bobbs-Merrill Co., 1971).

[19]Jack V. Hough, Jana L. Bagwell, and David R. Morgan, *The Relationship of Political and Personal Variables to the Roles of City Managers* (Norman: Bureau of Governmental Research, University of Oklahoma, 1973).

[20]Frederick C. Mosher, *Democracy and the Public Service* (New York: Oxford University Press, 1982), 6–8; David N. Ammons and Charldean Newell, *Leadership Roles, Work Characteristics, and Time Management* (Albany: State University of New York Press, 1989), 44–45.

[21]James H. Svara, *Official Leadership in the City: Patterns of Conflict and Cooperation* (New York: Oxford University Press, 1990).

[22]James H. Svara, "The Shifting Boundary between Elected Officials and City Managers in Large Council-Manager Cities," *Public Administration Review* 59, no. 1 (1999): 44–53.

[23]Practitioners point out that the blurring of lines is due not only to city managers' actions, but also to mayors and council members with a tendency toward micromanaging.

[24]Ruth DeHoog and Gordon P. Whitaker, "Political Conflict or Professional Advancement: Alternative Explanations of City Manager Turnover," *Journal of Urban Affairs* 12, no. 4 (1990): 361–377.

[25]Marie Montgomery, "Time to Move On, Popular Manager Says," *Public Management* 70 (April 1988): 25.

[26]Renner, "Local Government Management Profession," 39–40.

[27]James B. Kaatz, P. Edward French, and Hazel Prentiss-Cooper, "City Council Conflict as a Cause of Psychological Burnout and Voluntary Turnover among City Managers," *State and Local Government Review* 31 (Fall 1999): 162, 168.

[28]Feiock and Stream, "Explaining the Tenure," 124–125.

[29]Feiock et al., "Politics, Administration, and Manager Turnover," 10.

[30]Richard C. Feiock and Christopher Stream, "Local Government Structure, Council Change, and City Manager Turnover," in *The Future of Local Government Administration: The Hansell Symposium,* ed. H. George Frederickson and John Nalbandian (Washington, D.C.: ICMA, 2002), 121–122.

[31]Barbara C. McCabe et al., "Turnover among City Managers: The Role of Political and Economic Change," *Public Administration Review* 68, no. 2 (2008): 380–386.

[32]George L. Hanbury, Alka Sapat, and Charles W. Washington, "Know Yourself and Take Charge of Your Own Destiny: The 'Fit Model' of Leadership," *Public Administration Review* 64, no. 5 (2004): 568–569.

[33]Ibid., 572.

[34]Robert W. Kweit and Mary G. Kweit, *People and Politics in Urban America,* 2nd ed. (New York: Garland Publishing, 1999), 176–181.

[35]Amy Bridges, *Morning Glories: Municipal Reform in the Southwest* (Princeton, N.J.: Princeton University Press, 1997).

[36]Floyd Hunter, *Community Power Structure* (Chapel Hill: University of North Carolina Press, 1953), 102.

[37]Desmond King and Helen Margetts, "Rational Choice and Community Power Structures," *Political Studies* 43 (1995): 265–277; G. William Domhoff, *Who Rules America? Power and Politics in the Year 2000,* 3rd ed. (Mountain View, Calif.: Mayfield, 1998).

[38]Harvey Molotch, "The City as a Growth Machine: Toward a Political Economy of Place," *American Journal of Sociology* 82 (September 1976): 309–332; John R. Logan and Harvey Molotch, *Urban Fortunes: The Political Economy of Place* (Berkeley: California University Press, 1987).

[39]G. William Domhoff, "The Growth Machine and the Power Elite," in *Community Power: Directions for Future Research,* ed. Robert J. Waste (Beverly Hills, Calif.: Sage, 1986), 53–75.

[40]Peter Dreier, John Mollenkopf, and Todd Swanstrom, *Place Matters: Metropolitics for the Twenty-first Century* (Lawrence: University Press of Kansas, 2001), 164–171.

[41]Stephen L. Elkin, *City and Regime in the American Republic* (Chicago: Chicago University Press, 1987); Clarence N. Stone, *Regime Politics: Governing Atlanta 1946–1988* (Lawrence: University Press of Kansas, 1989); Larry Keating, *Atlanta: Race, Class and Urban Expansion* (Philadelphia: Temple University Press, 2001); Karen Mossberger and Gerry Stoker, "The Evolution of Urban Regime Theory: The Challenge of Conceptualization," *Urban Affairs Review* 36 (July 2001): 810–835; Clarence N. Stone, "Looking Back to Look Forward: Reflections on Urban Regime Analysis," *Urban Affairs Review* 40 (January 2005): 309–341.

[42]Keating, *Atlanta: Race, Class and Urban Expansion.*

[43]Robert A. Dahl, *Who Governs? Democracy and Power in an American City* (New Haven, Conn.: Yale University Press, 1961); Nelson W. Polsby, *Community Power and Political Theory,* 2nd ed. (New Haven, Conn.: Yale University Press, 1980); David Judge, "Pluralism," in *Theories of Urban Politics,* ed. David Judge, Gerry Stoker, and Harold Wolman (Thousand Oaks, Calif.: Sage, 1995), 13–34.

[44]Community power studies, especially on elite theory, have been criticized for their methodologies. Critics have charged that the research method chosen will lead to certain findings (see Robert Presthus, *Men at the Top: A Study in Community Power* [New York: Oxford University Press, 1964], 3–31). This study does not resolve the dispute; instead, it uses elitism and pluralism as possible patterns of community power.

[45]Frederick M. Wirth, *Power in the City: Decision-Making in San Francisco* (Berkeley: University of California Press, 1974); Douglas Yates, *The Ungovernable City: The Politics of Urban Problems and Policy Making* (Cambridge: MIT Press, 1978); Robert J. Waste, ed., *Community Power: Directions for Future Research* (Beverly Hills, Calif.: Sage, 1986).

[46]Heinz Eulau, "From Labyrinths to Networks: Political Representation in Urban Settings," in *Community Power: Directions for Future Research,* ed. Robert J. Waste (Beverly Hills, Calif.: Sage, 1986), 139–175.

[47]H. George Frederickson, "The Repositioning of American Public Administration," *PS: Political Science & Politics* 32 (December 1999): 701–711.

[48]Mark Considine and Jenny M. Lewis, "Governance at Ground Level: The Frontline Bureaucrat in the Age of Markets and Networks," *Public Administration Review* 59, no. 6 (1999): 467–481; Stephen Goldsmith and William D. Eggers, *Governing by Network: The New Shape of the Public*

Sector (Washington, D.C.: Brookings Institution Press, 2004); Siegrun F. Freyss, "Local Government Operations and Human Resource Policies: Trends and Transformations," in *The Municipal Year Book 2004* (Washington, D.C.: ICMA, 2004), 19.

[49]Longtime observers of local politics fear that elected officials are less and less able to exercise effective policy guidance—not only due to increased complexity, but also due to changes in the type of person willing to run for public office.

[50]Karen S. Christensen, *Cities and Complexity: Making Intergovernmental Decisions* (Thousand Oaks, Calif.: Sage, 1999).

[51]Gordon P. Whitakerand Ruth H. DeHoog, "City Managers under Fire: How Conflict Leads to Turnover," in *Ideal and Practice in Council-Manager Government*, 2nd ed., ed. H. George Frederickson (Washington, D.C.: ICMA, 1995), 142–156.

[52]Ammons and Newell, *Leadership Roles*, 10; Michael Vasu, Debra W. Stewart, and G. David Garson, *Organizational Behavior and Public Management*, 3rd ed. (New York: Marcel Dekker, 1998), 92.

[53]Anthony Downs, *Inside Bureaucracy* (Boston: Little, Brown, 1967).

[54]James H. Svara, "The Politics-Administration Dichotomy Model as Aberration," *Public Administration Review* 58, no. 1 (1998): 55.

[55]Ibid., 56. The latest code, revised in 2004, does not refer to city managers in particular and instead talks about "professional local government management": see the ICMA Code of Ethics with Guidelines at icma.org/main/.

[56]Bollens and Ries, *City Manager Profession*, 20.

[57]John Nalbandian, "Politics, Administration, and the City Manager," in *Ideal and Practice in Council-Manager Government* (see note 51), 84–94.

[58]Dahl, *Who Governs?*

[59]Craig M. Wheeland, "Identity and Excellence: Role Models for City Managers," *Administration & Society* 26 (November 1994): 291; Carl H. Neu, "The Manager as Coach: Increasing the Effectiveness of Elected Officials," *IQ Report* 35 (October 2003): 3–15.

[60]Robert B. Denhardt and Barry R. Hammond, *Public Administration in Action: Readings, Profiles, and Cases* (Pacific Grove, Calif.: Brooks/Cole, 1992), 142; David R. Morgan and Sheilah S. Watson, "Policy Leadership in Council-Manager Cities: Comparing Mayor and Manager," in *Ideal and Practice in Council-Manager Government* (see note 51), 76.

[61]Keith F. Mulrooney, "Prologue: Can City Managers Deal Effectively with Major Social Problems?" *Public Administration Review* 31, no. 1 (1971): 12; Charles T. Henry, "Urban Manager Roles in the 70's," *Public Administration Review* 31, no. 1 (1971): 25; Jeff S. Luke, "Finishing the Decade: Local Government to 1990," *State and Local Government Review* 18 (Fall 1986): 132–137; John Nalbandian, "Facilitating Community, Enabling Democracy: New Roles for Local Government Managers," *Public Administration Review* 59, no. 3 (1999): 187–197; Jane G. Kazman, *Working Together: A Guide for Elected and Appointed Officials* (Washington, D.C.: ICMA, 1999), 17.

[62]James H. Svara, "Policy and Administration: City Managers as Comprehensive Professional Leaders," in *Ideal and Practice in Council-Manager Government* (see note 51), 29–52.

[63]Camille C. Barnett, "What's a Nice Girl Like This Doing in a Business Like This," *PA Times* 17, no. 6 (1994): 9; Camille C. Barnett, "Barnett Outlines Urban Problems and Solutions," *PA Times* 17, no. 7 (1994): 13, 16. The degree of public attention depends to some extent on the media market in the region. Thus, according to Matthew Kridler, city manager of Springfield, Ohio, if the city is the center of a radio, TV, or newspaper market, reporters may call regularly, so the city needs a media-savvy spokesperson: see Matthew J. Kridler, "Response," in *The Future of Local Government Administration* (see note 30), 124–129.

[64]Mark H. Moore, *Creating Public Value: Strategic Management in Government* (Cambridge: Harvard University Press, 1995), 17, 20.

[65]For managers in transition to a new job, city manager Bill Kirchhoff adds a fourth and fifth management dimension—past workplace and the media, at both the old city and the new one. See William Kirchhoff, *Hitting the Beach! A Survival Handbook for the Job-Changing Public Manager* (Washington, D.C.: ICMA, 1994).

[66]Some observers suggest that candidates look at the leadership style of the previous city manager—and avoid it, since council members often seek a fresh face and a new start.

[67]All populations cited are from the Census Bureau's July 2007 estimates, census.gov/popest/estimates.php.

[68]Richard Marosi and Monte Morin, "Robles Is Fired in South Gate," *Los Angeles Times,* June 11, 2003, B1, articles.latimes.com/2003/jun/11/local/me-sogate11 (accessed September 30, 2008).

[69]Kevin Pang, "Ex-Compton Officials Are Sentenced," *Los Angeles Times,* May 15, 2004, B3, articles.latimes.com/2004/may/15/local/me-compton15 (accessed September 30, 2008).

[70]Wendy L. Hassett and Douglas J. Watson, "Long-Serving City Managers: Practical Application of the Academic Literature," *Public Administration Review* 62, no. 5 (2002): 624.

[71]Data available from factfinder.census.gov/home/saff/main.html?_lang=en.

[72]Web site of the city of Plano, Texas, plano.gov/City_Hall/CityGovernment/council/ (accessed October 5, 2008).

[73]Bollens and Ries, *City Manager Profession*, 36.

[74]Roger Fisher and William Ury, *Getting to Yes: Negotiating Agreement without Giving In*, 2nd ed. (New York: Penguin Books, 1991), 40–55.

[75]Jason Kosareff, "Rosemead City Manager Steps Down," *Pasadena Star-News*, January 31, 2006.

[76]David Lias, "Wal-Mart Given Green Light," *Plain Talk,* November 19, 2004.

[77]Randy Dockendorf, "New City Manager Charts Course in Vermillion," *Press & Dakotan*, March 18, 2005; repr. in *Public Management* 87 (July 2005): 31.

[78]Imran Ghori, "His Frugal Policy Yields Success in Highland," *Public Management* 83 (June 2001): 22.

[79]Edward C. Banfield, *Political Influence* (New York: Free Press, 1961), as cited in Clarence N. Stone, "Paradigms, Power, and Urban Leadership," in *Leadership and Politics: New Perspectives in Political Science*, ed. Bryan D. Jones (Lawrence: University Press of Kansas, 1989), 136.

[80]Patrick McGreevy and Michael Finnegan, "Villaraigosa Sets a Style: 'Hands-On,' " *Los Angeles Times*, June 28, 2005, B1, B6, articles.latimes.com/2005/jun/28/local/me-govern28 (accessed September 30, 2008).

[81]Neu, *The Manager as Coach*.

[82]Mulrooney, "Prologue," 6.

[83]Robert T. Golembiewski and Gerald Gabris, "Today's City Managers: A Legacy of Success-Becoming-Failure," *Public Administration Review* 54, no. 6 (1994): 525–531.

[84]Murray Edelman, *The Symbolic Uses of Politics* (Urbana: University of Illinois Press, 1964).

[85]Wayne F. Anderson, Chester A. Newland, and Richard R. Stillman II, *The Effective Local Government Manager* (Washington, D.C.: ICMA, 1983), 68; see also Robert T. Golembiewski and Gerald Gabris, "Tomorrow's City Management: Guides for Avoiding Success-Becoming-Failure," *Public Administration Review* 55, no. 3 (1995): 241.

[86]Emily Ramshaw, "Ascent to City Manager a Bumpy Ride," *Dallas Morning News,* February 6, 2006, 1.

[87]Robert D. Behn, "What Right Do Public Managers Have to Lead?" *Public Administration Review* 58, no. 3 (1998): 218.

[88]Peter M. Senge, *The Fifth Discipline: The Art and Practice of the Learning Organization* (London: Century Business, 1993), 14.

[89]Fred Rhynhart, "The City Manager: Public Trust Overrides Entrepreneurship," *PA Times* 16, no. 10 (1993): 8.

[90]Larry D. Terry, *Leadership of Public Bureaucracies*, 2nd ed. (Thousand Oaks, Calif.: Sage, 2002). Some experienced city managers see the roles of community builder, educator, etc., that are matched with hyperpluralistic conditions as too optimistic. In their view, to survive in a dysfunctional or toxic jurisdiction, city managers are inclined to become defensive: they "duck and cover" and become caretakers.

[91]Poul E. Mouritzen and James H. Svara, eds., *Leadership at the Apex: Politicians and Administrators in Western Local Governments* (Pittsburgh, Pa.: University of Pittsburgh Press, 2002).

[92]Goldsmith and Eggers, *Governing by Network*, 89.

[93]As discussed in Jack W. Meek, Keith Schildt, and Matthew Witt, "Local Government Administration in a Metropolitan Context," in *The Future of Local Government Administration* (see note 30), 145, network governance can go hand-in-hand with hyperpluralism or weak council leadership, in that networks of professionals may continue to do their work despite political turmoil and lack of policy direction from the top. We may see a politics/administration dichotomy in reality, even though it has been declared a myth in theory.

[94]"Durham's Community-Wide Efforts to Combat Gangs" (September 2005), durhamnc.gov/departments/manager/pdf/durham_combats_gangs_0905.pdf (accessed October 5, 2008).

[95]William H. Hansell, "Professionalism in Local Government Administration," in *The Future of Local Government Administration* (see note 30), 190.

[96]Kazman, *Working Together*, 1.

[97]William J. Pammer et al., "Managing Conflict and Building Cooperation in Council-Manager Cities: Insights on Establishing a Resolution Framework," *State and Local Government Review* 31, no. 3 (1999): 202–213, cviog.uga.edu/slgr/1999/3e.pdf (accessed October 25, 2008).

Cooperative Competition: Alternative Service Delivery, 2002–2007

Mildred E. Warner
Department of City and Regional Planning
Cornell University

Amir Hefetz
Faculty of Architecture and Town Planning
Technion–Israel Institute of Technology

Selected Findings

Intergovernmental contracting at 20% is the most common form of contracting reported in 2007, up from 17% in 2002.

Lack of competition has been a consistent problem for local governments, and it is getting worse: problems with an inadequate supply of competent private deliverers has grown from 25% in 1992 to 31% in 2007.

There is a lagged effect of monitoring rising after contracting has fallen and dropping when contracting rates go up, which suggests that managers need to couple contracting with effective monitoring; without adequate and consistent monitoring, contracting levels are unstable.

ICMA has been tracking local government use of alternative service delivery mechanisms since 1982. The 1997 survey showed a peak in for-profit contracting at 18% of service delivery; in the 2002 survey, however, contracting dropped and public delivery—either direct or mixed—rose. This reversal from contracting to more public forms of delivery reflected continuing government reform. It was not a return to the public bureaucracies of old but, rather, an effort to balance the benefits of markets with the need for citizen engagement and professional planning to ensure that public service delivery is efficient, equitable, and responsive to citizen concerns.[1]

Over the past decade, local governments have contracted out and back in as part of a continuing process of experimentation aimed at improving service delivery. Practice varies widely across jurisdictions as pragmatic government managers mix public delivery and contracting to address differences in citizen preference, local government expertise, and the level of competition and competence found in private markets at the local and metropolitan levels.

ICMA's surveys on alternative service delivery (ASD), conducted every five years since 1982, have enabled us to track this process of innovation and experimentation.[2] Data from the 2007 survey reveal that use of both direct public delivery and mixed public-private delivery has essentially fallen back to 1997 levels, while use of for-profit privatization and nonprofit contracting has held steady since 2002.[3] What *has* grown over the 2002–2007 period is intergovernmental contracting—from 17% to 20%. Intergovernmental contracting and for-profit contracting have always been the two most common alternative forms of service delivery measured by ICMA. But since 1997, for-profit contracting has typically been one or two percentage points higher than intergovernmental contracting. As revealed in findings from the 2007 survey, that is no longer the case.

ICMA would like to thank the Reason Foundation for its generous support for conducting the *2007 Alternative Service Delivery* survey.

What is intergovernmental contracting as compared to private contracting? Intergovernmental contracting represents a public market of cooperating governments—a form of "cooperative competition" in which governments join with their neighbors to achieve efficiency gains.[4] In contrast to the private market of competition between public and private suppliers, cooperative competition among governments offers many of the benefits of markets without the risks of losing control or ending up with a private monopoly. Both for-profit contracting and intermunicipal cooperation have been shown to achieve efficiency gains through economies of scale, but the public market of cooperative competition is more likely to give attention to service equity across the metropolitan region and to protect citizen interests.[5] Under intergovernmental contracting, public accountability procedures and open government rules apply, elected officials retain direct control over services, and the service remains public.

Citizens like local government because they like local control. This is why political consolidation has sparked so little interest over the years. And yet our fragmented local government system cries out for some form of regional integration. The 2007 survey results suggest that local government managers, having learned from their experience with for-profit and mixed contracting, are now using intergovernmental contracting as the preferred contracting alternative. Cooperative competition among neighboring governments promotes regional service integration while allowing participants to maintain local control. These are priority concerns of U.S. cities as they attempt to modernize service delivery to meet the demands of a more competitive economic system that requires a dynamic and coordinated metropolitan region.

But the 2007 survey also indicates problems on the horizon. While contracting is flat, monitoring is down. Lack of sufficient competition remains a problem, and monitoring service quality and citizen satisfaction are receiving less attention than they did in 2002. Over the last decade of ICMA ASD surveys, we have seen that monitoring typically lags behind contracting. When this happens, contracts are more likely to fail, and reductions in

contracting levels follow. Markets are not self-regulating; this is especially true of public service markets, where competition is low. Even in intergovernmental contracting, contracting and monitoring must go hand in hand. So while the 2007 ASD survey shows an important increase in use of cooperative contracting, it also reveals a continued need to give more attention to monitoring.

SURVEY RESPONSE AND METHODOLOGY

The 2007 ASD survey was sent to 6,095 cities and counties across the United States in the fall of 2007. Follow-up reminders were sent in late fall 2007 and again in January 2008. The survey was sent to the chief administrative officers in all cities with a population over 10,000 and all counties with a population of 25,000 and over. In addition, a random sample was drawn from one in four municipalities with a population of 2,500–9,999—for the 2007 survey, ICMA increased its sampled population by 725 localities, primarily among municipalities in the under-10,000 population group—and from one in four counties in the 2,500–24,999 population group.

Responses were received from 1,599 municipalities for an overall response rate of 26%. Although this total includes 316 more responses than were received in the 2002 survey, it reflects less representation from jurisdictions over 250,000 in population (66 in 2007 compared with 81 in 2002), and more representation from mid-sized cities (100,000–249,999) and small communities (under 5,000). As in 2002, suburban places continue to represent more than half of the sample, and independent (rural) localities represent a larger proportion than central (core metro) cities (see Table 2/1).[6]

In 2002 the ASD survey was conducted solely as a Web-based survey, and the number responding fell to 1,283. In 2007 the survey was conducted as a paper survey again, and the number responding rose to 1,599. As this is a very complex survey, covering 67 services and the factors motivating alternative delivery, ICMA researchers have found that public managers benefit from a paper copy,

Table 2/1 SURVEY RESPONSE RATE

Classification	2002 Response rate, %	2007 No. surveyed (A)	No. responding	% of (A)
All	24	6,095	1,599	26
Cities[1]	27	4,241	1,244	29
Counties[1]	18	1,854	355	19
Population group				
Over 1,000,000	40	37	9	24
500,000–1,000,000	24	86	18	21
250,000–499,999	31	146	39	27
100,000–249,999	29	454	157	35
50,000–99,999	23	793	190	24
25,000–49,999	22	1,420	350	25
10,000–24,999	24	2,032	525	26
5,000–9,999	24	599	156	26
2,500–4,999	20	528	155	29
Geographic division				
New England.	17	485	111	23
Mid-Atlantic	15	849	153	18
East North-Central	25	1,181	327	28
West North-Central	24	613	190	31
South Atlantic	32	875	287	33
East South-Central	12	459	63	14
West South-Central. . . .	21	654	141	22
Mountain	30	349	114	33
Pacific Coast	34	630	213	34
Metro status				
Central	28	993	274	28
Suburban	25	2,932	841	29
Independent	20	2,170	484	22

[1]For a definition of terms, please see "Inside the *Year Book,*" x.

which may be filled out over a series of days after they have had an opportunity to check with the relevant departments for details on each service.

As in the past, the response rate was higher among cities than counties. Responses were highest from the Pacific Coast, Mountain, South Atlantic, and West North-Central divisions, and lowest from the East South-Central and Mid-Atlantic divisions (Table 2/1).

LOCAL GOVERNMENT PROVISION AND DELIVERY OF SERVICES

The ASD survey asks local government managers how services are currently provided in their jurisdictions. First, it presents a list of 67 services, and for each service respondents are asked whether it is provided by the government, has never been provided by the government, or has been shed. Respondents are then asked whether public employees are used in delivery of the service and, if so, whether they are used entirely or only in part (mixed public-private delivery). Finally, for each service, the survey asks about the use of six different alternative forms of service delivery: intergovernmental contracting, private for-profit contracting, private nonprofit contracting, franchises, subsidies, and volunteers.

The survey also asks a series of questions about whether the local government has explored the option of alternative service delivery within the past five years, who was involved in evaluating the option, and whether steps have been taken to ensure success in implementing private service delivery. This year, two new questions were added to the survey: local governments that use intergovernmental contracting were asked to identify both the motivators for and the obstacles to using

this delivery approach; these questions provided a basis for comparison with the motivators for and obstacles to private contracting.

Most governments do not provide all 67 services listed by ICMA; on average, the typical government provides about half of these services. Of those who provide the services, not all respondents indicated *how* they provide the services—that is, how the services are delivered. ICMA treats the data on service provision separately from the data on service delivery. For each percentage reported in the three service delivery tables that follow (Tables 2/2, 2/3, and 2/4), the base is the number of governments reporting how they deliver the service, irrespective of whether they themselves provide it; in other words, in each case the relevant base is the number of respondents who checked at least one option about how the service is delivered. This number, which varies for each service, is presented in the first two columns of Table 2/2.

All percentages for specific factor questions or services are based on the number of respondents to that particular survey question (as shown), not on the entire sample. Thus, any comparison between services delivered and factors involved should be treated carefully because the base number reporting is different in each case.

Public Delivery Drops Slightly but Remains the Most Common Delivery Mode

On average, local governments in the 2007 ICMA sample reported providing 34 of the 67 services measured. Service provision had been shrinking among local governments from 1992, but from 2002 to 2007 it was stable (the average number of services provided actually rose from 33 to 34) (not shown). Most services show decreases in provision. Those services where provision dropped by more than 10% are tree trimming, inspection, crime

prevention, vehicle towing, recreation facilities, parks landscaping/maintenance, building maintenance and security, fleet maintenance, payroll, data processing, secretarial services, personnel services, and public relations (not shown). A smaller number of services show increases in provision; those with the largest increases (close to 10 percentage points) are operation and management of electric and gas utilities, day care facilities, hospitals, and homeless shelters, and these services are the ones more likely to be contracted out (not shown).

Direct public delivery remains the most common form of local government service delivery. The ICMA ASD survey identifies two forms of public service delivery: public employees entirely or public employees in part. Overall, the level of service delivery with public employees entirely fell from 52% in 2002 to 47% in 2007 (Table 2/2). The 2007 level is similar to that found in 1997. The highest levels of direct public provision (over 80%) are found in support functions (payroll, secretarial services, personnel services, and public relations), as well as in crime prevention, traffic control, and inspection; 65% or more of responding governments use public employees entirely for public works (street cleaning, snow plowing, water distribution and treatment, parking meters), public utility meter reading and billing, fire prevention, police/fire communications, recreation facilities, building security, and data processing. The lowest use of public employees entirely (below 35%) is found in solid-waste collection and disposal, transit and paratransit, hazardous materials disposal, operation and management of utilities, vehicle towing, most functions of health and human services, cultural and art programs, museums, and legal services.

In contrast to the 1997–2002 period, when public delivery increased, there were no significant increases in the use of public employees entirely from 2002 to 2007; however, there were significant decreases in use (by 10 percentage points or more) over that period in the areas of commercial and residential solid-waste collection, parking meters, operation and management of utilities, health and human services (insect control, animal shelters, day care facilities, hospitals, prisons, job training programs, and welfare programs), tax assessing and bill processing, and title records (Table 2/2). These are many of the same areas that had the highest increases in direct delivery in 2002.[7] As shown in Table 2/3, most of these services have gone to intergovernmental contracting; only waste collection, utilities, day care facilities, and hospitals show large increases in for-profit contracting. These trends reflect a continuing process of experimentation between direct public delivery and various alternatives over time.

Delivery with public employees in part involves a mix of both public and private production. Mixed public-private delivery is used to benchmark costs and production processes, to create competition, and to ensure citizen satisfaction with the service delivery process.[8] Mixed delivery showed the largest increase (6 percentage points) from 1997 to 2002 as complete contracting dropped, but for the 2002–2007 period, the level of mixed delivery dropped from its peak of 23% in 2002 back to 17% in 2007 (the level in 1997)[9] (Table 2/2). This up-and-down trend in mixed delivery mirrors the up-and-down trend in direct public delivery described

Table 2/2   USE OF DIRECT PUBLIC DELIVERY BY PUBLIC EMPLOYEES ENTIRELY OR IN PART, 2002–2007

Service	No. reporting 2002	No. reporting 2007	Public employees entirely 2002, %	2007, %	Percentage point change	Public employees in part 2002, %	2007, %	Percentage point change
Average[1]	596	779	52.0	47.2	−4.7	23.1	16.7	−6.4
Public works/transportation								
Residential solid-waste collection	620	932	44.5	33.9	−10.6	10.5	6.4	−4.0
Commercial solid-waste collection	408	699	33.3	22.2	−11.1	18.1	10.4	−7.7
Solid-waste disposal	504	851	32.7	25.9	−6.8	17.7	9.0	−8.7
Street repair	971	1,180	41.7	38.7	−3.0	52.9	51.5	−1.4
Street/parking lot cleaning	787	1,035	70.9	67.0	−3.9	18.8	18.6	−0.2
Snow plowing/sanding	739	917	75.2	74.2	−1.0	21.9	20.1	−1.8
Traffic sign/sign installation/maintenance	864	1,070	43.4	46.8	3.4	41.2	35.1	−6.1
Parking meter maintenance/collection	229	279	79.5	69.5	−10.0	14.8	11.5	−3.3
Tree trimming/planting on public rights-of-way	904	1,066	39.6	40.0	0.4	49.4	46.8	−2.6
Maintenance/administration of cemeteries	384	513	67.7	62.0	−5.7	21.6	17.2	−4.4
Inspection/code enforcement	981	1,146	82.3	81.8	−0.5	15.2	13.2	−2.0
Operation of parking lots/garages	379	454	65.4	63.7	−1.7	22.2	17.2	−5.0
Operation/maintenance of bus transit system	258	403	30.2	24.1	−6.1	21.3	9.2	−12.1
Operation/maintenance of paratransit system	240	366	30.4	21.6	−8.8	21.3	10.4	−10.9
Operation of airports	302	422	42.4	38.6	−3.8	28.5	20.4	−8.1
Water distribution	694	908	75.9	72.5	−3.4	14.3	9.1	−5.2
Water treatment	619	851	71.4	64.6	−6.8	12.3	7.4	−4.9
Sewage collection/treatment	743	942	60.8	58.1	−2.7	22.5	16.5	−6.0
Disposal of sludge	559	782	42.0	36.7	−5.3	19.3	13.9	−5.4
Disposal of hazardous materials	399	615	22.8	16.1	−6.7	31.6	20.7	−10.9
Public utilities								
Operation/management: electric	172	387	48.3	27.6	−20.7	8.7	3.9	−4.8
Operation/management: gas	113	315	28.3	14.6	−13.7	6.2	1.3	−4.9
Meter reading	593	794	77.6	68.8	−8.8	9.4	8.2	−1.2
Billing	637	818	76.1	69.6	−6.5	13.3	10.6	−2.7
Public safety								
Crime prevention/patrol	1,001	1,206	85.6	88.0	2.4	9.4	6.1	−3.3
Police/fire communications	925	1,157	69.1	66.5	−2.6	18.3	13.4	−4.9
Fire prevention/suppression	821	1,044	74.4	71.6	−2.8	12.3	8.5	−3.8
Emergency medical service	724	940	52.2	48.9	−3.3	28.5	18.6	−9.9
Ambulance service	575	860	45.9	40.5	−5.4	19.8	11.0	−8.8
Traffic control/parking enforcement	854	1,028	85.4	83.5	−1.9	9.8	8.0	−1.8
Vehicle towing and storage	473	422	7.2	12.3	5.1	13.3	13.3	0.0
Health and human services								
Sanitary inspection	520	731	59.0	56.8	−2.2	17.7	9.7	−8.0
Insect/rodent control	409	597	45.0	34.8	−10.2	27.1	14.6	−12.5
Animal control	809	1,022	63.4	57.9	−5.5	14.6	12.1	−2.5
Operation of animal shelters	508	772	44.5	33.5	−11.0	15.0	8.8	−6.2
Operation of day care facilities	124	320	29.0	13.8	−15.3	29.8	9.4	−20.4
Child welfare programs	248	411	28.2	21.2	−7.0	34.7	14.8	−19.9
Programs for the elderly	614	799	27.5	23.9	−3.6	51.3	42.4	−8.9
Operation/management of hospitals	67	253	14.9	2.8	−12.1	14.9	2.4	−12.5
Public health programs	350	512	30.9	24.6	−6.3	36.6	21.3	−15.3
Drug and alcohol treatment programs	256	395	9.4	7.1	−2.3	37.1	21.0	−16.1
Operation of mental health/mental retardation programs/facilities	201	369	14.9	6.8	−8.1	30.3	16.3	−14.0
Prisons/jails	457	648	61.3	48.0	−13.3	19.5	12.8	−6.7
Operation of homeless shelters	124	288	6.5	2.8	−3.7	16.1	5.9	−10.2
Workforce development/job training programs	261	409	18.8	9.0	−9.8	37.2	21.3	−15.9
Intake/eligibility determination for welfare programs	219	388	49.3	30.2	−19.1	19.2	7.7	−11.5
Parks and recreation								
Operation/maintenance of recreation facilities	940	1,130	70.0	72.7	2.7	26.4	22.2	−4.2
Parks landscaping/maintenance	949	1,141	66.3	67.7	1.4	27.7	25.2	−2.5
Operation of convention centers/auditoriums	274	381	54.7	50.7	−4.0	20.4	15.0	−5.4
Cultural and arts programs								
Operation of cultural and arts programs	417	567	23.7	26.6	2.9	49.2	34.2	−15.0
Operation of libraries	617	792	55.9	50.5	−5.4	13.1	9.3	−3.8
Operation of museums	290	433	24.8	23.8	−1.0	25.9	15.0	−10.9
Support functions								
Buildings/grounds maintenance	1,028	1,222	58.3	62.2	3.9	39.1	34.4	−4.7
Building security	799	958	70.8	70.1	−0.7	19.9	17.1	−2.8
Fleet management/vehicle maintenance:								
Heavy equipment	963	1,140	50.9	56.1	5.2	45.1	36.7	−8.4
Emergency vehicles	907	1,085	45.8	48.5	2.7	44.7	38.0	−6.7
All other vehicles	972	1,152	53.8	55.0	1.2	39.8	35.7	−4.1
Payroll	1,024	1,228	92.3	89.0	−3.3	5.8	7.4	1.6
Tax bill processing	674	903	66.8	56.1	−10.7	16.8	14.7	−2.1
Tax assessing	546	821	58.1	45.6	−12.5	13.6	11.7	−1.9
Data processing	938	1,090	74.0	74.6	0.6	22.8	19.7	−3.1
Collection of delinquent taxes	653	890	52.8	47.0	−5.8	23.3	18.7	−4.6
Title records/plat map maintenance	565	797	63.4	49.3	−14.1	21.4	18.4	−3.0
Legal services	838	1,042	31.9	31.0	−0.9	32.5	24.0	−8.5
Secretarial services	960	1,107	91.9	92.1	0.2	7.8	6.9	−0.9
Personnel services	982	898	88.0	88.5	0.5	10.8	10.6	−0.2
Public relations/public information	944	1,116	82.3	83.2	0.9	15.7	13.7	−2.0

[1]Averages are "by service" as the number of respondents differs for each service.

Table 2/3   USE OF ALTERNATIVE SERVICE DELIVERY, 2002–2007

Service	Another government or authority			Private for profit			Private nonprofit		
	2002, %	2007, %	Percentage point change	2002, %	2007, %	Percentage point change	2002, %	2007, %	Percentage point change
Average	16.5	19.9	3.4	18.0	17.8	−0.3	8.2	7.8	−0.4
Public works/transportation									
Residential solid-waste collection	3.5	5.0	1.5	39.4	47.4	8.1	0.6	1.5	0.9
Commercial solid-waste collection	3.9	4.9	1.0	43.1	56.2	13.1	0.2	1.7	1.5
Solid-waste disposal	18.1	20.7	2.6	38.1	42.7	4.6	1.4	1.8	0.4
Street repair	6.8	6.7	−0.1	35.3	30.6	−4.7	0.6	0.7	0.1
Street/parking lot cleaning	3.4	5.1	1.7	18.3	16.0	−2.3	0.9	0.7	−0.2
Snow plowing/sanding	6.2	7.2	1.0	12.6	9.6	−3.0	0.1	0.3	0.2
Traffic sign/sign installation/maintenance	17.5	16.4	−1.1	27.1	21.3	−5.8	0.2	0.4	0.2
Parking meter maintenance/collection	3.5	11.1	7.6	9.6	10.4	0.8	0.0	0.7	0.7
Tree trimming/planting on public rights-of-way	5.5	5.0	−0.5	38.3	32.5	−5.8	2.7	1.7	−1.0
Maintenance/administration of cemeteries	3.4	6.4	3.0	12.2	13.5	1.3	4.4	6.4	2.0
Inspection/code enforcement	5.4	5.0	−0.4	7.2	7.7	0.5	0.2	0.1	−0.1
Operation of parking lots/garages	4.2	8.6	4.4	20.6	18.5	−2.1	2.1	2.6	0.5
Operation/maintenance of bus transit system	34.5	39.7	5.2	20.9	18.6	−2.3	11.2	11.9	0.7
Operation/maintenance of paratransit system	32.1	36.6	4.5	19.2	18.0	−1.2	15.8	18.0	2.2
Operation of airports	25.8	33.9	8.1	20.5	13.0	−7.5	1.3	2.6	1.3
Water distribution	14.1	15.7	1.6	7.2	5.7	−1.5	0.4	1.7	1.3
Water treatment	17.9	24.2	6.3	6.3	5.5	−0.8	0.6	1.5	0.9
Sewage collection/treatment	25.7	27.1	1.4	8.3	7.1	−1.2	0.4	1.4	1.0
Disposal of sludge	20.4	24.9	4.5	30.8	28.9	−1.9	1.1	2.0	0.9
Disposal of hazardous materials	28.1	37.6	9.5	38.3	31.7	−6.6	4.3	3.6	−0.7
Public utilities									
Operation/management: electric	16.3	12.9	−3.4	26.7	47.8	21.1	4.1	4.9	0.8
Operation/management: gas	14.2	9.8	−4.4	42.5	60.3	17.8	3.5	5.7	2.2
Meter reading	6.6	7.1	0.5	12.1	17.8	5.7	1.3	1.8	0.5
Billing	7.8	6.4	−1.4	12.4	16.1	3.7	1.4	2.4	1.0
Public safety									
Crime prevention/patrol	8.1	8.2	0.1	0.1	0.5	0.4	0.4	0.2	−0.2
Police/fire communications	24.3	24.8	0.5	0.2	1.1	0.9	0.8	1.6	0.8
Fire prevention/suppression	10.4	11.6	1.2	0.7	0.8	0.1	1.8	2.5	0.7
Emergency medical service	15.3	17.3	2.0	12.6	16.9	4.3	8.4	2.3	−6.1
Ambulance service	14.8	18.0	3.2	20.5	22.2	1.7	8.3	9.5	1.2
Traffic control/parking enforcement	7.3	8.3	1.0	1.3	4.0	2.7	0.2	0.5	0.3
Vehicle towing and storage	3.8	6.4	2.6	79.5	65.4	−14.1	1.5	5.5	4.0
Health and human services									
Sanitary inspection	31.2	32.4	1.2	3.5	4.5	1.0	0.0	1.2	1.2
Insect/rodent control	31.8	35.0	3.2	16.4	21.1	4.7	0.2	3.2	3.0
Animal control	17.7	23.0	5.3	5.8	5.0	−0.8	8.8	7.6	−1.2
Operation of animal shelters	21.1	30.4	9.3	6.7	8.7	2.0	21.7	22.2	0.5
Operation of day care facilities	10.5	13.4	2.9	37.9	53.8	15.9	34.7	32.8	−1.9
Child welfare programs	37.5	52.6	15.1	11.3	9.7	−1.6	25.0	14.8	−10.2
Programs for the elderly	26.2	27.3	1.1	7.3	7.4	0.1	30.6	28.5	−2.1
Operation/management of hospitals	43.3	31.6	−11.7	25.4	39.5	14.1	28.4	37.5	9.1
Public health programs	44.6	52.0	7.4	11.1	6.1	−5.0	19.4	13.1	−6.3
Drug and alcohol treatment programs	38.3	48.6	10.3	18.4	20.3	1.9	46.5	35.9	−10.6
Operation of mental health/mental retardation programs/facilities	45.3	57.5	12.2	19.4	14.4	−5.0	36.3	32.2	−4.1
Prisons/jails	32.4	43.7	11.3	1.8	1.7	−0.1	1.1	1.1	0.0
Operation of homeless shelters	22.6	37.2	14.6	4.8	4.5	−0.3	62.1	56.3	−5.9
Workforce development/job training programs	48.3	58.9	10.6	11.5	6.6	−4.9	31.0	24.7	−6.3
Intake/eligibility determination for welfare programs	37.9	59.3	21.4	2.3	1.8	−0.5	9.6	7.7	−1.9
Parks and recreation									
Operation/maintenance of recreation facilities	8.4	7.1	−1.3	8.7	7.6	−1.1	7.3	3.7	−3.6
Parks landscaping/maintenance	5.6	5.0	−0.6	18.1	15.1	−3.0	2.0	1.2	−0.8
Operation of convention centers/auditoriums	18.2	21.5	3.3	15.3	15.5	0.2	9.1	6.3	−2.8
Cultural and arts programs									
Operation of cultural and arts programs	13.4	12.9	−0.5	9.8	6.9	−2.9	44.6	35.3	−9.3
Operation of libraries	28.5	33.8	5.3	0.5	1.4	0.9	6.5	6.4	−0.1
Operation of museums	12.4	20.3	7.9	4.5	3.9	−0.6	35.2	38.3	3.1
Support functions									
Buildings/grounds maintenance	1.8	1.2	−0.6	30.4	21.3	−9.1	1.9	1.5	−0.4
Building security	2.5	1.4	−1.1	19.1	18.8	−0.3	1.0	0.7	−0.3
Fleet management/vehicle maintenance:									
Heavy equipment	1.6	1.7	0.1	37.2	26.0	−11.2	0.6	1.1	0.5
Emergency vehicles	3.7	4.1	0.4	39.9	29.5	−10.4	0.9	1.7	0.8
All other vehicles	1.3	1.7	0.4	36.0	26.5	−9.5	0.6	1.0	0.4
Payroll	0.5	0.7	0.2	5.5	7.1	1.6	0.1	0.2	0.1
Tax bill processing	23.3	29.1	5.8	7.4	7.9	0.5	0.3	0.7	0.4
Tax assessing	29.5	40.3	10.8	8.2	7.9	−0.3	0.2	0.9	0.7
Data processing	3.8	5.0	1.2	17.3	10.7	−6.6	0.4	0.6	0.2
Collection of delinquent taxes	24.8	29.2	4.4	17.9	14.7	−3.2	0.6	0.8	0.2
Title records/plat map maintenance	25.3	34.4	9.1	6.4	8.3	1.9	0.0	0.8	0.8
Legal services	2.6	4.6	2.0	55.7	51.9	−3.8	1.7	2.7	1.0
Secretarial services	0.2	0.7	0.5	5.3	4.0	−1.3	0.1	0.3	0.2
Personnel services	0.9	1.2	0.3	8.6	5.8	−2.8	0.3	0.7	0.4
Public relations/public information	1.0	1.0	0.0	11.9	8.8	−3.1	1.4	1.3	−0.1

above. The services with the highest levels of mixed provision (over 34%) also have high levels of contracting (street repair, traffic signs, tree trimming, programs for the elderly, buildings and grounds maintenance, fleet management, and cultural and arts programs). Mixed delivery decreased for practically all services, but decreases were especially high (by 10 percentage points or more) in transit and paratransit, disposal of hazardous materials, cultural and arts programs, museums, and most human services—services for which, except in the case of hospitals, intergovernmental contracting increased.

Alternative Delivery Modes: For-Profit and Nonprofit Delivery Are Flat, Intergovernmental Contracting Is Rising

Of the six alternative delivery mechanisms measured by ICMA, intergovernmental contracting, for-profit contracting, and nonprofit contracting are the most common. Intergovernmental contracting grew on average from 17% in 2002 to 20% in 2007 (Table 2/3). The highest levels of cooperation (30% or more) were found in transit and paratransit, airports, disposal of hazardous materials, libraries, tax assessing, title records, and all but three health and human services.

About 80% of the services show increases in intergovernmental contracting, the largest of which (by 10 percentage points or more) are in health and human services, especially welfare intake/eligibility, child welfare programs, and homeless shelters. Most of these increases come from the nonprofit sector, which suggests that the nonprofit sector has difficulty achieving economies of scale and that further increases in efficiency can be gained by shifting to intergovernmental contracting. The only significantly large percentage point drop was in the operation and management of hospitals—from 43% in 2002 to 32% in 2007. Hospital service delivery appears to be bifurcating into three alternatives: intergovernmental contracting (32%), for-profit contracting (40%), or nonprofit contracting (38%) (Table 2/3).

For-profit privatization—at 18% on average—is roughly the same as in 2002. The highest levels of for-profit privatization (at 25% or more) are in solid-waste collection and disposal, street repair, tree trimming, disposal of sludge and hazardous materials, operation and management of utilities, vehicle towing, day care facilities, hospitals, fleet maintenance, and legal services. In general, the largest percentage point drops and increases are also found in this set of services. For-profit privatization dropped more than 10 percentage points in vehicle towing and fleet maintenance, which is surprising because these two services seem to be obvious candidates for contracting. It may be that governments view vehicle towing as a money maker: direct public delivery of this service increased by 5 percentage points over the five-year period. Information asymmetry, which occurs when governments lack complete information on costs and quality in their contractors, can lead to higher costs in contracted vehicle maintenance than will be incurred by in-house maintenance, and this may explain the drop in private delivery. Indeed, some of the highest rates of mixed delivery are found in fleet maintenance. Mixed delivery gives governments more

information because they maintain involvement in direct service delivery.

Nonprofit privatization also appears relatively stable over this period. The overall average decreased slightly in 2007 but still hovered around 8% (Table 2/3). Most services show little change. The highest levels of nonprofit contracting (35% or more) are found in day care facilities, drug and alcohol treatment programs, mental health programs, homeless shelters, cultural and arts programs, and museums. Interestingly, the largest decreases in nonprofit delivery are also concentrated in health and human services—notably, in hospitals, drug and alcohol programs, and child welfare programs (as well as in cultural and arts programs). As previously noted, except for the operation and management of hospitals, these health and human services are among the ones for which intergovernmental contracting increased. It appears that intergovernmental contracting is used to gain economies of scale that the nonprofit sector cannot achieve on its own.

Franchises, subsidies, and volunteers are the least common alternative modes of service delivery—accounting for only about 2% of service delivery overall (not shown). Table 2/4 shows those services for which at least one of these three alternatives is responsible for more than 3% of delivery. Overall, franchises dropped by almost half (from 2.2% to 1.3% of service delivery) from 2002 to 2007 (not shown). Franchises are most common in residential and commercial solid-waste collection and disposal, and in the operation and management of electric and gas utilities, but rates have dropped in each of these areas since 2002. Subsidies are most common in paratransit, child welfare programs, programs for the elderly, drug and alcohol programs, mental health programs, homeless shelters, cultural and arts programs, and museums, but local government reliance on subsidies has dropped by at least one-third in each of these areas since 2002. Volunteers are most common in fire prevention, programs for the elderly, cultural and arts programs, and museums.

Table 2/4 **USE OF FRANCHISES, SUBSIDIES, AND VOLUNTEERS FOR DELIVERY OF SELECTED SERVICES, 2002–2007**

Service	Franchises, %		Subsidies, %		Volunteers, %	
	2002	2007	2002	2007	2002	2007
Public works/transportation						
Residential solid-waste collection	15.6	13.5	0.3	0.2	0.0	0.2
Commercial solid-waste collection	19.9	13.6	0.0	0.0	0.0	0.0
Solid-waste disposal	9.7	8.7	1.0	0.0	0.0	0.1
Tree trimming/planting on public rights-of-way	1.4	0.1	0.7	0.1	3.4	3.4
Maintenance/administration of cemeteries	0.5	0.2	0.8	0.6	3.9	3.5
Operation/maintenance of bus transit system	1.9	1.2	5.4	4.0	0.4	0.2
Operation/maintenance of paratransit system	1.7	1.6	7.1	4.9	0.4	0.8
Public utilities						
Operation/management: electric	11.0	9.6	0.0	0.8	0.0	0.0
Operation/management: gas	19.5	11.4	0.0	1.0	0.0	0.0
Public safety						
Fire prevention/suppression	0.2	0.1	0.9	0.5	12.9	13.0
Emergency medical service	1.5	1.0	1.0	0.9	10.1	8.4
Ambulance service	2.4	1.9	1.6	1.4	11.3	8.1
Vehicle towing and storage	6.1	3.1	0.4	0.2	0.2	0.0
Health and human services						
Operation of animal shelters	0.2	0.8	2.6	1.6	5.9	3.6
Operation of day care facilities	1.6	1.9	11.3	3.1	2.4	1.6
Child welfare programs	0.8	0.5	10.1	4.9	7.3	2.7
Programs for the elderly	0.8	0.5	8.1	5.1	17.1	11.4
Operation/management of hospitals	1.5	0.0	1.5	3.2	1.5	0.4
Public health programs	1.7	0.2	6.3	3.1	5.7	2.1
Drug and alcohol treatment programs	2.0	0.5	12.1	5.3	5.5	2.0
Operation of mental health/mental retardation programs/facilities	2.5	0.3	10.4	5.1	4.5	1.4
Operation of homeless shelters	3.2	0.0	15.3	7.6	8.9	4.5
Parks and recreation						
Operation/maintenance of recreation facilities	3.3	0.8	1.7	0.4	8.6	5.3
Parks landscaping/maintenance	0.8	0.2	0.4	0.1	5.5	3.8
Cultural and arts programs						
Operation of cultural and arts programs	0.7	1.1	12.5	7.8	26.9	20.6
Operation of libraries	0.2	0.5	3.7	3.4	8.4	7.7
Operation of museums	1.0	0.2	12.1	6.2	30.7	19.4

Note: Services shown are those with delivery levels above 3% for any one of these alternatives.

Historically, such citizen participation has been common and popular in services that support a strong sense of community. It averaged 3% across all services in 2002 but dropped to 2% overall in 2007 (not shown), with especially large drops in museums, cultural and arts programs, homeless shelters, and programs for the elderly. This drop in volunteerism could become more of a challenge as baby boomers age and public financing for the arts falters.

What the data for 2007 seem to show is some specialization in service delivery. Direct public delivery is still the most common delivery method for most services, and where it is declining, the shift is toward intergovernmental contracting, which appears to be the primary delivery approach for health and human services. Nonprofit delivery is still very important in health and human services as well as in cultural and arts programs, but where there are shifts, they again appear to be toward intergovernmental contracting. These shifts account for much of the growth in intergovernmental contracting in 2007. For-profit is the primary form of service delivery for solid-waste collection and disposal, gas and electric utilities, day care facilities, hospitals, legal services, and vehicle towing. However, except for solid-waste collection and disposal, utilities, hospitals, and day care facilities—services that have a long tradition of alternative private suppliers in the market—for-profit contracting is not growing. With the exception of hospitals, the experimentation with private delivery in other new service areas has not proved stable.

FACTORS BEHIND CHOICE OF SERVICE DELIVERY ALTERNATIVE

The ASD survey asks about a series of factors that relate to local government use of alternative service delivery. It first asks whether a government has studied the feasibility of adopting private service delivery; it then asks who was involved in the decision, what obstacles have been encountered, what activities have been undertaken to ensure that private delivery is being implemented successfully, and what techniques are being used to evaluate private delivery. From 2002 to 2007, the proportion of local governments that studied feasibility (58% vs. 50%) and that undertook activities to ensure success (44% vs. 38%) dropped, but the percentages of governments that systematically evaluate private service delivery (47% vs. 45%) and that have encountered obstacles (41% vs. 39%) have been relatively stable (Figures 2/1–2/4). These trends suggest that city managers have learned how to assess and manage contracts and no longer see alternative service delivery as "new."

Each question leads to a series of subquestions, which shed more light on managers' thinking. Regarding factors underlying privatization, the primary reason cited is still internal attempts to decrease costs (87%), followed by external fiscal pressures, including restrictions placed on raising taxes (50%) (Figure 2/1). This indicates that city managers still primarily see alternative service delivery as a way to reduce costs and fiscal pressures. The only significant changes from 2002 are that fewer governments report unsolicited proposals from potential service deliverers and fewer report an active citizen group favoring privatiza-

tion. This suggests that managers may be under less political pressure from either vendors or citizens to privatize.

Who Evaluates the Feasibility of Adopting Private Delivery Alternatives

A more pragmatic, managerial approach to alternative service delivery is reflected in who inside government is involved in the decision to pursue this option. Managers and department heads are involved in about 80% of the cases, whereas elected officials are involved in fewer than half, and their rate of involvement is dropping (Table 2/5). The involvement of attorneys is dropping as well, and line employees are the least likely to be involved (14%). Increasingly, evaluation of the feasibility of private service delivery is primarily the concern of managers, department heads, and accounting officers.

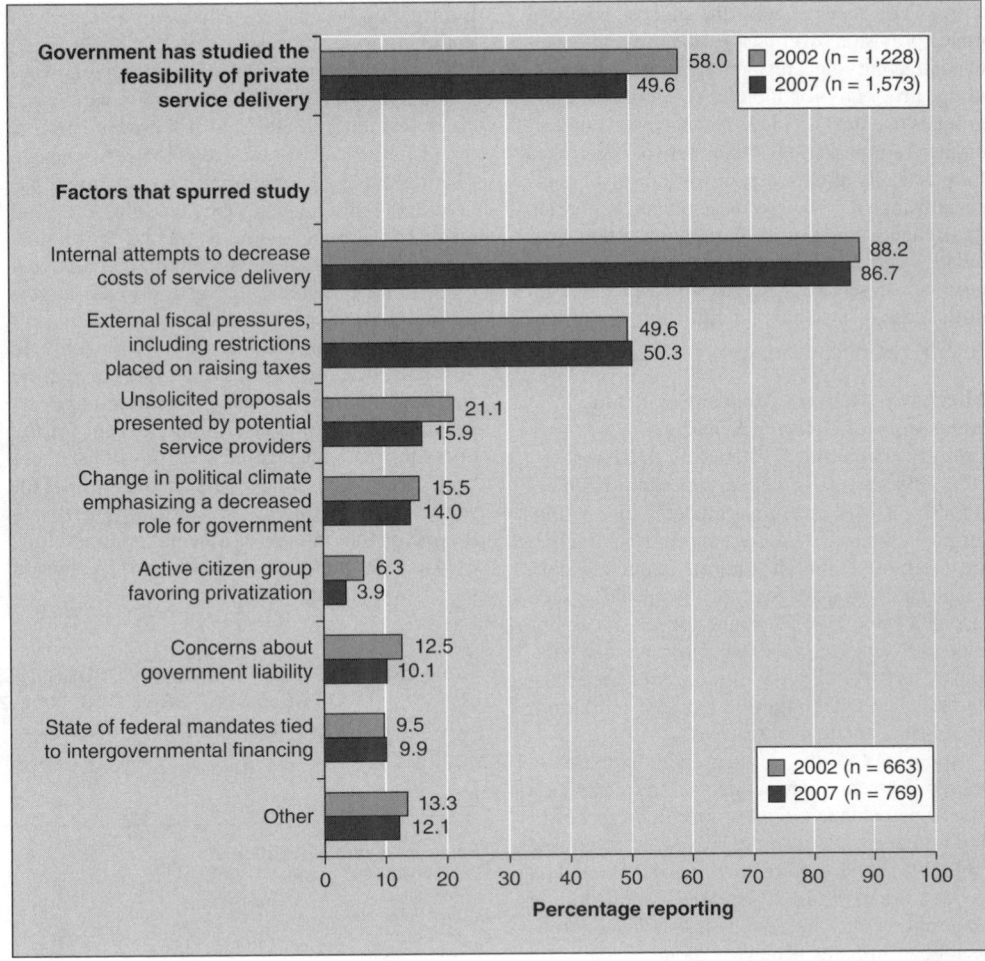

Figure 2/1 *Factors underlying study of the feasibility of private service delivery*

Table 2/5 INDIVIDUALS INVOLVED IN EVALUATING THE FEASIBILITY OF PRIVATE SERVICE DELIVERY

	2002	2007
Inside government	% (n = 622)	% (n = 778)
Manager/chief administrative officer (CAO)	86.9	87.0
Department heads	83.8	78.3
Finance/accounting officer	52.1	52.1
Elected officials	51.4	44.6
Assistant manager/CAO	39.9	38.0
Management and/or budget analysts	33.9	35.2
Attorney	36.3	30.5
Procurement/purchasing officer	21.4	18.9
Line employees	16.6	13.5
Other	4.3	2.1
Outside government	% (n = 645)	% (n = 612)
Potential service deliverers	53.6	61.6
Professionals/consultants with expertise in particular service areas	53.0	48.2
Managers/CAOs of other local governments who have experience using private service delivery	19.8	21.1
Citizen advisory committees	22.6	18.8
Service recipients/consumers	15.3	12.6
State agencies, leagues, or associations	9.8	8.5
Other	7.1	4.6

However, when we look at who *outside* government is involved in evaluating the feasibility of private service delivery, we see a significant increase since 2002 in the involvement of potential service deliverers (from 54% to 62%), while the role of professional consultants has dropped (from 53% to 48%) (Table 2/5). Some researchers have argued that alternative service delivery can increase the role for citizens in the service purchasing decision, but the findings from this survey do not support that conclusion. The involvement of both citizen advisory committees and service recipients is both small and dropping. Service delivery evaluation is mostly a professional activity among government managers, consultants, and private providers, which suggests that local governments may be enjoying more of a partnership relationship with contractors than one that keeps contractors at arm's length. This could result in improved communication and coordination between government and its contractors, but it also presents risks of collusion. Economist Elliott Sclar has recognized the appeal of relational contracting in reducing the transaction costs of contracting, but he has also warned that collusion may occur when contracts become partnerships, and government and its contractors become too close—especially regarding evaluation and monitoring.[10]

Obstacles to Private Service Delivery

The percentage of governments reporting obstacles to adopting private service delivery has remained relatively stable since 2002. Opposition is still highest from line employees (47%) and elected officials (39%), but these rates have dropped since 2002 (Figure 2/2). Restrictive labor agreements are also seen as a major obstacle (40%), more so than in 2002. Curiously, citizen opposition remains the same at about 29%, confirming that political opposition to privatization is still a factor.

But the obstacles reflect more than politics: they also measure market and management characteristics. Survey results show that problems with contract specification and monitoring are down, suggesting that managers have learned how to write contracts and build monitoring systems. That legal constraints are also down offers strong evidence of managerial learning about contracting over time.

However, there are two disturbing points in these data. First, the percentage of managers reporting a lack of empirical evidence on the effectiveness of private alternatives is up, especially among suburbs (not shown). This percentage had dropped from 28% in 1992 to 22% in 2002.[11] Although less than a quarter of all responding managers account for this reversal, it may reflect the increasing evidence that cost savings from privatization are not guaranteed. A recent empirical analysis of all published studies of privatization in water distribution and waste collection shows that privatization is not typically associated with cost savings, and when it is, the cost savings tend to erode over time.[12]

Second, nearly a third of local governments still have an insufficient supply of competent private deliverers to choose from. Lack of competition has been a consistent problem for local governments, as revealed across all the ICMA ASD

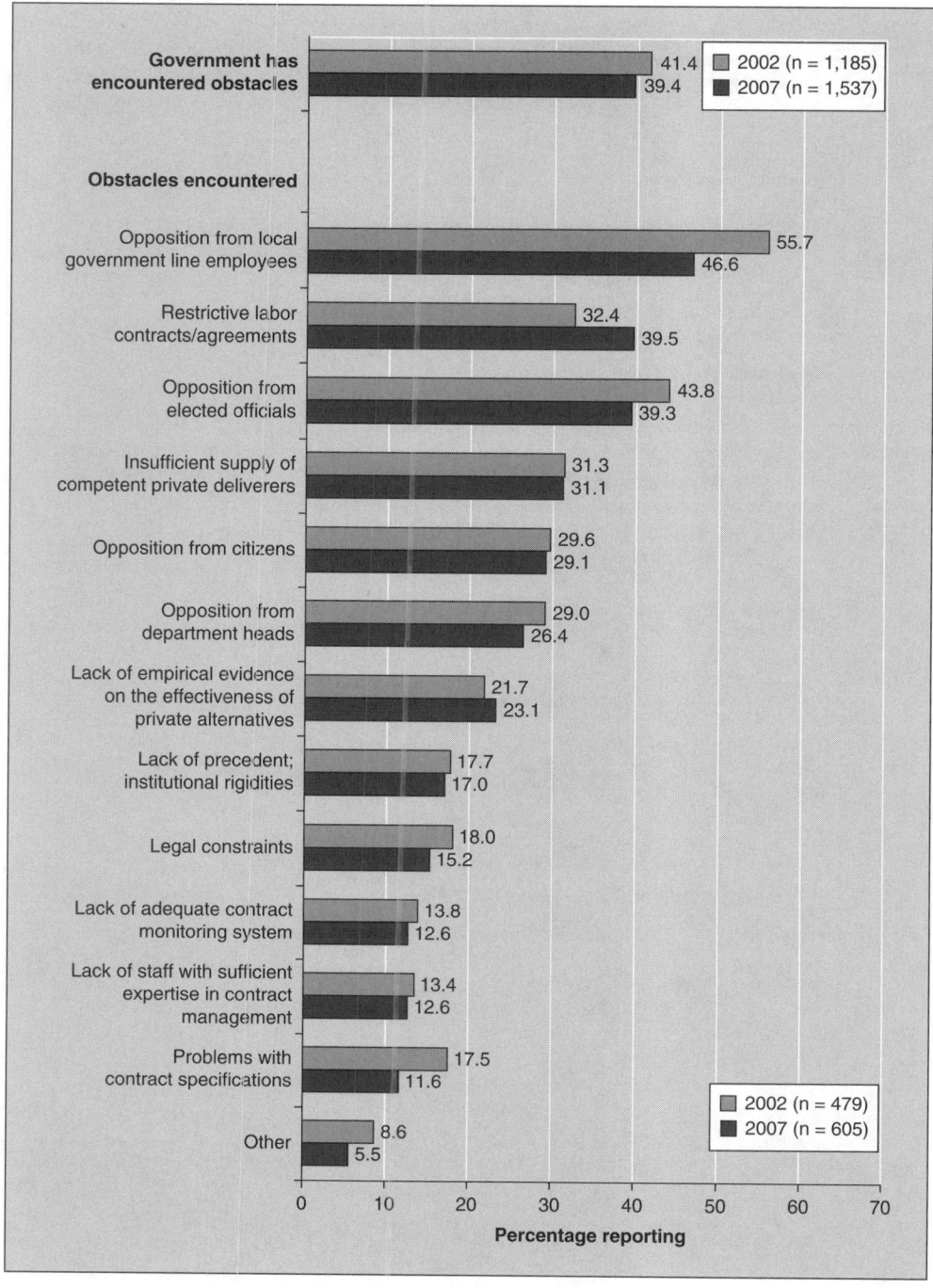

Figure 2/2   *Obstacles in adopting private service delivery*

surveys since 1982, and it is not getting better. Problems with an inadequate supply of competent private deliverers has grown from 25% in 1992 to 31% in 2007.[13] Given the long-standing experimentation with contracting, this lack of competition is surprising. In 2007, we conducted a special survey with ICMA that specifically asked managers about the level of competition they face for each service in their local or regional market.[14] The average number of alternative providers reported was fewer than one for most services. Of the 67 services measured, the only ones with more than two alternative providers were solid-waste collection, street repair, tree trimming, vehicle towing, insect and rodent control, hospital management, drug and alcohol programs, day care facilities, parks landscaping/maintenance, cultural and arts programs, building maintenance and se-

curity, legal services, data processing, secretarial services, and public relations (not shown). In general, these are the services for which contracting is highest. Contracting out in services for which there are fewer than two alternative providers is not likely to be effective. When a government contracts out a service without competition, it is merely substituting a private monopoly for a public one. Competition and efficiency are linked, and privatization without competition is not expected to yield cost savings.

Activities Undertaken to Ensure Success in Implementation

In 2007, fewer governments reported undertaking activities to ensure success when implementing private service delivery alternatives than in 2002. Among those that do, however, identifying

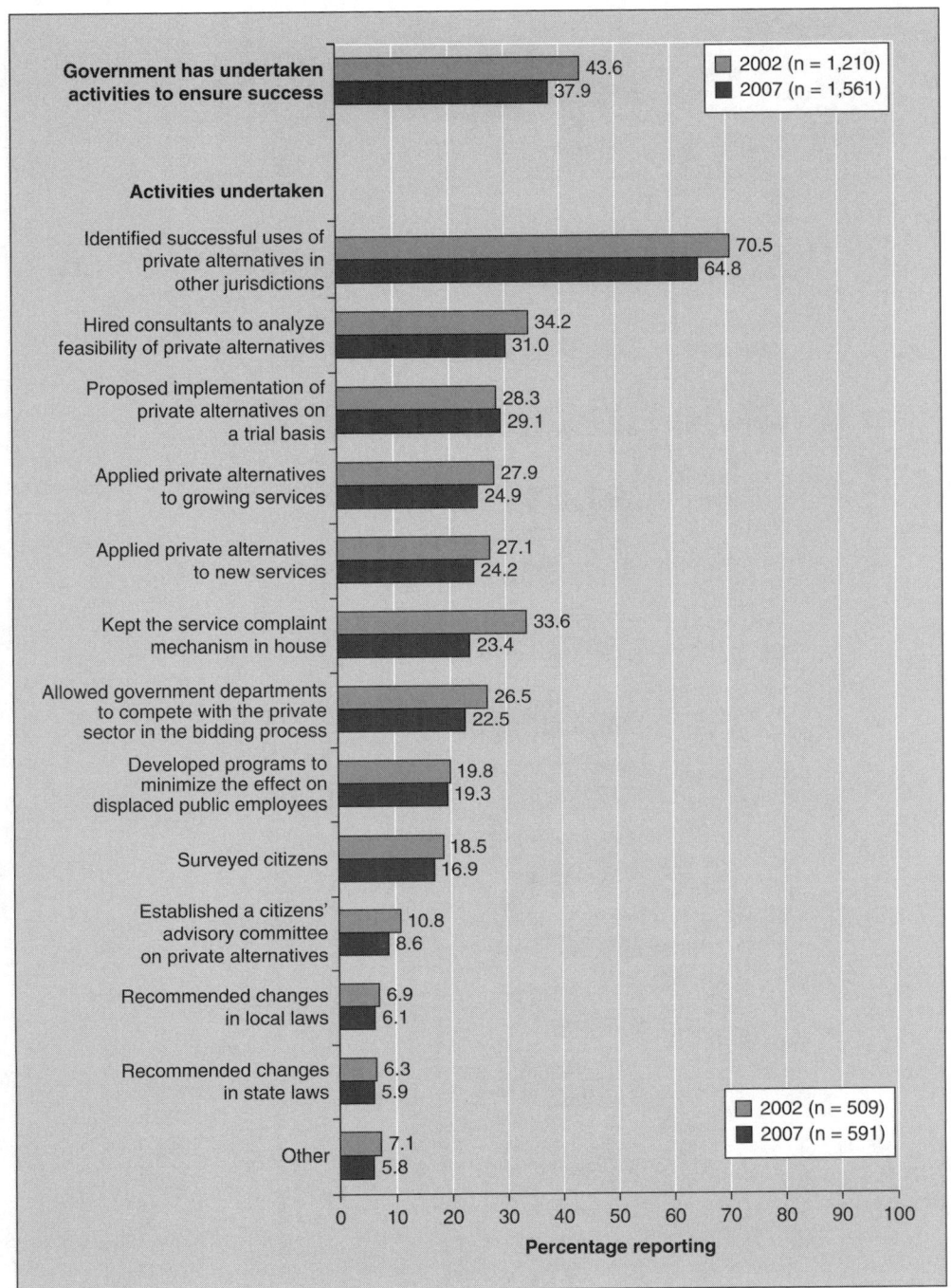

Figure 2/3   *Activities undertaken to ensure success in implementing private service delivery*

standards specified in the contract dropped from 84% of responding governments in 2002 to 78% in 2007. Attention to citizen satisfaction has also dropped—from 69% to 58%. Of the techniques used to evaluate private service delivery, monitoring citizen complaints is no longer the most common method used: more reliance is now given to analyzing data and records (72%) and to conducting field observations (70%). These findings, coupled with the increased outsourcing of the complaint mechanism revealed in Figure 2/3, raises concern about how service quality and citizen satisfaction will be maintained.

There is a disturbing pattern here. When contracting levels were at 20% in 1997, monitoring levels were at 69% (not shown). Contracting dropped in 2002 to 18%, and monitoring rose to 75%. Now in 2007 we see monitoring dropping again to 68%. While for-profit contracting levels overall are generally flat, this drop in monitoring might result in a drop in contracting again in 2012. This lagged effect of monitoring rising after contracting has already fallen back suggests that managers need to couple effective monitoring with contracting: without adequate and consistent monitoring, contracting levels are unstable.

A Focus on Intergovernmental Contracting
In the 2007 survey ICMA added two questions specifically about intergovernmental contracting, which, as has been noted, is currently the most common form of contracting reported. The first question asked about motivators for intergovernmental contracting, and the second asked about obstacles to it.

Intergovernmental contracting has been suggested as an alternative to consolidated regional government because it allows governments to coordinate and obtain economies of scale in those service areas where such advantages are most needed. Additionally, it offers the promise of efficiency gains, and unlike consolidation, it preserves local voice and local control. Indeed, as Table 2/6 shows, strengthening intergovernmental collaboration and promoting regional service integration were cited as reasons for intergovernmental contracting by 64% and 59% of responding governments, respectively. However, the primary motivators for intergovernmental contracting are to save money (80%) and to achieve economies of scale (77%).

The most important obstacle to intergovernmental contracting, cited by almost two thirds of respondents, is concern over the loss of community control. The next most important obstacles are opposition from employees and elected officials (43%) and concern about monitoring agreements (32%) (Table 2/6).

It is interesting to compare intergovernmental contracting with for-profit privatization, the two most common service delivery alternatives. The motivators for each are similar: to save money and promote efficiency. But privatization is also a response to fiscal pressures, whereas intergovernmental contracting is a response to regionalism. Both alternatives face similar levels of opposition from line employees and elected officials. However, citizen opposition to privatization is almost

a successful experience in other jurisdictions is still the most common method used (Figure 2/3). Governments learn from their neighbors. Although the use of consultants has decreased, it is still the second most common method used to ensure success. Allowing government departments to compete with the private sector in the bidding process has dropped from 27% to less than 23%. Since 2002, governments have also been less likely to apply contracting to new or growing services (down three percentage points in both cases). This may suggest that managers are clearer about which services they consider to be the best candidates for contracting and see less need to experiment and benchmark. The biggest drop is in keeping the complaint mechanism in house (from 34% to

23%). This reversal back to 1997 levels suggests that governments are outsourcing the complaint mechanism as well as the service delivery. If this is the case, it could create problems in the future as government does not have sufficient control over knowledge about the level of citizen satisfaction with service delivery.

Techniques Used to Evaluate Private Service Delivery
Monitoring is still reported by fewer than half of all responding governments. Of those who do monitor, the aspects they evaluate are all down from 2002. Cost, the most common criterion evaluated at 82%, is down from 87% (Figure 2/4). Measuring compliance with delivery

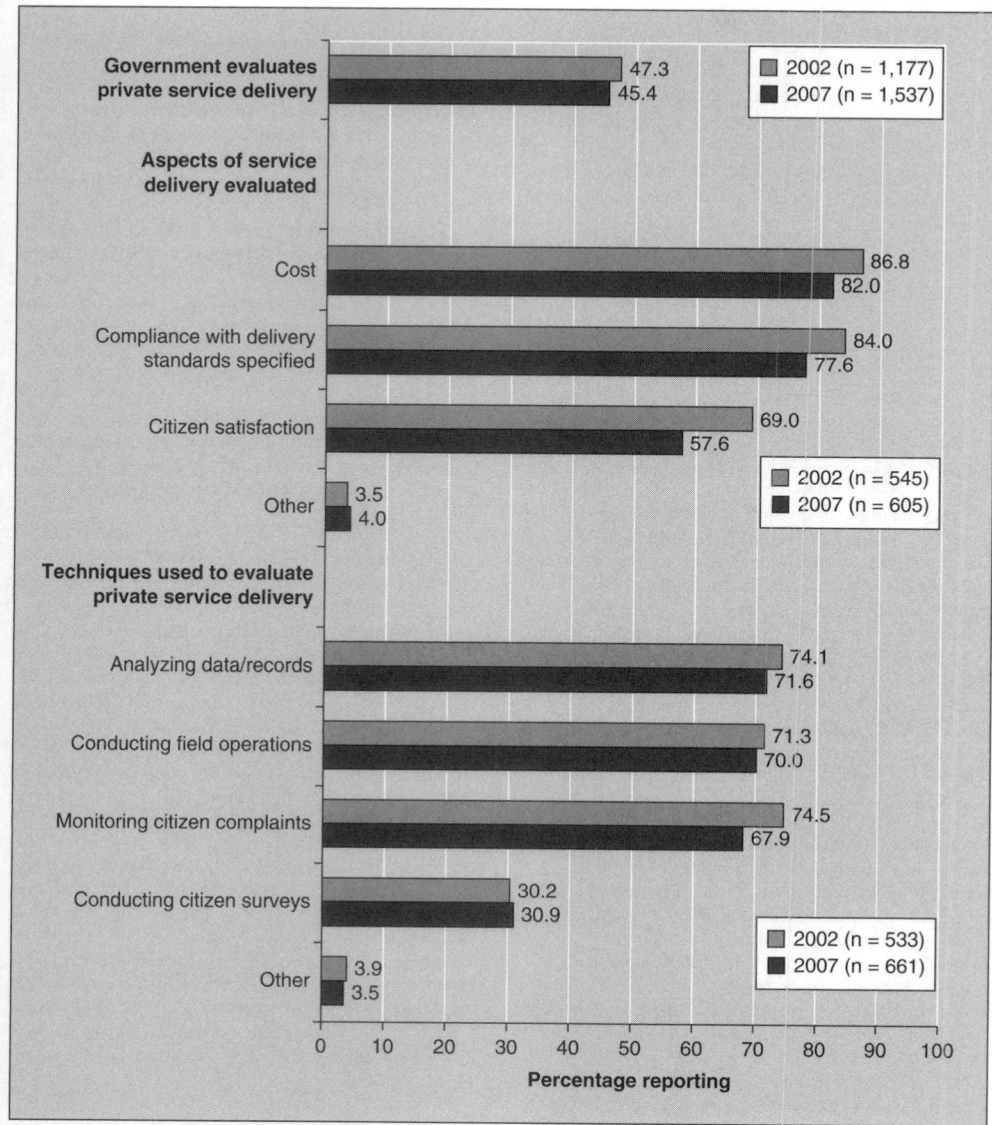

Figure 2/4   *Techniques used to evaluate private service delivery*

Reverse Contracting

Clearly, local government service delivery is a dynamic process. As managers experiment with alternative forms of delivery, we see shifts in levels of contracting among services. Beginning in 2002 ICMA added a question on the stability of alternative service delivery, asking governments if they had brought back in house services that had been previously contracted out. As in 2002, 22% of respondents in 2007 reported having brought previously contracted work back in house (Table 2/7). Of those, 61% reported problems with unsatisfactory service quality, 52% reported problems with insufficient cost savings, and 34% reported that internal government efficiency had improved. These percentages are similar to those reported in 2002 except for a drop in problems with service quality (from 73% to 61%). These factors indicate that poor performance by private deliverers is the primary reason for services being brought back in house. Some governments use contracting back in as a substitute for monitoring, but further analysis of reverse contracting has shown that it is also due to problems with markets (lack of competition) and concerns about citizen satisfaction.[16]

CONCLUSION

The ICMA ASD surveys show a dynamic pattern of shifting between private and public delivery. In 2002, the big story was the drop in contracting and the rise in direct public delivery and mixed public-private delivery. This was seen as a response to problems with service quality and lack of cost savings. Government raised its monitoring rates and increased its involvement in the market through direct and mixed delivery. In 2007, public delivery is down, and mixed delivery is down even more. But for-profit contracting is stable. Opposition in general is down, although opposition from labor and elected officials, as well as problems with restrictive labor agreements, continue to be the most important obstacles to privatization. Citizen opposition, at 29%, has barely moved since 1992—possibly because of persistent concerns over service quality and lack of cost savings. However, monitoring is also down from 2002, and competition has not increased: nearly a third of all respondents still face problems with lack of competent private deliverers. Without monitoring and competition, local governments should not expect efficiency gains from market provision.

On the other hand, the shifts in the 2007 survey show an increased use of intergovernmental contracting. Intergovernmental contracting offers a means to attain economies of scale. It reflects a cooperative market of public governments rather than a private market based primarily on competition. It also promotes regional service integration while retaining government control over the service delivery process. As a result, it faces less citizen opposition than privatization and can access more alternative suppliers (which means more competition). Moreover, as past research has shown, intergovernmental contracting

one-third higher than it is to intergovernmental contracting (29% vs. 19%), and problems with lack of alternative deliverers are twice as high for privatization (31%) as for intergovernmental contracting (17%). And intergovernmental contract-

ing is an especially attractive option for rural governments, whose small size and distance from urban centers make them less attractive to private suppliers than suburban governments are. This rural difference has been well documented.[15]

Table 2/6   MOTIVATORS FOR AND OBSTACLES TO INTERGOVERNMENTAL CONTRACTING, 2007

Motivators/obstacles	Percentage
Motivators for intergovernmental contracting (n = 1,253)	
Save money	80.2
Achieve economies of scale	77.4
Strengthen collaborative intergovernmental relations	63.7
Promote regional service integration	59.0
Access technical expertise	37.1
Avoid shedding services	7.3
There is a lack of private providers	7.0
Other	2.9
Obstacles to intergovernmental contracting (n = 746)	
Concern about loss of community control	64.1
Internal opposition from employees, elected officials	42.9
Concern about difficulty in monitoring intergovernmental agreements	32.4
External opposition from citizens	18.8
No neighboring government willing to enter into an agreement	16.5
Other	8.0

Table 2/7   REVERSE CONTRACTING, 2002 AND 2007

	2002	2007
Local government brought back in house services that were previously contracted out	% (n = 1,146)	% (n = 1,535)
	22.2	21.6
Factors that played a part in the decision to bring back services	% (n = 245)	% (n = 330)
Service quality was not satisfactory	72.7	61.2
Cost savings were insufficient	51.0	52.4
Local government efficiency improved	35.9	33.9
Problems monitoring the contract	20.4	17.0
Strong political support to bring back the service delivery	21.6	17.0
Problems with the contract specifications	15.1	10.0
Other	12.7	13.3

yields similar efficiency gains as for-profit privatization but performs better in terms of equity and citizen responsiveness:[17] for-profit privatization tends to favor richer suburbs whereas intergovernmental contracting is common among both suburbs and rural municipalities.[18] But recent analysis has found problems with accountability and monitoring in intergovernmental contracting as well as in for-profit contracts.[19] The 2007 survey shows that the loss of community control is the most important obstacle to intergovernmental contracting, and this may reflect a concern with monitoring.

What do these results suggest for future trends? The ICMA surveys suggest a disturbing pattern of monitoring lagging behind contracting. When contracting is up, monitoring is down, which is the opposite of what should be. Monitoring and contracting must go hand in hand. Local government managers must balance the use of market forms of delivery with attention to service quality, cost-efficiency, and citizen satisfaction. They are experienced contractors, and they have learned to use a variety of alternative survey delivery approaches. But failure to give consistent attention to monitoring service quality and citizen satisfaction undermines the potential efficiency gains and stability of those alternative approaches.

core, 53% suburb, and 29% independent in 2007. This reflects an increase in rural areas and a decline in the metro core and suburbs from 2002, when the percentages were 22%, 51%, and 27%, respectively. We adjusted the overall delivery data results in 2007 to be consistent with the 2002 composition by metro status, and found no difference in average level of public delivery or for-profit and only a one percentage point difference in intergovernmental contracts. The raw data in the tables in this report are not adjusted and reflect actual percentage responses from the 2002 and 2007 samples. A description of differences in alternative service delivery by metro status is found in a report published for the Reason Foundation: see Mildred E. Warner and Amir Hefetz, *Local Government Privatization and Alternative Service Delivery, 2002–2007: Innovation, Diffusion, and Learning,* Reason Foundation policy study (Los Angeles: Reason Foundation, 2009).

[1]Mildred E. Warner, "Reversing Privatization, Rebalancing Government Reform: Markets, Deliberation and Planning," *Policy and Society* 27, no. 2 (2008): 163–174.

[2]For a complete discussion of alternative service delivery trends from 1992 to 2002, see Mildred E. Warner, Michael J. Ballard, and Amir Hefetz, "Contracting Back In: When Privatization Fails," in *The Municipal Year Book 2003* (Washington, D.C.: ICMA, 2003), 30–36. A thorough analysis of mixed delivery is found in Mildred E. Warner and Amir Hefetz, "Managing Markets for Public Service: The Role of Mixed Public/Private Delivery of City Services," *Public Administration Review* 68, no. 1 (2008): 150–161; a thorough analysis of reverse contracting can be found in Amir Hefetz and Mildred E. Warner, "Beyond the Market vs. Planning Dichotomy: Understanding Privatisation and Its Reverse in US Cities," *Local Government Studies* 33, no. 4 (2007): 555–572.

[3]Data from 1992 and 1997 can be found in Mildred Warner and Amir Hefetz, "Pragmatism over Politics: Alternative Service Delivery in Local Government, 1992–2002," in *The Municipal Year Book 2004* (Washington, D.C.: ICMA, 2004), 8–16.

[4]Mildred E. Warner, "Competition, Cooperation, and Local Governance," in *Challenges for Rural America in the Twenty-First Century,* ed. David L. Brown and Louis E. Swanson (University Park: Pennsylvania State University Press, 2003), 252–262.

[5]Mildred E. Warner and Amir Hefetz, "Applying Market Solutions to Public Services: An Assessment of Efficiency, Equity, and Voice," *Urban Affairs Review* 38, no. 1 (2002): 70–89, government.cce.cornell.edu/doc/pdf/WarnerHefetz 2002UrbanAffairsReview.pdf (accessed January 2, 2009).

[6]There were 1,474 usable responses in the final set of respondents. Breakdowns by metro status show 18% metro

[7]Warner and Hefetz, "Pragmatism over Politics."

[8]Mildred E. Warner and Amir Hefetz, "Managing Markets for Public Service: The Role of Mixed Public/Private Delivery of City Services," *Public Administration Review* 68, no. 1 (2008): 150–161.

[9]Warner and Hefetz, "Pragmatism over Politics," 10.

[10]Elliott Sclar, *You Don't Always Get What You Pay For: The Economics of Privatization* (Ithaca, N.Y.: Cornell University Press, 2000).

[11]See Warner and Hefetz, "Pragmatism over Politics," 14.

[12]Germà Bel and Mildred E. Warner, "Does Privatization of Solid Waste and Water Services Reduce Costs? A Review of Empirical Studies," *Resources, Conservation & Recycling* 52, no. 12 (2008): 1337–1348.

[13]Ibid.

[14]Mildred E. Warner, "Civic Government or Market-Based Governance? The Limits of Privatization for Rural Local Governments," *Agriculture and Human Values* 26, no. 1 (2009).

[15]Mildred E. Warner, "Market-Based Governance and the Challenge for Rural Governments: U.S. Trends," *Social Policy and Administration: An International Journal of Policy and Research* 40, no. 6 (2006): 612–631; Mildred E. Warner and Amir Hefetz, "Rural-Urban Differences in Privatization: Limits to the Competitive State," *Environment and Planning C: Government and Policy* 21, no. 5 (2003).

[16]Hefetz and Warner, "Contracting Back In."

[17]Warner and Hefetz, "Applying Market Solutions to Public Services."

[18]Warner and Hefetz, "Rural-Urban Differences in Privatization"; and Warner, "Market-Based Governance."

[19]Mildred E. Warner, "Inter-municipal Cooperation in the U.S.: A Regional Governance Solution?" *Urban Public Economics Review/Revista de Economía Pública Urbana* 7 (2006): 132–151.

3

County Form of Government: Trends in Structure and Composition

Edgar E. Ramírez de la Cruz
Arizona State University

Selected Findings

County structure has changed marginally since 2002: the proportion of counties with the council-manager and council-administrator forms of government combined dropped by five percentage points, whereas the proportion of counties with the commission form increased by three percentage points.

The percentage of counties that reported having a CAO increased from 54% in 2002 to 56% in 2007.

The percentage of counties adopting direct democracy provisions has generally increased. Interestingly, however, the percentage of counties providing for recall dropped in all regions except the Northeast, where it increased from 9% to almost 18%.

The rich variety of structures in American counties is the result of diverse population changes that have required counties to fulfill different responsibilities and provide different types of services.[1] In general, counties provide two principal types of services. The first type includes services provided by the traditional county government as an arm of the state. In their original constitutions, many states saw counties as mere geographic subdivisions useful for providing state services, such as law enforcement, corrections, elections, civil records, and courts, which in many states are still the main responsibilities of counties and represent the most substantial part of their budgets. However, since the early 1900s and, more intensely, after World War II, the combined effects of growth, population pressures, urban sprawl, suburbanization, and the reform movement have demanded that counties provide new services as well, such as planning, zoning, libraries, hospitals, and parks. The provision of these new services, similar to those provided by cities, has created new responsibilities and required professional expertise, so counties have had to create new institutional arrangements to organize their activities.[2]

Yet some analysts still see counties as being poorly equipped to deal with the provision of modern services. Many studies have emerged with the general impression that county governments lack professional administration; are too inflexible to deal with the changing needs of the population; and are sometimes even inefficient, incompetent, or corrupt political machines.[3] But other studies have viewed counties from a more positive perspective as moving toward the professional administration of services, particularly in urban areas.

To uncover trends in the changing structure of local government, ICMA has been conducting surveys among counties since 1988. The 1988 and 2002 surveys on the county form of government offered important insights into those changes.[4] The 1988 survey reported an increasing variety in form of government as a result of home rule charters (discussed below) and the growing use of professional administrators. The 2002 survey also reported an increasing number of counties adopting the position of chief administrative

officer (CAO), as well as the continuing practice of electing various constitutional officers, such as prosecutors, recorders, and treasurers. This article presents a cross-sectional analysis of the current structure of county government based on a survey conducted in 2007. It describes the results in aggregated terms; for selected variables, the results are disaggregated by population size, region, and metropolitan status. It also identifies trends within some political institutions by comparing the 2007 results with results of previous surveys.

SURVEY METHODOLOGY

ICMA's *County Form of Government 2007* survey asked 20 questions covering such topics as form of government; county constitutional officers; appointed administrators and officials; governing bodies and their presiding officers; the provision of referenda, recall, and initiative; the selection of department heads; and the fiscal calendar.

The survey was mailed to 3,039 counties in August 2007. A follow-up survey was sent to those counties that did not respond to the first one. Final responses were received from 1,102 counties for a response rate of 36%. As shown in Table 3/1, the response rates are similar across the various population categories, with a marginally higher response from counties with a population over 1,000,000. In general, the response rate was slightly higher in 2007 than it was in 2002 (33%) (not shown).[5]

However, there are variations in the response rate by geographic division and metro status that need to be considered when making generalizations about national trends. Geographically, the highest response rate came from the West and the North-Central regions (42% each), while the lowest came from the East South-Central division (19%). The response rates from almost all the divisions improved over those reported in 2002; only the rates from the Mountain and Pacific Coast divisions did not improve, and the decline in the Mountain division was notable: from 52% in 2002 to 43% in 2007. In terms of metro status, the variation was small: 38% from central counties and 36% from suburban and independent counties each.

Table 3/1 SURVEY RESPONSE

Classification	No. of counties[1] surveyed (A)	Respondents No.	Respondents % of (A)
Total	3,039	1,102	36
Population group			
Over 1,000,000	28	12	43
500,000–1,000,000 ...	63	17	27
250,000–499,999	110	41	37
100,000–249,999	275	109	40
50,000–99,999	383	151	39
25,000–49,999	638	228	36
10,000–24,999	869	309	36
5,000–9,999	386	131	34
2,500–4,999	173	64	37
Under 2,500	114	40	35
Geographic region			
Northeast	189	53	28
North-Central	1,054	440	42
South...............	1,372	430	31
West	424	179	42
Geographic division			
New England	45	15	33
Mid-Atlantic	144	38	26
East North-Central ...	437	185	42
West North-Central ...	617	255	41
South Atlantic	545	234	43
East South-Central ...	360	70	19
West South-Central...	467	126	27
Mountain	276	119	43
Pacific Coast........	148	60	41
Metro status			
Central	457	172	38
Suburban	341	124	36
Independent	2,241	806	36

[1] For a definition of terms, please see "Inside the *Year Book*," xii.

HOME RULE CHARTER

To carry out new responsibilities and enhance their autonomy and flexibility, some counties have been granted discretion to transform their structures. After California passed a constitutional amendment in 1911 to give counties discretionary authority to form their home rule charter, 35 other states followed their lead.[6] Among these states, the level of flexibility given to counties to redefine their structures varies significantly. However, even states without home rule charter provisions have state legislation that gives counties

some level of extra authority to structure their governments.

Usually, a home rule charter allows counties to deviate from the commission form of government commonly prescribed by state constitutions—to change, in some cases, both the form of government and the duties and responsibilities of elected officers. But despite the potential benefits of adopting a charter, few counties have used that method to provide themselves with an adequate structure for fulfilling new responsibilities and roles. As in 2002, the vast majority of counties (78%) reported that their source of authority for the structure of government is state law (Table 3/2). Second in importance is the charter, which exists in only 9% of responding counties. Nevertheless, the charter is the most common source of authority for counties with a population of over 1,000,000; it is also the source of authority for at least 21% of counties in the next two highest population brackets (250,000–499,999 and 500,000–1,000,000). Finally, the charter as the source of authority is more common in central counties and in the Northeast region than in other metropolitan designations or regions in the country.

COUNTY FORM OF GOVERNMENT

The survey asked respondents to identify their form of county government among one of the following four options: commission, council-administrator, council-manager, and council–elected executive. The following definitions were provided to help respondents make the distinction:

- In the commission form of government, the elected commissioner or board member serves as director of one or more functional departments (e.g., public works or health and human services) in addition to his or her policy-making role. The presiding officer may be chosen from the board or elected directly.
- In the council-administrator form, the elected board sets policy, adopts legislation, and approves the budget. The commission appoints an administrator to conduct the day-to-day county business, to prepare the budget, to oversee department heads, and to recommend policy to the board.
- In the council-manager form, an elected board sets policy, adopts legislation, and approves the budget. The commission appoints a manager with broad executive authority to oversee and manage county departments, hire and fire most department directors, hire and fire county staff, prepare the budget, and recommend policy to the board.
- In the council–elected executive form, the elected board is responsible for making policy. The executive, elected at large, implements county board policies, prepares the budget, and acts as county spokesperson. The executive often has veto power, which can be overridden.

From these options, only 89% of the 1,102 respondents identified their form of government in the county (not shown). To facilitate comparisons between the 2002 and 2007 surveys, Table 3/3 shows the breakdown of these forms of government based on those 982 responses. Together, the council-administrator and council-manager forms of government account for 51% of the responding counties, the commission form was reported by 35%, and the council–elected executive form is found in 13%.[7] Compared with responses from the 2002 survey (Figure 3/1), the percentage of counties reporting the council–elected executive form of government did not change significantly; however, the proportion of counties with the council-administrator or council-manager forms combined dropped by five percentage points, while the proportion with the commission form increased by more than three percentage points.

In terms of population groups, a significant association appears to exist between form of government and county size (Table 3/3). Among responding counties up to 24,999 in population, the dominant form is the commission. The commission is also found in much as 71% of counties with a population between 2,500 and 4,999. However, in counties with populations of 25,000 or more, the most common form of government is either council-administrator or council-manager, found in at least 58% of the responding counties. The highest percentage of governments with a council and administrator or manager (80%) exists among counties with populations between 500,000 and 1,000,000. Of the 12 responding counties with populations above 1,000,000, 25% reported having a council–elected executive government, which is significantly higher than the proportion found in the other population groups. This association between population and form of government suggests that when counties cross the 25,000 population threshold, they are likely to change their structure.

Regionally, the commission form of government is the most common form among counties in the North-Central and West regions, with 47% and 43% reporting this form, respectively. In the Northeast region, the most prevalent form is the council-administrator, which is present in 51% of responding counties. In the South, 32% of the counties reported having council-administrator form of government, which, in conjunction with the council-manager form, is the most common form of government in the region at 61%.

The results from the 2007 survey are similar to those from the 2002 survey in terms of the relationship between metropolitan status and form of government. The 2007 survey reports that the council–elected executive form of government is rarely found in metropolitan regions. Instead, the most prevalent form in independent counties is the commission (43%); among suburban and central counties, it is the council-administrator (44% and 39%, respectively). Looking at central counties alone, if we add the 36% that reported having the council-manager form of government, we can say that 75% of these counties have some type of professional administrator in place. This is an increase of three percentage points over what was reported by central counties in 2002 (not shown), and it is consistent with the trends reported by previous surveys.[8]

County Constitutional Officers

One of the common criticisms of the original county structure of government is that authority was fragmented because of the large number of county constitutional officers—elected executives who, except in budgetary matters, are independent of the governing body.[9] Although the direct election of independent executives in the county

Table 3/2   METHOD OF ESTABLISHMENT

Classification	No. reporting (A)	Charter No.	Charter % of (A)	State law No.	State law % of (A)	Local ordinance No.	Local ordinance % of (A)	Council resolution No.	Council resolution % of (A)	Other No.	Other % of (A)
Total	1,039	97	9	814	78	41	4	68	7	19	2
Population group											
Over 1,000,000	12	6	50	5	42	0	0	1	8	0	0
500,000–1,000,000	17	4	24	13	77	0	0	0	0	0	0
250,000–499,999	38	8	21	25	66	2	5	3	8	0	0
100,000–249,999	105	14	13	82	78	5	5	3	3	1	1
50,000–99,999	145	13	9	113	78	5	3	11	8	3	2
25,000–49,999	220	20	9	170	77	12	6	14	6	4	2
10,000–24,999	282	25	9	226	80	12	4	13	5	6	2
5,000–9,999	123	5	4	105	85	4	3	7	6	2	2
2,500–4,999	59	1	3	46	78	1	2	9	15	2	3
Under 2,500	38	1	3	29	76	0	0	7	18	1	3
Geographic region											
Northeast	52	14	27	31	60	3	6	2	4	2	4
North-Central	416	12	3	347	83	11	3	38	9	8	2
South	400	55	14	296	74	23	6	18	5	8	2
West	171	16	9	140	82	4	2	10	6	1	1
Metro status											
Central	165	35	21	114	69	7	4	8	5	1	1
Suburban	120	10	8	97	81	4	3	8	7	1	1
Independent	754	52	7	603	80	30	4	52	7	17	2
Form of government											
County commission	333	10	3	282	85	5	2	32	10	4	1
Council-administrator	312	35	11	237	76	13	4	21	7	6	2
Council-manager	178	29	16	123	69	12	7	12	7	2	1
Council–elected executive	123	19	15	95	77	7	6	1	1	1	1
Did not report	93	4	4	77	83	4	4	2	2	6	7

Note: Percentages may exceed 100% because of rounding.

Table 3/3   FORM OF GOVERNMENT

Classification	No. reporting (A)	Commission No.	Commission % of (A)	Council-administrator No.	Council-administrator % of (A)	Council-manager No.	Council-manager % of (A)	Council-elected executive No.	Council-elected executive % of (A)
Total	982	348	35	326	33	181	18	127	13
Population group									
Over 1,000,000	12	1	8	4	33	4	33	3	25
500,000–1,000,000	15	1	7	7	47	5	33	2	13
250,000–499,999	40	5	13	17	43	13	33	5	13
100,000–249,999	103	14	14	38	37	40	39	11	11
50,000–99,999	140	32	23	60	43	35	25	13	9
25,000–49,999	206	57	28	75	36	45	22	29	14
10,000–24,999	264	104	39	91	35	34	13	35	13
5,000–9,999	111	70	63	21	19	3	3	17	15
2,500–4,999	56	40	71	6	11	1	2	9	16
Under 2,500	35	24	69	7	20	1	3	3	9
Geographic region									
Northeast	49	10	20	25	51	7	14	7	14
North-Central	386	181	47	136	35	23	6	46	12
South.	383	87	23	122	32	112	29	62	16
West	164	70	43	43	26	39	24	12	7
Metro status									
Central	163	18	11	63	39	59	36	23	14
Suburban	115	25	22	50	44	26	23	14	12
Independent	704	305	43	213	30	96	14	90	13

Table 3/4   DEPARTMENT HEADS APPOINTED OR ELECTED

Department head	No. reporting (A)	Appointed No.	Appointed % of (A)	Elected No.	Elected % of (A)
Clerk of the board	920	403	44	517	56
Clerk of the court.	1,007	240	24	767	76
Recorder	933	124	13	809	87
Treasurer.	1,007	164	16	843	84
Assessor	1,000	457	46	543	54
Prosecutor. . . .	983	70	7	913	93
Attorney.	663	437	66	226	34
Sheriff	1,083	10	1	1,073	99

is believed to hold them accountable to voters every election cycle, which may make them more responsive to their constituents, a high number of directly elected officials may create problems of coordination and command. This is particularly true when counties are seeking to provide new types of services, in which case the lack of centralized authority can obstruct unified formulation and implementation of county strategies. In the commission form of government, effective policy making requires such factors as strong, unified leadership and basic agreement about county policies, which are not easily achieved when authority resides with officials who are not answerable to the commission. In addition to a coordinated and unified approach, appointed department heads can bring professional experience and technical expertise to county administration, qualities that are particularly needed in such areas as finance management, tax collection, legal matters, planning, and property appraisal.

As survey findings reveal, whether specific county officers are elected or appointed varies widely. Although the specific activities performed by these officials vary considerably from state to state, the inherent tasks required for each position may influence the extent to which citizens prefer those officers to be directly accountable to them.[10] For each of the following eight county positions—assessor, prosecutor, attorney, sheriff, treasurer, recorder, clerk of the board, and clerk of the court—Table 3/4 shows the percentages overall that are appointed or elected. Reported percentages according to population, geographic region, metro status, or form of government, however, are not shown.

County clerks, court clerks, auditors, and recorders perform activities that could be unified in a single position or divided among various public officials, often depending on the size of the county. Common responsibilities of these officers include serving as secretary of the county board, keeping records of meetings, and setting the agenda. In some counties, these officials can also audit bills against the county, record legal documents such as property transfers, and serve in the court system as staff officer.

Fifty-six percent of responding counties reported electing the clerk of the governing board, but the percentage is higher in less populated counties. For instance, in counties with a population below 25,000, between 60% and 89% elect the county clerk; among counties over 100,000, however, almost 77% appoint the county clerk. If counties are differentiated by region and form of government, two other important differences stand out: 96% of counties in the Northeast region and 43% of those in the West region reported appointing the county clerk, compared with only 20% in the North-Central region. Counties with an appointed manager or administrator also appear more likely to appoint the county clerk, as reported by 59% and 72% of each, respectively.

The clerk of the court is elected in 76% of counties that reported having this position. This percentage is consistent across population and metro status, although there are considerable differences by region. Among counties that appoint this position, the percentage is lowest in the South region (4%) and the highest in the Northeast (57%), followed by the West and North-Central regions (44% and 33%, respectively). These results suggest that unlike counties in the other regions, those in the South may emphasize the administrative function of the court clerks over the policy-making function, which would pose less of a need for direct accountability to voters.

Although most counties (87%) elect the recorder, there is again variation by particular characteristics. In terms of the form of government, in 22% of council-administrator counties and 20% of council-manager counties, this position is appointed, compared with only 6% of counties with the commission form of government. Geographically, 26% of counties in the South region appoint this position, compared with 7% of counties in both the North-Central and West regions.

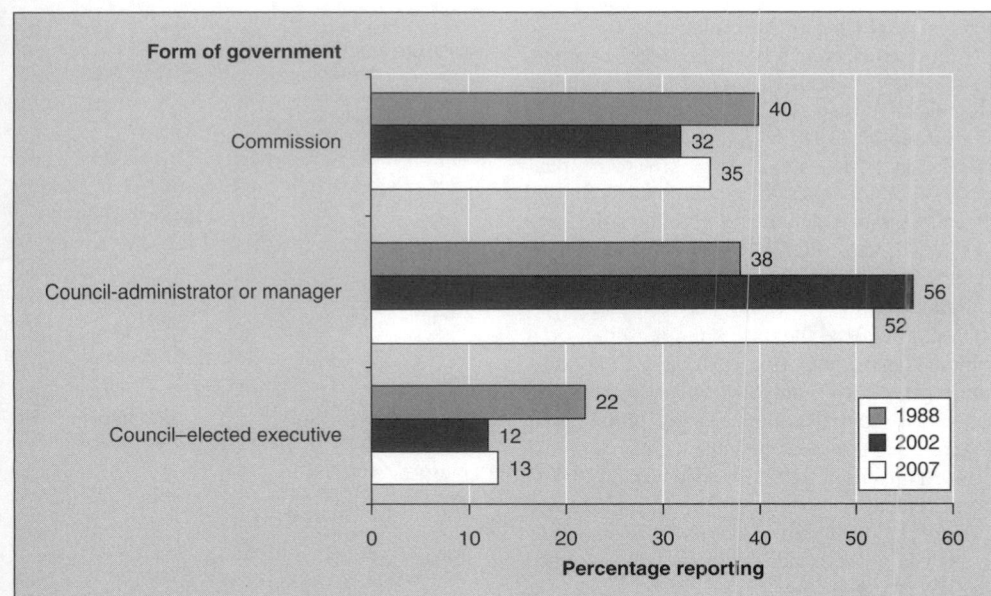

Figure 3/1   *Form of government, 1988–2007*

County treasurers receive money for the county from a variety of sources, keep records of banks, and balance the county financial funds. In some cases they can also invest county funds when such funds are not immediately needed. Since 84% of counties reported that their treasurers are elected, these officers appear to be highly accountable to the voters. The percentage is even higher in counties with a population under 10,000. Geographically, in the West and North-Central regions nearly every county elects the treasurer (94% and 97%, respectively), whereas in the Northeast and South regions, the treasurer is elected in only 77% and 64% of counties, respectively. The major difference by form of government exists between council-manager counties, only 61% of which reported electing the treasurer, and counties with a commission form of government, nearly all of which (96%) elect the treasurer.

County assessors usually appraise property values in order to evaluate the fiscal responsibilities of property owners. Assessors often update county maps and property records; They may also send tax notices and collect taxes and fees. Overall, 46% of responding counties appoint the assessor, but regionally this ranges from 94% of counties in the Northeast to only 6% in the West. The assessor is also more likely to be appointed in council-administrator and council–elected executive counties (60% and 56%, respectively) than in counties with a commission form of government (34%).

The county prosecutor and county attorney may be two separate individuals with distinct responsibilities, or the functions of these positions may reside in a single individual who serves in both capacities. In the latter case, the official serves as attorney to the county, providing advice in legal matters and representing the county in several types of legal cases, and also prosecutes persons in the name of the state, presenting the state's case at trial. Therefore, while as attorney this official is required to serve the council directly, as prosecutor he or she must also respond to the needs of the general population. These two capacities may be associated with different levels of direct accountability to voters, so reconciling them represents a major challenge when both functions are vested in the same official.

The great majority of counties that reported having the position of prosecutor also reported that the prosecutor is elected (93%), a finding that essentially holds true even when counties are disaggregated by the various classification categories (e.g., population, metro status). This suggests that county residents prefer to hold prosecutors accountable to them. However, the attorney position is appointed in 66% of the 663 counties that reported having it, and the percentage is higher (up to 83%) in cities with populations between 25,000 and 1,000,000. A significant regional difference exists as well: in the North-Central and South regions, the attorney is elected in 43% and 35% of counties, respectively, compared with only 6% of counties in the Northeast region.

County sheriffs provide law enforcement on highways; in addition, they provide police services in unincorporated areas and, in some states, in incorporated areas as well. Because they also arrest and are responsible for the custody of suspected criminals, they are in charge of administering and maintaining the county jail. In addition, they process paperwork in a number of court matters and can also act as officers of the court. Finally, they can participate in emergency management and response. Practically all counties (99%) elect the sheriff, a practice that is in no way correlated with a county's region, metro status, or form of government.

Theoretically, a system that is based solely on either appointing or electing department heads, like the officers just described above, can be expected to emphasize either unity of command or accountability. The survey asked counties whether all their department heads are either appointed or elected, or whether there is a mix of methods. The results indicate that 69% of counties have a system that combines these two mechanisms; however, there are some associations between the small percentages of counties that have all department heads either elected (12%) or appointed (19%) and their population size, region, and form of government (not shown). For instance, among counties with a population of 100,000 and above, only one county elects all its department heads, compared with between 19% and 31% of counties with a population below 5,000. In the South and Northeast regions, 28% and 33% of counties, respectively, reported appointing all departments heads, compared with only 7% in the North-Central region. As for form of government, 23% of council-administrator counties and 36% of council-manager counties appoint all their department heads, whereas 14% of counties with the council–elected executive form elect all department heads.

More than 900 counties reported that one or more of their department heads are appointed. In nearly half of those counties (53%), the council has the authority to appoint the department heads directly (not shown); in 12%, that authority rests with the appointed executive, and in another 12%, department heads are appointed by a combination of the council and the appointed executive.

Professional County Administrator

In some cases, the clerk of the board can perform tasks commonly associated with a county administrator, such as following up on board decisions, preparing the budget, and advising commissioners.[11] Most often, however, a professional manager or administrator is appointed to coordinate the implementation process among the various departments. Professional CAOs are able to act as consensus builders, relying on persuasion, communication, and collaborative leadership.[12] In addition, since they are often recruited on a national basis, they bring professional expertise and experience to—and can introduce innovations in—county administration. Usually, professional CAOs are highly educated and have spent most of their professional careers in various positions in local government, in both counties and cities. They often move from one jurisdiction to another in order to gain professional experience and advance in their careers.

The specific responsibilities of CAOs are defined in the charter or assigned by the commission, and they vary from county to county. Among their many responsibilities, county CAOs often implement regulations and ordinances passed by the council, organize the departments, conduct research on county issues, establish specific personnel policies, supervise department heads, suggest policies to the council to deal with current issues, and recommend and participate in the comprehensive plan of the county. In some cases, they are responsible for drafting the county budget and for appointing and firing department heads in consultation with the council. Having a county administrator allows the council to concentrate on legislative matters; at the same time, it helps commissioners signal their intention to separate policy and politics from administration. In addition, since CAOs serve at the pleasure of their councils or boards, they are relatively easy to replace if there is dissatisfaction with their performance.

Table 3/5 shows the presence of CAOs in 2007 by the various classification categories. The results indicate the continuing association between county population and the existence of a CAO. The percentage of counties that reported having a CAO increased from 54% in 2002 to 56% in 2007, with an increase apparent in almost every population bracket reported (not shown). In general, CAOs can be found in a majority of counties with populations of 10,000 and above. In the three population brackets under 10,000, the position is far less common. Nevertheless, even in these brackets, the percentages of counties that do not have a CAO are smaller than those reported in 2002.

The existence of a CAO is highly associated with county form of government. All council-

Table 3/5	POSITION OF CHIEF ADMINISTRATIVE OFFICER		

| | | Yes | |
Classification	No. reporting (A)	No.	% of (A)
Total	1,075	600	56
Population group			
Over 1,000,000	12	10	83
500,000–1,000,000	17	14	82
250,000–499,999	41	32	78
100,000–249,999	107	88	82
50,000–99,999	147	106	72
25,000–49,999	222	137	62
10,000–24,999	296	155	52
5,000–9,999	130	33	25
2,500–4,999	63	12	19
Under 2,500	40	13	33
Geographic region			
Northeast	52	44	85
North-Central	431	183	43
South	416	273	66
West	176	100	57
Metro status			
Central	171	136	80
Suburban	121	91	75
Independent	783	373	48
Form of government			
County commission	343	49	14
Council-administrator	325	324	100
Council-manager	181	181	100
Council–elected executive	125	25	20
Did not report	101	21	21

* = Less than 0.5%.

manager counties and all but one of the council-administrator counties have a CAO. And while the percentages for commission (14%) and council–elected executive (20%) counties are small, they are slightly higher than those reported in the 2002 survey (12% and 16%, respectively) (not shown), which confirms a trend that has often been noted. Finally, in the majority of counties that have a CAO (82%), the position is appointed by the commission, compared with only 9% in which the CAO is appointed by a combination of the presiding officer and the commission, and only 2% in which the CAO is appointed by the presiding officer alone (Figure 3/2).

COUNTY GOVERNING BOARDS

The responsibilities of county boards vary from state to state. Commonly, the board of commissioners has legislative authority to enact ordinances, adopt a budget, and set county tax rates. It may also have authority to appoint various employees, review license applications, and share responsibilities with other elected officials at the county level (mainly under the commission form of government). In the absence of county managers or elected executives, the council has additional responsibilities, such as preparing the budget, appointing department heads, and supervising the day-to-day operations of the county. In cases where the county has a charter, the charter is often used to define the board's additional responsibilities.

Size and Composition
Variation in council responsibilities may be associated with the significant variation in council size observed in the survey. On average, the council or board has 6 members, although some counties reported having as many as 39 members (not shown). The most common size of a council is 3 members, as reported by 36% of respondents, followed by 5 members, reported by 33%. Regionally, counties in the West have an average of 3.6 members compared with counties in the Northeast and North-Central regions, which have, on average, more than 7 members.

In general, council positions are dominated by men, who occupy 86% of the county board seats (not shown). However, women are better represented in the largest counties than in the smaller ones: in counties with populations of 250,000 and above, they occupy almost 30% of the seats on county commissions, and in counties with populations of 500,000 and above, that proportion rises to 35%. Regionally, women are better represented in the West, where they hold approximately 36% of the seats on county boards. They are also likely to hold a higher percentage of seats in central counties than in suburban or independent counties.

Term Limits and Vacancies
Finally, there are two other common characteristics of county boards. First is the lack of limits on the number of terms that members can serve: 94% of counties—a small increase over the 92% reported in 2002—do not have such a limit (not shown). The percentage of counties that do have a limit is relatively higher in counties with populations over 250,000, rising up to 21% in some brackets, as well as in counties with a council-manager form of government. The second additional characteristic involves how a vacancy on the county board is filled before an election: responding counties indicated that the two most common forms of filling a vacancy are through appointment by the political party or the governor (33%), or through appointment by the commission (27%) (Figure 3/3).

Presiding Officer
The presiding officer can assume various names, often depending on the type of services that were emphasized when the county was established in the state; in Kentucky, for example, the presiding officer is the judge executive and, as such, is responsible for the judicial services of the county. Even when the name of the position is similar, the position can carry different responsibilities and authority; for example, when the presiding officer is the county judge (as in some Texas and Alabama counties), the position brings with it significantly more authority because the judge has fiscal as well as judicial responsibilities.

Nevertheless, in a large percentage of counties where the presiding officer is not directly elected,

that officer cannot provide substantive leadership because of his or her limited authority over other commissioners and potentially short length of tenure. In nearly two-thirds of responding counties (62%), the presiding officer is selected by members of the commission, in 27%, the presiding officer is elected directly by voters, and in 1%, the presiding officer is the member of the commission who received the most votes in the general election (Table 3/6). Also in the majority of counties—92%, slightly less than in 2002—the presiding officer is a member of the commission. And only 6% of counties grant the presiding officer the authority to veto measures passed by the commission; in most counties where the presiding officer has such authority, it can be used to veto ordinances, resolutions, and appropriations passed by the council.

In half of the responding counties (52%), the presiding officer has a term length of one year; in 14% of counties, the term of office is two years, and in almost 30% it is four years (not shown). Recall attempts filed against the presiding officer continue to be uncommon—reported only in 4% of counties—and are rarely successful once filed (not shown). In absolute terms, among counties responding the survey, recalls have succeeded only twice since 2002.

Political Representation Systems
Members of the county board can be elected at large, by district, or by a mix of these two forms of political representation. The form through which members are elected can have important implications for the groups they represent. In cities, for example, scholars have suggested that district elections produce representatives who are likely to depend on support from groups and voters from specific areas and communities and thus will likely represent their particular interests.[13] On the other hand, representatives elected at large serve a countywide constituency, requiring council members to respond to a broader set of political interests than those present in a single district; as a result, at-large elections likely facilitate decision making because board members have similar policy preferences.

Counties responding to the 2007 survey reported few changes in their type of representation since 2002: 60% elect all their board members by district or ward, 25% elect all members at large, and 14% use a combination of these two forms of political representation (compared with 62%, 28%, and 11%, respectively, in 2002) (not shown). The small increase in mixed representation seems to come at the expense of at-large elections.

POLITICAL REFORM IN COUNTY GOVERNMENT

Although one of the main institutional advances accomplished by the reform movement in local government is the nonpartisan ballot, a majority of counties (83%) still show the political affiliation of candidates to the county commission on the ballot (not shown). This percentage is similar across the various classification categories. Nevertheless, in council-administrator or council-manager

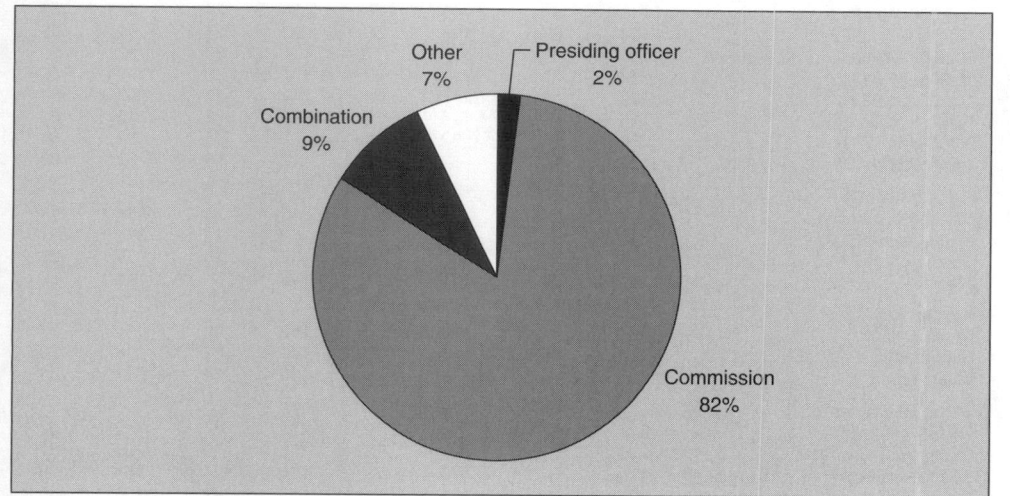

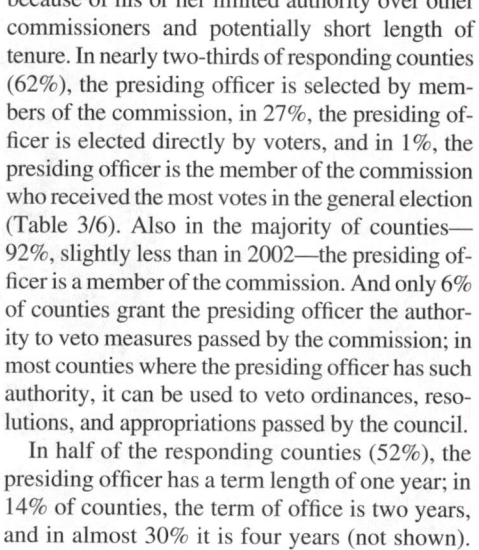

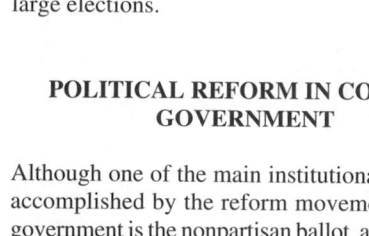

Figure 3/2 *Responsibility for appointing the chief administrative officer*

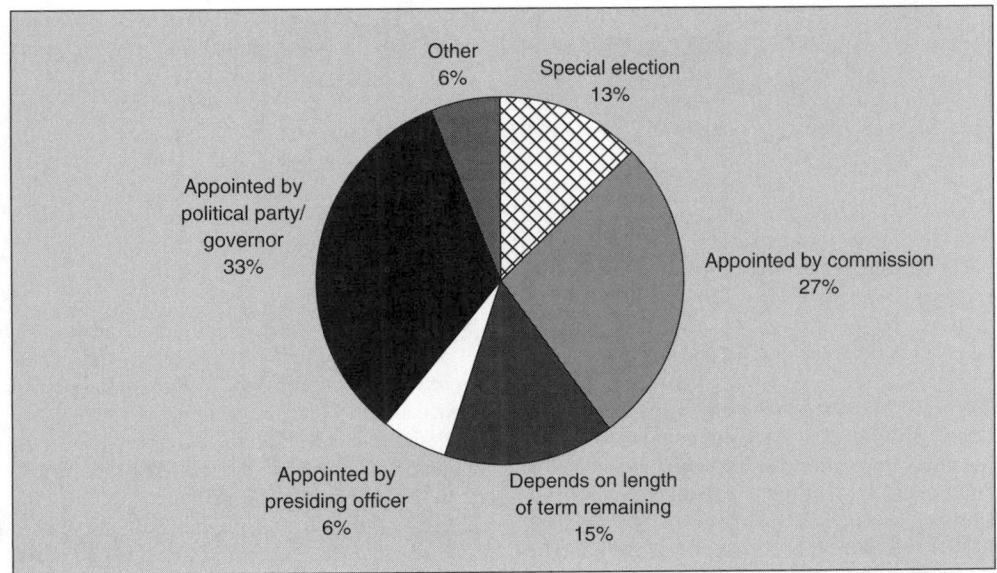

Figure 3/3   *Method of filling a vacated seat*

counties, the percentages are relatively lower than in other forms of government: 74% and 77%, respectively. These percentages are similar to those reported in the 1988 and 2002 surveys, which suggest that this reform does not seem to have had a major impact in counties (not shown).

Provisions for direct democracy, another product of the reform movement, allow citizens to propose legislation for enactment or rejection at the polls, with or without the intervention of the county board, or to approve or reject ordinances passed by the county board. Provisions for initiatives, recall of elected officials, and referendum tend to lower the costs (e.g., of media notification, phone calls, a meeting place) for residents and interest groups to organize themselves and influence the policy-making process. In general, these provisions can enhance responsiveness by county authorities: research on local government indicates that with access to direct democracy institutions, "not in my back yard" (NIMBY) and environmental groups are more likely to advance their

interests.[14] In regional terms, the West region has the highest rate of adoption of direct democracy instruments, which is consistent with the results of ICMA's 2002 survey.[15]

The adoption of these provisions varies significantly among counties. Overall, 40% reported allowing citizens to place initiatives in the ballot (Table 3/7). This provision is even more common among highly populated counties, with 83% of counties with populations above 1,000,000 reporting such provisions. Geographically, 64% of counties in the West region have a provision for the

initiative, compared with only 30% of counties in the South. Neither metro status nor form of government significantly predicts the adoption of the initiative. Among counties that provide the initiative, the majority (59%) require that any change proposed by citizens through a petition process must be placed directly on the ballot for a vote, while one third require that the commission consider the proposal *before* it is placed on the ballot (not shown); in both cases, the results of the vote are binding on the county government. The survey reports that increasing percentages of counties in all regions provide for the initiative, but most especially in the Northeast, where it jumped from 9% in 2002 to 34% in 2007.

More than 70% of counties overall reported having a provision for the legislative referendum, which allows the commission to place any question (e.g., local bond measures, charter amendments) on the ballot for voter approval (Table 3/7). The percentages are highest in both small (under 2,500) and very large counties (250,000 and above) and include all reporting counties with populations above 1,000,000. Regionally, the highest percentage of counties providing for a legislative referendum is in the West (81%). The legislative referendum is also associated with differences in the county form of government: 79% of council-manager counties compared with 61% of counties with the council–elected executive form. However, there are no significant differences by metro status.

The majority of counties (68%) do not allow for the popular referendum. Among those that do, the highest percentages are in the under-2,500 population bracket (56%) and in the West (51%),

Table 3/6   CHARACTERISTICS OF PRESIDING OFFICER, 1988–2007

	1988, %	2002, %	2007, %
Presiding officer selected by			
Voters	22	23	27
Commission.	69	64	62
Commission/highest no. of votes	na	na	1
Rotate	8	12	9
Member of the commission			
Yes	93	94	92
No	7	6	8
Authority to veto commission-passed measures			
Yes	8	5	6
No	92	95	94

Note: Percentages may not total 100% because of rounding.

Table 3/7   PROVISION FOR METHODS OF DIRECT DEMOCRACY

Classification	Initiative		Legislative referendum		Popular referendum		Recall	
	No reporting (A)	County offers, % of (A)	No reporting (B)	County offers, % of (B)	No reporting (C)	County offers, % of (C)	No reporting (D)	County offers, % of (D)
Total	981	40	1,001	71	896	32	941	55
Population group								
Over 1,000,000	12	83	12	100	11	36	12	75
500,000–1,000,000	14	43	16	88	13	46	10	70
250,000–499,999	40	40	41	78	38	29	37	62
100,000–249,999	104	37	106	68	97	24	101	55
50,000–99,999	131	41	137	77	121	25	132	50
25,000–49,999	210	35	211	69	197	28	197	48
10,000–24,999	269	39	277	69	244	37	253	51
5,000–9,999	115	43	115	67	97	32	115	60
2,500–4,999	56	50	53	59	51	45	52	64
Under 2,500.	30	60	33	79	27	56	32	88
Geographic region								
Northeast.	47	34	48	56	45	33	44	18
North-Central.	383	42	393	70	350	39	374	61
South.	390	30	395	69	355	18	359	38
West	161	64	165	81	146	51	164	87
Metro status								
Central.	161	41	168	76	156	30	154	63
Suburban.	114	40	117	75	101	27	106	50
Independent	706	40	716	69	639	34	681	54
Form of government								
County commission	312	47	314	72	279	37	300	57
Council-administrator	296	37	307	71	278	30	288	57
Council-manager.	170	31	173	79	164	24	167	58
Council–elected executive.	120	47	121	61	103	42	106	45
Did not report.	83	39	86	63	72	26	80	41

whereas lowest percentage is in the South (18%). Form of government is significantly associated with the adoption of the popular referendum, as counties with a council–elected executive have the highest adoption rate (42%) whereas council-manager counties have the lowest (24%).

More than half of the reporting counties provide for the recall of elected officials: 55% allow citizens to place a question on the ballot regarding whether an elected official should be removed from office. As with the provision for the legislative referendum, this percentage is highest in counties with populations of 250,000 and above as well as in counties under 2,500 in population. Region is also a predictor of adoption, with the highest percentages for the provision of recall in the West and North-Central regions (87% and 61%, respectively), and the lowest percentages in the Northeast and South regions (18% and 38%, respectively). Interestingly, the percentages of counties providing for recall dropped in all regions except the Northeast, where it increased by eight percentage points since 2002. Neither metro status nor form of government is significantly associated with the adoption rate of recall.

CONCLUSION

The numerous demographic, social, and political changes that have occurred in the United States over the years have forced local governments to develop institutional arrangements that help can them respond to a changing environment, and the various county government structures reflect the ongoing struggle to adapt those institutions to deal with the changing demands of citizens and to be more responsive, effective, and efficient in delivering new types of public services. Using findings from ICMA's *County Form of Government 2007* survey, this article has examined the structures of county governments as they relate to differences in county population size, region, and metro status. It has also identified some underlying trends in evidence since findings from the 2002 survey were reported.

While the prevalent political institutions in counties seem to be trending toward more professional administration, more research is needed to identify the extent to which the professional administration of counties is resulting in more efficient and effective government; also worth pursuing is whether the institutional arrangements associated with government reform are only legitimizing the expansion of county government. Despite concerns with testing on the county level theories that were developed at the city level,[16] several aspects of county government, including its structure and other political institutions, can be seen as facilitating collective decision making—among, for example, some interest groups seeking to advance their preferred policies—and can thus be subjected to similar analyses as those already conducted in cities.[17] In other words, any change in the structure of county government has clear implications for the policies that will be produced by such a structure and, by extension, for what interests will most likely be addressed. Future research should identify the extent to which, in order to protect their interests, some groups limit the adoption of new institutional arrangements that provide more professional administration in counties.

[1]Victor S. DeSantis, "County Government: A Century of Change," in *The Municipal Year Book 1989* (Washington, D.C.: ICMA, 1989), 55–84; Tanis J. Salant, "County Governments: An Overview," *Intergovernmental Perspective* (Washington, D.C.: Advisory Commission on Intergovernmental Relations, 1991).

[2]J. Edwin Benton, *Counties as Service Delivery Agents: Changing Expectations and Roles* (New York: Praeger, 2002); Vincent Marando and Mavis Mann Reeves, "County Government Structural Reform: Influence of State, Region, and Urbanization," *Publius: The Journal of Federalism* 23 (Winter 1993): 41–52.

[3]David R. Morgan and Kenneth Kickham, "Changing the Form of County Government: Effects on Revenue and Expenditure Policy," *Public Administration Review* 59, no. 4 (1999): 315–324; Victor S. DeSantis and Tari Renner, "The Impact of Political Structures on Public Policies in American Counties," *Public Administration Review* 54, no. 3 (1994): 291–295.

[4]DeSantis, "A Century of Change"; Tanis J. Salant, "Trends in County Government Structure," in *The Municipal Year Book 2004* (Washington, D.C.: ICMA, 2004), 35–41.

[5]Salant, "Trends in County Government Structure," 36.

[6]DeSantis, "A Century of Change."

[7]Taking into consideration the response rate, the results of this survey should be interpreted with caution. Based on data from the National Association of Counties (NACo) for all counties in 2001, the breakdown of the county structure was commission, 55% (n = 1,697); council-administrator/manager, 32% (n = 968), and council–elected executive, 13% (n = 398). These percentages are almost the opposite of those reported here for counties with a commission or a council-manager/administrator. The fact that the ICMA survey reports 22% more counties with a council-manager/administrator than NACo does suggests a possible nonresponse bias problem; that is, council-administrator/manager counties may have been more inclined to respond ICMA's survey than counties with the commission form of government. This expectation is plausible, given that county managers/administrators may be more interested than other county officials in participating in a survey from a professional association.

[8]Salant, "Trends in County Government Structure," 37; DeSantis, "A Century of Change."

[9]Herbert S. Duncombe, *Modern County Government* (Washington, D.C.: NACo, 1977).

[10]Ibid.

[11]Ibid.

[12]James H. Svara, "Leadership and Professionalism in County Government," in *The American County*, ed. Donald Menzel (Tuscaloosa: University of Alabama Press, 1996), 109–127.

[13]James C. Clingermayer and Richard C. Feiock, *Institutional Constraints and Policy Choice* (New York: SUNY Press, 2001).

[14]Elisabeth R. Gerber and Justin H. Phillips, "Direct Democracy and Land Use Policy: Exchanging Public Goods for Development Rights," *Urban Studies* 41, no. 2 (2004): 463–479.

[15]Salant, "Trends in County Government Structure," 40.

[16]Mark Schneider and Kee Ok Park, "Metropolitan Counties as Service Delivery Agents: The Still Forgotten Governments," *Public Administration Review* 49 (1989): 345–352.

[17]Clingermayer and Feiock, *Institutional Constraints and Policy Choice;* David R. Morgan and John P. Pelissero, "Urban Policy: Does Political Structure Matter?" *American Political Science Review* 74, no. 4 (1980): 999–1006.

A 4

Cities Leading the Way: The Use of Alternative Work Schedules

Rex L. Facer II
Chyleen A. Arbon
Lori L. Wadsworth
Romney Institute of Public Management Marriott School
Brigham Young University

Selected Findings

The most common type of alternative work schedule is the compressed workweek, offered by 46% of all responding cities; the next most common option is flextime, offered by 34%.

The most influential factors behind an organization's adoption of alternative work schedules are improved employee morale (48%) and employee work-life balance (46%). The two most significant drawbacks for organizations are increased scheduling difficulty (39%) and decreased face time with employees (24%).

For employees, the most commonly perceived benefit is improved work-life balance (74%), and the most significant drawback is longer workdays (38%).

Alternative work schedules are not a new idea, but they have recently been receiving a considerable amount of renewed attention. During the summer of 2008, as the price of gasoline escalated to over $4.00 per gallon, local governments and their employees sought ways to cope with rising fuel prices. One strategy that gained renewed attention was to change the number of days that employees work each week. For example, the city of Birmingham, Alabama, shifted from a traditional five-day workweek to a four-day workweek for its employees. Employees still work 40 hours per week, but now they compress those 40 hours into four days rather than five. This saves them 20% of their commuting costs (time and fuel). However, this approach does not address the organizational consequences of rising energy costs. To reduce those costs, some cities have chosen to close down their offices one day a week. Provo, Utah, adopted a four-day workweek several years ago, and most city departments in Provo are now closed on Fridays.

This summer, to further explore what cities are doing to combat rising energy costs, we surveyed U.S. cities with populations of 25,000 and above on their use of alternative work schedules. This article first identifies the various types of alternative work schedules in use; then, after a brief review of the pertinent literature, it presents data on the current prevalence of these arrangements among selected U.S. municipalities, discussing the factors that influence adoption of alternative work schedules and the benefits and drawbacks of those work schedules for employees and organizations. It then cites research findings and survey results with regard to one type of alternative work schedule in particular: the compressed workweek.

TYPES OF ALTERNATIVE WORK SCHEDULES

Alternative work schedules are schedules that do not fit the traditional eight-hour workday—typically from 8:00 AM to 5:00 PM, five days a week. Alternative work schedules come in many different formats. Flexibility varies within the categories, and each type has its advantages and disadvantages.

A *compressed workweek* schedules longer shifts for fewer days of the week. Although such schedules limit the free time that employees have available on working days, it allows them extra time off during the week to handle their personal affairs while also reducing travel time and expenses.

Flextime allows employees to start and finish work at times other than the traditional 8:00 AM to 5:00 PM time period. Most flextime schedules have certain constraints on acceptable stop and start times, and most organizations using flextime require all employees to be at work for the core hours of the workday (e.g., between 10:00 AM and 2:00 PM). Flextime is typically offered as a work-life balance option, but it also might help save employees commute time and gas consumption, as it allows them to choose to commute during less congested traffic periods.

Job sharing is an arrangement in which one job position is split between two or more workers. This is also often used as a work-life balance option for valued employees who prefer to change to part-time work. The tradeoff in some organizations is reduced benefits (medical, vacation time, sick leave, 401k, etc.) for employees working less than a 40-hour week.

Telecommuting allows employees to work from a remote location. This arrangement gives them autonomy so they can more efficiently balance their work and life priorities. In addition, the organization might realize cost savings as a result of lower overhead at the work site. There are some concerns, however, about employee productivity and decreased sense of camaraderie because of decreased face time with the employer and co-workers.

LITERATURE REVIEW

Much of the research on alternative work schedules dates back to the 1970s, when there was a major movement toward such innovative arrangements.[1] Many writers contend that there were several reasons for this movement, the most commonly cited being quality of work life and productivity improvements for employees and organizations. Since much of this surge occurred before the energy crisis of the 1970s, however, energy conservation was not a driving force. But whatever the reasons, Jon Pierce reports that by 1972, more than 700 companies were offering compressed workweeks to over 100,000 employees, and about 60 to 70 companies a month were shifting to that arrangement.[2] Some studies show that by 1974, the number of employees working four 10-hour days a week (4/10s) was approximately 853,000.[3] But this movement lost momentum for a variety of reasons, including union opposition. Research suggests that although some organizations have continued to offer alternative work schedules, it has often been as an informal benefit rather than as a formal program.

ICMA Project on Workforce Mobility

Cities and counties are exploring and implementing a host of strategies all designed to save money, improve performance, manage and make better use of employee talent, and improve customer satisfaction with local government service delivery. In 2008, ICMA, in collaboration with Runzheimer International, started a project to examine the workforce mobility elements that are vital to these strategies and the ways in which they are being put to use. Such elements include wireless and handheld technologies, geographic positioning systems (GPS), telecommuting options, fuel sharing, flexible vehicles, and tele- and video-conferencing. If done right, managing mobility can reduce budget expenditures, decrease energy consumption, and increase employee morale and productivity—as studies done in the private sector can confirm. More information on ICMA's ongoing project can be found at www.icma.org.

Over the last 30 years, however, discussion in the academic literature about alternative work schedules has been sparse, and despite the growing number of cities that offer such schedules, the vast majority of extant research on this topic has centered on private organizations. In our review of that literature, we found significant relationships between alternative work schedules and increased productivity and job performance,[4] decreased employee turnover,[5] and decreased levels of work-family conflict,[6] as well as an indirect relationship with job satisfaction and general health.[7] More specifically, the research shows that private sector employees participating in compressed workweek schedules report increased job satisfaction[8] and decreased levels of perceived anxiety and stress,[9] while organizations benefit from decreased absenteeism,[10] increased productivity,[11] and more favorable employee attitudes regarding both job and co-workers.[12]

But some research on alternative work schedules in the public sector does exist:[13] Samantha Durst has found, for example, that there are very few public organizations that have formally evaluated the benefits of these policies.[14] This article represents another contribution to that body of research.

RESEARCH DESIGN

Using current U.S. Census estimates for 2006, we identified all 1,375 U.S. cities with a population estimate of 25,000 or more. We then randomly selected 355 cities for inclusion in our sample. A member of our research team contacted each city's human resource (HR) professional (generally the HR director), who is considered to have the most knowledge about the organization's use of alternative work schedules. Usable survey responses were received from 151 cities, resulting in a response rate of 43%.

Responses came from cities in 38 of the 50 U.S. states. The highest number of cities from one state was in California, whose 33 responding cities represent 22% of our total; seven states (Idaho, Maryland, Massachusetts, Mississippi, New Mexico, Oregon, and Rhode Island) had only one responding city each (not shown). Yet as Tables 4/1 and 4/2 show, the regional and population distributions of responding cities are similar to those of all U.S. cities with populations of

Table 4/2 DISTRIBUTION BY POPULATION: REPORTING CITIES COMPARED TO ALL U.S. CITIES

Population	Reporting cities			All U.S. cities over 25,000*		
	No. (A)	% of (A)	Cumulative percentage	No. (B)	% of (B)	Cumulative percentage
Total	151	100	100	1,375	100	100
25,000–49,999	74	49	49	684	50	50
50,000–99,999	50	33	82	423	31	81
100,000–199,999	9	6	88	164	12	93
200,000–299,999	10	7	95	39	3	96
300,000 and over	8	5	100	65	5	101

Note: Percentages may exceed 100% because of rounding.
*Based on 2006 Census population estimates.

25,000 or more. This highlights the representativeness of our sample.

FINDINGS ON ALTERNATIVE WORK SCHEDULES

More than half (56%) of all cities surveyed reported that they currently offer their employees some type of alternative work schedule (Table 4/3). Another 5% reported that they currently have a firm plan to do so and that they will provide a range of options.

Geographically, the highest percentage of cities that offer alternative work schedules is in the West region, as reported by about 75% of western cities (Table 4/4), and the lowest percentage is in the South (35%). In both the Northeast and the North-Central regions, almost half of the responding cities (50% and 49%, respectively) reported offer-

Table 4/3 ALTERNATIVE WORK SCHEDULES OFFERED

Type	Cities reporting (n = 151)	
	No.	Percentage
Total	151	100
Offer alternative work schedule	85	56
Compressed workweek	70	46
Flextime	52	34
Job sharing	14	9
Telecommuting	15	10
Other	12	8
Do not offer	59	39
Definitely plan to offer	7	5

Note: Percentages may exceed 100% because of multiple responses.

ing this option. Not surprisingly, western cities also have the highest levels of employee participation in alternative work schedules, with almost 30% reporting participation by 71% or more of their employees. By comparison, cities in the other three regions have much lower rates of employee participation in alternative work schedules.

We also examined the prevalence of four basic types of alternative work schedules: compressed workweeks, flextime, job sharing, and telecommuting. The most common type of alternative work schedule reported by responding cities is the compressed workweek, with 46% of all cities reporting that they offer it to at least some of their employees (see Table 4/3). The next most common option is flextime, offered by more than one-third of responding cities (34%). The other three options (job sharing, telecommuting, and "other") are each offered by no more than 10% of cities.

Factors Influencing the Adoption of Alternative Work Schedules

Focusing on the 85 cities that reported offering alternative work schedules, we explored the factors that influenced its adoption. The most influential factor appears to be that alternative work schedules improve employee morale (48%), followed closely by the belief that such arrangements support employee work-life balance (46%), increase productivity (44%), and extend business hours (40%) (Figure 4/1). Respondents were also given the opportunity to provide their own reasons for adopting alternative work schedules, but while 35 respondents (41%) indicated that there were reasons other than those listed in the survey instrument—for example, reduce commuting time, provide better customer service, deal with increased gas prices, and reduce pollution—

Table 4/1 DISTRIBUTION OF CITIES WITH POPULATIONS OVER 25,000, BY REGION

Region[1]	Percentage of cities reporting (n = 151)	Percentage of all U.S. cities over 25,000 (n = 1,375)
Northeast	9	12
North-Central	29	27
South	29	30
West	34	32

Note: Percentages exceed 100% because of rounding.
[1]For the breakdown of states in each region, see "Inside the *Year Book*," xi.

Table 4/4 AVAILABILITY OF, AND EMPLOYEE PARTICIPATION IN, ALTERNATIVE WORK SCHEDULES, BY REGION

Region	No. cities reporting (A)	Alternative work schedules offered		Level of employee participation, by percentage				
		No.	% of (A)	None % of (A)	1–30 % of (A)	31–50 % of (A)	51–70 % of (A)	71–100 % of (A)
Northeast	14	7	50	50	43	0	7	0
North-Central	43	21	49	51	40	5	0	5
South	43	15	35	65	33	0	0	2
West	51	38	75	26	29	8	8	29

Note: Percentages may exceed 100% because of rounding.

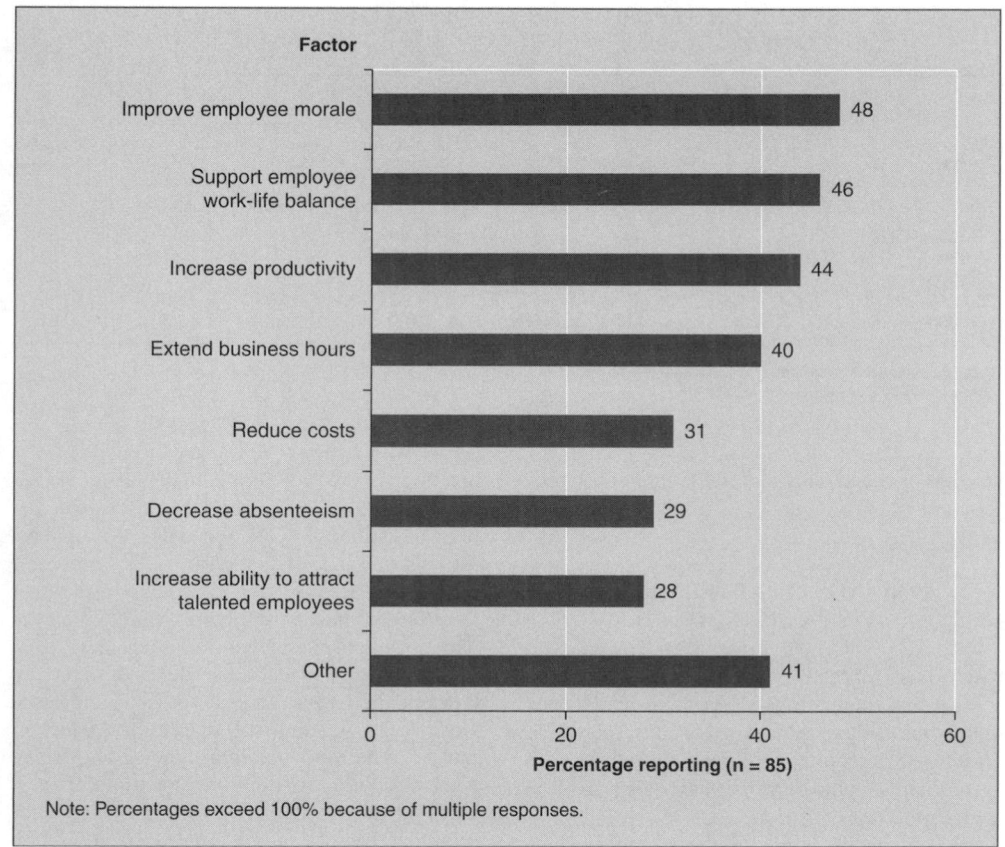

Figure 4/1 *Factors influencing the adoption of alternative work schedules*

there was not a strong or consistent pattern in their responses.

Organizational Benefits and Drawbacks
We asked the HR directors from those cities that offer some form of alternative work schedules to reflect on the benefits and drawbacks of such arrangements for the city. The most popular benefit that the HR directors identified is improved employee morale, reported by nearly two-thirds (64%) of the cities (Figure 4/2). The other benefit that was noted by more than half the cities is improved work-life balance for employees (54%). These benefits match the factors that influenced the cities' adoption of alternative work schedules. The third most cited benefit is improved customer service (46%), followed by increased productivity (41%). Among the 17% of respondents who identified benefits of alternative work schedules other than those listed in the survey, the one mentioned most often is energy conservation or reduced utility costs.

The most significant drawback that HR directors found with alternative work schedules is increased scheduling difficulty, reported by 33 of the 85 cities (39%) that implemented such schedules (Figure 4/3). The next most common drawback is decreased face time with employees (24%). All the other drawbacks were reported by fewer than 10% of respondents. However, nearly 25% of responding HR directors indicated that there were other drawbacks not mentioned in the survey. There was no common theme in the other drawback responses—for example, that alter-

native work schedules are not available for all employees, but are offered to only certain employees on a case-by-case basis; that they make it difficult to calculate payroll hours for employees; and that they exacerbate difficulties due to staff shortages. Perhaps the most interesting finding on the perceived drawbacks, however, was how few were reported relative to the perceived benefits.

Employee Benefits and Drawbacks
In addition to asking HR directors to reflect on the benefits to the organization, we asked them to respond from the perspective of employees—a reflection that HR directors are well suited to make: since their offices oversee alternative work schedules, these managers are the ones most likely to receive feedback from their employees. As they reported, the most commonly perceived benefit from the employee's perspective is improved work-life balance (74%) (Figure 4/4). Tied as the second most commonly perceived benefits, although with only half the strength as improved work-life balance, are decreased stress and reduced personal costs (39% each). Among other benefits identified that were not mentioned in the survey, HR directors noted employees' increased ability to enjoy their time off, increased educational opportunities, and increased job satisfaction.

As for the drawbacks that employees perceive from alternative work schedules, the one that the HR directors cited most often is longer workdays, reported by 32 of the 85 responding cities offering alternative work schedules (38%) (Figure 4/5).

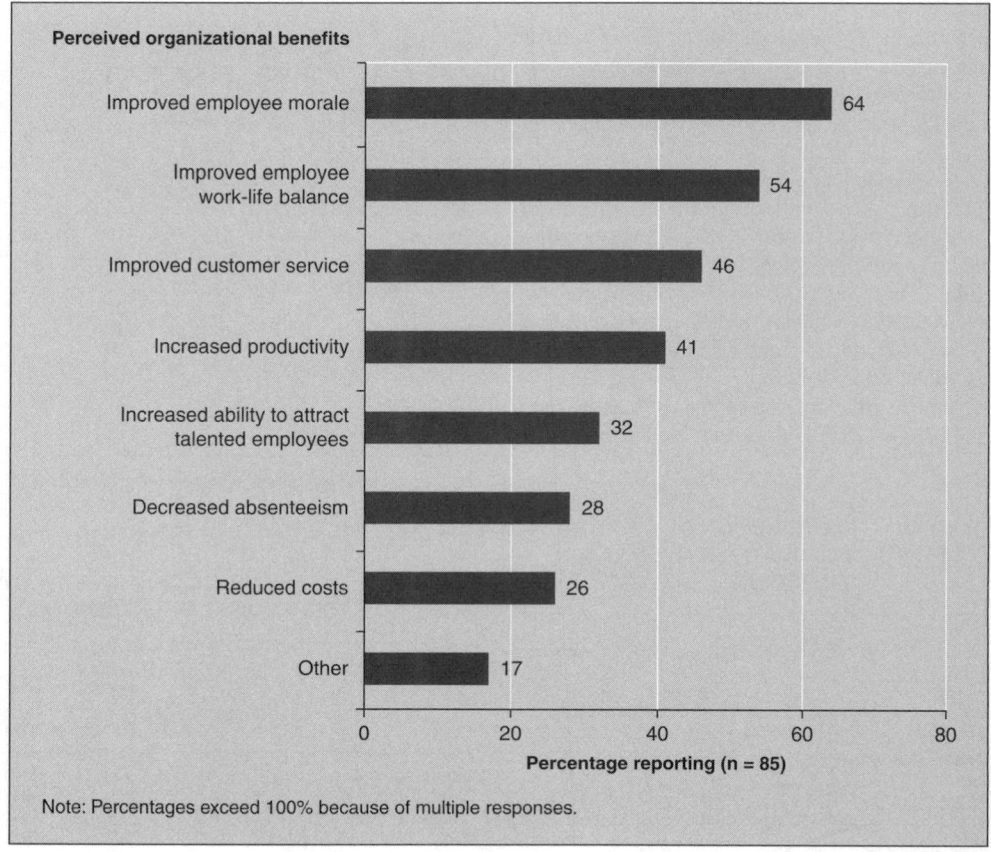

Figure 4/2 *Perceived benefits of alternative work schedules for organizations*

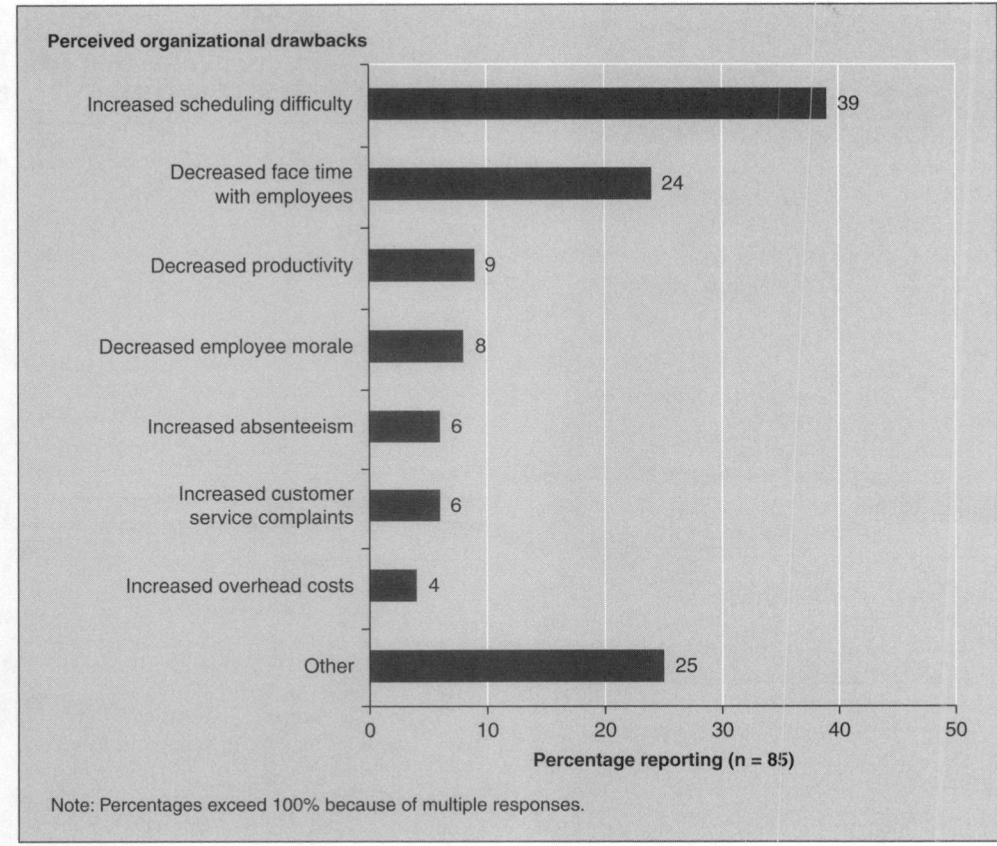

Figure 4/3   *Perceived drawbacks of alternative work schedules for organizations*

The next two most commonly reported drawbacks are related: increased isolation from colleagues (11%) and decreased face time with the employer (7%), both of which contribute to employee isolation. Notably, only one respondent found that the arrangement increased limitation on career advancement. Among drawbacks that were not listed in the survey, no clear pattern emerged: responses included internal friction between participating and nonparticipating employees over perceived inequity, a harder commute to work based on commute hours, the need to sacrifice pay increases to

implement alternative work schedules, issues with sick leave and holiday pay, and carpooling challenges.

COMPRESSED WORKWEEKS

Given that the most commonly offered alternative work schedule in U.S. cities is the compressed workweek, we turned our attention to this particular type of arrangement.

Prior Research Findings
From a specific focus on the research into the compressed workweek, we learn that the employee benefits they provide include increased job autonomy and job satisfaction, decreased absenteeism, and decreased transportation costs.[15] Job satisfaction is actually an important benefit for both the employee and the organization, as it is related to decreased turnover rates and improved recruitment.[16] Specifically, satisfied employees are less likely to leave their jobs, thereby saving recruitment and training costs for the organization. Furthermore, talented employees are likely to be drawn to organizations where employees are satisfied.[17]

An additional benefit for employees is increased work-family balance.[18] Research on work-family balance has found it to be positively related to increased productivity, decreased absenteeism and turnover,[19] and lower levels of psychological distress[20] and life stress.[21] Again, each of these outcomes can be beneficial not only to individuals but also to organizations.

In addition to higher levels of employee job satisfaction, as noted above, organizational benefits have been reported to include increased productivity, decreased absenteeism, and decreased transportation costs.[22] Regarding increased productivity, studies have shown that when employees have to spend fewer days at work, they spend less time on daily set-up and cleanup tasks. One deposit-support department for a large bank reported a tremendous morale boost, a turnover rate reduced to zero, many employees with perfect attendance records, and processing time for mortgage approvals reduced from eight days to three.[23]

As for decreased absenteeism, one study suggests that 63% of workers using compressed workweeks said that they were absent less often as a result.[24] Such work schedules can also lead to reduced use of leave, both annual and sick. Sick leave is conserved because employees are able to schedule routine medical and dental appointments on their days off, thereby reserving sick leave for use if they are actually incapacitated.[25]

Finally, compressed workweeks have been associated with decreased transportation concerns, benefiting the employees, the organization, and society as a whole. This occurs because employees participating in this schedule commute one less day of the week, which can decrease their transportation time and costs by 20%. In addition, these employees leave home and work after peak traffic hours, thereby decreasing traffic congestion.[26] One survey of commuters conducted by the Center for Urban Transportation Research in 2001 found that compressed workweek schedules reduce

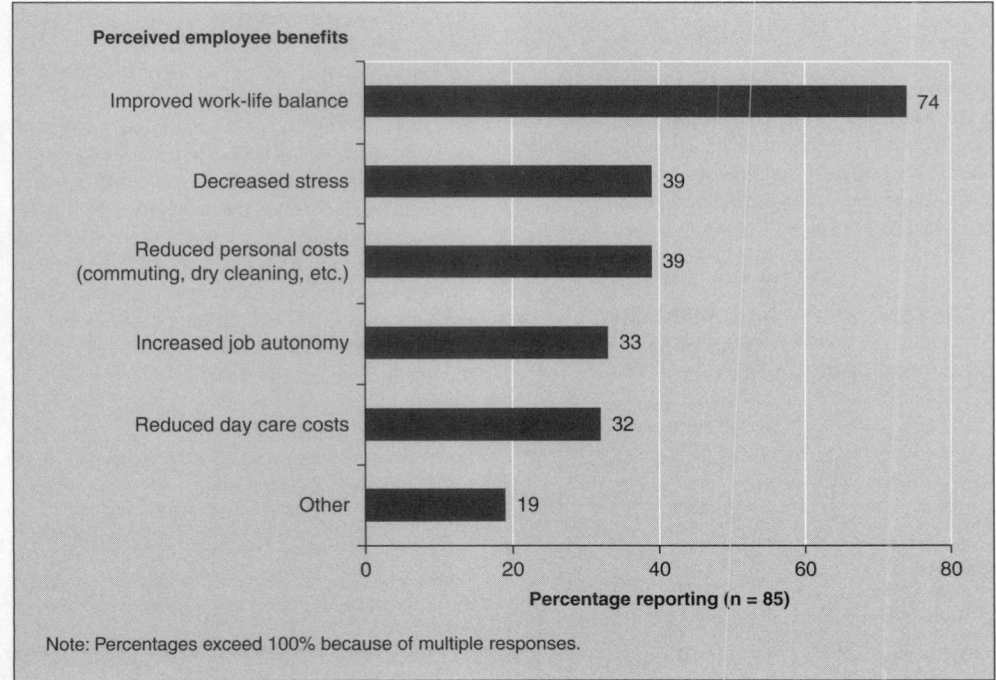

Figure 4/4   *Perceived benefits of alternative work schedules for employees*

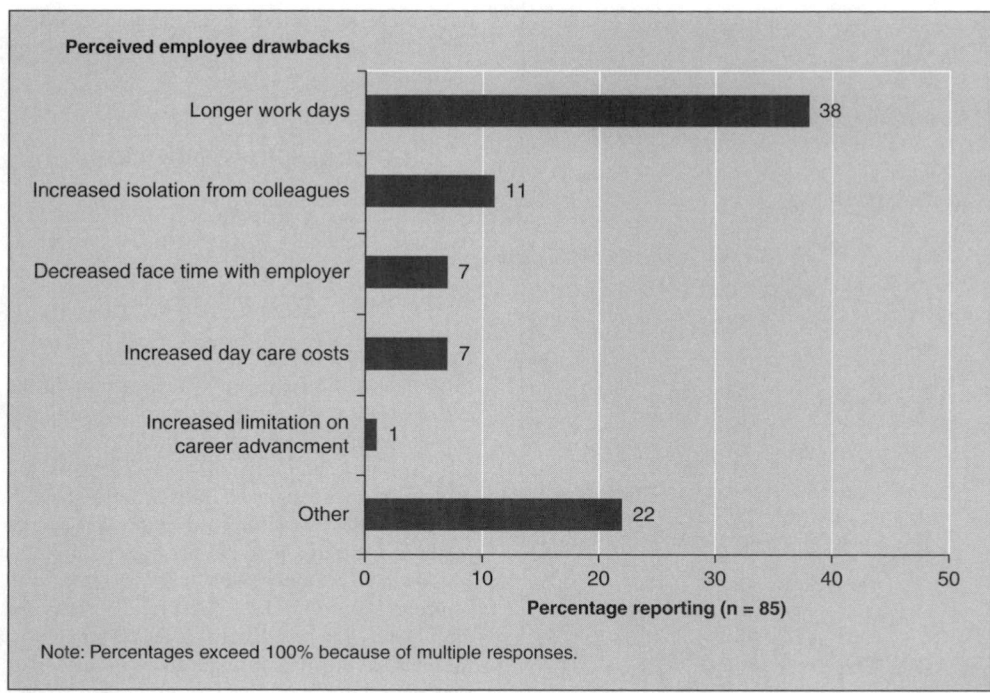

Perceived employee drawbacks

Note: Percentages exceed 100% because of multiple responses.

Figure 4/5   *Perceived drawbacks of alternative work schedules for employees*

automobile commutes by 7% to 10%, making it among the most effective commute trip reduction strategies considered.[27] In addition, Maralee Sundo and Satoshi Fujii found that such schedules significantly reduce participants' total commute time and increase the employees' personal time to devote to household activities or sleep.[28] Reducing long commuting times also has concrete consequences for organizations, as longer commutes yield increased stress, health complaints, absenteeism and tardiness, as well as decreased performance.[29]

Current Survey Findings

Compressed workweeks are generally offered in one of three schedules: 4/10s (working 10-hour shifts for four days with three days off each week), 9/80s (a two-week schedule of eight 9-hour workdays Monday through Thursday, one 8-hour Friday, and one Friday off every other week), and 3/36s (12-hour shifts for three days with four days off each week). We asked the responding cities about these three commonly used schedules: 49 cities reported offering a 4/10 schedule to their employees (33%), 34 cities offer a 9/80 schedule (23%), and 6 cities offer a 3/36 schedule (4.0%) (Table 4/5). Several cities offer multiple types of compressed schedules, as shown in Table 4/5.

Some organizations have allowed employees to choose whether to participate in a compressed workweek schedule, while others have made participation mandatory. As we tried to better understand the organizational experience with compressed workweeks, we were particularly interested in the process of implementing them. From our current study, we found that of those 70 cities offering some type of compressed workweek, 34% require it for at least a portion of their employees, while 66% offer it as an optional schedule for interested employees (not shown).

In addition, we looked at the regional distribution of cities offering compressed workweek schedules. As with alternative work schedules in general, cities in the West region are more likely to offer compressed workweeks than those in the other regions; the region least likely to do so is the Northeast (Table 4/6). Finally, in looking at compressed workweeks by size of the city as represented by the number of employees (Table 4/6), we found that there appears to be a slight correlation ($r = 0.147, p = 0.073$) between size of a city and the likelihood of that city offering a compressed workweek.

SUMMARY

Rising gas prices and environmental concerns have been just a few of the reasons behind the recent resurgence of interest in alternative work schedules. This research suggests that over half of the cities in the United States, and particularly those in the West region, are now offering some type of al-

Table 4/5   TYPES OF COMPRESSED WORKWEEK (CWW) SCHEDULES

Type of schedule	No.	Percentage of cities with CWW (n = 70)	Percentage of all reporting cities (n = 151)
Only 4/10	30	43	20
Only 9/80	16	23	11
Only 3/36	0	0	0
4/10 and 9/80	13	19	9
4/10 and 3/36	1	1	1
All three	5	7	3
Didn't specify	4	6	3
Do not offer a CWW	81	–	54

Note: Percentages may not total 100% because of rounding.

Table 4/6   AVAILABILITY OF COMPRESSED WORKWEEK (CWW) SCHEDULES, BY REGION AND NUMBER OF EMPLOYEES

	No. cities reporting (A)	Offer CWW	
		No.	% of (A)
Region (n = 151)			
Northwest	14	2	14
North-Central	43	10	23
South	43	15	35
West	51	22	43
No. employees[1] (n = 150)			
199 or fewer	21	12	57
200–399	56	18	32
400–599	21	11	52
600–799	16	9	56
800–999	9	6	67
1,000 or more	27	14	52

[1]One city did not indicate the number of employees so it is not included in this table. However, that city is not one that offers a compressed workweek.

ternative work schedule, and that the most common type offered is the compressed workweek.

The HR directors reported that alternative work schedules benefit organizations in several ways, including improved employee morale, employee work-life balance, customer service, productivity, and ability to attract talented employees. In contrast, a much smaller percentage of HR directors reported drawbacks; among those that did, the most commonly cited drawbacks are difficulties with scheduling and decreased face time with employees.

The HR directors also described their perception of employee benefits and drawbacks. The benefits that were cited most frequently are improved work-life balance, decreased stress, lower personal costs such as commuting and dry cleaning, and, to a lesser extent, increased job autonomy and reduced day care costs. The main drawback for employees is simply working a longer day. The other drawbacks were mentioned by 10% or fewer of the respondents.

Despite the increasing incidence of alternative work schedules, there has been very little research into these arrangements. One approach for additional research would be to conduct a similar study in other public sector settings. In addition, research is needed to understand the most effective way for an organization to change to an alternative work schedule. Although we know some of the benefits and drawbacks of alternative work schedules from the perspective of HR directors, additional research should be conducted by directly asking similar questions of employees.

[1]Randall B. Dunham and D. L. Hawk, "The Four-Day/Forty-Hour Week: Who Wants It?" *Academy of Management Journal* 20, no. 4 (1977): 644–655; James G. Goodale and A. K. Aagaard, "Factors Relating to Varying Reactions to the 4-Day Workweek," *Journal of Applied Psychology* 60, no. 1 (1975): 33–38; and John M. Ivancevich, "Effects of the Shorter Workweek on Selected Satisfaction and Performance Measures," *Journal of Applied Psychology* 59, no. 6 (1974): 717–721.

[2]Jon L. Pierce, *Alternative Work Schedules* (Boston: Allyn and Bacon, 1989).

[3]Janice Neipert Hedges, "How Many Days Make a Workweek," *Monthly Labor Review* 98, no. 4 (1975): 29–36.

[4]Patrick D. Lynch, Robert Eisenberger, and Stephen Armeli, "Perceived Organizational Support: Inferior versus Superior Performance by Wary Employees," *Journal of Applied Psychology* 84, no. 4 (1999): 467–483.

[5]Aaron Cohen, "Nonwork Influences on Withdrawal Cognitions: An Empirical Examination of an Overlooked Issue," *Human Relations* 50, no. 12 (1997): 1511–1536.

[6]T. D. Allen, "Examining the Impact of Family-Friendly Benefits: The Role of Organizational Support Perceptions" (paper presented at the annual meeting of the Academy of Management, Chicago, August 1999).

[7]Linda Thiede Thomas and Daniel C. Ganster, "Impact of Family-Supportive Work Variables on Work-Family Conflict and Strain: A Control Perspective," *Journal of Applied Psychology* 80, no. 1 (1995): 6–15.

[8]Dunham and Hawk, "The Four-Day/Forty-Hour Week."

[9]Ivancevich, "Effects of the Shorter Workweek."

[10]Goodale and Aagaard, "Factors Relating to Varying Reactions"; S. Ronen and S. B. Primps, "The Compressed Work Week as Organizational Change: Behavioral and Attitudinal Outcomes," *Academy of Management Review* 6, no. 1 (1981): 61–74.

[11]Duxbury and Haines, "Predicting Alternative Work Arrangements."

[12]M. Tippins and L. K. Stroh, "The 4/4 Work Schedule: Impact on Employee Productivity and Work Attitudes in a Continuous Operation Industry," *Journal of Applied Business Research* 9, no. 3 (1993): 131–35.

[13]Linda Duxbury and George Haines Jr., "Predicting Alternative Work Arrangements from Salient Attitudes: A Study of Decision Makers in the Public Sector," *Journal of Business Research* 23, no. 1 (1991): 83–97; Rex L. Facer and Lori L. Wadsworth, "Alternative Work Schedules and Work-Family Balance: A Research Note," *Review of Public Personnel Administration* 28, no. 2 (2008): 166–177.

[14]Samantha L. Durst, "Assessing the Effect of Family-Friendly Programs on Public Organizations," *Review of Public Personnel Administration* 19, no. 3 (1999): 19–33.

[15]Pierce, *Alternative Work Schedules;* Boris B. Baltes, "Flexible and Compressed Workweek Schedules: A Meta-Analysis of their Effects on Work-Related Criteria," *Journal of Applied Psychology* (1999): 496–513; Facer and Wadsworth, "Alternative Work Schedules and Work-Family Balance."

[16]Wendy R. Boswell, John W. Boudreau, and Jan Tichy, "The Relationship between Employee Job Changes and Job Satisfaction: The Honeymoon-Hangover Effect," *Journal of Applied Psychology* 90, no. 5 (2005): 882–892.

[17]Debra Shipman, "Can We Learn a Few Things from Google?" *Nursing Management* 37, no. 8 (2006): 10–12.

[18]Facer and Wadsworth, "Alternative Work Schedules and Work-Family Balance."

[19]Jennifer L. Glass and Sarah Beth Estes, "The Family Responsive Workplace," *Annual Review of Sociology* 23 (August 1997): 289–313.

[20]Michael R. Frone, Marcia Russell, and M. Lynne Cooper, "Antecedents and Outcomes of Work-Family Conflict: Testing a Model of the Work-Family Interface," *Journal of Applied Psychology* 77, no. 1 (1992): 65–78.

[21]Saroj Parasuraman, Jeffrey H. Greenhaus, and Cherlyn Skromme Granrose, "Role Stressors, Social Support, and Well-Being among Two-Career Couples," *Journal of Organizational Behavior* 13, no. 4 (1992): 339–356.

[22]Baltes, "Flexible and Compressed Workweek Schedules."

[23]Mary Williams Walsh, "Luring the Best in an Unsettled Time," *New York Times,* January 30, 2001.

[24]Norma Tombari and Nora Spinks, "The Work/Family Interface at Royal Bank Financial Group: Successful Solutions—A Retrospective Look at Lessons Learned," *Women in Management Review* 14, no. 5 (1999): 186–193.

[25]Box and Cox, *The Economist* 56 (1994).

[26]Rudy Hung, "An Annotated Bibliography of Compressed Workweeks," *International Journal of Manpower* 17, no. 6/7 (1996): 43–53.

[27]Satoshi Fujii, Tommy Gärling, and Ryuichi Kitamura, "Changes in Driver's Perceptions and Use of Public Transport during a Freeway Closure: Effects of Temporal Structural Change on Cooperation in a Real-Life Social Dilemma," *Environment and Behavior* 33, no. 6 (2001): 796–808.

[28]Maralee Sundo and Satoshi Fujii, "The Effects of a Compressed Working Week on Commuters' Daily Activity Patterns," *Transportation Research* 39, no. 10 (2005): 835–848.

[29]Giovanni Costa, Laurie Pickup, and Vittorio DiMartino, "Communicating: A Further Stress Factor for Working People: Evidence from the European Community," *International Archives of Occupational and Environmental Health* 60, no. 5 (1988): 377–385.

How Will Public Sector Retirement Withstand the Current Recession?

Gregory J. Dyson
Gordon Tiffany, CFP®
ICMA-RC

with
Craig Small
ICMA-RC
Kathy Harm, CFP®
Special advisor to ICMA-RC

Selected Findings

Depending on the depth and length of the market downturn, public sector employers may be required to make additional contributions to boost the funding levels of their pension plans. However, increasing mandated retirement contributions will mean less money to provide public services. It may also mean those closer to retirement will have their benefits protected, but newer workers may see significant changes.

With the cost of defined benefit plans for retiree health care now appearing directly on government balance sheets, governments are looking for defined contribution alternatives that can help employees pay for health care in retirement without increasing governments' liabilities.

State and local government leaders know that they need qualified and experienced employees to ensure essential public services. They have long recognized that public employee retirement systems are significant recruitment and retention tools, a key reason that public service is seen as an attractive lifetime career, and an essential element of the implied employment contract. But by the end of 2008, some observers were asking if mounting economic difficulties could threaten the continued viability of public retirement plans.

The defined benefit and defined contribution retirement plans that public employers and their employees count on as the foundation for their retirement security depend on investment earnings to build the asset base needed to pay expected benefits. In fact, most of the assets are expected to be derived from earnings, not contributions. Public employees planning for their own retirements have relied on expectations of reasonably predictable pension benefits, orderly financial markets, and the continuation of Medicare and Social Security.

For various reasons, retirement benefits for public sector workers are generally better than those available for private sector workers.[1] But requirements to fund promised public employee retirements compete directly with the need to fund vital public services. Every tax dollar used to meet retirement funding obligations is unavailable to support more police on the streets or to keep library doors open.

The last quarter of 2008 was a difficult time for the nation's economy. On December 1, 2008, the National Bureau of Economic Research (NBER) announced that an economic recession had been under way for a year.[2] Unemployment was up, economic growth down, credit markets nearly dysfunctional, and tax revenues for many state and local governments falling. Even if the economic situation unexpectedly brightens, this time of economic challenge is an opportunity to consider the implications that economic uncertainty may have for the financial commitments made by state and local government retirement plans during more prosperous times. In other words, it is important to ask whether the public retirement plans can withstand the economic storm that hit full force in 2008, and whether local and state governments will be able to sustain these plans even in less volatile times.

This review of the public sector retirement landscape is based on the familiar "three-legged stool" metaphor for retirement income. The three legs are employer-based retirement plans, government benefits (Social Security and Medicare), and individual savings. The metaphor is a model for retirement income diversification, with sources sponsored by the employer (retirement plans), the government (Social Security and Medicare), and the individual (savings). Another critical element of retirement security is retiree health care benefits, which are increasingly seen as a fourth leg, converting the metaphorical stool into a table. By the end of 2008, all parts of this model were challenged.

By analyzing how the sharp decline in the stock market will affect the public employee defined benefit pension systems and defined contribution plan investment accounts, the following article provides some insight into the current economic climate and the financial distress that it is causing those in state and local government. It first reviews the collapse of the housing bubble and its impact on individual retirement plans; it then examines the roles of Social Security, Medicare, personal savings, and retiree health care in shaping public sector retirement. The explanations contained within should guide the reader to a better understanding of how the public sector prepares for retirement, and how the severe economic situation has affected—and will continue to affect—both employers and employees.

THE ECONOMIC ENVIRONMENT: LATE 2008

Near the end of 2008, grim economic news swept across the country. The unemployment rate jumped to 6.7% in November, up by 1.7% since December 2007. During this same time frame, the number of unemployed persons increased by 2.7 million, a trend that continued through the end of the year.[3] City and county revenues across the country were flat or declining, and many officials had to make painful decisions to cut services, dip into rainy-day reserves, and/or selectively increase taxes and fees.[4] The impact of the nation's economic distress in such a relatively short period of time indicated to experts that the recession could be long lasting, and deep enough to have a further impact on local and state government employees and their retirement plans.

The current global economic downturn began as a relatively contained decline in housing prices in a few localities in the United States and then ballooned into a worldwide crisis. The enormous inventory of securitized mortgage debt that had built up since the early part of 2000 began to collide with falling housing prices.

Accounting rules forced banks and other financial institutions to write down the value of the mortgages they held. Once-iconic financial institutions, heavily invested in mortgage-backed securities, began to fail. Fearful of losing the value of their remaining assets, some banks virtually stopped lending. Economic activity slowed sharply, layoffs soared, and consumer spending fell. Negative effects spread quickly from the United States to economies linked around the globe, in part because many of the mortgage-backed securities were held by foreign investors. Only unprecedented government intervention prevented a freezing of credit markets.

Distress quickly found its way from the banking system into the broader economy. Consumer spending was down sharply in the third quarter of 2008. By early December, Federal Reserve chairman Ben Bernanke agreed with assessments that the recession would extend well into 2009.[5]

The downturn caused widespread investment losses. Including reinvested dividends, the Standard & Poor's 500-stock index, a broad measure of the nation's largest companies, was down more than 39% for the year as of the end of November 2008. Safe-haven investments were hard to find. The 10-year treasury note index fell 26% during the same period, and most commodities were

off sharply. Equity assets in all retirement plans dropped in value by about $4 trillion in the two years ending October 9, 2008,[6] with continuing losses in October and November.

The Investment Company Institute reported that as recently as March 2008, retirement assets accounted for 40% of Americans' net worth.[7] The value of these assets plummeted just as Americans' most common largest assets, their homes, were falling in value. The combined effect on household net worth was considerable and had a powerful psychological impact. Consumers cut spending and reconsidered their retirement prospects.

The stock market is considered a leading indicator, often beginning to decline before a recession starts and beginning to rebound before it ends. Financial analysts were divided about how long the drop in the financial markets would continue. Some noted that stock market recovery often begins at the time of worst news as those investors with a long view see bargains in depressed prices. Other observers argued that the current situation was unprecedented; some worried that it might signal a lengthy transition to a permanently less robust economy.

EARLIER RECESSIONS

There are various ways to define recession. A simple definition is two quarters in a row of negative economic growth. A more sophisticated definition takes into account a broad array of economic data. The NBER Business Cycle Dating Committee, a committee of experts, defines a recession as "a significant decline in economic activity spread across the economy, lasting more than a few months, normally visible in real GDP [gross domestic product], real [personal] income, employment [non-farm payrolls], industrial production, and wholesale-retail sales."[8] This definition requires data to be gathered and analyzed. It was not until December 1, 2008, that the NBER announced that the U.S. economy had entered into a recession 12 months earlier: "The Business Cycle Dating Committee of the National Bureau of Economic Research . . . determined that a peak in economic activity occurred in the U.S. economy in December 2007. The peak marks the end of the expansion that began in November 2001 and the beginning of a recession."[9]

In accordance with the NBER definition, there have been 21 recessions in the United States since 1900. They have lasted an average of 14 months, including the two (August 1929 to March 1933, lasting 43 months, and May 1937 to June 1938, lasting 13 months) that together are considered the Great Depression.[10] The 12 recessions that took place in the first half of the 20th century lasted, on average, more than 17 months each. During this 50-year period, which included the Great Depression, the U.S. economy was in recession more than a third of the time.

The Great Depression was far more severe than any economic dislocation experienced since. During the first of its two recessions (1929–1933), GDP fell by 30%. By contrast, during the worst post–World War II recession (1973–1975), GDP fell by less than 5%.

The second half of the 20th century saw enormous economic progress. With just seven recessions lasting a total of 75 months, the economy was in recession only 12.5% of the time, less than half the rate of the first 50 years. On average, these recessions were not only short and infrequent but also less severe than those common in earlier years. America had become a nation accustomed to economic growth, with interruptions to prosperity being relatively rare and inconsequential.

It is noteworthy that the economic turmoil of the first half of the 20th century directly brought about Social Security, arguably the greatest contribution to retirement economic security in the history of the United States. Further, the distress began a wave of legislation—including laws intended to stabilize and regulate previously freewheeling financial markets and loosely regulated banks—on which today's financial system is based. These laws include the Federal Home Loan Bank Act of 1932, the Banking Acts of 1933 and 1935, the Securities and Exchange Act of 1934, and the Federal Credit Union Act of 1934. This decade also saw the creation of the Federal Open Market Committee within the Federal Reserve System, the body that still directs the nation's monetary policy. The reforms that grew out of the economic distress have shaped the orderly financial markets on which today's institutional retirement systems and individual retirement planning depend. Thus, as the motive for reform, economic distress has resulted in greater retirement security.

THE FIRST LEG: RETIREMENT PLANS

The nation's public employee retirement plans serve more than 8 million state and local government employees. These plans are different in several important ways from those offered by private employers. The private sector has seen a dramatic shift in recent decades away from the defined benefit model as the 401(k) plan has emerged as the dominant private plan design. In contrast, the defined benefit model in the public sector has been resilient. According to one study, nearly 80% of state and local government workers were covered by a retirement plan in 2006, primarily of the defined benefit variety; in the private sector, on the other hand, only 45% of employees had any retirement plan at work, and figures from 2004 (see Figure 5/1) indicate that more than 60% of those workers relied solely on a defined contribution plan.[11]

In a 2007 *Issue in Brief* for the Center for Retirement Research at Boston College, Alicia Munnell and Mauricio Soto reported that some 98% of public sector defined benefit retirement plans have a cost-of-living adjustment, a benefit virtually unheard of in private sector plans. The relatively higher benefits are more expensive, as indicated by the average of $185,900 set aside for each state and local plan participant compared to $84,800 for each private sector retirement plan participant. In contrast, only 72% of state and local workers are included in the Social Security system, an almost universal private benefit.[12]

Public plans are not insured by the Pension Benefit Guarantee Corporation (PBGC). However, they are seen as having the taxing authority of the sponsoring government to guarantee their full benefits. PBGC ensures only a partial payment to eligible participants. Public entities are assumed to be perpetual, and their promised benefits not likely to disappear.

Defined Benefit Plans vs. Defined Contribution Plans

A primary distinction between defined benefit and defined contribution retirement plans is that the

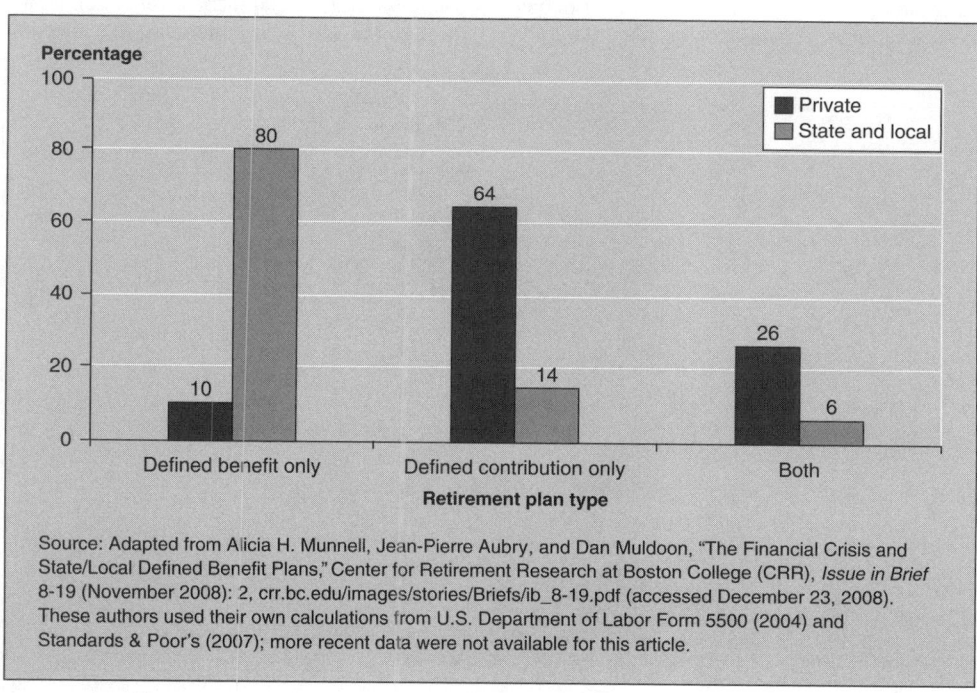

Source: Adapted from Alicia H. Munnell, Jean-Pierre Aubry, and Dan Muldoon, "The Financial Crisis and State/Local Defined Benefit Plans," Center for Retirement Research at Boston College (CRR), *Issue in Brief* 8-19 (November 2008): 2, crr.bc.edu/images/stories/Briefs/ib_8-19.pdf (accessed December 23, 2008). These authors used their own calculations from U.S. Department of Labor Form 5500 (2004) and Standards & Poor's (2007); more recent data were not available for this article.

Figure 5/1   *Percentage of workers covered by a pension, by pension type and sector, 2004*

defined benefit plan guarantees a payment amount based on a formula, whereas the payment available from a defined contribution plan is based on the value of the assets at the time of distribution. The assets held in a defined benefit plan are invested by the plan, following standards established by law and the plan's own investment policy. The plan itself, the employer, and ultimately the tax- or ratepayers bear the investment risk. While the individual retiree's pension is substantially shielded from the consequences of an investment decline, it will usually not increase if investment return is better than required to pay promised benefits. By contrast, the defined contribution model looks to the individual worker to make key investment decisions and to both bear the investment risk and enjoy the rewards.

Defined benefit plans (see Figure 5/2) and defined contribution plans typically build their asset base from employer contributions, from employee contributions, and, especially, through asset appreciation. Although both types rely on investment return to build the asset base, individual investment decisions made by defined contribution participants may be more problematic than the professionally overseen investment decisions made for defined benefit participants. This is because defined contribution plans, which have recently begun to provide participants with more investment help (offering target date funds and individual advice, for example), are more likely than professionally managed portfolios to be influenced by the emotions of the individual investor.

Public Sector Pension Plans and Market Fluctuations

Most of these pension plan investments consistently follow established policies, so they may not react as much to market turbulence as individual investments might. For example, after the 2001 recession and bear market, while individual investment decisions were apparently affected by short-term losses, the asset allocations of public plans were about the same as before. Since the mid-

1990s, "public officials . . . [have managed] their pensions on a business-like basis . . . [and] the funding status of public plans has looked very much like that of their private sector counterparts."[13]

Accounting rules mean that the impact of investment losses in defined benefit plans is not immediately apparent and may have little immediate impact on funding or benefits. Such pension plans have a long-term perspective, investing not for immediate return but to support promised benefits over many decades. They are generally invested to withstand short-term market volatility, diversifying their investments to lessen the impact of market fluctuations and providing a more predictable return over long periods than the more volatile financial markets. The strategy is built into the plans' actuarial assumptions.

Defined benefit plans' gains and losses are smoothed by averaging the market value over several years. But investment losses must eventually be made up. A recent sample of 120 public sector defined benefit plans showed that the funding level in 2007 was 87% but had declined to 65% by October 2008.[14] The impact of these losses will be recognized over time and mixed with future investment outcomes. However, for the older workers who plan to rely on defined contribution income—or, for that matter, on any invested account—the rate of return has more immediate importance: it will be more difficult for them to recover losses because there will be less time for them to do so. The recent steep declines in portfolio values will have more effect on these older workers, particularly if they have invested significantly in equities.

In a press statement released in September 2008, the National Association of State Retirement Administrators (NASRA) asserted that public pension funds maintain sufficient "liquidity needed to pay promised benefits for the near term, and the accumulated assets and funding mechanisms that will allow them to continue to do so indefinitely." Pointing out that the public pension system has endured past financial market crises going back through the 1970s, it concluded that the state

retirement systems are "expected to withstand the latest market turmoil."[15]

Even with the long-term perspective, however, the immediate impact of the economic downturn on public employee pension plans cannot be ignored as the plans must maintain an asset base adequate to meet the accumulated liability derived from the value of the promised benefits. State and local defined benefit plans together suffered investment losses of $1 trillion in the 12 months before October 9, 2008, and the markets continued to suffer some of their worst declines after that date (see Table 5/1).[16]

These losses matter since the plans are ultimately responsible for the promised benefits. Most plans have been able to assume that the asset base to pay benefits will consist mainly of accumulated investment earnings on contributions. Employers may have to increase their contributions to make up the current shortfalls unless the markets rally substantially before the end of their respective fiscal years. However, increased employer contributions, especially at a time when state and local revenues are declining, will have an unavoidable impact on public services.

As the nation's largest pension plan, the California Public Employees' Retirement System (CalPERS) has come under close scrutiny. Its performance is viewed as a bellwether of how the market downturn will affect pension funding levels and, as a consequence, employer contributions. CalPERS stated that from the end of its fiscal year on June 30, 2008, until October 10, 2008, its assets had declined by 20%, or at least $48 billion.[17] If that loss were to be sustained until the end of the next fiscal year, participating state agencies and local employers, needing to maintain the plan's funding level, would be faced with an increase in contributions of 2% to 4%—starting in July 2010 for two-thirds of its employers and in July 2011 for the remaining third.

While most pension plans entered the recent period with adequate funding, a few plans were below the levels considered acceptable even before the economic downturn, according to the General Accountability Office (GAO), the investigative

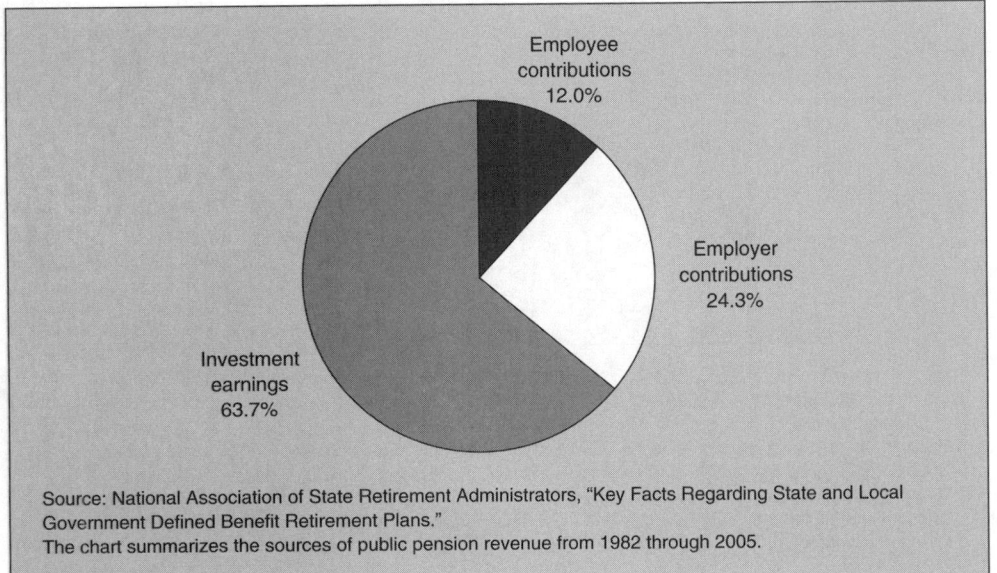

Source: National Association of State Retirement Administrators, "Key Facts Regarding State and Local Government Defined Benefit Retirement Plans."
The chart summarizes the sources of public pension revenue from 1982 through 2005.

Figure 5/2 *Funding of public benefit plans*

Table 5/1 EQUITY DECLINES FROM OCTOBER 9, 2007 (PEAK) TO OCTOBER 9, 2008

Pension sponsor	Decline[1] (in $ trillions)
Total	3.8
Defined benefit plans	
Private employer	0.9
State and local governments	1.0
Defined contribution plans	
Private employer	1.1
Individual retirement accounts	0.8
Federal government[2]	0.1

Source: Adapted from Alicia H. Munnell, Jean-Pierre Aubry, and Dan Muldoon, "The Financial Crisis and Private Defined Benefit Plans," CRR, *Issue in Brief* 8-19 (November 2008): 2, globalaging.org/pension/us/private/2008/benefitplans.pdf (accessed December 23, 2008).
[1]Figures do not add to total because of rounding.
[2]The Thrift Savings Plan accounts for slightly less than 20% of total federal pension assets, but it includes virtually all of the equity exposure.

arm of the U.S. Congress. Public plan experts consider 80% funding to be adequate for public plans.[18] The most recent data, from 2006, showed that 63% of public plans had a funding ratio of at least 80% and that 54% of these plans would be well funded by 2008 if assets were smoothed; however, only 9% would be adequately funded without smoothing (see Figure 5/3). Even before the significant drop in market returns, the GAO predicted that underfunded plans faced "tough choices" just to maintain the level of benefits promised to future retirees.[19]

THE SECOND LEG: GOVERNMENT BENEFITS

As has been noted, more than a quarter of state and local government employees are not covered by the Social Security system. Those not covered may qualify for the benefit from other work or as the spouse of a covered worker, although their payments will generally be calculated by a formula that reduces the benefit. However, they generally have compensation through a more generous defined benefit formula. The benefit multiplier for public workers who are covered by Social Security averages 1.9% per year of service. For those not covered it averages 2.2%; the higher resulting benefit is intended as compensation for not earning a Social Security check.[20]

The financial difficulties of Social Security are well known. According to the 2008 Social Security Trustee report, "Projected long run program costs are not sustainable under current financing arrangements. Social Security's current annual surpluses of tax income over expenditures will begin to

decline in 2011 and then turn into rapidly growing deficits as the baby boom generation retires."[21]

How the current economic situation may affect Social Security cannot be known immediately. It may be that workers delay retirement in response to financial stress and therefore postpone the age at which they begin to draw Social Security benefits. This delay will not greatly change the financial prospects for the system; benefits are adjusted by a more or less actuarially neutral formula for the age at which they begin to be drawn. A person retiring somewhat later in life will draw fewer checks, but those checks will be of a greater amount, and the net impact on the trust fund will be minimal.

What *will* have an impact, however, are reduced payroll taxes collected to support the system. If unemployment remains high for an extended period or if higher-paying jobs are lost permanently—as may happen, for example, with the demise or bankruptcy reorganization of major employers—the impact on the system may be significant, and long-term solutions may be more difficult. A prolonged recession could threaten Social Security benefits, especially for younger workers, as Congress considers alternatives to secure the system. Social Security, already doubted by many younger workers as a reliable source of income for their own retirements, could become even less dependable.

The financial difficulties of Medicare are less well known than those of Social Security, but according to the Social Security and Medicare Boards of Trustees, "Medicare's financial difficulties come sooner—and are much more severe—than those confronting Social Security."[22] Although differing in important ways from defined benefit pensions, Social Security is effectively a modified defined benefit program. This makes it a good deal more predictable than Medicare, which is a modified indemnity program. Medicare pays a portion of health care costs, not a predetermined dollar amount. Health care costs are difficult to predict: they continue to rise at rates greater than inflation as new treatments become available, individual health care use increases with age, and the baby boomer generation (defined as those born between 1946 and 1964) becomes Medicare eligible beginning in 2011. Together these developments make the financial situation of Medicare so severe that the trustees have issued an official funding warning for two years in a row—even before the current economic crisis.

During the current economic crisis, the existence of Medicare—despite uncertainties—is likely to have an impact on individual retirement timing decisions. Private market health insurance commonly costs more than $1,000 per month for a couple, even when they continue in an employer group plan using COBRA (Consolidated Omnibus Budget Reconciliation Act). Medicare supplement policies may cost half that amount, possibly less, depending on the policy and geographic location. With employer-supported retiree health care benefits potentially at risk and health care costs increasing, waiting to reach age 65 in order to retire with Medicare eligibility becomes a more compelling strategy than retiring earlier.

The two parts of the government-provided "leg"—Social Security and Medicare—present

challenges for individual retirement planning given that the timing and impact of possible solutions, particularly for Medicare, remain unknown. The rational planning response is for individuals to reserve more money from their retirement budgets to cover possible shortfalls in any Medicare benefits and to discount the amount of Social Security that they will be paid—especially younger workers. But with shrinking retirement portfolios in the current economic environment, that is very difficult to do.

THE THIRD LEG: PERSONAL SAVINGS

With defined benefit plans remaining a relatively firm leg on the retirement stool, and Social Security—assumed to be a valuable asset for those planning to retire in the next decade or two—and Medicare being somewhat problematic, there is another leg to consider. Personal savings is the third variable usually included in a solid retirement plan. How the current economic downturn affects two aspects of this savings component—retirement savings accounts for the group entering retirement age and the value of an individual investor's primary residence—is reviewed below.

Retirement Savings Accounts
In any study of retirement and personal savings, filtering public sector employees from the general population is difficult because the data are generally collected on an aggregate basis rather than by employer. Nonetheless, certain trends are similar in both the public and private sectors. (It should be noted, though, that the availability of defined benefit pension plans for most public employees makes those public employees less dependent on their accumulated savings as a factor in the retirement decision.)

Several studies offer a picture of the retirement situation for the baby boomers as they near the end of their working careers. According to one study, two-thirds of the oldest baby boomers are financially unprepared for retirement, and many are not even aware of their predicament. Noting that boomers have consumed more and saved less during their working lives than previous generations, the study found that the boomers' ratio of debt to net worth was 50% higher than that of the previous generation even before the recent financial turmoil.[23]

With the economic crisis of 2008, the situation is even more bleak. According to a report released by the Urban Institute, retirement accounts lost 18.3% of their value in the year since September 30, 2007, for a total loss of $1.6 trillion.[24] According to another study, the impact of the market downturn was exacerbated by the investment decisions of investors, including 27% who had over 90% of their accounts in equities, and a total of 48% who invested more than 70% in equities.[25]

The losses have had a significant impact on the retirement outlook for those nearing retirement age. According to a survey of 1,628 employed people over age 45, which was conducted by the American Association of Retired Persons in the three-week period ending September 21, 2008,

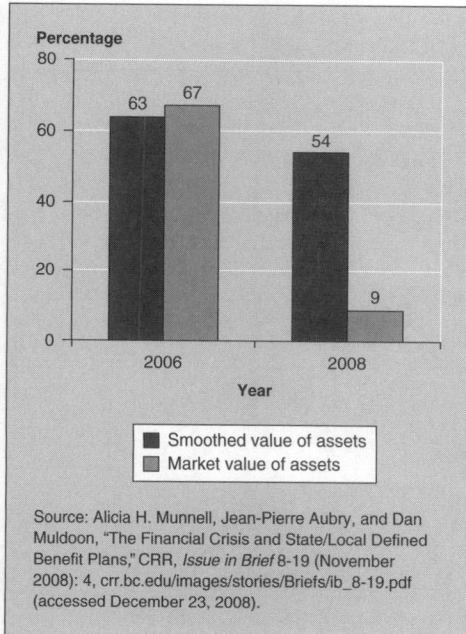

Percentage

Source: Alicia H. Munnell, Jean-Pierre Aubry, and Dan Muldoon, "The Financial Crisis and State/Local Defined Benefit Plans," CRR, *Issue in Brief* 8-19 (November 2008): 4, crr.bc.edu/images/stories/Briefs/ib_8-19.pdf (accessed December 23, 2008).

Figure 5/3   *Percentage of plans with funding ratios of 80% or more in 2006 and 2008, smoothed and market value of assets*

34% were considering postponing their retirement; 27% said that they were having trouble making rent or mortgage payments; 13% were withdrawing funds from their accounts prematurely (which can trigger special tax penalties and substantially reduce the ultimate payout of the retirement account); and 20% indicated that they were no longer contributing to their retirement accounts.[26]

Individuals learn from their own life experiences. Many of those who came of age during the Great Depression formed lifetime habits of frugality and conservative investing. Those who invested in technology stocks during the tech bubble of the 1990s learned other lessons, perhaps even that taking investment risks can have both large rewards and great hazards. It is possible that employees who have seen their defined contribution portfolios shrink in the current downturn may exhibit a lasting conservatism when it comes to investments. While this would minimize their exposure to loss, it would also limit their future returns and could thereby necessitate a higher contribution rate if they are to achieve desired asset growth.

It is not surprising, given the crisis atmosphere surrounding retirement plans, that Congress has started hearing legislative proposals ranging from fairly modest propositions, such as increasing opportunities to access retirement savings penalty-free, to the more radical concept of replacing all defined contribution plans with a universal government-run defined benefit plan. As of the publication of this article, no retirement-related legislative proposal had gained much of a following. However, it is fair to recall that the Great Depression served as the catalyst for major financial reform, including the creation of Social Security.

House Values
With retirement accounts clearly under stress, average American retirees once might have looked to the equity in their homes to back up their retirement income. However, home values have suffered greatly during the current downturn, a phenomenon not seen during previous recessions. Opportunities to borrow are fewer, and credit is tight, depressing sales activity and home prices.

Factors that have contributed significantly to the overall economic distress include riskier mortgage structures, such as interest-only and adjustable-rate mortgages, as well as the collapse in value of subprime mortgages, which were issued during a period of low interest rates and lax credit standards. Ultimately, the problem mortgages led to the failure of major financial institutions and the highest rate of mortgage foreclosures since the 1930s. Nearly 1.3 million U.S. housing properties were subject to foreclosure activity in 2007, up 79% from 2006.[27] During the second quarter of 2008, according to the Mortgage Bankers Association, a record 1.2 million homes were in foreclosure, and some analysts estimate that another 2 million families could face foreclosure in the next two years.[28]

Real estate markets are, by definition, local. Not all communities saw the extraordinary price gains that signaled a bubble. In fact, just a handful of states have accounted for the majority of foreclosures. In October 2008, for example,

seven states (Arizona, California, Florida, Illinois, Michigan, Nevada, and Ohio) accounted for more than 60% of the foreclosures; and at one time, according to RealtyTrac, an online real estate data source, California alone accounted for one in four foreclosures.[29] But the flood of foreclosures on the market hurts the national economy, depressing home values regionally and consumer spending nationally through a reverse wealth effect. One widely regarded index estimated that housing prices, which had gained 60% from 2000 until their peak in 2006, declined 24% from their peak in the first quarter of 2006 to the second quarter of 2008.[30] Even if a particular family's house had not dropped much in value, the news reports made it feel as though the "housing crisis" were everywhere.

For a large number of Americans, home equity is the largest component of their net worth. According to a 2008 study by Munnell and Soto, taking the value of both a pension and Social Security into account, housing in 2004 accounted for more than 20% of total assets for the typical household approaching retirement (age 55–64) (see Figure 5/4).[31] Without those two sources of income, the house accounted for half of the typical household's property and financial wealth.[32] Although there was much regional variation, many of those Americans who bought their homes in 2006 and 2007 with subprime loans found that their outstanding mortgages were greater than the newly depreciated value of their homes, leading to a negative contribution to net worth. Nationally, housing was estimated to have continued to drop by 2% per month since July 2008.[33] Potential buyers were understandably reluctant to purchase a home that they expected would continue to depreciate.

For many individuals, a major element in their retirement plans has been the anticipated equity

from the sale of their primary residences as they downsize to smaller homes. Those who intend to retire to a different state, however, may end up postponing their retirement plans if selling their primary residences is problematic. (The degree to which relocation may also be an important element is indicated by the percentage of individuals who are receiving retirement benefits in a state different from the one where those benefits were earned. The New York State and Local Retirement Systems [NYSLRS] and CalPERS pay 23% and 14%, respectively, of their benefits to retirees living outside those states.)[34] For retirees with the means, however, there are bargains to be found. Of the seven states with the most foreclosures, three (Arizona, California, and Nevada) are in traditional retirement areas, and the distressed housing prices in these states have created buying opportunities not seen for many years.

Not only has the housing downturn reduced the value of the asset, it has also restricted the cash flow of those individuals who have been using the equity in their homes to maintain their consumption levels, even at a time of diminished wage growth. Retirees today remain burdened by house payments well into their retirement years. The Federal Reserve reports that for households headed by a person age 65–74, more than 32% had mortgage debt in 2004, up from less than 19% in 1992.[35]

According to the *Federal Reserve Flow of Funds,* "total debt rose from about 60 percent of disposable personal income in 1983 to 80 percent in the early 1990s and soared to 120 percent of income in 2007" (see Figure 5/5).[36] A study of these patterns suggests that housing values rose by $6.4 trillion from 2001 to 2006, and that $1.2 trillion of the value was extracted through a financing mechanism and $410 billion was used to finance consumption.[37]

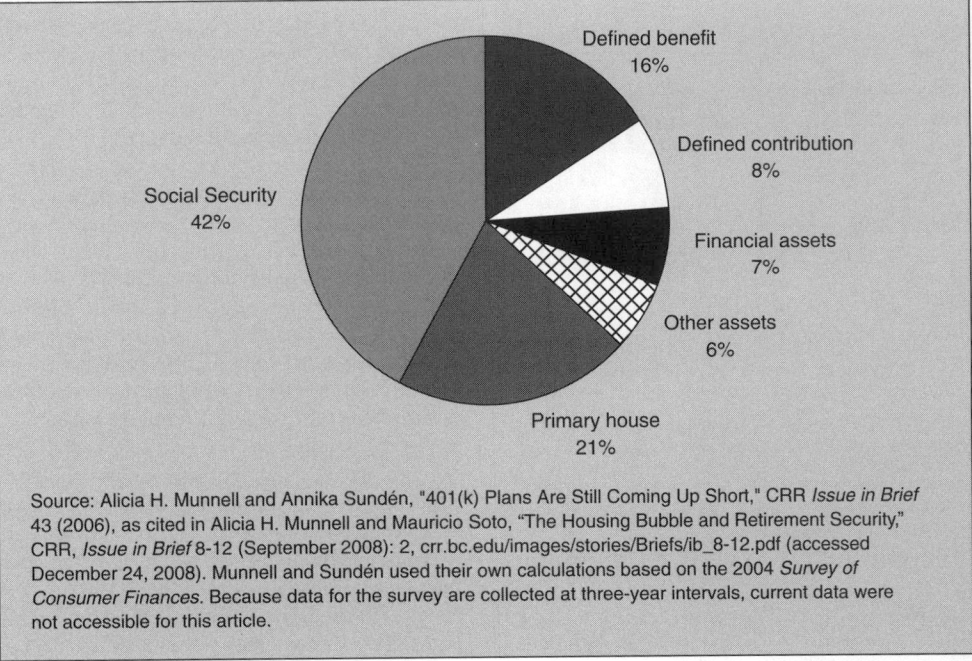

Source: Alicia H. Munnell and Annika Sundén, "401(k) Plans Are Still Coming Up Short," CRR *Issue in Brief* 43 (2006), as cited in Alicia H. Munnell and Mauricio Soto, "The Housing Bubble and Retirement Security," CRR, *Issue in Brief* 8-12 (September 2008): 2, crr.bc.edu/images/stories/Briefs/ib_8-12.pdf (accessed December 24, 2008). Munnell and Sundén used their own calculations based on the 2004 *Survey of Consumer Finances.* Because data for the survey are collected at three-year intervals, current data were not accessible for this article.

Figure 5/4   *Assets of a typical household age 55–64, 2004*

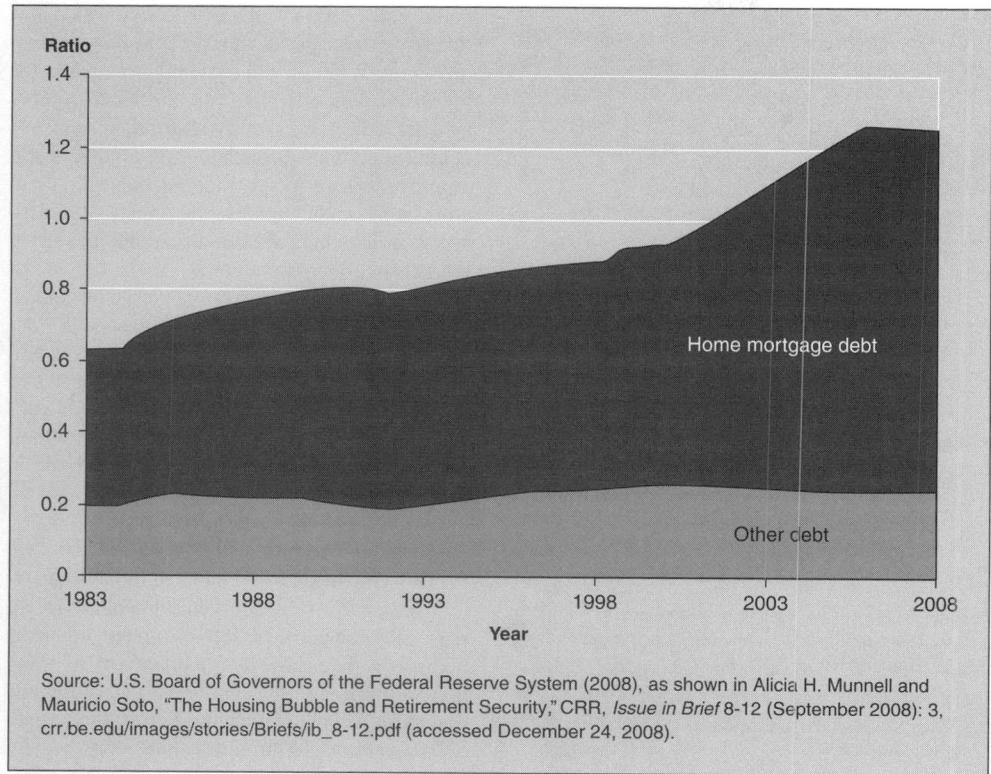

Figure 5/5 *Ratio of debt to income: all households, 1983–2008*

For the group nearing retirement, the consequences of this spending spree on their biggest pre-retirement asset has been significant. Homeowners aged 50–62 "extracted $380 billion from their primary residences and consumed $149 billion directly" (see Table 5/2).[38] According to Munnell and Soto, those pre-retirement households that extracted value from their primary residences have a net worth that is today about 14% lower than it was in 2001. Their report concludes that a considerable fraction of those entering retirement today "have a fragile balance sheet in a time of depressed home prices and poor financial market returns."[39]

Another report, published by the Center for Economic Policy and Research, arrives at a similar conclusion about the implications of the housing crash and finds that

inadequate saving is likely to be an especially serious problem for workers who are approaching retirement. These workers will have little opportunity to make up for the wealth lost in the collapse of the housing bubble. Many retirees will find themselves far more dependent on Social Security and Medicare than would have been the case if their savings behavior had not been affected by the stock and housing bubbles.[40]

A FOURTH LEG: RETIREE HEALTH CARE

While asset accumulation is a primary component of any retirement plan, an emerging consideration in retirement readiness is the ability to ensure proper health care coverage for the employee and family members after the period of employment. With assets diminished, the expense of health care during retirement takes on growing importance and can be a leading consideration for an employee trying to decide whether to leave the workforce.

Any decision about whether to retire must take into consideration expected expenses. In the past, a formula of perhaps 80% of pre-retirement income would be sufficient for the typical retiree to meet living expenses during retirement. But the rising cost of health care and the lack of individual health insurance policies at a reasonable cost, especially prior to Medicare eligibility at age 65,

have changed that formula. The percentage of local government employees with no access to retiree health benefits (aside from COBRA benefits for up to 18 months) is 35% for early retirees and 40% for retirees 65 and older.[41] For those who retire without group coverage, there may actually be no available coverage—or coverage may be cost-prohibitive. And where post-retirement coverage is available through the employer, the employee may be required to pay 100% of the cost for his or her own and spouse's coverage.

Even before the current recession, state and local governments and their retirees were increasingly concerned about the cost of retiree health care, for two reasons. First, health insurance premiums more than doubled from 1999 to 2007.[42] Second, the Governmental Accounting Standards Board is now requiring that, as active employees earn their benefits, the liability for future retiree health benefits is recognized in state and local governments' financial statements. This accounting change, occurring at a time when contributions to defined benefit plans are expected to increase and revenues are down, has led to increased scrutiny of retiree health care benefits by local governments and taxpayers. Many local governments are considering tightening eligibility criteria for those benefits, raising the share of premiums paid by retirees, or seeking other approaches to limiting the governmental liability for retiree health care.

Governments find themselves in a difficult position: trimming benefits upsets employees while raising taxes risks a taxpayer revolt; however, a government that takes no action could damage its operations, finances, or even its credit rating. One solution has been to develop defined contribution retiree health care programs that help employees without creating additional liabilities on the employers' financial statements. As the economic stress of the recession becomes more evident in the public sector, managers will likely become more interested in protecting their already strained balance sheets and may begin looking with increased favor on these defined contribution solutions.

LABOR FORCE PARTICIPATION

On an aggregate basis, the percentage of people age 55 and older who are in the workforce has been rising in recent years after a long period of decline (see Figure 5/6). A fact sheet published by the Urban Institute noted that "after declining for most of the 20th century, labor force participation rates for older men have been increasing during the past two decades.... Participation rates for older women were relatively constant between 1968 and the late 1980s, but they have been increasing steadily since 1988." Focusing specifically on the 15-year period between 1992 and 2007, it noted that participation rates for men age 62–64 increased from 41% to 51%, and those for men age 65–69 increased from 22% to 34%. Among women, the study looked at participation rates from 1988 through 2007 and found that rates for women age 55–61 increased from 44% to 64%; for women age 62–64 they in-

Table 5/2	AMOUNT EXTRACTED AND CONSUMED FROM INCREASES IN HOUSING WEALTH, BY AGE GROUP, 2001–2006		
Age in 2004	Housing gains (in $ billions)	Amount extracted from home equity (in $ billions)	Amount consumed from home equity (in $ billions)
<30	392	23	8
30–39	1,027	156	46
40–49	1,608	366	114
50–62	2,360	380	149
63–79	855	284	100
80+	510	15	1

Source: Adapted from Alicia H. Munnell and Mauricio Soto, "The Housing Bubble and Retirement Security," CRR, *Issue in Brief* 8-12 (September 2008): 7, crr.bc.edu/images/stories/Briefs/ib_8-12.pdf (accessed December 24, 2008).

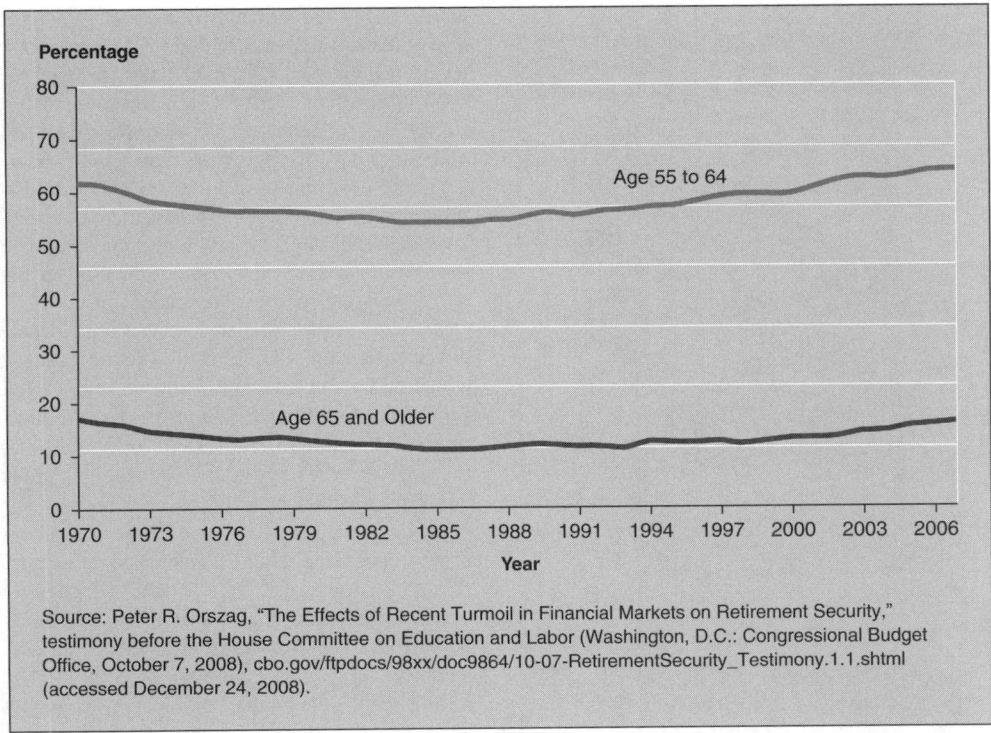

Figure 5/6   *Percentage of people age 55 and older participating in the workforce, 1970–2007*

creased from 25% to 42%; and for women age 65–69 and for women age 70 and above, they doubled to 26% and 8%, respectively.[43]

The reasons that workers give as to why they continue working vary. According to one survey, 85% of baby boomers said that they considered it at least somewhat likely that they would continue to work beyond the traditional retirement age. Nearly 40% said that it was extremely likely, and of those, two-thirds cited financial reasons.[44] Clearly, the deterioration in the economy will be a major consideration in, if not a determinant of, the retirement decision for those nearing retirement age.

As a rule, defined benefit plans with reasonable actuarial assumptions will not be affected by increasing retirement ages. If employees stay on the job longer, both they and their employers will be making contributions for additional periods, there will be less need for liquidity to make benefit payments, and the length of time during which they receive retirement benefits will be shortened. In plans with capped benefit formulas, additional years of service result in benefit increases only from higher salaries, in which case pension plans could benefit from delays in retirement. In plans that have incentives for early retirement, delayed retirement could actually benefit an employer.

Although delays in retirement may have no effect on defined contribution plans, they may result in slightly higher costs for employers since employers could be making additional retirement contributions at their employees' peak earning levels and incurring higher payroll costs because older workers are not being replaced by new, lower-paid recruits.

SUMMARIZING THE SITUATION

Most economists are predicting that the current recession will be long and deep. These are unusual times with all three levels of government having their revenues negatively affected simultaneously; in the past, it has been one or two out of three, but not all three. The economic downturn will continue to depress federal and state income tax revenues, while reduced consumer spending will continue to affect federal and state sales tax revenues. With home prices decreasing, local property tax receipts are decreasing as well.[45]

For public sector retirement leaders, the difficult economic scenario demands careful management. Policy makers will be forced to consider whether current state and local retirement plans can be sustained in the face of these economic challenges, whether changes are needed, and whether this is the time to seek them.

Pension Plan Funding
Despite the current economic climate, most defined benefit public pension plans will have adequate investing time and the means to mandate increased contributions, if needed, to avoid a crisis in meeting benefit payments. Depending on both the depth and length of the market downturn, public sector employers may be required to make additional contributions to boost the funding levels of their pension plans. But they will be hard-pressed to meet such a call, given the immediate effect of falling revenues from tax receipts. Increasing mandated retirement contributions will mean less money to provide public services.

An added difficulty awaits those pension plans that were already underfunded before the current recession. While most pension plans entered the recession with adequate funding levels, others now face an even greater shortfall because of market conditions. In all these cases, public sector employers need to set aside adequate funds to cover pension obligations over time or face difficulty selling their debt in an already unsettled market for government bonds.

The debate over the relative merits of defined benefit and defined contribution plans will continue. Advocates of the defined benefit model will point to its relative stability, while advocates of the defined contribution model will call on public employees to bear the investment risk for their own retirement, as employees commonly do in the private sector.

Retirement Patterns
While trying to discern reliable retirement behavior patterns from past economic downturns might reasonably be considered to be a relevant undertaking, the data show little evidence of anything that could provide predictive value. Each economic downturn has its own characteristics that do not offer much insight into future behavior.

Even before the current economic downturn, the pattern in the national workforce had shown an increase in the proportion of those who continue to work after age 55. A number of reasons may lie behind this trend, including the need for additional income or job satisfaction.

A distinguishing characteristic of the current recession is the impact of the collapse of the housing market on the retirement picture, as many prospective retirees find that their largest asset is worth much less than they had anticipated. Consequently, many governmental employees who are in or nearing retirement could find themselves more dependent on their governmental retirement plans (whether defined benefit or defined contribution), Social Security, and Medicare than they had planned.

Personal Investments
Given the precipitous fall in market values in 2008, retirees who were invested in equities suffered serious losses. More important, many may now find that returning to the equities market requires a greater degree of risk than they are willing to tolerate after such dislocation. For those with a significant number of work years before retirement, failing to invest in equities could mean that their accounts might not grow faster than the rate of inflation. The alternative to accepting prudent investment risk is simply to save more, something that many might find difficult or impossible to do.

Health Care Costs
While retirement planners have traditionally focused on asset accumulation and income generation, a growing area of interest is the expense side, especially the cost of health care during retirement. This component alone may be sufficient to prevent a worker from deciding to retire before Medicare eligibility.

In the public sector, defined benefit plans for retiree health care have been developed to help

workers meet these expenses. The cost of these plans is now appearing directly on government balance sheets. With other costs rising significantly, including the possible cost of increased pension plan funding, governments are looking for defined contribution alternatives that can help employees pay for health care in retirement without increasing governments' liabilities.

Federal Government Interventions

One major consequence of the economic crisis is the enormous financial interventions that the federal government has made to bolster the private economy. It is not possible to know yet what impact this may have on public sector retirement. While finding solutions to impending Social Security and Medicare shortfalls is becoming more urgent, it is made more difficult by the financial commitments made by the federal government in response to the crisis. A comprehensive national health care initiative also seems more challenging now.

On the state and local level, the need to increase retirement contributions at a time of falling revenue might precipitate reductions in benefits. If so, the pattern has been that those closer to retirement will have their benefits protected but newer workers may see significant changes.

CONCLUSION

While no one can know precisely what impact the economic turmoil of 2008 and beyond will have on public sector retirement, the findings and observations above suggest that the retirement picture will be changed in the years ahead. In coming years, state and local governments should be prepared to increase payments to their defined benefit pension plans as necessary to make up for underfunding caused by the precipitous drop in portfolio values. They should consider instituting defined contribution retirement and retiree health care options, as appropriate, to control future benefits costs. And public sector employees—even those who are pension-eligible—should consider how to craft a comfortable retirement at a time when the "three-legged stool" is decidedly less stable than it had appeared before the current recession.

[1] Alicia H. Munnell and Mauricio Soto, "State and Local Pensions Are Different from Private Plans," Center for Retirement Research at Boston College (CRR), *State and Local Pension Plans* 1 (November 2007), crr.bc.edu/images/stories/Briefs/slp_1.pdf?phpMyAdmin=43ac483c4de9t51d9eb41.

[2] National Bureau of Economic Research (NBER), "Determination of the December 2007 Peak in Economic Activity," wwwdev.nber.org/cycles/dec2008.html (accessed December 22, 2008); see also Neil Irwin, "NBER: U.S. in Recession That Began Last December," *Washington Post,* December 1, 2008, washingtonpost.com/wp-dyn/content/article/2008/12/01/AR2008120101365.html (accessed December 23, 2008).

[3] Bureau of Labor Statistics, "The Employment Situation," November 2008, bls.gov/news.release/empsit.nr0.htm (accessed December 23, 2008).

[4] Chris Hoene and Amanda M. Straub, "City Fiscal Conditions Take a Turn for the Worse," *Nation Cities Weekly,* September 15, 2008, nlc.org/articles/articleItems/NCW91508/fiscalreport2008.aspx (accessed December 24, 2008); Congressional Budget Office (CBO), *The Budget and Economic Outlook: An Update* (Washington, D.C.: CBO, September 2008), cbo.gov/ftpdocs/97xx/doc9706/09-08-Update.pdf (accessed December 24, 2008).

[5] Ben S. Bernanke, speech delivered to the Greater Austin Chamber of Commerce, Austin, Texas, December 1, 2008, federalreserve.gov/newsevents/speech/bernanke20081201a.htm (accessed December 24, 2008).

[6] Alicia H. Munnell, Jean-Pierre Aubry, and Dan Muldoon, "The Financial Crisis and State/Local Defined Benefit Plans," CRR, *Issue in Brief* 8–19 (November 2008), crr.bc.edu/images/stories/Briefs/ib_8-19.pdf (accessed December 23, 2008).

[7] Investment Company Institute, "The U.S. Retirement Market, First Quarter 2008," *Research Fundamentals* 17, no. 3-Q1 (October 2008): 1, ici.org/stats/mf/retmrkt_update.pdf (accessed December 24, 2008).

[8] NBER, "The NBER's Recession Dating Procedure," nber.org/cycles/recessions.html (accessed December 22, 2008).

[9] NBER, "December 2007 Peak in Economic Activity."

[10] NBER, "Business Cycle Expansions and Contractions," nber.org/cycles/main.html (accessed December 22, 2008).

[11] Munnell, Aubry, and Muldoon, "State/Local Defined Benefit Plans."

[12] Munnell and Soto, "State and Local Pensions Are Different," 2–4.

[13] Alicia H. Munnell et al., "The Miracle of Funding by State and Local Pension Plans," CRR, *State and Local Pension Plans* 5 (April 2008): 7, crr.bc.edu/images/stories/Briefs/slp_5.pdf?phpMyAdmin=43ac483c4de9t51d9eb41 (accessed December 24, 2008)

[14] Munnel, Aubry, and Muldoon, "State/Local Defined Benefit Plans," 3.

[15] National Association of State Retirement Administrators (NASRA), "State and Local Pensions Navigating the Storm," press statement, September 25, 2008, 2, sib.wa.gov/information/pr/NASRA_NCTR.pdf (accessed December 19, 2008).

[16] Munnel, Aubry, and Muldoon, "State/Local Defined Benefit Plans," 3.

[17] Craig Karmin et al., "Calpers Looks to Shore Up Assets," *Wall Street Journal,* October 23, 2008, sec.online.wsj.com/article/SB122469119659558689.html (accessed December 24, 2008).

[18] Munnell, Aubry, and Muldoon, "State/Local Defined Benefit Plans."

[19] U.S. General Accounting Office (GAO), *State and Local Government Retiree Benefits: Current Status of Benefit Structures, Protections, and Fiscal Outlook for Funding Future Costs,* GAO-07-1156 (Washington, D.C.: GAO, September 2007), 35, gao.gov/new.items/d071156.pdf (accessed December 24, 2008).

[20] Munnell and Soto, "State and Local Pensions Are Different," 3.

[21] Social Security Online, "Status of the Social Security and Medicare Programs," 2008 Social Security Trustee Report, ssa.gov/OACT/TRSUM/trsummary.html (accessed December 23, 2008).

[22] Ibid.

[23] Eric D. Beinhocker, Diana Farrell and Ezra Greenberg, "Why Baby Boomers Will Need to Work Longer," *McKinsey Quarterly* (November 2008): 1–10.

[24] Richard W. Johnson, Mauricio Soto, and Sheila Zedlewski, "How Is the Economic Turmoil Affecting Older Americans?" fact sheet on retirement policy (Washington, D.C.: Urban Institute, October 2008), 2, urban.org/UploadedPDF/411765_economic_turmoil.pdf (accessed December 24, 2008).

[25] Jack VanDerhei, "The Impact of the Financial Crisis on Workers' Retirement Security," testimony for House Education and Labor Committee, October 7, 2008, house.gov/ed_workforce/testimony/2008-10-07-JackVanDerhei.pdf (accessed December 24, 2008).

[26] William Bulkeley, "One in Five Baby Boomers Cuts Retirement Saving," *Wall Street Journal,* October 7, 2008, A10, online.wsj.com/article/SB122333045141409159.html (accessed December 23, 2008).

[27] RealtyTrac, "U.S. Foreclosure Activity Increases 75 Percent in 2007," press release, January 29, 2008, realtytrac.com/ContentManagement/pressrelease.aspx?ChannelID=9&ItemID=3988&accnt=64847 (accessed December 23, 2008).

[28] Tami Luhby, "FDIC's Bair Pushes Aggressive Mortgage Plan," *CNNMoney.com,* November 14, 2008), money.cnn.com/2008/11/14/news/economy/fdic_bair/?postversion=2008111416 (accessed December 24, 2008).

[29] RealtyTrac, "U.S. Foreclosure Activity Increases 5 Percent in October."

[30] CRR, "S&P/Case-Shiller U.S. National Home Price Index, 1990–Present,"crr.bc.edu/images/stories/case_shiller_11_25_2008.pdf (accessed December 23, 2008).

[31] The "typical household aged 55–64" refers to the mean of the middle 10% of the sample of households headed by an individual aged 55–64.

[32] Alicia H. Munnell and Mauricio Soto, "The Housing Bubble and Retirement Security," CRR, *Issue in Brief* 8–12 (September 2008): 2, crr.bc.edu/images/stories/Briefs/ib_8-12.pdf (accessed December 24, 2008).

[33] CRR, "U.S. National Home Price Index."

[34] The figure for New York State is derived from New York State and Local Retirement System, *Comprehensive Annual Financial Report for Fiscal Year Ended March 31, 2007* (Albany: Office of the New York State Comptroller, 2007), 23; the figure for CalPERS was provided to the authors by Ed Fong, information officer for the Office of the Chief Actuary for the pension system.

[35] Jonathan Clements, "Retiring with a Mortgage? Here's What to Do," *Wall Street Journal online,* September 20, 2007, realestatejournal.com/buysell/mortgages/20070920-clements.html (accessed December 24, 2008).

[36] Munnell and Soto, "Housing Bubble and Retirement Security," 2–3.

[37] Ibid., 6.

[38] Ibid., 7.

[39] Ibid., 8.

[40] Dean Baker and David Rosnick, "The Impact of the Housing Crash on Family Wealth" (Washington, D.C.: Center for Economic and Policy Research, July 2008), 7, cepr.net/documents/publications/wealth_2008_07.pdf (accessed December 23, 2008).

[41] Evelina R. Moulder, "Local Government Employee Health Insurance Programs," in *The Municipal Year Book 2008* (Washington, DC.: ICMA, 2008), 4.

[42] Kaiser Family Foundation and Health Research and Educational Trust, *Employer Health Benefits: 2007 Annual Survey* (Menlo Park, Calif., and Chicago: Henry J. Kaiser Foundation and the Health Research and Educational Trust, 2007), 1, kff.org/insurance/7672/upload/76723.pdf (accessed December 24, 2008).

[43] Richard W. Johnson, "Should People Work Longer, and Will They?" (Washington, D.C.: Urban Institute, December 2007), 4–5, urban.org/UploadedPDF/411584_work_longer.pdf (accessed December 24, 2008).

[44] Bienhocker, Farrell, and Greenberg, "Baby Boomers."

[45] CBO, *The Budget and Economic Outlook.*

6

Learning from Award-Winning Innovations in Local Government, 2008

Karen Thoreson
Alliance for Innovation
James H. Svara
Center for Urban Innovation
Arizona State University

Selected Findings

As part of its Supported Alternatives for Our Valued Youth (SAVY) initiative, Petersburg, Virginia, used a needs assessment to develop alternative programs and services for its youth, thereby reducing the use of secure detention among youths by 75% over a three-year period.

Sarasota County, Florida, has managed to hold its public works costs flat by seeking out innovative and smart applications to harness technology and by employing an asset management system to measures the results.

Having determined that acceptable levels of thermal comfort can be achieved in its downtown area through an integrated approach to the design of the urban environment, city staff and consultants in Phoenix, Arizona, developed a streamlined, form-based zoning code.

In uncertain times, innovation is more important than ever. In the current financial crisis, local governments face pressures to adjust their activities and reduce their budgets, but it is important that they do not simply retrench and cut back. Rather, they need to develop new policies, new programs, new processes, and new delivery methods that will allow them to meet the challenges inherent in this unpredictable environment while continuing to provide high-quality services to, and advance the interests of, their constituents.

And cities and counties all across the country are doing just that—developing new policies, administrative practices, and management techniques to solve tough problems, rethink traditional processes, or outperform established approaches. Unfortunately, even if a government has a creative solution to a problem, if no one else knows about it, the impact will be limited to that one community. In addition, many governments may be experiencing the same problem, but if they try to solve this problem in isolation, the process will be longer and is likely to be less effective than it would if they could benefit from the experience of another local government that has developed a promising approach.

The Alliance for Innovation (AFI)—a partnership of ICMA, Arizona State University (ASU) and the former Innovation Groups (IG)—is dedicated to promoting a "Community of Practice" comprised of local governments that seek to develop and share best practices across all realms of municipal and county organizations, and to disseminate information about these practices among academics who teach and conduct research related to local government.

One of the most important ways that information has been shared about innovations is through awards programs. A government that has what it considers to be an innovative approach can submit it for review in comparison with what others are doing. Although entering a competition is sometimes dismissed as just publicity seeking, sharing information is an important service that a jurisdiction makes to the local government community. Entering award competitions also sends a signal to staff that innovation is important. By selecting and publicizing the best submissions,

the awards process helps to disseminate information and promote the diffusion of innovation.

"Innovation" can take two forms. There are original, breakthrough ideas that open up new approaches or provide unique solutions. And there are new practices that can be adapted from other places with the intention of improving results or performance. Former *Governing* columnist Otis White recognizes this distinction when he says that innovation can be both "breakthrough" changes and efforts to promote "continuous improvement."[1] The cases presented here illustrate both the breakthrough type and leading examples of ideas that jurisdictions have transplanted, adapted, and recombined in order to address a pressing local need or pursue an opportunity in a creative way. Some of the cases are still emerging, and it is important for other governments to know about these pioneering efforts. Other cases are further developed, have been tested, and have already achieved clear results.

This article presents 23 cases that stand out as exemplary approaches in the following areas of local government: innovative approaches to strengthening the sense of community, remaking the locality, improving health and safety, promoting sustainability, expanding applications of

e-government, and improving organizational performance. Some of the programs described below have won or been finalists for national awards, or received special recognition, from AFI or ICMA in 2008; others have been selected as case studies for presentation at the AFI's 2008 Transforming Local Government (TLG) conference. The article concludes with an assessment of the common characteristics that helped these organizations succeed at innovation.

STRENGTHENING COMMUNITIES

Understanding that a community-centric approach helps improve the lives of citizens, the local governments highlighted below have found a variety of ways to transform neighborhoods and strengthen social connections.

Neighborhood Quality of Life Study
Chesapeake, Virginia (pop. 219,154)[2]
AFI Award Finalist

The merger between the City of South Norfolk and Norfolk County in 1963 to form the City of Chesapeake resulted in a diverse landscape of

Alliance for Innovation and ICMA Awards for Best Practices

A total of 243 submissions were received by AFI and ICMA. These were reviewed and evaluated by committees of local government practitioners, academics, and organizational staff.

The AFI case studies included here were presented at the 2008 Transforming Local Government conference, held in Greenville, South Carolina, in June, and can be accessed at transformgov.org in the Government News section. All submissions for selection as case study presenters or award recipients are available to members of the Alliance for Innovation at transformgov.org within the Knowledge Center under Learning Resources—"Havlick and Muelenbeck Award Submittals" and "Transforming Local Government Conference."

ICMA awards recognize both individual achievement and program excellence. All of the ICMA award winners received national recognition at the ICMA's 94th annual conference, held in Richmond, Virginia, in September 2008, and are featured in the October 2008 issue of PM *magazine.*

urban, suburban, and rural communities in a wide range of neighborhoods. Faced with the challenge of meeting the needs of so many different populations, the city embarked on the Neighborhood Quality of Life Study, an innovative and practical policy tool to guide the measurement of neighborhood-level quality of life conditions across the city.

Strong, livable, residential communities are the backbone of a successful city. The Chesapeake Neighborhood Quality of Life research model defines neighborhood quality of life as the intersection between social well-being, community design, crime, and economic vitality. Acknowledging how these components are interrelated was the first step in creating a program to routinely assess progress and focus efforts on addressing the individual needs of each neighborhood.

For statistical purposes, the city was divided into 172 neighborhood statistical areas (NSAs). Neighborhood statistical areas are defined as communities of interest consisting of one or more neighborhoods or subdivisions. After analyzing 23 variables, including crime, social, physical, and economic data, the study classified each NSA as "developing," "sustaining," or "revitalizing." The final analysis yielded 17 developing, 80 sustaining, and 20 revitalizing NSAs (55 neighborhoods were omitted from the analysis). This framework enabled the city to align specific NSAs with other NSAs of similar dynamics and facing similar challenges, and thus to target public actions to address neighborhood issues based on common concerns rather than on local geography.

The "Chesapeake Neighborhood Quality of Life Study," which was developed to aid community residents, elected officials, and local government staff, serves both diagnostic and implementation roles. Equipped with accessible and understandable information, neighborhood residents and city staffers can talk about concerns using the same framework of understanding. The ultimate goal of this project is to provide a tool that evaluates Chesapeake's neighborhoods in terms of long-term sustainability.

Contact: Mark S. Cox
Organization: City of Chesapeake
E-mail: Pubcomm@CityOfChesapeake.net
Web site: Chesapeake.va.us

Neighborhood Strength Index (NSi)
Arlington, Texas (pop. 371,038)
AFI Award Finalist

Crime is often a serious problem in declining neighborhoods, but it may be a cause or a consequence of other conditions. The police department in Arlington, Texas, has practiced the community-based policing philosophy for more than 20 years and has held to a geographic accountability system since 1996. In 2007, it began a change management initiative to develop a more proactive community policing approach—one that would try to identify a declining neighborhood before the threat of crime rose significantly.

Often in the community policing model, a police department may establish strong partnerships with its external stakeholders but overlook the valuable partnerships that could be established

internally, from within the city itself, with its fellow employees spread across various city departments. To remedy this situation in Arlington, the police department took the lead in establishing cross-departmental partnerships and citywide geographic accountability models: to streamline contacts and improve communication between city departments, it developed the Neighborhood Strength Index (NSi). With the information that is collected from throughout the city, the NSi identifies factors that contribute to a neighborhood's decline, mapping dense areas where these factors exist and illustrating them as "hot spots," so that management can clearly target and apply limited resources to areas of greatest need. This process supports intelligence-led policing and integrates it into the current geographic policing model.

The cost savings are difficult to calculate at this stage, but the results in terms of time and city resources allocated to specific neighborhoods, as well as the overall value of the benefits reaped from having law enforcement and community services work together, are considerable. The NSi project has helped the Arlington police department and other city departments focus on suspected problem locations and transform the city into a network of partnerships, actively engaged and participating in information sharing in order to achieve a safer community and strengthen the fight against crime.

Contact: Jacqueline Zee, crime and intelligence analyst
Organization: Arlington Police Department
E-mail: Jacqueline.Zee@arlingtontx.gov
Web site: arlingtontx.gov

Fairfax County's Magnet Housing Program
Fairfax County, Virginia (pop. 1,010,241)
AFI Muehlenbach Award Winner

Fairfax County is one of the key areas of job growth, not only in the Washington, D.C., area but also in the nation. The abundance of jobs and the resulting need for a skilled and available workforce demand that the county provide a range of affordable housing. The Magnet Housing Program is an innovative approach that addresses both issues. Magnet Housing works in partnership with employers to provide affordable, attractive housing to individuals moving from jobs to a careers, whether they are in training, participating in an apprenticeship program, starting at the entry level, or filling critical, hard-to-fill positions.

Fairfax County's Magnet Housing Program was the first of its kind in the nation: a program that is designed specifically to meet the housing needs of a local workforce and that includes partnerships with major area employers and an employer-sponsored training component for resident employees. It was initially implemented in 2004 as a pilot program with the county's fire and rescue department, offering 10 affordable dwelling units in one condominium development; the program has since expanded to a total of 48 units located throughout the county. In addition, innovative partnerships have been developed between the Fairfax County Redevelopment and Housing Authority (FCRHA) and the Fairfax County public schools, police department, sheriff's office, human resources, and Inova Health Systems.

Future plans for the Magnet Housing Program include the development of the Residences at the Government Center, a complex that will be affordable to households making between 50% and 100% of the area median income, and the construction by the FCRHA of a living/learning campus in the county near the Government Center. This campus will provide affordable housing to program participants, while partnerships with Inova Health Systems and other county employers provide training and career development.

The Magnet Housing Program provides affordable housing to the county's workforce—a group working in a location that, even in a cooling housing market, remains too expensive for many working families to afford. Funding for the program is nonfederal, which allows the program the flexibility it requires to meet employer and workforce needs.

Contact: Kristina Norvell, director of public affairs
Organization: Fairfax County Redevelopment and Housing Authority
E-mail: Kristina.norvell@fairfaxcounty.gov
Web site: fairfaxcounty.gov/rha

Delray Beach Community Land Trust
Delray Beach, Florida (pop. 64,112)
TLG Case Study, Alliance

As Delray Beach enjoyed revitalization and growth, the value of real property began to increase dramatically. By 2006, with a median home price of $479,000 and median household income just over $50,000, an estimated 90% of Palm Beach County households could not afford to purchase a single-family home. While some traditional subsidy programs were available to low- and moderate-income households, they generally provided that the homes could be resold at full market value after about 10 years. The community needed a more permanent and effective solution to address the lack of affordable housing.

The Delray Beach Community Land Trust (DBCLT) is one of several affordable workforce housing initiatives. The land trust was formed by community stakeholders in December 2005 to preserve affordable homeownership and rental units in the city of Delray Beach. Under the DBCLT program, individual families and the community at large share in the long-term affordability and wealth creation that results from the wise investment of public money in privately owned housing. A land-lease agreement enables the land trust to buy back each home for an amount determined by the DBCLT's resale formula, which gives homeowners a fair return for their investment while keeping the price affordable for other lower-income people.

During the first year, 16 homes were built; of those, 6 have been sold and occupied, another 6 are in the underwriting approval stage at the banks, and 2 have been leased with purchase options. The DBCLT has 160 applicants currently in the pipeline, and is working with builders and potential buyers for the construction of 20 new single-family homes. In addition, 34 rental units became available at the end of October 2007.

The city of Delray Beach and the Delray Beach Community Redevelopment Agency (CRA) played a crucial role in the development of the DBCLT. Both donated vacant lots to the land trust; the CRA has provided crucial operating funds along with acquisition and construction financing; and the city provides the DBCLT with office space, equipment and operating supplies, and priority assistance with permitting construction projects. Other collaborators have included Florida Atlantic University and the MacArthur Foundation.

Contact: Lula Butler
Organization: City of Delray Beach
E-mail: Butler@ci.delray-beach.fl.us
Web site: mydelraybeach.com

Supported Alternatives for Our Valued Youth
Petersburg, Virginia (pop. 32,885)
AFI Award Finalist

A vital element in the present and future of a community is its young people. The city of Petersburg has a number of indicators that suggest that its youth are struggling and stressed. It has the second-highest high school dropout rate in Virginia, and 81% of children entering school have unmarried mothers and no adult men in the household. With the highest teenage pregnancy rate in Virginia (80%), it holds one of the highest percentages of unwed mothers in the state (72%). The city's overall crime index is 2,678, more than twice the national average; there are three gangs linked to national groups; and the city's use of secure detention for youth offenders is high. The city of Petersburg is committed to reversing these dismal demographics.

The product of focused efforts, starting in 2001, to identify alternatives to secure detention for its youth offenders, Supported Alternatives for Our Valued Youth (SAVY) is a collaboration of over 20 city agencies and community partners with a core mission of enhancing the physical, mental, educational, and social well-being of the children and youth of Petersburg. Its main objectives are achieved by analyzing the needs and assets of existing programs while at the same time increasing communication within the community.

To create a foundation and road map to identify and address the diverse needs of the city's youth and children, SAVY invested in a comprehensive city-wide Youth Needs Assessment. Conducted by Virginia Polytechnic and State University and funded by the Cameron Foundation, a local charitable organization, the assessment produced some compelling findings. In response to those findings, Petersburg developed alternative programs and services that reduced the use of secure detention by 75% over a three-year period. Now the youth in the city, their caregivers, and city agencies benefit from a broader multidisciplinary approach to address a full range of issues affecting young people.

Contact: Eric Campbell, assistant city manager
Organization: City of Petersburg
E-mail: ctymgr@earthlink.net
Web site: petersburg-va.org/

REMAKING THE LOCALITY

Two very different cities—one a mill town and one a river town—had a similar problem: disinvestment and a changed economy demanded wholly new approaches to community development.

From Textiles to Biotech
Kannapolis, North Carolina (pop. 41,487)
TLG Case Study, Alliance

In 2003 there were 7 million square feet of vacant textile space over the entire downtown of Kannapolis, North Carolina, with no hope of another user. With the close of Pillowtex, the city's major employer, 4,500 residents had lost their jobs and 280 acres were left lifeless in the downtown area. In late 2004, California-based David Murdock, chief executive officer of Castle & Cooke, purchased the Pillowtex site and in September 2005, he developed a plan in partnership with the city and the University of North Carolina (UNC) system to redevelop downtown Kannapolis by launching the North Carolina Research Campus (NCRC).

When completed, the NCRC will be a $1.5 billion bioscience research campus of massive proportions. Plans include universities, a state-of-the-art laboratory and office space for biotech and life science firms, civic uses, and retail and residential development. With the removal of huge amounts of obsolete textile manufacturing equipment and facilities, the project will encompass the entire downtown of Kannapolis, making it one of the largest urban redevelopment projects on record in the United States. According to the impact analysis, the campus could generate 37,000 new jobs in the region 25 years after development is completed.

The main purpose of the NCRC will be to study nutrition and health, including new ways of cultivating and harvesting plants and vegetables, and of identifying the demographic and environmental factors that affect the efficacy of treatment for such major diseases as diabetes, brain disease, obesity, and cancer. Once completed in 2012, the campus will have 3.2 million square feet of office, lab, and civic space; 12 parking decks containing approximately 10,000 spaces; and nearly 1,000 on-campus dwelling units. It will also include a girl's science and math high school for students recruited from around the world. UNC–Chapel Hill, UNC–Greensboro, UNC–Charlotte, North Carolina State University, North Carolina Agricultural and Technical University, North Carolina Central, Duke University, and Appalachian State University will have facilities on the campus.

From the outset, the NCRC has been designed to be a live, work, play environment. The redevelopment plans include five parks, one of which will be a seven-acre courtyard in the heart of the campus. The campus will flow seamlessly into the existing downtown. Physical redevelopment has been supported by new initiatives to better serve the current and new diverse population.

Contact: Mike Legg
Organization: City of Kannapolis
E-mail: mlegg@ci.kannapolis.nc.us
Web site: ci.kannapolis.nc.us

Green City Initiative
Davenport, Iowa (pop. 98,975)
ICMA Community Sustainability Award

The largest Farm Belt city on the Mississippi, Davenport, Iowa, had a century-long history as a manufacturing and agricultural hub. But like many Midwest cities have come to acknowledge, economies change. That, coupled with 50 years of urban disinvestment, job loss, and double-digit population loss, emboldened Davenport's leaders to create the Green City Initiative to pursue comprehensive and fully integrated revitalization and sustainability strategies throughout the community. Their accomplishments can be described under the traditional three-legged sustainability stool of environmental preservation, economic competitiveness, and social equity.

Green City Initiative projects include the first LEED city building in Iowa, a hybrid municipal fleet, a wastewater plant that generates 90% of its own electricity from recovered methane, a regional park developed from a former brownfield, a dozen community gardens in underserved neighborhoods, and 800 new trees planted *annually* along major streets. Community cleanups, enhanced recycling, and a comprehensive compost facility connect the citizens with these environmental enhancements.

Revitalization of the city's core, an economic strategy that was approved by 73% of the voters in 2001, leveraged an initial $113 million in public and private redevelopment projects. These include adaptive reuse of vacant warehouses, development of downtown arts and culture establishments, a mixed-use commercial/housing complex, and the unique "Skybridge"—a pedestrian suspension bridge with a 600-foot span and glass walls.

Recognizing that the future depends on tomorrow's workforce, the Davenport Promise Task Force is currently refining a community revitalization and growth strategy to ensure that every student can have post–high school tuition (college, trade apprenticeship, or vocational training) paid for through an innovative community partnership.

By all measures, the impact of the city's revitalization and sustainability efforts have been extraordinary. The old riverfront is now a public showplace. New offices and lofts are being built in the downtown. Hundred-year-old neighborhoods are attracting new investment. And as to metrics, over the past five years, crime has dropped by one-third, the tax base has increased by more than a billion dollars, and the population is now growing.

Contact: Craig Malin
Organization: City of Davenport
E-mail: ctm@ci.davenport.ia.us
Web site: cityofdavenportiowa.com

IMPROVING HEALTH AND SAFETY

Health is not a traditional function of city government, but these cities, whether focusing internally or externally, have made the health and safety of employees one of their core responsibilities.

Health Care Management System by Prevention

Lewiston, Maine (pop. 35,234)
ICMA Strategic Leadership and Governance Award

While Lewiston, Maine, knew it could not control or influence the skyrocketing cost of health care for its employees and families, it did recognize that it could help curb the development of serious diseases and encourage healthy lifestyles. So in 2005, Lewiston entered into an agreement with the Central Maine Medical Center (CMMC) to develop and implement Health Care Management System by Prevention, a cutting-edge program that assesses the health risk behaviors of employees and their spouses; provides guidance to help them address at-risk behaviors, and helps them set and achieve reasonable, sustainable goals.

The program has many elements, including a CMMC city hall–based health educator, a 15% reduction in program participants' health insurance costs, and a Wellness Center membership for 150 employees and spouses. Participants are also provided with an annual comprehensive physical exam, a health risk assessment, a personal exercise program, health informational classes and body fat/waist management goals. For these services Lewiston pays CMMC quarterly payments of $5,409 and an annual fee of $7,762.

The benefits of the program are very telling. Lewiston's health insurance premiums remained stable except in 2008, when they decreased by nearly 5% ($350,000 annual saving). As Lewiston employees have become more educated about their health, they have used less municipal sick time, decreasing the average use from 8.18 days in 2006 to 6.75 in 2007. Weight loss among the municipal employees has been massive: as of February 1, 2007, 59% of employees and spouses lost a total of 1,962 pounds. One year later, 47% had lost an additional 1,402 pounds.

Becoming proactive in the health care management arena has increased productivity, reduced costs, and developed more educated, healthy employees. These successes prove that financially and healthwise, preventive care is far more effective than disease management.

Contact: James Bennett
Organization: City of Lewiston
E-mail: jbennett@ci.lewiston.me.us
Web site: ci.lewiston.me.us

Community Transportation Plan

Decatur, Georgia (pop. 19,168)
TLG Case Study, Alliance

There is increasing recognition of the link between the built environment and human health. How we live and travel affects not only our physical well-being but our mental, emotional, and spiritual state as well. The design of our environment also affects how we connect with each other and how we establish a sense of place and community. Regular physical activity has been proven to benefit people of all ages, having positive effects on self-image, self-esteem, physical and mental wellness, and overall health.

In May 2006, the city of Decatur, Georgia, set out on an ambitious project to develop a compre-hensive transportation plan for the city, shifting the emphasis from moving cars to creating a healthy and active built environment. This focus on an "active living" community was the foundation of the Decatur Community Transportation Plan (CTP). The CTP incorporated a wide range of technical analysis, tools, and strategies that helped integrate both traditional automobile planning and elements that are more important to pedestrians and cyclists.

Since its inception, the CTP has pursued a holistic effort to examine the city's infrastructure system, challenge the current allocation of roadway space, and develop a series of recommendations that advance Decatur into the current generation of active and healthy cities. The result is a comprehensive plan that includes a range of strategies, from educational programs for users of all modes of transportation to the redesign of intersections and the addition of sidewalks, bicycle lanes, and crosswalks. The plan also offered a health impact assessment workshop that convened health professionals, community leaders, and citizens to discuss the effects of the CTP's recommendations from a health perspective.

The transportation system envisioned through the CTP creates an environment that promotes the health and vitality of all citizens and visitors. It provides safe and reliable carfree options for everyone to become and stay active, both physically and socially, in the community. It is especially beneficial to the city's most vulnerable populations, such as low-income households, children, and older adults, all of whom have different physical, mental, and financial challenges to mobility. This inclusive participation provides immeasurable benefit not only to individual citizens, but also to the collective spirit of Decatur and the Atlanta region as a whole.

Contact: Amanda Thompson, planning director
Organization: Planning Department, City of Decatur
E-mail: Amanda.Thompson@decaturga.com
Web site: decaturga.com

Ambulance Safety Initiative

Winter Park, Florida (pop. 28,445)
ICMA Community Health and Safety Award

Paramedics are known for their life-saving skills, but often they are put at risk themselves as their ambulances hurtle across communities to reach an accident victim, or race to a medical facility with a patient in tow. During the 1990s, more than 300 fatal ambulance accidents occurred in the United States, most of which involved emergency medical service (EMS) personnel who were unrestrained in the vehicle. The dilemma of rendering care to their passengers while using radios and accessing medical equipment made it physically impossible for EMS personnel to use standard lap-type seat belts. Add to that their hesitancy to use any sort of restraint for fear that it would not allow them to perform their jobs properly, and the conundrum was clear.

Lt. Andrew Isaacs of the Winter Park Fire-Rescue Department (WPFD), being told that there was no design for a safety restraint on the market that could accommodate paramedic needs, set about studying and designing such a device. In 2004, he initiated the Ambulance Safety Initiative (ASI), an assessment of a restraint system that would allow for all EMS personnel to travel safely while performing the basic ergonomics of emergency medical care. He thoroughly researched the continuum of patient care from vehicle markings to equipment accessibility. His comprehensive approach to the problem ultimately led to the development of a five-point restraint system that offers greater security for the riders while allowing for the continued mobility needed to treat patients.

The city of Winter Park funds all activities of the fire-rescue department, and its Vehicle Replacement Fund (VRF) serves as the internal leasing function for city vehicles. Once specifications were drafted, the ASI units were advertised for competitive bid in adherence to the city's purchasing procedures and state law. Two manufacturers responded and agreed to change their ambulance design (there are currently five manufacturers producing similarly designed units). Within two years of the project's inception, a contract was signed to produce units meeting all specifications.

The single most important achievement of the ASI is the increased level of safety for EMS personnel. The attention that the WPFD paid to both safety and usability has resulted in what the industry calls "America's safest ambulance." The three measures used to evaluate success include personal compliance (now at 90%), reduction in worker's compensation (injuries from related travel dropped to 0%), and reduction in motor vehicle crashes (100% compliance with revised vehicle markings, lighting, and equipment location).

The ASI units designed by and produced for the WPFD are a first for the United States as they address the unique work of paramedics during transport. The WPFD's pioneering work is now considered the standard for the industry nationwide.

Contact: Randy Knight
Organization: City of Winter Park
E-mail: city.manager@cityofwinterpark.org
Web site: CityofWinterpark.org

PROMOTING SUSTAINABILITY

An encouraging development in the new millennium has been the rising interest among local governments in achieving greater environmental, economic, and social sustainability.

Turning Liabilities into Assets: A Class EQ Biosolid Fertilizer

Leesburg, Virginia (pop. 38,465)
TLG Case Study, Alliance

Disposal of organic solids presents a number of potential problems, including contaminants, pathogens, and odor. The water content of these solids creates problems in landfills, and incineration can create air emissions and ash waste.

Like many other communities, Leesburg, Virginia, opted in 1975 to implement a land application program for the treated biosolids it produced. The treated biosolids were applied at no cost to

local farms granted permits by the Virginia Department of Health. This program was successful for more than 20 years. But as the town's population and the resulting wastewater flows increased, the quantity of biosolids being produced also increased. During the same period, Loudoun County's population increased as well, with significant development occurring in the rural areas where the permitted farms are located, and several sites were lost to development.

Faced with a growing annual quantity of organic solid by-products from its wastewater system, Leesburg abandoned its aesthetically displeasing Class B land application method and instead produced an environmentally friendly and sustainable Class EQ (Exceptional Quality) biosolid fertilizer. In so doing, the town turned a potential liability into a tremendous asset for the region. It now operates a heat drying system that is the first of its kind for any government in Virginia, and it offers bags of the high-grade pellets to residents at no cost and to commercial users at a low cost. Leesburg has completed trademark protection on the product name.

This entrepreneurial program is saving taxpayers tens of thousands of dollars annually in fertilizer expenses for town-owned facilities. Managers of large-use areas, such as golf courses and farms, who acquire the product now have a low-cost and environmentally friendly alternative to inorganic fertilizers that can harm the Potomac River watershed.

Contact: Aref Etemadi
Organization: Town of Leesburg
E-mail: aetemadi@leesburgva.gov
Web site: leesburgva.gov

Using a Form-Based Zoning Code to Mitigate the Urban Heat Island
Phoenix, Arizona (pop. 1,552,259)
TLG Case Study, Alliance

A number of significant public projects have been completed in downtown Phoenix, Arizona, during the past 20 years, but the city has lacked a larger plan to guide development and create places rather than just projects. It has also been apparent that thermal comfort is a key to the success of the downtown: the extreme summer heat creates stressful street-level conditions to the extent that it has a negative impact on the development of a pedestrian-friendly public realm. City staff and a consultant team were charged with creating sustainability standards to provide more pedestrian shade and reduce the urban heat island effect as part of a new streamlined form-based code for downtown and of detailed master plans for parks and public spaces, circulation, and public art.

The Urban Form Plan is a major implementation step identified in Downtown Phoenix: A Strategic Vision and Blueprint for the Future, adopted by the city council in December 2004. It covers approximately 1,500 acres that constitute the geographic heart of the city. The strategic vision describes the downtown as a destination that integrates housing, employment, culture, entertainment, and shopping into a livable and sustainable environment; the area offers many types of urban housing choices; neighborhoods that encourage

adaptive reuse and uniqueness; quality building design; an active local arts and entertainment scene; distinctive retail experiences; and well-designed public spaces.

Participants in the Urban Form planning process determined that acceptable levels of thermal comfort can be achieved in the downtown area through an integrated approach to the design of the urban environment that includes street and building proportions, open space, urban forestry, building design, and the use of building and paving materials that reduce the absorption and retention of heat. This effort to create a desirable pedestrian environment called "the Connected Oasis"—a "green infrastructure" network of shaded pedestrian corridors that connect various downtown destinations with adjacent neighborhoods and, eventually, with a more far-reaching pedestrian network—will provide opportunities for both passive and active recreational facilities and activities.

With approval of the plan in 2008, Phoenix is the largest city in the country to make the shift from standard zoning to a form-based code in its downtown area, and it is the first city in the country to use that code as an urban heat island mitigation strategy.

Contact: Dean P. Brennan, FAICP,
    principal planner
Organization: Planning Department,
    City of Phoenix
E-mail: dean.brennan@phoenix.gov
Web site: phoenix.gov/planning

Comprehensive Approaches to Climate Change and Sustainability
Santa Rosa, California (pop. 154,241)
TLG Case Study

Berkeley, California (pop. 101,377)
TLG Case Study

Palo Alto, California (58,246)
AFI Award Finalist

Pinellas County, Florida (pop. 917,437)
TLG Case Study, Alliance

Sustainability has emerged as a major concern in American society, and local governments are developing a wide range of innovative approaches to reduce emissions and strengthen the environment, promote responsible development, and ensure that the needs of all residents are addressed equitably. The efforts highlighted below are presented in a composite description that focuses on specific methods used in particular communities while reflecting common themes. Taken together, they are illustrative of the high level of commitment that communities are displaying to advance sustainability,

Santa Rosa, California On August 2, 2005, the Santa Rosa city council passed a resolution to reduce greenhouse gas emissions from its municipal operations to 20% below 2000 levels by the year 2010. The city has since initiated many programs to save money, reduce greenhouse gasses, and generate clean, renewable energy. Major efforts include retrofitting all city buildings with high-efficiency lighting and appliances and cool roofs; buying hybrid and alternatively fueled vehicles; pursuing long-standing

and aggressive water conservation measures for residential, commercial, municipal, and industrial users; implementing the Santa Rosa Build It Green (SR BIG) program; installing five large solar energy (photovoltaic) arrays; adopting the Environmentally Preferred Purchasing Policy; and injecting 11 million gallons of recycled water into the Geysers Steam fields. The Geysers project produces more than 85 megawatts of clean green energy each year.

Contact: Dell Tredinnick
Organization: City of Santa Rosa
E-mail: Dtredinnick@srcity.org
Web site: santa-rosa.ca.us/Pages/default.aspx

Berkeley, California In November 2006, Berkeley voters issued a call to action on greenhouse gas emissions by overwhelmingly endorsing Measure G, a ballot initiative that set the goals of reducing the entire community's greenhouse gas emissions by 80% by the year 2050. Although the measure is technically advisory, the city of Berkeley is acting on it as if it is binding, and the steps it is taking illustrate how widespread community and local government involvement can support the development of a Climate Action Plan. The city hired a full-time "climate action coordinator," formed a cross-departmental project team to help identify and analyze potential and existing emissions reduction strategies, organized a six-month community engagement and input process, and conducted significant qualitative and quantitative research. Committed to producing and implementing a plan that reflects community diversity, expertise, ideas, and concerns, Berkeley is partnering with many community groups to host and actively participate in a series of events, focus groups, and workshops to ensure community participation in the plan's development and implementation. The city also launched a "community climate action forum" (BerkeleyClimateAction.org), an online resource for posting draft reports for public review, conducting public surveys, and further engaging and educating community members on the issue of climate change.

Contact: Timothy Burroughs
Organization: City of Berkeley
E-mail: tburroughs@ci.berkeley.ca.us
Web site: ci.berkeley.ca.us/Home.aspx

Palo Alto, California In 2006, the mayor of Palo Alto established the Green Ribbon Task Force on Climate Protection, whose report to the city council at the end of the year provided recommendations on various aspects of the community, including energy, transportation, the built environment, and citizen education. The council put global climate change on its list of the top four priorities, and a sustainability team of four existing staff members completed the Climate Protection Plan, which the council approved on December 3, 2007. The plan includes a detailed assessment of current greenhouse gas emissions from the city operations, Palo Alto residents, and nonresidents who work in or visit Palo Alto; an expanded methodology for incorporating the environmental impact of transportation, energy use, solid waste, and both "upstream" and "downstream" emissions into municipal and community

assessments; 120 recommendations for curtailing emissions; specific reduction targets that would bring the city and community above and beyond compliance with California's climate change legislation; and detailed cost-benefit assessments of many of those recommendations to allow the council and the public to assess their budgetary and carbon-cutting impacts. The "Education and Motivation" (community outreach) portion of the plan created the Community Environmental Action Partnership, which has representatives in the faith community, nonprofits, schools, businesses, government, and neighborhoods. The partnership determines how its members will implement emission reductions programs to reach the reduction targets set out in the plan.

Contact: Nancy Nagel and Karl van Orsdol
Organization: City of Palo Alto
E-mail: nancy.nagel@cityofpaloalto.org and
 karl.vanorsdol@cityofpaloalto.org
Web site: cityofpaloalto.org/knowzone/
 agendas/grtf.asp

Pinellas County, Florida Guided by the results of a community visioning process and surveys of citizens, Pinellas County has developed a comprehensive approach to advancing sustainability. The approach begins with a staff advisory team that draws on groups from within each department and on technical committees organized by themes, such as sustainable economy and business, to make recommendations, and with citizen focus groups to provide guidance. All the input that is received then flows through the county's Bushnell Center for Urban Sustainability, a partnership between the county and University of Florida's Cooperative Extension Service, which identifies and coordinates organization-wide sustainability programs and initiatives, such as energy independence and security, a green fleet program, and sustainable purchasing.

The center seeks to be a catalyst for creative problem solving and organizational management and innovation, as well as a conduit for strategic partnerships with external stakeholders (e.g., the Century Commission for a Sustainable Florida) and the University of Florida and other academic institutions. In its centralized coordination and leadership role, the Bushnell Center has been instrumental in assisting the county's strategic focus area teams to integrate their efforts under an overall sustainability umbrella. If several teams emerge with conflicting strategic goals or objectives, for instance, the Bushnell Center will facilitate a solution that creates an opportunity out of a potential conflict. In addition, the center has piloted the use of a net benefit analysis methodology for comparing the sustainability of alternative purchasing scenarios for products and services that the county acquires. In the long run, the Bushnell Center will work with the county to institutionalize and enhance this type of analysis in the decision-making process for county infrastructure.

Contact: Devesh Nirmul
Organization: Pinellas County Bushnell Center
 for Urban Sustainability
E-mail: dnirmul@pinellascounty.org
Web site: pinellascounty.org

EXPANDING APPLICATIONS OF E-GOVERNMENT

Technology has changed government in a dramatic fashion. New services, business processes, and community connections are important by-products.

Open eGov
Newport News, Virginia (pop. 179,153)
AFI Havlick Award Winner

Like other local governments, Newport News, Virginia, faced ongoing challenges in using information technology (IT). The city's Web site was fragmented and inconsistent, and the content was often out of date. User departments either had Web masters with knowledge and skills to update their department's Web pages or had to request service from the IT department. Governments were expected to keep up with the increasing demand for online services. Updating software for mainframe applications had a higher priority than replacing Web software.

To address all these needs, Newport News developed Open eGov, a Web software application offered free of charge and available to any other local government. In this collaborative approach, government organizations, nonprofits, and the private sector work together to share the cost of enhanced capabilities; by reducing or eliminating the duplication of effort between localities, they are thus able to deliver online Web services to citizens more effectively and efficiently.

Open eGov is flexible enough to handle common functions and services while allowing for personalization and customization. It enables the Web site to offer many fully executable online transactions, supporting interaction with citizens, businesses, and other government agencies. It also enables all departments to update their own content and publish it directly to the Web without going through IT. This capability has resulted in improved service delivery to the citizens in Newport News: by decentralizing the Web content, the departments were able to eliminate about a third of the Web pages, thereby improving citizens' ability to find the content relevant to them.

The collaborative approach may be especially beneficial to smaller localities that otherwise could not afford a Web content management system. All organizations benefit from the rapid growth in applications and tools that the participants provide. Citizens benefit from more functionality, faster deployment schedules, less cost, and more standardization of Web access to government. The new software is registered as an open-source general public license and is available as a free download.

Contact: Andy Stein
Organization: City of Newport News
E-mail: astein@nngov.com
Web site: nngov.com/egov/open-egov

Ask Arvada: Information and Service 24/7
Arvada, Colorado (pop. 106,328)
Alliance Award Finalist

Arvada, Colorado, a northwestern suburb in the Denver metro area, is committed to "Continuing to Build a Great Community." Because many of its citizens work outside the city proper and have limited access to city service during the traditional 8 AM–5 PM business day, Arvada undertook to developing a virtual city hall to give citizens access to city services 24 hours a day, seven days a week.

Arvada used the in-house knowledge of its staff and experienced vendors (Tele-works and Government Outreach) to plan and develop "Ask Arvada." Using existing information from a phone service that provided answers to frequently asked questions (FAQs), vendors and staff were able to identify the types of questions that citizens have and the types of service requests that are most typical. Standard forms from each department are available online for citizens who are unable to get to city hall during regular business hours. A citizen request-and-tracking system allows citizen contact information to be shared throughout the organization. A brief citizen survey enables managers and supervisors to review customer satisfaction with the service.

The result is a multimodal response-tracking system that has greatly improved service delivery, response time, and citizen satisfaction. City personnel received extensive training in the system before the new program was launched. When the system was ready to be deployed, the cross-departmental planning team reached out to all city departments and found that even those that desired not to participate had to comply as they received service requests.

As of November 2008 Arvada had engaged more than 150 staff who regularly respond to questions and requests for service, had answered more than 1,583 service requests, and had more than 24,827 inquires for information through the FAQs. Arvada sees "Ask Arvada" as a stepping-stone for development of a full 311 call system in the future.

Contact: Craig Kocian
Organization: Arvada, CO
E-mail: ckocian@arvada.org
Web site: arvada.org

DubLink
Dublin, Ohio (pop. 37,954)
Alliance Award Finalist

Dublin, Ohio, has long been viewed as an innovative and progressive community. Following passage of the Telecommunications Act of 1996, Dublin became the first city in the country to deploy fiber optics through its own sewer lines. That innovative strategy led to the development of a 25-mile multiconduit system throughout Dublin's commercial district in 1999, accommodating fiber-based services for voice, data, and video systems. Many more innovative technologies were deployed between 2000 and 2005 to bring high-speed capacity to public buildings, colleges and universities, hospitals, and public broadcasting.

Today, more than 1,600 miles of fiber create the Ohio Supercomputer Center (OSCnet) and the Central Ohio Research Network (CORN). These are linked to the institutional fiber networks of the city and to the Dublin city schools,

allowing for—among other benefits—streaming video for security at stadium events or distance learning with institutions of higher education. Additionally, the city deployed a four-square-mile WiFi area encompassing its commercial district and is currently deploying WiFi citywide (a 24-square-mile area). The hotspot network grid uses existing towers, buildings, sirens, traffic, and light poles in the rights-of-way and easements.

The city's use for the WiFi is focused toward mobile computing for emergency responders and other field staff. The WiFi is also being used during community events, such as the Dublin Irish Festival and Jack Nicklaus's PGA Memorial Golf Tournament, to scan tickets and provide reports on attendance. Corporate buildings and office parks, as well as small-business owners, are eligible to receive WiFi.

The city of Dublin's public/institutional plan is to own and use bandwidth, both optical fiber and wireless/WiFi to maximize communications for city operations and to establish point-to-point connectivity among facilities. The bandwidth has provided the community with flexibility, reliability, and numerous opportunities for economic development.

Contact: Dana L. McDaniel
Organization: City of Dublin
E-mail: dmcdaniel@dublin.oh.us
Web site: dublin.oh.us

IMPROVING ORGANIZATIONAL PERFORMANCE

Local governments have much to gain from making the organizations as effective as possible.

Harnessing the Volunteered Energy of Employees: The Strategic Change Team
Carlsbad, California (pop. 95,439)
TLG Case Study, Alliance

For an organization to be sustainable, it must challenge itself to learn, stay in touch with the community, update its skills, and find ever better ways to deliver service. In the mid-1990s, Ray Patchett, then city manager of Carlsbad, California, established the Strategic Change Team (SCT) to actively partner with his city's senior management in order to further Carlsbad's mission, values, and vision. In later years, the team expanded its purpose, embracing experiences rich in learning in order to enhance members' ability to contribute to the team and organization.

One of the SCT's most recent projects was a "Futuring" process called TREK 2017. Following a two-day conference that brought together city employees, the mayor, the city council, and citizens to look at what citizens and stakeholders envisioned the city to be in the coming decade, the TREK process engaged more than 100 participants in volunteer workgroups that refined and further developed insights from the conference. Strategic initiative teams are now translating that work into concrete plans for the future.

The SCT's impact on the organization has been more broad-based than this example suggests. The growth experience for members exerts a subtle but significant effect as participants bring their insights, expanded thinking, and broadened perspectives into the workplace. The city's deputy city manager has termed the effect "viral" to describe a systemically spreading positive contagion of beneficial ideas and ways of thinking.

The SCT offers forward-thinking, innovative employees an opportunity to find a supportive venue for learning and engagement. The team challenges the city, internally and externally, to be open to discussions about change, innovation, and sustainability for the organization and community.

Contact: Bonnie Elliott
Organization: City of Carlsbad
E-mail: belli@ci.carlsbad.ca.us
Web site: carlsbadca.gov

Organization and Employment Development Program
Polk County, Florida (pop. 574,746)
ICMA Strategic Leadership and Governance Award

While excellent customer service is often touted by business and government as being a priority, few organizations make the sustained investment in their workforce to achieve this goal. Not so Polk County, Florida, where County Manager Robert M. (Mike) Herr spearheaded a comprehensive program to (1) develop a high-performing workforce that delivers top-quality customer service, (2) engender a commitment to excellence within that workforce, and (3) foster a culture that focuses on results.

In 2003, Manager Herr created a new division within his organization, Organization and Employee Development (OED). The OED's mission is to achieve organizational excellence through the engagement, development, and recognition of employees, and to stimulate a culture shift that values employees as critical to organizational success.

OED put into place several programs that focus on employees from their first days on the job to their last days with the county. New Employee Orientation is a two-day program that serves to introduce new employees to the organization and its values. The Employee Development Program offers permanent employees more than 110 classroom sessions within four certification programs of study. An Emerging Leaders program was established to identify top performers, prepare them for leadership, and enable them to qualify for upcoming management vacancies. And a Succession Planning Program identifies potential candidates for critical positions and ensures that there are individual development plans to prepare them for candidacy.

Employees themselves were given responsibility for developing and promoting the organizational mission statement, vision statement, and values, as well as Kudos, an employee recognition program. They are also encouraged to engage within the organization through the SHINE

(*Suggestions Help Increase and Nurture Excellence*) program, in which cost-saving or process-improvement suggestions can earn the suggester anywhere from $25 to $3,000. Another initiative—Cheaper, Better, Faster—uses cross-departmental teams to identify and develop process improvement strategies for targeted service areas, such as e-payment options or capital improvement projects. Finally, an annual employee satisfaction survey, designed as a tool for open communication, was adopted to allow employees to express their feelings and analyze the composite results of the assessment.

OED has made incredible strides in changing the way employees think about themselves, their future, and their workplace. This translates into superior customer service and is the foundation for growth toward organizational greatness, one employee at a time.

Contact: Michael Herr
Organization: Polk County
E-mail: michaelherr@polk-county.net
Web site: polk-county.net

From "Trust Us" to a Performance-Based Organization
Fort Collins, Colorado (pop. 133,899)
TLG Case Study, Alliance

During the 1990s, Fort Collins, Colorado, enjoyed double-digit revenue growth and developed many new services for citizens. But as the national and local economy changed, so did the revenue picture. By 2003, expenses were outpacing projected revenues. When a new city manager and mayor arrived in 2005, they took steps to make local government more transparent, accountable, and financially sustainable. Rather than expecting citizens to "trust us," the city reestablished itself as a performance-based organization.

First, the city revamped the budgeting process. Rather than funding departments, as had always been the practice, the new process, Budgeting for Outcomes (BFO), focuses on funding services that are priorities of citizens. The city council identifies the priority outcomes, city staff put together proposals for the best ways to deliver the services, and a cross-departmental "results team" determines which offers will best achieve the desired outcomes. BFO ensures that every budget line item links directly to a service that the community wants.

BFO has provided several unexpected and positive results. It has encouraged employees to think creatively and cooperatively with other city departments, leading to increased sharing with, and capitalizing on the expertise of, other departments. It has strengthened the city's partnership with the city council and community, and helped all city employees better understand city finances and the cost of services.

At the same time that BFO was implemented, a whole new revenue forecasting system was put in place. Accuracy in forecasts is essential to creating sustainable services and building community credibility. Previous budgeting had relied on a generic forecast, which did not keep pace with the quick-changing nature of the economy. The

new system is customized, taking into account regional competition, performance of key retailers, and other elements.

Proving that local services are on par with those provided by similar communities is also important in building trust with citizens. ICMA's performance measurement program provided a credible benchmarking system. Now armed with hard facts, Fort Collins uses this information to implement best practices, evaluate services, and identify efficiencies.

The final component linked performance management with individual performance. The goals for every employee are linked to higher organizational objectives, and all are tied to the council-established priorities. The city uses a "total rewards" framework for its performance management system, which addresses attracting and retaining quality employees, building capacity, and engaging the workforce. Performance-based pay is one component of the new performance management system.

Fort Collins has long enjoyed a reputation of excellence. This performance-based approach has strengthened the city's credibility with elected officials and the community and will be the basis of the organization's success far into the future.

Contact: Darin Atteberry
Organization: City of Fort Collins
E-mail: datteberry@fcgov.com
Web site: fcgov.com

Flat Budget Spending in Public Works
Sarasota County, Florida (pop. 372,073)
TLG Case Study, Alliance

Although its road asset base has been growing every year, Sarasota County, Florida, has nevertheless been able to hold its public works costs flat. The traffic engineering and operations department has sought out innovative and smart applications to harness technology, and has measured the results of those efforts. Their asset management system (AMS) provides some interesting examples of how effectively this has been done.

Because signage degrades quickly in the harsh Florida sun, the AMS is used to measure orientation to the sun and predict when a sign will need replacing—an application that has resulted in a 10% reduction in signage replacement costs. Keeping track of where everything is speeds up a replacement or repair when needed. Connecting the geographic information system to the AMS helps locate job sites and reduces travel, resulting in a 10% increase in productivity. Equipping field staff with computers allows them to pull up work tickets in real-time and eliminate paperwork and secondary data entry, yielding another 11% cost reduction. Replacing 135-watt incandescent bulbs in traffic signals and streetlights with LED bulbs, which have a 500% longer life, has reduced required electrical power by 65%. Applying a video detection system at traffic signals allows signals to change more rapidly when conditions warrant, resulting in a 1% carbon reduction from less waiting time at traffic lights.

These are just some of the technologies that Sarasota County has deployed to provide improved service more efficiently and at a lower cost. Since maintaining a quality environment is also a community priority, the county has achieved quantifiable, sustainable gains in that area as well.

Contact: James L. Ley
Organization: Sarasota County
E-mail: jley@scgov.net
Web site: scgov.net

LESSONS LEARNED

Despite widespread perceptions that governments are reactive and lethargic, there is actually a high degree of experimentation with new approaches and ideas. The innovations described here are just a sampling of the many award-winning and recognized initiatives that were chosen from an even greater number of new local government programs and approaches submitted to the award competitions of the Alliance for Innovation and ICMA. Other general award programs are conducted by Harvard University's Ash Institute, the National Civic League, the National League of Cities, and the National Association of Counties, as well as by numerous associations that recognize accomplishment in specialized areas such as budgeting, housing, and information technology.

The question is, how can governments be more innovative? Examining the initiatives taken by a small number of jurisdictions does not clearly indicate which local governments will be innovators. The stories told in the award applications suggest, however, that there are certain characteristics that are shared by those governments that achieved exemplary change.

First, there is *leadership* that proposes new ideas and promotes an organizational culture that supports change. Scholar Sanford Borins has demonstrated that the ideas that lead to receiving the Ash Institute's Innovations in American Government Award come from both elected officials and staff, and that the staff members who start the ball rolling are more likely to be middle-level and front-line employees than to be agency heads.[3] It is also important for city and county managers and department heads to encourage the search for new approaches and support experimentation in order to foster a culture of innovation.[4] The innovations discussed here originated from many sources— mayors (Palo Alto), city councils (Phoenix), citizens (Berkeley), mayors and city managers (Fort Collins), managers (Polk County), department heads (Arlington), commissions (Delray Beach), other staff (Dublin, Newport News, and Winter Park), and individuals and organizations outside government (Kannapolis). Councils and managers provided critical support even if they were not the initiators.

Second, and growing out of this proactive leadership orientation, innovation requires *openness* and *creativity*. Participants in the process were encouraged to search for new approaches to reframe problems (Decatur), use new technologies (Leesburg), develop new solutions (Winter Park), adapt methods used in other local governments or in the private sector (Sarasota), create new coordinating mechanisms (Pinellas and Chesapeake), and use new processes to generate ideas (Carlsbad and Polk). Leaders support the spread of creativity throughout the organization by giving departments a high level of autonomy. Departments are encouraged to adapt city or countywide rules and regulations in a manner that best fits the needs of each department.

Third, these governments have achieved new levels of *collaboration* internally. The citizen relations program in Arvada was not viewed simply as an IT project but as a new way of conducting activities that affected the entire organization. The Arlington police created a tool for organizational change that includes other city departments in the fight against crime and the revitalization of neighborhoods, and Chesapeake developed a cabinet drawn from many departments to promote neighborhood quality of life. The Budgeting for Outcomes process in Fort Collins encourages employees to think creatively and cooperatively with other city departments in an effort to find more effective ways of accomplishing goals. Palo Alto's Sustainability Team was able to synthesize the expertise and experience of many departments with varying approaches to environmental programs. Cross-disciplinary involvement stimulates creativity and expands the capacity to solve problems. With collaboration, there is greater integration of the parts of the organization and stronger linkage between innovation goals and specific actions—a systemically spreading contagion of beneficial ideas and ways of thinking that Carlsbad labels "viral."

Fourth, the governments developed *partnerships,* thereby extending the collaborative spirit to a wide array of organizations outside the government. Delray worked with government and nonprofit organizations to create the Community Land Trust. Dublin developed a public-private partnership to create its WiFi system, and it uses the system to help small-business owners, assist with community events, support WiFi development in other cities, and connect Dublin city schools to the city and to the Central Ohio Research Network. The Fairfax County Magnet Housing Program grew out of agency collaboration and partnerships with other organizations whose recruits and new employees have housing needs. Lewiston's work with a local health provider enabled the tremendous leveraging of existing community resources. University partnerships were central to the Kannapolis and Pinellas efforts. Sustainability and climate change initiatives in Berkeley, Palo Alto, and Santa Rosa have depended on strong partnerships with community organizations. Arlington and Petersburg established coalitions of agencies to be part of their programs to support neighborhoods and young people.

Fifth, many of the successful innovations grew out of and depended on *strong linkages to citizens.* In Berkeley, a citizen referendum set the climate change target that provides the goal for city activities. Decatur and Phoenix have involved citizens in their assessment and planning. Kannapolis found that some longtime residents saw

the rebuilding of the town center as a loss of its heritage until they were involved more actively in the process. Fort Collins used citizen input to determine desired community outcomes. Davenport is relying on the Promise Task Force to bring forward the funding framework for their post-secondary access-for-all project. The success of the Leesburg biosolid fertilizer program depended on developing citizen acceptance and support.

These elements that accompany innovation—leadership, a search for new ideas, collaboration, partnerships, and citizen linkages—do not automatically lead to the discovery of new ways to better serve citizens and use resources. Nor do they guarantee that innovations will be implemented smoothly or achieve intended results. They are, however, the qualities that support an innovative organization. When communities foster these elements and look to other local governments for information and support, they are likely to find, as did the governments highlighted here, that they can do more and do better even in challenging and uncertain times.

[1]Otis White, "Seven Big Lessons for Local Governments," *Governing.Com,* posted January 3, 2006, governing .com/notebook.htm [accessed 11/13/08]

[2]All populations are July 2007 estimates from the U.S. Bureau of the Census.

[3]Sanford Borins, "Loose Cannons and Rule Breakers, or Enterprising Leaders? Some Evidence about Innovative Public Managers," *Public Administration Review* 60, no. 6 (2000): 500.

[4]Janet Vinzant Denhardt and Robert B. Denhardt, *Creating a Culture of Innovation: 10 Lessons from America's Best Run City* (Washington, D.C.: IBM Center for the Business of Government, 2001).

B The Intergovernmental Dimension

B 1

State-Local Relations: Authority and Finances

David R. Berman
Senior Research Fellow, Morrison Institute
Arizona State University

Selected Findings

Florida voters approved Amendment 1, whose tax-relief measures are expected to cost local governments billions of dollars in lost revenue over the next five years. A massive and complicated tax reform plan in Indiana cuts property taxes and replaces the lost revenue with sales, income, and other taxes.

California voters approved Proposition 99, a state constitutional amendment that gives them more protection against governmental use of eminent domain on behalf of private developers.

With states demanding more transparency from local governments in the way of open meetings information posted on public-access Web sites, Connecticut, Mississippi, New Hampshire, and Tennessee took action in 2008 to improve public access to local government records.

In 2008, responding to expected cuts in state aid, the mayor of a Connecticut town said, "We're on our own. . . . We're going to have to see what residents want to do. The community may not be able to afford the current level of services."[1] Local officials in much of the country shared these concerns.[2] By the end of 2008, local officials were not looking for or expecting more state aid; rather, they were hoping to minimize cuts in aid, stave off increases in unfunded mandates, avoid revenue takeaways, and somehow secure greater flexibility in raising revenues. Particularly in light of the economic downturn, local officials have ongoing reasons to be concerned about state mandates, prohibitions and preemptions, and the lack of state fiscal support for local government. This article provides an overview of conditions and developments in the areas of local authority and finance; it also considers significant ballot measures, judicial decisions, and legislation.

LOCAL AUTHORITY

In the mid-19th century, state legislatures were, in effect, "spasmodic city councils" that directly controlled the actions of local officials and interfered at will in local government affairs. In response, local officials and others began a long quest for home rule, which increases a local government's ability to initiate action and gives it greater protection from state interference in local affairs. Over the years, the view that local governments should have home rule has gained ground: some degree of home rule is available for municipalities in 48 states, and county governments have such powers in 37 of the 48 states with viable county governments.[3]

Although municipalities and counties with home rule authority are generally better off than those without, local governments with or without home rule have only limited power to initiate action and must spend much time and energy trying to ward off mandates, preemptions, and prohibitions that would further limit their authority. In practical terms, the amount of home rule authority depends not only on what is in state constitutions or laws, but also on how judges have interpreted those laws—and, perhaps most fundamentally, on how legislatures have chosen to live up to the spirit as well as the letter of the law.

Home Rule

Judges have claimed, at various times and in various places, that there is an inherent right of local self-government. The dominant legal view, however, has been that municipalities, counties, and other local units are the "legal creatures" of their states. In the words of Judge John F. Dillon, a much-quoted 19th-century authority on municipal law,

> *Municipal corporations owe their origin to, and derive their powers and rights wholly from, the legislature. It breathes into them the breath of life, without which they cannot exist. As it creates, so it may destroy. If it may destroy, it may abridge and control. . . . We know of no limitation of this right so far as corporations themselves are concerned. They are, so to phrase it, the mere tenants at will of the legislature.*[4]

Consistent with this view, courts have commonly limited the power of local governments by applying what has come to be known as "Dillon's Rule of strict construction":

> *It is a general and undisputed proposition of law that a municipal corporation possesses and can exercise the following powers, and no others: First, those granted in express words; second, those necessarily or fairly implied in or incident to the powers expressly granted; third, those essential to the accomplishment of declared objects and purposes of the corporation—not simply convenient, but indispensable. Any fair, reasonable doubt concerning the existence of power is resolved by courts against the corporation, and the power is denied.*[5]

Local governments in Dillon's Rule states must obtain specific legislative authority for virtually everything they wish to do. As a result, state legislators are busy passing bills that affect one or a few local governments and are immersed in minor local matters at the expense of policy issues of statewide interest. In New Hampshire, for example, municipalities have been compelled to secure state legislative approval for routine decisions—such as whether they can impose a user fee for trash removal, post warning signs on frozen ponds, or allow their citizens to pay municipal bills by credit card. In Arkansas, another Dillon's Rule state, the legislature busied itself in 2007 by giving municipalities specific powers—such as the authority to remove vehicles abandoned in the right-of-way.

To circumvent Dillon's Rule, several states have constitutional provisions or statutes that allow local governments to obtain home rule. The traditional and most common form of home rule (1) gives local governments that qualify under state constitutional or statutory provisions (e.g., a municipality over a certain population size) the right to make decisions without specific grants of authority on local matters and (2) limits the power of the state to intervene in local matters. In practice, however, courts have found it difficult to distinguish between what is a local affair and what is of statewide concern, and they have usually resolved uncertainties in favor of the states.

Other states where home rule exists, Alaska being an example, avoid the problem of distinguishing between state and local concerns by taking a devolution-of-powers approach, under which local units are authorized to carry out any function or exercise any power not expressly forbidden or preempted by the state (in essence, a reversal of Dillon's Rule). Even in these states, however, courts have tended to interpret the law to limit municipal action to what the courts define as the sphere of local affairs, and they often overturn municipal ordinances on the ground that such ordinances relate to a "statewide" rather than a "local" matter.[6] And in many of the states that have some form of official home rule, courts nevertheless continue to apply Dillon's Rule to limit the scope of municipal power.[7]

In addition to granting local governments the protection of home rule, many states prohibit special, or local, legislation—that is, acts that affect only a particular local jurisdiction. State constitutions commonly classify municipalities and counties by criteria such as population or total property value, and they require that the legislature treat all

jurisdictions in the same category equally. Prohibitions on local legislation, however, offer only limited protection, largely because legislatures are permitted to refine the scheme to the point where only one jurisdiction falls into a classification. Because of the classification schemes, state legislatures often have nearly as much freedom in dealing with their large cities as they did under the system of special legislation.

Local laws are common in some states, particularly in the South. For example, of the 139 bills that passed in the 2005 regular session of the Alabama legislature, 80 were local bills relating to such matters as fire protection fees, traffic laws, and the sale of draft beer. In Alabama, South Carolina, and other southern states, there is also a strong tradition of giving state legislators a great deal of control over legislation affecting the localities they represent. This practice effectively compels local elected officials to constantly go back to the legislative delegation for additional authority.

In 1973, South Carolina voters adopted the Home Rule Act, a constitutional amendment that prohibits special legislation. Since then, in keeping with the amendment, governors have regularly vetoed special legislation, but the legislature has just as routinely overridden the vetoes. Thus, the amendment has done little to prevent needless or harmful legislative interference in the affairs of specific local governments. To make matters worse, the South Carolina Supreme Court has interpreted the amendment in such a way as to prevent the legislature from delegating more authority to individual local governments. In 2007, for example, the court ruled in a 3–2 decision that a 2005 law transferring the power to appoint members of a recreation commission from Richland County's legislative delegation to the Richland county council violated the constitutional prohibition on special legislation. To comply with the court ruling, the legislature would have to pass legislation applying to all counties or all local governments. Coming up with general legislation of this nature is far more difficult than acting through special legislation. In 2008, South Carolina legislators gave some consideration to a proposed constitutional amendment that would have allowed the legislature to pass local or special legislation, thus removing a cornerstone of the 1973 act; pending the results of an in-depth study, however, no action has been taken.

Some states generally forbid their legislatures to pass legislation that affects only one locality, but they allow individual localities to petition the legislature for additional powers; this is considered acceptable because the action is initiated by the localities themselves and is therefore not an unwanted intrusion into local concerns. The legislators who represent the communities involved play a key role in determining the fate of the petitions. In Massachusetts, requests of this nature—known as home rule petitions—account for more than half of all laws passed by the legislature each year. Many of these requests for additional authority are denied; some are simply ignored; and still others are rejected not on their merits but because they get caught up in larger issues of state politics.[8] In each session, Massachusetts legislators

spend time deciding on matters that could just as easily have been left to local discretion in the first place.

Massachusetts employs the petition process in large part because the home rule provisions of state law actually give local governments little authority to act on their own. Because of the many exceptions in the 1960s laws that conferred home rule, and because of subsequent court decisions that undermined home rule, home rule in Massachusetts has been called "a myth."[9] Similarly, a recent study undertaken in North Carolina suggests that local governments' need for specific legislative authority to take action "limits flexibility, efficiency, and predictability."[10] The study recommends that the legislature (1) use broad language when drafting enabling legislation, (2) clarify the broad construction standard that courts must use to review challenges to local authority, and (3) delegate greater discretion to local entities. According to the study, unless changes are made, local authority in North Carolina will continue to depend on court decisions and special legislation.

In Ohio, meanwhile, critics have charged that a series of legislative acts have steadily chipped away at home rule authority. In recent years, the legislature has thrown out local ordinances imposing gun controls, residency requirements for police and firefighters, and anti-predatory-lending rules. The legislature has also attempted to stop localities from using red-light cameras to catch traffic offenders (the governor vetoed the measure), placed limits on the eminent domain powers of localities, and banned localities from filing lawsuits against lead-paint companies to help cover the cost of cleaning up lead paint in older buildings. State legislators are currently considering legislation that would override local laws regarding scrap-metal thievery. As discussed later in this article, many of these battles have moved from the legislature to the courts.[11]

The need for home rule has also been a rallying point for municipal officials in West Virginia: as Danny Jones, mayor of Charleston, declared in 2006, "Cities have to be able to have the power to govern themselves. . . . Every time we take a step, the state tells us how to take it."[12] This situation, however, may be greatly improving. In 2007, in response to complaints from local governments, the West Virginia legislature passed a bill allowing cities to experiment with home rule for five years—and, in the words of Lisa Dooley, executive director of the West Virginia Municipal League, "to prove the theory that home rule works."[13] A special panel selected four cities to participate in the program; on the basis of a wish list put together by the cities, the panel gave the jurisdictions authority to make decisions on a range of matters, including taxation, personnel, and administration.

Although many of the questions concerning local authority end up in court, state legislatures settle many more of them—not surprisingly, usually on the side of the state. Regardless of their constituencies, ideologies, or party identification, state legislators are generally reluctant to relinquish control over local governments. From where

they sit, local officials usually see more local autonomy as a good thing. From where *they* sit, state legislators tend to see local autonomy as a potential problem.[14] As an Alabama state senator said of county governments: "I oppose any Home Rule. We exist for checks and balances to keep county commissioners from doing anything unreasonable. Those good old boys back home can cook up things that might not be palatable to the local public."[15]

Businesses and various other interest groups also worry about local government discretion. Business groups often oppose home rule out of concern that local governments will use their new-found authority to impose more business taxes and regulations, or to take other steps that will adversely affect profits. When it comes to regulations, business groups find it easier to deal with a single state legislative body and a single set of standards than with a multitude of local governments imposing a variety of regulations. Builders, for example, have called on state legislatures to adopt statewide building codes so that they do not have to deal with building requirements that vary from locality to locality. Merchants who sell tobacco products also commonly favor statewide standards over local regulations. Likewise, those in the wireless communications industry, anxious to avoid a patchwork of municipal and county ordinances, have pressed for uniform statewide laws regarding the use of cell phones. In all these situations, local officials argue that important differences in local needs and conditions make varying regulations necessary.

Scope and Character of State Involvement

States routinely pass legislation that affects local authority, procedures, and finances. In fact, about one-fifth of the hundreds of measures introduced yearly in state legislatures significantly affect local governments. State laws determine the general level of local authority and the types of governmental structures that local governments can adopt. Other state laws concern elections, structure of government, incorporation, annexation, consolidation, and intergovernmental service agreements. In recent years, a number of new state laws have been passed that affect local government finances and personnel management. State laws often set debt limits, mandate public budget hearings, require a referendum for bond issues, and outline property assessment methods. Most local governments must abide by state laws that require employee training and workers' compensation. As indicated later in this article, recent state legislation has focused on transparency in local government operations, property taxes, eminent domain, cable regulation, and illegal immigration.

Given the importance of state legislative decisions to local governments' well-being, it comes as no surprise to find that local elected officials regularly take their case to state lawmakers. Sometimes they are on the offensive, trying to secure needed changes from the legislature. Perhaps even more often, though, local officials are on the defensive, trying to prevent cuts in state funding or to fend off costly mandates and unnecessary regulations. Often, local officials simply seek greater clarity in state law: in Utah in 2007, for

example, a legislative committee attempted to clear up confusion in state statutes concerning the roles of the mayor, the council, and administrators in local governance.

Some state legislation is the result of a genuine desire to make local government more accountable, effective, and efficient. For example, state legislators have long felt responsible for protecting citizens from dishonest or incompetent local officials. They also feel a duty to address problems that spill over local boundary lines, and to ensure fair treatment for all citizens with regard to education and other services. In an effort to maintain the health of the state's economy, many legislators have come to the aid of distressed localities. And in nearly every session, state legislators tinker with laws that they think will improve local government operations or service delivery. Nevertheless, in some cases, such tinkering, particularly in the case of mandates, may originate in a desire to shift program costs. And in the case of prohibitions, legislative action is often a matter of acceding to the demands of interest groups that are eager to avoid local taxes or regulations.

Mandates

State officials often rely on their legislative and regulatory authority to compel local units to follow certain procedures, make changes in existing programs, or assume new program responsibilities.[16] The matters addressed by mandates range from the important to the inconsequential, with the latter outnumbering the former.[17] Still, there are a considerable number of important and often costly mandates in each state. State mandates—whether in the form of statutes, executive orders, or administrative regulations—often create unfunded costs for local governments. Some mandates cost relatively little money, but their aggregate effects can be staggering, and the big-ticket items, in areas such as health care, education, land use, and environmental protection, can overwhelm local government budgets. Some of the largest costs stem from federal mandates—in areas such as education, environmental protection, and election administration—that are passed on to local units.

Transparency In recent years, states have begun demanding that local governments hold more open meetings, and that they make available more information about what they are doing, especially through public-access Web sites. Open-meeting requirements have been particularly burdensome, hamstringing local officials and their staffs and creating unreasonable criminal offenses. When it comes to open records, local officials have been concerned about covering the costs of searching for and reproducing whatever records that citizens or the media might demand.

In 2008, Mississippi lawmakers gave the state ethics commission the power to review alleged violations of the state's open-meeting and open-records laws and to fine local governments that violate these laws. Legislators also opened police incident reports to the public, freeing citizens and media organizations from having to file expensive lawsuits to secure such information. Meanwhile, in Tennessee, the general assembly updated the open-records law, making public

records more easily available to the public. The law created an ombudsman's office, the Office of Open Records Council, to help citizens secure access to public records held by local governments and to study problems such as excessive delays and overly high fees. Under a Connecticut law that went into effect in 2008, municipalities must put information about public board and commission meetings (including notices and minutes) on Web sites. New Hampshire also took action in 2008 with the passage of the Right to Know Law, which encourages public access to local governmental records. The law defines the records that are subject to the law; includes an explicit prohibition on conducting meetings by e-mail; and establishes standards for the retention, disclosure, and disposal of electronic records.

Employee Benefits Some expensive mandates are the products of end runs by local government employees who succeed in securing benefits through state legislation that they could not obtain through collective bargaining. For example, some states require local governments to pay police officers and firefighters what some observers consider to be overly generous pension benefits. (Although retirement benefits are set by state law, they are paid for out of local funds.) In a number of states—Florida, Illinois, Kentucky, New Jersey, Pennsylvania, and West Virginia among them—police and firefighter pension funds are underfunded or run the risk of being so. Overall, however, the funding of health care for police, fire, and other public-employee retiree programs is even more of a problem than pension funding.

In some states, wages and benefits for police officers and firefighters are determined by arbitrators appointed under the provisions of state law and are therefore outside the control of local elected officials. Moreover, the arbitrators' decisions tend to have a ripple effect, setting a higher standard for wages and benefits for other employees.[18] Binding arbitration has added to the burden of unfunded mandates in Connecticut, Michigan, and New York.

Local officials have, with varying degrees of success, sought legislation to reduce benefits or the conferral of new benefits. In 2008, New Jersey and New Hampshire passed such legislation despite the objections of public workers' unions. In West Virginia, municipal governments failed to obtain state financial assistance in funding police officers' and firefighters' pensions. Kentucky legislators made some changes that will affect benefits for county and municipal employees hired after September 2008, but they failed to overhaul the pension system. Illinois lawmakers made the pension system for emergency workers more transparent but did not take action to lower pension costs. In Indiana, as part of a broader tax-relief package, the state took over some pension payments from local governments. In Alaska, legislators helped out municipal governments and school districts by picking up a share of their ever-increasing retirement costs—which are projected to amount to around $450 million in 2009.[19] In 2008, the governor of Iowa vetoed a revision of the state bargaining-rights law that would have expanded the range of bargaining

issues to include matters relating to staffing levels and retirement.

Mandate Relief Even when local officials sympathize with the goals of state mandates, they are aware that all mandates distort local priorities and restrict local managerial flexibility. Nevertheless, local officials appear willing to live with most mandates if those mandates are at least partially funded; given local governments' financial constraints, they are hard put, without state funding, to both provide mandated services and address local priorities.[20]

When it comes to mandates, courts have been inclined to defer to the judgment of the legislatures, making it difficult for localities to challenge state mandates in the courts.[21] On the other hand, local governments have had some success in securing voter support for measures that are intended to reduce the number of mandates, or that require the states to pick up the costs of implementation. Voters appear to view such measures as a means of reducing local property taxes and preserving local control over spending priorities.[22]

Local officials and their associations regularly try to fend off mandates—or, failing that, to limit their financial impact. Local governments have sometimes obtained a pledge of additional state funds to cover the costs of new mandates—although, over time, states have not always been willing or able to live up to their agreements. Local governments have also sometimes succeeded in gaining the authority to raise the revenues needed to meet the costs of a new mandate; this outcome is not all that desirable, however, because local officials who raise taxes in order to comply with a mandate risk incurring the wrath of their taxpayers for programs demanded by the state.

Local officials have secured a number of legislative and administrative reforms that focus on the mandate process. Several states have statutory or constitutional provisions that limit their ability to impose mandates on local governments. Some laws call for full or partial state reimbursement of the costs of new mandates; others require that the state pick up the costs for mandated programs or give localities the authority to raise taxes to finance them. Under Proposition 1A, which California voters adopted in 2004, if the state fails to provide reimbursement within a year, local agencies may stop providing the mandated service. Explaining this provision, a representative for the California State Association of Counties said, "They've always said that they know they owe us the money, but the problem has been that they didn't ever allow us to not perform the mandate."[23]

More than 40 states have fiscal note requirements that call for state agencies (in some places, commissions on intergovernmental relations) to estimate the costs that state laws or regulations impose on localities. Several states combine fiscal notes with a requirement that the state reimburse localities, in full or in part, for the expense of undertaking the mandated activity. Other states use fiscal notes simply to call attention to the costs incurred by local governments. When employed alone (i.e., without a reimbursement requirement), fiscal notes appear to have only a limited effect on legislative behavior. Even if legislators are made more aware of the financial

burden they are passing on to local governments, they will not necessarily refuse to impose the costs—which are, after all, assumed not by the state but by local governments. As an anti-mandate strategy, the primary value of fiscal notes seems to be in providing local governments with lobbying ammunition. Moreover, fiscal notes have been criticized at times for failing to even come close to anticipating the actual costs of mandates.

As a deterrent to unfunded mandates, a statutory or constitutional requirement for reimbursement is more effective than a simple requirement for cost estimates. Moreover, reimbursement requirements added to the state constitution with the backing of the voters may initially be more effective in influencing legislative behavior than those created by statute. Legislatures in some states have simply ignored reimbursement requirements (there is no penalty for doing so) or gotten around them by earmarking as mandate reimbursement a part of the funding already allocated for state aid to localities—in effect, deducting mandate reimbursement costs from local aid programs.[24] Overall, extensive funding for mandates does not appear to be the major effect of reimbursement provisions; instead, the provisions seem more likely to deter mandates or to cause them to be modified so that they are less expensive.[25]

Despite occasional victories, laws protecting local governments against mandates rarely live up expectations. Massachusetts legislators, for example, have had little difficulty getting around a provision in Proposition 2½ that prevents them from imposing a direct service or cost obligation on a city or town without either obtaining local approval or paying the full cost of the mandate.[26] In New Jersey, despite a 1995 "state mandate, state pay" amendment to the state constitution, costly mandates continue to pile up—prompting some lawmakers to demand a reassessment of existing mandates and a freeze on new ones. New Jersey local officials, meanwhile, have contended that a state law requiring municipal governments to build affordable housing violates the 1995 constitutional provision because it does not provide the necessary funding (estimated at $6 billion statewide) for them to do so. The officials have taken their case to court and to the state Council on Local Mandates, which was established in 1995 to implement the mandate law, but the matter has yet to be resolved. The council did come through for small New Jersey municipalities on another matter in 2008, however, by deciding that a plan to make them start paying for state police coverage that they had been receiving free of charge amounted to an illegal unfunded mandate.

In 2008, Michigan local officials had some reason to cheer. A state court of appeals ruled that because the state had not reimbursed school districts for the cost of complying with data-reporting requirements it had imposed, the state had violated the 1978 Headlee Amendment to the state constitution. Although the amendment requires the state to provide funding for any new activity that it requires local governments to undertake, school district officials and the state had battled over the application of the law for more than 25 years.

Thus far, the Connecticut legislature has not considered the recommendations of a commis-

sion, appointed by the governor in 2005, that undertook a systematic review of state mandates and submitted a report early in 2007. The Connecticut Conference of Mayors, meanwhile, is seeking full reimbursement for state-mandated property tax exemptions and a prohibition against additional state mandates on municipalities unless they are accompanied by full state funding. By the conference's count, 1,200 unfunded mandates have been imposed on local governments, including 37 in 2007–2008 alone.[27] According to a 2006 survey of Connecticut municipal officials, the most burdensome mandates in that state have to do with education, prevailing wages, and binding arbitration. Half of the respondents said that hikes in property tax rates could be directly traced to these and other unfunded and underfunded state mandates.[28] In Florida, meanwhile, research indicates that between 1978 and 2008, the state imposed close to 2,000 unfunded or underfunded mandates on local governments, amounting to about $15 billion in costs for local governments over that period. Moreover, the number of mandates has increased in recent years: costs for local governments were estimated at $1 billion for 2008 alone.[29]

County officials in various parts of the nation find that state mandates account for 70% or more of their budgets, leaving little room for non-mandated programs such as veterans' services, senior services, and road paving. In 2008, county officials in New York State complained that 80% to 90% of their budgets were made up of, or were about to be made up of, state mandates. Officials from three counties formed the Upstate Mandate Relief Commission to explore ways of easing the mandate problem. Meanwhile, a county official in rural Mississippi told reporters that "We just can't handle those dadgum unfunded mandates."[30]

Prohibitions and Preemptions

Along with demands that they do certain things, local governments confront a range of "thou shalt not" directives. Localities may be prevented from taking certain actions because they conflict with state law. In other cases, local action may be preempted even if the state has not acted, simply because a given activity is reserved to the state.

Tax Exemptions Legislative prohibitions often reflect a particular group's desire to minimize, if not completely avoid, government taxation or regulation. In particular, local officials are continuously on guard against state legislation that would exempt certain businesses from local sales taxes or completely preempt local sales tax authority. In 2006, for example, the Oklahoma legislature considered no fewer than 36 requests for sales tax exemptions, many of which were granted. One Oklahoma municipal official likened the stream of sales tax exemptions to "death by a thousand duck bites."[31]

State legislators are attracted to certain proposals—such as raising the homestead exemption on property taxes or granting sales tax exemptions—both because they are politically popular and because they carry no costs to the state. But tax exemptions can significantly reduce the flow of funds into local treasuries and can be as financially devastating as unfunded mandates.

Local officials generally seek, but do not always receive, a guarantee of state reimbursement for any local revenues that are lost because of a state tax-exemption measure. When money lost as the result of exemptions is not reimbursed, local officials have to make up the difference by drawing on their own revenue sources, usually the property tax. And when the state grants exemptions from taxes on business property, local governments must often make up the difference by shifting the burden to those who own residential properties. In some places, such shifts have been dramatic.

Tobacco and Guns Some of the historic battles over preemption have involved the regulation of tobacco and guns. When it comes to tobacco, half the states preempt local ordinances that address youths' access to tobacco (laws that concern, for example, penalties for minors, the posting of signs, the fines that can be imposed on retailers who violate the law, and restrictions on vending machines and on the distribution of samples), and 15 states have laws preempting clean indoor-air ordinances.[32] Because it is easier and less expensive than going from locality to locality, the tobacco industry has directed its efforts to the state level. Anti-smoking coalitions, however, have enjoyed more success at the local level.[33]

Because of pressure from the tobacco industry and from groups such as restaurant associations, statewide smoking regulations are often less demanding than the local ordinances they replace. They often exempt various venues—such as taverns, casinos, lounges, and bowling alleys—from local as well as state smoking restrictions. From the local point of view, the best state laws serve as a "floor," not a "ceiling," and allow local communities to pass even stronger anti-smoking laws than those set by the state.

In tobacco-growing states, anti-smoking advocates have been especially concerned about preemptive state laws, believing that the strong influence of the tobacco industry in the state legislatures will yield state laws that are far less restrictive than those found in many localities. In South Carolina, such concerns have helped to stymie statewide legislation. Anti-smoking forces in that state received some good news in 2008, when the state supreme court ruled that local governments are not preempted from enacting and enforcing anti-smoking laws.

In 2008, Pennsylvania lawmakers adopted a statewide smoking ban that was diluted by a variety of exemptions. Although the new law allowed Philadelphia to keep its tighter ban—the only active local ban in the state—it prohibited other localities from taking action. A statewide ban that will go into effect in Nebraska in 2009, on other hand, does not preempt the passage of local anti-smoking laws.

Thanks in large part to the National Rifle Association, 46 states prohibit or restrict local gun-control ordinances. Some states prohibit local jurisdictions from imposing firearm ordinances that are more restrictive than state laws (Alaska imposed such a restriction in 2005), and others have rescinded local ordinances to ensure uniform firearms laws statewide. In five states, preemption

has come through judicial rulings rather than by statute. A growing number of states (which now make up a majority) have restricted local governments' authority to regulate the open carrying of guns and to determine where guns can be banned. Since 2006, in response to the events surrounding Hurricane Katrina, at least 20 states have passed legislation that prohibits local governments from attempting, during emergencies or natural disasters, to confiscate weapons from citizens who are legally permitted to possess them. The Wisconsin legislature passed such a law in 2008.

In 2008, local gun-control efforts in Ohio received a setback when the state supreme court ruled in a 4–3 decision that home rule municipalities did not have the right to bar people who are carrying concealed weapons from entering municipal parks. The court held that such regulations conflicted with state gun laws, and with the intent of the legislature that these laws be applied consistently statewide. The majority rejected the argument that gun control was a local issue, and that local governments should be free to pursue whatever policy works best in their communities. Local officials had argued that a special effort was needed to curb violence in urban areas heavily affected by crime, and that gun control was an important part of that effort.

During a gun epidemic, Jersey City, New Jersey, had enacted an ordinance limiting the number of handguns people can purchase. A lower court invalidated the ordinance, and in 2008, a New Jersey appellate court reached a similar decision, claiming that because this area of regulation had been preempted by the state, the city had no authority to act—even though the state had not yet acted. Critics of the decision argued that it violated the principle of local home rule and prevented localities from devising solutions to unique and severe problems. Although this was a setback for home rule, there has been some effort in the legislature to fill the void created by the decision by enacting a state law limiting the number of gun purchases per month.

Eminent Domain Courts have long recognized that under the power of eminent domain, local governments have broad authority to regulate the use of private property in the interests of public safety, health, and welfare. Specifically, local governments may confiscate private property for "public use" if the owner receives "just compensation." In recent years, however, eminent domain has been called into question: the issue is what constitutes public use. Traditionally, the power to take private land for public use has been restricted to purposes such as the revitalization of blighted areas, or the construction of roads and public buildings that will be owned or primarily used by the general public. The notion that public use should encompass takings for the purpose of general public benefits, such as increased tax revenues or economic development, is more controversial.

In 2005, in *Kelo v. City of New London*, the U.S. Supreme Court confirmed, by a 5–4 vote, a Connecticut Supreme Court decision that had upheld the right of a city to take private homes through eminent domain and sell the property for private development. The decision did not give municipalities new powers, but it did confirm the

existence of a power that some local governments had been exercising within the political limits established in their communities. Writing for the majority, Justice Paul Stevens noted that "promoting economic development is a traditional and long-accepted function of government" and that "local officials, not federal judges, know best in deciding whether a development project will benefit the community." The Court noted, however, that there was nothing in its decision to prevent states from restricting municipal use of the power of eminent domain.

The *Kelo* decision was in keeping with the rulings of several state courts that had defined public use broadly; other state courts, however, had limited local governments' power to confiscate private property for economic development. At the time of the decision, courts in about a dozen states had already prohibited state and local governments from using eminent domain to promote economic development unless the goal was to eliminate blight.

At least 40 states now have broad constitutional or statutory prohibitions on state and local governments' authority to take property and transfer it to a private party for economic development. Some states have restricted eminent domain in the context of urban redevelopment by specifying that the authority may be exercised only to take a parcel that is blighted. Other states have gone further, coupling restrictions on private use with narrower definitions of what constitutes "blight"—in effect, allowing condemnation only when the property poses a threat to public health and safety. In response to the *Kelo* decision, several states have altered the eminent domain process—by, for example, requiring that property owners receive earlier notification and more complete information. Some states have increased the amount of compensation given to people whose property is condemned.

In several states, various groups, some of which have a national base, have drawn upon the current outcry against eminent domain to promote a broader campaign for the protection of property rights. As part of this effort, property-rights advocates have been active in the courts, challenging zoning and other governmental restrictions on the use of private property by contending that such regulations diminish the value of their property and thus amount to unconstitutional takings. The goal of such litigation is to discourage local regulations by requiring localities to compensate property owners who are financially damaged by them.

Property-rights advocates, real estate agents, and developers have also pushed for state legislation and for voter-approved propositions that would require property owners to be compensated if state or local regulations limit the use of private property. Measure 37, approved by Oregon voters in 2004, was the result of such an effort. Under that measure, if zoning or other land use decisions diminish property values, state and local governments must either reimburse property owners or lift the restrictions. Local governments have generally chosen to waive restrictions in order to settle claims against them under Measure 37. One result of Measure 37 was to open the

door to the creation of large residential, commercial, and industrial developments on farm- and forestland. In 2007, Oregon voters modified the measure to curb such development through zoning restrictions and through limitations on the number of homes that landowners can build on their property as compensation for a regulatory taking.

In 2006, "*Kelo*-plus" propositions—measures that both limit eminent domain and restrict takings (along the lines of Measure 37)—were on the ballot in Arizona, California, and Idaho. Voters approved the proposition in Arizona but turned down those in California and Idaho. After passage of the Arizona proposition, a spokesperson for the Arizona Municipal League said that it "will have the effect of seriously slowing down or virtually stopping new zoning."[34] Opponents of takings measures have argued that such measures have the potential not only to severely cripple the enforcement of zoning regulations, but also to undermine environmental controls, smoking bans, living-wage laws, and restrictions on adult entertainment.

In June 2008, California voters approved Proposition 99, a state constitutional amendment that gives more protection against governmental use of eminent domain on behalf of private developers. Critics claimed, though, that the measure—which was backed by the California League of Cities and environmental groups—offers little real protection. In the same election, California voters turned down a proposition that would have more severely limited the ability of government to seize property. (The rejected measure also contained a provision that would have phased out rent controls in the state.)

On the judicial level, there were some decisions regarding the authority of local governments that local officials could cheer about in 2008. In Colorado, the state supreme court declared the Telluride Amendment—a state law that denied municipalities the power to condemn property beyond their boundaries for parks or open spaces—invalid because it infringed on the power of home rule cities. In Missouri, the state supreme court ruled that under existing law, all municipalities in the state, not just those with home rule charters, can use eminent domain powers to eradicate blight, provided they can prove that a property is blighted.

On the negative side, New Jersey courts have been inclined in recent years to rein in the ability of municipalities to seize property for large-scale redevelopment. In 2007, the state supreme court declared that a finding of actual blight was necessary before property could be taken. And in 2008, the state court of appeals, citing this decision, declared that the city of Long Branch failed to demonstrate that the homes it had condemned met the legal definition of *blighted*.

Telecommunications For some time, phone companies have been pressuring state legislatures for bills that would move cable-franchising authority to the state level—and in 20 states, they have succeeded. Previously, cable companies negotiated individual franchise contracts with each municipality in which they wished to operate; this arrangement allowed localities to collect

fees and to subject the cable companies to local regulations. Local officials are concerned that where statewide franchising bills become law, localities will not only lose franchise fees and regulatory authority, but also be unable to protect public rights-of-way and respond to consumer complaints. Another concern is that cable companies operating under state franchises will bypass low-income areas or small rural populations that they consider unprofitable. Local franchise agreements commonly avoid such problems through "build-out" provisions that require companies to provide service in every neighborhood. Local agreements also ensure that companies provide services such as educational and government-access channels; these, too, could be lost in the shift of franchising authority to the state level. Not all states that have shifted authority to state agencies have safeguarded local revenues, and only about half the states that have moved cable-franchising authority to the state level have included build-out provisions.

In 2005, the Texas legislature approved a statewide franchise system that could serve as a model for future action by other states. In response to local concerns, the legislature grandfathered existing franchise agreements and directed that future fees from statewide franchises be transferred to local governments. Although a California law adopted in 2006 transferred cable-franchising authority from local agencies to the state's public utility commission, local authorities continue to oversee customer service, retain limited control over rights-of-way, and receive a 5% franchise fee (the maximum amount allowed by the federal government). A comprehensive act adopted in Illinois in 2007 imposes state franchising but (1) requires cable providers to pay municipalities up to a 5% franchise fee, (2) requires cable providers to help pay for the cost of operating local government and public-access channels, (3) imposes regulations and fees on cable providers' use of rights-of-way, and (4) includes extensive consumer protections regarding matters such as rate increases, installation, and termination of service. As the result of a continuing campaign by AT&T, statewide cable franchising came to Tennessee in 2008. Thanks to some input from municipal officials, the law contains build-out requirements; it also preserves municipal control over rights-of-way and requires cable companies to pay 5% of gross revenues to municipalities as franchise fees.

Municipal officials in Louisiana and Wisconsin are less satisfied with cable-franchising laws passed in their states. The Louisiana law, known as the Consumer Choice for Television Act, makes it easy for cable companies to operate anywhere in the state. Rather than negotiating with separate localities, they simply have to touch base with the secretary of state's office, which has little discretion in how it performs its duties: it simply and routinely applies a few rules and regulations stipulated by state law. Moreover, the measure provides little oversight, lacks any provision for addressing consumer complaints, and does not require companies to serve any particular areas. Local governments may obtain the 5% franchise fee if they pass an ordinance stating that they want it. Wisconsin lawmakers, rejecting almost all changes sought by municipal officials, passed a similar measure.

Residency Requirements State prohibitions and preemptions often address everyday local government decisions on personnel and other internal matters. Of importance in several states have been the efforts, sometimes supported by groups of local employees such as police and firefighters, to eliminate local residency requirements for municipal workers. In 1999, the Minneapolis Police Federation led a successful effort in the state legislature to repeal the authorization for locally enacted residency requirements in Minneapolis and St. Paul. Also in 1999, a similar decision by the Michigan legislature, which ended the long-established local practice of requiring municipal employees to live inside municipal boundaries, helped prompt an unsuccessful effort to secure a constitutional amendment that would have made it tougher for the legislature to restrict or eliminate local laws.

In several states, legislatures have prohibited local residency requirements for schoolteachers. In 2000, for example, city council members in Providence, Rhode Island, voiced their displeasure with a recent state law that exempted teachers from the city's residency requirement, which was embedded in the city's charter. A year later, the Pennsylvania legislature prohibited Philadelphia and Pittsburgh from requiring teachers to live in the districts where they work.

The issue of residency requirements is alive and well in Ohio, where some municipalities have challenged a 2006 state law, supported by police and other city-employee unions, that prohibits municipalities from requiring their employees to live within municipal limits. The municipalities are arguing that their home rule powers give them the authority to set residency requirements. Several lower courts have ruled in favor of the municipalities, but the issue is before the state supreme court. Residency requirements are in effect in 124 Ohio municipalities.

Supporters of state actions to end residency requirements argue that the state has an interest in safeguarding employees' freedom of movement. Supporters also argue that ending residency requirements will help cities attract teachers, public safety officers, and other needed workers. Those in favor of residency requirements contend that being a part of the community they serve strengthens public employees' job performance and commitment to the community—which, in turn, helps foster positive attitudes among community residents toward municipal workers. Supporters of residency requirements also view them as a means of keeping well-paid, middle-class people in cities, and cite as an additional virtue the fact that residency requirements can help reduce response times during emergencies. More generally, state prohibitions are criticized on the ground that decisions regarding local residency requirements, whatever their merits, should be made not by the state but by the local governments involved.

Other Areas of Authority Other areas marked by contention over authority include predatory lending, illegal immigration, and the use of red-light cameras.

Local lending ordinances aimed at aggressive and deceptive marketing tactics that ignore the borrower's ability to pay have taken on particular salience in recent years because of the link between such lending practices and the high rate of housing foreclosures. For localities, foreclosures decrease property tax revenues and bring increased costs associated with safety, security, and maintenance of abandoned properties. However, state laws preempting anti-predatory-lending ordinances have limited the ability of local governments to act on the lending practices that contribute to foreclosures. Moreover, many local ordinances have been challenged in court.[35] Nevertheless, the foreclosure situation has encouraged legislators in California, Louisiana, Pennsylvania, Rhode Island, and other states to give local governments more authority to deal with the large number of vacant and untended foreclosed properties—by, for example, increasing fines on owners who fail to maintain their properties (i.e., on lenders who take back properties), compelling the owners to bring the properties up to code, or requiring owners to reimburse municipalities that do the work themselves.

Nationwide, some 80 municipalities have various types of sanctuary policies. For example, some municipalities have adopted ordinances or rules and regulations that prohibit police or other officials from questioning residents about their immigration status. Several states prohibit local governments from adopting policies that, in effect, hinder the enforcement of federal or state immigration laws. Other states not only prohibit the establishment of local sanctuaries but also require police to check the legal status of people they arrest, require judges to check the legal status of those seeking bail, and require jailers to check the legal status of inmates. Still other states require local officials to verify the legal status of those seeking public benefits or public employment, and further require that firms contracting with local government be prohibited from hiring illegal aliens. The Oklahoma Taxpayer and Citizen Protection Act of 2007 has served as a model for legislation designed to address states' concerns about illegal immigration. In 2008, Missouri, South Carolina, Virginia, and Utah passed similar legislation.

In several states, questions have arisen about local authority to use red-light and speed-enforcement cameras. In Ohio, courts have come down on the side of local government: the state supreme court ruled in 2008 that the use of such cameras is within the home rule authority of municipalities and does not conflict with state law. Municipalities came up with a similar victory in Iowa, where the state supreme court upheld the legality of a traffic-control camera system used by the city of Davenport, arguing that the legislature had given municipalities the authority to go beyond the traffic-enforcement procedures outlined in state law. In Missouri, a move in 2008 to prohibit municipalities from using red-light cameras came up short in the legislature. And in Indiana, the state attorney general issued an opinion to the effect that municipalities could use red-light cameras without specific legislative authorization to do so.

LOCAL FINANCES

Financing is an area in which local officials have relatively little control: the local government revenue base is largely what state officials want it to be. The state not only confers local revenue sources but also may reduce them or divert them to state uses. In recent years, with the states straining for revenues and being locked into costly "untouchables," such as education and health care, local officials have had to fight "takeaways"—state attempts to deprive them of revenue sources that local governments have long relied on. At the same time, state aid has been unreliable, to say the least. Although states have shown some tendency to assume more of the costs of government, this shift has often led to a loss of local control. States have also encouraged consolidation and service sharing at the local level as a means of achieving savings.

Financial Controls

State constitutions and statutes impose controls on nearly all aspects of local financial management: assessment, taxation, indebtedness, budgeting, accounting, auditing, and fiscal reporting. In the area of taxation, for example, states may prohibit certain types of local taxes (e.g., a sales tax or a graduated income tax) and may limit increases in tax rates or property tax assessments. In a half-dozen states, the amount of total revenue that can be raised is tied to measures such as inflation, population, and growth in personal income, and all funds raised over the limit have to be refunded to taxpayers. In some states, total expenditures are tied to a growth index. Finally, many states require voter approval for tax increases and for spending increases above a certain level.

Other state-imposed limitations on local finances have to do with local borrowing; such limitations may, for example, require a public referendum to permit the issuance of bonds, restrict the purposes for which localities may borrow, or limit the amount of debt that localities can incur. Debt limits apply to general-obligation bonds and may be expressed either as specific dollar amounts or as a percentage (from 15% to 25%) of the value of the property within the jurisdiction. One effect of debt limits is to encourage local governments to turn to more costly revenue bonds, which are supported only by the revenues derived from the project for which the money is borrowed.

Many state restrictions grew out of the Great Depression of the 1930s, which caused local financial operations to collapse throughout the nation. During that period, several states placed in receivership cities that faced financial emergencies. The depression brought a multitude of measures at the state level that were designed to head off future problems; it also gave birth to the idea of giving a state agency complete control over the financial management of all municipalities, although this actually occurred only in the few states where municipal default problems had been extensive. Among the powers given to state agencies in these places—of which New Jersey was one—was the authority to review local budgets before their adoption and to order changes to

avoid a deficit. New Jersey continues to exercise unique financial controls over local governments; North Carolina and Ohio are other prime examples of states where state agencies continuously monitor local government finances in an attempt to keep local governments from falling into financial distress. Monitoring can act as a form of credit enhancement, making investors more comfortable with municipal bonds and encouraging them to give the bonds a higher rating.

A more recent wave of restrictions has centered not so much on keeping local governments out of financial difficulty as on reducing the size of local government and local governments' demands on taxpayers. The modern "taxpayers' rebellion" has been built around tax and expenditure limitations (TELs). On the taxation side, most of the focus has been on the property tax. Proposition 13, which was adopted by California voters in 1978, has provided one popular model. Proposition 13 capped local property tax rates and limited increases in assessed property value unless the property was sold. Another model, Proposition 2½, took effect in Massachusetts in 1980, after having been adopted in a voter referendum. Proposition 2½ limits property tax increases to no more than 2.5% of the total value of the taxable property within a local jurisdiction; it also limits how much property taxes can increase each year without voter approval.

Expenditure limitations are less common than tax limitations. The most heavily promoted of these is the Taxpayers' Bill of Rights (TABOR), which was adopted by Colorado voters in 1992. In its original form, TABOR required voter approval of (1) any new state or local tax or any increase in an existing tax and (2) any state or local spending increase that exceeded a certain limit. The limits on state spending were tied to inflation and to changes in population; those on local government spending were tied to changes in population and in property values. Neither state nor local spending could increase by more than 6% annually, and revenues that exceeded the amount that state or local governments could spend had to be refunded to taxpayers unless voters decided otherwise.

In November 2005, confronted by a state budget crisis, the governor and the legislature asked voters to lift the state spending limits for five years, allowing the state government to keep $3.7 billion in revenues that existing taxes were expected to generate; this money would otherwise have had to be returned to taxpayers. Close to 52% of the voters approved this proposal, known as Referendum C. As a result of the voters' action, the legislature had an extra $800 million in 2006 for education, transportation, and health care—areas in which it had been forced to cut back because of recessionary conditions and limited funds.

In November 2008, however, Colorado voters rejected a proposal to take the revenues that exceed the amount that the state can spend under the TABOR provisions and permanently funnel them into a long-term savings account to be used exclusively for schools (preschool through 12th grade), instead of refunding them to taxpayers. The Savings Account for Education (SAFE) measure would also have ended a program, which voters approved in 2000 (Amendment 23), that requires

automatic increases in education spending to keep up with inflation.

National groups, including Americans for Limited Government and Americans for Tax Reform, continue to promote Colorado's TABOR plan, or versions thereof, in more than a dozen states—but, thus far, have had little to show for their efforts. Anti-tax sentiment, however, continues to run strong. Many of the current anti-tax efforts are focused on the property tax: groups in several states have proposed constitutional or statutory provisions that would limit increases in property tax rates, property assessments, and property tax levies.

The primary effect of the tax revolt of the past three decades has been to cut into local revenues. In some jurisdictions, however, there has been a secondary effect: because local officials have found it more difficult to meet matching requirements for state and federal grants, their ability to attract intergovernmental aid has been compromised. Often, local officials succeed in reducing their losses through productivity improvements or through targeted revenue increases, such as new or increased fees. They have also been encouraged to spend more time lobbying for increases in state aid. Because of such steps, TELs appear to have had little effect on total spending. They have, however, affected the composition of local revenues; specifically, they have decreased local governments' long-term reliance on the property tax and increased reliance on state aid and on regressive revenue sources, such as locally collected fees and sales taxes. Generally, TELs also appear, over the long run, to encourage centralization of authority at the state level.[36]

Locally Collected Revenues

Local governments in the United States raise around 62% of their general revenue. Most of the remaining revenue—some 34% of general revenue—comes from the states, while the federal government contributes the remaining 4%. Of the revenue that local governments raise on their own, about 45% comes from the property tax, 10% from locally adopted sales taxes, 3% from individual income taxes, and 26% from various charges (e.g., hospitals and sewage fees).[37] Municipalities have the most diversified revenue structure and, compared with counties, are far less dependent on state aid and the property tax.

Nationwide, property tax revenues increased by 6.3% in 2007 but are predicted to decline by 3.6% in 2008 because of the housing crisis. To help make up for this loss, many municipalities are looking for other revenue streams. Many have increased service fees and charges.[38] Others have looked to increased authority to levy sales taxes. In Kentucky, for example, an effort is under way for a state constitutional amendment to allow local-option sales taxes that, with voter approval, can be used to pay for specific projects. Thus far, however, the proposal has stalled in the legislature. A similar proposal failed in the Idaho legislature in 2008. In Iowa, meanwhile, the legislature turned down bills designed to substitute sources such as fees and local-option sales taxes for property taxes.

The Property Tax Historically, the property tax has been a rich and relatively stable source of income that local officials could pretty much call their own, increasing or decreasing the tax rate depending on their budgetary needs. However, this tax has become increasingly unpopular.[39] Public-choice theorists like the property tax because it gives citizens a highly visible "tax price" for the services that are being offered, thus clarifying citizens' choices. Yet, one might argue, it is the very visibility of the tax that makes it unpopular and encourages local officials to turn to less visible revenue sources.[40]

State and local officials commonly debate over who is responsible for the increases in property tax levels: state officials point to local governments' failure to tighten their belts sufficiently, and local officials contend that the state is responsible because it has cut aid, forcing localities to turn to the property tax, and has not allowed localities to seek out other locally collected revenue sources.

For a number of years, there has been considerable effort throughout the nation to end or greatly reduce reliance on the local property tax. The problem has been deciding what could or should be done. As the author of an alternative-revenue bill in Iowa put it in 2008, "Everybody knows that property taxes are a problem in Iowa, but everybody finds something wrong with every solution."[41]

Some of the pressure to abandon the property tax has come not from the state legislature but from court decisions. Courts in about half the states have found that reliance on the local property tax to finance education discriminates against students in areas where property values are the lowest, and thus violates state constitutional provisions.

State legislatures have used a number of methods to force or encourage local units to cut expenses, which indirectly reduces pressure on the property tax: among other means, state have imposed spending caps, set limitations on retirement benefits for local government workers, and encouraged sharing or consolidation of local services. States have also used more direct methods: granting property tax rebates, and freezing or capping increases in property tax rates or property assessments. However, severe state-imposed limits on property taxes make it more difficult for local officials to meet increased costs, including those costs mandated by the state, and ultimately lead to cutbacks in local services. Limits are easier to live with if they are accompanied by increases in state aid and/or by greater access to revenues from other local sources; giving voters the opportunity to override the limits also makes them more palatable.

Targeted relief and "tax swapping" (substituting one tax for another) are other common state responses to property tax pressure. Several states have adopted programs that provide tax relief for certain population groups on the basis of such factors as age, income, and disability. For example, some states have homestead exemption programs, under which a portion of the value of a home belonging to a member of a targeted group is exempt from the property tax. Still others have "circuitbreaker" programs that protect against property tax overload. Such programs provide automatic tax relief when property taxes exceed a certain percentage of household income; the critical percentage and the definition of household income vary from state to state, and tax relief generally comes in the form of direct tax reductions or rebates.[42]

States that cut property taxes generally replace at least some of the lost revenue through tax swapping or by temporarily drawing on state budget surpluses. Property tax cuts are sometimes accompanied by increases in state aid. Sometimes, too, local governments are given increased authority to raise revenue by other means, such as a local income tax. Several states have limited property tax cuts or rebates to primary residences or owner-occupied homes and excluded vacation homes and investment property. Given the extent of local government dependence on the property tax, whether and how states decide to replace revenues that are lost because of state-imposed property tax cuts are matters of vital concern to local governments.

Although sales tax revenues are the most common replacement for property taxes, other sources have not been ignored. In 2006, Texas lawmakers turned to a broad-based business tax to replace property tax revenues. In 2007, after allowing citizens to deduct up to $1,000 in property tax payments from their income taxes, North Dakota legislators filled the void by increasing taxes on oil and gas production. Also in 2007, South Dakota legislators offset a property tax reduction by increasing taxes on tobacco.

Late in 2007, the Washington State Supreme Court (holding that the voters had been misled by the wording of the proposition) overturned Initiative 747, a 2001 measure adopted by the voters to limit the annual growth in property tax revenue to 1% (the previous cap had been 6%). The legislature acted quickly, reinstating the measure just a few weeks later. In Missouri in 2008, in order to prevent localities from reaping windfalls in property taxes when property is reassessed, lawmakers passed a law requiring local governments to roll back their tax rate so that the total revenue equals that collected the previous year. Lawmakers also expanded the existing tax credit for low-income seniors and disabled residents. Dealing with the complicated problem of "appraisal creep" is also on the agenda of the Texas legislature. In Tennessee, local officials continue to have problems coping with revenue reductions stemming from 2007 legislation that limited property tax increases for senior citizens.

In 2007 and 2008, dramatic and more far-reaching actions regarding property tax relief took place in Florida and Indiana. In 2007, Florida lawmakers threatened the withdrawal of state aid to encourage localities to roll back property taxes to 2006 levels (revenues generated by new construction were excluded). The law requires localities to reduce their property taxes by up to 9% (depending on their recent property tax revenue history), and it applies to all local governments except those with severe financial difficulties and those that have experienced very slow growth in property tax revenues. Higher tax rates are permitted, however, with the approval of a supermajority of the city council or county commission, or through a voter referendum. Thus far, the law has prompted several communities to raise fees, to freeze or lay off staff, and to cut programs—especially quality-of-life programs such as libraries, parks, and special events. Local officials argued that decisions about taxes and service levels should rest primarily with voters and local officials, and that the law amounts to state interference.

On January 29, 2008, statewide voters in Florida went further by approving Amendment 1, which includes a smorgasbord of tax-relief measures, such as a general property tax cut; a doubling of the homestead exemption for nonschool taxes; and a provision, commonly known as "portability," that allows homeowners who are moving and buying a new home within the state to take with them up to $500,000 of the savings provided by the existing 3% cap on increases in property assessments. Fearing a massive loss of revenue, local officials had harshly criticized Amendment 1. The measure is expected to cost local governments billions of dollars in lost revenue over the next five years alone.

Florida officials dodged another proposal that could have added greatly to their burden when the state supreme court ruled that Amendment 5 could not appear on the November 2008 ballot because it was too complex to appear before the voters. The amendment would have eliminated the state-set property tax for schools and limited the annual increases in property assessments for businesses, rental units, and second homes to 5% (increases for primary homes were already capped at 3% by Amendment 1). The measure outlined several ways for the legislature to make up for the lost funds—for example, by raising the sales tax from 6% to 7%, eliminating various sales tax exemptions (if all were eliminated, the state would obtain an estimated $4 billion dollars more per year), levying new taxes, and cutting state spending.

In 2007, the Indiana legislature provided $300 million in property tax relief and gave local governments the option of increasing local income taxes to replace the lost revenue. Property tax relief also dominated the 2008 legislative session. The outcome was a massive and complicated tax reform plan that, at its core, cuts property taxes and replaces the lost revenue with sales, income, and other taxes. The law increases property tax deductions for homesteads and requires the following caps on property tax increases by 2010: homestead property taxes, 1%; rental and farm property taxes, 2%; and business and industry property taxes, 3%. To help offset the loss of property tax revenue at the local level, the state has assumed certain expenses now being borne by local governments, including child welfare, school operating costs, and pre-1977 police and fire pension funds. To pay for all this, the measure increases the sales tax rate from 6% to 7%, making it the highest among neighboring states. With the reform, the average homeowner's property tax bill was expected to drop about 30%. Local government officials predict, however, that to make up for the loss of property tax revenue, they will have to either raise other taxes, most likely local income taxes, or cut services. Thus far, many have been reluctant to go the route of raising taxes.

Local Sales Taxes Thirty-eight states allow a local sales tax. Many states permit counties, mu-

nicipalities, and special districts to levy the tax, while some restrict that right to either municipalities or counties. The sales tax has the advantage of shifting, or "exporting," part of the tax burden to nonresidents, but it tends to be regressive in its overall impact. And because the sales tax is also highly sensitive to changes in the economy, it promises periods of feast or famine.

Another disadvantage is that reliance on the sales tax encourages the "fiscalization of land use," also known as "zoning for dollars": land use decisions that favor sales-tax–generating developments, such as shopping centers, over housing or other nonretail activities. The quest for sales tax revenue not only conditions land use decisions but often throws local governments into intense, sometimes ruinous, competition for developments like shopping centers. In many cases, jurisdictions compete by attempting to offer retail developers the largest tax rebate. In some places, however, state legislatures have sought to prevent rebate offers, which they see as needless giveaways, by threatening to cut off state aid. Under an Arizona bill passed in 2007, for example, municipalities that are located in certain high-growth counties and that offer tax rebates to retail developers are penalized by losing state-shared revenue that is equivalent in amount to the incentives given to the developers. Local officials in the Phoenix metropolitan area pledged to avoid competing with each other by agreeing to share revenues from developments along common borders, but they failed to implement their agreements. While often acknowledging the ill effects of competition, local officials in Arizona and elsewhere believe that the root of the problem is a state-structured tax system that forces them to be excessively dependent on the sales tax. Many view tax rebates as an important economic development tool.

The idea of giving local governments the authority to impose a sales tax as a substitute for property taxes or state aid has been floated around the country, with varying results. Opponents have raised the concerns noted earlier (e.g., about the regressiveness of the sales tax), and expressed fears that a higher sales tax will depress retail business—automobile dealerships in particular—and drive shoppers to areas where tax rates are lower. There is also some concern about just how high sales taxes can go: combining increased local sales taxes with increased state sales taxes could eventually reach a tipping point and prompt a taxpayers' rebellion.

Income Taxes, User Fees, and Impact Fees Of the 18 states that authorize local income taxes, only a few—in particular, Ohio and Pennsylvania—rely on the tax to a significant extent. Apparently, many jurisdictions are afraid that a local income tax would hurt the development of the local economy.[43] On the administrative side, Pennsylvania lawmakers—in an effort to save money being lost to a highly fragmented tax collection system—consolidated income tax collection at the local level, reducing the number of income tax collectors from 560 to fewer than 70.

Several localities have taken advantage of new authority to collect fees for various services, such as police, fire, and ambulance. User fees have become a popular means of financing water and sewer service, transportation, and other services.

The notion that the direct user of a service should pay for it appears to be popular throughout the country. Because of this view, user fees are a relatively acceptable way of raising revenue. Local officials also find user fees attractive because they can usually be levied without permission from the state legislature. However, some courts have declared user fees (such as transportation utility fees, which are fees charged to private property owners to finance road repairs or improvements in their area) to be disguised taxes and therefore invalid in the absence of specific state authorization.

Close to half the states authorize local governments to impose impact fees on developers to help offset the costs engendered by the construction or expansion of roads, sewers, and parks. A study by the Brookings Institution found that impact fees have been a valuable tool for financing local infrastructure: in addition to making up for declines in federal and state assistance for construction projects, such fees have helped local governments avoid greater reliance on the property tax and have also made it possible to sustain community growth.[44]

Because those who benefit from the improvements pay for them, local officials see impact fees as an equitable means of helping to offset the costs of development. Builders commonly argue, however, that impact fees are excessive and far beyond the actual cost of providing new infrastructure. In recent years, several states have sided with builders' associations and enacted legislation that requires impact fees to be (1) reasonable and (2) related to reliable estimates of the impact of particular developments.

Meanwhile, builders' associations around the country have been waging state-level campaigns against various types of development fees. In 2004, as the result of such pressure, the Minnesota legislature passed a law requiring municipalities that charge a fee for reviewing or processing a development application to establish a demonstrable link between the fee levied and the actual cost of providing the service. In 2006, courts in Mississippi and North Carolina invalidated impact fees, holding that localities needed state enabling legislation to collect them. Also in 2006, at the request of the Wisconsin Builders Association, the Wisconsin legislature passed a law that limits the types of facilities that can be funded with impact fees.

Takeaways, Holdups, and Charges In recent years, many localities have struggled not only to obtain new revenue sources but also to protect the ones they have. For example, local governments have had to fight off tax exemptions adopted at the state level that reduce the intake from local property, sales, and other taxes. As noted earlier, fighting exemptions is often a losing battle. Another problem is that legislatures have, at times, simply dipped into local tax revenues and used them for their own purposes.

In 2007, South Carolina local officials were able to fend off state efforts to take fines paid by motorists who had been caught by red-light cameras (the fines had been used to support the operation of the camera systems) and deposit them in a state fund for schools. The Texas legislature, on the other hand, decided that municipalities must share the fines with the state. In Missouri in 2007,

municipalities won a major victory when a bill that had passed in the house failed in the senate; the bill would have prevented municipalities from going to court to collect taxes from cell phone companies. After failing to secure passage of the bill, the cell phone companies announced that they would negotiate a settlement with the municipalities. The resolution of this six-year-long battle could bring in hundreds of millions in municipal revenues.

Some of the most dramatic battles have been in California—where, beginning in 1992, municipalities, counties, and special districts lost close to $3 billion a year in property taxes because the legislature decided to draw on this source to pay for education. In the course of the decade, the legislature also took away other local taxes and fees—for example, on alcohol, cigarettes, and mobile homes—often without reimbursing local governments.

In 2003, faced with a $38 billion deficit, the California legislature took half of the municipal governments' sales tax revenues to balance the budget, promising (as it had in the past) to make it up later. In response, a coalition of local officials began an initiative campaign that ultimately resulted in a constitutional amendment, Proposition 1A, approved by California voters in 2004. Under Proposition 1A, the state is prohibited from borrowing property tax revenues from local governments unless the governor declares a fiscal emergency and two-thirds of the legislature agrees to the loan. In addition, the borrowed funds must be paid back, with interest, within five years. The proposition also prohibits the state from reducing local government sales tax revenues, and allows local governments to stop providing any mandated service for which the state fails to provide reimbursement within a year. With the greater security offered by Proposition 1A, several California cities decided in 2005–2006 to ask their voters to approve half-cent sales tax increases. Some local officials said that without passage of Proposition 1A, they would not have gone to the voters: "Why pass a sales tax increase if the state is just going to take it away?"[45]

In 2008, state officials grappling with a $15.2 billion deficit discussed borrowing from local property tax revenues or from local transportation sales tax revenues. In the end, state officials elected not to borrow from local governments; the budget did, however, include a one-year, nonrefundable seizure of $350 million of local redevelopment funds. The budget also deferred $75 million in state mandate repayments. Given the continuing state deficit, more raids may be coming.

Arizona municipal officials rejoiced when state budget negotiators promised not to cut revenues funneled to local governments through the urban revenue-sharing program. But most of what municipalities saved in shared revenues was taken away: in what looked more like a holdup than an ordinary takeaway, local officials were caught off guard by a provision in the 2008 state budget package ordering them to donate nearly $30 million to the state general fund—to the tune of $17 million from municipalities and $13 million from counties. The president of the League of Arizona Cities and Towns remarked, "I've never

seen anything like this before. . . . It's unusual and confusing. We don't know if it's a tax, a fee or an assessment or what the money will be used for."[46] In another interview, a lobbyist for the city of Phoenix added, "It's not so much about the dollars. . . . It's the principle that they can reach into our budget and take money."[47]

States have also tried to cope with their financial problems by upping their charges for local governments' use of state services, or by charging local governments for services they had been receiving for free—both highly controversial moves. In New Jersey, a proposal to start charging rural areas for state police services set off a storm of protest that has yet to be resolved. As one mayor said in 2008, "We've already told the state we're not gonna pay. . . . They're gonna have to put the whole township committee in jail."[48] As noted earlier, local government complaints led the state Council on Local Mandates to find that the proposed action amounted to an invalid unfunded mandate.

State Assistance

State financial aid to local governments consists of grants and shared taxes. Grants are usually for specific programs in areas such as education or transportation, although most states also provide unrestricted grants for general purposes. Much of the unrestricted aid comes to local governments as compensation for a state action—for example, to compensate for a state-required property tax exemption that reduces local revenues—or to help local governments pay for state-mandated services. In the case of shared taxes, states act as tax collectors, returning all or a portion of the yield to local governments according to an allocation formula or on the basis of the revenues' origin. Sales, income, and gasoline taxes are among the state taxes that are often shared. As they do with grants, states earmark much of the shared revenue for specific purposes—requiring, for example, that localities spend their share of the state gas tax on highway or street improvements. Some shared revenue, however, is unrestricted and can be spent as local officials see fit.

In addition to providing conventional aid, state governments have regularly come to the rescue of local governments facing fiscal distress. Legislatures have sometimes—usually in response to a request for help from a locality—developed ad hoc legislation for specific jurisdictions in dire financial straits, giving them financial and technical assistance and imposing various controls on their activities.

Taking a more comprehensive and proactive route, legislatures in some 20 states have passed financial-distress legislation that authorizes state agencies to monitor the fiscal affairs of local governments and to intervene in the affairs of those that, according to a set of indicators, appear to be heading toward financial trouble. The indicators that states use vary considerably; on the whole, though, the measures are not particularly helpful in detecting local financial problems before they become serious.[49] Under fiscal-distress legislation, localities that are found to be in fiscal trouble initially receive a mixture of aid and regulation. If these do not work, the agency or a state-appointed board or administrator may assume the reins of government—in other words, implement a state takeover.[50]

State aid is a major source of local revenue, accounting for more than one-third of all local general revenue. Over the years, the bulk of state aid (since 1975, between 60% and 64%) has gone to education.[51] A majority of the aid goes to school districts; counties come in second, and municipalities wind up third. More than 80% of all funds for education go to independent school districts; the rest go to municipal or county governments in the few states—including Maryland, North Carolina, and Virginia—where these units, rather than independent school districts, have responsibility for school systems. Counties receive the bulk of the state funds earmarked for welfare, health, and hospitals, while state aid for highways is relatively equally distributed between counties and municipalities. Municipalities receive 58% of all general, unrestricted support funds.[52] Overall, state aid has a modest equalizing effect, only somewhat reducing the revenue gap between poorer and wealthier localities. On the other hand, as noted earlier, states often assist financially distressed local governments when the need arises.

Although vital to local governments, state aid is not dependable—a characteristic that makes it more difficult for local governments to plan budgets and borrow money. The amount tends to ebb and flow with legislative moods and changing economic conditions. Because state aid is based largely on sales and income taxes, it can be relatively high in times of prosperity but relatively low when the economy is in trouble. Even in times of widespread prosperity, however, aid may be limited because it competes poorly with demands for tax relief and for other expenditures. Moreover, even in good economic times, state aid may not fare well because lawmakers, for ideological or political reasons, do not look favorably on the aid system; as a Wisconsin legislator declared nearly a decade ago, "I don't view my role as being an ATM machine for local governments."[53]

Some—perhaps many—state lawmakers are critical of state aid on principle: they see no reason for the state to raise money that local officials spend and have suggested that, as an alternative, the state give local officials greater authority to raise revenues. Critics of this approach argue that it overlooks the wide variation in localities' tax bases and revenue-raising ability. Increased authority to raise revenues is unlikely to be of much value in a jurisdiction with a limited tax base. State aid, on the other hand, can enable jurisdictions with lower tax bases to afford at least a minimal level of services. Because of structural changes in their economies, some jurisdictions have a particularly strong need for continued intergovernmental aid.

On the question of state aid, the debate has often proceeded as one might expect: state officials find state aid programs objectionable because they are the ones who must suffer the pain of raising revenues, while local officials get credit for providing the services that the aid supports. Along with this view comes the suspicion that local officials seek the aid only because they are afraid to ask their own taxpayers to support services and because they want to use state money to keep local tax rates low. Local officials, for their part, see state aid as justified because it offsets costly state mandates and makes up for state laws that limit local governments' ability to raise revenues. With state mandates in mind, local officials argue that when it comes to claiming credit for programs financed by other governments in order to keep their taxes low, the states are the guilty parties.

What happens when states decide to cut aid? Here is one local official's answer: "It's not rocket science. . . . It's pretty much raise taxes or cut services. That's what it boils down to."[54] Generally, municipal officials say that they are most likely to cut funds for general government (administration and personnel) or leisure and culture (parks and recreation, libraries), and least likely to cut funds for public safety (police, fire, and emergency medical services).[55] But whatever adjustments are made to compensate for cutbacks in state aid tend to be short term: rather than abandon or drastically revamp programs, local officials often try to maintain service levels by making temporary adjustments in funding—such as drawing on budget reserves, delaying capital purchases or construction projects, or cutting employee expenses—and hoping that these will suffice until aid is restored.[56] In recent years, many localities have attempted to cope by imposing new fees or increasing old ones.

Although matters became worse as the year ended, the state aid picture in 2008 was a mixed bag. In Virginia, budget cuts for 2008–2009 for all the cities and counties in the state amounted to $50 million. As in California, some of the first aid to go was that slated to pay for state mandates. New Jersey legislators cut $154 million in funding for municipal property tax relief. New York legislators made an across-the-board 6% cut in local aid for a wide variety of programs, saving $97 million in 2008–2009 and $160 million in 2009–2010. However, legislators managed to avoid cutting aid to local governments to support state-mandated programs, and spared several programs of value to municipalities, including the Aid and Incentives to Municipalities program, which provides property tax relief. The 2009 Maryland state budget preserved the local government share of total revenues, but a downturn in total revenues resulted in fewer dollars for local governments.

State assistance to local governments in Massachusetts increased $28 million in 2008—around 5%—but most of that increase was school aid rather than general municipal aid. Local officials in that state were bracing themselves for future cuts. Many, though, heaved a sign of relief in November 2008, when voters rejected Question One, which would have eliminated the state income tax—and brought drastic cuts in state aid. In 2008, despite a state budget deficit of $400 million, Michigan local governments got their first revenue-sharing increase in eight years—a 2% increase that amounted to $8 million. In oil-rich Alaska, lawmakers came up with a long-term community revenue-sharing program; under this law, local governments will receive an additional $60 million a year over a four-year period, depending on how much revenue is raised from a special tax on oil.

State Assumption of Financial Responsibility

Considering state aid in isolation gives an incomplete and somewhat misleading picture of

state efforts to ease financial pressures on local governments. For example, a state that provides minimal direct aid to local governments may actually provide more indirect aid than many or most states by assuming the cost of expensive functions that, in other states, are borne by local governments. Looking across the nation, the state share of total state and local spending is relatively high in Alaska, Vermont, and West Virginia, and relatively low in Florida, Nebraska, and Tennessee.[57] Much of the difference among states has to do with the proportion of spending on education that is borne by the state government.

Transferring education funding to the states has been an effective means of ensuring equity and providing overall support. It has also, however, created other difficulties. For one, it makes financial support of education less stable by tying it to the ups and downs in the fiscal health of the state—and, often, to revenue sources that are less dependable than the property tax, especially in a recessionary period. Pinning school funding to the sales tax, for example, makes support for education volatile. Even in good times, moreover, the level of support can vary significantly because education has to compete with a host of other demands on state funds.

The growth in state financial aid also has disadvantages for educators: namely, increases in state regulations and caps on local educational expenditures. States have become increasingly involved with curriculum, class size, and special education—and, in the interest of accountability, are more and more likely to impose statewide academic standards and mandated tests. As state funding of education has grown, so has state meddling in the details of educational policy. As one state legislator put it, "When we control the money, it's hard to get out of the details."[58] Overall, while local school officials are busier than ever before, their authority, particularly at the district level, has been increasingly undercut.

In recent years, states have not only picked up more of the costs of education but also taken on more financial responsibility for courts and corrections, health care for indigent citizens, mental health care, and cash welfare assistance. Generally, state assumption of expenditures can reduce the spending disparities that result from reliance on the local property tax and free up local property tax revenue for other local functions. Yet the price is likely to be a loss of local control and perhaps a decline in service quality. In fact, some programs that are now under state administration may be better off under direct local control. Some observers have suggested, for example, that a decentralized court system, which can allow more flexibility in judicial administration, may be preferable to a court system financed and administered by the state. Instead of assuming full financial and administrative responsibility for courts, states could provide relief through grants-in-aid and cost-reimbursement plans while giving local governments some control over the administration of the system.

Consolidation and Cooperation

In the interest of cost savings, states have occasionally encouraged the consolidation of local government units or greater service sharing between local governments. The consolidation of school districts, for example, has been viewed as a means of achieving economic efficiency and lowering property taxes; such consolidations are currently being contemplated in a number of states, including Arizona and New Jersey. In 2007, legislatures in Maine and South Dakota shrunk the number of school districts from more than 150 to about 80.

In recent years, several states, including New Jersey and Wisconsin, have used financial grants to encourage local governments to consolidate fire protection and other services, or to share costs for functions such as road construction and sanitation. In New Jersey, the governor has warned local officials to start combining essential services or risk a reduction in state aid. The Local Unit Alignment, Reorganization and Consolidation Commission has taken on the task of identifying opportunities for towns to combine services with other towns or with counties, or even to merge with other jurisdictions. In Indiana, the Indiana Commission on Local Government Reform recommended that township governments be eliminated; however, no action has been taken on that recommendation. In 2008, voters and the legislature did eliminate almost all township assessors, and generally shifted the task of property assessment from the township to the county level.

Rather than restructure local governments, state lawmakers have usually encouraged pragmatic responses to problems that spill over boundary lines. They have, for example, encouraged (1) the transfer of functions among jurisdictions (e.g., from city to county), (2) elaborate systems of interlocal contracts and agreements, (2) local government participation in metropolitan or regional councils of governments, and (4) the creation of special districts and authorities to deal with specific issues. States generally play a positive role in encouraging cooperative activities, and much can be accomplished through state passage of joint powers acts, which encourage cooperative ventures.

Local officials have shown a particular inclination to seek out partnerships with other local governments. Indeed, over the years, the tensions and uncertainties of dealing with the federal and state governments have encouraged local officials to look to each other for support and to come together to address common problems and operate more economically. As of 2003, for example, there were 3,332 cooperative agreements between local government entities in New York.[59] Local officials value the cooperative approach as a means of retaining local identity while preserving their ability to address problems that transcend their boundaries or that are beyond their individual financial or technical capabilities.

CONCLUDING NOTE

Although home rule remains important as a legal concept, the world of local officials is filled with state mandates, preemptions, and prohibitions. In addition, state aid programs—especially those under which state revenues are shared with local governments for unrestricted purposes—have become endangered.

The absence of broad and clear grants of local discretion means that local government authority is unstable—continually defined and redefined through litigation, and through an endless flow of special legislation. States would do well to clarify and strengthen home rule—and to increase, when possible, local discretion to deal with matters that are of no great concern to the state or that should be decided in light of the needs and priorities of particular communities. State intervention carries the double risk of transferring control to authorities that have little knowledge of local problems and of contributing to the neglect of what are properly state duties.

Municipal and county officials always have to worry about costly mandates and takeaways, but especially so when state lawmakers face budget deficits. Unfortunately, these are the very times when localities also face revenue shortfalls, and state actions make a bad local situation even worse. State officials think of mandates and takeaways as "burden sharing"; local officials think of them as "burden shifting."

Naturally, state officials give prime attention to state budgets, and local officials give prime attention to local budgets. The state, though, has the upper hand. For state budget makers, the task at hand is to balance state spending and revenues; they are not apt to worry excessively about local governments' budgetary problems or about the impact of their decisions on local entities. As a result, a single state budget problem may well become a hundred or so local government budget problems—and local officials have little choice but to adjust as well as they can.

States can take a number of steps to increase the financial stability of local governments. They could, for example, greatly ease the pressure on local property taxes by eliminating various mandates and tax exemptions and by expanding local revenue-raising powers. Mandate relief and increased revenue authority could go a long way toward helping localities to become more self-sufficient. They would also better equip localities to weather current and future economic downturns.[60] State governments can also help local officials meet their financial responsibilities by extending aid, picking up the costs of certain functions, and encouraging greater efficiency and cost sharing among local governments.

In building a revenue structure, localities need state cooperation to secure a balanced set of taxes—including sales or income taxes, which are plentiful when the economy is good but lose value when it is bad, and a property tax, which comes in handy during a recession but is not as responsive as other taxes to economic growth. Since the potential revenue bases of local jurisdictions vary widely, state aid is needed to upgrade and, through careful targeting, to equalize service levels.

[1]Quoted in Josh Kovner, "Town to Cut, Delay Projects," *Hartford Courant,* October 6, 2008, A3.

[2]Michael A. Pagano and Christopher W. Hoene, *City Fiscal Conditions in 2008* (Washington, D.C.: National League of Cities, September 2008).

[3]U.S. Advisory Commission on Intergovernmental Relations (ACIR), *Local Government Autonomy: Needs for State Constitutional Statutory and Judicial Clarification* (Washington, D.C.: U.S. Government Printing Office [GPO], October 1993); see also Dale Krane, Platon N. Rigos, and Melvin B. Hill Jr., *Home Rule in America: A Fifty-State Handbook* (Washington, D.C.: CQ Press, 2001).

[4]*City of Clinton v. Cedar Rapids and Missouri River Railroad,* 24 Iowa 455 @ 475 (1868).

[5]John F. Dillon, *Commentaries on the Law of Municipal Corporations* (Boston: Little, Brown, 1911), 145.

[6]Gordon L. Clark, *Judges and the Cities* (Chicago: University of Chicago Press, 1985), 78–79.

[7]See Jesse J. Richardson Jr., Meghan Zimmerman Gough, and Robert Puentes, "Is Home Rule the Answer? Clarifying the Influence of Dillon's Rule on Growth Management" (paper prepared for the Brookings Institution Center on Urban and Metropolitan Policy, January 2003), brookings.edu/reports/2003/01metropolitanpolicy_richardson.aspx?rssid=puentesr (accessed December 15, 2008); and David J. Barron, "Reclaiming Home Rule," *Harvard Law Review* 116 (June 2003): 2348–2386.

[8]David J. Barron, Gerald E. Frug, and Rick T. Su, *Dispelling the Myth of Home Rule: Local Power in Greater Boston* (Cambridge, Mass.: Rappaport Institute for Greater Boston, 2008), 13–15.

[9]Ibid.

[10]Frayda S. Bluestein, "Do North Carolina Local Governments Need More Home Rule?" *North Carolina Law Review* 84 (September 2006): 1983.

[11]Joe Hallett, Mark Niquette, and Alan Johnson, "Legislature Has Let Cities Down, Mayors Say," *Columbus Dispatch,* December 2, 2007, 13A.

[12]Quoted in Justin D. Anderson, "Jones Vows to Fight for W. Va. Cities; Mayor's Goal as President Is to Gain Home Rule for Municipalities," *Charleston Daily Mail,* August 21, 2006, 1D.

[13]Quoted in Brian Farkas, "Home-Rule Cities Promise Big Payoffs," *Charleston* (W. Va.) *Gazette,* February 10, 2008, P1A.

[14]David R. Berman, Lawrence L. Martin, and Laura Kajfez, "County Home Rule: Does Where You Stand Depend on Where You Sit?" *State and Local Review* 17 (Spring 1985): 232–234.

[15]Quoted in James W. Zumwalt, "The Local Government Role: Home Rule and Short Ballots," in *Proceedings: A Symposium on the Alabama Constitution* (Auburn, Ala.: Center for Governmental Services, Auburn University, February 15, 1996).

[16]What is included in the definition of a mandate varies from state to state. The Connecticut ACIR, for example, counts not only statutes or administrative regulations that directly require actions on the part of local governments, but also those that require actions if a local government chooses to perform a service that it is not actually required to perform. See Connecticut ACIR, *Compendium of Statutory and Regulatory Mandates on Municipalities in Connecticut* (Hartford: Connecticut ACIR, 2003). Some states regard prohibitions and preemptions as mandates; these are considered in a separate section of this article.

[17]A study of Kansas completed in the mid-1990s, for example, suggests that the state had a compelling interest in the adoption and enforcement of only about 100 of the 941 mandates it was imposing on local governments at the time. About 300 of those mandates were obsolete and widely ignored. One of these—more than a century old—required counties to pay the burial expenses of Civil War veterans and limited this payment to $20 per headstone. See Edward Flentje, "State Mandates as Family Values?" *Current Municipal Problems* 22 (1996): 510–512.

[18]Task Force on Local Government Services and Fiscal Stability, *Final Report to the Governor* (State and Local Government Team, Michigan State University Extension, May 2006).

[19]Anne Sutton, "Bill Aims to Plug Funding Holes," *Anchorage Daily News,* March 15, 2008, A1.

[20]State of Minnesota, Office of the Legislative Auditor, *State Mandates on Local Governments* (St. Paul: January 2000); see also Lawrence J. Grossback, "The Problem of State-Imposed Mandates: Lessons from Minnesota's Local Governments," *State and Local Government Review* 34 (Fall 2002): 183–197.

[21]Robert M. M. Shaffer, "Comment: Unfunded State Mandates and Local Governments," *University of Cincinnati Law Review* 64 (Spring 1996): 1057–1088.

[22]Susan A. MacManus, "Mad about Mandates: The Issue of Who Should Pay for What Resurfaces—in the 1990s," *Publius* 21 (Summer 1991): 59–75; see also Shaffer, "Unfunded State Mandates."

[23]Pat Leary, quoted in Alexa H. Bluth, "Cities May Get Some Clout," *Sacramento Bee,* October 25, 2004, 1A.

[24]See Richard H. Horte, "State Expenditures with Mandate Reimbursement," in *Coping with Mandates: What Are the Alternatives?* ed. Michael Fix and Daphne Kenyon (Washington, D.C.: Urban Institute Press, 1990), 23; and Janet M. Kelly, *State Mandates: Fiscal Notes, Reimbursement, and Anti-Mandate Strategies* (Washington, D.C.: National League of Cities, 1992).

[25]Virginia Legislature, Joint Legislative Audit and Review Commission, *Intergovernmental Mandates and Financial Aid to Local Governments,* House Document no. 56 (Richmond: 1992).

[26]Barron, Frug, and Su, *Dispelling the Myth.*

[27]Ken Dixon, "Cities Again Decry Property Tax," *Chronicle,* September 30, 2008, 7.

[28]Connecticut Business and Industry Association, "How State Mandates Affect Connecticut's Cities and Towns," cbia.com/newsroom/surveys/2006/municipalmandates report206.pdf (accessed December 15, 2008).

[29]Linda Kleindienst, "Local Governments Forced to Find Money for State Mandates," *Orlando Sentinel,* April 28, 2008, B4. This article draws on information gathered by Lance deHaven Smith, a professor of public administration at Florida State University.

[30]Quoted in Gary Pettus, "Taxes Rising across State," (Jackson, Miss.) *Clarion-Ledger,* September 21, 2008, 1A.

[31]Quoted in Janet Pearson, "City Gets Serious about Finding New Revenue," *Tulsa World,* July 9, 2006, G1.

[32]American Lung Association, *Summary Reports: Preemptive State Tobacco Control Laws and Affected Provisions* (New York: American Lung Association, July 14, 2008).

[33]Peter D. Jackson, Jeffrey Wasserman, and Kristiana Raube, "The Politics of Antismoking Legislation," *Journal of Health Politics, Policy, and Law* 18 (Winter 1993): 787–819.

[34]Quoted in Christian Parker, "Eminent Domain Issue Passes, Gets OK from Supreme Court," *Arizona Capitol Times,* November 10, 2006, 3–4.

[35]National League of Cities, *Anti-Predatory Lending Ordinances* (Washington, D.C.: National League of Cities, February 2008). In some states, such as Ohio, court decisions that municipalities could not regulate predatory lending practices have been followed by comprehensive state regulations to protect against predatory lending.

[36]ACIR, *Tax and Expenditure Limits on Local Governments* (Washington, D.C.: GPO, March 1995); see also Phillip G. Joyce and Daniel R. Mullins, "The Changing Fiscal Structure of the State and Local Public Sector: The Impact of Tax and Expenditure Limitations," *Public Administration Review* 51 (May–June 1991): 240–253; Daniel E. O'Toole and Brian Stipak, "Coping with State Tax and Expenditure Limitations: The Oregon Experience," *State and Local Government Review* 30 (Winter 1998): 9–16; Alvin D. Sokolow, "The Changing Property Tax and State-Local Relations," *Publius* 28 (Winter 1998): 165–187; and Jocelyn M. Johnston, Michael A. Pagano, and Philip A. Russo Jr., "State Limits and State Aid: An Exploratory Analysis of County Revenue Structure," *State and Local Government Review* 32 (Spring 2000): 86–97.

[37]U.S. Bureau of the Census, *State and Local Government Finances, 2005–2006* (Washington, D.C.: GPO, 2007).

[38]Pagano and Hoene, *City Fiscal Conditions.*

[39]Richard L. Cole and John Kincaid, "Public Opinion on U.S. Federal and Intergovernmental Issues in 2006: Continuity and Change," *Publius* 36 (Summer 2006): 443–459.

[40]This argument is made, for example, by Wallace E. Oates in "Local Property Taxation: An Assessment," *Land Lines* (May 1999).

[41]Quoted in Melissa Walker, "D. M. Lacks Legislative Support in Utility Fee Case," *Des Moines Register,* May 12, 2008, 1B.

[42]For a detailed analysis, see Stanley Chervin, *Property Tax Reduction and Relief Programs* (Nashville: Tennessee ACIR, June 2007).

[43]David Brunori, *Local Tax Policy: A Federalist Perspective* (Washington, D.C.: Urban Institute Press, 2003).

[44]Arthur C. Nelson and Mitch Moody, *Paying for Prosperity: Impact Fees and Job Growth* (Washington, D.C.: Brookings Institution, June 2003).

[45]Paul Brown, councilman, San Luis Obispo, quoted in Sally Connell, "Prop. 1A Greased Way for Tax Votes," (San Luis Obispo, Calif.) *Tribune,* August 13, 2006, A1.

[46]Quoted in Edythe Jensen, "City Is Stung by AZ Refund," *Chandler* (Ariz.) *Republic,* July 12, 2008, 1.

[47]Quoted in Mary Jo Pitzl, "New $9.9 Billion Budget: Some Pain, Gain," *Arizona Republic,* July 6, 2008, B1.

[48]Quoted in Paul Mulshine, "Small Towns Plan Big Revolt on State Police Fees," (Newark, N.J.) *Star-Ledger,* August 7, 2008, 19.

[49]Philip Kloha, Carol S. Weissert, and Robert Kleine, "Someone to Watch over Me: State Monitoring of Local Fiscal Conditions," *American Review of Public Administration* 35 (September 2005): 236–255.

[50]For a recent review of state practices, see Charles K. Coe, "Preventing Local Government Fiscal Crises: Emerging Best Practices," *Public Administration* Review (July/August 2008): 759–767. One example of general-distress legislation is the Pennsylvania Municipalities Financial Recovery Act of 1987, popularly known as Act 47, which applies to all cities except Philadelphia. Under Act 47, a state agency regularly collects financial information from the nearly 3,000 local governments in Pennsylvania, and evaluates it according to several indicators of distress, including operating deficits and defaults on obligations. The agency may declare a municipality officially distressed—although such a declaration is usually at the request of a local governing body—and appoint a state coordinator to develop and implement a plan to correct the problems. A municipality may reject this plan and develop its own, but the agency has to approve the municipality's plan. Until the agency approves a plan, it can withhold assistance that would otherwise have been provided under Act 47, and can also withhold some other revenues that the locality would otherwise have received as part of regular state funding. Since 1987, 23 municipalities have qualified as "financially distressed" under Pennsylvania's Act 47. Six of these have exited the program. Early in 2004, the city of Pittsburgh, having failed to secure help from the state legislature in its efforts to broaden its tax base, sought and received "distressed" status under Act 47. It continues to operate under state oversight.

[51]While the record varies from state to state, by some measurements state aid to education has generally declined in recent years. When one controls for inflation, for example, state aid per pupil dropped in the nation as a whole between 2002 and 2005. See Suho Bae and Thomas Gais, "State Fiscal Report: State-Specific Data Reveal Growing Differences in Education Resources since the Last Recession," *Rockefeller Institute Policy Brief* (Albany, N.Y.: July 12, 2007).

[52]See David R. Berman, *Local Government and the States: Autonomy, Politics and Policy* (Armonk, N.Y.: M. E. Sharpe, 2003).

[53]Representative John Gard, quoted in Amy Rinard, "State Lawmakers Cool to More Local Funding," *Milwaukee Journal Sentinel,* April 9, 1999, 1.

[54]Quoted in Kevin McDermott and Patrick J. Powers, "Illinois Cities Protest Plan to Cut Revenue Sharing," *St. Louis Post-Dispatch,* May 11, 2002, 12.

[55]Christopher Hoene, *Local Budget and Tax Policy in the U.S.: Perceptions of City Officials* (Washington, D.C.: National League of Cities, 2005).

[56]John R. Bartle, "Coping with Cutbacks: City Response to Aid Cuts in New York State," *State and Local Review* 28 (Winter 1996): 38–48.

[57]Congressional Quarterly, *State and Local Source Book 2005* (Washington, D.C.: Congressional Quarterly, 2006), 38.

[58]Quoted in Robert C. Johnson and Jessica L. Sandham, "States Increasingly Flexing Their Policy Muscle," *Education Week* 18, no. 31 (1999): 19–20.

[59]Ernest J. Strada, "Successful Strategies to Improve the Efficiency and Competitiveness of Local Government Entities in New York State" (testimony before the New York State Commission on Local Government Efficiency and Competitiveness, June 13, 2007, Saratoga Springs, N.Y.), 3, nyslocalgov.org/pdf/hearings/061307/Baynes.pdf (accessed December 15, 2008).

[60]Christopher Hoene and Michael A. Pagano, *Cities and State Fiscal Structure* (Washington, D.C.: National League of Cities, 2008).

THE *YEAR BOOK* STATE CORRESPONDENTS

Arkansas
Ken Wasson
Assistant Director
Arkansas Municipal League

Louisiana
George Marretta
Director of Research and Special Projects
Louisiana Municipal Association

Maryland
Thomas C. Reynolds
Manager, Research and Information
Maryland Municipal League

Missouri
Patrick Bonnot
Staff Associate, Legislation
Missouri Municipal League

New Hampshire
Cordell Johnson
Government Affairs Attorney
Local Government Center

Tennessee
John M. Holloway
Government Relations
Tennessee Municipal League

Texas
Bennett Sandlin
General Counsel
Texas City Management Association

Vermont
Steven E. Jeffrey
Executive Director
Vermont League of Cities and Towns

Virginia
Mary Jo Fields
Director of Research
Virginia Municipal League

B 2

Congressional Actions Affecting Local Government: The 110th Congress

Lydia Bjornlund
Bjornlund Communications

Selected Findings

In response to the meltdown of the financial market, Congress passed the Emergency Economic Stabilization Act of 2008 authorizing Secretary Paulson to spend up to $700 billion to purchase mortgage-backed securities and bail out financially distressed banks and other financial institutions.

The Second Chance Act, an unprecedented piece of legislation, authorizes $165 million in federal grants to government agencies and community and faith-based organizations to provide employment assistance, substance abuse treatment, housing, family programming, mentoring, victims support, and other services that can help reduce repeat offenses and violations of probation and parole.

As the Democrats expanded their leadership of Congress with the 2008 elections, they pledged to push an ambitious agenda to counter 14 years of Republican control. The war in Iraq had played center stage for much of the first session of the 110th Congress, but with success of the "surge" as well as increasing concerns about the economy at home, the focus of the American people and their legislators shifted to the economy—specifically, the housing and credit crisis. Then, in the months preceding the presidential election, a new crisis demanded their attention: the collapse of the stock market. The election of Barack Obama as well as enhanced Democratic majorities in both the House of Representatives and the Senate seemed to suggest that the American people were ready for a change from politics as usual.

THE ENVIRONMENT

With Democrats in control of Congress, energy and environmental issues became priorities. Early in 2007, Congress introduced and passed the Clean Energy Act (P.L. 110-140), comprehensive legislation intended "to move the United States toward greater energy independence and security, to increase the production of clean renewable fuels, to protect consumers, to increase the efficiency of products, buildings, and vehicles, to promote research on and deploy greenhouse gas capture and storage options, and to improve the energy performance of the Federal Government, and for other purposes."[1]

Among the provisions of the act were two new grant programs for local governments. The Energy Efficiency and Conservation Block Grant Program authorizes $2 billion annually over five years to help cities and counties address energy efficiency and emissions concerns. A second grant program creates demonstration grants to help local governments implement cost-effective technologies in local government buildings. The funding will be allotted through a cost-sharing program in which the federal government will assume 40% of expenses for new energy-saving efficiencies and the local government will assume the rest. Local government lobbyists have lauded the enactment of the grant programs; however, the 110th Congress failed to appropriate funds for them in 2008.

Congress's record on other environmental protection issues proved no better. The Clean Water State Revolving fund, a major source of water infrastructure funding for local governments, was cut in half and has been slated for elimination. Local government lobbyists have worked to establish a sustainable water trust fund to support infrastructure projects, and Congress asked the Government Accountability Office to provide a report on potential revenue sources for this purpose by spring 2009.

Congress also held a series of hearings on climate change. Although neither the House nor the Senate moved climate change bills, the issue appears to be gaining steam. Some pundits believe that climate change legislation will be a priority in the upcoming session.

In the continuing resolution that appropriated funds through March 2009, most federal energy and environmental programs were kept at current fiscal year (FY) 2008 levels. One change in environmental policy enacted in the legislation involves offshore drilling: the law removes the ban on offshore drilling in coastal waters more than 100 miles from the Atlantic and Pacific coasts and allows states to opt in a program to allow oil drilling 50–100 miles from shore. The bill also allows Colorado, Utah, and Wyoming to opt in oil shale leasing programs on federal lands.

PUBLIC SAFETY

Local government lobbying organizations continued to push for federal funding, program flexibility, and intergovernmental cooperation to address a wide range of public safety issues, including natural disaster preparedness emergency response, interoperable emergency communications, first-responder training and homeland security, and crime prevention.

Byrne/JAG Reauthorization

The Edward Byrne Memorial Justice Assistance Grant (Byrne/JAG) Program, the largest justice assistance grant to states, is the cornerstone of the federal government's criminal justice program. Administered by the Department of Justice, the program funds state and local government efforts in a broad range of activities, including drug treatment and enforcement, criminal reentry initiatives, crime prevention, and corrections. Forty percent of Byrne/JAG funds are sent directly to local law enforcement agencies; the remaining funds are distributed through state governments. Grants may be used to provide personnel, equipment, training, technical assistance, and information systems for the arrest, prosecution, adjudication, detention, and rehabilitation of offenders. State and local governments laud the flexible terms of the program, which allow them to target funds to address the shifting needs and priorities of their communities.

In the Consolidated Appropriations Act of 2008 (P.L. 110-161), signed into law on December 26, 2007, the Byrne/JAG program was cut by 67% from $520 million in FY 2007 to $170 million in FY 2008. Reauthorizing the program and increasing appropriations became a priority for state and local law enforcement lobbyists, but they were unsuccessful in remedying the funding gap.

Reauthorization legislation passed both houses of Congress in the summer of 2008 and was signed by President Bush—who had threatened to veto the legislation—on July 30, 2008, becoming Public Law 110-294. The reauthorization bill keeps the Byrne/JAG program from being abolished and funds the program at FY 2006 levels through FY 2012. With the passage of the authorization legislation, local government lobbyists have turned their attention to securing appropriations for 2009 and beyond.

The Second Chance Act

It has been estimated that more than two-thirds of people serving terms in local jails, state prisons, and juvenile facilities are rearrested within three years of their release. Local government lobbying organizations argue that this puts a strain on local resources. According to the Bureau of Justice Statistics, local governments spend over $95 billion annually on criminal justice. In addition to stepped-up law enforcement, the high rate of recidivism also contributes to increased needs for public health, human service programs, public

housing, and job training and employment programs. Local government organizations have called for assistance in reducing recidivism.

In April 9, 2008, the Second Chance Act (P.L. 110-199) was signed into law, authorizing $165 million for FY 2009 and FY 2010. This first-of-its-kind legislation authorizes federal grants to government agencies and community and faith-based organizations to provide employment assistance, substance abuse treatment, housing, family programming, mentoring, victims support, and other services that can help reduce repeat offenses and violations of probation and parole.

Both the House and Senate provided funding for Second Chance Act programs in their draft appropriations bills for FY 2009, but they failed to pass those bills before the start of the fiscal year. The continuing resolution provides no funding for new programs, including the Second Chance Act. Supporters of the act have vowed to urge Congress to appropriate funds for it early in the next session.

Reauthorization of the Mentally Ill Offender Treatment and Crime Reduction Act

The Mentally Ill Offender Treatment and Crime Reduction Act (MIOTCRA) of 2004 was intended to keep the mentally ill out of jail and juvenile detention centers and to get them the support that they need. Although the law authorizing funding through MIOTCRA is not scheduled to expire until 2009, both the House and Senate introduced bills late in 2007 to reauthorize and strengthen the law (S. 2304; H.R. 3992). Both versions of the legislation increased overall funding levels for MIOTCRA and included a new law enforcement grant program to fund collaborative initiatives between law enforcement and mental health agencies. The House and Senate hammered out the differences in their bills, and on October 14, 2008, President Bush signed the reauthorization legislation (P.L. 110-416).

The new legislation reauthorizes MIOTCRA through 2013 at a level of $50 million per year. Several provisions have been added, including training for law enforcement officers to help them respond appropriately to mentally ill individuals, and the development of law enforcement receiving centers to assess the mental health of individuals in custody. The law also encourages the use of computerized information systems and intergovernmental cooperative collaboration by allowing planning funds to be used for this purpose.

HEALTH AND HUMAN SERVICES

Reauthorization of the farm bill was passed in May 2008, leaving the 110th Congress time to address several smaller pieces of legislation, such as health insurance coverage for mental health and substance abuse disorders, and child welfare and adoption. Congress was unsuccessful, however, in securing reauthorization legislation of the State Children's Insurance Program, or SCHIP.

Farm Bill Reauthorization

The farm bill dates back to the Great Depression and is updated every five years. The subsidies included in the farm bills have always focused on traditional commodities—corn and other field crops, dairy, and sugar—with very limited funds going to other fruits and vegetables. Yet roughly 60% of the farm bill appropriation covers such nutrition programs as food stamps, designed to ensure that no Americans go hungry. The 2008 farm bill, for instance, includes about $209 billion for nutrition programs, compared with $35 billion for agricultural commodity programs.

As the five years covered by the 2002 farm bill came to a close, Congress struggled to come to consensus on reauthorization legislation. Near the end of 2007, Congress extended the 2002 law as it worked to iron out differences in the versions of the bill that passed the House and Senate. On May 14, 2008, the House passed its farm bill, H.R. 2419, by a vote of 318–106. The Senate passed the bill the following day by a vote of 81–19. President Bush, who had called for reform and cuts in the 2002 bill as well as in this proposed legislation, vetoed the $307 billion bill on May 21—the first time the farm bill had been vetoed since 1953. "At a time of high food prices and record farm income, this bill lacks program reform and fiscal discipline," Bush explained. "It continues subsidies for the wealthy and increases farm bill spending by more than $20 billion, while using budget gimmicks to hide much of the increase."[2]

By the next day, both the Senate and the House had overridden the president's veto in what the *Washington Post* called "the most significant legislative rebuff of Bush's presidency,"[3] and the Food, Conservation, and Energy Act of 2008 became Public Law 110-234. (P.L. 110-234 was replaced by P.L. 110-246, which added a title that had been unintentionally dropped from the initial legislation.)

The Food, Conservation, and Energy Act of 2008 expands many of the traditional farm bill programs. In addition to the extension of federal subsidies for agricultural commodities, the bill includes a $10.3 billion increase in spending on nutrition programs (including food stamps) and a $1.25 billion increase in food bank support over the next 10 years. The Supplemental Nutrition Assistance Program (SNAP) is an enhancement over the food stamp program: it raises the standard deduction and indexes it for inflation, and it eliminates the cap on the dependent care deduction. The law also includes new funding for organic agriculture, and requires country-of-origin labeling for meat and produce.

In addition, the law increases conservation program spending by $7.9 billion over previous authorized levels, and doubles the funding for the Farm Protection Program to protect agricultural lands from development pressure. Several provisions are included to encourage renewable energy, including $1 billion for programs that will help the renewable energy industry invest in new technologies that use a variety of sources beyond feed grains

Of particular interest to many local governments are the provisions included in the Rural Development Title (Title VI). This title, which addresses a wide range of policy issues concerning rural communities, has been part of the farm bill since 1973; in general it supports (1) infrastructure in rural areas, with traditional assistance for housing, electrical generation and transmission, water and wastewater, and community capacity; (2) agricultural development; and (3) rural business creation and expansion. The new farm bill restores to $150 million mandatory funding for rural development that had been eliminated during conference negotiations. It also reauthorizes with discretionary funding several programs that had been authorized with mandatory spending in the 2002 farm bill; these programs include the Rural Firefighters and Emergency Personnel grant program, the Rural Strategic Investment Program, the Rural Business Investment Program, and the Access to Broadband Services in Rural Areas. More recently, policy makers have pushed for programs that support innovative and alternative business development, as well as innovative mechanisms to finance it. Thus, along with expanding broadband access in rural areas, the new farm bill creates a new micro-entrepreneurial assistance program and a new rural collaborative investment program, and authorizes three new regional economic development commissions. It also authorizes $120 million for a one-time funding of pending water and wastewater infrastructure projects.

Immediately following passage of the new farm bill, local, state, and federal government agencies began work on its implementation. Among priorities for local governments will be to ensure that rural development and other local government–friendly provisions are funded at their maximum authorized levels.

Mental Health Parity and Addiction Equity Act

After more than a decade of struggle, Congress passed the Paul Wellstone and Pete Domenici Mental Health Parity and Addiction Equity Act of 2008 as part of the Emergency Economic Stabilization Act (see below). The Mental Health Parity and Addiction Equity Act requires most group health plans to provide more generous coverage for the treatment of mental illnesses and substance abuse disorders. It does not state that qualifying health plans must offer mental health or substance use disorder benefits, but it does mandate that group health plans that offer such benefits must do so in parity with medical/surgical benefits.

An estimated 35 million Americans suffer from mental illness. Supporters of the legislation say that mental illness is a medical condition and should be treated like any physical problem. Critics contend that the law goes too far in mandating what diseases and illnesses are covered by group insurance policies. The law exempts small businesses with fewer than 50 employees and individual health plans.

Americans with Disabilities Act Amendments

The Americans with Disabilities Act (ADA) was passed in 1990 to protect the rights of disabled Americans. Since then, a series of Supreme Court decisions have seriously undermined the initial intent of the ADA by narrowing the qualifications that define an "individual with a disability." For instance, the Court had ruled that a person who takes medication or uses technology (such as a prosthetic limb or hearing aid) to mitigate a disability should not be considered disabled. In September 2008, Congress passed and

President Bush signed the Americans with Disabilities Amendments Act (P.L. 100-325), which broadens the definition of a disability and clarifies when "reasonable accommodations" must be provided to disabled citizens.

Child Welfare

On October 7, 2008, President Bush signed the Fostering Connections to Success and Increasing Adoptions Act (P.L. 110-351) into law. The purpose of the law is to promote permanent families for children without parents through relative guardianship and adoption, and to improve education and health care for children in the foster care system. The legislation increases incentives to states to find adoptive families for children in foster care, especially those children with disabilities or other special needs. States can continue providing assistance to foster children up to age 21. The law also clarifies that states may waive non-safety-related licensing standards for relatives on a case-by-case basis.

Attempts to Reauthorize SCHIP

The State Children's Health Insurance Program (SCHIP) has been in place since 1997, when it was enacted as part of the Balanced Budget Act of 1997. Together with Medicaid, SCHIP has helped to reduce the number of low-income uninsured children by expanding eligibility levels and simplifying application procedures. In 2007, Congress passed two versions of the Children's Health Insurance Program Reauthorization Act (CHIPRA) to expand and extend SCHIP. However, President Bush vetoed both bills (H.R. 976 and H.R. 3963), and there were insufficient votes in the House to override the vetoes. In December 2007, Congress passed S. 2499, extending SCHIP through March 2009. Given that the legislation falls far short of the comprehensive SCHIP reauthorization efforts, lawmakers are expected to renew reauthorization efforts as the extension deadline nears, in anticipation of a better response from President Obama.

HOUSING AND HOMELESSNESS

In the spring of 2008, the subprime mortgage crisis called attention to housing issues. The Housing and Economic Recovery Act of 2008 (HERA), which was passed to provide short-term relief for the troubled market, also implemented a new Affordable Housing Trust Fund and increased authorized funding for the Community Development Block Grant (CDBG) program. Congress also considered legislation to reform Section 8 housing programs and to reauthorize the McKinney-Vento Homeless Assistance Act, but it failed to secure passage for either one.

Housing and Economic Recovery Act of 2008

The Housing and Economic Recovery Act of 2008 (HERA; P.L. 110-289) became law on July 30, 2008. Passed in response to the subprime mortgage crisis, HERA placed Fannie Mae and Freddie Mac under conservatorship—a legal status similar to Chapter 11 bankruptcy—and strengthened regulatory oversight over these and other government-sponsored enterprises. Fannie Mae and Freddie Mac had funded 70% of home loans at the beginning of 2008, and legislators believed that support of these two companies was crucial to the recovery of the housing market. The law responded to the immediate crisis by authorizing the Federal Housing Authority (FHA) to insure up to $300 billion of 30-year fixed-rate refinance loans for up to 90% of appraised value for distressed borrowers. It also authorizes states to refinance subprime loans using mortgage revenue bonds.

HERA also seeks to implement long-standing reform by reorganizing and modernizing the FHA, which includes the creation of a new independent agency charged with overseeing Fannie Mae, Freddie Mac, and other government-sponsored enterprises. The law also expands the types of mortgage products available through the agency.

As one provision of the act, Fannie Mae and Freddie Mac are required to contribute a portion of their mortgage purchases to a new Affordable Housing Trust Fund. This trust fund will be administered by the Department of Housing and Urban Development (HUD), which will distribute the funds in the form of grants to states for the construction, rehabilitation, and preservation of housing for low-income families. Only state governmental entities are authorized to receive trust fund grants, which are targeted for the lowest-income households with the greatest need for affordable housing. All the funds are required to go to people with incomes under 50% of the median income, and at least 90% of the funds must be used for rental housing.

HERA also includes $3.92 billion in additional funds for the CDBG program. The Bush administration opposed the CDBG provision and initially threatened to veto any legislation that included it, but the president did not carry through on this threat. The law provides pass-through funding for state and local governments on the basis of their home foreclosure percentages, the number of homes financed by subprime mortgage loans, and the number and percentage of homes in default or delinquency. The National Association of Counties (NACo) called CDBG funding "vital for local governments" because it provides them "with financial assistance to purchase and rehabilitate foreclosed homes."[4] The law also includes $180 million for housing counseling assistance programs.

Section 8 Housing

Section 8 was first included in the United States Housing Act of 1937. Legislators have called for reform of Section 8 housing for many years. The biggest complaint about today's program is that it has grown too large: it currently accounts for more than 60% of HUD's total budget. Critics aver that the funds are misspent and that the program has failed to meet the housing needs of poor families, particularly those who are elderly or disabled. In addition, to determine the allocation of funds, HUD employs a formula that uses 2004 data, which critics say cannot accurately target today's needs.

Among the housing reform bills Congress considered in this session was the Section 8 Voucher Act (SEVRA) of 2007 (H.R. 1851; S. 2684). Housing choice vouchers are the leading form of low-income housing assistance, serving nearly 2 million households, including families with children, the elderly, and people with disabilities. SEVRA would reform the program for the first time in 10 years, streamlining it and simplifying the rules governing the calculation of rents in public housing, project-based Section 8 properties, and the voucher program. Under SEVRA, funding for vouchers would be based on each public housing agency's actual spending for vouchers in the previous year. The bill would also reform the financing of "portability" moves so that families could more easily exercise their right to move with a voucher.

The House passed SEVRA in July 2007 by a strong bipartisan vote, 333–83, but the companion Senate bill failed to reach the floor. Advocates of Section 8 reform say they will introduce similar legislation in the next session.

Reauthorization of the McKinney-Vento Homeless Assistance Act

Several pieces of legislation were introduced to reauthorize the McKinney-Vento Homeless Assistance Act, which was initially passed in 1987. In the reauthorization legislation, Congress sought to consolidate and streamline several homeless assistance grant programs, as well as make the programs more flexible. In addition, some of the proposals would expand the definition of homelessness.

The House passed the Community Partnership to End Homelessness Act (H.R. 7221) on October 2, 2008. The Senate Banking, Housing, and Urban Affairs Committee had reported its version of the bill (S. 1518) on September 19, 2007, but it never reached the Senate floor for debate.

TRANSPORTATION

Congress dealt successfully with several short-term issues plaguing the transportation sector. In September 2008, a law (P.L. 110-318) transferred $8 billion from the General Fund to the Highway Trust Fund to make up for a shortfall in the trust fund that had threatened to reduce federal highway spending.

At the beginning of the 110th session, the authorization of two major transportation laws had lapsed: one governing the funding of Amtrak and another funding airport and aviation programs. Congress passed Amtrak reauthorization legislation for the first time since 1997, including important safety provisions in the wake of several rail accidents that experts say could have been prevented with better technologies. However, Congress failed to come to consensus on airport and aviation legislation, choosing instead to pass a series of short-term extensions of the current programs.

Amtrak Reauthorization and Rail Safety

For years Congress has struggled with how much federal funding should be used to support Amtrak. Some lawmakers, particularly those from the Northeast and Midwest, have championed providing financial support to Amtrak, while others have questioned whether taxpayers should subsidize Amtrak, which ran a $1 billion deficit in FY 2007. The Bush administration repeatedly

slashed funding in its proposed budget, and the president threatened to veto reauthorization legislation. However, Amtrak appropriations have remained relatively stable in recent years—$1.31 billion in FY 2006, $1.35 billion in FY 2008—while its ridership has increased: a record 28.7 million people rode Amtrak's trains in FY 2008. As concerns about climate change and gas prices have increased, so too has support among legislators for funding passenger rail service.

On October 16, 2008, the Rail Safety Improvement Act became law (P.L. 110-432). One half of the legislation reauthorizes Amtrak at $13 billion over the next five years—almost double its current level. The new law includes $5.3 billion for capital grants, $2.9 billion for operating grants, and $1.5 billion for new high-speed railways. About $1.9 billion would fund a matching-grant program to encourage states to invest in intercity passenger rail expansion and repair. Another $1.4 billion is authorized to help pay down Amtrak's debt, which currently amounts to more than $3 billion.

The other half of the legislation is designed to improve railroad safety. Of particular interest to local governments with commuter rail projects is a provision that will help mediate right-of-way disputes between commuter rail providers and freight railroads. The law also requires a "positive train control"—technology that automatically stops trains that run a stop signal—to be implemented on passenger trains and certain hazardous materials rail lines by 2015. This provision gained support in Congress after a train ran a stop sign in California on September 25, 2008, resulting in a crash that killed 25 people. Other safety provisions include a cap on railroad workers' shifts at 12 hours, and mandated 10-hour rest periods for train crews and signal employees.

Airport and Aviation Reauthorization

Since the latest authorization for federal airport and aviation programs expired on September 30, 2007, Congress has continued the programs with a series of short-term extensions. For several years, counties and other local and state government lobbying organizations have lobbied on behalf of an aviation reauthorization bill that would fully fund the Airport Improvement Program (AIP), the Essential Air Service (EAS) Program, and the Small Communities Air Service Development Program (SCASDP). The AIP, which is funded primarily through the Airport and Airway Trust Fund, currently provides about $3.5 billion annually in grants for capital improvements to commercial, cargo, and general aviation airports. The EAS Program, which provides subsidies to air carriers serving small and rural communities, has been funded at around $110 million. The SCASDP provides grants to small and rural communities to maintain and attract expanded air service through a variety of techniques, such as the marketing of the airports and air carriers and the subsidization of service.

In the fall of 2007, the House passed its airport and aviation reauthorization bill (H.R. 2881) by a vote of 267–151. The legislation, which authorizes funds through FY 2011, would have increased authorized funds for both the AIP and the EAS Program. But the reauthorization bill stalled

in the Senate as committees fought over financing of the modernization of the air traffic control system. On September 23, a six-month extension of the current airport and aviation legislation was enacted—the fifth such extension. Congress is expected to revisit the issue in 2009.

ANNUAL APPROPRIATIONS

On September 30, 2008—the last day of the fiscal year—President Bush signed the Consolidated Security, Disaster Assistance, and Continuing Appropriations Act of 2009 (P.L. 110-329). Passed as a continuing resolution, this legislation includes 3 of the 12 regular appropriations acts for FY 2009: the Department of Homeland Security (DHS), the Department of Veterans' Affairs, and the Department of Defense. In addition, it provides for continuing appropriations for the remaining 9 regular appropriations acts for that fiscal year, funding most of these programs at current levels until new spending bills are enacted, or March 6, 2009—a date that was selected to help smooth the transition for the new administration.

According to the Congressional Budget Office, enactment of the Consolidated Appropriations Act for FY 2009 brought total discretionary budget authority for the fiscal year to $1,089.6 billion: $993.7 billion in nonemergency spending and $95.9 billion in emergency spending. These amounts reflect $65.9 billion in emergency spending in a FY 2009 "bridge fund" for war activities (provided in P.L. 110-252), and $2.2 billion in nonemergency advance appropriations for Bioshield.[5] Total budget authority for the three regular appropriations acts included in the act amounted to $669.6 billion: $602.8 billion in nonemergency spending and $66.9 billion in emergency spending, mostly from the "bridge fund" provided in P.L. 110-252.

Department of Homeland Security Funding

The Consolidated Security, Disaster Assistance, and Continuing Appropriations Act appropriated $40 billion for DHS for FY 2009. The White House's proposed budget had recommended slashing some of the programs that support local governments' efforts to provide for the nation's security. The final bill includes DHS funding at the following levels:

- $950 million for the State Homeland Security Grant Program
- $838 million for the Urban Area Security Initiative Grant Program
- $750 million for the Assistance to Firefighters Grant Program.

The legislation increased funding over FY 2008 levels for state and local governments' immigration enforcement, training programs, emergency operation centers, and interoperable communication grants.

Disaster Funding

The Consolidated Appropriations Act provides $22.9 billion in emergency supplemental appropriations for disaster relief and recovery, including

$7.9 billion for the Federal Emergency Management Agency's Disaster Relief Fund and $1.5 billion to help New Orleans pay the local cost share of hurricane and storm damage reduction projects. Other disaster-related provisions include

- $6.5 billion for CDBGs to provide communities with flexible grants to help disaster recovery efforts such as temporary housing, the repair and/or replacement of damaged homes and public infrastructure, and economic development
- $1.3 billion for the Army Corps of Engineers to repair infrastructure damage caused by disasters
- $910 million for emergency wildfire suppression and related costs
- $850 million in Emergency Highway Relief to help repair roads and bridges damaged by recent disasters
- $799 million for Small Business Administration loans and for technical assistance to businesses and homeowners hit by disasters
- $600 million for Social Services Block Grants to provide states with flexible sources of funding to address disaster needs such as food and health care
- $400 million in Economic Development Assistance programs to help communities hit by disasters create strategies for economic recovery.

Other Funding

Most appropriations of interest to local governments were continued at FY 2008 levels, including most Department of Transportation, Department of Justice, and Department of Interior programs. The federal highway program is funded at roughly $41.2 billion (the full amount authorized under the Safe, Accountable, Flexible, Efficient Transportation Equity Act: A Legacy for Users [SAFETEA-LU]); the federal transit program at $9.35 billion; the AIP at $3.5 billion; the EAS Program (which the Bush administration had sought to eliminate) at $110 million; and Amtrak at $1.35 billion.

Most HUD programs, including the CDBG formula program and the HOME program, are also funded at current levels. FY 2009 appropriations for CDBG are $3.59 billion; the HOME program will receive $1.63 billion. A notable exception is the Low Income Home Energy Assistance Program (LIHEAP), which received a substantial increase from $2.6 billion in FY 2008 to $5.1 billion in FY 2009. The $5.1 billion appropriation allocates $4.5 billion into formula block grants to states, and $590 million to the emergency contingency fund. First implemented in 1982, LIHEAP helps pay the winter heating bills or summer cooling bills of low-income and elderly people.

Other Provisions

The Consolidated Appropriations Act halts a congressional moratorium on offshore oil exploration. The ban, which Congress first implemented in 1981, prohibits drilling within 200 miles of coastal states' shorelines. While the refusal of Congress to continue the moratorium signals a temporary end to the oil drilling debate in Congress, lawmakers from both parties acknowledge that there may be a need to clarify the nation's oil-drilling policies.

The legislation also includes funding for the transition to the new presidential administration.

Early in the next session, the 111th Congress will be tasked with addressing funding for the remaining fiscal year for the nine appropriations acts currently funded through March 2009.

FINANCE: THE EMERGENCY ECONOMIC STABILIZATION ACT OF 2008

The meltdown of the financial market escalated in September 2008 when several events—including the federal takeover of Fannie Mae and Freddie Mac, the bankruptcy of Lehman Brothers, an emergency Federal Reserve loan to the American International Group, and the merger of Merrill Lynch into Bank of America—signaled a growing crisis for the U.S. economy. Although there have been other financial crises in the past, the United States had not experienced one of this magnitude since the Great Depression. Some financial analysts said that this was simply the latest in a series of financial crises demonstrating that the U.S. economy was in trouble.

Treasury Secretary Henry Paulson introduced a measure that involved the government acquiring or insuring as much as $700 billion of troubled mortgage-backed securities with the goal of reducing the level of uncertainty regarding these assets and restoring confidence in the credit markets. The plan was immediately backed by President Bush, and negotiations began with congressional leaders to draft appropriate legislation. In testimony before Congress, Paulson explained that the legislation was needed to "avoid a continuing series of financial institution failures and frozen credit markets that threaten American families' financial well-being, the viability of businesses both small and large, and the very health of our economy."[6]

Lawmakers and the White House concurred that immediate relief was needed to restore consumer confidence; President Bush "lobbied furiously for the measure," which he believed was critical to economic recovery because "increasingly tight credit is not only stopping small business expansion, but in some respects is threatening the very ability of small businesses to exist."[7] Meanwhile, free-market advocates questioned the wisdom of bailing out the financial market, arguing that it should be allowed to run its course. Thus, a number of provisions were added to sweeten the deal for nay-sayers. Help for rural schools was aimed mainly at lawmakers in the West, for instance; disaster aid was included to appease lawmakers from disaster-stricken states in the Midwest and South; and the deductibility of state and local taxes for people in states without income taxes (including Florida and Texas) was extended.

The Emergency Economic Stabilization Act (EESA) of 2008 (P.L. 110-343) was passed on October 3, authorizing Secretary Paulson to spend up to $700 billion to purchase mortgage-backed securities and bail out financially distressed banks and other financial institutions. But the stock market continued to spiral downward. Sluggish sales over the fall and into the 2008 holiday season demonstrated that it may

take a long time for consumer confidence to be restored.

The financial bailout bill included several provisions that were among the priorities of NACo and other state and local government organizations. For instance, the Secure Rural Schools program was extended through 2011, and full funding for the Payment in Lieu of Taxes Program (PILT) was authorized through 2012.

Secure Rural Schools

The Secure Rural Schools and Community Self-Determination Act (SRS; P.L. 106-393) first became law in 2000 to address declining revenues from the timber harvest on federal lands. Many rural counties had relied on a share of receipts from timber harvests to supplement local funding for school systems and roads. Also known as the Payment to States Act, the SRS fundamentally changed the way the U.S. Forest Service returns a portion of its annual receipts to jurisdictions falling within national forest boundaries. The purpose of the act is to stabilize payments to counties that help support roads and schools, provide projects that enhance forest ecosystem health, and provide employment opportunities; and to improve cooperative relationships among federal land management agencies and local governments. Since 2000, SRS funds have been used to support more than 4,400 rural schools and to help maintain county roads.

SRS authorization ended on September 30, 2006, and President Bush proposed to phase out the Secure Rural Schools program in lieu of the sale of 300,000 acres of national forestland. Amid the contentious debates that followed, Congress ignored reauthorization legislation in favor of a one-year extension of the program. Proponents of SRS tacked on the reauthorization bill as an amendment to several other bills and finally secured its passage as an amendment to the EESA. The law reauthorizes the SRS through 2011.

With notable exceptions, the amended SRS act is similar to the original law. As with the 2000 authorization, counties will have to elect the kind of payment they will receive. The 2008 law establishes a new formula for calculation of state payments that is based on several factors, including acreage of federal land, previous payments, and per capita personal income. Calculations of each year's state payments are based on a "full funding amount" that will ramp down each succeeding year through 2011.

PILT

Like the SRS, the Payments in Lieu of Taxes (PILT) program is intended to help support rural counties with federal land. Since 1978, the program has helped to reimburse localities for the costs of providing services for a national park, wildlife refuge, or other federal lands. In recent years, PILT funding has been appropriated on a level less than authorized, and counties have made full funding of PILT a priority. Actions taken at the end of the 110th Congress achieved this goal: the EESA provides full mandatory funding for PILT through FY 2012. This represents a 65% increase (of $139 million) over FY 2008 levels.

Tax Extenders and Alternative Minimum Tax Relief Act

Incorporated into the EESA was the Tax Extenders and Alternative Minimum Tax Relief Act (S. 2), which includes $100 billion in tax breaks for businesses and the middle class. For over a year, businesses and industry groups had lobbied Congress to reauthorize dozens of expiring tax credits that they argued would provide both tax relief and job creation during a period of economic turmoil. The highlight of the tax package is a one-year "patch" that prevents the alternative minimum tax (AMT) from affecting 22 million Americans. This will cost an estimated $76.7 billion in fiscal year FY 2009, but it is expected to raise nearly $15 billion the following year for a net budget impact of $61.8 billion. In addition to the AMT fix, the tax package reauthorizes dozens of expired and expiring tax credits totaling more than $48 billion over 10 years.

The EESA includes two other tax provisions of particular interest to local governments: (1) a two-year extension of the optional deduction of state and local sales taxes on federal returns and (2) an option for homeowners who do not itemize federal income tax deductions to take a standard deduction for state and local property taxes.

Energy Improvement and Extension Act

After weeks of contentious negotiations, the Energy Improvement and Extension Act was passed on October 3 as part of the EESA. The main purpose of the act is to provide incentives for energy production and conservation. The bill extends production tax credits that were set to expire at the end of 2008 and expands federal energy tax incentives. In total, the legislation includes $17 billion in energy-related tax incentives, which are offset by freezing a scheduled tax deduction for certain profits deriving from oil and natural gas sales and exchange.

The new law extends the duration of the production tax credit for wind projects and provides an eight-year extension of investment tax credits for commercial and residential solar energy, fuel cell, and microturbine projects. It also provides a two-year extension of the production tax credit for biomass and other renewable fuel sources. Energy resources that qualify include closed-loop biomass (organic material from a plant that is grown exclusively to produce electricity), open-loop biomass (solid, nonhazardous, cellulosic waste material; lignin material; or agricultural livestock waste nutrients), geothermal energy, solar energy, small irrigation power, municipal solid waste, qualified hydropower production, and hydrokinetic energy.

The legislation increases the credit amounts for fuel cells; establishes new credits for small wind-energy, geothermal, and combined heat and power; extends eligibility of credits to public utilities; and allows taxpayers to take the credit against the alternative minimum tax.

The bill also extends incentives for energy efficiency. Tax credits for builders of new energy-efficient homes have been extended through 2009, and tax deductions for owners and designers of energy-efficient commercial buildings were extended through 2013. Additionally, some

residential energy-efficiency tax credits that had expired at the end of 2007 have been reinstated; energy-efficient home improvements that quality for these credits include windows, doors, roofs, insulation, HVAC, and non-solar water heaters. However, improvements made during 2008 are not eligible for a tax credit.

FAILED LEGISLATION

Several other pieces of legislation that Congress considered failed to make it to the floor. Of particular interest to local governments was a bill introduced by Rep. Barney Frank (D-Mass.) intended "to ensure uniform and accurate credit rating of municipal bonds and provide for a review of the municipal bond insurance industry." Among the provisions of the Municipal Bond Fairness Act (H.R. 6308) was a requirement for rating agencies to use the same rating scale for municipal and corporate bonds. Rating agencies often rate municipal bonds lower than corporate bonds, which increases the interest rates and costs of debt for issuers. The House Financial Services Committee approved the bill on July 30, but it failed to reach the floor for debate. Rep. Richard Neal (D-Mass.), a cosponsor of the bill, vowed to make the bill a priority in the next session.

Collective bargaining legislation also captured the attention of local government lobbyists. For almost a decade, Congress has threatened to pass legislation addressing collective bargaining rights for public safety employees. In the 110th session, both houses introduced the Public Safety Employer-Employee Cooperation Act (H.R. 980/S. 2123), which would have established minimum standards for state collective bargaining laws for public safety officers employed by state or local governments. The bill was intended to ensure the right of public safety employees to join a union and have the union recognized by the employer; the right of public safety officers to negotiate wages, hours, and working conditions; a dispute resolution mechanism; and the enforcement of contracts through state courts.

Thirty-five states currently have collective bargaining laws in place. Lobbying organizations for state and local governments—including NACo, the National League of Cities, the International Association of Chiefs of Police, National Sheriffs' Association, and the International Public Management Association for Human Resources—fought the bill on the premise that it preempted the power of states and localities to decide the nature and extent of collective bargaining rights.

The legislation passed the House of Representatives on July 17, 2007, by a vote of 314–97. The Senate began consideration of the bill during the week of May 12, 2008, but temporarily suspended debate on May 15. It vowed to take up the issue again when the 111th session of Congress convenes in 2009.

LOOKING TO THE FUTURE

The constitutional transfer of power and authority from an incumbent American president to a successor is a momentous occasion in American government. It is also a complex and multifaceted undertaking, as the outgoing administration concludes its affairs and the incoming administration gets organized. As the nation looks to its new leadership and a new direction, local governments are hoping to address some of the short- and long-term issues plaguing them. Among their concerns are forging a stronger intergovernmental cooperative relationship that avoids unfunded mandates and preemptive strikes on local and state authority.

One of the issues that Congress is certain to deal with is the economy. At the outset of 2009, Congress and the new Obama administration are expected to introduce economic recovery plans to help create jobs and restore economic stability. The federal government's approach to the collapse in America's housing market will likely have long-reaching repercussions for local governments.

In addition, the 111th Congress will have to face issues related to the war in Iraq and continued threats to homeland security. As local governments play a critical role in protecting the nation's citizens, they will watch closely to ensure that legislation strengthens intergovernmental partnerships and supports an "all-hazard" approach to public safety.

Congress also may take a new look at health care reform, including how to meet the needs of an estimated 46 million Americans who are uninsured, as well as of the families and children who have been affected by the slowing of the economy. Legislators are also expected to introduce major legislation on climate change, incorporating programs that will encourage energy efficiency, alternative energy, and environmental protection.

[1]U.S. Congress, House of Representatives, *Energy Independence and Security Act of 2007*, 110th Cong., 1st sess., 2007, H.R. 6, atvmloan.energy.gov/hr6.pdf (accessed January 13, 2009).

[2]The White House, "Farm Bill Veto Message," press release, May 21, 2008, whitehouse.gov/news/releases/2008/05/20080521-4.html (accessed January 14, 2009).

[3]Jonathan Weisman and Dan Morgan, "House Overrides Veto of Farm Bill," *Washington Post*, May 22, 2008, A01, washingtonpost.com/wp-dyn/content/article/2008/05/21/AR2008052101313.html (accessed January 14, 2009).

[4]Daria Daniel, "Bush Signs Housing Stimulus Package," National Association of Counties, n.d., naco.org/Template.cfm?Section=housing&template=/ContentManagement/ContentDisplay.cfm&ContentID=28324 (accessed January 14, 2009).

[5]Robert Keith, *Consolidated Appropriations Act for FY2009 (P.L. 110-329): An Overview*, CRS Report RL 34711 (Washington, D.C.: Congressional Research Service, November 3, 2008), CRS-11, assets.opencrs.com/rpts/RL34711_20081103.pdf (accessed January 13, 2009).

[6]U.S. Department of the Treasury, "Testimony by Secretary Henry M. Paulson, Jr. before the Senate Banking Committee on Turmoil in US Credit Markets: Recent Actions regarding Government Sponsored Entities, Investment Banks and Other Financial Institutions," press release, September 23, 2008, treas.gov/press/releases/hp1153.htm (accessed January 14, 2009).

[7]Charles Babington and Julie Hirschfeld Davis, "Bush: Lawmakers 'Must Listen' Vote Yes," Associated Press, October 2, 2008, azstarnet.com/sn/byauthor/260442 (accessed January 14, 2009).

B 3

Recent Supreme Court Cases Affecting Local Government

Shea Riggsbee Denning, Robert P. Joyce,
James M. Markham, Christopher B. McLaughlin,
and Jeffrey B. Welty
School of Government
University of North Carolina at Chapel Hill

Selected Findings

In a significant departure from its earlier Second Amendment jurisprudence, the Supreme Court held that the amendment protects an individual's right to possess and carry weapons, and that the District of Columbia's de facto ban on handguns was therefore unconstitutional.

An at-will public employee who was arbitrarily dismissed does not have a valid claim under the equal protection clause; however, employers—including local governments—have an increased burden in defending age discrimination claims brought under the theory of disparate impact.

The 2007–2008 term of the U.S. Supreme Court was notable for several opinions affecting local government. Among the matters addressed by the Court were the regulation of firearms, the right to counsel, search and seizure, the constitutionality of lethal injection, capital punishment, voting rights, elections law, campaign finance, disparate-impact claims, and taxation.

REGULATION OF FIREARMS

The Second Amendment protects an individual's right to possess a firearm unconnected with service in a militia. Although the right is not unlimited, a law that completely bans a jurisdiction's residents from possessing handguns is unconstitutional.

The District of Columbia prohibited residents from carrying handguns and required residents to keep all firearms, including long guns, unloaded and disassembled or bound by a trigger lock. In *District of Columbia v. Heller* (554 U.S. __, 128 S.Ct. 2783 [2008]), Dick Heller, a law enforcement officer authorized to carry a gun while on duty, challenged these mandates under the Second Amendment. He contended that they constituted a de facto handgun ban and that such a ban was unconstitutional.

The Second Amendment provides as follows: "A well regulated Militia, being necessary to the security of a free State, the right of the people to keep and bear Arms, shall not be infringed." The District of Columbia argued that the amendment protects only the right to bear arms in connection with service in a militia, and that its ban on the carrying of handguns for private purposes, such as self-defense, was therefore consistent with the amendment. In support of its argument, the District pointed to *United States v. Miller* (307 U.S. 174 [1939]), in which the U.S. Supreme Court upheld, against a Second Amendment challenge, a federal law prohibiting the possession of short-barreled shotguns. In *Miller,* the Court stated that the purpose of the Second Amendment was "to assure the continuation and render possible the effectiveness of" the militia, and that the amendment "must be interpreted and applied with that end in view." Because there was no "evidence tending to show that possession or use of a [sawed-off shotgun] . . . has some reasonable relationship to the preservation or efficiency of a well regulated militia," the ban on such weapons was held to be consistent with the Second Amendment.

The Supreme Court, in an opinion written by Justice Scalia, rejected the District's argument, holding that the Second Amendment's reference to a militia is merely a "prefatory clause" that does not limit the scope of the right guaranteed by the "operative clause" of the amendment. And the operative clause, the Court held, protects an individual's right to possess and carry weapons, apart from any service in a militia or similar organization. The Court reached this conclusion after a lengthy examination of the following: (1) the text of the amendment; (2) the way in which the key terms were used at the time the amendment was adopted; (3) the historical context in which the amendment was drafted; and (4) the opinions of legal scholars writing just after the ratification of the Constitution, virtually all of whom apparently viewed the Second Amendment as providing for an individual's right to bear arms.

The Court recognized several limitations on the right, however. First, it is limited to types of weapons typically possessed by law-abiding citizens for lawful purposes. The sawed-off shotguns at issue in *Miller,* therefore, may still be banned, as may machine guns and other weapons not typically owned by law-abiding citizens. Furthermore, the Court noted that certain persons, such as felons and people who are mentally ill, may properly be barred from owning weapons. Likewise, certain places, such as government buildings, may be declared off-limits to those carrying firearms.

Because none of these exceptions applied to Heller, the Court concluded that the District of Columbia improperly precluded him from carrying a handgun in his home for self-defense. It likewise held that the District's requirement that all firearms be kept disassembled or equipped with a trigger lock was unconstitutional, in that it effectively precluded Heller from using a firearm for the constitutionally protected purpose of self-defense.

Significantly, the Court did not strike down the District's annual licensing scheme, although the lower court had done so. Instead, based on Heller's representation that he did not object to the licensing requirement, the Court simply instructed the District to issue Heller a license for a handgun if he met all the usual criteria for licensing. By identifying exceptions to the right to bear arms and by declining to invalidate the District's licensing requirement, the Court indicated that municipalities have some latitude in regulating the possession of firearms. Exactly how much latitude will likely be determined by the future litigation that *Heller* will undoubtedly engender.

RIGHT TO COUNSEL

A defendant's Sixth Amendment right to counsel attaches at his initial appearance before a judicial official. Such an appearance marks the beginning of adversary judicial proceedings, regardless of whether a prosecutor is present for, or even aware of, the appearance.

Texas police wrongly believed that Walter Rothgery had a felony conviction. Partly on the basis of this erroneous belief, the police arrested Rothgery and charged him with being a felon in possession of a firearm. Pursuant to Texas procedure, the police brought Rothgery before a magistrate, who found probable cause to support the arrest, advised Rothgery of the charges against him, and set bond. Shortly thereafter, Rothgery posted bond and was released. Both at the proceeding before the magistrate and afterwards, Rothgery apparently requested that counsel be appointed to represent him, but local policy dictated that no lawyer be appointed unless and until an information (a charging document signed by a prosecutor rather than a grand jury) was filed or an indictment returned.

Thus, Rothgery remained unrepresented for several months until an indictment was returned against him. He was then re-arrested; his bond was increased to an amount he could not post;

and he was jailed. Because an indictment had been issued, a lawyer was appointed, and the lawyer assembled the paperwork showing that Rothgery had no felony convictions. The charges were dismissed, but not before Rothgery had spent three weeks in jail. Pursuant to 42 U.S.C. §1983, Rothgery sued the county where he had been charged, alleging that he had been deprived of his Sixth Amendment right to counsel when his requests for a lawyer at and after his initial appearance before the magistrate went unheeded, and that as a result of the county's refusal to appoint a lawyer, he had spent three needless weeks in jail.

The Sixth Amendment guarantees defendants the right to the assistance of counsel in "all criminal prosecutions." But because it applies only to "prosecutions"—and not, for example, to investigations—the right does not attach until "the initiation of adversary judicial . . . proceedings" (*Kirby v. Illinois,* 406 U.S. 682, 689 [1972]). Responding to Rothgery's lawsuit, the county argued that such proceedings did not begin until a prosecutor was involved in, or at least aware of, the charges against a defendant. Because no prosecutor was involved in Rothgery's initial appearance before the magistrate, Rothgery's Sixth Amendment rights had not yet attached and therefore could not have been violated. The trial court agreed and granted summary judgment in favor of the county; the intermediate appellate court affirmed.

The U.S. Supreme Court granted review on the issue of when the Sixth Amendment right to counsel attaches, and in *Rothgery v. Gillespie County* (542 U.S. __, 128 S.Ct. 2578 [2008]) it reversed the lower courts. The Court pointed to two earlier decisions—*Michigan v. Jackson* (475 U.S. 625 [1986]) and *Brewer v. Williams* (430 U.S. 387 [1977])—as evidence that "the right to counsel attaches at the initial appearance before a judicial officer." Although the earlier decisions involved somewhat different facts, the Court held that the reasoning in those opinions was applicable to Rothgery's case. Specifically, the earlier cases had found that by the time a defendant has been arrested and brought before a judicial official, he is embroiled in the complexities of the criminal justice system, is facing a deprivation of his liberty, and is in an adversary relationship with the state. In *Rothgery,* the Court observed that all of these things are true even if the defendant has not yet been indicted—and indeed, even if no prosecutor is aware of the proceedings. Furthermore, the Court noted, the federal government and almost all states take steps toward appointing counsel at or just after the initial appearance, suggesting a near consensus that the right to counsel should attach at that point.

The Court therefore determined that adversary judicial proceedings had commenced when Rothgery was brought before the magistrate, and that his Sixth Amendment right to counsel had attached at that time. It remanded the case for further proceedings, having undercut the lower courts' basis for ruling against Rothgery.

It is important to note that the Court did not hold that Rothgery had been deprived of his Sixth Amendment rights. A defendant is not necessarily

entitled to a lawyer as soon as his Sixth Amendment right to counsel attaches. Rather, according to the Court's precedents, he is entitled to a lawyer only after the right to counsel has attached and he is confronted with a "critical stage" of the case, such as trial, a pretrial interrogation by police, or some other proceeding that is of crucial importance to the case (see, e.g., *United States v. Wade,* 388 U.S. 218, 224 [1967]). An initial appearance is not a critical stage (see *Gerstein v. Pugh,* 420 U.S. 103 [1975]), so the fact that Rothgery was not represented before the magistrate does not mean that his Sixth Amendment rights were violated.

Rothgery had argued that his rights were violated by the county's failure to appoint counsel during the six months between his initial appearance and the return of the indictment. The lower courts never addressed this issue, and it was not before the Court. However, the majority opinion, by Justice Souter, suggested some sympathy for Rothgery's position when it stated that "counsel must be appointed within a reasonable time after attachment to allow for adequate representation at any critical stage before trial, as well as at trial itself." Justice Alito's concurring opinion evinced a different view: "It does not follow, and I do not understand the Court to hold, that the county had an obligation to appoint an attorney to represent petitioner within some specified period after [his appearance before the magistrate]." If the majority was, in fact, signaling that the Sixth Amendment requires the appointment of counsel shortly after the initial appearance, regardless of whether a critical stage is imminent, there will likely be a successor case to *Rothgery* addressing the issue more clearly.

Rothgery has at least one immediate consequence for law enforcement officers. In many jurisdictions, courts had previously ruled that the Sixth Amendment right to counsel did not attach at the initial appearance before a magistrate. Thus, if a defendant was taken before a magistrate and released on bond, officers could approach the defendant before his next court appearance and question him without warning him of his right to counsel: *Miranda* warnings were not required because the defendant was not in custody, and Sixth Amendment warnings were not required because the Sixth Amendment right to counsel had not yet attached. *Rothgery* makes clear that the Sixth Amendment right to counsel attaches at the initial appearance before a magistrate; because interrogation by the police is a critical stage, officers must therefore advise a defendant of his Sixth Amendment rights and obtain a waiver before questioning the defendant. Whether *Rothgery* will have implications beyond this investigative context remains to be seen.

SEARCH AND SEIZURE

A police officer may arrest a suspect if the officer has probable cause to believe that the suspect has committed a criminal offense. Even if the arrest violates state law—because the state requires the issuance of a citation for the offense in question—the arrest is not unreasonable under the Fourth Amendment.

Two police officers employed by a Virginia municipality stopped a car driven by David Moore because of doubts about the validity of his driver's license. After confirming their suspicions, the officers arrested Moore for the misdemeanor offense of driving on a suspended license—notwithstanding a Virginia statute that, with several exceptions not relevant in Moore's case, prohibits officers from arresting suspects for that offense and instead requires them to issue citations. The officers then conducted a search incident to arrest, and found that Moore was in possession of crack cocaine and a substantial amount of cash.

Prior to his trial on drug charges, Moore moved to suppress the results of the search, arguing that since the arrest was in violation of Virginia law, the search was the result of an unreasonable arrest—and therefore violated the Fourth Amendment's prohibition against unreasonable searches and seizures. The trial court denied Moore's motion, holding that an arrest made in violation of state law is not necessarily unreasonable under the Fourth Amendment. Moore was convicted, and he appealed. The state supreme court eventually ruled in Moore's favor.

The U.S. Supreme Court granted review, and in *Virginia v. Moore* (__ U.S. __ , 128 S.Ct. 1598 [2008]), it reversed the state supreme court. In an opinion written by Justice Scalia, the Court observed that as a general matter, an arrest is reasonable under the Fourth Amendment "when an officer has probable cause to believe a person committed even a minor crime in his presence." Arresting a suspect ensures that the suspect ceases his criminal activity and helps to guarantee that he will appear in court to answer criminal charges. Thus, unless the Fourth Amendment incorporates the statutory law of arrest into its reasonableness standard, the officers' arrest of Moore was reasonable. The Court held that the amendment does not incorporate the statutory law of arrest.

First, the Court examined the history of the Fourth Amendment, and found no evidence that the Framers intended for the scope of the amendment to incorporate the statutory law of arrest. If anything, the Court observed, the amendment was intended as a guarantee of rights separate and apart from whatever rights the legislative and executive branches of government saw fit to recognize.

Second, the Court pointed to several of its own decisions that suggested that Fourth Amendment reasonableness must be determined without reference to state search and seizure laws. Among these cases were *California v. Greenwood* (486 U.S. 35 [1988]), in which the Court held that a search of a suspect's garbage did not violate the Fourth Amendment even though it violated the California Constitution, and *Whren v. United States* (517 U.S. 806 [1996]), in which the Court upheld a traffic stop under the Fourth Amendment even though it violated regulations governing the conduct of plainclothes police officers.

Third, the Court noted that incorporating the statutory law of arrest into the Fourth Amendment would cause the scope of the amendment to vary from jurisdiction to jurisdiction because different states have different rules regarding arrests; the scope of the amendment would also vary from

officer to officer because a federal officer operating in, say, Virginia would not be subject to the state laws that would bind a state officer. This would make the amendment difficult for officers to apply in practice, and it would undermine the Court's efforts to establish simple, bright-line rules for officers to follow.

Of course, *Moore* does not mean that an officer may freely ignore the statutory law of arrest in his or her jurisdiction. Depending on the jurisdiction, an arrest that violates statutory law may still result in the suppression of evidence, or it may open the door to civil liability for the officer or to other problems. Thus, no matter how simple and bright-line the Fourth Amendment's rules may be under *Moore,* officers still need to understand the intricacies of the statutory law of arrest.

CONSTITUTIONALITY OF LETHAL INJECTION

Kentucky's lethal injection procedures do not violate the Eighth Amendment's prohibition against cruel and unusual punishment.

Two death row inmates, both convicted of double homicides, challenged the three-drug lethal injection protocol used to put inmates to death in Kentucky. Under that state's procedure, the first drug administered is a barbiturate (sodium thiopental, also known as Pentathol) that renders the inmate unconscious. The second drug (pancuronium bromide, also known as Pavulon) causes paralysis, and the third drug, potassium chloride, stops the heart. The inmates acknowledged that this procedure, if applied as intended, would result in a humane death, but they cited medical evidence that improper administration of the first drug would make injection of the other drugs severely painful. The inmates argued that the mere risk that the procedure would not be followed properly ran afoul of the Eighth Amendment's ban on cruel and unusual punishment. The U.S. Supreme Court disagreed, holding that the "risk of pain from maladministration of a concededly humane lethal injection protocol" did not violate the Constitution when there was "no substantial risk of severe pain," and as long as no alternative procedure has been identified that is "feasible, readily implemented, and in fact significantly reduce[s] a substantial risk of severe pain" (*Baze v. Rees,* 128 S.Ct. 1250 [2008]).

The inmates rested much of their case on an argument that they had identified a one-drug protocol that would reduce the risk of harm inherent in the three-drug procedure. The Court rejected this approach, declining to turn the courts into "boards of inquiry charged with determining 'best practices' for executions." Writing for a plurality, Chief Justice Roberts confirmed that the relevant inquiry is not, as the petitioners argued, whether a method of execution poses an "unnecessary risk," but whether it presents a "substantial risk of serious harm"—a risk that is "sure or very likely to cause serious illness and needless suffering" and that is deemed "objectively intolerable." As to the last point, the Court found it difficult to regard lethal injection as "objectively intolerable" when thirty-six states and the federal government use the specific three-drug combination used by Kentucky.

The rule from *Baze* is straightforward enough; the 97-page opinion, however, is not. The chief justice's opinion was joined in full by only two justices, Kennedy and Alito. Justice Alito filed a concurring opinion in which no other justice joined. Justices Stevens, Scalia, Thomas, and Breyer concurred in the judgment, but each wrote separately to express one concern or another. Justice Ginsburg dissented, joined by Justice Souter. Only Justices Souter and Kennedy chose not to write separately at all. Justice Ginsburg's dissent argued that Kentucky's protocol lacked basic safeguards used by other states to confirm that the first drug is working before the second and third drugs are administered. The dissenters would thus have remanded the case with instructions for the lower court to consider whether the omission of those safeguards poses a substantial—and readily avoidable—risk of severe and unnecessary pain.

The sharpest conflict between the justices was not, however, between the plurality and the dissent, but between Justices Stevens and Scalia. In his concurrence, Justice Stevens joined the plurality in deference to the Court's prior Eighth Amendment case law, but for the first time he stated his personal conclusion that the death penalty represents the "pointless and needless extinction of life with only marginal contributions to any discernible social or public purposes." Justice Scalia criticized this conclusion in his own concurrence, calling it "insupportable as an interpretation of the Constitution . . . the very text of [which] recognizes that the death penalty is a permissible legislative choice."

Although the Court's decision in *Baze* upheld the most commonly used method of execution and ended a six-month de facto moratorium on the death penalty, the divisions in the Court leave the states guessing about how to avoid litigation over execution methods, and ensure that the debate about capital punishment will go on unabated.

CAPITAL PUNISHMENT FOR CHILD RAPE

The Eighth Amendment bars Louisiana from imposing the death penalty for the rape of a child where the crime did not result, and was not intended to result, in the victim's death.

Patrick Kennedy was convicted of the rape of his eight-year-old stepdaughter. Under Louisiana law, capital punishment was authorized for the rape of a child under 12 years of age. Kennedy was sentenced to death. The Supreme Court of Louisiana affirmed the sentence, rejecting the defendant's argument that *Coker v. Georgia* (433 U.S. 584 [1977]) barred the death penalty for rape. The state high court said that *Coker* involved capital punishment for the rape of an adult, not a child. Acknowledging that Louisiana would be in the minority of jurisdictions that authorize the death penalty for child rape, the court determined the crime to be deserving of death.

The U.S. Supreme Court disagreed, ruling that capital punishment for child rape is unconstitutional under the Eighth Amendment (*Kennedy v. Louisiana,* 128 S.Ct. 2641 [2008]). Justice Kennedy wrote for a bare five-justice majority (made up of the liberal-leaning justices—Kennedy, Breyer, Ginsburg, Souter, and Stevens) in reversing the sentence. After walking through the history of capital punishment in America from 1925 to the present, the Court determined that in light of the "evolving standards of decency that mark the progress of a maturing society," the death penalty was disproportionate, and therefore unconstitutional, for child rape where the crime did not result, and was not intended to result, in the victim's death.

The crux of the Court's reasoning amounted, in large part, to nose-counting. How many jurisdictions allow death for child rape? Six. Forty-four states, meanwhile, have not made child rape a capital offense. Thus, under the approach used recently in *Atkins v. Virginia* (536 U.S. 304 [2002]) and *Roper v. Simmons* (543 U.S. 551 [2005]) to outlaw capital punishment for people who are mentally retarded and for defendants under 18 years of age at the time of their crime, respectively, the Court found a "national consensus" against the death penalty for child rape. The Court also applied "its own judgment" to determine that in most cases, the death penalty in child-rape cases is not in the best interests of the victims or of society at large.

Through a dissent authored by Justice Alito, the conservative justices—Chief Justice Roberts and Justices Alito, Scalia, and Thomas—disagreed. The dissent argued that many states have hesitated to enact capital punishment for child rape only because of a misreading of *Coker,* and that the majority's opinion therefore overstated the existence of a national consensus. If anything, the dissent pointed out, the national trend favors capital punishment for child rape: six states have enacted such laws since 1977—five in the past "few years." Justice Alito also expressed frustration with the Court's having injected "its own judgment" about the best interests of victims and society into what ought to be a legislative debate.

Shortly after the *Kennedy* decision was handed down, it came to light that in 2006, Congress and the president had updated the Uniform Code of Military Justice to authorize the death penalty for child rape. Given the Court's methodology in discerning a national consensus, failure to take account of this change was an embarrassing oversight. Nevertheless, only two Justices (Alito and Thomas) voted in favor of a motion to rehear the case in light of the error, and so the decision stands.

Alongside *Atkins* and *Roper, Kennedy* offers another bright line in the Court's otherwise murky death penalty jurisprudence. Although the Court continues to limit the states' discretion to apply capital punishment, it also makes clear—through its practice of polling state law to discern a consensus—that state legislatures will determine the future of the death penalty.

PHOTO IDENTIFICATION
AND VOTING RIGHTS

A state may require voters to show photo identification at the polls.

In 2007, Indiana enacted a law requiring in-person voters at primaries and general elections to show photo identification at the polls. A voter who lacked photo identification because of indigency or religious objection to being photographed could fill out a provisional ballot, which would be counted if the voter executed an affidavit before the circuit court clerk within 10 days. Similarly, a voter who had photo identification but was unable to produce it at the polls could fill out a provisional ballot that would be counted if the voter brought the photo identification to the clerk within 10 days. No photo identification was required for by-mail absentee voting. The state, through the motor vehicle bureau, would provide free photo identification cards to residents who did not have driver's licenses.

A number of plaintiffs, including the Indiana Democratic Party, joined together to file a lawsuit challenging the new law, arguing that the photo identification requirement arbitrarily disenfranchised qualified voters and placed an unjustified burden on those who could not readily obtain such identification.

In *Crawford v. Marion County Election Board* (128 S.Ct. 1610 [2008]), the U.S. Supreme Court held that the Indiana law does not violate any constitutional provision. According to the best available estimates, about 43,000 Indiana citizens of voting age do not have photo identification cards—about 1% of the voting-age population. While the requirement might put minor restrictions on the ability of a small number of voters to vote, those restrictions can be overcome, and they are justified by the state's interest in avoiding voter fraud (especially given the large number of names on Indiana's voter rolls of persons who either are deceased or no longer live in Indiana) and preserving public confidence in the voting process. These interests, coupled with the availability of provisional ballots and free photo identification cards, tilt the balance in the state's favor. As a result of this decision, states that impose photo identification requirements for voting may continue to enforce them, and states that have not imposed them may now do so if they choose.

DEFINING "FORCE AND EFFECT"
UNDER THE VOTING RIGHTS ACT

Under Section 5 of the Voting Rights Act of 1965, changes in elections law may require the approval of the U.S. Department of Justice. It is not always easy to determine, however, whether approval must be sought for a particular change.

Section 5 of the Voting Rights Act of 1965 does not apply everywhere in the country: it applies to a few states in their entirety, to parts of other states, and to some states not at all. Where it does apply, it requires that any change in any elections law must receive "preclearance" from the U.S. Department of Justice (or, much less frequently, from the federal district court in the District of Columbia) before it can go into effect. If the Justice Department objects to the change, the change is not precleared and cannot go into effect. Preclearance is required for any change in any elections law that (1) has itself has been precleared and (2) has actually been put into force or effect (or that has never been changed since the Voting Rights Act was enacted).

Alabama, a state covered in its entirety by Section 5, faced a complicated situation regarding the method of filling vacancies on the Mobile County Commission. When the Voting Rights Act was enacted, Alabama state law required that midterm vacancies on county boards of commissioners were to be filled through appointment by the governor. In 1985, the legislature passed a local law providing that such vacancies in Mobile County were to be filled by special election. That law, which constituted a change in the elections law, was submitted for preclearance and was precleared.

In 1987, a vacancy occurred, and a special election was scheduled in accordance with the new law. A lawsuit challenging the new law was filed—and, later that same year, after the election had already been held, the Alabama Supreme Court ruled that the 1985 law violated the Alabama constitution. In effect, the state supreme court ruling reinstated the original law, which called for an appointment by the governor. The court's decision was not submitted for preclearance.

In 2004, the Alabama legislature enacted a new law specifying that vacancies were to be filled through appointment by the governor unless a local law was in effect that called for special elections. The 2004 act was precleared. Did it revive the 1985 Mobile County law? When a vacancy again occurred in the Mobile County Commission, the following question arose: was there to be a special election under the 1985 law or a governor's appointment under the general law?

In a lawsuit brought to answer that question, the state supreme court ruled in 2005 that the 2004 act did not revive the 1985 law, so appointment by the governor was still the rule for Mobile County. The 2005 supreme court ruling was not submitted for preclearance. In accordance with the 2005 ruling, the governor filled the vacancy by appointment.

But then a new lawsuit was brought, this time under Section 5 of the Voting Rights Act. Since neither the 1987 nor the 2005 state supreme court decisions had been precleared, the lawsuit asserted, neither could be given effect. The last change in the law that had been precleared was the 1985 act calling for special elections.

The federal judges presiding over that lawsuit gave the state defendants time to submit the two supreme court rulings for preclearance. (Retroactive preclearance is possible and would have made the lawsuit unnecessary.) The Justice Department, however, refused to grant preclearance. Did that then mean that the 1985 act—which had been found to be unconstitutional by the state supreme court but was the last precleared change directly on point—was the law, and that the recent vacancy should have been filled by special election? Yes, according to the federal judges. The matter was then appealed to the U.S. Supreme Court.

The question to be decided by the Supreme Court in *Riley v. Kennedy* (128 S.Ct. 1970 [2008]) was what it meant for a law to be put into *force and effect.* The Supreme Court noted that since the state court decisions had never been precleared, the law reverted to the most recent law that had been precleared and was in force or effect. The 1985 law had certainly been precleared, the Supreme Court said, but it had never been in force or effect. It was challenged at the earliest proper moment by a lawsuit and was struck down by the state supreme court in a proper proceeding. Even though an election had actually been held under it, it was never *in force or effect.* Therefore, the latest proper law in force and effect was the pre-Voting Rights Act law, which called for the governor's appointment.

As this case demonstrates, it is not always easy to determine what constitutes a change that must be precleared by the Justice Department under Section 5. The prudent course for units of government is to submit all changes: better safe than sued.

VOTING IN PRIMARY ELECTIONS

Washington State's nonpartisan blanket primary is constitutional.

All states conduct primary elections in which the voters select the candidates to face one another in the general election, but there are different kinds of primaries. In a closed primary, only voters who are affiliated with a particular party may vote in that party's primary, and the primary winners become the parties' nominees. In an open primary, voters who are not affiliated with a particular party may vote in that party's primary, but they must cast their primary votes only within that party, regardless of the office. Thus, for example, a Democrat who chooses to vote in the Republican primary for governor may vote only in the Republican primary for all other races in that election. In a blanket primary, any voter, regardless of party affiliation, may vote for any party's nominee in any race.

Until the decision in *California Democratic Party v. Jones* (530 U.S. 567) in 2000, California used a blanket primary: all candidates from all parties appeared together on one primary ballot, and any voter could vote for any candidate in any race. The highest vote-getter in each party became the nominee of that party and was awarded a place on the ballot in the general election. In the *Jones* decision, the U.S. Supreme Court ruled that this system was unconstitutional, holding that the parties have constitutional rights of freedom of association, and that the blanket system violated those rights by allowing voters not affiliated with a party to choose the party's nominees.

Washington State's system had been essentially the same as California's—but as a result of the *Jones* decision, Washington changed its system in 2004. Under the new system, all candidates appear on the primary ballot and choose their own party affiliation. The two top vote-getters,

irrespective of party, move on to the general election; thus, the general election could have two Democrats or two Republicans squaring off against one another. In essence, the California system struck down by the Supreme Court in 2000 was a partisan blanket primary, and the Washington system adopted in 2004 is a non-partisan blanket primary.

Several political parties challenged the new non-partisan blanket primary, on two principal grounds. First, the parties argued that the system, like the unconstitutional California system in *Jones,* took away their constitutional right to freedom of association, under which they would be permitted to choose their own nominees. Second, since candidates were permitted to choose their own party affiliation on the ballot, candidates with whom a party strongly disagreed could nonetheless appear on the ballot as if affiliated with that party, creating the possibility that a party would be associated with candidates whom it found repugnant and potentially leading to confusion among voters.

When the case reached the U.S. Supreme Court, the Court noted that election regulations that impose a severe burden on the right of association are unconstitutional unless they can withstand strict scrutiny; that is, they are constitutional only if they are narrowly tailored to serve a compelling governmental interest (*Washington State Grange v. Washington State Republican Party,* 128 S.Ct. 1184 [2008]). If regulations impose a burden that is *less than severe,* however, they are more likely to be constitutional than those that impose a severe burden. Rather than serving a "compelling governmental interest," they need only serve "important regulatory" interests.

So, does Washington's nonpartisan blanket primary impose a *severe* burden on the political parties' right to association or a *less than severe* burden? The Court held that the burden is less than severe because, unlike the voters in California, those in the nonpartisan Washington primary are not choosing the nominees of the parties. The two top vote-getters move on the general election without regard to party; they do not move on to the general election as party nominees. Further, any speculation that the voters will be confused by the candidates' self-identification by party is just that—speculation: "There is simply no basis to presume that a well-informed electorate will interpret a candidate's party-preference designation to mean that the candidate is the party's chosen nominee or representative or that the party associates with or approves of the candidate." Since the burden is less than severe, it need merely serve important regulatory interests, which it does.

CAMPAIGN FINANCE REGULATION

The "Millionaire's Amendment," which was designed to help candidates facing wealthy opponents, is an unconstitutional burden on the right to free speech.

More than 30 years ago, the U.S. Supreme Court, in *Buckley v. Valeo* (424 U.S. 1 [1976]), set the basic constitutional limitations on laws that regulate fund-raising and spending by candidates in political campaigns. In essence, the Court held in *Buckley* that in the name of fighting corruption and the appearance of corruption, the legislature may limit the amount that contributors may *give* to a candidate, but that the legislature may not limit the amount that a candidate may *spend* in getting his or her message out. Further, the Court held that because limits on how much the candidates themselves may contribute to and spend on their own campaigns would violate the candidates' First Amendment right to free speech, no such limits may be imposed.

In line with the *Buckley* decision and others that have followed it, Congress has imposed contribution limits on candidates for federal office. For example, no individual may contribute more than $2,300 in an election cycle to any candidate. In light of the unlimited right of candidates to finance their own campaigns, Congress included the so-called Millionaire's Amendment in the Bipartisan Campaign Finance Reform Act of 2002. Under that provision, if Candidate A has a self-funded opponent (i.e., "the millionaire") who spends more than $350,000 of personal funds on a campaign, certain restrictions on contribution limits for Candidate A are relaxed; for example, Candidate A may accept a contribution of up to $6,900 from any one individual—triple the regular limit of $2,300. The contribution restrictions for the self-funded candidate, however, remain unchanged.

A self-funded candidate for a seat in the U.S. House of Representatives sued to challenge the Millionaire's Amendment—arguing, under *Buckley,* that it acted as an unconstitutional burden on his right to free speech. The U.S. Supreme Court agreed, and struck down the Millionaire's Amendment (*Davis v. Federal Election Commission,* 128 S.Ct. 2759 [2008]). If the law had provided that the contribution limits for both candidates went up when the self-funded candidate contributed a certain amount of his or her own money, the Court said, there would be no constitutional problem. The problem arises because the contribution limits are increased for Candidate A but not for the self-funded candidate. Thus, the law compels the self-funded candidate to make a choice that is too difficult: limit the spending of his or her own funds, or face an opponent who has the advantage of relaxed contribution limits.

The Court rejected the argument that the difference in contribution limits is justified by a desire by Congress "to reduce the natural advantage that wealthy individuals possess in campaigns for federal office" or "to level electoral opportunities." According to the Court, such a desire is not a legitimate governmental objective. Different candidates have different advantages: some are wealthy; others are celebrities; still others have well-known family names. It is up to the voters to judge among these advantages; it is not up to Congress "to abrogate the voters' authority to evaluate the strengths of candidates competing for office." In this case, the Supreme Court has reinforced the basic constitutional principles that have governed campaign finance regulation since the *Buckley* decision: limitations on contributions may be constitutionally imposed, but limitations on spending may not.

AT-WILL EMPLOYMENT IN GOVERNMENT AGENCIES

A public employee whose dismissal was arbitrary does not have a valid claim under the equal protection clause.

May an at-will employee be dismissed by a public employer maliciously, on a whim, or with careless indifference to the truth of any allegations against the employee? Yes, according to the U.S. Supreme Court in *Engquist v. Oregon Department of Agriculture* (128 S.Ct. 2146): that is the nature of at-will employment.

Suppose one group of public employees is treated differently from another group: for example, city residents are given preference over nonresidents in hiring decisions. Courts have long held that in order to withstand a challenge under the equal protection clause of the Fourteenth Amendment to the U.S. Constitution, such differential treatment of groups of people must be at least rationally related to a legitimate governmental objective; that is, the difference must not be irrational or arbitrary. In recent years, the notion that governmental distinctions between *groups* must not be irrational or arbitrary has been extended by the courts—including the Supreme Court—to embrace distinctions between *individuals.* Where one resident was required to give a 33-foot easement to obtain city water service but all others were required to give only 15-foot easements, for example, and there was no rational reason related to a legitimate governmental objective for the difference, the Supreme Court held that the one resident had a valid equal protection claim, even though she did not assert that she was part of a group of individuals that were being treated differently (*Village of Willowbrook v. Olech,* 528 U.S. 562 [2000]). Someone pursuing such an equal protection claim is said to be using the "class of one" equal protection theory.

In the *Engquist* case, an employee who had been dismissed from a state agency claimed that the dismissal was arbitrary, vindictive, and malicious, and was not rationally related to any legitimate governmental objective. That is, she claimed that her dismissal violated the equal protection clause under the class-of-one theory.

The Supreme Court denied her claim. The Court said that to recognize a claim that the government treated an employee differently from others for a bad reason or for no reason at all—the class-of-one claim—would be "simply contrary to the concept of at-will employment. The Constitution does not require repudiating that familiar doctrine."

DISPARATE-IMPACT CLAIMS AND THE AGE DISCRIMINATION IN EMPLOYMENT ACT

An employer defending against an age discrimination claim made under the disparate-impact theory of unintentional discrimination must prove that its actions were reasonable.

Courts have long held that it is possible for an employer to violate Title VII of the Civil Rights

Act of 1964—that is, to discriminate unlawfully on the grounds of race, color, religion, sex, or national origin—even in the absence of an intent to discriminate. Under the disparate-impact theory of liability, even if an employer has no intent to discriminate, it can be found to have violated Title VII if its employment practices have an adverse affect on a group that is identifiable by race, sex, color, religion, or national origin.

In 2005, the U.S. Supreme Court ruled in *Smith v. City of Jackson* (544 U.S. 228 [2005]) that the disparate-impact theory was *also* available to plaintiffs claiming unlawful age discrimination under the Age Discrimination in Employment Act (ADEA). However, one question was left open by that decision. Under the ADEA, an employer is exempt from liability for actions that would appear to violate the ADEA but are "based on reasonable factors other than age." How is this exception to be dealt with in a disparate-impact case—where, by the very nature of the claim, the employer has not acted *because of age* but because of some other factors, with a resulting age-related impact?

In *Meacham v. Knolls Atomic Power Laboratory* (128 S.Ct. 2395 [2008]), the Supreme Court held that the exception for "reasonable factors other than age" provides an affirmative defense; in other words, the burden of persuasion rests with the party raising the defense—in this case, the employer. Thus, if the employer wishes to avoid liability in a disparate-impact case by asserting that its actions were based on "reasonable factors other than age," it must prove that its actions were reasonable; the plaintiff does not have to prove that the use of the other factors was unreasonable.

The Court noted that this holding may make it more difficult for employers to defend disparate-impact age discrimination cases: "[T]here is no denying that putting employers to the work of persuading [juries] that their choices are reasonable makes it harder and costlier to defend" against age claims. "[N]or do we doubt that this will sometimes affect the way employers do business with their employees." The Court implied that the law may not be ideal; nonetheless, "We have to read it the way Congress wrote it."

A CIVIL WAR–ERA STATUTE AND EMPLOYMENT DISCRIMINATION

A Civil War–era discrimination statute permits lawsuits for retaliation.

There are two distinct kinds of employment discrimination: one is based directly on a protected characteristic, and the other is retaliation against an employee who complains about discriminatory treatment.

Under Title VII of the Civil Rights Act of 1964, both kinds of discrimination are unlawful and can be challenged in court. But what about 42 U.S.C. §1981—a statute dating from the period just after the Civil War, which guarantees to all citizens the same right "to make and enforce contracts . . . as is enjoyed by white people"? The U.S. Supreme Court held long ago that direct race discrimination in employment violates §1981 as well as Title VII. But what about retaliation?

In *CBOCS West Inc. v. Humphries* (128 S.Ct. 1951 [2008]), the U.S. Supreme Court held that §1981 does in fact prohibit discrimination in the form of retaliation. The practical effect is that some retaliation lawsuits that would have been barred by the tight time schedule for filing charges of discrimination under Title VII may still be successfully brought under §1981.

TAXATION OF MULTISTATE BUSINESSES

A state may constitutionally tax the apportioned value derived from a unitary business operated within and outside the state—but, in the absence of a unitary business, the fact that an asset serves an operational function does not provide an independent ground for the taxation of that asset by a state other than the one in which the asset is situated.

Both the due process clause and the commerce clause of the U.S. Constitution restrict a state's ability to tax out-of-state activities. The due process clause requires some minimum connection between a state and the person, property, or transaction it seeks to tax, along with a rational relationship between the income attributed to the taxing state and the value of the corporate business within the state. The commerce clause bars states from imposing taxes that discriminate against interstate commerce or that burden it by subjecting interstate activities to unfairly apportioned taxation.

The U.S. Supreme Court has held that the due process clause and the commerce clause do not require a state to isolate a corporation's income-producing activities within the state before imposing an income tax on an out-of-state corporation operating within its jurisdiction. Instead, the Constitution permits the state to tax an apportioned sum of the out-of-state corporation's multistate business that is carried on in the taxing state. A state may not, however, tax any portion of the income that the out-of-state corporation earns from an unrelated business activity that constitutes a discrete business enterprise. This way of allocating the income of a multistate business is know as the unitary business principle.

When the Mead Corporation (Mead), an Ohio corporation, sold the electronic research service Lexis/Nexis to a third party for $1.5 billion in 1994, realizing more than $1 billion in capital gains, it did not report any of the gains as business income on its Illinois tax returns, despite the fact that it did significant business in Illinois. Instead, Mead asserted that the gain was income unrelated to the business it conducted in Illinois, and that it was therefore taxable only by Ohio, its state of domicile.

Illinois disagreed and assessed approximately $4 million in additional taxes and penalties against Mead. Mead (now a subsidiary of the petitioner, MeadWestvaco Corporation) paid under protest and sued. Both the trial court and the Appellate Court of Illinois ruled that Illinois was constitutionally entitled to tax an apportioned share of the gain. In *MeadWestvaco Corp. v. Illinois Department of Revenue* (128 S.Ct. 1498 [2008]), the Supreme Court vacated the state courts' judgment in a unanimous opinion.

There was no dispute that Mead had done business in Illinois. Thus, the question was not whether Illinois could impose a tax on Mead, but what portion of Mead's income Illinois could tax. The Court thus applied the unitary business principle to determine whether the Lexis/Nexis business was (1) part of Mead's multistate—or unitary—business, including the business it conducted in Illinois, or (2) a discrete business enterprise operated out of state.

The latest iteration of the unitary business principle was articulated in *Allied-Signal, Inc., v. Director, Div. of Taxation* (504 U.S. 768 [1992]), in which the Court noted that an asset could form part of a taxpayer's unitary business if it served an operational rather than an investment function. For example, a manufacturing company's purchase and sale of futures contracts is operational if the futures are purchased as a form of insurance against price increases in the supply of products to be manufactured. In the absence of such a relationship, the company's purchase of futures contracts is an investment activity. Value associated with an asset held for an operational purpose may be subject to apportioned taxation by a state other than the state where the corporation is domiciled, even if the corporation does not have a unitary relationship with the entity holding the asset.

The Supreme Court rejected the state court's interpretation in *MeadWestvaco* that operational function could serve as a basis for apportionment in cases where there was no unitary relationship. The Court explained that an asset's operational function is relevant only to determining whether the asset is a unitary part of the business being conducted in the taxing state; it does not answer the question of whether the asset is a discrete asset to which the state has no claim.

The Court then turned to the capital gains at issue in the case at hand, noting that while the trial court had found none of the hallmarks of a unitary relationship—functional integration, centralized management, and economies of scale—in the relationship between Mead and Lexis/Nexis, the appellate court, believing that the basis for apportionment could be satisfied by confirming the operational function of Lexis/Nexis, had made no such determination. Therefore, the Court vacated the judgment of the appellate court and remanded the case for further proceedings, to determine whether Mead and Lexis/Nexis formed a unitary business.

The Court declined to uphold the lower court's ruling on the alternative ground urged by Illinois and its amici ("friends of the court")—namely, that the substantial business Lexis/Nexis conducted in Illinois justified the apportionment of Mead's capital gain—noting that this issue had not been raised before the lower courts and that such a ruling might call into question the constitutionality of the tax schemes of other jurisdictions.

The Court's ruling is of interest to local governments because many local governments receive funding from states or share in a designated portion of state government revenues—which, of course, include revenues from corporate income taxes.

TAX VALUATION OF RAILROAD PROPERTY

Under the federal law that prohibits states from taxing railroad property more heavily than other commercial property, railroads may challenge a state's choice of valuation methodologies as well as the application of those methodologies.

More than 30 years ago, Congress enacted the Railroad Revitalization and Regulatory Reform Act ("the 4-R Act"), which bars states from discriminatory taxation of property owned by railroads (49 U.S.C. §11501). Among its several provisions, the 4-R Act prohibits a state from assessing railroad property in such a way that the property's tax-value-to-market-value ratio is higher than that applied to other commercial and industrial property in the state. If a railroad's ratio exceeds that applied to other commercial and industrial property by 5% or more, the railroad may seek an injunction against the tax in federal court.

In 1987, in *Burlington Northern R. Co. v. Oklahoma Tax Comm'n* (107 S.Ct. 1855 [1987]), the U.S. Supreme Court held that the 4-R Act permits a railroad to challenge a state's valuation of its property for tax purposes. In that case, however, the railroad had challenged only the state's application of its valuation methodology, not the methodology itself, and the Court did not extend its opinion to address challenges to a state's choice of methodologies. A split subsequently developed among the federal circuit courts of appeals on the issue of whether 4-R Act challenges are limited to the application of valuation methodologies and exclude the selection of those methodologies. In late 2007, the Supreme Court resolved this uncertainty with its unanimous opinion in *CSX Transportation, Inc., v. Georgia State Board of Equalization et al.* (128 S.Ct. 467 [2007]). The Court made clear that in an action under the 4-R Act, a railroad may challenge a state's choice of valuation methodologies and not just the application of those methodologies.

Between 2001 and 2002, the state property tax bill of CSX Transportation, Inc., jumped 41%, primarily because of the state's decision to use a different combination of valuation methodologies.

CSX promptly sued the state of Georgia under the 4-R Act, alleging that the state had grossly overestimated the market value of the railroad's in-state property and that its tax-value-to-market-value ratio was at least 5% greater than the ratio for other commercial and industrial property in Georgia. To support its 4-R Act claims, CSX offered evidence attacking the valuation methodologies that had produced the substantially higher 2002 tax levy. The railroad submitted the testimony of its own expert appraiser, who used a different valuation methodology than that used by the state—which, not surprisingly, yielded a much lower market value for CSX's property than the state's methodology had.

The federal district court and the Court of Appeals for the Eleventh Circuit rejected CSX's argument, holding that the 4-R Act does not permit challenges to a state's choice of valuation methodologies as long as those methodologies are rational and not motivated by discriminatory intent. The Supreme Court disagreed and unanimously reversed the lower courts' rulings, finding no relevant distinction under the 4-R Act between a state's choice of valuation methodologies and their application. Because the 4-R Act requires that a railroad's property be valued at its true market value, a court must be permitted to evaluate a state's valuation methodologies as well as the application of those methods: "Valuation is not just a matter of mathematics, as if the district court could prevent discriminatory taxation simply by double-checking the state's assessment calculations. . . . Given the extent to which the chosen methods can affect the determination of value, preventing courts from scrutinizing state valuation methodologies would render [the 4-R Act] a largely empty command."

SUMMARY

Many of the cases decided by the Court in the 2007–2008 term were closely watched, and some of the ensuing opinions closely divided, with the 97-page opinion in *Baze v. Rees* serving as the most extreme example. Those looking for cohesion may be heartened to note that in at least one area of primary concern to local government—the interpretation of constitutional principles and statutes governing taxation, albeit at the state rather than the local level—the Court issued unanimous opinions.

In time, the Court's opinion in *District of Columbia v. Heller* may prove to be among those widely recognized by name alone—along with *Miranda v. Arizona, Roe v. Wade,* and *Bush v. Gore.* In a significant departure from its earlier Second Amendment jurisprudence, the Court held that the amendment protects an individual's right to possess and carry weapons, and that a de facto ban on handguns enacted by the District of Columbia was therefore unconstitutional. Local governing bodies will find their ability to restrict the possession and carrying of certain types of weapons severely curtailed by the opinion.

Law enforcement officers and judicial officials at all levels will find *Rothgery v. Gillespie County* significant for its holding that a defendant's Sixth Amendment right to counsel attaches at the defendant's initial appearance before a judicial official.

Local governments may be relieved to learn, on the one hand, that under *Engquist v. Oregon Department of Agriculture,* a public employee who was arbitrarily dismissed does not have a valid claim under the equal protection clause. On the other hand, under *Meacham v. Knolls Atomic Power Laboratory,* employers—including local governments—have an increased burden in defending age discrimination claims brought under the theory of disparate impact.

The Court also weighed in on two significant issues in the arena of criminal sentencing, rejecting challenges to lethal injection as cruel and unusual punishment and thereby ending a de facto death penalty moratorium, and ruling capital punishment unconstitutional in cases in which child rape does not result, and is not intended to result, in the child's death.

Significantly, some of the Court's opinions from the 2007–2008 term appear to be but the first step in establishing the parameters of broader constitutional principles, such as the right to bear arms and the right to counsel; successor cases are almost sure to follow. Local government officials and others will have to stay tuned for the next installment.

C Staffing and Compensation

C 1

Salaries of Municipal Officials, 2008

Rollie O. Waters and Joyce C. Powell
The Waters Consulting Group, Inc.

Selected Findings

The highest percentage of increase in average salary using the same cities from 2007 to 2008 is for the position of chief administrative officer (CAO)/city manager (5.6%); the lowest is for the position of human services director (2.4%).

The highest average salary shown is for the combined position of CAO/city manager ($100,151).

The position of primary assistant manager/CAO showed the greatest shift in average salaries by region, from $55,275 in the Northeast to $114,242 in the West—a difference of $58,967.

The position with the greatest spread (50%) between average salary range minimum and maximum is fire chief. The position with the least range spread (16%) is chief elected official.

This article and the accompanying tables present the results of ICMA's 2008 survey of salaries of local government officials in cities. In 2008, the survey instrument collected salary information on 23 positions that are common to municipal and county governments, as well as on 52 management and professional positions. Data reported in the *Municipal Year Book* cover the 23 positions of local government officials.

Local government salaries are affected by several variables other than individual expertise, including population, geographic region, and service delivery. Cities that have ports, military bases, or universities and that are full service will typically have higher salaries than those that do not have these characteristics.

SURVEY METHODOLOGY

This is the fifth year that ICMA has offered Survey Navigator™ for ICMA, a Web-based interactive version of the annual survey. This system is managed and operated by the Waters Consulting Group, Inc. Prior to SurveyNavigator™, data were collected in the summer and fall months and made available in a summary format through ICMA's *Municipal Year Book,* which is published in the spring of the following year; a printed version and a disk of the survey data were also made available for a fee through the ICMA bookstore. Now, with SurveyNavigator™ for ICMA, an online version is updated weekly as changes are made by each participating local government.

In July 2008, survey notices were mailed to all municipal and county governments with populations of 2,500 and above, and to those under 2,500 that are recognized by ICMA as having a council-manager form of government or as providing for an appointed general management (chief administrative officer, or CAO) position. The survey notice gave the Web address for SurveyNavigator™ (surveynavigator.com/icma) and provided a unique identification number and password for the local government choosing to participate. A second, abbreviated paper survey was mailed and/or e-mailed to those local governments that had not responded to the first mailing or had not provided the information online. The overall city response rate to the 2008 survey was 19% as of December 20, 2008 (Table 1/1), 3% lower than the response rate in 2007. However, the structure of the new online survey tool allows for weekly updates and additional data to be entered at any time by participating local governments.

AVERAGE SALARIES

Using the exact same cities and titles to ensure comparability between 2007 and 2008, Table 1/2 shows the percentage of change in average salary for all 23 positions over the preceding year. This year the highest percentage of increase in average salary overall is 5.6% for the position of CAO/city manager, followed by 5.4% for the position of information services director; the lowest is 2.4% for the position of human services director.

When all data from 2008 are used irrespective of the cities that reported in 2007, the highest average salary shown is for the combined position of CAO/city manager ($100,151) (Table 1/3), which is consistent with prior years and not surprising given the level of responsibility the position holds. The next highest average salary is for the primary assistant manager/CAO ($90,644), followed closely by the average salary for the engineer ($85,342).

Population size has a major influence on local government salaries, in part because larger populations usually require more services to meet citizen demands and thus require more employees to provide those services. The complexity of managing cities with larger populations requires a salary commensurate with the level of expertise and experience demanded of the job. Unfortunately, a drop in survey participation resulted in fewer than three cities reporting for two population groups, so no calculations could be made for positions in these population groups. However, the breakout of average salaries by population group shown in Table 1/3 provides a picture of change in the average salary for smaller cities.

Geographic region also affects salaries. Historically, the highest salaries are typically found in the West, and this data collection cycle shows no exception. For twenty-two of the twenty-three positions included in the survey, the highest average salary among all cities is found in the West region (Table 1/4). The one exception is the position of

Table 1/1 SURVEY RESPONSE

Classification	No. of cities[1] surveyed (A)	Respondents No.	Respondents % of (A)
Total	8,675	1,642	19
Population group			
Over 1,000,000	9	2	22
500,000–1,000,000	23	2	9
250,000–499,999	36	9	25
100,000–249,999	179	34	19
50,000–99,999	407	89	22
25,000–49,999	775	146	19
10,000–24,999	1,821	365	20
5,000–9,999	1,883	300	16
2,500–4,999	2,003	325	16
Under 2,500	1,539	370	24
Geographic region			
Northeast	2,134	167	8
North-Central	2,669	704	26
South	2,660	561	21
West	1,212	210	17
Geographic division			
New England	838	61	7
Mid-Atlantic	1,296	106	8
East North-Central	1,550	281	18
West North-Central	1,119	423	38
South Atlantic	1,170	334	29
East South-Central	492	47	10
West South-Central	998	180	18
Mountain	455	119	26
Pacific Coast	757	91	12
Form of government			
Mayor-council	3,945	677	17
Council-manager	4,126	910	22
Commission	152	19	13
Town meeting	387	29	7
Representative town meeting	65	7	11
Metro status			
Central	540	114	21
Independent	3,346	845	25
Suburban	4,789	683	14

[1]For a definition of terms, please see "Inside the *Year Book,*" x.

Table 1/2 CHANGE IN AVERAGE SALARY, 2007 TO 2008

Position	2007 average salary ($)	2008 average salary ($)	Percentage of change (%)
Chief administrative officer/city manager	94,372	99,619	5.6
Chief elected official	44,315	46,097	4.0
Chief financial officer	76,852	80,702	5.0
Chief law enforcement official	72,689	76,417	5.1
Chief librarian	58,062	60,819	4.7
Clerk	50,354	52,647	4.6
Economic development director	71,294	74,769	4.9
Engineer	84,763	89,208	5.2
Fire chief	77,514	81,633	5.3
Health officer	71,324	74,213	4.1
Human resources director	76,749	80,770	5.2
Human services director	80,474	82,371	2.4
Information services director	79,954	84,257	5.4
Parks and recreation director	70,517	74,275	5.3
Parks superintendent	54,279	56,700	4.5
Planning director	73,178	76,998	5.2
Primary assistant manager/CAO	88,550	93,177	5.2
Public safety director	92,875	95,830	3.2
Public works director	71,900	74,870	4.1
Purchasing director	65,541	68,308	4.2
Recreation director	56,236	58,069	3.3
Risk manager	69,252	72,096	4.1
Treasurer	47,938	50,038	4.4

Note: This table compares the average pay change for position using the exact same cities and titles used in *The Municipal Year Book 2007*. Where cities that reported last year did not report this year, they were excluded from the calculations for both years shown above.

chief elected official, for which the highest average salary is found in the Northeast region.

A close look at the average salaries on a regional basis for the positions of public works director and economic development director provides a clear example of this regional influence. For the position of public works director (Table 1/5), the highest average salary for 2008 ($99,381) is found in the West region. This is $30,097 higher than the lowest average salary for the same position ($69,284), found in the South. For the position of economic development director (Table 1/6), the lowest average salary is in the North-Central region ($66,875) and the highest is again in the West ($97,653), a difference of $30,778.

Figure 1/1 illustrates the variation among geographic regions for several positions. Of interest is the average salary for the chief librarian, which continues to be lower than that for other positions throughout the regions.

City governments often want to know how competitive their salary ranges are when compared with those of other local governments; both salary ranges and the salaries themselves influence a

Table 1/3 AVERAGE SALARY ($) FOR POSITION, BY POPULATION GROUP, 2008

Job title	Total	Greater than 1,000,000	500,000– 1,000,000	250,000– 499,999	100,000– 249,999	50,000– 99,999	25,000– 49,999	10,000– 24,999	5,000– 9,999	2,500– 4,999	Less than 2,500
Chief administrative officer/city manager	100,151	...	...	184,634	180,184	142,477	140,315	112,967	93,087	75,732	61,784
Chief elected official	49,224	...	...	64,920	46,698	64,139	52,689	49,978	37,898	29,528	49,596
Chief financial officer	82,125	...	...	132,290	126,026	106,814	105,131	84,687	69,126	57,993	50,652
Chief law enforcement official	78,118	...	...	140,340	133,260	113,288	111,063	89,987	72,622	57,915	49,435
Chief librarian	60,632	...	...	102,458	101,402	89,119	79,972	64,266	49,556	39,912	29,842
Clerk	53,289	...	...	103,622	87,269	70,556	70,538	58,397	52,595	44,785	37,046
Economic development director	76,075	...	...	106,113	105,737	92,360	90,292	77,760	63,354	48,111	41,488
Engineer	85,342	...	...	104,687	102,787	97,157	93,855	79,657	74,275	58,333	56,284
Fire chief	81,699	...	...	132,161	128,238	106,314	102,420	80,597	61,992	50,733	50,429
Health officer	73,335	...	...	113,946	102,391	84,712	83,298	59,106	48,955	47,717	...
Human resources director	79,131	...	...	119,097	113,730	97,256	90,644	69,078	58,388	49,031	45,619
Human services director	75,910	...	...	102,500	103,247	80,585	86,757	67,095	46,007	56,410	...
Information services director	84,649	...	...	124,161	113,115	92,537	89,832	70,324	63,857	50,697	55,763
Parks and recreation director	74,277	...	...	131,140	112,942	98,564	93,800	72,973	58,503	46,045	34,793
Parks superintendent	55,891	...	...	86,270	78,107	67,937	66,144	52,757	46,156	36,109	38,137
Planning director	78,861	...	...	121,486	109,624	95,471	92,727	75,941	65,451	55,553	51,934
Primary assistant manager/CAO	90,644	...	...	135,133	127,707	116,340	107,121	83,827	73,074	57,201	51,151
Public safety director	77,163	...	...	...	...	94,844	104,244	74,130	70,741	57,672	51,886
Public works director	75,904	...	...	127,884	124,031	109,808	106,825	84,306	70,076	57,116	48,410
Purchasing director	66,355	...	...	94,208	80,981	72,375	67,874	52,793	45,317	35,317	...
Recreation director	59,163	...	...	91,195	78,653	73,694	68,109	55,118	43,888	38,737	55,222
Risk manager	72,029	...	...	87,282	86,808	71,605	72,587	61,986	64,255	...	...
Treasurer	51,728	...	...	93,115	98,442	80,725	73,484	57,333	51,714	43,393	37,638

Note: (. . .) indicates that fewer than three municipalities reported, so meaningful statistics could not be computed.

Table 1/4   AVERAGE SALARY ($) FOR POSITION, BY REGION, 2008

Job title	Region				
	Total	Northeast	North-Central	South	West
Chief administrative officer/ city manager	100,151	85,458	90,839	98,808	135,650
Chief elected official	49,224	59,696	48,519	46,772	48,501
Chief financial officer	82,125	74,343	80,252	75,734	103,449
Chief law enforcement official	78,118	82,816	72,894	72,062	108,872
Chief librarian	60,632	60,333	51,586	61,126	79,796
Clerk	53,289	51,334	49,411	50,535	72,490
Economic development director	76,075	67,325	66,875	77,501	97,653
Engineer	85,342	76,302	83,140	84,950	93,052
Fire chief	81,699	76,489	82,507	73,801	107,731
Health officer	73,335	67,440	70,453	75,472	111,105
Human resources director	79,131	68,420	78,155	73,194	94,434
Human services director	75,910	68,492	70,897	71,972	100,030
Information services director	84,649	76,039	84,064	81,859	94,853
Parks and recreation director	74,277	64,593	67,579	70,573	101,492
Parks superintendent	55,891	57,467	57,772	49,550	66,877
Planning director	78,861	70,114	75,615	74,033	96,021
Primary assistant manager/CAO	90,644	55,275	79,209	96,842	114,242
Public safety director	77,163	52,013	73,215	84,725	92,935
Public works director	75,904	70,149	74,473	69,284	99,381
Purchasing director	66,355	69,178	62,607	62,723	82,812
Recreation director	59,163	53,420	54,193	55,870	74,218
Risk manager	72,029	78,561	74,898	65,400	80,185
Treasurer	51,728	49,933	46,538	61,988	71,064

Table 1/5   AVERAGE SALARY FOR PUBLIC WORKS DIRECTOR, BY REGION, 2007 AND 2008

Region	2007		2008	
	No. reporting	Average salary ($)	No. reporting	Average salary ($)
Total	1,312	71,165	1,225	75,904
Northeast	144	69,803	136	70,149
North-Central	485	71,102	473	74,473
South	577	67,914	432	69,284
West	106	90,996	184	99,381

Table 1/6   AVERAGE SALARY FOR ECONOMIC DEVELOPMENT DIRECTOR, BY REGION, 2007 AND 2008

Region	2007		2008	
	No. reporting	Average salary ($)	No. reporting	Average salary ($)
Total	337	74,451	333	76,075
Northeast	24	67,557	20	67,325
North-Central	121	62,880	145	66,875
South	154	76,693	105	77,501
West	38	106,558	63	97,653

local government's ability to attract and retain quality employees. Table 1/7 shows the average salary range minimums, maximums, and spreads for all 23 full-time positions surveyed in 2008. The position of fire chief has the greatest range spread (50%), and the position of chief elected official has the least range spread (16%). Figure 1/2 shows the actual average salaries for selected positions in conjunction with the average salary ranges for those positions.

Table 1/8 lists the average, median, and first- and third-quartile salaries for all 23 position where there were enough responses to compute the information. Again, the low participation rate for this year's survey resulted in fewer than three cities reporting for the largest two population groups (greater than 1,000,000 and 500,000–1,000,000), so no calculations could be made for positions in those groups.

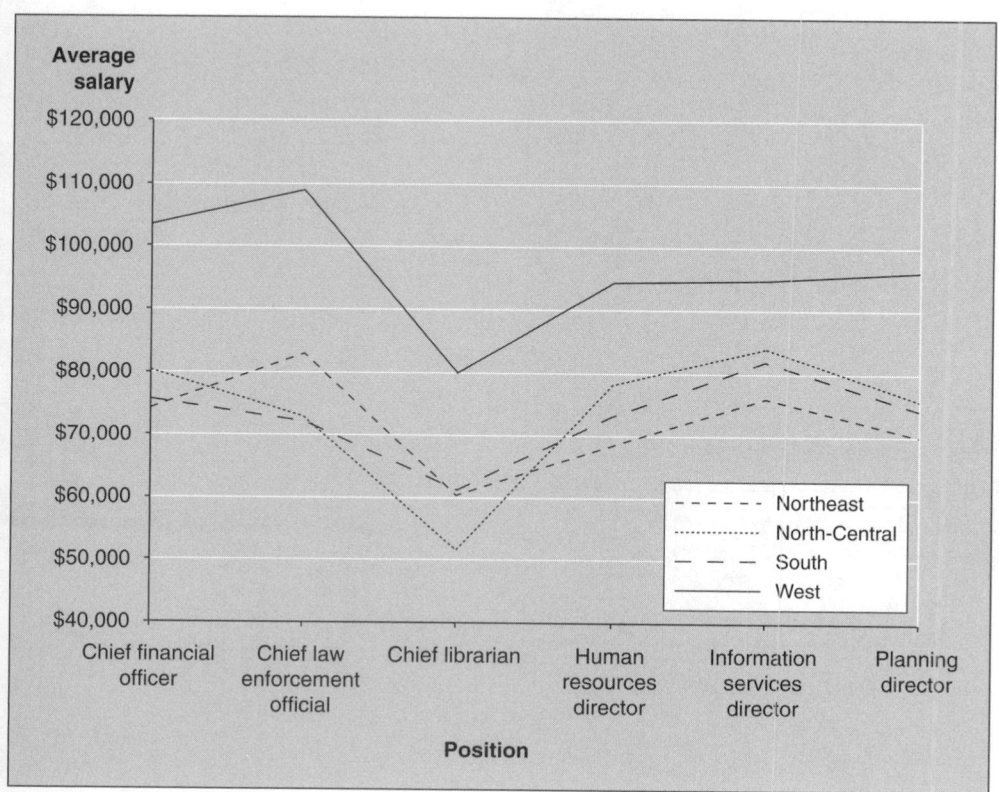

Figure 1/1   *Average salaries for six selected municipal positions, by geographic region, 2008*

Table 1/7   AVERAGE PAY STRUCTURE RANGES, 2008

Position	No. reporting	Average minimum ($)	Average maximum ($)	Average range spread (%)
Chief administrative officer/city manager .	470	78,972	105,699	34
Chief elected official	23	56,918	66,241	16
Chief financial officer	654	66,949	93,613	40
Chief law enforcement official	226	53,915	75,304	40
Chief librarian	614	47,476	66,810	41
Clerk	206	66,019	91,194	38
Economic development director	334	68,517	96,741	41
Engineer	491	68,295	96,468	41
Fire chief	50	58,414	87,873	50
Health officer	415	64,434	92,109	43
Human resources director	46	65,706	93,205	42
Human services director	262	67,081	96,763	44
Information services director	417	63,237	89,496	42
Parks and recreation director	323	47,076	67,236	43
Parks superintendent	418	64,541	91,852	42
Planning director	776	66,885	92,655	39
Primary assistant manager/CAO	262	76,052	106,127	40
Public safety director	60	67,021	96,114	43
Public works director	753	65,118	91,214	40
Purchasing director	104	55,218	80,910	47
Recreation director	198	50,626	72,105	42
Risk manager	138	54,927	80,859	47
Treasurer	175	47,936	65,426	36

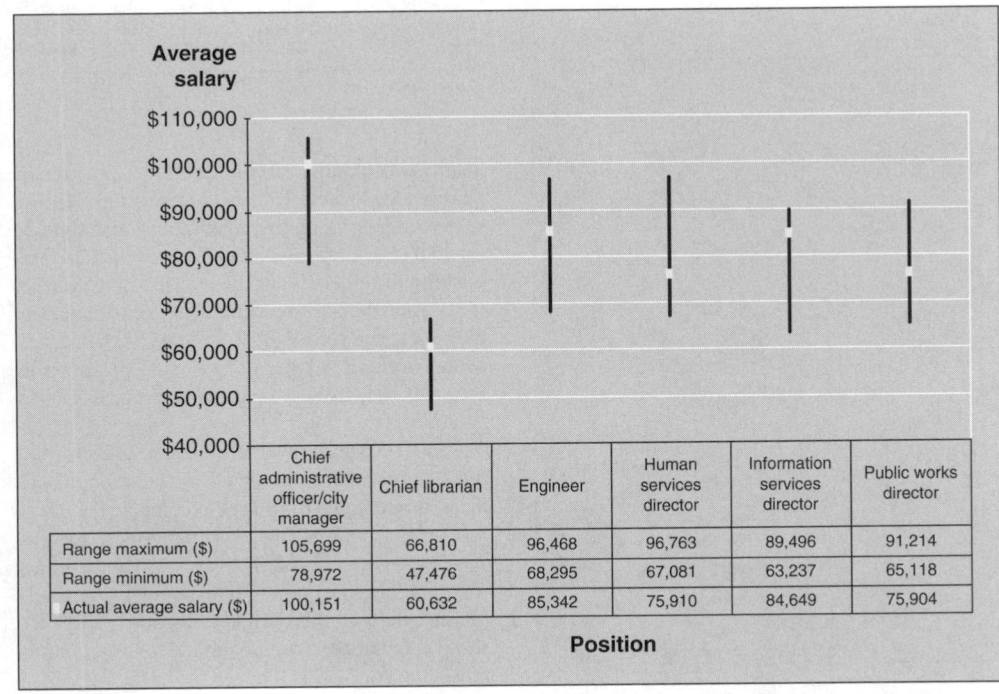

Figure 1/2   *Actual average salaries and salary ranges for six selected municipal positions, 2008*

Table 1/8   SALARIES OF MUNICIPAL OFFICIALS: JULY–DECEMBER 2008

Salary data for the municipal positions in this table are based on information reported by municipal officials between late July 2008 and mid December 2008. Data are reported by position title only. Although job responsibilities are generally similar, the titles do not necessarily indicate identical duties and responsibilities.

This table includes salaries for only full-time personnel. Salaries are presented by ten population groups and are further classified by geographic region, city type, and form of government. In some instances, form-of-government informa-

tion is missing; therefore, the number of municipalities reporting by form of government might not always match the total number of municipalities reporting.

Classifications having fewer than three municipalities reporting are excluded because meaningful statistics cannot be computed. Consequently, the number reporting in some subcategories does not always equal the total reporting. The median represents either the value of the middle observation or, when there is an even number of observations, the mean of the two middle obser-

vations. The first- and third-quartile observations represent the value of the observation below which 25% and 75% of the number of observations fall, respectively, and are calculated around the median, such that an equal number of observations fall between the median and the first quartile and between the median and the third quartile.

(. . .) indicates that fewer than three municipalities reported, so meaningful statistics could not be computed.

Title of official	Number of municipalities reporting	Distribution of 2008 salaries			
		Mean ($)	First quartile ($)	Median ($)	Third quartile ($)
All cities					
Chief admin. officer/city manager					
Total	1,233	100,151	70,000	94,992	123,480
Geographic region					
Northeast	109	85,458	62,000	81,000	102,253
North-Central	488	90,839	68,579	85,661	110,646
South	446	98,808	66,251	94,478	124,900
West	190	135,650	102,891	130,389	161,906
Metro type					
Central	101	147,634	122,190	146,224	168,324
Suburban	688	105,205	75,004	100,000	128,674
Independent	444	81,519	59,850	78,685	101,331
Form of government					
Mayor-council	331	83,123	61,911	79,477	102,022
Council-manager	873	107,189	75,000	102,000	133,715
Commission	10	98,088	85,166	92,734	100,795
Town meeting	18	74,904	56,537	68,850	96,238
Chief elected official					
Total	271	49,224	21,074	44,928	68,750
Geographic region					
Northeast	32	59,696	33,500	64,250	78,103
North-Central	106	48,519	22,415	47,214	65,000
South	95	46,772	20,600	41,600	60,000
West	38	48,501	20,226	33,872	77,328
Metro type					
Central	63	60,553	24,860	51,750	94,022
Suburban	126	47,754	20,050	43,962	65,750
Independent	82	42,778	22,605	44,065	55,000
Form of government					
Mayor-council	180	55,714	30,000	52,000	74,287
Council-manager	78	30,996	16,020	22,194	36,810
Commission	3	25,030	21,587	25,000	28,458
Town meeting	8	82,553	74,494	76,003	94,467
Chief financial officer					
Total	926	82,125	61,669	79,045	101,785
Geographic region					
Northeast	85	74,343	56,732	73,187	88,315
North-Central	324	80,252	63,702	78,984	95,945
South	352	75,734	55,680	72,556	92,502
West	165	103,449	81,834	103,328	123,132
Metro type					
Central	104	107,706	91,225	105,115	123,349
Suburban	527	85,482	66,345	84,662	104,402
Independent	295	67,110	50,752	65,832	80,181
Form of government					
Mayor-council	264	72,273	52,132	71,005	89,873
Council-manager	634	86,287	65,131	84,050	105,410
Commission	9	77,144	69,571	76,312	93,275
Town meeting	15	82,116	66,873	86,000	90,500
Rep. town meeting . .	4	84,080	68,468	87,362	102,974
Chief law enforcement official					
Total	1,334	78,118	54,143	73,034	97,855
Geographic region					
Northeast	130	82,816	64,125	78,815	98,797
North-Central	553	72,894	53,206	68,682	90,577
South	482	72,062	49,019	66,400	90,706
West	169	108,872	82,742	106,464	131,088
Metro type					
Central	109	114,194	95,964	106,536	128,724
Suburban	673	86,621	63,202	84,456	106,684
Independent	552	60,628	45,304	58,168	72,291

Title of official	Number of municipalities reporting	Distribution of 2008 salaries			
		Mean ($)	First quartile ($)	Median ($)	Third quartile ($)
All cities continued					
Form of government					
Mayor-council	532	66,524	46,306	62,680	83,493
Council-manager	757	86,201	60,122	81,786	106,698
Commission	18	72,546	59,888	67,614	82,677
Town meeting	20	82,516	66,080	80,187	104,415
Rep. town meeting . .	7	86,880	59,096	69,948	102,948
Chief librarian					
Total	368	60,632	40,000	57,163	78,288
Geographic region					
Northeast	51	60,333	47,925	59,759	71,570
North-Central	144	51,586	34,525	47,195	62,988
South	107	61,126	42,339	57,090	75,814
West	66	79,796	56,422	77,770	100,846
Metro type					
Central	50	91,222	74,779	90,687	101,675
Suburban	166	64,046	46,701	58,718	79,859
Independent	152	46,841	31,868	44,101	58,912
Form of government					
Mayor-council	116	51,823	34,762	47,409	64,730
Council-manager	229	65,549	44,554	60,720	83,671
Commission	3	47,269	42,044	53,970	55,845
Town meeting	17	55,284	40,000	58,936	70,785
Rep. town meeting . .	3	69,561	56,682	69,060	82,190
Clerk					
Total	1,166	53,289	38,234	49,414	64,861
Geographic region					
Northeast	110	51,334	35,263	48,164	61,787
North-Central	424	49,411	36,037	46,350	61,588
South	468	50,535	37,000	47,325	59,576
West	164	72,490	53,271	71,898	89,535
Metro type					
Central	99	72,027	55,761	70,525	82,692
Suburban	580	58,991	43,645	56,088	71,566
Independent	487	42,690	32,327	41,000	50,907
Form of government					
Mayor-council	460	45,594	32,782	42,213	55,659
Council-manager	667	58,646	42,956	54,911	71,721
Commission	10	58,979	48,688	53,682	67,453
Town meeting	22	49,887	42,331	51,949	60,126
Rep. town meeting . .	7	51,140	45,129	46,462	54,375
Economic development director					
Total	333	76,075	55,577	73,590	91,281
Geographic region					
Northeast	20	67,325	49,537	68,644	79,464
North-Central	145	66,875	52,000	66,705	80,954
South	105	77,501	54,079	72,000	99,750
West	63	97,653	79,494	92,915	115,888
Metro type					
Central	50	97,840	78,866	92,564	121,150
Suburban	181	79,828	65,004	79,078	93,654
Independent	102	58,747	45,392	56,256	69,720
Form of government					
Mayor-council	110	68,764	51,024	67,191	84,885
Council-manager	214	80,385	60,610	77,962	99,140
Town meeting	5	53,788	43,701	50,000	73,000
Engineer					
Total	443	85,342	71,112	85,424	101,365
Geographic region					
Northeast	35	76,302	61,670	76,145	95,633
North-Central	162	83,140	71,456	85,259	98,692
South	151	84,950	70,512	83,699	99,951
West	95	93,052	74,972	91,701	108,710

Table 1/8 SALARIES OF MUNICIPAL OFFICIALS: JULY–DECEMBER 2008
continued

Title of official	Number of municipalities reporting	Mean ($)	First quartile ($)	Median ($)	Third quartile ($)	Title of official	Number of municipalities reporting	Mean ($)	First quartile ($)	Median ($)	Third quartile ($)
All cities continued						**All cities continued**					
Metro type						Metro type					
Central	90	94,801	80,888	92,877	106,517	Central	94	97,298	78,355	94,316	117,329
Suburban	240	87,810	73,101	89,248	104,795	Suburban	180	84,205	68,384	83,200	98,435
Independent	113	72,568	60,256	72,800	85,925	Independent	67	68,096	53,634	67,587	80,345
Form of government						Form of government					
Mayor-council	118	74,599	63,622	75,765	88,974	Mayor-council	70	77,581	59,891	77,480	91,089
Council-manager	311	89,767	73,547	89,861	105,178	Council-manager	259	87,044	67,753	85,328	100,868
Commission	3	82,937	77,226	77,232	85,796	Commission	4	76,547	68,340	78,579	86,785
Town meeting	7	69,321	56,948	72,923	81,200	Town meeting	5	70,212	62,008	67,000	80,951
Rep. town meeting . .	4	88,113	80,808	95,578	102,883	Rep. town meeting . .	3	77,654	62,569	78,728	93,276
Fire chief						**Parks and recreation director**					
Total	716	81,699	60,000	79,123	100,811	Total	623	74,277	50,405	71,593	94,420
Geographic region						Geographic region					
Northeast	58	76,489	63,540	75,391	90,536	Northeast	55	64,593	45,838	66,066	79,314
North-Central	238	82,507	63,662	83,668	99,936	North-Central	214	67,579	46,702	65,304	88,478
South	319	73,801	52,999	71,956	91,204	South	248	70,573	50,703	68,312	88,349
West	101	107,731	81,164	104,915	130,836	West	106	101,492	82,973	100,164	122,036
Metro type						Metro type					
Central	107	107,662	92,148	101,928	120,783	Central	95	96,923	78,201	94,931	110,429
Suburban	356	87,362	66,726	86,575	104,986	Suburban	328	78,301	56,348	76,907	98,239
Independent	253	62,750	48,410	61,863	75,067	Independent	200	56,922	42,360	53,864	71,271
Form of government						Form of government					
Mayor-council	234	72,609	52,353	71,041	89,963	Mayor-council	177	59,328	38,542	56,511	76,377
Council-manager	453	86,896	63,697	84,594	107,712	Council-manager	430	80,939	59,842	79,221	99,786
Commission	11	75,259	60,807	68,964	93,004	Commission	3	73,042	56,502	65,004	85,563
Town meeting	13	68,652	47,424	65,270	99,680	Town meeting	10	57,766	49,822	66,152	73,173
Rep. town meeting . .	5	84,323	73,859	90,064	90,694	Rep. town meeting . .	3	57,625	46,813	47,216	63,232
Health officer						**Parks superintendent**					
Total	82	73,335	50,587	70,966	92,098	Total	429	55,891	42,840	54,511	67,408
Geographic region						Geographic region					
Northeast	29	67,440	53,956	63,115	78,199	Northeast	20	57,467	47,650	55,854	64,774
North-Central	24	70,453	49,989	70,700	91,506	North-Central	124	57,772	44,070	58,360	68,662
South	24	75,472	50,399	73,725	92,934	South	196	49,550	37,947	48,483	59,673
West	5	111,105	90,756	93,870	137,097	West	89	66,877	53,273	65,836	84,924
Metro type						Metro type					
Central	27	94,851	73,833	91,548	106,155	Central	75	67,255	56,229	66,179	74,487
Suburban	36	68,967	46,922	68,098	88,547	Suburban	205	59,256	45,054	58,623	71,598
Independent	19	51,037	38,779	50,310	57,962	Independent	149	45,540	36,225	45,427	54,800
Form of government						Form of government					
Mayor-council	24	67,267	48,549	58,381	80,018	Mayor-council	113	50,566	38,126	48,731	62,556
Council-manager	44	80,848	57,178	77,756	95,155	Council-manager	305	57,846	44,075	56,000	70,065
Town meeting	10	60,689	50,429	63,455	74,750	Commission	4	53,658	45,053	53,891	62,496
Human resources director						Town meeting	4	51,284	46,775	48,790	53,299
Total	539	79,131	58,780	78,234	97,902	Rep. town meeting . .	3	66,717	57,657	64,314	74,575
Geographic region						**Planning director**					
Northeast	41	68,420	49,424	67,524	80,547	Total	570	78,861	58,459	77,717	94,928
North-Central	145	78,155	60,008	79,518	97,032	Geographic region					
South	227	73,194	52,668	70,491	91,652	Northeast	56	70,114	53,138	65,054	82,613
West	126	94,434	75,611	92,296	112,806	North-Central	141	75,615	57,491	76,172	92,178
Metro type						South	248	74,033	55,544	72,297	89,805
Central	106	96,114	79,930	93,097	110,887	West	125	96,021	76,020	97,224	118,008
Suburban	283	81,364	62,234	79,726	99,778	Metro type					
Independent	150	62,917	46,696	62,933	79,159	Central	96	96,631	81,773	94,397	109,881
Form of government						Suburban	329	79,658	60,700	79,306	95,002
Mayor-council	137	69,020	50,086	67,676	84,645	Independent	145	65,287	50,362	62,262	77,662
Council-manager	389	83,154	64,330	82,560	101,052	Form of government					
Commission	3	71,574	61,235	81,078	86,665	Mayor-council	133	69,265	51,148	69,192	84,587
Town meeting	7	58,018	39,619	50,000	73,040	Council-manager	414	82,629	62,066	81,754	98,997
Rep. town meeting . .	3	76,009	63,232	78,234	89,898	Commission	5	74,545	54,648	81,816	88,502
Human services director						Town meeting	14	63,898	52,529	60,020	67,576
Total	75	75,910	60,602	75,961	88,298	Rep. town meeting . .	4	65,764	47,715	64,894	82,944
Geographic region						**Primary asst. manager/CAO**					
Northeast	15	68,492	61,020	68,250	81,876	Total	369	90,644	65,562	89,000	113,925
North-Central	16	70,897	44,992	76,132	89,103	Geographic region					
South	31	71,972	60,602	74,569	84,721	Northeast	33	55,275	44,265	56,300	61,800
West	13	100,030	76,124	102,212	113,499	North-Central	119	79,209	61,760	78,518	98,026
Metro type						South	149	96,842	76,377	95,222	119,729
Central	21	92,207	76,124	86,856	102,212	West	68	114,242	94,186	112,694	138,276
Suburban	42	73,293	60,200	73,215	86,344	Metro type					
Independent	12	56,547	37,126	49,505	77,427	Central	69	117,641	98,642	115,332	135,336
Form of government						Suburban	222	90,632	66,486	89,020	112,239
Mayor-council	17	56,855	38,800	61,216	74,569	Independent	78	66,799	45,573	66,810	87,027
Council-manager	51	83,508	69,788	84,240	93,207	Form of government					
Town meeting	6	63,559	60,441	64,118	67,702	Mayor-council	63	70,075	47,014	69,512	89,473
Information services director						Council-manager	298	96,136	69,727	94,458	118,020
Total	341	84,649	65,124	83,000	100,000	Town meeting	5	37,122	31,408	33,613	46,099
Geographic region						**Public safety director**					
Northeast	34	76,039	62,045	77,020	92,831	Total	126	77,163	55,304	73,124	96,951
North-Central	91	84,064	69,580	83,000	96,422	Geographic region					
South	143	81,859	61,563	78,802	95,193	Northeast	6	52,013	45,746	48,488	56,585
West	73	94,853	78,171	97,572	110,066	North-Central	75	73,215	54,558	71,000	95,575

Table 1/8   SALARIES OF MUNICIPAL OFFICIALS: JULY–DECEMBER 2008
continued

Title of official	Number of municipalities reporting	Distribution of 2008 salaries			
		Mean ($)	First quartile ($)	Median ($)	Third quartile ($)
All cities continued					
South	32	84,726	65,913	78,359	101,333
West	13	92,935	65,000	94,908	113,509
Metro type					
Central	12	104,610	75,820	104,315	118,840
Suburban	82	77,058	52,048	73,739	98,137
Independent	32	67,141	54,598	65,690	79,198
Form of government					
Mayor-council	54	63,725	45,166	58,696	77,165
Council-manager	71	87,826	69,005	83,004	104,790
Public works director					
Total	1,225	75,904	53,789	71,427	95,029
Geographic region					
Northeast	136	70,149	51,930	65,811	86,721
North-Central	473	74,473	55,744	70,584	91,611
South	432	69,284	47,097	64,167	87,108
West	184	99,381	76,790	99,170	121,093
Metro type					
Central	99	108,820	90,933	108,300	124,293
Suburban	670	81,323	59,607	78,055	99,368
Independent	456	60,797	44,455	58,400	74,098
Form of government					
Mayor-council	438	65,678	47,115	61,826	80,995
Council-manager	744	82,090	58,950	78,823	101,483
Commission	15	73,486	61,791	65,333	83,575
Town meeting	22	71,958	50,465	79,446	89,556
Rep. town meeting . .	6	75,890	59,246	73,908	85,300
Purchasing director					
Total	149	66,355	52,166	67,330	82,745
Geographic region					
Northeast	16	69,178	57,187	68,078	85,167
North-Central	35	62,607	43,113	62,875	83,172
South	76	62,723	51,324	63,231	71,646
West	22	82,812	72,383	84,972	96,647
Metro type					
Central	63	75,747	62,142	70,268	88,069
Suburban	59	64,859	51,459	66,893	79,423
Independent	27	47,708	30,715	48,000	58,135
Form of government					
Mayor-council	42	60,493	44,198	63,595	71,790
Council-manager	104	69,155	55,247	68,696	84,720
Recreation director					
Total	269	59,163	42,079	56,992	74,544
Geographic region					
Northeast	33	53,420	42,951	51,429	63,783
North-Central	80	54,193	37,401	53,279	68,325
South	96	55,870	42,387	52,435	66,030
West	60	74,218	58,167	76,570	92,190
Metro type					
Central	49	74,304	60,601	70,818	88,527
Suburban	139	60,944	42,710	60,070	76,465
Independent	81	46,949	36,732	44,384	53,765
Form of government					
Mayor-council	78	52,200	36,825	48,602	63,597
Council-manager	182	62,774	45,081	61,686	77,285
Town meeting	5	44,349	42,951	43,181	46,000
Risk manager					
Total	163	72,029	57,445	70,938	85,093
Geographic region					
Northeast	5	78,561	72,927	78,234	78,575
North-Central	29	74,898	64,259	77,333	83,589
South	79	65,400	52,870	62,569	78,008
West	50	80,185	61,974	77,648	96,323
Metro type					
Central	66	72,144	57,402	71,218	86,357
Suburban	72	78,155	63,641	76,662	87,939
Independent	25	54,084	45,590	51,563	63,661
Form of government					
Mayor-council	28	67,266	58,345	69,590	77,887
Council-manager	131	73,081	57,445	71,498	86,525
Treasurer					
Total	378	51,728	33,337	46,020	64,293
Geographic region					
Northeast	53	49,933	33,433	45,066	61,614
North-Central	232	46,538	32,322	43,568	55,117
South	55	61,988	32,172	48,847	80,818
West	38	71,064	48,294	66,972	83,900
Metro type					
Central	37	86,715	69,803	84,120	105,465
Suburban	153	54,706	37,482	47,549	69,869
Independent	188	42,419	30,550	41,402	51,638

Title of official	Number of municipalities reporting	Distribution of 2008 salaries			
		Mean ($)	First quartile ($)	Median ($)	Third quartile ($)
All cities continued					
Form of government					
Mayor-council	197	45,072	31,000	41,500	52,512
Council-manager	166	59,414	39,188	54,108	74,378
Commission	5	61,928	45,566	46,822	83,048
Town meeting	8	43,590	32,075	36,453	55,968
Over 1,000,000					
Chief admin. officer/city manager					
Total	. . .	. . .	. . .	. . .	. . .
Geographic region	. . .	. . .	. . .	. . .	. . .
Metro type	. . .	. . .	. . .	. . .	. . .
Form of government	. . .	. . .	. . .	. . .	. . .
Chief elected official					
Total	. . .	. . .	. . .	. . .	. . .
Geographic region	. . .	. . .	. . .	. . .	. . .
Metro type	. . .	. . .	. . .	. . .	. . .
Form of government	. . .	. . .	. . .	. . .	. . .
Chief financial officer					
Total	. . .	. . .	. . .	. . .	. . .
Geographic region	. . .	. . .	. . .	. . .	. . .
Metro type	. . .	. . .	. . .	. . .	. . .
Form of government	. . .	. . .	. . .	. . .	. . .
Chief law enforcement official					
Total	. . .	. . .	. . .	. . .	. . .
Geographic region	. . .	. . .	. . .	. . .	. . .
Metro type	. . .	. . .	. . .	. . .	. . .
Form of government	. . .	. . .	. . .	. . .	. . .
Chief librarian					
Total	. . .	. . .	. . .	. . .	. . .
Geographic region	. . .	. . .	. . .	. . .	. . .
Metro type	. . .	. . .	. . .	. . .	. . .
Form of government	. . .	. . .	. . .	. . .	. . .
Clerk					
Total	. . .	. . .	. . .	. . .	. . .
Geographic region	. . .	. . .	. . .	. . .	. . .
Metro type	. . .	. . .	. . .	. . .	. . .
Form of government	. . .	. . .	. . .	. . .	. . .
Economic development director					
Total	. . .	. . .	. . .	. . .	. . .
Geographic region	. . .	. . .	. . .	. . .	. . .
Metro type	. . .	. . .	. . .	. . .	. . .
Form of government	. . .	. . .	. . .	. . .	. . .
Engineer					
Total	. . .	. . .	. . .	. . .	. . .
Geographic region	. . .	. . .	. . .	. . .	. . .
Metro type	. . .	. . .	. . .	. . .	. . .
Form of government	. . .	. . .	. . .	. . .	. . .
Fire chief					
Total	. . .	. . .	. . .	. . .	. . .
Geographic region	. . .	. . .	. . .	. . .	. . .
Metro type	. . .	. . .	. . .	. . .	. . .
Form of government	. . .	. . .	. . .	. . .	. . .
Health officer					
Total	. . .	. . .	. . .	. . .	. . .
Geographic region	. . .	. . .	. . .	. . .	. . .
Metro type	. . .	. . .	. . .	. . .	. . .
Form of government	. . .	. . .	. . .	. . .	. . .
Human resources director					
Total	. . .	. . .	. . .	. . .	. . .
Geographic region	. . .	. . .	. . .	. . .	. . .
Metro type	. . .	. . .	. . .	. . .	. . .
Form of government	. . .	. . .	. . .	. . .	. . .
Human services director					
Total	. . .	. . .	. . .	. . .	. . .
Geographic region	. . .	. . .	. . .	. . .	. . .
Metro type	. . .	. . .	. . .	. . .	. . .
Form of government	. . .	. . .	. . .	. . .	. . .
Information services director					
Total	. . .	. . .	. . .	. . .	. . .
Geographic region	. . .	. . .	. . .	. . .	. . .
Metro type	. . .	. . .	. . .	. . .	. . .
Form of government	. . .	. . .	. . .	. . .	. . .
Parks and recreation director					
Total	. . .	. . .	. . .	. . .	. . .
Geographic region	. . .	. . .	. . .	. . .	. . .
Metro type	. . .	. . .	. . .	. . .	. . .
Form of government	. . .	. . .	. . .	. . .	. . .
Parks superintendent					
Total	. . .	. . .	. . .	. . .	. . .

Table 1/8   SALARIES OF MUNICIPAL OFFICIALS: JULY–NOVEMBER 2008
continued

Title of official	Number of municipalities reporting	Mean ($)	First quartile ($)	Median ($)	Third quartile ($)
Over 1,000,000 continued					
Geographic region	...	...	...	...	...
Metro type	...	...	...	...	...
Form of government	...	...	...	...	...
Planning director					
Total	...	...	...	...	...
Geographic region	...	...	...	...	...
Metro type	...	...	...	...	...
Form of government	...	...	...	...	...
Primary asst. manager/CAO					
Total	...	...	...	...	...
Geographic region	...	...	...	...	...
Metro type	...	...	...	...	...
Form of government	...	...	...	...	...
Public safety director					
Total	...	...	...	...	...
Geographic region	...	...	...	...	...
Metro type	...	...	...	...	...
Form of government	...	...	...	...	...
Public works director					
Total	...	...	...	...	...
Geographic region	...	...	...	...	...
Metro type	...	...	...	...	...
Form of government	...	...	...	...	...
Purchasing director					
Total	...	...	...	...	...
Geographic region	...	...	...	...	...
Metro type	...	...	...	...	...
Form of government	...	...	...	...	...
Recreation director					
Total	...	...	...	...	...
Geographic region	...	...	...	...	...
Metro type	...	...	...	...	...
Form of government	...	...	...	...	...
Risk manager					
Total	...	...	...	...	...
Geographic region	...	...	...	...	...
Metro type	...	...	...	...	...
Form of government	...	...	...	...	...
Treasurer					
Total	...	...	...	...	...
Geographic region	...	...	...	...	...
Metro type	...	...	...	...	...
Form of government	...	...	...	...	...
500,000–1,000,000					
Chief admin. officer/city manager					
Total	...	...	...	...	...
Geographic region	...	...	...	...	...
Metro type	...	...	...	...	...
Form of government	...	...	...	...	...
Chief elected official					
Total	...	...	...	...	...
Geographic region	...	...	...	...	...
Metro type	...	...	...	...	...
Form of government	...	...	...	...	...
Chief financial officer					
Total	...	...	...	...	...
Geographic region	...	...	...	...	...
Metro type	...	...	...	...	...
Form of government	...	...	...	...	...
Chief law enforcement official					
Total	...	...	...	...	...
Geographic region	...	...	...	...	...
Metro type	...	...	...	...	...
Form of government	...	...	...	...	...
Chief librarian					
Total	...	...	...	...	...
Geographic region	...	...	...	...	...
Metro type	...	...	...	...	...
Form of government	...	...	...	...	...
Clerk					
Total	...	...	...	...	...
Geographic region	...	...	...	...	...
Metro type	...	...	...	...	...
Form of government	...	...	...	...	...
Economic development director					
Total	...	...	...	...	...
Geographic region	...	...	...	...	...
Metro type	...	...	...	...	...
Form of government	...	...	...	...	...

Title of official	Number of municipalities reporting	Mean ($)	First quartile ($)	Median ($)	Third quartile ($)
500,000–1,000,000 continued					
Engineer					
Total	...	...	...	...	...
Geographic region	...	...	...	...	...
Metro type	...	...	...	...	...
Form of government	...	...	...	...	...
Fire chief					
Total	...	...	...	...	...
Geographic region	...	...	...	...	...
Metro type	...	...	...	...	...
Form of government	...	...	...	...	...
Health officer					
Total	...	...	...	...	...
Geographic region	...	...	...	...	...
Metro type	...	...	...	...	...
Form of government	...	...	...	...	...
Human resources director					
Total	...	...	...	...	...
Geographic region	...	...	...	...	...
Metro type	...	...	...	...	...
Form of government	...	...	...	...	...
Human services director					
Total	...	...	...	...	...
Geographic region	...	...	...	...	...
Metro type	...	...	...	...	...
Form of government	...	...	...	...	...
Information services director					
Total	...	...	...	...	...
Geographic region	...	...	...	...	...
Metro type	...	...	...	...	...
Form of government	...	...	...	...	...
Parks and recreation director					
Total	...	...	...	...	...
Geographic region	...	...	...	...	...
Metro type	...	...	...	...	...
Form of government	...	...	...	...	...
Parks superintendent					
Total	...	...	...	...	...
Geographic region	...	...	...	...	...
Metro type	...	...	...	...	...
Form of government	...	...	...	...	...
Planning director					
Total	...	...	...	...	...
Geographic region	...	...	...	...	...
Metro type	...	...	...	...	...
Form of government	...	...	...	...	...
Primary asst. manager/CAO					
Total	...	...	...	...	...
Geographic region	...	...	...	...	...
Metro type	...	...	...	...	...
Form of government	...	...	...	...	...
Public safety director					
Total	...	...	...	...	...
Geographic region	...	...	...	...	...
Metro type	...	...	...	...	...
Form of government	...	...	...	...	...
Public works director					
Total	...	...	...	...	...
Geographic region	...	...	...	...	...
Metro type	...	...	...	...	...
Form of government	...	...	...	...	...
Purchasing director					
Total	...	...	...	...	...
Geographic region	...	...	...	...	...
Metro type	...	...	...	...	...
Form of government	...	...	...	...	...
Recreation director					
Total	...	...	...	...	...
Geographic region	...	...	...	...	...
Metro type	...	...	...	...	...
Form of government	...	...	...	...	...
Risk manager					
Total	...	...	...	...	...
Geographic region	...	...	...	...	...
Metro type	...	...	...	...	...
Form of government	...	...	...	...	...
Treasurer					
Total	...	...	...	...	...
Geographic region	...	...	...	...	...
Metro type	...	...	...	...	...
Form of government	...	...	...	...	...

Table 1/8 SALARIES OF MUNICIPAL OFFICIALS: JULY–NOVEMBER 2008
continued

Title of official	Number of municipalities reporting	Distribution of 2008 salaries			
		Mean ($)	First quartile ($)	Median ($)	Third quartile ($)
250,000–499,999					
Chief admin. officer/city manager					
Total	8	184,634	182,848	198,106	210,000
Geographic region					
North-Central	3	148,739	124,494	140,488	168,858
West	3	201,984	197,976	198,984	204,492
Metro type					
Central	8	184,634	182,848	198,106	210,000
Form of government					
Council-manager	6	204,680	197,667	204,492	210,000
Chief elected official					
Total	7	64,920	31,972	43,470	99,626
Geographic region					
North-Central	3	110,675	99,626	101,220	116,998
Metro type					
Central	7	64,920	31,972	43,470	99,626
Form of government					
Council-manager	5	44,727	28,000	35,944	43,470
Chief financial officer					
Total	9	132,290	123,132	130,006	145,903
Geographic region					
North-Central	4	123,518	117,497	125,221	131,242
West	3	140,211	135,395	147,657	148,751
Metro type					
Central	9	132,290	123,132	130,006	145,903
Form of government					
Mayor-council	3	117,981	112,832	122,163	125,221
Council-manager	6	139,445	132,537	143,017	147,219
Chief law enforcement official					
Total	9	140,340	136,875	141,234	147,280
Geographic region					
North-Central	4	122,773	106,453	123,156	139,476
West	3	164,484	159,180	171,360	173,226
Metro type					
Central	9	140,340	136,875	141,234	147,280
Form of government					
Mayor-council	3	114,604	103,469	109,437	123,156
Council-manager	6	153,208	142,676	147,140	165,340
Chief librarian					
Total	3	102,458	88,684	101,244	115,625
Geographic region	...	...	...	...	...
Metro type					
Central	3	102,458	88,684	101,244	115,625
Form of government					
Council-manager	3	102,458	88,684	101,244	115,625
Clerk					
Total	8	103,622	94,119	103,548	113,740
Geographic region					
North-Central	3	86,699	82,388	90,514	92,917
West	3	116,527	108,893	112,486	122,141
Metro type					
Central	8	103,622	94,119	103,548	113,740
Form of government					
Council-manager	6	107,190	102,672	108,893	116,247
Economic development director					
Total	7	106,113	88,160	112,297	121,389
Geographic region					
North-Central	3	108,728	101,526	119,646	121,389
West	3	91,092	80,490	92,915	102,606
Metro type					
Central	7	106,113	88,160	112,297	121,389
Form of government					
Council-manager	5	100,003	83,405	92,915	112,297
Engineer					
Total	6	104,687	105,805	112,364	118,770
Geographic region					
North-Central	3	89,109	80,260	105,471	106,140
Metro type					
Central	6	104,687	105,805	112,364	118,770
Form of government					
Council-manager	4	103,961	102,202	118,487	120,246
Fire chief					
Total	9	132,161	122,448	140,043	147,657
Geographic region					
North-Central	4	118,688	111,444	119,604	126,847
West	3	149,723	148,751	149,844	150,756
Metro type					
Central	9	132,161	122,448	140,043	147,657
Form of government					
Mayor-council	3	111,569	106,130	116,759	119,604
Council-manager	6	142,457	140,383	144,530	149,297

Title of official	Number of municipalities reporting	Distribution of 2008 salaries			
		Mean ($)	First quartile ($)	Median ($)	Third quartile ($)
250,000–499,999 continued					
Health officer					
Total	4	113,946	102,486	106,256	117,717
Geographic region					
North-Central	3	121,168	106,256	106,625	128,808
Metro type					
Central	4	113,946	102,486	106,256	117,717
Form of government	...	...	...	...	...
Human resources director					
Total	8	119,097	108,996	124,623	130,647
Geographic region					
North-Central	3	114,374	105,276	119,466	126,018
West	3	116,623	106,572	111,420	124,073
Metro type					
Central	8	119,097	108,996	124,623	130,647
Form of government					
Council-manager	6	123,704	116,010	129,893	131,928
Human services director					
Total	3	102,500	94,812	113,499	115,687
Geographic region	...	...	...	...	...
Metro type					
Central	3	102,500	94,812	113,499	115,687
Form of government					
Council-manager	3	102,500	94,812	113,499	115,687
Information services director					
Total	8	124,161	115,470	130,117	135,195
Geographic region					
North-Central	3	127,777	118,680	129,193	137,582
West	3	115,772	99,829	117,904	132,780
Metro type					
Central	8	124,161	115,470	130,117	135,195
Form of government					
Council-manager	6	125,988	121,188	131,322	142,380
Parks and recreation director					
Total	7	131,140	122,081	136,464	136,923
Geographic region					
West	3	131,351	128,664	136,464	136,595
Metro type					
Central	7	131,140	122,081	136,464	136,923
Form of government					
Council-manager	6	134,244	126,589	136,595	137,021
Parks superintendent					
Total	6	86,270	71,581	92,814	105,018
Geographic region	...	...	...	...	...
Metro type					
Central	6	86,270	71,581	92,814	105,018
Form of government					
Council-manager	5	83,683	66,634	86,424	106,956
Planning director					
Total	8	121,486	117,495	125,529	129,594
Geographic region					
North-Central	3	111,493	102,363	109,726	119,740
West	3	128,783	124,812	129,540	133,133
Metro type					
Central	8	121,486	117,495	125,529	129,594
Form of government					
Council-manager	6	127,860	124,264	128,799	129,701
Primary asst. manager/CAO					
Total	6	135,133	118,456	140,659	156,002
Geographic region					
West	3	138,444	126,454	158,022	160,222
Metro type					
Central	6	135,133	118,456	140,659	156,002
Form of government					
Council-manager	5	139,330	131,375	149,942	158,022
Public safety director					
Total	...	...	...	...	...
Geographic region	...	...	...	...	...
Metro type	...	...	...	...	...
Form of government	...	...	...	...	...
Public works director					
Total	9	127,884	119,645	135,313	140,938
Geographic region					
North-Central	4	119,549	111,809	127,290	135,030
West	3	130,958	116,619	147,657	153,647
Metro type					
Central	9	127,884	119,645	135,313	140,938
Form of government					
Mayor-council	3	114,419	103,973	119,645	127,479
Council-manager	6	134,617	135,940	139,946	145,977

Table 1/8   SALARIES OF MUNICIPAL OFFICIALS: JULY–NOVEMBER 2008
continued

Title of official	Number of municipalities reporting	Distribution of 2008 salaries			
		Mean ($)	First quartile ($)	Median ($)	Third quartile ($)
250,000–499,999 continued					
Purchasing director					
Total	7	94,208	87,696	96,465	102,258
Geographic region					
North-Central	3	90,619	87,696	89,664	93,065
West	3	93,549	86,843	97,561	102,261
Metro type					
Central	7	94,208	87,696	96,465	102,258
Form of government					
Council-manager	5	96,813	96,465	97,561	106,956
Recreation director					
Total	4	91,195	88,425	92,642	95,412
Geographic region	. . .	. . .	. . .	. . .	. . .
Metro type					
Central	4	91,195	88,425	92,642	95,412
Form of government					
Council-manager	3	91,594	89,492	95,284	95,541
Risk manager					
Total	6	87,282	74,816	89,427	93,394
Geographic region	. . .	. . .	. . .	. . .	. . .
Metro type					
Central	6	87,282	74,816	89,427	93,394
Form of government					
Council-manager	4	85,839	68,453	81,589	98,975
Treasurer					
Total	5	93,115	85,463	91,292	105,465
Geographic region					
North-Central	3	94,073	88,378	91,292	98,378
Metro type					
Central	5	93,115	85,463	91,292	105,465
Form of government					
Council-manager	3	96,273	79,816	105,465	117,325
100,000–249,999					
Chief admin. officer/city manager					
Total	31	180,184	161,850	176,455	199,832
Geographic region					
North-Central	4	154,806	146,715	154,434	162,524
South	13	180,356	164,171	171,127	212,598
West	14	187,276	175,370	184,296	200,141
Metro type					
Central	21	173,798	152,688	166,567	198,640
Suburban	10	193,595	177,255	187,298	207,556
Form of government					
Council-manager	28	183,393	163,553	180,279	202,922
Chief elected official					
Total	17	46,698	27,000	37,260	64,459
Geographic region					
North-Central	5	49,851	35,000	39,141	41,200
South	6	48,713	26,959	45,730	72,999
West	6	42,056	29,145	37,170	45,315
Metro type					
Central	12	46,357	30,687	38,201	67,306
Suburban	5	47,516	26,500	37,080	48,000
Form of government					
Council-manager	14	41,211	26,959	37,170	46,300
Chief financial officer					
Total	32	126,026	109,954	123,901	136,686
Geographic region					
North-Central	6	119,198	108,217	117,307	123,028
South	11	120,175	103,760	121,039	133,412
West	15	133,047	123,393	128,918	142,458
Metro type					
Central	20	126,443	108,467	121,516	145,939
Suburban	12	125,331	119,824	128,905	131,391
Form of government					
Mayor-council	3	121,697	116,921	129,800	130,524
Council-manager	28	127,200	113,462	123,901	141,237
Chief law enforcement official					
Total	33	133,260	117,832	125,145	150,001
Geographic region					
North-Central	6	126,185	108,555	123,954	145,307
South	13	121,437	109,367	121,492	129,600
West	14	147,271	126,753	143,622	167,052
Metro type					
Central	22	131,700	115,424	123,954	149,930
Suburban	11	136,380	123,417	141,312	150,548
Form of government					
Council-manager	30	135,889	121,387	130,806	151,557

Title of official	Number of municipalities reporting	Distribution of 2008 salaries			
		Mean ($)	First quartile ($)	Median ($)	Third quartile ($)
100,000–249,999 continued					
Chief librarian					
Total	19	101,402	89,734	99,292	118,326
Geographic region					
South	8	94,366	82,618	92,214	104,746
West	9	109,364	98,000	118,320	120,000
Metro type					
Central	12	98,665	89,849	98,646	108,628
Suburban	7	106,092	92,239	118,320	119,166
Form of government					
Council-manager	18	102,139	91,776	99,885	118,328
Clerk					
Total	33	87,269	74,500	86,237	97,368
Geographic region					
North-Central	6	79,952	75,820	81,337	83,077
South	12	77,681	62,370	72,558	96,108
West	15	97,867	87,848	92,020	104,892
Metro type					
Central	21	83,772	70,408	79,778	92,020
Suburban	12	93,389	87,184	92,285	103,788
Form of government					
Mayor-council	3	68,136	66,254	70,408	71,154
Council-manager	29	89,391	78,258	89,460	101,244
Economic development director					
Total	20	105,737	89,534	109,517	132,318
Geographic region					
North-Central	4	101,815	84,048	89,808	107,575
South	9	96,704	63,246	108,696	121,209
West	7	119,590	103,411	129,459	133,880
Metro type					
Central	14	106,697	84,731	121,091	134,000
Suburban	6	103,496	92,424	102,590	109,928
Form of government					
Council-manager	18	106,765	91,975	115,655	133,199
Engineer					
Total	29	102,787	89,353	102,165	112,507
Geographic region					
North-Central	5	104,338	91,707	109,017	110,255
South	12	94,989	86,411	94,556	101,679
West	12	109,939	101,844	108,937	123,025
Metro type					
Central	19	97,686	85,961	95,308	109,636
Suburban	10	112,480	104,474	108,937	125,217
Form of government					
Council-manager	27	103,988	91,579	104,388	116,584
Fire chief					
Total	29	128,238	111,426	127,951	145,933
Geographic region					
North-Central	5	116,020	111,426	114,502	117,190
South	13	113,576	97,829	114,546	127,951
West	11	151,119	140,496	146,304	156,408
Metro type					
Central	21	125,237	111,394	117,190	133,855
Suburban	8	136,116	134,534	140,496	146,026
Form of government					
Council-manager	26	131,635	114,513	130,522	146,157
Health officer					
Total	7	102,391	81,960	94,891	99,618
Geographic region					
South	6	88,342	79,636	90,749	96,294
Metro type					
Central	7	102,391	81,960	94,891	99,618
Form of government					
Council-manager	7	102,391	81,960	94,891	99,618
Human resources director					
Total	33	113,730	100,235	113,269	132,000
Geographic region					
North-Central	6	108,303	89,273	109,406	118,750
South	13	103,752	93,600	104,555	116,965
West	14	125,322	109,453	124,198	136,668
Metro type					
Central	22	111,924	92,504	106,295	128,352
Suburban	11	117,342	110,725	115,892	126,852
Form of government					
Council-manager	30	115,985	103,894	114,555	132,379
Human services director					
Total	5	103,247	93,600	98,340	102,212
Geographic region					
South	3	87,151	81,557	93,600	95,970
Metro type					
Central	5	103,247	93,600	98,340	102,212

Table 1/8   SALARIES OF MUNICIPAL OFFICIALS: JULY–NOVEMBER 2008
continued

Title of official	Number of municipalities reporting	Distribution of 2008 salaries			
		Mean ($)	First quartile ($)	Median ($)	Third quartile ($)
100,000–249,999 continued					
Form of government					
Council-manager	5	103,247	93,600	98,340	102,212
Information services director					
Total	32	113,115	99,975	113,870	127,422
Geographic region					
North-Central	6	106,861	104,389	108,953	112,999
South	13	105,043	93,600	110,886	122,806
West	13	124,074	105,000	124,595	130,373
Metro type					
Central	22	113,193	100,328	113,061	129,475
Suburban	10	112,944	101,433	115,753	124,192
Form of government					
Council-manager	29	114,009	100,244	114,336	129,348
Parks and recreation director					
Total	28	112,942	99,372	110,751	122,346
Geographic region					
North-Central	3	99,311	95,906	103,812	104,967
South	13	105,928	96,600	110,166	112,914
West	12	123,947	101,290	123,096	131,756
Metro type					
Central	19	108,096	96,390	103,812	112,832
Suburban	9	123,172	120,328	124,595	130,363
Form of government					
Council-manager	26	113,393	97,524	112,043	123,845
Parks superintendent					
Total	25	78,107	64,922	80,112	88,893
Geographic region					
North-Central	3	86,692	84,964	86,790	88,469
South	13	67,517	64,236	66,937	72,945
West	9	90,543	84,924	90,667	96,949
Metro type					
Central	17	73,448	64,357	70,321	83,138
Suburban	8	88,009	86,698	90,407	95,416
Form of government					
Council-manager	22	78,598	65,426	78,277	88,367
Planning director					
Total	31	109,624	94,194	103,188	125,097
Geographic region					
North-Central	6	102,439	95,020	98,628	109,672
South	12	98,233	90,487	95,507	105,277
West	13	123,455	103,188	125,304	138,600
Metro type					
Central	19	108,292	94,194	98,343	121,479
Suburban	12	111,734	98,442	106,159	126,343
Form of government					
Mayor-council	3	107,796	96,070	100,000	115,624
Council-manager	27	110,409	94,712	104,183	125,097
Primary asst. manager/CAO					
Total	23	127,707	113,824	130,223	144,912
Geographic region					
South	11	119,869	115,214	124,564	139,475
West	10	136,567	117,416	144,860	154,386
Metro type					
Central	15	123,570	112,789	124,564	139,819
Suburban	8	135,465	125,954	143,365	147,664
Form of government					
Council-manager	21	132,863	119,350	137,840	145,800
Public safety director					
Total	...	...	...	...	...
Geographic region	...	...	...	...	...
Metro type	...	...	...	...	...
Form of government	...	...	...	...	...
Public works director					
Total	30	124,031	115,079	123,250	129,420
Geographic region					
North-Central	6	120,859	111,234	120,398	132,427
South	10	114,448	108,512	118,476	127,198
West	14	132,235	121,742	127,684	137,389
Metro type					
Central	19	122,880	111,355	120,511	131,376
Suburban	11	126,019	122,112	128,107	129,253
Form of government					
Council-manager	27	125,250	117,164	125,000	131,970
Purchasing director					
Total	20	80,981	67,558	84,154	91,801
Geographic region					
North-Central	3	89,297	83,420	91,439	96,246
South	10	74,984	62,109	76,295	85,973
West	7	85,984	80,789	91,728	94,695

Title of official	Number of municipalities reporting	Distribution of 2008 salaries			
		Mean ($)	First quartile ($)	Median ($)	Third quartile ($)
100,000–249,999 continued					
Metro type					
Central	16	81,601	67,558	84,154	92,561
Suburban	4	78,504	74,071	84,046	88,479
Form of government					
Council-manager	18	82,236	71,713	85,471	91,947
Recreation director					
Total	17	78,653	64,922	77,667	87,764
Geographic region					
South	10	64,584	58,006	65,280	73,276
West	7	98,752	86,574	92,020	95,357
Metro type					
Central	14	76,492	62,508	72,032	85,640
Suburban	3	88,737	84,097	85,384	91,700
Form of government					
Council-manager	16	78,715	64,117	76,894	88,828
Risk manager					
Total	23	86,808	80,011	86,499	97,789
Geographic region					
North-Central	4	90,414	80,860	90,706	100,260
South	9	81,399	73,452	84,061	87,124
West	10	90,233	84,917	88,511	98,596
Metro type					
Central	15	85,641	77,103	86,499	93,432
Suburban	8	88,995	83,595	86,785	99,552
Form of government					
Council-manager	22	87,153	80,964	86,812	98,596
Treasurer					
Total	15	98,442	77,135	92,618	128,128
Geographic region					
North-Central	4	87,183	81,400	91,671	97,454
South	6	103,274	74,374	111,933	132,995
West	5	101,650	83,239	87,912	125,008
Metro type					
Central	10	104,788	88,480	98,666	132,995
Suburban	5	85,750	68,292	83,239	87,912
Form of government					
Council-manager	12	98,736	80,187	90,265	127,150
50,000–99,999					
Chief admin. officer/city manager					
Total	75	142,477	128,629	143,950	158,963
Geographic region					
Northeast	5	110,590	62,000	137,351	147,933
North-Central	27	132,713	120,740	133,780	143,995
South	28	150,548	135,912	150,741	167,615
West	15	155,613	140,145	158,496	173,000
Metro type					
Central	44	137,443	115,357	139,753	158,826
Suburban	30	149,534	134,673	144,121	165,684
Form of government					
Mayor-council	15	112,672	106,779	112,898	135,837
Council-manager	59	150,514	135,070	149,568	166,597
Chief elected official					
Total	41	64,139	18,630	63,500	100,000
Geographic region					
Northeast	6	68,029	54,875	70,500	94,375
North-Central	17	57,379	24,720	46,900	90,020
South	10	72,014	16,848	100,000	105,642
West	8	65,741	18,398	63,172	89,700
Metro type					
Central	26	67,914	18,671	77,750	100,131
Suburban	15	57,595	22,050	49,992	80,217
Form of government					
Mayor-council	23	94,693	77,750	100,000	109,484
Council-manager	17	25,504	15,600	17,700	26,400
Chief financial officer					
Total	78	106,814	94,945	105,861	118,230
Geographic region					
Northeast	6	106,936	90,199	112,835	127,888
North-Central	26	108,096	97,342	106,891	114,839
South	30	100,781	90,823	103,462	110,714
West	16	115,998	104,769	114,212	126,736
Metro type					
Central	46	102,069	92,155	102,134	110,661
Suburban	31	113,966	104,712	115,107	126,967
Form of government					
Mayor-council	23	101,179	91,778	99,023	108,250
Council-manager	54	109,440	101,377	109,737	124,508

Table 1/8   SALARIES OF MUNICIPAL OFFICIALS: JULY–NOVEMBER 2008
continued

Title of official	Number of municipalities reporting	Distribution of 2008 salaries			
		Mean ($)	First quartile ($)	Median ($)	Third quartile ($)
50,000–99,999 continued					
Chief law enforcement official					
Total	81	113,288	99,902	111,894	123,618
Geographic region					
Northeast	6	124,510	111,886	125,529	138,531
North-Central	27	111,653	97,839	118,955	122,966
South	31	107,485	100,951	105,492	119,643
West	17	122,506	109,633	122,820	135,688
Metro type					
Central	48	105,927	96,633	104,084	118,800
Suburban	32	124,374	117,454	123,166	134,785
Form of government					
Mayor-council	24	103,086	90,923	101,790	116,992
Council-manager	56	118,218	105,873	119,562	129,412
Chief librarian					
Total	33	89,119	78,708	87,387	101,773
Geographic region					
Northeast	3	97,713	92,618	98,057	102,980
North-Central	11	86,427	81,229	88,275	98,079
South	12	86,197	70,978	83,607	101,479
West	7	94,677	76,004	94,602	103,944
Metro type					
Central	23	87,378	76,004	87,387	100,839
Suburban	10	93,124	80,852	88,661	109,188
Form of government					
Mayor-council	13	90,542	78,708	90,035	106,015
Council-manager	20	88,194	77,862	86,220	101,479
Clerk					
Total	74	70,556	60,485	72,309	82,537
Geographic region					
Northeast	6	83,395	68,437	82,903	91,424
North-Central	28	69,494	63,134	71,425	76,939
South	28	69,478	56,395	71,206	82,179
West	12	69,132	58,562	72,705	79,836
Metro type					
Central	45	65,008	55,692	63,985	74,268
Suburban	28	78,997	73,041	78,708	90,060
Form of government					
Mayor-council	22	65,298	54,371	64,532	75,880
Council-manager	52	72,781	62,077	74,266	84,288
Economic development director					
Total	35	92,360	78,181	89,313	103,866
Geographic region					
Northeast	3	101,376	87,689	91,054	109,902
North-Central	10	84,178	77,027	84,115	87,739
South	11	90,356	75,598	89,313	98,288
West	11	99,344	84,645	101,580	111,622
Metro type					
Central	16	90,285	78,051	90,059	97,421
Suburban	18	93,143	79,019	87,125	108,121
Form of government					
Mayor-council	11	94,172	86,346	92,388	98,288
Council-manager	24	91,530	76,385	85,866	109,452
Engineer					
Total	65	97,157	88,000	100,615	108,564
Geographic region					
Northeast	5	102,365	91,872	108,282	117,249
North-Central	23	100,642	93,155	101,136	108,692
South	25	94,905	80,880	95,904	105,009
West	12	93,001	83,853	94,993	106,175
Metro type					
Central	43	92,749	82,363	91,872	102,640
Suburban	21	105,984	104,012	108,438	112,472
Form of government					
Mayor-council	18	88,410	76,015	88,100	100,997
Council-manager	46	100,641	91,492	101,928	108,821
Fire chief					
Total	77	106,314	95,236	105,491	118,248
Geographic region					
Northeast	4	110,336	99,652	113,621	124,304
North-Central	28	104,143	94,690	105,692	112,797
South	31	103,870	92,334	101,928	114,852
West	14	114,918	101,655	115,460	121,289
Metro type					
Central	50	101,918	92,266	101,082	110,978
Suburban	26	114,358	105,537	113,758	124,524
Form of government					
Mayor-council	24	99,563	88,144	98,796	109,160
Council-manager	52	109,684	98,921	109,160	120,697
Health officer					
Total	16	84,712	72,200	78,236	93,194
Geographic region					
Northeast	3	85,512	75,056	77,447	91,935

Title of official	Number of municipalities reporting	Distribution of 2008 salaries			
		Mean ($)	First quartile ($)	Median ($)	Third quartile ($)
50,000–99,999 continued					
North-Central	6	92,309	80,292	89,040	96,105
South	7	77,857	58,715	75,000	85,158
Metro type					
Central	12	81,434	69,406	77,576	93,194
Suburban	4	94,546	83,743	89,040	99,843
Form of government					
Mayor-council	4	77,372	67,737	75,056	84,691
Council-manager	11	88,018	72,903	88,055	94,840
Human resources director					
Total	80	97,256	86,471	96,647	106,447
Geographic region					
Northeast	6	94,520	81,498	84,383	108,664
North-Central	28	97,746	87,499	98,575	106,312
South	31	95,128	88,130	94,562	104,532
West	15	101,834	91,372	101,580	113,847
Metro type					
Central	47	92,559	82,970	92,252	102,288
Suburban	32	104,172	93,452	104,425	115,235
Form of government					
Mayor-council	24	90,705	79,139	88,172	98,946
Council-manager	55	100,205	89,802	100,234	111,926
Human services director					
Total	16	80,585	74,985	80,696	87,053
Geographic region					
North-Central	4	86,199	83,367	87,963	90,795
South	10	80,463	74,931	80,696	85,953
Metro type					
Central	10	80,747	75,697	80,696	85,953
Suburban	6	80,314	75,254	81,012	89,084
Form of government					
Mayor-council	4	70,559	65,046	71,152	76,665
Council-manager	12	83,927	79,046	84,483	88,284
Information services director					
Total	69	92,537	80,775	92,171	103,108
Geographic region					
Northeast	6	96,627	86,280	94,635	103,418
North-Central	22	91,335	80,274	87,721	100,011
South	28	91,402	80,195	92,077	103,026
West	13	95,131	87,123	99,216	106,221
Metro type					
Central	44	90,758	79,786	90,028	103,026
Suburban	24	95,228	83,145	95,062	101,974
Form of government					
Mayor-council	20	87,250	74,654	84,094	95,800
Council-manager	48	95,068	84,999	96,561	106,639
Parks and recreation director					
Total	66	98,564	84,551	98,801	111,866
Geographic region					
Northeast	6	99,782	83,706	100,787	117,422
North-Central	19	99,870	90,449	100,440	108,862
South	27	89,849	81,054	91,548	97,924
West	14	113,076	101,811	113,742	129,775
Metro type					
Central	41	91,933	77,339	90,194	101,580
Suburban	25	109,438	100,440	109,317	121,519
Form of government					
Mayor-council	17	90,025	76,925	83,500	102,624
Council-manager	49	101,526	90,020	99,923	116,791
Parks superintendent					
Total	58	67,937	59,262	68,307	74,876
Geographic region					
Northeast	3	73,614	69,932	73,708	77,344
North-Central	19	74,571	67,098	71,598	78,597
South	26	59,216	53,984	59,296	66,112
West	10	76,300	68,688	78,060	86,523
Metro type					
Central	37	65,889	59,228	63,630	70,630
Suburban	21	71,543	64,210	71,856	80,980
Form of government					
Mayor-council	15	70,355	66,167	68,746	74,487
Council-manager	43	67,093	57,432	64,210	74,859
Planning director					
Total	71	95,471	83,953	92,929	105,465
Geographic region					
Northeast	6	95,148	81,806	88,700	104,463
North-Central	21	94,125	85,924	92,048	99,060
South	29	90,719	82,884	91,884	105,000
West	15	106,673	94,372	101,580	122,638
Metro type					
Central	44	91,972	82,507	92,033	101,740
Suburban	26	101,170	86,469	98,396	114,444

Table 1/8   SALARIES OF MUNICIPAL OFFICIALS: JULY–NOVEMBER 2008
continued

Title of official	Number of municipalities reporting	Distribution of 2008 salaries			
		Mean ($)	First quartile ($)	Median ($)	Third quartile ($)
50,000–99,999 continued					
Form of government					
Mayor-council	19	90,505	77,020	86,858	95,522
Council-manager	51	97,458	86,366	98,116	109,755
Primary asst. manager/CAO					
Total	52	116,340	105,122	115,818	128,774
Geographic region					
North-Central	17	109,017	101,000	108,782	120,434
South	25	123,557	113,400	118,027	134,576
West	8	120,214	111,098	122,093	125,961
Metro type					
Central	31	116,353	104,966	115,291	129,997
Suburban	21	116,321	105,857	117,998	125,000
Form of government					
Mayor-council	7	107,036	94,769	106,638	120,144
Council-manager	45	117,787	105,857	117,420	129,842
Public safety director					
Total	4	94,844	89,125	102,987	108,707
Geographic region					
North-Central	3	91,960	75,772	102,477	113,407
Metro type					
Central	3	85,013	75,772	102,477	102,987
Form of government	. . .	. . .	. . .	. . .	. . .
Public works director					
Total	77	109,808	96,455	110,692	124,992
Geographic region					
Northeast	6	110,865	97,585	113,584	127,532
North-Central	25	111,838	99,000	114,288	121,519
South	28	104,044	91,393	105,394	114,114
West	18	115,605	102,993	118,624	131,795
Metro type					
Central	44	103,749	91,393	101,946	115,124
Suburban	32	118,088	109,797	119,154	128,302
Form of government					
Mayor-council	22	101,507	91,996	97,728	113,091
Council-manager	54	113,732	105,850	114,916	127,473
Purchasing director					
Total	40	72,375	63,288	69,433	80,925
Geographic region					
Northeast	6	79,736	67,116	76,989	90,803
North-Central	8	75,702	63,042	68,100	83,506
South	22	67,541	60,220	68,685	72,494
West	4	81,270	73,652	80,643	88,262
Metro type					
Central	27	69,630	61,651	68,064	72,379
Suburban	12	78,182	68,538	76,632	84,962
Form of government					
Mayor-council	10	70,814	62,693	68,212	80,730
Council-manager	30	72,896	64,137	69,433	79,752
Recreation director					
Total	44	73,694	60,460	71,934	85,878
Geographic region					
North-Central	15	75,856	63,353	77,339	88,599
South	19	66,400	57,876	63,522	74,892
West	8	88,464	77,413	85,695	97,201
Metro type					
Central	26	70,697	60,179	67,712	82,755
Suburban	18	78,022	64,296	78,078	85,909
Form of government					
Mayor-council	11	69,655	57,519	72,467	80,904
Council-manager	33	75,040	63,064	71,401	85,924
Risk manager					
Total	44	71,605	56,793	71,218	83,793
Geographic region					
North-Central	8	80,408	72,619	81,124	86,607
South	23	65,271	53,971	60,974	80,231
West	11	77,872	61,755	74,412	97,256
Metro type					
Central	33	65,849	54,202	63,396	77,765
Suburban	11	88,873	80,848	85,665	96,949
Form of government					
Mayor-council	12	72,627	64,763	72,675	79,981
Council-manager	32	71,221	55,626	70,012	84,160
Treasurer					
Total	20	80,725	70,591	79,234	100,615
Geographic region					
Northeast	3	103,254	92,938	103,961	113,924
North-Central	8	83,124	74,179	79,234	86,542
South	6	71,547	51,313	73,812	98,215
West	3	70,156	63,174	69,803	76,962
Metro type					
Central	14	76,731	70,066	76,438	83,569
Suburban	6	90,045	79,896	90,861	102,846

Title of official	Number of municipalities reporting	Distribution of 2008 salaries			
		Mean ($)	First quartile ($)	Median ($)	Third quartile ($)
50,000–99,999 continued					
Form of government					
Mayor-council	9	79,980	69,803	81,915	104,827
Council-manager	11	81,335	72,041	79,120	90,861
25,000–49,999					
Chief admin. officer/city manager					
Total	129	140,315	120,085	139,727	155,000
Geographic region					
Northeast	6	127,726	116,800	124,600	129,822
North-Central	52	127,625	112,048	130,303	143,431
South	33	140,265	128,454	141,627	154,507
West	38	159,712	140,022	152,579	185,535
Metro type					
Central	18	128,537	115,489	133,134	145,436
Suburban	87	148,971	126,902	143,786	160,491
Independent	24	117,771	105,614	115,209	141,085
Form of government					
Mayor-council	19	111,281	85,332	115,000	135,351
Council-manager	110	145,330	125,814	141,267	155,968
Chief elected official					
Total	45	52,689	20,000	50,000	79,911
Geographic region					
Northeast	5	66,666	25,000	79,911	93,022
North-Central	17	53,162	20,000	60,100	78,737
South	15	40,719	18,806	25,000	55,000
West	8	65,391	26,237	62,286	107,803
Metro type					
Central	13	51,199	21,148	48,000	79,911
Suburban	22	51,619	15,997	40,900	87,433
Independent	10	56,978	25,832	62,233	73,334
Form of government					
Mayor-council	26	70,658	52,501	75,508	93,548
Council-manager	18	24,492	15,328	20,100	24,366
Chief financial officer					
Total	122	105,131	91,943	105,622	116,604
Geographic region					
Northeast	7	105,390	88,996	105,350	120,894
North-Central	48	99,389	86,101	103,551	111,212
South	34	100,505	89,900	100,876	111,285
West	33	118,195	103,938	116,352	129,828
Metro type					
Central	19	92,431	79,888	91,578	105,509
Suburban	81	110,510	95,940	109,725	122,824
Independent	22	96,296	87,890	100,089	108,330
Form of government					
Mayor-council	24	94,573	73,883	95,850	108,673
Council-manager	96	107,769	95,006	108,119	117,021
Chief law enforcement official					
Total	121	111,063	95,451	109,832	130,151
Geographic region					
Northeast	7	110,686	88,008	97,224	133,225
North-Central	45	104,225	89,000	105,996	119,616
South	35	102,501	93,396	100,443	117,218
West	34	129,005	111,885	130,375	138,675
Metro type					
Central	21	98,331	86,156	96,990	105,000
Suburban	75	120,142	102,550	118,609	133,920
Independent	25	94,522	80,994	96,595	111,576
Form of government					
Mayor-council	29	96,938	86,156	95,917	107,172
Council-manager	90	115,253	99,070	115,133	132,723
Chief librarian					
Total	48	79,972	68,319	79,988	92,253
Geographic region					
Northeast	5	81,412	69,060	88,196	93,360
North-Central	13	76,719	68,907	82,800	90,779
South	17	71,665	60,008	72,585	80,000
West	13	93,535	76,368	91,884	108,744
Metro type					
Central	8	74,966	66,564	76,281	84,802
Suburban	29	83,415	69,060	82,800	93,360
Independent	11	74,537	64,687	69,624	82,723
Form of government					
Mayor-council	6	66,974	52,702	75,489	83,764
Council-manager	40	81,811	68,435	79,988	92,513
Clerk					
Total	113	70,538	56,000	69,888	83,203
Geographic region					
Northeast	7	79,641	64,686	73,303	87,648
North-Central	44	61,813	53,251	65,959	72,472

Table 1/8 SALARIES OF MUNICIPAL OFFICIALS: JULY–NOVEMBER 2008
continued

Title of official	Number of municipalities reporting	Mean ($)	First quartile ($)	Median ($)	Third quartile ($)
25,000–49,999 continued					
South	32	66,333	51,830	59,146	81,660
West	30	85,698	74,434	89,154	97,953
Metro type					
Central	17	61,323	51,853	63,000	70,548
Suburban	78	74,672	59,255	73,530	88,761
Independent	18	61,330	44,942	61,052	72,753
Form of government					
Mayor-council	19	63,298	46,351	59,134	75,272
Council-manager	92	72,099	57,172	71,473	85,028
Economic development director					
Total	57	90,292	70,093	88,392	104,520
Geographic region					
North-Central	26	76,330	63,777	72,247	89,049
South	14	94,797	72,850	96,448	110,500
West	16	109,617	96,183	103,751	129,788
Metro type					
Central	8	77,659	70,332	80,564	83,067
Suburban	39	95,580	71,270	99,750	112,766
Independent	10	79,774	65,618	83,654	97,865
Form of government					
Mayor-council	14	81,646	64,128	76,028	100,023
Council-manager	42	93,394	73,123	93,082	109,790
Engineer					
Total	96	93,855	80,441	93,711	104,606
Geographic region					
Northeast	5	92,551	82,311	90,454	100,702
North-Central	39	91,591	80,220	93,948	101,869
South	29	91,230	80,912	90,000	98,262
West	23	101,287	84,264	99,923	110,406
Metro type					
Central	16	90,228	79,664	87,815	99,861
Suburban	62	98,325	86,419	97,707	108,511
Independent	18	81,681	73,739	80,166	93,776
Form of government					
Mayor-council	20	83,890	74,284	82,927	97,661
Council-manager	74	96,502	84,889	93,949	105,803
Fire chief					
Total	106	102,420	86,197	100,182	114,828
Geographic region					
Northeast	5	86,102	75,221	78,854	90,064
North-Central	46	96,943	87,301	97,100	106,878
South	32	99,476	84,929	98,907	111,516
West	23	121,017	107,356	123,385	130,206
Metro type					
Central	18	94,490	84,774	92,933	99,002
Suburban	66	108,471	92,252	105,927	121,768
Independent	22	90,753	74,498	93,595	108,102
Form of government					
Mayor-council	24	90,201	72,792	89,098	99,174
Council-manager	80	106,057	91,514	103,899	118,137
Health officer					
Total	9	83,298	70,595	71,640	93,870
Geographic region					
North-Central	4	58,833	58,439	70,861	71,255
Metro type					
Suburban	6	98,514	71,694	82,865	126,290
Form of government					
Mayor-council	4	76,023	55,020	68,316	89,319
Council-manager	5	89,119	71,640	71,859	93,870
Human resources director					
Total	117	90,644	76,440	91,164	101,920
Geographic region					
Northeast	6	85,491	71,258	88,290	98,346
North-Central	42	85,101	70,663	87,671	99,330
South	34	83,863	74,863	85,636	94,326
West	35	104,767	91,686	104,988	116,428
Metro type					
Central	20	79,345	69,465	79,277	91,431
Suburban	76	95,627	82,121	97,354	109,499
Independent	21	83,373	71,386	85,812	95,321
Form of government					
Mayor-council	26	81,679	65,823	79,277	99,213
Council-manager	89	93,280	80,300	92,928	104,988
Human services director					
Total	15	86,757	78,585	87,861	95,579
Geographic region					
Northeast	3	88,667	86,230	86,459	90,001
North-Central	4	77,853	75,197	88,298	90,955
South	3	71,713	61,134	62,280	77,576
West	5	101,761	84,240	105,000	109,540
Metro type					
Suburban	12	92,953	85,560	90,366	99,461
25,000–49,999 continued					
Form of government					
Council-manager	12	90,007	81,413	88,298	96,407
Information services director					
Total	82	89,832	78,255	89,802	100,000
Geographic region					
Northeast	7	79,831	76,716	78,728	92,232
North-Central	32	87,043	78,390	84,622	93,183
South	25	90,793	79,996	91,786	97,850
West	18	97,346	86,818	98,443	106,758
Metro type					
Central	13	68,990	60,028	68,141	79,996
Suburban	60	94,050	79,948	91,620	101,590
Independent	9	91,821	85,702	96,101	100,000
Form of government					
Mayor-council	14	85,937	76,788	87,848	99,049
Council-manager	66	90,554	78,613	90,910	99,963
Parks and recreation director					
Total	101	93,800	76,781	93,197	111,484
Geographic region					
Northeast	6	96,990	81,195	91,177	109,945
North-Central	35	88,258	71,835	92,146	106,725
South	32	86,261	76,553	81,916	93,648
West	28	108,659	94,668	113,217	122,637
Metro type					
Central	19	84,693	75,431	82,378	91,333
Suburban	63	100,165	87,832	101,296	114,221
Independent	19	81,801	68,373	81,477	94,986
Form of government					
Mayor-council	24	81,296	66,774	78,650	93,480
Council-manager	76	97,940	82,954	96,508	112,483
Parks superintendent					
Total	74	66,144	53,832	65,894	73,891
Geographic region					
North-Central	21	66,201	61,505	66,872	73,199
South	29	56,991	47,139	53,480	63,974
West	22	76,913	65,831	78,076	87,768
Metro type					
Central	10	55,833	46,666	50,688	63,743
Suburban	50	69,359	60,301	68,299	77,248
Independent	14	62,027	51,053	65,833	71,864
Form of government					
Mayor-council	14	61,018	47,455	62,341	65,921
Council-manager	59	67,044	56,406	66,872	73,832
Planning director					
Total	92	92,727	80,697	89,993	106,992
Geographic region					
Northeast	8	85,979	78,742	84,329	92,487
North-Central	30	84,799	70,252	89,042	95,081
South	27	86,633	80,649	85,238	97,058
West	27	109,630	94,864	111,576	126,635
Metro type					
Central	16	83,033	67,628	86,438	96,843
Suburban	61	97,284	82,833	93,216	109,312
Independent	15	84,538	57,669	87,110	108,306
Form of government					
Mayor-council	21	77,062	63,372	77,092	94,536
Council-manager	69	97,738	85,238	92,504	112,882
Primary asst. manager/CAO					
Total	60	107,121	89,267	104,178	122,191
Geographic region					
North-Central	20	94,274	83,520	97,898	103,786
South	24	109,019	89,267	109,562	123,637
West	14	128,217	103,756	118,901	149,370
Metro type					
Central	12	93,939	79,716	90,740	116,965
Suburban	42	114,138	96,552	108,837	130,854
Independent	6	84,368	80,339	90,253	103,994
Form of government					
Mayor-council	8	86,305	74,661	85,387	113,865
Council-manager	52	110,324	93,922	105,980	123,704
Public safety director					
Total	18	104,244	95,448	103,927	112,957
Geographic region					
North-Central	14	98,482	95,448	101,745	108,333
Metro type					
Suburban	13	110,591	100,612	109,400	115,627
Independent	3	89,132	86,038	94,908	95,115
Form of government					
Mayor-council	4	81,173	74,424	77,812	84,561
Council-manager	14	110,836	98,989	107,267	115,098

Table 1/8   SALARIES OF MUNICIPAL OFFICIALS: JULY–NOVEMBER 2008
continued

Title of official	Number of municipalities reporting	Mean ($)	First quartile ($)	Median ($)	Third quartile ($)
25,000–49,999 continued					
Public works director					
Total	124	106,825	93,180	107,946	123,510
Geographic region					
Northeast	8	102,227	82,855	99,877	117,527
North-Central	50	102,036	92,931	106,005	114,855
South	31	100,413	82,840	99,195	111,754
West	35	120,398	104,060	121,763	131,164
Metro type					
Central	19	96,947	82,310	97,296	109,843
Suburban	84	112,639	98,527	111,285	126,074
Independent	21	92,508	82,892	98,176	105,040
Form of government					
Mayor-council	23	95,123	77,758	98,328	117,975
Council-manager	99	109,715	96,678	108,127	124,796
Purchasing director					
Total	27	67,874	58,791	69,093	71,499
Geographic region					
Northeast	3	74,157	61,467	70,000	84,769
North-Central	5	55,115	42,276	54,568	59,796
South	14	67,191	60,940	68,867	70,060
West	5	78,777	69,756	71,136	94,474
Metro type					
Central	8	62,443	57,303	64,445	69,863
Suburban	16	70,131	62,453	69,492	73,458
Independent	3	70,321	58,244	58,822	76,648
Form of government					
Mayor-council	8	68,207	60,640	69,547	73,082
Council-manager	19	67,734	58,791	68,641	70,661
Recreation director					
Total	47	68,109	54,133	65,322	81,842
Geographic region					
Northeast	4	78,070	72,658	77,756	83,168
North-Central	16	57,861	53,047	57,835	64,309
South	14	64,651	51,497	63,790	72,526
West	13	81,381	67,020	90,697	93,388
Metro type					
Central	3	69,159	57,045	66,472	79,930
Suburban	35	68,764	53,703	65,322	85,128
Independent	9	65,211	61,584	62,300	76,460
Form of government					
Mayor-council	10	57,171	51,830	60,045	66,596
Council-manager	36	70,960	56,353	65,718	89,861
Risk manager					
Total	39	72,587	60,956	69,490	78,401
Geographic region					
North-Central	5	66,983	60,591	64,259	73,465
South	17	64,444	59,897	63,661	71,872
West	15	83,283	66,253	78,568	96,743
Metro type					
Central	7	56,698	51,147	60,591	62,653
Suburban	26	79,157	68,398	73,425	83,856
Independent	6	62,651	63,892	64,620	65,819
Form of government					
Mayor-council	4	59,574	55,770	61,763	65,567
Council-manager	34	73,951	61,427	70,836	80,068
Treasurer					
Total	23	73,484	48,602	70,096	90,269
Geographic region					
North-Central	9	48,961	42,517	49,280	57,200
South	4	72,587	63,484	74,353	83,456
West	8	96,364	67,856	99,847	133,274
Metro type					
Central	4	56,543	46,612	61,243	71,174
Suburban	13	87,045	70,096	86,820	122,256
Independent	6	55,394	44,648	52,562	60,151
Form of government					
Mayor-council	5	56,705	47,924	49,280	68,670
Council-manager	17	76,776	53,816	77,438	93,718
10,000–24,999					
Chief admin. officer/city manager					
Total	299	112,967	95,000	108,675	124,984
Geographic region					
Northeast	45	99,470	83,200	99,988	113,000
North-Central	103	106,095	92,779	105,837	116,006
South	110	111,794	97,683	108,243	125,963
West	41	148,193	120,578	142,833	164,208
Metro type					
Central	5	106,783	97,887	106,002	110,917
Suburban	189	118,279	97,614	113,194	134,550
Independent	105	103,700	92,592	104,128	115,885

Title of official	Number of municipalities reporting	Mean ($)	First quartile ($)	Median ($)	Third quartile ($)
10,000–24,999 continued					
Form of government					
Mayor-council	66	97,434	81,090	101,358	113,572
Council-manager	221	118,414	99,988	112,611	131,904
Commission	7	87,928	85,269	91,832	95,028
Town meeting	5	112,326	96,650	110,000	115,679
Chief elected official					
Total	78	49,978	22,057	51,829	66,875
Geographic region					
Northeast	15	59,800	36,338	65,000	75,427
North-Central	35	49,294	24,500	51,659	65,000
South	23	48,173	18,439	52,000	59,504
West	5	33,605	17,000	21,735	36,000
Metro type					
Suburban	49	50,917	21,735	54,002	71,736
Independent	28	48,263	22,093	46,751	59,755
Form of government					
Mayor-council	58	50,747	38,952	53,001	65,000
Council-manager	13	31,502	15,750	17,760	34,000
Town meeting	5	91,088	75,853	94,289	95,000
Chief financial officer					
Total	303	84,687	70,854	83,782	95,874
Geographic region					
Northeast	51	75,770	59,679	77,500	87,546
North-Central	102	83,318	73,673	85,880	94,439
South	107	81,556	69,094	78,229	90,812
West	43	106,303	85,918	97,116	123,996
Metro type					
Central	5	78,168	71,542	74,706	81,000
Suburban	197	89,059	74,000	88,315	100,417
Independent	101	76,482	65,523	77,292	87,903
Form of government					
Mayor-council	80	79,137	68,712	78,577	91,500
Council-manager	204	87,177	72,101	85,880	97,624
Commission	6	70,660	61,150	74,656	78,451
Town meeting	11	90,491	79,897	87,734	98,025
Chief law enforcement official					
Total	328	89,987	75,596	88,467	102,307
Geographic region					
Northeast	56	92,849	79,844	89,071	103,023
North-Central	124	87,624	76,468	88,598	99,860
South	111	83,681	69,708	83,000	94,228
West	37	112,493	91,680	104,189	126,240
Metro type					
Central	4	83,794	79,732	84,374	88,436
Suburban	209	96,739	83,486	95,638	107,474
Independent	115	77,931	67,754	77,937	88,038
Form of government					
Mayor-council	103	83,811	70,128	83,760	95,378
Council-manager	204	93,034	78,722	90,214	104,024
Commission	9	76,646	70,560	77,220	84,456
Town meeting	9	108,759	100,200	110,000	117,850
Rep. town meeting . .	3	78,560	63,474	69,948	89,341
Chief librarian					
Total	88	64,266	53,226	60,860	72,285
Geographic region					
Northeast	21	65,743	57,509	62,361	72,265
North-Central	24	66,174	57,371	64,526	79,586
South	31	56,606	50,084	53,706	61,969
West	12	77,656	56,033	79,470	90,573
Metro type					
Suburban	47	66,792	53,422	61,570	78,915
Independent	40	61,589	52,898	60,240	69,965
Form of government					
Mayor-council	21	64,511	53,706	64,416	69,826
Council-manager	57	64,494	51,209	60,000	73,486
Commission	3	47,269	42,044	53,970	55,845
Town meeting	7	68,961	59,540	70,785	71,570
Clerk					
Total	250	58,397	45,993	56,079	67,723
Geographic region					
Northeast	41	54,333	42,424	53,833	61,800
North-Central	71	55,476	46,527	56,820	65,655
South	107	56,328	45,481	53,460	63,243
West	31	77,607	65,095	75,012	91,686
Metro type					
Central	3	52,294	43,081	47,181	58,951
Suburban	162	62,151	48,842	60,828	72,376
Independent	85	51,460	43,175	52,104	58,598
Form of government					
Mayor-council	71	53,727	40,291	51,064	67,223
Council-manager	161	60,821	48,651	57,626	69,468

Table 1/8   SALARIES OF MUNICIPAL OFFICIALS: JULY–NOVEMBER 2008
continued

Title of official	Number of municipalities reporting	Mean ($)	First quartile ($)	Median ($)	Third quartile ($)
10,000–24,999 continued					
Commission	5	56,659	52,395	53,531	53,833
Town meeting	10	57,198	54,031	59,780	63,474
Rep. town meeting ..	3	45,752	45,129	45,667	46,334
Economic development director					
Total	94	77,760	65,246	76,976	87,926
Geographic region					
Northeast	11	66,681	65,979	68,675	74,145
North-Central	37	73,390	65,099	76,876	82,104
South	33	78,779	64,011	78,354	95,963
West	13	96,985	78,000	88,560	109,618
Metro type					
Suburban	61	79,237	66,271	79,685	88,404
Independent	31	73,250	64,606	70,824	79,948
Form of government					
Mayor-council	28	74,705	63,116	71,263	83,399
Council-manager	60	80,430	67,851	77,771	89,229
Town meeting	3	58,413	49,975	73,000	74,145
Engineer					
Total	155	79,657	68,494	78,000	90,024
Geographic region					
Northeast	21	70,819	51,870	72,273	82,400
North-Central	60	79,185	69,348	82,661	89,779
South	49	78,063	68,500	73,712	83,699
West	25	91,339	70,452	89,398	111,279
Metro type					
Central	3	69,456	68,958	69,628	70,040
Suburban	98	83,158	70,236	82,604	98,227
Independent	54	73,871	61,820	72,811	85,670
Form of government					
Mayor-council	39	71,867	64,296	74,622	84,452
Council-manager	106	82,809	69,543	82,090	95,742
Town meeting	6	75,101	66,231	76,462	81,800
Fire chief					
Total	248	80,597	67,772	78,300	90,676
Geographic region					
Northeast	36	81,824	69,488	80,003	91,335
North-Central	90	81,063	67,665	81,908	90,918
South	99	74,982	65,446	73,044	83,568
West	23	101,020	84,042	94,729	110,008
Metro type					
Central	5	68,870	65,295	68,214	74,829
Suburban	141	87,123	71,956	86,316	98,259
Independent	102	72,150	63,484	72,470	80,538
Form of government					
Mayor-council	85	78,406	66,234	78,410	87,576
Council-manager	146	82,474	68,886	79,410	91,952
Commission	6	70,250	56,267	64,740	86,957
Town meeting	8	80,775	64,693	85,015	104,043
Rep. town meeting ..	3	71,518	61,930	73,859	82,276
Health officer					
Total	31	59,106	42,754	54,345	78,035
Geographic region					
Northeast	18	64,405	45,813	61,058	85,349
North-Central	8	54,069	48,358	51,655	55,199
South	4	37,418	36,051	38,408	39,775
Metro type					
Suburban	21	61,481	43,099	58,656	78,199
Independent	10	54,119	39,775	49,669	55,394
Form of government					
Mayor-council	8	53,624	48,358	51,655	58,072
Council-manager	12	62,689	38,597	48,722	90,901
Town meeting	8	61,731	46,405	64,253	81,548
Human resources director					
Total	186	69,078	54,835	69,150	81,060
Geographic region					
Northeast	25	61,679	49,057	58,474	73,008
North-Central	44	67,804	54,152	69,737	81,785
South	85	67,091	55,944	67,738	78,221
West	32	81,889	70,166	78,578	87,398
Metro type					
Central	5	59,701	50,100	64,330	65,080
Suburban	105	72,164	55,228	71,491	86,300
Independent	76	65,432	55,319	66,595	77,902
Form of government					
Mayor-council	49	61,838	47,046	64,302	72,610
Council-manager	129	72,549	59,444	71,865	83,262
Town meeting	6	61,664	44,821	58,890	75,670
Human services director					
Total	20	67,095	50,861	65,198	82,790
Geographic region					
Northeast	7	70,662	64,118	68,250	75,440

Title of official	Number of municipalities reporting	Mean ($)	First quartile ($)	Median ($)	Third quartile ($)
10,000–24,999 continued					
North-Central	6	59,697	40,431	45,929	59,887
South	6	66,389	53,249	69,331	83,225
Metro type					
Suburban	14	68,400	57,032	65,198	76,410
Independent	6	64,051	39,777	65,661	87,052
Form of government					
Mayor-council	5	46,585	38,800	45,322	46,536
Council-manager	10	77,525	60,442	83,007	87,052
Town meeting	5	66,746	62,179	66,058	68,250
Information services director					
Total	109	70,324	58,000	67,735	84,177
Geographic region					
Northeast	19	70,764	59,562	67,000	84,842
North-Central	21	68,822	58,932	67,587	80,898
South	52	66,904	54,885	64,725	75,546
West	17	82,148	73,320	84,984	87,214
Metro type					
Central	3	53,858	48,226	54,931	60,027
Suburban	66	73,867	60,575	71,490	87,332
Independent	40	65,712	51,881	66,294	77,429
Form of government					
Mayor-council	22	60,914	50,323	58,720	69,764
Council-manager	80	73,092	60,547	70,595	85,105
Town meeting	5	70,212	62,008	67,000	80,951
Parks and recreation director					
Total	200	72,973	60,970	69,998	86,142
Geographic region					
Northeast	30	61,721	48,742	66,381	73,614
North-Central	68	70,148	57,126	66,902	85,532
South	78	72,671	61,870	69,998	83,049
West	24	96,024	81,000	93,072	106,614
Metro type					
Central	5	73,006	61,960	72,690	76,201
Suburban	124	75,682	61,069	75,285	89,030
Independent	71	68,240	60,486	67,350	76,455
Form of government					
Mayor-council	50	60,823	50,118	61,374	73,248
Council-manager	140	78,111	63,973	75,383	89,030
Town meeting	7	65,503	66,152	68,142	75,469
Parks superintendent					
Total	136	52,757	44,007	52,642	60,265
Geographic region					
Northeast	12	52,155	46,761	54,025	59,406
North-Central	38	56,401	48,499	55,899	64,209
South	63	46,972	39,492	46,835	53,785
West	23	62,899	54,540	60,520	72,098
Metro type					
Central	3	47,521	36,080	36,339	53,372
Suburban	70	56,413	46,522	56,179	66,584
Independent	63	48,946	42,445	50,586	55,482
Form of government					
Mayor-council	31	49,888	43,771	53,273	58,779
Council-manager	98	53,794	43,983	52,078	61,311
Commission	3	43,831	37,939	52,166	53,891
Planning director					
Total	176	75,941	61,892	73,742	87,906
Geographic region					
Northeast	31	68,181	54,908	64,636	79,396
North-Central	43	68,402	56,936	67,951	81,177
South	77	77,197	64,147	74,280	88,451
West	25	94,661	84,120	98,571	101,064
Metro type					
Central	4	73,747	70,683	72,774	75,839
Suburban	115	78,139	63,362	75,000	91,854
Independent	57	71,660	58,989	69,803	84,120
Form of government					
Mayor-council	39	67,804	54,775	65,217	82,446
Council-manager	125	79,260	66,227	76,535	91,336
Town meeting	9	69,890	54,487	63,593	79,486
Primary asst. manager/CAO					
Total	116	83,827	66,486	80,623	95,604
Geographic region					
Northeast	17	63,622	52,403	59,496	69,863
North-Central	44	74,411	65,449	72,698	87,325
South	42	92,511	78,103	89,884	105,807
West	13	114,062	106,428	108,451	127,812
Metro type					
Suburban	89	85,824	66,063	80,929	103,695
Independent	25	77,782	67,500	76,648	89,789

Table 1/8 SALARIES OF MUNICIPAL OFFICIALS: JULY–NOVEMBER 2008
continued

Title of official	Number of municipalities reporting	Mean ($)	First quartile ($)	Median ($)	Third quartile ($)
10,000–24,999 continued					
Form of government					
Mayor-council	18	68,062	60,440	70,582	76,816
Council-manager	98	86,722	67,921	86,382	101,348
Public safety director					
Total	51	74,130	58,696	74,520	92,730
Geographic region					
Northeast	4	56,767	49,847	54,796	61,715
North-Central	29	69,947	59,016	73,289	89,482
South	14	81,917	74,007	80,710	96,509
West	4	94,563	73,537	88,763	109,789
Metro type					
Suburban	35	75,341	54,487	77,155	93,735
Independent	15	71,011	59,947	73,289	83,303
Form of government					
Mayor-council	20	61,228	44,102	61,871	77,531
Council-manager	30	83,678	70,032	80,710	99,601
Public works director					
Total	312	84,306	71,214	85,088	96,272
Geographic region					
Northeast	57	78,601	64,613	81,678	90,068
North-Central	112	84,802	74,562	85,588	96,763
South	106	79,418	67,375	77,990	91,623
West	37	105,598	93,348	100,872	117,288
Metro type					
Central	4	83,936	74,523	83,670	93,084
Suburban	200	88,293	74,976	87,988	100,085
Independent	108	76,938	66,170	76,150	89,341
Form of government					
Mayor-council	91	79,685	70,817	81,005	92,239
Council-manager	200	86,716	71,401	87,131	97,907
Commission	8	73,886	63,906	69,891	87,138
Town meeting	11	88,587	82,580	87,500	96,007
Purchasing director					
Total	31	52,793	40,286	51,438	64,014
Geographic region					
Northeast	7	57,993	45,464	58,605	68,844
North-Central	7	53,141	44,876	49,728	61,596
South	16	48,235	36,824	49,794	55,542
Metro type					
Suburban	18	55,437	40,883	52,524	68,941
Independent	12	48,361	40,028	49,128	53,776
Form of government					
Mayor-council	11	55,159	44,706	53,568	67,344
Council-manager	18	52,844	42,137	50,583	61,874
Recreation director					
Total	81	55,118	42,420	53,765	65,988
Geographic region					
Northeast	18	53,285	42,625	50,397	60,643
North-Central	26	50,393	40,124	46,265	62,522
South	23	50,680	42,305	46,872	58,580
West	14	73,540	61,733	67,427	79,092
Metro type					
Suburban	49	60,244	46,000	60,129	70,319
Independent	31	47,126	41,820	44,701	54,296
Form of government					
Mayor-council	26	51,397	40,124	48,949	59,911
Council-manager	50	58,445	43,768	59,660	67,951
Risk manager					
Total	36	61,986	45,585	55,925	73,806
Geographic region					
North-Central	7	67,162	52,703	74,700	80,291
South	19	52,842	43,893	48,096	60,126
West	9	73,912	51,591	63,540	73,508
Metro type					
Suburban	22	71,946	56,283	65,650	30,797
Independent	12	45,473	41,372	46,049	48,963
Form of government					
Mayor-council	8	54,886	40,308	58,270	67,539
Council-manager	26	64,082	46,694	55,925	76,833
Treasurer					
Total	50	57,333	44,896	56,262	69,241
Geographic region					
Northeast	15	51,867	42,533	56,300	61,505
North-Central	23	56,434	43,599	53,117	68,037
South	10	65,199	45,683	66,047	80,532
Metro type					
Suburban	29	55,092	39,144	54,002	65,000
Independent	20	60,120	51,651	58,922	70,626

Title of official	Number of municipalities reporting	Mean ($)	First quartile ($)	Median ($)	Third quartile ($)
10,000–24,999 continued					
Form of government					
Mayor-council	17	47,599	40,000	45,698	56,224
Council-manager	28	62,357	47,838	60,492	72,480
Town meeting	4	57,099	48,860	57,855	66,094
5,000–9,999					
Chief admin. officer/city manager					
Total	233	93,087	77,000	91,500	106,506
Geographic region					
Northeast	29	72,434	64,297	72,093	80,600
North-Central	82	89,764	79,998	87,265	99,373
South	84	95,190	76,564	94,115	111,135
West	38	111,371	96,501	105,000	119,243
Metro type					
Suburban	134	97,271	79,364	95,934	110,688
Independent	99	87,425	76,344	87,294	97,750
Form of government					
Mayor-council	75	86,515	72,750	84,604	100,299
Council-manager	153	96,835	80,000	94,992	108,747
Town meeting	5	76,990	67,000	74,700	82,542
Chief elected official					
Total	50	37,898	21,378	33,762	53,061
Geographic region					
Northeast	5	51,451	34,523	55,856	72,975
North-Central	17	35,319	16,800	33,000	52,165
South	22	41,864	30,000	40,035	53,046
West	6	19,366	15,949	19,899	21,750
Metro type					
Suburban	23	38,218	18,274	31,200	56,689
Independent	27	37,625	25,000	34,523	50,750
Form of government					
Mayor-council	41	38,050	24,000	35,000	52,165
Council-manager	6	21,642	19,263	21,085	24,043
Town meeting	3	68,328	64,415	72,975	74,564
Chief financial officer					
Total	182	69,126	56,454	68,730	79,684
Geographic region					
Northeast	14	52,511	41,177	51,269	67,155
North-Central	64	70,052	60,006	70,720	79,566
South	74	67,313	54,624	64,695	75,734
West	30	79,378	62,964	79,242	91,669
Metro type					
Suburban	103	71,382	57,702	72,665	84,364
Independent	79	66,186	55,322	64,575	75,342
Form of government					
Mayor-council	58	64,958	52,443	66,948	77,639
Council-manager	120	71,159	57,916	69,947	81,236
Town meeting	3	68,249	56,873	68,746	79,873
Chief law enforcement official					
Total	257	72,622	59,395	71,388	82,659
Geographic region					
Northeast	29	76,582	66,780	72,754	80,089
North-Central	95	72,549	60,004	71,423	81,802
South	98	67,000	52,308	64,206	76,779
West	35	85,279	74,081	82,659	99,323
Metro type					
Suburban	133	80,064	67,839	77,293	91,229
Independent	124	64,640	53,683	64,589	73,661
Form of government					
Mayor-council	113	69,738	51,500	69,347	81,203
Council-manager	134	75,296	62,204	72,493	83,714
Commission	4	62,537	60,824	62,739	64,452
Town meeting	5	76,496	74,173	76,332	80,089
Chief librarian					
Total	73	49,556	40,000	50,440	57,380
Geographic region					
Northeast	16	49,508	38,497	51,644	60,152
North-Central	25	49,995	44,075	53,694	57,176
South	20	44,947	35,369	43,805	49,590
West	12	56,384	41,730	55,790	69,645
Metro type					
Suburban	34	53,924	44,158	55,746	60,297
Independent	39	45,747	36,655	44,554	53,658
Form of government					
Mayor-council	28	47,501	39,951	49,236	54,616
Council-manager	38	50,381	40,228	49,787	57,388
Town meeting	7	53,294	40,986	58,936	66,273
Clerk					
Total	210	52,595	41,458	50,776	62,493
Geographic region					
Northeast	29	46,595	35,000	45,677	55,436
North-Central	58	52,568	43,184	53,882	62,524

Table 1/8 **SALARIES OF MUNICIPAL OFFICIALS: JULY–NOVEMBER 2008**
continued

Title of official	Number of municipalities reporting	Mean ($)	First quartile ($)	Median ($)	Third quartile ($)
5,000–9,999 continued					
South	88	50,155	38,280	47,811	58,181
West	35	63,747	50,722	60,029	71,680
Metro type					
Suburban	114	57,421	46,378	56,396	67,541
Independent	96	46,865	38,684	44,938	53,799
Form of government					
Mayor-council	76	50,925	39,044	49,993	60,623
Council-manager	123	53,605	41,964	52,083	62,832
Town meeting	8	50,531	45,508	48,219	54,925
Economic development director					
Total	59	63,354	50,653	61,221	75,315
Geographic region					
Northeast	4	44,459	42,032	44,594	47,022
North-Central	30	65,346	57,394	63,571	73,770
South	18	58,253	44,358	54,488	69,525
West	7	78,732	56,250	84,760	89,977
Metro type					
Suburban	34	71,979	62,000	73,037	81,561
Independent	25	51,624	45,488	52,291	57,924
Form of government					
Mayor-council	22	64,035	53,467	63,993	76,058
Council-manager	36	63,484	49,500	60,148	74,682
Engineer					
Total	59	74,275	63,401	71,488	87,909
Geographic region					
Northeast	3	64,881	49,821	65,000	80,000
North-Central	21	69,764	63,800	72,518	78,420
South	24	79,394	62,788	69,638	95,856
West	11	74,277	62,544	72,588	87,176
Metro type					
Suburban	34	75,056	63,559	73,987	90,910
Independent	25	73,212	63,324	70,453	78,420
Form of government					
Mayor-council	21	69,285	63,800	70,000	77,854
Council-manager	37	78,178	63,324	75,456	91,513
Fire chief					
Total	149	61,992	48,410	60,180	76,565
Geographic region					
Northeast	9	48,891	40,000	48,735	62,179
North-Central	47	62,226	48,705	60,000	74,226
South	74	59,970	46,363	57,294	70,640
West	19	75,496	61,143	68,244	85,380
Metro type					
Suburban	73	70,345	57,385	63,901	85,600
Independent	76	53,969	45,189	53,862	62,941
Form of government					
Mayor-council	61	56,736	44,500	55,167	66,000
Council-manager	81	66,361	53,768	62,294	77,766
Commission	3	67,291	61,911	62,724	70,388
Town meeting	4	49,713	36,548	44,368	57,532
Health officer					
Total	7	48,955	38,886	49,253	57,741
Geographic region					
Northeast	4	57,132	53,790	57,741	61,084
Metro type					
Independent	6	48,905	38,828	47,151	58,961
Form of government					
Council-manager	4	42,364	38,174	38,886	43,076
Human resources director					
Total	80	58,388	43,994	55,611	68,521
Geographic region					
Northeast	3	46,666	41,361	46,579	51,929
North-Central	14	53,844	48,183	52,771	58,797
South	45	54,724	41,928	50,134	61,741
West	18	73,038	68,023	73,222	84,673
Metro type					
Suburban	42	60,825	45,623	57,770	68,377
Independent	38	55,696	39,948	51,591	69,209
Form of government					
Mayor-council	23	51,287	41,695	50,086	57,586
Council-manager	56	61,702	46,556	57,371	74,747
Human services director					
Total	7	46,007	32,631	47,626	60,428
Geographic region					
South	4	54,745	53,560	60,428	61,613
Metro type					
Suburban	6	49,425	38,395	53,633	60,822
Form of government					
Mayor-council	3	40,678	30,409	35,318	48,267
Council-manager	3	50,796	44,792	59,640	61,223

Title of official	Number of municipalities reporting	Mean ($)	First quartile ($)	Median ($)	Third quartile ($)
5,000–9,999 continued					
Information services director					
Total	25	63,857	49,754	59,382	77,283
Geographic region					
North-Central	4	58,491	55,267	58,843	62,067
South	16	66,746	49,938	67,138	77,587
West	5	58,904	49,754	59,151	59,251
Metro type					
Suburban	13	63,667	46,000	60,030	78,404
Independent	12	64,063	50,876	58,777	71,144
Form of government					
Mayor-council	6	64,888	58,573	59,706	75,956
Council-manager	19	63,531	47,877	59,251	75,930
Parks and recreation director					
Total	115	58,503	45,193	52,530	69,828
Geographic region					
Northeast	9	42,040	38,813	44,558	48,248
North-Central	40	55,455	45,474	53,916	65,768
South	50	57,293	45,042	51,320	68,269
West	16	79,164	62,841	78,492	95,062
Metro type					
Suburban	62	62,190	46,366	60,210	74,396
Independent	53	54,189	44,460	48,714	59,176
Form of government					
Mayor-council	45	50,869	38,542	47,634	61,200
Council-manager	67	64,472	48,669	58,368	74,093
Town meeting	3	39,713	32,299	48,248	51,396
Parks superintendent					
Total	70	46,156	34,657	45,936	54,435
Geographic region					
Northeast	3	47,679	46,402	47,750	48,991
North-Central	19	47,852	40,776	45,600	56,901
South	33	41,256	31,538	38,064	49,302
West	15	54,481	46,484	54,580	61,173
Metro type					
Suburban	29	49,989	42,657	49,920	59,530
Independent	41	43,444	33,114	42,598	50,344
Form of government					
Mayor-council	28	42,787	33,750	41,338	47,995
Council-manager	40	48,439	35,965	49,611	55,491
Planning director					
Total	103	65,451	51,068	62,262	77,639
Geographic region					
Northeast	9	49,373	41,995	50,636	52,187
North-Central	22	63,070	43,828	67,608	78,575
South	50	64,104	51,648	62,131	75,357
West	22	77,470	60,667	70,734	88,047
Metro type					
Suburban	65	68,045	50,636	64,312	79,830
Independent	38	61,013	51,648	61,515	72,369
Form of government					
Mayor-council	28	58,943	44,516	61,656	72,529
Council-manager	69	69,265	52,577	67,446	80,208
Town meeting	5	53,111	52,017	52,187	58,040
Primary asst. manager/CAO					
Total	52	73,074	52,944	76,910	93,625
Geographic region					
Northeast	3	45,045	44,372	46,099	46,245
North-Central	13	69,028	56,196	61,320	85,130
South	26	73,199	55,509	78,377	91,649
West	10	86,416	66,144	93,750	96,793
Metro type					
Suburban	31	78,317	59,660	83,108	94,518
Independent	21	65,335	46,392	60,194	84,277
Form of government					
Mayor-council	12	64,362	46,678	60,408	84,581
Council-manager	37	77,806	60,036	83,994	96,366
Public safety director					
Total	19	70,741	60,306	68,954	73,825
Geographic region					
North-Central	12	63,717	60,000	65,275	71,250
South	5	87,629	68,954	75,496	81,702
Metro type					
Suburban	15	71,657	63,036	69,756	73,825
Independent	4	67,308	58,261	60,306	69,352
Form of government					
Mayor-council	7	59,267	56,523	60,000	65,412
Council-manager	12	77,435	65,410	71,577	77,450
Public works director					
Total	241	70,076	58,497	68,256	80,966
Geographic region					
Northeast	30	61,505	52,156	61,880	66,770
North-Central	84	71,989	61,524	70,012	80,254

Table 1/8   SALARIES OF MUNICIPAL OFFICIALS: JULY–NOVEMBER 2008
continued

Title of official	Number of municipalities reporting	Distribution of 2008 salaries			
		Mean ($)	First quartile ($)	Median ($)	Third quartile ($)
5,000–9,999 continued					
South	90	65,833	51,186	63,098	78,421
West	37	83,005	69,192	86,458	97,380
Metro type					
Suburban	143	74,547	60,397	70,345	86,457
Independent	98	63,552	48,798	63,907	74,018
Form of government					
Mayor-council	98	66,355	52,455	67,071	76,912
Council-manager	131	73,583	60,319	69,996	83,225
Commission	4	61,176	57,981	60,021	63,216
Town meeting	7	64,277	51,780	59,853	70,848
Purchasing director					
Total	13	45,317	27,036	33,030	51,376
Geographic region					
North-Central	5	44,787	27,036	29,988	62,875
South	8	45,648	30,087	35,265	48,844
Metro type					
Suburban	6	49,813	31,866	44,438	60,000
Independent	7	41,463	25,262	31,248	40,515
Form of government					
Mayor-council	5	33,001	23,920	31,248	33,030
Council-manager	8	53,014	29,250	42,750	61,058
Recreation director					
Total	47	43,888	34,095	41,168	49,083
Geographic region					
Northeast	6	34,941	22,731	41,976	43,124
North-Central	13	42,835	25,887	36,000	52,354
South	17	43,454	36,732	42,079	46,787
West	11	50,686	36,231	48,197	56,929
Metro type					
Suburban	26	44,712	35,311	42,060	51,057
Independent	21	42,869	30,264	40,679	48,630
Form of government					
Mayor-council	17	41,813	33,655	41,168	48,630
Council-manager	28	45,207	33,696	40,840	49,595
Risk manager					
Total	8	64,255	56,855	60,154	61,819
Geographic region					
South	5	66,151	53,821	57,866	61,298
Metro type					
Suburban	3	61,858	61,399	61,500	62,137
Independent	5	65,693	53,821	57,866	59,010
Form of government					
Council-manager	8	64,255	56,855	60,154	61,819
Treasurer					
Total	59	51,714	40,246	48,847	62,838
Geographic region					
Northeast	15	48,960	39,646	43,680	55,038
North-Central	29	51,569	41,004	51,355	58,117
South	6	45,075	28,308	38,740	62,537
West	9	61,194	47,925	50,000	67,392
Metro type					
Suburban	34	55,229	40,806	48,700	70,043
Independent	25	46,933	40,123	48,847	53,200
Form of government					
Mayor-council	27	51,985	40,174	51,355	64,534
Council-manager	29	52,125	40,368	47,549	67,100
2,500–4,999					
Chief admin. officer/city manager					
Total	237	75,732	61,421	73,279	88,940
Geographic region					
Northeast	15	63,715	53,480	59,060	72,500
North-Central	109	75,701	65,957	75,005	85,405
South	92	71,337	58,304	68,049	85,863
West	21	103,728	80,000	102,169	122,800
Metro type					
Suburban	133	79,989	64,420	78,000	92,195
Independent	103	70,253	58,578	69,449	80,065
Form of government					
Mayor-council	91	70,770	56,591	71,390	83,013
Council-manager	141	79,533	65,851	75,000	91,835
Town meeting	5	58,837	55,830	58,656	67,700
Chief elected official					
Total	23	29,528	16,607	23,145	38,800
Geographic region					
North-Central	9	25,414	18,000	22,500	26,400
South	12	33,827	16,268	35,500	47,376
Metro type					
Suburban	8	27,228	19,156	24,450	31,250
Independent	15	30,755	15,946	23,145	43,800
Form of government					
Mayor-council	22	30,183	16,967	24,773	40,200

Title of official	Number of municipalities reporting	Distribution of 2008 salaries			
		Mean ($)	First quartile ($)	Median ($)	Third quartile ($)
2,500–4,999 continued					
Chief financial officer					
Total	122	57,993	45,050	56,734	69,102
Geographic region					
Northeast	7	48,621	41,967	46,100	56,517
North-Central	51	58,035	48,703	57,353	69,031
South	48	52,495	40,356	50,517	61,948
West	16	78,455	67,915	74,454	96,731
Metro type					
Suburban	71	61,912	48,542	61,601	71,264
Independent	50	52,842	40,252	51,536	62,930
Form of government					
Mayor-council	44	51,248	39,430	50,340	61,669
Council-manager	77	62,191	48,000	62,052	71,637
Chief law enforcement official					
Total	265	57,915	46,845	57,000	65,000
Geographic region					
Northeast	25	59,199	48,886	55,000	64,500
North-Central	125	59,613	48,800	59,446	66,430
South	97	52,599	41,800	52,221	60,252
West	18	72,981	59,631	70,944	81,314
Metro type					
Suburban	126	64,454	53,693	62,675	74,170
Independent	138	51,914	43,730	52,098	59,986
Form of government					
Mayor-council	136	54,395	43,910	54,040	64,087
Council-manager	123	62,003	52,531	60,000	68,182
Town meeting	4	54,774	48,602	51,037	57,209
Chief librarian					
Total	60	39,912	30,330	39,846	48,011
Geographic region					
Northeast	5	34,684	22,247	30,000	40,000
North-Central	33	41,008	33,966	42,515	47,944
South	13	32,295	28,739	30,379	37,398
West	9	49,795	40,000	51,771	56,016
Metro type					
Suburban	21	46,483	40,000	44,200	51,584
Independent	39	36,373	29,507	35,227	43,493
Form of government					
Mayor-council	26	36,127	30,046	36,094	42,451
Council-manager	31	44,237	33,744	44,658	52,634
Town meeting	3	28,016	22,024	22,247	31,124
Clerk					
Total	213	44,785	35,671	43,909	52,000
Geographic region					
Northeast	20	38,086	30,000	33,636	45,673
North-Central	78	46,155	38,950	44,381	53,745
South	92	42,216	35,327	42,682	49,245
West	23	56,235	37,233	55,661	73,644
Metro type					
Suburban	106	48,240	37,000	46,671	55,991
Independent	106	41,414	33,559	41,399	50,070
Form of government					
Mayor-council	107	41,751	33,672	40,883	49,358
Council-manager	103	48,127	39,104	47,202	55,130
Economic development director					
Total	39	48,111	37,012	48,000	56,759
Geographic region					
North-Central	20	45,950	37,018	47,899	56,168
South	14	46,052	34,226	42,653	49,989
West	4	65,656	47,567	65,407	83,497
Metro type					
Suburban	15	50,815	36,250	50,804	65,795
Independent	24	46,422	37,018	47,871	50,500
Form of government					
Mayor-council	19	43,901	34,382	45,000	51,547
Council-manager	19	52,223	38,306	49,916	60,764
Engineer					
Total	23	58,333	41,366	57,886	72,057
Geographic region					
North-Central	10	55,934	46,750	53,874	67,899
South	6	57,404	39,673	52,888	64,387
West	6	70,627	66,604	70,309	82,234
Metro type					
Suburban	11	62,770	52,374	66,225	78,295
Independent	12	54,266	36,623	50,249	63,428
Form of government					
Mayor-council	12	57,490	36,623	56,443	68,614
Council-manager	11	59,253	45,249	60,278	77,939

Table 1/8   SALARIES OF MUNICIPAL OFFICIALS: JULY–NOVEMBER 2008
continued

Title of official	Number of municipalities reporting	Distribution of 2008 salaries			
		Mean ($)	First quartile ($)	Median ($)	Third quartile ($)
2,500–4,999 continued					
Fire chief					
Total	69	50,733	36,066	49,490	59,514
Geographic region					
Northeast	3	43,957	36,212	47,424	53,436
North-Central	13	54,000	35,164	53,400	68,448
South	46	47,790	37,221	48,323	54,998
West	7	66,915	58,128	62,712	79,876
Metro type					
Suburban	31	60,568	49,231	54,600	69,193
Independent	38	42,710	32,684	43,142	54,733
Form of government					
Mayor-council	24	49,027	32,735	44,008	62,255
Council-manager	44	51,740	40,798	52,490	59,465
Health officer					
Total	6	47,717	40,422	49,266	59,125
Geographic region	. . .	. . .	. . .	. . .	. . .
Metro type					
Suburban	4	43,298	32,504	42,652	53,447
Form of government					
Mayor-council	4	38,040	32,504	42,652	48,189
Human resources director					
Total	26	49,031	36,818	44,118	53,262
Geographic region					
North-Central	6	31,883	25,583	29,590	34,737
South	12	46,324	42,209	44,566	49,729
West	7	69,205	54,569	77,128	85,231
Metro type					
Suburban	14	59,303	43,985	51,490	75,167
Independent	12	37,048	28,597	37,937	43,891
Form of government					
Mayor-council	8	40,246	30,719	34,771	49,102
Council-manager	18	52,936	42,728	44,566	62,967
Human services director					
Total	6	56,410	39,622	61,875	71,492
Geographic region					
South	4	53,678	34,511	53,451	72,619
Metro type					
Independent	4	57,890	48,575	61,875	71,189
Form of government					
Council-manager	5	52,778	34,934	53,687	70,062
Information services director					
Total	8	50,697	41,716	53,847	60,777
Geographic region					
West	3	49,890	37,552	45,880	60,222
Metro type					
Suburban	3	57,665	49,216	52,552	63,558
Independent	5	46,516	29,225	55,142	58,887
Form of government					
Council-manager	6	53,967	48,195	57,015	64,558
Parks and recreation director					
Total	76	46,045	35,880	44,772	52,078
Geographic region					
Northeast	4	35,498	31,077	39,664	44,085
North-Central	34	42,517	30,305	43,538	47,941
South	32	45,785	36,420	44,772	52,866
West	6	74,456	53,610	73,237	91,684
Metro type					
Suburban	37	53,152	38,750	50,629	64,676
Independent	38	39,328	30,108	42,876	46,954
Form of government					
Mayor-council	26	36,493	26,968	35,761	45,321
Council-manager	50	51,012	42,746	47,728	58,279
Parks superintendent					
Total	42	36,109	29,746	34,876	43,538
Geographic region					
North-Central	15	39,560	32,916	37,856	43,863
South	22	33,907	26,582	32,410	41,763
West	5	35,448	30,011	32,864	39,645
Metro type					
Suburban	22	38,821	31,632	38,667	43,969
Independent	20	33,126	27,094	30,663	38,880
Form of government					
Mayor-council	16	36,660	29,384	36,001	43,988
Council-manager	26	35,770	29,746	34,834	41,763
Planning director					
Total	58	55,553	44,607	51,974	65,174
Geographic region					
North-Central	11	52,272	48,512	52,244	58,243
South	34	51,347	39,654	49,955	60,983
West	11	71,959	57,382	65,952	88,302

Title of official	Number of municipalities reporting	Distribution of 2008 salaries			
		Mean ($)	First quartile ($)	Median ($)	Third quartile ($)
2,500–4,999 continued					
Metro type					
Suburban	32	59,551	46,325	59,730	68,688
Independent	25	51,178	43,742	49,910	55,764
Form of government					
Mayor-council	13	49,620	42,744	45,559	60,000
Council-manager	45	57,267	46,000	53,378	65,952
Primary asst. manager/CAO					
Total	34	57,201	43,242	55,539	68,310
Geographic region					
Northeast	7	38,820	32,511	35,715	44,893
North-Central	13	57,523	49,878	59,078	64,917
South	9	57,126	48,927	60,043	68,655
West	5	82,231	67,275	83,600	108,056
Metro type					
Suburban	18	60,512	44,839	54,801	72,132
Independent	16	53,477	36,198	56,022	64,930
Form of government					
Mayor-council	11	52,188	38,177	46,350	61,288
Council-manager	21	62,179	49,878	61,222	69,867
Public safety director					
Total	24	57,672	39,049	53,256	69,776
Geographic region					
North-Central	14	53,853	45,166	50,515	56,433
South	5	64,111	57,286	70,000	75,316
West	4	67,597	38,071	54,074	83,600
Metro type					
Suburban	15	59,198	42,012	49,632	65,968
Independent	9	55,129	38,448	57,286	69,701
Form of government					
Mayor-council	15	48,516	38,424	46,342	55,494
Council-manager	9	72,933	57,286	70,000	85,287
Public works director					
Total	225	57,116	46,345	55,931	67,000
Geographic region					
Northeast	27	50,509	38,802	46,280	56,030
North-Central	92	61,102	52,840	61,111	68,746
South	84	51,080	41,000	50,564	59,359
West	22	71,600	62,616	68,500	78,588
Metro type					
Suburban	121	60,633	50,004	59,272	70,518
Independent	103	53,014	42,543	52,000	62,522
Form of government					
Mayor-council	100	54,073	45,633	52,427	63,954
Council-manager	123	59,797	48,730	59,155	69,020
Purchasing director					
Total	5	35,317	30,181	35,736	43,950
Geographic region					
North-Central	3	32,802	27,228	35,736	39,843
Metro type					
Independent	3	32,300	24,451	30,181	39,091
Form of government					
Council-manager	3	40,710	37,066	43,950	45,975
Recreation director					
Total	25	38,737	31,500	35,381	41,620
Geographic region					
North-Central	9	34,973	32,372	35,381	37,500
South	10	35,917	30,135	33,495	40,940
West	4	49,884	30,700	36,371	55,555
Metro type					
Suburban	8	34,913	30,858	34,548	40,105
Independent	17	40,537	31,500	35,381	46,523
Form of government					
Mayor-council	11	37,356	32,086	37,105	41,205
Council-manager	14	39,823	30,920	33,938	40,940
Risk manager					
Total	. . .	. . .	. . .	. . .	. . .
Geographic region	. . .	. . .	. . .	. . .	. . .
Metro type	. . .	. . .	. . .	. . .	. . .
Form of government	. . .	. . .	. . .	. . .	. . .
Treasurer					
Total	73	43,393	33,322	43,300	49,236
Geographic region					
Northeast	13	37,736	29,120	35,340	44,000
North-Central	43	45,258	38,531	45,566	53,879
South	12	40,545	28,502	39,362	45,487
West	5	48,892	37,482	47,112	56,016
Metro type					
Suburban	37	42,919	33,433	39,915	48,321
Independent	36	43,880	33,241	44,204	50,015

Table 1/8   SALARIES OF MUNICIPAL OFFICIALS: JULY–NOVEMBER 2008
continued

Title of official	Number of municipalities reporting	Distribution of 2008 salaries			
		Mean ($)	First quartile ($)	Median ($)	Third quartile ($)
2,500–4,999 continued					
Form of government					
Mayor-council	41	42,255	32,240	44,000	48,321
Council-manager	28	45,987	36,560	43,441	58,010
West	11	71,959	57,382	65,952	88,302
Less than 2,500					
Chief admin. officer/city manager					
Total	217	61,784	49,005	59,397	73,050
Geographic region					
Northeast	9	51,469	37,500	50,700	58,767
North-Central	108	60,228	49,207	58,870	70,075
South	81	61,857	47,426	58,270	76,125
West	19	75,205	63,654	70,000	82,000
Metro type					
Suburban	105	66,390	52,437	66,496	79,900
Independent	112	57,466	46,263	56,591	66,713
Form of government					
Mayor-council	60	60,669	50,559	58,585	70,075
Council-manager	152	62,543	49,105	59,700	74,739
Town meeting	3	35,833	33,750	37,500	38,750
Chief elected official					
Total	6	49,596	42,302	48,334	57,285
Geographic region					
North-Central	3	42,696	40,280	40,560	44,044
Metro type					
Suburban	4	47,022	40,420	44,044	50,646
Form of government					
Mayor-council	5	49,688	40,560	47,528	60,000
Chief financial officer					
Total	74	50,652	37,447	48,354	63,604
Geographic region					
North-Central	23	55,203	48,108	53,498	68,773
South	43	45,325	35,633	45,000	52,042
West	8	66,207	47,348	68,903	82,573
Metro type					
Suburban	32	55,253	45,115	51,959	68,753
Independent	42	47,147	35,446	45,625	53,574
Form of government					
Mayor-council	28	45,295	32,822	43,900	53,734
Council-manager	46	53,914	40,362	50,888	64,452
Chief law enforcement official					
Total	236	49,435	40,360	47,715	56,401
Geographic region					
Northeast	7	49,116	44,129	49,378	56,071
North-Central	127	48,411	39,728	48,006	54,643
South	92	48,309	40,149	45,534	54,759
West	10	73,030	59,038	63,966	85,261
Metro type					
Suburban	87	55,364	45,431	51,989	61,307
Independent	149	45,974	37,390	44,616	54,163
Form of government					
Mayor-council	121	45,052	36,462	44,616	51,989
Council-manager	111	54,344	43,110	51,500	59,284
Chief librarian					
Total	41	29,842	21,504	30,181	36,691
Geographic region					
North-Central	36	30,601	21,479	30,894	37,596
South	3	21,932	21,062	21,504	22,589
Metro type					
Suburban	18	32,773	25,638	35,434	40,107
Independent	23	27,549	21,352	25,471	31,875
Form of government					
Mayor-council	20	29,509	21,028	28,147	37,965
Council-manager	20	29,453	22,416	29,289	35,631
Clerk					
Total	261	37,046	29,515	35,360	42,890
Geographic region					
Northeast	7	35,465	27,319	31,200	40,102
North-Central	136	36,447	29,005	33,907	42,286
South	104	36,687	30,000	36,053	42,562
West	14	46,318	37,326	44,176	56,911
Metro type					
Suburban	80	41,625	34,412	39,178	47,088
Independent	181	35,022	28,600	33,153	40,850
Form of government					
Mayor-council	159	35,794	28,870	33,907	41,711
Council-manager	98	39,176	31,207	38,263	45,193
Economic development director					
Total	19	41,488	32,173	37,260	47,758
Geographic region					
North-Central	15	36,154	29,526	36,361	37,395

Title of official	Number of municipalities reporting	Distribution of 2008 salaries			
		Mean ($)	First quartile ($)	Median ($)	Third quartile ($)
Less than 2,500 continued					
Metro type					
Suburban	8	47,594	23,455	47,728	68,130
Independent	11	37,048	34,032	36,483	37,395
Form of government					
Mayor-council	11	45,202	34,820	37,308	54,643
Council-manager	8	36,382	27,240	36,022	43,280
Engineer					
Total	7	56,284	34,338	50,000	83,604
Geographic region					
West	4	76,979	70,898	83,604	89,684
Metro type					
Suburban	4	58,993	41,850	63,932	81,075
Independent	3	52,673	34,338	34,476	61,909
Form of government					
Mayor-council	3	28,692	25,800	34,200	34,338
Council-manager	4	76,979	70,898	83,604	89,684
Fire chief					
Total	25	50,429	39,048	46,879	58,261
Geographic region					
North-Central	5	56,861	34,899	58,126	58,782
South	19	48,918	39,224	42,686	57,142
Metro type					
Suburban	11	52,947	40,106	52,000	61,373
Independent	14	48,451	36,180	42,561	55,858
Form of government					
Mayor-council	10	47,894	37,751	41,246	48,513
Council-manager	15	52,120	40,106	52,000	61,112
Health officer					
Total	. . .	. . .	. . .	. . .	. . .
Geographic region	. . .	. . .	. . .	. . .	. . .
Metro type	. . .	. . .	. . .	. . .	. . .
Form of government	. . .	. . .	. . .	. . .	. . .
Human resources director					
Total	5	45,619	32,067	46,045	50,000
Geographic region	. . .	. . .	. . .	. . .	. . .
Metro type					
Suburban	3	57,335	48,023	50,000	62,981
Form of government					
Council-manager	3	42,704	39,056	46,045	48,023
Human services director					
Total	. . .	. . .	. . .	. . .	. . .
Geographic region	. . .	. . .	. . .	. . .	. . .
Metro type	. . .	. . .	. . .	. . .	. . .
Form of government	. . .	. . .	. . .	. . .	. . .
Information services director					
Total	4	55,763	41,123	55,664	70,304
Geographic region	. . .	. . .	. . .	. . .	. . .
Metro type					
Suburban	4	55,763	41,123	55,664	70,304
Form of government	. . .	. . .	. . .	. . .	. . .
Parks and recreation director					
Total	27	34,793	25,994	37,232	41,676
Geographic region					
North-Central	13	36,923	27,540	37,960	47,216
South	12	32,219	24,712	33,750	39,576
Metro type					
Suburban	8	40,092	36,705	40,924	47,512
Independent	19	32,562	24,576	29,453	39,146
Form of government					
Mayor-council	12	33,104	24,788	37,596	38,521
Council-manager	14	35,353	27,125	33,750	43,535
Parks superintendent					
Total	16	38,137	30,720	38,929	43,350
Geographic region					
North-Central	7	37,881	35,412	40,082	43,282
South	6	36,788	28,539	32,319	37,765
West	3	41,431	38,226	43,136	45,489
Metro type					
Suburban	5	44,074	39,458	42,572	43,992
Independent	11	35,439	30,073	35,858	41,609
Form of government					
Mayor-council	5	33,259	28,781	31,366	39,458
Council-manager	11	40,354	34,587	40,082	44,068
Planning director					
Total	27	51,934	40,248	53,847	63,281
Geographic region					
North-Central	5	57,628	32,000	60,000	75,961
South	14	47,563	40,735	50,097	54,869
West	8	56,025	47,500	59,842	66,943

Table 1/8   SALARIES OF MUNICIPAL OFFICIALS: JULY–NOVEMBER 2008
continued

Title of official	Number of municipalities reporting	Distribution of 2008 salaries			
		Mean ($)	First quartile ($)	Median ($)	Third quartile ($)
Less than 2,500 continued					
Metro type					
Suburban	18	54,864	42,565	54,784	65,326
Independent	9	46,076	36,400	48,194	54,080
Form of government					
Mayor-council	7	41,071	33,576	36,400	40,248
Council-manager	19	55,836	49,097	54,953	66,193
Primary asst. manager/CAO					
Total	23	51,151	31,947	35,892	73,457
Geographic region					
North-Central	9	44,523	32,049	35,600	53,256
South	8	56,480	33,750	54,759	81,209
West	4	66,090	32,654	57,375	90,811
Metro type					
Suburban	13	49,581	28,100	50,000	68,055
Independent	10	53,192	32,430	34,800	68,116
Form of government					
Mayor-council	4	35,561	29,771	33,024	38,814
Council-manager	16	53,972	32,141	38,677	78,960
Public safety director					
Total	4	51,886	47,407	52,272	56,750
Geographic region	. . .	. . .	. . .	. . .	. . .
Metro type					
Suburban	3	52,333	46,000	54,000	59,500
Form of government	. . .	. . .	. . .	. . .	. . .
Public works director					
Total	204	48,410	39,955	46,000	55,808
Geographic region					
Northeast	8	46,017	38,619	44,207	53,219
North-Central	100	49,581	41,116	47,486	56,772
South	79	44,573	39,358	42,736	51,257
West	17	60,473	46,632	58,800	69,000
Metro type					
Suburban	79	53,219	44,704	50,195	60,707
Independent	125	45,370	37,066	42,736	54,288

Title of official	Number of municipalities reporting	Distribution of 2008 salaries			
		Mean ($)	First quartile ($)	Median ($)	Third quartile ($)
Less than 2,500 continued					
Form of government					
Mayor-council	98	45,368	39,343	43,316	54,096
Council-manager	102	51,302	41,344	49,770	57,199
Purchasing director					
Total	. . .	. . .	. . .	. . .	. . .
Geographic region	. . .	. . .	. . .	. . .	. . .
Metro type	. . .	. . .	. . .	. . .	. . .
Form of government	. . .	. . .	. . .	. . .	. . .
Recreation director					
Total	3	55,222	38,832	51,429	69,715
Geographic region	. . .	. . .	. . .	. . .	. . .
Metro type					
Independent	3	55,222	38,832	51,429	69,715
Form of government	. . .	. . .	. . .	. . .	. . .
Risk manager					
Total	. . .	. . .	. . .	. . .	. . .
Geographic region	. . .	. . .	. . .	. . .	. . .
Metro type	. . .	. . .	. . .	. . .	. . .
Form of government	. . .	. . .	. . .	. . .	. . .
Treasurer					
Total	130	37,638	28,678	35,703	44,954
Geographic region					
Northeast	5	29,105	18,600	18,720	32,378
North-Central	113	38,237	29,146	37,045	45,510
South	7	29,121	27,723	29,196	32,172
West	5	44,559	30,015	39,330	53,748
Metro type					
Suburban	29	41,586	32,000	39,499	48,111
Independent	101	36,504	27,560	34,840	44,117
Form of government					
Mayor-council	93	36,854	28,080	35,152	43,971
Council-manager	36	40,189	29,451	36,992	50,134

Salaries of County Officials, 2008

Rollie O. Waters and Joyce C. Powell
The Waters Consulting Group, Inc.

Selected Findings

The highest percentages of increase in average salary using the same counties from 2007 to 2008 are for the positions of chief administrative officer (CAO)/county manager, chief financial officer, and fire chief (5.4% each); the lowest is for the position of recreation director (3.2%).

The highest average salary shown is for the combined position of CAO/county manager ($107,855).

The position with the greatest spread (62%) between average salary range minimum and maximum is fire chief. The position with the least range spread (38%) is chief elected official.

This article and the accompanying tables present the results of ICMA's 2008 survey of salaries of local government officials in counties. In 2008, the survey instrument collected salary information on 23 positions that are common to municipal and county governments.

SURVEY METHODOLOGY

This is the fifth year that ICMA has offered SurveyNavigator™ for ICMA, a Web-based interactive version of the annual survey. This system is managed and operated by the Waters Consulting Group, Inc. Prior to SurveyNavigator™, data were collected in the summer and fall months and made available in a summary format through ICMA's *Municipal Year Book,* which is published in the spring of the following year; a printed version and a disk of the survey data were also made available for a fee through the ICMA bookstore. Now, with SurveyNavigator™ for ICMA, an online version is updated weekly as changes are made by each participating local government.

In July 2008, survey notices were mailed to all municipal and county governments with populations of 2,500 and above, and to those under 2,500 that are recognized by ICMA as having a council-manager form of government or as providing for an appointed general management (chief administrative officer, or CAO) position. The survey notice gave the Web address for SurveyNavigator™ (surveynavigator.com/icma) and provided a unique identification number and password for the local government choosing to participate. A second, abbreviated paper survey was mailed and/or e-mailed to those local governments that had not responded to the first mailing or had not provided the information online. The overall county response rate to the 2008 survey was 11% as of December 20, 2008 (Table 2/1), 7% lower than the response rate in 2007. However, the structure of the new online survey tool allows for updates and additional data to be entered at any time by participating local governments.

Table 2/1 SURVEY RESPONSE

Classification	No. of counties surveyed (A)	Respondents No.	Respondents % of (A)
Total	3,040	343	11
Population group			
Over 1,000,000	28	6	21
500,000–1,000,000 . .	63	5	8
250,000–499,999 . . .	110	16	15
100,000–249,999 . . .	276	27	10
50,000–99,999	383	37	10
25,000–49,999	638	71	11
10,000–24,999	869	105	12
5,000–9,999	386	40	10
2,500–4,999	173	24	14
Under–2,500	114	12	11
Geographic region			
Northeast	190	11	6
North-Central	1,054	173	16
South	1,372	118	9
West	424	41	10
Geographic division			
New England	46	2	4
Mid-Atlantic	144	9	6
East North-Central . .	437	59	14
West North-Central . .	617	114	18
South Atlantic	545	68	12
East South-Central . .	360	14	4
West South-Central . .	467	36	8
Mountain	276	24	9
Pacific Coast	148	17	11
Form of government			
County commission . .	2,191	230	10
Council-manager/ admin.	371	60	16
Council–elected executive	478	53	11
Metro status			
Central	458	56	12
Independent	2,241	251	11
Suburban	341	36	11
County type			
Metro	799	92	12
Nonmetro	2,241	251	11

AVERAGE SALARIES

Using the exact same counties and titles to ensure comparability between 2007 and 2008, Table 2/2 shows the percentage of change in average salary

for all 23 positions over the preceding year. Overall, the highest percentages of increase in average salary from 2007 to 2008 are for the positions of CAO/county manager, chief financial officer, and fire chief (5.4% each); the lowest is for the position of recreation director (3.2%).

Many factors influence the salaries of top local government officials. One is the type of services delivered. Some county services, for example, include an airport and/or a seaport. Some counties provide refuse collection and disposal for all cities and towns within their boundaries; others provide parks and recreation services, but the solid-waste collection is provided by the cities within the county.

Another factor influencing local government salaries is population. This is true, in part, because larger populations usually mean larger budgets, more services to meet citizen demands, and more employees to be managed. The complexity of managing counties with larger populations requires a salary commensurate with the level of expertise and experience demanded of the job. An example of the variation in average salaries among population groups is shown in Table 2/3, where the difference between the highest and lowest average salaries for the chief financial officer position is $128,947.

Regional variations also affect average salaries. For more than half of the positions surveyed, the highest average salaries in 2008 appear in the West region; for more than three-quarters of the positions, the lowest average salaries are found in the North-Central region (Table 2/4). Figure 2/1 shows the regional differences and similarities in average salaries for six selected positions.

County governments often want to know how competitive their salary ranges are when compared with those of other local governments; both salary ranges and the salaries themselves influence a county's ability to attract and retain quality employees. Table 2/5 shows the average salary range minimums, maximums, and spreads for all 23 full-time positions surveyed in 2008. The position of fire chief has the greatest range spread (62%), and the position of chief elected official has the least range spread (38%), followed closely

Table 2/2   CHANGE IN AVERAGE SALARY, 2007 TO 2008

Position	2007 average salary ($)	2008 average salary ($)	Percentage of change (%)
Chief admin. officer/county manager	97,740	103,029	5.4
Chief elected official	41,284	43,166	4.6
Chief financial officer	75,770	79,838	5.4
Chief law enforcement official	62,999	66,270	5.2
Chief librarian	62,359	65,081	4.4
Clerk	43,735	45,732	4.6
Economic development director	73,322	76,540	4.4
Engineer	76,208	79,668	4.5
Fire chief	81,380	85,789	5.4
Health officer	61,776	65,005	5.2
Human resources director	73,667	77,605	5.3
Human services director	76,782	80,485	4.8
Information services director	69,883	73,563	5.3
Parks and recreation director	64,912	68,217	5.1
Parks superintendent	48,198	50,130	4.0
Planning director	58,274	61,159	5.0
Primary assistant manager/CAO	81,942	86,136	5.1
Public safety director	55,812	58,306	4.5
Public works director	82,228	86,532	5.2
Purchasing director	60,424	63,535	5.1
Recreation director	53,460	55,154	3.2
Risk manager	56,476	59,122	4.7
Treasurer	48,107	50,494	5.0

Note: This table compares the average pay change for position using the exact same counties and titles used in *The Municipal Year Book 2008.* Where counties that reported last year did not report this year, they were excluded from the calculations for both years shown above.

Table 2/3   AVERAGE SALARY FOR CHIEF FINANCIAL OFFICER, BY POPULATION GROUP, 2008

Population group	No. reporting	Average salary ($)
Total	105	82,273
Over 1,000,000	4	163,759
500,000–1,000,000	4	136,886
250,000–499,999	15	110,393
100,000–249,999	17	104,502
50,000–99,999	16	71,855
25,000–49,999	22	72,121
10,000–24,999	23	52,718
5,000–9,999	4	34,812
2,500–4,999[1]	. . .	. . .
Under 2,500	. . .	. . .

[1]Because meaningful statistics cannot be computed for classifications having fewer than three counties reporting, no average salary data are available for this population group.

by the positions of chief law enforcement official and treasurer (39% each). Figure 2/2 shows the actual average salaries for six selected positions in conjunction with the average salary ranges for those positions.

Table 2/6 lists the average, median, and first- and third-quartile salaries for all 23 position where there were enough responses to compute the information. For some positions, such as chief librarian in counties with populations over 1 million, there were fewer than three counties reporting, so no calculation could be made.

Table 2/4   AVERAGE SALARY ($) FOR POSITION, BY REGION, 2008

Job title	Total	Region			
		Northeast	North-Central	South	West
Chief admin. officer/county manager	107,855	87,552	91,032	114,891	122,298
Chief elected official	46,229	66,284	29,510	54,020	63,895
Chief financial officer	82,273	111,408	69,370	85,867	86,728
Chief law enforcement official	65,892	54,654	59,904	72,618	77,062
Chief librarian	68,531	71,872	72,149	66,848	70,647
Clerk	48,035	56,742	43,973	48,393	58,296
Economic development director	82,679	82,975	66,700	88,114	88,162
Engineer	82,103	. . .	80,262	80,450	91,294
Fire chief	71,487	. . .	. . .	72,768	75,144
Health officer	69,092	72,871	58,164	86,617	93,070
Human resources director	72,827	67,532	64,980	72,922	86,493
Human services director	85,442	85,608	77,290	87,311	103,132
Information services director	79,548	66,889	65,217	89,593	92,999
Parks and recreation director	65,435	. . .	52,579	73,117	97,798
Parks superintendent	53,602	52,776	50,849	56,743	57,096
Planning director	67,652	66,784	51,484	79,894	74,981
Primary assistant manager/CAO	94,727	67,850	84,252	97,244	103,536
Public safety director	67,060	55,099	41,978	82,092	54,696
Public works director	84,081	87,157	69,216	85,737	105,697
Purchasing director	70,826	. . .	62,917	74,249	65,455
Recreation director	53,680	. . .	38,552	57,130	. . .
Risk manager	69,184	. . .	61,659	69,751	77,863
Treasurer	51,455	58,253	45,514	57,489	65,696

Note: (. . .) indicates that fewer than three counties reported, so meaningful statistics could not be computed.

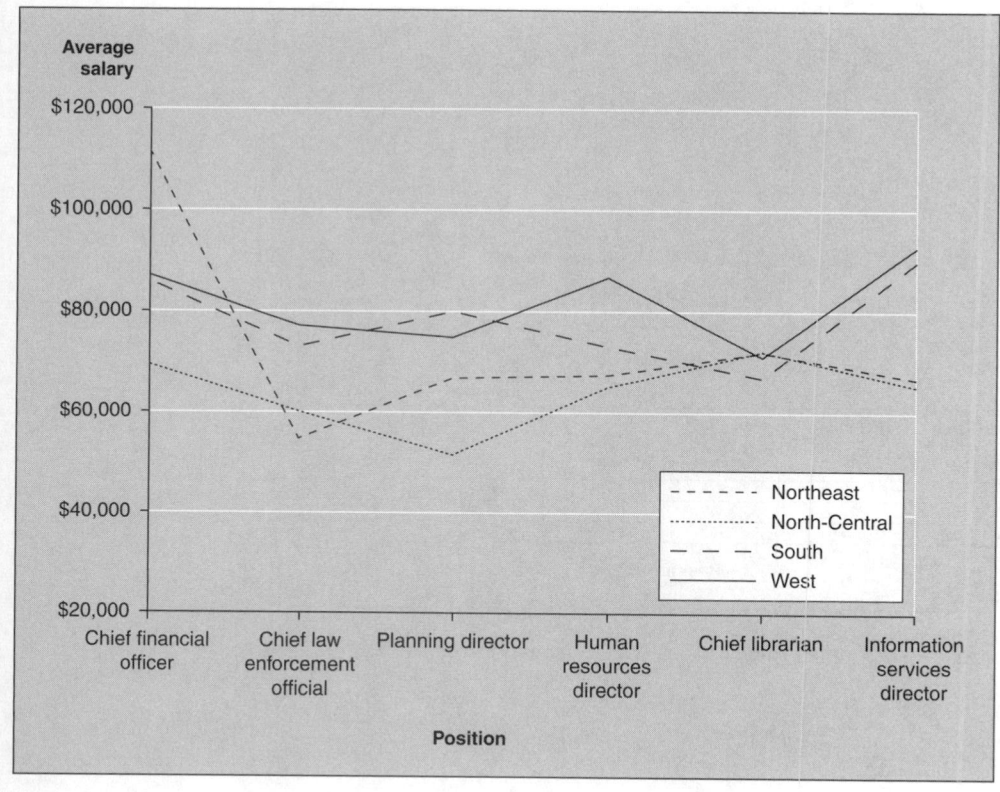

Figure 2/1 *Average salaries for six selected county positions, by geographic region, 2008*

Table 2/5   AVERAGE PAY STRUCTURE RANGES, 2008

Position	No. reporting	Average minimum ($)	Average maximum ($)	Average range spread (%)
Chief admin. officer/county manager	56	81,814	119,800	46
Chief elected official	16	34,067	47,169	38
Chief financial officer	74	69,694	103,762	49
Chief law enforcement official	61	63,376	88,302	39
Chief librarian	37	60,623	90,391	49
Clerk	70	36,870	53,419	45
Economic development director	37	69,611	106,888	54
Engineer	55	63,453	93,871	48
Fire chief	27	55,439	89,578	62
Health officer	44	69,185	96,716	40
Human resources director	93	58,695	88,805	51
Human services director	47	72,322	106,471	47
Information services director	84	65,044	96,321	48
Parks and recreation director	51	60,446	92,226	53
Parks superintendent	30	47,191	69,641	48
Planning director	75	60,603	91,521	51
Primary assistant manager/CAO	35	77,558	114,016	47
Public safety director	24	59,142	88,893	50
Public works director	57	70,595	105,791	50
Purchasing director	36	54,905	85,080	55
Recreation director	16	47,741	72,733	52
Risk manager	41	56,383	84,259	49
Treasurer	43	47,641	66,093	39

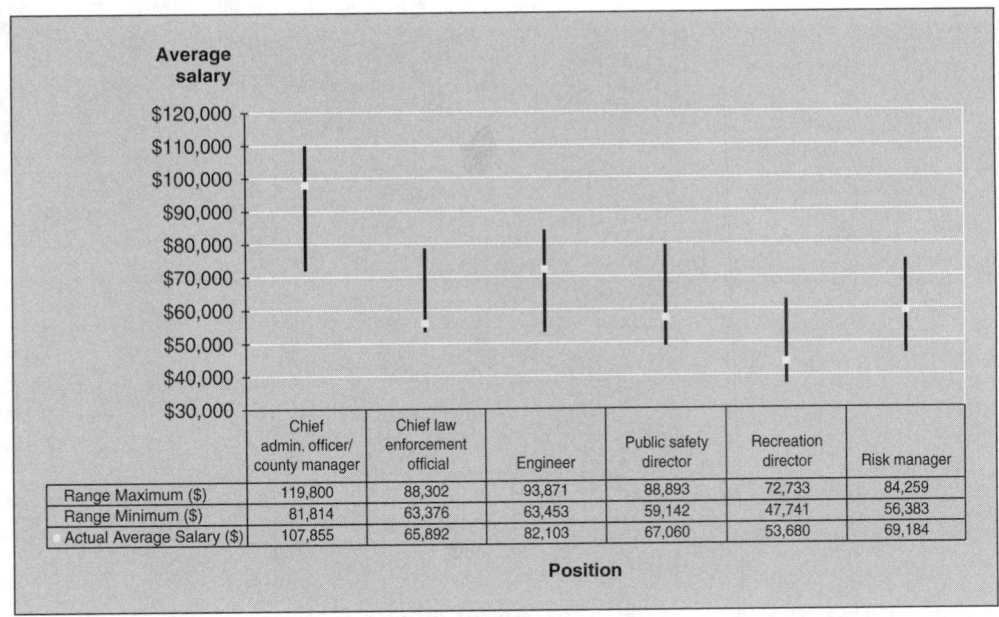

Figure 2/2   *Actual average salaries and salary ranges for six selected county positions, 2008*

	Chief admin. officer/ county manager	Chief law enforcement official	Engineer	Public safety director	Recreation director	Risk manager
Range Maximum ($)	119,800	88,302	93,871	88,893	72,733	84,259
Range Minimum ($)	81,814	63,376	63,453	59,142	47,741	56,383
Actual Average Salary ($)	107,855	65,892	82,103	67,060	53,680	69,184

Table 2/6   SALARIES OF COUNTY OFFICIALS: JULY–DECEMBER 2008

Salary data for the county positions in this table are based on information reported by county officials between late July 2008 and mid December 2008. Data are reported by position title only. Although job responsibilities are generally similar, the titles do not necessarily indicate identical duties and responsibilities.

For the position of county manager, data are shown for only those counties recognized by ICMA as having the council-manager form of government. For the position of chief administrative officer, data are shown for all other reporting counties.

Salaries are presented by ten population groups and are further classified by geographic region and form of government. In some instances, form-of-government information is missing; therefore, the number of counties reporting by form of government might not always match the total number of counties reporting. For all positions, only full time positions are reported on the table.

Classifications having fewer than three counties reporting are excluded because meaningful statistics cannot be computed. Consequently, the number reporting in some subcategories does not always equal the total reporting. Quartiles are not shown when only three counties reported. The median represents either the value of the middle observation or, when there is an even number of observations, the mean of the two middle observations. The first- and third-quartile observations represent the value of the observation below which 25% and 75% of the number of observations fall, respectively, and are calculated around the median, such that an equal number of observations fall between the median and the first quartile and the median and the third quartile.

(. . .) indicates that fewer than three counties reported, so meaningful statistics could not be computed.

Title of official	Number of counties reporting	Distribution of 2008 salaries			
		Mean ($)	First quartile ($)	Median ($)	Third quartile ($)
All counties					
Chief admin. officer/county manager					
Total	135	107,855	76,381	100,000	134,784
Geographic region					
Northeast	7	87,552	53,798	76,070	117,952
North-Central	38	91,032	76,156	84,758	113,829
South	70	114,891	79,698	103,719	143,625
West	20	122,298	83,750	117,000	157,002
County type					
Metro	65	137,118	103,261	128,378	158,631
Nonmetro	70	80,682	62,750	81,532	98,903
Form of government					
Commission	63	81,261	55,455	80,458	99,776
Council-manager/admin	39	133,483	97,424	127,000	156,673
Council–elected executive ..	33	128,336	100,779	120,809	150,095
Chief elected official					
Total	126	46,229	23,914	35,610	59,430
Geographic region					
Northeast	3	66,284	33,529	44,953	88,373
North-Central	48	29,510	19,520	24,304	31,516
South	59	54,020	34,520	49,400	63,862
West	16	63,895	28,386	59,372	95,902

Title of official	Number of counties reporting	Distribution of 2008 salaries			
		Mean ($)	First quartile ($)	Median ($)	Third quartile ($)
All counties continued					
County type					
Metro	43	59,063	26,471	53,365	84,176
Nonmetro	83	39,580	22,971	33,240	48,567
Form of government					
Commission	92	42,971	23,987	34,520	53,677
Council-manager/admin	10	33,321	17,862	26,223	45,015
Council–elected executive ..	24	64,094	25,696	56,582	95,142
Chief financial officer					
Total	107	82,273	55,475	77,991	107,841
Geographic region					
Northeast	3	111,408	104,252	112,245	118,982
North-Central	29	69,370	44,982	62,795	94,107
South	55	85,867	61,417	78,964	103,571
West	20	86,728	58,110	91,159	115,460
County type					
Metro	57	102,506	77,624	101,977	121,098
Nonmetro	50	59,207	44,725	56,356	73,899
Form of government					
Commission	46	70,100	44,039	63,197	93,696
Council-manager/admin	31	95,651	72,327	89,217	120,769
Council–elected executive ..	30	87,113	57,125	84,044	114,360

Table 2/6 SALARIES OF COUNTY OFFICIALS: JULY–DECEMBER 2008
continued

Title of official	Number of counties reporting	Mean ($)	First quartile ($)	Median ($)	Third quartile ($)
All counties continued					
Chief law enforcement official					
Total	279	65,892	46,149	58,544	76,108
Geographic region					
Northeast	7	54,654	42,058	46,075	62,295
North-Central	151	59,904	45,658	57,000	71,233
South	83	72,618	46,142	65,671	88,625
West	38	77,062	49,562	65,954	93,194
County type					
Metro	69	97,423	75,593	95,568	111,234
Nonmetro	210	55,532	44,231	55,142	64,961
Form of government					
Commission	206	57,458	44,165	55,865	66,438
Council-manager/admin	35	94,474	75,590	93,993	108,011
Council–elected executive	38	85,285	58,259	76,933	99,755
Chief librarian					
Total	66	68,531	47,123	66,512	90,560
Geographic region					
Northeast	4	71,872	55,080	76,934	93,726
North-Central	10	72,149	54,824	71,500	92,201
South	42	66,848	47,123	63,214	77,559
West	10	70,647	39,834	68,046	97,262
County type					
Metro	35	84,152	64,216	83,203	98,707
Nonmetro	31	50,895	37,010	49,982	65,542
Form of government					
Commission	28	48,037	33,956	47,914	62,506
Council-manager/admin	21	84,064	61,620	83,203	95,200
Council–elected executive	17	83,098	69,185	75,274	98,813
Clerk					
Total	243	48,035	35,029	43,545	53,637
Geographic region					
Northeast	8	56,742	39,390	55,022	64,490
North-Central	111	43,973	34,064	40,498	48,192
South	90	48,393	34,638	43,527	53,408
West	34	58,296	44,396	53,236	62,542
County type					
Metro	64	63,189	45,007	58,010	73,188
Nonmetro	179	42,616	34,050	40,685	48,039
Form of government					
Commission	177	45,225	34,100	42,173	51,432
Council-manager/admin	29	56,688	43,000	48,172	71,388
Council–elected executive	37	54,694	39,271	48,202	63,524
Economic development director					
Total	54	82,679	56,369	78,486	105,219
Geographic region					
Northeast	3	82,975	68,340	110,693	111,469
North-Central	13	66,700	44,750	60,216	71,345
South	32	88,114	63,364	80,653	101,237
West	6	88,162	62,094	101,662	110,278
County type					
Metro	28	103,806	80,918	101,576	117,126
Nonmetro	26	59,926	43,445	57,213	74,367
Form of government					
Commission	21	65,953	40,896	50,420	80,121
Council-manager/admin	18	91,608	67,405	91,778	109,290
Council–elected executive	15	95,379	76,275	89,500	109,256
Engineer					
Total	123	82,103	66,545	84,701	93,692
Geographic region					
North-Central	73	80,262	66,500	84,701	92,324
South	36	80,450	64,574	80,833	92,253
West	12	91,294	76,716	94,699	103,956
County type					
Metro	46	88,572	69,183	90,446	104,213
Nonmetro	77	78,238	66,457	81,131	91,500
Form of government					
Commission	83	80,521	66,500	83,740	92,162
Council-manager/admin	23	90,756	77,787	92,040	100,548
Council–elected executive	17	78,123	63,295	70,813	101,209
Fire chief					
Total	40	71,487	46,524	60,673	81,111
Geographic region					
South	33	72,768	45,000	59,545	80,493
West	3	75,144	57,007	82,963	97,192
County type					
Metro	26	81,925	50,840	69,170	105,680
Nonmetro	14	52,104	37,229	48,096	60,623
Form of government					
Commission	19	57,842	37,713	48,942	64,547
Council-manager/admin	12	80,233	58,931	70,776	94,647
Council–elected executive	9	88,634	53,900	77,897	111,420

Title of official	Number of counties reporting	Mean ($)	First quartile ($)	Median ($)	Third quartile ($)
All counties continued					
Health officer					
Total	100	69,092	39,694	63,603	90,134
Geographic region					
Northeast	3	72,871	53,804	77,608	94,307
North-Central	64	58,164	34,508	55,000	77,339
South	16	86,617	69,949	77,649	100,366
West	17	93,070	39,591	87,237	139,543
County type					
Metro	38	96,150	74,781	92,405	119,317
Nonmetro	62	52,508	32,543	46,545	68,091
Form of government					
Commission	63	54,166	33,086	47,961	70,725
Council-manager/admin	12	117,871	86,827	111,490	148,677
Council–elected executive	25	83,292	59,762	77,608	109,488
Human resources director					
Total	126	72,827	47,212	65,532	94,420
Geographic region					
Northeast	5	67,532	38,955	51,037	104,000
North-Central	34	64,980	45,862	61,963	86,103
South	66	72,922	48,326	66,057	84,511
West	21	86,493	63,690	90,952	111,635
County type					
Metro	68	91,808	67,908	87,737	112,454
Nonmetro	58	50,573	34,135	51,592	63,459
Form of government					
Commission	59	57,696	37,393	52,903	70,325
Council-manager/admin	33	87,483	65,723	82,239	111,635
Council–elected executive	34	84,857	58,340	82,255	109,114
Human services director					
Total	75	85,442	62,070	83,803	109,177
Geographic region					
Northeast	3	85,608	72,289	86,744	99,494
North-Central	34	77,290	58,144	75,465	97,998
South	25	87,311	64,575	85,467	108,870
West	13	103,132	85,524	109,483	119,320
County type					
Metro	35	107,457	87,099	108,870	120,777
Nonmetro	40	66,179	47,722	64,048	77,456
Form of government					
Commission	36	70,352	47,722	68,185	79,971
Council-manager/admin	23	95,628	80,243	97,843	109,286
Council–elected executive	16	104,752	85,365	110,864	119,339
Information services director					
Total	117	79,548	53,832	76,526	96,763
Geographic region					
Northeast	6	66,889	47,685	68,018	85,834
North-Central	45	65,217	48,384	55,541	85,072
South	49	89,593	63,600	86,272	100,534
West	17	92,999	77,525	94,524	106,318
County type					
Metro	64	96,514	81,169	89,474	112,290
Nonmetro	53	59,061	47,250	55,170	70,469
Form of government					
Commission	57	69,074	48,384	58,860	82,451
Council-manager/admin	28	97,763	78,282	93,822	116,279
Council–elected executive	32	82,266	54,836	85,270	101,641
Parks and recreation direction					
Total	94	65,435	40,463	57,255	83,414
Geographic region					
North-Central	44	52,579	38,049	45,496	62,276
South	42	73,117	50,796	63,960	91,103
West	6	97,798	90,674	98,501	116,203
County type					
Metro	43	89,373	69,495	86,859	109,085
Nonmetro	51	45,251	37,182	41,888	53,565
Form of government					
Commission	56	53,829	36,653	45,555	59,303
Council-manager/admin	19	83,488	66,242	77,213	91,268
Council–elected executive	19	81,588	59,811	88,576	103,491
Parks superintendent					
Total	46	53,602	39,280	50,892	70,994
Geographic region					
Northeast	4	52,776	38,850	56,483	70,409
North-Central	22	50,849	34,244	45,776	70,222
South	17	56,743	47,624	51,796	75,144
West	3	57,096	48,953	56,510	64,946
County type					
Metro	27	61,099	49,126	60,333	74,263
Nonmetro	19	42,948	32,117	41,904	47,085

Table 2/6 SALARIES OF COUNTY OFFICIALS: JULY–DECEMBER 2008
continued

Title of official	Number of counties reporting	Distribution of 2008 salaries			
		Mean ($)	First quartile ($)	Median ($)	Third quartile ($)
All counties continued					
Form of government					
Commission	23	45,187	30,851	42,786	56,490
Council-manager/admin	12	56,092	45,206	50,892	69,308
Council–elected executive . .	11	68,481	55,472	71,099	78,003
Planning director					
Total	125	67,652	42,848	63,033	87,831
Geographic region					
Northeast	7	66,784	45,475	64,168	84,605
North-Central	47	51,484	35,160	44,193	63,278
South	50	79,894	58,825	78,073	95,425
West	21	74,981	45,860	65,604	99,428
County type					
Metro	52	88,991	70,503	87,988	109,638
Nonmetro	73	52,452	37,852	50,000	63,699
Form of government					
Commission	71	56,474	36,943	50,650	69,199
Council-manager/admin	30	82,244	64,640	81,624	99,986
Council–elected executive . .	24	82,481	55,204	78,677	110,554
Primary assistant manager/CAO					
Total	54	94,727	57,536	97,025	126,069
Geographic region					
Northeast	3	67,850	37,087	44,495	86,935
North-Central	9	84,252	72,367	82,918	116,917
South	31	97,244	58,073	96,532	129,189
West	11	103,536	80,281	99,000	132,420
County type					
Metro	32	117,438	94,939	118,270	144,295
Nonmetro	22	61,694	40,239	57,623	81,015
Form of government					
Commission	17	58,639	35,137	55,800	78,814
Council-manager/admin	20	120,639	100,897	115,629	145,573
Council–elected executive . .	17	100,331	75,500	96,532	131,976
Public safety director					
Total	34	67,060	44,327	61,743	93,511
Geographic region					
Northeast	4	55,099	41,817	43,525	56,806
North-Central	8	41,978	28,916	36,622	50,164
South	19	82,092	61,743	70,000	110,003
West	3	54,696	40,820	44,460	63,454
County type					
Metro	17	85,358	60,527	94,183	111,841
Nonmetro	17	48,763	38,970	47,718	62,958
Form of government					
Commission	16	45,256	36,565	43,525	50,164
Council-manager/admin	14	87,215	64,966	86,971	110,922
Council–elected executive . .	4	83,737	59,023	77,355	102,069
Public works director					
Total	96	84,081	52,805	83,225	111,716
Geographic region					
Northeast	3	87,157	74,613	97,226	104,735
North-Central	28	69,216	35,708	62,705	101,728
South	50	85,737	58,371	82,814	105,134
West	15	105,697	72,998	112,608	133,623
County type					
Metro	49	107,400	83,450	107,578	126,881
Nonmetro	47	59,770	37,986	55,000	80,940
Form of government					
Commission	48	68,668	40,662	58,542	87,142
Council-manager/admin	22	99,495	76,087	104,725	121,729
Council–elected executive . .	26	99,492	78,849	100,098	119,368
Purchasing director					
Total	47	70,826	52,835	66,717	86,207
Geographic region					
North-Central	8	62,917	34,581	81,076	86,092
South	32	74,249	53,842	66,412	86,840
West	5	65,455	59,651	63,264	86,278
County type					
Metro	31	84,860	67,070	83,424	90,791
Nonmetro	16	43,634	30,567	47,238	55,774
Form of government					
Commission	19	60,791	40,171	53,749	67,953
Council-manager/admin	16	79,977	66,565	78,714	87,738
Council–elected executive . .	12	74,513	60,538	71,188	87,369
Recreation director					
Total	28	53,680	35,941	49,485	68,689
Geographic region					
North-Central	5	38,552	28,398	33,575	35,000
South	21	57,130	37,224	51,917	69,879
All counties continued					
County type					
Metro	15	67,102	52,052	58,228	75,339
Nonmetro	13	38,193	33,280	35,616	40,199
Form of government					
Commission	11	45,272	30,839	35,000	46,058
Council-manager/admin	8	65,524	50,180	70,279	76,554
Council–elected executive . .	9	53,429	44,632	52,335	58,228
Risk manager					
Total	56	69,184	53,503	66,270	79,224
Geographic region					
North-Central	16	61,659	45,277	62,274	76,156
South	30	69,751	52,722	64,465	78,273
West	8	77,863	69,033	73,302	82,817
County type					
Metro	45	75,061	61,550	69,828	86,521
Nonmetro	11	45,142	33,975	37,983	50,423
Form of government					
Commission	20	60,443	39,002	52,463	64,361
Council-manager/admin	16	77,735	64,609	77,211	91,487
Council–elected executive . .	20	71,086	61,549	70,814	77,676
Treasurer					
Total	260	51,455	37,476	44,692	57,317
Geographic region					
Northeast	5	58,253	46,075	46,402	78,566
North-Central	156	45,514	35,757	43,240	49,702
South	63	57,489	38,965	48,437	69,497
West	36	65,696	45,073	56,708	85,253
County type					
Metro	60	75,581	55,859	75,253	91,589
Nonmetro	200	44,217	36,314	42,847	49,018
Form of government					
Commission	206	46,417	36,493	44,167	51,266
Council-manager/admin	24	77,359	59,622	77,759	94,890
Council–elected executive . .	30	65,326	37,822	53,379	90,381
Over 1,000,000					
Chief admin. officer/county manager					
Total	4	189,158	149,946	182,031	221,243
Geographic region	. . .	. . .	. . .	. . .	. . .
County type					
Metro	4	189,158	149,946	182,031	221,243
Form of government	. . .	. . .	. . .	. . .	. . .
Chief elected official					
Total	. . .	. . .	. . .	. . .	. . .
Geographic region	. . .	. . .	. . .	. . .	. . .
County type	. . .	. . .	. . .	. . .	. . .
Form of government	. . .	. . .	. . .	. . .	. . .
Chief financial officer					
Total	4	163,759	139,975	166,013	189,797
Geographic region					
South	3	179,990	166,013	183,749	195,846
County type					
Metro	4	163,759	139,975	166,013	189,797
Form of government	. . .	. . .	. . .	. . .	. . .
Chief law enforcement official					
Total	3	145,664	105,352	117,287	171,787
Geographic region	. . .	. . .	. . .	. . .	. . .
County type					
Metro	3	145,664	105,352	117,287	171,787
Form of government	. . .	. . .	. . .	. . .	. . .
Chief librarian					
Total	. . .	. . .	. . .	. . .	. . .
Geographic region	. . .	. . .	. . .	. . .	. . .
County type	. . .	. . .	. . .	. . .	. . .
Form of government	. . .	. . .	. . .	. . .	. . .
Clerk					
Total	3	92,995	53,175	54,142	113,389
Geographic region	. . .	. . .	. . .	. . .	. . .
County type					
Metro	3	92,995	53,175	54,142	113,389
Form of government	. . .	. . .	. . .	. . .	. . .
Economic development director					
Total	4	132,622	105,035	131,155	158,742
Geographic region					
South	3	153,048	131,155	146,045	171,439
County type					
Metro	4	132,622	105,035	131,155	158,742
Form of government	. . .	. . .	. . .	. . .	. . .

Table 2/6   SALARIES OF COUNTY OFFICIALS: JULY–DECEMBER 2008
continued

Title of official	Number of counties reporting	Distribution of 2008 salaries			
		Mean ($)	First quartile ($)	Median ($)	Third quartile ($)
Over 1,000,000 continued					
Engineer					
Total	...	...	...	...	...
Geographic region	...	...	...	...	...
County type	...	...	...	...	...
Form of government	...	...	...	...	...
Fire chief					
Total	...	...	...	...	...
Geographic region	...	...	...	...	...
County type	...	...	...	...	...
Form of government	...	...	...	...	...
Health officer					
Total	...	...	...	...	...
Geographic region	...	...	...	...	...
County type	...	...	...	...	...
Form of government	...	...	...	...	...
Human resources director					
Total	6	123,723	102,920	115,090	125,553
Geographic region					
South	4	133,053	110,204	123,977	146,826
County type					
Metro	6	123,723	102,920	115,090	125,553
Form of government	...	...	...	...	...
Human services director					
Total	5	128,230	123,688	124,856	125,654
Geographic region					
South	3	130,213	110,952	123,688	146,211
County type					
Metro	5	128,230	123,688	124,856	125,654
Form of government	...	...	...	...	...
Information services director					
Total	6	137,260	112,817	143,619	153,132
Geographic region					
South	4	158,517	146,429	151,834	163,922
County type					
Metro	6	137,260	112,817	143,619	153,132
Form of government	...	...	...	...	...
Parks and recreation direction					
Total	4	148,028	131,979	146,017	162,066
Geographic region					
South	3	161,721	146,017	151,711	172,420
County type					
Metro	4	148,028	131,979	146,017	162,066
Form of government	...	...	...	...	...
Parks superintendent					
Total	...	...	...	...	...
Geographic region	...	...	...	...	...
County type	...	...	...	...	...
Form of government	...	...	...	...	...
Planning director					
Total	3	134,916	106,124	109,520	151,009
Geographic region	...	...	...	...	...
County type					
Metro	3	134,916	106,124	109,520	151,009
Form of government	...	...	...	...	...
Primary assistant manager/CAO					
Total	3	157,253	138,213	159,509	177,421
Geographic region	...	...	...	...	...
County type					
Metro	3	157,253	138,213	159,509	177,421
Form of government	...	...	...	...	...
Public safety director					
Total	...	...	...	...	...
Geographic region	...	...	...	...	...
County type	...	...	...	...	...
Form of government	...	...	...	...	...
Public works director					
Total	5	143,082	130,365	145,533	166,256
Geographic region					
South	3	163,805	148,310	166,256	180,525
County type					
Metro	5	143,082	130,365	145,533	166,256
Form of government	...	...	...	...	...
Purchasing director					
Total	6	116,550	89,374	103,737	130,459
Geographic region					
South	4	132,822	109,864	125,917	148,875
County type					
Metro	6	116,550	89,374	103,737	130,459
Form of government	...	...	...	...	...

Title of official	Number of counties reporting	Distribution of 2008 salaries			
		Mean ($)	First quartile ($)	Median ($)	Third quartile ($)
Over 1,000,000 continued					
Recreation director					
Total	...	...	...	...	...
Geographic region	...	...	...	...	...
County type	...	...	...	...	...
Form of government	...	...	...	...	...
Risk manager					
Total	5	107,227	86,521	91,699	116,000
Geographic region					
South	3	129,356	103,849	116,000	148,185
County type					
Metro	5	107,227	86,521	91,699	116,000
Form of government	...	...	...	...	...
Treasurer					
Total	...	...	...	...	...
Geographic region	...	...	...	...	...
County type	...	...	...	...	...
Form of government	...	...	...	...	...
500,000–1,000,000					
Chief admin. officer/county manager					
Total	3	180,988	153,326	156,752	196,532
Geographic region	...	...	...	...	...
County type					
Metro	3	180,988	153,326	156,752	196,532
Form of government	...	...	...	...	...
Chief elected official					
Total	4	105,358	79,750	116,968	142,576
Geographic region	...	...	...	...	...
County type					
Metro	4	105,358	79,750	116,968	142,576
Form of government	...	...	...	...	...
Chief financial officer					
Total	4	136,886	129,103	137,176	144,959
Geographic region	...	...	...	...	...
County type					
Metro	4	136,886	129,103	137,176	144,959
Form of government	...	...	...	...	...
Chief law enforcement official					
Total	4	125,342	112,486	115,922	128,778
Geographic region	...	...	...	...	...
County type					
Metro	4	125,342	112,486	115,922	128,778
Form of government	...	...	...	...	...
Chief librarian					
Total	...	...	...	...	...
Geographic region	...	...	...	...	...
County type	...	...	...	...	...
Form of government	...	...	...	...	...
Clerk					
Total	3	99,117	95,303	97,300	102,023
Geographic region	...	...	...	...	...
County type					
Metro	3	99,117	95,303	97,300	102,023
Form of government	...	...	...	...	...
Economic development director					
Total	4	102,572	92,886	101,278	110,963
Geographic region	...	...	...	...	...
County type					
Metro	4	102,572	92,886	101,278	110,963
Form of government	...	...	...	...	...
Engineer					
Total	3	104,207	91,798	100,296	114,661
Geographic region	...	...	...	...	...
County type					
Metro	3	104,207	91,798	100,296	114,661
Form of government	...	...	...	...	...
Fire chief					
Total	...	...	...	...	...
Geographic region	...	...	...	...	...
County type	...	...	...	...	...
Form of government	...	...	...	...	...
Health officer					
Total	...	...	...	...	...
Geographic region	...	...	...	...	...
County type	...	...	...	...	...
Form of government	...	...	...	...	...

Table 2/6 continued SALARIES OF COUNTY OFFICIALS: JULY–DECEMBER 2008

Title of official	Number of counties reporting	Distribution of 2008 salaries			
		Mean ($)	First quartile ($)	Median ($)	Third quartile ($)
500,000–1,000,000 continued					
Human resources director					
Total	4	127,414	116,588	123,905	134,732
Geographic region	...	...	...	...	...
County type					
Metro	4	127,414	116,588	123,905	134,732
Form of government	...	...	...	...	...
Human services director					
Total	...	...	...	...	...
Geographic region	...	...	...	...	...
County type	...	...	...	...	...
Form of government	...	...	...	...	...
Information services director					
Total	4	121,612	109,134	113,380	125,857
Geographic region	...	...	...	...	...
County type					
Metro	4	121,612	109,134	113,380	125,857
Form of government	...	...	...	...	...
Parks and recreation direction					
Total	4	100,817	89,868	101,782	112,732
Geographic region	...	...	...	...	...
County type					
Metro	4	100,817	89,868	101,782	112,732
Form of government	...	...	...	...	...
Parks superintendent					
Total	...	...	...	...	...
Geographic region	...	...	...	...	...
County type	...	...	...	...	...
Form of government	...	...	...	...	...
Planning director					
Total	3	117,117	104,568	125,233	133,723
Geographic region	...	...	...	...	...
County type					
Metro	3	117,117	104,568	125,233	133,723
Form of government	...	...	...	...	...
Primary assistant manager/CAO					
Total	...	...	...	...	...
Geographic region	...	...	...	...	...
County type	...	...	...	...	...
Form of government	...	...	...	...	...
Public safety director					
Total	...	...	...	...	...
Geographic region	...	...	...	...	...
County type	...	...	...	...	...
Form of government	...	...	...	...	...
Public works director					
Total	4	134,016	118,185	133,886	149,717
Geographic region	...	...	...	...	...
County type					
Metro	4	134,016	118,185	133,886	149,717
Form of government	...	...	...	...	...
Purchasing director					
Total	3	89,643	86,285	86,670	91,515
Geographic region	...	...	...	...	...
County type					
Metro	3	89,643	86,285	86,670	91,515
Form of government	...	...	...	...	...
Recreation director					
Total	...	...	...	...	...
Geographic region	...	...	...	...	...
County type	...	...	...	...	...
Form of government	...	...	...	...	...
Risk manager					
Total	4	81,292	69,345	82,905	94,852
Geographic region	...	...	...	...	...
County type					
Metro	4	81,292	69,345	82,905	94,852
Form of government	...	...	...	...	...
Treasurer					
Total	3	97,384	92,703	93,306	100,026
Geographic region	...	...	...	...	...
County type					
Metro	3	97,384	92,703	93,306	100,026
Form of government	...	...	...	...	...
250,000–499,999					
Chief admin. officer/county manager					
Total	13	180,971	149,344	179,307	214,614
Geographic region					
Northeast	3	132,070	117,952	124,171	142,239
South	6	211,312	184,295	203,381	232,874

Title of official	Number of counties reporting	Distribution of 2008 salaries			
		Mean ($)	First quartile ($)	Median ($)	Third quartile ($)
250,000–499,999 continued					
County type					
Metro	13	180,971	149,344	179,307	214,614
Form of government					
Council-manager/admin.	6	205,422	182,517	203,381	230,619
Council–elected executive	5	169,610	144,608	158,631	181,678
Chief elected official					
Total	10	67,848	32,285	60,788	92,846
Geographic region					
South	4	48,185	26,167	41,132	63,150
West	3	93,858	80,586	95,568	107,984
County type					
Metro	10	67,848	32,285	60,788	92,846
Form of government					
Council-manager/admin.	3	44,010	38,030	50,265	53,119
Council–elected executive	5	91,747	84,683	95,568	120,401
Chief financial officer					
Total	15	110,393	99,064	116,177	125,969
Geographic region					
Northeast	3	111,408	104,252	112,245	118,982
South	6	110,472	89,497	122,221	125,501
West	4	103,626	94,087	108,636	118,174
County type					
Metro	15	110,393	99,064	116,177	125,969
Form of government					
Commission	3	107,949	99,064	101,867	113,793
Council-manager/admin.	6	118,714	121,659	124,914	127,738
Council–elected executive	6	103,293	87,284	113,825	115,984
Chief law enforcement official					
Total	12	129,611	107,988	128,873	151,946
Geographic region					
South	6	138,129	130,018	140,654	160,195
West	3	127,223	103,334	111,100	143,051
County type					
Metro	12	129,611	107,988	128,873	151,946
Form of government					
Council-manager/admin.	5	147,499	128,885	133,488	171,260
Council–elected executive	5	121,618	95,568	117,357	147,821
Chief librarian					
Total	11	95,042	87,860	95,200	108,254
Geographic region					
Northeast	3	84,157	76,934	92,102	95,351
South	5	91,800	83,617	93,600	117,694
County type					
Metro	11	95,042	87,860	95,200	108,254
Form of government					
Council-manager/admin.	5	96,375	83,617	95,200	117,694
Council–elected executive	4	100,804	93,225	96,207	103,785
Clerk					
Total	12	81,292	69,124	79,076	91,518
Geographic region					
Northeast	3	75,084	61,821	62,332	81,972
South	5	77,513	71,388	71,413	72,141
West	3	87,220	86,656	87,300	87,825
County type					
Metro	12	81,292	69,124	79,076	91,518
Form of government					
Commission	3	70,314	61,821	62,332	74,816
Council-manager/admin.	3	85,277	71,764	72,141	92,222
Council–elected executive	6	84,788	75,062	87,181	97,855
Economic development director					
Total	4	128,361	107,025	111,469	132,805
Geographic region	...	...	...	...	...
County type					
Metro	4	128,361	107,025	111,469	132,805
Form of government	...	...	...	...	...
Engineer					
Total	10	99,479	91,703	101,827	108,516
Geographic region					
South	5	87,521	80,555	90,718	94,659
County type					
Metro	10	99,479	91,703	101,827	108,516
Form of government					
Council-manager/admin.	4	92,908	88,177	92,689	97,420
Council–elected executive	4	97,260	91,461	105,331	111,130
Fire chief					
Total	5	106,104	66,194	111,197	129,265
Geographic region					
South	4	116,082	98,284	120,231	138,029
County type					
Metro	5	106,104	66,194	111,197	129,265

Table 2/6   SALARIES OF COUNTY OFFICIALS: JULY–DECEMBER 2008
continued

Title of official	Number of counties reporting	Mean ($)	First quartile ($)	Median ($)	Third quartile ($)
250,000–499,999 continued					
Form of government					
Council-manager/admin. . . .	3	100,002	85,371	111,197	120,231
Health officer					
Total	9	121,371	109,488	116,177	120,000
Geographic region					
West	3	142,341	114,744	120,000	158,768
County type					
Metro	9	121,371	109,488	116,177	120,000
Form of government					
Council-manager/admin. . . .	3	146,189	120,516	147,811	172,674
Council–elected executive . .	4	105,692	101,518	112,833	117,007
Human resources director					
Total	15	114,818	99,570	112,245	124,278
Geographic region					
South	7	113,798	88,281	111,527	134,346
West	4	115,220	104,035	112,184	123,369
County type					
Metro	15	114,818	99,570	112,245	124,278
Form of government					
Council-manager/admin. . . .	6	129,581	114,318	122,889	139,941
Council–elected executive . .	7	103,545	86,187	108,395	118,858
Human services director					
Total	7	111,464	110,973	116,177	116,612
Geographic region	. . .	. . .	. . .	. . .	. . .
County type					
Metro	7	111,464	110,973	116,177	116,612
Form of government					
Council-manager/admin. . . .	3	116,153	113,151	116,600	119,379
Council–elected executive . .	3	115,015	114,211	116,177	116,401
Information services director					
Total	14	111,651	99,299	108,276	126,617
Geographic region					
Northeast	3	90,704	85,556	86,112	93,556
South	7	121,088	104,156	129,265	139,358
West	3	108,952	104,090	106,971	112,823
County type					
Metro	14	111,651	99,299	108,276	126,617
Form of government					
Commission	3	101,558	93,000	101,000	109,838
Council-manager/admin. . . .	4	126,678	121,632	133,936	138,982
Council–elected executive . .	7	107,390	93,661	106,971	113,059
Parks and recreation direction					
Total	9	104,818	92,123	113,520	116,177
Geographic region					
South	3	107,934	103,545	114,967	115,840
County type					
Metro	9	104,818	92,123	113,520	116,177
Form of government					
Council-manager/admin. . . .	3	106,870	102,822	113,520	114,244
Council–elected executive . .	4	108,084	105,296	113,523	116,311
Parks superintendent					
Total	8	64,824	55,674	69,515	72,541
Geographic region					
Northeast	3	61,355	56,483	70,179	70,639
County type					
Metro	8	64,824	55,674	69,515	72,541
Form of government					
Council–elected executive . .	4	70,904	67,452	73,982	77,433
Planning director					
Total	11	100,883	88,616	107,638	118,441
Geographic region					
Northeast	3	93,818	84,605	88,000	100,122
South	7	100,425	94,992	107,638	118,441
County type					
Metro	11	100,883	88,616	107,638	118,441
Form of government					
Council-manager/admin. . . .	4	113,975	105,916	114,062	122,121
Council–elected executive . .	5	96,921	89,232	112,245	116,396
Primary assistant manager/CAO					
Total	9	143,607	129,375	142,424	171,475
Geographic region					
South	5	158,836	142,424	155,019	180,274
County type					
Metro	9	143,607	129,375	142,424	171,475
Form of government					
Council-manager/admin. . . .	5	154,853	142,424	155,019	171,475
Council–elected executive . .	3	129,609	102,172	131,976	158,231
Public safety director					
Total	4	104,515	93,656	103,109	113,968
Geographic region					
South	3	107,895	101,668	111,841	116,095

Title of official	Number of counties reporting	Mean ($)	First quartile ($)	Median ($)	Third quartile ($)
250,000–499,999 continued					
County type					
Metro	4	104,515	93,656	103,109	113,968
Form of government					
Council-manager/admin. . . .	3	107,895	101,668	111,841	116,095
Public works director					
Total	11	119,627	106,634	117,322	134,302
Geographic region					
South	5	124,119	123,197	126,881	141,724
County type					
Metro	11	119,627	106,634	117,322	134,302
Form of government					
Council-manager/admin. . . .	5	133,406	123,197	126,881	148,788
Council–elected executive . .	5	110,328	101,023	112,245	116,643
Purchasing director					
Total	8	79,277	65,739	80,108	86,317
Geographic region					
South	5	85,442	76,793	83,424	90,942
County type					
Metro	8	79,277	65,739	80,108	86,317
Form of government					
Council-manager/admin. . . .	3	83,720	80,108	83,424	87,183
Council–elected executive . .	3	86,942	71,139	84,776	101,663
Recreation director					
Total	. . .	. . .	. . .	. . .	. . .
Geographic region	. . .	. . .	. . .	. . .	. . .
County type	. . .	. . .	. . .	. . .	. . .
Form of government	. . .	. . .	. . .	. . .	. . .
Risk manager					
Total	12	82,194	72,483	80,142	90,626
Geographic region					
South	5	89,164	78,294	91,416	92,558
West	3	68,728	66,465	66,647	69,951
County type					
Metro	12	82,194	72,483	80,142	90,626
Form of government					
Council-manager/admin. . . .	4	87,090	84,143	88,755	91,702
Council–elected executive . .	6	80,220	70,940	74,564	80,461
Treasurer					
Total	13	93,949	78,829	86,011	98,080
Geographic region					
South	5	91,698	74,618	81,693	97,468
West	4	106,844	86,978	97,728	117,594
County type					
Metro	13	93,949	78,829	86,011	98,080
Form of government					
Commission	3	81,955	79,283	80,000	83,650
Council-manager/admin. . . .	5	91,530	78,829	81,693	97,468
Council–elected executive . .	5	103,565	86,011	98,080	108,155
100,000–249,999					
Chief admin. officer/county manager					
Total	25	132,592	98,758	135,693	155,593
Geographic region					
North-Central	8	109,043	84,533	108,584	128,495
South	11	147,535	136,689	152,009	161,716
West	4	168,978	145,881	169,656	192,753
County type					
Metro	22	135,033	103,683	140,202	155,445
Nonmetro	3	114,697	93,169	110,268	134,010
Form of government					
Commission	7	104,576	83,825	98,758	122,276
Council-manager/admin. . . .	10	143,812	145,404	153,505	157,212
Council–elected executive . .	8	143,082	122,585	132,036	171,500
Chief elected official					
Total	14	51,225	17,062	37,132	85,140
Geographic region					
North-Central	3	20,054	15,449	16,761	23,013
South	8	48,910	17,587	35,826	57,712
West	3	88,569	74,959	96,904	106,346
County type					
Metro	13	46,259	16,800	29,264	53,014
Form of government					
Commission	3	80,113	54,993	95,849	113,101
Council-manager/admin. . . .	5	20,861	16,761	17,849	26,651
Council–elected executive . .	6	62,084	45,000	49,007	85,932

Table 2/6　　SALARIES OF COUNTY OFFICIALS: JULY–DECEMBER 2008
continued

Title of official	Number of counties reporting	Mean ($)	First quartile ($)	Median ($)	Third quartile ($)
100,000–249,999 continued					
Chief financial officer					
Total	17	104,502	94,107	105,164	115,627
Geographic region					
North-Central	3	98,090	94,351	94,594	100,082
South	11	102,051	88,244	105,164	115,139
West	3	119,901	110,332	115,627	127,333
County type					
Metro	16	104,468	92,885	105,367	115,984
Form of government					
Commission	4	94,713	87,667	99,636	106,682
Council-manager/admin.	6	105,462	93,305	109,395	116,097
Council–elected executive	7	109,271	97,247	105,036	125,645
Chief law enforcement official					
Total	22	104,658	94,006	101,025	110,398
Geographic region					
North-Central	8	97,369	90,571	98,113	105,153
South	9	100,290	94,601	100,000	104,939
West	4	139,912	130,167	145,834	155,578
County type					
Metro	19	104,914	94,205	100,000	106,693
Nonmetro	3	103,037	86,347	111,420	123,918
Form of government					
Commission	8	94,279	83,922	100,652	106,095
Council-manager/admin.	8	104,024	94,114	99,629	106,829
Council–elected executive	6	119,343	99,264	105,710	144,293
Chief librarian					
Total	10	84,732	69,800	81,976	99,152
Geographic region					
South	6	74,319	67,406	69,968	85,520
County type					
Metro	10	84,732	69,800	81,976	99,152
Form of government					
Commission	3	63,573	58,680	66,664	70,012
Council-manager/admin.	4	92,787	85,352	94,309	101,744
Council–elected executive	3	95,153	84,916	99,527	107,577
Clerk					
Total	16	68,282	60,063	66,707	75,840
Geographic region					
North-Central	6	71,432	65,571	72,093	77,105
South	8	58,238	48,796	57,793	65,617
County type					
Metro	14	63,892	55,523	64,059	73,639
Form of government					
Commission	5	69,088	63,682	68,979	71,895
Council-manager/admin.	7	66,443	50,774	64,435	75,979
Council–elected executive	4	70,495	59,884	69,366	79,976
Economic development director					
Total	10	103,639	98,061	104,262	118,102
Geographic region					
South	7	98,105	90,509	102,255	109,769
County type					
Metro	9	104,364	100,897	106,268	119,713
Form of government					
Council-manager/admin.	5	101,125	100,897	102,255	113,270
Council–elected executive	4	112,661	103,980	112,991	121,671
Engineer					
Total	13	81,201	69,052	83,740	93,590
Geographic region					
South	10	76,676	67,392	79,379	91,743
County type					
Metro	13	81,201	69,052	83,740	93,590
Form of government					
Commission	4	76,260	62,604	76,396	90,052
Council-manager/admin.	6	84,648	70,585	83,529	93,203
Council–elected executive	3	80,897	67,099	90,851	99,672
Fire chief					
Total	7	81,116	63,297	80,493	100,182
Geographic region					
South	6	76,066	61,213	73,980	86,971
County type					
Metro	6	76,066	61,213	73,980	86,971
Form of government					
Commission	3	73,101	54,035	59,128	85,181
Council-manager/admin.	3	79,030	73,980	80,493	84,812
Health officer					
Total	11	116,309	91,529	108,544	144,065
Geographic region					
North-Central	5	96,969	91,468	91,589	103,717
South	3	118,383	99,117	108,544	132,730
West	3	146,469	144,065	147,805	149,541
County type					
Metro	10	112,812	91,498	106,131	133,853
100,000–249,999 continued					
Form of government					
Commission	3	92,980	87,612	91,589	97,653
Council-manager/admin.	4	132,793	112,962	132,856	152,687
Council–elected executive	4	117,322	91,023	115,897	142,195
Human resources director					
Total	23	88,823	75,266	88,366	106,278
Geographic region					
North-Central	5	85,056	72,964	87,108	94,107
South	13	85,393	77,567	83,450	89,905
West	4	114,128	106,899	111,966	119,195
County type					
Metro	21	87,161	72,964	87,108	104,068
Form of government					
Commission	6	74,233	54,555	73,564	92,857
Council-manager/admin.	9	86,857	77,567	82,978	89,905
Council–elected executive	8	101,978	86,194	107,514	119,195
Human services director					
Total	12	111,132	95,246	105,751	122,152
Geographic region					
North-Central	4	104,458	96,451	105,751	113,759
South	5	98,612	87,453	97,843	102,900
West	3	140,898	133,562	147,805	151,686
County type					
Metro	11	107,092	92,648	103,297	119,358
Form of government					
Council-manager/admin.	6	108,349	90,051	100,371	123,538
Council–elected executive	5	115,057	103,297	119,320	119,396
Information services director					
Total	23	93,689	85,870	89,227	97,922
Geographic region					
North-Central	7	89,746	84,506	88,004	88,954
South	12	97,115	87,800	89,315	97,343
West	3	103,400	88,779	100,032	116,337
County type					
Metro	21	94,156	86,272	89,227	96,763
Form of government					
Commission	6	86,307	83,507	88,836	89,533
Council-manager/admin.	10	95,298	86,705	88,768	96,693
Council–elected executive	7	97,717	86,288	89,274	116,337
Parks and recreation direction					
Total	13	86,831	71,105	90,412	98,051
Geographic region					
North-Central	4	69,300	65,744	69,151	72,706
South	7	93,515	81,677	91,333	101,060
County type					
Metro	12	85,731	70,869	85,376	97,240
Form of government					
Commission	5	79,795	68,140	70,161	98,051
Council-manager/admin.	4	78,700	72,482	76,641	82,858
Council–elected executive	4	103,758	95,560	98,501	106,698
Parks superintendent					
Total	10	63,048	50,889	58,424	74,704
Geographic region					
South	7	63,856	49,126	60,333	79,274
County type					
Metro	10	63,048	50,889	58,424	74,704
Form of government					
Council-manager/admin.	4	52,838	45,687	49,126	56,276
Council–elected executive	4	69,804	58,649	66,858	78,013
Planning director					
Total	18	93,742	74,045	94,193	107,987
Geographic region					
North-Central	3	71,089	68,920	70,798	73,113
South	11	94,396	83,716	95,285	105,082
West	3	126,577	115,236	128,495	138,878
County type					
Metro	17	93,258	73,584	93,101	109,991
Form of government					
Commission	3	75,267	65,164	70,798	83,135
Council-manager/admin.	8	87,838	74,966	90,538	96,507
Council–elected executive	7	108,408	90,716	109,991	131,082
Primary assistant manager/CAO					
Total	16	99,655	81,876	100,406	128,065
Geographic region					
South	8	99,843	92,086	105,284	121,317
West	4	126,386	98,629	124,454	152,211
County type					
Metro	13	104,113	82,918	108,757	133,052
Nonmetro	3	80,337	71,006	97,517	98,259

Table 2/6 SALARIES OF COUNTY OFFICIALS: JULY–DECEMBER 2008
continued

Title of official	Number of counties reporting	Mean ($)	First quartile ($)	Median ($)	Third quartile ($)
100,000–249,999 continued					
Form of government					
Commission	3	53,745	39,158	44,495	63,707
Council-manager/admin.	6	114,535	103,548	114,190	124,707
Council–elected executive	7	106,577	87,641	99,000	141,480
Public safety director					
Total	7	91,898	70,985	94,183	116,946
Geographic region					
South	7	91,898	70,985	94,183	116,946
County type					
Metro	7	91,898	70,985	94,183	116,946
Form of government					
Council-manager/admin.	5	84,675	66,210	75,760	108,165
Public works director					
Total	17	109,575	99,047	111,234	119,892
Geographic region					
North-Central	3	109,265	102,291	117,797	120,505
South	10	100,994	87,349	104,725	110,320
West	4	131,260	112,311	129,184	148,133
County type					
Metro	15	109,250	92,916	107,578	121,552
Form of government					
Commission	3	85,634	72,835	86,785	99,010
Council-manager/admin.	7	104,197	101,476	105,544	110,093
Council–elected executive	7	125,213	114,609	119,892	144,340
Purchasing director					
Total	10	77,303	68,173	77,497	86,243
Geographic region					
South	8	77,936	69,674	77,497	88,288
County type					
Metro	10	77,303	68,173	77,497	86,243
Form of government					
Council-manager/admin.	5	82,059	74,359	80,635	86,136
Council–elected executive	3	81,429	74,771	86,278	90,512
Recreation director					
Total	7	69,109	52,126	56,979	69,086
Geographic region					
South	6	71,905	53,182	62,636	69,482
County type					
Metro	7	69,109	52,126	56,979	69,086
Form of government					
Council–elected executive	3	59,202	54,657	56,979	62,636
Risk manager					
Total	15	67,877	59,902	64,753	77,168
Geographic region					
North-Central	3	61,204	53,742	60,231	68,180
South	9	65,281	59,573	64,176	66,257
West	3	82,338	74,065	78,302	88,593
County type					
Metro	14	67,132	59,738	64,465	74,553
Form of government					
Commission	3	61,897	53,742	60,231	69,220
Council-manager/admin.	7	65,932	61,875	64,753	71,193
Council–elected executive	5	74,188	60,333	69,828	95,304
Treasurer					
Total	16	79,656	62,094	76,924	92,432
Geographic region					
North-Central	7	71,109	62,101	63,682	82,330
South	6	73,000	59,900	69,221	87,591
West	3	112,914	108,656	113,571	117,501
County type					
Metro	15	78,051	61,855	76,109	89,345
Form of government					
Commission	5	66,742	62,333	62,826	63,682
Council-manager/admin.	6	71,938	59,661	68,743	77,331
Council–elected executive	5	101,833	91,418	95,472	113,571
50,000–99,999					
Chief admin. officer/county manager					
Total	23	102,162	90,763	104,803	113,274
Geographic region					
North-Central	7	87,311	80,089	85,000	108,218
South	14	108,097	100,992	107,484	114,247
County type					
Metro	10	109,982	103,647	108,197	114,890
Nonmetro	13	96,147	85,000	100,456	111,633
Form of government					
Commission	11	93,969	84,805	100,456	111,514
Council-manager/admin.	4	112,230	102,734	109,902	119,398
Council–elected executive	8	108,394	98,200	106,615	117,446

Title of official	Number of counties reporting	Mean ($)	First quartile ($)	Median ($)	Third quartile ($)
50,000–99,999 continued					
Chief elected official					
Total	11	47,217	24,075	53,365	59,744
Geographic region					
South	8	45,094	26,975	46,946	55,745
County type					
Metro	8	55,395	47,524	56,907	65,250
Nonmetro	3	25,410	17,853	17,900	29,213
Form of government					
Commission	9	53,743	40,526	54,326	60,000
Chief financial officer					
Total	16	71,855	60,509	65,097	83,672
Geographic region					
North-Central	4	65,357	58,533	62,252	69,075
South	8	73,124	62,015	69,102	86,465
West	4	75,815	60,569	74,123	89,369
County type					
Metro	9	74,399	63,345	65,790	83,088
Nonmetro	7	68,583	53,831	60,645	86,022
Form of government					
Commission	8	71,595	63,328	70,325	83,197
Council-manager/admin.	3	70,902	61,559	62,472	76,031
Council–elected executive	5	72,842	53,836	63,345	83,088
Chief law enforcement official					
Total	25	76,193	67,686	72,676	82,000
Geographic region					
North-Central	8	80,321	71,850	76,383	81,728
South	12	70,200	57,970	67,851	78,294
West	4	89,137	74,748	79,908	94,296
County type					
Metro	14	75,839	68,331	72,543	77,793
Nonmetro	11	76,644	67,052	72,676	82,658
Form of government					
Commission	14	71,120	64,829	74,135	77,793
Council-manager/admin.	4	90,193	68,561	88,638	110,270
Council–elected executive	7	78,340	67,851	68,842	79,530
Chief librarian					
Total	14	64,807	57,571	66,935	69,732
Geographic region					
South	11	66,628	58,143	64,724	71,003
County type					
Metro	5	58,976	59,285	61,703	69,145
Nonmetro	9	68,046	57,000	69,641	72,274
Form of government					
Commission	5	57,605	49,497	64,724	69,145
Council-manager/admin.	3	69,112	64,509	69,732	74,026
Council–elected executive	6	68,656	58,176	65,718	71,639
Clerk					
Total	28	54,961	43,354	51,788	60,497
Geographic region					
North-Central	9	56,288	40,823	55,522	65,000
South	15	51,098	43,349	47,906	52,431
West	3	72,375	58,994	59,488	79,313
County type					
Metro	15	55,066	44,259	51,775	61,874
Nonmetro	13	54,840	40,823	51,800	58,500
Form of government					
Commission	16	57,783	47,386	56,818	63,707
Council-manager/admin.	3	39,453	36,938	43,358	43,920
Council–elected executive	9	55,115	45,159	48,202	53,544
Economic development director					
Total	6	72,332	56,851	68,992	86,413
Geographic region					
South	6	72,332	56,851	68,992	86,413
County type					
Nonmetro	5	74,632	55,524	77,152	89,500
Form of government					
Council-manager/admin.	3	70,780	58,178	60,831	78,409
Council–elected executive	3	73,884	66,076	77,152	83,326
Engineer					
Total	14	85,934	82,133	88,530	92,608
Geographic region					
North-Central	5	95,747	88,594	90,174	104,803
South	8	81,867	75,631	86,856	92,045
County type					
Metro	9	82,736	69,410	86,628	92,890
Nonmetro	5	91,690	88,466	88,594	91,763
Form of government					
Commission	10	89,327	85,592	89,384	92,608
Council-manager/admin.	3	84,169	73,853	88,466	96,635

Table 2/6   SALARIES OF COUNTY OFFICIALS: JULY–DECEMBER 2008
continued

Title of official	Number of counties reporting	Distribution of 2008 salaries			
		Mean ($)	First quartile ($)	Median ($)	Third quartile ($)
50,000–99,999 continued					
Fire chief					
Total	10	56,373	44,186	52,368	68,606
Geographic region					
South	8	53,030	43,096	46,601	64,069
County type					
Metro	7	54,948	42,821	48,202	63,704
Nonmetro	3	59,698	52,857	61,800	67,591
Form of government					
Commission	6	54,476	41,731	50,767	67,289
Council–elected executive	3	64,322	55,001	61,800	72,382
Health officer					
Total	16	74,440	62,200	76,868	87,312
Geographic region					
North-Central	5	64,411	58,000	63,600	78,476
South	7	76,517	73,592	77,152	82,841
West	3	101,121	81,911	87,237	113,390
County type					
Metro	10	73,926	59,400	73,592	78,393
Nonmetro	6	75,296	76,726	82,195	87,461
Form of government					
Commission	8	58,435	43,471	60,800	77,057
Council–elected executive	6	92,979	74,667	86,753	97,318
Human resources director					
Total	25	63,260	54,000	63,690	70,838
Geographic region					
North-Central	5	63,666	54,000	63,523	63,720
South	16	59,580	53,299	61,091	68,389
West	4	77,475	69,051	75,843	84,267
County type					
Metro	12	67,015	61,268	66,504	76,599
Nonmetro	13	59,794	54,000	60,861	66,827
Form of government					
Commission	13	61,564	54,000	63,690	70,838
Council-manager/admin.	3	70,451	67,504	68,180	72,263
Council–elected executive	9	63,314	54,000	57,678	64,827
Human services director					
Total	10	79,325	65,934	78,633	85,408
Geographic region					
North-Central	3	82,900	71,948	73,884	89,344
South	4	72,123	62,300	73,978	83,800
West	3	85,353	73,289	85,524	97,504
County type					
Metro	6	87,770	76,258	84,220	99,867
Nonmetro	4	66,657	59,659	62,814	69,812
Form of government					
Commission	4	72,618	67,773	71,948	76,794
Council-manager/admin.	3	81,220	69,429	83,381	94,092
Council–elected executive	3	86,372	74,817	85,058	97,271
Information services director					
Total	25	66,779	53,000	65,520	78,418
Geographic region					
North-Central	7	66,873	50,641	68,473	78,980
South	14	62,586	50,221	59,024	69,089
West	4	81,290	75,904	80,083	85,469
County type					
Metro	12	70,228	55,589	62,008	89,372
Nonmetro	13	63,595	48,282	68,473	70,469
Form of government					
Commission	13	66,408	56,452	70,279	77,715
Council-manager/admin.	4	80,269	63,937	80,676	97,008
Council–elected executive	8	60,637	47,352	51,381	70,534
Parks and recreation direction					
Total	10	59,833	53,848	59,016	69,512
Geographic region					
North-Central	3	66,301	56,022	57,116	71,988
South	7	57,061	46,546	60,915	67,951
County type					
Metro	6	61,767	55,474	60,972	69,512
Nonmetro	4	56,931	50,017	57,202	64,115
Form of government					
Commission	4	53,822	49,067	54,208	58,964
Council–elected executive	4	58,816	52,738	60,972	67,049
Parks superintendent					
Total	4	64,416	54,377	64,259	74,297
Geographic region	...	...	...	...	...
County type					
Nonmetro	4	64,416	54,377	64,259	74,297
Form of government					
Commission	3	69,851	64,259	72,051	76,544

Title of official	Number of counties reporting	Distribution of 2008 salaries			
		Mean ($)	First quartile ($)	Median ($)	Third quartile ($)
50,000–99,999 continued					
Planning director					
Total	17	69,947	58,600	69,617	81,241
Geographic region					
North-Central	6	66,247	50,381	67,262	80,218
South	10	71,778	60,096	68,446	80,493
County type					
Metro	6	79,350	69,963	79,416	93,832
Nonmetro	11	64,818	58,583	64,584	76,040
Form of government					
Commission	10	71,086	64,461	72,416	82,778
Council-manager/admin.	4	77,070	68,359	73,933	82,644
Council–elected executive	3	56,651	55,677	58,566	58,583
Primary assistant manager/CAO					
Total	7	82,289	68,865	75,500	95,881
Geographic region					
South	5	77,527	64,273	75,500	89,472
County type					
Nonmetro	5	77,527	64,273	75,500	89,472
Form of government					
Council–elected executive	4	86,044	72,693	82,486	95,837
Public safety director					
Total	3	59,991	57,518	60,527	62,732
Geographic region					
South	3	59,991	57,518	60,527	62,732
County type	...	...	...	...	...
Form of government	...	...	...	...	...
Public works director					
Total	16	83,067	67,603	84,410	99,834
Geographic region					
North-Central	3	90,887	84,410	85,820	94,831
South	10	78,485	63,675	78,576	90,199
County type					
Metro	7	80,587	59,956	83,000	97,134
Nonmetro	9	84,996	75,621	85,820	98,889
Form of government					
Commission	10	82,964	64,684	84,410	101,724
Council–elected executive	4	90,524	81,892	88,799	97,432
Purchasing director					
Total	5	52,621	49,993	51,921	54,482
Geographic region					
South	5	52,621	49,993	51,921	54,482
County type					
Nonmetro	5	52,621	49,993	51,921	54,482
Form of government	...	...	...	...	...
Recreation director					
Total	...	...	...	...	...
Geographic region	...	...	...	...	...
County type	...	...	...	...	...
Form of government	...	...	...	...	...
Risk manager					
Total	7	55,064	44,834	53,893	65,950
Geographic region					
South	4	52,257	46,896	52,104	57,465
County type					
Metro	6	58,135	51,210	58,807	67,065
Form of government					
Commission	5	48,784	39,354	50,315	53,893
Treasurer					
Total	21	63,214	53,214	58,474	72,500
Geographic region					
North-Central	11	60,298	53,064	53,544	70,444
South	7	62,717	51,440	58,113	70,793
West	3	75,063	62,230	65,960	83,345
County type					
Metro	10	66,680	54,529	67,043	75,041
Nonmetro	11	60,063	53,064	54,060	62,230
Form of government					
Commission	16	59,360	52,036	58,294	66,742
Council–elected executive	4	70,844	53,462	64,716	82,099
25,000–49,999					
Chief admin. officer/county manager					
Total	30	87,988	79,533	87,516	101,676
Geographic region					
North-Central	9	77,341	79,800	82,606	88,296
South	15	93,708	81,422	96,290	113,190
West	4	116,237	91,958	107,158	131,437

Table 2/6 SALARIES OF COUNTY OFFICIALS: JULY–DECEMBER 2008
continued

Title of official	Number of counties reporting	Distribution of 2008 salaries			
		Mean ($)	First quartile ($)	Median ($)	Third quartile ($)
25,000–49,999 continued					
County type					
Metro	7	104,666	92,168	120,809	127,000
Nonmetro	23	82,911	78,068	84,906	92,565
Form of government					
Commission	19	77,840	56,744	82,606	90,517
Council–manager/admin.	8	104,638	84,658	99,045	127,000
Council–elected executive	3	107,854	101,377	101,975	111,392
Chief elected official					
Total	26	43,975	28,457	44,861	59,971
Geographic region					
North-Central	8	29,268	23,317	29,285	34,037
South	16	53,131	46,428	55,546	64,739
County type					
Metro	4	54,234	42,507	54,006	65,733
Nonmetro	22	42,110	25,492	44,739	56,589
Form of government					
Commission	21	41,043	27,629	44,769	53,461
Council–elected executive	4	50,616	38,766	53,884	65,733
Chief financial officer					
Total	22	72,121	58,125	74,692	84,059
Geographic region					
North-Central	7	55,568	44,406	54,600	70,431
South	12	79,138	72,316	79,454	86,265
West	3	82,677	63,640	94,000	107,375
County type					
Metro	5	89,810	85,000	90,060	96,794
Nonmetro	17	66,918	54,600	67,754	78,250
Form of government					
Commission	11	65,887	49,215	63,600	77,171
Council–manager/admin.	7	79,592	74,692	78,250	85,359
Council–elected executive	4	76,192	69,739	81,496	87,948
Chief law enforcement official					
Total	60	62,845	46,072	62,200	74,602
Geographic region					
Northeast	4	39,835	37,453	42,058	44,441
North-Central	25	68,158	57,968	70,000	76,047
South	25	59,965	43,320	56,502	70,340
West	6	68,048	52,264	73,814	81,760
County type					
Metro	11	72,739	55,537	78,085	91,029
Nonmetro	49	60,624	46,075	59,500	70,982
Form of government					
Commission	49	59,668	46,062	59,500	70,982
Council–manager/admin.	8	82,070	71,126	86,997	97,793
Council–elected executive	3	63,462	56,790	70,977	73,892
Chief librarian					
Total	12	58,827	49,069	60,432	67,066
Geographic region					
South	9	58,746	46,331	60,000	69,185
County type					
Metro	3	69,088	65,995	70,371	72,822
Nonmetro	9	55,406	46,331	56,151	60,863
Form of government					
Commission	6	54,953	47,244	54,991	60,647
Council–manager/admin.	3	62,714	58,886	61,620	65,995
Council–elected executive	3	62,688	56,395	69,185	72,230
Clerk					
Total	56	43,572	36,368	42,183	51,939
Geographic region					
Northeast	4	44,988	34,677	38,009	48,320
North-Central	21	43,813	36,742	44,818	49,240
South	25	40,239	34,121	40,577	48,400
West	6	55,667	46,699	59,080	62,542
County type					
Metro	11	42,749	34,080	40,772	52,397
Nonmetro	45	43,773	36,951	42,192	51,432
Form of government					
Commission	46	43,510	35,620	41,587	52,953
Council–manager/admin.	6	45,043	41,210	43,371	51,833
Council–elected executive	4	42,070	37,038	41,414	46,446
Economic development director					
Total	11	65,841	55,000	71,273	80,382
Geographic region					
North-Central	4	56,616	47,248	58,100	67,468
South	6	78,634	77,938	80,382	84,856
County type					
Metro	4	83,603	80,783	83,632	86,452
Nonmetro	7	55,692	44,496	60,000	68,737

Title of official	Number of counties reporting	Distribution of 2008 salaries			
		Mean ($)	First quartile ($)	Median ($)	Third quartile ($)
25,000–49,999 continued					
Form of government					
Commission	5	52,490	38,992	60,000	66,200
Council-manager/admin.	3	84,410	82,830	86,080	86,825
Council–elected executive	3	69,525	63,696	77,391	79,288
Engineer					
Total	32	79,112	65,742	83,350	91,229
Geographic region					
North-Central	19	79,788	73,571	84,701	90,912
South	10	73,065	63,721	66,290	81,453
West	3	94,992	86,581	93,794	102,805
County type					
Metro	8	77,750	61,934	75,728	89,789
Nonmetro	24	79,566	66,372	84,229	91,229
Form of government					
Commission	24	78,621	65,742	83,350	90,798
Council-manager/admin.	5	88,796	84,701	91,500	93,055
Council–elected executive	3	66,899	64,943	66,590	68,702
Fire chief					
Total	7	50,245	36,777	53,900	63,321
Geographic region					
South	7	50,245	36,777	53,900	63,321
County type					
Nonmetro	5	49,873	49,100	53,900	57,090
Form of government					
Commission	3	31,093	22,090	24,453	36,777
Health officer					
Total	24	53,801	27,263	57,723	76,932
Geographic region					
North-Central	17	51,681	21,706	56,326	75,552
South	3	56,014	45,560	59,119	68,021
West	4	61,152	34,578	61,843	88,417
County type					
Metro	4	39,167	16,092	31,925	55,000
Nonmetro	20	56,728	30,922	59,739	76,932
Form of government					
Commission	20	51,617	27,263	51,663	75,437
Human resources director					
Total	30	53,061	38,239	51,640	65,627
Geographic region					
North-Central	10	46,292	36,271	49,299	59,031
South	15	56,588	40,250	53,040	69,219
West	3	69,900	60,046	69,811	79,711
County type					
Metro	8	65,752	57,394	68,886	77,905
Nonmetro	22	48,446	38,239	49,299	59,031
Form of government					
Commission	19	46,305	35,777	45,000	53,020
Council-manager/admin.	7	65,207	57,658	64,806	68,886
Council–elected executive	4	63,895	58,133	72,144	77,905
Human services director					
Total	17	77,104	57,834	77,104	89,353
Geographic region					
North-Central	7	69,332	59,765	75,446	82,802
South	7	79,567	54,557	81,379	96,337
County type					
Metro	3	109,497	96,337	108,870	122,345
Nonmetro	14	70,163	49,709	73,988	86,720
Form of government					
Commission	10	66,545	41,200	65,182	85,876
Council-manager/admin.	6	93,991	78,779	86,152	103,778
Information services director					
Total	21	63,409	52,339	58,471	75,720
Geographic region					
North-Central	10	56,649	50,160	54,351	57,679
South	7	71,772	62,575	67,469	82,819
County type					
Metro	6	73,623	63,763	74,467	84,961
Nonmetro	15	59,324	48,787	55,170	65,535
Form of government					
Commission	13	60,350	48,384	55,300	70,400
Council-manager/admin.	4	77,631	72,169	82,819	88,280
Council–elected executive	4	59,132	54,462	58,360	63,030
Parks and recreation direction					
Total	19	53,296	44,434	53,641	63,491
Geographic region					
North-Central	7	45,628	35,865	45,535	55,705
South	11	58,422	52,085	55,000	69,859

Table 2/6 **SALARIES OF COUNTY OFFICIALS: JULY–DECEMBER 2008**
continued

Left table:

Title of official	Number of counties reporting	Mean ($)	First quartile ($)	Median ($)	Third quartile ($)
25,000–49,999 continued					
County type					
Metro	5	74,301	66,720	77,213	81,820
Nonmetro	14	45,795	36,588	48,731	54,551
Form of government					
Commission	13	45,755	34,340	46,933	54,854
Council-manager/admin.	4	68,373	58,986	69,509	78,896
Parks superintendent					
Total	8	37,859	30,944	38,194	46,025
Geographic region					
North-Central	3	35,450	30,430	38,574	42,033
South	4	42,369	36,422	42,719	48,667
County type					
Metro	3	45,998	43,099	47,624	49,710
Nonmetro	5	32,975	27,041	32,244	37,814
Form of government					
Commission	4	33,348	25,852	32,808	40,304
Council-manager/admin.	4	42,369	36,422	42,719	48,667
Planning director					
Total	32	56,373	41,856	51,929	67,308
Geographic region					
Northeast	3	43,342	32,928	34,940	49,554
North-Central	16	45,612	37,402	43,615	51,112
South	9	69,681	54,871	74,460	77,897
West	4	79,246	60,123	78,279	97,403
County type					
Metro	7	68,235	54,658	74,460	81,449
Nonmetro	25	53,051	37,852	50,650	64,168
Form of government					
Commission	23	52,103	36,951	44,382	64,551
Council-manager/admin.	6	67,782	55,939	61,976	79,952
Council–elected executive	3	66,291	60,488	74,460	76,179
Primary assistant manager/CAO					
Total	9	68,709	38,821	78,814	90,158
Geographic region					
South	6	71,146	44,615	76,079	97,048
County type					
Metro	3	96,972	94,751	99,344	100,379
Nonmetro	6	54,577	36,058	50,410	74,611
Form of government					
Commission	6	54,577	36,058	50,410	74,611
Public safety director					
Total	6	46,283	39,919	43,525	51,665
Geographic region					
Northeast	3	42,006	40,868	42,766	43,525
County type					
Nonmetro	4	50,482	42,955	49,204	56,732
Form of government					
Commission	5	42,629	38,970	42,766	44,283
Public works director					
Total	11	82,808	71,206	84,200	89,106
Geographic region					
South	8	78,106	61,591	84,111	88,658
County type					
Metro	4	89,349	85,078	88,022	92,293
Nonmetro	7	79,070	61,120	80,350	86,206
Form of government					
Commission	6	82,218	66,634	82,275	87,208
Council-manager/admin.	3	76,133	71,178	82,177	84,111
Purchasing director					
Total	9	56,642	51,000	61,550	63,600
Geographic region					
South	7	58,798	56,275	61,916	64,300
County type					
Metro	4	63,796	61,825	63,458	65,429
Nonmetro	5	50,919	41,800	51,000	59,651
Form of government					
Commission	5	50,919	41,800	51,000	59,651
Recreation director					
Total	6	44,776	30,311	41,551	50,798
Geographic region					
South	4	53,787	44,302	49,550	59,035
County type					
Nonmetro	4	35,401	27,576	32,224	40,049
Form of government					
Commission	3	29,852	26,753	28,398	32,224
Risk manager					
Total	8	47,760	36,659	45,187	62,075
Geographic region					
North-Central	3	40,325	34,972	39,342	45,187
South	5	52,222	37,983	61,550	63,648

Right table:

Title of official	Number of counties reporting	Mean ($)	First quartile ($)	Median ($)	Third quartile ($)
25,000–49,999 continued					
County type					
Metro	4	60,368	58,921	62,599	64,046
Nonmetro	4	35,153	32,165	35,335	38,323
Form of government					
Commission	4	40,261	36,659	38,663	42,265
Council–elected executive	3	52,464	46,076	61,550	63,395
Treasurer					
Total	55	51,198	40,788	46,916	57,016
Geographic region					
Northeast	3	44,233	43,148	46,075	46,239
North-Central	28	48,404	42,172	46,936	53,744
South	18	54,310	40,479	46,328	62,160
West	6	58,385	47,448	60,844	70,757
County type					
Metro	11	58,025	34,522	56,532	71,007
Nonmetro	44	49,491	41,879	46,239	53,967
Form of government					
Commission	49	48,693	40,577	46,402	54,477
Council-manager/admin.	4	86,905	77,925	87,609	96,590
10,000–24,999					
Chief admin. officer/county manager					
Total	29	74,784	62,000	74,084	95,062
Geographic region					
North-Central	8	62,136	47,671	73,396	78,444
South	18	78,909	63,300	75,391	97,592
West	3	83,762	58,705	65,000	99,438
County type					
Metro	5	78,446	53,560	76,697	100,000
Nonmetro	24	74,021	62,000	73,572	86,883
Form of government					
Commission	18	62,739	52,569	66,100	73,828
Council-manager/admin.	6	105,881	98,742	104,465	109,733
Council–elected executive	5	80,832	75,000	76,697	95,062
Chief elected official					
Total	37	39,409	22,164	29,390	44,887
Geographic region					
North-Central	20	26,723	20,466	24,304	29,537
South	14	61,133	35,835	46,310	65,789
West	3	22,604	20,766	21,174	23,727
County type					
Nonmetro	36	40,054	23,375	29,684	45,173
Form of government					
Commission	36	39,959	23,375	29,684	45,173
Chief financial officer					
Total	23	52,718	44,683	50,500	61,784
Geographic region					
North-Central	7	52,135	45,251	46,001	59,346
South	13	51,789	44,700	50,500	60,773
West	3	58,106	43,000	59,791	74,055
County type					
Metro	3	52,665	47,600	50,500	56,647
Nonmetro	20	52,726	43,313	52,314	61,319
Form of government					
Commission	13	48,074	34,625	45,836	58,560
Council-manager/admin.	5	66,608	60,773	62,958	70,491
Council–elected executive	5	50,903	45,045	46,001	55,051
Chief law enforcement official					
Total	90	57,645	49,648	57,624	64,740
Geographic region					
North-Central	58	57,865	52,526	58,099	62,922
South	22	57,072	46,498	58,580	66,875
West	10	57,632	50,198	55,348	59,088
County type					
Metro	5	68,844	63,613	65,709	75,000
Nonmetro	85	56,987	48,597	57,244	62,687
Form of government					
Commission	75	56,118	48,844	56,851	61,825
Council-manager/admin.	6	75,083	75,427	76,585	81,202
Council–elected executive	9	58,752	48,174	59,074	62,897
Chief librarian					
Total	9	44,148	32,130	40,000	52,811
Geographic region					
South	7	36,294	30,915	34,564	41,250
County type					
Nonmetro	7	42,881	30,915	34,564	47,656
Form of government					
Commission	6	34,951	30,307	33,347	40,516
Council-manager/admin.	3	62,543	48,582	57,164	73,815

Table 2/6   SALARIES OF COUNTY OFFICIALS: JULY–DECEMBER 2008
continued

Title of official	Number of counties reporting	Mean ($)	First quartile ($)	Median ($)	Third quartile ($)
10,000–24,999 continued					
Clerk					
Total	69	43,631	34,100	42,693	47,663
Geographic region					
North-Central	35	40,151	34,119	40,839	44,976
South	25	45,862	33,351	37,122	48,437
West	9	50,963	46,350	51,539	55,285
County type					
Metro	5	50,383	33,351	36,778	43,000
Nonmetro	64	43,103	34,129	42,847	47,792
Form of government					
Commission	56	43,441	34,400	43,077	47,792
Council–manager/admin.	6	51,996	37,005	44,127	49,813
Council–elected executive	7	37,976	33,463	34,138	40,668
Economic development director					
Total	14	55,999	43,445	49,410	64,187
Geographic region					
North-Central	4	51,191	43,787	51,826	59,230
South	7	54,446	43,630	48,400	69,300
West	3	66,035	43,235	50,420	81,028
County type					
Nonmetro	12	55,513	42,669	49,410	61,540
Form of government					
Commission	9	44,238	40,896	44,000	48,400
Council–manager/admin.	4	77,613	64,187	69,300	82,726
Engineer					
Total	37	79,532	66,489	80,570	94,100
Geographic region					
North-Central	34	79,516	66,742	80,834	93,656
County type					
Nonmetro	36	79,895	67,239	80,851	94,476
Form of government					
Commission	32	80,410	69,872	80,851	92,768
Council–elected executive	3	57,724	52,837	65,673	66,587
Fire chief					
Total	7	41,465	30,225	35,000	47,062
Geographic region					
South	5	42,423	29,400	35,000	47,032
County type					
Nonmetro	5	37,915	31,050	35,000	47,032
Form of government					
Commission	4	35,635	30,638	33,025	38,023
Health officer					
Total	24	44,807	29,401	46,545	56,515
Geographic region					
North-Central	22	45,024	31,568	46,545	55,324
County type					
Nonmetro	23	43,969	28,102	46,115	55,216
Form of government					
Commission	19	46,398	32,436	46,115	59,269
Council–elected executive	5	38,763	17,212	46,976	55,000
Human resources director					
Total	19	46,444	31,257	37,787	62,021
Geographic region					
North-Central	6	47,010	33,212	47,327	62,312
South	10	42,001	31,152	36,766	57,280
West	3	60,124	34,369	41,828	76,732
County type					
Nonmetro	17	45,548	30,826	37,787	60,773
Form of government					
Commission	12	38,092	27,850	34,565	43,071
Council–manager/admin.	4	67,055	53,502	62,450	76,004
Council–elected executive	3	52,372	46,700	56,867	60,292
Human services director					
Total	18	63,052	52,992	63,303	75,691
Geographic region					
North-Central	13	66,606	56,496	66,369	75,760
South	3	40,192	29,902	32,000	46,387
County type					
Nonmetro	17	63,050	51,825	63,520	75,760
Form of government					
Commission	14	58,596	48,928	61,070	74,112
Council–manager/admin.	3	83,691	75,097	89,420	95,150
Information services director					
Total	21	53,734	44,218	53,832	58,150
Geographic region					
North-Central	14	47,321	42,572	49,366	55,436
South	4	65,362	54,471	65,545	76,436
West	3	68,156	49,075	58,150	82,234

Title of official	Number of counties reporting	Mean ($)	First quartile ($)	Median ($)	Third quartile ($)
10,000–24,999 continued					
County type					
Nonmetro	20	54,320	44,569	54,258	58,724
Form of government					
Commission	16	48,465	41,887	49,366	55,226
Council–manager/admin.	3	81,096	68,485	76,526	91,422
Parks and recreation direction					
Total	29	43,865	38,176	40,991	50,000
Geographic region					
North-Central	19	42,267	37,485	40,445	45,555
South	10	46,900	38,388	45,660	55,342
County type					
Metro	3	44,474	31,212	39,023	55,012
Nonmetro	26	43,794	38,182	41,155	49,250
Form of government					
Commission	24	42,737	36,653	40,718	47,750
Council–manager/admin.	3	55,627	47,941	56,591	63,796
Parks superintendent					
Total	11	37,431	30,851	41,397	44,642
Geographic region					
North-Central	10	37,034	30,282	37,352	44,663
County type					
Nonmetro	10	39,347	32,193	41,650	44,663
Form of government					
Commission	10	35,730	30,282	37,098	43,926
Planning director					
Total	30	49,551	34,977	44,810	60,500
Geographic region					
North-Central	15	41,004	34,386	39,420	45,600
South	9	56,089	45,427	53,357	60,833
West	6	61,113	43,779	57,194	74,717
County type					
Metro	3	55,650	45,333	59,500	67,892
Nonmetro	27	48,874	35,160	44,193	57,095
Form of government					
Commission	22	47,398	34,977	44,810	53,248
Council–manager/admin.	4	67,484	53,972	68,558	82,069
Council–elected executive	4	43,460	38,079	40,101	45,482
Primary assistant manager/CAO					
Total	9	50,906	29,000	51,333	57,000
Geographic region					
South	5	50,456	51,333	55,800	57,000
West	3	62,127	37,373	46,350	78,993
County type					
Nonmetro	8	50,145	28,849	48,842	56,636
Form of government					
Commission	5	43,738	29,000	46,350	55,800
Council–manager/admin.	3	73,323	54,167	57,000	84,318
Public safety director					
Total	9	49,238	38,520	45,656	62,958
Geographic region					
North-Central	3	29,969	25,693	34,724	36,622
South	4	56,583	47,203	55,338	64,719
County type					
Nonmetro	9	49,238	38,520	45,656	62,958
Form of government					
Commission	6	41,670	35,673	41,490	45,357
Council–manager/admin.	3	64,375	55,338	62,958	72,703
Public works director					
Total	15	49,211	41,000	47,006	54,726
Geographic region					
North-Central	4	48,853	37,500	43,503	54,856
South	9	50,401	42,000	53,073	55,000
County type					
Nonmetro	13	49,545	42,000	47,006	54,451
Form of government					
Commission	11	49,422	41,000	45,884	53,500
Council–elected executive	3	45,841	41,537	53,073	53,762
Purchasing director					
Total	5	32,743	21,722	22,698	33,190
Geographic region					
South	3	39,766	26,595	33,190	49,649
County type					
Nonmetro	5	32,743	21,722	22,698	33,190
Form of government					
Commission	3	24,971	20,861	21,722	27,456
Recreation director					
Total	8	40,486	34,644	35,866	37,968
Geographic region					
South	6	42,553	35,741	36,670	39,455

Table 2/6   SALARIES OF COUNTY OFFICIALS: JULY–DECEMBER 2008
continued

Title of official	Number of counties reporting	Distribution of 2008 salaries			
		Mean ($)	First quartile ($)	Median ($)	Third quartile ($)
10,000–24,999 continued					
County type					
Nonmetro	7	41,111	34,288	35,616	38,712
Form of government					
Commission	4	35,514	33,501	34,288	36,300
Risk manager					
Total	3	45,369	39,106	42,949	50,423
Geographic region	...	...	...	...	...
County type					
Nonmetro	3	45,369	39,106	42,949	50,423
Form of government	...	...	...	...	...
Treasurer					
Total	85	44,678	39,157	44,339	48,732
Geographic region					
North-Central	57	43,413	39,313	44,554	48,383
South	17	43,078	33,457	37,122	44,121
West	11	53,709	45,417	52,410	56,271
County type					
Metro	4	46,414	33,430	39,877	52,861
Nonmetro	81	44,593	39,194	44,339	48,732
Form of government					
Commission	74	44,022	39,360	44,447	48,685
Council-manager/admin.	5	66,895	59,800	69,293	77,780
Council–elected executive	6	34,257	29,455	33,798	36,854
5,000–9,999					
Chief admin. officer/county manager					
Total	4	58,951	43,003	48,875	64,824
Geographic region	...	...	...	...	...
County type					
Nonmetro	4	58,951	43,003	48,875	64,824
Form of government	...	...	...	...	...
Chief elected official					
Total	18	35,749	22,331	28,768	55,981
Geographic region					
North-Central	9	21,918	19,204	21,804	25,443
South	6	46,777	34,615	48,450	60,263
West	3	55,187	52,706	59,256	59,703
County type					
Nonmetro	17	34,059	21,804	28,400	46,156
Form of government					
Commission	15	34,835	21,439	28,400	52,706
Council–elected executive	3	40,320	30,405	36,900	48,525
Chief financial officer					
Total	4	34,812	33,810	36,613	37,615
Geographic region	...	...	...	...	...
County type					
Nonmetro	3	34,341	31,782	37,001	38,229
Form of government					
Commission	3	34,082	31,394	36,225	37,841
Chief law enforcement official					
Total	34	46,701	41,049	46,671	51,122
Geographic region					
North-Central	25	44,622	40,565	44,518	50,000
South	5	44,462	33,853	44,000	57,477
West	4	62,489	50,685	52,965	64,769
County type					
Nonmetro	33	47,238	42,500	46,920	51,246
Form of government					
Commission	27	44,807	38,859	44,518	50,998
Council–elected executive	5	55,170	42,840	47,125	48,362
Chief librarian					
Total	3	32,479	28,234	39,456	40,212
Geographic region	...	...	...	...	...
County type					
Nonmetro	3	32,479	28,234	39,456	40,212
Form of government					
Commission	3	32,479	28,234	39,456	40,212
Clerk					
Total	28	39,289	36,640	38,160	43,751
Geographic region					
North-Central	18	37,502	36,213	37,783	39,818
South	7	42,266	35,377	48,180	49,090
West	3	43,062	40,762	44,000	45,832
County type					
Nonmetro	28	39,289	36,640	38,160	43,751
Form of government					
Commission	22	39,073	36,213	37,783	44,296
Council–elected executive	5	39,294	36,900	39,271	42,500

Title of official	Number of counties reporting	Distribution of 2008 salaries			
		Mean ($)	First quartile ($)	Median ($)	Third quartile ($)
5,000–9,999 continued					
Economic development director					
Total	...	...	...	...	...
Geographic region	...	...	...	...	...
County type	...	...	...	...	...
Form of government	...	...	...	...	...
Engineer					
Total	10	63,591	49,036	64,500	74,979
Geographic region					
North-Central	8	63,600	46,298	64,500	77,715
County type					
Nonmetro	10	63,591	49,036	64,500	74,979
Form of government					
Commission	7	62,031	44,548	62,500	76,813
Fire chief					
Total	...	...	...	...	...
Geographic region	...	...	...	...	...
County type	...	...	...	...	...
Form of government	...	...	...	...	...
Health officer					
Total	6	47,516	44,086	44,536	54,247
Geographic region					
North-Central	5	44,042	44,033	44,244	44,827
County type					
Nonmetro	6	47,516	44,086	44,536	54,247
Form of government					
Commission	4	44,044	40,613	44,536	47,967
Human resources director					
Total	4	25,804	18,113	22,300	29,991
Geographic region	...	...	...	...	...
County type					
Nonmetro	4	25,804	18,113	22,300	29,991
Form of government					
Commission	3	26,071	16,625	19,600	32,282
Human services director					
Total	...	...	...	...	...
Geographic region	...	...	...	...	...
County type	...	...	...	...	...
Form of government	...	...	...	...	...
Information services director					
Total	3	49,895	38,320	40,639	56,843
Geographic region	...	...	...	...	...
County type					
Nonmetro	3	49,895	38,320	40,639	56,843
Form of government	...	...	...	...	...
Parks and recreation direction					
Total	6	33,379	26,324	35,791	39,785
Geographic region					
North-Central	6	33,379	26,324	35,791	39,785
County type					
Nonmetro	6	33,379	26,324	35,791	39,785
Form of government					
Commission	5	31,952	23,769	33,988	37,594
Parks superintendent					
Total	...	...	...	...	...
Geographic region	...	...	...	...	...
County type	...	...	...	...	...
Form of government	...	...	...	...	...
Planning director					
Total	7	37,922	26,215	38,774	46,445
Geographic region					
North-Central	3	28,184	20,831	27,901	35,396
West	3	52,125	44,387	50,000	58,800
County type					
Nonmetro	6	40,154	30,619	40,832	48,223
Form of government					
Commission	6	35,909	25,372	33,338	41,861
Primary assistant manager/CAO					
Total	...	...	...	...	...
Geographic region	...	...	...	...	...
County type	...	...	...	...	...
Form of government	...	...	...	...	...
Public safety director					
Total	...	...	...	...	...
Geographic region	...	...	...	...	...
County type	...	...	...	...	...
Form of government	...	...	...	...	...

Table 2/6 SALARIES OF COUNTY OFFICIALS: JULY–DECEMBER 2008
continued

Title of official	Number of counties reporting	Distribution of 2008 salaries Mean ($)	First quartile ($)	Median ($)	Third quartile ($)
5,000–9,999 continued					
Public works director					
Total	7	46,588	39,546	41,828	53,343
Geographic region					
North-Central	4	40,772	37,836	40,019	42,956
County type					
Nonmetro	6	47,539	39,115	44,083	56,847
Form of government					
Commission	5	45,522	40,883	41,828	46,337
Purchasing director					
Total	. . .	. . .	. . .	. . .	. . .
Geographic region	. . .	. . .	. . .	. . .	. . .
County type	. . .	. . .	. . .	. . .	. . .
Form of government	. . .	. . .	. . .	. . .	. . .
Recreation director					
Total	. . .	. . .	. . .	. . .	. . .
Geographic region	. . .	. . .	. . .	. . .	. . .
County type	. . .	. . .	. . .	. . .	. . .
Form of government	. . .	. . .	. . .	. . .	. . .
Risk manager					
Total	. . .	. . .	. . .	. . .	. . .
Geographic region	. . .	. . .	. . .	. . .	. . .
County type	. . .	. . .	. . .	. . .	. . .
Form of government	. . .	. . .	. . .	. . .	. . .
Treasurer					
Total	37	39,081	35,024	37,825	42,240
Geographic region					
North-Central	27	37,131	34,805	37,594	40,069
South	7	41,663	35,528	42,240	46,120
West	3	50,605	45,832	47,664	53,907
County type					
Nonmetro	36	39,218	35,216	38,160	42,305
Form of government					
Commission	28	38,176	34,478	37,667	41,039
Council–elected executive ..	7	41,849	36,609	39,271	43,084
2,500–4,999					
Chief admin. officer/county manager					
Total	. . .	. . .	. . .	. . .	. . .
Geographic region	. . .	. . .	. . .	. . .	. . .
County type	. . .	. . .	. . .	. . .	. . .
Form of government	. . .	. . .	. . .	. . .	. . .
Chief elected official					
Total	3	29,916	21,728	29,088	37,690
Geographic region	. . .	. . .	. . .	. . .	. . .
County type					
Nonmetro	3	29,916	21,728	29,088	37,690
Form of government					
Commission	3	29,916	21,728	29,088	37,690
Chief financial officer					
Total	. . .	. . .	. . .	. . .	. . .
Geographic region	. . .	. . .	. . .	. . .	. . .
County type	. . .	. . .	. . .	. . .	. . .
Form of government	. . .	. . .	. . .	. . .	. . .
Chief law enforcement official					
Total	19	38,501	32,875	36,712	40,686
Geographic region					
North-Central	17	36,686	32,000	35,811	37,312
County type					
Nonmetro	19	38,501	32,875	36,712	40,686
Form of government					
Commission	19	38,501	32,875	36,712	40,686
Chief librarian					
Total	. . .	. . .	. . .	. . .	. . .
Geographic region	. . .	. . .	. . .	. . .	. . .
County type	. . .	. . .	. . .	. . .	. . .
Form of government	. . .	. . .	. . .	. . .	. . .
Clerk					
Total	18	31,527	27,253	31,965	33,646
Geographic region					
North-Central	14	31,387	28,200	31,965	33,287
South	3	26,799	22,672	23,504	29,278
County type					
Nonmetro	18	31,527	27,253	31,965	33,646
Form of government					
Commission	17	31,999	27,600	32,000	33,750
Economic development director					
Total	. . .	. . .	. . .	. . .	. . .
Geographic region	. . .	. . .	. . .	. . .	. . .
County type	. . .	. . .	. . .	. . .	. . .
Form of government	. . .	. . .	. . .	. . .	. . .

Title of official	Number of counties reporting	Distribution of 2008 salaries Mean ($)	First quartile ($)	Median ($)	Third quartile ($)
2,500–4,999 continued					
Engineer					
Total	. . .	. . .	. . .	. . .	. . .
Geographic region	. . .	. . .	. . .	. . .	. . .
County type	. . .	. . .	. . .	. . .	. . .
Form of government	. . .	. . .	. . .	. . .	. . .
Fire chief					
Total	. . .	. . .	. . .	. . .	. . .
Geographic region	. . .	. . .	. . .	. . .	. . .
County type	. . .	. . .	. . .	. . .	. . .
Form of government	. . .	. . .	. . .	. . .	. . .
Health officer					
Total	3	34,662	33,278	34,620	36,026
Geographic region					
North-Central	3	34,662	33,278	34,620	36,026
County type					
Nonmetro	3	34,662	33,278	34,620	36,026
Form of government					
Commission	3	34,662	33,278	34,620	36,026
Human resources director					
Total	. . .	. . .	. . .	. . .	. . .
Geographic region	. . .	. . .	. . .	. . .	. . .
County type	. . .	. . .	. . .	. . .	. . .
Form of government	. . .	. . .	. . .	. . .	. . .
Human services director					
Total	. . .	. . .	. . .	. . .	. . .
Geographic region	. . .	. . .	. . .	. . .	. . .
County type	. . .	. . .	. . .	. . .	. . .
Form of government	. . .	. . .	. . .	. . .	. . .
Information services director					
Total	. . .	. . .	. . .	. . .	. . .
Geographic region	. . .	. . .	. . .	. . .	. . .
County type	. . .	. . .	. . .	. . .	. . .
Form of government	. . .	. . .	. . .	. . .	. . .
Parks and recreation direction					
Total	. . .	. . .	. . .	. . .	. . .
Geographic region	. . .	. . .	. . .	. . .	. . .
County type	. . .	. . .	. . .	. . .	. . .
Form of government	. . .	. . .	. . .	. . .	. . .
Parks superintendent					
Total	. . .	. . .	. . .	. . .	. . .
Geographic region	. . .	. . .	. . .	. . .	. . .
County type	. . .	. . .	. . .	. . .	. . .
Form of government	. . .	. . .	. . .	. . .	. . .
Planning director					
Total	. . .	. . .	. . .	. . .	. . .
Geographic region	. . .	. . .	. . .	. . .	. . .
County type	. . .	. . .	. . .	. . .	. . .
Form of government	. . .	. . .	. . .	. . .	. . .
Primary assistant manager/CAO					
Total	. . .	. . .	. . .	. . .	. . .
Geographic region	. . .	. . .	. . .	. . .	. . .
County type	. . .	. . .	. . .	. . .	. . .
Form of government	. . .	. . .	. . .	. . .	. . .
Public safety director					
Total	. . .	. . .	. . .	. . .	. . .
Geographic region	. . .	. . .	. . .	. . .	. . .
County type	. . .	. . .	. . .	. . .	. . .
Form of government	. . .	. . .	. . .	. . .	. . .
Public works director					
Total	7	30,295	28,875	31,188	32,183
Geographic region					
North-Central	5	31,820	30,732	31,188	32,401
County type					
Nonmetro	7	30,295	28,875	31,188	32,183
Form of government					
Commission	6	30,017	27,946	30,960	32,098
Purchasing director					
Total	. . .	. . .	. . .	. . .	. . .
Geographic region	. . .	. . .	. . .	. . .	. . .
County type	. . .	. . .	. . .	. . .	. . .
Form of government	. . .	. . .	. . .	. . .	. . .
Recreation director					
Total	. . .	. . .	. . .	. . .	. . .
Geographic region	. . .	. . .	. . .	. . .	. . .
County type	. . .	. . .	. . .	. . .	. . .
Form of government	. . .	. . .	. . .	. . .	. . .
Risk manager					
Total	. . .	. . .	. . .	. . .	. . .
Geographic region	. . .	. . .	. . .	. . .	. . .
County type	. . .	. . .	. . .	. . .	. . .
Form of government	. . .	. . .	. . .	. . .	. . .

Table 2/6   SALARIES OF COUNTY OFFICIALS: JULY–DECEMBER 2008
continued

Title of official	Number of counties reporting	Distribution of 2008 salaries			
		Mean ($)	First quartile ($)	Median ($)	Third quartile ($)
2,500–4,999 continued					
Treasurer					
Total	19	32,900	30,321	31,596	33,543
Geographic region					
North-Central	17	31,692	30,094	31,188	32,000
County type					
Nonmetro	19	32,900	30,321	31,596	33,543
Form of government					
Commission	19	32,900	30,321	31,596	33,543
Less than 2,500					
Chief admin. officer/county manager					
Total	...	...	...	...	...
Geographic region	...	...	...	...	...
County type	...	...	...	...	...
Form of government	...	...	...	...	...
Chief elected official					
Total	...	...	...	...	...
Geographic region	...	...	...	...	...
County type	...	...	...	...	...
Form of government	...	...	...	...	...
Chief financial officer					
Total	...	...	...	...	...
Geographic region	...	...	...	...	...
County type	...	...	...	...	...
Form of government	...	...	...	...	...
Chief law enforcement official					
Total	10	40,468	33,433	40,022	46,405
Geographic region					
North-Central	4	35,834	32,446	33,522	36,910
West	5	43,068	37,773	42,272	48,695
County type					
Nonmetro	10	40,468	33,433	40,022	46,405
Form of government					
Commission	9	38,298	33,344	37,773	46,000
Chief librarian					
Total	3	23,023	22,177	23,657	24,187
Geographic region	...	...	...	...	...
County type					
Nonmetro	3	23,023	22,177	23,657	24,187
Form of government					
Commission	3	23,023	22,177	23,657	24,187
Clerk					
Total	10	37,104	30,567	35,799	42,930
Geographic region					
North-Central	3	31,542	28,810	29,422	33,214
West	6	40,403	36,380	42,532	46,961
County type					
Nonmetro	9	35,713	29,422	34,594	41,737
Form of government					
Commission	9	35,875	29,422	34,594	41,737
Economic development director					
Total	...	...	...	...	...
Geographic region	...	...	...	...	...
County type	...	...	...	...	...
Form of government	...	...	...	...	...
Engineer					
Total	...	...	...	...	...
Geographic region	...	...	...	...	...
County type	...	...	...	...	...
Form of government	...	...	...	...	...
Fire chief					
Total	...	...	...	...	...
Geographic region	...	...	...	...	...
County type	...	...	...	...	...
Form of government	...	...	...	...	...
Health officer					
Total	3	39,183	38,911	39,591	39,660
Geographic region	...	...	...	...	...
County type					
Nonmetro	3	39,183	38,911	39,591	39,660
Form of government					
Commission	3	39,183	38,911	39,591	39,660

Title of official	Number of counties reporting	Distribution of 2008 salaries			
		Mean ($)	First quartile ($)	Median ($)	Third quartile ($)
Less than 2,500 continued					
Human resources director					
Total	...	...	...	...	...
Geographic region	...	...	...	...	...
County type	...	...	...	...	...
Form of government	...	...	...	...	...
Human services director					
Total	...	...	...	...	...
Geographic region	...	...	...	...	...
County type	...	...	...	...	...
Form of government	...	...	...	...	...
Information services director					
Total	...	...	...	...	...
Geographic region	...	...	...	...	...
County type	...	...	...	...	...
Form of government	...	...	...	...	...
Parks and recreation direction					
Total	...	...	...	...	...
Geographic region	...	...	...	...	...
County type	...	...	...	...	...
Form of government	...	...	...	...	...
Parks superintendent					
Total	...	...	...	...	...
Geographic region	...	...	...	...	...
County type	...	...	...	...	...
Form of government	...	...	...	...	...
Planning director					
Total	...	...	...	...	...
Geographic region	...	...	...	...	...
County type	...	...	...	...	...
Form of government	...	...	...	...	...
Primary assistant manager/CAO					
Total	...	...	...	...	...
Geographic region	...	...	...	...	...
County type	...	...	...	...	...
Form of government	...	...	...	...	...
Public safety director					
Total	...	...	...	...	...
Geographic region	...	...	...	...	...
County type	...	...	...	...	...
Form of government	...	...	...	...	...
Public works director					
Total	3	41,783	32,674	32,692	46,346
Geographic region	...	...	...	...	...
County type					
Nonmetro	3	41,783	32,674	32,692	46,346
Form of government	...	...	...	...	...
Purchasing director					
Total	...	...	...	...	...
Geographic region	...	...	...	...	...
County type	...	...	...	...	...
Form of government	...	...	...	...	...
Recreation director					
Total	...	...	...	...	...
Geographic region	...	...	...	...	...
County type	...	...	...	...	...
Form of government	...	...	...	...	...
Risk manager					
Total	...	...	...	...	...
Geographic region	...	...	...	...	...
County type	...	...	...	...	...
Form of government	...	...	...	...	...
Treasurer					
Total	9	32,716	28,198	31,423	36,485
Geographic region					
North-Central	4	30,896	28,018	29,810	32,689
West	4	34,965	32,186	36,453	39,233
County type					
Nonmetro	8	31,557	28,018	31,212	35,067
Form of government					
Commission	9	32,716	28,198	31,423	36,485

Police and Fire Personnel, Salaries, and Expenditures for 2008

Evelina R. Moulder
ICMA

Selected Findings

The average numbers of uniformed personnel are 91 for police and 76 for fire departments.

The average entrance salaries are $41,620 for police and $38,889 for fire personnel.

The mean per capita total departmental expenditures are $257.70 for police and $209.57 for fire departments.

With cities across the country facing overwhelming budget shortfalls, police and fire services will probably not be immune to cost-saving measures. News reports indicate that hiring freezes and capital expenditures are among the options under consideration.

This article examines the current cross-sectional patterns and longitudinal trends in U.S. municipalities' police and fire departmental personnel, salaries, and expenditures.

METHODOLOGY

The data in this research were collected from responses to ICMA's annual *Police and Fire Personnel, Salaries, and Expenditures* survey, which was mailed in February 2008 to 3,271 municipalities with populations of 10,000 or more (Table 3/1). Respondents had a choice of completing and submitting the survey on the Web or by mail. A total of 1,320 jurisdictions submitted surveys for an overall response rate of 40%, which is close to last year's response rate.

The survey response patterns are presented in Table 3/1 by population group, geographic region, geographic division, and metropolitan status. There is variation in the response patterns by population size, with a low of 17% in cities with 500,000–1,000,000 in population, and a high of 41% in those with a population under 250,000. The patterns by geographic division show that New England and East South-Central jurisdictions were the least likely to complete the questionnaire (25% each), while West North-Central, South Atlantic, West South-Central, and Mountain jurisdictions were the most likely to do so (50%–52% in each division). There is minimal variation by metropolitan status.

ADMINISTRATION

Respondents were asked several questions about service provision and delivery. Virtually all the jurisdictions responding to the 2008 survey (97%) indicated that they provide police services, and 85% reported that they provide fire services (not

Table 3/1   SURVEY RESPONSE

	No. of municipalities surveyed (A)	Respondents No.	Respondents % of (A)
Total	3,271	1,320	40
Population group			
Over 1,000,000	9	3	33
500,000–1,000,000 . .	23	4	17
250,000–499,999 . . .	36	12	33
100,000–249,999 . . .	179	73	41
50,000–99,999	413	169	41
25,000–49,999	785	316	40
10,000–24,999	1,826	743	41
Geographic region			
Northeast	887	252	28
North-Central	916	385	42
South	844	383	45
West	624	300	48
Geographic division			
New England	352	89	25
Mid-Atlantic	535	163	31
East North-Central . .	669	256	38
West North-Central . .	248	129	52
South Atlantic	386	196	51
East South-Central . .	169	43	25
West South-Central .	288	144	50
Mountain	161	84	52
Pacific Coast	463	216	47
Metro status			
Central	539	208	39
Suburban	2,113	848	40
Independent	619	264	43

shown)—figures that have remained almost identical for several years. Twenty-six jurisdictions reported having a public safety department. To be counted among these respondents, a city had to report "public safety department" as the type of service for both police and fire (see sidebar).

These data on cities that provide police and fire services do not necessarily mean that all these cities actually deliver each service: 4% of jurisdictions reported contracting with another government for police service delivery (not shown). The highest percentage of cities reporting this arrangement is in the Pacific Coast division (18%). Among the 36 cities that do not provide police services, 42 answered the question about how the services *are* provided, and of those, the majority (25), all of which are under 250,000 in popula-

Cities that reported a public safety department (consolidated police and fire)

Sunnyvale	*CA*
Greenacres	*FL*
Bainbridge	*GA*
Storm Lake	*IA*
East Grand Rapids	*MI*
Escanaba	*MI*
Ionia	*MI*
Farmington	*MI*
Grand Haven	*MI*
Oak Park	*MI*
Cottage Grove	*MN*
Maryville	*MO*
Mexico	*MO*
Sikeston	*MO*
West Plains	*MO*
Kinston	*NC*
Morganton	*NC*
Alamogordo	*NM*
Brook Park	*OH*
Grants Pass	*OR*
Harrisburg	*PA*
Cayce	*SC*
North Myrtle Beach	*SC*
Spartanburg	*SC*
Mitchell	*SD*
Ashwaubenon	*WI*

tion, reported that the county provides the service (not shown). Three cities reported a regional police service; one reported a special district.

Of the cities that provide fire protection services, the majority (62%) reported having a full-time paid or a full-time and part-time paid fire department, 19% reported a combination of paid and volunteer fire personnel, 13% reported an all-volunteer fire department, and the remaining cities said they contract out for such services or provide

them in some other way (not shown). Among the 192 cities that do not provide fire services, 162 provided information on how the services are provided, and of those, 53% reported that services are provided by a special district and 27% indicated that the county provides the service. Regional fire services were reported by 7%.

PERSONNEL

The average size of the full-time paid workforce for both police and fire departments is presented in Table 3/2. The data include both uniformed and civilian, or nonuniformed, personnel. The average number of total police department employees, 109, represents a decrease in the average number of police personnel reported in 2007, which was 122. The average number of fire personnel is 83, compared with 84 in 2007. As with all averages in this article, these fluctuate depending on which cities report information each year.

The average numbers of full-time paid police employees show a decrease with population size for all reporting jurisdictions. However, because there are relatively few cities over 1,000,000 in population, findings from cities of that size can fluctuate significantly, depending on the cities that responded and their population size. In 2006 only Los Angeles and Philadelphia returned surveys. In 2007, Phoenix, Philadelphia, San Diego, and Dallas returned surveys. Since none of these cities has a population as high as that of Los Angeles, the average number of full-time paid police personnel was noticeably lower in 2007 than it was in 2006. In 2008, Los Angeles, Phoenix, and San Diego submitted surveys, although we do not have the number of full-time, paid police personnel for Los Angeles.

The average numbers of full-time police personnel by population category in 2008 also differ somewhat from the 2007 figures. For example, cities over 1,000,000 in population show an average of 3,412 police personnel (Table 3/2), compared with 4,462 in 2007; cities in the 500,000–1,000,000 population group show an average of 2,145 police personnel in 2008, compared with 2,027 police employees in 2007.

The patterns for fire departments are similar to those for police departments: the average numbers of full-time paid fire employees decrease with the population size of the reporting communities. Cities over 1,000,000 in population show an average of 2,286 fire employees (Table 3/2), compared with 1,912 in 2007, while cities in the population group of 500,000–1,000,000 show an average of 1,178 fire employees in 2008, compared with 1,043 in 2007. Continuing down in population, the average for communities in the 10,000–24,999 population group (27) is almost identical to the 2007 average (26).

Per capita figures per 1,000 population are important because they "normalize" the data. This is apparent in Table 3/2 because although the average numbers of personnel per capita generally decrease, they are comparable averages.

The cross-sectional patterns by geographic division indicate that municipalities in the Mountain division show the highest average number of full-time police employees (204) and that those in the New England division show the lowest (53) (Table 3/2). Regarding full-time paid fire employees, the highest average number is in the Pacific Coast division (162), and the lowest average numbers are in the Mid-Atlantic and East North-Central divisions (46 each). As in 2007, the South Atlantic and East South-Central divisions, respectively, show the highest average numbers of police and fire full-time paid personnel per capita per 1,000 population.

Not surprisingly, metropolitan status patterns indicate that central cities have larger police and fire departments than either independent or suburban cities. In 2008, central cities averaged 321 full-time paid police department personnel, compared with 73 and 53 for suburban and independent communities, respectively (Table 3/2). The figures for full-time paid fire department personnel show a similar pattern, as the central cities show an average of 214, compared with 55 for suburban cities and 37 for independent cities. These differences, of course, reflect population differences in the communities served and are consistent with the patterns reported in previous surveys. The per capita figures per 1,000 population show the highest per capita full-time paid police and fire department personnel in central and independent jurisdictions.

Figure 3/1 shows the changes over ten years in the average number of full-time employees per 1,000 population for both services.

Table 3/3 presents the average numbers of full-time uniformed, or sworn, personnel in police and fire departments as of January 1, 2008. Among reporting cities, these numbers are 91 for police departments and 76 for fire departments, representing a decrease for both services. Among the cities with over 1,000,000 in population, the average number of sworn police personnel reported in 2008 is 4,934; in 2007, the figure was 3,512. Predictably, the remaining averages are consistently correlated with the population size of the responding jurisdictions: the police department averages range from 1,700 for cities of 500,000–1,000,000 to 34 for cities of 10,000–24,999. The figures per 1,000 population show a high of 2.61 for cities of 500,000–1,000,000 in population and a low of 1.80 for cities of 100,000–249,999.

For fire departments in cities over 1,000,000 in population, the average number of sworn personnel reported in 2008 is 2,085, compared with 1,480 in 2007. As with the average number of sworn police personnel, the remaining averages decline from 1,060 for cities in the 500,000–1,000,000 population group to 26 for cities in the 10,000–24,999 population group. The figures per 1,000 population show a high of 1.81 for cities in the 50,000–99,999 population range and a low of 1.02 for cities of over 1,000,000.

The Pacific Coast division shows the highest average number of sworn full-time police personnel (167), followed by the Mountain division (147), while the New England division shows the lowest (45) (Table 3/3). When per capita per 1,000 population figures are reviewed, the South Atlantic (2.87) and East South-Central (2.84) divisions are the highest, and the Pacific Coast division is the lowest (1.51), which was also the case in 2007. For fire personnel, the Pacific Coast and Mountain divisions again show the highest average numbers of uniformed personnel per capita (137 and 110, respectively), while the East North-Central and Mid-Atlantic divisions show the lowest (45 and 46, respectively). When per capita per 1,000 population figures are reviewed, the East South-Central division shows the highest average (2.38) and the West North-Central shows the lowest (1.12). The differences by metropolitan status show that independent cities have slightly higher per capita numbers of uniformed personnel in both services than central cities and that suburban communities' per capita numbers are the lowest.

Table 3/2   FULL-TIME PAID PERSONNEL, 2008

Classification	Police			Fire		
	No. reporting	Mean	Per capita per 1,000 population	No. reporting	Mean	Per capita per 1,000 population
Total	1,117	109	2.62	866	83	1.71
Population group						
Over 1,000,000	2	3,412	2.66	3	2,286	1.12
500,000–1,000,000	4	2,145	3.30	4	1,178	1.85
250,000–499,999	9	942	2.55	9	437	1.18
100,000–249,999	62	365	2.49	56	228	1.54
50,000–99,999	139	176	2.52	124	143	1.95
25,000–49,999	268	91	2.57	222	60	1.70
10,000–24,999	633	42	2.67	448	27	1.68
Geographic division						
New England	77	53	2.23	63	48	1.84
Mid-Atlantic	135	57	2.25	54	46	1.33
East North-Central	230	67	2.35	190	46	1.46
West North-Central	109	83	2.27	84	50	1.12
South Atlantic	160	166	3.67	138	109	2.32
East South-Central	37	96	3.48	36	68	2.47
West South-Central	134	119	2.83	127	79	1.78
Mountain	75	204	3.02	57	117	1.63
Pacific Coast	160	152	2.14	117	162	1.65
Metro status						
Central	183	321	2.88	173	214	1.84
Suburban	694	73	2.50	483	55	1.62
Independent	240	53	2.78	210	37	1.81

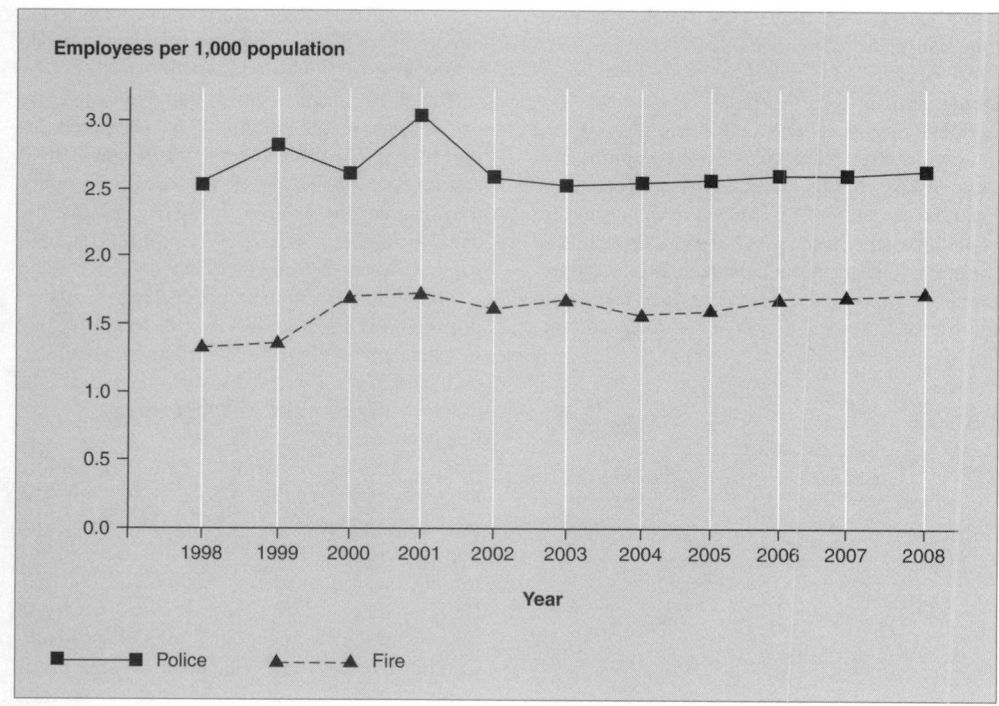

Figure 3/1   *Police and fire trends in employees per 1,000 population, 1998–2008.*

Table 3/3   UNIFORMED SWORN PERSONNEL, 2008

	Police			Fire		
Classification	No. reporting	Mean	Per capita per 1,000 population	No. reporting	Mean	Per capita per 1,000 population
Total	1,127	91	2.06	849	76	1.61
Population group						
Over 1,000,000	3	4,934	2.22	3	2,085	1.02
500,000–1,000,000	4	1,700	2.61	4	1,060	1.66
250,000–499,999	9	676	1.83	8	415	1.13
100,000–249,999	62	268	1.80	57	201	1.35
50,000–99,999	139	129	1.84	120	131	1.81
25,000–49,999	274	70	1.98	219	57	1.61
10,000–24,999	636	34	2.16	438	26	1.60
Geographic division						
New England	78	45	1.89	61	47	1.72
Mid-Atlantic	133	50	1.95	50	46	1.31
East North-Central	232	53	1.89	182	45	1.45
West North-Central	111	64	1.85	83	50	1.12
South Atlantic	165	123	2.87	140	100	2.16
East South-Central	37	77	2.84	37	65	2.38
West South-Central	135	91	2.12	127	73	1.64
Mountain	75	147	2.15	57	110	1.48
Pacific Coast	161	167	1.51	112	137	1.38
Metro status						
Central	185	291	2.18	173	197	1.72
Suburban	703	56	1.97	468	50	1.51
Independent	239	42	2.21	208	36	1.73

HOURS WORKED PER SHIFT

Several questions were asked regarding the average number of hours worked per week and per shift for both services. The results, which are not displayed, are as expected. Approximately 74% of jurisdictions reported that their police department employees work 40 hours a week, and 18% reported a 42-hour workweek. Fire departments had more varied responses to the workweek question: 23% indicated that their workweek is 56 hours, and only 5% reported a 40-hour workweek. Eighteen percent reported a 50- to 54-hour workweek in 2008, which is a slight increase over that reported in 2007.

The average number of hours worked per shift also varies between the services. Forty-one percent of the cities indicated that their police officers work an 8-hour shift, and 54% reported 10- or 12-hour shifts. Fire departments, on the other hand, are most likely to have 24-hour shifts (78%), unchanged from 2007.

SALARY AND LONGEVITY PAY

Tables 3/5 through 3/8 present various salary and longevity pay data for full-time police officers and firefighters.

Minimum and Maximum Salaries

Tables 3/5 and 3/6 present detailed entrance and maximum salary data for police officers and firefighters, respectively, as well as the average number of years required for each to reach the maximum. In addition to the measures of central tendency (mean and median) for the salary data, the first and third quartiles are included to indicate the degree of dispersion. The annual base salaries are the entrance salaries paid to sworn police officers or firefighters within their first 12 months of employment. Each reported amount excludes uniform allowances, holiday pay, hazardous duty pay, and any other form of additional compensation. The maximum is the highest annual base salary paid to uniformed personnel who do not hold any promotional rank.

The median entrance salary for police personnel is $40,822 and the mean is $41,620 (Table 3/5). The median maximum salary for police is $57,341 and the mean is $59,385. The entrance salary for firefighters tends to be lower than that for police, with a median of $37,476 and a mean of $38,889 (Table 3/6). The maximum fire salary median and mean are $52,259 and $53,517, respectively. For both police and fire, the mean is higher than the median salary. This means that some higher salaries are positively skewing the mean.

The highest average entrance salaries for both police personnel and firefighters are found in suburban cities and the Pacific Coast division. The highest average maximum salaries for both groups of personnel are also found in suburban cities; geographically, however, the highest average maximum salary for firefighters is again in the Pacific Coast division while that for police personnel is in the Mid-Atlantic division, followed closely by the Pacific Coast division. The lowest average en-

STAFFING REQUIREMENTS FOR FIRE PERSONNEL

All reporting jurisdictions with a population of 250,000 and over reported minimum staffing requirements, as did 81% of reporting jurisdictions overall (not shown). The responses by geographic division indicate that the majority of jurisdictions in all areas of the country have a minimum requirement and that more than 80% of cities in the South Atlantic, Pacific Coast, East South-Central, Mountain, and West South-Central divisions have requirements or policies advising minimum staffing per shift. This pattern is similar to that reported in previous surveys, as are the differences by metropolitan status, which range from a low of 77% for suburban cities to a high of 93% for central cities.

The average minimum staffing for apparatus—pumpers, ladders, and other equipment—is presented in Table 3/4. For pumpers, ladders, and rescue units, the average minimum crew is highest for cities over 500,000 in population.

trance and maximum salaries for both police personnel and firefighters are found in independent cities and in the East South-Central division. For both services, the difference between the highest and lowest average entrance salaries among the geographic divisions is substantial: $25,597 for police and $23,805 for fire. The difference between the highest and lowest average maximum salaries among the geographic divisions is $30,490 for police, compared with $26,671 for firefighters.

For both police and fire services, an average of seven years of service is required to reach the maximum salary, with larger cities tending to have longer service requirements.

Longevity Pay

Longevity pay is defined as compensation beyond the regular maximum salary based on number of years of service. Longevity serves as an economic incentive to decrease employee turnover and reward those employees who have already achieved the maximum salary and now have limited opportunities for promotion. Longevity pay can be administered in several ways—a flat dollar amount, a percentage of the base salary, a percentage of the maximum pay, or a step increase in the basic salary plan.

Tables 3/7 and 3/8 show a range of longevity pay data for police and firefighter personnel, respectively. The tables cover whether personnel can receive longevity pay, the maximum salary they can receive including longevity pay, and the average number of years of service that is required for them to receive longevity pay.

Sixty-five percent of all police departments reporting have a system that awards longevity pay to their personnel (Table 3/7). The Mid-Atlantic and West South-Central divisions show the highest percentage of cities with longevity pay for police personnel (93% each).

The average maximum salary including longevity pay for police officers is $63,949. The figures range from a low of $61,551 for cities with populations of 10,000–24,999 to a high of $76,941 for cities with populations of 500,000–1,000,000. Geographic divisions show a clear disparity in this regard. Once again, cities in the East South-Central division show the lowest average maximum of $45,571, while the highest average maximums are $79,641 for Mid-Atlantic and $78,630 for Pacific Coast jurisdictions. And again, suburban cities have a higher average maximum salary with longevity pay ($68,787) than either central ($58,789) or independent ($50,732) cities.

The longevity pay patterns for firefighters (Table 3/8) are similar to those for police officers. Sixty-three percent of jurisdictions reported longevity pay for fire personnel, including 92% of jurisdictions in the West South-Central division (the high) and 33% of those in the East South-Central division (the low). Central jurisdictions (66%) are slightly ahead of suburban (62%) and independent (60%) jurisdictions in offering longevity pay for firefighters.

Table 3/4   MINIMUM CREW PER FIRE APPARATUS, 2008

Classification	Pumpers No. reporting	Pumpers Average minimum crew	Ladders No. reporting	Ladders Average minimum crew	Rescue units No. reporting	Rescue units Average minimum crew
Total	606	3.1	530	3.1	441	2.6
Population group						
Over 1,000,000	3	4.0	3	4.7	2	2.0
500,000–1,000,000	3	4.0	3	4.3	2	4.0
250,000–499,999	10	3.3	11	3.4	7	2.4
100,000–249,999	44	3.5	44	3.3	30	2.7
50,000–99,999	97	3.1	93	3.1	75	2.5
25,000–49,999	158	3.0	147	3.0	111	2.5
10,000–24,999	291	3.1	229	3.1	214	2.7
Geographic division						
New England	31	2.7	30	2.5	25	2.2
Mid-Atlantic	62	3.4	56	3.5	44	3.3
East North-Central	101	3.0	84	2.8	87	2.5
West North-Central	63	3.4	55	3.3	49	2.8
South Atlantic	111	3.0	98	2.9	71	2.3
East South-Central	24	3.1	20	3.3	13	2.3
West South-Central	82	3.1	68	3.1	55	2.5
Mountain	36	3.8	35	3.7	29	2.7
Pacific Coast	96	3.0	84	3.2	68	2.5
Metro status						
Central	143	3.2	136	3.1	101	2.5
Suburban	338	3.1	295	3.1	256	2.6
Independent	125	3.0	99	3.0	84	2.7

Table 3/5   POLICE OFFICERS' ANNUAL BASE SALARY, JANUARY 1, 2008

Classification	Entrance salary No. of cities reporting	Entrance salary Mean ($)	Entrance salary First quartile ($)	Entrance salary Median ($)	Entrance salary Third quartile ($)	Maximum salary No. of cities reporting	Maximum salary Mean ($)	Maximum salary First quartile ($)	Maximum salary Median ($)	Maximum salary Third quartile ($)	No. of years to reach maximum No. of cities reporting	Mean
Total	1,146	41,620	34,533	40,822	46,986	1,124	59,385	49,287	57,341	67,552	924	7
Population group												
Over 1,000,000	2	48,510	44,504	48,510	52,516	2	72,854	68,147	72,854	77,560	2	8
500,000–1,000,000	4	50,152	39,316	49,282	60,117	4	68,074	59,762	70,916	79,230	3	13
250,000–499,999	10	46,163	38,743	42,612	54,954	10	64,499	56,678	65,934	72,796	7	7
100,000–249,999	64	47,778	39,438	45,392	54,613	64	67,555	57,673	66,245	73,280	55	9
50,000–99,999	139	46,125	38,222	44,270	52,156	136	64,371	55,348	64,061	72,596	112	8
25,000–49,999	276	42,414	35,683	41,986	47,682	274	60,412	50,576	58,436	68,598	227	7
10,000–24,999	651	39,573	32,966	39,104	45,410	634	56,868	46,759	55,024	64,398	518	7
Geographic division												
New England	78	42,459	38,592	41,400	45,694	77	54,301	49,455	52,874	58,309	74	6
Mid-Atlantic	146	42,151	36,895	41,986	47,014	146	73,471	60,540	71,070	84,011	144	6
East North-Central	230	43,058	38,219	42,997	47,232	227	59,246	51,896	59,064	66,641	221	6
West North-Central	111	38,044	32,592	38,230	43,782	111	52,138	44,458	53,477	59,858	85	7
South Atlantic	168	34,814	30,955	33,500	38,018	159	54,810	47,173	54,003	60,890	77	14
East South-Central	39	29,780	26,202	29,087	32,112	38	42,981	36,528	42,864	49,593	31	12
West South-Central	133	36,920	31,423	37,246	42,182	130	49,422	41,176	50,242	57,888	93	9
Mountain	79	40,674	34,920	40,955	45,208	76	58,053	50,825	58,064	64,591	51	9
Pacific Coast	162	55,377	48,862	54,498	60,960	160	71,372	62,094	69,924	78,664	148	5
Metro status												
Central	188	40,923	33,810	39,774	45,206	185	58,222	49,523	56,451	65,138	145	9
Suburban	717	44,014	37,404	43,231	49,192	702	63,575	53,948	61,886	71,032	604	7
Independent	241	35,044	29,774	33,697	39,690	237	47,880	40,164	46,356	53,872	175	8

Table 3/6 FIREFIGHTERS' ANNUAL BASE SALARY, JANUARY 1, 2008

Classification	Entrance salary					Maximum salary					No. of years to reach maximum	
	No. of cities reporting	Mean ($)	First quartile ($)	Median ($)	Third quartile ($)	No. of cities reporting	Mean ($)	First quartile ($)	Median ($)	Third quartile ($)	No. of cities reporting	Mean
Total	817	38,889	31,940	37,476	44,349	797	53,517	45,100	52,259	61,593	634	7
Population group												
Over 1,000,000	2	45,860	41,908	45,860	49,813	2	71,065	65,192	71,065	76,938	2	11
500,000–1,000,000	4	49,049	33,675	46,708	62,082	4	68,306	52,804	63,230	78,733	3	5
250,000–499,999	10	43,470	36,760	42,341	51,836	10	60,650	53,730	58,808	69,247	7	8
100,000–249,999	56	43,383	35,450	39,654	50,152	56	61,618	51,381	59,594	67,496	46	9
50,000–99,999	118	42,646	35,157	40,516	47,748	115	58,892	50,764	57,484	66,088	96	7
25,000–49,999	211	39,458	32,658	39,273	44,970	210	54,597	47,518	53,135	61,805	174	7
10,000–24,999	416	36,689	29,680	35,760	42,000	400	49,856	41,328	48,766	56,225	306	7
Geographic division												
New England	62	40,091	36,654	39,513	42,886	60	50,547	46,394	49,174	53,252	53	6
Mid-Atlantic	50	38,720	34,525	38,040	43,358	50	59,364	49,855	54,090	71,309	43	6
East North-Central	177	41,636	36,288	41,016	45,966	173	55,549	48,079	54,975	62,930	167	6
West North-Central	73	36,309	30,253	35,100	41,282	72	49,722	42,705	48,923	55,120	56	8
South Atlantic	135	31,377	27,622	30,801	33,983	127	49,435	42,024	49,344	55,468	55	14
East South-Central	38	29,311	25,368	28,451	31,633	38	41,917	35,504	40,812	49,612	30	12
West South-Central	121	34,785	29,000	33,859	39,257	118	45,519	37,528	45,549	53,138	91	8
Mountain	52	38,119	33,623	38,480	42,736	50	54,869	47,191	55,501	59,615	34	9
Pacific Coast	109	53,116	46,668	51,889	57,907	109	68,588	61,106	67,636	74,495	105	5
Metro status												
Central	176	38,644	31,971	36,736	43,483	173	53,933	46,797	52,486	60,977	138	8
Suburban	436	41,894	34,358	41,029	47,667	424	57,431	48,766	55,837	64,867	346	6
Independent	205	32,709	26,849	31,331	37,338	200	44,858	37,343	43,236	50,421	150	8

Table 3/7 LONGEVITY PAY FOR POLICE OFFICERS, JANUARY 1, 2008

Classification	No. reporting	Personnel can receive longevity pay				Maximum salary including longevity pay					No. of years of service to receive longevity pay	
		Yes		No		No. of cities reporting	Mean ($)	First quartile ($)	Median ($)	Third quartile ($)	No. of cities reporting	Mean
		No.	% of (A)	No.	% of (A)							
Total	1,165	757	65	408	35	572	63,949	52,034	60,750	72,247	694	6
Population group												
Over 1,000,000	3	1	33	2	67	1	67,440	67,440	67,440	67,440	1	7
500,000–1,000,000	3	2	67	1	33	2	76,941	71,734	76,941	82,148	2	16
250,000–499,999	10	6	60	4	40	4	61,840	58,585	62,412	65,667	6	6
100,000–249,999	63	36	57	27	43	29	68,139	58,532	66,525	74,603	33	6
50,000–99,999	142	94	66	48	34	76	69,165	57,675	69,792	77,923	90	7
25,000–49,999	281	186	66	95	34	144	65,468	54,744	61,115	72,849	169	5
10,000–24,999	663	432	65	231	35	316	61,551	49,138	58,178	68,880	393	6
Geographic division												
New England	79	65	82	14	18	51	58,119	51,576	54,809	62,172	58	8
Mid-Atlantic	148	138	93	10	7	111	79,641	62,071	76,403	91,256	131	6
East North-Central	233	175	75	58	25	140	60,682	52,608	60,158	69,060	165	6
West North-Central	116	63	54	53	46	47	56,874	48,060	57,047	67,267	61	6
South Atlantic	168	74	44	94	56	46	58,879	47,224	56,785	70,257	57	8
East South-Central	40	13	33	27	68	9	45,571	40,293	43,335	51,655	13	6
West South-Central	137	127	93	10	7	85	51,315	43,522	52,158	59,609	118	2
Mountain	79	27	34	52	66	21	59,544	53,333	59,721	67,341	23	7
Pacific Coast	165	75	46	90	55	62	78,630	69,797	76,916	85,482	68	9
Metro status												
Central	188	120	64	68	36	89	58,789	51,655	57,065	65,025	112	6
Suburban	729	488	67	241	33	379	68,787	56,906	66,898	76,171	450	6
Independent	248	149	60	99	40	104	50,732	43,012	48,302	55,009	132	5

The average maximum salary with longevity pay for firefighters is $54,687. Among population groups, the two cities with populations of over 1,000,000 show the highest average maximum salary with longevity pay ($76,185), while cities with populations of 10,000–24,999 show the lowest ($50,177). Geographically, Pacific Coast jurisdictions show the highest average maximum salary with longevity pay ($76,753), and East South-Central communities again show the lowest ($45,631). Suburban communities show a higher average maximum salary ($58,204) than either central ($55,079) or independent ($45,117) cities.

Overall, the length of service required for police and firefighters to receive longevity pay is six years for both, which is identical to the number reported in 2007. However, the number of years varies somewhat within the classification categories. In the Pacific Coast division, for example, both groups of personnel serve a well-above-average number of years to qualify for longevity pay: police serve an average of 9 years and firefighters serve an average of 10.

Table 3/8   LONGEVITY PAY FOR FIREFIGHTERS, JANUARY 1, 2008

Classification	No. reporting	Personnel can receive longevity pay				Maximum salary including longevity pay					No. of years of service to receive longevity pay	
		Yes		No		No. of cities reporting	Mean ($)	First quartile ($)	Median ($)	Third quartile ($)	No. of cities reporting	Mean
		No.	% of (A)	No.	% of (A)							
Total	923	577	63	346	38	415	54,687	46,600	53,736	63,912	515	6
Population group												
Over 1,000,000	3	2	67	1	33	2	76,185	69,752	76,185	82,618	2	8
500,000–1,000,000	3	2	67	1	33	2	72,125	66,188	72,125	78,062	2	5
250,000–499,999	10	5	50	5	50	3	56,107	53,736	56,691	58,769	5	7
100,000–249,999	58	33	57	25	43	28	63,741	51,900	61,948	69,911	32	6
50,000–99,999	122	81	66	41	34	63	61,049	51,685	59,553	70,938	78	6
25,000–49,999	230	156	68	74	32	114	56,257	49,463	54,542	64,691	138	5
10,000–24,999	497	298	60	199	40	203	50,177	41,885	49,694	59,002	258	5
Geographic division												
New England	66	53	80	13	20	37	54,086	48,519	51,509	56,899	50	8
Mid-Atlantic	79	56	71	23	29	41	55,551	49,657	55,271	77,578	45	5
East North-Central	200	148	74	52	26	113	55,938	48,635	56,736	65,138	139	5
West North-Central	94	46	49	48	51	29	48,224	41,686	50,368	56,175	39	6
South Atlantic	137	64	47	73	53	41	53,523	43,894	51,715	62,768	52	7
East South-Central	39	13	33	26	67	9	45,631	40,807	43,335	51,655	13	6
West South-Central	132	122	92	10	8	89	46,278	38,542	49,250	54,686	115	2
Mountain	58	24	41	34	59	17	54,028	47,442	57,855	63,320	21	8
Pacific Coast	118	51	43	67	57	41	76,753	69,316	73,134	84,000	41	10
Metro status												
Central	177	116	66	61	35	86	55,079	49,349	52,827	60,252	110	6
Suburban	519	324	62	195	38	238	58,204	50,464	58,574	69,293	287	6
Independent	227	137	60	90	40	91	45,117	39,982	45,231	50,524	118	5

Table 3/9   EXPENDITURES FOR SALARIES AND WAGES (CIVILIAN AND UNIFORMED), 2008

Classification	Police			Fire		
	No. of cities reporting	Mean ($)	Per capita ($)	No. of cities reporting	Mean ($)	Per capita ($)
Total	1,068	7,011,342	155.64	850	5,383,773	102.58
Population group						
Over 1,000,000	2	252,461,100	197.40	2	155,744,812	122.72
500,000–1,000,000	3	203,088,600	289.26	3	94,467,348	139.57
250,000–499,999	10	60,005,980	171.12	10	30,551,383	86.85
100,000–249,999	61	23,856,335	167.96	56	15,929,358	109.79
50,000–99,999	131	11,329,885	161.04	117	11,683,178	155.33
25,000–49,999	248	5,417,201	154.33	207	3,668,552	103.22
10,000–24,999	613	2,432,215	152.76	455	1,444,913	87.86
Geographic division						
New England	71	4,190,557	151.91	64	3,368,041	112.65
Mid-Atlantic	134	4,521,148	178.99	55	3,234,830	86.06
East North-Central	219	4,474,020	151.09	188	3,173,074	96.87
West North-Central	107	4,749,090	119.32	92	2,737,541	56.77
South Atlantic	158	9,122,354	176.49	138	6,048,944	113.59
East South-Central	35	3,687,142	139.02	33	2,883,901	103.92
West South-Central	123	5,632,655	132.14	119	3,952,183	88.12
Mountain	71	11,928,400	158.81	55	8,504,772	97.62
Pacific Coast	150	13,244,477	168.82	106	13,833,489	159.05
Metro status						
Central	179	20,622,665	164.96	171	12,819,672	110.08
Suburban	657	4,890,659	162.53	464	4,349,550	109.38
Independent	232	2,515,056	128.97	215	1,701,637	81.95

EXPENDITURES

Respondents were asked to provide expenditure (not budget) figures for their department's most recently completed fiscal year. The items include salaries and wages for all department personnel, contributions for employee benefits, capital outlays, and all other departmental expenditures. Average expenditures are presented in Tables 3/9 through 3/15. Per capita expenditures are shown in addition to average expenditures. Per capita presentations are useful because they normalize the information.

Salaries and Wages

Part of ICMA's process of reviewing survey results is to design logic checks that will identify problematic values. One logic check is that total expenditures for salaries and wages must be greater than the minimum salary for police (or fire) sworn personnel multiplied by the number of sworn personnel reported. For those jurisdictions reporting total expenditures for salaries and wages below that amount, the total salary and wage expenditures amount was removed.

Table 3/9 shows that the average per capita expenditure for civilian and uniformed police personnel in 2008 was $155.64, an increase from the 2007 average of $150.19. As population decreases, average per capita expenditures also generally decrease. So, too, do average salary and wage expenditures for police: from $252,461,100 for cities with populations over 1,000,000 to $2,432,215 for cities of 10,000–24,999 in population (Table 3/9). The average expenditure decrease is more pronounced than the average per capita decrease among population groups, which is to be expected.

Overall, the spread of average per capita salary and wage expenditures is greater for police departments than for fire departments. The average per capita police expenditures show a low of $152.76 in cities of 10,000–24,999 in population and a high of $289.26 in cities of 500,000–1,000,000 in population (Table 3/9). For firefighters, the average per capita expenditures range from a low of $86.85 in cities with populations of 250,000–499,999 to a high of $155.33 in cities with populations of 50,000–99,999.

Geographically, Mid-Atlantic jurisdictions show the highest average per capita salary and wage expenditure for police personnel ($178.99), and Pacific Coast jurisdictions show the highest for firefighters ($159.05). Cities in the West North-Central division show the lowest for both police ($119.32) and for fire personnel ($56.77).

Social Security and Retirement Benefits

The average expenditures for municipal contributions to federal social security and other employee

retirement programs are reported in Table 3/10. These expenditures are for both uniformed and civilian personnel. The table shows combined retirement and social security contributions because some states opt out of social security programs for local government employees, relying instead on an employee-sponsored retirement program. Zeros have been removed from the calculations because although zero is a legitimate answer, it skews the averages.

The average per capita expenditure for employee social security and retirement benefits for police in 2008 ($31.78) is up from the 2007 amount ($28.93). Among the population groups, the highest average police per capita expenditure for social security and retirement ($49.46) is in the 500,000–1,000,000 population group, but only two cities reported. Geographically, the highest average police department per capita expenditure for these benefits is found in the Pacific Coast division ($41.80); the lowest is in the West North-Central division ($19.52). Suburban cities show a slightly higher average per capita municipal contribution ($33.49) than central cities ($33.34); independent cities show a lower amount ($26.74).

The average per capita expenditure for social security and retirement benefits for fire departments in 2008 was $20.44 (Table 3/10), compared with $19.53 in 2007. The per capita amounts fluctuate among the population groups. Among the geographic divisions, the highest average fire department per capita expenditure for social security and retirement benefits is found in the South Atlantic cities ($25.88), and the lowest is in the West North-Central ($13.78) cities. Suburban cities show the highest average per capita expenditures at $21.47.

Health, Hospitalization, Disability, and Life Insurance

Table 3/11 shows the average total municipal contributions for health, hospitalization, disability, and life insurance programs. The mean per capita expenditures for 2008 increased to $27.88 for police and $18.77 for fire. In 2007, they were $24.48 for police and $16.37 for fire.

Total Personnel Expenditures

Table 3/12 shows the total personnel expenditures for civilian and uniformed employees for both police and fire services. These data represent total salaries and wages; contributions for federal social security and other retirement programs; and contributions to health, hospitalization, disability, and life insurance programs. To be included in this table, the jurisdiction had to provide each of these expenditures. Those who reported an amount of zero were excluded from the table. Again, although zero is a legitimate amount, it negatively skews the average.

For fire services in particular, the workforce composition affects personnel expenditures. Departments that rely heavily on volunteers have significantly lower personnel expenditures than those who use paid staff.

The mean per capita personnel expenditure amounts are $211.40 for police and $131.33 for fire (Table 3/12), up from $201.17 and $127.61, respectively, in 2007. For police departments,

these amounts generally decline from the larger to the smaller cities. Among the geographic divisions, the high for police is in the South Atlantic division ($240.70), followed by the Pacific Coast division ($234.73); the low is in the West North-Central division ($157.96).

For fire departments, the mean per capita personnel expenditures vary noticeably among population groups—from a high of $197.14 for cities with populations of 500,000–1,000,000, to a low

of $109.46 for cities of 250,000–499,999 in population. Geographically, the average per capita high is again seen in the South Atlantic division ($152.85), and the low is again seen in the West North-Central division ($80.65). The highest average per capita personnel expenditure for police departments is found in suburban cities; for fire, the highest is in central cities. For both services, independent cities have the lowest average per capita personnel expenditures.

Table 3/10 TOTAL MUNICIPAL CONTRIBUTIONS TO SOCIAL SECURITY AND STATE/CITY-ADMINISTERED EMPLOYEE RETIREMENT SYSTEMS, 2008

	Police			Fire		
Classification	No. of cities reporting	Mean ($)	Per capita ($)	No. of cities reporting	Mean ($)	Per capita ($)
Total	803	1,345,604	31.78	645	903,085	20.44
Population group						
Over 1,000,000	1	52,209,077	39.52	1	2,658,831	2.01
500,000–1,000,000	2	31,398,973	49.46	2	14,158,828	22.47
250,000–499,999	7	11,893,723	29.96	7	6,490,198	16.19
100,000–249,999	43	4,903,590	33.14	42	3,310,798	21.91
50,000–99,999	90	2,652,391	38.23	83	1,556,607	22.99
25,000–49,999	192	1,111,384	31.90	162	833,431	23.38
10,000–24,999	468	468,593	30.31	348	295,444	18.41
Geographic division						
New England	33	585,191	25.02	24	421,636	16.08
Mid-Atlantic	87	716,092	33.15	32	543,321	19.94
East North-Central	142	1,032,588	34.11	131	806,749	23.72
West North-Central	101	796,749	19.52	84	692,480	13.78
South Atlantic	149	2,115,131	40.13	127	1,297,666	25.88
East South-Central	31	721,817	27.40	30	575,916	21.35
West South-Central	115	1,066,295	24.52	107	727,396	15.66
Mountain	61	2,367,279	30.15	46	1,125,283	16.11
Pacific Coast	84	1,991,078	41.80	64	1,241,510	24.19
Metro status						
Central	137	3,714,077	33.34	131	2,076,229	21.09
Suburban	466	1,002,756	33.49	334	710,798	21.47
Independent	200	522,036	26.74	180	406,097	18.04

Table 3/11 TOTAL MUNICIPAL CONTRIBUTIONS FOR HEALTH, HOSPITALIZATION, DISABILITY, AND LIFE INSURANCE PROGRAMS, 2008

	Police			Fire		
Classification	No. of cities reporting	Mean ($)	Per capita ($)	No. of cities reporting	Mean ($)	Per capita ($)
Total	946	1,192,868	27.88	759	956,103	18.77
Population group						
Over 1,000,000	1	50,458,269	38.20	1	27,297,629	20.66
500,000–1,000,000	2	20,712,716	31.59	2	12,143,063	18.38
250,000–499,999	10	7,713,526	22.32	10	4,062,483	11.49
100,000–249,999	56	3,934,060	27.80	51	2,494,978	17.32
50,000–99,999	116	2,664,798	38.27	103	2,829,922	38.36
25,000–49,999	224	928,954	26.41	187	644,440	18.13
10,000–24,999	537	413,268	26.33	405	232,685	14.44
Geographic division						
New England	39	643,063	26.88	34	514,057	19.39
Mid-Atlantic	109	628,035	29.44	48	359,550	13.11
East North-Central	191	888,165	29.15	164	661,311	18.94
West North-Central	100	746,544	19.37	87	466,044	10.10
South Atlantic	152	1,133,501	27.44	129	773,723	17.64
East South-Central	32	551,474	20.18	31	436,422	15.50
West South-Central	119	1,568,569	30.46	119	1,250,385	22.67
Mountain	67	2,033,399	27.68	51	1,493,880	16.08
Pacific Coast	137	2,027,645	31.52	96	2,121,060	28.14
Metro status						
Central	163	2,813,286	25.89	154	1,772,288	16.89
Suburban	569	1,007,131	30.11	408	965,599	21.53
Independent	214	452,478	23.46	197	298,402	14.52

Table 3/12   TOTAL PERSONNEL EXPENDITURES, 2008

	Police			Fire		
Classification	No. of cities reporting	Mean ($)	Per capita ($)	No. of cities reporting	Mean ($)	Per capita ($)
Total	782	8,672,370	211.40	622	6,054,765	131.33
Population group						
Over 1,000,000	1	399,405,326	302.34	1	181,731,002	137.57
500,000–1,000,000	1	171,397,616	304.23	1	111,065,946	197.14
250,000–499,999	7	83,097,788	218.12	7	42,271,678	109.46
100,000–249,999	43	32,527,304	221.38	42	22,127,621	147.95
50,000–99,999	90	15,094,114	215.23	83	9,627,983	140.94
25,000–49,999	188	7,457,082	212.79	156	5,125,610	144.56
10,000–24,999	452	3,252,721	208.59	332	1,955,685	120.85
Geographic division						
New England	31	4,938,080	202.95	23	3,909,002	144.22
Mid-Atlantic	82	5,062,777	230.96	28	3,482,240	122.93
East North-Central	139	6,977,242	222.43	126	4,979,607	141.70
West North-Central	98	6,486,208	157.96	82	4,132,507	80.65
South Atlantic	148	10,087,482	240.70	125	6,623,054	152.85
East South-Central	29	5,381,802	192.56	27	4,278,409	144.56
West South-Central	110	7,629,592	175.13	102	5,393,462	115.79
Mountain	61	17,157,771	221.21	46	12,150,872	135.46
Pacific Coast	84	12,775,969	234.73	63	8,887,084	149.35
Metro status						
Central	136	22,856,700	213.02	129	14,440,121	139.06
Suburban	453	6,579,813	223.25	320	4,612,636	136.79
Independent	193	3,588,740	182.44	173	2,469,623	115.46

Table 3/13   MUNICIPAL EXPENDITURES FOR CAPITAL OUTLAYS, 2008

	Police			Fire		
Classification	No. of cities reporting	Mean ($)	Per capita ($)	No. of cities reporting	Mean ($)	Per capita ($)
Total	943	556,621	14.69	743	640,692	16.71
Population group						
Over 1,000,000	2	6,756,103	5.20	2	6,836,355	5.26
500,000–1,000,000	3	17,839,782	27.06	3	12,189,373	16.72
250,000–499,999	10	3,134,982	8.15	10	4,098,040	12.50
100,000–249,999	54	1,066,319	7.52	52	781,531	5.85
50,000–99,999	122	1,022,294	15.15	107	1,256,750	17.25
25,000–49,999	216	532,254	15.32	174	399,401	11.63
10,000–24,999	536	241,127	15.14	395	354,951	20.39
Geographic division						
New England	57	133,368	6.15	45	183,176	8.41
Mid-Atlantic	109	402,896	19.35	62	275,513	16.65
East North-Central	188	279,405	10.15	149	266,023	9.67
West North-Central	97	213,188	7.93	73	291,327	8.87
South Atlantic	148	838,166	16.10	123	1,127,148	34.85
East South-Central	32	716,460	17.99	33	1,548,405	28.67
West South-Central . . .	117	712,513	15.32	112	357,842	11.11
Mountain	67	1,048,479	24.33	53	1,054,243	24.19
Pacific Coast	128	777,976	18.25	93	1,119,521	12.43
Metro status						
Central	161	1,247,571	10.51	157	1,241,826	10.61
Suburban	572	487,621	16.95	406	578,650	21.00
Independent	210	214,833	11.74	180	256,310	12.35

Capital Outlays

Table 3/13 shows departmental expenditures for capital outlays. These outlays include the purchase and replacement of equipment, the purchase of land and existing structures, and construction. The amounts include the capital expenditures within individual departmental budgets as well as those expenditures included in citywide capital budgets designated for departmental programs or equipment. Total capital outlay expenditures may fluctuate dramatically from one year to the next for both police and fire

departments. This is because the cost of individual capital projects varies widely among communities as well as within the same community over time. Whereas the number of employees, which relates to population size, determines personnel expenditures, fire equipment such as pumpers will cost the same regardless of the size of the community. Thus, the per capita cost for the pumpers will necessarily be higher among cities with fewer people.

The 2008 average municipal capital outlay expenditures per capita were $14.69 for police,

an increase over the $11.07 shown in 2007, and $16.71 for fire, which is above the 2007 figure of $11.09. For police, the highest average capital outlay expenditures per capita are in cities with populations of 500,000–1,000,000 ($27.06) and cities in the Mountain division ($24.33). For fire services, the average capital outlays per capita are highest in cities with populations of 10,000–24,999 ($20.39) as well as cities in the South Atlantic division ($34.85). For both services, the lowest average capital outlays per capita are in New England division cities.

OTHER EXPENDITURES

Table 3/14 presents the data for all other departmental expenditures not accounted for in the previous tables. These include ongoing maintenance, utilities, fuel, supplies, and other miscellaneous items.

The average per capita expenditures in 2008 were $35.60 for police and $23.77 for fire. These figures represent an increase in the per capita average expenditures over those reported in 2007 ($32.51 and $20.89, respectively).

TOTAL DEPARTMENTAL EXPENDITURES

Table 3/15 shows the combined personnel, capital outlay, and all other departmental expenditures. The average per capita figures for 2008 are $257.70 and $209.57 for police and fire, respectively—an increase over the $242.17 for police personnel and $144.60 for fire personnel reported in 2007.

Not all cities include the same expenditures in their budgets. Of the 772 jurisdictions providing information about services included in the fire department budget, 48% cited ambulance personnel and 51% cited ambulance equipment (not shown). Emergency medical training (EMT) personnel were included by 91%, and EMT equipment was included by 93%. This does not necessarily mean, however, that these are the only jurisdictions that provide EMT and ambulance services; these are just the cities that reported having these services in the fire department budget.

CONCLUSION

This report has examined the cross-sectional and longitudinal patterns found in the responses to ICMA's annual *Police and Fire Personnel, Salaries, and Expenditures* survey. Most of the changes over time in police and fire employment and expenditures have been small, incremental shifts. It is not uncommon for one year to show increases and the next to show decreases in average expenditures.

Although using per capita figures instead of absolute numbers reduces the skew of the data, any analysis of the reported changes must control for population size of the responding jurisdictions. Another influential factor is a significant difference in the number reporting in any population group. Any major increase or decrease in that number can affect the average.

Table 3/14   ALL OTHER DEPARTMENT EXPENDITURES, 2008

Classification	Police			Fire		
	No. of cities reporting	Mean ($)	Per capita ($)	No. of cities reporting	Mean ($)	Per capita ($)
Total	1,014	1,615,923	35.60	843	1,145,325	23.77
Population group						
Over 1,000,000	2	45,955,120	36.22	2	28,573,834	22.49
500,000–1,000,000	3	40,718,426	62.69	3	16,244,443	26.14
250,000–499,999	8	17,395,482	47.70	8	4,885,509	14.56
100,000–249,999	57	5,654,283	40.44	52	3,740,653	24.43
50,000–99,999	127	2,867,781	40.66	112	2,946,149	42.60
25,000–49,999	238	1,253,374	35.77	202	703,543	19.92
10,000–24,999	579	519,018	33.64	464	331,779	20.97
Geographic division						
New England	67	397,998	16.85	62	449,910	17.73
Mid-Atlantic	122	437,419	19.90	81	319,164	14.32
East North-Central	207	797,333	29.25	173	551,781	19.34
West North-Central	103	1,193,620	29.03	90	537,175	14.01
South Atlantic	151	2,423,988	49.38	130	1,625,454	29.09
East South-Central	34	972,757	34.27	34	2,582,698	50.84
West South-Central ...	122	1,102,547	27.71	122	1,250,183	25.97
Mountain	67	2,818,625	40.40	52	1,812,204	26.14
Pacific Coast	141	3,887,022	62.35	99	2,243,238	31.63
Metro status						
Central	171	4,670,961	39.64	163	2,876,702	26.86
Suburban	624	1,128,840	35.75	475	877,524	24.55
Independent	219	618,338	32.05	205	389,182	19.50

Table 3/15   TOTAL DEPARTMENTAL EXPENDITURES, 2008

Classification	Police			Fire		
	No. of cities reporting	Mean ($)	Per capita ($)	No. of cities reporting	Mean ($)	Per capita ($)
Total	1,012	11,459,681	257.70	856	11,377,619	209.57
Population group						
Over 1,000,000	2	417,848,560	327.81	2	240,844,609	189.72
500,000–1,000,000	3	294,612,347	424.35	3	139,899,447	206.08
250,000–499,999	9	99,876,124	274.92	9	51,109,254	142.11
100,000–249,999	57	38,020,096	269.40	52	24,591,017	170.87
50,000–99,999	129	18,610,060	264.79	115	41,103,463	572.98
25,000–49,999	235	8,922,830	253.17	202	6,407,257	180.42
10,000–24,999	577	4,010,519	255.43	473	2,279,014	139.31
Geographic division						
New England	64	5,008,787	201.66	59	3,735,452	144.43
Mid-Atlantic	120	6,439,923	271.92	88	3,371,737	112.57
East North-Central	212	7,045,762	240.81	178	5,656,424	173.58
West North-Central	104	7,647,938	191.99	90	4,528,010	98.92
South Atlantic	151	14,756,923	313.49	130	9,545,801	192.28
East South-Central	33	6,519,488	226.27	34	41,321,006	687.94
West South-Central	120	9,221,274	231.81	120	16,689,134	295.62
Mountain	66	20,551,813	275.92	53	14,278,607	174.64
Pacific Coast	142	23,298,211	305.68	104	23,100,402	269.72
Metro status						
Central	172	32,983,030	267.28	165	27,239,976	279.98
Suburban	622	8,003,798	266.50	484	9,527,549	212.71
Independent	218	4,338,319	225.04	207	3,059,477	146.11

Table 3/16 **POLICE DEPARTMENT PERSONNEL, SALARIES, AND EXPENDITURES FOR CITIES 10,000 AND OVER: 2008**

This table comprises 1,407 cities 10,000 and over in population (based on U.S. Bureau of the Census 2000 counts). The information in the table was collected in the spring of 2008 in a survey conducted by ICMA. Refer to the accompanying article for the survey methodology. The information is presented in two separate tables—one for police (Table 3/16) and one for fire (Table 3/17). The following definitions apply to both tables.

Type: letter identifies municipal designation: c, city; v, village; b, borough; t, town; tp, township.

Service provision: the number in this column indicates how the service is provided.
1 Full-time paid
2 All volunteer
3 Combined paid and volunteer
4 Public safety department (consolidated police and fire department)
5 Contract with county or other government entity for service
6 Contract with private company for service
7 Other

Full-time paid personnel: the number in this column shows the actual (not authorized) number of full-time paid employees.

Full-time uniformed personnel: the number in this column shows the number of sworn/uniformed employees.

Duty hours per week: shows the average number of hours worked per week.

Minimum base salary ($): shows the minimum base salary paid to full-time sworn/uniformed personnel. This amount does not include uniform allowance, holiday pay, hazard pay, or any other additional compensation.

Maximum base salary ($): shows the maximum base salary paid to full-time sworn/uniformed personnel. This amount does not include uniform allowance, holiday pay, hazard pay, or any other additional compensation.

Longevity pay: shows whether personnel can receive longevity pay: y, yes; n, no.

Maximum salary with longevity ($): shows the maximum salary with longevity pay included.

Years of service for longevity: shows the number of years of service required before personnel can receive longevity pay.

Total expenditures (A) ($): shows total departmental expenditures for the most recently completed fiscal year.

Total personnel expenditures (B) ($): shows total expenditures for salaries and wages (C); city contribution to retirement and social security (D); and city contribution to health, hospitalization, disability, and life insurance programs (E).

(B) as % of (A): shows total personnel expenditures as a percentage of total departmental expenditures. In some instances, the percentage equals or exceeds 100%. For some cities the retirement expenditures are in other accounts, so although they are reported as costs, they do not come out of the departmental budget. This accounts for the percentage in excess of 100.

Salaries and wages (C) ($): shows the amount of salaries and wages for all departmental personnel—regular, temporary, full time, and part time—and of stipends for volunteers. This is a gross amount, including longevity pay, hazard pay, and holiday pay, without deduction of withholding for income tax or employee contributions to social security or retirement coverage.

City contribution to retirement and social security (D) ($): shows city contributions only.

City contribution to insurance (E) ($): shows city contribution to health, hospitalization, disability, and life insurance programs.

Capital outlay (F) ($): Shows amount spent on purchases of equipment, land and existing structures, and construction.

All other (G) ($): shows amount of expenditures other than those described in (B) through (F) above. Expenditures include fuel, utilities, supplies, etc.

(—) Indicates data not reported.

City	State	Type	Service provision	Full-time paid personnel	Full-time uniformed personnel	Duty hours per week	Minimum base salary ($)	Maximum base salary ($)	Longevity pay	Maximum salary with longevity ($)	Years of service for longevity	Reported expenditures (in $000)							
												Total expenditures (A) ($)	Total personnel expenditures (B) ($)	(B) as % of (A)	Salaries and wages (C) ($)	City contribution to retirement and social security (D) ($)	City contribution to insurance (E) ($)	Capital outlay (F) ($)	All other (G) ($)
Over 1,000,000																			
LOS ANGELES	CA	c	1	—	9,605	other	56,522	82,267	n	—	—	—	—	—	—	—	—	—	—
PHOENIX	AZ	c	1	4,242	3,226	40	40,498	63,440	y	67,440	7	454,652	399,405	88	296,738	52,209	50,458	10,818	44,437
SAN DIEGO	CA	c	3	2,583	1,970	40	—	—	n	—	—	381,045	—	—	208,184	—	—	2,694	47,474
500,000–1,000,000																			
BALTIMORE	MD	c	1	3,595	3,013	42	41,058	66,527	y	66,527	26	347,073	—	—	234,252	52,414	—	43,903	64,663
EL PASO	TX	c	1	1,525	1,177	56	34,092	39,465	—	—	—	—	—	—	—	—	—	—	—
SAN JOSE	CA	c	1	1,764	1,393	40	67,953	91,000	n	—	—	323,492	—	—	239,693	—	15,732	5,027	20,208
SEATTLE	WA	c	1	1,697	1,216	40	57,505	75,306	y	87,355	7	213,272	171,398	80	135,321	10,383	25,693	4,589	37,285
250,000–499,999																			
ALBUQUERQUE	NM	c	1	1,415	1,008	40	39,520	43,826	y	51,935	4	145,763	98,282	67	70,889	17,340	10,052	10,100	37,381
ANCHORAGE	AK	c	—	—	—	—	—	—	—	—	—	—	—	—	—	—	—	—	—
AURORA	CO	c	1	778	642	40	45,268	69,101	y	70,601	5	71,105	77,277	109	62,461	5,284	9,531	25	5,120
CINCINNATI	OH	c	—	—	—	—	—	—	—	—	—	—	—	—	—	—	—	—	—
FRESNO	CA	c	3	1,249	834	40	57,348	73,212	n	—	—	123,013	99,306	81	78,180	17,828	3,297	12,465	—
MINNEAPOLIS	MN	c	1	1,085	619	40	47,771	71,547	y	—	7	123,613	95,843	78	73,820	9,594	12,428	201	27,569
OMAHA	NE	c	1	906	746	40	36,227	57,360	y	60,802	7	93,729	85,022	91	63,714	13,534	7,773	411	8,296
RALEIGH	NC	c	1	—	—	42	32,649	62,767	y	64,022	5	—	—	—	44,866	—	4,127	5,009	—
RIVERSIDE	CA	c	3	566	397	40	61,068	77,940	n	—	—	86,205	—	—	51,850	—	6,386	934	14,374
SANTA ANA	CA	c	3	663	362	40	63,336	76,980	n	—	—	108,131	—	—	59,972	—	11,566	210	27,045
VIRGINIA BEACH	VA	c	1	976	814	40	38,484	55,802	n	—	—	80,726	69,384	86	52,376	12,034	4,973	55	11,287
WICHITA	KS	c	1	844	661	40	39,957	56,451	y	—	6	66,600	56,572	85	41,931	7,638	7,002	1,938	8,090
100,000–249,999																			
ABILENE	TX	c	1	230	172	40	39,736	51,085	y	63,085	—	19,084	15,536	81	12,344	2,220	972	1,182	2,367
AKRON	OH	c	1	519	473	40	43,659	50,981	y	53,071	5	50,949	43,610	86	31,207	6,111	6,292	1,552	5,787
ALLENTOWN	PA	c	1	312	197	40	42,059	56,245	y	58,670	5	30,999	—	—	28,763	—	268	75	1,274
AMARILLO	TX	c	1	—	297	40	38,736	52,500	y	54,890	1	30,911	26,177	85	20,021	3,446	2,710	495	4,239
ANN ARBOR	MI	c	1	207	150	40	41,018	65,246	y	65,746	5	25,802	22,262	86	15,915	2,147	4,199	42	3,498
ARVADA	CO	c	1	230	157	40	49,667	68,135	n	—	—	22,756	—	—	14,296	—	2,185	—	4,779
BAKERSFIELD	CA	c	1	491	347	40	50,365	61,345	y	—	—	51,748	—	—	29,230	—	6,022	240	7,391
BATON ROUGE– EAST BATON ROUGE	LA	c	1	794	629	40	31,390	43,450	y	52,141	10	69,749	54,944	79	41,286	6,004	7,652	8,146	6,660

Table 3/16
continued

POLICE DEPARTMENT PERSONNEL, SALARIES, AND EXPENDITURES FOR CITIES 10,000 AND OVER: 2008

												Reported expenditures (in $000)							
City	State	Type	Service provision	Full-time paid personnel	Full-time uniformed personnel	Duty hours per week	Minimum base salary ($)	Maximum base salary ($)	Longevity pay	Maximum salary with longevity ($)	Years of service for longevity	Total expenditures (A) ($)	Total personnel expenditures (B) ($)	(B) as % of (A)	Salaries and wages (C) ($)	City contribution to retirement and social security (D) ($)	City contribution to insurance (E) ($)	Capital outlay (F) ($)	All other (G) ($)
100,000–249,999 continued																			
BERKELEY	CA	c	1	287	188	40	61,980	100,584	y	—	19	48,956	—	—	28,044	—	7,801	224	4,338
BROWNSVILLE	TX	c	1	308	236	40	28,131	78,360	y	79,560	1	25,188	28,662	114	22,031	3,326	3,304	810	2,347
CAMBRIDGE	MA	c	—	—	—	—	—	—	—	—	—	—	—	—	—	—	—	—	—
CAPE CORAL	FL	c	3	359	254	other	43,992	64,084	n	—	—	35,331	28,828	82	19,448	5,987	3,392	3,045	3,459
CARROLLTON	TX	c	1	161	132	40	—	—	—	—	—	—	—	—	—	—	—	—	—
CHESAPEAKE	VA	c	1	521	380	40	35,843	69,063	n	—	—	45,802	35,751	78	25,641	6,010	4,100	1,093	8,958
CLEARWATER	FL	c	3	373	203	40	42,761	63,328	n	—	—	36,188	29,833	82	22,698	4,121	3,014	218	6,137
COLUMBIA	SC	c	1	382	—	40	30,461	48,737	n	—	—	26,019	21,821	84	16,183	2,908	2,730	1,203	2,995
COLUMBUS–MUSCOGEE CONSOLIDATED	GA	c	1	467	374	42	30,152	46,797	n	—	—	25,278	22,172	88	15,809	4,514	1,849	809	2,297
CONCORD	CA	c	1	214	155	40	60,421	73,449	n	—	—	38,056	30,902	81	18,943	7,019	4,939	1,292	5,862
CORAL SPRINGS	FL	c	1	198	198	40	48,378	71,818	y	73,318	10	36,268	30,810	85	20,751	6,516	3,543	654	4,803
COSTA MESA	CA	c	3	174	156	40	71,028	95,184	n	—	—	38,263	—	—	23,420	—	2,566	1,223	5,899
EL MONTE	CA	c	3	224	149	40	60,228	73,224	y	77,616	5	31,693	—	—	19,443	—	2,329	1,112	3,317
FAYETTEVILLE	NC	c	1	499	273	40	33,151	56,805	n	—	—	40,796	30,491	75	22,713	3,997	3,780	3,564	6,741
FULLERTON	CA	c	3	228	154	40	61,995	79,123	n	—	—	36,266	30,704	85	20,770	5,821	4,112	277	5,285
GARLAND	TX	c	3	453	276	40	48,892	66,202	y	67,477	3	41,845	37,286	89	29,304	5,267	2,714	50	4,509
GILBERT	AZ	t	1	—	—	40	49,544	69,361	n	—	—	33,890	28,642	85	21,244	3,356	4,042	573	4,674
GLENDALE	AZ	c	3	550	382	40	49,992	68,418	y	69,218	—	—	—	—	—	—	—	—	—
GRAND PRAIRIE	TX	c	3	221	221	40	48,641	66,821	y	68,501	1	29,547	25,296	86	19,102	3,937	2,257	582	3,668
GRAND RAPIDS	MI	c	1	388	319	42	36,884	57,032	y	58,532	5	42,048	35,567	85	26,442	1,450	7,674	10	6,471
HAMPTON	VA	c	1	334	272	40	36,700	59,905	y	—	3	20,301	—	—	16,095	—	—	171	4,035
HENDERSON	NV	c	1	547	358	40	53,451	78,956	n	—	—	33,339	29,575	89	21,524	5,367	2,684	526	3,237
HUNTINGTON BEACH	CA	c	1	364	280	40	68,994	103,958	y	—	5	—	—	—	27,834	—	—	—	—
IRVINE	CA	c	1	174	174	40	59,342	92,019	n	—	—	47,157	—	—	24,631	—	8,410	7	6,770
JOLIET	IL	c	1	387	303	40	42,506	76,548	y	—	15	—	41,396	—	30,833	5,518	5,043	—	—
LAKEWOOD	CO	c	1	422	294	40	55,141	72,114	n	—	—	—	—	—	—	—	—	—	—
LAREDO	TX	c	1	443	437	40	43,930	61,901	y	63,398	1	39,821	33,902	85	25,931	5,817	2,153	47	5,872
LUBBOCK	TX	c	1	533	375	40	45,558	54,625	y	54,817	1	41,820	35,964	86	25,651	5,964	4,348	3	5,854
McALLEN	TX	c	1	392	259	40	41,558	41,558	y	54,142	1	26,145	22,504	86	17,356	2,678	2,469	263	3,379
MESQUITE	TX	c	1	—	—	40	—	—	—	—	—	—	—	—	—	—	—	—	—
NAPERVILLE	IL	c	1	302	190	40	54,437	76,502	y	79,002	10	33,486	31,302	93	23,690	4,177	3,434	122	2,062
NORFOLK	VA	c	1	816	687	40	36,516	57,887	n	—	—	60,882	55,908	92	45,286	6,539	4,082	753	4,221
NORWALK	CA	c	5	—	—	—	—	—	—	—	—	—	—	—	—	—	—	—	—
OCEANSIDE	CA	c	1	313	216	40	55,392	78,816	n	—	—	52,577	—	—	34,583	—	—	—	14,355
ONTARIO	CA	c	3	329	269	40	53,273	64,753	y	74,142	8	62,706	47,014	75	32,590	5,416	9,008	3,982	11,710
OVERLAND PARK	KS	c	3	340	260	40	39,672	66,288	n	—	—	30,207	25,664	85	19,317	3,133	3,214	1,491	3,052
PALMDALE	CA	c	—	—	—	—	—	—	—	—	—	—	—	—	—	—	—	—	—
PASADENA	CA	c	3	382	250	42	63,116	77,286	n	—	—	53,318	—	—	27,463	—	3,757	148	14,640
PASADENA	TX	c	1	342	262	40	43,231	63,662	y	—	1	41,143	30,378	74	21,281	4,739	4,359	5,836	4,929
PEMBROKE PINES	FL	c	1	315	243	40	48,755	68,702	y	74,198	10	40,856	36,238	89	21,868	9,908	4,462	1,626	2,992
PEORIA	AZ	c	1	286	189	40	49,233	69,264	n	—	—	34,824	26,411	76	19,419	3,762	3,230	155	8,262
PROVIDENCE	RI	c	1	—	—	other	47,273	59,932	y	66,525	5	—	—	—	37,665	—	—	—	—
RICHMOND	VA	c	—	—	—	—	—	—	—	—	—	—	—	—	—	—	—	—	—
SALEM	OR	c	1	232	186	40	46,883	59,800	n	—	—	35,569	28,433	80	19,267	5,565	3,600	96	7,040
SALINAS	CA	c	1	267	198	40	63,960	81,648	y	85,730	20	35,509	26,451	74	21,103	1,068	4,279	4,535	4,523
SALT LAKE CITY	UT	c	1	594	439	40	37,565	60,653	y	62,153	6	50,470	45,034	89	29,747	10,196	5,091	642	4,793
SAN BUENAVENTURA (VENTURA)	CA	c	1	188	140	40	60,238	73,221	n	—	—	27,974	—	—	15,008	—	3,057	463	2,911
SANTA CLARA	CA	c	3	187	129	40	92,892	112,872	y	118,524	10	36,871	—	—	24,306	—	—	—	3,977
SAVANNAH	GA	c	1	800	540	40	34,115	50,475	n	—	—	59,721	46,838	78	35,696	5,102	6,040	92	12,791
SOUTH BEND	IN	c	1	320	251	48	41,000	43,496	y	49,546	10	28,897	—	—	17,934	—	2,125	3,201	—
SPRINGFIELD	MA	c	—	—	—	—	—	—	—	—	—	—	—	—	—	—	—	—	—
STERLING HEIGHTS	MI	c	1	223	171	40	45,225	70,154	y	75,654	5	28,925	25,912	90	17,979	2,041	5,891	2,142	871
ST. PETERSBURG	FL	c	1	773	495	40	40,305	60,891	n	—	—	83,532	71,527	86	47,107	16,818	7,601	744	11,709
SUNNYVALE	CA	c	4	280	49	56	80,678	117,268	n	—	—	56,501	—	—	29,299	—	5,865	26	8,655
TACOMA	WA	c	1	419	378	40	57,075	69,077	y	74,603	5	—	—	—	—	—	—	—	—
TALLAHASSEE	FL	c	1	352	352	40	38,065	62,224	y	65,025	13	45,205	—	—	29,633	—	2,693	209	8,899
THORNTON	IL	tp	—	—	—	—	—	—	—	—	—	—	—	—	—	—	—	—	—
THOUSAND OAKS	CA	c	5	—	—	48	—	—	—	—	—	—	—	—	—	—	—	—	—
TOPEKA	KS	c	1	327	273	40	35,838	58,115	n	—	—	27,796	21,775	78	17,296	2,661	1,817	—	6,021
VANCOUVER	WA	c	1	234	201	40	53,016	71,052	n	—	—	30,075	22,995	76	19,391	1,050	2,553	57	7,022
WACO	TX	c	1	328	235	40	40,718	53,924	y	55,124	1	25,997	21,913	84	16,862	3,753	1,297	67	4,017
WEST COVINA	CA	c	1	176	122	40	62,736	76,272	y	81,611	10	26,753	31,427	117	22,458	4,464	4,504	1,439	16,345
WEST VALLEY CITY	UT	c	1	231	186	40	37,800	56,174	n	—	—	18,005	—	—	11,818	—	1,182	44	2,597
WICHITA FALLS	TX	c	1	263	198	40	40,402	55,463	y	—	1	17,331	15,378	89	11,758	2,278	1,342	62	1,891
WINSTON–SALEM	NC	c	1	636	291	40	32,100	68,680	n	—	—	—	45,441	—	30,512	8,660	6,269	160	5,107
50,000–99,999																			
ALHAMBRA	CA	c	1	128	82	40	59,052	71,796	n	—	—	20,993	15,400	73	10,221	3,054	2,125	585	5,008
ANTIOCH	CA	c	1	166	116	40	64,752	78,708	y	84,611	10	25,599	—	—	13,738	—	2,084	—	6,186
BAYTOWN	TX	c	1	180	112	40	39,354	56,620	y	57,820	1	15,768	12,753	81	9,217	2,065	1,471	735	2,280

Table 3/16 continued — POLICE DEPARTMENT PERSONNEL, SALARIES, AND EXPENDITURES FOR CITIES 10,000 AND OVER: 2008

City	State	Type	Service provision	Full-time paid personnel	Full-time uniformed personnel	Duty hours per week	Minimum base salary ($)	Maximum base salary ($)	Longevity pay	Maximum salary with longevity ($)	Years of service for longevity	Total expenditures (A) ($)	Total personnel expenditures (B) ($)	(B) as % of (A)	Salaries and wages (C) ($)	City contribution to retirement and social security (D) ($)	City contribution to insurance (E) ($)	Capital outlay (F) ($)	All other (G) ($)
50,000–99,999 continued																			
BELLINGHAM	WA	c	1	165	111	40	53,220	72,564	y	77,643	5	20,876	14,724	71	11,097	1,924	1,702	321	5,832
BETHLEHEM	PA	c	1	160	154	40	40,324	53,539	y	57,822	4	13,950	—	—	9,588	—	1,655	346	668
BLOOMINGTON	MN	c	1	132	115	42	45,516	70,908	n	—	—	19,336	14,135	73	11,046	1,434	1,654	57	5,144
BOSSIER CITY	LA	c	3	235	177	40	32,796	39,504	y	—	3	16,993	13,937	82	10,593	1,881	1,463	668	2,387
BOULDER	CO	c	1	267	157	40	44,917	66,548	y	—	—	26,442	21,913	83	16,895	1,725	3,292	395	4,134
BOWIE	MD	c	1	32	28	40	41,300	71,242	n	—	—	2,487	622	25	515	40	66	871	994
BRICK	NJ	tp	1	175	130	40	46,369	102,169	y	113,918	5	16,171	18,186	112	13,507	2,420	2,258	—	243
BRYAN	TX	c	1	144	109	40	38,667	58,573	y	59,773	1	12,829	10,309	80	7,744	1,597	968	364	2,156
BUENA PARK	CA	c	1	141	89	40	59,232	75,600	y	79,380	20	22,179	19,441	88	12,556	4,714	2,170	407	2,332
BURNSVILLE	MN	c	1	85	75	40	44,724	63,792	y	69,528	12	10,505	8,245	78	6,496	767	982	214	2,047
CAMARILLO	CA	c	5	—	—	40	—	—	—	—	—	13,070	—	—	178	—	28	—	12,842
CANTON	OH	c	1	188	168	40	38,255	47,311	y	49,111	3	17,867	—	—	10,713	—	—	391	1,878
CARSON	CA	c	1	208	170	40	80,882	85,810	y	95,650	19	—	—	—	—	—	—	—	—
CARY	NC	t	1	199	165	42	36,462	—	n	—	—	15,159	13,030	86	9,991	2,313	726	—	1,501
CHARLESTON	WV	c	1	211	183	other	32,005	32,005	y	39,133	1	15,649	13,864	89	9,968	2,064	1,831	901	884
CHINO	CA	c	3	141	95	40	60,816	73,920	n	—	—	26,034	—	—	12,206	—	2,870	91	6,450
CHINO HILLS	CA	c	5	—	—	—	—	—	—	—	—	—	—	—	—	—	—	—	—
CITRUS HEIGHTS	CA	c	3	131	84	40	53,151	63,781	n	—	—	13,537	—	—	9,715	1,964	1,858	—	—
CLINTON	MI	tp	1	143	110	40	43,843	69,858	y	71,158	5	18,960	16,606	88	10,552	2,300	3,754	245	2,108
COLERAIN TOWNSHIP	OH	tp	1	35	32	42	42,739	58,990	n	—	—	4,100	—	—	2,224	—	538	164	827
CORVALLIS	OR	c	1	80	54	40	45,854	62,675	n	—	—	10,279	7,312	71	5,276	837	1,199	232	2,735
DAVIS	CA	c	1	—	—	56	58,185	70,724	y	—	5	—	—	—	—	—	—	—	—
DAYTONA BEACH	FL	c	1	293	242	40	33,629	56,957	n	—	—	31,742	25,199	79	17,055	5,714	2,429	844	5,700
DECATUR	IL	c	1	162	153	40	—	—	—	—	—	18,441	—	—	11,841	—	2,278	—	1,682
DELRAY BEACH	FL	c	1	224	120	40	42,203	76,357	n	—	—	—	20,298	—	14,629	3,682	1,986	—	—
DELTONA	FL	c	5	—	—	—	—	—	—	—	—	—	—	—	—	—	—	—	—
DES PLAINES	IL	c	1	127	103	40	52,293	72,928	y	75,386	10	15,279	16,481	108	9,570	4,870	2,041	334	1,012
DIAMOND BAR	CA	c	5	—	—	—	—	—	—	—	—	—	—	—	—	—	—	—	—
DOTHAN	AL	c	3	212	141	42	29,340	45,011	n	—	—	28,070	12,256	44	8,469	2,257	1,531	13,725	2,089
DUBUQUE	IA	c	1	101	95	40	43,264	48,048	y	50,450	6	9,457	7,174	76	5,834	147	1,192	1,076	1,207
EAGAN	MN	c	1	87	70	40	46,862	64,605	y	70,429	5	10,845	—	—	7,959	—	1,082	1,804	
EDEN PRAIRIE	MN	c	1	89	65	40	48,693	67,350	n	—	—	9,363	7,989	85	6,639	840	510	500	1,147
EDMOND	OK	c	1	135	112	42	—	—	y	—	4	—	—	—	—	94,530	34,204	—	—
ELGIN	IL	c	1	247	185	42	53,916	74,124	y	75,324	10	29,497	27,542	93	21,874	1,919	3,749	54	1,900
EVANSTON	IL	c	—	—	—	—	—	—	—	—	—	—	—	—	—	—	—	—	—
FARMINGTON HILLS	MI	c	1	167	89	40	44,078	63,460	y	69,806	3	18,893	17,406	92	11,654	3,906	1,846	312	1,175
FEDERAL WAY	WA	c	1	153	124	40	50,832	68,208	y	72,471	15	22,151	—	—	11,807	—	1,860	2,738	4,358
FLAGSTAFF	AZ	c	1	152	101	40	41,233	56,889	n	—	—	14,907	11,596	78	8,625	1,619	1,352	965	2,346
FLOWER MOUND	TX	t	1	107	69	40	48,191	60,977	y	62,177	1	8,759	8,040	92	6,033	936	1,071	2	717
FOLSOM	CA	c	3	121	58	40	57,243	74,696	y	80,298	10	—	—	—	—	—	—	—	—
FREDERICK	MD	c	1	181	139	42	40,106	64,211	n	—	—	—	—	—	—	—	—	—	—
GAITHERSBURG	MD	c	1	51	45	40	44,817	76,980	n	—	—	6,078	5,106	84	3,873	877	355	406	566
GARDENA	CA	c	1	191	80	—	56,640	68,844	y	79,171	5	19,180	—	—	10,588	—	3,887	1,171	—
GASTONIA	NC	c	1	179	154	40	29,796	54,054	y	—	—	13,834	11,362	82	9,330	1,026	1,005	40	2,432
GREAT FALLS	MT	c	1	129	80	other	38,352	—	y	—	1	9,309	7,134	77	5,178	851	1,105	101	2,074
GREELEY	CO	c	1	241	141	40	47,919	67,770	n	—	—	21,114	—	—	18,050	—	—	313	2,751
GREEN	OH	tp	7	29	27	40	42,202	61,444	y	—	10	3,220	—	—	3,100	—	—	125	—
GREENVILLE	NC	c	1	210	170	40	33,000	50,000	n	—	—	18,000	21,500	119	10,000	11,000	500	88	3,000
HAMILTON	NJ	tp	1	—	—	—	—	—	—	—	—	—	—	—	—	—	—	—	—
HAMILTON	OH	c	1	158	125	40	42,058	54,309	y	58,656	5	15,903	13,538	85	9,830	1,862	1,845	454	1,911
HAMMOND	IN	c	—	—	—	—	—	—	—	—	—	—	—	—	—	—	—	—	—
HARLINGEN	TX	c	1	162	125	40	31,800	41,800	y	43,000	1	11,011	8,542	78	6,382	1,337	822	755	1,714
HAWTHORNE	CA	c	1	153	134	42	58,356	81,996	y	91,016	26	27,748	20,419	74	13,966	3,143	3,310	39	7,290
HESPERIA	CA	c	5	—	—	—	—	—	—	—	—	—	—	—	—	—	—	—	—
HILLSBORO	OR	c	1	156	117	40	48,384	60,924	n	—	—	20,380	14,586	72	10,342	2,501	1,743	380	5,414
HOOVER	AL	c	1	215	157	42	40,456	57,595	n	—	—	24,220	17,479	72	13,449	2,124	1,906	2,055	4,686
HUNTINGTON PARK	CA	c	3	107	65	40	50,235	83,130	y	140,725	20	15,657	—	—	9,968	—	3,116	659	1,914
IDAHO FALLS	ID	c	1	124	88	40	37,003	51,043	y	53,690	3	10,442	—	—	6,323	—	—	124	1,028
IOWA CITY	IA	c	—	—	—	—	—	—	—	—	—	—	—	—	—	—	—	—	—
IRONDEQUOIT	NY	t	1	70	58	40	38,004	67,727	y	72,637	4	7,817	—	—	5,463	—	716	164	565
IRVINGTON	NJ	tp	1	211	183	42	37,887	83,150	y	91,465	5	17,727	—	—	17,331	—	—	—	396
JACKSONVILLE	NC	c	1	145	101	42	33,829	69,080	y	71,480	5	11,194	7,877	70	5,915	1,172	790	567	2,750
KALAMAZOO	MI	c	4	301	247	42	46,454	70,412	y	72,812	6	32,355	—	—	20,703	—	—	472	3,157
KENNEWICK	WA	c	1	108	89	42	54,732	63,348	y	71,076	15	14,811	10,621	72	7,874	986	1,759	277	3,914
KENT	WA	c	1	186	130	40	54,444	68,532	y	74,816	30	25,105	18,429	73	13,958	1,812	2,659	248	6,378
KILLEEN	TX	c	3	262	201	40	37,704	55,560	y	57,240	1	18,076	15,690	87	12,353	2,493	843	936	1,451
LA CROSSE	WI	c	1	117	95	other	40,676	48,870	y	59,834	10	10,461	9,612	92	5,828	1,582	2,201	210	640
LA HABRA	CA	c	1	105	71	40	57,262	74,651	n	—	—	14,215	—	—	8,016	—	—	28	2,848
LAGUNA NIGUEL	CA	c	5	—	—	—	—	—	—	—	—	—	—	—	—	—	—	—	—
LAKE FOREST	CA	c	5	—	—	—	—	—	—	—	—	—	—	—	—	—	—	—	—
LAKELAND	FL	c	1	341	224	42	40,011	60,890	y	61,370	10	30,429	—	—	19,057	—	1,657	420	6,845
LAKEWOOD	CA	c	—	—	—	—	—	—	—	—	—	—	—	—	—	—	—	—	—
LAS CRUCES	NM	c	1	248	—	40	38,569	—	y	53,252	20	13,724	7,996	58	1,414	4,574	2,007	135	3,588

Table 3/16 continued POLICE DEPARTMENT PERSONNEL, SALARIES, AND EXPENDITURES FOR CITIES 10,000 AND OVER: 2008

City	State	Type	Service provision	Full-time paid personnel	Full-time uniformed personnel	Duty hours per week	Minimum base salary ($)	Maximum base salary ($)	Longevity pay	Maximum salary with longevity ($)	Years of service for longevity	Total expenditures (A) ($)	Total personnel expenditures (B) ($)	(B) as % of (A)	Salaries and wages (C) ($)	City contribution to retirement and social security (D) ($)	City contribution to insurance (E) ($)	Capital outlay (F) ($)	All other (G) ($)
50,000–99,999 continued																			
LAUDERHILL	FL	c	1	—	—	42	—	—	y	—		13,807	14,221	103	8,713	3,798	1,709	887	1,613
LAWTON	OK	c	3	223	158	40	28,642	44,387	y	47,450	—	16,234	14,029	86	11,100	1,630	1,299	757	1,448
LAYTON	UT	c	1	103	76	40	34,779	58,535	n	—	—	9,115	6,492	71	4,954	745	793	821	—
LEWISVILLE	TX	c	1	202	139	40	49,832	60,537	y	61,737	1	16,299	—	—	10,559	—	1,544	115	2,750
LIVERMORE	CA	c	1	133	91	40	66,822	81,172	y	85,231	5	23,492	—	—	12,771	—	2,787	25	4,355
LODI	CA	c	1	113	56	48	53,114	64,557	n	—	—	13,135	—	—	7,956	—	1,663	439	883
LYNCHBURG	VA	c	1	183	156	40	30,618	57,387	n	—	—	13,225	11,543	87	8,638	2,114	790	17	1,543
LYNWOOD	CA	c	5	—	—	40	—	—	—	—		—	—		—	—	—	—	—
MANCHESTER	CT	t	1	151	110	40	46,530	64,100	y	64,600	10	16,476	14,507	88	10,222	2,531	1,753	370	1,598
MARGATE	FL	c	1	179	114	40	46,846	67,395	y	70,395	10	17,992	16,809	93	11,155	2,813	2,841	287	895
MARIETTA	GA	c	1	167	134	42	34,029	50,773	y	51,073	5	13,004	—	—	10,811	—	—	419	1,774
McKINNEY	TX	c	1	189	132	40	48,292	61,547	y	62,747	1	17,384	13,973	80	10,531	1,926	1,515	1,097	2,315
MEDFORD	OR	c	3	157	100	40	45,737	55,388	n	—	—	16,818	14,365	85	10,161	2,246	1,958	205	707
MIAMI BEACH	FL	c	1	569	396	40	44,000	72,800	y	80,860	25	74,541	58,185	78	41,532	14,193	2,460	160	15,196
MIDDLETOWN	OH	c	—	—	—	—	—	—	—	—		—	—		—	—	—	—	—
MILPITAS	CA	c	1	112	87	40	78,566	95,496	y	109,916	9	—	—		—	—	—	—	—
MINNETONKA	MN	c	1	76	57	42	51,209	64,022	n	—	—	7,589	6,539	86	5,173	692	673	34	1,015
MISSOURI CITY	TX	c	1	96	72	40	41,500	58,100	y	42,460	1	—	—		—	—	—	—	—
MONTEBELLO	CA	c	1	119	84	40	50,904	64,980	n	—	—	15,951	13,321	84	8,676	2,418	2,227	383	2,246
MONTEREY PARK	CA	c	3	109	74	40	59,628	72,480	n	—	—	15,694	—	—	8,789	—	1,422	1,605	2,163
MOUNTAIN VIEW	CA	c	1	171	93	40	80,689	97,984	n	—	—	23,628	—	—	15,804	—	2,629	62	2,592
MUNCIE	IN	c	1	106	106	40	41,971	41,971	y	44,271	4	9,429	—	—	6,070	—	—	156	1,047
MURFREESBORO	TN	c	1	257	210	other	31,200	48,800	y	—	1	—	—		—	—	—	—	—
NEW ROCHELLE	NY	c	1	225	181	other	44,562	75,803	y	76,828	5	29,316	26,343	90	20,102	3,766	2,474	9	2,964
NORMAN	OK	c	1	168	135	42	37,332	53,155	y	53,155	5	14,921	12,510	84	9,346	1,720	1,444	705	1,705
NORTH CHARLESTON	SC	c	1	372	290	42	32,429	45,401	y	—	10	23,527	19,428	83	13,277	2,370	3,781	1,135	2,964
NORTH RICHLAND HILLS	TX	c	1	—	—	40	—	—	—	—		—	—		—	—	—	—	—
OAK PARK	IL	tp	—	—	—	—	—	—	—	—		—	—		—	—	—	—	—
OGDEN CITY	UT	c	1	205	139	48	34,924	47,586	n	—	—	14,187	11,821	83	8,134	2,121	1,565	31	2,336
OLATHE	KS	c	1	217	177	40	35,940	49,186	n	—	—	24,903	20,905	84	16,680	2,409	1,815	131	3,867
OLD BRIDGE	NJ	tp	1	105	—	other	41,606	84,089	y	46,702	5	—	—		—	—	—	—	—
ORLAND PARK	IL	v	1	124	95	40	41,969	70,004	y	71,704	5	15,573	—	—	10,254	—	—	1,063	1,013
PALATINE	IL	v	1	151	112	40	55,288	77,115	y	78,115	8	16,384	14,455	88	10,463	2,296	1,695	369	1,559
PALM BAY	FL	c	1	274	166	40	35,811	57,467	y	—	5	20,571	16,916	82	12,449	2,343	2,123	703	2,952
PAWTUCKET	RI	c	1	189	153	40	44,545	52,234	y	57,849	4	17,988	16,442	91	11,504	2,729	2,209	197	1,349
PENSACOLA	FL	c	1	216	154	40	32,968	56,243	y	61,867	5	17,027	12,728	75	8,981	2,761	986	5	4,294
PETALUMA	CA	c	—	—	—	—	—	—	—	—		—	—		—	—	—	—	—
PITTSBURG	CA	c	1	101	75	40	63,372	77,028	n	—	—	16,949	15,071	89	8,471	4,695	1,904	27	1,850
PLAIN	OH	tp	5	—	—	40	—	—	—	—		1,641	—	—	—	—	—	31	1,610
PLANTATION	FL	c	1	295	187	40	50,826	72,092	y	74,192	10	31,313	28,445	91	19,523	5,003	3,919	998	1,869
PLYMOUTH	MN	c	1	85	70	40	46,446	68,723	n	—	—	9,182	7,230	79	5,739	751	740	19	1,933
POMPANO BEACH	FL	c	—	—	—	—	—	—	—	—		—	—		—	—	—	—	—
PORT ST. LUCIE	FL	c	3	363	307	40	38,608	60,208	y	61,408	10	35,900	28,998	81	20,305	4,285	4,407	1,888	5,013
PORTLAND	ME	c	1	219	165	40	31,975	45,678	n	—	—	13,898	—	—	11,358	—	—	259	2,282
QUINCY	MA	c	1	234	203	40	41,028	51,992	y	42,528	5	19,948	—	—	19,388	—	—	224	336
READING	PA	c	1	—	239	40	51,273	56,823	y	—	3	—	—		—	—	—	—	—
REDDING	CA	c	1	171	121	40	51,106	71,904	n	—	—	24,132	18,205	75	11,847	3,838	2,520	748	5,172
REDLANDS	CA	c	3	147	89	40	54,674	66,456	y	69,779	20	25,492	19,839	78	13,317	4,172	2,350	1,601	4,052
REDONDO BEACH	CA	c	3	154	96	40	54,263	65,982	y	77,859	10	33,878	18,990	56	13,590	3,656	1,743	1,232	13,656
RICHARDSON	TX	c	1	236	144	40	—	—	y	—	1	19,083	18,114	95	13,943	2,903	1,267	16	983
ROANOKE	VA	c	1	325	271	48	31,993	51,190	n	—	—	22,600	18,496	82	13,289	2,993	2,214	62	4,042
ROCHESTER HILLS	MI	c	5	62	60	40	—	—	—	—		8,092	—		—	—	—	—	—
ROCKY MOUNT	NC	c	1	176	70	48	30,369	45,553	y	—	5	10,869	9,565	88	7,285	1,242	1,038	345	959
ROSEVILLE	CA	c	1	188	122	40	50,480	72,690	y	76,325	10	—	—		16,254	—	2,528	—	—
ROSWELL	GA	c	1	194	126	40	35,000	56,690	n	—	—	17,608	13,701	78	10,083	1,614	2,004	993	2,915
ROUND ROCK	TX	c	1	187	138	40	44,096	65,624	y	67,244	1	17,903	14,282	80	10,801	2,107	1,374	1,239	2,381
ROYAL OAK	MI	c	1	110	89	40	39,153	55,228	y	60,750	5	10,947	10,365	95	7,225	1,566	1,573	5	577
SAN ANGELO	TX	c	1	175	140	40	30,960	47,820	y	—	2	12,772	10,485	82	7,782	1,874	829	706	1,580
SAN LEANDRO	CA	c	1	—	90	40	73,607	89,469	y	92,153	1	24,579	15,647	64	8,528	5,689	1,430	53	8,879
SAN MARCOS	CA	c	5	—	—	—	—	—	—	—		—	—		—	—	—	—	—
SAN MATEO	CA	c	1	151	113	40	74,485	88,754	n	—	—	—	—		—	—	—	3,909	3,495
SANDY CITY	UT	c	3	—	—	—	—	—	—	—		—	—		—	—	—	—	—
SANDY SPRINGS	GA	c	1	103	92	42	44,270	58,745	n	—	—	15,687	8,038	51	5,931	1,249	857	3,870	9,710
SANTA MARIA	CA	c	1	152	103	40	61,202	74,392	n	—	—	20,680	18,522	90	13,003	3,438	2,080	93	2,066
SANTA MONICA	CA	c	1	406	216	40	65,192	80,481	y	87,000	5	63,626	—	—	39,709	—	6,557	1,588	5,032
SANTEE	CA	c	—	—	—	—	—	—	—	—		—	—		—	—	—	—	—
SARASOTA	FL	c	—	253	190	—	36,579	65,138	n	—	—	27,774	28,024	101	16,274	7,847	3,902	—	3,082
SCHENECTADY	NY	c	1	207	161	40	29,717	53,141	y	56,994	1	14,750	—	—	13,727	—	—	229	794
SHORELINE	WA	c	5	—	—	—	—	—	—	—		—	—		—	—	—	—	—
SIOUX CITY	IA	c	1	152	126	40	40,497	55,049	y	57,065	5	16,267	13,080	80	8,843	2,224	2,013	58	3,129
SOUTH GATE	CA	c	1	137	89	40	61,845	90,775	y	106,207	5	21,154	—	—	12,173	—	1,770	526	2,365
SPARKS	NV	c	1	165	114	40	47,798	62,271	y	64,771	5	20,221	—	—	11,409	—	2,072	159	3,584

Table 3/16 continued — **POLICE DEPARTMENT PERSONNEL, SALARIES, AND EXPENDITURES FOR CITIES 10,000 AND OVER: 2008**

City	State	Type	Service provision	Full-time paid personnel	Full-time uniformed personnel	Duty hours per week	Minimum base salary ($)	Maximum base salary ($)	Longevity pay	Maximum salary with longevity ($)	Years of service for longevity	Total expenditures (A) ($)	Total personnel expenditures (B) ($)	(B) as % of (A)	Salaries and wages (C) ($)	City contribution to retirement and social security (D) ($)	City contribution to insurance (E) ($)	Capital outlay (F) ($)	All other (G) ($)
50,000–99,999 continued																			
SPRINGFIELD	OH	c	1	148	128	40	39,811	52,000	y	—	5	11,777	10,821	92	7,960	1,426	1,435	30	926
ST. JOSEPH	MO	c	1	164	118	40	32,253	45,863	n	—	—	11,373	9,864	87	6,775	1,904	1,184	542	1,268
SUNRISE	FL	c	1	280	165	40	52,019	73,502	y	79,153	10	27,188	23,527	87	16,516	4,825	2,185	1,894	1,768
TEMPLE	TX	c	1	155	130	40	38,188	53,642	y	54,842	1	—	12,242	—	9,270	1,870	1,102	584	453
TRENTON	NJ	c	1	409	358	40	26,203	66,136	y	—	5	42,501	—	—	34,824	—	—	135	1,346
TURLOCK	CA	c	1	123	80	40	46,992	66,120	n	—	—	20,485	12,786	62	8,318	2,056	2,411	3,901	3,798
TUSCALOOSA	AL	c	1	340	260	40	38,475	51,055	y	51,655	5	24,583	19,539	79	15,373	2,247	1,919	1,212	3,832
TUSTIN	CA	c	1	146	96	40	65,673	80,194	n	—	—	19,654	—	—	11,980	—	2,328	—	2,813
TYLER	TX	c	1	229	177	40	38,563	56,921	y	58,121	1	—	—	—	—	—	—	—	—
UNION CITY	CA	c	1	109	79	40	71,352	85,440	y	89,712	19	18,948	—	—	10,682	—	3,626	2,056	2,472
UPLAND	CA	c	1	125	66	40	57,249	69,586	y	71,326	5	15,181	—	—	7,976	—	420	72	4,514
VACAVILLE	CA	c	1	184	117	40	72,600	88,194	n	—	—	26,710	—	—	16,327	—	4,810	260	2,269
VICTORIA	TX	c	1	146	107	48	39,041	45,088	y	46,288	1	—	—	—	—	—	—	—	—
VISTA	CA	c	5	—	—	42	—	—				—	—	—	—	—	—	—	—
WALNUT CREEK	CA	c	1	107	73	40	70,637	85,821	n	—	—	20,083	17,002	85	10,768	4,507	1,726	—	3,082
WEST CHESTER	OH	tp	1	—	—	40	47,071	61,329	y	—	5	11,598	—	—	6,890	—	1,249	469	1,861
WHITE PLAINS	NY	c	1	254	215	40	51,114	76,657	y	80,073	5	29,795	—	—	28,387	—	—	13	901
WILMINGTON	NC	c	1	305	250	42	31,610	57,816	n	—	—	27,333	16,912	62	13,400	2,027	1,485	6,429	3,992
YORBA LINDA	CA	c	5	—	—	40	—	—				—	—	—	—	—	—	—	—
YUBA CITY	CA	c	3	99	71	40	51,816	66,132	n	—	—	11,513	9,626	84	6,275	2,302	1,049	118	1,768
YUMA	AZ	c	1	248	164	40	42,746	59,845	n	—	—	22,161	17,638	80	13,574	2,412	1,650	952	3,572
25,000–49,999																			
ALAMOGORDO	NM	c	4	116	83	40	32,241	41,569	n	—	—	7,121	5,682	80	3,769	1,140	772	242	974
ALBANY	OR	c	1	87	62	42	43,644	54,960	y	56,052	10	10,384	7,305	70	5,385	644	1,276	118	2,961
ALEXANDRIA	LA	c	1	223	167	—	29,340	68,773	n	—	—	15,194	11,641	77	9,283	1,284	1,073	1,036	2,517
ALPHARETTA	GA	c	1	139	104	42	36,750	66,150	n	—	—	8,532	6,866	80	4,911	938	1,017	929	737
ALTAMONTE SPRINGS	FL	c	1	124	104	40	36,000	52,200	n	—	—	9,612	8,470	88	6,543	1,387	540	634	508
ANDOVER	MA	t	1	73	53	other	43,000	50,564	y	53,092	5	6,517	—	—	5,755	—	—	—	762
ANDOVER	MN	c	—	—	—		—	—				—	—	—	—	—	—	—	—
ANKENY	IA	c	1	56	47	other	38,982	54,852	y	56,852	3	6,189	4,090	66	2,654	812	624	1,527	572
ATASCADERO	CA	c	1	—	—	40	—	—				—	—	—	—	—	—	—	—
AUBURN	AL	c	1	199	189	42	35,654	53,930	n	—	—	7,527	6,520	87	5,435	786	298	330	676
AUBURN	NY	c	1	76	66	other	37,079	54,591	y	—	4	6,041	—	—	4,627	—	—	137	427
AVONDALE	AZ	c	3	160	94	40	47,840	69,264	n	—	—	14,081	10,867	77	8,355	1,363	1,149	436	2,779
BALLWIN	MO	c	1	61	51	40	40,070	59,829	n	—	—	—	—	—	—	—	—	—	—
BARTLESVILLE	OK	c	3	69	52	40	32,614	43,701	y	45,501	5	4,720	3,865	82	2,875	547	443	289	566
BARTLETT	IL	v	1	71	56	40	50,108	70,977	y	74,526	10	9,104	7,840	86	5,630	1,486	724	139	1,125
BELL	CA	c	3	48	37	40	60,708	73,800	n	—	—	6,507	—	—	4,498	—	487	—	827
BELMONT	CA	c	1	44	28	56	—	—	n	—	—	—	—	—	—	—	—	—	—
BELOIT	WI	c	1	99	62	42	37,756	55,004	y	—	0	10,963	9,495	87	5,546	1,507	2,442	479	889
BEVERLY	MA	c	1	72	69	40	48,996	53,853	y	54,953	10	6,522	—	—	5,911	—	—	119	492
BIG SPRING	TX	c	3	—	—	48	32,427	32,427	y	—	1	—	—	—	—	—	—	—	—
BLAINE	MN	c	1	70	60	40	—	—		—	—	7,402	5,866	79	4,559	641	665	488	648
BLUE SPRINGS	MO	c	1	117	83	48	35,651	53,477	n	—	—	—	—	—	—	—	—	—	—
BONITA SPRINGS	FL	c	—	—	—		—	—				—	—	—	—	—	—	—	—
BOTHELL	WA	c	1	78	54	42	53,700	69,660	y	76,626	5	9,959	8,353	84	6,368	708	1,277	6	1,599
BOUNTIFUL	UT	c	—	—	—		—	—				—	—	—	—	—	—	—	—
BROOKFIELD	WI	c	1	83	65	other	48,200	63,353	n	—	—	8,468	7,486	88	5,225	1,341	920	294	687
BROOKLYN CENTER	MN	c	1	54	44	40	44,505	65,448	y	67,752	12	5,454	4,591	84	3,538	486	566	5	859
BROOMFIELD	CO	c	1	195	146	40	44,366	66,768	n	—	—	18,453	16,242	88	13,361	1,408	1,472	49	2,162
BRUNSWICK	OH	c	1	40	39	40	37,794	54,205	y	56,063	4	5,906	—	—	3,101	—	856	197	874
BULLHEAD CITY	AZ	c	1	137	83	40	40,408	58,264	y	59,721	10	12,635	9,953	79	7,577	789	1,587	145	2,537
BURLINGTON	NC	c	1	140	107	40	32,253	53,236	y	—	5	10,083	8,036	80	6,383	767	887	308	1,739
CALEXICO	CA	c	1	65	47	40	47,160	57,336	y	57,576	5	6,641	5,371	81	3,678	922	771	143	1,126
CAMPBELL	CA	c	1	65	43	40	77,355	99,757	n	—	—	11,670	10,347	89	6,788	1,813	1,745	—	1,323
CAROL STREAM	IL	v	1	86	52	40	50,292	72,541	n	—	—	10,723	9,170	86	6,613	1,442	1,115	260	1,292
CARPENTERSVILLE	IL	v	1	82	68	40	51,564	72,852	y	73,652	1	10,162	8,687	85	6,557	1,252	878	135	1,340
CASA GRANDE	AZ	c	1	122	79	40	44,000	129,576	n	—	—	—	10,718	—	6,806	2,932	980	849	701
CASPER	WY	c	1	108	91	40	44,533	54,163	n	—	—	9,677	7,242	75	5,745	580	916	649	1,786
CEDAR FALLS	IA	c	3	46	43	48	36,011	46,912	y	48,292	4	3,844	3,269	85	2,130	581	557	33	542
CEDAR HILL	TX	c	3	83	65	other	42,937	54,800	y	54,800	1	8,065	5,932	74	4,217	820	894	48	2,085
CHELTENHAM	PA	tp	1	113	84	40	54,502	68,128	y	68,528	5	12,299	11,166	91	7,407	1,806	1,952	413	720
CLEARFIELD	UT	c	1	45	31	40	40,955	58,489	n	—	—	3,624	3,015	83	2,185	437	393	91	517
CLEBURNE	TX	c	1	70	55	40	44,999	54,955	y	59,576	1	5,514	4,903	89	3,607	775	521	18	593
CLEVELAND HEIGHTS	OH	c	1	113	104	40	49,611	56,437	y	58,437	5	10,928	10,732	98	7,042	2,439	1,250	—	1,150
CLINTON	IA	c	1	54	46	42	34,985	55,198	n	—	—	5,130	4,265	83	2,870	703	692	—	865
CLOVIS	NM	c	1	77	52	40	32,136	37,253	n	—	—	6,562	4,931	75	3,430	762	738	169	1,462
COCONUT CREEK	FL	c	1	134	89	42	42,633	74,676	y	75,526	3	—	—	—	—	—	—	—	—
COEUR D'ALENE	ID	c	1	86	67	40	51,532	57,865	n	—	—	8,069	7,222	90	5,165	931	1,126	144	703
COLLIERVILLE	TN	t	1	122	88	42	28,286	48,263	n	—	—	8,669	7,441	86	5,388	1,010	1,042	520	708
COLTON	CA	c	1	104	71	40	58,200	70,716	n	—	—	16,433	—	—	8,515	—	—	672	4,347
COLUMBIA	TN	c	3	94	85	40	24,939	38,293	y	40,293	3	6,379	4,886	77	3,780	693	413	355	1,138

Table 3/16 continued **POLICE DEPARTMENT PERSONNEL, SALARIES, AND EXPENDITURES FOR CITIES 10,000 AND OVER: 2008**

City	State	Type	Service provision	Full-time paid personnel	Full-time uniformed personnel	Duty hours per week	Minimum base salary ($)	Maximum base salary ($)	Longevity pay	Maximum salary with longevity ($)	Years of service for longevity	Total expenditures (A) ($)	Total personnel expenditures (B) ($)	(B) as % of (A)	Salaries and wages (C) ($)	City contribution to retirement and social security (D) ($)	City contribution to insurance (E) ($)	Capital outlay (F) ($)	All other (G) ($)
25,000–49,999 continued																			
COLUMBUS	MS	c	3	67	57	42	29,196	32,677	y	—	0	—	—	—	—	—	—	—	—
CONROE	TX	c	3	139	102	40	39,416	53,720	y	54,920	1	11,850	10,278	87	7,617	1,504	1,157	298	1,274
CONWAY	AR	c	1	137	105	40	29,145	39,372	n	—	—	8,042	6,706	83	4,879	1,285	542	442	893
COPPELL	TX	c	1	76	61	40	42,598	62,275	y	—	0	8,333	—	—	4,858	—	511	1,717	706
CORTLANDT	NY	t	7	—	—	—	—	—	—	—	—	—	—	—	—	—	—	—	—
COTTAGE GROVE	MN	c	4	—	—	40	—	—	—	—	—	—	—	—	—	—	—	—	—
CRYSTAL LAKE	IL	c	1	72	61	40	46,134	71,572	y	—	20	7,624	—	—	5,386	—	668	217	1,353
CULVER CITY	CA	c	1	156	109	40	60,002	77,657	n	—	—	27,613	24,137	87	15,508	4,210	4,417	77	3,400
CYPRESS	CA	c	3	70	55	40	60,684	77,436	n	—	—	15,631	—	—	9,691	—	—	1,068	3,270
DANVERS	MA	t	1	59	56	40	41,518	51,185	y	52,208	5	5,028	—	—	4,515	—	—	105	409
DANVILLE	IL	c	1	80	65	42	41,613	52,016	y	60,339	4	8,189	6,436	79	4,486	1,291	659	150	1,753
DANVILLE	VA	c	3	—	137	42	31,842	49,855	n	—	—	—	—	—	—	—	—	—	—
DE SOTO	TX	c	1	86	67	40	43,716	57,132	y	58,332	1	7,036	6,462	92	4,732	1,008	722	378	196
DEER PARK	TX	c	1	78	47	40	42,536	58,531	y	—	—	—	—	—	3,334	431	—	158	515
DELHI	OH	tp	1	31	29	40	46,893	58,863	y	60,363	2	3,216	—	—	1,591	—	324	90	880
DERRY	NH	t	1	72	57	40	40,477	49,873	y	—	5	7,170	6,710	94	5,261	577	872	246	214
DES MOINES	WA	c	3	56	41	56	42,876	71,352	n	—	—	—	—	—	—	—	—	—	—
DODGE CITY	KS	c	1	62	48	40	33,904	43,659	y	44,659	1	4,161	3,480	84	2,331	605	543	137	545
DOVER	DE	c	1	120	—	42	40,673	88,176	y	93,376	9	10,356	10,171	98	7,440	1,409	1,322	321	10,035
DRACUT	MA	t	1	51	48	40	40,195	46,583	y	47,083	—	5,314	5,130	97	3,079	151	1,900	96	88
DUBLIN	OH	c	1	87	65	40	45,341	67,557	y	68,931	4	9,403	8,732	93	6,267	1,128	1,337	63	608
DUNCANVILLE	TX	c	1	68	55	40	45,099	58,383	y	59,583	1	7,550	5,978	79	4,506	971	500	223	1,352
EAST BRUNSWICK	NJ	tp	1	120	93	40	47,377	95,229	y	106,656	5	—	15,859	—	11,813	2,650	1,395	120	1,275
EAST LANSING	MI	c	1	92	62	40	40,061	53,768	y	55,058	5	4,353	4,353	100	2,303	1,199	850	—	—
EAST POINT	GA	c	1	138	125	40	34,500	48,171	n	—	—	—	—	—	—	—	—	—	—
EASTPOINTE	MI	c	1	52	—	40	39,744	57,175	y	—	5	—	—	—	—	—	—	—	—
EGG HARBOR	NJ	tp	1	130	102	other	36,870	78,080	y	81,984	5	11,838	11,158	94	9,659	1,383	116	164	516
ELK GROVE VILLAGE	IL	v	1	127	94	40	53,601	71,504	y	72,329	10	12,530	11,045	88	8,391	1,415	1,238	131	1,354
ELMWOOD PARK	IL	v	1	43	36	40	51,426	64,967	y	70,164	3	4,925	4,494	91	3,024	1,121	348	142	289
EMPORIA	KS	c	1	68	46	40	—	—	n	—	—	4,222	3,318	79	2,691	409	218	72	832
ENID	OK	c	1	124	86	40	28,422	47,005	y	48,605	5	7,463	6,337	85	5,698	567	71	74	1,052
EULESS	TX	c	1	144	85	40	47,962	60,544	y	—	1	8,541	8,031	94	6,126	935	970	150	359
EUREKA	CA	c	1	80	47	42	45,192	54,960	n	—	—	7,846	—	—	4,528	—	1,009	172	1,108
FAIRBORN	OH	c	1	60	43	40	42,661	58,531	y	59,994	5	5,587	4,914	88	3,746	712	455	104	569
FARMERS BRANCH	TX	c	1	106	73	42	47,664	64,877	y	66,377	1	—	—	—	—	—	—	—	—
FARMINGTON	NM	c	1	165	127	40	44,488	50,072	y	54,578	5	8,015	6,541	82	5,111	841	589	84	1,391
FINDLAY	OH	c	1	85	70	40	35,568	51,792	y	—	8	6,647	—	—	4,253	—	796	—	798
FISHERS	IN	t	1	94	82	42	38,528	53,939	y	—	—	5,660	8,727	154	5,551	1,385	1,790	460	2,025
FITCHBURG	MA	c	1	97	88	40	37,793	42,334	y	44,401	5	—	—	—	6,929	—	—	—	615
FLORENCE	SC	c	1	121	110	42	28,015	40,813	y	40,186	25	7,457	6,599	88	4,904	865	829	—	858
FOND DU LAC	WI	c	1	76	71	40	38,967	54,881	n	—	—	8,327	6,848	82	4,778	1,244	825	539	940
FOSTER CITY	CA	c	1	51	—	40	—	—	y	—	—	8,370	—	—	7,192	—	—	—	1,178
FREEHOLD	NJ	tp	1	95	70	40	33,000	90,910	y	95,310	5	11,036	10,484	95	7,694	1,401	1,389	56	496
FREMONT	NE	c	1	50	41	40	33,156	46,644	n	—	—	—	—	—	—	—	—	—	—
FRIDLEY	MN	c	3	45	39	40	40,789	62,691	y	68,349	4	—	—	—	3,279	—	—	—	—
FRIENDSWOOD	TX	c	1	73	56	40	43,243	64,875	y	—	1	5,833	5,052	87	3,735	752	564	30	794
GALLOWAY	NJ	tp	1	92	73	40	39,280	75,246	y	84,087	5	7,918	8,653	109	6,296	1,205	1,152	781	384
GARFIELD	NJ	c	1	—	36	40	25,886	93,465	y	111,532	5	9,373	9,001	96	7,371	563	1,066	163	209
GARFIELD HEIGHTS	OH	c	1	75	63	40	44,316	57,970	y	60,495	5	6,973	—	—	5,123	—	924	—	161
GEORGETOWN	TX	c	1	82	60	40	38,783	57,720	y	61,416	0	7,641	5,790	76	4,388	839	563	626	1,225
GLADSTONE	MO	c	—	—	—	—	—	—	—	—	—	—	—	—	—	—	—	—	—
GLASTONBURY	CT	t	1	75	59	40	53,253	68,574	y	69,074	5	7,980	—	—	5,576	—	—	209	542
GLEN ELLYN	IL	v	1	47	38	40	46,342	71,074	n	—	—	5,626	4,596	82	3,345	825	426	316	715
GOLDSBORO	NC	c	1	107	97	42	33,500	47,858	y	49,772	5	6,978	5,669	81	4,361	751	556	47	1,261
GOOSE CREEK	SC	c	3	71	54	40	29,717	45,218	n	—	—	4,736	3,485	74	2,848	368	268	169	1,082
GRAND BLANC	MI	tp	1	53	46	40	37,176	54,687	y	57,087	6	16,591	—	—	3,354	—	535	1,024	11,421
GRAND FORKS	ND	c	1	94	79	40	36,832	55,248	y	56,268	6	7,400	6,504	88	5,085	930	488	149	746
GRAND JUNCTION	CO	c	1	187	107	40	51,869	62,904	n	—	—	24,950	13,321	53	10,769	1,065	1,487	6,906	4,723
GRANTS PASS	OR	c	—	—	—	40	—	—	—	—	—	—	—	—	—	—	—	—	—
GRAPEVINE	TX	c	1	125	87	40	47,826	61,040	y	62,240	1	10,541	—	—	8,206	1,146	—	—	1,189
GREENACRES	FL	c	4	—	—	42	—	—	—	—	—	—	—	—	—	—	—	—	—
GREENFIELD	WI	c	3	114	59	other	44,684	61,205	y	61,457	5	13,276	7,245	55	5,068	1,236	940	5,373	159
GREENVILLE	MS	c	3	139	94	42	22,500	29,000	y	—	—	8,459	7,081	84	5,709	800	571	128	1,251
GROTON	CT	t	1	74	69	40	46,384	56,410	y	57,370	6	7,987	7,228	90	5,454	419	1,354	148	611
GROVE CITY	OH	c	1	59	59	40	43,160	69,077	y	70,377	5	7,936	7,760	98	5,742	1,078	939	433	822
HALTOM CITY	TX	c	1	97	72	40	45,981	54,657	y	—	1	7,029	—	—	4,726	—	634	116	909
HANFORD	CA	c	3	74	54	40	43,826	52,811	n	—	—	7,293	5,713	78	3,983	1,276	453	233	1,347
HANOVER PARK	IL	v	1	76	52	40	49,317	71,968	n	—	—	9,162	8,124	89	5,771	1,456	897	—	1,038
HARRISBURG	PA	c	4	—	—	40	—	—	—	—	—	—	—	—	—	—	—	—	—
HARRISONBURG	VA	c	1	100	84	40	31,429	57,158	y	—	—	6,816	5,646	83	4,178	885	582	318	852
HAZELWOOD	MO	c	1	78	65	40	43,704	56,815	n	—	—	—	—	—	—	—	—	—	—
HELENA	MT	c	1	84	53	40	36,789	45,611	y	48,190	2	5,371	4,414	82	3,456	479	478	221	737
HENDERSONVILLE	TN	c	1	113	86	42	31,694	48,227	y	50,127	2	7,165	5,936	83	4,475	966	495	482	747

Table 3/16 continued **POLICE DEPARTMENT PERSONNEL, SALARIES, AND EXPENDITURES FOR CITIES 10,000 AND OVER: 2008**

Reported expenditures (in $000)

City	State	Type	Service provision	Full-time paid personnel	Full-time uniformed personnel	Duty hours per week	Minimum base salary ($)	Maximum base salary ($)	Longevity pay	Maximum salary with longevity ($)	Years of service for longevity	Total expenditures (A) ($)	Total personnel expenditures (B) ($)	(B) as % of (A)	Salaries and wages (C) ($)	City contribution to retirement and social security (D) ($)	City contribution to insurance (E) ($)	Capital outlay (F) ($)	All other (G) ($)
25,000–49,999 continued																			
HILTON HEAD ISLAND	SC	t	—	—	—	—	—	—	—	—	—	—	—	—	—	—	—	—	—
HINESVILLE	GA	c	1	105	81	other	31,460	—	n	—	—	—	—	87	—	—	—	—	—
HOBART	IN	c	1	70	55	40	32,048	44,748	y	47,398	1	4,899	4,269	87	3,176	598	494	94	535
HOMESTEAD	FL	c	1	148	105	40	45,323	89,241	y	96,381	5	22,581	14,145	63	9,518	3,043	1,584	2,512	5,924
HOT SPRINGS	AR	c	1	128	98	40	33,697	36,475	y	37,375	1	9,720	7,604	78	5,373	1,518	712	151	1,965
HOWELL	NJ	tp	1	114	97	40	35,028	94,198	y	132,150	5	—	—	—	—	—	—	—	—
HUBER HEIGHTS	OH	c	1	65	47	48	42,711	60,642	n	—	—	6,552	5,412	83	3,788	775	848	297	843
HURST	TX	c	1	120	72	40	56,971	62,379	y	64,899	1	13,434	9,670	72	7,046	1,610	1,013	145	3,619
IMPERIAL BEACH	CA	c	—	—	—	—	—	—	—	—	—	—	—	—	—	—	—	—	—
INVER GROVE HEIGHTS	MN	c	1	41	34	other	44,180	61,380	y	66,905	4	3,935	3,566	91	2,933	316	317	4	365
ITHACA	NY	c	1	89	72	40	38,651	60,461	y	62,011	10	9,956	8,522	86	5,736	1,229	1,556	246	1,188
JACKSON	NJ	tp	1	—	88	40	43,326	98,055	y	121,803	0	13,745	12,886	94	9,595	1,616	1,674	533	326
JACKSONVILLE	AR	c	1	82	70	40	27,592	35,348	y	35,948	3	5,410	4,632	86	3,023	970	638	132	647
JAMESTOWN	NY	c	1	72	63	40	40,868	59,316	y	62,131	8	7,154	6,867	96	4,689	1,514	664	55	231
JOPLIN	MO	c	1	107	97	40	29,719	42,295	y	—	5	8,663	5,184	60	3,785	684	715	592	2,886
KELLER	TX	c	1	80	53	40	45,739	60,133	y	60,133	1	7,221	6,331	88	4,043	1,804	482	727	163
KINGSPORT	TN	c	1	163	105	40	30,408	42,394	n	—	—	9,102	8,082	89	5,889	1,363	829	—	1,020
KISSIMMEE	FL	c	1	251	134	40	37,170	57,450	y	58,050	10	17,714	13,912	79	9,880	2,369	1,662	1,619	2,183
KOKOMO	IN	c	1	150	103	40	45,163	53,292	y	55,892	1	12,495	11,052	88	7,907	1,160	1,983	488	955
LA GRANGE	GA	c	1	95	81	42	35,048	45,885	n	—	—	6,633	4,951	75	3,808	479	663	213	1,469
LA PUENTE	CA	c	5	—	—	—	—	—	—	—	—	—	—	—	—	—	—	—	—
LA VERNE	CA	c	1	68	43	40	59,224	71,987	n	—	—	—	—	—	6,320	—	887	—	—
LACEY	WA	c	3	72	55	42	51,892	67,648	y	70,354	11	8,511	5,875	69	4,754	277	843	94	2,543
LAKE HAVASU CITY	AZ	c	1	121	87	40	44,470	61,360	y	61,860	5	10,283	9,719	95	7,513	924	1,281	564	—
LANCASTER	TX	c	3	—	—	40	—	—	—	—	—	—	—	—	—	—	—	—	—
LARAMIE	WY	c	1	80	50	40	42,263	56,853	n	—	—	6,206	4,597	74	3,451	479	666	603	1,006
LEAWOOD	KS	c	1	81	61	40	36,150	51,584	y	—	4	7,321	6,065	83	4,655	879	530	316	941
LEESBURG	VA	t	1	95	76	40	43,894	72,424	n	—	—	8,811	7,438	84	5,396	1,103	938	576	797
LENEXA	KS	c	1	131	88	40	37,779	56,966	n	—	—	12,660	10,026	79	7,449	1,076	1,500	341	1,294
LEWISTON	ME	c	1	93	82	40	30,943	47,445	n	—	—	5,507	4,934	90	4,096	247	590	114	458
LIBERTY	MO	c	1	56	39	40	35,964	50,340	n	—	—	4,431	3,789	86	2,845	409	535	113	529
LIMA	OH	c	1	102	80	40	37,107	44,470	y	46,509	8	7,779	—	—	4,976	—	1,385	6	490
LITTLETON	CO	c	1	96	71	40	47,521	67,341	y	67,341	30	10,094	8,416	83	6,628	705	1,083	108	1,571
LOMBARD	IL	v	1	92	76	42	49,817	70,193	n	—	—	10,776	9,194	85	6,826	1,692	675	—	1,582
LOMPOC	CA	c	3	68	47	40	51,660	69,240	n	—	—	8,571	—	—	5,223	—	944	153	1,098
LONG BEACH	NY	c	1	77	77	40	44,185	98,954	y	104,254	6	11,608	—	—	10,181	1,890	—	200	1,427
LONGVIEW	WA	c	1	66	48	40	52,144	72,168	y	75,054	10	—	—	—	—	—	—	—	—
LOS ALTOS	CA	c	3	—	29	48	69,342	84,292	n	—	—	7,439	—	—	4,245	—	629	109	1,058
LOS BANOS	CA	c	3	67	45	40	50,412	61,332	n	—	—	8,863	6,832	77	4,056	1,795	981	879	1,152
LOWER MAKEFIELD	PA	tp	1	34	34	40	39,944	66,629	y	—	20	—	3,774	—	2,631	789	354	481	—
LUFKIN	TX	c	1	98	75	40	34,320	43,576	y	43,756	1	7,473	5,882	79	4,387	930	565	304	1,287
LYNNWOOD	WA	c	1	86	71	40	57,325	69,451	y	72,220	5	11,229	9,004	80	6,722	830	1,452	175	2,050
MADERA	CA	c	1	76	58	42	45,504	61,056	n	—	—	8,027	—	—	4,506	—	2,416	61	1,043
MAMARONECK	NY	t	1	41	40	40	44,000	87,000	y	90,000	—	—	—	—	3,800	—	—	—	—
MANASSAS	VA	c	1	116	92	40	40,997	68,474	n	—	—	13,265	9,914	75	7,325	1,501	1,087	368	2,984
MANHATTAN	KS	c	—	—	—	—	—	—	—	—	—	—	—	—	—	—	—	—	—
MANHEIM	PA	tp	1	68	53	40	40,212	66,366	y	69,966	5	7,088	6,032	85	4,050	942	1,040	248	1,056
MANKATO	MN	c	1	71	51	40	45,826	54,742	y	60,216	5	—	—	—	3,819	432	—	—	—
MANSFIELD	OH	c	1	148	96	40	35,208	48,258	y	—	1	12,299	10,511	85	7,497	1,901	1,112	589	1,199
MANSFIELD	TX	c	1	116	71	40	46,075	79,876	y	—	1	9,554	—	—	7,713	—	616	1,144	—
MARION	IA	c	1	47	38	40	35,796	49,728	y	50,928	5	4,382	3,701	84	2,571	649	481	267	414
MARLBORO	NJ	tp	1	94	72	other	43,240	91,418	y	102,845	5	—	—	—	8,524	—	—	585	585
MARYLAND HEIGHTS	MO	c	3	96	78	40	49,730	65,441	y	67,398	4	8,929	8,023	90	6,109	1,082	832	232	674
MARYSVILLE	WA	c	3	82	6	42	48,984	67,872	y	76,017	5	10,482	7,471	71	5,721	716	1,033	—	3,011
MASON CITY	IA	c	1	51	47	other	38,230	48,651	n	—	—	4,473	3,701	83	2,704	687	310	195	576
McCANDLESS	PA	t	1	30	28	40	41,000	69,992	y	73,621	1	3,268	2,887	88	2,267	165	454	94	287
MENOMONEE FALLS	WI	v	1	81	57	40	51,183	61,149	n	—	—	7,135	6,553	92	4,485	1,129	938	100	482
MERIDIAN	ID	tp	1	—	44	40	35,009	55,173	y	56,453	5	4,989	4,434	89	3,240	757	437	—	555
MERIDIAN	MS	c	1	111	93	42	23,281	34,922	n	—	—	8,581	5,503	64	4,048	789	665	25	3,054
MICHIGAN CITY	IN	c	1	109	86	40	39,822	39,822	y	47,786	3	5,659	7,668	136	5,413	1,088	1,168	894	247
MIDLAND	MI	c	1	49	47	42	40,027	61,816	y	66,761	5	—	—	—	—	—	—	—	—
MILLVILLE	NJ	c	1	93	76	40	30,081	61,683	y	66,155	5	8,112	7,872	97	5,625	1,045	1,200	—	240
MILTON	MA	t	1	56	47	40	35,769	50,190	y	—	10	5,804	—	—	5,183	—	—	114	507
MINOT	ND	c	1	81	62	40	33,224	49,321	n	—	—	5,026	4,148	83	3,365	439	343	200	679
MISHAWAKA	IN	c	1	130	102	48	46,465	48,465	n	—	—	9,431	8,918	95	6,326	1,486	1,106	320	193
MISSION	TX	c	1	160	115	40	37,000	37,000	y	38,200	—	10,270	8,983	87	6,649	1,140	1,193	439	848
MOLINE	IL	c	1	110	82	40	41,820	64,576	n	—	—	11,260	9,762	87	6,946	1,415	1,401	—	1,497
MONROE	NC	c	3	90	80	42	31,429	47,819	n	—	—	7,536	6,041	80	4,670	785	585	412	1,083
MONROVIA	CA	c	3	83	54	40	56,395	71,976	y	74,135	5	11,968	—	—	6,153	—	1,148	466	1,816
MONTCLAIR	NJ	tp	1	135	110	42	29,641	81,371	y	89,508	5	—	—	—	—	—	—	—	—
MOORE	OK	c	1	75	69	40	36,247	50,613	y	57,295	3	6,131	5,663	92	4,338	833	492	80	389
MOORHEAD	MN	c	1	68	52	40	41,343	49,523	y	51,504	29	6,480	4,229	65	3,339	446	444	95	2,156

Table 3/16
continued

POLICE DEPARTMENT PERSONNEL, SALARIES, AND EXPENDITURES FOR CITIES 10,000 AND OVER: 2008

City	State	Type	Service provision	Full-time paid personnel	Full-time uniformed personnel	Duty hours per week	Minimum base salary ($)	Maximum base salary ($)	Longevity pay	Maximum salary with longevity ($)	Years of service for longevity	Total expenditures (A) ($)	Total personnel expenditures (B) ($)	(B) as % of (A)	Salaries and wages (C) ($)	City contribution to retirement and social security (D) ($)	City contribution to insurance (E) ($)	Capital outlay (F) ($)	All other (G) ($)
25,000–49,999 continued																			
MOORPARK	CA	c	5	26	23	42	63,894	88,043	n	—	—	5,775	—	—	5,239	—	168	14	355
MOUNT LAUREL	NJ	tp	1	81	55	42	39,370	88,097	y	123,624	10	—	—	—	—	—	—	—	—
MOUNT LEBANON	PA	c	1	60	42	40	48,452	69,101	y	80,010	4	6,861	6,328	92	4,496	967	864	—	533
MOUNT VERNON	WA	c	1	52	41	40	52,678	65,851	y	78,954	10	5,910	4,649	79	3,577	453	619	49	1,212
MUNDELEIN	IL	v	1	48	48	40	54,908	75,145	n	—	—	—	—	—	—	—	—	—	—
MURRAY	UT	c	1	—	—	40	32,656	48,984	n	—	—	—	—	—	—	—	—	—	—
MURRIETA	CA	c	1	134	92	40	60,709	88,686	n	—	—	—	—	—	—	—	—	—	—
MUSKEGON	MI	c	1	91	80	40	33,753	50,556	y	52,056	5	8,284	7,126	86	5,134	1,067	924	65	1,093
NAUGATUCK	CT	t	—	66	54	40	49,981	56,189	y	50,486	—	—	—	—	—	—	—	—	—
NEW BRAUNFELS	TX	c	1	114	92	40	42,934	53,619	y	55,569	1	8,958	7,720	86	5,634	1,133	953	222	1,017
NEWARK	DE	c	1	81	65	40	44,318	61,342	y	62,342	8	7,773	6,906	89	5,232	742	931	119	748
NILES	IL	v	1	78	61	40	54,021	74,203	y	77,057	8	11,872	10,030	84	7,103	1,409	1,518	368	1,474
NORMAL	IL	t	1	89	77	40	41,543	63,912	n	—	—	8,633	7,287	84	5,191	1,342	753	21	1,325
NORTH ANDOVER	MA	t	1	53	46	40	38,033	47,996	y	—	5	—	—	—	—	—	—	—	—
NORTH BRUNSWICK	NJ	tp	1	83	83	40	33,288	85,712	y	102,602	8	13,717	12,990	95	9,401	2,514	1,075	200	526
NORTH CHICAGO	IL	c	1	73	58	40	45,824	66,635	n	—	—	6,959	6,291	90	5,072	735	483	31	638
NORTH LAUDERDALE	FL	c	5	—	—	40	—	—	—	—	—	—	—	—	—	—	—	—	—
NORTH ROYALTON	OH	c	1	42	37	40	49,005	60,590	y	62,590	5	4,818	—	—	2,903	—	667	218	521
NORTHBROOK	IL	v	1	92	65	40	47,802	75,115	y	76,915	5	—	—	—	—	—	—	—	—
NOVATO	CA	c	1	78	56	40	63,670	77,400	y	—	—	12,303	—	—	7,575	—	1,352	74	1,668
NOVI	MI	c	1	97	69	42	45,379	66,061	n	—	—	11,131	9,582	86	6,516	1,935	1,130	451	1,048
O'FALLON	MO	c	1	134	102	40	44,220	60,361	n	—	—	10,949	9,716	89	7,772	1,381	562	525	709
OAK CREEK	WI	c	1	78	57	40	42,320	61,703	n	—	—	8,235	8,545	104	4,888	2,789	866	—	801
OAK PARK	MI	c	4	75	63	42	48,529	69,327	y	71,027	—	10,413	9,827	94	5,862	3,008	957	—	586
OAK RIDGE	TN	c	1	144	130	40	33,238	49,857	y	52,357	5	5,364	4,571	85	3,381	654	536	81	713
OAKLEY	CA	c	5	—	27	—	65,412	81,492	y	85,566	15	—	—	—	—	—	—	—	—
OCALA	FL	c	1	229	147	40	30,957	47,704	y	49,135	1	22,420	16,861	75	11,882	3,035	1,943	1,275	4,285
ORO VALLEY	AZ	t	1	142	107	40	44,075	60,278	n	—	—	—	—	—	—	—	—	—	—
PACIFICA	CA	c	1	50	37	40	67,272	88,296	y	91,824	5	8,293	—	—	4,924	—	—	49	1,033
PALM COAST	FL	c	—	—	—	—	—	—	—	—	—	—	—	—	—	—	—	—	—
PALM DESERT	CA	c	5	—	—	—	—	—	—	—	—	—	—	—	—	—	—	—	—
PALM SPRINGS	CA	c	1	156	156	40	56,304	68,604	y	—	15	19,375	—	—	10,123	—	2,787	—	3,543
PARADISE	CA	t	1	—	—	40	—	—	—	—	—	—	—	—	—	—	—	—	—
PASCAGOULA	MS	c	1	—	—	42	—	—	—	—	—	—	—	—	—	—	—	—	—
PASCO	WA	c	1	70	59	40	51,626	62,525	n	—	—	10,149	6,747	66	5,379	667	700	188	3,214
PEABODY	MA	c	1	109	92	40	44,546	51,228	y	79,678	5	8,783	—	—	8,124	—	—	90	659
PEACHTREE CITY	GA	c	1	62	58	40	33,158	53,396	n	—	—	5,619	4,155	74	2,965	662	528	711	753
PEARLAND	TX	c	1	141	114	40	42,880	59,355	y	—	1	10,830	9,104	84	7,106	1,248	750	586	1,139
PENFIELD	NY	t	—	—	—	—	—	—	—	—	—	—	—	—	—	—	—	—	—
PHARR	TX	c	1	144	92	40	25,000	36,000	y	—	1	—	—	—	—	—	—	—	—
PHENIX CITY	AL	c	1	101	79	42	27,850	45,272	n	—	—	5,414	4,674	86	3,529	556	589	254	485
PITTSFIELD CHARTER TOWNSHIP	MI	tp	1	50	38	40	39,011	56,207	y	58,107	5	4,085	3,480	85	2,595	422	463	224	381
PLAINFIELD	MI	tp	—	—	—	—	—	—	—	—	—	—	—	—	—	—	—	—	—
PORT HURON	MI	c	1	67	51	40	40,974	54,632	n	—	—	7,714	—	—	4,224	—	—	3	924
PORT ORANGE	FL	c	3	93	83	42	34,792	57,040	n	—	—	10,932	6,751	62	5,021	513	1,217	491	3,690
QUEENSBURY	NY	t	—	—	—	—	—	—	—	—	—	—	—	—	—	—	—	—	—
QUINCY	IL	c	1	91	77	40	39,743	54,802	y	55,076	20	8,544	7,664	90	5,519	1,284	860	128	752
REDMOND	WA	c	1	118	80	40	56,784	65,796	y	68,428	5	13,395	—	—	8,603	—	1,466	3,910	2,251
REVERE	MA	c	—	—	—	—	—	—	—	—	—	—	—	—	—	—	—	—	—
REYNOLDSBURG	OH	c	1	70	55	40	41,267	64,958	y	66,208	4	6,698	—	—	4,230	—	808	196	694
RICHFIELD	MN	c	1	51	44	40	48,516	64,403	n	—	—	—	—	—	—	—	—	—	—
RIVERTON	UT	c	5	—	—	—	—	—	—	—	—	—	—	—	—	—	—	—	—
RIVIERA BEACH	FL	c	1	143	109	42	38,469	54,265	y	54,265	0	16,145	12,083	75	8,355	2,707	1,021	465	3,597
ROCK HILL	SC	c	1	—	—	40	31,013	43,410	n	—	—	10,614	7,981	75	5,994	1,117	871	183	245
ROME	GA	c	1	111	96	40	28,000	42,000	n	—	—	7,865	6,220	79	4,673	779	768	461	1,185
ROSWELL	NM	c	1	102	84	42	29,774	45,749	y	—	3	—	—	—	—	—	—	—	—
ROWLETT	TX	c	1	—	—	40	49,192	58,737	y	—	1	8,990	—	—	6,420	—	911	—	881
ROY	UT	c	1	43	38	40	34,486	50,336	n	—	—	3,687	3,054	83	2,222	564	268	362	271
SAGINAW	MI	tp	1	52	47	40	35,989	54,683	n	—	—	5,135	4,083	80	2,846	599	637	136	916
SALEM	NH	t	1	70	52	40	38,075	54,828	y	—	—	7,356	6,706	91	4,905	615	1,186	129	521
SALINA	KS	c	1	104	78	40	37,918	64,834	y	—	5	—	—	—	—	—	—	—	—
SALISBURY	NC	c	1	106	80	42	29,042	54,469	y	—	—	7,229	5,478	76	4,092	693	693	202	1,549
SAN CARLOS	CA	c	3	44	29	40	70,912	86,181	n	—	—	13,281	5,844	44	4,164	1,194	486	39	7,398
SAN JUAN	TX	c	1	48	48	42	32,269	32,269	y	32,365	1	—	—	—	—	—	—	—	—
SAN JUAN CAPISTRANO	CA	c	—	—	—	—	—	—	—	—	—	—	—	—	—	—	—	—	—
SAN LUIS OBISPO	CA	c	1	90	59	40	57,824	78,650	y	—	—	11,739	10,358	88	7,021	2,092	1,246	499	882
SAN RAMON	CA	c	1	75	56	40	76,428	—	n	—	—	13,674	—	—	6,988	—	2,242	192	2,417
SANDUSKY	OH	c	1	49	47	40	31,641	46,245	y	47,870	3	5,957	5,073	85	3,593	665	814	53	832
SEASIDE	CA	c	1	72	44	40	62,741	76,242	y	78,148	10	8,674	—	—	4,303	—	1,163	333	1,605
SEATAC	WA	c	—	—	—	—	—	—	—	—	—	—	—	—	—	—	—	—	—

Reported expenditures (in $000)

Table 3/16 continued POLICE DEPARTMENT PERSONNEL, SALARIES, AND EXPENDITURES FOR CITIES 10,000 AND OVER: 2008

Reported expenditures (in $000)

City	State	Type	Service provision	Full-time paid personnel	Full-time uniformed personnel	Duty hours per week	Minimum base salary ($)	Maximum base salary ($)	Longevity pay	Maximum salary with longevity ($)	Years of service for longevity	Total expenditures (A) ($)	Total personnel expenditures (B) ($)	(B) as % of (A)	Salaries and wages (C) ($)	City contribution to retirement and social security (D) ($)	City contribution to insurance (E) ($)	Capital outlay (F) ($)	All other (G) ($)
25,000–49,999 continued																			
SHAKER HEIGHTS	OH	c	1	96	69	40	41,239	66,185	y	—	7	11,237	9,685	86	7,306	1,192	1,186	114	1,438
SHERMAN	TX	c	1	64	64	40	37,246	50,908	y	52,158	1	—	—	—	—	—	—	—	—
SHREWSBURY	MA	t	1	59	43	other	43,894	50,085	n	—	—	4,110	—	—	3,633	—	—	64	413
SIERRA VISTA	AZ	c	1	101	73	40	42,918	64,388	n	—	—	10,806	7,470	69	5,608	1,175	687	2,812	524
SOUTH JORDAN	UT	c	1	55	49	40	33,197	47,133	n	—	—	—	—	—	2,620	—	—	—	—
SPARTANBURG	SC	c	4	—	—	42	—	—	—	—	—	—	—	—	—	—	—	—	—
SPRING VALLEY	NY	v	1	—	58	40	41,972	87,638	y	93,798	3	7,566	—	—	6,083	—	—	930	187
STANTON	CA	c	5	—	—	40	—	—	—	—	—	7,375	—	—	—	—	—	—	—
STATE COLLEGE	PA	b	1	79	65	40	47,050	58,802	y	65,646	5	7,556	6,326	84	4,909	409	1,007	384	846
ST. GEORGE	UT	c	3	109	101	40	35,052	53,385	y	54,987	10	11,436	7,865	69	5,145	1,562	1,158	1,350	2,221
STILLWATER	OK	c	1	116	76	40	35,693	60,174	y	61,612	5	9,108	7,436	82	5,834	748	854	223	753
STOW	OH	c	1	—	—	40	43,222	56,056	y	56,472	5	5,586	4,891	88	3,570	657	664	7	688
STREAMWOOD	IL	v	1	71	59	40	50,463	68,597	n	—	—	14,925	7,391	50	5,518	936	936	6,737	797
SUISUN CITY	CA	c	1	34	23	40	—	—	n	—	—	3,673	—	—	2,410	631	632	111	858
SURPRISE	AZ	t	3	170	127	40	50,814	71,157	y	74,003	8	33,589	11,323	34	8,667	1,354	1,302	20,037	2,228
SYLVANIA	OH	tp	1	60	44	40	54,246	54,246	y	56,959	5	6,758	—	—	3,744	—	609	165	1,402
TEXARKANA	TX	c	1	100	89	40	33,885	44,296	y	45,496	1	7,943	6,187	78	4,766	818	602	240	1,517
TEXAS CITY	TX	c	1	110	86	40	34,000	52,000	y	—	1	8,420	—	—	5,290	—	969	—	1,370
THE COLONY	TX	c	1	73	52	42	—	—	y	—	1	5,217	4,666	89	3,608	723	334	—	551
TINLEY PARK	IL	v	1	108	77	40	51,625	71,032	y	72,592	5	14,216	12,382	87	9,187	1,616	1,579	860	974
TROY	NY	c	1	154	128	40	36,453	54,089	y	56,089	5	14,580	12,741	87	9,026	2,136	1,579	369	1,370
TRUMBULL	CT	t	1	82	72	other	42,500	60,000	y	98,500	15	7,757	7,161	92	5,765	1,337	59	184	412
TULARE	CA	c	1	101	66	40	45,915	55,810	n	—	—	9,635	8,003	83	5,261	1,562	1,180	54	1,578
TUPELO	MS	c	1	127	115	40	32,618	39,468	n	—	—	8,450	—	—	4,771	—	540	581	2,471
UPPER ARLINGTON	OH	c	1	62	49	40	43,514	68,598	y	71,198	4	6,870	—	—	4,621	—	887	145	297
UPPER DUBLIN	PA	tp	1	48	40	40	47,204	72,621	y	—	5	5,478	4,982	91	3,910	169	902	373	123
URBANA	IL	c	1	68	55	40	48,818	50,232	y	60,814	2	7,779	—	—	4,498	—	338	350	918
WALLINGFORD	CT	t	1	98	76	40	49,788	59,474	y	60,224	5	9,014	7,789	86	6,026	558	1,205	254	971
WALNUT	CA	c	5	—	—	40	—	—	—	—	—	—	—	—	—	—	—	—	—
WARMINSTER	PA	tp	1	55	47	40	42,000	67,549	y	69,549	5	6,821	—	—	4,152	—	1,538	119	935
WARREN	OH	c	1	99	80	40	31,325	44,762	y	—	—	10,100	—	—	5,553	—	1,099	150	1,804
WATERTOWN	NY	c	1	74	70	40	41,579	52,166	y	53,216	6	6,359	5,329	84	3,855	812	662	19	1,010
WATSONVILLE	CA	c	1	85	67	40	65,864	88,264	n	—	—	13,396	9,976	74	6,963	2,239	774	449	2,970
WELLINGTON	FL	v	—	—	—	—	—	—	—	—	—	—	—	—	—	—	—	—	—
WEST BEND	WI	c	1	73	55	40	45,894	57,488	y	58,148	5	6,754	6,275	93	4,272	1,056	947	67	412
WEST HOLLYWOOD	CA	c	—	—	—	—	—	—	—	—	—	—	—	—	—	—	—	—	—
WEST SACRAMENTO	CA	c	1	107	71	40	56,052	68,136	n	—	—	15,111	9,295	62	6,265	2,333	696	3,903	1,913
WEST SPRINGFIELD	MA	t	1	—	80	40	40,147	53,636	y	—	—	—	—	—	—	—	—	—	—
WESTERVILLE	OH	c	1	88	73	40	47,736	68,640	y	70,290	5	9,793	—	—	6,398	—	899	—	1,312
WESTFIELD	MA	c	1	90	79	40	40,833	44,886	y	48,331	5	8,282	7,720	93	5,494	708	1,517	84	478
WESTFIELD	NJ	t	1	68	59	40	36,487	80,486	y	—	—	6,154	—	—	5,561	—	—	152	441
WESTLAKE	OH	c	1	—	52	40	53,827	63,940	y	66,440	5	7,155	—	—	4,579	—	841	222	691
WHEAT RIDGE	CO	c	1	102	73	40	46,934	67,246	n	—	—	—	8,896	—	6,391	664	1,840	85	691
WILDWOOD	MO	c	—	—	—	—	—	—	—	—	—	—	—	—	—	—	—	—	—
WILLINGBORO	NJ	tp	1	86	73	40	38,606	69,928	y	104,381	8	—	9,510	—	6,152	457	2,900	169	372
WILMETTE	IL	v	1	63	46	40	58,902	74,107	y	81,636	5	8,876	14,858	167	7,767	4,727	2,364	227	—
WILSON	NC	c	1	136	114	40	32,896	49,344	y	51,811	—	10,640	7,904	74	5,889	1,010	1,005	371	2,365
WINTER SPRINGS	FL	c	1	90	69	42	32,850	50,015	y	—	—	6,851	5,539	81	4,180	816	542	648	665
WOODRIDGE	IL	v	1	86	60	40	47,860	73,944	n	—	—	7,849	7,521	96	5,769	1,173	578	139	189
YUCAIPA	CA	c	—	—	—	—	—	—	—	—	—	—	—	—	—	—	—	—	—
ZANESVILLE	OH	c	1	72	56	40	29,744	45,838	y	48,415	5	5,702	—	—	3,364	—	939	16	521
10,000–24,999																			
ABERDEEN	NJ	tp	1	42	30	40	39,841	100,812	n	—	—	—	—	—	3,054	—	—	—	—
ADDISON	TX	t	1	66	57	40	43,285	63,939	y	65,619	1	6,601	5,289	80	3,915	627	747	483	829
ADRIAN	MI	c	1	36	33	40	38,752	52,478	n	—	—	2,921	2,390	82	1,735	280	374	99	433
AGOURA HILLS	CA	c	5	—	—	—	—	—	—	—	—	2,689	—	—	—	—	—	—	—
ALBEMARLE	NC	c	1	51	45	42	28,995	47,549	y	49,926	5	3,428	2,855	83	2,133	344	377	105	469
ALBERT LEA	MN	c	1	29	29	40	46,758	52,562	n	—	—	3,407	2,947	87	2,191	281	475	19	413
ALGONQUIN	IL	v	1	—	49	40	47,815	74,740	y	75,674	9	6,496	5,202	80	3,993	816	393	134	1,160
ALICE	TX	c	1	50	36	40	30,264	35,838	y	37,038	1	3,292	2,742	83	2,120	326	296	253	297
ALLIANCE	OH	c	3	40	—	40	37,981	41,933	y	43,253	4	3,794	—	—	2,338	—	587	194	289
ALPENA	MI	c	1	19	18	40	32,323	42,785	y	45,352	8	1,580	—	—	985	—	17	36	227
ALTUS	OK	c	1	55	42	40	27,914	44,691	n	—	—	3,252	2,678	82	2,016	368	294	100	474
AMERICUS	GA	c	1	51	19	42	26,082	36,515	y	—	—	3,122	2,330	75	1,767	212	349	185	607
AMESBURY	MA	t	1	33	31	other	38,548	48,423	y	55,686	10	—	—	—	—	—	—	—	—
ANGLETON	TX	c	3	55	36	40	32,947	40,165	y	—	1	3,208	2,794	87	2,052	371	370	252	163
ANOKA	MN	c	1	34	27	40	43,562	62,231	y	67,832	4	3,604	2,933	81	2,420	289	224	7	664
ANSONIA	CT	c	1	61	44	40	45,950	52,874	y	53,196	—	—	3,925	—	2,629	267	1,028	—	—
ARKANSAS CITY	KS	c	3	35	24	42	31,078	39,770	y	—	3	2,571	2,220	86	1,558	314	347	75	275
ARLINGTON	WA	c	1	33	25	56	51,384	64,680	y	65,880	5	3,670	2,550	69	2,109	319	122	—	659
ARNOLD	MO	c	1	57	46	40	35,818	53,227	y	55,356	10	4,789	4,347	91	3,005	770	571	12	430
ARROYO GRANDE	CA	c	3	27	27	40	52,032	63,264	n	—	—	5,567	4,942	89	3,039	1,288	614	125	500

Table 3/16 continued — POLICE DEPARTMENT PERSONNEL, SALARIES, AND EXPENDITURES FOR CITIES 10,000 AND OVER: 2008

City	State	Type	Service provision	Full-time paid personnel	Full-time uniformed personnel	Duty hours per week	Minimum base salary ($)	Maximum base salary ($)	Longevity pay	Maximum salary with longevity ($)	Years of service for longevity	Total expenditures (A) ($)	Total personnel expenditures (B) ($)	(B) as % of (A)	Salaries and wages (C) ($)	City contribution to retirement and social security (D) ($)	City contribution to insurance (E) ($)	Capital outlay (F) ($)	All other (G) ($)
10,000–24,999 continued																			
ARTESIA	NM	c	3	44	31	40	30,528	45,804	y	48,684	5	—	—	—	—	—	—	—	—
ARVIN	CA	c	1	16	—	48	42,390	54,100	y	—	7	1,765	—	—	994	—	143	92	115
ASHEBORO	NC	c	1	83	77	40	31,940	48,244	n	—	—	5,285	4,038	76	3,286	497	254	249	997
ASHLAND	MA	t	1	31	27	40	42,307	52,809	y	53,809	20	2,616	—	—	2,426	—	—	118	72
ASHLAND	OH	c	1	38	29	40	36,670	44,554	y	45,891	5	3,143	2,797	89	2,112	396	289	23	324
ASHLAND	OR	c	1	38	28	40	45,336	57,595	n	—	—	4,671	3,149	67	2,180	566	402	—	1,523
ASHWAUBENON	WI	v	4	56	46	other	46,748	66,647	y	—	20	7,661	6,750	88	4,814	1,083	853	112	799
ATCHISON	KS	c	1	24	23	40	27,934	37,378	y	38,378	5	1,517	1,345	89	962	195	187	45	127
ATHENS	AL	c	3	54	43	40	27,284	44,129	n	—	—	—	—	—	—	—	—	—	—
ATHENS	TN	c	1	33	31	40	30,156	45,205	y	—	—	2,085	1,622	78	1,247	236	138	212	251
AUBURN	CA	c	1	32	21	42	39,192	98,544	y	113,325	7	4,328	—	—	3,423	—	—	289	—
AUBURN	MA	t	1	48	37	other	38,387	51,369	n	—	—	3,200	—	—	2,898	—	—	54	248
AUBURN	ME	c	1	52	48	40	—	—	—	—	—	3,957	—	—	3,084	—	123	431	319
AUBURNDALE	FL	c	—	—	—	—	—	—	—	—	—	—	—	—	—	—	—	—	—
AURORA	OH	c	3	34	26	40	50,524	60,403	y	62,443	5	3,353	—	—	2,069	—	576	110	203
AUSTIN	MN	c	1	34	31	40	45,594	54,850	y	57,318	7	3,575	2,713	76	2,087	265	360	136	727
AVENAL	CA	c	5	—	—	—	—	—	—	—	—	—	—	—	—	—	—	—	—
AVENTURA	FL	c	1	119	80	40	46,062	68,055	n	—	—	12,980	10,266	79	7,115	1,719	1,432	1,450	1,264
AVON	CT	t	1	43	35	40	53,366	67,554	n	—	—	5,135	4,484	87	3,041	913	530	65	586
AVON LAKE	OH	c	1	34	29	40	49,486	65,837	y	67,487	6	3,991	—	—	2,544	—	375	171	387
BABYLON	NY	v	—	—	—	—	—	—	—	—	—	—	—	—	—	—	—	—	—
BAINBRIDGE	GA	c	4	55	42	42	—	—	n	—	—	3,889	2,728	70	2,149	233	345	468	693
BARRINGTON	IL	v	1	41	34	42	51,128	73,382	n	—	—	—	—	—	—	—	—	—	—
BATAVIA	IL	c	1	52	33	40	54,656	75,362	n	—	—	7,472	6,419	86	4,417	983	1,018	80	973
BAY VILLAGE	OH	c	1	27	23	40	43,116	61,611	y	64,611	5	2,858	—	—	1,956	—	401	21	155
BEACH PARK	IL	v	5	—	—	40	—	—	—	—	—	—	—	—	—	—	—	—	—
BEACHWOOD	NJ	b	1	20	18	40	—	—	n	—	—	1,906	1,720	90	1,471	128	120	50	136
BEACHWOOD	OH	c	1	57	43	40	56,504	69,446	y	70,946	7	7,121	6,286	88	4,601	725	959	127	708
BEACON	NY	c	1	34	34	40	51,739	65,243	y	—	17	—	—	—	—	—	—	—	—
BEAUFORT	SC	c	1	—	—	42	34,889	—	y	—	2	3,983	3,168	80	2,279	433	456	200	615
BEECH GROVE	IN	c	1	35	32	42	—	—	—	—	—	—	—	—	—	—	—	—	—
BEEVILLE	TX	c	1	32	26	40	27,782	30,588	y	—	10	1,506	1,220	81	939	98	182	84	203
BEL AIR	MD	t	1	45	31	40	39,689	44,208	n	—	—	3,594	3,027	84	2,200	417	410	210	357
BELLE GLADE	FL	c	—	—	—	—	—	—	—	—	—	—	—	—	—	—	—	—	—
BELLMAWR	NJ	b	1	—	23	—	45,754	74,589	y	79,064	1	2,903	2,729	94	1,925	277	527	—	173
BELTON	MO	c	1	66	45	40	34,887	46,751	y	—	—	4,471	3,901	87	2,894	481	526	4	566
BELTON	TX	c	1	38	29	40	35,300	41,960	y	—	—	—	—	—	—	—	—	—	—
BELVIDERE	IL	c	1	50	47	42	39,806	60,784	n	—	—	3,870	—	—	2,811	—	54	152	505
BEMIDJI	MN	c	3	32	29	other	41,974	48,934	n	—	—	2,872	2,379	83	1,861	215	302	144	350
BENBROOK	TX	c	1	48	35	40	42,001	56,285	y	57,485	1	4,342	3,933	91	2,948	640	345	98	310
BENTONVILLE	AR	c	1	77	53	40	29,411	47,932	y	47,932	—	5,268	4,394	83	3,342	642	409	167	717
BEREA	OH	c	1	40	33	40	46,605	57,969	y	—	5	—	—	—	2,770	—	567	—	—
BERKELEY	MO	c	3	—	—	40	32,619	40,810	n	—	—	3,261	2,767	85	2,346	173	248	109	385
BERKELEY HEIGHTS	NJ	tp	1	29	27	48	48,109	140,000	y	121,570	5	3,337	—	—	2,820	432	—	—	85
BERLIN	CT	t	1	54	40	40	50,133	71,180	y	71,880	5	5,632	5,187	92	3,860	654	672	241	204
BERLIN	NH	c	1	30	22	40	42,328	48,277	y	50,152	5	2,295	1,994	87	1,264	605	124	18	847
BETHANY	OK	c	1	37	27	40	33,216	51,132	y	—	3	2,782	2,469	89	1,793	372	304	69	243
BETHLEHEM	PA	tp	1	34	34	40	51,958	55,968	y	58,468	5	3,818	3,554	93	2,266	843	444	120	145
BIDDEFORD	ME	c	1	66	46	40	41,933	54,683	y	—	—	4,869	4,311	89	3,394	349	567	124	434
BIRMINGHAM	MI	c	3	47	35	40	39,287	62,687	y	68,956	5	6,028	5,270	87	3,647	681	941	77	681
BIXBY	OK	c	1	34	21	40	30,565	36,050	y	36,050	—	2,081	1,664	80	1,229	173	261	168	248
BLOOMINGDALE	IL	v	1	65	48	40	48,422	71,254	y	—	8	7,043	6,397	91	4,769	814	813	209	438
BLYTHE	CA	c	1	41	27	40	49,525	66,602	y	69,852	5	4,846	4,289	88	2,640	963	685	8	550
BOONE	IA	c	1	25	16	40	37,389	45,487	n	—	—	1,843	1,495	81	947	250	298	79	269
BOONE	NC	t	1	35	35	42	32,117	48,176	y	48,176	12	2,393	1,992	83	1,611	199	182	83	318
BORGER	TX	c	1	26	26	40	31,800	36,491	y	—	1	2,041	1,726	85	1,288	228	210	57	258
BOULDER CITY	NV	c	1	44	33	40	49,920	66,456	n	—	—	4,509	3,769	84	2,562	712	494	85	656
BOURNE	MA	t	1	45	45	40	36,587	53,760	y	—	10	—	—	—	2,663	—	—	107	253
BRAINERD	MN	c	1	37	26	40	—	—	y	—	8	2,910	2,374	82	1,799	230	345	161	375
BRECKSVILLE	OH	c	1	36	29	40	50,011	65,858	y	69,608	2	3,411	—	—	2,834	331	—	167	79
BRENTWOOD	PA	b	1	14	—	40	67,000	67,000	y	—	—	1,467	—	—	1,006	—	—	188	—
BRENTWOOD	TN	c	1	61	58	40	32,531	52,748	y	—	5	—	—	—	—	—	—	—	—
BRIDGETON	MO	c	1	66	53	40	37,086	54,142	n	—	—	5,880	5,240	89	3,708	769	763	167	472
BRIDGETON	NJ	c	1	—	17	40	34,611	67,307	y	71,009	5	6,088	6,088	100	4,712	676	700	—	—
BRIGHAM CITY	UT	c	1	30	25	40	30,181	51,736	n	—	—	2,494	1,959	79	1,340	348	270	49	575
BRIGHTON	CO	c	3	—	58	40	44,304	60,696	n	—	—	6,527	—	—	4,129	—	669	431	957
BRISTOL	RI	t	1	—	39	40	43,030	56,227	y	60,724	5	3,062	4,590	150	2,731	964	895	238	332
BROOK PARK	OH	c	4	—	—	40	—	—	—	—	—	—	—	—	—	—	—	—	—
BROOKINGS	SD	c	3	37	28	40	36,628	44,553	y	46,533	5	2,642	2,361	89	1,705	248	407	92	188
BROWNSVILLE	TN	t	1	36	28	40	26,280	32,080	n	—	—	1,056	—	—	932	—	64	40	124
BUCKINGHAM	PA	tp	1	24	22	42	36,789	67,552	y	—	20	3,119	2,272	73	1,481	326	465	126	717
BUENA VISTA	MI	tp	1	18	16	42	32,985	47,840	n	—	—	—	—	—	—	—	—	—	—
BUFORD	GA	c	—	—	—	—	—	—	—	—	—	—	—	—	—	—	—	—	—

Table 3/16 continued   POLICE DEPARTMENT PERSONNEL, SALARIES, AND EXPENDITURES FOR CITIES 10,000 AND OVER: 2008

City	State	Type	Service provision	Full-time paid personnel	Full-time uniformed personnel	Duty hours per week	Minimum base salary ($)	Maximum base salary ($)	Longevity pay	Maximum salary with longevity ($)	Years of service for longevity	Total expenditures (A) ($)	Total personnel expenditures (B) ($)	(B) as % of (A)	Salaries and wages (C) ($)	City contribution to retirement and social security (D) ($)	City contribution to insurance (E) ($)	Capital outlay (F) ($)	All other (G) ($)
10,000–24,999 continued																			
BURLESON	TX	c	1	71	54	40	44,572	57,944	y	59,144	1	5,731	4,814	84	3,762	637	414	183	734
BUTLER	PA	tp	1	—	21	40	30,000	59,037	y	—	—	—	—	—	1,532	—	—	310	75
CADILLAC	MI	c	1	17	15	42	39,769	44,406	y	—	—	—	—	—	—	—	—	—	—
CALABASAS	CA	c	—	—	—	—	—	—	—	—	—	—	—	—	—	—	—	—	—
CALHOUN	GA	c	1	53	45	42	32,234	37,969	n	—	—	—	—	—	—	—	—	—	—
CALLAWAY	FL	c	—	—	—	—	—	—	—	—	—	—	—	—	—	—	—	—	—
CALN	PA	tp	1	19	17	42	45,720	65,314	y	68,114	5	2,068	—	—	1,441	—	436	25	77
CAMAS	WA	c	1	31	25	42	54,552	65,148	y	77,503	6	4,772	3,689	77	3,142	192	355	65	1,018
CAMBRIDGE	OH	c	1	27	24	40	36,212	40,227	y	41,475	5	—	—	—	1,391	—	—	—	—
CAMDEN	AR	c	1	34	19	56	24,232	25,210	n	—	—	1,488	1,171	79	947	26	197	57	260
CANANDAIGUA	NY	c	1	30	26	other	42,094	52,885	y	53,910	5	2,774	2,504	90	1,875	367	262	85	185
CANBY	OR	c	1	28	23	40	49,332	59,964	y	62,962	5	—	3,471	—	2,754	269	448	150	292
CANON CITY	CO	c	3	49	36	40	32,541	52,333	y	53,333	5	3,684	3,022	82	2,358	243	420	174	488
CANTON	MA	t	1	43	42	40	38,521	49,870	y	50,670	5	4,693	—	—	3,289	—	478	239	261
CANYON	TX	c	1	—	—	40	—	—	—	—	—	—	—	—	—	—	—	—	—
CAPITOLA	CA	c	3	32	22	40	56,244	71,772	n	—	—	5,606	3,640	65	2,461	934	245	127	1,839
CARBONDALE	IL	c	1	82	64	40	37,333	48,817	y	54,079	15	6,547	5,623	86	3,915	1,046	662	107	817
CARPINTERIA	CA	c	5	—	—	—	—	—	—	—	—	—	—	—	—	—	—	—	—
CARRBORO	NC	t	1	42	39	42	34,898	54,091	y	—	5	—	—	—	—	—	—	—	—
CARROLL	IA	c	1	16	15	40	32,458	40,572	y	41,172	5	2,001	1,040	52	689	190	160	857	104
CARTERET	NJ	b	1	74	64	40	36,346	76,437	y	85,609	5	7,986	—	—	5,198	—	1,805	100	162
CASCADE CHARTER	MI	tp	—	—	—	40	—	—	—	—	—	661	—	—	636	—	—	—	25
CASSELBERRY	FL	c	1	66	66	40	34,875	—	n	—	—	5,848	4,803	82	3,420	843	539	14	1,031
CAYCE	SC	c	4	63	54	42	28,374	42,970	n	—	—	3,531	2,846	81	2,371	403	71	117	568
CEDAR CITY	UT	c	1	41	34	40	32,670	48,826	n	—	—	3,585	2,666	74	1,681	479	505	352	567
CENTERVILLE	OH	c	1	54	40	40	47,195	66,456	y	66,936	6	5,707	—	—	3,596	—	552	98	783
CENTERVILLE	UT	c	1	21	17	42	34,916	58,698	n	—	—	1,850	1,465	79	954	299	211	177	209
CENTRAL POINT	OR	c	1	28	23	48	41,340	50,244	n	—	—	3,326	2,912	88	1,559	984	368	379	35
CENTRALIA	IL	c	1	36	27	40	37,706	40,606	y	48,728	—	2,501	2,158	86	1,441	439	277	68	275
CENTRALIA	WA	c	3	35	28	42	50,340	59,820	y	61,914	6	4,313	3,140	73	2,482	175	482	125	1,048
CHAMBERSBURG	PA	b	1	37	33	40	40,914	53,872	y	53,872	1	3,917	3,287	84	2,113	627	547	89	540
CHAMPLIN	MN	c	1	30	26	40	40,930	63,169	y	68,854	16	—	2,370	—	1,921	249	200	—	—
CHANHASSEN	MN	c	5	—	—	40	—	—	—	—	—	—	—	—	—	—	—	—	—
CHARLESTON	IL	c	1	37	31	42	33,396	56,292	y	—	1	2,509	—	—	1,967	—	179	111	251
CHARLTON	MA	t	1	22	17	40	44,774	53,724	y	53,924	11	2,359	2,183	93	1,746	218	218	—	176
CHICKASHA	OK	c	1	38	29	40	25,225	35,672	y	37,352	4	2,290	2,051	90	1,393	234	423	7	233
CHILLICOTHE	OH	c	1	52	47	40	32,344	41,662	y	43,062	2	5,028	4,242	84	2,680	651	910	196	590
CHRISTIANSBURG	VA	t	1	68	51	40	33,971	43,782	y	—	—	4,317	3,390	79	2,522	527	340	274	653
CIRCLEVILLE	OH	c	1	31	24	40	31,054	41,308	y	42,808	5	2,708	—	—	1,549	—	284	127	334
CLAREMORE	OK	c	1	53	37	40	35,096	44,540	n	—	—	3,722	3,068	82	2,119	557	392	161	493
CLARKSBURG	WV	c	1	—	42	40	27,753	30,217	y	—	2	3,297	2,562	78	1,632	624	305	188	547
CLAWSON	MI	c	1	18	17	40	39,506	59,064	n	—	—	2,218	1,836	83	1,195	348	292	53	1,523
CLAYTON	CA	c	3	12	10	40	52,596	63,924	n	—	—	1,890	1,540	81	998	360	181	87	263
CLAYTON	MO	c	1	55	50	40	43,860	61,869	n	—	—	4,914	4,306	88	3,246	697	362	70	538
CLAYTON	OH	c	1	14	14	42	36,594	55,041	n	—	—	1,630	1,386	85	982	181	223	7	236
CLEARLAKE	CA	c	3	29	21	40	34,690	48,811	y	—	—	3,517	2,774	79	1,677	531	566	159	667
CLEMMONS	NC	v	5	—	—	—	—	—	—	—	—	726	—	—	—	—	—	—	726
CLINTON	MS	c	1	72	48	42	24,969	41,271	n	—	—	3,934	3,043	77	2,259	439	345	147	743
CLINTON	NJ	tp	1	27	24	other	44,087	83,777	y	96,441	5	3,033	2,739	90	2,159	313	266	96	199
CLINTON	UT	c	3	19	17	40	35,901	52,312	n	—	—	1,578	1,199	76	771	229	199	29	349
CLIVE	IA	c	1	27	24	40	41,325	56,472	n	—	—	2,918	—	—	1,536	—	340	297	—
COCOA	FL	c	1	71	67	40	36,433	51,457	n	—	—	6,372	5,016	79	3,560	736	720	547	809
COHOES	NY	c	1	48	35	40	39,810	55,475	y	58,475	5	2,700	—	—	—	—	408	389	—
COLCHESTER	VT	t	1	27	26	40	—	—	—	—	—	2,510	2,189	87	1,567	215	407	57	264
COLDWATER	MI	c	1	19	—	40	—	—	y	—	5	1,675	1,436	86	1,153	99	183	50	189
COLLEGE PARK	MD	c	—	—	—	—	—	—	—	—	—	—	—	—	—	—	—	—	—
COLLINSVILLE	IL	c	1	54	40	40	54,662	54,662	y	60,694	2	5,746	4,818	84	3,508	637	673	226	702
CONCORD	MA	t	1	43	35	40	38,725	50,799	y	52,799	20	3,461	—	—	3,224	—	—	101	136
CONNERSVILLE	IN	c	1	33	31	40	33,380	39,360	y	42,860	1	2,783	2,646	95	1,732	292	622	8	129
CONWAY	SC	c	1	71	58	42	30,341	45,512	y	—	—	3,787	3,118	82	2,207	386	525	191	478
CONYERS	GA	c	1	—	49	40	33,040	46,491	y	46,491	8	2,812	2,684	95	2,129	321	234	23	105
COOS BAY	OR	c	3	34	23	40	40,812	52,092	y	55,738	15	—	2,906	—	1,890	552	464	—	—
COPLEY	OH	tp	1	22	20	40	44,266	58,450	y	—	3	2,467	2,127	86	1,669	138	320	97	243
CORALVILLE	IA	c	1	34	31	40	38,219	54,073	y	—	—	3,025	2,493	82	1,810	289	394	59	473
CORCORAN	CA	c	1	32	19	40	37,068	45,252	y	—	—	2,806	2,227	79	1,483	475	269	71	508
CORNELIUS	NC	t	1	—	—	42	21,866	48,075	y	—	—	3,040	2,118	70	1,647	258	213	56	867
CORNING	NY	c	1	27	23	40	34,198	53,388	y	55,513	10	10,803	3,371	31	1,071	2,024	276	27	154
COSHOCTON	OH	c	5	—	—	—	—	—	—	—	—	—	—	—	—	—	—	—	—
COVENTRY	CT	t	1	19	14	40	50,710	61,526	y	63,026	3	2,075	1,757	85	1,201	276	280	138	181
COVINGTON	GA	c	1	64	56	42	28,234	46,420	n	—	—	5,335	3,761	71	2,912	430	419	138	1,440
CRANBERRY	PA	tp	1	31	28	42	45,015	68,873	y	76,313	6	2,125	—	—	1,596	443	—	198	—
CRAWFORDSVILLE	IN	c	1	66	32	40	39,115	52,471	y	52,471	1	3,128	2,687	86	2,007	345	334	96	345
CRESTVIEW	FL	c	1	—	63	40	26,624	—	y	60,879	—	—	—	—	3,301	—	—	—	—

Table 3/16 continued

POLICE DEPARTMENT PERSONNEL, SALARIES, AND EXPENDITURES FOR CITIES 10,000 AND OVER: 2008

City	State	Type	Service provision	Full-time paid personnel	Full-time uniformed personnel	Duty hours per week	Minimum base salary ($)	Maximum base salary ($)	Longevity pay	Maximum salary with longevity ($)	Years of service for longevity	Total expenditures (A) ($)	Total personnel expenditures (B) ($)	(B) as % of (A)	Salaries and wages (C) ($)	City contribution to retirement and social security (D) ($)	City contribution to insurance (E) ($)	Capital outlay (F) ($)	All other (G) ($)
10,000–24,999 continued																			
CRESTWOOD	MO	c	1	38	29	40	45,963	57,326	n	—	—	2,980	2,487	83	1,920	294	272	87	407
CROMWELL	CT	t	1	34	25	42	45,310	61,450	n	—	—	3,152	—	—	2,486	358	—	85	224
CROWN POINT	IN	c	1	50	37	40	38,840	50,146	y	50,606	—	3,972	3,409	86	2,617	434	357	228	336
CRYSTAL	MN	c	1	—	—	40	40,500	62,267	y	67,872	16	3,795	2,870	76	2,257	305	307	171	714
CULLMAN	AL	c	1	57	57	40	25,865	36,421	n	—	—	5,013	3,743	75	2,902	460	380	437	834
CUMBERLAND	MD	c	1	56	51	40	33,864	41,297	y	41,297	25	4,316	3,773	87	2,444	546	783	150	693
CUMRU	PA	tp	1	25	22	40	63,210	69,013	y	69,203	3	3,015	2,788	92	1,948	394	445	88	139
DALLAS	OR	c	1	22	18	40	47,316	55,344	n	—	—	2,545	1,905	75	1,274	343	287	88	552
DAPHNE	AL	t	1	75	44	42	34,407	53,540	n	—	—	4,664	3,641	78	2,711	374	555	267	756
DARIEN	IL	c	3	—	40	40	42,436	66,433	n	—	—	—	—	—	—	—	—	—	—
DE BARY	FL	c	5	—	—	48	—	—	—	—	—	2,326	—	—	—	—	—	—	—
DE LAND	FL	c	1	79	60	42	31,602	45,824	y	46,424	8	6,990	5,273	75	3,709	1,002	561	229	1,488
DEERFIELD	IL	v	1	52	39	40	54,270	75,062	y	80,316	9	7,438	6,401	86	4,667	928	806	214	822
DEFIANCE	OH	c	3	28	28	40	35,168	48,163	y	—	5	3,130	—	—	1,622	—	452	87	662
DEMING	NM	c	1	40	34	42	33,320	42,392	y	45,411	8	2,787	1,852	66	1,445	233	173	62	873
DENISON	TX	c	1	55	40	42	37,998	46,987	y	48,487	1	3,742	3,400	91	2,517	503	379	—	342
DERRY	PA	tp	1	45	38	40	43,923	60,215	y	67,980	5	5,316	4,681	88	3,308	752	620	88	547
DESTIN	FL	c	—	—	—	40	—	—	—	—	—	—	—	—	—	—	—	—	—
DEWITT	MI	tp	1	16	15	40	37,309	51,153	y	52,653	10	1,402	—	—	838	—	—	62	112
DICKINSON	TX	c	1	41	36	48	31,345	39,707	y	40,187	1	3,557	—	—	2,618	—	61	22	640
DICKSON	TN	t	1	50	44	40	26,125	39,690	y	41,190	3	3,213	2,817	88	1,973	502	341	91	306
DINUBA	CA	c	1	50	38	40	49,728	60,444	n	—	—	4,952	—	—	2,976	—	566	80	731
DIXON	CA	c	3	32	26	40	49,488	63,156	n	—	—	3,948	3,289	83	2,205	759	324	3	656
DORAL	FL	c	1	—	93	40	44,500	68,500	n	—	—	—	—	—	—	—	—	—	—
DOUGLAS	GA	c	1	39	33	42	27,343	40,691	n	—	—	2,405	2,133	89	1,453	316	363	2	272
DOVER	NJ	t	1	41	36	40	44,122	82,138	n	—	—	3,321	—	—	3,119	—	—	27	174
DOVER	OH	c	1	22	21	40	45,198	45,198	y	—	7	1,914	—	—	1,227	—	297	—	389
DOVER	PA	tp	—	—	—	—	—	—	—	—	—	—	—	—	—	—	—	—	—
DOYLESTOWN	PA	tp	1	24	22	other	41,381	66,789	y	—	1	3,033	2,585	85	1,813	363	408	123	325
DUMAS	TX	c	1	28	24	42	32,585	59,218	y	60,178	1	1,878	1,442	77	1,129	201	111	71	322
DUNCAN	OK	c	1	46	42	42	30,653	32,185	y	33,865	3	3,450	2,542	74	2,225	76	241	197	711
DUNKIRK	NY	c	1	34	33	40	47,098	62,047	y	—	2	4,067	3,873	95	2,879	594	399	4,067	194
DURANT	OK	c	3	46	33	40	29,914	42,269	y	44,911	1	2,946	2,507	85	1,794	330	383	122	317
DURHAM	NH	t	1	21	19	40	37,220	48,825	n	—	—	2,104	1,917	91	1,452	176	289	—	206
EASLEY	SC	c	1	54	42	42	30,223	—	n	—	—	4,014	—	—	3,052	777	185	283	125
EAST GRAND RAPIDS	MI	c	4	32	29	56	46,469	56,117	y	57,117	5	3,816	3,409	89	2,167	622	620	32	375
EAST GREENWICH	RI	t	1	33	33	42	45,786	51,948	y	57,142	3	—	—	—	—	—	—	—	—
EAST HAMPTON	CT	t	1	17	15	40	47,720	65,763	y	66,388	5	—	—	—	—	—	—	—	—
EAST LAMPETER	PA	tp	1	44	40	40	40,948	60,734	y	83,052	4	4,201	3,659	87	2,502	573	584	174	368
EAST LIVERPOOL	OH	c	1	18	17	40	26,644	41,579	y	42,479	5	1,589	—	—	1,035	—	223	—	136
EAST LONGMEADOW	MA	t	1	25	23	40	46,525	49,455	y	51,705	10	2,063	—	—	1,962	—	—	—	101
EAST PEORIA	IL	c	1	40	37	40	33,592	63,745	y	70,119	3	—	—	—	2,440	—	—	—	—
EAST ROCKAWAY	NY	v	—	—	—	—	—	—	—	—	—	—	—	—	—	—	—	—	—
EASTHAMPTON	MA	t	1	33	27	40	39,472	44,047	n	—	—	1,999	—	—	1,902	—	—	97	—
EASTON	MA	t	1	38	31	40	41,350	54,409	y	54,809	5	3,290	—	—	2,904	—	—	89	298
EATONTOWN	NJ	b	1	56	38	40	45,175	95,548	y	105,103	5	5,599	5,126	92	4,260	587	278	295	178
EDEN	NC	c	1	55	46	42	30,276	53,105	n	—	—	4,083	3,193	78	2,295	436	461	279	611
EL CAMPO	TX	c	1	33	26	42	33,750	48,119	y	—	0	1,810	1,414	78	1,187	205	21	75	321
EL CERRITO	CA	c	1	51	42	40	60,526	94,164	y	100,755	7	7,546	6,156	82	3,958	1,361	836	60	1,330
EL DORADO	KS	c	3	28	25	48	26,669	38,394	y	39,354	5	1,674	1,443	86	1,134	153	156	—	230
EL RENO	OK	c	1	41	27	40	29,432	41,122	y	43,522	3	2,428	1,754	72	1,339	230	184	362	312
ELIZABETH	PA	tp	1	12	—	40	—	25,851	y	54,621	—	1,267	976	77	805	119	52	—	291
ELIZABETH CITY	NC	c	1	71	59	40	33,446	41,335	y	—	—	4,891	3,596	74	2,699	558	339	237	1,058
ELIZABETHTOWN	PA	b	1	18	16	40	38,935	59,900	y	—	5	1,594	1,847	116	1,296	258	292	73	225
ELKO	NV	c	3	46	40	other	44,786	56,678	y	58,178	8	4,674	3,796	81	2,616	734	446	167	711
ELKTON	MD	t	1	48	36	42	38,002	53,501	n	—	—	—	—	—	—	—	—	—	—
ELMWOOD PARK	NJ	b	1	44	42	40	25,010	100,795	y	108,856	3	5,762	—	—	4,461	—	335	—	210
ENDICOTT	NY	v	1	35	—	40	33,176	54,577	n	—	—	4,346	3,751	86	2,403	583	765	154	441
ENNIS	TX	c	3	40	34	40	38,314	47,902	y	49,488	1	3,305	2,761	84	1,978	381	403	241	302
ENTERPRISE	AL	c	3	88	53	42	24,814	37,502	y	38,702	10	—	3,042	—	2,387	310	345	—	—
ESCANABA	MI	c	4	44	34	42	41,387	51,761	y	52,161	5	4,106	3,631	88	2,457	660	514	49	425
EUSTIS	FL	c	1	56	44	42	31,953	48,706	—	—	—	4,462	3,760	84	2,620	702	438	320	381
EVANSTON	WY	c	1	89	28	40	36,345	52,639	n	—	—	2,523	2,090	83	1,510	255	325	137	296
EVERGREEN PARK	IL	v	1	69	58	40	44,791	71,060	y	—	15	—	—	—	—	—	—	—	—
EXETER	PA	tp	1	34	32	42	60,235	65,717	y	—	3	4,049	3,510	87	2,659	206	644	137	402
FAIRFAX	VA	c	1	74	61	42	48,368	71,462	y	75,035	15	11,064	—	—	7,351	—	—	—	1,075
FAIRHAVEN	MA	t	1	46	37	48	43,493	64,147	y	65,147	5	—	—	—	—	—	—	—	—
FAIRMONT	MN	c	1	19	17	40	54,107	55,307	y	57,047	4	2,195	1,806	82	1,235	359	213	15	334
FAIRVIEW HEIGHTS	IL	c	1	50	40	42	51,828	55,512	y	68,649	3	4,475	—	—	3,299	—	—	—	360
FALLS CHURCH	VA	c	1	54	33	40	42,913	83,426	n	—	—	—	—	—	—	—	—	—	—
FARIBAULT	MN	c	1	41	33	40	—	55,390	y	57,606	5	3,887	3,037	78	2,416	300	320	43	808
FARMINGTON	MI	c	4	30	23	40	41,497	62,689	y	64,439	4	2,965	2,649	89	1,902	376	371	91	225
FARMINGTON	MN	c	1	27	24	40	47,840	56,618	y	—	7	3,172	2,300	73	1,810	239	250	143	729

Table 3/16 continued — POLICE DEPARTMENT PERSONNEL, SALARIES, AND EXPENDITURES FOR CITIES 10,000 AND OVER: 2008

City	State	Type	Service provision	Full-time paid personnel	Full-time uniformed personnel	Duty hours per week	Minimum base salary ($)	Maximum base salary ($)	Longevity pay	Maximum salary with longevity ($)	Years of service for longevity	Total expenditures (A) ($)	Total personnel expenditures (B) ($)	(B) as % of (A)	Salaries and wages (C) ($)	City contribution to retirement and social security (D) ($)	City contribution to insurance (E) ($)	Capital outlay (F) ($)	All other (G) ($)
10,000–24,999 continued																			
FARMINGTON	MO	c	1	32	24	40	28,458	35,139	n	—	—	1,922	1,587	83	1,148	188	251	110	225
FARMINGTON	UT	c	1	16	13	40	34,154	48,319	y	—	1	1,619	—	—	875	—	—	220	220
FARRAGUT	TN	t	—	—	—	—	—	—	—	—	—	—	—	—	—	—	—	—	—
FAYETTEVILLE	GA	c	1	48	44	40	32,472	53,732	n	—	—	3,718	3,012	81	2,142	375	495	235	471
FERGUSON	PA	tp	1	19	19	40	38,567	57,136	y	59,084	6	2,490	—	—	1,189	—	99	—	879
FERNANDINA BEACH	FL	c	1	43	34	48	35,237	50,255	y	51,503	5	3,966	2,734	69	2,035	332	367	232	1,000
FILLMORE	CA	c	5	7	6	other	61,400	84,600	n	—	—	2,961	—	—	2,961	—	—	—	—
FLORENCE	NJ	tp	1	31	25	40	42,980	75,637	y	78,662	3	3,497	3,259	93	2,547	331	381	45	193
FOREST ACRES	SC	c	1	33	28	42	—	—	—	—	—	—	—	—	—	—	—	—	—
FOREST GROVE	OR	c	1	30	26	40	46,044	59,640	n	—	—	3,671	3,076	84	2,128	501	446	159	435
FOREST HILL	TX	c	1	36	26	40	41,336	41,336	y	45,836	1	2,611	2,141	82	1,611	268	262	70	400
FOREST PARK	IL	v	1	50	36	40	45,809	68,049	y	68,531	20	5,031	—	—	—	588	—	77	859
FORREST CITY	AR	c	1	45	35	42	24,372	28,844	y	30,644	5	2,488	1,709	69	1,332	284	93	327	452
FORT MORGAN	CO	c	1	35	28	42	36,840	50,988	n	—	—	2,700	2,235	83	1,457	241	537	99	366
FORT WALTON BEACH	FL	c	1	65	54	40	31,500	54,620	y	55,520	—	5,245	4,377	83	3,309	574	494	207	710
FOUNTAIN	CO	c	1	54	40	42	41,434	63,419	n	—	—	4,362	3,722	85	2,947	232	542	191	449
FOUNTAIN HILLS	AZ	t	5	—	—	—	—	—	—	—	—	—	—	—	—	—	—	—	—
FRANCONIA	PA	tp	1	14	13	40	68,500	73,000	y	—	5	1,400	—	—	1,100	—	—	300	300
FRANKFORT	IL	v	1	29	—	40	37,179	60,500	n	—	—	4,684	—	—	2,101	—	367	146	1,912
FRANKFORT	IN	c	1	38	29	other	37,638	—	n	—	—	1,974	—	—	1,488	—	—	—	261
FRANKLIN	NJ	tp	1	33	30	40	43,556	75,015	n	—	—	—	—	—	—	—	—	—	—
FREEHOLD	NJ	b	1	—	35	40	34,713	84,969	y	88,819	5	5,943	5,299	89	3,684	469	1,145	109	535
GAFFNEY	SC	c	1	40	38	42	25,800	32,250	n	—	—	—	—	—	—	—	—	—	—
GALENA PARK	TX	c	1	22	18	40	38,443	40,876	y	—	1	1,606	1,348	84	926	189	233	78	180
GALION	OH	c	1	20	17	40	28,558	32,968	y	—	1	—	—	—	728	—	—	—	—
GARDEN CITY	ID	c	1	35	26	42	34,008	58,531	n	—	—	3,053	2,577	84	1,975	359	243	155	321
GARDEN CITY	NY	v	1	—	—	other	39,020	97,527	y	133,415	6	—	—	—	7,542	—	—	—	—
GATESVILLE	TX	c	1	22	16	40	26,749	—	n	—	—	1,327	959	72	717	102	139	175	194
GENEVA	NY	c	1	42	37	40	38,814	54,222	y	55,322	5	3,437	3,208	93	2,305	555	347	44	185
GLASSBORO	NJ	b	1	44	44	—	62,961	80,160	y	103,797	6	5,250	—	—	4,634	—	10	—	606
GLOVERSVILLE	NY	c	1	34	32	—	35,381	47,362	y	49,362	5	24,481	—	—	1,959	380	—	40	69
GOLDEN	CO	c	3	60	44	40	45,400	65,200	n	—	—	5,989	4,991	83	3,852	578	561	49	950
GOODYEAR	AZ	c	3	123	90	40	46,715	67,660	y	68,660	—	11,542	8,211	71	6,352	1,056	802	1,269	2,062
GRAFTON	MA	t	1	23	18	40	34,801	50,923	y	51,448	7	1,815	—	—	1,557	—	—	—	258
GRAFTON	WI	v	1	28	21	42	45,879	61,173	y	61,623	1	4,517	2,342	52	1,613	353	376	1,831	344
GRANBY	CT	t	1	19	14	40	51,979	66,310	y	67,060	5	2,121	1,883	89	1,395	237	250	79	160
GRAND HAVEN	MI	c	4	37	31	42	34,111	55,727	n	—	—	3,480	2,912	84	2,223	282	407	234	344
GRAND RAPIDS	MI	tp	5	—	—	42	—	—	—	—	—	—	—	—	—	—	—	—	—
GRANDVIEW	MO	c	1	63	50	40	35,797	50,088	y	50,952	3	5,057	4,021	80	3,263	324	433	261	775
GRANDVILLE	MI	c	1	28	26	40	40,007	53,964	y	55,164	15	2,809	—	—	1,666	—	—	6	460
GRASS VALLEY	CA	c	1	39	28	42	44,592	57,036	n	—	—	4,662	3,854	83	2,462	854	538	219	589
GREEN RIVER	WY	c	1	41	31	40	39,690	53,581	y	—	—	4,059	3,553	88	2,342	534	678	212	294
GREENFIELD	CA	c	1	19	16	40	42,912	52,164	n	—	—	2,499	1,733	69	1,179	224	330	19	746
GREENFIELD	IN	c	1	46	35	40	35,002	39,548	n	—	—	—	—	—	1,891	—	—	341	352
GREENVILLE	TX	c	1	72	51	40	40,026	53,859	y	55,359	1	5,181	4,749	92	3,335	758	656	—	432
GREENWOOD	MS	c	1	61	49	40	20,842	29,245	n	—	—	3,610	2,884	80	2,049	367	467	144	582
GREENWOOD	SC	c	1	61	47	42	28,184	39,499	n	—	—	3,772	2,688	71	1,984	355	349	149	935
GRIFFIN	GA	c	1	115	98	42	27,352	41,947	n	—	—	—	—	—	4,704	—	—	—	—
GRIFFITH	IN	t	—	40	31	40	40,960	49,556	y	—	3	—	—	—	2,154	—	—	—	—
GROVER BEACH	CA	c	1	—	—	48	—	—	—	—	—	—	—	—	—	—	—	—	—
HAINES CITY	FL	c	1	69	48	40	34,898	52,349	y	—	5	4,434	3,307	75	2,557	348	401	303	825
HALF MOON BAY	CA	c	3	20	15	40	72,192	87,719	y	94,298	5	4,104	—	—	2,357	—	415	77	626
HAMBURG	NY	v	1	22	16	40	49,472	65,963	y	68,463	5	1,917	1,834	96	1,233	256	344	—	83
HAMPTON	PA	tp	1	19	17	40	50,438	68,769	y	70,209	5	2,251	2,028	90	1,547	208	272	96	127
HANNIBAL	MO	c	1	—	—	40	29,557	56,443	n	—	—	2,530	—	—	1,808	297	424	43	357
HARKER HEIGHTS	TX	c	1	54	43	40	41,160	64,368	y	64,368	1	3,404	2,567	75	2,021	368	178	203	634
HARPER WOODS	MI	c	1	39	33	40	37,908	56,366	y	60,593	4	5,015	—	—	3,213	—	1,125	112	370
HARTFORD	VT	t	1	23	21	40	37,110	55,390	n	—	—	2,022	1,647	81	1,219	154	273	113	263
HASTINGS	MN	c	3	—	30	40	39,936	61,422	y	62,633	4	3,560	2,678	75	2,171	289	218	247	635
HASTINGS	NE	c	1	44	36	40	32,105	44,814	n	—	—	3,001	2,583	86	1,841	243	498	—	418
HATFIELD	PA	tp	1	31	26	40	39,392	72,422	y	76,722	4	3,684	—	—	2,272	—	214	449	—
HAVELOCK	NC	c	1	36	29	42	29,052	46,196	n	—	—	1,856	1,478	80	1,038	180	260	165	214
HAVERSTRAW	NY	v	—	—	—	—	—	—	—	—	—	—	—	—	—	—	—	—	—
HAWAIIAN GARDENS	CA	c	—	—	—	—	—	—	—	—	—	—	—	—	—	—	—	—	—
HAYS	KS	c	1	49	30	40	28,596	48,936	y	—	5	—	—	—	—	—	—	—	—
HAZEL CREST	IL	v	1	36	29	40	44,358	67,496	y	—	5	—	—	—	—	—	—	—	—
HAZEL PARK	MI	c	1	49	36	40	40,310	57,135	y	—	5	4,102	3,739	91	2,932	399	407	21	342
HAZLET	NJ	tp	1	52	45	40	51,000	85,705	y	87,055	5	—	—	—	4,563	—	—	—	—
HEALDSBURG	CA	c	3	30	17	40	61,008	74,448	y	80,616	5	—	—	—	2,450	—	449	—	—
HENDERSON	TX	c	3	42	32	40	35,275	38,275	y	39,475	1	2,535	2,331	92	1,691	270	369	92	113
HENDERSONVILLE	NC	c	1	50	38	42	29,548	44,958	y	46,082	5	3,450	2,812	82	2,154	345	313	205	433
HERMOSA BEACH	CA	c	1	51	38	other	58,404	67,596	y	81,113	5	9,945	6,620	67	3,854	2,307	458	71	3,253

Table 3/16
continued

POLICE DEPARTMENT PERSONNEL, SALARIES, AND EXPENDITURES FOR CITIES 10,000 AND OVER: 2008

Reported expenditures (in $000)

City	State	Type	Service provision	Full-time paid personnel	Full-time uniformed personnel	Duty hours per week	Minimum base salary ($)	Maximum base salary ($)	Longevity pay	Maximum salary with longevity ($)	Years of service for longevity	Total expenditures (A) ($)	Total personnel expenditures (B) ($)	(B) as % of (A)	Salaries and wages (C) ($)	City contribution to retirement and social security (D) ($)	City contribution to insurance (E) ($)	Capital outlay (F) ($)	All other (G) ($)
10,000–24,999 continued																			
HERNDON	VA	t	1	74	58	40	45,741	74,508	n	—	—	8,068	7,110	88	5,384	1,065	661	385	572
HEWITT	TX	c	1	31	22	40	28,920	46,800	y	48,000	1	1,678	1,341	80	1,039	178	123	113	224
HIBBING	MN	c	1	34	31	40	39,987	42,800	y	46,224	5	3,294	2,403	73	1,684	210	509	—	568
HIGHLAND VILLAGE	TX	c	1	35	27	40	45,806	56,312	y	—	2	2,669	2,318	87	1,839	186	292	145	206
HILLIARD	OH	c	1	—	50	40	39,285	63,036	y	64,796	5	7,178	—	—	4,682	—	1,166	991	339
HILLSBOROUGH	CA	t	1	36	27	40	71,656	87,126	n	—	—	5,790	5,177	89	3,194	1,129	853	24	589
HILLSIDE	NJ	tp	1	73	—	other	28,700	74,660	y	86,000	5	6,848	—	—	6,846	—	—	—	214
HILLTOWN	PA	tp	1	22	19	42	47,476	70,041	y	75,000	5	2,840	2,556	90	1,638	369	548	72	212
HINGHAM	MA	t	1	48	46	40	41,727	53,866	y	54,466	10	4,322	—	—	3,771	—	218	252	299
HOLBROOK	MA	t	1	22	20	other	39,308	53,214	y	53,614	5	—	—	—	1,800	—	—	50	60
HOLLY HILL	FL	c	1	34	31	40	31,365	50,142	n	—	—	2,687	2,257	84	1,518	522	216	85	382
HOMER GLEN	IL	v	—	—	—	—	—	—		—	—	—	—	—	—	—	—	—	—
HOMEWOOD	IL	v	1	43	39	40	52,524	69,310	y	70,810	6	—	—	—	3,940	—	—	—	—
HOPE	AR	c	1	36	25	42	26,925	29,192	y	30,232	5	2,287	1,529	67	1,098	205	226	248	503
HOPEWELL	PA	tp	1	14	—	40	31,500	52,500	y	53,500	5	1,478	—	—	946	—	156	89	228
HOPEWELL	VA	c	1	66	52	40	33,335	61,809	n	—	—	5,733	4,644	81	3,614	668	361	187	902
HOPKINS	MN	c	1	38	25	40	50,600	63,337	y	69,680	4	4,144	3,325	80	2,591	327	407	204	616
HOWARD	WI	v	5	—	—	other	—	—	y	—	—	1,246	—	—	—	—	—	54	1,192
HUDSON	NH	t	1	55	43	40	41,142	55,557	n	—	—	5,626	4,838	86	3,703	463	672	—	757
HUDSON	OH	c	1	36	28	40	42,245	—	y	64,018	3	3,647	3,051	84	2,350	376	324	57	539
HUEYTOWN	AL	c	1	39	32	40	31,450	48,755	n	—	—	—	—	—	—	—	—	—	—
HUMBLE	TX	c	1	73	57	40	40,356	53,568	y	—	1	6,798	5,459	80	4,084	742	632	164	1,175
HUNTERSVILLE	NC	t	1	80	71	42	33,737	52,292	—	—	—	8,115	4,116	51	3,277	403	435	771	3,228
HUNTINGTON	IN	c	1	34	31	other	38,178	38,178	y	46,196	1	2,388	2,070	87	1,787	280	2	133	185
HUTCHINSON	MN	c	1	32	22	40	40,705	58,512	n	—	—	3,160	2,675	85	2,078	218	379	75	410
INDIAN TRAIL	NC	t	—	—	—	—	—	—		—	—	—	—	—	—	—	—	—	—
INDIANOLA	IA	c	1	21	19	40	37,734	46,552	y	46,952	5	1,882	1,496	79	995	263	237	79	307
IONIA	MI	c	4	19	17	42	30,697	46,782	y	48,887	2	2,271	1,722	76	1,171	290	260	252	297
ISSAQUAH	WA	c	1	—	—	48	55,488	68,436	n	—	—	—	—	—	—	—	—	—	—
JACKSONVILLE BEACH	FL	c	1	79	57	40	35,568	57,928	n	—	—	7,317	5,641	77	4,476	690	475	354	1,322
JUNCTION CITY	KS	c	1	49	49	40	22,947	43,127	y	—	5	3,662	—	—	2,739	—	—	35	888
KATY	TX	c	1	59	1	40	48,000	—	y	—	1	—	—	—	—	—	—	—	—
KENMORE	WA	c	5	—	—	40	—	—		—	—	—	—	—	—	—	—	—	—
KENNESAW	GA	c	1	70	54	42	28,620	58,240	n	—	—	4,599	3,719	81	2,543	366	809	113	766
KENNETT	MO	c	1	26	21	40	22,000	—	n	—	—	1,219	979	80	755	91	133	26	214
KERRVILLE	TX	c	1	70	53	40	37,335	51,095	y	52,295	1	4,790	4,075	85	2,828	590	657	216	499
KEWANEE	IL	c	1	32	24	40	37,248	46,305	y	48,805	5	2,658	2,274	86	1,710	225	339	99	285
KILGORE	TX	c	3	43	33	42	32,555	43,965	y	—	1	2,786	2,270	81	1,544	365	361	94	421
KILLINGLY	CT	t	7	—	—	—	—	—		—	—	—	—	—	—	—	—	—	—
KINGMAN	AZ	c	1	86	57	other	39,924	56,176	n	—	—	8,091	6,404	79	4,660	828	916	257	1,429
KINGSLAND	GA	c	1	45	42	42	26,603	37,526	n	—	—	2,865	1,952	68	1,508	182	262	218	695
KINSTON	NC	c	4	130	121	42	—	45,882	y	—	5	7,914	7,337	93	5,970	750	617	577	—
KIRKSVILLE	MO	c	1	28	25	40	26,669	30,073	n	—	—	1,647	1,293	79	1,013	126	153	73	281
KLAMATH FALLS	OR	c	1	46	40	42	39,540	—	n	—	—	5,189	—	—	2,818	—	420	—	1,049
LA GRANDE	OR	c	1	34	18	40	29,963	38,190	n	—	—	4,002	3,349	84	2,563	337	448	365	288
LA GRANGE	IL	v	3	38	28	42	47,245	67,453	y	—	—	3,692	3,378	92	2,478	623	277	107	206
LA MARQUE	TX	c	1	38	28	40	38,316	50,184	y	—	1	2,749	2,238	81	1,885	303	49	178	333
LA PALMA	CA	c	3	33	27	40	52,786	70,738	n	—	—	5,038	—	—	2,608	—	—	503	315
LA PORTE	IN	c	1	52	43	40	34,180	37,915	y	41,416	3	2,472	—	—	2,071	—	—	22	267
LA QUINTA	CA	c	5	46	42	48	52,151	77,682	n	—	—	—	—	—	—	—	—	—	—
LA VISTA	NE	c	1	35	31	40	37,627	53,622	y	56,035	7	2,718	2,453	90	1,910	254	289	31	234
LACKAWANNA	NY	c	1	47	47	40	42,404	50,403	y	51,503	5	4,741	4,543	96	3,324	846	373	58	139
LADY LAKE	FL	t	1	44	29	42	36,894	56,347	n	—	—	3,673	2,492	68	1,748	376	368	614	567
LAFAYETTE	CO	c	1	48	36	40	45,149	48,365	y	62,424	2	—	—	—	3,105	—	167	—	88
LAKE FOREST PARK	WA	c	1	26	19	40	45,444	61,236	y	66,653	5	15,124	—	—	1,240	—	220	3,460	11,664
LAKE MARY	FL	c	1	54	38	42	37,019	55,539	y	—	3	4,309	3,310	77	2,414	569	326	135	865
LAKE ST. LOUIS	MO	c	1	40	30	40	42,191	42,191	n	—	—	—	—	—	—	—	—	—	—
LAKE STATION	IN	c	1	28	24	40	34,862	44,539	y	47,039	—	—	—	—	—	—	—	—	—
LAKE WALES	FL	c	1	44	42	42	32,127	—	—	—	—	4,696	3,796	81	2,485	532	778	239	661
LAKE ZURICH	IL	v	1	55	38	40	50,854	72,765	y	73,765	20	6,627	5,777	87	4,489	539	749	113	737
LEBANON	MO	c	1	—	—	40	28,260	34,880	y	36,700	5	1,579	—	—	1,222	—	—	64	220
LEESBURG	FL	c	1	107	77	40	32,635	47,923	n	—	—	9,128	7,126	78	4,768	1,871	486	668	—
LEMON GROVE	CA	c	5	—	—	—	—	—		—	—	—	—	—	—	—	—	—	—
LEMOORE	CA	c	1	34	28	48	38,100	48,888	y	—	5	3,521	2,594	74	1,895	531	168	266	661
LENOIR	NC	c	1	71	54	42	23,398	—	n	—	—	4,254	3,153	74	2,184	637	331	46	1,054
LEVELLAND	TX	c	3	31	22	40	35,714	35,714	y	36,914	1	1,865	1,498	80	1,112	225	161	138	229
LEXINGTON	NC	c	1	70	56	40	25,669	45,762	y	46,906	3	4,890	4,163	85	3,028	493	642	138	589
LEXINGTON	NE	c	1	17	15	40	27,955	41,746	n	—	—	1,111	926	83	667	88	170	12	173
LIBERTYVILLE	IL	v	1	58	41	40	51,862	77,053	n	—	—	6,732	6,292	93	4,644	942	706	7	433
LILBURN	GA	c	1	38	27	40	37,122	55,684	n	—	—	26,347	2,207	8	1,748	240	219	49	377
LINCOLN PARK	NJ	b	1	32	26	48	19,998	98,943	n	—	—	3,777	—	—	3,046	559	—	1	170
LINCOLNWOOD	IL	v	1	49	34	40	51,708	72,615	n	—	—	5,491	5,074	92	3,494	984	595	85	333

Table 3/16 continued — POLICE DEPARTMENT PERSONNEL, SALARIES, AND EXPENDITURES FOR CITIES 10,000 AND OVER: 2008

City	State	Type	Service provision	Full-time paid personnel	Full-time uniformed personnel	Duty hours per week	Minimum base salary ($)	Maximum base salary ($)	Longevity pay	Maximum salary with longevity ($)	Years of service for longevity	Total expenditures (A) ($)	Total personnel expenditures (B) ($)	(B) as % of (A)	Salaries and wages (C) ($)	City contribution to retirement and social security (D) ($)	City contribution to insurance (E) ($)	Capital outlay (F) ($)	All other (G) ($)
10,000–24,999 continued																			
LINDENHURST	IL	v	1	18	16	40	47,000	66,000	n	—	—	2,476	—	—	1,460	—	—	200	364
LINDENWOLD	NJ	b	1	55	40	40	41,460	74,142	y	79,332	5	5,131	4,880	95	3,606	666	608	35	215
LINO LAKES	MN	c	1	29	27	40	—	—	n	—	—	2,957	2,488	84	1,967	239	282	135	334
LITTLE CHUTE	WI	v	1	29	26	40	32,302	53,310	y	53,310	3	2,647	2,265	86	1,512	353	398	19	363
LOCKHART	TX	c	1	24	23	40	33,500	37,000	y	38,200	1	1,857	1,504	81	1,133	189	182	156	197
LOGAN	PA	tp	1	16	—	40	27,019	50,544	y	52,060	5	1,631	1,420	87	983	193	243	54	157
LOMA LINDA	CA	c	5	—	—	—	—	—	—	—	—	—	—	—	—	—	—	—	—
LOMITA	CA	c	5	—	—	—	—	—	—	—	—	—	—	—	—	—	—	—	—
LONDONDERRY	NH	t	—	—	—	—	—	—	—	—	—	—	—	—	—	—	—	—	—
LOVELAND	OH	c	3	18	16	40	55,598	59,794	y	—	12	2,510	1,898	76	1,396	310	192	106	506
LOWER	NJ	tp	1	45	40	42	41,027	79,982	y	—	5	6,488	—	—	4,545	—	464	1,007	129
LOWER ALLEN	PA	tp	1	23	21	40	47,955	61,203	y	65,203	5	2,611	2,305	88	1,647	279	379	105	201
LOWER GWYNEDD	PA	tp	1	19	18	40	49,775	71,107	y	76,796	5	2,522	2,247	89	1,501	347	397	97	178
LOWER MACUNGIE	PA	tp	—	—	—	—	—	—	—	—	—	—	—	—	—	—	—	—	—
LOWER MORELAND	PA	tp	1	26	21	40	50,028	68,813	y	75,695	4	2,602	2,372	91	2,009	45	318	134	96
LOWER SOUTHAMPTON	PA	tp	1	—	30	40	34,095	—	y	—	4	—	—	—	2,345	—	—	—	—
LUMBERTON	NC	c	1	80	69	42	24,663	27,905	y	27,955	1	4,882	4,217	86	3,122	539	556	320	344
LYNBROOK	NY	v	—	48	—	40	48,871	139,627	y	139,627	—	8,171	—	—	7,760	—	901	—	465
LYNDHURST	NJ	tp	1	50	50	40	25,531	94,994	y	100,694	4	—	8,167	—	5,598	1,318	1,250	1,325	750
LYNDHURST	OH	c	1	40	30	40	51,879	66,538	y	69,865	5	4,073	3,452	85	2,596	490	366	143	478
LYNN HAVEN	FL	c	1	39	26	42	31,013	48,681	n	—	—	—	—	—	—	—	—	—	—
LYONS	IL	v	1	35	28	48	—	—	—	—	—	3,444	3,268	95	2,764	48	455	15	161
MAITLAND	FL	c	1	51	41	40	36,134	55,013	n	—	—	4,182	3,798	91	2,593	824	380	216	231
MAMARONECK	NY	v	1	51	—	40	43,957	105,369	y	107,094	—	5,903	—	—	5,301	—	—	—	602
MANDEVILLE	LA	c	1	54	37	40	28,850	46,073	n	—	—	4,610	3,674	80	2,421	656	596	235	701
MANVILLE	NJ	b	1	22	—	40	88,000	120,000	y	—	5	—	—	—	2,605	—	—	—	—
MAPLE VALLEY	WA	c	5	—	—	—	—	—	—	—	—	—	—	—	—	—	—	—	—
MAPLEWOOD	NJ	tp	1	77	65	42	42,572	74,327	y	84,287	5	27,967	—	—	5,342	—	763	20,932	232
MARANA	AZ	t		—	—	40	51,570	58,506	n	—	—	8,222	6,841	83	5,477	873	490	888	493
MARQUETTE	MI	c	1	38	32	40	32,428	43,264	y	43,694	5	2,972	2,702	91	1,903	332	467	23	247
MARSHALL	MO	c	3	35	22	40	28,725	31,346	n	—	—	1,744	1,515	87	1,169	107	238	—	229
MARTINSVILLE	IN	c	1	30	21	40	—	—	—	—	—	2,602	2,065	79	1,289	226	550	106	450
MARTINSVILLE	VA	c	1	58	52	40	31,220	47,767	y	33,720	40	4,199	3,551	85	2,677	665	209	159	489
MARYSVILLE	OH	c	1	37	31	40	36,587	54,212	y	55,062	3	2,654	—	—	1,900	—	—	154	253
MARYVILLE	MO	c	4	26	21	40	24,980	40,164	y	—	3	1,150	1,007	88	727	268	11	153	206
MARYVILLE	TN	c	1	59	52	40	30,804	55,286	n	—	—	4,768	3,554	75	2,471	460	623	150	1,064
MASON	OH	c	1	45	41	other	42,994	60,840	n	—	—	—	—	—	—	—	—	—	—
MATTOON	IL	c	1	55	42	42	39,175	49,066	y	63,592	4	4,637	4,126	89	2,793	930	403	97	413
MAUMEE	OH	c	1	62	46	40	45,018	57,275	y	46,818	5	6,957	—	—	3,922	—	832	51	1,436
McCOMB	MS	c	1	—	—	42	—	—	—	—	—	—	—	—	—	—	—	—	—
McMINNVILLE	TN	c	1	42	36	42	27,912	27,913	n	—	—	1,686	—	—	1,405	—	—	68	213
MEDFORD	NJ	tp	1	—	43	40	44,861	85,923	n	—	—	5,580	5,105	91	4,022	542	540	126	277
MEDWAY	MA	t	1	—	17	40	50,000	—	y	—	—	—	—	—	—	—	—	—	—
MELROSE PARK	IL	v	1	86	75	40	31,000	71,769	y	74,269	15	8,262	—	—	5,632	—	1,622	143	316
MENASHA	WI	t	1	43	26	40	—	—	n	—	—	2,637	2,552	97	1,743	393	415	85	—
MEQUON	WI	c	1	46	38	other	45,218	60,619	y	—	30	—	—	—	—	—	—	—	—
MERRIAM	KS	c	1	33	28	40	37,894	56,841	n	—	—	2,883	2,593	90	1,921	389	282	—	290
MEXICO	MO	c	4	37	35	40	26,000	35,650	n	—	—	2,059	1,764	86	1,263	245	256	62	1,996
MIAMI	OK	c	1	31	—	—	—	—	n	—	—	—	—	—	1,452	188	—	60	164
MIDDLEBURG HEIGHTS	OH	c	1	38	31	40	47,923	64,626	y	—	5	4,246	—	—	2,862	—	465	104	315
MIDDLETOWN	PA	tp	7	—	—	—	—	—	—	—	—	—	—	—	—	—	—	—	—
MILFORD	NH	t	1	30	25	40	36,448	51,385	—	—	—	2,209	—	—	1,671	219	—	116	203
MILL VALLEY	CA	c	1	—	—	42	—	—	—	—	—	—	—	—	—	—	—	—	—
MILLBROOK	AL	c	1	—	—	48	25,376	—	n	—	—	1,899	1,567	83	1,324	169	73	—	332
MILLBURY	MA	t	1	25	—	40	56,525	75,946	y	—	10	2,173	—	—	1,747	—	14	215	72
MILLEDGEVILLE	GA	c	1	56	43	42	29,242	44,495	n	—	—	3,231	2,418	75	1,714	277	427	562	251
MINEOLA	NY	v	—	—	—	—	—	—	—	—	—	—	—	—	—	—	—	—	—
MINT HILL	NC	t	1	26	26	42	31,614	50,540	n	—	—	—	—	—	—	—	—	—	—
MITCHELL	SD	c	4	—	—	40	—	—	—	—	—	—	—	—	—	—	—	—	—
MOBERLY	MO	c	1	—	—	—	—	—	n	—	—	2,437	2,109	87	1,491	186	432	94	233
MONROE	GA	c	1	44	38	42	29,714	44,472	n	—	—	3,425	2,623	77	1,814	389	421	102	699
MONROE	MI	c	1	—	—	40	—	—	—	—	—	—	—	—	—	—	—	—	—
MONROE	WA	c	1	51	37	40	51,072	62,100	y	64,214	5	—	4,599	—	3,496	800	302	748	138
MONTGOMERY	OH	c	1	24	21	40	48,256	62,650	y	—	5	2,723	2,283	84	1,726	310	247	125	325
MONTROSE	CO	c	1	50	38	40	41,046	52,342	n	—	—	4,686	3,333	71	2,528	307	498	89	1,264
MONTVILLE	NJ	tp	1	44	41	40	37,451	87,602	y	93,737	5	6,217	—	—	4,587	—	736	25	284
MORGAN CITY	LA	c	1	51	48	42	24,660	24,660	y	—	1	3,021	2,420	80	1,891	243	285	142	458
MORGANTON	NC	c	4	88	75	42	—	—	y	—	—	6,591	5,368	81	3,961	601	806	323	899
MORRO BAY	CA	c	1	22	16	40	48,822	135,864	n	—	—	2,837	—	—	1,639	—	291	—	333
MOUNT CLEMENS	MI	c	5	—	—	40	—	—	—	—	—	—	—	—	—	—	—	—	—
MOUNT OLIVE	NJ	tp	1	63	54	40	39,478	81,916	y	86,831	7	5,935	—	—	5,091	—	21	77	263

Table 3/16 continued

POLICE DEPARTMENT PERSONNEL, SALARIES, AND EXPENDITURES FOR CITIES 10,000 AND OVER: 2008

City	State	Type	Service provision	Full-time paid personnel	Full-time uniformed personnel	Duty hours per week	Minimum base salary ($)	Maximum base salary ($)	Longevity pay	Maximum salary with longevity ($)	Years of service for longevity	Total expenditures (A) ($)	Total personnel expenditures (B) ($)	(B) as % of (A)	Salaries and wages (C) ($)	City contribution to retirement and social security (D) ($)	City contribution to insurance (E) ($)	Capital outlay (F) ($)	All other (G) ($)
10,000–24,999 continued																			
MOUNT PLEASANT	TX	c	1	39	28	40	31,705	42,486	y	—	1	2,255	1,870	83	1,394	276	199	70	315
MOUNT VERNON	OH	c	1	27	25	40	37,294	50,960	y	52,832	5	2,502	—	—	1,274	—	226	343	659
MOUNTAIN BROOK	AL	c	—	—	—	other	34,507	53,477	y	58,023	20	6,117	5,010	82	3,775	714	520	460	647
MOUNTAIN HOME	AR	c	3	—	—	40	—	—		—		—	—	—	—	—	—	—	—
MUKILTEO	WA	c	1	29	23	40	51,431	66,496	n	—	—	3,753	2,988	80	2,250	320	418	10	755
MUNSTER	IN	t	1	50	39	40	37,398	52,354	y	55,144	6	3,856	3,514	91	2,578	512	423	86	256
MURRYSVILLE	PA	c	—	21	—	40	49,005	61,256	y	—	1	2,625	2,517	96	1,664	473	380	99	2,118
NAPLES	FL	c	1	115	75	42	46,536	66,843	y	69,843	11	11,517	9,082	79	6,768	1,244	1,070	523	1,912
NARRAGANSETT	RI	t	1	52	41	other	36,237	53,056	y	60,749	3	4,940	4,172	84	3,033	900	239	15	647
NEDERLAND	TX	c	1	—	23	40	39,416	44,824	y	46,504	1	2,726	2,197	81	1,540	364	293	75	453
NEW BERN	NC	c	1	135	82	42	29,896	65,909	y	65,909	5	8,678	6,787	78	4,964	881	942	35	1,856
NEW BRIGHTON	MN	c	1	33	27	40	40,987	63,057	y	68,732	4	3,496	2,727	78	2,185	278	264	330	438
NEW CANAAN	CT	t	1	50	46	40	50,691	70,178	y	—	5	6,190	—	—	435	—	900	224	409
NEW HOPE	MN	c	1	36	29	40	40,593	68,071	y	—	4	3,900	3,515	90	2,924	297	293	110	865
NEW LENOX	IL	v	1	—	50	40	46,259	76,086	n	—	—	4,857	—	—	3,926	—	—	154	777
NEW MILFORD	NJ	b	1	36	33	40	31,516	88,374	y	—	20	—	—	—	—	—	—	—	—
NEW PORT RICHEY	FL	c	1	52	37	40	40,216	57,662	n	—	—	4,843	4,218	87	2,744	1,185	289	153	471
NEW ULM	MN	c	1	25	22	40	44,283	52,354	n	—	—	2,098	1,807	86	1,364	166	277	43	248
NEWBERG	OR	c	1	40	29	40	43,152	60,732	y	61,932	10	3,904	2,936	75	1,939	504	493	127	841
NEWBERRY	SC	c	1	34	31	42	29,079	42,165	y	—	—	1,873	1,572	84	1,231	218	123	83	218
NEWTON	KS	c	1	36	32	42	30,253	39,711	y	40,335	2	2,849	2,416	85	1,824	250	342	—	432
NEWTON	NC	c	1	43	34	42	30,950	45,947	n	—	—	3,120	2,260	72	1,678	277	305	227	633
NEWTOWN TOWNSHIP	PA	tp	1	28	28	48	28,675	73,834	n	—	—	4,167	3,802	91	2,632	572	598	108	258
NILES	MI	c	1	31	23	40	38,051	48,186	y	53,044	5	2,718	2,371	87	1,820	159	392	—	347
NIXA	MO	c	1	32	21	40	29,646	39,036	n	—	—	1,589	1,308	82	982	151	174	24	257
NORCO	CA	c	5	—	—		—	—		—		—	—	—	—	—	—	—	—
NORFOLK	MA	t	1	23	17	other	40,646	58,479	y	—	3	—	—	—	1,544	—	134	81	—
NORRIDGE	IL	v	1	54	39	40	45,261	79,747	n	—	—	6,917	5,504	80	4,007	610	886	937	476
NORTH AUGUSTA	SC	c	4	68	11	48	39,726	55,616	n	—	—	4,583	3,825	83	2,941	518	366	13	745
NORTH BRANFORD	CT	t	1	24	23	40	45,031	58,309	y	60,109	5	3,003	2,658	89	1,616	582	460	65	279
NORTH FAYETTE	PA	tp	1	29	20	40	50,384	67,178	y	71,209	5	2,532	2,490	98	1,680	376	433	87	1,636
NORTH MANKATO	MN	c	1	14	12	42	44,520	54,780	y	—	—	1,304	1,052	81	813	104	134	26	226
NORTH MYRTLE BEACH	SC	c	4	—	—	42	—	—		—		—	—	—	—	—	—	—	—
NORTH OGDEN	UT	c	1	20	18	42	30,427	49,333	n	—	—	1,396	1,178	84	777	182	219	18	976
NORTH READING	MA	t	1	—	30	40	38,804	46,528	y	48,328	5	—	—	—	2,762	—	—	74	259
NORTH ST. PAUL	MN	c	1	—	—	42	—	—		—		—	—	—	—	—	—	—	—
NORTH STRABANE	PA	tp	1	20	20	40	51,958	51,958	y	54,556	2	1,790	1,553	87	1,010	192	351	89	147
NORTHBRIDGE	MA	t	1	26	18	40	—	—		—		—	—	—	—	—	—	—	—
NORTHVILLE	MI	tp	1	46	33	40	47,588	67,873	y	69,373	5	—	—	—	—	—	—	—	—
NORTON	MA	t	1	28	—	40	37,356	51,268	y	51,968	25	2,307	—	—	2,056	—	—	85	166
NORTON SHORES	MI	c	1	31	30	42	46,934	54,338	y	55,338	—	3,785	—	—	1,856	1,008	—	158	502
NORWOOD	OH	c	1	—	52	42	49,325	—	y	—	5	—	—	—	4,058	—	—	—	—
OCOEE	FL	c	1	91	66	42	36,414	55,245	n	—	—	—	6,002	—	4,079	1,133	790	—	—
OCONOMOWOC	WI	c	1	21	21	40	47,154	59,280	n	—	—	2,676	2,337	87	1,602	358	377	88	250
OIL CITY	PA	c	1	18	—	40	29,614	39,484	y	40,669	5	1,202	—	—	789	—	180	23	209
ONALASKA	WI	c	1	24	24	other	42,629	47,599	y	49,979	10	—	—	—	—	—	—	—	—
ONTARIO	OR	c	3	29	27	40	38,196	46,356	n	—	—	—	—	—	—	—	—	—	—
ORANGE	TX	c	1	54	40	40	40,310	50,294	y	51,494	1	4,150	3,947	95	2,721	677	549	56	147
ORINDA	CA	c	5	16	14	40	—	—		—		—	—	—	—	—	—	—	—
OSWEGO	IL	v	1	64	53	40	46,000	72,215	n	—	—	7,426	6,078	82	4,263	1,090	725	316	1,032
OTTAWA	IL	c	1	33	30	42	37,707	43,506	y	50,506	1	—	—	—	—	—	—	—	—
OTTUMWA	IA	c	1	45	36	40	39,104	43,805	y	45,614	5	3,228	2,893	90	2,043	479	371	93	241
OWATONNA	MN	c	1	38	35	40	45,062	53,004	n	—	—	3,788	3,054	81	2,330	292	432	47	688
OXFORD	MS	c	1	66	58	other	29,087	36,847	n	—	—	3,059	—	—	2,219	412	—	147	281
OXFORD	OH	c	1	44	27	40	46,749	54,999	y	56,099	5	3,045	2,805	92	2,072	532	201	—	240
OZARK	AL	c	1	40	34	40	25,249	35,676	y	34,457	10	2,237	1,538	69	1,186	156	196	5	694
PALATKA	FL	c	1	43	36	40	31,421	—	y	—	10	3,836	2,714	71	1,940	455	318	48	1,075
PALISADES PARK	NJ	b	1	39	32	40	30,139	101,477	y	119,004	20	5,507	—	—	4,092	—	348	83	370
PALMER	PA	tp	1	36	33	40	51,711	60,253	y	63,868	5	—	—	—	—	—	—	—	—
PALMETTO	FL	c	1	48	31	42	33,236	49,864	y	52,900	14	3,744	2,900	77	2,198	319	382	382	463
PALOS HEIGHTS	IL	c	1	31	29	42	45,252	77,619	n	—	—	3,983	3,504	88	2,348	527	629	32	446
PALOS VERDES ESTATES	CA	c	1	32	22	other	53,364	70,188	y	77,206	5	5,208	—	—	3,018	—	385	288	475
PAPILLION	NE	c	1	42	38	40	38,293	55,390	y	66,324	6	3,587	2,897	81	2,223	334	340	36	653
PARK FOREST	IL	v	1	50	34	40	43,731	66,336	n	—	—	5,751	4,637	81	3,492	714	431	194	920
PARKER	CO	t	1	77	58	40	49,194	65,998	n	—	—	7,451	5,852	79	4,786	510	556	427	1,172
PARLIER	CA	c	1	18	15	48	36,775	41,600	n	—	—	1,415	1,051	74	778	153	120	15	349
PARSONS	KS	c	1	—	33	42	31,655	36,141	n	—	—	—	—	—	—	—	—	—	—
PATTERSON	CA	c	5	—	—		—	—		—		2,285	—	—	—	—	—	—	2,285
PATTON	PA	tp	1	19	17	40	40,352	59,342	y	60,542	6	1,905	1,616	85	1,181	230	204	43	333
PAYSON	AZ	t	1	35	27	40	41,494	62,241	n	—	—	4,865	3,505	72	2,759	269	476	355	551

Table 3/16 continued

POLICE DEPARTMENT PERSONNEL, SALARIES, AND EXPENDITURES FOR CITIES 10,000 AND OVER: 2008

City	State	Type	Service provision	Full-time paid personnel	Full-time uniformed personnel	Duty hours per week	Minimum base salary ($)	Maximum base salary ($)	Longevity pay	Maximum salary with longevity ($)	Years of service for longevity	Total expenditures (A) ($)	Total personnel expenditures (B) ($)	(B) as % of (A)	Salaries and wages (C) ($)	City contribution to retirement and social security (D) ($)	City contribution to insurance (E) ($)	Capital outlay (F) ($)	All other (G) ($)
10,000–24,999 continued																			
PELHAM	AL	t	1	80	65	40	48,895	56,190	n	—	—	—	5,742	—	4,394	845	502	133	464
PENDLETON	OR	c	1	28	26	42	38,388	48,576	y	51,004	15	—	2,328	—	1,597	467	264	17	920
PERRYSBURG	OH	c	1	39	39	40	43,000	55,000	y	56,000	10	4,238	3,494	82	2,870	119	505	295	449
PETERS	PA	tp	1	23	21	42	51,210	64,013	y	66,524	5	2,299	2,159	94	1,606	296	257	50	89
PFLUGERVILLE	TX	c	1	80	58	40	38,906	62,250	y	—	—	—	—	—	—	—	—	—	—
PIEDMONT	CA	c	1	—	—	40													
PINECREST	FL	v	1	77	54	40	48,204	69,078	n	—	—	7,186	—	—	3,972	—	898	912	1,006
PLAINSBORO	NJ	tp	1	60	45	40	45,893	81,302	y	84,852	7	—	—	—	—	—	—	—	—
PLAINVIEW	TX	c	1	42	33	40	31,324	36,316	y	—	25	2,857	2,316	81	1,730	336	250	332	208
PLEASANT PRAIRIE	WI	v	1	30	29	40	46,571	58,198	n	—	—	2,760	2,434	88	1,707	392	334	78	248
PLUMSTEAD	PA	tp	1	15	—	40	38,392	66,191	y	—	10	2,276	1,895	83	1,269	337	288	160	220
POINT PLEASANT	NJ	b	1	46	36	40	31,975	90,693	y	99,762	7	5,107	4,930	97	3,885	672	373	9	168
POPLAR BLUFF	MO	c	1	—	—	42													
POQUOSON	VA	c	3	26	22	40	30,666	42,031	n	—	—	2,327	1,692	73	1,252	239	200	100	535
PORT ANGELES	WA	c	3	57	32	40	49,620	59,088	y	54,263	5	6,812	4,908	72	3,653	508	746	86	1,049
PORT LAVACA	TX	c	3	26	20	42	29,843	40,375	y	43,103	1	1,286	1,061	82	885	111	65	24	201
PORTALES	NM	c	1	39	23	42	24,819	39,681	y	—	10	2,145	2,721	127	1,896	631	194	238	249
PORTLAND	TX	c	1	32	26	40	32,186	36,050	y	37,250	1	2,534	1,943	77	1,376	254	313	71	520
PORTSMOUTH	NH	c	1	88	66	40	40,763	54,886	y	—	5	7,721	6,996	91	5,204	555	1,238	28	697
PRESCOTT VALLEY	AZ	t	3	83	67	40	42,622	59,670	n	—	—	—	5,435	—	4,194	285	955	—	—
PRINCETON	NJ	b	1	37	34	40	53,720	86,710	y	91,046	5	—	4,154	—	3,394	295	464	167	181
PRIOR LAKE	MN	c	1	26	23	40	44,748	62,304	y	67,911	16	2,755	2,396	87	1,939	246	211	72	286
PROSPECT HEIGHTS	IL	c	1	27	27	40	51,196	118,241	y	118,991	—	3,997	3,573	89	2,567	606	400	16	407
PULLMAN	WA	c	1	39	28	40	46,812	63,372	n	—	—	4,306	—	—	2,335	—	—	44	936
PUNTA GORDA	FL	c	1	53	37	42	40,000	56,586	n	—	—	4,837	3,979	82	2,555	1,150	273	497	1,321
RAMSEY	MN	c	1	27	22	40	42,041	62,298	y	65,930	16	2,582	2,143	83	1,745	224	173	162	278
RAMSEY	NJ	b	1	—	32	40	35,000	93,525	y	102,878	4	—	—	—	3,820	—	—	—	—
RAYMORE	MO	c	1	39	27	42	30,303	44,182	n	—	—	2,766	—	—	—	—	—	36	—
READING	MA	t	1	42	40	other	38,758	73,082	n	—	—	3,320	—	—	3,111	—	—	—	208
RED BANK	NJ	b	1	48	41	40	44,799	83,401	y	89,656	5	5,652	5,306	94	4,080	570	656	150	200
RED BANK	TN	c	3	23	21	40	27,366	31,683	n	—	—	1,325	—	—	844	158	—	5	518
RED WING	MN	c	1	33	27	40	48,381	59,030	n	—	—	3,125	2,621	84	1,999	250	371	85	420
REIDSVILLE	NC	c	1	56	49	42	30,117	45,176	y	46,676	2	4,115	2,883	70	2,196	388	299	308	924
RICHMOND	TX	t	1	—	—	40	36,920	56,768	y	—	1	—	—	—	—	—	—	—	—
RICHMOND HEIGHTS	OH	c	1	29	20	40	45,790	60,445	y	63,467	5	3,326	—	—	2,189	—	246	51	383
RINGWOOD	NJ	b	1	25	20	other	36,722	105,749	y	116,324	5	3,661	3,547	97	2,587	504	456	—	137
RIPON	CA	c	1	26	—	42	52,404	63,697	n	—	—	—	3,809	—	2,908	424	477	6,000	635
RIVER FALLS	WI	c	1	24	16	40	44,491	54,392	n	—	—	2,436	2,154	88	1,490	323	341	25	257
RIVER FOREST	IL	v	1	34	34	40	—	—	—	—	—	3,846	3,528	92	2,380	683	465	68	250
RIVERBANK	CA	c	5	—	—	40													
RIVERSIDE	OH	c	1	33	32	40	44,512	57,346	y	58,178	5	3,646	2,872	79	2,112	416	344	172	602
RIVERVIEW	MI	c	1	45	—	40	—	—	—	—	—	3,317	3,148	95	2,192	608	348	12	157
ROANOKE RAPIDS	NC	c	1	39	36	42	27,536	40,899	y	41,599	2	—	1,422	—	959	367	96	122	1,461
ROBINSON	PA	tp	1	31	26	40	49,000	78,000	y	73,000	5	—	—	—	—	—	222	—	—
ROCHESTER	MI	c	1	25	19	40	38,207	59,141	y	61,941	5	2,866	2,211	77	1,548	153	510	125	531
ROCK SPRINGS	WY	c	1	66	43	40	44,385	55,431	n	—	—	5,746	4,933	86	3,552	675	705	205	609
ROCKLEDGE	FL	c	1	71	51	42	33,500	51,650	y	52,450	5	4,330	3,767	87	2,946	392	430	167	396
ROLLA	MO	c	1	34	31	48	26,943	35,682	n	—	—	2,175	1,600	74	1,260	164	175	103	472
ROLLING MEADOWS	IL	c	1	83	56	other	57,120	81,600	y	84,048	10	9,622	8,214	85	6,722	682	810	233	1,175
ROSEBURG	OR	c	3	40	35	40	41,400	55,476	n	—	—	4,464	3,753	84	2,405	790	558	15	695
ROSENBERG	TX	c	1	85	77	40	37,752	50,960	y	51,050	1	5,601	4,724	84	3,581	678	465	45	832
ROXBURY	NJ	tp	1	48	—	40	39,294	82,609	y	—	5	—	—	—	4,299	—	775	—	291
SACO	ME	c	1	46	34	40	40,934	45,094	y	48,811	4	2,832	—	—	2,408	—	—	—	410
SAFETY HARBOR	FL	c	5	—	—		—	—		—	—	—							—
SAGINAW	TX	c	1	37	37	48	37,938	56,905	y	—	1	2,479	2,350	95	1,950	383	16	—	130
SALEM	OH	c	3	24	23	40	26,811	45,094	y	46,906	5	1,915	—	—	1,140	—	464	—	97
SALISBURY	MD	c	1	87	—	40	37,122	56,231	n	—	—	7,836	6,879	88	4,638	1,452	787	—	958
SALISBURY	PA	tp	1	25	16	40	42,019	57,348	y	—	5	1,319	1,140	86	984	111	44	67	112
SAN ANSELMO	CA	c	1	26	19	40	59,472	72,288	y	75,902	2	3,750	3,331	89	2,201	878	251	109	310
SAN BENITO	TX	c	1	54	47	40	31,625	33,767	y	—	1	3,070	2,619	85	2,041	348	229	78	373
SAN FERNANDO	CA	c	3	56	34	40	50,988	63,156	y	69,472	4	5,947	—	—	4,043	—	519	498	830
SAN MARINO	CA	c	1	37	25	40	59,100	72,096	n	—	—	4,636	—	—	2,858	—	239	37	829
SAND SPRINGS	OK	c	1	37	34	40	33,862	44,189	y	46,109	2								
SANFORD	NC	c	1	95	78	42	32,243	49,062	y	—	5	6,936	5,147	74	4,137	502	508	531	1,257
SAPULPA	OK	c	1	59	46	40	24,000	41,400	n	—	—	4,245	3,746	88	2,737	330	678	159	341
SAULT STE. MARIE	MI	c	1	27	25	40	36,607	46,358	n	—	—	2,803	2,575	92	1,694	486	394	73	155
SCHERERVILLE	IN	t	1	73	63	42	40,994	51,062	y	52,862	3	5,122	4,332	85	3,078	640	614	—	789
SCHERTZ	TX	c	1	65	47	40	36,678	48,396	y	—	1	3,354	3,004	90	2,305	410	288	172	179
SCOTTS VALLEY	CA	c	3	24	18	42	49,944	66,936	n	—	—	3,431	3,156	92	2,084	717	354	24	251
SEBASTIAN	FL	c	3	53	40	40	34,678	62,632	y	77,942	10	4,798	4,134	86	2,810	767	557	308	445
SEDALIA	MO	c	3	57	44	40	30,152	45,228	n	—	—	3,215	2,504	78	2,048	191	264	167	544
SEDONA	AZ	c	1	—	—	other	—	—	—	—	—	—	—	—	—	—	—	—	—
SEEKONK	MA	t	1	35	32	40	40,750	49,397	y	51,867	25	2,730	—	—	2,525	—	—	—	205

Table 3/16
continued

POLICE DEPARTMENT PERSONNEL, SALARIES, AND EXPENDITURES FOR CITIES 10,000 AND OVER: 2008

Reported expenditures (in $000)

City	State	Type	Service provision	Full-time paid personnel	Full-time uniformed personnel	Duty hours per week	Minimum base salary ($)	Maximum base salary ($)	Longevity pay	Maximum salary with longevity ($)	Years of service for longevity	Total expenditures (A) ($)	Total personnel expenditures (B) ($)	(B) as % of (A)	Salaries and wages (C) ($)	City contribution to retirement and social security (D) ($)	City contribution to insurance (E) ($)	Capital outlay (F) ($)	All other (G) ($)
10,000–24,999 continued																			
SEGUIN	TX	c	3	62	46	40	37,315	50,190	y	51,390	1	7,560	3,517	47	2,709	488	319	3,733	310
SELMA	CA	c	3	56	37	40	40,104	48,732	y	—	—	4,242	3,491	82	2,397	642	451	—	750
SEMINOLE	FL	c	5	—	—														
SHERIDAN	WY	c	1	54	27	40	35,437	53,921	n	—	—								
SIKESTON	MO	c	4	82	74	42	28,663	34,268	n	—	—	5,615	4,477	80	3,171	481	824	412	727
SILOAM SPRINGS	AR	c	1	29	29	42	29,312	44,416	y	43,545	2	2,685	2,133	79	1,630	305	197	133	419
SMITHFIELD	RI	t	1	—	—	40	42,954	51,310	y	103,537	5	4,215	—	—	3,599	—	—	168	449
SNELLVILLE	GA	c	1	—	59	40	35,000	59,968	y										
SNYDER	TX	c	1	20	18	40	30,192	32,988	y	34,188	1	1,324	975	74	813	156	5	112	1,213
SODDY—DAISY	TN	c	1	25	—	40	—	—	n	—	—	1,817	1,488	82	1,113	215	160	160	170
SOMERSET	MA	t	1	33	32	40	34,357	42,946	y	—	5	2,017	—	—	1,895	—	—	—	122
SOUTH ELGIN	IL	v	1	41	32	40	46,675	66,602	n	—	—	4,806	4,101	85	2,954	680	466	98	607
SOUTH EUCLID	OH	c	1	41	38	40	46,278	63,213	y	82,462	5	—	—	—	3,136	—	—	—	—
SOUTH LAKE TAHOE	CA	c	3	60	27	40	50,782	61,737	n	—	—	8,241	6,693	81	4,178	1,357	1,158	347	1,200
SOUTH LYON	MI	c	1	20	18	40	38,853	59,085	y	59,885	—	2,138	1,841	86	1,313	236	292	43	254
SOUTH MILWAUKEE	WI	c	1	38	32	40	48,617	60,021	y	60,321	5	—	—	—	2,397	—	—	—	—
SOUTH OGDEN	UT	c	1	29	26	40	35,318	42,140	n	—	—								
SOUTH RIVER	NJ	b	1	32	30	40	47,828	77,577	y	88,461	6	4,545	3,813	84	2,792	358	663	641	91
SOUTH SALT LAKE	UT	c	1	67	57	40	34,356	60,168	y	—	—	7,891	5,207	66	3,655	1,021	530	505	753
SOUTH SIOUX CITY	NE	c	1	29	28	40	38,453	49,130	y	50,690	10	2,449	2,020	82	1,490	205	325	163	266
SOUTH ST. PAUL	MN	c	1	33	26	40	50,296	62,869	y	66,642	5	3,510	—	—	2,050	—	333	95	671
SOUTH WHITEHALL	PA	tp	1	37	37	40	45,730	55,888	y	57,288	2	3,462	—	—	2,565	—	449	160	96
SPANISH FORK	UT	c	1	33	28	40	36,000	—	n	—	—	2,801	2,188	78	1,517	452	219	128	485
SPARTA	NJ	tp	1	40	40	42	45,211	79,119	y	133,003	16	6,037	5,695	94	4,053	803	839	174	168
SPEEDWAY	IN	t	3	46	34	40	43,470	47,017	y	48,942	1	3,469	3,094	89	2,347	377	370	—	376
SPENCER	IA	c	1	26	18	42	39,099	46,928	y	47,828	10	1,725	—	—	1,193	247	—	90	195
SPENCER	MA	t	1	21	17	40	38,117	46,325	y	46,975	10	1,459	1,584	109	1,230	150	204	79	150
SPRINGBORO	OH	c	1	28	22	40	42,162	53,943	n	—	—								
SPRINGDALE	OH	c	1	44	38	42	50,935	61,903	y	63,653	5	4,759	—	—	2,749	—	78	101	1,318
SPRINGETTSBURY	PA	tp	1	34	31	40	36,971	63,848	y	66,898	5	3,438	3,166	92	2,218	636	311	83	189
SPRINGFIELD	TN	c	1	53	38	42	28,704	39,187	y	—	5	3,508	3,032	86	2,135	402	495	201	275
SPRINGVILLE	UT	c	1	35	25	40	34,100	52,500	n	—	—	3,045	—	—	1,254	—	780	392	619
ST. ANN	MO	c	1	48	39	42	33,787	39,831	y	—	5	2,992	—	—	2,115	365	—	172	338
ST. AUGUSTINE	FL	c	1	60	48	40	36,634	54,003	n	—	—	4,889	4,068	83	2,969	629	470	245	573
ST. CLOUD	FL	c	1	—	66	42	35,000	52,500	—	—	—	6,792	5,670	83	3,944	1,039	687	247	875
STAFFORD	CT	t	7	2	—	40	—	—	y	—	5								
STAFFORD	TX	t	1	58	44	40	36,408	48,863	y	—	1	41,816	3,663	9	2,431	490	742	180	853
STATESVILLE	NC	c	1	91	69	40	34,649	57,171	n	—	—	5,996	4,612	77	3,495	645	472	507	877
STAUNTON	VA	c	1	57	53	42	30,513	52,930	n	—	—	4,295	3,578	83	2,532	614	432	80	637
STERLING	CO	c	1	24	22	42	32,552	43,364	n	—	—	1,459	1,215	83	925	91	198	104	139
STERLING	IL	c	1	41	28	40	34,079	49,945	n	—	—	2,556	—	—	2,123	—	—	100	332
STONEHAM	MA	t	1	37	35	other	41,451	52,888	n	—	—	3,610	—	—	2,897	—	431	—	282
STORM LAKE	IA	c	4	—	—	42													
STREETSBORO	OH	c	1	33	26	40	36,046	56,576	y	57,836	3	3,381	—	—	2,367	—	281	263	137
SUDBURY	MA	t	1	33	27	other	43,543	47,545	y	48,045	7	2,505	—	—	2,143	—	—	121	241
SUFFERN	NY	v	1	32	27	40	44,000	97,000	y	—	3	4,565	—	—	3,247	—	393	—	207
SUGAR HILL	GA	c	—	—	—														
SULPHUR	LA	c	1	61	44	40	—	—	y	—	1	4,162	—	—	2,325	—	260	408	834
SUMMIT	NJ	c	1	57	48	other	46,905	91,233	n	—	—								
SUN PRAIRIE	WI	c	1	73	36	other	43,310	50,661	y	—	20	5,923	5,313	90	3,810	840	662	72	539
SUNNYSIDE	WA	c	1	—	—	48	46,812	56,904	y	58,178	20								
SWANSEA	IL	v	1	22	22	40	54,454	54,454	y	58,226	4	2,454	—	—	1,572	—	235	123	93
SYLACAUGA	AL	c	1	48	40	42	26,895	42,342	n	—	—	3,250	2,427	75	1,859	238	329	188	636
TAKOMA PARK	MD	c	1	—	41	40	41,381	55,036	y	—	—	6,230	4,505	72	3,275	743	486	772	953
TARBORO	NC	t	1	34	29	42	28,042	44,566	y	46,348	5	2,186	1,901	87	1,446	293	161	24	261
TARPON SPRINGS	FL	c	1	71	47	42	41,906	67,507	n	—	—	5,700	4,498	79	3,492	678	327	112	1,091
TARRYTOWN	NY	v	1	42	36	40	42,836	82,855	y	84,555	5	5,749	5,412	94	4,009	857	546	58	280
TAYLOR	TX	c	1	35	27	42	39,755	50,739	y	51,651	1	2,287	1,960	86	1,516	269	175	15	311
THE DALLES	OR	c	1	23	22	40	40,764	48,672	n	—	—	—	—	—	1,219	—	231	231	—
THIBODAUX	LA	c	1	56	40	42	26,582	42,141	n	—	—	3,263	2,412	74	1,806	302	304	32	818
TIFFIN	OH	c	1	42	29	40	38,750	48,984	y	53,882	4	3,308	—	—	2,148	—	458	117	273
TIFTON	GA	c	1	57	45	40	25,513	38,270	n	—	—	1,412	1,398	99	1,013	231	154	14	—
TINTON FALLS	NJ	b	1	42	41	—	30,577	100,215	n	—	—	5,662	5,303	94	3,949	838	516	100	259
TOLLAND	CT	t	7	5	—	40	—	—	n	—	—								
TONAWANDA	NY	c	1	33	28	40	42,812	52,774	y	54,474	5								
TOWAMENCIN	PA	tp	1	24	20	40	35,995	72,803	y	77,899	5	3,198	2,895	91	1,921	581	393	86	217
TOWN & COUNTRY	MO	c	1	42	34	40	45,864	64,896	y	73,821	5	3,993	3,905	98	2,623	984	298	267	1,103
TRAVERSE CITY	MI	c	1	35	32	40	37,565	42,702	y	45,698	10	3,724	2,815	76	1,940	562	312	—	909
TRENTON	MI	c	1	36	36	40	40,933	56,844	y	—	5	4,646	4,259	92	3,009	675	574	22	365
TROUTDALE	OR	c	3	26	22	40	46,968	57,096	y	59,380	5	3,290	2,346	71	1,716	279	350	173	770
TROY	OH	c	3	45	42	40	41,580	57,564	y	63,320	5	4,843	4,054	84	2,946	579	528	323	467
TRUSSVILLE	AL	c	1	54	42	42	34,445	53,394	n	—	—	4,488	4,288	96	2,980	1,086	222	115	531
TUALATIN	OR	c	1	42	35	42	47,174	62,078	n	—	—								

Table 3/16 continued POLICE DEPARTMENT PERSONNEL, SALARIES, AND EXPENDITURES FOR CITIES 10,000 AND OVER: 2008

City	State	Type	Service provision	Full-time paid personnel	Full-time uniformed personnel	Duty hours per week	Minimum base salary ($)	Maximum base salary ($)	Longevity pay	Maximum salary with longevity ($)	Years of service for longevity	Total expenditures (A) ($)	Total personnel expenditures (B) ($)	(B) as % of (A)	Salaries and wages (C) ($)	City contribution to retirement and social security (D) ($)	City contribution to insurance (E) ($)	Capital outlay (F) ($)	All other (G) ($)
10,000–24,999 continued																			
TWENTYNINE PALMS	CA	c	5	—	—	—	—	—	—	—	—	—	—	—	—	—	—	—	—
UKIAH	CA	c	1	38	27	—	46,011	64,742	n	—	—	5,051	—	—	4,108	—	520	40	943
UNIVERSAL CITY	TX	c	1	39	29	40	33,987	—	y	34,035	1	2,212	—	—	1,544	231	—	95	342
UNIVERSITY PARK	TX	c	1	51	40	40	51,132	65,256	y	66,456	1	5,664	4,692	83	3,459	744	488	79	893
UPPER ALLEN	PA	tp	1	18	4	40	60,476	60,476	y	61,686	5	2,070	1,819	88	1,253	310	256	144	250
UPPER GWYNEDD	PA	tp	1	24	21	42	39,764	72,298	y	—	5	2,893	2,664	92	1,796	267	600	42	187
UPPER PROVIDENCE	PA	tp	1	23	21	40	50,923	63,654	y	66,154	6	2,995	2,588	86	1,661	354	574	151	216
UPPER ST. CLAIR	PA	tp	1	35	28	40	44,762	71,032	y	74,932	4	4,338	3,948	91	2,685	666	596	175	215
UVALDE	TX	c	1	39	30	40	26,374	39,208	y	39,208	1	2,225	—	—	1,575	190	—	153	306
VAN WERT	OH	c	1	23	23	40	32,385	42,661	y	43,911	5	2,315	—	—	1,437	—	301	190	183
VANDALIA	OH	c	1	40	31	40	46,291	61,690	n	—	—	4,213	3,584	85	2,645	512	426	305	323
VENICE	FL	c	3	67	48	40	38,110	58,750	y	—	10	7,292	6,270	86	4,236	940	1,094	294	728
VERO BEACH	FL	c	—	86	62	40	36,254	57,948	n	—	—	7,185	6,061	84	4,740	650	670	215	909
VILLA PARK	IL	v	1	55	40	40	54,200	72,448	y	73,098	7	5,500	—	—	4,131	—	571	11	786
WALPOLE	MA	t	1	44	36	40	40,906	60,675	y	61,550	5	4,862	4,439	91	3,526	449	464	144	280
WANTAGE	NJ	tp	7	—	—	—	—	—	—	—	—	—	—	—	—	—	—	—	—
WARREN	PA	c	1	21	16	40	31,025	36,500	y	39,000	5	1,177	—	—	742	—	249	33	137
WARREN	RI	t	1	29	23	40	35,857	45,673	y	57,908	5	1,898	—	—	1,670	—	—	45	184
WARRENSBURG	MO	c	1	38	34	40	29,201	44,363	y	44,383	5	2,133	1,602	75	1,204	184	213	165	366
WARRENSVILLE HEIGHTS	OH	c	1	50	37	40	45,600	64,408	y	68,560	1	5,264	4,135	79	2,857	546	731	154	1,010
WARRENVILLE	IL	c	1	37	28	42	51,664	75,469	n	—	—	4,610	3,905	85	2,803	683	419	98	606
WARSAW	IN	c	1	42	35	40	36,660	41,003	y	49,203	1	3,515	2,879	82	2,036	385	458	103	533
WARWICK	PA	tp	1	20	18	40	40,856	67,771	y	—	4	2,561	2,274	89	1,575	278	421	88	200
WASHINGTON	IL	c	1	25	19	40	36,885	52,249	n	—	—	2,272	1,954	86	1,383	259	312	6	312
WASHINGTON (MORRIS)	NJ	tp	1	35	32	40	45,885	85,941	y	87,941	5	4,147	3,898	94	2,896	607	394	45	204
WATAUGA	TX	c	1	54	37	48	42,926	56,009	y	59,609	1	3,575	2,974	83	2,418	278	277	164	438
WEATHERFORD	TX	c	1	83	59	40	42,182	59,055	y	60,255	1	6,221	5,117	82	3,856	826	434	159	944
WEBSTER	MA	t	3	—	—	40	—	—	—	—	—	—	—	—	—	—	—	—	—
WEBSTER GROVES	MO	c	1	50	46	40	41,735	58,429	n	—	—	4,116	3,483	85	2,816	319	347	80	552
WEST BRADFORD	PA	tp	7	—	—	—	—	—	—	—	—	—	—	—	—	—	—	—	—
WEST CHESTER	PA	b	1	—	—	40	46,003	66,465	y	—	5	4,871	—	—	3,549	—	—	226	476
WEST COLUMBIA	SC	c	1	72	54	42	29,756	85,171	n	—	—	4,449	3,307	74	2,450	443	414	222	920
WEST DEER	PA	tp	1	12	12	40	33,896	52,147	y	52,771	4	1,119	—	—	757	—	89	15	199
WEST LAMPETER	PA	tp	1	16	15	40	42,358	56,477	y	59,477	5	1,550	1,324	85	889	179	256	84	142
WEST MANCHESTER	PA	tp	1	29	26	40	42,140	63,708	y	74,283	20	2,076	—	—	1,722	—	169	—	355
WEST PLAINS	MO	c	4	—	—	42	—	—	—	—	—	—	—	—	—	—	—	—	—
WEST WHITELAND	PA	tp	1	30	28	42	37,404	71,593	y	74,321	5	4,022	3,483	87	2,503	485	494	136	403
WESTBOROUGH	MA	t	1	35	34	40	45,419	51,467	y	57,893	25	2,810	2,674	95	2,275	199	200	55	81
WESTCHESTER	IL	v	1	47	35	40	48,300	70,424	n	—	—	5,170	4,694	91	3,470	561	663	87	389
WESTERN SPRINGS	IL	v	1	29	21	40	46,677	65,736	n	—	—	2,998	2,710	90	2,006	498	206	122	166
WHITE	PA	tp	7	—	—	—	—	—	—	—	—	—	—	—	—	—	—	—	—
WHITE BEAR LAKE	MN	c	1	—	38	40	38,926	59,886	y	67,136	4	2,901	2,420	83	1,933	236	252	156	325
WHITEFISH BAY	WI	v	1	27	25	42	44,504	59,485	y	59,460	5	2,657	2,404	90	1,723	364	316	80	174
WHITEHALL	PA	b	1	20	20	40	50,454	72,078	y	76,403	5	2,236	—	—	1,612	—	231	47	335
WHITPAIN	PA	tp	1	38	31	40	47,970	76,995	y	84,694	5	4,081	3,576	88	2,770	311	495	81	3,275
WILLIAMSBURG	VA	c	3	54	36	40	32,760	55,224	n	—	—	4,339	3,435	79	2,506	547	381	310	595
WILLOWICK	OH	c	1	35	25	40	48,069	65,187	y	67,184	5	3,188	—	—	2,235	—	396	—	231
WILTON	CT	t	1	44	38	other	48,877	66,922	y	67,572	10	—	—	—	—	—	—	—	—
WILTON MANORS	FL	c	1	42	32	40	45,316	68,139	n	—	—	—	5,057	—	2,715	1,524	817	—	619
WINCHESTER	KY	c	1	38	34	40	26,664	43,335	y	43,335	4	3,142	2,667	85	1,711	574	382	93	382
WINCHESTER	VA	c	1	79	66	40	32,815	57,865	n	—	—	6,216	5,422	87	4,066	785	570	181	612
WINDHAM	ME	t	1	28	26	40	36,658	45,732	y	46,732	12	1,607	—	—	1,500	—	—	33	75
WINDHAM	NH	t	1	20	18	40	40,188	48,473	n	—	—	2,116	1,801	85	1,346	155	300	72	243
WINDSOR	CA	t	5	—	—	—	—	—	—	—	—	4,549	—	—	—	—	—	—	—
WINDSOR LOCKS	CT	t	1	33	25	other	53,802	62,193	y	62,793	5	3,758	3,524	94	2,641	367	515	78	156
WINFIELD	KS	c	3	32	23	40	28,496	38,230	n	—	—	2,029	1,759	87	1,267	285	206	80	190
WINTER GARDEN	FL	c	1	81	62	42	40,394	—	n	—	—	7,586	5,419	71	3,873	888	658	1,162	950
WIXOM	MI	c	1	25	21	40	38,255	61,791	y	63,954	15	3,274	—	—	1,875	—	—	90	485
WOODBURN	OR	c	1	40	32	42	42,984	54,696	n	—	—	4,234	3,385	80	2,403	491	491	2,286	966
WOODHAVEN	MI	c	1	34	30	40	41,163	63,814	n	—	—	—	—	—	—	—	—	—	—
WOODSTOCK	GA	c	1	47	44	42	32,576	49,569	n	—	—	3,513	2,804	80	2,144	469	191	222	487
WOODSTOCK	IL	c	1	54	41	40	46,200	74,587	n	—	—	4,972	—	—	3,721	—	774	12	415
WOODWARD	OK	c	3	36	25	40	31,423	40,584	y	—	1	1,251	1,083	87	762	114	207	121	47
WORTH	IL	v	1	26	24	42	42,305	66,496	y	—	20	2,458	2,273	92	1,722	258	292	52	425
WORTHINGTON	MN	c	1	24	—	40	44,904	52,838	y	53,858	5	2,217	1,937	87	1,487	188	262	40	240
WORTHINGTON	OH	c	1	48	34	40	43,786	67,379	y	68,679	5	4,905	—	—	3,285	—	638	141	264
WYLIE	TX	c	1	46	42	42	49,000	65,913	y	—	—	4,123	3,288	80	2,503	362	422	417	418
XENIA	OH	c	1	53	47	40	41,371	56,950	n	—	—	5,109	—	—	3,225	—	655	201	520
YANKTON	SD	c	1	26	26	40	32,566	44,058	y	—	5	2,343	1,946	83	1,499	222	225	88	309
YARMOUTH	MA	t	1	85	59	42	40,980	53,751	y	54,701	5	6,459	—	—	5,690	—	311	206	193
YAZOO CITY	MS	c	1	—	41	42	31,669	32,600	n	—	—	2,289	—	—	1,479	—	175	119	402
YUCCA VALLEY	CA	t	5	—	—	40	—	—	—	—	—	—	—	—	—	—	—	—	—
ZEPHYRHILLS	FL	c	1	54	34	42	35,485	53,227	n	—	—	4,116	3,168	77	2,219	775	173	383	595

Table 3/17   **FIRE DEPARTMENT PERSONNEL, SALARIES, AND EXPENDITURES FOR CITIES 10,000 AND OVER: 2008**

This table comprises 1,407 cities 10,000 and over in population (based on U.S. Bureau of the Census 2000 counts). The information in the table was collected in the spring of 2008 in a survey conducted by ICMA. Refer to the accompanying article for the survey methodology. The information is presented in two separate tables—one for police (Table 3/16) and one for fire (Table 3/17). The following definitions apply to both tables.

Type: letter identifies municipal designation: c, city; v, village; b, borough; t, town; tp, township.

Service provision: the number in this column indicates how the service is provided.
1 Full-time paid
2 All volunteer
3 Combined paid and volunteer
4 Public safety department (consolidated police and fire department)
5 Contract with county or other government entity for service
6 Contract with private company for service
7 Other

Full-time paid personnel: the number in this column shows the actual (not authorized) number of full-time paid employees.

Full-time uniformed personnel: the number in this column shows the number of sworn/uniformed employees.

Duty hours per week: shows the average number of hours worked per week.

Minimum base salary ($): shows the minimum base salary paid to full-time sworn/uniformed personnel. This amount does not include uniform allowance, holiday pay, hazard pay, or any other additional compensation.

Maximum base salary ($): shows the maximum base salary paid to full-time sworn/uniformed personnel. This amount does not include uniform allowance, holiday pay, hazard pay, or any other additional compensation.

Longevity pay: shows whether personnel can receive longevity pay: y, yes; n, no.

Maximum salary with longevity ($): shows the maximum salary with longevity pay included.

Years of service for longevity: shows the number of years of service required before personnel can receive longevity pay.

Total expenditures (A) ($): shows total departmental expenditures for the most recently completed fiscal year.

Total personnel expenditures (B) ($): shows total expenditures for salaries and wages (C); city contribution to retirement and social security (D); and city contribution to health, hospitalization, disability, and life insurance programs (E).

(B) as % of (A): shows total personnel expenditures as a percentage of total departmental expenditures. In some instances, the percentage equals or exceeds 100%. For some cities the retirement expenditures are in other accounts, so although they are reported as costs, they do not come out of the departmental budget. This accounts for the percentage in excess of 100.

Salaries and wages (C) ($): shows the amount of salaries and wages for all departmental personnel—regular, temporary, full time, and part time—and of stipends for volunteers. This is a gross amount, including longevity pay, hazard pay, and holiday pay, without deduction of withholding for income tax or employee contributions to social security or retirement coverage.

City contribution to retirement and social security (D) ($): shows city contributions only.

City contribution to insurance (E) ($): shows city contribution to health, hospitalization, disability, and life insurance programs.

Capital outlay (F) ($): Shows amount spent on purchases of equipment, land and existing structures, and construction.

All other (G) ($): shows amount of expenditures other than those described in (B) through (F) above. Expenditures include fuel, utilities, supplies, etc.

(—) Indicates data not reported.

											Reported expenditures (in $000)						
City	State	Type	Service provision	Full-time paid personnel	Full-time uniformed personnel	Duty hours per week	Minimum base salary ($)	Maximum base salary ($)	Longevity pay	Maximum salary with longevity ($)	Years of service for longevity	Total expenditures (A) ($)	Total personnel expenditures (B) ($)	(B) as % of (A)	Salaries and wages (C) ($)	City contribution to retirement and social security (D) ($)	City contribution to insurance (E) ($)	Capital outlay (F) ($)	All other (G) ($)
Over 1,000,000																			
LOS ANGELES	CA	c	1	3,939	3,586	56	53,766	82,810	y	89,050	10	—	—	—	—	—	—	—	—
PHOENIX	AZ	c	1	1,747	1,747	56	37,955	59,320	y	63,320	7	236,642	181,731	77	151,775	2,658	27,298	10,991	28,584
SAN DIEGO	CA	c	1	1,173	922	56	—	—	n	—	—	245,047	—	—	159,715	—	—	2,682	28,563
500,000–1,000,000																			
BALTIMORE	MD	c	1	1,731	1,701	42	32,038	51,939	y	60,250	5	137,761	—	—	101,900	22,231	—	19,553	14,969
EL PASO	TX	c	1	945	868	56	34,221	53,092	—	—	—	—	—	—	—	—	—	—	—
SAN JOSE	CA	c	1	849	744	56	70,740	94,827	n	—	—	142,608	—	—	91,155	—	9,653	15,294	6,822
SEATTLE	WA	c	1	1,189	927	other	59,196	73,368	y	84,000	5	139,329	111,066	80	90,347	6,085	14,633	1,721	26,942
250,000–499,999																			
ALBUQUERQUE	NM	c	1	692	659	56	43,097	46,592	y	50,782	8	66,528	56,864	85	38,210	12,091	6,563	6,318	3,346
ANCHORAGE	AK	c	1	—	—	56	—	—	—	—	—	—	—	—	—	—	—	—	—
AURORA	CO	c	1	329	311	56	41,585	67,791	n	—	—	31,836	28,614	90	22,956	1,974	3,683	83	3,739
CINCINNATI	OH	c	—	—	—	—	—	—	—	—	—	—	—	—	—	—	—	—	—
FRESNO	CA	c	1	424	—	56	54,672	69,732	n	—	—	54,038	37,700	70	30,134	6,294	1,271	4,292	—
MINNEAPOLIS	MN	c	1	452	430	50–54	43,654	60,242	y	—	7	49,730	39,822	80	29,685	3,781	6,355	427	9,481
OMAHA	NE	c	1	649	640	56	34,223	57,375	y	60,847	7	75,908	65,700	87	48,904	10,886	5,909	6,536	3,671
RALEIGH	NC	c	1	—	—	50–54	31,117	55,580	y	56,691	5	—	—	—	29,045	—	2,120	3,398	—
RIVERSIDE	CA	c	1	235	209	56	54,564	73,068	n	—	—	57,055	—	—	25,188	—	2,736	14,715	8,198
SANTA ANA	CA	c	1	242	213	56	58,008	70,512	n	—	—	46,600	—	—	30,743	—	5,836	258	4,515
VIRGINIA BEACH	VA	c	3	477	435	56	36,630	53,113	n	—	—	44,039	36,051	82	27,403	6,272	2,376	4,352	3,636
WICHITA	KS	c	1	432	425	56	37,149	52,499	y	—	6	34,249	31,152	91	23,247	4,130	3,774	600	2,497
100,000–249,999																			
ABILENE	TX	c	1	177	171	56	34,226	48,253	y	60,253	—	13,312	12,391	93	9,868	1,860	662	85	836
AKRON	OH	c	1	381	353	48	44,970	52,520	y	55,671	5	40,190	35,872	89	25,282	5,852	4,738	909	3,419
ALLENTOWN	PA	c	1	140	135	42	40,611	55,593	y	57,418	5	15,773	—	—	14,784	—	137	116	289
AMARILLO	TX	c	1	—	227	56	34,752	49,296	y	51,096	1	20,318	17,480	86	13,587	2,187	1,705	370	2,468
ANN ARBOR	MI	c	1	94	79	50–54	44,784	63,175	y	63,675	7	12,657	11,118	88	7,564	865	2,688	85	1,454
ARVADA	CO	c	—	—	—	—	—	—	—	—	—	—	—	—	—	—	—	—	—
BAKERSFIELD	CA	c	1	210	183	56	50,511	61,496	y	64,571	15	24,376	—	—	15,047	—	2,852	134	2,526
BATON ROUGE–EAST BATON ROUGE	LA	c	1	554	553	56	28,102	41,269	y	49,522	10	48,653	42,825	88	32,308	4,491	6,025	2,807	3,022

Table 3/17 continued — **FIRE DEPARTMENT PERSONNEL, SALARIES, AND EXPENDITURES FOR CITIES 10,000 AND OVER: 2008**

City	State	Type	Service provision	Full-time paid personnel	Full-time uniformed personnel	Duty hours per week	Minimum base salary ($)	Maximum base salary ($)	Longevity pay	Maximum salary with longevity ($)	Years of service for longevity	Total expenditures (A) ($)	Total personnel expenditures (B) ($)	(B) as % of (A)	Salaries and wages (C) ($)	City contribution to retirement and social security (D) ($)	City contribution to insurance (E) ($)	Capital outlay (F) ($)	All other (G) ($)
100,000–249,999 continued																			
BERKELEY	CA	c	1	137	125	—	75,180	94,716	n	—	—	25,245	—	—	14,657	—	4,329	102	2,566
BROWNSVILLE	TX	c	1	197	187	50–54	27,922	62,387	y	63,011	1	18,051	21,380	118	16,501	2,541	2,337	8	1,542
CAMBRIDGE	MA	c	—	—	—	—	—	—	—	—	—	—	—	—	—	—	—	—	—
CAPE CORAL	FL	c	1	207	192	48	44,229	59,005	n	—	—	29,842	21,765	73	13,846	4,669	3,249	5,781	2,297
CARROLLTON	TX	c	1	129	36	—	—	—	—	—	—	—	—	—	—	—	—	—	—
CHESAPEAKE	VA	c	1	438	425	56	39,182	67,434	n	—	—	39,636	33,986	86	24,692	5,381	3,913	75	5,575
CLEARWATER	FL	c	1	212	193	50–54	35,323	52,486	n	—	—	23,786	20,032	84	13,464	4,590	1,978	59	3,695
COLUMBIA	SC	c	1	444	423	other	29,894	46,270	n	—	—	31,582	27,048	86	19,967	3,551	3,530	521	4,012
COLUMBUS–MUSCOGEE CONSOLIDATED	GA	c	1	377	367	56	27,316	46,797	n	—	—	22,292	20,545	92	14,566	4,191	1,788	96	1,651
CONCORD	CA	c	—	—	—	—	—	—	—	—	—	—	—	—	—	—	—	—	—
CORAL SPRINGS	FL	c	1	191	157	48	48,919	66,400	y	73,040	5	21,353	16,175	76	11,865	2,411	1,898	1,875	3,303
COSTA MESA	CA	c	1	101	93	56	63,816	85,524	n	—	—	19,367	—	—	13,224	—	1,376	334	1,673
EL MONTE	CA	c	5	—	—	—	—	—	—	—	—	—	—	—	—	—	—	—	—
FAYETTEVILLE	NC	c	1	284	148	56	27,967	47,329	y	50,878	5	21,581	16,245	75	12,147	1,466	2,631	2,497	2,839
FULLERTON	CA	c	1	94	89	56	51,684	69,253	n	—	—	15,775	13,649	87	9,638	2,759	1,251	219	1,908
GARLAND	TX	c	3	261	124	56	49,412	62,435	y	63,710	3	25,738	23,639	92	18,943	3,169	1,526	327	1,773
GILBERT	AZ	t	1	—	—	56	43,565	60,990	n	—	—	20,565	17,427	85	13,707	1,230	2,490	74	3,064
GLENDALE	AZ	c	3	272	219	other	40,126	59,284	y	60,884	3	—	—	—	—	—	—	—	—
GRAND PRAIRIE	TX	c	3	209	20	56	46,520	63,916	y	65,596	1	22,503	18,451	82	14,080	2,960	1,410	2,630	1,423
GRAND RAPIDS	MI	c	1	234	234	50–54	36,604	55,922	y	56,912	5	23,999	20,930	87	17,796	2,974	160	1,195	1,874
HAMPTON	VA	c	3	268	257	50–54	36,700	59,905	y	—	3	16,286	—	—	13,506	—	—	341	2,439
HENDERSON	NV	c	1	207	190	56	51,309	75,828	n	—	—	69,371	59,538	86	41,066	10,947	7,524	1,458	8,376
HUNTINGTON BEACH	CA	c	1	148	126	56	57,450	106,563	n	—	—	—	—	—	13,098	—	—	—	—
IRVINE	CA	c	—	—	—	—	—	—	—	—	—	—	—	—	—	—	—	—	—
JOLIET	IL	c	1	215	211	50–54	47,089	73,173	y	—	15	—	28,991	—	20,439	4,917	3,635	—	—
LAKEWOOD	CO	c	—	—	—	—	—	—	—	—	—	—	—	—	—	—	—	—	—
LAREDO	TX	c	1	350	337	56	37,827	48,796	y	50,152	1	31,266	29,190	93	22,813	4,069	2,307	6	2,070
LUBBOCK	TX	c	1	330	300	56	38,697	48,998	y	50,198	1	26,701	25,079	94	18,125	4,080	2,873	11	1,911
McALLEN	TX	c	1	160	150	56	36,962	36,962	y	51,962	1	14,159	10,605	75	8,147	618	1,840	1,944	1,611
MESQUITE	TX	c	1	—	—	56	—	—	—	—	—	—	—	—	—	—	—	—	—
NAPERVILLE	IL	c	1	213	202	56	55,635	76,062	y	77,562	10	25,909	23,387	90	17,195	3,513	2,679	38	2,484
NORFOLK	VA	c	1	517	499	56	35,492	54,008	n	—	—	38,065	35,347	93	28,598	4,035	2,713	106	2,612
NORWALK	CA	c	—	—	—	—	—	—	—	—	—	—	—	—	—	—	—	—	—
OCEANSIDE	CA	c	1	116	105	56	—	—	n	—	—	23,566	—	—	17,453	—	—	31	4,255
ONTARIO	CA	c	1	153	140	56	54,911	66,744	y	80,093	10	35,605	29,883	84	20,121	3,390	6,370	2,784	2,939
OVERLAND PARK	KS	c	1	159	129	56	37,476	64,392	n	—	—	17,300	16,290	94	10,918	3,594	1,777	150	1,855
PALMDALE	CA	c	—	—	—	—	—	—	—	—	—	—	—	—	—	—	—	—	—
PASADENA	CA	c	1	187	167	56	50,033	80,021	n	—	—	36,798	—	—	18,982	—	1,956	411	12,231
PASADENA	TX	c	3	14	7	other	35,993	53,990	y	—	1	4,787	984	21	685	146	152	258	3,545
PEMBROKE PINES	FL	c	1	255	228	other	—	—	y	—	10	34,426	30,784	89	18,529	8,375	3,879	1,679	1,963
PEORIA	AZ	c	1	157	133	56	33,284	57,279	n	—	—	20,569	16,209	79	13,028	1,105	2,075	192	4,168
PROVIDENCE	RI	c	1	—	—	48	43,426	56,908	y	63,167	5	—	—	—	27,840	—	—	—	—
RICHMOND	VA	c	—	—	—	—	—	—	—	—	—	—	—	—	—	—	—	—	—
SALEM	OR	c	1	165	158	56	44,146	62,375	n	—	—	24,334	18,047	74	12,084	3,687	2,275	1,128	5,160
SALINAS	CA	c	1	96	89	56	62,436	79,704	y	83,689	20	14,882	12,079	81	8,853	452	2,774	2,014	789
SALT LAKE CITY	UT	c	1	369	335	—	36,358	57,177	y	58,677	20	30,396	27,584	91	22,050	2,495	3,039	69	2,742
SAN BUENAVENTURA (VENTURA)	CA	c	1	114	79	56	53,317	68,047	n	—	—	17,894	—	—	9,727	—	1,417	115	2,046
SANTA CLARA	CA	c	3	160	150	56	90,312	109,812	y	115,212	10	29,794	—	—	21,066	—	—	27	2,043
SAVANNAH	GA	c	1	333	300	56	32,471	48,782	n	—	—	21,984	18,053	82	14,048	1,873	2,131	133	3,797
SOUTH BEND	IN	c	1	260	244	56	35,535	48,270	n	—	—	23,027	—	—	14,159	—	1,925	3,069	—
SPRINGFIELD	MA	c	—	—	—	—	—	—	—	—	—	—	—	—	—	—	—	—	—
STERLING HEIGHTS	MI	c	1	107	100	56	40,497	64,818	y	68,868	5	16,088	14,110	88	9,593	1,181	3,335	1,260	718
ST. PETERSBURG	FL	c	1	345	319	50–54	34,826	54,455	n	—	—	44,563	39,821	89	23,548	11,661	4,612	1,406	43,157
SUNNYVALE	CA	c	4	—	—	50–54	—	—	—	—	—	—	—	—	—	—	—	—	—
TACOMA	WA	c	1	443	411	other	51,418	67,683	y	73,098	5	—	—	—	—	—	—	—	—
TALLAHASSEE	FL	c	1	263	249	50–54	32,148	51,470	n	—	—	24,944	—	—	14,748	—	1,777	104	6,184
THORNTON	IL	tp	—	—	—	—	—	—	—	—	—	—	—	—	—	—	—	—	—
THOUSAND OAKS	CA	c	—	—	—	—	—	—	—	—	—	—	—	—	—	—	—	—	—
TOPEKA	KS	c	1	249	233	56	37,136	37,136	y	39,427	5	19,031	17,642	93	13,854	2,138	1,649	—	1,389
VANCOUVER	WA	c	3	215	182	48	57,312	72,444	n	—	—	30,038	23,032	77	18,976	1,019	3,037	1,152	5,854
WACO	TX	c	1	196	190	56	38,036	50,369	y	51,714	1	16,971	14,333	84	10,955	2,441	936	58	258
WEST COVINA	CA	c	1	85	80	56	65,124	79,164	y	84,705	10	14,567	16,720	115	12,425	2,810	1,485	185	10,087
WEST VALLEY CITY	UT	c	1	97	94	56	34,200	55,708	n	—	—	7,595	—	—	4,474	—	447	126	1,654
WICHITA FALLS	TX	c	1	160	158	56	37,233	51,113	y	—	1	11,223	10,342	92	8,094	1,434	813	6	876
WINSTON–SALEM	NC	c	1	346	182	56	29,040	60,720	n	—	—	—	20,358	—	15,316	1,906	3,136	84	2,089
50,000–99,999																			
ALHAMBRA	CA	c	1	74	66	56	53,844	68,724	n	—	—	14,104	11,033	78	7,576	2,272	1,185	939	2,132
ANTIOCH	CA	c	—	—	—	—	—	—	—	—	—	—	—	—	—	—	—	—	—
BAYTOWN	TX	c	1	96	90	56	35,861	49,906	y	51,106	1	9,571	7,205	75	5,235	1,175	794	1,084	1,282

Table 3/17 continued   FIRE DEPARTMENT PERSONNEL, SALARIES, AND EXPENDITURES FOR CITIES 10,000 AND OVER: 2008

City	State	Type	Service provision	Full-time paid personnel	Full-time uniformed personnel	Duty hours per week	Minimum base salary ($)	Maximum base salary ($)	Longevity pay	Maximum salary with longevity ($)	Years of service for longevity	Reported expenditures (in $000)							
												Total expenditures (A) ($)	Total personnel expenditures (B) ($)	(B) as % of (A)	Salaries and wages (C) ($)	City contribution to retirement and social security (D) ($)	City contribution to insurance (E) ($)	Capital outlay (F) ($)	All other (G) ($)
50,000–99,999 continued																			
BELLINGHAM	WA	c	1	164	145	48	53,382	67,733	y	70,104	5	22,620	16,727	74	12,319	2,136	2,271	491	5,402
BETHLEHEM	PA	c	1	114	113	42	35,524	50,771	y	55,271	4	8,670	—	—	6,159	—	1,210	66	190
BLOOMINGTON	MN	c	2	3	—	other	—	—	n	—	—	2,804	931	33	852	27	52	219	1,653
BOSSIER CITY	LA	c	1	228	185	56	32,616	32,616	y	—	3	10,251	14,918	146	10,251	3,114	1,552	1,727	—
BOULDER	CO	c	1	124	102	56	44,310	57,484	y	—	4	13,040	11,089	85	8,595	869	1,625	654	1,296
BOWIE	MD	c	—	—	—	—	—	—	—	—	—	—	—	—	—	—	—	—	—
BRICK	NJ	tp	2	—	—	—	—	—	—	—	—	—	—	—	—	—	—	—	—
BRYAN	TX	c	1	97	92	56	37,012	42,952	y	44,152	1	8,525	7,138	84	5,358	1,105	676	125	1,262
BUENA PARK	CA	c	5	—	—	—	—	—	—	—	—	—	—	—	—	—	—	—	—
BURNSVILLE	MN	c	1	41	39	56	50,808	67,884	y	71,952	4	4,728	4,133	87	3,242	382	509	46	549
CAMARILLO	CA	c	—	—	—	—	—	—	—	—	—	—	—	—	—	—	—	—	—
CANTON	OH	c	1	173	170	40	38,626	47,770	y	49,570	3	15,676	—	—	9,218	—	—	296	3,961
CARSON	CA	c	1	3,926	2,788	56	49,643	72,571	y	90,375	10	814,432	—	—	467,251	—	83,036	31,691	—
CARY	NC	t	1	202	188	50–54	33,072	51,251	n	—	—	16,499	12,658	77	10,336	2,044	278	1,746	1,303
CHARLESTON	WV	c	1	203	198	56	29,688	32,705	y	36,844	1	16,022	13,781	86	9,116	2,972	1,693	1,108	1,133
CHINO	CA	c	—	—	—	—	—	—	—	—	—	—	—	—	—	—	—	—	—
CHINO HILLS	CA	c	—	—	—	—	—	—	—	—	—	—	—	—	—	—	—	—	—
CITRUS HEIGHTS	CA	c	—	—	—	—	—	—	—	—	—	—	—	—	—	—	—	—	—
CLINTON	MI	tp	1	96	92	56	42,699	70,895	y	72,195	5	14,971	12,676	85	7,688	2,356	2,632	257	2,020
COLERAIN TOWNSHIP	OH	tp	1	55	52	50–54	40,576	65,628	n	—	—	10,757	7,701	72	5,675	1,142	884	—	3,056
CORVALLIS	OR	c	3	68	65	56	46,793	61,156	n	—	—	8,848	6,860	78	4,897	964	999	348	1,639
DAVIS	CA	c	1	—	—	56	65,602	87,714	—	—	—	—	—	—	—	—	—	—	—
DAYTONA BEACH	FL	c	1	122	114	40	30,801	53,276	n	—	—	11,840	10,056	85	6,725	2,037	1,294	305	1,479
DECATUR	IL	c	1	116	114	56	41,461	52,910	y	59,259	25	17,210	—	—	7,435	—	5,739	—	1,172
DELRAY BEACH	FL	c	1	152	144	48	39,888	61,058	n	—	—	—	17,241	—	12,108	3,369	1,763	—	—
DELTONA	FL	c	1	81	70	48	32,558	57,673	y	—	—	9,119	—	—	4,901	—	—	—	—
DES PLAINES	IL	c	1	107	104	48	50,793	74,061	y	76,061	10	15,122	14,681	97	8,666	4,383	1,631	1,501	669
DIAMOND BAR	CA	c	—	—	—	—	—	—	—	—	—	—	—	—	—	—	—	—	—
DOTHAN	AL	c	1	167	160	56	28,662	43,908	n	—	—	11,695	10,635	91	7,351	2,027	1,257	58	1,001
DUBUQUE	IA	c	1	90	89	56	40,855	48,048	y	51,411	5	8,839	7,284	82	4,951	1,373	960	633	922
EAGAN	MN	c	2	5	—	—	—	—	n	—	—	2,141	—	—	1,068	—	—	557	516
EDEN PRAIRIE	MN	c	2	8	—	other	54,725	69,306	n	—	—	2,944	1,016	35	881	81	53	877	1,051
EDMOND	OK	c	1	118	114	56	—	—	y	—	4	1,298,779	—	—	—	—	88,249	—	80,773
ELGIN	IL	c	1	137	135	50–54	53,033	70,685	y	72,285	10	15,958	15,056	94	11,338	1,531	2,186	341	561
EVANSTON	IL	c	—	—	—	—	—	—	—	—	—	—	—	—	—	—	—	—	—
FARMINGTON HILLS	MI	c	3	48	34	42	44,335	66,490	y	71,809	3	8,348	7,193	86	5,264	1,248	681	112	1,042
FEDERAL WAY	WA	c	—	—	—	—	—	—	—	—	—	—	—	—	—	—	—	—	—
FLAGSTAFF	AZ	c	1	97	95	56	38,897	53,674	n	—	—	9,218	8,150	88	6,560	765	825	233	834
FLOWER MOUND	TX	t	1	72	60	56	46,117	58,353	y	59,553	1	6,603	5,787	88	4,359	709	718	93	723
FOLSOM	CA	c	1	76	35	48	64,432	78,297	y	84,169	10	—	—	—	—	—	—	—	—
FREDERICK	MD	c	—	—	—	—	—	—	—	—	—	—	—	—	—	—	—	—	—
GAITHERSBURG	MD	c	—	—	—	—	—	—	—	—	—	—	—	—	—	—	—	—	—
GARDENA	CA	c	—	—	—	—	—	—	—	—	—	—	—	—	—	—	—	—	—
GASTONIA	NC	c	1	141	139	56	27,014	42,016	y	—	—	9,439	8,115	86	6,543	685	886	6	1,318
GREAT FALLS	MT	c	1	68	65	48	36,384	—	y	—	1	5,508	4,429	80	3,233	545	651	87	992
GREELEY	CO	c	1	108	101	56	42,595	59,713	n	—	—	11,073	—	—	9,639	—	—	70	1,364
GREEN	OH	tp	1	41	39	56	48,390	58,263	y	—	10	6,509	—	—	6,199	—	—	310	—
GREENVILLE	NC	c	1	128	125	56	30,000	63,000	n	—	—	10,000	8,800	88	7,000	800	1,000	77	900
HAMILTON	NJ	tp	—	—	—	—	—	—	—	—	—	—	—	—	—	—	—	—	—
HAMILTON	OH	c	1	114	113	50–54	43,056	55,640	y	61,214	5	12,360	11,305	91	7,971	1,954	1,379	69	986
HAMMOND	IN	c	—	—	—	—	—	—	—	—	—	—	—	—	—	—	—	—	—
HARLINGEN	TX	c	1	111	108	56	29,000	35,500	y	36,700	1	6,901	5,930	86	4,728	627	574	117	854
HAWTHORNE	CA	c	—	—	—	—	—	—	—	—	—	—	—	—	—	—	—	—	—
HESPERIA	CA	c	5	47	41	56	33,696	43,139	n	—	—	7,566	—	—	4,042	—	815	535	1,181
HILLSBORO	OR	c	3	87	79	50–54	—	—	n	—	—	12,465	9,473	76	7,100	1,405	968	314	2,677
HOOVER	AL	c	1	153	152	50–54	40,456	57,595	n	—	—	17,035	14,294	84	10,951	1,721	1,622	1,171	1,571
HUNTINGTON PARK	CA	c	—	—	—	—	—	—	—	—	—	—	—	—	—	—	—	—	—
IDAHO FALLS	ID	c	1	102	99	56	37,722	51,091	y	53,398	3	11,109	—	—	6,088	—	—	267	1,211
IOWA CITY	IA	c	—	—	—	—	—	—	—	—	—	—	—	—	—	—	—	—	—
IRONDEQUOIT	NY	t	2	—	—	—	—	—	—	—	—	—	—	—	—	—	—	—	—
IRVINGTON	NJ	tp	—	139	134	48	39,898	78,603	y	86,463	5	12,085	—	—	11,676	—	—	—	409
JACKSONVILLE	NC	c	1	77	75	56	29,222	56,832	y	59,232	5	5,213	4,104	79	3,084	469	550	212	897
KALAMAZOO	MI	c	4	—	—	56	—	—	—	—	—	—	—	—	—	—	—	—	—
KENNEWICK	WA	c	1	79	77	50–54	47,736	62,808	y	67,833	28	9,308	7,604	82	6,256	376	971	56	1,648
KENT	WA	c	1	176	163	56	57,156	76,212	y	83,076	25	23,188	18,355	79	14,937	920	2,497	763	4,071
KILLEEN	TX	c	1	193	190	50–54	34,395	51,592	y	53,272	1	11,458	9,995	87	7,824	1,607	564	207	1,256
LA CROSSE	WI	c	1	96	95	56	38,646	47,991	y	53,736	10	9,345	8,867	95	5,578	1,233	2,055	85	393
LA HABRA	CA	c	—	—	—	—	—	—	—	—	—	—	—	—	—	—	—	—	—
LAGUNA NIGUEL	CA	c	—	—	—	—	—	—	—	—	—	—	—	—	—	—	—	—	—
LAKE FOREST	CA	c	5	—	—	—	—	—	—	—	—	—	—	—	—	—	—	—	—
LAKELAND	FL	c	1	148	132	50–54	36,403	51,235	y	51,715	10	11,781	—	—	8,433	—	722	395	1,100
LAKEWOOD	CA	c	—	—	—	—	—	—	—	—	—	—	—	—	—	—	—	—	—
LAS CRUCES	NM	c	1	125	122	56	37,201	—	y	52,346	21	10,975	9,179	84	6,856	1,284	1,038	91	1,707

Table 3/17 continued — FIRE DEPARTMENT PERSONNEL, SALARIES, AND EXPENDITURES FOR CITIES 10,000 AND OVER: 2008

City	State	Type	Service provision	Full-time paid personnel	Full-time uniformed personnel	Duty hours per week	Minimum base salary ($)	Maximum base salary ($)	Longevity pay	Maximum salary with longevity ($)	Years of service for longevity	Total expenditures (A) ($)	Total personnel expenditures (B) ($)	(B) as % of (A)	Salaries and wages (C) ($)	City contribution to retirement and social security (D) ($)	City contribution to insurance (E) ($)	Capital outlay (F) ($)	All other (G) ($)
50,000–99,999 continued																			
LAUDERHILL	FL	c	1	103	100	48	46,630	65,612	y	68,236	10	11,524	10,481	91	7,286	2,393	801	193	850
LAWTON	OK	c	1	125	123	56	26,557	44,466	y	47,688	—	10,083	8,894	88	7,023	1,053	818	644	545
LAYTON	UT	c	1	49	45	56	33,710	53,003	n	—	—	5,855	3,906	67	3,355	235	315	491	—
LEWISVILLE	TX	c	1	135	127	56	46,801	56,854	y	58,054	1	13,236	—	—	8,787	—	1,075	218	2,025
LIVERMORE	CA	c	—	—	—	—	—	—		—	—	—	—	—	—	—	—	—	—
LODI	CA	c	1	56	55	48	47,752	63,991	n	—	—	8,442	—	—	5,113	—	949	24	911
LYNCHBURG	VA	c	1	183	183	56	30,618	57,387	n	—	—	14,001	12,882	92	9,633	2,334	914	25	1,094
LYNWOOD	CA	c	5	—	—	56	—	—		—	—	—	—	—	—	—	—	—	—
MANCHESTER	CT	t	1	84	80	42	44,833	62,188	y	62,588	10	11,843	8,838	75	6,419	905	1,513	696	2,310
MARGATE	FL	c	1	111	109	56	38,396	61,434	y	64,434	10	13,303	12,085	91	8,020	2,235	1,829	450	768
MARIETTA	GA	c	1	135	130	56	34,012	50,756	y	51,056	5	11,359	—	—	9,645	—	—	662	10,511
McKINNEY	TX	c	1	160	148	56	48,292	64,547	y	62,747	1	18,625	12,842	69	9,754	1,775	1,312	4,173	1,610
MEDFORD	OR	c	3	78	72	56	53,407	62,307	n	—	—	9,211	8,190	89	5,727	1,324	1,138	37	49
MIAMI BEACH	FL	c	1	231	205	48	42,301	70,046	y	77,751	7	36,903	—	—	21,782	—	2,044	92	4,995
MIDDLETOWN	OH	c	—	—	—	—	—	—		—	—	—	—	—	—	—	—	—	—
MILPITAS	CA	c	1	66	62	—	81,209	98,176	y	113,001	9	—	—	—	—	—	—	—	—
MINNETONKA	MN	c	1	7	7	40	47,000	74,782	n	—	—	2,137	973	46	815	85	73	490	674
MISSOURI CITY	TX	c	1	60	60	50–54	36,520	—	y	37,480	1	—	—	—	—	—	—	—	—
MONTEBELLO	CA	c	1	65	58	56	46,740	59,700	n	—	—	11,636	9,613	83	6,620	1,520	1,472	95	1,928
MONTEREY PARK	CA	c	3	61	57	56	59,652	72,504	n	—	—	9,145	—	—	6,068	—	787	109	1,062
MOUNTAIN VIEW	CA	c	1	89	69	56	78,663	95,624	n	—	—	15,562	—	—	10,822	—	1,710	115	956
MUNCIE	IN	c	1	108	108	56	41,971	41,971	y	44,271	4	7,795	—	—	5,512	—	—	20	437
MURFREESBORO	TN	c	1	190	190	50–54	31,200	48,800	y	—	1	1,260,460	—	—	—	—	—	41,670	70,789
NEW ROCHELLE	NY	c	1	170	167	other	38,061	72,703	y	74,263	5	23,697	20,106	85	13,905	3,363	2,838	867	2,704
NORMAN	OK	c	1	133	129	56	38,567	54,914	y	54,914	5	11,067	10,192	92	7,892	1,048	1,252	206	669
NORTH CHARLESTON	SC	c	1	212	198	50–54	27,642	38,699	y	—	10	12,355	10,633	86	7,014	1,275	2,344	840	882
NORTH RICHLAND HILLS	TX	c	—	—	—	—	—	—		—	—	—	—	—	—	—	—	—	—
OAK PARK	IL	tp	—	—	—	—	—	—		—	—	—	—	—	—	—	—	—	—
OGDEN CITY	UT	c	1	123	121	56	34,038	46,865	n	—	—	10,733	8,360	78	6,005	1,235	1,120	267	2,116
OLATHE	KS	c	1	122	115	50–54	35,100	48,037	n	—	—	16,165	14,284	88	11,195	1,643	1,445	72	1,809
OLD BRIDGE	NJ	tp	—	—	—	—	—	—		—	—	—	—	—	—	—	—	—	—
ORLAND PARK	IL	v	—	—	—	—	—	—		—	—	—	—	—	—	—	—	—	—
PALATINE	IL	v	1	99	95	50–54	45,970	65,014	y	66,014	8	14,994	11,809	79	8,694	1,734	1,381	2,183	1,001
PALM BAY	FL	c	1	139	119	48	35,878	54,268	y	—	5	13,174	11,616	88	8,584	1,800	1,232	514	1,044
PAWTUCKET	RI	c	1	150	147	42	45,398	50,129	y	55,393	5	16,893	15,005	89	10,688	2,337	1,980	114	1,774
PENSACOLA	FL	c	1	136	123	56	30,050	46,196	y	50,816	5	12,393	10,774	87	6,994	3,121	658	—	1,620
PETALUMA	CA	c	—	—	—	—	—	—		—	—	—	—	—	—	—	—	—	—
PITTSBURG	CA	c	—	—	—	—	—	—		—	—	—	—	—	—	—	—	—	—
PLAIN	OH	tp	3	35	29	50–54	36,349	52,616	y	54,341	2	4,030	3,308	82	2,265	519	524	302	420
PLANTATION	FL	c	2	79	65	—	—	—		—	—	3,357	1,720	51	1,176	226	318	97	1,540
PLYMOUTH	MN	c	1	7	5	other	40,710	52,684	n	—	—	1,811	1,062	59	907	96	58	—	750
POMPANO BEACH	FL	c	1	191	181	48	44,430	62,518	y	—	14	27,273	—	—	20,293	—	—	1,043	5,937
PORT ST. LUCIE	FL	c	—	—	—	—	—	—		—	—	—	—	—	—	—	—	—	—
PORTLAND	ME	c	1	252	243	42	29,047	43,527	n	—	—	17,890	—	—	12,413	—	—	20	5,457
QUINCY	MA	c	1	216	208	42	38,800	53,560	y	53,910	5	—	—	—	16,000	—	—	1,250	—
READING	PA	c	3	148	133	42	50,180	53,446	y	—	5	10,465	10,469	100	7,839	476	2,153	979	954
REDDING	CA	c	1	84	77	56	47,786	60,977	n	—	—	15,023	11,223	75	7,862	2,057	1,304	496	3,304
REDLANDS	CA	c	3	67	63	56	51,889	63,072	y	66,226	20	12,829	11,102	87	7,624	2,732	746	133	1,594
REDONDO BEACH	CA	c	1	67	61	48	51,252	61,872	y	71,772	5	14,452	11,161	77	7,879	2,152	1,130	51	1,239
RICHARDSON	TX	c	1	148	145	56	—	—	y	1,200	1	14,867	13,968	94	10,868	2,291	809	—	895
ROANOKE	VA	c	1	272	264	56	31,993	51,190	n	—	—	20,147	17,084	85	12,779	2,890	1,414	60	3,003
ROCHESTER HILLS	MI	c	1	49	—	56	39,911	61,876	y	65,280	5	7,530	4,874	65	3,429	707	738	714	1,943
ROCKY MOUNT	NC	c	1	48	48	56	28,923	43,384	y	—	5	8,861	7,897	89	6,294	998	604	155	809
ROSEVILLE	CA	c	1	121	104	56	50,997	71,758	y	75,346	10	—	—	—	14,076	—	1,437	—	—
ROSWELL	GA	c	3	16	10	other	—	—	n	—	—	6,253	4,200	67	3,608	353	238	709	1,344
ROUND ROCK	TX	c	1	126	120	56	43,913	52,502	y	60,122	1	10,603	8,667	82	6,526	1,269	871	444	1,492
ROYAL OAK	MI	c	1	65	64	50–54	38,661	55,226	y	60,748	5	7,117	6,780	95	4,600	1,064	1,115	—	337
SAN ANGELO	TX	c	1	171	168	56	30,960	43,740	y	—	1	10,358	9,958	96	7,628	1,613	717	297	103
SAN LEANDRO	CA	c	—	—	—	—	—	—		—	—	—	—	—	—	—	—	—	—
SAN MARCOS	CA	c	1	72	62	56	—	—		—	—	11,798	9,676	82	7,011	1,877	788	321	1,800
SAN MATEO	CA	c	1	87	81	56	77,197	92,077	n	—	—	—	—	—	—	—	—	158	1,316
SANDY CITY	UT	c	3	—	—	—	—	—		—	—	—	—	—	—	—	—	—	—
SANDY SPRINGS	GA	c	1	82	71	56	32,445	45,423	n	—	—	14,516	3,291	23	2,429	432	429	5,445	8,210
SANTA MARIA	CA	c	1	47	45	56	54,040	65,687	n	—	—	8,714	13,260	152	5,614	6,876	769	74	942
SANTA MONICA	CA	c	1	110	102	56	61,708	76,188	y	—	0	24,545	—	—	14,930	—	2,224	2,234	1,654
SANTEE	CA	c	1	64	58	56	46,046	68,679	n	—	—	9,717	—	—	6,133	—	709	16	1,246
SARASOTA	FL	c	—	—	—	—	—	—		—	—	—	—	—	—	—	—	—	—
SCHENECTADY	NY	c	1	120	114	42	35,096	54,644	y	58,425	5	8,236	—	—	7,819	—	—	9	407
SHORELINE	WA	c	—	—	—	—	—	—		—	—	—	—	—	—	—	—	—	—
SIOUX CITY	IA	c	1	115	111	56	40,120	54,850	y	56,981	5	11,854	10,450	88	7,013	1,854	1,582	78	1,326
SOUTH GATE	CA	c	—	—	—	—	—	—		—	—	—	—	—	—	—	—	—	—
SPARKS	NV	c	1	114	100	other	50,940	61,271	y	63,771	5	17,803	—	—	9,576	—	1,534	1,818	2,192

Table 3/17 continued

FIRE DEPARTMENT PERSONNEL, SALARIES, AND EXPENDITURES FOR CITIES 10,000 AND OVER: 2008

City	State	Type	Service provision	Full-time paid personnel	Full-time uniformed personnel	Duty hours per week	Minimum base salary ($)	Maximum base salary ($)	Longevity pay	Maximum salary with longevity ($)	Years of service for longevity	Total expenditures (A) ($)	Total personnel expenditures (B) ($)	(B) as % of (A)	Salaries and wages (C) ($)	City contribution to retirement and social security (D) ($)	City contribution to insurance (E) ($)	Capital outlay (F) ($)	All other (G) ($)
50,000–99,999 continued																			
SPRINGFIELD	OH	c	1	132	130	50–54	41,225	53,181	y	—	5	11,698	10,831	93	7,736	1,711	1,382	—	867
ST. JOSEPH	MO	c	1	134	131	other	30,032	42,705	n			10,155	9,569	94	6,105	2,430	1,034	—	587
SUNRISE	FL	c	1	150	138	48	40,432	60,021	y	64,635	10	19,244	17,286	90	12,487	3,153	1,645	524	1,434
TEMPLE	TX	c	1	103	100	56	35,337	47,355	y	48,555	1	—	9,098	—	6,977	1,318	802	404	49
TRENTON	NJ	c	1	235	220	40	27,321	63,569	y		5	26,855	—	—	21,407	—	—	33	547
TURLOCK	CA	c	1	47	44	56	47,112	57,252	n	—	—	9,391	5,990	64	3,951	1,098	941	1,892	1,508
TUSCALOOSA	AL	c	1	234	230	42	38,475	51,055	y	51,655	5	17,071	13,498	79	10,697	1,576	1,225	1,373	2,200
TUSTIN	CA	c	5	—	—	—	—	—				—	—	—	—	—	—	—	—
TYLER	TX	c	1	149	145	56	36,743	48,091	y	49,291	1	—	—	—	—	—	—	—	—
UNION CITY	CA	c	1	53	50	56	65,784	81,648	y	85,730	19	11,335	—	—	6,904	—	2,086	1,509	836
UPLAND	CA	c	1	47	36	56	55,805	67,832	y	69,528	5	7,936	—	—	4,554	—	157	148	1,967
VACAVILLE	CA	c	1	87	82	56	75,674	91,982	n	—	—	17,730	—	—	11,090	—	2,511	336	1,463
VICTORIA	TX	c	1	118	114	56	35,328	43,497	y	44,697	1	—	—	—	—	—	—	—	—
VISTA	CA	c	1	81	76	56	47,676	70,464	n	—	—	15,105	—	—	8,051	—	1,188	1,097	3,083
WALNUT CREEK	CA	c		—	—	—	—	—				—	—	—	—	—	—	—	—
WEST CHESTER	OH	tp	1	—	—	50–54	46,199	60,381	y	—	5	7,245	—	—	4,528	—	1,747	51	942
WHITE PLAINS	NY	c	1	171	170	40	51,114	76,657	y	80,073	5	22,136	—	—	20,950	—	—	358	326
WILMINGTON	NC	c	1	227	218	56	25,661	40,545	n	—	—	16,139	11,172	69	8,662	1,389	1,120	3,316	1,651
YORBA LINDA	CA	c	5	—	—	—	—	—				—	—	—	—	—	—	—	—
YUBA CITY	CA	c	3	50	47	56	46,668	70,356	n	—	—	8,298	7,080	85	4,771	1,703	606	121	1,097
YUMA	AZ	c	1	125	107	56	39,694	55,571	n	—	—	11,266	8,565	76	6,604	1,175	785	796	1,905
25,000–49,999																			
ALAMOGORDO	NM	c	4	—	—	56	25,255	29,803	n	—	—	1,122	827	74	534	169	124	25	269
ALBANY	OR	c	1	76	39	48	46,500	58,788	y	64,080	20	9,757	6,450	66	4,992	603	854	39	3,269
ALEXANDRIA	LA	c	1	128	111	40	23,833	61,593	n	—	—	10,094	—	—	6,049	—	842	357	1,998
ALPHARETTA	GA	c	1	97	96	50–54	36,750	66,150	n	—	—	7,290	6,756	93	4,657	914	1,184	291	243
ALTAMONTE SPRINGS	FL	c	—	—	—	—	—	—				—	—	—	—	—	—	—	—
ANDOVER	MA	t	1	72	70	42	42,940	49,844	y	52,356	5	5,829	—	—	5,507	—	—	—	322
ANDOVER	MN	c	2	3	2	other	—	—				—	—	—	—	—	—	—	—
ANKENY	IA	c	3	12	11	56		—	—			3,273	1,832	56	1,313	283	236	1,041	400
ATASCADERO	CA	c	1	—	—	48	—	—				—	—	—	—	—	—	—	—
AUBURN	AL	c	1	98	98	other	33,936	51,332	n	—	—	4,500	3,042	68	2,560	347	134	1,019	440
AUBURN	NY	c	1	73	71	48	36,363	53,536	y	—	4	5,641	—	—	4,460	—	—	18	249
AVONDALE	AZ	c	1	65	56	56	42,615	61,720	n	—	—	7,266	5,449	75	4,526	345	578	401	1,417
BALLWIN	MO	c	—	—	—	—	—	—				—	—	—	—	—	—	—	—
BARTLESVILLE	OK	c	1	71	66	56	30,925	39,516	y	41,316	5	5,315	4,768	90	3,275	446	1,046	118	429
BARTLETT	IL	v	—	—	—	—	—	—				—	—	—	—	—	—	—	—
BELL	CA	c	—	—	—	—	—	—				—	—	—	—	—	—	—	—
BELMONT	CA	c	7	41	36	56	—	—	n	—	—	—	—	—	—	—	—	—	—
BELOIT	WI	c	1	68	55	50–54	36,730	51,423	y	—	0	8,218	7,408	90	4,469	1,001	1,937	299	511
BEVERLY	MA	c	1	69	62	42	48,331	53,366	y	54,466	10	5,399	—	—	5,027	—	—	21	351
BIG SPRING	TX	c	1	—	—	56	26,499	35,162	y	—	1	—	—	—	—	—	—	—	—
BLAINE	MN	c	—	—	—	—	—	—				—	—	—	—	—	—	—	—
BLUE SPRINGS	MO	c	—	—	—	—	—	—				—	—	—	—	—	—	—	—
BONITA SPRINGS	FL	c	—	—	—	—	—	—				—	—	—	—	—	—	—	—
BOTHELL	WA	c	1	62	56	50–54	52,992	75,708	y	83,279	5	8,131	6,963	86	5,623	316	1,023	62	1,106
BOUNTIFUL	UT	c	—	—	—	—	—	—				—	—	—	—	—	—	—	—
BROOKFIELD	WI	c	1	58	57	56	43,902	63,296	n	—	—	6,900	6,175	89	4,432	964	779	34	691
BROOKLYN CENTER	MN	c	2	2	1	—	—	—	y			925	570	62	355	172	42	—	355
BROOMFIELD	CO	c	—	—	—	—	—	—				—	—	—	—	—	—	—	—
BRUNSWICK	OH	c	1	28	26	48	35,593	50,868	y	52,673	4	3,778	2,642	70	1,607	573	461	779	357
BULLHEAD CITY	AZ	c	—	—	—	—	—	—				—	—	—	—	—	—	—	—
BURLINGTON	NC	c	1	92	90	56	30,847	50,878	y	—	5	5,372	4,557	85	3,554	447	556	120	693
CALEXICO	CA	c	1	35	34	56	41,244	52,632	y	52,932	5	4,276	3,203	75	2,249	499	454	278	795
CAMPBELL	CA	c	5	—	—	—	—	—				—	—	—	—	—	—	—	—
CAROL STREAM	IL	v	—	—	—	—	—	—				—	—	—	—	—	—	—	—
CARPENTERSVILLE	IL	v	1	41	40	50–54	48,719	67,855	y	68,655	1	5,825	4,657	80	3,630	589	437	562	606
CASA GRANDE	AZ	c	1	63	59	48	41,096	126,687	n	—	—	—	5,219	—	3,557	1,169	493	485	209
CASPER	WY	c	1	75	73	56	40,395	49,098	n	—	—	7,352	5,721	78	4,512	553	656	820	812
CEDAR FALLS	IA	c	3	34	34	50–54	33,929	46,130	y	47,510	4	3,113	2,701	87	1,709	458	533	86	326
CEDAR HILL	TX	c	1	62	61	56	42,060	53,680	y	53,680	1	6,175	4,821	78	3,468	675	677	224	1,129
CHELTENHAM	PA	tp	2	—	—	other	—	—	y			—	—	—	—	—	—	—	—
CLEARFIELD	UT	c	—	—	—	—	—	—				—	—	—	—	—	—	—	—
CLEBURNE	TX	c	1	56	55	56	44,057	54,583	y	59,383	1	5,029	4,515	90	3,341	692	482	8	506
CLEVELAND HEIGHTS	OH	c	1	80	79	50–54	53,348	61,406	y	63,406	5	9,218	9,785	106	6,129	2,253	1,402	—	551
CLINTON	IA	c	1	45	45	50–54	30,465	50,397	n	—	—	3,912	3,502	90	2,328	627	547	—	410
CLOVIS	NM	c	1	78	74	56	—	—	n	—	—	6,259	4,499	72	3,019	692	787	987	874
COCONUT CREEK	FL	c	5	—	34	48	51,200	74,200	y	77,200	10	—	—	—	—	—	—	—	—
COEUR D'ALENE	ID	c	1	55	53	56	44,000	53,522	n	—	—	8,020	4,891	61	3,109	1,072	710	3,972	2,756
COLLIERVILLE	TN	t	1	70	60	56	31,078	48,263	n	—	—	5,872	5,165	88	3,819	701	644	213	493
COLTON	CA	c	1	50	45	56	52,104	63,312	n	—	—	10,634	—	—	6,032	—	—	879	2,114
COLUMBIA	TN	c	1	90	88	50–54	25,263	38,807	y	40,807	3	6,237	5,261	84	4,081	754	426	439	537

Table 3/17 continued   FIRE DEPARTMENT PERSONNEL, SALARIES, AND EXPENDITURES FOR CITIES 10,000 AND OVER: 2008

City	State	Type	Service provision	Full-time paid personnel	Full-time uniformed personnel	Duty hours per week	Minimum base salary ($)	Maximum base salary ($)	Longevity pay	Maximum salary with longevity ($)	Years of service for longevity	Total expenditures (A) ($)	Total personnel expenditures (B) ($)	(B) as % of (A)	Salaries and wages (C) ($)	City contribution to retirement and social security (D) ($)	City contribution to insurance (E) ($)	Capital outlay (F) ($)	All other (G) ($)
25,000–49,999 continued																			
COLUMBUS	MS	c	1	72	71	48	29,519	30,695	y	—	0	—	—	—	—	—	—	—	—
CONROE	TX	c	1	87	84	48	39,000	53,153	y	54,353	1	7,670	6,839	89	5,077	958	804	35	796
CONWAY	AR	c	1	97	95	50–54	29,145	39,372	n	—	—	7,035	6,072	86	4,679	794	598	226	737
COPPELL	TX	c	1	78	74	48	—	—	y	—	0	8,810	—	—	5,775	—	484	1,237	674
CORTLANDT	NY	t	—	—	—	—	—	—	—	—	—	—	—	—	—	—	—	—	—
COTTAGE GROVE	MN	c	4	—	—	40	—	—	—	—	—	—	—	—	—	—	—	—	—
CRYSTAL LAKE	IL	c	1	55	52	50–54	47,333	69,841	n	—	—	6,852	—	—	4,340	—	541	1,164	807
CULVER CITY	CA	c	1	71	62	56	62,454	79,771	n	—	—	14,808	12,557	85	8,451	2,109	1,995	660	1,592
CYPRESS	CA	c	—	—	—	—	—	—	—	—	—	—	—	—	—	—	—	—	—
DANVERS	MA	t	1	51	50	42	41,720	50,564	y	51,349	10	—	—	—	3,571	—	—	12	243
DANVILLE	IL	c	1	60	59	other	36,995	49,326	y	57,218	4	5,970	5,758	96	3,557	1,626	575	40	212
DANVILLE	VA	c	1	123	122	50–54	30,336	47,480	n	—	—	—	—	—	4,917	685	—	217	640
DE SOTO	TX	c	1	66	66	50–54	44,112	54,840	y	56,040	1	5,808	5,209	90	3,899	795	514	238	361
DEER PARK	TX	c	2	6	—	other	35,000	48,110	y	—	—	—	—	—	222	27	—	360	163
DELHI	OH	tp	1	24	22	50–54	45,895	57,914	y	59,414	2	3,662	2,961	81	2,301	418	242	—	700
DERRY	NH	t	1	84	77	42	38,963	45,100	y	—	5	9,775	8,578	88	6,103	945	1,530	62	1,136
DES MOINES	WA	c	—	—	—	—	—	—	—	—	—	—	—	—	—	—	—	—	—
DODGE CITY	KS	c	1	25	25	56	34,979	42,618	y	43,618	1	1,668	1,564	94	1,047	288	229	7	96
DOVER	DE	c	3	—	—	other	31,595	41,413	y	—	9	563	337	60	238	62	36	303	563
DRACUT	MA	t	1	42	41	42	30,585	45,017	y	45,847	—	4,561	—	—	2,497	—	1,850	71	38
DUBLIN	OH	c	—	—	—	—	—	—	—	—	—	—	—	—	—	—	—	—	—
DUNCANVILLE	TX	c	1	51	49	56	41,586	53,257	y	54,457	1	5,176	4,528	87	3,428	746	353	125	523
EAST BRUNSWICK	NJ	tp	2	—	—	other	—	—	—	—	—	—	—	—	—	—	—	—	—
EAST LANSING	MI	c	1	52	51	50–54	41,016	53,071	y	54,355	5	2,328	2,328	100	946	854	527	—	—
EAST POINT	GA	c	1	124	124	other	30,886	48,171	n	—	5	—	—	—	—	—	—	—	—
EASTPOINTE	MI	c	1	26	—	56	45,966	55,966	y	—	5	—	—	—	—	—	—	—	—
EGG HARBOR	NJ	tp	2	2	—	other	—	—	y	—	0	925	173	19	152	17	2	248	504
ELK GROVE VILLAGE	IL	v	1	100	89	50–54	47,433	69,056	y	69,881	10	121,128	10,884	9	8,145	1,418	1,320	350	1,210
ELMWOOD PARK	IL	v	1	26	26	50–54	52,766	66,364	y	71,673	3	3,942	3,242	82	1,878	1,071	291	82	619
EMPORIA	KS	c	1	53	48	50–54	—	—	n	—	—	3,986	2,964	74	2,377	376	211	51	971
ENID	OK	c	1	82	80	56	39,480	43,342	y	44,942	5	6,369	5,166	81	4,537	551	78	727	476
EULESS	TX	c	1	71	70	56	48,266	62,114	y	—	1	6,392	5,981	94	4,569	692	719	172	239
EUREKA	CA	c	1	41	39	48	40,008	48,660	n	—	—	4,242	—	—	2,623	—	567	84	332
FAIRBORN	OH	c	1	52	51	50–54	41,058	59,783	y	61,277	5	5,633	5,119	91	3,730	886	502	—	514
FARMERS BRANCH	TX	c	1	78	73	56	48,616	60,584	y	62,084	1	—	—	—	—	—	—	—	—
FARMINGTON	NM	c	1	93	85	56	26,011	67,484	y	34,029	6	4,473	3,953	88	3,027	563	363	—	520
FINDLAY	OH	c	1	78	75	48	33,320	49,298	y	—	10	6,619	—	—	4,229	—	725	—	690
FISHERS	IN	t	1	119	113	other	38,528	53,939	y	—	—	—	10,962	—	6,957	1,859	2,144	437	1,000
FITCHBURG	MA	c	1	87	84	42	39,777	44,109	y	—	5	6,300	—	—	6,000	—	—	—	300
FLORENCE	SC	c	1	68	67	42	25,410	37,018	y	36,484	25	4,655	3,554	76	2,614	462	477	768	333
FOND DU LAC	WI	c	1	67	65	56	43,946	53,219	y	54,239	5	7,136	6,100	85	4,346	939	815	190	847
FOSTER CITY	CA	c	1	34	—	56	—	—	y	—	—	7,213	—	—	6,432	—	—	—	781
FREEHOLD	NJ	tp	—	—	—	—	—	—	—	—	—	—	—	—	—	—	—	—	—
FREMONT	NE	c	1	30	29	50–54	30,828	43,380	n	—	—	—	—	—	—	—	—	—	—
FRIDLEY	MN	c	1	8	7	56	48,718	59,259	n	—	—	—	—	—	—	—	—	—	—
FRIENDSWOOD	TX	c	6	—	—	—	—	—	y	—	—	—	—	—	—	—	—	—	—
GALLOWAY	NJ	tp	2	1	—	other	—	—	y	—	0	1,253	677	54	37	626	13	1,285	363
GARFIELD	NJ	c	2	—	—	other	—	—	n	—	—	326	—	—	—	—	—	66	262
GARFIELD HEIGHTS	OH	c	1	—	47	50–54	42,824	56,439	y	58,964	5	4,458	—	—	3,158	—	735	—	97
GEORGETOWN	TX	c	3	58	56	56	33,000	52,051	y	55,747	0	5,678	3,997	70	3,077	570	350	936	744
GLADSTONE	MO	c	—	—	—	other	—	—	—	—	—	—	—	—	—	—	—	—	—
GLASTONBURY	CT	t	3	2	1	other	—	—	n	—	—	959	—	—	373	—	27	90	442
GLEN ELLYN	IL	v	3	—	—	—	—	—	—	—	—	—	—	—	—	—	—	—	—
GOLDSBORO	NC	c	1	82	80	56	31,905	45,579	y	47,402	5	4,576	4,152	91	3,327	410	415	10	414
GOOSE CREEK	SC	c	3	39	34	40	29,717	45,218	n	—	—	2,952	1,967	67	1,586	229	151	496	489
GRAND BLANC	MI	tp	2	2	1	other	—	—	—	—	—	715	—	—	—	—	—	—	—
GRAND FORKS	ND	c	1	66	64	50–54	36,832	55,248	y	56,268	6	4,762	4,476	94	3,389	690	396	26	260
GRAND JUNCTION	CO	c	1	116	103	56	48,148	58,392	n	—	—	11,289	8,872	79	7,178	666	1,027	295	2,123
GRANTS PASS	OR	c	—	—	—	56	—	—	—	—	—	—	—	—	—	—	—	—	—
GRAPEVINE	TX	c	1	99	—	56	—	—	—	—	—	8,512	—	—	6,833	942	—	—	737
GREENACRES	FL	c	4	—	—	56	—	—	—	—	—	—	—	—	—	—	—	—	—
GREENFIELD	WI	c	1	52	51	56	40,551	60,735	y	61,335	5	5,104	4,555	89	2,932	908	714	154	395
GREENVILLE	MS	c	1	85	82	56	22,500	27,232	n	—	—	4,809	4,532	94	3,616	508	408	50	227
GROTON	CT	t	—	—	—	—	—	—	—	—	—	—	—	—	—	—	—	—	—
GROVE CITY	OH	c	—	—	—	—	—	—	—	—	—	—	—	—	—	—	—	—	—
HALTOM CITY	TX	c	1	51	46	56	45,981	54,657	y	—	1	4,503	—	—	2,971	—	359	368	394
HANFORD	CA	c	3	32	30	56	41,904	50,494	n	—	—	3,859	2,777	72	1,872	670	234	678	404
HANOVER PARK	IL	v	1	36	35	50–54	—	—	y	—	10	4,402	3,712	84	2,862	431	419	—	690
HARRISBURG	PA	c	4	—	—	42	—	—	—	—	—	—	—	—	—	—	—	—	—
HARRISONBURG	VA	c	1	81	75	50–54	31,859	57,158	y	—	—	5,926	4,554	77	3,369	719	466	702	670
HAZELWOOD	MO	c	1	38	37	other	46,149	59,994	n	—	—	—	—	—	—	—	—	—	—
HELENA	MT	c	1	36	35	other	39,933	46,271	y	47,442	1	3,171	2,646	83	2,075	305	265	81	444
HENDERSONVILLE	TN	c	3	94	91	other	31,694	48,227	y	50,127	2	6,457	5,899	91	4,420	977	502	55	502

Table 3/17 continued   FIRE DEPARTMENT PERSONNEL, SALARIES, AND EXPENDITURES FOR CITIES 10,000 AND OVER: 2008

City	State	Type	Service provision	Full-time paid personnel	Full-time uniformed personnel	Duty hours per week	Minimum base salary ($)	Maximum base salary ($)	Longevity pay	Maximum salary with longevity ($)	Years of service for longevity	Reported expenditures (in $000)							
												Total expenditures (A) ($)	Total personnel expenditures (B) ($)	(B) as % of (A)	Salaries and wages (C) ($)	City contribution to retirement and social security (D) ($)	City contribution to insurance (E) ($)	Capital outlay (F) ($)	All other (G) ($)
25,000–49,999 continued																			
HILTON HEAD ISLAND	SC	t	1	146	120	56	37,845	56,767	y	56,767	—	12,631	10,784	85	8,720	1,140	923	310	1,537
HINESVILLE	GA	c	3	49	47	other	29,962	—	n	—	—	—	—	—	—	—	—	—	—
HOBART	IN	c	1	52	51	other	31,285	43,791	y	46,441	1	3,863	3,402	88	2,561	475	367	9	451
HOMESTEAD	FL	c	—	—	—	—	—	—	—	—	—	—	—	—	—	—	—	—	—
HOT SPRINGS	AR	c	1	78	77	50–54	30,746	37,339	y	38,239	1	7,002	6,137	88	3,831	1,768	538	56	808
HOWELL	NJ	tp	3	5	4	other	—	—	—	—	—	—	—	—	—	—	—	—	—
HUBER HEIGHTS	OH	c	1	56	51	other	39,653	57,628	n	—	—	5,975	5,189	87	3,483	879	826	262	523
HURST	TX	c	1	57	56	50–54	56,451	61,833	y	64,353	1	6,725	5,841	87	4,265	995	580	4	880
IMPERIAL BEACH	CA	c	1	13	12	56	45,228	57,732	n	—	—	1,797	1,642	91	875	503	263	—	—
INVER GROVE HEIGHTS	MN	c	7	2	—	other	—	—	y	—	—	490	341	69	304	23	13	—	150
ITHACA	NY	c	3	76	72	40	34,787	63,254	y	64,804	10	9,205	7,136	78	5,031	971	1,134	184	1,884
JACKSON	NJ	tp	2	—	—	other	—	—	y	—	—	—	—	—	—	—	—	—	—
JACKSONVILLE	AR	c	1	60	59	56	27,280	34,771	y	35,371	3	3,796	3,484	92	2,062	995	426	12	300
JAMESTOWN	NY	c	1	69	68	42	38,837	65,750	y	65,386	4	6,578	6,384	97	4,396	1,375	613	33	161
JOPLIN	MO	c	1	77	76	50–54	26,923	38,319	y	—	5	5,096	4,333	85	3,022	550	760	267	496
KELLER	TX	c	1	59	57	56	43,534	57,250	y	57,250	1	5,489	4,679	85	3,021	1,299	358	499	310
KINGSPORT	TN	c	1	103	101	56	28,943	40,351	n	—	—	6,313	5,542	88	4,037	855	650	—	771
KISSIMMEE	FL	c	1	101	91	56	34,944	54,018	y	54,618	10	10,401	8,885	85	6,115	1,556	1,212	136	1,380
KOKOMO	IN	c	1	121	119	56	41,340	50,985	y	53,585	3	10,550	9,585	91	6,594	1,115	1,876	365	600
LA GRANGE	GA	c	1	60	60	50–54	27,603	39,761	n	—	—	3,450	2,941	85	2,263	282	395	31	479
LA PUENTE	CA	c	5	—	—	—	—	—	—	—	—	—	—	—	—	—	—	—	—
LA VERNE	CA	c	1	35	30	56	57,907	70,387	n	—	—	—	—	—	4,593	—	511	—	—
LACEY	WA	c	—	—	—	—	—	—	—	—	—	—	—	—	—	—	—	—	—
LAKE HAVASU CITY	AZ	c	1	94	85	56	41,671	58,356	y	58,856	5	8,329	7,446	89	5,847	537	1,061	883	—
LANCASTER	TX	c	1	—	—	56	—	—	—	—	—	—	—	—	—	—	—	—	—
LARAMIE	WY	c	1	50	40	50–54	39,310	52,867	n	—	—	4,500	3,714	83	2,775	474	464	87	699
LEAWOOD	KS	c	1	55	54	50–54	32,162	49,029	y	—	4	4,818	4,166	86	3,153	658	354	236	417
LEESBURG	VA	t	—	—	—	—	—	—	—	—	—	—	—	—	—	—	—	—	—
LENEXA	KS	c	1	90	88	other	35,096	52,259	n	—	—	8,963	8,066	90	5,234	1,589	1,243	426	471
LEWISTON	ME	c	1	80	75	42	30,030	46,345	—	—	—	5,420	4,528	84	3,852	161	513	32	860
LIBERTY	MO	c	1	50	49	50–54	—	—	n	—	—	3,798	3,246	85	2,324	416	506	148	404
LIMA	OH	c	1	66	65	50–54	38,994	45,617	y	48,505	8	6,778	—	—	4,293	—	1,013	25	435
LITTLETON	CO	c	1	151	138	56	43,938	64,246	y	66,046	30	18,824	15,624	83	12,227	1,216	2,181	610	2,590
LOMBARD	IL	v	1	79	65	50–54	48,382	66,905	n	—	—	9,890	8,516	86	6,478	1,324	714	—	1,374
LOMPOC	CA	c	1	25	21	56	46,260	61,992	n	—	—	3,710	—	—	2,317	—	397	106	390
LONG BEACH	NY	c	3	27	27	40	38,497	89,226	y	97,278	6	3,248	—	—	2,745	605	—	100	503
LONGVIEW	WA	c	1	44	37	50–54	49,844	66,458	y	69,780	10	—	—	—	—	—	—	—	—
LOS ALTOS	CA	c	—	—	—	—	—	—	—	—	—	—	—	—	—	—	—	—	—
LOS BANOS	CA	c	3	20	18	56	44,112	53,628	n	—	—	3,356	1,977	59	1,186	524	267	968	411
LOWER MAKEFIELD	PA	tp	—	—	—	—	—	—	—	—	—	—	—	—	—	—	—	—	—
LUFKIN	TX	c	5	82	78	48	31,849	38,093	y	38,293	1	6,268	4,978	79	3,944	591	443	481	808
LYNNWOOD	WA	c	1	56	54	48	58,459	69,089	y	74,193	5	7,757	6,536	84	4,819	313	1,404	33	1,188
MADERA	CA	c	—	—	—	—	—	—	—	—	—	—	—	—	—	—	—	—	—
MAMARONECK	NY	t	3	14	14	42	35,000	82,000	y	83,500	—	—	—	—	1,600	—	—	—	—
MANASSAS	VA	c	3	8	8	50–54	40,997	68,474	n	—	—	715	702	98	509	109	83	—	12
MANHATTAN	KS	c	1	—	80	56	32,906	62,078	y	—	5	4,397	13,938	317	3,209	10,194	535	405	139
MANHEIM	PA	tp	2	—	—	other	—	—	—	—	—	—	—	—	—	—	—	—	—
MANKATO	MN	c	3	18	18	50–54	42,675	51,069	y	56,175	5	—	—		1,281	137	—	—	—
MANSFIELD	OH	c	1	99	96	48	36,452	48,648	y	—	1	10,086	8,765	87	6,127	1,530	1,108	89	1,232
MANSFIELD	TX	c	1	81	79	48	40,000	62,045	y	—	1	6,427	—	—	4,346	—	454	771	2,082
MARION	IA	c	1	28	28	56	37,002	46,062	y	47,262	5	2,608	2,303	88	1,554	438	311	157	148
MARLBORO	NJ	tp	—	—	—	—	—	—	—	—	—	—	—	—	—	—	—	—	—
MARYLAND HEIGHTS	MO	c	—	—	—	—	—	—	—	—	—	—	—	—	—	—	—	—	—
MARYSVILLE	WA	c	—	—	—	—	—	—	—	—	—	—	—	—	—	—	—	—	—
MASON CITY	IA	c	1	46	44	56	30,638	46,405	n	—	—	3,966	3,224	81	2,318	599	307	615	127
McCANDLESS	PA	t	2	—	—	—	—	—	—	—	—	—	—	—	—	—	—	—	—
MENOMONEE FALLS	WI	v	3	15	14	50–54	47,794	62,723	n	—	—	2,135	1,789	84	1,273	310	205	8	338
MERIDIAN	MI	tp	—	—	41	50–54	34,632	53,117	y	54,397	5	4,361	3,900	89	2,590	854	454	—	461
MERIDIAN	MS	c	1	113	106	56	22,574	33,861	n	—	—	6,298	5,050	80	3,563	694	792	795	453
MICHIGAN CITY	IN	c	1	83	81	56	39,822	39,822	y	47,786	3	5,334	7,030	132	5,139	977	913	808	204
MIDLAND	MI	c	1	46	45	56	34,437	55,563	y	60,008	5	—	—	—	—	—	—	—	—
MILLVILLE	NJ	c	3	13	13	50–54	26,746	62,604	y	67,143	5	1,329	1,242	93	837	184	220	—	87
MILTON	MA	t	1	56	55	42	34,935	49,081	y	—	10	4,160	—	—	3,876	—	—	46	—
MINOT	ND	c	1	50	49	56	33,224	49,321	n	—	—	3,252	—	—	2,232	—	264	250	212
MISHAWAKA	IN	c	1	109	107	48	46,079	48,079	n	—	—	7,780	7,149	92	4,940	1,173	1,036	423	208
MISSION	TX	c	3	70	64	50–54	33,000	33,000	y	34,200	3	4,160	3,443	83	2,578	429	435	380	336
MOLINE	IL	c	1	70	69	50–54	41,567	42,815	n	—	—	9,720	7,251	75	4,798	1,390	1,063	886	1,582
MONROE	NC	c	3	81	79	56	21,195	32,198	n	—	—	5,904	4,559	77	3,466	586	507	563	782
MONROVIA	CA	c	3	40	38	56	57,876	73,866	y	76,082	5	8,258	—	—	4,887	—	285	157	1,250
MONTCLAIR	NJ	tp	1	90	89	42	28,177	80,172	y	88,189	5	—	—	—	—	—	—	—	—
MOORE	OK	c	1	59	58	56	32,634	61,270	y	66,175	3	5,065	4,860	96	3,898	531	431	17	187
MOORHEAD	MN	c	1	34	1	other	43,935	49,261	y	51,231	29	2,957	2,288	77	1,792	229	266	51	618

Table 3/17
continued

FIRE DEPARTMENT PERSONNEL, SALARIES, AND EXPENDITURES FOR CITIES 10,000 AND OVER: 2008

City	State	Type	Service provision	Full-time paid personnel	Full-time uniformed personnel	Duty hours per week	Minimum base salary ($)	Maximum base salary ($)	Longevity pay	Maximum salary with longevity ($)	Years of service for longevity	Total expenditures (A) ($)	Total personnel expenditures (B) ($)	(B) as % of (A)	Salaries and wages (C) ($)	City contribution to retirement and social security (D) ($)	City contribution to insurance (E) ($)	Capital outlay (F) ($)	All other (G) ($)
25,000–49,999 continued																			
MOORPARK	CA	c	—	—	—	—	—	—	—	—	—	—	—	—	—	—	—	—	—
MOUNT LAUREL	NJ	tp	—	—	—	—	—	—	—	—	—	—	—	—	—	—	—	—	—
MOUNT LEBANON	PA	c	3	18	17	40	57,356	75,686	y	77,578	4	2,885	2,161	75	1,602	245	314	—	727
MOUNT VERNON	WA	c	3	37	34	48	53,703	65,491	y	73,134	5	4,039	3,404	84	2,764	181	459	75	560
MUNDELEIN	IL	v	3	21	21	50–54	55,978	76,610	n			—	—	—	—	—	—	—	—
MURRAY	UT	c	1	—	—	50–54	32,656	48,984	n			—	—	—	—	—	—	—	—
MURRIETA	CA	c	1	59	51	56	61,293	74,495	n			—	—	—	—	—	—	—	—
MUSKEGON	MI	c	1	40	38	50–54	31,491	80,025	y	50,525	5	4,619	4,108	89	2,878	687	543	60	451
NAUGATUCK	CT	t	1	42	41	42	42,988	49,578	y	42,988	15	—	—	—	—	—	—	—	—
NEW BRAUNFELS	TX	c	1	105	100	50–54	40,865	51,035	y	52,985	1	7,983	6,922	87	5,088	1,032	801	—	1,061
NEWARK	DE	c	—	—	—	—	—	—	—	—	—	—	—	—	—	—	—	—	—
NILES	IL	v	1	57	54	50–54	54,021	56,722	n			8,589	7,164	83	5,239	820	1,104	864	561
NORMAL	IL	t	1	66	62	50–54	41,462	66,857	n			6,208	5,533	89	3,734	1,145	653	14	662
NORTH ANDOVER	MA	t	1	56	55	42	39,273	47,342	y		5	—	—	—	—	—	—	—	—
NORTH BRUNSWICK	NJ	tp	2	—	—	—	—	—	—	—	—	—	—	—	—	—	—	—	—
NORTH CHICAGO	IL	c	1	33	27	40	36,288	56,211	n			2,937	2,793	95	2,008	533	251	—	144
NORTH LAUDERDALE	FL	c	1	46	45	48	—	—	—			4,819	3,729	77	2,515	705	508	53	1,038
NORTH ROYALTON	OH	c	1	35	34	48	45,615	60,648	y	62,648	5	4,208	—	—	2,731	—	530	229	124
NORTHBROOK	IL	v	1	75	69	56	—	—	y	72,887	5	—	—	—	—	—	—	—	—
NOVATO	CA	c	—	—	—	—	—	—	—	—	—	—	—	—	—	—	—	—	—
NOVI	MI	c	1	31	30	48	35,010	57,215	n			5,047	3,952	78	2,909	568	474	645	450
O'FALLON	MO	c	—	—	—	—	—	—	—	—	—	—	—	—	—	—	—	—	—
OAK CREEK	WI	c	1	52	51	56	42,317	60,316	y	60,556	5	6,275	6,434	103	3,585	2,147	701	—	440
OAK PARK	MI	c	4	—	—	42	—	—	—	—	—	—	—	—	—	—	—	—	—
OAK RIDGE	TN	c	1	—	—	56	33,255	49,882	y	52,382	5	4,003	3,306	83	2,494	487	326	65	631
OAKLEY	CA	c	—	—	—	—	—	—	—	—	—	—	—	—	—	—	—	—	—
OCALA	FL	c	1	139	128	other	30,881	48,439	y	49,892	1	13,831	10,709	77	7,244	2,053	1,411	603	2,518
ORO VALLEY	AZ	t	—	—	—	—	—	—	—	—	—	—	—	—	—	—	—	—	—
PACIFICA	CA	c	1	29	26	56	63,528	85,092	y	95,736	5	6,158	—	—	3,970	—	—	51	352
PALM COAST	FL	c	3	49	47	56	32,659	55,150	n			5,242	3,726	71	2,386	878	462	84	1,432
PALM DESERT	CA	c	5	—	—	—	—	—	—	—	—	—	—	—	—	—	—	—	—
PALM SPRINGS	CA	c	1	65	65	—	52,296	63,732	y			10,709	—	—	5,568	—	1,318	522	1,752
PARADISE	CA	t	3	—	—	56	—	—	—	—	—	—	—	—	—	—	—	—	—
PASCAGOULA	MS	c	1	—	—	50–54	—	—	—	—	—	—	—	—	—	—	—	—	—
PASCO	WA	c	1	48	48	50–54	48,646	60,034	y	62,426	20	5,637	4,691	83	3,984	205	502	89	856
PEABODY	MA	c	1	100	97	40	42,723	48,464	y	71,098	5	7,053	—	—	6,645	—	—	107	301
PEACHTREE CITY	GA	c	3	58	56	48	33,158	53,396	n			5,078	4,169	82	2,947	768	453	165	694
PEARLAND	TX	c	3	20	18	48	32,585	43,993	y	—	1	709	—	—	—	10	5	152	463
PENFIELD	NY	t	—	—	—	—	—	—	—	—	—	—	—	—	—	—	—	—	—
PHARR	TX	c	1	60	30	50–54	27,100	34,162	y	—	1	—	—	—	—	—	—	—	—
PHENIX CITY	AL	c	1	62	57	50–54	27,850	45,272	n			3,583	3,126	87	2,332	365	428	136	321
PITTSFIELD CHARTER TOWNSHIP	MI	tp	1	20	20	50–54	35,821	48,120	y	49,320	5	2,584	1,944	75	1,478	202	263	150	490
PLAINFIELD	MI	tp	1	15	14	56	39,651	55,681	n			2,564	1,737	68	1,374	200	163	408	419
PORT HURON	MI	c	1	45	42	56	39,751	53,001	n			5,546	—	—	3,075	—	—	19	607
PORT ORANGE	FL	c	1	66	63	56	33,371	55,357	n			7,585	5,673	75	3,981	455	1,236	327	1,585
QUEENSBURY	NY	t	—	—	—	—	—	—	—	—	—	—	—	—	—	—	—	—	—
QUINCY	IL	c	1	72	69	50–54	34,261	49,879	y	52,756	23	7,014	6,450	92	4,105	1,568	776	11	553
REDMOND	WA	c	1	169	—	56	54,708	74,904	y	80,147	5	16,738	—	—	11,387	—	2,102	1,546	1,908
REVERE	MA	c	—	—	—	—	—	—	—	—	—	—	—	—	—	—	—	—	—
REYNOLDSBURG	OH	c	—	—	—	—	—	—	—	—	—	—	—	—	—	—	—	—	—
RICHFIELD	MN	c	1	26	26	56	52,277	64,627	y	68,589	25	—	—	—	—	—	—	—	—
RIVERTON	UT	c	5	—	—	—	—	—	—	—	—	—	—	—	—	—	—	—	—
RIVIERA BEACH	FL	c	1	82	80	48	37,052	60,354	y	62,768	4	11,038	7,829	71	4,610	2,696	522	148	3,062
ROCK HILL	SC	c	1	—	—	50–54	27,997	39,187	n			6,001	5,016	84	3,804	678	535	119	865
ROME	GA	c	1	157	153	56	28,000	42,000	n			11,047	8,609	78	6,864	789	955	392	2,046
ROSWELL	NM	c	1	87	86	56	29,345	39,325	y	—	3	—	—	—	—	—	—	—	—
ROWLETT	TX	c	1	—	—	other	—	—	y	—	1	7,121	—	—	4,970	—	666	—	877
ROY	UT	c	1	31	30	56	—	—	—	—	—	2,661	2,290	86	1,705	366	218	26	345
SAGINAW	MI	tp	2	7	—	other	—	—	—	—	—	1,419	823	58	632	123	67	168	428
SALEM	NH	t	1	68	54	42	38,447	45,569	y	—	5	7,219	6,584	91	4,604	752	1,228	—	636
SALINA	KS	c	1	98	94	56	36,895	57,200	y	—	5	—	—	—	—	—	—	—	—
SALISBURY	NC	c	1	77	68	50–54	24,632	49,196	n			4,859	3,685	76	2,904	254	526	71	1,102
SAN CARLOS	CA	c	—	—	—	—	—	—	—	—	—	—	—	—	—	—	—	—	—
SAN JUAN	TX	c	3	11	10	50–54	25,685	28,441	—			—	—	—	459	—	—	171	60
SAN JUAN CAPISTRANO	CA	c	—	—	—	—	—	—	—	—	—	—	—	—	—	—	—	—	—
SAN LUIS OBISPO	CA	c	1	52	45	56	50,882	69,420	y	—	—	9,921	8,764	88	5,941	1,962	861	502	655
SAN RAMON	CA	c	—	—	—	—	—	—	—	—	—	—	—	—	—	—	—	—	—
SANDUSKY	OH	c	1	53	50	50–54	32,221	48,441	y	50,066	3	5,825	4,811	83	3,264	782	764	57	957
SEASIDE	CA	c	1	36	25	50–54	55,637	67,625	y	69,316	10	5,048	—	—	2,401	—	594	702	616
SEATAC	WA	c	1	53	47	50–54	50,460	69,120	y	92,172	5	6,673	5,336	80	4,061	454	821	838	499

Table 3/17
continued

FIRE DEPARTMENT PERSONNEL, SALARIES, AND EXPENDITURES FOR CITIES 10,000 AND OVER: 2008

Reported expenditures (in $000)

City	State	Type	Service provision	Full-time paid personnel	Full-time uniformed personnel	Duty hours per week	Minimum base salary ($)	Maximum base salary ($)	Longevity pay	Maximum salary with longevity ($)	Years of service for longevity	Total expenditures (A) ($)	Total personnel expenditures (B) ($)	(B) as % of (A)	Salaries and wages (C) ($)	City contribution to retirement and social security (D) ($)	City contribution to insurance (E) ($)	Capital outlay (F) ($)	All other (G) ($)
25,000–49,999 continued																			
SHAKER HEIGHTS	OH	c	1	70	67	50–54	44,711	66,187	y	—	7	7,763	7,151	92	5,205	1,022	924	116	446
SHERMAN	TX	c	1	74	74	56	35,190	41,680	y	42,930	1	—	—	—	—	—	—	—	—
SHREWSBURY	MA	t	1	37	35	42	43,906	50,086	y	50,436	5	2,608	—	—	2,446	—	—	—	163
SIERRA VISTA	AZ	c	1	60	50	56	38,933	58,410	n	—	—	7,514	3,358	45	2,744	277	336	3,701	456
SOUTH JORDAN	UT	c	1	48	47	other	33,197	47,133	n	—	—	—	—	—	2,398	—	—	—	—
SPARTANBURG	SC	c	4	—	—	48	—	—	—	—	—	—	—	—	—	—	—	—	—
SPRING VALLEY	NY	v	2	—	—	other	—	—	—	—	—	301	—	—	—	—	—	—	301
STANTON	CA	c	5	—	—	56	—	—	—	—	—	3,262	—	—	—	—	—	—	—
STATE COLLEGE	PA	b	—	—	—	—	—	—	—	—	—	—	—	—	—	—	—	—	—
ST. GEORGE	UT	c	3	23	22	48	33,363	41,704	y	42,955	10	2,711	2,092	77	1,142	242	707	181	437
STILLWATER	OK	c	1	73	71	56	32,393	51,589	y	53,989	5	7,956	5,988	75	4,725	597	665	154	704
STOW	OH	c	1	—	—	50–54	42,890	55,619	y	56,035	5	9,510	5,536	58	3,845	922	768	6	3,967
STREAMWOOD	IL	v	1	49	47	48	54,016	71,994	n	—	—	6,707	5,235	78	3,644	687	904	1,120	352
SUISUN CITY	CA	c	3	—	3	50–54	—	—	n	—	—	809	—	—	397	—	68	10	260
SURPRISE	AZ	t	3	122	103	56	46,301	60,948	y	63,386	8	22,431	8,885	40	7,414	472	998	11,672	1,873
SYLVANIA	OH	tp	3	56	55	50–54	52,475	53,525	y	56,736	5	6,418	—	—	3,593	—	834	50	1,078
TEXARKANA	TX	c	1	79	77	56	32,983	40,899	y	42,099	1	5,157	4,721	92	3,716	563	442	173	262
TEXAS CITY	TX	c	1	76	45	50–54	—	—	y	—	1	5,470	—	—	3,140	—	497	238	1,160
THE COLONY	TX	c	1	49	48	56	45,360	48,204	y	51,204	1	3,863	3,305	86	2,508	554	241	142	406
TINLEY PARK	IL	v	3	—	—	other	—	—	y	—	—	2,960	2,205	74	1,950	250	5	286	469
TROY	NY	c	1	132	129	40	28,937	48,842	y	50,842	5	12,900	12,090	94	8,069	2,452	1,568	226	584
TRUMBULL	CT	t	—	—	—	—	—	—	—	—	—	—	—	—	—	—	—	—	—
TULARE	CA	c	1	49	38	56	41,556	50,512	n	—	5	4,718	3,896	83	2,563	836	497	200	621
TUPELO	MS	c	1	90	89	56	26,804	35,447	n	—	—	4,976	—	—	3,546	—	405	255	721
UPPER ARLINGTON	OH	c	1	64	61	50–54	—	—	y	—	4	7,890	—	—	4,778	—	941	159	438
UPPER DUBLIN	PA	tp	2	—	—	other	—	—	—	—	—	369	—	—	—	—	18	88	263
URBANA	IL	c	1	59	57	56	43,861	43,861	y	59,417	1	5,677	—	—	3,612	—	302	158	547
WALLINGFORD	CT	t	3	67	64	42	43,552	56,149	y	56,899	5	7,043	6,138	87	4,741	448	948	193	712
WALNUT	CA	c	5	—	—	—	—	—	—	—	—	—	—	—	—	—	—	—	—
WARMINSTER	PA	tp	2	—	—	—	—	—	—	—	—	—	—	—	—	—	—	—	—
WARREN	OH	c	1	77	75	50–54	33,962	48,483	y	—	5	7,154	—	—	4,391	—	847	21	668
WATERTOWN	NY	c	1	81	80	40	39,600	49,178	y	50,228	6	7,163	6,627	93	4,621	1,170	835	—	537
WATSONVILLE	CA	c	1	33	32	56	56,900	76,252	n	—	—	5,768	5,188	90	3,647	1,219	321	33	547
WELLINGTON	FL	v	—	—	—	—	—	—	—	—	—	—	—	—	—	—	—	—	—
WEST BEND	WI	c	1	40	40	56	41,102	51,131	y	51,791	5	3,923	3,774	96	2,621	572	581	—	149
WEST HOLLYWOOD	CA	c	—	—	—	—	—	—	—	—	—	—	—	—	—	—	—	—	—
WEST SACRAMENTO	CA	c	1	70	57	56	58,957	68,993	n	—	—	8,697	7,344	84	4,904	1,971	469	175	1,177
WEST SPRINGFIELD	MA	t	—	—	67	42	42,436	50,009	y	51,509	15	—	—	—	—	—	—	—	—
WESTERVILLE	OH	c	1	90	88	50–54	46,458	63,225	y	64,875	5	10,338	8,865	86	6,486	1,460	919	—	1,472
WESTFIELD	MA	c	1	88	85	48	35,955	41,699	y	46,895	5	8,406	7,892	94	5,711	762	1,418	131	383
WESTFIELD	NJ	t	3	41	40	48	46,929	80,992	y	—	—	3,695	—	—	3,222	—	—	—	473
WESTLAKE	OH	c	1	49	42	48	53,828	63,941	y	66,441	5	5,623	—	—	3,633	—	728	62	423
WHEAT RIDGE	CO	c	—	—	—	—	—	—	—	—	—	—	—	—	—	—	—	—	—
WILDWOOD	MO	c	—	—	—	—	—	—	—	—	—	—	—	—	—	—	—	—	—
WILLINGBORO	NJ	tp	3	19	19	50–54	44,632	67,454	y	101,068	8	—	—	—	1,216	—	—	175	228
WILMETTE	IL	v	1	47	44	50–54	58,901	74,107	y	81,636	5	7,131	13,057	183	6,386	4,447	2,224	461	—
WILSON	NC	c	1	92	88	56	32,896	49,344	y	51,811	—	6,412	5,574	87	4,144	711	719	18	820
WINTER SPRINGS	FL	c	1	51	49	56	32,850	47,633	y	—	—	4,065	3,577	88	2,658	530	388	119	370
WOODRIDGE	IL	v	—	—	—	—	—	—	—	—	—	—	—	—	—	—	—	—	—
YUCAIPA	CA	c	—	—	—	—	—	—	—	—	—	—	—	—	—	—	—	—	—
ZANESVILLE	OH	c	1	48	43	56	34,311	45,741	y	47,938	5	4,329	—	—	2,484	—	757	143	167
10,000–24,999																			
ABERDEEN	NJ	tp	2	—	—	—	—	—	—	—	—	—	—	—	—	—	—	—	—
ADDISON	TX	t	1	55	54	56	43,709	60,599	y	62,279	1	5,701	—	—	3,543	—	622	381	554
ADRIAN	MI	c	1	19	19	50–54	35,678	50,052	n	—	—	1,675	1,256	75	919	127	210	191	128
AGOURA HILLS	CA	c	—	—	—	—	—	—	—	—	—	—	—	—	—	—	—	—	—
ALBEMARLE	NC	c	1	42	42	56	26,270	43,077	y	45,231	5	2,956	2,196	74	1,637	197	362	315	445
ALBERT LEA	MN	c	1	17	17	56	53,820	88,654	n	—	—	1,537	1,304	85	948	115	240	84	143
ALGONQUIN	IL	v	—	—	—	—	—	—	—	—	—	—	—	—	—	—	—	—	—
ALICE	TX	c	3	32	32	50–54	28,485	34,517	y	35,717	1	2,101	1,546	74	1,186	183	177	350	205
ALLIANCE	OH	c	1	33	—	48	39,736	41,708	y	43,028	4	2,667	—	—	1,694	—	395	64	135
ALPENA	MI	c	1	24	23	56	35,206	40,302	y	42,720	8	2,442	1,709	70	1,217	475	17	11	721
ALTUS	OK	c	1	52	29	48	25,713	42,806	n	—	—	2,240	1,881	84	1,457	233	190	194	165
AMERICUS	GA	c	1	—	22	50–54	25,111	35,156	y	—	—	3,061	2,439	80	1,863	225	351	138	484
AMESBURY	MA	t	1	34	34	42	36,295	45,973	y	52,869	7	—	—	—	—	—	—	—	—
ANGLETON	TX	c	2	1	—	—	—	—	y	60	1	103	56	54	44	5	6	—	47
ANOKA	MN	c	3	4	4	56	37,746	42,853	n	—	—	1,452	776	53	469	267	40	487	189
ANSONIA	CT	c	2	1	—	—	—	—	n	—	—	—	131	—	93	13	25	—	—
ARKANSAS CITY	KS	c	3	23	23	56	—	—	y	—	3	1,973	1,711	87	1,194	265	252	101	161
ARLINGTON	WA	c	3	28	26	56	50,952	67,944	y	69,144	5	4,061	2,850	70	2,377	362	110	—	854
ARNOLD	MO	c	—	—	—	—	—	—	—	—	—	—	—	—	—	—	—	—	—
ARROYO GRANDE	CA	c	3	9	8	56	47,496	57,720	n	—	—	1,570	1,395	89	969	280	146	40	135

Table 3/17 continued **FIRE DEPARTMENT PERSONNEL, SALARIES, AND EXPENDITURES FOR CITIES 10,000 AND OVER: 2008**

City	State	Type	Service provision	Full-time paid personnel	Full-time uniformed personnel	Duty hours per week	Minimum base salary ($)	Maximum base salary ($)	Longevity pay	Maximum salary with longevity ($)	Years of service for longevity	Reported expenditures (in $000)							
												Total expenditures (A) ($)	Total personnel expenditures (B) ($)	(B) as % of (A)	Salaries and wages (C) ($)	City contribution to retirement and social security (D) ($)	City contribution to insurance (E) ($)	Capital outlay (F) ($)	All other (G) ($)
10,000–24,999 continued																			
ARTESIA	NM	c	1	21	20	56	25,692	39,492	y	42,372	5	—	—	—	—	—	—	—	—
ARVIN	CA	c	—	—	—	—	—	—	—	—	—	—	—	—	—	—	—	—	—
ASHEBORO	NC	c	1	50	49	56	31,940	46,086	n	—	—	2,819	2,369	84	1,951	210	208	40	409
ASHLAND	MA	t	1	23	22	42	41,512	53,098	y	54,298	20	2,150	—	—	1,935	—	—	85	131
ASHLAND	OH	c	1	38	37	50–54	41,588	45,508	y	46,758	7	2,970	2,666	90	1,969	479	217	28	276
ASHLAND	OR	c	1	34	26	56	50,292	62,424	n	—	—	5,177	3,427	66	2,346	646	434	394	1,356
ASHWAUBENON	WI	v	4	—	—	other	—	—	—	—	—	—	—	—	—	—	—	—	—
ATCHISON	KS	c	1	19	18	56	26,703	35,585	y	36,585	5	1,055	—	—	656	—	162	44	88
ATHENS	AL	c	1	38	37	48	24,589	40,353	n	—	—	—	—	—	—	—	—	—	—
ATHENS	TN	c	3	21	19	50–54	25,778	38,669	n	—	—	1,400	1,122	80	864	161	96	163	114
AUBURN	CA	c	3	14	14	56	42,828	61,920	y	71,208	7	1,773	—	—	1,296	—	—	244	—
AUBURN	MA	t	1	57	31	48	42,357	52,840	n	—	—	2,062	—	—	1,903	—	—	—	159
AUBURN	ME	c	1	64	63	42	—	—	—	—	—	2,744	—	—	2,282	—	91	89	282
AUBURNDALE	FL	c	—	—	—	—	—	—	—	—	—	—	—	—	—	—	—	—	—
AURORA	OH	c	1	18	17	56	50,899	58,500	y	60,300	6	2,522	2,287	91	1,558	336	392	67	169
AUSTIN	MN	c	1	10	10	56	40,685	48,901	y	50,368	7	1,267	847	67	557	110	179	16	403
AVENAL	CA	c	—	—	—	—	—	—	—	—	—	—	—	—	—	—	—	—	—
AVENTURA	FL	c	—	—	—	—	—	—	—	—	—	—	—	—	—	—	—	—	—
AVON	CT	t	2	—	—	—	—	—	—	—	—	1,501	289	19	201	44	44	—	1,212
AVON LAKE	OH	c	1	30	27	50–54	49,418	65,834	y	67,434	6	3,470	3,145	91	2,257	558	329	122	203
BABYLON	NY	v	2	—	—	other	—	—	—	—	—	383	—	—	—	—	—	28	354
BAINBRIDGE	GA	c	4	—	—	42	—	—	—	—	—	—	—	—	—	—	—	—	—
BARRINGTON	IL	v	1	41	39	50–54	—	—	—	—	—	—	—	—	—	—	—	—	—
BATAVIA	IL	c	1	24	23	50–54	50,400	69,494	n	—	—	4,559	3,544	78	2,510	496	537	187	828
BAY VILLAGE	OH	c	1	26	26	50–54	43,116	61,611	y	64,611	5	2,977	—	—	2,011	—	357	21	140
BEACH PARK	IL	v	—	—	—	—	—	—	—	—	—	—	—	—	—	—	—	—	—
BEACHWOOD	NJ	b	2	—	—	other	—	—	n	—	—	73	—	—	—	—	—	25	48
BEACHWOOD	OH	c	1	44	40	other	56,504	69,446	y	70,946	7	5,109	4,811	94	3,301	785	725	24	273
BEACON	NY	c	3	13	13	48	44,206	52,888	y	—	18	—	—	—	—	—	—	—	—
BEAUFORT	SC	c	3	—	—	other	26,714	—	y	—	2	3,094	2,184	71	1,598	280	305	568	342
BEECH GROVE	IN	c	1	40	30	48	—	—	—	—	—	—	—	—	—	—	—	—	—
BEEVILLE	TX	c	2	—	—	other	—	—	—	—	—	227	—	—	74	—	2	37	113
BEL AIR	MD	t	—	—	—	—	—	—	—	—	—	—	—	—	—	—	—	—	—
BELLE GLADE	FL	c	—	—	—	—	—	—	—	—	—	—	—	—	—	—	—	—	—
BELLMAWR	NJ	b	2	—	—	—	—	—	—	—	—	171	—	—	—	—	—	66	106
BELTON	MO	c	1	46	45	other	34,887	46,751	y	—	—	3,422	2,982	87	2,188	391	403	—	440
BELTON	TX	c	3	27	24	other	35,360	41,643	y	—	—	—	—	—	—	—	—	—	—
BELVIDERE	IL	c	1	32	30	50–54	38,932	54,844	y	57,998	3	2,569	—	—	1,853	—	34	50	284
BEMIDJI	MN	c	3	8	8	48	34,740	45,672	n	—	—	889	559	63	435	51	72	252	78
BENBROOK	TX	c	3	16	16	50–54	42,001	56,285	y	58,493	1	1,739	1,454	84	1,119	215	120	34	252
BENTONVILLE	AR	c	1	71	64	56	30,259	49,694	y	49,694	—	8,424	4,424	53	3,312	646	466	3,374	627
BEREA	OH	c	1	23	23	50–54	46,314	57,658	y	—	5	—	—	—	1,769	—	395	—	—
BERKELEY	MO	c	1	—	—	50–54	33,459	43,078	n	—	—	1,702	—	—	1,260	—	105	47	197
BERKELEY HEIGHTS	NJ	tp	2	—	—	other	—	—	n	—	—	—	—	—	—	—	—	—	—
BERLIN	CT	t	2	—	—	other	—	—	y	—	—	665	133	20	108	8	17	185	347
BERLIN	NH	c	1	20	20	42	36,525	44,096	y	45,596	5	1,615	1,682	104	1,020	515	146	12	421
BETHANY	OK	c	1	23	22	50–54	27,624	42,564	y	—	3	1,717	1,498	87	1,150	157	191	2	217
BETHLEHEM	PA	tp	2	—	—	other	—	—	y	—	0	—	—	—	—	—	—	—	—
BIDDEFORD	ME	c	3	45	43	42	32,760	38,329	y	41,012	5	3,119	2,733	88	2,152	219	362	70	316
BIRMINGHAM	MI	c	3	36	36	56	38,088	62,930	y	69,224	5	4,648	4,096	88	2,879	470	747	57	495
BIXBY	OK	c	—	23	21	50–54	27,593	31,973	y	36,028	1	2,412	1,233	51	889	123	220	956	223
BLOOMINGDALE	IL	v	—	—	—	—	—	—	—	—	—	—	—	—	—	—	—	—	—
BLYTHE	CA	c	3	—	—	other	—	—	y	—	—	421	194	46	157	13	23	34	193
BOONE	IA	c	1	14	14	50–54	37,320	47,306	y	48,278	3	1,207	1,168	97	728	198	241	13	27
BOONE	NC	t	3	15	14	50–54	—	—	—	—	—	1,034	787	76	640	76	71	—	247
BORGER	TX	c	1	—	17	50–54	28,800	31,790	y	—	1	1,431	1,244	87	954	170	120	58	129
BOULDER CITY	NV	c	1	22	20	56	52,649	70,383	n	—	—	2,551	2,348	92	1,608	453	287	8	195
BOURNE	MA	t	1	39	38	42	39,830	47,636	y	—	10	—	—	—	2,757	—	—	219	314
BRAINERD	MN	c	3	9	8	56	45,165	53,028	y	55,415	8	1,254	867	69	615	125	126	203	184
BRECKSVILLE	OH	c	1	17	16	50–54	51,592	65,841	y	69,591	2	2,194	—	—	1,494	303	—	200	197
BRENTWOOD	PA	b	2	—	—	other	—	—	—	—	—	—	—	—	—	—	—	—	—
BRENTWOOD	TN	c	1	59	58	40	32,531	52,748	y	—	5	—	—	—	—	—	—	—	—
BRIDGETON	MO	c	—	—	—	—	—	—	—	—	—	—	—	—	—	—	—	—	—
BRIDGETON	NJ	c	1	16	4	56	42,383	63,571	y	65,696	5	1,398	1,548	111	1,124	184	240	—	—
BRIGHAM CITY	UT	c	1	—	—	other	—	—	n	—	—	487	—	—	159	—	66	50	200
BRIGHTON	CO	c	—	—	—	—	—	—	—	—	—	—	—	—	—	—	—	—	—
BRISTOL	RI	t	3	2	2	other	41,763	70,000	y	44,478	5	385	319	83	224	41	54	247	161
BROOK PARK	OH	c	4	—	—	48	—	—	—	—	—	—	—	—	—	—	—	—	—
BROOKINGS	SD	c	3	3	2	other	—	—	y	—	0	691	207	30	146	21	40	168	315
BROWNSVILLE	TN	t	1	25	25	56	26,080	30,080	n	—	—	825	—	—	825	—	57	40	—
BUCKINGHAM	PA	tp	2	—	—	—	—	—	—	—	—	—	—	—	—	—	—	—	—
BUENA VISTA	MI	tp	1	9	9	50–54	35,417	41,399	n	—	—	—	—	—	—	—	—	—	—
BUFORD	GA	c	—	—	—	—	—	—	—	—	—	—	—	—	—	—	—	—	—

Table 3/17
continued

FIRE DEPARTMENT PERSONNEL, SALARIES, AND EXPENDITURES FOR CITIES 10,000 AND OVER: 2008

City	State	Type	Service provision	Full-time paid personnel	Full-time uniformed personnel	Duty hours per week	Minimum base salary ($)	Maximum base salary ($)	Longevity pay	Maximum salary with longevity ($)	Years of service for longevity	Total expenditures (A) ($)	Total personnel expenditures (B) ($)	(B) as % of (A)	Salaries and wages (C) ($)	City contribution to retirement and social security (D) ($)	City contribution to insurance (E) ($)	Capital outlay (F) ($)	All other (G) ($)
10,000–24,999 continued																			
BURLESON	TX	c	3	39	27	48	44,572	57,944	y	59,144	1	3,123	1,968	63	1,539	264	164	782	373
BUTLER	PA	tp	2	—	—	—	—	—	—	—	—	—	—	—	—	—	—	—	—
CADILLAC	MI	c	1	11	10	50–54	38,208	42,325	y	—	—	—	—	—	—	—	—	—	—
CALABASAS	CA	c	—	—	—	—	—	—	—	—	—	—	—	—	—	—	—	—	—
CALHOUN	GA	c	1	40	40	50–54	23,702	33,678	n	—	—	—	—	—	—	—	—	—	—
CALLAWAY	FL	c	—	—	—	—	—	—	—	—	—	—	—	—	—	—	—	—	—
CALN	PA	tp	3	1	—	40	50,876	50,876	n	—	—	249	—	—	50	—	23	—	173
CAMAS	WA	c	1	39	36	48	61,800	73,812	y	—	—	3,626	—	—	2,158	—	526	160	611
CAMBRIDGE	OH	c	1	20	20	other	37,003	40,350	y	41,598	5	—	—	—	1,093	—	—	—	—
CAMDEN	AR	c	1	30	29	56	23,950	26,154	n	—	—	1,603	1,184	74	888	113	182	267	152
CANANDAIGUA	NY	c	3	16	16	40	39,219	49,923	y	50,973	5	1,888	1,683	89	1,228	248	207	39	166
CANBY	OR	c	—	—	—	—	—	—	—	—	—	—	—	—	—	—	—	—	—
CANON CITY	CO	c	—	—	—	—	—	—	—	—	—	—	—	—	—	—	—	—	—
CANTON	MA	t	1	53	52	42	38,545	49,884	y	50,734	5	6,361	—	—	3,697	—	623	1,224	373
CANYON	TX	c	3	5	4	40	31,692	42,624	y	—	1	—	—	—	289	—	28	27	—
CAPITOLA	CA	c	—	—	—	—	—	—	—	—	—	—	—	—	—	—	—	—	—
CARBONDALE	IL	c	1	32	30	50–54	34,704	46,853	y	—	—	2,742	2,508	91	1,594	547	366	15	219
CARPINTERIA	CA	c	—	—	—	—	—	—	—	—	—	—	—	—	—	—	—	—	—
CARRBORO	NC	t	1	33	33	56	31,619	49,010	y	—	5	—	—	—	—	—	—	—	—
CARROLL	IA	c	2	—	—	other	—	—	n	—	—	758	46	6	38	3	4	688	25
CARTERET	NJ	b	3	24	20	42	39,662	75,682	y	87,034	5	3,022	—	—	1,740	—	604	70	366
CASCADE CHARTER	MI	tp	3	—	18	50–54	35,000	53,765	n	—	—	1,924	1,225	64	1,073	124	28	196	513
CASSELBERRY	FL	c	1	51	51	56	33,042	—	n	—	—	4,405	3,901	89	2,752	723	426	9	495
CAYCE	SC	c	4	—	7	48	28,374	38,778	n	—	—	—	—	—	—	—	—	—	—
CEDAR CITY	UT	c	3	7	7	40	30,888	43,644	n	—	—	934	669	72	438	194	36	92	174
CENTERVILLE	OH	c	—	—	—	—	—	—	—	—	—	—	—	—	—	—	—	—	—
CENTERVILLE	UT	c	—	—	—	—	—	—	—	—	—	—	—	—	—	—	—	—	—
CENTRAL POINT	OR	c	—	—	—	—	—	—	—	—	—	—	—	—	—	—	—	—	—
CENTRALIA	IL	c	1	23	22	50–54	37,152	40,366	y	48,635	5	2,008	1,713	85	1,166	308	238	59	236
CENTRALIA	WA	c	—	—	—	—	—	—	—	—	—	—	—	—	—	—	—	—	—
CHAMBERSBURG	PA	b	3	24	22	other	37,338	49,657	y	49,657	1	2,456	1,563	64	1,066	215	282	124	768
CHAMPLIN	MN	c	—	—	—	—	—	—	—	—	—	—	—	—	—	—	—	—	—
CHANHASSEN	MN	c	2	—	—	other	—	—	—	—	—	—	—	—	—	—	—	—	—
CHARLESTON	IL	c	1	32	32	50–54	32,448	53,568	y	—	1	2,659	—	—	1,846	—	167	265	380
CHARLTON	MA	t	1	15	14	42	45,313	45,313	y	45,713	11	1,562	1,315	84	1,073	134	108	—	247
CHICKASHA	OK	c	1	37	35	56	25,742	37,041	y	38,721	1	2,880	2,392	83	1,861	229	302	3	485
CHILLICOTHE	OH	c	1	44	43	56	—	—	y	—	5	6,407	4,136	65	2,622	807	707	1,972	299
CHRISTIANSBURG	VA	t	3	1	—	other	—	—	—	—	—	753	327	43	228	59	39	286	200
CIRCLEVILLE	OH	c	1	16	16	56	30,383	34,792	y	36,292	5	1,613	—	—	862	—	158	59	256
CLAREMORE	OK	c	1	44	40	other	26,979	33,654	y	33,771	3	3,360	2,972	88	2,217	396	359	17	371
CLARKSBURG	WV	c	1	42	42	other	27,753	30,217	y	—	2	3,158	2,478	78	1,536	608	334	18	662
CLAWSON	MI	c	2	—	—	other	—	—	n	—	—	440	306	69	36	249	20	48	122
CLAYTON	CA	c	—	—	—	—	—	—	—	—	—	—	—	—	—	—	—	—	—
CLAYTON	MO	c	1	36	35	56	41,246	61,869	n	—	—	3,180	3,039	96	2,318	477	243	2	139
CLAYTON	OH	c	1	—	7	50–54	40,822	52,385	n	—	—	1,239	986	80	752	130	104	17	237
CLEARLAKE	CA	c	—	—	—	—	—	—	—	—	—	—	—	—	—	—	—	—	—
CLEMMONS	NC	v	—	—	—	—	—	—	—	—	—	—	—	—	—	—	—	—	—
CLINTON	MS	c	1	50	49	50–54	24,969	41,271	n	—	—	3,316	2,553	77	1,871	406	275	301	462
CLINTON	NJ	tp	2	—	—	other	—	—	y	—	—	1,614	—	—	—	—	—	1,520	94
CLINTON	UT	c	3	8	8	50–54	41,835	60,945	n	—	—	906	659	73	447	89	122	38	209
CLIVE	IA	c	1	8	7	48	41,150	51,060	n	—	—	2,037	—	—	1,062	—	103	93	—
COCOA	FL	c	1	39	39	50–54	32,893	48,143	n	—	—	3,363	2,868	85	1,832	637	399	61	434
COHOES	NY	c	1	—	38	48	31,999	50,640	y	53,440	5	2,900	—	—	—	—	425	347	—
COLCHESTER	VT	t	2	—	—	—	—	—	—	—	—	—	—	—	—	—	—	—	—
COLDWATER	MI	c	3	15	—	50–54	—	—	y	—	5	1,500	1,222	81	920	117	184	—	279
COLLEGE PARK	MD	c	—	—	—	—	—	—	—	—	—	—	—	—	—	—	—	—	—
COLLINSVILLE	IL	c	1	30	29	42	47,524	48,332	y	53,159	4	3,433	3,022	88	2,175	422	425	126	285
CONCORD	MA	t	1	39	38	42	41,435	56,205	y	58,205	20	3,271	—	—	2,976	—	—	107	187
CONNERSVILLE	IN	c	1	32	32	56	38,301	38,922	y	42,422	1	2,748	2,626	96	1,707	276	643	—	121
CONWAY	SC	c	1	34	33	50–54	26,209	39,314	y	—	—	1,742	1,425	82	1,032	177	215	21	296
CONYERS	GA	c	—	—	—	—	—	—	—	—	—	—	—	—	—	—	—	—	—
COOS BAY	OR	c	3	17	16	56	42,480	54,216	y	—	—	—	1,589	—	1,083	302	204	—	—
COPLEY	OH	tp	1	16	15	50–54	44,266	58,450	y	—	3	2,013	1,762	88	1,329	177	255	47	204
CORALVILLE	IA	c	3	3	3	40	42,447	56,465	n	—	—	635	243	38	163	26	54	218	174
CORCORAN	CA	c	—	—	—	—	—	—	—	—	—	—	—	—	—	—	—	—	—
CORNELIUS	NC	t	2	—	—	other	—	—	—	—	—	—	—	—	—	—	—	—	—
CORNING	NY	c	1	25	25	42	35,403	49,505	y	49,505	3	2,263	2,098	93	1,477	355	264	39	127
COSHOCTON	OH	c	1	18	—	42	29,135	35,534	y	35,534	—	1,529	—	—	854	—	257	153	101
COVENTRY	CT	t	2	—	—	—	—	—	—	—	—	666	—	—	—	—	—	297	369
COVINGTON	GA	c	1	57	56	50–54	26,762	44,000	n	—	—	5,066	3,440	68	2,603	378	458	609	1,017
CRANBERRY	PA	tp	2	1	—	—	38,304	38,304	n	—	—	38,283	—	—	25	12	—	8	—
CRAWFORDSVILLE	IN	c	1	37	36	56	38,149	47,617	y	47,617	1	2,649	2,405	91	1,668	367	369	32	212
CRESTVIEW	FL	c	1	—	45	56	21,932	—	y	124,937	—	—	—	—	2,720	—	—	—	—

Table 3/17   FIRE DEPARTMENT PERSONNEL, SALARIES, AND EXPENDITURES FOR
continued   CITIES 10,000 AND OVER: 2008

City	State	Type	Service provision	Full-time paid personnel	Full-time uniformed personnel	Duty hours per week	Minimum base salary ($)	Maximum base salary ($)	Longevity pay	Maximum salary with longevity ($)	Years of service for longevity	Reported expenditures (in $000)							
												Total expenditures (A) ($)	Total personnel expenditures (B) ($)	(B) as % of (A)	Salaries and wages (C) ($)	City contribution to retirement and social security (D) ($)	City contribution to insurance (E) ($)	Capital outlay (F) ($)	All other (G) ($)
10,000–24,999 continued																			
CRESTWOOD	MO	c	1	27	26	56	48,485	54,053	n	—	—	2,595	2,180	84	1,634	265	281	—	415
CROMWELL	CT	t	3	—	—	—	—	—	—	—	—	—	—	—	—	—	—	—	—
CROWN POINT	IN	c	3	21	20	56	38,840	50,146	y	50,606	—	2,042	1,818	89	1,423	234	161	69	155
CRYSTAL	MN	c	2	—	—	other	—	—	—	—	—	—	—	—	—	—	—	—	—
CULLMAN	AL	c	1	34	33	50–54	25,865	36,421	n	—	—	2,331	2,007	86	1,547	248	212	28	296
CUMBERLAND	MD	c	1	65	64	48	32,218	39,889	y	39,889	25	4,865	4,312	89	2,833	430	1,048	151	402
CUMRU	PA	tp	2	—	—	—	—	—	—	—	—	—	—	—	—	—	—	—	—
DALLAS	OR	c	3	4	3	40	—	—	n	—	—	719	333	46	214	56	62	—	338
DAPHNE	AL	t	3	30	29	56	34,407	53,540	n	—	—	2,438	1,732	71	1,327	182	222	212	493
DARIEN	IL	c	—																
DE BARY	FL	c	5	—	—	56	—	—	—	—	—	938	—	—	—	—	—	—	—
DE LAND	FL	c	1	46	45	other	29,379	42,608	y	43,208	8	4,539	2,549	56	1,868	406	276	61,233	757
DEERFIELD	IL	v	—																
DEFIANCE	OH	c	1	19	19	56	35,030	44,767	y	—	5	1,937	—	91	1,188	—	278	23	167
DEMING	NM	c	1	20	20	56	28,478	36,232	y	38,812	8	1,241	1,126	91	866	156	105	9	105
DENISON	TX	c	1	57	52	56	32,629	36,859	y	38,364	1	2,298	2,037	89	1,597	264	176	43	218
DERRY	PA	tp	2	—	—	—	—	—	y	—	—	425	—	—	—	—	19	10	396
DESTIN	FL	c	—																
DEWITT	MI	tp	1	2	2	40	35,508	44,367	n	—	—	854	—	—	214	—	—	478	85
DICKINSON	TX	c	2	3	2	42	32,513	48,770	y	49,250	1	519	387	75	336	26	24	—	131
DICKSON	TN	t	1	38	34	50–54	23,867	39,690	y	41,190	3	2,463	—	—	—	389	254	12	1,496
DINUBA	CA	c	1	26	22	56	50,724	61,656	n	—	—	3,357	2,172	65	1,565	311	296	200	985
DIXON	CA	c	3	23	20	56	49,656	63,360	n	—	—	3,508	2,643	75	1,908	446	289	401	464
DORAL	FL	c	—																
DOUGLAS	GA	c	3	38	37	56	25,388	38,731	n	—	—	2,333	1,846	79	1,265	257	324	346	141
DOVER	NJ	t	1	6	6	48	48,097	70,623	n	—	—	594	—	—	444	—	—	69	82
DOVER	OH	c	1	18	17	56	42,894	42,894	y	—	5	1,727	—	—	1,002	—	233	—	492
DOVER	PA	tp	2	—															
DOYLESTOWN	PA	tp	2	—	—	—	—	—	—	—	—	—	—	—	—	—	—	—	—
DUMAS	TX	c	1	16	16	50–54	24,143	52,201	y	53,161	1	1,011	793	78	612	111	69	38	166
DUNCAN	OK	c	1	40	39	56	30,261	39,604	y	41,101	3	3,031	2,393	79	2,096	37	260	360	278
DUNKIRK	NY	c	3	29	28	40	34,882	49,832	y	—	25	2,361	2,232	95	1,662	379	191	—	129
DURANT	OK	c	1	35	33	56	26,379	31,733	y	36,176	1	1,976	1,760	89	1,321	171	267	106	110
DURHAM	NH	t	1	20	19	42	37,326	46,630	n	—	—	2,628	2,291	87	1,680	279	331	38	300
EASLEY	SC	c	3	50	24	other	26,676	—	n	—	—	—	2,549	—	2,047	404	97	138	400
EAST GRAND RAPIDS	MI	c	4	—	—	56	—	—	—	—	—	—	—	—	—	—	—	—	—
EAST GREENWICH	RI	t	1	42	12	42	32,869	48,506	y	—	5	—	—	—	—	—	—	—	—
EAST HAMPTON	CT	t	2	—															
EAST LAMPETER	PA	tp	2	—	—	other	—	—	—	y	—	—	385	—	—	—	—	—	18	367
EAST LIVERPOOL	OH	c	1	18	16	56	34,711	44,204	y	45,104	5	1,503	—	—	972	—	222	—	23
EAST LONGMEADOW	MA	t	3	8	8	40	41,000	44,300	y	—	5	632	—	—	578	—	—	—	54
EAST PEORIA	IL	c	1	40	37	56	29,000	61,974	y	71,404	3	—	—	—	2,310	—	—	—	—
EAST ROCKAWAY	NY	v	2	—															
EASTHAMPTON	MA	t	1	26	—	42	37,776	43,989	y	—	10	1,698	—	—	1,588	—	—	—	111
EASTON	MA	t	1	37	36	42	38,612	50,805	y	51,205	5	2,829	—	—	2,567	—	—	—	262
EATONTOWN	NJ	b	3	1	—	other	—	—	—	—	—	168	—	—	—	—	—	56	108
EDEN	NC	c	3	17	17	50–54	28,834	50,576	n	—	—	1,552	1,059	68	764	132	164	235	258
EL CAMPO	TX	c	2	—	—	other	—	—	—	y	—	0	221	—	—	—	—	3	7	182
EL CERRITO	CA	c	1	36	35	56	59,885	88,414	y	88,414	—	6,495	5,876	90	3,956	1,242	677	46	574
EL DORADO	KS	c	3	16	16	50–54	27,605	39,752	y	40,712	5	976	832	85	635	79	118	—	145
EL RENO	OK	c	1	19	17	50–54	28,080	39,340	y	42,340	5	1,373	1,147	84	906	108	132	123	102
ELIZABETH	PA	tp	2	—	—	other	—	—	—	n	—	—	398	—	—	—	—	—	—	—
ELIZABETH CITY	NC	c	—	46	40	56	28,280	41,434	y	—	—	3,235	2,428	75	1,864	320	243	—	807
ELIZABETHTOWN	PA	b	—																
ELKO	NV	c	3	22	18	other	44,649	56,455	y	57,855	8	3,969	—	—	1,556	—	288	1,255	445
ELKTON	MD	t	—																
ELMWOOD PARK	NJ	b	2	—	—	—	—	—	—	—	—	70	—	—	70	—	—	—	—
ENDICOTT	NY	v	1	35	—	42	32,061	49,023	n	—	—	4,248	3,567	84	2,111	490	965	561	120
ENNIS	TX	c	3	29	28	50–54	39,257	49,094	y	50,680	1	2,804	2,109	75	1,473	304	332	458	237
ENTERPRISE	AL	c	1	38	37	50–54	24,814	37,502	y	38,702	10	—	1,659	—	1,264	163	232	—	—
ESCANABA	MI	c	4	—	—	42	—	—	—	y	—	—	—	—	—	—	—	—	—
EUSTIS	FL	c	1	32	30	50–54	29,900	45,500	—	—	—	1,749	1,479	85	1,073	218	187	99	170
EVANSTON	WY	c	—																
EVERGREEN PARK	IL	v	1	4	—	40	—	—	y	—	5	—	—	—	—	—	—	—	—
EXETER	PA	tp	2	2	2	other	—	—	y	—	—	263	—	—	48	9	—	58	147
FAIRFAX	VA	c	3	76	64	56	46,870	69,249	y	72,711	15	12,017	—	—	7,686	—	—	206	1,361
FAIRHAVEN	MA	t	1	24	22	48	38,626	46,904	y	47,904	5	—	—	—	—	—	—	—	—
FAIRMONT	MN	c	2	—	—	other	—	—	n	—	—	391	177	45	82	41	54	107	106
FAIRVIEW HEIGHTS	IL	c	—																
FALLS CHURCH	VA	c	2	—	—	other	—	—	n	—	—	—	—	—	—	—	—	—	—
FARIBAULT	MN	c	1	11	9	56	48,144	53,493	y	55,633	5	1,316	1,039	79	802	101	136	104	173
FARMINGTON	MI	c	4	—	—	other	—	—	y	—	—	—	—	—	—	—	—	—	—
FARMINGTON	MN	c	7	1	—	other	—	—	n	—	—	617	374	61	179	115	79	—	243

Table 3/17
continued

FIRE DEPARTMENT PERSONNEL, SALARIES, AND EXPENDITURES FOR
CITIES 10,000 AND OVER: 2008

City	State	Type	Service provision	Full-time paid personnel	Full-time uniformed personnel	Duty hours per week	Minimum base salary ($)	Maximum base salary ($)	Longevity pay	Maximum salary with longevity ($)	Years of service for longevity	Total expenditures (A) ($)	Total personnel expenditures (B) ($)	(B) as % of (A)	Salaries and wages (C) ($)	City contribution to retirement and social security (D) ($)	City contribution to insurance (E) ($)	Capital outlay (F) ($)	All other (G) ($)
10,000–24,999 continued																			
FARMINGTON	MO	c	1	11	9	other	24,965	29,733	n	—	—	829	642	77	466	86	90	85	19
FARMINGTON	UT	c	3	1	1	—	—	—	—	—	—	469	—	—	282	—	—	71	66
FARRAGUT	TN	t	—																
FAYETTEVILLE	GA	c	3	25	24	56	32,472	53,732	n	—	—	1,841	1,633	89	1,164	206	263	—	208
FERGUSON	PA	tp	—																
FERNANDINA BEACH	FL	c	1	31	29	56	33,954	67,527	y	67,627	5	2,738	2,121	77	1,591	273	256	260	358
FILLMORE	CA	c	3	5	—	40	36,384	44,220	n	—	—	552	404	73	238	135	31	—	148
FLORENCE	NJ	tp	3	6	6	other	44,000	62,000	y	64,000	5	1,546	875	57	577	173	125	27	644
FOREST ACRES	SC	c	—																
FOREST GROVE	OR	c	3	18	17	56	49,788	61,764	n	—	—	2,496	1,846	74	1,291	306	249	228	422
FOREST HILL	TX	c	1	17	17	56	41,336	41,336	y	45,836	1	1,482	1,108	75	817	136	155	115	259
FOREST PARK	IL	v	1	23	23	other	45,947	73,039	y	73,556	20	2,550	—	—	1,938	477	—	134	563
FORREST CITY	AR	c	3	20	20	other	23,564	26,458	y	28,258	5	1,314	895	68	718	99	77	247	890
FORT MORGAN	CO	c	3	4	1	other	—	—	n	—	—	568	426	75	189	167	70	77	164
FORT WALTON BEACH	FL	c	1	39	37	56	28,593	49,581	y	50,481	—	3,238	2,592	80	1,946	337	308	65	582
FOUNTAIN	CO	c	3	30	26	50–54	38,064	58,198	n	—	—	2,710	1,430	53	1,125	85	219	990	290
FOUNTAIN HILLS	AZ	t	6																
FRANCONIA	PA	tp	—																
FRANKFORT	IL	v	—																
FRANKFORT	IN	c	1	41	38	56	37,638	—	n	—	—	1,992	—	—	1,608	—	—	—	155
FRANKLIN	NJ	tp	2	—	—	other	—	—	—	—	—	—	—	—	—	—	—	—	—
FREEHOLD	NJ	b	2	—	4	other	—	—	n	—	—	451	189	42	129	12	47	51	210
GAFFNEY	SC	c	1	34	32	—	23,049	28,811	n	—	—	—	—	—	—	—	—	—	—
GALENA PARK	TX	c	3	7	5	50–54	34,037	34,037	n	—	—	588	488	83	338	64	85	3	97
GALION	OH	c	1	16	16	48	29,186	33,844	y	—	1	—	—	—	787	—	—	—	—
GARDEN CITY	ID	c	—																
GARDEN CITY	NY	v	3	35	35	42	38,020	76,916	y	78,216	8	5,051	5,315	105	3,344	1,643	327	847	298
GATESVILLE	TX	c	2	—	—	other	—	—	n	—	—	169	—	—	—	17	50	100	
GENEVA	NY	c	3	21	19	40	41,431	52,926	y	54,026	5	1,991	1,732	87	1,241	274	216	3	256
GLASSBORO	NJ	b	—	5	5	40	44,595	51,803	y	52,814	3	480	—	—	410	—	1	—	69
GLOVERSVILLE	NY	c	1	32	32	42	29,400	49,078	y	—	1	2,336	—	—	1,936	366	—	—	43
GOLDEN	CO	c	3	9	6	other	—	—	n	—	—	3,516	779	22	498	201	81	2,340	396
GOODYEAR	AZ	c	3	113	93	56	43,183	62,543	y	63,543	—	9,597	7,073	74	5,928	408	736	752	1,773
GRAFTON	MA	t	2	—	—	other	—	—	n	—	—	359	—	—	129	—	—	—	150
GRAFTON	WI	v	2																
GRANBY	CT	t	—																
GRAND HAVEN	MI	c	4	—	—	42	—	—	—	—	—	—	—	—	—	—	—	—	—
GRAND RAPIDS	MI	tp	3	6	—	56	35,995	41,703	n	—	—	735	550	75	427	70	52	77	535
GRANDVIEW	MO	c	1	41	40	56	33,089	52,024	y	52,888	3	3,169	2,791	88	2,203	232	355	31	347
GRANDVILLE	MI	c	3	8	7	42	34,054	44,270	y	45,377	15	836	—	—	480	—	—	15	165
GRASS VALLEY	CA	c	1	17	15	56	39,504	48,036	n	—	—	2,044	1,608	79	1,102	233	272	1	436
GREEN RIVER	WY	c	2	2	2	other	—	—	y	—	—	828	418	51	334	47	37	311	99
GREENFIELD	CA	c	—																
GREENFIELD	IN	c	3	45	45	48	35,002	39,548	n	—	—	—	—	—	2,169	—	—	79	423
GREENVILLE	TX	c	1	49	48	56	40,136	48,763	y	50,263	1	3,867	3,463	90	2,631	382	451	—	348
GREENWOOD	MS	c	1	55	54	other	23,675	28,488	n	—	—	2,620	2,333	89	1,631	303	399	131	156
GREENWOOD	SC	c	1	50	49	40	24,939	34,882	n	—	—	2,560	2,366	92	1,765	284	316	69	125
GRIFFIN	GA	c	1	65	64	other	28,575	45,675	—	—	—	—	—	—	2,330	—	—	—	—
GRIFFITH	IN	t	2	—	—	other	—	—	n	—	—	—	—	—	—	—	—	—	—
GROVER BEACH	CA	c	1	—	—	other	—	—	—	—	—	—	—	—	—	—	—	—	—
HAINES CITY	FL	c	1	31	30	56	31,655	47,483	y	—	5	2,439	1,546	63	1,177	183	185	597	296
HALF MOON BAY	CA	c	—																
HAMBURG	NY	v	2	—	—	other	—	—	n	—	—	470	—	—	—	—	74	—	332
HAMPTON	PA	tp	2	—	—	other	—	—	—	—	—	—	—	—	—	—	—	—	—
HANNIBAL	MO	c	1	40	40	48	27,328	56,443	n	—	—	—	2,302	—	1,645	264	392	106	154
HARKER HEIGHTS	TX	c	1	39	37	50–54	—	—	y	—	1	2,165	1,861	86	1,473	270	117	31	274
HARPER WOODS	MI	c	1	14	14	56	37,001	52,495	y	55,645	4	1,700	—	—	1,128	—	395	64	48
HARTFORD	VT	t	1	22	20	48	37,110	55,390	n	—	—	2,762	1,942	70	1,326	181	436	352	468
HASTINGS	MN	c	3	—	15	56	41,282	55,078	y	56,730	5	2,881	1,679	58	1,419	170	90	438	764
HASTINGS	NE	c	3	28	27	50–54	29,891	42,008	n	—	—	1,897	1,683	89	1,216	163	303	—	213
HATFIELD	PA	tp	2																
HAVELOCK	NC	c	3	12	12	50–54	30,504	58,960	n	—	—	781	574	73	445	76	52	39	168
HAVERSTRAW	NY	v	2																
HAWAIIAN GARDENS	CA	c	—																
HAYS	KS	c	3	24	23	56	27,204	46,572	y	—	5	—	—	—	—	—	—	—	—
HAZEL CREST	IL	v	1	22	17	50–54	44,349	62,261	y	—	5	—	—	—	—	—	—	—	—
HAZEL PARK	MI	c	1	23	23	50–54	34,213	54,125	y	—	5	2,384	2,072	87	1,616	194	262	139	173
HAZLET	NJ	tp	1																
HEALDSBURG	CA	c	3	12	6	56	59,808	72,984	y	77,472	5	—	—	—	1,032	—	179	—	—
HENDERSON	TX	c	1	21	20	48	33,777	36,777	y	37,977	1	1,170	1,046	89	744	119	183	84	40
HENDERSONVILLE	NC	c	1	17	—	50–54	28,141	42,823	y	43,894	5	1,747	1,155	66	897	107	151	45	547
HERMOSA BEACH	CA	c	1	19	18	56	51,360	65,544	y	72,100	15	5,071	3,587	71	2,378	986	222	67	1,419

Table 3/17 continued   FIRE DEPARTMENT PERSONNEL, SALARIES, AND EXPENDITURES FOR CITIES 10,000 AND OVER: 2008

City	State	Type	Service provision	Full-time paid personnel	Full-time uniformed personnel	Duty hours per week	Minimum base salary ($)	Maximum base salary ($)	Longevity pay	Maximum salary with longevity ($)	Years of service for longevity	Total expenditures (A) ($)	Total personnel expenditures (B) ($)	(B) as % of (A)	Salaries and wages (C) ($)	City contribution to retirement and social security (D) ($)	City contribution to insurance (E) ($)	Capital outlay (F) ($)	All other (G) ($)
10,000–24,999 continued																			
HERNDON	VA	t	—	—	—	—	—	—	—	—	—	—	—	—	—	—	—	—	—
HEWITT	TX	c	1	10	10	40	28,920	46,800	y	48,000	1	303	223	74	173	29	20	25	55
HIBBING	MN	c	3	26	26	50–54	39,782	46,802	y	50,546	5	3,851	2,467	64	1,744	216	507	—	393
HIGHLAND VILLAGE	TX	c	3	12	11	50–54	—	—	y	—	2	1,124	867	77	701	69	97	—	257
HILLIARD	OH	c	—	—	—	—	—	—	—	—	—	—	—	—	—	—	—	—	—
HILLSBOROUGH	CA	t	1	31	29	56	75,723	92,133	n	—	—	6,356	5,590	88	3,741	803	1,046	445	320
HILLSIDE	NJ	tp	1	47	—	other	28,700	74,660	y	86,000	5	4,862	—	—	4,745	—	—	—	117
HILLTOWN	PA	tp	—	—	—	—	—	—	—	—	—	—	—	—	—	—	—	—	—
HINGHAM	MA	t	1	50	45	42	39,021	63,025	y	63,825	10	4,051	—	—	3,591	—	191	202	258
HOLBROOK	MA	t	1	26	20	42	39,308	53,214	y	53,614	5	—	—	—	1,846	—	—	109	53
HOLLY HILL	FL	c	1	14	13	56	29,792	47,626	n	—	—	1,478	1,262	85	840	291	131	86	130
HOMER GLEN	IL	v	—	—	—	—	—	—	—	—	—	—	—	—	—	—	—	—	—
HOMEWOOD	IL	v	3	19	17	50–54	49,992	66,972	y	68,122	6	—	—	—	1,913	—	—	—	—
HOPE	AR	c	1	16	16	56	21,578	23,791	n	—	—	896	659	74	491	64	104	44	194
HOPEWELL	PA	tp	2	—	—	other	—	—	n	—	—	247	—	—	—	—	—	—	245
HOPEWELL	VA	c	1	39	38	56	33,335	61,809	n	—	—	2,737	2,425	89	1,808	377	239	7	305
HOPKINS	MN	c	2	1	1	other	—	—	n	—	—	856	385	45	343	14	27	30	441
HOWARD	WI	v	3	1	—	other	65,354	—	y	—	5	958	250	26	201	30	18	203	505
HUDSON	NH	t	3	47	45	42	30,925	47,043	n	—	—	4,166	3,594	86	2,680	423	491	—	572
HUDSON	OH	c	3	5	4	40	42,182	—	n	—	—	960	645	67	475	73	97	93	222
HUEYTOWN	AL	c	1	33	33	50–54	31,450	48,755	n	—	—	—	—	—	—	—	—	—	—
HUMBLE	TX	c	1	16	14	56	40,356	53,568	y	—	1	1,707	1,387	81	1,045	192	150	57	262
HUNTERSVILLE	NC	t	2	—	—	—	—	—	—	—	—	—	—	—	—	—	—	—	—
HUNTINGTON	IN	c	1	43	41	56	38,178	38,178	y	46,196	1	2,622	2,359	90	1,977	381	2	128	134
HUTCHINSON	MN	c	3	2	2	other	—	—	n	—	—	465	368	79	201	126	41	7	91
INDIAN TRAIL	NC	t	—	—	—	—	—	—	—	—	—	—	—	—	—	—	—	—	—
INDIANOLA	IA	c	3	9	9	50–54	33,128	46,552	y	46,952	5	1,079	785	73	563	91	130	109	186
IONIA	MI	c	4	—	—	other	—	—	n	—	—	29	—	—	29	—	—	—	—
ISSAQUAH	WA	c	—	—	—	—	—	—	—	—	—	—	—	—	—	—	—	—	—
JACKSONVILLE BEACH	FL	c	1	32	31	56	34,187	36,225	n	—	—	3,041	2,471	81	1,877	365	228	512	59
JUNCTION CITY	KS	c	1	49	48	56	—	—	y	—	5	2,610	—	—	2,366	—	—	32	212
KATY	TX	c	3	2	1	40	48,000	—	y	—	1	—	—	—	—	—	—	—	—
KENMORE	WA	c	—	—	—	—	—	—	—	—	—	—	—	—	—	—	—	—	—
KENNESAW	GA	c	—	—	—	—	—	—	—	—	—	—	—	—	—	—	—	—	—
KENNETT	MO	c	1	10	7	50–54	28,000	—	n	—	—	583	454	78	356	42	55	16	113
KERRVILLE	TX	c	3	52	24	56	36,232	45,845	y	47,045	1	3,404	2,896	85	2,149	453	293	104	268
KEWANEE	IL	c	1	19	18	other	30,268	38,136	y	40,296	5	1,492	1,362	91	942	188	233	31	98
KILGORE	TX	c	1	36	33	50–54	32,555	43,965	y	—	1	1,965	1,746	89	1,195	272	279	—	219
KILLINGLY	CT	t	—	—	—	—	—	—	—	—	—	—	—	—	—	—	—	—	—
KINGMAN	AZ	c	1	65	57	56	38,022	53,501	—	—	—	5,649	4,682	83	3,563	454	665	710	259
KINGSLAND	GA	c	3	21	21	—	22,742	32,080	n	—	—	1,517	1,127	74	901	99	127	—	390
KINSTON	NC	c	4	—	—	56	—	—	—	—	—	—	—	—	—	—	—	—	—
KIRKSVILLE	MO	c	1	22	21	50–54	26,336	31,776	n	—	—	1,402	1,037	74	842	78	117	191	174
KLAMATH FALLS	OR	c	—	—	—	—	—	—	—	—	—	—	—	—	—	—	—	—	—
LA GRANDE	OR	c	1	16	13	56	27,729	35,329	n	—	—	2,407	2,045	85	1,573	213	259	30	332
LA GRANGE	IL	v	1	21	20	50–54	50,045	69,275	n	—	—	2,382	2,192	92	1,489	505	187	85	115
LA MARQUE	TX	c	1	18	16	50–54	33,455	46,345	y	—	1	1,737	1,330	77	997	160	172	42	365
LA PALMA	CA	c	—	—	—	—	—	—	—	—	—	—	—	—	—	—	—	—	—
LA PORTE	IN	c	1	43	43	50–54	34,180	37,915	y	41,416	3	2,307	—	—	1,966	—	—	—	209
LA QUINTA	CA	c	5	26	25	other	53,942	61,106	y	65,383	17	—	—	—	—	—	—	—	—
LA VISTA	NE	c	3	2	1	other	—	—	y	—	—	315	91	29	62	10	19	24	201
LACKAWANNA	NY	c	1	43	43	40	37,760	47,802	y	48,802	5	4,411	4,141	94	3,097	757	287	73	197
LADY LAKE	FL	t	5	—	—	—	—	—	—	—	—	—	—	—	—	—	—	—	—
LAFAYETTE	CO	c	3	14	13	56	—	—	y	—	—	—	—	—	—	—	—	—	—
LAKE FOREST PARK	WA	c	—	—	—	—	—	—	—	—	—	—	—	—	—	—	—	—	—
LAKE MARY	FL	c	1	38	37	56	—	—	y	—	3	3,863	3,235	84	2,409	508	318	16	612
LAKE ST. LOUIS	MO	c	—	—	—	—	—	—	—	—	—	—	—	—	—	—	—	—	—
LAKE STATION	IN	c	2	—	—	other	—	—	—	—	—	—	—	—	—	—	—	—	—
LAKE WALES	FL	c	1	24	21	56	29,448	—	—	—	—	2,200	1,885	86	1,219	343	322	58	256
LAKE ZURICH	IL	v	1	61	57	48	49,450	71,258	y	72,758	15	7,787	6,486	83	5,096	657	733	354	947
LEBANON	MO	c	1	—	17	50–54	17,500	22,600	y	23,506	5	922	—	—	642	—	—	46	196
LEESBURG	FL	c	1	69	68	56	34,216	49,446	n	—	—	6,675	5,301	79	3,581	1,398	322	524	—
LEMON GROVE	CA	c	1	20	18	56	52,881	64,298	n	—	—	3,360	—	—	1,865	981	—	226	307
LEMOORE	CA	c	2	1	—	—	—	—	n	—	—	691	67	10	49	14	3	322	302
LENOIR	NC	c	1	57	57	56	21,223	—	n	—	—	3,622	2,544	70	1,872	345	325	3	479
LEVELLAND	TX	c	3	8	8	56	35,731	35,731	y	36,931	1	686	476	69	352	69	55	129	81
LEXINGTON	NC	c	1	47	46	56	20,112	35,856	y	36,752	3	2,936	2,485	85	1,793	292	400	8	443
LEXINGTON	NE	c	2	—	—	other	—	—	—	—	—	125	35	28	13	17	4	16	75
LIBERTYVILLE	IL	v	1	39	35	50–54	52,345	77,326	n	—	—	5,693	4,023	71	2,885	652	485	127	1,543
LILBURN	GA	c	—	—	—	—	—	—	—	—	—	—	—	—	—	—	—	—	—
LINCOLN PARK	NJ	b	2	—	—	other	—	—	n	—	—	253	—	—	—	—	—	92	160
LINCOLNWOOD	IL	v	6	29	28	56	—	—	—	—	—	2,622	—	—	—	6	7	78	2,469

Table 3/17 continued FIRE DEPARTMENT PERSONNEL, SALARIES, AND EXPENDITURES FOR CITIES 10,000 AND OVER: 2008

City	State	Type	Service provision	Full-time paid personnel	Full-time uniformed personnel	Duty hours per week	Minimum base salary ($)	Maximum base salary ($)	Longevity pay	Maximum salary with longevity ($)	Years of service for longevity	Total expenditures (A) ($)	Total personnel expenditures (B) ($)	(B) as % of (A)	Salaries and wages (C) ($)	City contribution to retirement and social security (D) ($)	City contribution to insurance (E) ($)	Capital outlay (F) ($)	All other (G) ($)
10,000–24,999 continued																			
LINDENHURST	IL	v	—	—	—	—	—	—	—	—	—	—	—	—	—	—	—	—	—
LINDENWOLD	NJ	b	—	—	—	—	—	—	—	—	—	—	—	—	—	—	—	—	—
LINO LAKES	MN	c	5	4	2	other	—	—	—	—	—	—	—	—	—	—	—	—	—
LITTLE CHUTE	WI	v	2	—	—	other	—	—	y	—	0	497	77	16	19	49	8	—	412
LOCKHART	TX	c	3	17	17	48	31,521	33,773	y	34,973	1	863	735	85	555	91	88	10	119
LOGAN	PA	tp	2	—	—	other	—	—	—	—	—	365	—	—	—	—	19	63	283
LOMA LINDA	CA	c	1	32	29	56	54,287	67,636	y	71,060	11	—	—	—	—	—	—	—	—
LOMITA	CA	c	5	—	—	—	—	—	—	—	—	—	—	—	—	—	—	—	—
LONDONDERRY	NH	t	—	—	—	—	—	—	—	—	—	—	—	—	—	—	—	—	—
LOVELAND	OH	c	6	—	—	—	—	—	—	—	—	—	—	—	—	—	—	—	—
LOWER	NJ	tp	2	—	—	other	—	—	—	—	—	—	—	—	—	—	—	—	—
LOWER ALLEN	PA	tp	2	—	—	other	—	—	n	—	—	244	—	—	—	—	2	—	224
LOWER GWYNEDD	PA	tp	2	—	—	other	—	—	—	—	—	—	—	—	—	—	—	—	—
LOWER MACUNGIE	PA	tp	2	—	—	—	—	—	—	—	—	—	—	—	—	—	—	—	—
LOWER MORELAND	PA	tp	2	—	—	—	—	—	—	—	—	—	—	—	—	—	—	—	—
LOWER SOUTHAMPTON	PA	tp	2	—	—	—	—	—	—	—	—	—	—	—	—	—	—	—	—
LUMBERTON	NC	c	3	52	52	56	22,344	25,912	y	25,952	1	3,761	2,638	70	1,964	324	349	70	1,053
LYNBROOK	NY	v	2	—	—	—	—	—	—	—	—	—	—	—	—	—	—	—	—
LYNDHURST	NJ	tp	2	—	—	other	—	—	—	—	—	744	—	—	—	—	—	194	500
LYNDHURST	OH	c	1	26	26	48	51,867	66,536	y	69,863	5	3,107	2,864	92	2,111	456	296	23	220
LYNN HAVEN	FL	c	1	22	21	other	22,838	35,868	n	—	—	—	—	—	—	—	—	—	—
LYONS	IL	v	3	3	3	40	—	—	—	—	—	1,267	705	56	403	37	264	—	564
MAITLAND	FL	c	1	44	42	56	33,698	51,359	n	—	—	3,835	3,191	83	2,110	774	307	341	303
MAMARONECK	NY	v	2	—	—	—	—	—	y	—	—	672	—	—	—	—	—	—	672
MANDEVILLE	LA	c	—	—	—	—	—	—	—	—	—	—	—	—	—	—	—	—	—
MANVILLE	NJ	b	2	—	—	40	—	—	—	—	—	117	—	—	96	—	—	—	—
MAPLE VALLEY	WA	c	—	—	—	—	—	—	—	—	—	—	—	—	—	—	—	—	—
MAPLEWOOD	NJ	tp	1	43	41	42	33,584	71,538	y	82,627	5	5,285	—	—	3,425	—	546	477	276
MARANA	AZ	t	—	—	—	—	—	—	—	—	—	—	—	—	—	—	—	—	—
MARQUETTE	MI	c	1	25	25	50–54	30,005	48,190	y	48,620	5	1,966	1,779	90	1,186	220	372	—	187
MARSHALL	MO	c	1	18	18	56	27,023	31,303	n	—	—	1,044	852	82	655	63	134	—	192
MARTINSVILLE	IN	c	1	17	17	56	38,698	38,698	y	—	5	—	—	—	957	—	132	211	—
MARTINSVILLE	VA	c	3	57	28	56	24,408	37,344	y	26,908	40	2,100	1,722	82	1,281	312	128	132	246
MARYSVILLE	OH	c	1	29	28	50–54	40,984	54,975	y	55,825	3	2,734	—	—	1,851	—	—	205	255
MARYVILLE	MO	c	4	—	—	40	—	—	—	—	—	137	112	82	79	31	2	18	32
MARYVILLE	TN	c	1	41	38	other	29,328	52,665	n	—	—	3,809	2,753	72	1,890	348	514	525	531
MASON	OH	c	1	30	29	50–54	43,214	51,317	n	—	—	—	—	—	—	—	—	—	—
MATTOON	IL	c	1	38	38	50–54	33,965	48,586	y	61,233	4	4,107	3,736	91	2,270	1,001	465	187	183
MAUMEE	OH	c	1	24	—	40	—	—	y	—	0	2,577	2,179	85	1,579	195	404	40	358
McCOMB	MS	c	1	—	—	50–54	—	—	—	—	—	—	—	—	—	—	—	—	—
McMINNVILLE	TN	c	1	32	32	48	24,729	24,729	n	—	—	1,288	—	—	1,063	—	—	48	177
MEDFORD	NJ	tp	3	—	5	40	37,980	48,112	n	—	—	672	399	59	304	49	46	127	145
MEDWAY	MA	t	1	—	4	42	50,000	—	y	—	—	—	—	—	—	—	—	—	—
MELROSE PARK	IL	v	1	61	59	56	34,000	71,769	y	74,269	15	6,482	—	—	4,238	—	1,250	14	258
MENASHA	WI	t	3	4	4	other	39,617	50,449	n	—	—	791	600	76	461	79	59	191	—
MEQUON	WI	c	7	1	—	other	—	—	n	—	—	—	—	—	—	—	—	—	—
MERRIAM	KS	c	3	22	22	48	33,141	49,712	n	—	—	1,856	1,748	94	1,262	265	221	—	108
MEXICO	MO	c	4	—	—	40	26,000	35,650	n	—	—	—	—	—	—	—	—	2	—
MIAMI	OK	c	1	30	29	56	25,776	33,865	n	—	—	1,365	—	—	1,301	—	50	25	53
MIDDLEBURG HEIGHTS	OH	c	1	25	25	48	46,575	64,572	y	—	5	3,215	—	—	2,056	—	323	85	291
MIDDLETOWN	PA	tp	2	—	—	—	—	—	—	—	—	171	—	—	—	—	—	—	—
MILFORD	NH	t	3	4	—	40	—	—	—	—	—	484	—	—	340	34	—	8	102
MILL VALLEY	CA	c	1	—	—	56	—	—	—	—	—	—	—	—	—	—	—	—	—
MILLBROOK	AL	c	3	2	2	other	—	—	n	—	—	662	392	59	330	42	20	—	170
MILLBURY	MA	t	3	—	—	other	—	—	—	—	—	6	—	—	—	—	—	110	250
MILLEDGEVILLE	GA	c	1	33	28	50–54	26,491	40,310	n	—	—	1,807	1,525	84	1,090	169	266	89	193
MINEOLA	NY	v	2	—	—	—	—	—	—	—	—	—	—	—	—	—	—	—	—
MINT HILL	NC	t	—	—	—	—	—	—	—	—	—	—	—	—	—	—	—	—	—
MITCHELL	SD	c	4	—	—	50–54	—	—	—	—	—	—	—	—	—	—	—	—	—
MOBERLY	MO	c	1	—	—	—	—	—	n	—	—	1,273	1,087	85	760	97	229	104	83
MONROE	GA	c	1	23	22	48	29,714	44,472	n	—	—	1,534	1,330	87	913	202	215	—	204
MONROE	MI	c	1	—	—	50–54	—	—	—	—	—	—	—	—	—	—	—	—	—
MONROE	WA	c	—	—	—	—	—	—	—	—	—	—	—	—	—	—	—	—	—
MONTGOMERY	OH	c	1	7	7	50–54	48,185	61,705	y	—	5	1,889	1,361	72	1,085	182	93	321	207
MONTROSE	CO	c	—	—	—	—	—	—	—	—	—	—	—	—	—	—	—	—	—
MONTVILLE	NJ	tp	2	—	—	—	—	—	—	—	—	—	—	—	—	—	—	—	—
MORGAN CITY	LA	c	1	39	38	other	22,440	22,440	y	—	1	2,105	1,821	87	1,363	201	256	115	168
MORGANTON	NC	c	4	—	—	42	—	—	—	—	—	—	—	—	—	—	—	—	—
MORRO BAY	CA	c	1	11	10	50–54	42,984	121,255	n	—	—	1,677	—	—	955	—	261	—	150
MOUNT CLEMENS	MI	c	3	—	—	56	39,548	52,384	y	54,084	5	1,423	—	—	1,059	—	151	79	116
MOUNT OLIVE	NJ	tp	—	—	—	—	—	—	—	—	—	—	—	—	—	—	—	—	—

Table 3/17   FIRE DEPARTMENT PERSONNEL, SALARIES, AND EXPENDITURES FOR
continued   CITIES 10,000 AND OVER: 2008

City	State	Type	Service provision	Full-time paid personnel	Full-time uniformed personnel	Duty hours per week	Minimum base salary ($)	Maximum base salary ($)	Longevity pay	Maximum salary with longevity ($)	Years of service for longevity	Reported expenditures (in $000)						
												Total expenditures (A) ($)	Total personnel expenditures (B) ($)	(B) as % of (A)	Salaries and wages (C) ($)	City contribution to retirement and social security (D) ($)	City contribution to insurance (E) ($)	Capital outlay (F) ($)	All other (G) ($)
10,000–24,999 continued																			
MOUNT PLEASANT	TX	c	3	23	22	56	29,606	39,673	y	—	1	1,518	1,299	86	975	178	145	—	220
MOUNT VERNON	OH	c	1	40	34	48	37,465	51,393	y	—	5	3,598	—	—	2,356	—	375	476	340
MOUNTAIN BROOK	AL	c	1	—	—	56	34,507	53,477	y	58,023	20	5,956	4,898	82	3,720	700	477	666	392
MOUNTAIN HOME	AR	c	3	—	—	other	—	—	—	—	—	—	—	—	—	—	—	—	—
MUKILTEO	WA	c	3	20	18	other	53,232	66,609	n	—	—	3,355	2,110	63	1,677	120	312	256	990
MUNSTER	IN	t	2	—	—	other	—	—	y	—	6	901	277	31	234	41	1	552	72
MURRYSVILLE	PA	c	—	—	—	—	—	—	—	—	—	—	—	—	—	—	—	—	—
NAPLES	FL	c	1	61	55	50–54	38,792	60,782	y	63,782	11	7,377	5,840	79	4,302	891	647	124	1,412
NARRAGANSETT	RI	t	1	34	34	42	46,410	46,410	y	53,139	3	4,707	3,918	83	2,931	428	558	351	438
NEDERLAND	TX	c	3	—	14	50–54	37,398	45,253	y	46,933	1	1,621	1,169	72	816	189	164	67	385
NEW BERN	NC	c	3	69	67	56	28,455	59,709	y	59,709	5	5,278	3,641	69	2,655	469	516	611	1,026
NEW BRIGHTON	MN	c	2	—	—	other	—	—	—	—	—	809	560	69	345	190	24	160	89
NEW CANAAN	CT	t	1	28	28	42	47,664	65,120	y	—	5	3,309	—	—	2,341	—	447	—	257
NEW HOPE	MN	c	—	—	—	—	—	—	—	—	—	—	—	—	—	—	—	—	—
NEW LENOX	IL	v	—	—	—	—	—	—	—	—	—	—	—	—	—	—	—	—	—
NEW MILFORD	NJ	b	2	—	—	other	—	—	—	—	—	180	—	—	—	—	—	50	125
NEW PORT RICHEY	FL	c	1	26	24	56	—	54,264	n	—	—	2,289	1,968	86	1,388	431	148	67	254
NEW ULM	MN	c	2	—	—	other	—	—	—	—	—	315	224	71	67	129	28	—	91
NEWBERG	OR	c	1	22	17	50–54	44,964	57,072	y	58,272	10	3,114	2,390	77	1,729	369	291	229	496
NEWBERRY	SC	c	1	20	19	48	27,405	39,737	y	—	—	1,074	884	82	681	121	82	25	166
NEWTON	KS	c	1	47	45	50–54	30,253	39,711	y	40,335	2	3,475	3,083	89	2,238	341	503	63	329
NEWTON	NC	c	1	48	25	50–54	24,773	36,754	n	—	—	1,693	1,374	81	1,046	115	212	6	313
NEWTOWN TOWNSHIP	PA	tp	3	9	9	48	43,683	54,680	n	—	—	934	878	94	561	162	154	18	38
NILES	MI	c	1	14	14	50–54	29,705	45,258	y	49,783	5	1,306	1,365	104	839	327	198	84	120
NIXA	MO	c	—	—	—	—	—	—	—	—	—	—	—	—	—	—	—	—	—
NORCO	CA	c	—	30	28	56	54,708	66,504	y	70,494	5	—	3,711	—	3,071	309	332	—	—
NORFOLK	MA	t	1	19	13	42	48,157	54,513	y	—	3	1,201	—	—	1,073	—	72	—	128
NORRIDGE	IL	v	—	—	—	—	—	—	—	—	—	—	—	—	—	—	—	—	—
NORTH AUGUSTA	SC	c	3	—	—	48	—	—	—	—	—	—	—	—	—	—	—	—	—
NORTH BRANFORD	CT	t	2	—	—	—	—	—	—	—	—	678	262	39	120	106	35	238	179
NORTH FAYETTE	PA	tp	2	—	—	—	—	—	—	—	—	—	—	—	—	—	—	—	—
NORTH MANKATO	MN	c	2	—	—	other	—	—	y	—	—	326	145	45	118	21	5	72	109
NORTH MYRTLE BEACH	SC	c	4	—	—	56	—	—	—	—	—	—	—	—	—	—	—	—	—
NORTH OGDEN	UT	c	5	—	—	—	—	—	—	—	—	—	—	—	—	—	—	—	—
NORTH READING	MA	t	1	—	—	42	41,845	49,577	y	51,377	5	—	—	—	1,845	—	—	46	215
NORTH ST. PAUL	MN	c	2	—	—	other	—	—	—	—	—	—	—	—	—	—	—	—	—
NORTH STRABANE	PA	tp	3	3	3	40	33,800	37,440	n	—	—	1,140	191	17	126	22	43	918	31
NORTHBRIDGE	MA	t	1	62	12	40	—	—	—	—	—	—	—	—	—	—	—	—	—
NORTHVILLE	MI	tp	1	23	23	50–54	42,480	60,686	y	61,686	5	—	—	—	—	—	—	—	—
NORTON	MA	t	1	30	27	42	36,838	49,268	y	49,668	5	2,485	—	—	2,268	—	—	115	102
NORTON SHORES	MI	c	1	17	16	50–54	36,880	48,161	y	49,161	—	2,211	—	—	1,198	136	—	92	266
NORWOOD	OH	c	1	—	55	other	44,493	—	y	—	5	—	—	—	4,572	—	—	—	—
OCOEE	FL	c	1	51	49	56	36,177	56,362	n	—	—	—	5,196	—	2,760	1,885	551	—	—
OCONOMOWOC	WI	c	3	3	3	other	49,521	55,583	n	—	—	1,035	299	29	236	38	26	31	704
OIL CITY	PA	c	1	16	—	48	35,873	40,560	y	41,878	5	951	—	—	651	—	181	5	60
ONALASKA	WI	c	1	9	5	48	37,096	45,154	y	47,412	10	—	—	—	—	—	—	—	—
ONTARIO	OR	c	3	9	—	56	41,297	48,544	n	—	—	—	—	—	—	—	—	—	—
ORANGE	TX	c	1	38	37	50–54	34,037	46,604	y	47,804	1	2,958	2,587	87	1,790	394	403	244	127
ORINDA	CA	c	1	72	47	40	—	—	—	—	—	—	—	—	—	—	—	—	—
OSWEGO	IL	v	—	—	—	—	—	—	—	—	—	—	—	—	—	—	—	—	—
OTTAWA	IL	c	1	29	27	50–54	—	—	y	50,680	1	—	—	—	—	—	—	—	—
OTTUMWA	IA	c	1	33	33	50–54	33,197	40,768	y	41,380	5	2,418	2,292	95	1,479	410	402	—	126
OWATONNA	MN	c	1	10	8	50–54	42,864	47,627	n	—	—	1,300	939	72	707	50	181	50	281
OXFORD	MS	c	—	61	60	50–54	28,240	30,859	n	—	—	2,480	—	—	1,933	361	—	60	126
OXFORD	OH	c	3	2	2	other	76,495	84,995	y	86,070	5	417	309	74	227	45	36	8	100
OZARK	AL	c	1	46	46	50–54	25,249	35,676	y	34,457	10	1,980	1,527	77	1,157	153	216	45	408
PALATKA	FL	c	1	20	20	56	27,112	—	y	—	10	1,742	1,425	82	1,038	212	174	26	291
PALISADES PARK	NJ	b	2	—	—	—	—	—	—	—	—	465	—	—	275	—	—	—	190
PALMER	PA	tp	7	1	1	—	—	—	—	—	—	—	—	—	—	—	—	—	—
PALMETTO	FL	c	—	—	—	—	—	—	—	—	—	—	—	—	—	—	—	—	—
PALOS HEIGHTS	IL	c	—	—	—	—	—	—	—	—	—	—	—	—	—	—	—	—	—
PALOS VERDES ESTATES	CA	c	5	—	—	—	—	—	—	—	—	—	—	—	—	—	—	—	—
PAPILLION	NE	c	3	26	25	56	36,596	48,945	y	62,602	6	2,349	1,583	67	1,199	166	219	38	727
PARK FOREST	IL	v	1	25	21	56	44,694	64,702	n	—	—	2,847	2,481	87	1,780	516	184	90	276
PARKER	CO	t	—	—	—	—	—	—	—	—	—	—	—	—	—	—	—	—	—
PARLIER	CA	c	5	—	—	other	—	—	—	—	—	225	—	—	—	—	—	—	—
PARSONS	KS	c	1	—	19	56	26,849	30,654	n	—	—	—	—	—	—	—	—	—	—
PATTERSON	CA	c	3	12	9	56	39,288	47,760	y	—	—	1,189	855	72	531	177	147	93	241
PATTON	PA	tp	—	—	—	—	—	—	—	—	—	—	—	—	—	—	—	—	—
PAYSON	AZ	t	1	25	24	56	35,780	53,670	n	—	—	3,184	2,233	70	1,676	264	293	40	884

Table 3/17 continued   FIRE DEPARTMENT PERSONNEL, SALARIES, AND EXPENDITURES FOR CITIES 10,000 AND OVER: 2008

City	State	Type	Service provision	Full-time paid personnel	Full-time uniformed personnel	Duty hours per week	Minimum base salary ($)	Maximum base salary ($)	Longevity pay	Maximum salary with longevity ($)	Years of service for longevity	Total expenditures (A) ($)	Total personnel expenditures (B) ($)	(B) as % of (A)	Salaries and wages (C) ($)	City contribution to retirement and social security (D) ($)	City contribution to insurance (E) ($)	Capital outlay (F) ($)	All other (G) ($)
10,000–24,999 continued																			
PELHAM	AL	t	1	79	78	other	48,895	56,190	n	—	—	—	6,168	—	4,712	901	554	43	304
PENDLETON	OR	c	3	30	20	56	42,501	55,686	y	58,470	15	2,762	2,311	84	1,656	405	250	6	445
PERRYSBURG	OH	c	1	22	22	50–54	42,000	56,000	y	58,000	10	2,372	1,868	79	1,576	237	55	64	440
PETERS	PA	tp	3	9	9	50–54	41,652	52,078	y	54,548	10	1,094	710	65	538	83	89	26	358
PFLUGERVILLE	TX	c	—	—	—	—	—	—	—	—	—	—	—	—	—	—	—	—	—
PIEDMONT	CA	c	1	—	—	56	—	—	—	—	—	—	—	—	—	—	—	—	—
PINECREST	FL	v	—	—	—	—	—	—	—	—	—	—	—	—	—	—	—	—	—
PLAINSBORO	NJ	tp	2	—	—	—	—	—	—	—	—	—	—	—	—	—	—	—	—
PLAINVIEW	TX	c	1	36	35	56	31,331	36,295	y	—	25	2,692	2,058	76	1,607	243	208	194	440
PLEASANT PRAIRIE	WI	v	1	19	18	56	40,690	56,047	n	—	—	2,571	1,909	74	1,380	302	227	190	472
PLUMSTEAD	PA	tp	2	—	—	other	—	—	n	—	—	—	—	—	—	—	—	—	—
POINT PLEASANT	NJ	b	2	—	—	—	—	—	—	—	—	292	—	—	—	—	—	110	182
POPLAR BLUFF	MO	c	1	—	—	other	—	—	—	—	—	—	—	—	—	—	—	—	—
POQUOSON	VA	c	3	29	27	50–54	30,666	42,031	n	—	—	2,268	1,896	84	1,365	267	263	36	336
PORT ANGELES	WA	c	1	24	23	56	50,244	64,476	y	—	1	3,342	2,333	70	1,871	113	349	—	1,009
PORT LAVACA	TX	c	3	16	16	48	28,421	38,453	y	41,892	1	1,063	685	64	581	73	31	250	128
PORTALES	NM	c	1	23	21	56	23,500	33,355	y	—	10	1,617	2,068	128	1,404	485	177	96	212
PORTLAND	TX	c	1	16	15	other	28,083	32,182	y	33,382	1	1,228	799	65	569	108	121	167	263
PORTSMOUTH	NH	c	1	61	60	42	36,562	47,786	y	—	5	6,110	5,442	89	4,129	598	713	3	666
PRESCOTT VALLEY	AZ	t	—	—	—	—	—	—	—	—	—	—	—	—	—	—	—	—	—
PRINCETON	NJ	b	2	—	—	other	—	—	n	—	—	475	46	10	36	4	6	206	223
PRIOR LAKE	MN	c	2	—	—	other	—	—	n	—	—	627	415	66	207	198	9	47	165
PROSPECT HEIGHTS	IL	c	—	—	—	—	—	—	—	—	—	—	—	—	—	—	—	—	—
PULLMAN	WA	c	3	32	31	50–54	45,096	54,156	n	—	—	3,649	—	—	2,258	—	—	18	570
PUNTA GORDA	FL	c	3	30	27	56	—	—	n	—	—	2,832	2,474	87	1,591	727	155	337	631
RAMSEY	MN	c	3	3	2	other	51,856	94,867	n	—	—	859	530	62	455	43	31	53	277
RAMSEY	NJ	b	2	—	—	other	—	—	n	—	—	—	—	—	104	—	—	—	—
RAYMORE	MO	c	—	—	—	—	—	—	—	—	—	—	—	—	—	—	—	—	—
READING	MA	t	1	46	45	42	39,334	66,075	—	—	—	3,335	—	—	3,244	—	—	—	95
RED BANK	NJ	b	2	—	—	—	—	—	—	—	—	—	—	—	—	—	—	—	—
RED BANK	TN	c	3	10	10	50–54	28,928	28,928	n	—	—	808	—	—	511	77	—	9	211
RED WING	MN	c	3	21	21	56	41,475	50,606	n	—	—	3,914	2,046	52	1,448	272	326	—	1,867
REIDSVILLE	NC	c	1	27	27	50–54	26,016	39,024	y	40,524	2	1,720	1,400	81	1,073	177	149	16	305
RICHMOND	TX	t	3	—	—	56	33,859	49,892	y	—	1	—	—	—	—	—	—	—	—
RICHMOND HEIGHTS	OH	c	1	19	18	50–54	45,790	60,445	y	63,467	5	2,801	2,246	80	1,679	324	242	395	159
RINGWOOD	NJ	b	2	—	—	—	—	—	—	—	—	—	—	—	—	—	—	—	—
RIPON	CA	c	—	—	—	—	—	—	—	—	—	—	—	—	—	—	—	—	—
RIVER FALLS	WI	c	2	—	—	other	—	—	—	—	—	355	—	—	221	13	—	5	115
RIVER FOREST	IL	v	1	22	22	other	44,027	70,831	n	—	—	3,031	—	—	2,022	—	330	81	133
RIVERBANK	CA	c	4	—	—	other	—	—	—	—	—	—	—	—	—	—	—	—	—
RIVERSIDE	OH	c	3	17	17	56	41,666	54,616	n	—	—	2,201	1,732	79	1,260	259	212	202	267
RIVERVIEW	MI	c	1	1	—	other	—	—	—	—	—	1,315	—	—	935	—	20	161	122
ROANOKE RAPIDS	NC	c	1	28	27	50–54	26,216	38,930	y	39,630	2	—	908	—	645	221	42	83	952
ROBINSON	PA	tp	2	—	—	—	—	—	—	—	—	—	—	—	—	—	—	—	—
ROCHESTER	MI	c	2	1	—	—	—	—	n	—	—	424	169	40	105	21	42	57	198
ROCK SPRINGS	WY	c	1	36	35	50–54	44,385	55,431	n	—	—	3,730	3,342	90	2,474	395	473	174	214
ROCKLEDGE	FL	c	1	40	39	—	32,000	50,300	y	51,100	5	3,132	2,808	90	2,108	283	416	139	185
ROLLA	MO	c	1	28	27	50–54	26,763	35,444	n	—	—	2,805	1,572	56	1,128	262	182	882	351
ROLLING MEADOWS	IL	c	1	51	49	50–54	57,400	82,000	y	84,460	10	7,013	5,934	85	4,785	561	586	200	960
ROSEBURG	OR	c	1	43	34	56	45,408	55,188	n	—	—	3,937	3,536	90	2,320	773	442	28	372
ROSENBERG	TX	c	1	36	34	50–54	37,151	50,159	y	50,219	1	2,620	2,199	84	1,677	311	210	24	397
ROXBURY	NJ	tp	2	—	—	other	—	—	—	—	—	229	—	—	—	—	—	—	229
SACO	ME	c	3	—	35	42	—	—	—	—	—	—	—	—	1,911	—	—	—	285
SAFETY HARBOR	FL	c	1	35	33	56	36,603	54,163	y	57,663	5	3,649	3,327	91	2,233	614	480	16	307
SAGINAW	TX	c	1	27	27	50–54	37,935	56,905	y	—	1	1,821	1,494	82	1,228	253	12	98	229
SALEM	OH	c	1	16	16	50–54	27,123	42,491	y	44,301	5	1,272	—	—	755	—	210	4	52
SALISBURY	MD	c	3	66	64	42	34,746	55,637	—	—	—	5,354	4,277	80	2,780	969	527	—	1,096
SALISBURY	PA	tp	2	—	—	—	—	—	—	—	—	—	—	—	—	—	—	—	—
SAN ANSELMO	CA	c	—	—	—	—	—	—	—	—	—	—	—	—	—	—	—	—	—
SAN BENITO	TX	c	1	29	28	50–54	31,827	31,827	y	—	1	1,712	1,561	91	1,226	214	121	32	119
SAN FERNANDO	CA	c	5	—	—	—	—	—	y	—	—	2,914	—	—	—	—	—	—	2,914
SAN MARINO	CA	c	1	19	18	56	68,268	82,032	n	—	—	3,320	—	—	2,249	—	60	20	553
SAND SPRINGS	OK	c	1	34	33	56	33,201	38,655	y	41,130	2	—	—	—	—	—	—	—	—
SANFORD	NC	c	1	51	50	56	30,680	46,684	y	—	5	3,273	2,774	85	2,189	262	322	33	466
SAPULPA	OK	c	1	52	51	56	22,500	30,360	n	—	—	3,786	3,537	93	2,834	375	327	79	171
SAULT STE. MARIE	MI	c	1	19	18	56	41,082	45,904	n	—	—	3,047	2,043	67	1,337	394	311	183	821
SCHERERVILLE	IN	t	1	12	12	48	40,994	51,062	y	52,862	3	837	665	79	499	83	82	—	172
SCHERTZ	TX	c	1	30	30	50–54	31,304	41,305	y	—	1	2,173	1,890	87	1,458	263	168	174	110
SCOTTS VALLEY	CA	c	—	—	—	—	—	—	—	—	—	—	—	—	—	—	—	—	—
SEBASTIAN	FL	c	—	—	—	—	—	—	—	—	—	—	—	—	—	—	—	—	—
SEDALIA	MO	c	1	40	40	—	30,152	45,228	n	—	—	2,407	1,998	83	1,618	139	240	307	102
SEDONA	AZ	c	—	—	—	—	—	—	—	—	—	—	—	—	—	—	—	—	—
SEEKONK	MA	t	3	27	26	42	36,065	47,816	n	—	—	1,748	—	—	1,628	—	—	—	120

Table 3/17 continued   FIRE DEPARTMENT PERSONNEL, SALARIES, AND EXPENDITURES FOR CITIES 10,000 AND OVER: 2008

City	State	Type	Service provision	Full-time paid personnel	Full-time uniformed personnel	Duty hours per week	Minimum base salary ($)	Maximum base salary ($)	Longevity pay	Maximum salary with longevity ($)	Years of service for longevity	Total expenditures (A) ($)	Total personnel expenditures (B) ($)	(B) as % of (A)	Salaries and wages (C) ($)	City contribution to retirement and social security (D) ($)	City contribution to insurance (E) ($)	Capital outlay (F) ($)	All other (G) ($)
10,000–24,999 continued																			
SEGUIN	TX	c	3	50	46	50–54	37,315	50,190	y	51,390	1	5,047	2,795	55	2,160	396	238	1,587	665
SELMA	CA	c	3	33	25	50–54	39,408	47,892	y	—	—	2,829	2,203	78	1,526	434	243	—	626
SEMINOLE	FL	c	1	86	78	56	36,922	53,372	y	54,372	5	9,537	8,173	86	5,093	2,102	977	190	1,174
SHERIDAN	WY	c	1	32	30	56	35,340	47,364	y	—	5	—	—	—	—	—	—	—	—
SIKESTON	MO	c	4	—	—	50–54	—	—	—	—	—	—	—	—	—	—	—	—	—
SILOAM SPRINGS	AR	c	1	48	46	56	28,141	42,874	y	42,033	2	3,290	2,540	77	1,989	318	233	137	613
SMITHFIELD	RI	t	1	—3,599,677		42	36,593	47,374	y	102,759	5	4,583	—	—	3,810	—	—	187	586
SNELLVILLE	GA	c	—	—	—	—	—	—	—	—	—	—	—	—	—	—	—	—	—
SNYDER	TX	c	3	9	9	50–54	30,192	32,988	y	34,188	1	818	474	58	395	76	2	163	655
SODDY—DAISY	TN	c	2	—	—	other	—	—	—	—	—	220	—	—	—	—	—	94	126
SOMERSET	MA	t	3	32	31	42	35,739	44,674	y	—	5	1,527	—	—	1,450	—	—	—	77
SOUTH ELGIN	IL	v	—	—	—	—	—	—	—	—	—	—	—	—	—	—	—	—	—
SOUTH EUCLID	OH	c	1	38	36	50–54	45,083	62,376	y	80,022	5	—	—	—	2,628	—	—	—	—
SOUTH LAKE TAHOE	CA	c	3	38	18	56	41,125	51,979	n	—	—	5,617	4,557	81	2,725	1,122	710	198	862
SOUTH LYON	MI	c	2	—	—	other	—	—	n	—	—	482	—	—	213	—	—	20	225
SOUTH MILWAUKEE	WI	c	3	27	26	—	47,214	58,290	y	58,590	5	—	—	—	1,742	—	—	—	—
SOUTH OGDEN	UT	c	1	15	14	56	30,123	33,044	n	—	—	—	—	—	—	—	—	—	—
SOUTH RIVER	NJ	b	2	—	—	other	—	—	y	—	0	212	—	—	—	—	—	33	91
SOUTH SALT LAKE	UT	c	1	40	39	56	—	—	n	—	—	4,065	3,438	85	2,615	492	330	137	490
SOUTH SIOUX CITY	NE	c	1	—	—	other	—	—	y	—	—	173	—	—	20	—	3	—	140
SOUTH ST. PAUL	MN	c	—	—	—	—	—	—	—	—	—	—	—	—	—	—	—	—	—
SOUTH WHITEHALL	PA	tp	2	—	—	other	—	—	—	—	—	307	—	—	—	—	12	3	293
SPANISH FORK	UT	c	2	—	—	other	—	—	—	—	—	2,801	126	4	107	16	3	82	2,593
SPARTA	NJ	tp	2	—	—	—	—	—	n	—	—	576	—	—	—	—	—	497	79
SPEEDWAY	IN	t	1	34	34	other	36,169	46,915	y	48,789	1	2,747	2,584	94	1,806	464	314	—	163
SPENCER	IA	c	3	5	5	50–54	35,320	42,705	y	43,605	10	402	—	—	276	65	—	7	54
SPENCER	MA	t	3	1	1	40	55,000	55,000	n	—	—	311	—	—	180	—	1	21	109
SPRINGBORO	OH	c	—	—	—	—	—	—	—	—	—	—	—	—	—	—	—	—	—
SPRINGDALE	OH	c	1	26	26	50–54	49,608	63,388	y	65,138	5	2,987	2,546	85	2,078	418	49	64	376
SPRINGETTSBURY	PA	tp	3	26	17	50–54	29,852	56,519	y	57,719	5	2,381	2,006	84	1,487	310	208	76	299
SPRINGFIELD	TN	c	1	30	30	50–54	28,704	39,187	y	—	5	2,063	1,685	82	1,185	222	277	211	168
SPRINGVILLE	UT	c	3	2	2	40	34,100	52,500	n	—	—	601	—	—	214	—	54	231	103
ST. ANN	MO	c	—	—	—	—	—	—	—	—	—	—	—	—	—	—	—	—	—
ST. AUGUSTINE	FL	c	1	33	32	56	37,010	53,916	n	—	—	2,745	2,462	90	1,551	620	291	86	198
ST. CLOUD	FL	c	1	58	53	56	33,000	49,500	—			4,351	3,780	87	2,610	704	466	111	461
STAFFORD	CT	t	2	—	—	—	—	—	—	—	—	—	—	—	—	—	—	—	—
STAFFORD	TX	t	3	2	2	other	—	—	y	—	1	1,113	684	61	632	32	19	371	58
STATESVILLE	NC	c	1	54	53	50–54	28,506	47,034	n	—	—	3,664	2,792	76	2,217	273	301	439	433
STAUNTON	VA	c	1	32	30	other	29,045	52,930	n	—	—	2,134	1,943	91	1,376	335	232	28	163
STERLING	CO	c	3	14	14	50–54	32,343	43,091	n	—	—	1,336	989	74	713	111	164	101	246
STERLING	IL	c	1	24	23	50–54	35,223	54,437	n	—	—	1,680	—	—	1,295	—	—	296	89
STONEHAM	MA	t	1	34	33	42	41,451	52,569	n	—	—	2,688	—	—	2,163	—	369	—	155
STORM LAKE	IA	c	4	—	—	40	—	—	—	—	—	—	—	—	—	—	—	—	—
STREETSBORO	OH	c	1	37	18	50–54	32,560	47,671	y	48,931	8	2,501	2,157	86	1,720	246	190	155	189
SUDBURY	MA	t	1	36	34	48	42,006	48,019	y	48,519	7	2,659	—	—	2,388	—	—	44	228
SUFFERN	NY	v	2	—	—	other	—	—	—	—	—	373	—	—	—	—	92	92	190
SUGAR HILL	GA	c	—	—	—	—	—	—	—	—	—	—	—	—	—	—	—	—	—
SULPHUR	LA	c	1	69	63	56	—	—	y	—	1	4,088	—	—	2,351	—	260	597	496
SUMMIT	NJ	c	1	32	28	42	56,196	81,211	n	—	—	—	—	—	—	—	—	—	—
SUN PRAIRIE	WI	c	6	—	—	—	—	—	—	—	—	—	—	—	—	—	—	—	—
SUNNYSIDE	WA	c	1	14	12	50–54	44,016	50,952	n	—	—	—	—	—	—	—	—	—	—
SWANSEA	IL	v	1	2	2	40	—	—	n	—	—	713	—	—	122	—	21	490	58
SYLACAUGA	AL	c	1	19	19	56	28,205	43,762	n	—	—	1,339	1,118	84	865	111	141	77	143
TAKOMA PARK	MD	c	—	—	—	—	—	—	—	—	—	—	—	—	—	—	—	—	—
TARBORO	NC	t	3	21	21	50–54	26,706	44,566	y	46,348	5	1,286	1,150	89	882	165	101	—	136
TARPON SPRINGS	FL	c	1	40	36	56	45,160	67,496	n	—	—	3,952	3,337	84	2,551	580	206	39	576
TARRYTOWN	NY	v	2	—	—	other	—	—	—	—	—	4,545	—	—	—	—	77	4,006	461
TAYLOR	TX	c	1	26	24	56	33,465	42,710	y	43,622	1	1,533	1,276	83	975	175	125	26	232
THE DALLES	OR	c	—	—	—	—	—	—	—	—	—	—	—	—	—	—	—	—	—
THIBODAUX	LA	c	2	—	—	—	—	—	n	—	—	405	—	—	—	—	13	46	346
TIFFIN	OH	c	1	40	39	50–54	33,293	41,426	y	45,568	4	3,140	—	—	2,042	—	483	44	170
TIFTON	GA	c	3	38	36	other	24,284	36,426	n	—	—	867	867	100	630	143	93	—	—
TINTON FALLS	NJ	b	—	—	—	—	—	—	—	—	—	—	—	—	—	—	—	—	—
TOLLAND	CT	t	3	4	—	40	35,214	—	n	—	—	1	—	—	—	—	—	—	—
TONAWANDA	NY	c	3	28	27	42	34,438	51,879	y	53,579	5	—	—	—	—	—	—	—	—
TOWAMENCIN	PA	tp	2	—	—	—	—	—	—	—	—	164	—	—	—	—	9	—	155
TOWN & COUNTRY	MO	c	5	—	—	—	—	—	—	—	—	—	—	—	—	—	—	—	—
TRAVERSE CITY	MI	c	1	31	29	56	34,886	40,011	y	42,806	8	3,323	2,526	76	1,727	544	255	—	797
TRENTON	MI	c	1	33	33	50–54	—	—	y	—	5	3,629	3,359	93	2,299	595	465	40	229
TROUTDALE	OR	c	5	—	—	—	—	—	—	—	—	1,296	—	—	—	—	—	—	1,296
TROY	OH	c	1	41	40	50–54	41,580	57,564	y	63,320	5	4,314	3,683	85	2,594	647	442	223	407
TRUSSVILLE	AL	c	3	35	30	48	34,445	53,394	n	—	—	2,836	2,315	82	1,592	610	114	150	603
TUALATIN	OR	c	—	—	—	—	—	—	—	—	—	—	—	—	—	—	—	—	—

Table 3/17
continued

FIRE DEPARTMENT PERSONNEL, SALARIES, AND EXPENDITURES FOR CITIES 10,000 AND OVER: 2008

City	State	Type	Service provision	Full-time paid personnel	Full-time uniformed personnel	Duty hours per week	Minimum base salary ($)	Maximum base salary ($)	Longevity pay	Maximum salary with longevity ($)	Years of service for longevity	Total expenditures (A) ($)	Total personnel expenditures (B) ($)	(B) as % of (A)	Salaries and wages (C) ($)	City contribution to retirement and social security (D) ($)	City contribution to insurance (E) ($)	Capital outlay (F) ($)	All other (G) ($)
10,000–24,999 continued																			
TWENTYNINE PALMS	CA	c	—	—	—	—	—	—	—	—	—	—	—	—	—	—	—	—	—
UKIAH	CA	c	3	22	20	56	36,236	54,952	n	—	—	3,235	—	—	2,134	—	285	39	1,101
UNIVERSAL CITY	TX	c	1	21	20	56	33,624	—	y	33,672	1	1,324	—	—	826	124	—	31	343
UNIVERSITY PARK	TX	c	1	34	33	56	48,804	62,304	y	63,504	1	4,291	3,693	86	2,729	598	366	138	465
UPPER ALLEN	PA	tp	2	—	—	other	—	—	n	—	—	214	—	—	—	—	—	17	197
UPPER GWYNEDD	PA	tp	2	—	—	other	—	—	y	—	—	99	—	—	—	—	11	—	87
UPPER PROVIDENCE	PA	tp	2	—	—	other	—	—	—	—	—	468	—	—	—	—	—	35	432
UPPER ST. CLAIR	PA	tp	2	—	—	other	—	—	y	—	0	218	—	—	—	—	29	—	189
UVALDE	TX	c	3	4	4	40	26,374	39,208	y	39,208	1	241	—	—	122	15	—	36	68
VAN WERT	OH	c	1	—	21	56	34,775	46,772	y	48,022	5	1,803	1,877	104	1,135	514	228	606	155
VANDALIA	OH	c	3	9	8	50–54	46,432	59,176	n	—	—	2,068	1,310	63	1,005	179	125	522	237
VENICE	FL	c	1	46	42	50–54	—	—	y	1,200	6	5,087	4,616	91	2,948	1,013	654	26	445
VERO BEACH	FL	c	1	—	—	—	—	—	—	—	—	—	—	—	—	—	—	—	—
VILLA PARK	IL	v	1	26	25	50–54	49,932	69,705	y	70,205	7	2,473	—	—	1,871	—	286	40	275
WALPOLE	MA	t	1	35	34	42	39,524	64,293	y	65,093	5	3,685	3,363	91	2,632	336	395	70	251
WANTAGE	NJ	tp	2	—	—	—	—	—	—	—	—	—	—	—	—	—	—	—	—
WARREN	PA	tp	2	18	17	56	28,248	32,947	y	35,912	2	1,787	1,264	71	839	139	285	368	155
WARREN	RI	t	2	1	—	—	—	—	y	—	5	472	—	—	161	—	—	106	205
WARRENSBURG	MO	c	1	25	23	56	26,990	41,666	y	41,686	5	2,406	1,247	52	942	133	172	805	354
WARRENSVILLE HEIGHTS	OH	c	1	36	34	48	32,601	59,769	y	64,551	1	3,629	3,385	93	2,382	572	431	7	238
WARRENVILLE	IL	c	—	—	—	—	—	—	—	—	—	—	—	—	—	—	—	—	—
WARSAW	IN	c	3	31	30	56	37,083	41,003	y	49,203	1	2,485	2,119	85	1,421	317	380	54	312
WARWICK	PA	tp	2	—	—	—	—	—	—	—	—	—	—	—	—	—	—	—	—
WASHINGTON	IL	c	6	—	—	—	—	—	—	—	—	—	—	—	—	—	—	—	—
WASHINGTON (MORRIS)	NJ	tp	2	—	—	—	—	—	—	—	—	181	—	—	—	—	—	43	138
WATAUGA	TX	c	3	20	20	other	42,926	56,009	y	59,609	1	1,408	1,226	87	1,013	115	98	—	182
WEATHERFORD	TX	c	3	52	51	56	40,227	56,318	y	57,518	1	3,549	3,067	86	2,325	492	249	94	389
WEBSTER	MA	t	7	—	—	other	—	—	—	—	—	—	—	—	—	—	—	—	—
WEBSTER GROVES	MO	c	1	37	—	56	41,609	58,252	n	—	—	3,502	3,323	95	2,674	279	370	15	164
WEST BRADFORD	PA	tp	2	—	—	—	—	—	—	—	—	—	—	—	—	—	—	—	—
WEST CHESTER	PA	b	2	—	—	—	—	—	—	—	—	982	—	—	—	—	—	692	290
WEST COLUMBIA	SC	c	1	24	23	56	23,851	67,912	n	—	—	2,401	1,300	54	969	150	180	911	191
WEST DEER	PA	tp	2	—	—	—	—	—	—	—	—	—	—	—	—	—	—	—	—
WEST LAMPETER	PA	tp	2	—	—	—	—	—	—	—	—	—	—	—	—	—	—	—	—
WEST MANCHESTER	PA	tp	2	—	1	other	—	—	n	—	—	205	—	—	63	—	—	45	142
WEST PLAINS	MO	c	4	—	—	48	—	—	—	—	—	—	—	—	—	—	—	—	—
WEST WHITELAND	PA	tp	2	—	—	other	—	—	—	—	—	—	—	—	—	—	—	—	—
WESTBOROUGH	MA	t	1	36	36	42	45,207	52,048	y	58,559	25	3,357	2,981	89	2,536	222	222	101	275
WESTCHESTER	IL	v	1	28	27	other	42,588	68,524	n	—	—	3,238	2,867	89	2,006	393	468	166	205
WESTERN SPRINGS	IL	v	3	3	—	—	—	—	n	—	—	1,385	825	60	700	100	24	21	539
WHITE	PA	tp	—	—	—	—	—	—	—	—	—	—	—	—	—	—	—	—	—
WHITE BEAR LAKE	MN	c	2	—	4	other	—	—	n	—	—	849	523	62	217	237	68	80	246
WHITEFISH BAY	WI	v	—	—	—	—	—	—	—	—	—	—	—	—	—	—	—	—	—
WHITEHALL	PA	b	2	—	—	—	—	—	y	—	—	—	—	—	—	—	—	—	—
WHITPAIN	PA	tp	3	4	4	40	48,672	50,835	y	53,235	5	531	—	—	356	—	97	—	51
WILLIAMSBURG	VA	c	1	37	36	56	32,760	55,224	n	—	—	3,466	2,628	76	1,916	425	286	402	436
WILLOWICK	OH	c	1	3	2	other	—	—	—	—	—	760	668	88	592	57	18	—	93
WILTON	CT	t	1	28	24	42	48,787	61,678	y	62,328	10	—	—	—	—	—	—	—	—
WILTON MANORS	FL	c	—	—	—	—	—	—	—	—	—	—	—	—	—	—	—	—	—
WINCHESTER	KY	c	1	56	55	56	26,664	43,335	y	43,335	4	5,548	3,905	70	2,491	873	541	900	744
WINCHESTER	VA	c	3	54	51	48	27,352	45,926	n	—	—	3,953	3,355	85	2,512	509	333	235	363
WINDHAM	ME	t	1	2	—	other	35,906	42,070	y	43,070	12	1,322	—	—	923	—	—	234	165
WINDHAM	NH	t	1	20	18	42	39,502	48,624	y	49,374	25	2,260	1,949	86	1,402	216	329	97	214
WINDSOR	CA	t	—	—	—	—	—	—	—	—	—	—	—	—	—	—	—	—	—
WINDSOR LOCKS	CT	t	2	—	—	other	—	—	n	—	—	475	—	—	198	—	51	55	159
WINFIELD	KS	c	3	20	18	56	23,762	36,108	n	—	—	1,814	1,388	77	1,010	253	125	56	370
WINTER GARDEN	FL	c	1	37	32	50–54	34,936	—	n	—	—	4,197	2,941	70	2,035	512	394	711	545
WIXOM	MI	c	1	2	1	other	—	—	n	—	—	1,909	—	—	565	—	—	990	260
WOODBURN	OR	c	—	—	—	—	—	—	—	—	—	—	—	—	—	—	—	—	—
WOODHAVEN	MI	c	1	8	7	40	38,938	61,651	n	—	—	—	—	—	—	—	—	—	—
WOODSTOCK	GA	c	1	46	45	48	32,576	49,569	n	—	—	2,942	2,649	90	2,102	372	175	126	167
WOODSTOCK	IL	c	—	—	—	—	—	—	—	—	—	—	—	—	—	—	—	—	—
WOODWARD	OK	c	3	36	17	56	26,321	38,526	y	—	1	882	799	91	495	96	207	53	29
WORTH	IL	v	1	13	13	50–54	38,670	60,889	n	—	—	1,220	1,181	97	815	204	162	18	21
WORTHINGTON	MN	c	2	—	—	—	—	—	y	—	—	195	134	69	44	84	6	—	61
WORTHINGTON	OH	c	1	41	36	50–54	42,752	57,559	y	58,859	5	5,515	4,649	84	3,069	996	583	394	472
WYLIE	TX	c	3	35	33	50–54	46,680	62,783	y	—	—	3,945	3,279	83	2,563	361	354	143	523
XENIA	OH	c	1	43	42	56	42,781	53,690	n	—	—	4,266	—	—	2,684	—	537	97	441
YANKTON	SD	c	7	2	2	other	—	—	y	—	5	547	171	31	137	17	17	299	77
YARMOUTH	MA	t	1	69	67	42	40,880	48,118	y	48,943	5	6,402	—	—	5,165	—	358	380	458
YAZOO CITY	MS	c	1	—	29	50–54	25,682	32,400	n	—	—	1,225	—	—	926	—	110	84	34
YUCCA VALLEY	CA	t	—	—	—	—	—	—	—	—	—	—	—	—	—	—	—	—	—
ZEPHYRHILLS	FL	c	3	26	25	50–54	—	—	—	—	—	2,294	1,810	79	1,232	484	92	345	186

D Directories

The *Year Book* Directories

The directories in this section of the *Year Book* contain the names of municipal and county officials in the United States as reported at the end of 2008. In addition, this section includes directories for U.S. state municipal leagues; provincial and territorial associations and unions in Canada; state agencies for community affairs; provincial and territorial agencies for local affairs in Canada; U.S. municipal management associations; international municipal management associations; state associations of counties; and U.S. councils of governments recognized by ICMA.

The names of municipal and county managers and other chief appointed management executives for the United States are shown in Directories 1/9 and 1/10. Information on recognized places, including legal basis, title of position, form of government, and year of recognition, plus the number of administrators the community has had and information on the current administrator, is presented in the annual ICMA publication *ICMA Member Roster* (formerly *Who's Who in Local Government Management*).

Information in Directories 1/1 through 1/8 was obtained from the National League of Cities (1/1), the Federation of Canadian Municipalities (1/2), the Council of State Community Development Agencies (1/3), the Ontario Ministry of Municipal Affairs (1/4), ICMA files (1/5, 1/6, and 1/8), and the National Association of Counties (1/7), and is current as of December 31, 2008, unless otherwise indicated.

Information for Directory 1/9 was obtained from the ICMA database of local government employees. The database comprises all cities 2,500 and over in population and all cities under 2,500 that are recognized by ICMA as having a council-manager form of government or as providing for an appointed general management (chief administrative officer) position. Each July local governments in the database are notified to update their information by completing an online update form. Those that have provided updated information are designated with an asterisk (*). Information for Directory 1/10 was obtained in the same way for all county-type governments in the ICMA database, which in fact includes all U.S. counties.

The phone numbers in Directories 1/9 and 1/10 are for the city hall, municipal building, or county building, or for some municipal or county official such as the manager, clerk, or mayor.

U.S. State Municipal Leagues

Directory 1/1 shows 49 state leagues of municipalities serving 49 states. (Hawaii does not have a league.) Information includes league address and Web site, name of the executive director, phone number, and fax number. State municipal leagues provide a wide range of research, consulting, training, publications, and legislative representation services for their clients.

Provincial and Territorial Associations and Unions in Canada

Directory 1/2 shows the associations and unions serving the provinces and territories of Canada. Included are the association's/union's Web site; the name of the president; and the name and title of a permanent officer along with his or her address, phone number, fax number, and e-mail address.

State Agencies for Community Affairs

Directory 1/3 shows the name, address, and Web site of 48 agencies for community affairs in the United States, as well as that for Puerto Rico. It includes the name and title of the head of the agency, along with the agency phone number and fax number. These agencies of state governments offer a variety of research, financial information, and coordination services for cities and other local governments.

Provincial and Territorial Agencies for Local Affairs in Canada

Directory 1/4 shows agencies for local affairs serving provinces and territories of Canada. The directory lists the name and address of the minister, the minister's phone number and fax number, and the agency's Web site.

U.S. Municipal Management Associations

Directory 1/5 shows the name, president, address, e-mail address, phone number, and fax

number of municipal management associations serving 48 of the United States. (The states of Wyoming, Idaho, Montana, North Dakota, and South Dakota are served by the Great Open Spaces City Management Association; Idaho and South Dakota are also served by their own associations; and neither Hawaii nor Louisiana has an association.)

International Municipal Management Associations

Directory 1/6 shows the name, president, address, e-mail address, phone number, and fax number of municipal management associations serving Canada and 17 other countries.

U.S. State Associations of Counties

Directory 1/7 shows the name, address, Web site, name of the executive director, phone number, and fax number for 53 county associations serving 47 states. (Two associations serve the states of Arizona, South Dakota, Washington, and West Virginia; three associations serve the state of Illinois; and three states—Connecticut, Rhode Island, and Vermont—do not have associations.) Like their municipal league counterparts, these associations provide a wide range of research, training, consulting, publications, and legislative representation services.

U.S. Councils of Governments Recognized by ICMA

Directory 1/8 gives the official name, appointed administrator, and telephone number for 96 councils of governments recognized by ICMA.

Officials in U.S. Municipalities

Directory 1/9 lists, alphabetically by state, all incorporated municipalities in the United States 2,500 and over in population, and those municipalities under 2,500 recognized by ICMA. It shows the current form of government; population (in thousands) according to the 2000 Census of Population; municipal phone number; and names of the mayor, appointed administrator, clerk of the governing board, chief finance officer, public works director, police chief, and fire

chief. Leaders (. .) in the population column mean that the population of the municipality is under 500.

Officials in U.S. Counties

Directory 1/10 lists, alphabetically by state, all county-type governments in the United States. It shows the population (in thousands) according to the 2000 Census of Population; the county telephone number; the name of the board chairman, county judge, or president; and the names of the appointed administrator, clerk of the governing board, chief financial officer, chief law enforcement official, and director of personnel. Leaders (. .) in the population column mean that the population of the county is under 500.

Other Local Government Directories

The names of municipal officials not reported in the *Year Book* are available in many states through directories published by state municipal leagues, state municipal management associations, and state associations of counties. Names and addresses of these leagues and associations are shown in Directories 1/1, 1/5, and 1/7. In some states the secretary of state, the state agency for community affairs (Directory 1/3), or another state agency publishes a directory that includes municipal and county officials. In addition, several directories with national coverage are published for health officers, welfare workers, housing and urban renewal officials, and other professional groups.

Directory 1/1   U.S. STATE MUNICIPAL LEAGUES

State	Municipal league, headquarters address, and Web site	Executive director (ED)	Phone number Fax number
Alabama	Alabama League of Municipalities, 535 Adams Avenue, Montgomery 36104 alalm.org	Perry C. Roquemore Jr.	334 262-2566 334 263-0200
Alaska	Alaska Municipal League, 217 Second Street, Suite 200, Juneau 99801-1267 akml.org	Kathie Wasserman	907 586-1325 907 463-5480
Arizona	League of Arizona Cities and Towns, 1820 West Washington Street, Phoenix 85007 azleague.org	Kenneth L. Strobeck	602 258-5786 602 253-3874
Arkansas	Arkansas Municipal League, P.O. Box 38, North Little Rock 72115 arml.org	Don A. Zimmerman	501 374-3484 501 374-0541
California	League of California Cities, 1400 K Street, Suite 400, Sacramento 95814 cacities.org	Chris McKenzie	916 658-8200 916 658-8240
Colorado	Colorado Municipal League, 1144 Sherman Street, Denver 80203 cml.org	Sam Mamet	303 831-6411 303 860-8175
Connecticut	Connecticut Conference of Municipalities, 900 Chapel Street, 9th Floor, New Haven 06510-2807 ccm-ct.org	James Finley Jr.	203 498-3000 203 562-6314
Delaware	Delaware League of Local Governments, P.O. Box 484, Dover 19903-0484 dllg.org/about.html	George C. Wright	302 678-0991 302 678-4777
Florida	Florida League of Cities, 301 S. Bronough Street, Suite 300, Tallahassee 32301 flcities.com	Michael Sittig	850 222-9684 850 222-3806
Georgia	Georgia Municipal Association, 201 Pryor Street, S.W., Atlanta 30303 gmanet.com/home	Jim Higdon	404 688-0472 678 686-6289
Idaho	Association of Idaho Cities, 3100 South Vista Avenue, Suite 310, Boise 83705 idahocities.org	Ken Harward	208 344-8594 208 344-8677
Illinois	Illinois Municipal League, East Capitol Avenue, Springfield 62705-5180 iml.org	Larry Frang	217 525-1220 217 525-7438
Indiana	Indiana Association of Cities and Towns, 200 South Meridian, Suite 340, Indianapolis 46225 citiesandtowns.org	Matthew C. Greller	317 237-6200 317 237-6206
Iowa	Iowa League of Cities, 317 Sixth Avenue, Suite 800, Des Moines 50309-4111 iowaleague.org	Alan Kemp	515 244-7282 515 244-0740
Kansas	League of Kansas Municipalities, 300 S.W. Eighth Avenue, Topeka 66603-3912 lkm.org	Don Moler	785 354-9565 785 354-4186
Kentucky	Kentucky League of Cities, 100 East Vine Street, Suite 800, Lexington 40507-3700 klc.org	Sylvia L. Lovely	859 977-3700 859 977-3703
Louisiana	Louisiana Municipal Association, 700 North 10th Street, Baton Rouge 70802 lamunis.org	Tom Ed McHugh	225 344-5001 225 344-3057
Maine	Maine Municipal Association, 60 Community Drive, Augusta 04330 memun.org	Christopher G. Lockwood	207 623-8428 207 626-5947
Maryland	Maryland Municipal League, 1212 West Street, Annapolis 21401 mdmunicipal.org	Scott A. Hancock	410 268-5514 410 268-7004
Massachusetts	Massachusetts Municipal Association, One Winthrop Square, Boston 02110 mma.org	Geoffrey Beckwith	617 426-7272 617 695-1314
Michigan	Michigan Municipal League, 1675 Green Road, Ann Arbor 48105 mml.org	Daniel P. Gilmartin	734 662-3246 734 662-8083
Minnesota	League of Minnesota Cities, 145 University Avenue West, St. Paul 55103-2044 lmnc.org	James F. Miller	651 281-1200 651 281-1299
Mississippi	Mississippi Municipal League, 600 East Amite Street, Suite 104, Jackson 39201 mmlonline.com	George E. Lewis	601 353-5854 601 353-6980
Missouri	Missouri Municipal League, 1727 Southridge Drive, Jefferson City 65109 mocities.com	Gary Markenson	573 635-9134 573 635-9009
Montana	Montana League of Cities and Towns, 208 North Montana Avenue, Suite 201, Helena 59601 mlct.org	Alec N. Hansen	406 442-8768 406 442-9231
Nebraska	League of Nebraska Municipalities, 1335 L Street, Lincoln 68508 lonm.org	L. Lynn Rex	402 476-2829 402 476-7052
Nevada	Nevada League of Cities and Municipalities, 310 South Curry Street, Carson City 89703 nvleague.org	David Fraser	775 882-2121 775 882-2813

Directory 1/1   U.S. STATE MUNICIPAL LEAGUES
continued

State	Municipal league, headquarters address, and Web site	Executive director (ED)	Phone number Fax number
New Hampshire	New Hampshire Local Government Center, 25 Triangle Park, Concord 03302-0617 nhlgc.org/LGCWebsite/index.asp	John B. Andrews	603 224-7447 603 224-5406
New Jersey.	New Jersey State League of Municipalities, 222 West State Street, Trenton 08608 njslom.com	William G. Dressel	609 695-3481 609 695-0151
New Mexico	New Mexico Municipal League, 1229 Paseo de Peralta, Santa Fe 87501 nmml.org	William F. Fulginiti	800 432-2036 505 984-1392
New York	New York State Conference of Mayors and Municipal Officials, 119 Washington Avenue, Albany 12210 nycom.org	Peter A. Baynes	518 463-1185 518 463-1190
North Carolina	North Carolina League of Municipalities, P.O. Box 3069, Raleigh 27602-3069 nclm.org	S. Ellis Hankins	919 715-4000 919 733-9519
North Dakota	North Dakota League of Cities, 410 East Front Avenue, Bismarck 58504-5641 ndlc.org	Connie Sprynczynatyk	701 223-3518 701 223-5174
Ohio	Ohio Municipal League, 175 South Third Street, Suite 510, Columbus 43215 omlohio.org	Susan J. Cave	614 221-4349 614 221-4390
Oklahoma.	Oklahoma Municipal League, 201 Northeast 23rd Street, Oklahoma City 73105 oml.org	Carolyn Stager	405 528-7515 405 528-7560
Oregon	League of Oregon Cities, 1201 Court Street, N.E., Suite 200, Salem 97301 orcities.org	Mike McCauley	503 588-6550 503 399-4863
Pennsylvania	Pennsylvania League of Cities and Municipalities, 414 North Second Street, Harrisburg 17101 plcm.org	John A. Garner Jr.	717 236-9469 717 236-6716
Rhode Island	Rhode Island League of Cities and Towns, One State Street, Suite 502, Providence 02908 rileague.org	Daniel L. Beardsley Jr.	401 272-3434 401 421-0824
South Carolina	Municipal Association of South Carolina, 1411 Gervais Street, Columbia 29211 masc.sc	Miriam Hair	803 799-9574 803 933-1299
South Dakota	South Dakota Municipal League, 214 East Capitol Avenue, Pierre 57501 sdmunicipalleague.org	Yvonne Taylor	605 224-8654 605 224-8655
Tennessee	Tennessee Municipal League, 226 Capitol Boulevard, Suite 710, Nashville 37219-1894 tml1.org	Margaret Mahery	615 255-6416 615 255-4752
Texas	Texas Municipal League, 1821 Rutherford Lane, Suite 400, Austin 78754-5128 tml.org	Frank J. Sturzl	512 231-7400 512 231-7490
Utah	Utah League of Cities and Towns, 50 South 600 East, Suite 150, Salt Lake City 84102 ulct.org	Ken Bullock	801 328-1601 801 531-1872
Vermont	Vermont League of Cities and Towns, 89 Main Street, Suite 4, Montpelier 05602-2948 vlct.org	Steven E. Jeffrey	802 229-9111 802 229-2211
Virginia	Virginia Municipal League, 13 E. Franklin Street, Richmond 23241 vml.org	R. Michael Amyx	804 649-8471 804 343-3758
Washington.	Association of Washington Cities, 1076 Franklin Street, S.E., Olympia 98501-1346 awcnet.org	Stan Finkelstein	360 753-4137 360 753-0149
West Virginia	West Virginia Municipal League, 2020 Kanawha Boulevard East, Charleston 25311 wvml.org	Lisa Dooley	304 342-5564 304 342-5586
Wisconsin.	League of Wisconsin Municipalities, 122 W. Washington Ave, Suite 300, Madison 53703-2215 lwm-info.org	Dan Thompson	608 267-2380 608 267-0645
Wyoming.	Wyoming Association of Municipalities, 315 West 27th Street, Cheyenne 82001 wyomuni.org	George Parks	307 632-0398 307 632-1942

Directory 1/2   PROVINCIAL AND TERRITORIAL ASSOCIATIONS AND UNIONS IN CANADA

Province or territory	Association/union and Web site	President	Permanent officer and contact information
Alberta.	Alberta Association of Municipal Districts and Counties aamdc.com	Donald Johnson	Gerald Rhodes, Executive Director 2510 Sparrow Drive Nisku T9E 8N5 Phone: 780 955-3639 Fax: 780 955-3615 E-mail: gerald@aamdc.com
	Alberta Urban Municipalities Association munilink.net/live/	Lloyd Bertschi	John McGowan, Chief Executive Officer 10507 Saskatchewan Drive, N.W. Edmonton T6E 4S1 Phone: 780 433-4431 Fax: 780 433-4454 E-mail: jmcgowan@auma.ca
British Columbia	Union of British Columbia Municipalities civicnet.bc.ca/ubcm	Susan Gimse	Gary MacIsaac, Executive Director 10551 Shellbridge Way, Suite 60 Richmond V6X 2W9 Phone: 604 270-8226 Fax: 604 270-9116 E-mail: gmacisaac@civicnet.bc.ca

Directory 1/2   **PROVINCIAL AND TERRITORIAL ASSOCIATIONS AND UNIONS IN CANADA**
continued

Province or territory	Association/union and Web site	President	Permanent officer and contact information
Manitoba	Association of Manitoba Municipalities amm.mb.ca	Ron Bell	Joe Masi, Executive Director 1910 Saskatchewan Avenue West Portage-la-Prairie R1N 0P1 Phone: 204 857-8666 Fax: 204 856-2370 E-mail: jmasi@amm.mb.ca
New Brunswick	Association Francophone des Municipalités du Nouveau-Brunswick afmnb.org	Jean-Paul Savoie	Lise Ouellette, Directrice-Générale 702 rue Principale, bureau 322 Petit-Rocher E8J 1V1 Phone: 506 542-2622 Fax: 506 542-2618 E-mail: afmnb@nbaibn.com
	Cities of New Brunswick Association	Joel Richardson	Sandra Mark, Executive Director P.O. Box 1421, Station A Fredericton E3B 5E3 Phone: 506 357-4242 Fax: 506 357-4243 E-mail: cnbacnb@nbnet.nb.ca
Newfoundland and Labrador. . .	Newfoundland and Labrador Federation of Municipalities nlfm.ca/default.php?display=cid96&mid=879	Wayne Ruth	Craig Pollett, Executive Director 460 Torbay Road St. John's A1A 5J3 Phone: 709 753-6820 Fax: 709 738-0071 E-mail: executivedirector@nlfm.ca
Northwest Territories.	Northwest Territories Association of Communities nwtac.com	Gordon Van Tighem	Yvette Gonzalez, Chief Executive Officer 5105-50th Street, Suite 200 Yellowknife X1A 1S1 Phone: 867 873-8359 Fax: 867 873-3042 E-mail: yvette@nwtac.com
Nova Scotia.	Union of Nova Scotia Municipalities unsm.ca	Warden Lloyd Hines	Kenneth R. B. Simpson, Executive Director 1809 Barrington Street, Suite 1106 Halifax B3J 3K8 Phone: 902 423-8331 Fax: 902 425-5592 E-mail: ksimpson@eastlink.ca
Ontario	Association of Municipalities of Ontario amo.on.ca	Peter Hume	Pat Vanini, Executive Director 200 University Avenue, Suite 801 Toronto M5H 3C6 Phone: 416 971-9856 Fax: 416 971-6191 E-mail: pvanini@amo.on.ca
	Federation of Canadian Municipalities fcm.ca	Jean Perrault	Brock Carlton, Chief Executive Officer 24 Clarence Street Ottawa K1N 5P3 Phone: 613 241-5221 Fax: 613 241-7440
Prince Edward Island	Federation of Prince Edward Island Municipalities fpeim.ca	Bruce MacDougall	John Dewey, Executive Director 1 Kirkdale Road Charlottetown C1E 1R3 Phone: 902 566-1493 Fax: 902 566-2880 E-mail: jdewey@fpeim.ca
Québec	Union des Municipalités du Québec umq.qc.ca	Robert Coulombe	Peggy Bachman, Directeur-Général 680 rue Sherbrook Ouest, bureau 680 Montreal H3A 2M7 Phone: 514 282-7700 Fax: 514 282-8893 E-mail: pbeachman@umq.qc.ca
Saskatchewan.	Saskatchewan Association of Rural Municipalities sarm.ca/	David Marit	Ken Engel, Executive Director 2075 Hamilton Street Regina S4P 2E1 Phone: 306 757-3577 Fax: 306 565-2141 E-mail: kengel@sarm.ca
	Saskatchewan Urban Municipalities Association suma.org/siteengine/activepage.asp?PageID=1	Allan Earle	Laurent Mougeot, Executive Director 2222 13th Avenue, Suite 200 Regina S4P 3M7 Phone: 306 525-3727 Fax: 306 525-4373 E-mail: lmougeot@suma.org
Yukon	Association of Yukon Communities ayc.yk.ca	Bev Buckway	Tom Paterson, Executive Director 1114 First Avenue, #15 Whitehorse Y1A 1A3 Phone: 867 668-4388 Fax: 867 668-7574 E-mail: ayced@northwestel.net

DIRECTORY 1/3 STATE AGENCIES FOR COMMUNITY AFFAIRS

State or territory	Agency, address, and Web site	Name and title of agency head	Phone number Fax number
Alabama	Department of Economic and Community Affairs, 401 Adams Street, Montgomery 36104 adeca.state.al.us	Bill Johnson Director	334 242-5591 334 242-5099
Alaska	Department of Commerce, Community and Economic Development, P.O. Box 110800, Juneau 99811-0800 dced.state.ak.us	Emil Notti Commissioner	907 465-2500 907 465-5442
Arizona	Department of Commerce, 1700 West Washington, Suite 600, Phoenix 85007 azcommerce.com	Marco A. López Jr. Director	602 771-1160
Arkansas	Department of Economic Development, One Capitol Mall, Little Rock 72201 1800arkansas.com	Maria Haley Executive Director	501 682-7351 501 682-7394
California	Department of Housing and Community Development, 1800 Third Street, Sacramento 95811-6942 hcd.ca.gov	Lynn L. Jacobs Director	916 445-4775 916 324-5107
Colorado	Colorado Department of Local Affairs, 1313 Sherman Street, Suite 500, Denver 80203 dola.state.co.us	Susan Kirkpatrick Executive Director	303 866-4904 303 866-4317
Connecticut	Department of Economic and Community Development, Business and Housing Development, 505 Hudson Street, Hartford 06106-7106 ct.gov/ecd/site/default.asp	Joan McDonald Commissioner	860 270-8000 860 270-8008
Delaware	State Housing Authority, 18 The Green, Dover 19901 destatehousing.com/	Saundra R. Johnson Director	302 739-4263 302 739-6122
Florida	Department of Community Affairs, 2555 Shumard Oak Boulevard, Tallahassee 32399-2100 dca.state.fl.us	Thomas G. Pelham Secretary	850 488-8466 850 921-9781
Georgia	Department of Community Affairs, 60 Executive Park South, N.E., Atlanta 30329 dca.state.ga.us	Mike Beatty Commissioner	404 679-4940 404 679-0646
Idaho	Department of Commerce, 700 West State Street, Boise 83720-0093 commerce.idaho.gov	Don Dietrich Director	208 334-2470 208 334-2631
Illinois	Department of Commerce and Economic Opportunity, James R. Thompson Center, 100 West Randolph, Chicago 60601 illinoisbiz.biz/dceox	James Thompson Director	312 814-7179
Indiana	Indiana Housing and Community Development Authority, 30 South Meridian, Suite 1000, Indianapolis 46204 in.gov/ihfa	Sherry Seiwert Executive Director	317 232-7777 317 232-7778
Iowa	Department of Economic Development, 200 East Grand Avenue, Des Moines 50309 iowalifechanging.com	Mike Tramontina Director	515 242-4700 515 242-4809
Kansas	Department of Commerce, Division of Community Development, 1000 S.W. Jackson Street, Suite 100, Topeka 66612-1354 kdoch.state.ks.us/public	Carole Jordan Director	785 296-3481 785 296-3776
Kentucky	Governor's Office for Local Government, Division of Grants, 1024 Capital Center Drive, Frankfort 40601 gold.ky.gov	Tony Wilder Commissioner	502 573-2382 502 573-2939
Louisiana	Office of Community Development, Division of Administration, P.O. Box 94095, Baton Rouge 70804 doa.louisiana.gov/cdbg/cdbg.htm	Paul Rainwater Executive Director	225 342-7412 225 342-1947
Maine	Department of Economic and Community Development, 59 State House Station, Augusta 04333-0059 econdevmaine.com	John Richardson Commissioner	207 624-9800 207 287-8070
Maryland	Department of Housing and Community Development, 100 Community Place, Crownsville 21032-2023 dhcd.state.md.us	Raymond Skinner Secretary	410 514-7000 410 987-4070
Michigan	Michigan Economic Development Corporation, 300 North Washington Square, Lansing 48913 medc.michigan.org	James C. Epolito Chief Executive Officer	888 522-0103 517 241-3683
Minnesota	Department of Employment and Economic Development, First National Bank Building, 332 Minnesota Street, Suite E200, St. Paul 55101-1351 deed.state.mn.us	Dan McElroy Commissioner	651 259-7114 651 296-1290
Mississippi	Mississippi Development Authority, P.O. Box 849, Jackson 39205 Mississippi.org	Gray Swoope Executive Director	601 359-3449 601 359-3613
Missouri	Department of Economic Development, P.O. Box 1157, Jefferson City 65102-1157 ded.mo.gov	Garry Taylor Interim Director	573 751-4962 573 526-7700
Montana	Department of Commerce, Local Government Assistance Division, P.O. Box 200501, Helena 59620 commerce.mt.gov/	Anthony Preite Director	406 841-2700 406 841-2701
Nebraska	Department of Economic Development, P.O. Box 94666, 301 Centennial Mall South, Lincoln 68509-4666 neded.org	Richard Baier Director	402 471-3747 402 471-3778
Nevada	Commission on Economic Development, 108 East Proctor Street, Carson City 89701 expand2nevada.com	Tim Rubald Director	775 687-4325 775 687-4450
New Hampshire	Office of Energy and Planning, 4 Chenell Drive, Concord 03301-8501 nh.gov/oep	Amy Ignatius Director	603 271-2155 603 271-2615
New Jersey	Department of Community Affairs, P.O. Box 800, 101 South Broad Street, Trenton 08625-0800 state.nj.us/dca	Joseph Doria Jr. Commissioner	609 292-6055 609 984-6696
New Mexico	Department of Finance and Administration, Local Government Division, 402 Don Gaspar, Santa Fe 87501 local.nmdfa.state.nm.us	Robert Apodaca Director	505 827-4950 505 827-4948
New York	Division of Housing and Community Renewal, Hampton Plaza, 38-40 State Street, Albany 12207 dhcr.state.ny.us	Deborah VanAmerongen Commissioner	518 473-2526 518 473-9462
North Carolina	Department of Commerce, 301 North Wilmington Street, Raleigh 27601-1058 nccommerce.com/en	Jim Fain Secretary	919 733-4151 919 715-9593
North Dakota	Division of Community Services, 1600 East Century Avenue, Suite 2, Bismarck 58503 state.nd.us/dcs	Paul Govig Director	701 328-4499 701 328-5320

Directory 1/3   STATE AGENCIES FOR COMMUNITY AFFAIRS
continued

State or territory	Agency, address, and Web site	Name and title of agency head	Phone number Fax number
Ohio............	Department of Development, 77 South High Street, Columbus 43216-1001 odod.state.oh.us	Lee Fisher Director	614 466-3379 614 644-0745
Oklahoma	Department of Commerce, 900 North Stiles Avenue, Oklahoma City 73104-3234 okcommerce.gov	Natalie Shirley Oklahoma Secretary of Commerce and Tourism	405 815-6552 405 815-5290
Oregon..........	Department of Economic and Community Development, 775 Summer Street, N.E., Suite 200, Salem 97301-1280 econ.oregon.gov	Tim McCabe Director	503 986-0123 503 581-5115
Pennsylvania.....	Department of Community and Economic Development, 400 North Street, 4th Floor, Commonwealth Keystone Building, Harrisburg 17120-0225 newpa.com/default.aspx?id=223	John Blake Acting Secretary	717 787-3003 717 787-6866
Puerto Rico	Office of the Commissioner of Municipal Affairs, P.O. Box 70167, San Juan 00936-8167 ocam.gobierno.pr	Ángel Castillo Rodriguez Commissioner	787 754-1600 787 753-8254
Rhode Island.....	Office of Housing and Community Development, One Capitol Hill, 3rd Floor, Providence 02908 muni-info.ri.gov	Norene Shawcross Chief Executive Officer	401 222-5766 401 222-2083
South Carolina....	Department of Commerce, 1201 Main Street, Suite 1600, Columbia 29201-3200 sccommerce.com	Joe E. Taylor Jr. Secretary	803 737-0400 803 737-0418
South Dakota.....	Department of Tourism and State Development, 711 East Wells Avenue, Pierre 57501-3369 sdreadytowork.com	Richard Benda Secretary	605 773-3301 605 773-3256
Tennessee.......	Housing Development Agency, 404 James Robertson Parkway, Suite 1200 Nashville 37243-0900 state.tn.us/thda	Ted R. Fellman Executive Director	615 815-2015 615 564-2700
Texas...........	Department of Housing and Community Affairs, P.O. Box 13941, Austin 78711-3941 tdhca.state.tx.us	Michael Gerber Executive Director	512 475-3930 512 469-9606
Utah............	Governor's Office of Economic Development, 324 South State Street, Suite 500, Salt Lake City 84111 goed.utah.gov	Jason Perry Executive Director	801 538-8700 801 538-8888
	The Utah Department of Community and Culture, 324 South State Street, Suite 500, Salt Lake City 84111 community.utah.gov	Palmer DePaulis Executive Director	801 538-8700 801 538-8888
Vermont.........	Department of Housing and Community Affairs, National Life Building, 6th Floor, One National Life Drive, Montpelier 05620-0501 dhca.state.vt.us	Tayt Brooks Deputy Commissioner	802 828-5216 802 828-5218
Virginia..........	Department of Housing and Community Development, The Jackson Center, 501 North Second Street, Richmond 23219-1321 dhcd.virginia.gov	Bill Shelton Director	804 371-7000 804 371-7090
Washington	Department of Community, Trade and Economic Development, P.O. Box 42525, 128 Tenth Avenue, S.W., Olympia 98504-2525 cted.wa.gov	Julie Wilkerson Director	360 725-4000 360 586-8440
West Virginia	Department of Commerce, Capitol Complex, Building 6, 1900 Kanawha Boulevard East, Charleston 25305-0311 wvdo.org	Kelly Goes Executive Director	304 558-2234 304 558-0449
Wisconsin	Department of Commerce, 201 West Washington Avenue, Madison 53703-7970 commerce.state.wi.us	Dick Leinenkugel Secretary	608 266-7088 608 226-8969

Directory 1/4   PROVINCIAL AND TERRITORIAL AGENCIES FOR LOCAL AFFAIRS IN CANADA

Providence or territory	Minister, address, and Web site	Phone number Fax number	Providence or territory	Minister, address, and Web site	Phone number Fax number
Alberta.............	Hon. Ray Danyluk Alberta Municipal Affairs and Housing Communications Branch 18th Floor, Commerce Place 10155-102 Street Edmonton T5J 4L4 municipalaffairs.gov.ab.ca	780 427-2732 780 422-1419	New Brunswick	Hon. Rick Brewer Minister of Human Resources, Minister responsible for the Aboriginal Affairs Secretariat, 4th Floor P.O. Box 6000 Fredericton E3B 5H1 Hon. Rick Brewer gnb.ca/0016/index-e.asp	506 453-2506 506 453-7154
British Columbia	Honourable Blair Lekstrom Minister of Community Services and Minister Responsible for Seniors' and Women's Issues P.O. Box 9056 STN PROV GOVT Victoria V8W 9E2 gov.bc.ca/cserv/index.html	250 387-2283 250 387-4312	Newfoundland and Labrador	Hon. Dianne Whalen Minister of Municipal Affairs Main Floor, West Block Confederation Building P.O. Box 8700 St. John's A1B 4J6 gov.nf.ca/mpa	709 729-3048 709 729-0943
Manitoba	Hon. Oscar Lathlin Minister of Aboriginal and Northern Affairs 344-450 Broadway Winnipeg R3C 0V8 gov.mb.ca/ana	204 945-3719 204 945-8374	Northwest Territories..	Hon. Jackson Lafferty Minister of Education, Culture, and Employment P.O. Box 1320 Yellowknife X1A 2L9 ece.gov.nt.ca	867 669-2399 867 873-0169

Directory 1/4 **PROVINCIAL AND TERRITORIAL AGENCIES FOR LOCAL AFFAIRS IN CANADA**
continued

Providence or territory	Minister, address, and Web site	Phone number / Fax number	Providence or territory	Minister, address, and Web site	Phone number / Fax number
Nova Scotia.	Hon. Jamie Muir Minister of Service and Municipal Relations P.O. Box 1003 Halifax B3J 2X1 gov.ns.ca/snsmr/muns/link	902 424-5200 902 424-0720	Québec	Nathalie Normandeau Ministre des Affaires Municipales 10, rue Pierre-Olivier-Chauveau Québec G1R 4J3 mamm.gouv.qc.ca/accueil.asp	418 691-2050 418 643-1795
Ontario	Hon. Jim Watson Minister of Municipal Affairs and Housing 777 Bay Street, 17th Floor Toronto M5G 2E5 mah.gov.on.ca	416 585-6226 416 585-6882	Saskatchewan.	Hon. Wyane Elhard Minister of Public Service Commission 2100 Broad Street Regina S4P 1Y5 gov.sk.ca/deptsorgs/overviews/?75	204 787-6447 202 787-1736
Prince Edward Island . .	Hon. Carolyn Bertram Minister of Community and Cultural Affairs P.O. Box 2000 Charlottetown C1A 7N8 gov.pe.ca/commcul/index.php3	902 368-5250 902 368-4121	Yukon	Hon. Archie Lang Minister of Community Services P.O. Box 2703 Whitehorse Y1A 2C6 community.gov.yk.ca/	867 667-5811 867 393-6295

Directory 1/5 **U.S. MUNICIPAL MANAGEMENT ASSOCIATIONS**

State	Association and Web site	President, address, and e-mail	Phone number / Fax number
Alabama.	Alabama City/County Management Association accma-online.org/	Sherrie Y. Kelley (until 10/09) County Administrator County of Coosa P.O. Box 10 Rockford 35136 skelleyadm@hotmail.com	256 377-1350 256 377-2524
Alaska	Alaska Municipal Management Association akml.org/amma.html	Denise Michels (until 11/09) Mayor City of Nome P.O. Box 281 Nome 99762 mayor@ci.nome.ak.us	907 443-5231 907 443-5349
Arizona.	Arizona City/County Management Association azmanagement.org/	Pam Kavanaugh (until 2/10) Assistant City Manager City of Glendale 5850 West Glendale Avenue Glendale 85301 pam@glendaleaz.com	623 930-2000
Arkansas	Arkansas City/County Management Association	Jimmy W. Bolt (until 6/09) City Manager City of Arkadelphia 700 Clay Street Arkadelphia 71923-5963 jimmy@cityofarkadelphia.com	870 246-9864 870 246-1813
		Ward J. Hanna (as of 7/09) Assistant Director City of Little Rock Little Rock City Hall 500 West Markham Street Little Rock 72201-1415 whanna@littlerock.org	501 371-6809 501 371-4498
California	City Manager's Department, League of California Cities cacities.org	Jeffrey C. Kolin (until 9/09) City Manager City of Santa Rosa P.O. Box 1678 Santa Rosa 95402-1678 jkolin@ci.santa-rosa.ca.us	707 543-3020 707 543-3030
		Ken Pulskamp (as of 10/09) City Manager City of Santa Clarita 23920 Valencia Boulevard, Suite 300 Santa Clarita 91355 kpulskamp@santa-clarita.com	661 255-4905
	Cal-ICMA www2.icma.org/cal-icma	Roderick (Rod) J. Wood (until 7/09) City Manager City of Beverly Hills 455 North Rexford Drive Beverly Hills 90211 rwood@beverlyhills.org	310 285-1012 310 273-1250
Colorado.	Colorado City and County Management Association cml.org/cccma/cccma.aspx	Nicholas (Nick) J. Meier (until 2/10) Town Manager Town of Platteville 400 Grand Avenue Platteville 80651-7503 nmeier@plattevillegov.org	970 785-2245 970 785-2476

Directory 1/5 **U.S. MUNICIPAL MANAGEMENT ASSOCIATIONS**
continued

State	Association and Web site	President, address, and e-mail	Phone number / Fax number
Connecticut	Connecticut Town and City Management Association	Barbara R. Gilbert (until 7/09) Town Manager Town of Rocky Hill 761 Old Main Street Rocky Hill 06067-1519 Bgilbert@ci.rocky-hill.ct.us	860 258-2700 860 258-7638
Delaware	City Management Association of Delaware	Rebecca Greene (until 1/11) Town Manager Town of Felton P.O. Box 329 Felton 19943 rgreene@townoffelton.com	302 284-9365
Florida	Florida City and County Management Association fccma.org/	Edward R Mitchell (until 6/09) City Administrator City of West Palm Beach P.O. Box 3366 West Palm Beach 33402-3366 emitchel@wpb.org	561 822-1400 561 822-1424
		Joseph Gallegos (as of 7/09) City Manager City of Wilton Manors City Hall 524 N.E. 21 Court Wilton Manors 33305 jgallegos@wiltonmanors.com	954 390-2122
Georgia	Georgia City-County Management Association gccma.com	Isaiah Hugley (until 4/09) City Manager Columbus–Muscogee Consolidated Government P.O. Box 1340 Columbus 31902-1340 ihugley@columbusga.org	706 653-4029 706 653-4032
		Lee Gilmour (as of 5/09) City Manager City of Perry P.O. Box 2030 Perry 31069-2700 Lee.Gilmour@perry-ga.gov	478 988-2703 478 988-2705
Idaho	Idaho City/County Management Association	Eric A. Keck (until 1/11) City Administrator City of Post Falls 408 Spokane Street Post Falls 83854-7538 ekeck@postfallsidaho.org	208 292-2310 208 773-8362
Illinois	Illinois City/County Management Association ilcma.org/	Patrick Urich (until 6/09) County Administrator County of Peoria 324 Main Street, Room 502 Peoria 61602-1319 purich@co.peoria.il.us	309 672-6056 309 672-6054
		James Norris (as of 7/09) Village Manager Village of Hoffman Estates 1900 Hassell Rdoad Hoffman Estates 60169 jim.norris@hoffmanestates.org	309 672-6056 309 672-6054
Indiana	Indiana Municipal Management Association citiesandtowns.org/content/affiliated/IMMA_DHT.htm	Gary A. Huff (until 11/09) Town Manager Town of Fishers 1 Municipal Drive Town Hall Fishers 46038-1574 huffg@fishers.in.us	317 595-3101 317 595-3110
Iowa	Iowa City/County Management Association iaccmanagement.govoffice2.com	Alan D. Johnson (until 6/09) City Manager City of Independence 331 First Street East Independence 50644-2814 citymgr@indytel.com	515 279-3662 515 279-3664
		Marketa Oliver (as of 7/09) City Administrator 1133 66th Street Windsor Heights 50311 moliver@windsorheights.org	
Kansas	Kansas Association of City/County Management accesskansas.org/kacm/	Matthew C. Allen (until 11/09) Assistant City Manager City of Garden City 301 North 8th Street Garden City 67846-5340 mallen@garden-city.org	620 276-1160 620 276-1169

Directory 1/5   U.S. MUNICIPAL MANAGEMENT ASSOCIATIONS
continued

State	Association and Web site	President, address, and e-mail	Phone number / Fax number
Kentucky	Kentucky City/County Management Association kccma.org/	James W. Zumwalt (until 9/09) City Manager City of Paducah P.O. Box 2267 Paducah 42002-2267 jzumwalt@ci.paducah.ky.us	270 444-8503 270 443-5058
		Dan Groth (as of 10/09) City Manager City of Independence 5409 Madison Pike Independence 41051 dgroth@cityofindependence.org	859 356-5302 859 356-6843
Maine	Maine Town and City Management Association mtcma.org	John P. Anderson (until 8/09) Town Manager Town of Boothbay P.O. Box 459 East Boothbay 04544-0459 townmanager@town.boothbay.me.us	207 633-2051 207 633-6620
Maryland	Maryland City and County Management Association icma.org/mccma/	Elaine M. Murphy (until 5/09; successor to be elected) City Administrator City of Hyattsville 4310 Gallatin Street Hyattsville 20781-2050 emurphy@hyattsville.org	301 985-5000 301 985-5007
Massachusetts	Massachusetts Municipal Management Association mma.org	Bruce Tobey (until 12/09) Councillor City of Gloucester 16 Montvale Avenue Gloucester 01930-1827 btobey@ci.gloucester.ma.us	978 282-0001
Michigan	Michigan Local Government Management Association mlgma.org	Theodore J. Staton (until 2/10) City Manager City of East Lansing 410 Abbot Road East Lansing 48823 tstaton@cityofeastlansing.com	517 337-1731 517 337-1559
Minnesota	Minnesota City/County Management Association mncma.org	Kris M. Busse (until 5/09) City Administrator City of Owatonna 540 West Hills Circle Owatonna 55060-4701 Kris.busse@ci.owatonna.mn.us	507 444-4300 507 444-4394
		Heather M. Worthington (as of 6/09) Assistant City Manager City of Edina 4801 West 50th Street Edina 55424-1394 hworthington@ci.edina.mn.us	952 826-0415 952 826-0390
Mississippi	Mississippi City/County Management Association	Gary A. Suddith (until 4/09) Small Business Development Director Jones County Junior College 900 Court Street Ellisville 39437 crc@jcjc.cc.ms.us	601 477-4165 601 477-4166
Missouri	Missouri City Management Association momanagers.org/	Richard R. Noll (until 5/09) Assistant City Manager City of Kansas City 414 East 12th Street, 29th Floor Kansas City 64106-2748 rich_noll@kcmo.org	816 513-1408 816 513-1363
		Barry Alexander (as of 6/09) City Administrator City of Shrewsbury 5200 Shrewsbury Avenue Shrewsbury 63119-4349 balexander@cityofshrewsbury.com	314 647-5795 314 647-1811
Nebraska	Nebraska Association of City and County Management nebraskacma.org/	Joseph P. Pepplitsch (until 10/09) City Manager City of Lexington P.O. Box 70 Lexington 68850-0070 jpepp@cityoflex.com	308 324-2341 308 324-4590
		Philip C. Green (as of 11/09) Assistant City Administrator City of Blair 218 South 16th Street Blair 68008-2010 PCGreen@ci.blair.ne.us	402 426-6691 402 426-4195

Directory 1/5   U.S. MUNICIPAL MANAGEMENT ASSOCIATIONS
continued

State	Association and Web site	President, address, and e-mail	Phone number Fax number
Nevada	Local Government Managers Association of Nevada nevadalogman.org/	Elizabeth N. Fretwell (until 6/09) City Manager City of Las Vegas 400 Stewart Avenue, Floor 8 Las Vegas 89101-2927 bfretwell@lasvegasnevada.gov	702 229-6501 702 464-5710
New Hampshire	New Hampshire Municipal Management Association nhmunicipal.org/LGCWebsite/index.asp	Jessie W. Levine (until 11/09) Town Administrator Town of New London 375 Main Street New London 03257 townadmin@nl-nh.com	603 526-4821 603 526-9494
New Jersey	New Jersey Municipal Management Association njmma.org/	Jasmine L. Lim (until 1/10) Business Administrator Township of Parsippany–Troy Hills 1001 Parsippany Boulevard Parsippany 07054 LimJ@Parsippany.net	973 263-4391 973 541-9416
New Mexico	New Mexico City Management Association	Matt J. McNeile (until 9/09) Acting City Manager City of Alamogordo 1376 East 9th Street Alamogordo 88310 mmcneile@ci.alamogordo.nm.us	505 439-4324 505 439-4394
New York	New York State City County Management Association nyscma.govoffice.com/	Harold J. Porr III (until 6/09) Village Administrator Village of Bronxville Village Hall 200 Pondfield Road Bronxville 10708-4832 hporr3@optonline.net	914 337-6500 914 337-2683
		Ingrid M. Richards (as of 7/09) Assistant Village Manager Village of Briarcliff Manor 1111 Pleasantville Road Briarcliff Manor 10510-1603 irichards@briarcliffmanor.org	914 944-2782 914 944-4837
North Carolina	North Carolina City and County Management Association ncmanagers.org/	David C. Cooke (until 5/09) County Manager County of Wake P.O. Box 550 Raleigh 27602-0550 dcooke@co.wake.nc.us	919 856-5555 919 856-6168
		Michael Dula (as of 6/09) Town of Elon College P.O. Box 595 Elon College 27244-0595 mdula@ci.elon.nc.us	336 584-3601 336 584-5334
Ohio	Ohio City/County Management Association ocmaohio.org/	Brian Humphress (until 6/09) City Manager City of Willard 710 Kennedy Drive Willard 44890-9413 manager@willard-oh.com	419 933-2591 419 933-4545
		Robert W. Harrison (as of 7/09) City Manager City of Wyoming 800 Oak Avenue Wyoming 45215-2720 harrison@wyoming.oh.us	513 821-7600 513 821-7952
Oklahoma	City Management Association of Oklahoma oml.org/dbs/CMAO/index.cfm	Steven Whitlock (until 8/09) City Manager City of Coweta P.O. Box 850 Coweta 74429-0850 swhitlock@coweta.lib.ok.us	918 486-2189 918 486-5366
Oregon	Oregon City/County Management Association occma.org/DesktopDefault.aspx	Nancy Boyer (until 12/09) Executive Director Mid-Willamette Valley Council of Governments 105 High Street N.E. Salem 97301 nboyer@mwvcog.org	503 588-6177

Directory 1/5   **U.S. MUNICIPAL MANAGEMENT ASSOCIATIONS**
continued

State	Association and Web site	President, address, and e-mail	Phone number / Fax number
Pennsylvania	Association for Pennsylvania Municipal Management apmm.govoffice.com/	Larry M. Comunale (until 5/09) Township Manager Township of Lower Gwynedd P.O. Box 625 Spring House 19477-0625 lcomunale@lowergwynedd.org	215 646-5302 215 646-3357
		Kenneth E. Myers (as of 6/09) Borough Manager Borough of Huntingdon 531 Washington Street P.O. Box 592 Huntingdon 16652 kmyers@huntingdonboro.com	814 643-3966 814 643-2644
Rhode Island	Rhode Island City and Town Management Association	Peter A. Deangelis Jr. Town Manager Town of Barrington 283 County Road Barrington 02806 pdeangelis@barrington.ri.gov	401 247-1900, x308 401 247-3765
South Carolina	South Carolina City and County Management Association ipspr.sc.edu/scccma	Roger P. LeDuc (until 6/09) City Manager City of Aiken P.O. Box 1177 Aiken 29802-1177 rleduc@cityofaikensc.gov	803 642-7654 803 642-7646
		Jason Ward (as of 7/09) County Administrator Dorchester County KFW Building 201 Johnston Street St. George 29477 wardj@dorchestercounty.net	843 563-0100 843 563-0137
South Dakota	South Dakota City Management Association sdmunicipalleague.org/	John C. Prescott (until 9/09) City Manager City of Vermillion 25 Center St Vermillion 57069-2101 johnp@cityofvermillion.com	605 677-7050 605 677-5461
		Jeffrey W. Weldon (as of 10/09) City Manager City of Brookings 311 Third Avenue Brookings 57006-0270 jweldon@cityofbrookings.org	605 692-6281 605 692-6907
Tennessee	Tennessee City Management Association tncma.org/	Kevin L. Helms (until 6/09) In transition	931 433-4445
		Lewis J. (Jody) Baltz III (as of 7/09) City Administrator City of Tullahoma P.O. Box 807 Tullahoma 37388-0807 jbaltz@tullahoma-tn.com	931 455-2648 931 455-0038
Texas	Texas City Management Association tcma.org/	Paul L. Parker (until 6/09) City Manager City of Lufkin 300 East Shepherd Street, Room 141 Lufkin 75901 pparker@cityoflufkin.com	936 633-0211 936 634-4774
		Courtney B. Sharp (as of 7/09) City Manager City of Midland P.O. Box 1152 Midland 79702-1152 csharp@midlandtexas.gov	432 685-7200 432 686-1600
Utah	Utah City Management Association ucma-utah.org/	Mark J Christensen (until 9/09) City Manager City of Washington Terrace 5249 South Southpointe Drive Washington Terrace 84405 markc@washingtonterracecity.org	801 395-8282 801 393-1921
Vermont	Vermont Town and City Management Association	Peter B. Webster (until 5/10) Town Manager Town of Norwich P.O. Box 376 Norwich 05055-0376 manager@norwich.vt.us	802 649-0127

Directory 1/5   U.S. MUNICIPAL MANAGEMENT ASSOCIATIONS
continued

State	Association and Web site	President, address, and e-mail	Phone number Fax number
Virginia	Virginia Local Government Management Association vlgma.org	Kathleen D. Guzi (until 6/09) County Administrator County of Bedford 122 East Main Street, Suite 202 Bedford 24523-2000 k.guzi@co.bedford.va.us	540 586-7601 540 586-0406
		Peter M. Stephenson (as of 7/09) Town Manager Town of Smithfield P.O. Box 246 Smithfield 23431 pstephenson@smithfieldva.gov	757 365-4200 757 365-9508
Washington	Washington City/County Management Association wccma.org	Bunyamin (Ben) B. Yazici (until 9/09) City Manager City of Sammamish 801 228th Avenue, S.E. Sammamish 98075 byazici@ci.sammamish.wa.us	425 836-7902 425 295-0600
West Virginia	West Virginia City Management Association	John A. DeStefano (until 8/09) City Manager City of Follansbee P.O. Box 606 Follansbee 26037-0606 jdestefano@1st.net	304 527-1330 304 527-2615
Wisconsin.	Wisconsin City/County Management Association wcma-wi.org	Lisa A. Kuss (until 6/09) City Administrator City of Clintonville 50 10th Street Clintonville 54929-1513 lkuss@clintonvillewi.org	715 823-7600 715 823-1352
		Mark A. Rohloff (as of 7/09) City Manager City of Oshkosh 215 Church Avenue Oshkosh 54901-4747 mrohloff@ci.oshkosh.wi.us	920 236-5000 920 236-5039
Wyoming, Idaho, ... Montana, North Dakota, and South Dakota	Great Open Spaces City Management Association	David W. Waind (until 5/09) City Manager City of Minot 515 2nd Avenue, S.W. Minot 58701-3739 waind@web.ci.minot.nd.us	701 857-4750 701 857-4751
		Chris A. Kukulski (as of 6/09) City Manager City of Bozeman P.O. Box 1230 Bozeman 59771-1230 ckukulski@bozeman.net	406 582-2306

Directory 1/6   INTERNATIONAL MUNICIPAL MANAGEMENT ASSOCIATIONS

State, province, or country	Association and Web site	President, address, e-mail address	Phone number Fax number
Australia	Local Government Managers Australia (LGMA) lgma.org.au	Ray Pincombe President/CEO City of Unley, South Australia P.O. Box 1 Unley, SA 5061 rpincombe@unley.sa.gov.au	08 83-72 5111 08 82-71-4886
Canada	Canadian Association of Municipal Administrators (CAMA) camacam.ca	Owen Tobert City of Calgary P.O. Box 2100 Postal Station M #8003 Calgary, AB T2P 2M5 owen.tobert@calgary.ca	403 268-8163 403 537-3027
Denmark	National Association of Chief Executives in Danish Municipalities (KOMDIR) komdir.dk	Jens Chr. Birch President Naestved Municipality Teatergade 8 4700 Naestved Jebir@naestved.dk	45-5588-500
India	City Managers' Association Gujarat cmag-india.com	R. Tripathi President City Managers' Association Gujarat Ahmedabad Municipal Corporation Office West Zone Usmanpura Crossroad, Ahmedabad 380013	91-079-27561184 91-079-27551595

Directory 1/6   **INTERNATIONAL MUNICIPAL MANAGEMENT ASSOCIATIONS**
continued

State, province, or country	Association and Web site	President, address, e-mail address	Phone number Fax number
	City Managers' Association Karnataka cmakarnataka.com	Dr. S Subramanya, IAS President City Managers' Association Karnataka 21st Floor, Public Utility Building, M.G. Road Bangalore 560001 cmakar@gmail.com	080-25590333 080-25590332
	City Managers' Association Orissa	Shri. Deoranjan Kumar Singh, IAS Vice Chairman Bhubaneswar Development Authority Sachibalaya Marg Bhubaneswar 751001 cmao@sancharnet.in	91-674-2395614 91-674-2390633
Indonesia	Association of Indonesia Municipalities (APEKS) apeksi.or.id	Dr. H. Jusuf SK President Contact: Dr. H Sarimun Hadisaputra Executive Director Century Tower, Lt. 10 R. 1006 Gedung ASPACK Kuningan Jl. Rasuna Said DAv. X-2 No.4 Jakarta Selatan 12950 Staff Liaison Rusfi Yunairi: rusfi@apeksi.or.id	62-21-5226773 62-21-5226775
Ireland.	County and City Managers' Association	Ms. Anne O'Keeffe Director Office for Local Authority Management County and City Manager's Association Floor 2, Cumberland House Fenian Street Dublin 2 aokeeffe@lgmsb.ie	35-31-609-5960
Israel.	Union of Local Authorities in Israel ulai.org.il	Avi Rabinovitch Deputy Director General Rehov Ha'Arbaa 19, 10th Floor Tel Aviv 64739 int@ulai.org.il	972-3-684-4210 972-3-684-4211
Mexico	Mexican Association of Municipalities (AMMAC) ammac.org.mx	Ruben Fernandez Executive Director Adolfo Prieto 1634, Colonia Del Valle Distrito Federa 03100 rfernandez@ammac.org.mx	55-55-24-4020
Nepal	Municipal Association of Nepal muannepal.org.np	Sushil Gyewali Executive Secretary 190 Niketan Marg, Dillibazar Kathmandu muan@ntc.net.np	97-71-443-6725 97-71-441-8671
Netherlands	Dutch City Managers Association gemeentesecretaris.nl	Piet J. Buytels President P.O. Box 1501 3100 EA Schiedam Schiedam vgs@vng.nl	31-10-246-5711
New Zealand.	New Zealand Society of Local Government Managers solgm.org.nz	Steve Parry Chief Executive Gore District Council 29 Civic Avenue P.O. Box 8 Gore sparry@goredc.govt.nz	03 209 0330 03 209 0357
Norway	Norwegian Forum of Municipal Executives	Finn Brevig Executive Director	47-21-50-20-20 47-41-50-20-20
Russia.	Local Government Research Center	Victor Pankraschenko President/CEO 6 Zubovskaya Street, Suite 314 Moscow 199121 ceo@rncm.ru	7-495-229-00-58
Slovakia	Slovak City Managers' Association apums.sk	Peter Agh City Manager City of Nove Zamky Hlavne namestie 10 94035 Nove Zamky Slovakia, E.U. Peter.agh@novezamky.sk	42-1-902-987-601
	Local Government Development Center apums.sk	Luba Vavrova Program Coordinator Centrum rozvoja samospráv Local Government Development Center Laurinská 2 811 01 Bratislava vavrova@crs.sk	4-21-2-54-248-024 4-21-2-54-248-264

Directory 1/6 **INTERNATIONAL MUNICIPAL MANAGEMENT ASSOCIATIONS**
continued

State, province, or country	Association and Web site	President, address, e-mail address	Phone number Fax number
South Africa	Institute for Local Government Management of South Africa ilgm.co.za	Pumza Macozoma Acting Executive Director 2 President Street Newtown, Johannesburg P.O. Box 30761 Braamfontein 2017 admin@ilgm.co.za macozomap@ilgm.co.za	27-11-838-800 27-11-298-5293
South Korea	Korean Urban Management Association kruma.org	Choon Hee Ro Chairman Kyonggi Research Institute 179-26, Pajang-Dong, Jangan-Gu Seoul City, Kyonggi Province 440-290 choonr@kangnam.ac.kr	82-331-222-4800 82-331-224-5434
Sweden.	Association of Swedish City Managers	Anna Sandborgh Chair Karlstads kommun Kommunledningskontoret 651 84 Karlstad anna.sandborgh@karlstad.se	46-5-429-5102
United Kingdom	Society of Local Authority Chief Executives (SOLACE) solace.org.uk	Byron Davies President/Chief Executive City of Cardiff County Hall, Atlantic Wharf Cardiff, WL CF10 4UW bdavies@cardiff.gov.uk	44-29-2087-2401

Directory 1/7 **U.S. STATE ASSOCIATIONS OF COUNTIES**

State	State association, address, and Web site	Executive director	Phone number Fax number
Alabama	Association of County Commissioners of Alabama, 100 North Jackson Street, Montgomery 36104 acca-online.org	O. H. Sharpless	334 263-7594 334 263-7678
Alaska	Alaska Municipal League, 217 Second Street, Suite 200, Juneau 99801-1267 akml.org	Kathie Wasserman	907 586-1325 907 463-5480
Arizona	Arizona Association of Counties, 1910 West Jefferson, Suite 1, Phoenix 85009-5223 azcounties.org	Nicole Stickler	602 252-6563 602 254-0969
	County Supervisors Association of Arizona, 1905 West Washington Street, Suite 100, Phoenix 85009-5274 countysupervisors.org	Craig Sullivan	602 252-5521 602 253-3227
Arkansas	Association of Arkansas Counties, 1415 West Third Street, Little Rock 72201-1810 arcounties.org	Eddie Jones	501 372-7550 501 372-0611
California	California State Association of Counties, 1100 K Street, Suite 101, Sacramento 95814-3932 csac.counties.org	Paul McIntosh	916 327-7500 916 441-5507
Colorado	Colorado Counties, Inc., 800 Grant Street, Suite 500, Denver 80203 ccionline.org	Larry Kallenberger	303 861-4076 303 861-2818
Delaware	Delaware Association of Counties, 12 North Washington Avenue, Lewes 19958-1806	Richard Cecil	302 645-0432 302 645-2232
Florida	Florida Association of Counties, P.O. Box 549, Tallahassee 32302-0549 fl-counties.com	Christopher Holley	850 922-4300 850 488-7501
Georgia	Association County Commissioners of Georgia, 50 Hurt Plaza, Suite 1000, Atlanta 30303-2954 accg.org	Jerry Griffin	404 522-5022 404 525-2477
Hawaii	Hawaii State Association of Counties, 4396 Rice Street, Suite 206, Lihue 96766 hawaii-county.com/	Michael Victorino	808 270-7760 808 270-7639
Idaho	Idaho Association of Counties, P.O. Box 1623, Boise 83701-1623 idcounties.org	Daniel Chadwick	208 345-9126 208 345-0379
Illinois	Illinois Association of County Board Members, 413 West Monroe Street, 2nd Floor, Springfield 62704-1959 ilcounty.org/	Kelly Murray	217 528-5331 217 528-5562
	Metro Counties of Illinois, 1303 Brandywine Road, Libertyville 60048-3000	Dwight Magalis	847 816-0889 847 247-9915
	United Counties Council of Illinois, 217 East Monroe Street, Suite 101, Springfield 62701-1743 unitedcounties.com/default.asp	W. Michael McCreery	217 544-5585 217 544-5571
Indiana	Association of Indiana Counties, 101 West Ohio Street, Suite 1575, Indianapolis 46204-1970 indianacounties.org	David Bottorff	317 684-3710 317 684-3713
Iowa	Iowa State Association of Counties, 501 S.W. Seventh Street, Suite Q, Des Moines 50309-4540 iowacounties.org	William Peterson	515 244-7181 515 244-6397
Kansas	Kansas Association of Counties, 300 S.W. Eighth Street, 3rd Floor, Topeka 66603-3912 kansascounties.org	Randall Allen	785 272-2585 785 272-3585

Directory 1/7   **U.S. STATE ASSOCIATIONS OF COUNTIES**
continued

State	State association, address, and Web site	Executive director	Phone number / Fax number
Kentucky	Kentucky Association of Counties, 380 King's Daughter Drive, Frankfort 40601-4106 kaco.org	Bob Arnold	502 223-7667 502 223-1502
Louisiana	Police Jury Association of Louisiana, 707 North Seventh Street, Baton Rouge 70802-5327 lpgov.org	Roland Dartez	225 343-2835 225 336-1344
Maine	Maine County Commissioners Association, 11 Columbia Street, Augusta 04330-6809 mainecounties.org	Robert Howe	207 623-4697 207 622-4437
Maryland	Maryland Association of Counties, 169 Conduit Street, Annapolis 21401-2512 mdcounties.org	Michael Sanderson	410 269-0043 410 268-1775
Massachusetts	Massachusetts Association of County Commissioners, 614 High Street, Dedham 02027-0310	Peter Collins	781 461-6105 781 326-6480
Michigan	Michigan Association of Counties, 935 North Washington Avenue, Lansing 48906-5137 micounties.org	Timothy K. McGuire	517 372-5374 517 482-4599
Minnesota	Association of Minnesota Counties, 125 Charles Avenue, St. Paul 55103-2108 mncounties.org	James A. Mulder	651 789-4325 651 224-6540
Mississippi	Mississippi Association of Supervisors, 793 North President Street, Jackson 39202-3002 masnetwork.org	Derrick Surrette	601 353-2741 601 353-2749
Missouri	Missouri Association of Counties, 516 East Capitol Avenue, P.O. Box 234, Jefferson City 65102-0234 mocounties.com	Dick Burke	573 634-2120 573 634-3549
Montana	Montana Association of Counties, 2715 Skyway Drive, Helena 59602-1213 maco.cog.mt.us	L. Harold Blattie	406 444-4360 406 442-5238
Nebraska	Nebraska Association of County Officials, 625 South 14th Street, Lincoln 68508-2749 nacone.org	Larry Dix	402 434-5660 402 434-5673
Nevada	Nevada Association of Counties, 201 South Roop Street, Suite 101, Carson City 89701-4790 nvnaco.org	Jeffrey Fontaine	775 883-7863 775 883-7398
New Hampshire	New Hampshire Association of Counties, 46 Donovan Street, Suite 2, Concord 03301-2624 nhcounties.org	Betsy B. Miller	603 224-9222 603 224-8312
New Jersey	New Jersey Association of Counties, 150 West State Street, Trenton 08608-1105 njac.org	Celeste Carpiano	609 394-3467 609 989-8567
New Mexico	New Mexico Association of Counties, 613 Old Santa Fe Trail, Santa Fe 87501-0308 nmcounties.org	Paul Gutierrez	505 983-2101 505 983-4396
New York	New York State Association of Counties, 540 Broadway, 5th Floor, Albany 12207-2737 nysac.org	Stephen J. Acquario	518 465-1473 518 465-0506
North Carolina	North Carolina Association of County Commissioners, 215 North Dawson Street, Raleigh 27603-1311 ncacc.org	David F. Thompson	919 715-2893 919 733-1065
North Dakota	North Dakota Association of Counties, 1661 Capitol Way, Bismarck 58502-0877 ndaco.org	Mark Johnson	701 328-7300 701 328-7308
Ohio	County Commissioners Association of Ohio, 209 East State Street, Columbus 43215-4309 ccao.org	Larry L. Long	614 221-5627 614 221-6986
Oklahoma	Association of County Commissioners of Oklahoma City, 429 N.E. 50th Street, Oklahoma City 73105-1815 okacco.com	Gayle Ward	405 516-5313 405 516-5333
Oregon	Association of Oregon Counties, P.O. Box 12729, Salem 97309-0729 aocweb.org	Mike McArthur	503 585-8351 503 373-7876
Pennsylvania	County Commissioners Association of Pennsylvania, P.O. Box 60769, Harrisburg 17106-0769 pacounties.org	Douglas E. Hill	717 232-7554 717 232-2162
South Carolina	South Carolina Association of Counties, 1919 Thurmond Mall, Columbia 29202-8207 sccounties.org	Michael B. Cone	803 252-7255 803 252-0379
South Dakota	South Dakota Association of County Officials, 300 East Capitol Avenue, Suite 2, Pierre 57501-3160 sdcounties.org	Eric Erickson	605 224-1968 605 224-9128
	South Dakota Association of County Commissioners, 222 East Capitol Avenue, Suite 1, Pierre 57501 sdcc.govoffice2.com	Bob Wilcox	605 224-4554 605 224-4833
Tennessee	Tennessee County Services Association, 226 Capitol Boulevard, Suite 700, Nashville 37219-1896 tncounties.org	David Seivers	615 532-3767 615 532-3769
Texas	Texas Association of Counties, 1210 San Antonio Street, Austin 78701 county.org	Karen Norris	512 478-8753 512 478-0519
Utah	Utah Association of Counties, 5397 South Vine Street, Salt Lake City 84107-6757 uacnet.org	L. Brent Gardner	801 265-1331 801 265-9485
Virginia	Virginia Association of Counties, 1001 East Broad Street, Suite LL20, Richmond 23219-1929 vaco.org	James Campbell	804 788-6652 804 788-0083
Washington	Washington Association of County Officials, 206 Tenth Avenue, S.E., Olympia 98501-1333 wacounties.org/waco	Deborah D. Wilke	360 753-7319 360 664-2812
	Washington State Association of Counties, 206 Tenth Avenue, S.E., Olympia 98501-1333 wacounties.org/wsac	Eric Johnson	360 753-1886 360 753-2842
West Virginia	County Commissioners' Association of West Virginia, 2309 Washington Street East, Charleston 25311-2312 polsci.wvu.edu/wv	Vivian G. Parsons	304 345-4639 304 346-3512
	West Virginia Association of Counties, 2211 Washington Street East, Charleston 25311-2218 wvcounties.org	Patricia Hamilton	304 346-0591 304 346-0592
Wisconsin	Wisconsin Counties Association, 22 East Mifflin Street, Suite 900, Madison 53703-4247 wicounties.org	Mark D. O'Connell	608 663-7188 608 663-7189
Wyoming	Wyoming County Commissioners Association, P.O. Box 86, Cheyenne 82003-0086 wyo-wcca.org	Joseph Evans	307 632-5409 307 632-6533

Directory 1/8   U.S. COUNCILS OF GOVERNMENTS RECOGNIZED BY ICMA

Local government	Appointed administrator	Phone number
ALABAMA–4		
Central Alabama Regional Planning and Development Commission	Bob Grasser	334 262-4300
East Alabama Regional Planning and Development Commission	James W. Curtis	256 237-6741
Regional Planning Commission of Greater Birmingham	Charles E. Ball	205 251-8139
South Central Alabama Development Commission	Tyson Howard	334 244-6903
ARIZONA–2		
Maricopa Association of Governments	Dennis Smith	602 254-6300
Pima Association of Governments	Gary G. Hayes, AICP	520 792-1093
ARKANSAS–3		
Metroplan	Jim McKenzie	501 372-3300
Northwest Arkansas Regional Planning Commission	Jeff Hawkins	479 751-7125
White River Planning & Development District	Van C. Thomas	870 793-5233
CALIFORNIA–10		
Association of Bay Area Governments	Henry L. Gardner	510 464-7900
Council of Fresno County Governments	Barbara Goodwin	559 233-4148
Sacramento Area Council of Governments	Mike McKeever	916 321-9000
Sacramento Transportation Authority	Brian Williams	916 323-0080
San Bernardino Associated Governments	Deborah Robinson Barmack	909 884-8276
San Diego Association of Governments	Kenneth E. Sulzer	619 595-5300
Santa Barbara County Association of Governments	Jim Kemp	805 961-8900
Southern California Association of Governments	Mark Pisano	818 236-1800
Stanislaus Area Association of Governments	Vince Harris	209 558-7830
Western Riverside Council of Governments	Rick Bishop	909 955-7985
COLORADO–1		
Denver Regional Council of Governments	Jennifer Schaufele	303 455-1000
DISTRICT OF COLUMBIA–1		
Metropolitan Washington Council of Governments	David J. Robertson	202 962-3200
FLORIDA–2		
Solid Waste Authority of Palm Beach County	John Booth	561 640-4000
Tampa Bay Regional Planning Council	Manny L. Pumariega	727 570-5151
GEORGIA–3		
Atlanta Regional Commission	Charles C. Krautler	404 463-3100
Middle Georgia Regional Development Center	James C. Tonn	478 751-6160
Southeast Georgia Regional Development Center	Lace Futch	912 285-6097
IDAHO–1		
Panhandle Area Council	James Deffenbaugh	208 772-0584
ILLINOIS–9		
Bi-State Regional Commission	Denise Bulat	309 793-6300
Champaign County Regional Planning Commission	Denny Inman	217 328-3313
DuPage Mayors and Managers Conference	Mark Baloga	630 571-0480
Lake County Municipal League	Christine D. Wilson	847 543-8160
North Central Illinois Council of Governments	Nora Fesco-Ballerine	815 875-3396
Northwest Municipal Conference	Mark Fowler	847 296-9200
South Central Illinois Regional Planning and Development Commission	Fred Walker	618 548-4234
Southwestern Illinois Metropolitan and Regional Planning Commission	Kevin Terveer	618 344-4250
Tri-County Regional Planning Commission	Terry D. Kohlbuss	309 694-9330
IOWA–1		
Midas Council of Governments	Stephen F. Hoesel	515 576-7183
KENTUCKY–4		
Barren River Area Development District	Dot Darby-Paschall	270 781-2381
Big Sandy Area Development District	Sandy Runyon	606 886-2374
Lincoln Trail Area Development District	James E. Greer	270 769-2393
Northern Kentucky Area Development District	John Mays	859 283-1885

Local government	Appointed administrator	Phone number
MARYLAND–2		
Baltimore Metropolitan Council	Larry Klimovitz	410 732-9570
Tri-County Council For Southern Maryland	David M. Jenkins	301 274-1922
MICHIGAN–1		
Southeast Michigan Council of Governments	Paul Tait	313 961-4266
MISSISSIPPI–1		
Central Mississippi Planning and Development District	F. Clarke Holmes	601 981-1511
MISSOURI–3		
East-West Gateway Coordinating Council	Les Sterman	314 421-4220
Mid-America Regional Council	David A. Warm	816 474-4240
South Central Ozark Council of Governments	James T. Dancy	417 256-4226
NEW MEXICO–2		
Middle Rio Grande Council of Governments	Lawrence D. Rael	505 247-1750
Southwest New Mexico Council of Governments	Don Rauch	505 388-1509
NEW YORK–1		
Capital District Regional Planning Commission	Chungchin Chen	518 453-0850
NORTH CAROLINA–5		
Centralina Council of Governments	Albert R. Sharp Jr.	704 372-2416
Lumber River Council of Governments	James B. Perry	910 618-5533
Piedmont Triad Council of Governments	Randall L. Billings	336 294-4950
Region L-Upper Coastal Plain Council of Governments	Greg T. Godard	252 446-0411
Region P-Eastern Carolina Council of Governments	Larry Moolenaar	258 638-3185
OHIO–4		
Miami Valley Regional Planning Commission	P. Michael Robinette	937 223-6323
Ohio-Kentucky-Indiana Regional Council of Governments	James Q. Duane	513 621-6300
Ohio Mid-Eastern Governments Association	John A. Quinlan	740 439-4471
Toledo Metropolitan Area Council of Governments	Anthony L. Reams	419 241-9155
OKLAHOMA–2		
Association of Central Oklahoma Governments	Zach D. Taylor	405 234-2264
Central Oklahoma Economic Development District	Wayne J. Manley	405 273-6410
OREGON–3		
Lane Council of Governments	George W. Kloeppel	541 687-4283
Mid-Columbia Economic Development District	Lee Curtis	541 296-2266
Oregon Cascades West Council of Governments	William R. Wagner	541 967-8720
SOUTH CAROLINA–3		
Central Midlands Council of Governments	Norman Whitaker III	803 376-5390
South Carolina Appalachian Council of Governments	Robert M. Strother	864 242-9733
Upper Savannah Council of Governments	Patricia C. Hartung	864 941-8050
SOUTH DAKOTA–2		
Northeast Council of Governments	Eric Senger	605 622-2595
Planning and Development District III	Greg Henderson	605 665-4408
TEXAS–15		
Alamo Area Council of Governments	Gloria C. Arriaga	210 362-5200
Ark-Tex Council of Governments	L. D. Williamson	903 832-8636
Capital Area Planning Council	Betty Voights	512 916-6000
Central Texas Council of Governments	Jim Reed	254 939-1801
Coastal Bend Council of Governments	John P. Buckner	361 883-5743
Concho Valley Council of Governments	Jeffrey K. Sutton	915 944-9666
Deep East Texas Council of Governments	Walter G. Diggles	409 384-5704
Heart of Texas Council of Governments	Kenneth L. Simmons	254 756-6631
Houston-Galveston Area Council	Jack Steele	713 627-3200
Nortex Regional Planning Commission	Dennis Wilde	940 322-5281
North Central Texas Council of Governments	R. Michael Eastland	817 640-3300
Panhandle Regional Planning Commission	Gary Pitner	806 372-3381
South Plains Association of Governments	Tim Pierce	806 762-8721

Directory 1/8   **U.S. COUNCILS OF GOVERNMENTS RECOGNIZED BY ICMA**
continued

Local government	Appointed administrator	Phone number
Texoma Council of Governments	Frances Pelley	903 893-2161
West Central Texas Council of Governments	Brad Helbert	325 672-8544
UTAH–1		
Five County Association of Governments .	John S. Williams	435 673-3548
VIRGINIA–5		
Crater Planning District Commission	Dennis K. Morris	804 861-1666
Hampton Roads Planning District Commission	Dwight L. Farmer	757 461-3200
Northern Neck Planning District Commission	Jerry W. Davis	804 333-1900
Northern Virginia Planning District Commission	G. Mark Gibb	703 642-0700

Local government	Appointed administrator	Phone number
West Piedmont Planning District Commission	Robert W. Dowd	276 638-3987
WASHINGTON–1		
Benton-Franklin Regional Council	Gwen Rasmussen	509 943-9185
WEST VIRGINIA–3		
Bel-O-Mar Regional Council	William C. Phipps	304 242-1800
Mid-Ohio Valley Regional Council	Jim Mylott	304 422-4993
Region One Planning and Development Council	Norman L. Kirkham	304 431-7225
WISCONSIN–1		
East Central Wisconsin Regional Planning Commission	Harlan P. Kiesow	920 751-4770

Directory 1/9   **OFFICIALS IN U.S. MUNICIPALITIES 2,500 AND OVER IN POPULATION**

Data collection

The names appearing in this directory were obtained from the ICMA database of local government employees. Local governments that have provided updated information are designated by an asterisk (*). For those that have not, the directories show the names of officials from the most recent update.

Form of government

CM   Council-manager
CO   Commission

MC   Mayor-council
RT   Representative town meeting
TM   Town meeting

Municipal designation

b   borough
c   city
d   district
pl   plantation
t   town
tp   township
v   village

Population

Population figures are rounded; 14,500 will appear as 15.

(..) Less than 500 population

Other codes

. . . Data not reported or not applicable

Jurisdiction	Type	Form of govern- ment	2000 Popu- lation	Main telephone number	Chief elected official	Appointed administrator	Clerk of the governing board	Chief financial officer	Fire chief	Police chief	Public works director
ALABAMA											
Abbeville	* c	MC	2	(334) 585-6444	Ryan Blalock	James Giganti	. . .	. . .	Ryan Feggin	Mike Jones	Robert Wright
Alabaster	c	MC	22	(205) 664-6800	Steven Rauch	. . .	Marsha Massey	. . .	John Cochran	Larry Rollen	Charles Howell
Albertville	c	MC	17	(256) 891-8282	Carl Pruett	. . .	Carolyn Camp	Jonathan Howard	Johnny Hix	Benny Womack	Chuck Rogers
Alexander City	c	MC	15	(256) 329-6730	Donald McClellan	. . .	Luise Hardman	. . .	Ronnie Betts	James Hardman	M. Brewer
Aliceville	* c	MC	2	(205) 373-6611	William McKinzey	Mary Bess Paluzzi	. . .	. . .	David Jackson	Tonnie Jones	Leroy Holladay
Andalusia	c	MC	8	(334) 222-3312	Jerry Andrews	. . .	Pam Steele	. . .	Ethan Dorsey	Wilbur Williams	James Hogg
Anniston	c	CM	24	(256) 231-7705	Hoyt Howell	. . .	Alan Atkinson	George Vick	William Fincher	John Dryden	Dale Garrett
Arab	t	MC	7	(256) 586-8128	. . .	. . .	. . .	. . .			
Athens	c	MC	18	(256) 233-8727	James Williams	. . .	John Hamilton	. . .	Cliff Christopher	Wayne Harper	James Rich
Atmore	c	MC	7	(251) 368-2253	Howard Shell	. . .	Rebecca Smith	. . .	Gerry McGhee	Jason Dean	Don Whatley
Attalla	* c	MC	6	(256) 538-9986	Jane Phillips	. . .	Sharon Jones	. . .	Robert Dillard	Joe Hereford	James Bohannon
Auburn	c	CM	42	(334) 501-7260	. . .	Charles Duggan	. . .	Andrea Jackson	Larry Langley	. . .	Jeffery Ramsey
Bay Minette	c	MC	7	(251) 580-1619	William Dobbins	. . .	Rita Findley	. . .	Jesse Gregson	Michael Rowland	Lamar Hadley
Bessemer	c	CO	29	(205) 424-4060	Edward May	. . .	. . .	. . .	Chester Kendrick	Oliver Adams	Frank Thompson
Birmingham	c	MC	242	(205) 254-2431	Bernard Kincaid	. . .	Paula Smith	Michael Johnson	Dwayne Murray	Annetta Nunn	Stephen Fancher
Boaz	* c	MC	7	(256) 593-9537	Timothy Walker	. . .	Jill Bright	. . .	Olen Morrison	Terry Davis	Jackie Pullen
Brent	c	MC	4	(205) 926-4643	Jerry Pow	. . .	Linda Cox	. . .	Dennis Stripling	. . .	Bill Hubbard
Brewton	c	MC	5	(251) 809-1770	Ted Jennings	John Angel	. . .	. . .	Lawrence Weaver	Monte McGougin	Danny Howard
Bridgeport	t	MC	2	(256) 495-3892	. . .	. . .	. . .	. . .			
Brighton	c	MC	3	(205) 428-9547	Eddie Cooper	. . .	Viola Jones	. . .	. . .	Samuel Greene	. . .
Brundidge	* c	MC	2	(334) 735-2321	Jimmy Ramage	William Thomas	. . .	. . .	. . .	Moses Davenport	Bobby Ellsworth
Calera	c	MC	3	(205) 668-3500	. . .	. . .	. . .	. . .			
Centreville	c	MC	2	(205) 926-4995	Debbie Martin	Donald Penny	Tina Crumpler	. . .	. . .	Mike Nichols	Roger Burnett
Chickasaw	c	MC	6	(251) 452-6550	Jim Trout	. . .	Mary McLean	. . .	. . .	Clarence Hollinghead	Sam Rawls
Childersburg	c	MC	4	(256) 378-5521	Billy Meeks	. . .	Sandra Donahoo	. . .	Douglas Blair	Charles Brown	. . .
Citronelle	c	MC	3	(251) 866-7973	Rannel Presnell	. . .	Diane Barnett	. . .	. . .	Raymond Reid	. . .
Clanton	* c	MC	7	(205) 755-1105	Billy Joe Driver	. . .	Debra Orange	. . .	David Driver	Brian Stilwell	. . .
Columbiana	c	MC	3	(205) 669-5800	J. Allan Lowe	. . .	Teresa Collum	. . .	. . .	Michael Lann	Lewis King
Cordova	t	MC	2	(205) 483-9266	Jack Scott	. . .	Elaine Stover	. . .	Dean Harbison	John Bentley	. . .
Cullman	c	MC	13	(256) 775-7124	Donald Green	. . .	Lucille Galin	. . .	Dennis Murray	Kenny Culpepper	Peter Nassetta
Dadeville	c	MC	3	(256) 825-9242	. . .	. . .	. . .	. . .	. . .	. . .	Mike Gilley
Daleville	* c	MC	4	(334) 598-2345	Wess Etheredge	. . .	Angelia Filmore	. . .	. . .	. . .	. . .
Daphne	t	CO	16	(251) 621-9000	Fred Small	. . .	David Cohen	Kimberly Briley	Andrew Hanson	David Carpenter	Kenneth Eslava
Decatur	c	MC	53	(256) 341-4500	Don Kyle	. . .	Gail Busbey	Tony Stapler	Charlie Johnson	Joel Gilliam	Brent Mullins
Demopolis	c	MC	7	(334) 289-0577	Austin Caldwell	. . .	Vickie Taylor	. . .	George Davenport	Jeff Manuel	Clarence Brooker
Dothan	* c	CM	57	(334) 615-3000	Pat Thomas	Michael West	Pam McCoy	Angela Palmer	Larry Williams	John Powell	Jerry Corbin
East Brewton	c	MC	2	(251) 867-6092	Terry Clark	. . .	Karen Singleton	. . .	Joey Shell	Wilson Mallard	William Dunaway
Elba	c	MC	4	(334) 897-2333	James Grimes	Wayne Grantham	. . .	. . .	Danny Jordan	Freddy Hanchey	. . .
Enterprise	c	MC	21	(334) 347-1211	Kenneth Boswell	. . .	Steven Hicks	. . .	Byron Herring	Thomas Jones	James Kilgore
Eufaula	* c	MC	13	(334) 688-2000	Jay Jaxon	. . .	Joy White	. . .	Lamar Register	J. C. West	Tim Brannon
Evergreen	c	MC	3	(251) 578-1574	. . .	. . .	. . .	. . .			
Fairfield	c	MC	12	(205) 788-2492	Larry Langford	. . .	Melvin Turner	. . .	Earl Allred	Laird Sharpe	Daniel Fields
Fairhope	c	MC	12	(251) 928-2136	. . .	. . .	. . .	. . .	. . .	. . .	. . .
Fayette	c	MC	4	(205) 932-5367	Ray Nelson	. . .	Dawn Clapp	. . .	Robert Fulmer	Euel Hall	. . .
Florence	c	MC	36	(256) 760-6400	James Frost	. . .	. . .	Dan Barger	Charles Cochran	Ricky Singleton	. . .
Foley	c	MC	7	(251) 943-1545	R. Timothy Russell	A. Perry Wilbourne	. . .	. . .	James Hinton	. . .	. . .
Fort Payne	c	MC	12	(256) 845-1524	J. Stout	. . .	James McGee	. . .	Arthur Hill	John Walker	. . .
Fultondale	c	MC	6	(205) 841-4481	James Lowery	. . .	Jane Hicks	. . .	. . .	Byron Pigg	. . .
Gadsden	c	CO	38	(205) 549-4550	Steve Means	Eugene Harrell	Iva Nelson	Lisa Rosser	Stephan Carroll	Richard Crouch	Brian Stovall
Gardendale	c	MC	11	(205) 631-8789	Kenneth Clemons	. . .	Keith Mosley	. . .	Clinton Doss	Mike Walker	Jeff Holliyan
Geneva	c	MC	4	(334) 684-2485	Karen Simmons	. . .	Lisa Johnson	. . .	Ben Latimer	Louis Lindsey	Donald Campbell
Glencoe	t	MC	5	(205) 492-1424	. . .	. . .	. . .	. . .	. . .	. . .	. . .
Graysville	c	MC	2	(205) 674-5643	. . .	. . .	Judy Flippo	. . .	Jeffrey Wesley	. . .	. . .
Greensboro	c	MC	2	(334) 624-8119	John Owens	. . .	. . .	. . .	. . .	Claude Hamilton	. . .
Greenville	c	MC	7	(334) 382-2647	Dexter McLendon	. . .	Linda Vanden Bosch	. . .	Michael Phillips	William Ingram	Milton Luckie
Gulf Shores	c	MC	5	(251) 968-2425	David Bodenhamer	Stephen Garman	Renee Moore	Shirley Bowyer	Joseph McClusky	Arthur Bourne	Charles Hamilton
Guntersville	c	MC	7	(256) 571-7560	James Townson	. . .	Betty Jones	. . .	James Brown	J. Scott Walls	Mike Bush
Haleyville	c	MC	4	(205) 486-3121	Larry Albright	. . .	. . .	. . .	Ralph Edwards	Kyle Reogas	Mike Taylor
Hamilton	t	MC	6	(205) 921-2121	Ray Harper	. . .	Sue Page	. . .	Barron Wiginton	Billy Owen	Steve Cox
Hartford	c	MC	2	(334) 588-2245	Gene Brannon	. . .	Vicky Marsh	. . .	. . .	Greg Adams	Jimmy Bottoms
Hartselle	* c	MC	12	(256) 773-2565	Dwight Tankersley	. . .	Rita Lee	. . .	Steve Shelton	Ronald Puckett	Byron Turney
Headland	c	MC	3	(334) 693-3365	Donald Smith	Jack Manley	Elizabeth White	. . .	Eric Lawrence	Fred Williams	Daniel Vinson
Heflin	c	MC	3	(256) 463-2290	Anna Berry	. . .	Terri Daulton	. . .	Rudy Rooks	Neil Payne	. . .
Helena	* c	MC	10	(205) 663-2161	Charles Penhale	. . .	Amanda Traywick	. . .	Peter Valenti	Douglas Jones	Brian Hinds
Hokes Bluff	t	MC	4	(205) 492-2414	Tim Langdale	S. Hamilton-Burns	. . .	. . .	Mike Howington	Harvey Scales	Wade Reed
Homewood	c	MC	25	(205) 877-8600	Barry McCulley	. . .	Linda Cook	Danny Panos	John Bresnan	Burke Swearingen	David McAshe
Hoover	c	MC	62	(205) 444-7500	Tony Petelos	. . .	Linda Crump	Robert Yeager	Thomas Bradley	Robert Berry	Thomas Daniel
Hueytown	c	MC	15	(205) 491-7010	Delor Baumann	. . .	Janice Wilhite	. . .	James Shelton	Doug McBee	Willie Hegler
Huntsville	c	MC	158	(256) 427-5000	Loretta Spencer	Terry Hatfield	. . .	Randall Taylor	Phillip Underwood	Rex Reynolds	Michael Abbott
Irondale	c	MC	9	(205) 956-9200	Tommy Alexander	Glenda Crowe	Glenda Cox	. . .	Randy Davis	Jerry McIntosh	Dexter Davis
Jackson	c	MC	5	(251) 246-2461	. . .	Jesse Miller	Betty Powell	. . .	. . .	Charles Burge	Kevin Woodson
Jacksonville	c	MC	8	(205) 435-7611	Jerry Smith	. . .	. . .	Rita Spruiell	Michael Daugherty	Thomas Thompson	Stanley Carr
Jasper	c	MC	14	(205) 221-2100	V. L. Posey	. . .	Kathy Chambless	. . .	Calvin Kluesner	Robert Cain	Glenn Ferguson
Kellyton	t	MC	..	(256) 234-4784	. . .	. . .	. . .	. . .	. . .	. . .	. . .
Lafayette	c	MC	3	(334) 864-9812	Robert Finley	. . .	. . .	. . .	Anthony Wolkerson	Eddie Ware	. . .
Lanett	c	CM	7	(334) 644-2141	Oscar Crawley	Joel Holley	Deborah Daniel	. . .	Tim Jennings	Teddy Morris	Mike Bass
Leeds	* c	MC	10	(205) 699-2585	James Whitfield	. . .	Helen Veasey	. . .	Allen Pierce	Charles Hudson	. . .
Lincoln	c	MC	4	(205) 763-7777	Carroll Watson	. . .	Laura Carmack	. . .	Mike Wesley	Dennis Surrett	Chip Chandler

Directory 1/9 continued — OFFICIALS IN U.S. MUNICIPALITIES 2,500 AND OVER IN POPULATION

Jurisdiction	Type	Form of govern-ment	2000 Popu-lation	Main telephone number	Chief elected official	Appointed administrator	Clerk of the governing board	Chief financial officer	Fire chief	Police chief	Public works director
ALABAMA continued											
Linden	c	MC	2	(334) 295-5051	...	Cheryl Hall	Pamela Duke	...	...	...	Terrence Tyson
Lipscomb	c	MC	2	(205) 428-6374	Simon Speights	Geneva Varnon	...	Deborah Miller	David Horn	Conlin Payne	Charles Burgin
Livingston	c	CM	3	(205) 652-2505	Thomas Tartt	Johnny Meadows	...	...	Terry Peeler	...	James Dial
Luverne	c	MC	2	(334) 335-3741	Joe Sport	...	Charlotte Flynn	...	...	Robert Davis	Guy Simmons
Madison	c	MC	29	(256) 772-5600	Charles Yancura	...	...	Lillie Causey	Ralph Cobb	Cecil Moses	Merlyn Adkins
Marion	c	MC	3	(334) 683-6545	Edward Daniel	...	Carolyn Thomas	...	...	Daron Mack	Jackie Nichols
Midfield	c	MC	5	(205) 923-7578	Carlton McWhorter	James Rhodes	...	...	...	James White	Gary Pratt
Millbrook	c	MC	10	(334) 285-6428	Robert Kelley	...	Teresa Mercer	...	Larry Brown	Kenneth Bradley	...
Mobile *	c	MC	198	(251) 208-7777	Samuel Jones	Alfred Stokes	...	Barbara Malkove	Stephen Dean	Phillip Garrett	John Bell
Monroeville	c	MC	6	(251) 575-2081	Anne Farish	...	Toni McKelvey	...	Eddie Everette	Rudolph Munnerlyn	Robert Sims
Montevallo	c	MC	4	(205) 665-2555	Grady Parker	...	Stephen Gibbs	John Abercrombie	...	Steve Southerland	Raymond Cardwell
Montgomery	c	MC	201	(334) 241-4400	Bobby Bright	...	Brenda Blalock	Lloyd Faulkner	John McKee	John Wilson	...
Moulton	t	MC	3	(256) 974-5191	...	...	Shirley Gilley	...	...	Edward Weatherford	...
Mountain Brook *	c	CM	20	(205) 870-3532	Lawrence Oden	Sam Gaston	...	Steven Boone	Robert Ezekiel	Johnny Stanley	Eddy Tate
Muscle Shoals	t	CO	11	(256) 383-5675	David Bradford	...	Ricky Williams	...	Paul McDougle	Robert Evans	Butch Fleming
Northport	c	CM	19	(205) 339-7000	Harvey Fretwell	Charles Swann	...	...	Daryl Patterson	William Galloway	Larry Boshell
Oneonta *	c	MC	5	(205) 274-2141	Darryl Ray	Edward Lowe	Tammie Noland	...	David Osborn	James Chapman	...
Opelika	c	MC	23	(334) 705-5130	Gary Fuller	John Seymour	Robert Shuman	Robert Price	Terry Adkins	Thomas Mangham	Mike Hilyer
Opp	c	MC	6	(334) 493-4572	...	...	...	...	...	...	...
Orange Beach	c	CM	3	(251) 981-6979	Stephen Russo	...	Cathy Larrimore	...	Michael Robinson	Robert Vinson	William Silvers
Oxford	t	MC	14	(256) 831-7510	Leon Smith	...	Shirley Henson	...	Eugene Smallwood	Stanley Merrill	...
Ozark	c	MC	15	(334) 774-5393	Willis Bunting	...	William Blackwell	...	Dempson Barefield	Tony Spivey	Steven Price
Pelham	t	MC	14	(205) 620-6400	Bobby Hayes	...	Donna Treslar	Tom Seale	Gary Waters	...	Ken Holler
Pell City	c	MC	9	(205) 338-3330	Adam Stocks	...	Marinda Gipson	...	Michael Sewell	Gregory Turley	Mike Martin
Phenix City	c	CM	28	(334) 291-4706	Jeff Hardin	H. H. Roberts	Martha Harris	Steve Smith	Wallace Hunter	Preston Robinson	...
Piedmont	c	MC	5	(256) 447-9007	Charles Fagan	...	William Fann	...	Robert Holbrook	Jimmy Trammell	...
Pleasant Grove	c	MC	9	(205) 744-7221	...	...	...	...	...	...	...
Prattville	c	MC	24	(334) 361-3609	...	...	...	...	Stanley Gann	Alfred Wadsworth	...
Prichard	c	MC	28	(251) 457-3381	...	...	...	...	...	...	...
Rainbow City *	c	MC	8	(256) 442-2511	Terry Calhoun	...	Barbara Wester	...	Melvin Potter	Allan Ragan	...
Rainsville	c	MC	4	(256) 638-6331	Roy Sanderson	...	Judy Lewis	...	Ronnie Helton	Roger Byrd	Rickey Dobbins
Red Bay *	c	MC	3	(256) 356-4473	Bobby Forsythe	...	Linda Holcomb	...	Thomas Strickland	Patrick Creel	...
Roanoke	c	MC	6	(334) 863-4129	...	...	...	...	...	...	...
Russellville	c	MC	8	(256) 332-6060	Johnny Brown	...	Kimberly Wright	...	Joe Mansell	Chris Hargett	...
Saraland	c	MC	12	(251) 675-5103	Thomas Williams	...	Denise Jernigan	...	Ravon Allen	...	Robert Lee
Satsuma	c	MC	5	(251) 675-1440	William Bush	...	Vicki Miller	...	Carey Parker	David Benefield	James Elmore
Scottsboro	c	MC	14	(256) 574-3100	Louis Price	...	Gail Duffey	...	Lonnie Webb	Ralph Dawe	William Johnson
Selma	c	MC	20	(334) 874-2110	James Perkins	...	...	Vickey Locke	Henry Allen	Robert Green	Tommy Smith
Sheffield	c	CO	9	(205) 383-0250	Ian Sanford	...	...	...	Tom Isbell	Warren Aycock	...
Slocomb	c	MC	2	(334) 886-2334	James West	Steve Turkoski	Jo Ann Lindsey	...	Kenneth Ball	...	...
Southside	t	MC	7	(256) 442-9775	Wally Burns	...	Cynthia Osborne	...	...	Charles Diggs	Jimmy Whittemore
Spanish Fort	c	MC	5	(251) 626-4884	W. Carter	Mary Williams	...	...	...	...	...
Stevenson	c	MC	1	(256) 437-3000	J. Ricky Steele	...	...	...	Chad McCrary	Danny Winters	Jimmy Guess
Sumiton	t	MC	2	(205) 648-3262	Harry Ellis	...	Judy Glover	...	David Waid	Terry Burnett	George Woods
Sylacauga	c	MC	12	(256) 401-2400	Sam Wright	...	Patricia Carden	...	Thomas Abrams	Louis Zook	Ralph Woolley
Talladega	c	CM	15	(256) 362-8186	Brian York	Michael Stampfler	...	Terri St. James	Danny Warrick	Alan Watson	James Swinford
Tallassee	c	MC	4	(334) 283-6571	Robert Payne	...	Barbara Garnett	...	Steve Dennis	Randy Yarbrough	Donald Haynes
Tarrant City	c	MC	8	(205) 841-2758	Loxcil Tuck	...	...	...	William Hewitt	Jesse Sprayberry	James Phillips
Thomasville *	c	MC	4	(334) 636-5827	Sheldon Day	...	Deborah Ballard	...	Mark Sims	William Hicks	Ronnie McClure
Troy *	c	CO	13	(334) 566-0177	Jimmy Lunsford	...	Alton Starling	...	Thomas Outlaw	Anthony Everage	Vaughn Daniels
Trussville	c	MC	12	(205) 655-7478	Eugene Melton	...	Lynn Porter	...	Russell Ledbetter	Don Sivley	Lewis Simpson
Tuscaloosa	c	MC	77	(205) 349-0125	Alvin DuPont	...	Stan McCracken	Mike Wright	Alan Martin	Ken Swindle	Richard Curry
Tuscumbia	c	CO	7	(256) 383-5463	Billy Shoemaker	...	Carolyn Burns	...	David Cole	Terry Sherron	Hugh Stanley
Tuskegee	c	CM	11	(334) 727-2180	...	Alfred Davis	...	...	...	...	...
Union Springs *	c	MC	3	(334) 738-2720	John McGowan	Cathy Dickerson	Presetta Walker	...	...	Clarence Wheeler	Billy Gholston
Valley *	c	MC	9	(334) 756-5225	Arnold Leak	James Bryan	Martha Cato	...	...	Michael Taylor	John McConnell
Vernon *	c	MC	2	(205) 695-7718	Mary Jones	...	Rebecca Cantrell	...	Larry DuBose	Ted Collins	...
Vestavia Hills	c	MC	24	(205) 978-0100	Charles McCallum	...	Rebecca Leavings	Melvin Turner	Alberto Zaragoza	James Wilson	Perry Glass
Warrior	c	MC	3	(205) 647-0521	Rena Hudson	Nancy Evans	...	...	Tommy Hale	Ray Horn	Frank Coffey
Weaver	c	MC	2	(256) 820-1125	William Kimbrough	...	Teresa Summerlin	...	...	Oscar Bush	Steven Mitchell
Wetumpka	c	MC	5	(334) 567-5147	R. Scott Golden	...	Velma Gober	...	Keith Gilmore	William Pertree	Randy Logan
Winfield	c	MC	4	(205) 487-4337	William West	...	Candace Reed	...	Keith Waldrop	Patrick Creel	...
York	c	MC	2	(205) 392-5231	Howard Kennedy	...	Janice Pringle	...	Cornelius Robinson	...	Ernie Truelove
ALASKA											
Akutan *	c	MC	..	(907) 274-7565	Joe Bereskin	Hermann Scanlan	A. Tcheripanoff	...	...	...	...
Anchorage	c	MC	260	(907) 343-4431	Mark Begich	...	Barbara Gruenstein	Jeffrey Sinz	Craig Goodrich	Walter Monegan	...
Barrow	c	CM	4	(907) 852-5211	Jim Vonderstrasse	...	Gwen Edwardson	Lucy Okpik	...	...	Jeff Leavitt
Bethel	c	CM	5	(907) 543-2047	Hugh Dyment	...	Sandra Modigh	...	George Young	Ben Dudley	Wayne Ogle
Chignik	c	MC	..	(907) 749-2280	Richard Sharpe	...	...	...	...	...	...
Cordova	c	CM	2	(907) 424-6200	Edward Zeine	Scott Hahn	Dixie Lambert	...	Robert Plumb	Kevin Clayton	...
Dillingham	c	CM	2	(907) 842-5211	Alice Ruby	Janice Shilanski	...	Staci Fieser	Norman Heyano	...	Ramon Roque
Fairbanks	c	MC	30	(907) 459-6881	James Hayes	Mark Boyer	Nancy Deleon	Jeffrey Brunsdon	Warren Cummings	James Welch	Dave Jacoby
Fort Yukon	c	CM	..	(907) 662-2479	Antoinette Peter	Richard Carron	Tina Herbert	Jennifer Cannon	G. Benjamin	Lance Fairchild	Grafton Bergman
Galena	c	CM	..	(907) 656-1301	Russ Sweetsir	Walter Wilcox	Jill Chadbourne	Joseph Smith	...	...	Stephen Grube
Homer	c	CM	3	(907) 235-8121	James Hornaday	Walt Wrede	Mary Calhoun	Regina Harville	Robert Painter	Mark Robl	Carey Meyer
Hoonah	c	MC	..	(907) 945-3663	Dennis Gray	Jerry Medina	Georgina Glover	...	Bill Wolfe	...	Mike Morrison
Juneau	c	CM	30	(907) 586-5250	Sarah Smith	Roddy Swope	Laurie Sica	Craig Duncan	Michael Doyle	Richard Gummow	Joseph Buck
Kenai *	c	CM	6	(907) 283-7535	Patricia Porter	Rick Koch	Carol Freas	Terry Eubank	Mike Tilley	Gus Sandahl	Wayne Ogle
Ketchikan	c	CM	7	(907) 228-5631	Robert Weinstein	Karl Amylon	Katherine Suiter	Robert Newell	Richard Leipfert	Gerald Sirevog	Harvey Hansen
King Cove	c	CM	..	(907) 497-2340	...	...	...	...	...	...	...
Kodiak *	c	CM	6	(907) 486-8640	Carolyn Floyd	Linda Freed	Debra Marlar	Mary Munk	Rome Kamai	Charles Kamai	Mark Kozak
Kotzebue	c	CM	3	(907) 442-3401	Frank Greene	Rick Walker	Linda Greene	...	Ronald Monson	Paul Nolton	Herman Reich
Mountain Village	c	MC	..	(907) 591-2929	Harry Wilde	Carol Myre	Melanie Dela Rosa	...	...	Ronald Self	...
Nome	c	CM	3	(907) 443-6600	Denise Michels	R. Romenesko	Leslee Wessel	Caroline Kauer	Wesley Perkins	Craig Moates	...
Palmer	c	CM	4	(907) 745-3271	John Combs	Tom Healy	Janette Bower	Allan Ossakow	Daniel Contini	George Boatright	...
Petersburg *	c	CM	3	(907) 772-4519	Al Dwyer	Richard Underkofler	Kathy O'Rear	Jody Tow	Jerod Cook	Dale Stone	Karl Hagerman
Saint Paul	c	CM	..	(907) 546-2331	...	Linda Snow	...	...	...	...	...
Sand Point	c	CM	..	(907) 383-2696	...	...	...	...	...	...	...
Saxman	c	MC	..	(907) 225-4166	Joe Williams	K. Ludwig-Johnson	Leona Casey	Nancy Nurmi	...	...	Horace Clark
Seldovia	c	CM	..	(907) 234-7643	Tim Volstad	...	Susan Elzig	...	Kim Buchman	Andy Anderson	...
Seward	c	CM	2	(907) 224-4047	...	...	Jean Lewis	Kristin Erchinger	David Squires	Thomas Clemons	William Casey

Directory 1/9 continued **OFFICIALS IN U.S. MUNICIPALITIES 2,500 AND OVER IN POPULATION**

Jurisdiction	Type	Form of govern-ment	2000 Popu-lation	Main telephone number	Chief elected official	Appointed administrator	Clerk of the governing board	Chief financial officer	Fire chief	Police chief	Public works director
ALASKA continued											
Sitka	* c	CO	8	(907) 747-1808	Scott McAdams	James Dinley	Colleen Pellett	Dave Wolff	Scott Elmer	Sheldon Schmitt	Mary Larsen
Skagway	c	CM	..	(907) 983-2297	Tim Bourcy	Robert Ward	Marjorie Harris	...	Martin Beckner	Dennis Spurrier	Grant Lawson
Soldotna	c	CM	3	(907) 262-9107	David Carey	Lawrence Semmens	Teresa Fahning	Joan Miller	...	John Lucking	Stephen Bonebrake
St. Mary'S	c	CM	..	(907) 438-2617	...	Walton Smith	Geraldine Sparks	Richard Alstrom	...	Lee Lamm	Allan Paukan
Unalakleet	c	CM	..	(907) 624-3531	Doris Ivanoff	...	...	...	...	John Wilson	Jay Freytag
Unalaska	c	CM	4	(907) 581-1251	...	...	Debra Mack	...	...	...	Dave Kemp
Valdez	c	CM	4	(907) 835-4313	...	John Hozey	Sheri Pierce	Tom Schantz	George Keeney	William Comer	Robert Thompson
Wasilla	c	MC	5	(907) 373-9055	Dianne Keller	Sandra Garley	Kristie Smithers	Susan Colligan	...	Angella Long	Archie Giddings
Whittier	c	CM	..	(907) 472-2327	Lester Lunceford	...	Brenda Krol	Donald Grande	Doug Maliski	...	Jim Spain
Wrangell	c	CM	2	(907) 874-2381	Valery McCandless	Robert Prunella	Christie Jamieson	Jeffery Jabusch	Timothy Buness	Arlen McCloskey	Robert Caldwell
ARIZONA											
Apache Junction	c	CM	31	(480) 982-8002	...	George Hoffman	Kathleen Connelly	J. Keith Lewis	...	...	Douglas Dobson
Avondale	c	CM	35	(623) 333-1000	Ronald Drake	Charles McClendon	Linda Farris	Kevin Artz	Paul Adams	Stephen MacKinnon	Janet Stewart
Benson	* c	CM	4	(520) 586-2245	Mark Fenn	Glenn Nichols	Vicki Vivian	Jim Cox	Keith Spangler	Glenn Nichols	Bradley Hamilton
Bisbee	* c	CM	6	(520) 432-6000	W. J. Porter	Stephen Pauken	Sharyl Honstein	Dee Flanagan	Jack Earnest	James Elkins	Russell McConnell
Buckeye	t	CM	6	(623) 386-4691	Dustin Hull	Jeanine Guy	Linda Garrison	...	Christine Dunnington	...	Ron Long
Bullhead City	* c	CM	33	(928) 763-9400	...	Timothy Ernster	Diane Heilmann	Rudy Vera	...	Rodney Head	Douglas Lutz
Camp Verde	t	CM	9	(928) 567-6631	...	Michael Scannell	...	...	...	...	...
Carefree	* t	CM	2	(480) 488-3686	Edward Morgan	Jonathan Pearson	Elizabeth Wise	...	...	...	...
Casa Grande	* c	CM	25	(520) 421-8600	Robert Jackson	James Thompson	Gloria Leija	Diane Archer	Scott Miller	Robert Huddleston	Kevin Louis
Cave Creek	t	CM	3	(480) 488-1400	Vincent Francia	Usama Abujbarah	Carrie Dyrek	Marian Groeneveld	...	Adam Stein	Roger Kindsfater
Chandler	c	CM	176	(480) 786-2000	...	W. Pentz	Maria Paddock	...	...	...	Robert Zeder
Chino Valley	t	CM	7	(928) 636-2646	Karen Fann	Gerald Stricklin	Jami Lewis	Linda York	...	Patricia Huntsman	James Confer
Clarkdale	t	CM	3	(928) 634-9591	...	Gayle Mabery	...	Carlton Woodruff	Jerry Doerksen	Pat Haynie	Steve Burroughs
Clifton	t	CM	2	(928) 865-4146	David McCullar	Ray Pini	E. Castaneda	...	...	...	Nazario Hernandez
Coolidge	c	CM	7	(520) 723-5361	Wilbur Wuertz	Robert Flatley	Norma Ortiz	Lisa Pannella	Michael McHugh	James Palmer	Donald Peters
Cottonwood	c	CM	9	(928) 634-5526	Ruben Jauvegui	...	Marianne Jimenez	Jesus Rodriguez	William Casson	Pat Spence	Timothy Costello
Dewey-Humboldt	* t	CM	6	(928) 632-7362	Earl Goodwin	William Emerson	Judy Morgan	Jane Fuller	...	Marc Schmidt	Kevin Manley
Douglas	c	CM	14	(520) 805-5507	Raymond Borane	Curtis Shook	Leticia Rodriguez	Regina Pace	...	Charles Austin	Carlos De La Torre
Duncan	t	CM	..	(928) 359-2791	Randall Norton	Alan Baker	Cynthia Nichols	...	Kelly Cambern	...	Lupe Madrigal
Eagar	t	CM	4	(928) 333-4128	Sandra Burke	William Greenwood	Judy Slade	Ricky Pinckard	...	Benjamin Garms	Elwin Browning
El Mirage	c	CM	7	(623) 972-8116	Fred Waterman	William Cornwall	Edith Hoover	Larry Price	Scott Alvord	Brian Beamish	Chris Young
Eloy	c	CM	10	(520) 466-9201	Manuel Salas	...	Mary Ridgell	Brian Wright	...	William Pitman	...
Flagstaff	c	CM	52	(928) 779-7685	Joe Donaldson	Kevin Burke	Elizabeth Burke	Mary Jenkins	Mike Iacona	J. McCann	Bill Menard
Florence	t	CM	17	(520) 868-7500	Patsy Williams	Himanshu Patel	Lisa Garcia	Rebecca Guilin	Donald Lowry	Robert Ingulli	Wayne Costa
Fountain Hills	* t	CM	20	(480) 816-5100	Jay Schlum	Richard Davis	Bevelyn Bender	Julie Ghetti	Scott LaGreca	...	Thomas Ward
Gila Bend	* t	MC	1	(928) 683-2255	...	Frederick Buss	Beverly Turner	Stacey Young	David Birchfield	...	Houshang Parsi
Gilbert	* t	CM	109	(480) 503-6000	Steven Berman	George Pettit	Catherine Templeton	Cindi Mattheisen	Collin Dewitt	Timothy Dorn	Lonnie Frost
Glendale	c	CM	218	(623) 930-2000	Elaine Scruggs	Edward Beasley	...	Ray Shuey	Mark Burdick	Steve Conrad	Roger Bailey
Globe	c	CM	7	(928) 425-7146	David Franquero	...	...	Teresa Williams	Martin Ricklefs	...	Joe Alvarez
Goodyear	c	CM	18	(623) 932-3910	James Cavanaugh	John Fischbach	Dortzal Cockrum	Larry Lange	Mark Gaillard	Peter Nick	Cato Esquivel
Guadalupe	* t	CM	5	(480) 730-3080	Francisco Montiel	Mark Johnson	...	...	Wayne Clement	...	Jim Ricker
Hayden	t	CM	..	(520) 356-7801	...	...	...	...	...	...	...
Holbrook	c	CM	4	(928) 524-6225	Bryan Smithson	David Newlin	Cheryl Millage	...	Jack Brooks	DWayne Hartup	Richard Young
Jerome	t	CM	..	(928) 634-7943	...	...	...	...	...	...	...
Kearny	t	CM	2	(520) 363-5547	Debra Sommers	Gary Eide	Margaret Gaston	...	Kenneth Piggott	Joeseph Martinez	Ramon Camcho
Kingman	c	CM	20	(928) 753-5561	Monica Gates	Jack Kramer	Toni Weddle	Coral Loyd	Charles Osterman	Robert Devries	...
Lake Havasu City	c	CM	41	(928) 453-4143	Mark Nexsen	Richard Kaffenberger	Carla Simendich	Gayle Whittle	Dennis Mueller	Daniel Doyle	Kevin Murphy
Litchfield Park	* c	CM	3	(623) 935-5033	Thomas Schoaf	Darryl Crossman	Mary Evans	Benjamin Ronquillo	...	...	Charles Ransom
Mammoth	t	MC	1	(520) 487-2331	...	...	Patsy Large	...	...	...	Juan Ponce
Marana	* t	CM	13	(520) 382-1900	Ed Honea	Gilbert Davidson	Jocelyn Bronson	Erik Montague	...	Terry Tometich	Barbara Johnson
Maricopa	c	CM	4	(520) 568-9098	...	Kevin Evans	Vanessa Bueras	Roger Kolman	...	...	Bob Jackson
Mesa	c	CM	396	(480) 644-2059	Keno Hawker	Christopher Brady	Barbara Jones	Bryan Raines	Harry Beck	Dennis Donna	Jack Friedline
Miami	t	MC	1	(928) 473-4403	Paul Licano	Robert Mawson	...	...	...	Dan Rodriguez	John Encizo
Nogales	c	MC	20	(520) 287-6571	Albert Kramer	Jaime Fontes	Leticia Robinson	Charles Diamond	Lorenzo Rodriquez	John Kissinger	Manuel Tapia
Oro Valley	t	CM	29	(520) 229-4700	Paul Loomis	David Andrews	Kathi Cuvelier	...	...	Daniel Sharp	...
Page	c	CM	6	(928) 645-8861	William Justice	Everett Thomas	Lori Anderson	Linda Watson	Larry Clark	Tom Hain	...
Paradise Valley	t	CM	13	(480) 948-7411	Marvin Davis	James Bacon	...	Lenore Lancaster	...	...	William Mead
Parker	t	MC	3	(928) 669-9265	D. L. Wilson	...	Candy Cockrell	Lori Wedemeyer	...	Rod Mendoza	...
Payson	* t	CM	13	(928) 474-5242	Kenny Evans	Debra Galbraith	Silvia Smith	...	Martin deMasi	Don Engler	LaRon Garrett
Peoria	c	CM	108	(623) 773-7100	John Keegan	Carl Swenson	Mary Jo Kief	John Wenderski	Robert McKibben	David Leonardo	Neil Mann
Phoenix	c	CM	1321	(602) 262-6609	Phil Gordon	Frank Fairbanks	Mario Paniagua	...	Alan Brunacini	Jack Harris	Mark Leonard
Pinetop-Lakeside	* t	CM	3	(928) 368-8696	Barbara Teague	L. Udall	Lu Anne Frost	John Brooksby	...	Sherwood Eldredge	Tommy Thomas
Prescott	c	CM	33	(928) 777-1100	...	Steven Norwood	Elizabeth Burke	Marklyn Woodfill	Darrell Willis	Randy Oaks	Craig McConnell
Prescott Valley	* t	CM	23	(928) 759-3000	Harvey Skoog	Larry Tarkowski	Diane Russell	William Kauppi	...	James Maxson	Norm Davis
Quartzsite	t	CM	3	(928) 927-4333	Patty Bergen	Jay Howe	Kay Kreun	Barbara Jones	...	Glenn Nichols	T. Collier
Queen Creek	* t	CM	4	(480) 358-3000	Arthur Sanders	Walter Kross	Jennifer Robinson	Patrick Flynn	Van Summers	Dante Proto	...
Safford	c	CM	9	(928) 348-3100	Van Talley	...	Sharon French	Carlos Vessels	Mike Rhodes	John Griffin	Robert Porter
Sahuarita	t	CM	3	(520) 822-8800	Lynne Skelton	James Stahle	Sandra Olivas	A. C. Marriotti	...	John Harris	Robert Welch
San Luis	c	CM	15	(928) 627-2027	Alex Harper	Jeffrey Philpot	...	Kerry Jones	Othon Luna	Heriberto Bejarano	David Ford
Scottsdale	c	CM	202	(480) 312-2491	Mary Manross	Janet Dolan	Carolyn Jagger	Craig Clifford	William McDonald	Alan Rodbell	Alvis Dreska
Sedona	* c	CM	10	(928) 204-7189	Pud Colquitt	Alison Zelms	Cherry Lawson	Barbara Ashley	Matt Shobert	Joe Vernier	...
Show Low	* c	CM	7	(928) 532-4000	Gene Kelley	Ed Muder	Ann Kurasaki	Larry Ploughe	...	...	Kenneth Patterson
Sierra Vista	* c	CM	37	(520) 458-3315	Robert Strain	Charles Potucek	Jill Adams	David Felix	Randy Redmond	Kenneth Kimmel	Michael Hemesath
Snowflake	t	CM	4	(928) 536-7103	John Stewart	Brian Richards	...	...	Brian Hancock	David Adams	Gary Fenstermaker
Somerton	c	CM	7	(928) 627-8866	Miguel Villalpando	...	...	...	Paul DeAnda	Terry Hollis	Eddie Mendez
South Tucson	c	CM	5	(520) 792-2424	Shirley Villegas	...	Dolores Robles	Ruben Villa	Larry Anderson	Sixto Molina	Angel Lopez
Springerville	t	CM	1	(928) 333-2656	Kay Dyson	Scott Garms	Valentina Cordova	Karen Asquith	Max Sadler	Steve West	Tom Malone
St. Johns	* c	CM	3	(928) 337-4517	Ross Overson	Gregory Martin	Holly Wagoner	Amy Bigelow	Gary Liston	Roy Melnick	Paul Ramsey
Star Valley	* t	CM	2	(928) 472-7752	Chuck Heron	...	Sarah Luckie	...	...	...	...
Superior	t	MC	3	(520) 689-5752	...	...	...	...	...	...	...
Surprise	* t	CM	30	(623) 222-1000	...	Charles Oliver	Sherry Aguilar	Robert Nilles	Michael White	Daniel Hughes	Robert Beckley
Taylor	* t	CM	3	(928) 536-7366	John Cole	Eric Duthie	Kelly Jones	Gus Lundberg	Clay Woods	Jerry Van Winkle	Ron Solomon
Tempe	* c	CM	158	(480) 350-8278	Hugh Hallman	Charles Meyer	Jan Hort	Jerry Hart	Cliff Jones	Thomas Ryff	Glenn Kephart
Thatcher	t	CM	4	(928) 428-2290	...	Terrel Hinton	...	...	...	Michael McEuen	...
Tolleson	c	CM	4	(623) 936-7111	Adolfo Gamez	Reyes Medrano	C. Hagen-Hurley	Steven Baumgardt	Donald Garcia	Lawrence Rodriguez	Mark Berrelez
Tucson	c	CM	486	(520) 791-4241	Robert Walkup	Mike Hein	Kathleen Detrick	J. Scott Douthitt	Dan Newburn	Richard Miranda	...
Wickenburg	* t	CM	5	(928) 684-5451	Ron Badowski	Gary Edwards	Donna Riffel	Stephanie Wojcik	Ed Temerowski	Anthony Melendez	Rick Austin
Willcox	c	CM	3	(520) 384-4271	Marlin Easthouse	Pat McCourt	Christina Whelan	Jeffrey Palmer	...	...	...
Williams	c	CM	2	(928) 635-4451	Kenneth Edes	J. Wells	Eleanor Addison	Joe Duffy	Joe Schulte	Frank Manson	Glenn Cornwell
Winslow	c	MC	9	(928) 289-2422	...	...	Linda Samson	Regina Reffner	Boney Candelaria	Stephen Garnett	...
Youngtown	* t	CM	3	(623) 933-8286	Michael LeVault	Lloyce Robinson	Letty Goldberg	Jackie Hoffman	...	Kimberly Johnson	Mark Hannah
Yuma	* c	CM	77	(928) 373-5000	Lawrence Nelson	Mark Watson	Brigitta Stanz	Donald Wicks	Jack McArthur	William Robinson	...

Directory 1/9 continued — OFFICIALS IN U.S. MUNICIPALITIES 2,500 AND OVER IN POPULATION

Jurisdiction	Type	Form of govern-ment	2000 Popu-lation	Main telephone number	Chief elected official	Appointed administrator	Clerk of the governing board	Chief financial officer	Fire chief	Police chief	Public works director
ARKANSAS											
Alma	c	MC	4	(479) 632-4110	John Ballentine	. . .	Christina Inge	. . .	Steve Meadors	Russell White	Mark Yardley
Arkadelphia	c	CM	10	(870) 246-9864	C. Hollingshead	Jimmy Bolt	. . .	. . .	Jerry Sullivan	Al Harris	. . .
Ashdown	c	MC	4	(870) 898-2622	Hoyt Johnson	. . .	Sandra Patterson	. . .	. . .	Ben McCraw	. . .
Atkins	c	MC	2	(479) 641-2900	. . .	. . .	. . .	. . .	. . .	. . .	. . .
Augusta	c	MC	2	(870) 347-5656	Jimmy Rhodes	. . .	. . .	. . .	. . .	Charles Allen	. . .
Bald Knob	c	MC	3	(501) 724-6371	Doyle Wallace	. . .	. . .	. . .	Danny Holobaugh	Larry Landis	. . .
Barling *	c	CM	4	(479) 452-1556	Jerry Barling	Ray Caruthers	Kristi St. Cyr	. . .	Lewis Haggard	Tracy Powell	Steve Core
Batesville	c	MC	9	(870) 698-2400	Rick Elumbaugh	. . .	Denise Johnston	. . .	Danny Russell	. . .	Sanford St. John
Beebe	c	MC	4	(501) 882-6295	Michael Robertson	Jackie Young	. . .	. . .	William Nick	S. Wayne Ballew	Dwight Oxner
Benton *	c	MC	21	(501) 776-5900	Richard Holland	. . .	Cindy Stracener	. . .	Ben Blankenship	Kirk Lane	. . .
Bentonville	c	MC	19	(479) 271-3191	Terry Coberly	. . .	Suzanne Grider	Stewart Smith	Dan White	James Allen	Britt Vance
Berryville	c	MC	4	(870) 423-4414	Tim McKinney	. . .	Sherry Clark	. . .	Gene Chafin	David Muniz	Dwayne Allen
Blytheville	c	MC	18	(870) 763-3602	. . .	. . .	. . .	. . .	Gary Perry	. . .	. . .
Booneville	c	MC	4	(479) 675-3811	Jerry Wilkins	. . .	Melinda Smith	. . .	Mike Talley	Stanley Campbell	. . .
Brinkley	c	CM	3	(870) 734-1382	. . .	. . .	. . .	. . .	. . .	. . .	. . .
Bryant	c	MC	9	(501) 847-0292	Paul Halley	. . .	Brenda Cockerham	Marilyn Payne	Randy Cox	Frank Gonzales	William Lasage
Cabot	c	MC	15	(501) 843-3566	Eddie Williams	Karen Davis	. . .	. . .	Phillip Robinson	Jackie Davis	Jerrel Maxwell
Camden	c	MC	13	(870) 836-6436	Chris Claybaker	. . .	. . .	. . .	William Seaton	Elisha Cochran	Bill Braswell
Carlisle *	c	MC	2	(870) 552-3120	Ray Glover	. . .	. . .	. . .	Marvin Reid	Eric Frank	Richard Sumner
Cherokee Village *	c	MC	4	(870) 257-5522	Lloyd Hefley	. . .	Phyllis Endrihs	. . .	Michael Taylor	Jason French	. . .
Clarksville	c	MC	7	(479) 754-6486	Billy Helms	. . .	. . .	. . .	Ron Wylie	Jimmy Ralph	Hugh Harrison
Conway	c	MC	43	(501) 450-6110	Tab Townsell	Donald Crain	Michael Garrett	Perry Faulkner	Bart Castleberry	Jerry Snowden	. . .
Corning	c	MC	3	(870) 857-6001	James Ermert	Allen Warmath	Frances Edwards	. . .	Donnie Kirby	Jim Groning	. . .
Crossett	c	MC	6	(870) 364-4825	Marshall McCormick	. . .	Jesse Walthall	Heath White	James Launius	Thomas Sturgeon	Thomas Goree
Dardanelle *	c	MC	4	(479) 229-4500	Carolyn McGee	. . .	Mary Martin	. . .	Carl Cross	Montie Sims	. . .
De Queen	c	CM	5	(870) 584-3445	Dale Kesner	. . .	. . .	Donna Jones	. . .	Richard McKinley	. . .
De Witt	c	MC	3	(870) 946-1776	Carroll Lester	Shirley Parker	Liz Ferguson	. . .	Ronnie Danner	Bob Paxton	Bill Paxton
Dermott	c	MC	3	(870) 538-5251	. . .	. . .	. . .	. . .	. . .	Carl McCree	. . .
Dumas *	c	MC	5	(870) 382-2121	Marion Gill	. . .	Johnny Brigham	. . .	David Byrd	Everett Cox	. . .
Earle	c	MC	3	(870) 792-8909	. . .	. . .	. . .	. . .	. . .	. . .	. . .
El Dorado	c	MC	21	(870) 881-4865	Mike Dumas	. . .	John Wells	. . .	Floyd McAdoo	Ricky Roberts	Charles Atkinson
England	c	MC	2	(501) 842-3911	Ruth Baker	Tammie Jinks	. . .	. . .	Bob Winkler	Nathan Cook	Roy Talley
Eudora	c	MC	2	(870) 355-4436	. . .	. . .	. . .	. . .	. . .	. . .	. . .
Eureka Springs	c	MC	2	(479) 253-9703	Kathy Harrison	. . .	MaryJane Sell	. . .	David Stoppel	Earl Hyatt	. . .
Fayetteville	c	CM	58	(479) 575-8330	Dan Coody	. . .	Sondra Smith	Stephen Davis	Chris Bosch	Rick Hoyt	. . .
Fordyce	c	MC	4	(870) 352-2198	William Lyon	. . .	Janice McDaniel	. . .	Roy Moseley	Joe Pennington	. . .
Forrest City	c	MC	14	(870) 633-1315	Larry Bryant	. . .	Marie Todd	. . .	Dan Curtner	Clarence McNeary	Clovis Macon
Fort Smith *	c	CM	80	(479) 785-2801	Ray Baker	Dennis Kelly	Cindy Remler	Kara Bushkuhl	Jerry Tomlin	. . .	Steve Parke
Gosnell	c	MC	3	(870) 532-8544	Dick Reams	. . .	. . .	Nola King	. . .	Michael Kelly	Charles Cobb
Gravette	c	MC	1	(479) 787-5757	. . .	. . .	. . .	. . .	. . .	. . .	. . .
Greenwood	c	MC	7	(479) 996-2742	Garry Campbell	. . .	Wilma Cabe	Dallas Melvin	Don Oliver	Keith Jackson	. . .
Gurdon	c	MC	2	(870) 353-2514	Rick Smith	. . .	Tambra Smith	. . .	Jake McBride	. . .	. . .
Hamburg	c	MC	3	(870) 853-5300	Gordon Hennington	. . .	. . .	. . .	Steve Cypert	Tommy Breedlove	Jimmy Hargis
Harrison	c	MC	12	(870) 741-2525	. . .	. . .	. . .	. . .	. . .	. . .	. . .
Heber Springs	c	MC	6	(501) 362-3635	Edward Roper	. . .	Norma Martin	. . .	Steve Haile	David Smith	. . .
Helena	c	MC	6	(870) 572-2528	Robert Miller	. . .	Sandra Ramsey	. . .	Reginald Wilson	Vincent Bell	. . .
Hope	c	CM	10	(870) 777-6701	Dennis Ramsey	Catherine Cook	Loreta Hare	Debra Hall	Bo Watkins	William Brinkworth	. . .
Hot Springs *	c	CM	33	(501) 321-6800	Mike Bush	. . .	. . .	Linda Baker	Arval Sanders	Bobby Southard	Ronald Kohler
Hoxie	c	MC	2	(870) 886-2742	Paul Hendrix	. . .	Katie Smith	. . .	David Mason	Kenny Jones	. . .
Jacksonville	c	MC	29	(501) 982-4671	Tommy Swaim	. . .	Susan Davitt	Paul Mushrush	John Vanderhoof	Larry Hibbs	Jimmy Oakley
Jonesboro *	c	MC	55	(870) 933-4640	Harold Perrin	. . .	Donna Jackson	Jim Barksdale	Leonard Jadrich	Michael Yates	Erick Woodruff
Lake Village	c	MC	2	(870) 265-2228	Joanne Bush	. . .	Harolyn Keith	. . .	. . .	Percy Wilburn	. . .
Little Rock *	c	CM	183	(501) 371-4590	Mark Stodola	Bruce Moore	Nancy Wood	Robert Biles	Rhoda Kerr	Stuart Thomas	. . .
Lonoke	c	MC	4	(501) 676-2588	Thomas Privett	. . .	Billie Uzzell	. . .	Scott Williams	Ronald Campbell	Tony Scroggins
Magnolia	c	MC	10	(870) 234-1375	Lane Jean	. . .	Judy Whitelaw	. . .	Herschel Hampton	Robert Gorum	Ricky Wilson
Malvern	c	MC	9	(501) 332-3638	. . .	. . .	. . .	. . .	Orlen Wiley	. . .	. . .
Manila	c	MC	3	(870) 561-4437	Melvin Browning	. . .	Rachael Scott	. . .	Don Nunnally	Jackie Hill	. . .
Marianna	c	MC	5	(870) 295-6089	Robert Taylor	. . .	. . .	. . .	Mark Andrews	Walter Johnson	Jack Dilks
Marion	c	MC	8	(870) 739-3071	. . .	. . .	. . .	. . .	. . .	. . .	. . .
Marked Tree	c	MC	2	(870) 358-3216	Lawrence Ashlock	. . .	Pamela Wright	. . .	Danny Johnson	Orbie Crum	Clifton Parham
Maumelle	c	CM	5	(501) 851-2500	Mike Watson	. . .	Joshua Clausen	Tyler Winningham	George Glenn	Sam Williams	Robert Cogdell
Mc Gehee	c	MC	4	(870) 222-3160	. . .	. . .	. . .	. . .	. . .	. . .	. . .
Mena	c	MC	5	(479) 394-3141	George McKee	. . .	Regina Walker	. . .	. . .	Russell Nichols	. . .
Monticello *	c	MC	9	(870) 367-4400	Joe Rogers	. . .	Patricia Nelson	Kimberly Fletcher	Steven Faulkner	Robert Rosegrant	Lennie Wood
Morrilton	c	MC	6	(501) 354-3484	Stewart Nelson	. . .	Charlotte Kindle	. . .	. . .	Norbert Gunderman	Charles Edwards
Mountain Home *	c	MC	11	(870) 425-5116	David Osmon	. . .	Karen Collins	. . .	Ken Williams	Carry Manuel	Alma Clark
Nashville	c	MC	4	(870) 845-7400	Mike Reese	. . .	Kelly Sherman	Pam McLaughlin	Jerry Harwell	Larry Yates	. . .
Newport	c	MC	7	(870) 523-6568	David Stewart	. . .	Linda Treadway	. . .	Michael Mink	Michael Scudder	Burt Willard
North Little Rock	c	MC	60	(501) 975-8855	Patrick Hays	Joseph Smith	Diane Whitbey	Robert Sisson	Joe McCall	Danny Bradley	Bobby Ward
Osceola	c	MC	8	(870) 563-5102	. . .	. . .	. . .	. . .	. . .	. . .	. . .
Ozark	c	MC	3	(479) 667-2238	. . .	. . .	. . .	. . .	. . .	. . .	. . .
Paragould	c	MC	22	(870) 239-7510	Winston Gaskill	. . .	Goldie Wise	. . .	William Brown	Dennis Hyde	Sandra Meeker
Paris	c	MC	3	(479) 963-2450	Jim Clay	. . .	Billy Rhinehart	Jewell White	Edward Boyd	Hershel Hice	Jimmy O'Bar
Pea Ridge	c	MC	2	(479) 451-1424	. . .	. . .	. . .	. . .	. . .	. . .	. . .
Piggott	c	MC	3	(870) 598-3791	Gerald Morris	. . .	Judy Parker	. . .	John Harlan	William Alstadt	Teddy Bellers
Pine Bluff	c	MC	55	(870) 543-1840	Francis King	. . .	Sharon Hagan	Edward Bogy	David Parsley	Daniel Moses	. . .
Pocahontas	c	MC	6	(870) 892-3924	Gary Crocker	. . .	. . .	. . .	Scott Baltz	Chad Mulligan	. . .
Prescott	c	MC	3	(870) 887-2210	. . .	. . .	. . .	. . .	. . .	. . .	. . .
Rogers	c	MC	38	(479) 621-1117	Stephen Womack	. . .	Sandra Fearman	. . .	Wesley Lewis	Timothy Keck	. . .
Russellville	c	MC	23	(479) 968-2098	Raye Turner	. . .	Kathy Collins	. . .	Dennis Miller	James Bacon	Morgan Barrett
Searcy *	c	MC	18	(501) 268-2483	Belinda LaForce	. . .	Peggy Meads	. . .	Bill Baldridge	J. R. Thomas	. . .
Sheridan	c	MC	3	(870) 942-3921	. . .	. . .	. . .	. . .	. . .	. . .	. . .
Sherwood	c	MC	21	(501) 833-3703	Bill Harmon	. . .	Virginia Hillman	. . .	. . .	James Thomas	Denver Gentry
Siloam Springs	c	CM	10	(479) 524-5136	M. L. VanPouke	David Cameron	Peggy Woody	Paul Calloway	Jimmy Harris	Jerry Toler	. . .
Springdale *	c	MC	45	(479) 750-8535	Doug Sprouse	. . .	Denise Pearce	. . .	E. Duane Atha	Kathy O'Kelley	Sam Goade
Stamps	c	MC	2	(870) 533-2965	E. W. Johnson	. . .	. . .	. . .	. . .	Robert Drake	. . .
Stuttgart	c	MC	9	(870) 673-8817	Harry Richenback	. . .	Mitri Greenhill	Jane Jackson	George Jackson	David Cowart	. . .
Texarkana	c	CM	26	(870) 779-4991	Horace Shipp	Harold Boldt	Patti Grey	. . .	Bobby Honea	Robert Harrison	Rachael Kaplan
Trumann	t	MC	6	(870) 483-5355	Jack Coggins	Patricia Powell	Patsy Bullock	. . .	Gary Anderson	R. Richardson	Bill Matthews
Van Buren	c	MC	18	(479) 474-8936	John Riggs	Vivian Mitchell	Barbie Curtis	. . .	Teasie Harris	Kenneth Bell	Don Mullens
Waldron *	c	MC	3	(479) 637-3181	Randy Butler	. . .	Sherry Johnston	. . .	Wayne Watkins	David Millard	Tomas Starr
Walnut Ridge	c	MC	4	(870) 886-6638	Junior Rogers	. . .	Carolyn Hayes	. . .	Wayne Masterson	Dan Webb	. . .
Warren *	c	MC	6	(870) 226-6743	Bryan Martin	. . .	Jeanie Reep	. . .	Howard Edwards	Randy Peek	Steven Rand
West Helena	c	MC	8	(870) 572-2528	. . .	. . .	. . .	. . .	. . .	. . .	. . .

Directory 1/9 continued   OFFICIALS IN U.S. MUNICIPALITIES 2,500 AND OVER IN POPULATION

Jurisdiction	Type	Form of govern-ment	2000 Popu-lation	Main telephone number	Chief elected official	Appointed administrator	Clerk of the governing board	Chief financial officer	Fire chief	Police chief	Public works director
ARKANSAS continued											
West Memphis	c	MC	27	(870) 732-7500	William Johnson	...	Phillip Para	Robert Gunter	Arburt Robinson	Robert Paudert	...
White Hall *	c	MC	4	(870) 247-2399	James Morgan	...	...	...	Sandy Castleberry	Noel Foster	...
Wynne	c	MC	8	(870) 238-9171	...	...	...	...	...	...	...
CALIFORNIA											
Adelanto *	c	CM	18	(760) 246-2300	Charley Glasper	D. Hart	Cindy Herrera	William Aylward	John Salvate	Lee Watkins	...
Agoura Hills	c	CM	20	(818) 597-7300	...	Greg Ramirez	Kimberly Rodrigues	Georgette Holt	...	...	...
Alameda	c	CM	72	(510) 748-4505	Beverly Johnson	Debra Kurita	Lara Weisiger	Zenda James	James Christiansen	Burnham Matthews	Matthew Naclerio
Albany	c	CM	16	(510) 528-5710	Peggy Thomsen	Beth Pollard	Jackie Bucholz	Joan Streit	Marc McGinn	Larry Murdo	Ann Chaney
Alhambra	c	CM	85	(626) 570-5095	Talmage Burke	Julio Fuentes	Frances Moore	Howard Longballa	Vincent Kemp	...	Mary Swink
Aliso Viejo *	c	CM	40	(949) 425-2500	Donald Garcia	Mark Pulone	Susan Ramos	Gina Tharani	Ed Fleming	Richard Paddock	John Whitman
Alturas	c	MC	2	(530) 233-2512	George Andreasen	...	Cary Baker	...	Keith Jacques	Ken Barnes	Chester Robertson
American Canyon	c	CM	9	(707) 647-4361	Cecil Shaver	Richard Ramirez	Kay Woodson	Pete Kolf	Keith Caldwell	Douglas Koford	Robert Weil
Anaheim	c	CM	328	(714) 765-5100	...	David Morgan	Sheryll Schroeder	William Sweeney	Roger Smith	John Welter	Gary Johnson
Anderson	c	CM	9	(530) 378-6626	Keith Webster	R Scott Morgan	...	L. Watkins-Gallino	...	Dale Webb	Richard Barchus
Angels Camp	c	CM	2	(209) 736-2181	...	Timothy Shearer	...	...	...	...	...
Antioch	c	CM	90	(925) 779-7000	Don Freitas	...	Jolene Martin	John Tasker	...	Mark Moczulski	Phil Harrington
Apple Valley	t	CM	54	(760) 240-7000	...	Frank Robinson	La Vonda Pearson	Kevin Smith	...	...	...
Arcadia	c	CM	53	(626) 574-5405	Gary Kovack	Donald Penman	June Alford	...	David Lugo	David Hinig	Patrick Malloy
Arcata	c	CM	16	(707) 822-5953	Harmony Groves	Michael Hackett	...	Janet Luzzi	John McFarland	Randal Mendosa	Doby Class
Arroyo Grande	c	CM	15	(805) 473-5400	Tony Ferrara	Steven Adams	Kelly Wetmore	Angela Kraetsch	Terry Fibich	...	Don Spagnolo
Artesia	c	CM	16	(562) 865-6262	Tony Mendoza	Maria Dadian	...	...	...	...	...
Arvin	c	CM	12	(661) 854-3134	Tim Tarver	Alan Christensen	Cecilia Vela	David Powell	...	Tommy Tunson	Bob Feulner
Atascadero *	c	CM	26	(805) 461-5000	Ellen Beraud	Wade McKinney	...	...	Kurt Stone	Jim Mulhall	...
Atherton	t	CM	7	(650) 752-0500	Kathy McKeithen	Jerome Gruber	...	John Johns	...	Robert Brennan	Duncan Jones
Atwater	c	CM	23	(209) 357-6300	Rudy Trevino	Gregory Wellman	...	...	Dennis Sparks	Jerry Moore	Frank Lozano
Auburn	c	CM	12	(530) 823-4211	...	Robert Richardson	Joseph Labrie	Richard Loomis	Mark D'Ambrogi	...	Thomas Fossum
Avalon	c	CM	3	(310) 510-0220	...	Thomas Sullivan	Shirley Davy	Betty Jo Garcia	Steven Hoefs	...	Pastor Lopez
Avenal	c	CM	14	(559) 386-5766	...	Melissa Whitten	Nina Garza	Esther Strong	...	Dave Putnam	Jerry Watson
Azusa *	c	CM	44	(626) 812-5027	Cristina Cruz-Madrid	Francis Delach	Vera Mendoza	Alan Kreimeier	...	Robert Garcia	Bill Nakasone
Bakersfield	c	CM	247	(661) 326-3006	Harvey Hall	Alan Tandy	Pamela McCarthy	Gregory Klimko	Ron Fraze	Eric Matlock	Raul Rojas
Baldwin Park	c	CM	75	(626) 960-4011	Manuel Lozano	Vijay Singhal	Kathryn Tizcareno	Hennie Apodaca	...	Mark Kling	Shafique Naiyer
Banning *	c	CM	23	(951) 922-3105	Robert Botts	Brian Nakamura	Marie Calderon	Bonnie Johnson	...	Leonard Purvis	Duane Burk
Barstow	c	CM	21	(760) 256-3531	Lawrence Dale	Richard Rowe	Joanne Cousino	Gil Olivarez	...	Dianne Burns	...
Beaumont *	c	CM	11	(951) 769-8520	Brian DeForge	...	Karen Thompson	William Aylward	...	Frank Coe	Deepak Moorjani
Bell	c	CM	36	(323) 588-6211	George Cole	Robert Rizzo	...	...	...	Michael Trevis	...
Bell Gardens	c	CM	44	(562) 806-7700	Jennifer Rodriquez	John Ornelas	Marta Solano	Misty Cheng	...	Keith Kilmer	John Oropeza
Bellflower	c	CM	72	(562) 804-1424	Ray Smith	Michael Egan	Debra Bauchop	Tae Rhee	...	...	...
Belmont	c	CM	25	(650) 595-7413	Paul Wright	Jack Crist	Teresa Cook	Thomas Fil	...	Greg Janke	Ray Davis
Belvedere	c	CM	2	(415) 435-3838	Barbara Morrison	George Rodericks	...	Rebecca Eastman	Rich Pearce	Mark Campbell	...
Benicia	c	CM	26	(707) 746-4200	Steven Messina	James Erickson	Linda Purdy	...	Ken Hanley	Sandra Spagnoli	...
Berkeley	c	CM	102	(510) 981-2489	Tom Bates	...	Sherry Kelly	...	Reginald Garcia	Roy Meisner	Rene Cardinaux
Beverly Hills	c	CM	33	(310) 285-1000	Mark Egerman	Roderick Wood	Nina Webster	Don Oblander	Pete Bonano	David Snowden	Rob Beste
Big Bear Lake	c	CM	5	(909) 866-5831	Elizabeth Harris	Jeffrey Mathieu	Katherine Jeffries	...	Kenneth Hammond	...	...
Bishop	c	CM	3	(760) 873-5863	Kathryn Henderson	Richard Pucci	...	...	Ray Seguine	...	David Grah
Blue Lake	c	CM	1	(707) 668-5655	...	...	...	...	...	...	...
Blythe	c	CM	12	(760) 922-6161	Robert Crain	David Lane	...	Helen Colbert	Curtis Crecelius	Robert Grady	James Rodkey
Bradbury *	c	CM	..	(626) 358-3218	Richard Barakat	Michelle Keith	Claudia Sandana	...	...	...	...
Brawley	c	CM	22	(760) 344-9111	...	Gary Burroughs	Janet Smith	Fredrick Selk	Frank Contreras	Henry Graham	Yazmin Arellano
Brea	c	CM	35	(714) 990-7600	Marty Simonoff	Tim O'Donnell	Lucinda Williams	William Gallardo	Alford Nero	Mike Messina	...
Brentwood	c	CM	23	(925) 516-5400	Brian Swisher	Donna Landeros	Margaret Wimberly	Pamela Ehler	...	Michael Davies	Paul Zolfarelli
Brisbane	c	CM	3	(415) 508-2100	...	Clayton Holstine	Sheri Schroeder	...	...	Thomas Hitchcock	Randy Breault
Brooktrails (Csd)	tp	CM	2	(707) 459-2494	George Skezas	Michael Chapman	...	...	Daryl Schoeppner	...	Wendell Wilson
Buellton	c	CM	3	(805) 688-5177	Victoria Pointer	Steven Thompson	Birgit Cripe	Kathryn Wollin	...	...	Bill Albrecht
Buena Park	c	CM	78	(714) 562-3500	Steve Berry	...	Shalice Reynoso	Sung Hyun	...	Gary Hicken	James Biery
Burbank	c	CM	100	(818) 238-5800	Stacey Murphy	Mary Alvord	Margarita Campos	Derek Hanway	Michael Davis	Thomas Hoefel	...
Burlingame	c	CM	28	(650) 558-7200	...	James Nantell	...	Jesus Nava	...	Gary Missel	...
Calabasas *	c	CM	20	(818) 224-1600	Mary Sue Maurer	Anthony Coroalles	Gwen Peirce	Gary Lysik	Joseph Graham	...	Robert Yalda
Calexico	c	CM	27	(760) 768-2110	...	Luis Estrada	Lourdes Cordova	Veronica Alvarado	Carlos Escalante	Tommy Tunson	Mariano Martinez
California City	c	CM	8	(760) 373-8661	Larry Adams	...	Helen Dennis	Terry Hicks	Mike Antonucci	Wayne Dickerson	Ron Wallace
Calimesa *	c	CM	7	(909) 795-9801	Shenna Moqeet	Randy Anstine	Darlene Gerdes	Debbie Cain	Craig Anthony	Ronald Wade	Elroy Kiepke
Calipatria	c	MC	7	(760) 348-2293	...	Romualdo Medina	...	...	Chris Hall	...	...
Calistoga	c	CM	5	(707) 942-2754	Andrew Alexander	...	...	...	Gary Kraus	Mike Dick	Paul Wade
Camarillo *	c	CM	57	(805) 388-5307	Don Waunch	Jerry Bankston	Jeffrie Madland	Ronnie Campbell	Robert Roper	Steve DeCesari	Thomas Fox
Campbell	c	CM	38	(408) 866-2100	Daniel Furtado	Daniel Rich	Anne Bybee	Jesse Takahashi	...	David Gullo	Robert Kass
Canyon Lake	c	CM	9	(909) 244-2955	Cora Barrett	...	Kathy Bennett	...	...	...	...
Capitola *	c	CM	10	(831) 475-7300	Dennis Norton	Richard Hill	Pamela Greeninger	...	...	Richard Ehle	Steven Jesberg
Carlsbad	c	CM	78	(760) 602-2440	Claude Lewis	Lisa Hildabrand	...	...	D. Van Der Maaten	Robert Vales	Lloyd Hubbs
Carmel-By-The-Sea	c	CM	4	(831) 620-2000	Sue McCloud	Richard Guillen	Karen Crouch	...	...	George Rawson	James Cullem
Carpinteria *	c	CM	14	(805) 684-5405	...	David Durflinger	Jayne Diza	...	...	...	...
Carson	c	CM	89	(310) 830-7600	...	Jerome Groomes	Helen Kawagoe	...	...	...	Kenneth Boyce
Cathedral City *	c	CM	42	(760) 770-0340	Kathleen DeRosa	Donald Bradley	Pat Hammers	...	William Soqui	Stanley Henry	Patrick Milos
Ceres	c	CM	34	(209) 538-5700	...	Brad Kilger	...	...	...	...	Joachim Hollstein
Cerritos	c	CM	51	(562) 860-0311	...	Art Gallucci	Josephine Triggs	...	...	...	Hal Arbogast
Chico	c	CM	59	(530) 896-7200	...	David Burkland	Deborah Presson	Jennifer Hennessy	John Brown	Bruce Hagerty	...
Chino	c	CM	67	(909) 591-9800	...	Patrick Glover	Lenna Tanner	David Cain	...	Eugene Hernandez	...
Chino Hills	c	MC	66	(909) 364-2600	Gwenn Norton-Perry	Douglas La Belle	Mary McDuffe	Judy Lancaster	...	Rick Carr	Patricia Hagler
Chowchilla *	c	CM	11	(559) 665-8615	Justin White	Nancy Red	Rebekah Barr	Connie Wright	Harry Turner	Jay Varney	...
Chula Vista	c	CM	173	(619) 691-5096	Shirley Horton	...	Susan Bigelow	Maria Kachadoorian	Douglas Perry	John Kaheny	John Lippitt
Citrus Heights	c	CM	85	(916) 725-2448	William Hughes	Henry Tingle	Lillian Hare	Stefani Daniell	...	Dan Drummond	Pete Santina
Claremont	c	CM	33	(909) 399-5460	...	Jeffrey Parker	Lynne Pahner	...	...	Paul Cooper	...
Clayton *	c	CM	10	(925) 673-7300	Gregory Manning	Gary Napper	Laci Jackson	Merry Pelletier	...	Dan Lawrence	...
Clearlake	c	CM	13	(707) 994-8201	James McMurray	Robert Van Nort	...	Michael Vivrette	...	Robert Chalk	...
Cloverdale *	c	CM	6	(707) 894-2521	Jessalee Raymond	Nina Regor	M. Winterbottom	...	...	Mark Tuma	...
Clovis *	c	CM	68	(559) 324-2000	Nathan Magsig	Kathleen Millison	John Holt	Robert Woolley	Samuel Aston	Jim Zulim	Mike Leonardo
Coachella	c	CM	22	(760) 398-3502	Eduardo Garcia	Timothy Brown	Isabel Castillon	John Gerardi	Alex Gregg	Colleen Walker	Paul Toor
Coalinga *	c	CM	11	(559) 935-1533	Trish Hill	Stephen Julian	Cindy Johnson	Robert Barron	Daniel Hernandez	Calvin Minor	Randy Arp
Colma *	t	CM	1	(650) 997-8300	Helen Fisicaro	Laura Allen	...	...	...	Robert Lotti	...
Colton	c	CM	47	(909) 370-5099	Helen Ramos	Daryl Parrish	Caroline Barrera	Dilu DeAlwis	Tom Hendrix	Kenneth Rulon	John Hutton
Colusa	c	CM	5	(530) 458-4740	Pamela Crippen	...	...	...	Randy Dunn	Lyle Montgomery	Patty Hickle
Commerce *	c	CM	12	(323) 722-4805	Hugo Argumedo	Jorge Rifa	Linda Olivieri	Vilko Domic	...	...	...
Compton	c	CM	93	(310) 605-5535	Omar Bradley	...	Charles Davis	Marilynn Horne	Milford Fonza	Ramon Allen	Angel Espiritu
Concord *	c	CM	121	(925) 671-3000	Helen Allen	Daniel Keen	Mary Rae Lehman	Peggy Lefebvre	...	David Livingston	Qamar Khan
Corcoran *	c	CM	14	(559) 992-2151	...	Ronald Hoggard	Lorraine Lopez	Joyce Venegas	...	...	Steven Kroeker

Directory 1/9 continued   OFFICIALS IN U.S. MUNICIPALITIES 2,500 AND OVER IN POPULATION

Jurisdiction	Type	Form of govern-ment	2000 Popu-lation	Main telephone number	Chief elected official	Appointed administrator	Clerk of the governing board	Chief financial officer	Fire chief	Police chief	Public works director
CALIFORNIA continued											
Corning *	c	CM	6	(530) 824-7034	. . .	Stephen Kimbrough	Lisa Linnet	. . .	Martin Spannaus	Anthony Cardenas	Tom Russ
Corona	c	CM	124	(909) 736-2209	. . .	. . .	Victoria Wasko	. . .	Mike Warren	Richard Gonzales	John Licata
Coronado *	c	CM	24	(619) 522-7300	Casey Tanaka	Mark Ochenduszko	Linda Hascup	. . .	Kim Raddatz	Louis Scanlon	Scott Huth
Corte Madera	t	CM	9	(415) 927-5050	. . .	. . .	. . .	George Warman	Robert Fox	. . .	. . .
Costa Mesa *	c	CM	108	(714) 754-5350	Alan Mansoor	Allan Roeder	Julie Folcik	Marc Puckett	Michael Morgan	Christopher Shawkey	Peter Naghavi
Cotati	c	CM	6	(707) 792-4600	Geoff Fox	Dianne Thompson	Tamara Taylor	Jone Hayes	. . .	Robert Stewart	Steve Nommsen
Covina *	c	CM	46	(626) 331-0114	Kevin Stapleton	. . .	Rosie Fabian	. . .	. . .	Kim Raney	Steve Henley
Crescent City *	c	CM	4	(707) 464-7483	Dennis Burns	Michael Young	L. Nickerson	Ken McDonald	Stephen Wakefield	Douglas Plack	James Barnts
Cudahy	c	CM	24	(323) 773-5143	. . .	George Perez	. . .	Aurora Martinez	. . .	. . .	. . .
Culver City	c	CM	38	(310) 253-6000	Steve Rose	Jerry Fulwood	Tom Crunk	Eric Shapiro	Michael Thompson	Ted Cooke	James Davis
Cupertino	c	CM	50	(408) 777-3227	. . .	David Knapp	Kimberly Smith	David Woo	. . .	. . .	Ralph Qualls
Cypress *	c	CM	46	(714) 229-6700	Todd Seymore	John Bahorski	Denise Basham	Richard Storey	. . .	Mark Yokoyama	Doug Dancs
Daly City	c	CM	103	(650) 991-8127	Carol Klatt	Patricia Martel	Maria Cortes	Donald McVey	Ron Myers	. . .	D. P. Gleichenhaus
Dana Point *	c	CM	35	(949) 248-3500	Lisa Bartlett	Doug Chotkevys	Kathy Ward	. . .	Rick Robinson	Mark Levy	Brad Fowler
Danville	t	CM	41	(925) 314-3300	Mike Shimansky	Joseph Calabrigo	Marie Sunseri	Elizabeth Hudson	. . .	. . .	. . .
Davis	c	CM	60	(530) 757-5644	Lois Wolk	William Emlen	Bette Racki	. . .	Rose Conroy	James Hyde	Robert Weir
Del Mar	c	CM	4	(858) 755-9313	Carl Hilliard	Karen Brust	Mercedes Martin	Kim Krause	David Ott	. . .	David Scherer
Del Rey Oaks	c	CM	1	(408) 394-8511	Jack Barlich	. . .	. . .	. . .	. . .	Ron Langford	. . .
Delano *	c	CM	38	(661) 721-3300	Grace Vallejo	Abdel Salem	Phyllia Kraft	. . .	. . .	Mark DeRosia	Kim Domingo
Desert Hot Springs	c	CM	16	(760) 329-6411	. . .	Richard Daniels	Rossie Stobbs	. . .	. . .	Patrick Williams	. . .
Diamond Bar	c	CM	56	(900) 860-2489	. . .	. . .	Lynda Burgess	Linda Magnuson	. . .	. . .	David Liu
Dinuba	c	CM	16	(559) 591-5900	Mike Smith	J. Todd	Linda Barkley	. . .	Myles Chute	Myron Galchutt	Blanca Beltran
Dixon	c	CM	16	(707) 678-7000	Mary Ann Courville	Nancy Huston	Janice Beaman	Joan Streit	. . .	Donald Mort	David Melilli
Dos Palos	c	CM	4	(209) 392-2174	Jerry Westlake	Darrell Fonseca	Alice Thompson	Manuela Sousa	Dewayne Jones	Paul Lopez	Hub Ballinger
Downey	c	CM	107	(562) 904-7293	Gary McCaughan	Gerald Caton	. . .	Lowell Williams	Ronald Irwin	Gregory Caldwell	Richard Redmayne
Duarte	c	CM	21	(626) 357-7931	. . .	. . .	. . .	. . .	. . .	. . .	. . .
Dublin	c	CM	29	(925) 833-6600	. . .	Joni Pattillo	Carolyn Parkinson	. . .	William McCannon	Gary Thuman	Lee Thompson
Dunsmuir	c	CM	1	(530) 235-4822	Ivan Young	Patricia Hall	Kathryn Wilson	J. Anderson	Daniel Madilla	Craig Dilley	Carl Morzenti
East Palo Alto	c	CM	29	(650) 853-3100	Rose Gibson	Alvin James	Salani Wendt	Amy Rio	. . .	Wesley Bowling	David Miller
El Cajon *	c	CM	94	(619) 441-1736	Mark Lewis	Kathleen Henry	Kathie Rutledge	Michael Shelton	Mike Scott	Patrick Sprecco	George Turner
El Centro *	c	CM	37	(760) 337-4540	Ben Solomon	Ruben Duran	Diane Caldwell	Leti Salcido	Chris Petree	Harold Carter	Terry Hagen
El Cerrito *	c	CM	23	(510) 215-4300	William Jones	Scott Hanin	Cheryl Morse	Mary Dodge	Mark Scott	Scott Kirkand	Dan Clark
El Monte	c	CM	115	(626) 580-2001	Ernest Gutierrez	Juan Mireles	Lorene Gutierrez	Marcie Medina	. . .	Kenneth Weldon	. . .
El Paso De Robles *	c	CM	24	(805) 237-3888	Frank Mecham	James App	Dennis Fansler	. . .	Ken Johnson	Lisa Solomon	Douglass Monn
El Segundo	c	CM	16	(310) 524-2300	Kelly McDowell	. . .	Cynthia Mortesen	. . .	Norm Angelo	Jack Wayt	Steve Finton
Elk Grove	c	CM	17	(916) 683-7111	Rick Soares	Laura Gill	Peggy Jackson	. . .	. . .	. . .	. . .
Emeryville	c	CM	6	(510) 596-4300	John Flores	. . .	. . .	. . .	Stephen Cutright	Kenneth James	Henry Van Dyke
Encinitas *	c	CM	58	(760) 633-2600	Maggie Houlihan	Phillip Cotton	Deborah Cervone	Jennifer Smith	Mark Muir	. . .	Larry Watt
Escalon	c	CM	5	(209) 838-4100	. . .	Carl Greeson	Lisa Nebe	Ricky Gibbs	. . .	Douglas Dunford	. . .
Escondido	c	CM	133	(760) 839-4643	Lori Pfeiler	Clayton Phillips	Marsha Whalen	Gil Rojas	Victor Reed	Duane White	Patrick Thomas
Eureka	c	CM	26	(707) 441-4144	. . .	David Tyson	K. Franco Simmons	Carolyn Thomas	Eric Smith	David Douglas	Mike Knight
Exeter	c	CM	9	(559) 592-9224	Charlie Norman	. . .	. . .	Sheri Emerson	. . .	Clifton Bush	Felix Ortiz
Fairfax *	t	CM	7	(415) 453-1584	David Weinsoff	Michael Rock	Judith Anderson	. . .	. . .	Ken Hughes	Kathleen Wilkie
Fairfield	c	CM	96	(707) 428-7394	Karin MacMillan	Sean Quinn	Claudia Archer	Robert Leland	. . .	William Gresham	Charles Beck
Farmersville	c	CM	8	(209) 747-0458	Paul Boyer	. . .	Rosemary Silva	Rene Miller	William Lindquist	Mario Krstic	Eliseo Martinez
Ferndale *	c	CM	1	(707) 786-4224	Jeff Farley	Jay Parrish	Frances Scalvini	Debbie Austrus	. . .	Karl Poppelreiter	Tim Miranda
Fillmore	c	CM	13	(805) 524-3701	Evaristo Barajas	Thomas Ristau	Shirley Spitler	Barbara Smith	Patrick Askren	. . .	John Kozar
Firebaugh	c	CM	5	(559) 659-2043	Marcia Sablan	Jose Ramirez	Dorice Fannon	Patricia Barboza	. . .	Rod Lake	Wilson David
Folsom	c	CM	51	(916) 355-7208	Andy Morin	Kerry Miller	Christa Schmidt	James Francis	Dan Haverty	Sam Spiegel	Richard Lorenz
Fontana	c	CM	128	(909) 350-7650	Mack Nuaimi	Kenneth Hunt	Beatrice Watson	Lisa Strong	. . .	Frank Scialdone	Curtis Aaron
Fort Bragg	c	CM	7	(707) 961-2823	Jere Melo	Linda Ruffing	Cynthia VanWormer	. . .	. . .	. . .	Dave Goble
Fortuna *	c	CM	10	(707) 725-7600	Patrick Whitchurch	Duane Rigge	. . .	Robert Sousa	Robert Sommerville	Kent Bradshaw	Charles Clark
Foster City	c	CM	28	(650) 286-3200	Marland Townsend	James Hardy	Therese Tahir	Ricardo Santiago	Philip Torre	Randy Sonnenberg	John Lisenko
Fountain Valley	c	CM	54	(714) 593-4400	Laurann Cook	Raymond Kromer	. . .	Elizabeth Fox	. . .	Elvin Miali	Wayne Osborne
Fowler	c	CM	3	(559) 834-3113	. . .	David Elias	Jeannie Davis	Helen Harding	. . .	Darrell Jamgochian	. . .
Fremont *	c	CM	203	(510) 494-4660	Bob Wasserman	Frederick Diaz	Dawn Abrahamson	Harriet Commons	Bruce Martin	Craig Steckler	Jill Keimach
Fresno	c	CM	427	(559) 498-4591	Alan Autry	Andrew Souza	Rebecca Klisch	. . .	. . .	Jerry Dyer	. . .
Fullerton	c	CM	126	(714) 738-6310	Don Bankhead	Christopher Meyer	. . .	Glenn Steinbrink	James Reed	Patrick McKinley	Robert Savage
Galt	c	CM	19	(209) 745-4695	Christina De La Cruz	Ted Anderson	Liz Aguire	Inez Kiriu	. . .	Doug Matthews	Robert Kawasaki
Garden Grove	c	CM	165	(714) 741-5000	Bill Dalton	George Tindall	Ruth Smith	Kingsley Okereke	Keith Osborn	Joseph Polisar	Keith Jones
Gardena *	c	CM	57	(310) 217-9500	Paul Tanaka	Mitchell Lansdell	Maria Marquez	. . .	Robert Valdillez	Edward Medrano	Bruce Pollack
Gilroy	c	CM	41	(408) 846-0228	. . .	Thomas Haglund	Rhonda Pellin	Cindy Murphy	Dale Foster	Gregory Giusiana	. . .
Glendale	c	CM	194	(818) 548-2110	Gus Gomez	James Starbird	Doris Twedt	Robert Franz	Richard Hinz	Russell Siverling	Kerry Morford
Glendora *	c	CM	49	(626) 914-8200	Karen Davis	Chris Jeffers	Kathleen Sessman	Josh Betta	. . .	Charles Montoya	David Davies
Goleta	c	CM	55	(805) 961-7500	Jonny Wallis	Daniel Singer	Deborah Constantino	Zenda James	Martin Johnson	Chris Pappas	Steven Wagner
Gonzales *	c	CM	7	(831) 675-5000	Maria Orozco	Rene Mendez	. . .	. . .	Rick Rubbo	Paulette Cudio	Carlos Lopez
Grand Terrace	c	CM	11	(909) 824-6621	Lee Ann Garcia	Thomas Schwab	Brenda Stanfill	Larry Ronnow	. . .	. . .	Jerry Glander
Grass Valley	c	CM	10	(530) 274-4309	. . .	Daniel Holler	Kristi Bashor	Carol Fish	Jim Marquis	John Foster	. . .
Greenfield *	c	CM	12	(831) 674-5591	John Huerta	Roger Wong	. . .	Ann Rathbun	John Sims	Joe Grebmeier	Glen Rudy
Gridley	c	CM	5	(530) 846-5695	Frank Cook	Randy Johnsen	. . .	. . .	. . .	Jack Storne	Ed Melton
Grover Beach	c	CM	13	(805) 473-4567	Stephen Lieberman	Robert Perrault	D. McMahon	Gayla Chapman	Michael Hubert	James Copsey	. . .
Guadalupe	c	CM	5	(805) 343-1340	Sam Arca	Frank Usher	. . .	Carolyn Cooper	Henry Lawrence	William Tucker	Samuel Angulo
Gustine *	c	CM	4	(209) 854-6471	Rich Ford	Margaret Silveira	Kelly Buendia	Roberta Casteel	Pat Borrelli	Richard Calderon	Ernie Garza
Half Moon Bay *	c	CM	11	(650) 726-8270	Bonnie McClung	. . .	Siobhan Smith	Hector Lwin	. . .	Don O'Keefe	. . .
Hanford	c	CM	41	(559) 585-2500	. . .	Gary Misenhimer	Karen McAlister	Tom Dibble	Timothy Teronimo	Carlos Mestas	. . .
Hawaiian Gardens	c	CM	14	(562) 420-2641	Ralph Cesena	Ernesto Marquez	Domenic Ruggeri	Michael Fresques	. . .	. . .	Joe Vasquez
Hawthorne	c	CM	84	(310) 349-2900	Larry Guidi	Jag Pathirana	Angie English	. . .	. . .	Michael Heffner	Arnold Shadbehr
Hayward	c	CM	140	(510) 583-4000	Roberta Cooper	Gregory Jones	Angelina Reyes	Debra Auker	Larry Arfsten	Lloyd Lowe	Robert Bauman
Healdsburg	c	CM	10	(707) 431-3317	Jason Liles	Chet Wystepek	Maria Curiel	Tamera Haas	Randy Collins	Susan Jones	George Hicks
Hemet	c	CM	58	(909) 765-2300	C. Robin Lowe	Stephen Harding	Gene Graves	. . .	Dave Vanverst	Lee Evanson	Juan Perez
Hercules	c	CM	19	(510) 799-8299	Terry Segerberg	Michael Sakamoto	. . .	Marie Simons	Gary Boyles	Michael Tye	Sharad Pandya
Hermosa Beach	c	CM	18	(310) 318-0239	Sam Edgerton	Stephen Burrell	Elaine Doerfling	Viki Copeland	Russell Tingley	Greg Savelli	Richard Morgan
Hesperia *	c	CM	62	(760) 947-1000	Thurston Smith	Michael Podegracz	Vicki Soderquist	. . .	Tim Wessel	Lance Clark	Dale Burke
Highland	c	CM	44	(909) 864-6861	Ross Jones	. . .	Betty Hughes	Chuck Dantnow	Jim Rissmiller	Sheree Stewart	Ernie Wong
Hillsborough	t	CM	10	(650) 375-7400	D. Regan	A. Constantouros	Rachelle Ungaretti	Edna Masbad	Dave Milanese	Matthew O'Connor	Martha DeBry
Hollister	c	CM	34	(831) 636-4300	. . .	. . .	. . .	Barbara Mulholland	William Garringer	Larry Todd	Clint Quilter
Holtville	c	CM	5	(760) 356-2912	Ira Hearen	Laura Fischer	. . .	Rosa Ramirez	David Lantzer	John Myers	Gerald Peacher
Hughson	c	CM	3	(209) 883-4055	Thomas Crowder	Joseph Donabed	Mary Jane Cantrell	. . .	. . .	. . .	Ron Bremer
Huntington Beach	c	CM	189	(714) 536-5491	Janet Lockhart	Frederick Wilson	Joan Flynn	Daniel Villella	Duane Olson	Kenneth Small	Robert Beardsley
Huntington Park	c	CM	61	(323) 582-6161	Elba Guerrero	Gregory Korduner	Rosanna Ramirez	Don Pruyn	. . .	Michael Trevis	Neil Poole
Huron *	c	CM	6	(559) 945-2241	Ramon Dominguez	. . .	. . .	. . .	. . .	Frank Steenport	Nick Escandon
Imperial	c	CM	7	(760) 355-4371	Mark Gran	Marlene Best	Debra Jackson	. . .	. . .	. . .	Joel Hamby
Imperial Beach *	c	CM	26	(619) 423-8300	Jim Janney	Gary Brown	Jacque Hald	. . .	. . .	Octavia Parker	Hank Levien
Indian Wells	c	CM	3	(760) 346-2489	. . .	Greg Johnson	. . .	Kevin McCarthy	. . .	. . .	William Hughes
Indio	c	CM	49	(760) 391-4000	Ben Godfrey	Glenn Southard	Cynthia Hernandez	Susan Mahoney	Ray Paiz	Bradley Ramos	Jim Smith

Directory 1/9 continued — OFFICIALS IN U.S. MUNICIPALITIES 2,500 AND OVER IN POPULATION

Jurisdiction		Type	Form of govern-ment	2000 Popu-lation	Main telephone number	Chief elected official	Appointed administrator	Clerk of the governing board	Chief financial officer	Fire chief	Police chief	Public works director
CALIFORNIA continued												
Industry		c	CM	. .	(626) 333-2211	David Perez	Philip Iriarte	Jodi Scrivens	Victoria Gallo	. . .	. . .	. . .
Inglewood		c	CM	112	(310) 412-5111	Roosevelt Dorn	Mark Weinberg	Yvonne Horton	. . .	. . .	Ronald Bank	William Mahar
Ione	*	c	CM	7	(209) 274-2412	. . .	Kimberly Kerr	Janice Traverso	Mark Smith	Ken Mackey	Michael Johnson	. . .
Irvine		c	CM	143	(949) 724-6000	Beth Krom	Sean Joyce	Pamyla Means	. . .	. . .	. . .	Marty Bryant
Irwindale		c	CM	1	(626) 430-2200	Manuel Almazan	Robert Griego	. . .	Abraham Dedios	. . .	Julian Miranda	Rod Posada
Jackson	*	c	CM	3	(209) 223-1646	Rosalie Escamilla	Michael Daly	Gisele Cangelosi	. . .	Mark Morton	Scott Morrison	. . .
Kerman		c	CM	8	(559) 846-9384	. . .	Ron Manfredi	Edith Forsstrom	. . .	. . .	William Newton	Alan Jacobsen
King City	*	c	CM	11	(408) 385-3281	Jeff Pereria	Michael Powers	. . .	Jim Larson	Danny Conaster	Nick Baldiviez	Sal Morales
Kingsburg	*	c	CM	9	(559) 897-5821	Leland Bergstrom	Donald Pauley	Sue Bauch	. . .	Gary Rocha	Jim Taylor	. . .
La Canada Flintridge	*	c	CM	20	(818) 790-8880	. . .	Mark Alexander	Kathleen Sessman	. . .	. . .	. . .	Steven Castellanos
La Habra		c	CM	58	(562) 905-9700	. . .	Donald Hannah	Sharie Apodaca	. . .	. . .	Dennis Kies	. . .
La Habra Heights		c	CM	5	(562) 694-6302	Stan Carroll	Shauna Clark	. . .	. . .	John Nielsen	. . .	. . .
La Mesa	*	c	CM	54	(619) 667-1179	Arthur Madrid	Sandra Kerl	Mary Kennedy	. . .	David Burk	Cliff Resch	Gregory Humora
La Mirada	*	c	CM	46	(562) 943-0131	Hal Malkin	Andrea Travis	Susan Ramos	Kevin Prelgovisk	. . .	. . .	Steve Forster
La Palma	*	c	CM	15	(714) 690-3330	G. Henry Charoen	Dominic Lazzaretto	. . .	Keith Neves	. . .	Ed Ethell	Jeff Moneda
La Puente	*	c	CM	41	(626) 855-1500	Louie Lujan	. . .	Amy Turner	Young Kim	. . .	. . .	Rene Salas
La Quinta	*	c	CM	23	(760) 777-7000	Don Adolph	Thomas Genovese	Veronica Montecino	John Falconer	Dorian Cooley	Colleen Walker	Timothy Jonasson
La Verne		c	CM	31	(909) 596-8726	Jon Blickenstaff	Martin Lomeli	Kathleen Hamm	Ronald Clark	John Breaux	Ronald Ingels	Dan Keesey
Lafayette		c	CM	23	(925) 284-1968	Don Tatzin	Steven Falk	Joanne Robbins	Gonzalo Silva	. . .	Mike Hubbard	Ron Lefler
Laguna Beach		c	CM	23	(949) 497-3311	Toni Iseman	Kenneth Frank	Verna Rollinger	. . .	Ken MacLeod	James Spreine	. . .
Laguna Hills	*	c	CM	31	(949) 707-2600	L. Allan Songstad	Bruce Channing	Peggy Johns	. . .	. . .	Steven Doan	Kenneth Rosenfield
Laguna Niguel		c	CM	61	(949) 362-4300	Mike Whipple	Timothy Casey	. . .	Dennis Miura	. . .	. . .	K. Montgomery
Lake Elsinore		c	CM	28	(909) 674-3124	Pamela Brinley	Robert Brady	Vicki Kasad	Matt Pressey	. . .	. . .	David Sapp
Lake Forest	*	c	CM	73	(949) 461-3400	Mark Tettemer	Robert Dunek	Sherry Wentz	Liz Andrew	. . .	. . .	Robert Woodings
Lakeport		c	MC	4	(707) 263-5615	Richard Lamkin	. . .	Janel Chapman	. . .	. . .	Thomas Engstrom	. . .
Lakewood	*	c	CM	79	(562) 866-9771	. . .	Howard Chambers	Denise Hayward	Diane Perkin	. . .	. . .	Lisa Rapp
Lancaster		c	CM	118	(805) 723-6000	Frank Roberts	. . .	Geri Bryan	Gary Hill	. . .	. . .	Jeffrey Long
Larkspur		c	CM	12	(415) 927-5110	. . .	Jean Bonander	Cynthia Huisman	Amy Koenig	Robert Sinnott	Phillip Green	Hamid Shamsapour
Lathrop		c	CM	10	(209) 941-7200	Kristy Sayles	Yvonne Quiring	Arthur Caldeira	Terri Vigna	. . .	Dolores Delgado	Cary Keaton
Lawndale	*	c	CM	31	(310) 973-3200	Harold Hofmann	Keith Breskin	Pamela Giamario	Ken Louie	. . .	. . .	Marlene Miyoshi
Lemon Grove	*	c	CM	24	(619) 825-3800	Mary Sessom	Graham Mitchell	Susan Garcia	Betty Hofman	Tim Smith	. . .	Patrick Lund
Lemoore	*	c	CM	19	(559) 924-6700	John Murray	Jeff Briltz	Nanci Lima	Nancy Cota	John Gibson	Kimberly Morrell	David Wlaschin
Lincoln		c	CM	11	(916) 645-3314	Kent Nakata	James Estep	Pat Avila	. . .	David Whitt	Brian Vizzusi	John Pedri
Lindsay	*	c	CM	10	(559) 562-7103	Ed Murray	Scot Townsend	. . .	Kenny Walker	. . .	. . .	Michael Camarena
Live Oak		c	CM	6	(530) 695-2112	. . .	Rob Hickey	Melissa Dempsey	Satwant Takhar	C. Vanevenhoven	. . .	Michael Bohlander
Livermore	*	c	CM	73	(925) 960-4100	Marshall Kamena	Linda Barton	. . .	Monica Potter	William Code	Steven Sweeney	Daniel McIntyre
Livingston		c	CM	10	(209) 394-8041	Gurpal Samra	Richard Warne	Martha Nateras	. . .	Gordon Wilkerson	William Eldridge	Paul Creighton
Lodi		c	CM	56	(209) 333-6800	Susan Hitchcock	Blair King	Randi Johl	James Krueger	Michael Pretz	Jerry Adams	Richard Prima
Loma Linda		c	CM	18	(909) 799-2810	. . .	Dennis Halloway	Pamela O'Camb	Rita Shirley-West	. . .	. . .	T. Jarb Thaipejr
Lomita	*	c	CM	20	(310) 325-7110	Margaret Estrada	Tom Odom	Dawn Tomita	. . .	. . .	. . .	Wendell Johnson
Lompoc		c	CM	41	(805) 736-1261	Dick Dewees	. . .	Jane Green	John Walk	Linual White	William Brown	Larry Bean
Long Beach		c	CM	461	(562) 570-6621	Beverly O'Neill	. . .	Larry Herrera	Michael Killebrew	David Ellis	Anthony Batts	Christine Andersen
Loomis	*	t	CM	6	(916) 652-1840	Walt Scherer	Perry Beck	Crickett Strock	Roger Carroll	Dave Wheeler	Dave Harris	Brian Fragiao
Los Alamitos		c	CM	11	(562) 431-3538	Frederick Freeman	. . .	Sue Vanderpool	. . .	. . .	Michael McCrary	. . .
Los Altos		c	CM	27	(650) 947-2740	Curtis Cole	. . .	Susan Kitchens	Starla Robinson	. . .	. . .	. . .
Los Altos Hills		t	CM	7	(650) 941-7222	Dean Warshawsky	Carl Cahill	Karen Jost	Sarah Ragsdale	. . .	. . .	Henry Louie
Los Angeles		c	MC	3694	(213) 485-2881	Richard Riordan	. . .	J. Carey	. . .	William Bamattre	Bernard Parks	. . .
Los Banos	*	c	CM	25	(209) 827-7000	Tommy Jones	Stephen Rath	. . .	Melinda Wall	Chet Guintini	Michael Hughes	. . .
Los Gatos	*	t	CM	28	(408) 354-6832	Mike Wasserman	Greg Larson	. . .	Stephen Conway	. . .	Scott Seaman	Todd Capurso
Lynwood		c	CM	69	(310) 603-0220	Fernando Pedroza	Roger Haley	Andrea Hooper	Robert Torrez	. . .	. . .	Paul Nguyen
Madera	*	c	CM	43	(559) 661-5400	. . .	David Tooley	Sonia Alvarez	David Coff	. . .	Michael Kime	Matthew Bullis
Malibu	*	c	CM	12	(310) 456-2489	Pamela Ulich	Jim Thorsen	Lisa Pope	. . .	. . .	. . .	Robert Brager
Mammoth Lakes		t	CM	7	(760) 934-8989	Rick Wood	Rob Clark	Anita Hatter	Brad Koehn	. . .	Michael Donnelly	Raymond Jarvis
Manhattan Beach		c	CM	33	(310) 802-5000	Linda Wilson	G. Dolan	Liza Tamura	. . .	Dennis Groat	Ernest Klevesahl	Neil Miller
Manteca		c	CM	49	(209) 239-8414	Willie Weatherford	Steven Pinkerton	Joann Tilton	Suzanne Mutimer	George Quaresma	Charles Halford	Mark Houghton
Marina		c	CM	25	(831) 884-1211	I. Mettee-McCutchon	Anthony Altfeld	Joy Junsay	. . .	Harold Kelley	. . .	Charles Johnson
Martinez		c	CM	35	(510) 372-3522	. . .	Philip Vince	. . .	. . .	. . .	. . .	. . .
Marysville		c	CM	12	(530) 749-3901	Bill Harris	Stephen Casey	Billie Fangman	Dixon Coulter	. . .	Bret Smith	David Lamon
Maywood		c	CM	28	(323) 562-5000	. . .	Edward Ahrens	Jose Ceja	. . .	. . .	Bruce Leflar	. . .
Mc Farland		c	CM	9	(805) 792-3091	. . .	. . .	. . .	. . .	. . .	. . .	. . .
Mendota		c	MC	7	(559) 655-3291	Joseph Riofrio	Gabriel Gonzalez	Brenda Carter	. . .	Doug Hicks	. . .	Domingo Morales
Menlo Park		c	CM	30	(650) 858-3370	Nicholas Jellins	Glen Rojas	. . .	Carol Augustine	. . .	Christopher Boyd	. . .
Merced		c	CM	63	(209) 385-6834	. . .	John Bramble	. . .	Bradley Grant	Kenneth Mitten	Mark Dossetti	John Raggio
Mill Valley		c	CM	13	(415) 388-4033	Christopher Raker	Anne Montgomery	Mary Herr	Eric Erikson	. . .	. . .	Wayne Bush
Millbrae		c	CM	20	(650) 259-2334	Robert Gottschalk	. . .	Deborah Konkol	. . .	Dennis Haag	Thomas Hitchcock	Ron Popp
Milpitas	*	c	CM	62	(408) 586-3090	Jose Esteves	. . .	Gail Blalock	Emma Karlen	Bill Weisgerber	Charles Lawson	Greg Armendariz
Mission Viejo	*	c	CM	93	(949) 470-3000	Frank Ury	Dennis Wilberg	Karen Hamman	. . .	. . .	Steve Bernardi	Mark Chagnon
Modesto	*	c	CM	188	(209) 577-5402	Jim Ridenour	Gregory Nyhoff	Stephanie Lopez	Wayne Padilla	James Miguel	Roy Wasden	Nicholas Pinhey
Monrovia	*	c	CM	36	(626) 932-5550	Robert Hammond	Scott Ochoa	Linda Proctor	. . .	C. Donovan	Roger Johnson	Ron Bow
Montclair	*	c	CM	33	(909) 626-8571	Paul Eaton	Lee McDougal	Donna Jackson	Richard Beltran	Troy Ament	. . .	Marilyn Staats
Monte Sereno		c	CM	3	(408) 354-7635	Erin Garner	Brian Loventhal	A. Chelemengos	Sue L'Heureux	. . .	. . .	. . .
Montebello		c	CM	62	(323) 887-1200	Ed Vasquez	Richard Torres	Robert King	Chickwan Tam	Jim Cox	G. Couso-Vasquez	Ted Spaceff
Monterey		c	CM	29	(831) 646-3765	Daniel Albert	Fred Meurer	Bonnie Gawf	Don Rhoads	Gregory Glass	. . .	Bill Reichmuth
Monterey Park		c	CM	60	(626) 307-1410	Betty Chu	June Yotsuya	David Barron	David Dong	Cathy Orchard	Jones Moy	Ronald Merry
Moorpark	*	c	CM	31	(805) 517-6200	Janice Parvin	Steven Kueny	. . .	Ron Ahlers	Robert Roper	Bob Brooks	Ken Gilbert
Moraga	*	t	CM	16	(925) 888-7022	Dave Trotter	. . .	. . .	Joan Streit	. . .	Mark Ruppenthal	Jill Mercurio
Moreno Valley		c	CM	142	(909) 413-3000	. . .	Robert Gutierrez	Alice Reed	Steve Chapman	. . .	. . .	Trent Pulliam
Morgan Hill	*	c	CM	33	(408) 779-7278	Dennis Kennedy	J. Tewes	Irma Torrez	John Dilles	. . .	Bruce Cumming	James Ashcraft
Morro Bay	*	c	CM	10	(805) 772-6200	Janice Peters	Andrea Lueker	Bridgett Bauer	Susan Slayton	Mike Pond	John DeRohan	Bruce Ambo
Mount Shasta	*	c	CM	3	(530) 926-7510	Timothy Stearns	Kevin Plett	Prudence Kennedy	Theodore Marconi	Matt Melo	Parish Cross	Rod Bryan
Mountain View	*	c	CM	70	(650) 903-6309	. . .	Kevin Duggan	Angee Salvador	Patty Kong	. . .	Scott Vermeer	Cathy Lazarus
Murrieta	*	c	MC	44	(951) 304-2489	. . .	Rick Dudley	Kay Vinson	Suzanne Wellcome	Paul Chrisman	Mark Wright	Patrick Thomas
Napa		c	CM	72	(707) 257-9500	Ed Henderson	Michael Parness	Pam Nigliazzo	Jed Christensen	. . .	Dan Monez	Mike O'Bryon
National City		c	CM	54	(619) 336-4300	Nicholas Inzunza	Chris Zapata	Michael Dalla	Bill Yeoman	Rod Juniel	Adolfo Gonzales	Roberto Saucedo
Needles		c	CM	4	(760) 326-2113	Pete Dwyer	. . .	. . .	Virginia Tasker	Robert Lyons	Mark Taylor	. . .
Nevada City	*	c	CM	3	(530) 265-2496	. . .	Gene Albaugh	Barbara Coffman	Catrina Andes	Sam Goodspeed	Louis Trovato	Verne Taylor
Newark	*	c	CM	42	(510) 578-4267	David Smith	John Becker	Sheila Harrington	Dennis Jones	Demetrious Shaffer	Ray Samuels	. . .
Newman		c	CM	7	(209) 862-3725	John Fantazia	Michael Holland	. . .	. . .	Melvin Souza	Michael Brady	Ernie Garza
Newport Beach		c	CM	70	(949) 644-3300	Steve Bromberg	Homer Bludau	Lavonne Harkless	. . .	Timothy Riley	Robert McDonell	Steve Badum
Norco		c	CM	24	(951) 735-3900	Herbert Higgins	Jeffery Allred	Debra McNay	. . .	Jack Frye	. . .	Bill Thompson
Norwalk	*	c	CM	103	(562) 929-5700	Michael Mendez	Ernie Garcia	Theresa Devoy	. . .	. . .	. . .	Grissel Chavez
Novato	*	c	CM	47	(415) 899-8900	. . .	Patricia Thompson	Shirley Gremmels	. . .	. . .	Joseph Kreins	Glenn Young
Oakdale	*	c	CM	15	(209) 845-3571	Farrell Jackson	Steven Hallam	Nancy Lilly	Albert Auila	Michael Botto	Marty West	. . .
Oakland		c	MC	399	(510) 238-3301	Jerry Brown	. . .	Ceda Floyd	William Noland	Gerald Simon	Richard Word	. . .
Oakley	*	c	CM	25	(925) 625-7007	Bruce Connelley	Bryan Montgomery	Nancy Ortenblad	Paul Abelson	. . .	Chris Thorsen	. . .

Directory 1/9 continued — OFFICIALS IN U.S. MUNICIPALITIES 2,500 AND OVER IN POPULATION

Jurisdiction	Type	Form of govern-ment	2000 Popu-lation	Main telephone number	Chief elected official	Appointed administrator	Clerk of the governing board	Chief financial officer	Fire chief	Police chief	Public works director
CALIFORNIA continued											
Oceanside *	c	CM	161	(760) 435-3500	James Wood	Peter Weiss	Barbara Wayne	Teri Fero	Terry Garrison	Frank McCoy	Joseph Arranga
Ojai	c	CM	7	(805) 646-5581	Sue Horgan	Jere Kersnar	Carlon Strobel	Susie Mears	...	Bruce Norris	Mike Culver
Ontario	c	CM	158	(909) 395-2442	Gary Ovitt	Gregory Devereaux	Traci McGinley	Yee Grant	Jim Bowman	James Doyle	Kenneth Jeske
Orange	c	CM	128	(714) 744-5500	Mark Murphy	John Sibley	Cassandra Cathcart	...	Vince Bonacker	Andy Romero	Harry Thomas
Orange Cove	c	CM	7	(559) 626-4488	Victor Lopez	Alan Bengyel	June Bracamontes	Ross Holliday	Bob Terry	L. Wright	...
Orinda *	c	CM	17	(925) 253-4220	Victoria Smith	Janet Keeter	Michele Olsen	...	Pete Nowicki	...	Rudi Golnik
Orland *	c	CM	6	(530) 865-1600	Paul Barr	Paul Poczobut	...	Daryl Brock	Jeff Gomes	Robert Pasero	Jere Schmitke
Oroville	c	CM	13	(530) 538-2407	...	Sharon Atteberry	...	Diane MacMillan	David Pittman	Mitchel Brown	Eric Teitelman
Oxnard *	c	CM	170	(805) 385-7590	Manuel Lopez	Edmund Sotelo	Daniel Martinez	Susan Winder	W. Milligan	Arthur Lopez	Granville Bowman
Pacific Grove *	c	CM	15	(831) 648-3100	Daniel Cort	...	Ann O'Rourke	James Becklenberg	...	Darius Engles	Celia Martinez
Pacifica *	c	CM	38	(650) 738-7301	...	Stephen Rhodes	Kathy O'Connell	...	Ron Myers	James Saunders	Van Ocampo
Palm Desert	c	CM	41	(760) 346-0611	Jean Benson	Carlos Ortega	Sheila Gilligan	Paul Gibson	...	...	Mark Greenwood
Palm Springs	c	CM	42	(760) 323-8200	William Kleindienst	David Ready	Patricia Sanders	Thomas Kanarr	Bary Freet	Gary Jeandron	David Barakian
Palmdale *	c	CM	116	(661) 267-5400	...	Stephen Williams	Victoria Hancock	Elizabeth St. John	...	...	Leon Swain
Palo Alto	c	CM	58	(650) 329-2376	...	James Keene	Donna Rogers	...	Nicholas Marinaro	Lynne Johnson	Glenn Roberts
Palos Verdes Estates *	c	CM	13	(310) 378-0383	Joseph Sherwood	Joseph Hoefgen	...	...	...	Dan Dreiling	Allan Rigg
Paradise	t	CM	26	(530) 872-6291	Daniel Wentland	Charles Rough	Frankie Rutledge	Rodney Davenport	Jim Broshears	...	Albert McGreehan
Paramount	c	CM	55	(562) 220-2027	Gene Daniels	...	Lana Chikami	Jose Gomez	...	...	Christopher Cash
Parlier *	c	CM	11	(559) 646-3545	Armando Lopez	Lou Martinez	Dorothy Garza	Patricia Barboza	...	Ismael Soliz	Rudy Vela
Pasadena	c	CM	133	(626) 405-4000	Johnny Isbell	Bernard Melekian	...	Steven Stark	...	...	Arlington Rodgers
Patterson	c	CM	11	(209) 892-8000	David Keller	M. Morris	Maricela Vela	Margaret Souza	James Kinnear	Tyrone Spencer	Ignacio Lopez
Perris	c	CM	36	(951) 943-6100	Daryl Busch	Richard Belmudez	Margaret Rey	Ron Carr	Tim Williams	Guy Kestell	Ahmad Ansari
Petaluma	c	CM	54	(707) 778-4340	...	John Brown	Gayle Peterson	William Thomas	Chris Albertson	...	Richard Skladzien
Pico Rivera *	c	CM	63	(562) 942-2000	...	Charles Fuentes	Daryl Betancur	John Herrera	...	Michael Rothans	Michael Moore
Piedmont	c	MC	10	(510) 420-3040	...	...	Ann Swift	Mark Bichsel	John Speakman	John Moilan	Larry Rosenberg
Pinole	c	CM	19	(510) 724-9000	Maria Alegria	...	Elizabeth Grimes	Catherine Heater	James Parrott	Theodore Barnes	Gordon Freeman
Pismo Beach	c	CM	8	(805) 773-4657	Mary Ann Reiss	Kevin Rice	Lori Grigsby	...	Matt Jenkins	Joseph Cortez	Dennis Delzeit
Pittsburg *	c	CM	56	(925) 252-4878	Will Casey	Marc Grisham	Alice Evenson	Marie Simons	...	Aaron Baker	...
Placentia *	c	CM	46	(714) 993-8117	Scott Brady	Troy Butzlaff	Patrick Melia	Steven Brisco	Chip Prather	James Anderson	...
Placerville	c	CM	9	(530) 642-5200	...	John Driscoll	...	...	...	Steve Brown	Gary Valladao
Pleasant Hill	c	CM	32	(925) 671-5270	Suzanne Angeli	...	Doris Nilsen	Richard Ricci	...	Michael Phalen	Leary Wong
Pleasanton	c	CM	63	(925) 931-5048	Jennifer Hosterman	Nelson Fialho	Karen Diaz	David Culver	William Cody	Michael Fraser	Robert Wilson
Plymouth *	c	CM	..	(209) 245-6941	Jon Colburn	Dixon Flynn	...	Jeffrey Gardner	...	Martin Ryan	Selby Beck
Pomona	c	CM	149	(909) 620-2491	Edward Cortez	Linda Lowry	Elizabeth Villeral	Paula Chamberlain	...	James Lewis	Chris Vogt
Port Hueneme	c	CM	21	(805) 986-6500	Maricela Morales	David Norman	...	Robert Bravo	...	Fernando Estrella	Andres Santamaria
Porterville	c	CM	39	(209) 782-7466	Gordon Woods	John Longley	...	...	S. Guyton	Silver Rodriguez	...
Portola	c	CM	2	(530) 832-4216	Bill Adamson	James Murphy	...	...	Curtis Marshall	...	Bill Whitener
Portola Valley *	t	MC	4	(650) 851-1700	...	Angela Howard	Sharon Hanlon	...	...	...	Howard Young
Poway *	c	CM	48	(858) 668-4400	Michael Cafagna	Rodney Gould	Linda Troyan	Andrew White	...	Todd Frank	Kevin Haupt
Rancho Cordova *	c	CM	57	(916) 851-8700	Linda Budge	Ted Gaebler	Mindy Cuppy	Donna Silva	...	Reuben Meeks	Cyrus Abhar
Rancho Cucamonga *	c	CM	127	(909) 477-2700	Donald Kurth	Jack Lam	Janice Reynolds	Tamara Layne	Peter Bryan	...	Dave Blevins
Rancho Mirage	c	CM	13	(760) 324-4511	G. Hobart	Patrick Pratt	Elena Keeran	Scott Morgan	...	...	Bruce Harry
Rancho Palos Verdes	c	CM	41	(310) 377-0360	Larry Clark	Carolyn Lehr	...	Dennis McLean	...	...	Dean Allison
Rancho Santa Margarita *	c	CM	47	(949) 635-1800	Jerry Holloway	Steven Hayman	Molly McLaughlin	...	...	Chuck Wilmot	Tom Wheeler
Red Bluff *	c	CM	13	(530) 527-2605	Wayne Brown	Martin Nichols	Gloria Shepard	M. Vanwamerdam	Michael Bachmeyer	Scott Capilla	Mark Barthel
Redding	c	CM	80	(530) 225-4065	Dick Dickerson	Kurt Starman	C. Strohmayer	Stephen Strong	Gilbert Fry	Leonard Moty	...
Redlands *	c	CM	63	(909) 798-7510	Jon Harrison	Nabar Martinez	Lorrie Poyzer	Tina Kundig	Jeff Frazier	James Bueermann	Rosemary Hoerning
Redondo Beach	c	CM	63	(310) 372-1171	Gregory Hill	William Workman	Sandy Forest	Diana Moreno	Anthon Beck	Robert Luman	Sylvia Glazer
Redwood City	c	CM	75	(650) 780-7000	...	Peter Ingram	Silvia Vonderlinden	Brian Ponty	Gerald Kohlmann	Carlos Bolanos	...
Reedley	c	CM	20	(559) 637-4200	Ray Soleno	Rocky Rogers	Elizabeth Vines	Lori Oken	David Powell	Douglas Johnson	...
Rialto	c	CM	91	(909) 820-2525	Grace Vargas	Henry Garcia	Barbara McGee	June Overholt	Stephen Wells	Michael Meyers	Robert Harary
Richmond	c	CM	99	(510) 620-6602	Irma Anderson	William Lindsay	Delores Holmes	James Goins	Michael Banks	Chris Magnus	Willie Haywood
Ridgecrest *	c	CM	24	(760) 499-5000	Marshall Holloway	Michael Avery	Rita Gable	...	...	Ronald Strand	Dennis Speer
Rio Dell	c	CM	3	(707) 764-3532	...	...	...	...	...	Pat Medina	...
Rio Vista	c	CM	4	(707) 374-6451	...	Hector De La Rosa	Kathleen Smith	Misty Cheng	Keith Tadewald	Larry Profitt	David Melilli
Ripon	c	CM	10	(209) 599-2108	Charles Winn	Everett Compton	Lynette Van Laar	...	...	Richard Bull	Ted Johnston
Riverbank	c	CM	15	(209) 869-7101	Chris Crifasi	Richard Holmer	...	...	...	Art Voortman	Laurie Barton
Riverside	c	CM	255	(951) 826-5553	Ronald Loveridge	...	Colleen Nicol	Paul Sundeen	Dave Carlson	Russ Leach	Siobhan Foster
Rocklin *	c	CM	36	(916) 625-5000	Peter Hill	Carlos Urrutia	Barbara Ivanusich	Kimberly Sarkovich	Bill Mikesell	Mark Siemens	Kent Foster
Rohnert Park *	c	CM	42	(707) 588-2227	Jake Mackenzie	Stephen Donley	Judy Hauff	Sandra Lipitz	Jack Rosevear	...	John McArthur
Rolling Hills	c	CM	1	(310) 377-1521	...	Anton Dahlerbruch	Marilyn Kern	Nan Huang	...	...	...
Rolling Hills Estates	c	CM	7	(310) 377-1577	Susan Seamans	Douglas Prichard	...	...	...	...	...
Rosemead	c	CM	53	(626) 569-2100	John Tran	Oliver Chi	Nina Castruita	...	...	...	...
Roseville	c	CM	79	(916) 774-5475	...	W. Robinson	Sonia Orozco	...	Ken Wagner	Joel Neves	Robert Jensen
Ross *	t	MC	2	(415) 453-1453	...	Gary Broad	...	...	Thomas Vallee	James Reis	Mel Jarjoura
Sacramento	c	CM	407	(916) 264-5726	Heather Fargo	Ray Kerridge	Valerie Burrowes	Thomas Sinclair	Dennis Smith	Arturo Venegas	Michael Kashiwagi
Salinas	c	CM	151	(831) 758-7254	...	Artie Fields	Ann Camel	John Copeland	Daniel Hernandez	Juan Ruiz	...
San Anselmo	c	CM	12	(415) 258-4600	...	Debra Stutsman	...	Janet Pendoley	...	Charles Maynard	Rabi Elias
San Bernardino	c	MC	185	(909) 384-5161	Judith Valles	...	Rachel Clark	Barbara Pachon	Larry Pitzer	...	Michael Hays
San Bruno	c	CM	40	(650) 616-7056	Larry Franzella	Constance Jackson	Carol Bonner	John O'Leary	Dan Voreyer	Lee Violett	...
San Buenaventura (Ventura)	c	CM	100	(805) 654-7853	Carl Morehouse	Rick Cole	Mabi Plisky	Jay Panzic	Mike Lavery	Pat Miller	Ronald Calkins
San Carlos *	c	CM	27	(650) 802-4100	...	Mark Weiss	Christine Boland	R. Mendenhall	Doug Fry	Greg Rothaus	Robert Weil
San Clemente *	c	CM	49	(949) 361-8324	Joe Anderson	G. Scarborough	Joanne Baade	Thomas Rendina	...	...	...
San Diego	c	MC	1223	(619) 236-6363	Susan Golding	Jay Goldstone	Charles Abdelnour	...	Jeff Bowman	William Lansdowne	...
San Dimas	c	CM	34	(909) 394-6200	Curtis Morris	Blaine Michaelis	Ina Rios	...	...	...	Krishna Patel
San Fernando	c	CM	23	(818) 898-1200	Julie Ruelas	Jose Pulido	Elena Chavez	Lorena Quijano	...	Anthony Alba	...
San Francisco	c	MC	776	(415) 557-4800	Willie Brown	Edwin Lee	Gloria Young	Chris Vein	Paul Tabacco	Fred Lau	...
San Gabriel	c	CM	39	(626) 308-2800	...	P. Paules	Cynthia Trujillo	Thomas Marston	Joseph Nestor	David Lawton	...
San Jacinto *	c	CM	23	(951) 654-7337	Jim Ayres	Barry McClellan	Dorothy Chouinard	C. Rogers-Elmore	Bob Michaels	William Tyler	Michael Emberton
San Jose	c	CM	894	(408) 277-4000	Ron Gonzales	Debra Figone	Patricia O'Hearn	Scott Johnson	Dale Foster	Tom Wheatley	Katy Allen
San Juan Bautista	c	CM	1	(831) 623-4661	Arturo Medina	Jennifer Coile	Shawna Serna	Janet Locey	Rick Cokley	Curtis Hill	...
San Juan Capistrano	c	CM	33	(949) 493-1171	...	Dave Adams	Margaret Monahan	Cynthia Russell	...	...	Amy Amirani
San Leandro	c	CM	79	(510) 577-3358	Sheila Young	...	Gayle Petersen	Jesse Balola	...	Joseph Kitchen	Robert Rockett
San Luis Obispo	c	CM	44	(805) 781-7100	David Romero	Kenneth Hampian	Lee Price	William Statler	Wolfgang Knabe	Deborah Linden	...
San Marcos	c	CM	54	(760) 744-1050	F. Smith	R. Gittings	Susan Vasquez	Liliane Serio	Larry Webb	Kim Quaco	Michael Mercereau
San Marino	c	CM	12	(626) 300-0700	...	...	Carol Robb	Lisa Bailey	John Penido	Arl Farris	John Alderson
San Mateo	c	CM	92	(650) 522-7260	...	Susan Loftus	Norma Gomez	Hossein Golestan	Brian Kelly	Susan Manheimer	Larry Patterson
San Pablo *	c	CM	30	(510) 215-3000	Leonard McNeil	Brock Arner	Lehny Corbin	Bradley Ward	...	Douglas Krathwohl	Adele Ho
San Rafael *	c	CM	56	(415) 485-3063	Al Boro	Kenneth Nordhoff	...	...	Robert Marcucci	Michael Cronin	...
San Ramon *	c	CM	44	(925) 973-2500	...	Herbert Moniz	Patricia Edwards	...	...	Scott Holder	Joye Fukuda
Sand City	c	CM	..	(831) 394-3054	David Pendergrass	Kelly Morgan	...	...	...	...	...
Sanger	c	CM	18	(559) 876-6303	...	Eugene Drinkhouse	Barbara Mergan	Carlos Sanchez	Clyde Clinton	Thomas Klose	John White
Santa Ana	c	CM	337	(714) 647-5340	Miguel Pulido	David Ream	Janice Guy	Francisco Gutierrez	Marc Martin	Paul Walters	Jim Ross
Santa Barbara	c	CM	92	(805) 564-5316	Martha Blum	James Armstrong	Cynthia Rodriguez	Bob Peirson	Ronald Prince	Camerino Sanchez	...

Directory 1/9 continued **OFFICIALS IN U.S. MUNICIPALITIES 2,500 AND OVER IN POPULATION**

Jurisdiction	Type	Form of govern-ment	2000 Popu-lation	Main telephone number	Chief elected official	Appointed administrator	Clerk of the governing board	Chief financial officer	Fire chief	Police chief	Public works director
CALIFORNIA continued											
Santa Clara	c	CM	102	(408) 615-2080	Patricia Mahan	Jennifer Sparacino	Rod Diridon	Mary Ann Parrot	Phillip Kleinheinz	Stephen Lodge	Stephen Yoshino
Santa Clarita	c	CM	151	(661) 259-2489	...	Kenneth Pulskamp	...	...	...	...	...
Santa Cruz	c	CM	54	(831) 420-5040	Emily Reilly	Richard Wilson	Leslie Cook	David Culver	Ron Prince	Steve Belcher	Mark Dettle
Santa Fe Springs	c	CM	17	(562) 868-0511	Joseph Serrano	Frederick Latham	Barbara Earl	Jose Gomez	Alex Rodriguez	...	Donald Jensen
Santa Maria *	c	CM	77	(805) 925-0951	Laurence Lavagnino	Tim Ness	Patti Rodriguez	...	Frank Ortiz	Danny Macagni	David Whitehead
Santa Monica	c	CM	84	(310) 393-9975	Richard Bloom	P. Ewell	Maria Stewart	Carol Swindell	...	James Butts	Craig Perkins
Santa Paula *	c	CM	28	(805) 525-4478	Richard Cook	Walter Bobkiewicz	Josie Herrera	John Quinn	Richard Araiza	Stephen MacKinnon	Clifford Finley
Santa Rosa	c	CM	147	(707) 543-3060	Michael Martini	Jeffrey Kolin	...	Ronald Bosworth	Tony Pini	Michael Dunbaugh	Rick Moshier
Santee	c	CM	52	(619) 258-4100	Randy Voepel	Keith Till	Linda Troyan	Tim McDermott	Mike Rottenberg	...	...
Saratoga *	c	CM	29	(408) 868-1200	Chuck Page	Dave Anderson	Ann Sullivan	...	...	...	John Cherbone
Sausalito *	c	CM	7	(415) 289-4100	...	Adam Politzer	...	...	...	Scott Paulin	Jonathon Goldman
Scotts Valley	c	CM	11	(831) 440-5600	Randy Johnson	Charles Comstock	Judi Coffman	Steve Ando	...	Steven Lind	Kenneth Anderson
Seal Beach	c	CM	24	(562) 431-2527	John Larson	David Carmany	Linda Devine	Greg Beaubien	...	Jeff Kirkpatrick	Mark Vukojevic
Seaside	c	CM	31	(831) 899-6700	Ralph Rubio	Ray Corpuz	Joyce Newsome	Daphne Hodgson	Jerry Wombacher	Anthony Sollicito	Diana Ingersoll
Sebastapol	c	CM	7	(707) 823-1153	...	David Brennan	Hollie Fiori	Ronald Puccinelli	John Zanzi	Jeffrey Weaver	Richard Emig
Selma *	c	CM	19	(559) 891-2200	...	D.-Bruce Heusser	Melanie Carter	Roberta Araki	Jeffrey Kestly	Thomas Whiteside	Robert Weaver
Shafter *	c	CM	12	(661) 746-5000	Cathy Prout	John Guinn	Christine Wilson	Jo Barrick	...	Charlie Fivecoat	Michael James
Shasta Lake	c	MC	9	(530) 275-7400	Debra Duryee	Don Moore	Eula Morrow	Carol Martin	...	...	Dennis Daily
Sierra Madre	c	CM	10	(626) 355-7135	John Buchanan	...	N. Shollenberger	...	Roger Lowe	Marilyn Diaz	Bruce Inman
Signal Hill	c	CM	9	(562) 989-7304	...	Kenneth Farfsing	...	Dennis MacArthur	...	Thomas Sonoff	...
Simi Valley	c	CM	111	(805) 583-6700	Paul Miller	Michael Sedell	...	...	...	Mark Laynew	Timothy Nanson
Solana Beach *	c	CM	12	(858) 720-2400	...	David Ott	Angela Ivey	Dennis Coleman	...	...	M. Sammak
Soledad	c	CM	11	(831) 678-3963	...	...	...	...	Jesse Casillas	Richard Cox	Clif Price
Solvang	c	CM	5	(805) 688-5575	Ken Palmer	Bradley Vidro	Lynne Bartz	Dana Waite	...	...	Tom Rowe
Sonoma *	c	CM	9	(707) 938-3681	Ken Brown	Linda Kelly	Gay Rainsbarger	...	Phillip Garcia	Bret Sackett	Milenka Bates
Sonora	c	CM	4	(209) 532-4541	...	Greg Applegate	...	Karen Stark	Mike Barrows	Mace McIntosh	...
South El Monte	c	CM	21	(626) 579-6540	...	Gary Chicots	Kathy Gonzales	Maria Zamora	...	...	...
South Gate	c	CM	96	(323) 563-9501	Hector De La Torre	Ronald Bates	Carmen Avalos	Kenneth Louie	...	...	Joseph Comstock
South Lake Tahoe	c	CM	23	(530) 542-6000	...	David Jinkens	Suzan Alessi	Christine Vuletich	Michael Chandler	Donald Muren	...
South Pasadena *	c	CM	24	(626) 403-7200	David Sifuentes	Lilian Myers	Sally Kilby	Tracey Hause	Jerry Wallace	Daniel Watson	Matthew Sweeney
South San Francisco	c	CM	60	(650) 877-8500	Joseph Fernekes	Barry Nagel	Sylvia Payne	Jim Steele	Russell Lee	Mark Raffaelli	Terry White
St. Helena	c	CM	5	(707) 967-2792	...	...	...	Tamera Haas	...	Bert Johansson	Myke Praul
Stanton	c	CM	37	(714) 379-9222	David Shawver	John Wager	Brenda Green	...	...	Robert Eason	...
Stockton	c	CM	243	(209) 937-8212	Gary Podesto	J Palmer	Katherine Meissner	Mark Moses	William Gillis	Mark Herder	James Giottonini
Suisun City *	c	CM	26	(707) 421-7300	Pete Sanchez	Suzanne Bragdon	Linda Hobson	Mark Joseph	Michael O'Brian	Edmond Dadisho	...
Sunnyvale *	c	CM	131	(408) 730-7480	Otto Lee	Gary Luebbers	Gail Borowski	Mary Bradley	...	...	Marvin Rose
Susanville	c	CM	13	(530) 252-5100	Rodney De Boer	Luann Rainey	Debra Magginetti	Robert Porfiri	Stuart Ratner	C. Gallagher	Craig Platt
Sutter Creek	c	CM	2	(209) 267-5647	Brent Parsons	J. Duke	Judy Allen	...	Butch Martin	...	George Christner
Taft	c	CM	6	(661) 763-1222	Cliff Thompson	...	Louise Hudgens	Teresa Statler	Ken Scott	Bertus Pumphrey	Gary Dabbs
Tehachapi	c	CM	10	(661) 822-2200	Philip Smith	...	Jeanette Kelley	Ronald Cunningham	Tim McLaughlin	...	Dennis Wahlstrom
Temecula	c	CM	57	(951) 506-5100	Chuck Washington	Shawn Nelson	Susan Jones	Genie Roberts	Glenn Patterson	Jerry Williams	William Hughes
Temple City	c	CM	33	(626) 285-2171	Peter Zovak	Charles Martin	Mary Flandrick	...	...	...	Janice Stroud
Thousand Oaks *	c	CM	117	(805) 449-2144	Jacqui Irwin	Scott Mitnick	Linda Lawrence	Candis Hong	Michael LaPlant	Dennis Carpenter	Mark Watkins
Tiburon *	t	CM	8	(415) 435-7373	Alice Fredericks	Margaret Curran	Diane Crane	...	...	Michael Cronin	Nicholas Nguyen
Torrance	c	CM	137	(310) 618-2960	...	LeRoy Jackson	Sue Herbers	Eric Tsao	Rick Bongard	James Herren	Brooks Bell
Tracy	c	CM	56	(209) 831-4100	George Bilbrey	R. Churchill	...	Zane Johnston	...	David Krauss	Nicholas Pinhey
Truckee	t	CM	13	(530) 582-7700	...	...	Patricia Osborne	Jill Olsen	...	Dan Boon	Daniel Wilkins
Tulare *	c	CM	43	(559) 684-4200	Richard Ortega	Darrel Pyle	Anna Vital	Darlene Thompson	Michael Threlkeld	Roger Hill	Lew Nelson
Turlock	c	CM	55	(209) 668-5540	...	...	...	...	Mark Langley	Lonald Lott	Cliff Martin
Tustin	c	CM	67	(714) 573-3000	Tracy Worley	William Huston	Maria Huizar	Ronald Nault	...	Steve Foster	Tim Serlet
Twentynine Palms	c	CM	14	(760) 367-6799	...	Michael Tree	Charlene Sherwood	Ronald Peck	...	...	Bobby Matz
Ukiah *	c	CM	15	(707) 463-6200	Phil Baldwin	Jane Chambers	Linda Brown	Gordon Elton	...	...	Tim Eriksen
Union City	c	CM	66	(510) 471-3232	Mark Green	Larry Cheeves	...	...	Gerald Simon	Randy Ulibarri	...
Upland	c	CM	68	(909) 931-4100	John Pomierski	Robb Quincey	Stephanie Rios	Stephen Dunn	John Scanlon	Martin Thouvenell	George Turner
Vacaville *	c	CM	88	(707) 449-5100	Leonard Augustine	Laura Kuhn	Michelle Thornbrugh	Ken Campo	Brian Preciado	Rich Word	Dale Pfeiffer
Vallejo	c	CM	116	(707) 648-4527	Anthony Intintoli	Joseph Tanner	Allison Villarante	Frederick Wright	Donald Parker	Robert Nichelini	Mark Akuba
Victorville *	c	CM	64	(760) 955-5000	...	Jon Roberts	Carolee Bates	...	...	...	Amer Jahker
Villa Park	c	CM	5	(714) 998-1500	...	...	...	...	...	...	...
Visalia	c	CM	91	(559) 713-4300	Jesus Gamboa	Steven Salomon	Randy Groom	...	George Sandoval	Jerry Barker	Russ Webber
Vista *	c	CM	89	(760) 726-1340	...	Rita Geldert	Marci Kilian	Tom Gardner	Gary Fisher	Tim Curran	Mauro Garcia
Walnut	c	CM	30	(909) 595-7543	Joaquin Lim	...	Teresa DeDios	Christine Londo	...	...	Mary Rooney
Walnut Creek	c	CM	64	(925) 943-5899	Gary Skrel	Gary Pokorny	...	...	...	Thomas Soberanes	Daniel Richardson
Wasco *	c	CM	21	(661) 758-7200	Cherylee Wegman	Ronald Mittag	Vickie Hight	Jim Zerivs	Dennis Thompson	J. R. Rodriguez	Dan Allen
Waterford	c	MC	6	(209) 874-2328	Charles Turner	Charles Deschenes	Lori Martin	...	...	...	Matt Erickson
Watsonville	c	CM	44	(831) 768-3010	Antonio Rivas	Carlos Palacios	L. Washington	Marc Pimentel	Mark Bisbee	Terrence Medina	David Koch
Weed *	c	CM	2	(530) 938-5020	Chuck Sutton	Earl Wilson	Deborah Salvestrin	Kelly McKinnis	Darin Quigley	Martin Nicholas	Craig Sharp
West Covina	c	CM	105	(626) 939-8450	Steve Herfert	Andrew Pasmant	Janet Berry	Thomas Bachman	Richard Greene	Frank Willis	Shannon Yauchzee
West Hollywood	c	CM	35	(323) 848-6400	...	Paul Arevalo	...	Anil Gandhy	...	...	...
West Sacramento	c	CM	31	(916) 617-4500	...	Toby Ross	Kryss Rankin	Leigh Keicher	Frederick Postel	Dan Drummond	...
Westlake Village	c	CM	8	(818) 706-1613	Christopher Mann	Raymond Taylor	Beth Schott	...	...	...	...
Westminster *	c	CM	88	(714) 898-3311	Margie Rice	Ramon Silver	Marian Contreras	Paul Espinoza	...	Andrew Hall	Brad Fowler
Wheatland *	c	CM	2	(530) 633-2761	Enita Elphick	Stephen Wright	Lisa Thomason	Rex Miller	Robert Verburg	Mike McCrary	Larry Panteloglow
Whittier *	c	CM	83	(562) 464-3340	David Butler	Stephen Helvey	Kathryn Marshall	Rod Hill	...	David Singer	David Mochizuki
Wildomar	c	CM	14	(951) 677-7751	Bob Cashman	John Danielson	...	...	...	...	...
Williams	c	MC	3	(530) 473-2445	...	...	...	...	...	...	...
Willits	c	CM	5	(707) 459-4601	Thomas Lucier	Gordon Logan	Frances Schatz	Patricia Frost	...	John Brown	David Madrigal
Willows *	c	CM	6	(530) 934-7041	Peter Towne	Stephen Holsinger	Natalie Butler	Timothy Sailsbery	Wayne Peabody	William Spears	Greg Tyhurst
Windsor *	t	CM	22	(707) 838-5311	Robin Goble	J. Mullan	Maria Delao	...	...	Steve Freitas	Richard Burtt
Winters *	c	CM	6	(530) 795-4910	Harold Anderson	John Donlevy	...	Shelly Gunby	...	Bruce Muramoto	...
Woodlake	c	CM	6	(559) 564-8055	Jack Ritchie	Bill Lewis	Ruth Gonzalez	...	...	John Zapalac	Ruben De Leon
Woodland *	c	CM	49	(530) 661-5800	...	Mark Deven	Sue Vannucci	...	Tod Reddish	Carey Sullivan	Greg Meyer
Woodside *	t	CM	5	(650) 851-6790	...	Susan George	Janet Koelsch	...	...	...	...
Yorba Linda *	c	CM	58	(714) 961-7100	Mark Schwing	William Kelly	Kathie Mendoza	Susan Hartman	...	Billy Hutchinson	Mark Stowell
Yountville	t	CM	2	(707) 944-8851	Cynthia Saucerman	Steven Rogers	Michelle Price	Richard Stranzl	Ernie Loveless	Doug Koford	Myke Praul
Yreka	c	CM	7	(530) 841-2324	Rory McNeil	Brian Meek	Elizabeth Casson	Rhetta Hogan	Peter Suter	Brian Bowles	Steven Neill
Yuba City *	c	CM	60	(530) 822-4602	Bob Barkhouse	Steven Jepsen	Terrel Locke	Robin Bertagna	Marc Boomgaarden	Richard Doscher	George Musallam
Yucaipa *	c	CM	41	(909) 797-2489	...	Raymond Casey	Jennifer Shankland	...	...	...	William Hemsley
Yucca Valley *	t	CM	16	(760) 369-7207	Frank Luckino	Andrew Takata	Janet Anderson	...	...	...	Art da Rosa
COLORADO											
Alamosa	c	CM	7	(719) 589-2593	Farris Bervig	Nathan Cherpeski	...	Hector Chavez	Donald Clayton	Ron Lindsey	Don Koskelin
Arvada *	c	CM	102	(720) 898-7000	Bob Frie	Craig Kocian	Christine Koch	Victoria Runkle	...	Don Wick	James Root
Aspen	c	CM	5	(970) 920-5241	Rachel Richards	Steve Barwick	Kathryn Koch	...	...	Thomas Stephenson	Brian Pettet
Aurora	c	CM	276	(303) 739-7000	Paul Tauer	Ronald Miller	Debra Johnson	John Gross	Casey Jones	Ricky Bennett	Darrell Hogan
Avon	t	CM	5	(970) 748-4000	Albert Reynolds	Larry Brooks	Patty McKenny	Scott Wright	...	Jeffrey Layman	Robert Reed
Basalt	t	CM	2	(970) 927-4701	Rick Stevens	Elizabeth Suerth	Pamela Schilling	Renae Gustine	...	Keith Ikeda	Bentley Henderson

Directory 1/9 continued

OFFICIALS IN U.S. MUNICIPALITIES 2,500 AND OVER IN POPULATION

Jurisdiction		Type	Form of govern-ment	2000 Popu-lation	Main telephone number	Chief elected official	Appointed administrator	Clerk of the governing board	Chief financial officer	Fire chief	Police chief	Public works director
COLORADO continued												
Bayfield		t	MC	1	(970) 884-9544	James Harrmann	. . .	. . .	. . .	. . .	Jim Harrington	Robert Ludwig
Berthoud	*	t	MC	4	(970) 532-2643	Milan Karspeck	James White	Mary Cowdin	. . .	Steve Charles	William Wegener	Jose Huerta
Black Hawk	*	c	CM	. .	(303) 582-2292	David Spellman	Richard Lessner	Jeanie Magno	. . .	Robert Norris	Stephen Cole	Thomas Isbester
Boulder		c	CM	94	(303) 441-3090	Mark Ruzzin	Jane Brautigam	Alisa Lewis	Robert Eichem	Larry Donner	Mark Beckner	Maureen Rait
Breckenridge	*	t	CM	2	(970) 547-3159	John Warner	Timothy Gagen	Mary Loufek	Brian Waldes	. . .	Rick Holman	Terry Perkins
Brighton	*	c	CM	20	(303) 655-2000	Janice Pawlowski	Manuel Esquibel	Gayle Martinez	Bernadette Kimmey	. . .	Clint Blackhurst	Jim Landeck
Broomfield		c	CM	38	(303) 469-3301	Karen Stuart	George Di Ciero	Russell Ragsdale	Gregory Demko	. . .	Thomas Deland	Dorian Brown
Brush		c	MC	5	(970) 842-5001	Daniel Scalise	Monty Torres	Cathryn Smith	Alta Gosselink	Eric Ruhl	Mark Thomas	Rowena Pennell
Buena Vista		t	CM	2	(719) 395-8643	Cara Russell	Jerry L'Estrange	Diane Spomer	. . .	Darryl Pratt	Jimmy Tidwell	Roy Gertson
Burlington		c	MC	3	(719) 346-8652	Thomas Jacobucci	. . .	Patricia Maldonado	. . .	. . .	Randall Millburn	Tracy Tillman
Calhan	*	t	MC	. .	(719) 347-2586	Blair Bartling	. . .	Cindy Tompkins	. . .	. . .	Buddy Johnson	Ryan Miller
Canon City		c	CM	15	(719) 269-9011	William Jackson	Steven Rabe	Rebecca Worthen	Hasmukh Patel	. . .	Daniel Shull	. . .
Carbondale		t	CM	5	(970) 963-2733	Michael Hassig	Tom Baker	Marcia Walter	Nancy Barnett	. . .	Eugene Schilling	Larry Ballenger
Castle Rock		t	CM	20	(303) 660-1015	. . .	Mark Stevens	Sally Misare	Pam Brockhaus	Arturo Morales	Joseph Lane	Bob Watts
Centennial	*	c	MC	107	(303) 734-4567	Randy Pye	J. Wedding-Scott	Linda Gawlik	. . .	. . .	Grayson Robinson	Dave Zelenok
Central City		c	CM	. .	(303) 582-5251	Bruce Schmalzr	Lynnette Hailey	Jennifer Novak	Cheryl McEachran	Gary Allen	James Saunders	Larry Wallerich
Cherry Hills Village		c	CM	5	(303) 789-2541	Doug Scott	Eric Ensey	Jennifer Pettinger	Karen Proctor	. . .	John Patterson	Kevin Louis
Collbran	*	t	MC	. .	(970) 487-3751	Bradford Osburn	. . .	. . .	. . .	. . .	. . .	. . .
Colorado Springs	*	c	CM	360	(719) 385-5900	Lionel Rivera	P. Culbreth-Graft	Kathryn Young	Terri Velasquez	Steven Cox	Richard Myers	. . .
Commerce City	*	c	CM	20	(303) 289-3612	Paul Natale	Gerald Flannery	Laura Bauer	Roger Tinklenberg	. . .	Phillip Baca	Gregg Clements
Cortez	*	c	CM	7	(970) 565-3402	Orly Lucero	Jay Harrington	Linda Smith	Kathi Moss	. . .	Roy Lane	Bruce Smart
Craig		c	CM	9	(970) 824-8151	Don Jones	James Ferree	Shirley Seely	Bruce Nelson	. . .	Walter Vanatta	William Earley
Crested Butte		t	CM	1	(970) 349-5338	. . .	Susan Parker	Eileen Hughes	Lois Rozman	. . .	Thomas Martin	Robert Gillie
Cripple Creek	*	c	MC	1	(719) 689-2502	Ed Libby	Bill McPherson	Debra Blevins	Paul Harris	Randle Baldwin	Gary Hamilton	Chip Huffman
Dacono		c	MC	3	(303) 833-2317	Wade Carlson	. . .	Nancy Elliott	. . .	. . .	Thomas Davis	Jon Rabas
Del Norte		t	CM	1	(719) 657-2708	Dennis Murphy	Patsy Moreland	. . .	. . .	. . .	Jeffrey Sailee	Jack Glover
Delta	*	c	CM	6	(970) 874-7566	Mary Cooper	Lanny Sloan	Jolene Nelson	Tod DeZeeuw	. . .	Robert Thomas	James Hatheway
Denver		c	MC	554	(303) 640-2613	John Hickenlooper	. . .	Sherry Jackson	Margaret Browne	Roderick Juniel	Jerry Whitman	. . .
Dillon	*	t	CM	. .	(970) 468-2403	Barbara Davis	C. Granbery	Jan Thomas	. . .	. . .	Joe Wray	J. Eric Holgerson
Durango		c	CM	13	(970) 375-5050	Sidny Zink	Ronald LeBlanc	Amy Phillips	Sherry Eilbes	. . .	Albert Bell	Otha Rogers
Eagle	*	t	CM	3	(970) 328-6354	Ed Woodland	William Powell	Marilene Miller	. . .	. . .	Rodger McLaughlin	Dustin Walls
Eaton	*	t	CM	2	(970) 454-3338	Scott Moser	Gary Carsten	Erica Bagley	. . .	. . .	Randall Jacobson	George Spaedt
Edgewater	*	c	MC	5	(303) 238-7803	Bonnie McNulty	. . .	Beth Hedberg	. . .	. . .	Dan Keough	Mike Ball
Elizabeth	*	t	CM	1	(303) 646-4166	Jon Gleiforst	Christopher LaMay	Serena Brooks	. . .	. . .	Michael Phibbs	Billy Holschuh
Englewood		c	CM	31	(303) 762-2300	Beverly Bradshaw	Gary Sears	Louchrisha Ellis	Francis Gryglewicz	Keith Lockwood	Chris Olson	Kenneth Ross
Erie		t	CM	6	(303) 926-2700	. . .	Mike Acimovic	. . .	. . .	. . .	Stephen Hasler	Judy Ding
Estes Park	*	t	CM	5	(970) 586-5331	John Baudek	Jacqueline Halburnt	J. Williamson	Steve McFarland	Scott Dorman	Wesley Kufeld	Scott Zurn
Evans	*	c	CM	9	(970) 339-5344	Lyle Achziger	Aden Hogan	Kim Betz	Jessica Gonifas	Warren Jones	Rick Brandt	Earl Smith
Federal Heights	*	c	MC	12	(303) 412-3520	Joyce Thomas	David Blanchard	Phyllis Schott	Gordon Maddock	Andrew Marsh	Lester Acker	. . .
Firestone		t	CM	1	(303) 833-3291	Chad Auer	Wesley LaVanchy	Judy Hegwood	Carl Nelson	. . .	. . .	. . .
Florence		c	CM	3	(719) 784-4848	Merle Strickland	Tom Piltingsrud	Dori Williams	Patricia Mock	. . .	Guy Orazem	Martin Duran
Fort Collins		c	CM	118	(970) 221-6505	Ray Martinez	Darin Atteberry	Wanda Krajicek	Michael Freeman	John Mulligan	Stephen Roy	. . .
Fort Lupton		c	MC	6	(303) 857-6694	Shannon Crespin	Mike Konefal	Barbara Rodgers	Claud Hanes	. . .	. . .	Ramon Hernandez
Fort Morgan		c	MC	11	(970) 867-4310	Jack Darnell	. . .	Nancy Lockwood	. . .	Michael Kirkendall	Keith Kuretich	. . .
Fountain	*	c	CM	15	(719) 382-8521	Jeri Howells	Scott Trainor	Sharon Mosley	Kathleen Kuberka	Darin Anstine	. . .	Duane Greenwood
Fraser		t	CM	. .	(970) 726-5491	Dennis Soles	Jeffrey Durbin	Molly McCandless	. . .	. . .	. . .	Allen Nordin
Frederick		t	CM	2	(303) 833-2388	Eric Doering	Derek Todd	Nanette Fornoff	Marcia Lierman	. . .	Gary Barbour	Allen Conway
Frisco		t	CM	2	(970) 668-5276	Bernie Zurbriggen	Michael Penny	Jo-Anne Tyson	Theresa Casey	. . .	Tom Wickman	Timothy Mack
Fruita		c	CM	6	(970) 858-3663	. . .	Clinton Kinney	. . .	Margaret Steelman	. . .	Mark Angelo	Tom Huston
Georgetown		t	CM	1	(303) 569-2555	Lynn Granger	. . .	Merinel Williams	. . .	. . .	Dave Forristal	Howard Kimbrel
Glendale		c	CM	4	(303) 759-1513	Joe Rice	Jerry Peters	Theresa Teeters	Doris Williams	Richard McGowan	Ken Burge	. . .
Glenwood Springs		c	CM	7	(970) 384-6400	Bruce Christensen	Jeffrey Hecksel	Robin Clemons	Michael Harman	Michael Piper	Terry Wilson	Robin Millyard
Golden		c	CM	17	(303) 384-8000	Charles Baroch	Michael Bestor	Susan Brooks	Jeffrey Hansen	John Bales	William Kilpatrick	Daniel Hartman
Granby	*	t	CM	1	(970) 887-2501	Jynnifer Pierro	Don Baird	Debbie Hess	Sharon Spurlin	. . .	Bill Housley	Scott Holley
Grand Junction	*	c	CM	41	(970) 244-1512	Gregg Palmer	Laurie Kadrich	Stephanie Tuin	Jodi Romero	Ken Watkins	Bill Gardner	. . .
Grand Lake	*	c	MC	. .	(970) 627-3435	. . .	Shane Hale	Ronda Kolinske	. . .	. . .	. . .	Bernie McGinn
Greeley	*	c	CM	76	(970) 350-9710	Ed Clark	Roy Otto	Betsy Holder	Timothy Nash	Dennis Hixon	Jerry Garner	Joel Hemesath
Greenwood Village	*	c	CM	11	(303) 773-0252	Nancy Sharpe	James Sanderson	Susan Phillips	Craig Larson	. . .	. . .	John Sheldon
Gunnison		c	CM	5	(970) 641-8070	Stu Ferguson	Kenneth Coleman	Gail Davidson	Wendy Hanson	Dennis Spritzer	Greg Anderson	Tex Bradford
Gypsum	*	t	CM	3	(970) 524-7514	Steve Carver	Jeffrey Shroll	Danette Schlegel	Mark Silverthorn	. . .	. . .	Jeff Shreeve
Hayden	*	t	CM	1	(970) 276-3741	Charles Grobe	Russell Martin	Susan Irvine	Lisa Dowling	. . .	Ray Birch	Franklin Fox
Hudson		t	MC	1	(303) 536-9311	Neal Pontius	Joseph Racine	Judy Larson	. . .	. . .	. . .	. . .
Ignacio		t	CM	. .	(970) 563-9494	Katherine Gurule	Miguel Sandoval	Georgann Valdez	. . .	. . .	Kirk Phillips	. . .
Johnstown		t	CM	3	(970) 587-5957	. . .	. . .	Diana Seele	. . .	. . .	Troy Krenning	Donald Gardner
Julesburg		t	CM	1	(970) 474-3344	Philip Mollendor	. . .	Murial Nelson	. . .	Todd Blochowitz	. . .	Allen Coyne
Kersey		t	CM	1	(970) 353-1681	Gilbert Marin	. . .	Julie Piper	. . .	. . .	Pat Carey	Derrick Arens
Kiowa	*	t	MC	. .	(303) 621-2366	Luke Bond	Lyn Boswell	Michelle Oeser	. . .	. . .	Michael Root	Zach Hackett
Kremmling		t	CM	1	(970) 724-3249	. . .	. . .	Sharon Cesar	. . .	. . .	Bob Bodemann	James Hursh
La Jara		t	MC	. .	(719) 274-0553	. . .	William Yohey	. . .	. . .	. . .	. . .	. . .
La Junta		c	CM	7	(719) 384-5991	Don Rizzuto	Rick Klein	Jan Schooley	Patty Hurt	Jerald Bradfield	Charles Widup	Joe Kelley
Lafayette		c	CM	23	(303) 665-5588	Chris Berry	Gary Klaphake	Susan Koster	Robert Wright	Gerald Morrell	Paul Schultz	Doug Short
Lakewood		c	CM	144	(303) 987-7700	Stephen Burkholder	Michael Rock	Margy Greer	. . .	. . .	Ron Burns	Richard Plastino
Lamar	*	c	CM	8	(719) 336-4376	Nelva Heath	Ronald Stock	Maribeth Kemp	. . .	Marshall Cook	Brian Phillips	Rick Akers
Las Animas		c	MC	2	(719) 456-0422	. . .	. . .	. . .	. . .	. . .	. . .	. . .
Leadville		c	MC	2	(719) 486-0549	Pete Moore	. . .	Eva Fenske	. . .	Michael Osborn	James Zoller	Scott Marcella
Limon	*	t	CM	2	(719) 775-2346	Del Beattie	. . .	Chris Snyder	. . .	. . .	Lynn Yowell	. . .
Littleton		c	CM	40	(303) 795-3720	James Taylor	James Woods	Julie Bower	. . .	John Mullin	. . .	Charles Blosten
Lochbuie		t	MC	2	(303) 655-3908	William Norris	. . .	Stacey Aranda	. . .	. . .	Gardner Mendenhall	Mike Hutto
Lone Tree	*	c	CM	4	(303) 708-1818	. . .	Jack Hidahl	. . .	. . .	. . .	Stephen Hasler	. . .
Longmont		c	CM	71	(303) 776-6050	Julia Pirnack	Gordon Pedrow	Valeria Skitt	Jim Golden	Steve Trunck	Mike Butler	. . .
Louisville		c	CM	18	(303) 335-4500	Charles Sisk	Malcolm Fleming	Nancy Varra	Patty Leslie	. . .	Bruce Goodman	Thomas Phare
Loveland		c	CM	50	(970) 962-2000	Larry Walsh	Don Williams	Teressa Andrews	. . .	Michael Chard	Luke Hecker	Keith Reester
Lyons		t	CM	1	(303) 823-6622	Timothy Kyer	Howard Armstrong	Debra Anthony	Janice Saeger	. . .	Dan Barber	Scott Daniels
Mancos		t	CM	1	(970) 533-7725	Greg Rath	Thomas Yennerell	Georgette Welage	. . .	. . .	. . .	Robin Schmittel
Manitou Springs		c	CM	4	(719) 685-5596	Bill Koerner	Dan Wecks	Lois Greenman	Fred Burmont	. . .	Jeff Nohr	Gary Smith
Mead	*	t	CM	2	(970) 535-4477	Richard Kraemer	Dan Dean	Charlene Reed	. . .	. . .	. . .	Daniel Dennison
Meeker		t	CM	2	(970) 878-5344	Steve Loshbaugh	Sharon Day	Lisa Cook	. . .	. . .	Bob Hervey	Russell Overton
Milliken		t	CM	2	(970) 587-4331	Linda Measner	Sheryl Trent	Gayle Martinez	Diana Vasquez	. . .	James Burack	Michael Woodruff
Minturn	*	t	CM	1	(970) 827-5645	Earle Bidez	. . .	Carrie Kendall	. . .	. . .	Lorenzo Martinez	Rod Cordova
Monte Vista		c	CM	4	(719) 852-2692	Donald Schall	Donald Vanwormer	Lucille Duran	Debbie Phillips	Charles Archer	Jim Gallegos	Randy Martinez
Montrose		c	CM	12	(970) 240-1400	Noelle Hagan	Mary Watt	Sharleen Walker	Shani Wittenberg	. . .	Tom Chinn	James Hougnon
Monument		t	MC	1	(719) 884-8012	Elizabeth Konarski	. . .	Anne Holliday	. . .	. . .	Joe Kissell	Tom Wall
Morrison		t	MC	. .	(303) 697-8749	Kathy Dichter	Jerry Smith	Elizabeth Hedberg	Donna Beckman	. . .	Robert Wasko	Buck Wenger
Mountain Village		t	MC	. .	(970) 369-6412	. . .	Greg Sparks	. . .	Steven Wilson	. . .	. . .	. . .
Nederland		t	CM	1	(303) 258-3266	. . .	James Stevens	Sheridan Garcia	. . .	. . .	Ken Robinson	Tim Underwood
New Castle		t	MC	1	(970) 984-2311	Frank Breslin	Andrew Barton	Lisa Cain	Lyle Layton	. . .	Chris Sadler	. . .

Directory 1/9 continued — OFFICIALS IN U.S. MUNICIPALITIES 2,500 AND OVER IN POPULATION

Jurisdiction	Type	Form of govern-ment	2000 Popu-lation	Main telephone number	Chief elected official	Appointed administrator	Clerk of the governing board	Chief financial officer	Fire chief	Police chief	Public works director
COLORADO continued											
Northglenn	c	CM	31	(303) 451-8326	. . .	. . .	Diana Lentz	Brent Worthington	. . .	Russ VanHouten	. . .
Orchard City	t	CM	2	(970) 835-3337	Thomas Huerkamp	David Varley	. . .	. . .	. . .	. . .	. . .
Ouray *	c	CM	. .	(970) 325-7211	Bob Risch	Patrick Rondinelli	. . .	. . .	Adam Kunz	Leo Rasmusson	Daniel Fossey
Pagosa Springs *	t	CM	1	(970) 264-4151	Ross Aragon	Mark Garcia	Deanna Jaramillo	. . .	. . .	Donald Volger	Chris Gallegos
Palisade *	t	CM	2	(970) 464-5602	David Walker	Tim Sarmo	Carol Speakman	. . .	Richard Rupp	Carroll Quarles	Frank Watt
Parker	t	CM	23	(303) 805-3117	. . .	Jeannene Bragg	Carol Baumgartner	Michael Farina	. . .	. . .	Michael Sutherland
Platteville	t	CM	2	(970) 785-2245	Steve Shafer	Nicholas Meier	Leah Heneger	. . .	. . .	. . .	Efren Rodriguez
Pueblo	c	CM	102	(719) 553-2633	Mike Occhiato	David Galli	Gina Dutcher	Robert Hain	Greg Miller	Jim Billings	Tom Cvar
Rangely	t	CM	2	(970) 675-8476	Valerie Mallett	. . .	Christine Brasfield	Karen Ewall	. . .	Flint Chambers	John Kenney
Ridgway	t	MC	. .	(970) 626-5308	Pat Willits	Greg Clifton	Pam Kraft	. . .	. . .	David Scott	Dan Bartashius
Rifle	c	CM	6	(970) 625-2121	. . .	John Hier	Wanda Nelson	Nancy Black	. . .	Daryl Meisner	Bill Sappington
Rocky Ford	c	MC	4	(719) 254-7414	Randy Hamilton	Daniel Hyatt	Cheryl Grasmick	Cathy Clevenger	Gary Cox	Frank Gallegos	Cy Chavez
Salida	c	CM	5	(719) 539-4555	. . .	Michael Copp	Deanna De Luca	. . .	. . .	Darwin Hibbs	Tom Shilling
Sheridan	c	CM	5	(303) 762-2200	Mary Carter	. . .	Arlene Sagee	Judy Dahl	Ronald Carter	Ray Sample	Randy Mouring
Silverthorne *	t	CM	3	(970) 262-7300	Dave Koop	Kevin Batchelder	Michele Karlin	. . .	. . .	Mark Hanschmidt	William Linfield
Silverton	t	CM	. .	(970) 387-5522	Jim Huffman	. . .	Linda Davis	. . .	. . .	. . .	Gilbert Archuleta
Snowmass Village	t	CM	1	(970) 923-3777	T. Manchester	Russel Forrest	. . .	Marianne Rakowski	. . .	Art Smythe	Hunt Walker
South Fork	t	MC	. .	(719) 873-0152	. . .	. . .	. . .	. . .	. . .	. . .	. . .
Steamboat Springs *	c	CM	9	(970) 879-2060	Loui Antonnuci	. . .	Julie Jordan	Don Taylor	Robert Struble	. . .	Philo Shelton
Sterling	c	CM	11	(970) 522-9700	Dan Jones	Joseph Kiolbasa	. . .	Debra Forbes	Robert Olme	Roy Breivik	James Allen
Superior *	t	CM	9	(303) 499-3675	. . .	Scott Randall	Phyllis Hardin	Paul Nilles	. . .	. . .	Jon Hakuaas
Telluride	t	CM	2	(970) 728-3071	John Steel	Frank Bell	Mary Schillaci	Lynne Beck	. . .	James Kolar	Stanford Berryman
Thornton	c	CM	82	(303) 538-7200	Noel Busck	Jack Ethredge	Nancy Vincent	David Boyd	Gregory Sheehan	James Nursey	Chester Elliot
Timnath	t	MC	. .	(970) 224-3211	. . .	Becky Davidson	Linda Salas	. . .	. . .	. . .	. . .
Trinidad *	c	CM	9	(719) 846-9843	Joseph Reorda	. . .	Lydia Shea	Rose Blatnik	James Bulson	Charles Glorioso	Michael Valentine
Vail	t	CM	4	(970) 479-2100	. . .	Stanley Zemler	Lorelei Donaldson	Judy Camp	John Gulick	Dwight Henninger	Greg Hall
Walsenburg	c	MC	4	(719) 738-1048	Jay Crook	. . .	Paula Sterkconder	H. C. Summers	Gilbert Pedraza	Glyn Ramsey	. . .
Wellington	t	CM	2	(970) 568-3381	Donald Irwin	. . .	. . .	Mike Cummins	Steve Sarno	. . .	Bill Bodkins
Westminster	c	CM	100	(303) 430-2400	Edward Moss	J. McFall	Linda Yeager	Tammy Hitchens	Jim Cloud	Daniel Montgomery	Ron Hellbusch
Wheat Ridge *	c	CM	32	(303) 234-5900	. . .	G. Young	Wanda Sang	. . .	. . .	Jack Hurst	Timothy Paranto
Windsor *	t	CM	9	(970) 686-7476	John Vazquez	Kelly Arnold	Patti Garcia	Dean Moyer	. . .	John Michaels	Terry Walker
Winter Park	t	CM	. .	(970) 726-8081	Harold Teverbaugh	. . .	Nancy Anderson	. . .	. . .	. . .	James Cordell
Woodland Park *	c	CM	6	(719) 687-9246	Steve Randolph	David Buttery	Cindy Morse	Kellie Case	. . .	Robert Larson	William Alspach
Wray	c	CM	2	(970) 332-4431	Danny Prather	Stanley Holmes	Ida Peery	. . .	Terry Jay	Richard Crays	Randy Wells
Yuma	c	CM	3	(970) 848-3878	Robert Harper	Doug Sanderson	Karma Wells	. . .	Daniel Lehman	Joseph Maier	William Eastin
CONNECTICUT											
Ansonia	c	MC	18	(203) 736-5930	James DellaVolpe	Linda Gentile	Elizabeth Lynch	Joseph Miller	Robert Caruso	Kevin Hale	Joseph Maffeo
Ashford	t	TM	4	(860) 487-4400	Ralph Fletcher	. . .	Barbara Metsack	. . .	Wayne Fletcher	. . .	Joseph Kalinowski
Avon *	t	CM	15	(860) 409-4300	. . .	Philip Schenck	Ann Dearstyne	Margaret Colligan	Jamie DiPace	Mark Rinaldo	Bruce Williams
Barkhamsted *	t	TM	3	(860) 379-8285	Donald Stein	Deborah Gilpin	Maria Mullady	. . .	. . .	. . .	Richard Novak
Beacon Falls	t	TM	5	(203) 729-4340	Susan Cable	. . .	Paula Balanda	. . .	Theodore Smith	. . .	Frank Delvecchio
Berlin *	t	TM	18	(860) 828-7002	. . .	Denise McNair	Kathryn Wall	Anna Johnson	Steve Waznia	Paul Fitzgerald	Arthur Simonian
Bethany	t	TM	5	(203) 393-2100	. . .	. . .	. . .	. . .	. . .	. . .	. . .
Bethel	t	MC	18	(203) 794-8505	. . .	. . .	Sheila Zelensky	. . .	. . .	. . .	. . .
Bethlehem	t	TM	3	(203) 266-7677	. . .	. . .	. . .	. . .	. . .	. . .	James Kacerguis
Bloomfield *	t	CM	19	(860) 769-3500	Sydney Schulman	Louie Chapman	Marguerite Phillips	Daniel Costello	. . .	Betsy J. S. Hard	David Gofstein
Bolton	t	MC	5	(860) 649-8066	Robert Morra	Joyce Stille	Susan Depold	Jerry McCall	Jim Preuss	. . .	Danato Rattazzi
Branford	t	RT	28	(203) 488-8394	John Opie	. . .	Georgette Laske	James Finch	Jack Ahern	Robert Gill	Edward Masotta
Bridgeport *	c	MC	139	(203) 576-7200	Bill Finch	Andrew Nunn	Hector Diaz	Michael Feeney	Michael Maglione	Hector Torress	John Marsillio
Bristol	c	MC	60	(860) 584-7600	. . .	. . .	Therese Pac	Glenn Klocko	Joe Pose	John DiVenere	Walter Veselka
Brookfield	t	TM	15	(203) 775-7300	Martin Foncello	. . .	Joan Locke	Richard Haley	Wayne Gravis	Robin Montgomery	Ronald Klimas
Brooklyn	t	TM	7	(860) 779-3411	Donald Francis	. . .	Leona Mainville	Steven Townsend	. . .	. . .	Leonard Albee
Burlington	t	TM	8	(860) 673-6789	Theodore Scheidel	. . .	. . .	. . .	. . .	. . .	Albert Wilusz
Canterbury	t	TM	4	(860) 546-9377	Neil Dupont	. . .	Sheila Mason Gale	. . .	. . .	. . .	David Veit
Canton	t	CM	8	(860) 693-7839	Mary Tomolonius	Robert Skinner	Linda Smith	. . .	Richard Hutchings	Lowell Humphrey	Walter LeGeyt
Cheshire	t	CM	28	(203) 271-6660	Matt Hall	Michael Milone	Carolyn Soltis	Patti-Lynn Ryan	Jack Casner	Michael Cruess	J. Michelangelo
Chester	t	TM	3	(860) 526-0013	Martin Heft	Lynne Jacques	Debra Calamari	. . .	. . .	. . .	John Divis
Clinton	t	TM	13	(860) 669-9333	William Fritz	. . .	Karen Marsden	Rosemary Faulkner	Jeff Heser	Joseph Faughnan	Edward Vailette
Colchester	t	TM	14	(860) 537-3461	. . .	. . .	. . .	. . .	. . .	. . .	. . .
Columbia	t	TM	4	(860) 228-0110	Adella Urban	Cindy Laquire	. . .	William Heldmann	. . .	. . .	Peter Naumec
Coventry	t	CM	11	(860) 742-6324	James Clark	John Elsesser	Susan Cyr	Elizabeth Bauer	. . .	Beau Thurnauer	. . .
Cromwell	t	TM	12	(860) 632-3497	Stanley Terry	. . .	Darlene Di Proto	Edward Alsup	. . .	Anthony Salvatore	Robert Jahn
Danbury	c	MC	74	(203) 797-4598	Mark Boughton	Michael McLachlan	Helena Abrantes	David St. Hilaire	Peter Siecienski	Robert Paquette	William Buckley
Danielson	b	CM	4	(860) 774-2527	Elaine Lippke	. . .	R. Duchesneau	. . .	Richard Levola	. . .	. . .
Darien	t	RT	19	(203) 656-7300	Evonne Klein	Karl Kilduff	Donna Rajczewski	Kathleen Clarke	. . .	Duane Lovello	Robert Steeger
Deep River	t	TM	4	(860) 526-6020	Richard Smith	Gina Sopneski	Jeanne Nickse	. . .	. . .	. . .	. . .
Derby	c	MC	12	(203) 736-1450	Tony Staffieri	. . .	Laura Wabno	. . .	. . .	Andrew Cota	Gary Parker
Durham	t	TM	6	(860) 349-3625	Henry Robinson	. . .	Marjorie Hatch	Maryjane Parsons	Steven Levy	. . .	Ralph Zimbouski
East Granby	t	TM	4	(860) 653-2576	. . .	. . .	. . .	. . .	. . .	. . .	. . .
East Haddam	t	TM	8	(860) 873-5020	Susan Merrow	. . .	Maryjane Plude	. . .	John Blaschik	. . .	Mark Kiefer
East Hampton *	t	CM	13	(860) 267-4468	Christopher Goff	Jeffery O'Keefe	Sandra Wieleba	Jeffery Jylkka	Gregory Voelker	Matthew Reimondo	Robert Drewry
East Hartford	t	MC	49	(860) 291-7200	Timothy Larson	John Choquette	. . .	Michael Walsh	David Dagon	Mark Sirois	Billy Taylor
East Haven	t	MC	28	(203) 468-3204	Joseph Maturo	Arthur DeSorbo	Elizabeth Leary	Paul Rizza	Wayne Sandford	Leonard Gallo	Fred Parlato
East Lyme	t	TM	18	(860) 739-6931	. . .	. . .	. . .	. . .	. . .	. . .	. . .
East Windsor	t	TM	9	(860) 623-8122	Linda Roberts	. . .	Karen Gaudreau	. . .	Blaine Simpkins	Edward DeMarco	Leonard Norton
Easton *	t	TM	7	(203) 268-6291	William Kupinse	. . .	W. D. Buckley	Grace Stanczyk	Martin Ohradan	John Solomon	Edward Nagy
Ellington	t	TM	12	(860) 870-3100	Michael Stupinski	. . .	Diane McKeegan	Nicholas Dicorleto	. . .	. . .	Peter Michaud
Enfield	t	CM	45	(860) 253-6300	. . .	Matthew Coppler	Suzanne Olechnicki	Gregory Simmons	. . .	Carl Sferrazza	Piya Hawkes
Essex	t	TM	6	(860) 767-4348	. . .	. . .	Betty Gaudenzi	. . .	Paul Fazzino	. . .	David Caroline
Fairfield *	t	RT	57	(203) 256-3057	Kenneth Flatto	Thomas Bremer	Elizabeth Browne	Paul Hiller	Richard Felner	Dave Peck	Richard White
Farmington	t	CM	23	(860) 675-2300	Arline Whitaker	Kathleen Eagen	Paula Ray	Daniel Costello	. . .	Michael Whalen	John McGrane
Glastonbury	t	CM	31	(860) 657-7710	. . .	Richard Johnson	Joyce Mascena	Diane Waldron	Matthew Nelson	Thomas Sweeney	Daniel Pennington
Granby *	t	CM	10	(860) 844-5300	John Adams	William Smith	. . .	Barbarajean Sibelli	. . .	David Watkins	James Klase
Greenwich *	t	RT	61	(203) 622-7734	Peter Tesei	John Crary	Carmella Budkins	Peter Mynarski	Peter Siecienski	David Ridberg	Amy Siebert
Griswold	t	TM	10	(860) 376-7060	Paul Brycki	. . .	Ellen Dupont	William Donovan	. . .	. . .	. . .
Groton	c	MC	10	(860) 446-4103	Dennis Popp	. . .	Debra Patrick	Anthony Timpano	Nick Delia	Larry Gurish	Robert Morse
Groton	t	CM	39	(860) 441-6630	. . .	Mark Oefinger	Barbara Tarbox	Salvatore Pandolfo	. . .	David Vanasse	Gary Schneider
Guilford *	t	TM	21	(203) 453-8015	Carl Balestracci	. . .	Janice Teft	Sheila Riegelmann	Charles Herrschaft	Thomas Terribile	John Volpe
Haddam	t	TM	7	(860) 345-8531	Anthony Bondi	. . .	Ann Huffstetler	. . .	. . .	. . .	Philip Goff
Hamden	t	MC	56	(203) 287-2500	Carl Amento	Michael Brandi	Vera Morrison	James Hliva	James Leddy	Robert Nolan	Joseph Celotto
Hartford *	c	MC	121	(860) 757-9511	Eddie Perez	Lee Erdmann	Daniel Carey	Christian Johnson	Charles Teale	Daryl Roberts	Bhupen Patel
Harwinton	t	TM	5	(860) 485-9051	Marie Knudsen	. . .	Patricia Williamsen	. . .	. . .	. . .	John Fredsall
Hebron *	t	TM	8	(860) 228-5971	. . .	Jared Clark	Carla Pomprowicz	. . .	Paul Burton	. . .	Andrew Tierney

Directory 1/9 continued

OFFICIALS IN U.S. MUNICIPALITIES 2,500 AND OVER IN POPULATION

Jurisdiction	Type	Form of govern-ment	2000 Popu-lation	Main telephone number	Chief elected official	Appointed administrator	Clerk of the governing board	Chief financial officer	Fire chief	Police chief	Public works director
CONNECTICUT continued											
Jewett City *	b	MC	3	(860) 376-7060	Cynthia Kata	Leona Sharkey	Valerie Pudvah	...	...	...	...
Kent	t	TM	2	(860) 927-3433	...	...	...	...	...	...	...
Killingly	t	CM	16	(860) 779-5335	Janice Thurlow	Bruce Benway	MaryEllen Heckler	James Day	...	...	...
Killingworth	t	TM	6	(860) 663-1765	David Denoir	...	Susan Adinolfo	...	...	...	James Ward
Lebanon	t	TM	6	(860) 642-6100	Daniel McGuire	...	Joyce McGillicuddy	Barbara Griffin	Robert Cady	...	Ronald Ives
Ledyard	t	MC	14	(860) 464-8740	Fred Allyn	...	Calvin Brouwer	Diane Napier	...	...	Steven Masalin
Lisbon	t	TM	4	(860) 376-7856	Thomas Sparkman	...	Marlene LePine	...	...	...	...
Litchfield	t	TM	8	(860) 567-7550	Leo Paul	...	Evelyn Goodwin	Cynthia Politano	Thomas O'Hare	Roger Doyle	James Koser
Madison	t	TM	17	(203) 245-5603	Thomas Scarpati	...	Dorothy Bean	Dorothy Bavin	Robert Gerard	Paul Jakubson	Donald Mac Millan
Manchester	t	CM	54	(860) 647-5235	Steve Cassano	Scott Shanley	Joe Camposeo	Alan Desmarais	Thomas Weber	Gerald Aponte	Mark Carlino
Mansfield	t	CM	20	(860) 429-3336	Elizabeth Paterson	Matthew Hart	Joan Gerdsen	Jeffery Smith	...	...	Lon Hultgren
Marlborough	t	TM	5	(860) 295-6204	Howard Dean	...	Nancy Dickson	...	...	...	Thomas Giola
Meriden	c	CM	58	(203) 630-4123	Joseph Marinan	...	Irene Masse	Edward Murphy	William Dunn	Robert Kosienski	Mark Zebora
Middlebury	t	TM	6	(203) 758-1779	Edward St. John	Claudia Tata	Alicia Ostar	Michael Belden	...	Patrick Bona	...
Middlefield	t	MC	4	(860) 349-7114	Charles Augur	...	Donna Golub	Joseph Geruch	Stan Atwell	...	John Wyskiel
Middletown	c	MC	43	(860) 344-3487	D. Thornton	...	Sandra Hutton	Carl Erlacher	Gary Ouellette	J. Brymer	William Russo
Milford *	c	MC	48	(203) 783-3220	James Richetelli	...	Alan Jepson	Judy Doneiko	Louis LaVecchia	Keith Mello	Bruce Kolwicz
Monroe *	t	MC	19	(203) 452-5400	Tom Buzi	...	Marsha Motter	Carl Tomchik	William Davin	John Salvatore	Arthur Baker
Montville *	t	MC	18	(860) 848-3030	Joseph Jaskiewicz	...	Lisa Terry	Terry Fafard	...	...	Donald Bourdeau
Naugatuck *	t	MC	30	(203) 729-4571	Michael Bronko	Aldo Pistarelli	Sophie Morton	Wayne McAllister	Charles Doback	Christopher Edson	Henry Witkoski
New Britain *	c	MC	71	(860) 826-3408	Timothy Stewart	Lisa Carver	Peter Denuzze	Robert Curry	Mark Carr	William Gagliardi	Mark Moriarty
New Canaan	t	TM	19	(203) 972-2350	Richard Bond	Peter Murphy	Claudia Weber	Gary Conrad	...	Christopher Lynch	Frank De Nicola
New Fairfield	t	TM	13	(203) 312-5660	Margaret Katkocin	...	Diana Peck	Mary Anne Weisner	...	...	Robert Rzasa
New Hartford	t	TM	6	(860) 379-3389	...	...	...	...	...	...	...
New Haven	c	MC	123	(203) 946-8252	John Destefano	...	Ronald Smith	Mark Pietrosimone	Michael Grant	Francisco Ortiz	Richard Miller
New London	c	CM	25	(860) 447-5210	Ernest Hewett	Martin Berliner	Michael Tranchida	Donald Goodrich	Ronald Samul	Bruce Rinehart	Edward Steward
New Milford	t	MC	27	(860) 355-6010	Patricia Murphy	...	George Buckbee	R. Jankowski	William May	Colin McCormack	Patrick Hackett
Newington *	t	CM	29	(860) 665-8500	Jeff Wright	John Salomone	Tanya Lane	Ann Harter	Chris Schroeder	Richard Mulhall	...
Newtown	t	MC	25	(203) 270-4201	Herbert Rosenthal	...	Cynthia Simon	Benjamin Spragg	William Halstead	Michael Kehoe	Fred Hurley
North Branford	t	CM	13	(203) 315-6000	Jo Anne Wentworth	Richard Branigan	Lisa Valenti	Anthony Esposito	Ralph Thomas	Matthew Canelli	Francis Merola
North Canaan	t	TM	3	(860) 824-7313	Douglas Humes	Dorothy Paviol	Carolyn O'Connor	Wheaton Byers	Charles Perotti	...	Brad Shook
North Haven	t	TM	22	(203) 239-5321	Kevin Kopetz	...	Elinor Pedalino	...	Vincent Landisio	James Dicarlo	...
North Stonington	t	TM	4	(860) 535-2877	...	...	...	...	Timothy Main	...	...
Norwalk	c	MC	82	(203) 854-7716	Richard Moccia	...	Mary Roman	Tom Hamilton	Denis McCarthy	Harry Rilling	Harold Alvord
Norwich	c	CM	36	(860) 823-3700	Arthur Lathrop	Alan Bergren	Dee Anne Brennan	Joseph Ruffo	James Walsh	Louis Fusaro	Joseph Loyacano
Old Lyme	t	TM	7	(860) 434-1605	Timothy Griswold	...	Irene Carnell	Doris Johnson	...	...	John Roach
Old Saybrook	t	TM	10	(860) 395-3123	Susan Townsley	...	Sarah Becker	...	David Heiney	Edmund Mosca	Ronald Baldi
Orange *	t	TM	12	(203) 891-2122	James Zeoli	...	Patrick O'Sullivan	Pamela Mangini	Charles Sherwood	Robert Gagne	Edwin Lieberman
Oxford	t	TM	9	(203) 888-2543	Katherine Johnson	Beverly Hanna	...	Carl Serus	...	...	George Swift
Plainfield	t	TM	14	(860) 564-4071	...	...	...	...	...	...	...
Plainville *	t	CM	17	(860) 793-0221	C. Wazorko	Robert Lee	Carol Skultety	Robert Buden	Raymond Swanson	Daniel Coppinger	Carmen Matteo
Plymouth	t	MC	11	(860) 585-4002	David Denis	...	Janet Scoville	Manuel Gomes	Mark Sekorski	...	Anthony Lorenzetti
Pomfret	t	TM	3	(860) 974-0191	...	...	Nora Johnson	...	...	...	...
Portland	t	TM	8	(860) 342-6700	Edward Kalinowski	...	Bernadette Dillon	...	...	...	Richard Kelsey
Preston *	t	TM	4	(860) 887-5581	Robert Congdon	...	Hattie Wucik	...	Tom Casey	...	Robert Boyd
Prospect	t	MC	8	(203) 758-4461	...	...	...	...	...	...	...
Putnam *	d	MC	9	(860) 963-6807	Robert Viens	...	Lucille Herrick	Paula LaJeunesse	...	Edward Perron	Gerard Beausoleil
Putnam *	t	TM	9	(860) 963-6800	...	Douglas Cutler	Sara D'Elia	...	...	...	...
Redding	t	TM	8	(203) 938-2002	Natalie Ketcham	...	Michele Grande	Mary Anne Wiesner	...	...	Roger Harker
Ridgefield	t	TM	23	(203) 431-2700	Rudy Marconi	...	Barbara Serfilippi	Jay Wahlberg	Heather Burford	Richard Ligi	Peter Hill
Rocky Hill	t	CM	17	(860) 258-2700	Barbara Surwilo	Barbara Gilbert	Ronald McNamara	John Mehr	Joseph Kochanek	Michael Custer	...
Salisbury	t	TM	3	(860) 435-9140	...	...	...	...	...	...	...
Seymour	t	TM	15	(203) 888-2511	Scott Barton	...	Esther Rozum	Douglas Thomas	Michael Driscoll	Michael Metzler	Dennis Rozum
Sharon	t	MC	2	(860) 364-5789	P. Moeller	...	Linda Amerrghi	...	Thomas Casey	...	...
Shelton	c	MC	38	(203) 924-1555	Mark Lauretti	Sandra Nesteriak	...	Louis Marusic	...	Robert Voccola	William Mooney
Simsbury	t	TM	23	(860) 658-3230	Thomas Vincent	...	Carolyn Keily	Kevin Kane	James Baldis	Peter Ingvertsen	...
Somers	t	TM	10	(860) 763-8200	Richard Jackson	...	Ann Marie Logan	Edward Sullivan	Bill Meier	...	Kenneth Anderson
South Windsor	t	CM	24	(860) 644-2511	...	Matthew Galligan	Gretchen Bickford	Melanie Crucitti	Philip Crombie	Gary Tyler	Michael Gantick
Southbury	t	TM	18	(203) 262-0600	Mark Cooper	...	Virginia Salisbury	...	John Stanko	...	George Metcalf
Southington	t	CM	39	(860) 276-6222	Edward Malczyk	John Weichsel	Leslie Cotton	Emilia Portelinha	Richard McDonough	John Daly	Steven Wlodkowski
Sprague	t	TM	2	(860) 822-3000	Dennison Allen	...	Claire Glaude	...	Daniel Nagle	...	Mark Benson
Stafford	t	TM	11	(860) 684-1778	Gordon Frassinelli	Michael Waugh	Carol Davis	...	...	...	Alan Wytas
Stamford	c	MC	117	(203) 977-5397	Dannel Malloy	...	Donna Loglisci	Lisa Reynolds	Robert McGrath	Louis Decarlo	Timothy Curtin
Stonington	t	TM	17	(860) 535-4721	Peter Dibble	George Sylvestre	Cynthia Ladwig	Marianna Stevens	...	Dave Erskine	...
Stratford	t	MC	49	(203) 385-4007	...	...	Patricia Ulatowski	Allen Moore	Ronald Nattrass	Robert Mossman	Michael Hudzik
Suffield *	t	TM	13	(860) 668-3838	Scott Lingenfelter	...	Elaine O'Brien	Deborah Cerrato	Thomas Bellmore	Michael Manzi	Jack Muska
Thomaston	t	TM	7	(860) 283-9678	Clifford Brammer	...	...	Susan Whitney	...	Edward Grabherr	Gerald Grohoski
Thompson	t	TM	8	(860) 923-9561	A. David Babbitt	...	...	Michael Martin	...	...	Leo Adams
Tolland	t	CM	13	(860) 871-3600	...	Steven Werbner	Meg DeVito	Christine Hutton	John Littell	...	John Bock
Torrington	c	MC	35	(860) 489-2228	...	...	...	...	...	...	...
Trumbull *	t	MC	34	(203) 452-5000	Raymond Baldwin	...	Rose Lodice	Lynn Heim	Robert Pescatore	Thomas Kiely	John Del Vecchio
Vernon	t	MC	28	(860) 870-3599	Ellen Marmer	...	...	James Luddecke	Robert Kelley	Rudolf Rossmy	George Fetko
Wallingford	t	MC	43	(203) 294-2070	William Dickinson	...	Rosemary Rascati	James Bowes	Wayne Lefebvre	Douglas Dortenzio	Henry McCully
Washington	t	TM	3	(860) 868-2259	Alan Chapin	...	Sheila Anson	...	Alden Johnson	...	...
Waterbury	c	MC	107	(203) 574-6761	Michael Jarjura	Sheila O'Malley	...	Patrick Jones	James Cavanaugh	Neil O'Leary	John Lawlor
Waterford	t	RT	19	(860) 442-0553	Paul Eccard	...	Robert Nye	Ruth Beers	Bruce Miller	Murray Pendleton	Ronald Cusano
Watertown	t	CM	21	(860) 945-5255	...	...	Virginia Stewart	Frank Nardelli	Larry Black	John Carroll	Roy Cavanaugh
West Hartford	t	CM	60	(860) 561-7460	Jonathan Harris	...	Norma Cronin	Chris Johnson	William Austin	James Strillacci	Dana Hallenbeck
West Haven *	c	MC	52	(203) 937-3560	John Picard	James Burns	Deborah Collins	Robert Barron	...	Ronald Quagliani	Beth Sabo
Westbrook	t	TM	6	(860) 399-3040	Tony Palermo	...	Lori Baldi	...	Clifford Spencer	...	John Riggio
Weston	t	TM	10	(203) 222-2677	...	Thomas Landry	Cynthia Williams	Richard Darling	...	Anthony Land	Joseph Lametta
Westport	t	RT	25	(203) 341-1000	Diane Farrell	...	Patricia Strauss	Donald Miklus	Denis McCarthy	William Chiarenzelli	Stephen Edwards
Wethersfield	t	CM	26	(860) 721-2801	Andrew Adil	Bonnie Therrien	Dolores Sassano	Lisa Hancock	Charles Flynn	James Cetran	Michael Turner
Willimantic	c	TM	14	(860) 465-3013	...	...	...	...	...	...	...
Willington *	t	TM	5	(860) 487-3100	...	...	...	...	...	...	...
Wilton *	t	TM	17	(203) 563-0100	William Brennan	...	Bettye Ragognetti	Joseph Dolan	Paul Milositz	Edward Kulhawik	Thomas Thurkettle
Winchester *	t	CM	10	(860) 379-2713	Kenneth Fracasso	Keith Robbins	Sheila Sedlack	Henry Centrella	Robert Shopey	Nicholas Guerriero	Patrick Hague
Windham	t	MC	22	(860) 465-3007	Michael Paulhus	...	Ann Bushey	Robert Buden	John Walsh	Lisa Maruzo-Bolduc	Brad Wojick
Windsor	t	CM	28	(860) 285-1900	Francis Brady	Peter Souza	Kathleen Quin	D. Cunningham	Dale Smith	Kevin Searles	Wayne Radke
Windsor Locks	t	TM	12	(860) 627-1444	Edward Ferrari	...	William Hamel	Barbara Bertrand	...	John Suchocki	Scott Lappen
Winsted	c	CM	7	(860) 379-2713	MaryAnn Welcome	Owen Quinn	...	...	...	...	...
Wolcott	t	MC	15	(203) 879-4666	...	...	...	...	...	...	...
Woodbridge *	t	TM	8	(203) 389-3400	Edward Sheehy	Joseph Hellauer	Stephanie Ciarleglio	Anthony Genovese	Andrew Esposito	Eugene Marcucci	Warren Connors
Woodbury	t	TM	9	(203) 263-2141	Richard Crane	...	Rita Connelly	Richard Hubbard	...	...	David Monckton
Woodstock	t	TM	7	(860) 928-0208	Delpha Very	...	Judy Alberts	...	...	...	Dwight Ryniewicz

Directory 1/9 continued — OFFICIALS IN U.S. MUNICIPALITIES 2,500 AND OVER IN POPULATION

Jurisdiction	Type	Form of govern-ment	2000 Popu-lation	Main telephone number	Chief elected official	Appointed administrator	Clerk of the governing board	Chief financial officer	Fire chief	Police chief	Public works director
DELAWARE											
Bethany Beach	t	CM	..	(302) 539-8011	Charles Bartlett	Clifford Graviet	Lisa Kail	Madalyn Forrest	...	...	James Seabrease
Cheswold	t	CM	..	(302) 734-6991	...	...	...	...	...	...	...
Dewey Beach	t	CM	..	(302) 227-6363	Robert Frederick	...	...	...	...	Raymond Morrison	...
Dover	c	CM	32	(302) 736-7073	...	Anthony DePrima	Janice Green	Donna Mitchell	...	Jeffrey Horvath	Scott Koenig
Elsmere	t	CM	5	(302) 998-2215	Charles Cavanaugh	John Giles	...	David Jaeger	George Giles	...	Joseph Cherneski
Fenwick Island	t	MC	..	(302) 539-3011	...	...	...	...	...	...	...
Georgetown *	t	CM	4	(302) 856-7391	Edwin Lambden	Eugene Dvornick	Angela Townsend	...	...	William Topping	William Bradley
Greenwood	t	MC	..	(302) 349-4534	Donald Donovan	Michael O'Gara	Doris Adkins	...	...	Brian Parsons	...
Harrington	c	MC	3	(302) 398-3530	...	...	Charlyne Hughes	Chris Truitt	...	John Horsman	Alan Moore
Laurel	t	MC	3	(302) 875-2277	John Shwed	...	Donna Adkins	Mary Introcaso	Jeff Hill	Donald McGinty	Allen Atkins
Lewes *	c	MC	2	(302) 645-7777	James Ford	...	Alice Erickson	E. Lorraine McCabe	...	...	...
Middletown	t	MC	6	(302) 378-2711	Kenneth Branner	Morris Deputy	Rebecca Ennis	Louis Vitola	...	...	...
Milford *	c	CM	6	(302) 422-6616	Daniel Marabello	David Baird	Teresa Hudson	Jeffrey Portmann	...	E. Keith Hudson	...
New Castle *	c	CM	4	(302) 322-9812	John Klingmeyer	Cathryn Thomas	Jill DiAngelo	Marian Delaney	...	Kevin McDerby	Joseph Freebery
Newark *	c	CM	28	(302) 366-7020	Vance Funk	Kyle Sonnenberg	Patricia Fogg	Dennis McFarland	...	Paul Tiernan	Richard Lapointe
Newport	t	CM	1	(302) 994-6403	...	Rita Shade	...	...	...	...	...
Ocean View	t	MC	1	(302) 539-9797	Gary Meredith	Kathy Roth	Marie Thomas	...	...	K. McLaughlin	Charles McMullen
Rehoboth Beach	c	CM	1	(302) 227-6181	Samuel Cooper	Gregory Ferrese	...	...	...	Keith Banks	Melbourne Craig
Seaford	c	CM	6	(302) 629-9173	Daniel Short	Dolores Slatcher	...	June Merritt	...	Gary Morris	Robert Nibblett
Smyrna	t	CM	5	(302) 653-3483	Mark Schaeffer	David Hugg	Carol McKinney	Gary Stulir	...	Richard Baldwin	Joseph Heeger
Wilmington	c	MC	72	(302) 576-2100	James Baker	W. Montgomery	Maribel Ruiz	Ronald Morris	James Ford	Michael Szczerba	Kash Srinivasan
DISTRICT OF COLUMBIA											
Columbia	d	MC	572	(202) 727-1000	Adrian Fenty	Dan Tangherlini	...	Natwar Gandhi	Adrian Thompson	Charles Ramsey	...
FLORIDA											
Alachua	c	CM	6	(386) 462-1231	Bonnie Burgess	...	...	Marcian Brown	...	Robert Jernigan	Oren Paulsen
Altamonte Springs	c	CM	41	(407) 571-8000	Russel Hauck	Phillip Penland	Patsy Wainright	Mark Debord	...	Robert Merchant	John Peters
Apalachicola	c	MC	2	(850) 653-9319	...	Betty Taylor-Webb	...	...	...	Anderson Williams	...
Apopka	c	MC	26	(407) 703-1700	John Land	Richard Anderson	Janice Goebel	...	Randall Fernandez	Charles Vavrek	...
Arcadia	c	CM	6	(941) 494-4114	...	...	...	...	...	...	...
Archer *	c	CM	1	(352) 495-2880	Laurie Costello	James Drymon	...	...	...	...	...
Astatula	t	MC	1	(352) 742-1100	...	...	Maria Montalvo	...	...	Carson Sink	Horace Mauldin
Atlantic Beach *	c	CM	13	(904) 247-5800	John Meserve	James Hanson	Donna Bussey	Fredrik Van Liere	...	Mike Classey	Ricky Carper
Atlantis *	c	CM	2	(561) 965-1744	Manuel Fernandez	Mo Thornton	Joan Cannata-Fox	...	...	Robert Mangold	Steven Hazuk
Auburndale	c	CM	11	(863) 965-5530	Marvin Wiley	Robert Green	...	Shirley Lowrance	Sam Efurd	Dean Longo	Mickey Etherton
Aventura	c	CM	14	(305) 466-8900	Susan Gottlieb	Eric Soroka	Teresa Soroka	Brian Raducci	...	Steve Steinberg	Alan Levine
Avon Park	c	CM	8	(863) 452-4400	Sharon Schuler	C. Shirey	...	Renee Green	Terry Feickert	Frank Mercurio	Theodore Long
Bal Harbour *	v	CM	3	(305) 866-4633	Daniel Tankleff	Alfred Treppeda	Ellisa Horvath	...	...	Thomas Hunker	Walter Mathews
Bartow *	c	CM	15	(863) 534-0100	Leo Longworth	George Long	Linda Culpepper	David Wright	James Robinson	...	William Pickard
Bay Harbor Islands	t	CM	4	(305) 866-6241	Isaac Salver	Ronald Wasson	Marlene Marante	Alan Short	...	John Ross	Joseph Fox
Bay Lake	c	CM	..	(407) 828-2241	Orville Bell	Mickey Shiver	Kathy Ludwig	Ann Blakeslee	...	...	...
Bell *	t	CM	..	(352) 463-6288	Darryl Bryan	Dan Cavanah	...	...	...	...	...
Belle Glade	c	CM	14	(561) 996-0100	Steve Wilson	...	Debra Buff	...	Stephen Rice	...	...
Belle Isle	c	CM	5	(407) 851-7730	William Brooks	Lawrence Williams	Belinda Bateman	...	...	...	James Sapp
Belleair	t	CM	4	(727) 588-3769	...	Micah Maxwell	Donna Carlen	...	...	...	...
Belleair Beach *	c	CM	1	(727) 595-4646	Lynn Rives	Nancy McCollum	Patricia Gentry	Maria Kemp	...	...	...
Belleair Bluffs	c	MC	2	(727) 584-2151	...	...	Debra Sullivan	...	...	...	Robert David
Biscayne Park	v	CO	3	(305) 899-8000	John Hornbuckle	Frank Spence	Ann Harper	Holly Hugdahl	...	Mitchell Glansberg	Joseph Fisher
Blountstown	c	CM	2	(850) 674-5488	...	...	...	...	...	...	...
Boca Raton	c	CM	74	(561) 393-7803	Steven Abrams	Leif Ahnell	S. Carannante	Mervyn Timberlake	Bruce Silk	Andrew Scott	R. DiChristopher
Bonifay	c	MC	4	(850) 547-4238	James Sims	...	Shirley Mitchell	...	Roy Messer	Ronnie Bennett	Jack Marell
Bonita Springs *	c	CM	32	(239) 949-6262	...	Gary Price	Dianne Lynn	...	...	...	Daryl Walk
Boynton Beach	c	CM	60	(561) 742-6000	Gerald Broening	Kurt Bressner	Janet Prainito	Diane Reese	William Bingham	Marshall Gage	Jeffrey Livergood
Bradenton	c	MC	49	(941) 708-6200	Wayne Poston	...	...	...	Mark Souders	Michael Radzilowski	John Cumming
Brooksville	c	CM	7	(352) 544-5407	Ernest Wever	T. Norman-Vacha	Karen Phillips	S. Baumgartner	James Daugherty	Boyce Tincher	Emory Pierce
Bunnell	c	CM	2	(386) 437-7500	Joann King	...	Ronya Johnson	...	Gary Hughes	Michael Ignasiak	Eric Crandall
Bushnell	c	CM	2	(352) 793-2591	...	Vince Ruano	...	N. Joy Coleman	...	Joyce Wells	Ronald Pitts
Callaway	c	CM	14	(850) 871-6000	Kenneth Meer	Judy Whitis	Genette Bernal	Alice Bennett	Jack McKinney	...	John Adams
Cape Canaveral *	c	CM	8	(321) 868-1221	Rocky Randels	Bennett Boucher	Susan Stills	...	David Sargeant	Doug Scragg	Walter Bandish
Cape Coral	c	CM	102	(239) 574-0450	Eric Feichthaler	Terrance Stewart	Bonnie Vent	Mark Mason	William Van Helden	Daniel Alexander	Charles Pavlos
Casselberry *	c	CM	22	(407) 262-7700	Charlene Glancy	Barbara Lipscomb	Donna Gardner	James Newlon	Donald Harkins	James Ruf	Eduardo Torres
Chattahoochee	c	CM	3	(850) 663-4046	James Atkins	Elmon Garner	Gayle Lanier	...	...	Edward Pullen	...
Chiefland	c	MC	1	(352) 493-6711	Matthew Pomeroy	Grady Hartzog	...	...	...	Robert Douglas	...
Chipley	c	CM	3	(850) 638-6350	Tommy McDonald	Jim Morris	Patrice Yates	...	Kevan Parker	Kevin Crews	Charles Barfield
Cinco Bayou	t	CM	..	(850) 833-3405	Michael Iovieno	Nell Dykes	...	...	...	...	...
Clearwater *	c	CM	108	(727) 562-4055	Frank Hibbard	William Horne	Cynthia Goudeau	Margaret Simmons	Jamie Geer	Sidney Klein	Tracy Mercer
Clermont	c	CM	9	(352) 394-4081	Harold Turville	David Saunders	...	Joseph Van Zile	Carle Bishop	Randall Story	Elbert Davis
Clewiston *	c	CO	6	(863) 983-1484	Mali Chamness	Wendell Johnson	Marilyn McCorvey	Ted Byrd	William Pelham	Don Gutshall	Sean Scheffler
Cocoa	c	CM	16	(321) 639-7585	Judy Parrish	James Holt	Joan Clark	Walter Mack	Arthur Romprey	Phillip Ludos	Michael DeVillo
Cocoa Beach *	c	CM	12	(321) 868-3306	Leon Beeler	Charles Billias	Loredana Kalaghchy	Kenneth Killgore	Scott Shear	James Scragg	Robert Torres
Coconut Creek	c	CM	43	(954) 973-6770	Becky Tooley	David Rivera	Barbara Price	Karen Brooks	...	George Raggio	J. Sundermeier
Cooper City *	c	CM	27	(954) 434-4300	Debby Eisinger	Bruce Loucks	Susan Poling	Horacio DeOca	Michael Campbell	John Hale	James Bowman
Coral Gables	c	CM	40	(305) 446-6800	Don Slesnick	David Brown	Walter Foeman	Donald Nelson	Richard Cook	M. Hammerschmidt	Alberto Delgado
Coral Springs	c	CM	117	(954) 344-1000	John Sommerer	Michael Levinson	...	David Russek	Donald Haupt	Roy Arigo	Rich Michaud
Crescent City	c	MC	1	(386) 698-2525	Howard Kinsella	Patrick Kennedy	...	Gay Harris	Allen Peacock	George Penley	Michael Ijames
Crestview	c	MC	14	(850) 682-1560	George Whitehurst	...	Janice Young	Patti Mann	Joseph Traylor	Travis Gillihan	General Cox
Crystal River *	c	CM	3	(352) 795-4216	Ronald Kitchen	Andrew Houston	Carol Harrington	Mark Thiele	...	...	John Lettow
Cutler Bay	t	CM	37	(305) 234-4262	...	Steven Alexander	...	...	...	...	...
Dade City *	c	CM	6	(352) 523-5050	Scott Black	William Poe	James Class	...	...	Raymond Velboom	...
Dania Beach	c	CM	20	(954) 924-3600	Robert Anton	Colin Donnelly	Louise Stilson	Patricia Varney	...	Donn Peterson	Dominic Orlando
Davenport *	c	CM	1	(863) 419-3300	Peter Rust	Amy Arrington	Raquel Castillo	David Dyer	Donald Pelt	Lloyd Clements	...
Davie	t	CM	75	(954) 797-1000	Thomas Trues	Gary Shimun	Russell Muniz	...	Donald DiPetrillo	John George	Bruce Bernard
Daytona Beach	c	CM	64	(386) 671-8000	Baron Asher	James Chisholm	Jennifer Thomas	James Maniak	Lawrence Taft	Dennis Jones	Stan Lemke
Daytona Beach Shores	c	CM	4	(386) 763-5373	Greg Northrup	Michael Booker	Cheri Schwab	Steve Whitmer	...	Stephan Dembinsky	Fred Hiatt
De Bary *	c	CM	15	(386) 668-2040	Bob Garcia	Maryann Courson	Stacy Tebo	James Seelbinder	...	...	...
De Funiak Springs *	c	CM	5	(850) 892-8500	C. Harold Carpenter	Kim Kirby	Vanessa Mitchell	Sara Bowers	Brian Coley	...	...
De Land	c	CM	20	(386) 740-5700	Robert Apgar	Michael Pleus	Julie Hennessy	Kevin Lewis	Patrick Kelly	Edward Overman	Marvin Williams
Deerfield Beach	c	CM	64	(954) 480-4200	Albert Capellini	Michael Mahaney	A. Graham-Johnson	Sally Siegel	Gary Lother	George Brennan	Donald Freedland
Delray Beach *	c	CM	60	(561) 243-7084	Rita Ellis	David Harden	Chevelle Nubin	Joseph Safford	David James	Anthony Strianese	Jim Schmitz
Deltona	c	CM	69	(386) 561-2100	John Masiarczyk	Faith Miller	...	...	Francis Ennist	...	Glenn Kerns
Destin	c	CM	11	(850) 837-4242	Craig Barker	Gregory Kisela	Dana Williams	Lisa Rolan	...	...	Timothy Shockley
Doral	c	CM	20	(305) 470-6840	...	Sergio Purrinos	...	...	...	...	Eric Carpenter
Dundee	t	CM	2	(863) 419-3100	Linda Riner-Mizell	Charles Saddler	Stephanie Diaz	Pamela Lawson	Chip Johnson	Sammy Taylor	C. J. Johnson
Dunedin	c	CM	35	(727) 733-4151	John Doglione	Robert DiSpirito	Sandra Woodall	...	Clarence Meyer	...	Douglas Hutchens

Directory 1/9 continued — OFFICIALS IN U.S. MUNICIPALITIES 2,500 AND OVER IN POPULATION

Jurisdiction	Type	Form of govern-ment	2000 Popu-lation	Main telephone number	Chief elected official	Appointed administrator	Clerk of the governing board	Chief financial officer	Fire chief	Police chief	Public works director
FLORIDA continued											
Dunnellon *	c	CM	1	(352) 465-8500	Fred Ward	...	Dawn Bowne	Jan Smith	Joseph Campfield	Roger Free	...
Eagle Lake *	c	CM	2	(863) 293-4141	Melinda Thomas	Peter Gardner	Dawn Osterhout	...	...	James Sullivan	Brian Fletcher
Eatonville *	t	MC	2	(407) 623-1313	...	...	Kathy Williams	Katherina Gibson	...	...	...
Edgewater	c	CM	18	(386) 424-2400	Donald Schmidt	Tracy Barlow	Susan Wadsworth	...	...	Michael Ignasiak	Terry Wadsworth
El Portal	v	MC	2	(305) 795-7880	...	...	Lenore Milan	...	...	...	...
Eustis	c	CM	15	(352) 483-5430	...	Paul Berg	...	Jim Myers	Roy Tremain	...	John Futch
Fellsmere *	c	CM	3	(772) 571-1616	Sara Savage	Jason Nunemaker	Debbie Krages	Larry Napier	...	Scott Melanson	Bud Roode
Fernandina Beach	c	CM	10	(904) 277-7305	Joe Gerity	Michael Czymbor	Cassandra Mitchell	Patricia Clifford	Daniel Leeper	...	...
Flagler Beach *	c	MC	4	(386) 517-2000	Alice Baker	Bernard Murphy	Angela Apperson	Kathleen Doyle	Martin Roberts	Richard Cody	Robert Smith
Florida City	c	CM	5	(305) 247-8221	Otis Wallace	Sylvestor Jackson	Sheila Paul	Desmond Chin	...	Pedro Taylor	Darin Baldwin
Fort Lauderdale *	c	CM	152	(954) 828-5300	Jim Naugle	George Gretsas	Jonda Joseph	Michael Kinneer	James Eddy	Frank Adderley	Albert Carbon
Fort Meade	c	CM	5	(863) 285-1100	...	Frederick Hilliard	Delores Avery	...	...	Irvin Heathcote	Glenn Curlee
Fort Myers	c	MC	48	(941) 332-6775	Bruce Grady	William Mitchell	Marie Adams	Maria Joyner	Richard Chappelle	...	Emmette Waite
Fort Myers Beach *	t	CM	6	(239) 765-0202	...	William Janke	Michelle Mayher	Evelyn Wicks	...	...	Jack Green
Fort Pierce	c	CM	37	(772) 460-2200	Edward Enns	David Recor	Cassandra Steele	George Bergalis	...	Eugene Savage	Gary Ferch
Fort Walton Beach *	c	CM	19	(850) 833-9504	Michael Anderson	Joyce Shanahan	Helen Spencer	Brandy Wunker	Michael Dutton	Theodore Litschauer	Thomas Murray
Frostproof *	c	CM	2	(863) 635-7855	Larry Sullivan	Tenny Croley	Ann Bass	Melody Zobel	William Lord	...	James Keene
Fruitland Park	c	CM	3	(352) 360-6727	Christopher Bell	Ralph Bowers	Linda Rodrick	...	Thomas Gamble	J. Isom	John Bostic
Gainesville *	c	CM	95	(352) 334-5077	...	Russell Blackburn	Kurt Lannon	Mark Benton	William Northcutt	Norman Botsford	Teresa Scott
Golden Beach *	t	MC	..	(305) 932-0744	Glenn Singer	Alexander Diaz	Elizabeth Sewell	Maria Camacho	...	James Skinner	Riley Crews
Golf	v	CM	..	(561) 732-0236	...	Mark Hull	Carol Marciano	...	...	...	Ron Lupo
Graceville	c	CM	2	(850) 263-3250	Guyton Williams	Michael Underwood	Kathleen Turner	...	Tracy Dennis	Daniel Ward	Eddie King
Grant-Valkaria *	t	CM	3	(321) 951-1380	Delbert Yonts	Richard Hood	Susanne Krueger	...	...	...	...
Green Cove Springs	c	CM	5	(904) 529-2200	Deborah Ricks	Don Bowles	Marjorie Robertson	...	...	Robert Musco	Bob Gamble
Greenacres *	c	CM	27	(561) 642-2000	Samuel Ferreri	Wadie Atallah	Sondra Hill	Jeffrey Price	...	...	Dennis Rogan
Greenville	t	CM	..	(850) 948-2251	...	...	...	...	...	...	...
Gretna *	c	CM	1	(850) 856-5257	...	Antonio Jefferson	Karen Fitzgerald	Dianne Formman	...	...	Bill Revels
Groveland	c	CM	2	(352) 429-2141	Matthew Bauman	Ralph Hester	Anne Sasser	Dolly Miller	Willie Morgan	Thomas Merrill	Larry Walker
Gulf Breeze *	c	CM	5	(850) 934-5115	Lane Gilchrist	Edwin Eddy	Marita Rhodes	Nancy Millay	C. Carmichael	Peter Paulding	Vernon Prather
Gulf Stream	t	CM	..	(561) 276-5116	William Koch	William Thrasher	Rita Taylor	...	...	Garrett Ward	...
Gulfport *	c	CM	12	(727) 893-1021	...	Thomas Brobeil	Louise Spence	William Kucera	...	...	Don Sopak
Haines City *	c	CM	13	(863) 421-3600	Herman Tyler	E. Toney-Deal	Cherry Dowdy	Donald Carter	Lon Cheney	...	...
Hallandale Beach *	c	CM	34	(954) 457-1348	Joy Cooper	Dwayne Good	Edward McGough	Mark Antonio	Daniel Sullivan	Thomas Magill	William Brant
Havana	t	CM	1	(850) 539-6493	...	Susan Freiden	...	Karen Myrick	Don Vickers	Brian Mitchell	...
Haverhill	t	MC	1	(561) 689-3070	...	...	...	...	...	...	...
Hawthorne	c	CM	1	(352) 481-2432	John Martin	Chad Shryock	...	Lakesha McGruder	...	...	William Cuthbert
Hialeah	c	MC	188	(305) 883-8050	Julio Robaina	...	...	...	Otto Drozd	Rolando Bolanos	Armando Vidal
Hialeah Gardens	c	MC	7	(305) 558-4114	Yioset Delacruz	...	Maria Joffer	Marcos Piloto	...	H. Keith Joy	Phillip Sheffield
High Springs	c	MC	3	(386) 454-1416	Byran Williams	James Drumm	...	Helen McIver	...	...	LaVerne Hodge
Highland Beach *	t	CM	3	(561) 278-4548	Jim Newill	Dale Sugerman	Beverly Brown	Cale Curtis	David James	Craig Hartmann	Jack Lee
Hillsboro Beach	t	MC	2	(954) 427-4011	Carmen McGarry	...	Cathy Deckert	Dan Dodge	...	Felix Brugnoni	...
Holly Hill *	c	CM	12	(386) 248-9420	Roland Via	Tim Harbuck	Valerie Manning	Kurt Swartzlander	Ron Spencer	...	Chris Hurst
Hollywood	c	CM	139	(954) 921-3201	Mara Giulianti	Cameron Benson	Patricia Cerny	Carlos Garcia	...	James Scarberry	Gregory Turek
Holmes Beach	c	MC	4	(941) 708-5800	Rich Bohnenberger	...	Brooke Bennett	Richard Ashley	...	Jay Romine	Joe Duennes
Homestead *	c	CM	31	(305) 224-4400	Lynda Bell	Mohd Shehadeh	Sheila Paul	Janette Smith	...	Alexander Rolle	Julio Brea
Indialantic *	t	CM	2	(321) 723-2242	David Berkman	Christopher Chinault	Laura Eaton	...	Jon MacDonald	Troy Morris	Ronald Cassedy
Indian Creek *	v	CM	..	(305) 865-4121	...	Samuel Kissinger	Marilane Lima	...	...	Clarke Maher	...
Indian Harbor Beach	c	CM	8	(321) 773-3181	Jim Nolan	Jacqueline Burns	Debra Maliska	Richard Anderson	Todd Scaldo	Robert Sullivan	Louis Giacona
Indian River Shores	t	CM	3	(772) 231-1771	Thomas Cadden	Robert Bradshaw	Laura Aldrich	...	...	...	Edward Morris
Indian Rocks Beach *	c	CM	5	(727) 595-2517	R. Johnson	...	Deanne O'Reilly	...	...	...	Dean Scharmen
Inverness *	c	CM	6	(352) 726-2611	...	Frank DiGiovanni	Debbie Davis	Donna Kilbury	...	...	Russ Kreager
Islamorada Village of Islands *	v	CM	6	(305) 664-6400	Cathi Hill	Kenneth Fields	Beverly Raddatz	Cindy Lawson	William Wagner	Don Fanelli	Myles Milander
Jacksonville	c	MC	735	(904) 630-1178	John Peyton	Alan Mosley	...	Calvin Ray	...	John Rutherford	Lynn Westbrook
Jacksonville Beach *	c	CM	20	(904) 270-1655	Fland Sharp	George Forbes	Heidi Reagan	Harry Royal	Gary Frazier	Bruce Thomason	William Edwards
Jasper	c	CM	1	(386) 792-1212	Matthew Hawkins	...	Jennifer Cone	Margaret Harper	William Trinder	Jeff McGuire	Walter Davis
Juno Beach	t	CM	3	(561) 626-1122	Linda Hodgkins	...	Allison Fay	Joseph Lo Bello	...	Halifax Clark	Anthony Meriano
Jupiter	t	CM	39	(561) 746-5134	...	Andrew Lukasik	Sally Boylan	...	...	Frank Kitzerow	Thomas Driscoll
Jupiter Island	t	CM	..	(772) 545-0100	Joseph Connolly	...	Antonia Wickes	Connie Holloman	...	...	...
Kenneth City	t	MC	4	(727) 544-6655	William Smith	...	Nancy Beelman	...	...	James Ernst	Albert Carrier
Key Biscayne	v	CM	8	(305) 365-5511	Joe Rasco	Genaro Iglesias	Conchita Alvarez	...	John Gilbert	Michael Flaherty	...
Key West	c	CM	25	(305) 292-8202	Jimmy Weekley	James Scholl	Cheryl Smith	Roger Wittenberg	William Wardlow	Gordon Dillion	Richard Knowles
Keystone Heights *	c	MC	1	(352) 473-4807	Mary Lou Hildreth	Kenneth Venables	Karen Nelson	...	...	...	Lee Edgy
Kissimmee *	c	CM	47	(407) 518-2110	George Gant	Mark Durbin	...	Amy Ady	Robert King	Fran Iwanski	David Derrick
Lady Lake	t	CM	11	(352) 751-1505	Michael Francis	William Vance	Deborah Gay	Karen Rickelman	...	...	Warren Blakeley
Lake Alfred *	c	CM	3	(863) 291-5747	Lowell Schmidt	Jan Shockley	Valerie Way	Amber Pennington	Roger Pridgen	Art Bodenheimer	Larry Harbuck
Lake Buena Vista	c	CM	..	(407) 828-2241	William Sterner	...	...	...	...	...	...
Lake Butler	c	CM	1	(386) 496-3401	Brantley Crawford	John Berchtold	...	...	...	...	Hardy Clyatt
Lake City	c	CM	9	(386) 752-2031	Steven Witt	Grayson Carson	Audrey Sikes	James Minchin	Alphonso Wilson	David Allbritton	William Dow
Lake Clarke Shores	t	CM	3	(561) 964-1515	Robert Shalhoub	Joann Hatton	Jo Plyler	William Thrasher	...	William Smith	Kevin Varney
Lake Helen	c	MC	2	(386) 228-2121	Mark Shuttleworth	Don Findell	J. Grammatikas	...	...	Keith Chester	Rick Mullen
Lake Mary	c	CM	11	(407) 585-1419	...	John Litton	Carol Foster	Jacqueline Sova	Craig Haun	Richard Beary	Bruce Paster
Lake Park *	t	CM	8	(561) 881-3300	Desca Dubois	Maria Davis	Vivian Mendez	Anne Costello	...	...	...
Lake Wales *	c	CM	10	(863) 678-4182	Lee Wheeler	Anthony Otte	Diane Smith	...	Thomas Tucker	Mark Levine	Ray Creel
Lake Worth	c	CM	35	(561) 586-1600	Rodney Romano	Robert Baldwin	Pamela Lopez	Mark Bates	Paul Blockson	William Smith	Dirk Bane
Lakeland	c	CM	78	(863) 834-6007	...	Douglas Thomas	Kelly Koos	Jerry Reynolds	Michael Mohler	Roger Bootnor	Richard Lilyquist
Lantana	t	CM	9	(561) 540-5000	...	Michael Bornstein	Darla Levy	Barbara Hastings	...	Richard Lincoln	Tom Lundquist
Largo *	c	CM	69	(727) 587-6700	Patricia Gerard	Norton Craig	Diane Bruner	Kimball Adams	Michael Wallace	Lester Aradi	Brian Ushers
Lauderdale Lakes	c	MC	31	(954) 535-2700	Samuel Brown	Anita Taylor	...	Donald St. Georges	Richard Sievers	...	...
Lauderdale-By-The-Sea	t	CM	2	(954) 776-0576	Oliver Parker	Esther Colon	Jonda Joseph	...	Jon Case	Edward Patten	William Mason
Lauderhill *	c	CM	57	(954) 730-3000	...	Charles Faranda	Andrea Anderson	Kennie Hobbs	Edward Curran	Kenneth Patchnek	Charles Cuyler
Leesburg	c	CM	15	(352) 728-9700	John Christian	Jay Evans	Betty Richardson	William Pfeilsticker	Dennis Sargent	H. Idell	...
Lighthouse Point	c	MC	10	(954) 943-6500	Fred Schorr	John Lavisky	Carol Landau	Terry Sharp	David Donzella	Ross Licata	Arthur Graham
Live Oak	c	CM	6	(386) 362-2276	...	...	William McCullers	Deborah Davis	George Croft	Nolan McLeod	Willard Hewiett
Longboat Key	t	CM	7	(941) 316-1999	...	Bruce St. Denis	Jane O'Connor	Terence Sullivan	Julius Halas	Al Hogle	Juan Florensa
Longwood	c	CM	13	(407) 260-3440	Paul Lovestrand	...	Geri Zambri	Carol Rogers	Charles Chapman	Tom Jackson	...
Lynn Haven	c	CM	12	(850) 265-2121	Walter Kelley	John Lynch	...	...	Richard Morrison	David Messer	Robert Olson
Macclenny	c	CM	4	(904) 259-6261	Gary Dopson	Gerald Dopson	...	Kathy Woods	Daniel Dugger	...	David Mette
Madeira Beach	c	CM	4	(727) 391-9951	Charles Parker	W. Higginbotham	Denise Schlegel	Monica Mitchell	Derryl O'Neal	...	Michael Maxemow
Madison *	c	CM	3	(850) 973-5081	...	Harold Emrich	Lee Hall	...	Aubrey Blanton	Fred Davis	...
Maitland	c	CM	12	(407) 539-6222	Doug Kinson	James Williams	Maria Waldrop	Sharon Anselmo	Kenneth Neuhard	Gary Calhoun	Anthony Leffin
Malabar *	t	CM	1	(321) 727-7764	Thomas Eschenberg	B. Wilbanks-Free	Debby Franklin	...	Joseph Gianantonio	Jack Parker	Carl Beatty
Manalapan	t	CM	..	(561) 585-9477	William Benjamin	Gregory Dunham	...	...	...	...	...
Mangonia Park	t	CM	1	(561) 848-1235	William Albury	...	Sherry Albury	...	...	Rodney Thomas	Peter LaMendola
Marathon	c	CM	10	(305) 743-0033	John Bartus	Michael Puto	Cindy Ecklund	Peter Rosasco	Hans Wagner	...	...
Marco Island *	c	CM	14	(239) 389-5000	William Trotter	Steven Thompson	Laura Litzan	...	Michael Murphy	Thomas Carr	A. Joel

Directory 1/9 continued **OFFICIALS IN U.S. MUNICIPALITIES 2,500 AND OVER IN POPULATION**

Jurisdiction	Type	Form of govern-ment	2000 Popu-lation	Main telephone number	Chief elected official	Appointed administrator	Clerk of the governing board	Chief financial officer	Fire chief	Police chief	Public works director
FLORIDA continued											
Margate	c	CM	53	(954) 972-6454	Arthur Bross	Leonard Golub	Shirley Baughman	Gail Gargano	. . .	Jerry Blough	James Hinds
Marianna	c	CM	6	(850) 482-4353	Paul Donofro	Louy Harris	Daniele Pippin	. . .	Jack Barwick	. . .	. . .
Mary Esther	c	CM	4	(850) 243-3566	Margaret McLemore	John Lulue	Lynne Oler	Tim Spellman	Ronald McArtor	. . .	Lee Iferd
Mascotte *	c	CM	2	(352) 429-3341	. . .	Marge Strausbaugh	Dana Waters	Art Bisner	Randy Brasher	Steven Allen	Henry Sharpe
Melbourne	c	CM	71	(321) 953-6350	Harry Goode	Jack Schluckebier	Cathleen Wysor	Michelle Ennis	Paul Forsberg	Donald Carey	Robert Klaproth
Melbourne Beach *	t	CM	3	(321) 724-5860	Rita Karpie	James Bursick	Christina Hoffkins	Jane Antonsen	Seth Stark	Ronald Krueger	. . .
Mexico Beach	c	CM	1	(850) 648-5700	. . .	. . .	. . .	. . .	. . .	. . .	. . .
Miami	c	MC	358	(305) 416-2100	Manuel Diaz	Pedro Hernandez	Priscilla Thompson	Diana Gomez	William Bryson	John Timney	Stephanie Grindell
Miami Beach *	c	CM	92	(305) 673-7000	Matti Herrera-Bower	Jorge Gonzalez	Robert Parcher	Patricia Walker	Eric Yuhr	Carlos Noriega	Fred Beckmann
Miami Gardens	c	CM	101	(305) 622-8000	Shirley Gibson	Danny Crew	Ronetta Taylor	Chris Wallace	. . .	. . .	Tom Ruiz
Miami Lakes	t	CM	12	(305) 364-6100	Wayne Slaton	Alex Rey	Debra Eastman	Alfredo Acin	. . .	. . .	Osdel Larrea
Miami Shores *	v	CM	10	(305) 795-2207	Herta Holly	Thomas Benton	Barbara Fugazzi	Holly Hugdahl	. . .	Kevin Lystad	Scott Davis
Miami Springs	c	CM	13	(305) 805-5000	Billy Bain	James Borgmann	Magali Valls	Charles Marshall	. . .	H. Dilling	Denise Yoezle
Midway	c	CM	1	(850) 574-2355	Delores Madison	. . .	Frances Harrell	. . .	. . .	Gregory Gardner	. . .
Milton	c	CM	7	(850) 983-5400	Guy Thompson	Donna Adams	Dewitt Nobles	. . .	John Reble	W. Markopoulos	Anthony Thomsen
Minneola *	c	CM	5	(352) 394-3598	. . .	Samuel Oppelaar	Jan McDaniel	Laura Zielonka	David Dobrzykowski	Greg Link	Mark Odell
Miramar	c	CM	72	(954) 967-1500	Lori Mosely	Robert Payton	. . .	John Merrell	James Hunt	Melvin Standley	Vernon Hargray
Monticello	c	MC	2	(850) 342-0153	. . .	Donald Anderson	Julie Clark	. . .	. . .	. . .	. . .
Mount Dora	c	CM	9	(352) 735-7186	James Yatsuk	Michael Quinn	. . .	Robert Brekelbaum	Ronald Snowberger	T. Scoggins	Gary Hammond
Mulberry *	c	CM	3	(863) 425-1125	Mark Seigler	Frank Thomas	Vanessa Baker	Blake Rane	Steven Peacock	Lynn Dumbrowski	Victor Harris
Naples *	c	CM	20	(239) 213-1810	Bill Barnett	A. Moss	Tara Norman	Ann Marie Ricardi	James McEvoy	. . .	Bob Middleton
Neptune Beach	c	CM	7	(904) 270-2400	Richard Brown	James Jarboe	Lisa Volpe	Steven Ramsey	. . .	. . .	Leon Smith
New Port Richey	c	CM	16	(727) 841-4500	Frank Parker	. . .	Victoria McDonald	Richard Snyder	Daniel Azzariti	Aage Madsen	Thomas O'Neill
New Smyrna Beach	c	CM	20	(386) 424-2100	. . .	. . .	. . .	Bill Poling	Timothy Hawver	Ronald Pagano	Mel Phillips
Newberry *	c	CM	3	(352) 472-2161	John Glanzer	Keith Ashby	Gayle Pons	. . .	David Rodriguez	. . .	Blaine Suggs
Niceville	c	CM	11	(850) 729-4008	. . .	Lannie Corbin	Daniel Doucet	. . .	Michael Wright	Brian Cruttenden	Bruce Price
North Bay Village	c	CM	5	(305) 756-7171	. . .	. . .	Yvonne Hamilton	Robert Lange	. . .	Scott Israel	. . .
North Lauderdale	c	CM	32	(954) 722-0900	Gary Frankel	Richard Sala	Carmela Dyer	Brian Raducci	. . .	. . .	Michael Shields
North Miami	c	CM	59	(305) 893-6511	Joe Celestin	Clarance Patterson	Simon Bloom	Carlos Perez	. . .	G. Boyd-Savage	Mark Collins
North Miami Beach	c	CM	35	(305) 948-2900	Jeffrey Mischon	Kelvin Baker	Solomon Odenz	Marilyn Spencer	. . .	William Berger	. . .
North Palm Beach *	v	CM	12	(561) 841-3355	Bill Manuel	Jimmy Knight	Melissa Teal	Samia Janjua	John Armstrong	. . .	Wiley Livingston
North Port *	c	CM	22	(941) 429-7000	Vanessa Carusone	Steven Crowell	Helen Raimbeau	Teresa Gould	William Taaffe	Terry Lewis	Branford Adumuah
North Redington Beach *	t	MC	1	(727) 391-4848	William Queen	. . .	Mari Campbell	. . .	. . .	. . .	Bruce Mercer
Oakland	c	CM	. .	(407) 656-1117	Kathy Stark	Maureen Rischitelli	Linda Balsavage	Elaine Strickland	. . .	Timothy Driscoll	Louis Marinaro
Oakland Park	c	CM	30	(954) 561-6250	Caryl Stevens	John Stunson	. . .	Elbert Wrains	Jim Henson	Edward Overman	. . .
Ocala *	c	CM	45	(352) 351-6663	Gerald Ergle	Ricky Horst	Valerie Forster	. . .	Danny Gentry	Samuel Williams	Glenn Kerns
Ocean Ridge	t	CM	1	(561) 732-2635	Gail Aaskov	. . .	Karen Hancsak	. . .	. . .	. . .	. . .
Ocoee *	c	CM	24	(409) 905-3100	Scott Vandergrift	Robert Frank	Jean Grafton	Wanda Horton	Richard Firstner	Charlie Brown	Steve Krug
Okeechobee	c	CM	5	(863) 763-3372	James Kirk	V. Whitehall	Lane Gamiotea	. . .	Herb Smith	Dennis Davis	Donnie Robertson
Oldsmar	c	CM	11	(813) 749-1100	Jim Ronecker	Bruce Haddock	Lisa Lene	. . .	Scott McGuff	. . .	John Mulvihill
Opa-Locka	c	CM	15	(305) 688-4611	. . .	Newall Daughtrey	Deborah Irby	Winston Mottley	. . .	Ronald Wilson	Amir Shafi
Orange City *	c	CM	6	(386) 775-5408	Albert Erwin	Chester Murray	Debbie Renner	Christine Davis	Herbert Hoffman	Jeffrey Baskoff	Paul Johnson
Orange Park	t	CM	9	(904) 264-9565	. . .	John Bowles	Joyce Bryan	Dorothy Mollnow	Harvey Silcox	James Boivin	William White
Orchid *	t	CM	. .	(772) 569-7686	Richard Dunlop	Maria Aguilar	. . .	. . .	. . .	Philip Redstone	. . .
Orlando	c	MC	185	(407) 246-2235	Buddy Dyer	Byron Brooks	Grace Chewning	G. Miller	Donald Harkins	. . .	. . .
Ormond Beach *	c	CM	36	(386) 676-3202	Frederick Costello	. . .	Veronica Patterson	Kelly McGuire	Barry Baker	Michael Longfellow	. . .
Oviedo	c	CM	26	(407) 977-6000	. . .	Richard Gestrich	Barbara Barbour	Michelle Greco	Wayne Martin	Dennis Peterson	Charles Smith
Pahokee	t	CM	5	(561) 924-5534	James Sasser	Matthew Brock	Raquel Diaz	Derrek Moore	. . .	. . .	Art Cobb
Palatka *	c	CM	10	(386) 329-0100	Karl Flagg	Elwin Boynton	Elizabeth Jordan	Ruby Williams	Mike Lambert	Gary Getchell	. . .
Palm Bay *	c	CM	79	(321) 952-3400	John Mazziotti	Lee Feldman	Alice Passmore	Yvonne McDonald	Steve Abraira	William Berger	James Proce
Palm Beach	t	CM	10	(561) 838-5410	. . .	Peter Elwell	Mary Pollitt	Jane Skittone	Kent Koelz	Michael Reiter	. . .
Palm Beach Gardens *	c	CM	35	(561) 799-4110	Eric Jablin	Ronald Ferris	Patricia Snider	Allan Owens	Peter Bergel	Stephen Stepp	Michael Morrow
Palm Coast *	c	CM	32	(386) 986-3700	Jon Netts	James Landon	Clare Hoeni	Ray Britt	Michael Beadle	. . .	Richard Adams
Palm Springs *	v	CM	11	(561) 965-4010	John Davis	Karl Umberger	Virginia Walton	Rebecca Morse	. . .	. . .	William Davis
Palmetto *	c	MC	12	(941) 723-4570	Shirley Bryant	. . .	James Freeman	Karen Simpson	. . .	James Lowe	Allen Tusing
Palmetto Bay	v	CM	25	(305) 259-1234	Eugene Flinn	Ron Williams	Meighan Pier	Alfredo Acin	. . .	Michael Mouring	. . .
Panama City *	c	CM	36	(850) 872-3010	Scott Clemons	Kenneth Hammons	. . .	. . .	Jerry Prater	John Van Etten	Neil Fravel
Panama City Beach	c	MC	7	(850) 233-5100	Gayle Oberst	Richard Jackson	Holly White	. . .	John Daly	R. H. Harding	Paul Castro
Parker *	c	MC	4	(850) 871-4104	Brenda Hendricks	. . .	Adonna Mullen	. . .	Andrew Kelley	Charles Sweat	. . .
Parkland *	c	CM	13	(954) 753-5040	Michael Udine	C. Gardner-Young	Sandra Couzzo	Barbara Hastings	Mark Curren	Paul O'Connell	Jim Berkman
Pembroke Park	t	CM	6	(954) 966-4600	John Lyons	Robert Levy	. . .	Georgina Rodriguez	Timothy Keefe	. . .	. . .
Pembroke Pines	c	CM	137	(954) 435-6505	Frank Ortis	Charles Dodge	Judy Neugent	Rene Gonzalez	John Picarello	Daniel Giustino	Shawn Denton
Pensacola	c	CM	56	(850) 435-1720	John Fogg	. . .	Shirley White	Richard Barker	James Dixon	John Mathis	Alfred Garza
Perry	c	CM	6	(850) 584-7161	. . .	. . .	. . .	Sarah Drawdy	Rodney Lytle	Herman Putnal	Barney Johnson
Pinecrest *	v	CM	19	(305) 234-2121	Cindy Lerner	Peter Lombardi	Guido Inguanzo	Gary Clinton	. . .	John Hohensee	Daniel Moretti
Pinellas Park	c	CM	45	(727) 541-0700	William Mischler	Michael Gustafson	Diane Corna	Ronald Miller	Douglas Lewis	Dorene Thomas	Thomas Nicholls
Plant City *	c	CM	29	(813) 659-4200	Rick Lott	David Sollenberger	Virginia Helper	Martin Wisgerhof	George Shiley	Bill McDaniel	G. Nabong
Plantation	c	MC	82	(954) 797-2240	Rae Armstrong	. . .	Susan Slattery	Herbert Herriman	Robert Pudney	Larry Massey	Frank Decelles
Polk City *	t	CM	1	(863) 984-1375	Donald Penton	Cory Carrier	Patricia Jackson	Pamela Lawson	. . .	. . .	Gene Kniffin
Pompano Beach *	c	CM	78	(954) 786-4626	Lamar Fisher	Garland Chadwell	Mary Chambers	Suzette Sibble	Harry Small	William Knowles	Robert McCaughan
Ponce Inlet	t	CM	2	(386) 322-6711	Nancy Epps	Kassandra Blissett	Jeaneen Clauss	. . .	Dan Scales	Steven Thomas	Ralph Schoenherr
Port Orange	c	CM	45	(386) 506-5500	Allen Green	Kenneth Parker	. . .	John Shelley	Thomas Weber	Gerald Monahan	Warren Pike
Port Richey	c	CM	3	(727) 816-1900	Mark Abbott	. . .	Shirley Dresch	Annette Perez	Timothy Fussell	William Sager	Allen Foley
Port St. Joe	c	CM	3	(386) 229-8261	Frank Pate	Lee Vincent	. . .	. . .	John Ford	. . .	Terry McDaniels
Port St. Lucie	c	CM	88	(772) 871-5225	Patricia Christensen	Donald Cooper	Karen Phillips	Marcia Dedert	Ron Parrish	John Skinner	Donald Freedland
Punta Gorda	c	CM	14	(941) 575-3308	Stephen Fabian	Howard Kunik	Susan Foster	David Drury	Robert Naylor	Charles Rinehart	Richard Keeney
Quincy	c	CM	6	(850) 627-7681	. . .	Willie Banks	Sylvia Hicks	Neva Reed	Leonard Griffiss	Gerald McSwain	Gene Tucker
Redington Beach	t	MC	1	(727) 391-3875	Bob Fountaine	. . .	Larry Bittner	Tim Gregson	. . .	. . .	Mark Davis
Redington Shores	t	MC	2	(727) 397-5538	. . .	. . .	. . .	. . .	. . .	. . .	. . .
Riviera Beach	c	CM	29	(561) 845-4000	Shelby Lowe	William Wilkins	Carrie Ward	Jeffrey Williams	Troy Perry	Clarence Williams	Vincent Akhimie
Rockledge	c	CM	20	(321) 690-3978	Larry Schultz	James McKnight	Mary Moist	. . .	Richard Allen	John Shockey	Jimmy Gilliard
Royal Palm Beach	v	CM	21	(561) 790-5100	David Lodwick	David Farber	Mary Anne Gould	Stanley Hochman	Thomas Vreeland	Michael Bruscell	Robert Hill
Safety Harbor *	c	CM	17	(727) 724-1555	Andy Steingold	Matthew Spoor	Cathy Benson	June Solanes	William Stout	. . .	Ray Boler
Sanford	c	CM	38	(407) 330-5602	Linda Kuhn	Robert Yehl	Janet Dougherty	James Poulalion	Gerard Ransom	Brian Todley	Thomas George
Sanibel	c	CM	6	(239) 472-3700	Stephen Brown	Judith Zimomra	. . .	Renee Lynch	. . .	William Tomlinson	Gates Castle
Sarasota	c	CM	52	(941) 951-3634	Lou Ann Palmer	Robert Bartolotta	Billy Robinson	Gibson Mitchell	. . .	Peter Abbott	William Hallisey
Satellite Beach	c	CM	9	(321) 773-4407	Harold Bolin	Michael Crotty	Barbara Boyens	Brenda Raver	Daniel Rocque	Lionel Cote	Robert Stowe
Sebastian	c	CM	16	(772) 589-5330	Brian Burkeen	Alfred Minner	Sally Maio	Shai Francis	. . .	James Davis	Jerry Converse
Sebring	c	MC	9	(863) 471-5100	George Hensley	Robert Hoffman	Kathy Haley	C Michael Eastman	Brad Batz	Thomas Dettman	. . .
Seminole *	c	MC	10	(727) 391-0204	James Johnson	Frank Edmunds	Lesley DeMuth	Christine Trovato	Daniel Graves	. . .	Allen Godfrey
Sewall'S Point	t	MC	1	(772) 287-2455	Jon Chicky	Robert Kellogg	Joan Barrow	. . .	. . .	Larry McCarty	. . .
South Bay	c	CM	3	(561) 996-6751	. . .	. . .	Virginia Walker	Gloria Ramos	. . .	. . .	Theodore Green
South Daytona *	c	CM	13	(386) 322-3068	Blaine O'Neal	Joseph Yarbrough	Debolena Moore	C. Campbell	. . .	Bill Hall	Mark Juliano
South Miami	c	CM	10	(305) 663-6338	Anna Price	W. Balogun	Ronetta Taylor	Hakeem Oshikoya	. . .	Cokes Watson	. . .
South Palm Beach	t	CM	. .	(561) 588-8889	Beverly Savin	Rex Taylor	Barbara Nock	. . .	Nicholas Alvaro	. . .	. . .

Directory 1/9 continued — OFFICIALS IN U.S. MUNICIPALITIES 2,500 AND OVER IN POPULATION

Jurisdiction	Type	Form of govern- ment	2000 Popu- lation	Main telephone number	Chief elected official	Appointed administrator	Clerk of the governing board	Chief financial officer	Fire chief	Police chief	Public works director
FLORIDA continued											
South Pasadena	c	CO	5	(727) 347-4171	. . .	. . .	Mary Braisted	James Graham	. . .	. . .	Gary Anderson
Southwest Ranches	t	CM	7	(954) 434-0008	. . .	. . .	. . .	. . .	. . .	. . .	. . .
Springfield	c	MC	8	(850) 872-7570	Robert Walker	. . .	Rhonda Taylor	. . .	Jeremy Adams	Sam Slay	Lee French
St. Augustine *	c	CM	11	(904) 825-1006	Joseph Boles	William Harriss	Karen Rogers	Mark Litzinger	Michael Arnold	Loran Lueders	Martha Campbell
St. Augustine Beach	c	CM	4	(904) 471-2122	. . .	Max Royle	. . .	. . .	. . .	Richard Hedges	Marcus Chattin
St. Cloud	c	CM	20	(409) 957-7209	Donna Hart	Thomas Hurt	Linda Jaworski	Michael Turner	Charlie Lewis	Mark Faucett	Robert MacKichan
St. Pete Beach *	c	CM	9	(727) 367-2735	Ward Friszolowski	Michael Bonfield	Theresa McMaster	Stephen Gallaher	Herman Golliner	Charles Romine	Scott Graubard
St. Petersburg *	c	CO	248	(727) 893-7171	Rick Baker	Patricia Elston	Evangelina Andujar	Jeffrey Spies	James Large	Charles Harmon	George Cassady
Starke	c	CO	5	(904) 964-5027	. . .	. . .	Linda Johns	. . .	Dwayne Hardee	Gordon Smith	Ricky Thompson
Stuart	c	CM	14	(772) 288-5313	Karl Krueger	Daniel Hudson	Cheryl White	. . .	Larry Massing	Edward Morley	Samuel Amerson
Sunny Isles Beach	c	CM	11	(305) 947-0606	David Samson	Anthony Szerlag	Richard Brown	Jean Watson	. . .	Fred Maas	Rick Conner
Sunrise *	c	CM	85	(954) 838-4522	Steven Feren	Bruce Moeller	Felicia Bravo	Laura Toebe	Norman Rynning	John Brooks	. . .
Surfside *	t	CM	4	(305) 861-4863	Charles Burkett	Gary Word	Beatris Arguelles	Martin Sherwood	. . .	David Allen	F. Rodriguez
Sweetwater	c	MC	13	(305) 221-0411	Jose Diaz	. . .	Marie Schmidt	Michael Lavin	. . .	Jesus Mencoal	Antero Espinosa
Tallahassee	c	CM	150	(850) 891-0000	John Marks	A. F. Thompson	. . .	David Reid	Thomas Quillin	Walter McNeil	. . .
Tamarac *	c	CM	55	(954) 597-3505	Joseph Schreiber	Jeffrey Miller	Marion Swenson	. . .	James Budzinski	Marc Duguay	Jack Strain
Tampa *	c	MC	303	(813) 274-8041	Pam Iorio	Darrell Smith	S. Foxx-Knowles	Bonnie Wise	Dennis Jones	Steve Hogue	Irvin Lee
Tarpon Springs	c	MC	21	(727) 938-3711	Beverley Billiris	. . .	Irene Jacobs	Arie Walker	Stephen Moreno	Mark Lecouris	Juan Cruz
Tavares	c	CM	9	(352) 742-6211	Ted Wicks	John Drury	Nancy Barnett	Lori Houghton	Emory Kendrick	Stoney Lubins	C. Frederick
Temple Terrace	c	CM	20	(813) 989-7100	. . .	Kim Leinbach	Sydney Barkholz	Lee Huffstutler	Clyde Hiers	Anthony Velong	Woodrow Garcia
Tequesta	v	CM	5	(561) 575-6200	Jim Humpage	Michael Couzzo	Gwen Carlisle	Jody Forsythe	James Weinand	Stephen Allison	Gary Preston
Titusville	c	CM	40	(321) 383-5775	Ronald Swank	Mark Ryan	Wanda Wells	Robert Erickson	. . .	Anthony Bollinger	James Herron
Treasure Island	c	CM	7	(727) 547-4575	Mary Maloof	Reid Silverboard	Jennifer Nye	Darren La France	Charles Fant	Joseph Pelkington	Donald Hambidge
Trenton *	c	CM	1	(352) 463-4000	Glen Thigpen	Jered Ottenwess	. . .	. . .	. . .	. . .	. . .
Umatilla	c	CM	2	(352) 669-3125	. . .	Glenn Irby	. . .	. . .	. . .	. . .	. . .
Valparaiso	c	MC	6	(850) 729-5402	John Arnold	Paul Maryeski	Tammy Johnson	. . .	Charles Frank	Joseph Hart	Anthony Piper
Venice	c	CM	17	(941) 486-2626	R. Hammett	. . .	Lori Stelzer	Jeffrey Snyder	John Reed	Julie Williams	Lawrence Heath
Vero Beach	c	CM	17	(772) 978-5151	Sandra Bowdent	. . .	Tammy Vock	Stephen Maillet	. . .	James Gabbard	Clifford Suthard
Waldo	c	MC	. .	(352) 468-1001	Frank Davis	Kim Worley	. . .	Chuck Hall	Edward Burkhalter	Alvin Smith	Bernard Carter
Wauchula	c	MC	4	(863) 773-3131	Henry Graham	Richard Giroux	Crissy Abbott	. . .	. . .	William Beattie	Luther McClellan
Wellington	v	CM	38	(561) 791-4000	Thomas Wenham	Franklin Schofield	Awilda Rodriguez	Francine Ramaglia	. . .	. . .	Kenneth Roundtree
West Melbourne	c	CM	9	(321) 727-7700	Shirley Bradshaw	David Reynal	Markae Rupp	Charlotte Luikart	. . .	Brian Lock	Barry Bartolino
West Miami	c	CM	5	(305) 266-1122	V. Yedra Chruszcz	Yolanda Aguilar	Felix Diaz	Mercedez Leon	. . .	Patrick Kiel	Juan Pena
West Palm Beach *	c	CO	82	(561) 822-1400	Lois Frankel	Edward Mitchell	Blane Kauthen	Thomas Harris	Phil Webb	Delsa Bush	John Alford
West Park	c	CM	12	(954) 963-5955	Eric Jones	Russell Benford	. . .	. . .	. . .	. . .	. . .
Weston *	c	CM	49	(954) 385-2000	Eric Hersh	John Flint	Patricia Bates	. . .	Craig Otten	Greg Page	Brad Kaine
White Springs	t	CM	. .	(386) 397-2310	Joseph McKire	Robert Townsend	Shirley Heath	Pam Tomlinson	Gerald Ford	Joe Subic	K. Hutcherson
Wildwood *	c	CM	3	(352) 330-1330	D. Wolf	James Stevens	. . .	Joseph Jacobs	. . .	. . .	R. Kornegay
Williston	c	CM	2	(352) 528-3060	. . .	. . .	. . .	. . .	. . .	. . .	. . .
Wilton Manors	c	CM	12	(954) 390-2100	Jim Stork	Joseph Gallegos	Angela Scott	Lisa Rabon	. . .	Richard Wierzbicki	David Archacki
Windermere *	t	MC	1	(407) 876-2563	Gary Bruhn	Cecilia Bernier	Dorothy Burkhalter	Linda Harrison	. . .	Daniel Saylor	Craig McNeal
Winter Garden *	c	CM	14	(407) 656-4111	John Rees	Michael Bollhoefer	Kathleen Golden	Robin Hayes	John Williamson	George Brennan	. . .
Winter Haven	c	CM	26	(863) 291-5600	Murray Easterling	David Greene	Barbara McKenzie	Calvin Bowen	Tony Jackson	Paul Goward	Anthony Viola
Winter Park *	c	CM	24	(407) 599-3292	David Strong	Randy Knight	Cynthia Bonham	Charles Hamil	James White	Douglas Ball	Troy Attaway
Winter Springs	c	CM	31	(407) 327-1800	Paul Parlyka	Ronald McLemore	Andrea Luaces	. . .	Timothy Lallathin	Daniel Kerr	Kipton Lockcuff
Zephyrhills	c	CM	10	(813) 780-0000	Clifford Mc Duffie	Steven Spina	Linda Boan	Cathy Familo	Robert Hartwig	Russell Barnes	Richard Moore
GEORGIA											
Acworth *	c	MC	13	(770) 974-3112	Thomas Allegood	Brian Bulthuis	Regina Russell	. . .	. . .	Michael Wilkie	Mark Hipp
Adel	c	CM	5	(229) 896-4504	Richard Barr	Jerry Permenter	. . .	. . .	Jimmy Walker	Scott Gore	Wayne Giddens
Albany	c	CM	76	(229) 431-3234	Willie Adams	Alfred Lott	Sue Hammond	Shirley Smith	James Arrowood	. . .	Phillip Roberson
Alma *	c	CM	3	(912) 632-8072	Wayne Williams	Nicholas Overstreet	Jackie Madders	. . .	Robert Taylor	Thomas Taggart	Carl Leggett
Alpharetta	c	CM	34	(678) 297-6000	Arthur Letchas	Robert Regus	Marilyn Rainwater	. . .	Keith Sanders	Ed Densmore	John Moskaluk
Alto *	t	MC	. .	(706) 778-8035	Audrey Turner	. . .	Penny Rogers	Lisa Turner	. . .	Lonnie Kidd	Wiley Cook
Americus *	c	MC	17	(229) 924-4411	Barry Blount	Charlotte Cotton	Charlotte Blanton	Suzanne Freeman	Allen Erkhart	James Green	Jess Grace
Ashburn	c	MC	4	(229) 567-3431	Robert Hunnicutt	Jerry Grimes	Sandra Lumpkin	Tina Mauldin	Brian Meadows	Ben Sumner	Carlton Webb
Athens–Clarke County	c	CM	90	(706) 613-3090	Erwin Eldridge	W. Reddish	Gloria Spratlin	John Culpepper	Wendell Faulkner	Joseph Lumpkin	David Clark
Atlanta	c	MC	416	(404) 330-6377	Shirley Franklin	Lynnette Young	Rhonda Johnson	Richard Anderson	. . .	Richard Pennington	David Scott
Auburn	c	MC	6	(770) 963-4002	Harold Money	Ron Griffith	. . .	Dee Hickman	. . .	. . .	. . .
Austell	c	MC	5	(770) 944-4300	Joe Jerkins	. . .	Carolyn Duncan	Brenda Norton	Timothy Williams	Bob Starrett	Randy Bowens
Avondale Estates *	c	CM	2	(404) 294-5400	Ed Rieker	Clai Brown	Juliette Sims	Kenneth Turner	. . .	Gary Broden	Bryan Armstead
Bainbridge	c	CM	11	(229) 248-2000	Billy Reynolds	Christopher Hobby	. . .	Steven McKown	Dennis Mock	. . .	Tommy King
Barnesville	c	CM	5	(770) 358-0181	James Matthews	Kenneth Roberts	Carolyn Parker	. . .	Robert Devane	. . .	William Johnson
Baxley	c	CM	4	(912) 367-8300	Steve Rigdon	Jeffrey Baxley	Von Spell	. . .	Jim Ammons	James Godfrey	Gary Patterson
Blackshear	c	MC	3	(912) 449-7000	Preston Hampton	. . .	Myra Bolden	. . .	. . .	George Smiley	Herbert Barber
Blakely	c	MC	5	(229) 723-3677	Ric Hall	. . .	. . .	. . .	Kenneth Jones	. . .	James Allen
Bowdon	c	MC	1	(770) 258-8980	. . .	. . .	. . .	. . .	. . .	Burl Langley	Jerry Langley
Braselton *	t	CM	1	(706) 654-3915	Patricia Graham	. . .	Jennifer Dees	Nan Edwards	. . .	Terry Esco	Ken Robbins
Bremen	c	MC	4	(770) 537-2331	Barbara Rivers	Kim Jones	. . .	Beverly Cash	Raymond Morton	Larry Henbree	. . .
Brunswick	c	CM	15	(912) 267-5500	Bradford Brown	Roosevelt Harris	Georgia Marion	James Bradley	Lee Stewart	Thomas Cowan	John Butts
Buford	c	CM	10	(770) 945-6761	Phillip Beard	Bryan Kerlin	. . .	Mike Brown	. . .	Nelson Stanley	Lamar Sudderth
Cairo *	c	CM	9	(229) 377-1722	R. VanLandingham	. . .	Carolyn Lee	Miriam Faircloth	Don Towne	Keith Sandefur	Charles Stokes
Calhoun *	c	MC	10	(706) 629-0151	Jimmy Palmer	Eddie Peterson	Heather Evans	Alicia Stewart	Leonard Nesbitt	Garry Moss	. . .
Camilla	c	CM	5	(229) 336-2220	Alfred Powell	Michael Scott	Kathy Baker	Jimmy Douglas	David Irwin	Raybun Folsom	James Watson
Canton	c	CM	7	(770) 704-1500	Cecil Pruett	. . .	Diana Threewitt	Robert Logan	Dean Floyd	Billy Cantrell	Larry Wilson
Carrollton	c	CM	19	(770) 830-2000	Wayne Garner	Casey Coleman	. . .	Jim Triplett	Jimmy Bearden	Joel Richards	Mike Green
Cartersville	c	CM	15	(770) 387-5616	Michael Fields	Samuel Grove	Sandra Cline	. . .	Norris Westbrooks	Michael McCain	Bobby Elliott
Cedartown	c	CM	9	(770) 748-3220	John Barrett	Barry Atkison	Carol Crawford	. . .	Sammy Stephens	Keith Barber	. . .
Centerville	c	MC	4	(478) 953-4734	Harold Edwards	Patrick Eidson	Krista Bedingfield	Dwight Williams	Frank Wadsworth	Michael Sullivan	Mike Brumfield
Chamblee	c	MC	9	(770) 986-5010	Evelyn Kennedy	James Gleason	Kathy Brannon	. . .	. . .	. . .	William Hannon
Chatsworth *	c	MC	3	(706) 695-2834	Tyson Haynes	. . .	Wilma Nolan	. . .	Mike Baxter	Terry Martin	Everett Jones
Clarkston	c	MC	7	(404) 296-6489	Lee Swaney	. . .	Tracy Ashby	Juliette Paxton	. . .	Tony Scipio	Mike Shipman
Claxton	c	MC	2	(912) 739-1712	Perry DeLoach	Gayle Durrence	. . .	. . .	Larry Rogers	Edward Oglesbee	. . .
Cochran	c	MC	4	(478) 934-6346	Charles Killebrew	. . .	Matthew Turknett	. . .	. . .	Robert Schmitz	Keith White
College Park	c	CM	20	(404) 767-1537	Jack Longino	. . .	Lakeitha Reeves	. . .	Henry Argo	Gary Yandura	Charles Brewer
Colquitt	c	CM	1	(229) 758-3412	Luther Clearman	Cory Thomas	Vicki Phillips	. . .	Craig Tully	Scott Worsley	Sam Gardner
Columbus–Muscogee Consolidated	c	CM	178	(706) 653-4000	Jim Wetherington	Isaiah Hugley	Tiny Washington	Pamela Hodge	Jeff Meyer	Richard Boren	Gary Stickles
Commerce	c	CM	5	(706) 335-3164	Charles Hardy	Clarence Bryant	Shirley Willis	Kathy Clark	Johnny Eubanks	John Gaissert	Thomas Harvey
Conyers *	c	CM	10	(770) 483-4411	Randal Mills	Antony Lucas	Patricia Smith	. . .	. . .	David Cathcarat	Brad Sutton
Cordele	c	CM	11	(229) 273-3102	. . .	Jean Burnette	. . .	Allen Fulford	Eugene Stephens	William Orrick	James Watson
Cornelia *	c	CM	3	(706) 778-8585	Margaret Ballard	Dee Anderson	Janie Henderson	. . .	Frankie Smith	Rick Darby	Keith Ethridge
Covington *	c	CM	11	(770) 385-2000	Kim Carter	Frank Turner	Tonya Grier	. . .	Don Floyd	Stacey Cotton	Billy Bouchillon
Cuthbert	c	MC	3	(229) 732-3161	. . .	. . .	. . .	. . .	. . .	. . .	. . .
Dahlonega *	c	CM	3	(706) 864-6133	Gary McCullough	William Lewis	Janet Jarrard	Christopher Austin	. . .	. . .	C. L. Grizzle

Directory 1/9 continued — OFFICIALS IN U.S. MUNICIPALITIES 2,500 AND OVER IN POPULATION

Jurisdiction	Type	Form of govern-ment	2000 Popu-lation	Main telephone number	Chief elected official	Appointed administrator	Clerk of the governing board	Chief financial officer	Fire chief	Police chief	Public works director
GEORGIA continued											
Dallas	c	CM	5	(770) 443-8110	. . .	Ken Elsberry	Sarah Ruff	Lloyd Williamson	. . .	Scot Halter	Kendall Smith
Dalton	c	MC	27	(706) 278-9500	Raymond Elrod	James Sanders	Bernadette Chattam	Cindy Jackson	Barry Gober	James Chadwick	Benny Dunn
Darien	c	MC	1	(912) 437-6686	David Bluestein	Christopher Cook	Colleen Jolley	. . .	. . .	. . .	Donnie Howard
Dawson	c	CM	5	(229) 995-4444	Robert Albritten	David Bell	Sheri Howard	. . .	Don Laye	Ernest Webb	. . .
Decatur *	c	CM	18	(404) 370-4102	William Floyd	Peggy Merriss	Karen Des Islets	. . .	Jerry Malone	Michael Booker	. . .
Donalsonville	c	MC	2	(229) 524-2118	David Fain	H. M. Shingler	Linda Gray	. . .	E. Brooks	Jimmy Holt	Donald Gambrell
Doraville	c	MC	9	(770) 451-8745	Ray Jenkins	. . .	Betty Cloer	. . .	. . .	Tommy McElroy	. . .
Douglas *	c	CM	10	(912) 389-3401	Jackie Wilson	Terrell Jacobs	Wynetta Gaskins	Joyce Cliett	Timothy White	Clifford Thomas	Anthony Kirkland
Douglasville	c	CM	20	(770) 920-3000	Mickey Thompson	William Osborne	Joyce Stone	Karin Callan	. . .	J. Whisenant	Greg Roberts
Dublin	c	CM	15	(478) 272-1620	. . .	George Roussel	. . .	Joseph Kinard	Robert Drew	Wayne Cain	Jimmy Sawyer
Duluth *	c	CM	22	(770) 476-3434	Shirley Lasseter	Euel McLemore	Teresa Lynn	Ken Sakmar	. . .	Randall Belcher	Audrey Turner
Dunwoody	c	CM	32	(678) 382-6700	. . .	Warren Hutmacher	. . .	. . .	. . .	. . .	. . .
East Dublin	c	MC	2	(478) 272-6883	George Gornto	Larry Drew	Terrie Drew	. . .	Doyle Tanner	William Luecke	H. Scarborough
East Point	c	CM	39	(404) 209-5160	Patsy Hilliard	. . .	Bobbie Jones	William Epps	. . .	Frank Brown	Derek Bogan
Eastman *	c	CM	5	(478) 374-7721	W. Jack Burnham	James Wright	Ivelyn Lampkin	. . .	Carl Johnson	Furman Wiggins	Royce Williams
Eatonton *	c	MC	6	(706) 485-3311	John Reid	Martin Elmore	Sarah Abrams	. . .	Steve Reid	Kent Lawrence	Gary Meese
Elberton	c	CM	4	(706) 213-3100	Iola Stone	Lanier Dunn	Cindy Churney	Lynn Saxon	Russell Guest	Mark Welsh	Jimmy Welborn
Fairburn *	c	CM	5	(770) 964-2244	Betty Hannah	James Williams	Nancy Williams	William Gregory	Harold Weller	James McCarthy	Troy Besseche
Fayetteville *	c	MC	11	(770) 461-6029	Kenneth Steele	William Morton	Judy Stephens	Lorri Robinson	Alan Jones	Steven Heaton	Charles Stanley
Fitzgerald	c	CM	8	(229) 426-5060	Gerald Thompson	Henry Tyson	Linda Saunders	Kathy Young	Roger Coleman	William Smallwood	Waymon Walker
Forest Park	c	CM	21	(404) 366-4720	Corine Deyton	Johnny Parker	. . .	M. Blandenburg	Eddie Buckholts	Dwayne Hobbs	Michael Gippert
Forsyth	c	MC	3	(478) 994-5649	James Pace	. . .	Janice Hall	. . .	Walter Carter	Benjamin Ponder	Alvin Randall
Fort Oglethorpe	c	CM	6	(706) 866-2544	Judson Burkhart	Jim Dinley	Harold Silcox	Pam Travillian	Bruce Ballew	Larry Black	Phillip Parker
Fort Valley	c	MC	8	(478) 825-8261	John Ezell	Richard Little	. . .	Linda Peterman	Gary Moye	. . .	George Clark
Gainesville *	c	CM	25	(770) 535-6887	Myrtle Figueras	. . .	Denise Jordan	Melody Marlowe	Jon Canada	Roy Hooper	. . .
Garden City	c	MC	11	(912) 966-7777	Andy Quinney	Brian Johnson	Rhonda Ferrell	Clara Rouse	James Crosby	David Lyons	Thomas Griffin
Glennville *	c	MC	3	(912) 654-2461	Jean Bridges	Amy Murray	Teresa Pazderski	. . .	Bobby Brannen	Mickey Anderson	Stan Dansby
Gordon	t	MC	2	(478) 628-2222	Kenneth Turner	. . .	Towana Brown	. . .	Terry Eady	Mike Hall	George Wynn
Grantville *	c	CM	1	(770) 583-2289	Casey Houston	Scott Starnes	Tonya Wheelus	. . .	. . .	Winston Allen	Joe Jones
Greensboro *	c	MC	3	(706) 453-7967	Glenn Wright	Larry Postell	. . .	. . .	Fred Cook	Ossie Mapp	Bill Shirley
Griffin	c	CM	23	(770) 229-6400	Bill Landrum	Kenny Smith	. . .	. . .	Tommy Jones	Frank Strickland	Brant Keller
Grovetown	c	MC	6	(706) 863-4576	. . .	. . .	. . .	. . .	. . .	. . .	. . .
Hampton	c	CM	3	(770) 946-4306	. . .	. . .	. . .	. . .	. . .	. . .	. . .
Hapeville	c	MC	6	(404) 669-2100	C. Martin	William Werner	. . .	Michael Rast	William Edwards	Dewey Attaway	James Griffith
Hartwell *	c	CM	4	(706) 376-4756	Matt Beasley	David Aldrich	Jean Turner	Joan Hughes	Terry Vickery	Cecil Reno	Dennis White
Hawkinsville	c	CM	3	(478) 892-3240	Henry Cravey	Jerry Murkerson	Evelyn Herrington	. . .	. . .	Samuel Tripp	Johnny Gordon
Hazlehurst *	c	MC	3	(912) 375-6680	R. Stone	. . .	Ethelyn Creech	. . .	Charles Wasdin	Steve Land	Jeff Jones
Helen	c	CM	. .	(706) 878-2733	. . .	Jerry Elkins	Kimberly Smith	Terri Caporale	. . .	Ted Ray	Joseph Hewell
Hinesville	c	MC	30	(912) 876-3564	Thomas Ratcliffe	Billy Edwards	Sarah Lumpkin	Kimberly Davis	Lamar Cook	George Stagmeier	. . .
Hogansville	c	CM	2	(706) 637-8629	Wilson St. Clair	Randall Jordan	Dianne Carter	. . .	. . .	Hilton Odom	. . .
Holly Springs *	c	MC	3	(770) 345-5546	Tim Downing	Robert Rokovitz	Marie Johnson	Robert Porche	Steve Pigott	Ken Ball	Chris Keown
Homerville *	c	MC	2	(912) 487-2375	Carol Chambers	Albert Thornton	Shirley Delk	. . .	Danny Strickland	Mark Register	. . .
Jackson	c	MC	3	(770) 775-7535	Charles Brown	. . .	Lara Brewer	. . .	Harvey Norris	Michael Riley	Dawson Heath
Jefferson *	c	CM	3	(706) 367-7207	. . .	. . .	Elizabeth McDonald	. . .	Bobby Gooch	Joe Wirthman	Jeff Killip
Jesup	c	CM	9	(912) 427-1313	Herb Shaw	Richard Deal	Onda Woodard	. . .	Julian Brinkley	Wayne Hutcheson	Eddie Williams
Jonesboro	c	MC	3	(770) 478-3800	Joy Day	. . .	Joan Jones	Stacey Inglis	. . .	Jim Roberts	Sam Durrance
Kennesaw	c	MC	21	(770) 424-8274	Leonard Church	Lewis Kennedy	Debra Taylor	Kenneth Turner	. . .	Tim Callahan	Woody McFarlin
Kingsland	c	MC	10	(912) 729-5613	Kenneth Smith	Gwendolyn Mungin	Shirley Bryan	Tamra Edwards	Morris Peeples	J. Franks Waits	William Coleman
La Fayette *	c	CM	6	(706) 639-1501	Neal Florence	Johnnie Arnold	Brenda Anderson	. . .	. . .	. . .	Richard Moore
La Grange	c	CM	25	(706) 883-2010	Jeff Lukken	Thomas Hall	. . .	. . .	Chris Smith	Louis Dekmar	David Brown
Lake City	c	MC	2	(404) 366-8080	Willie Oswalt	Gerald Garr	. . .	. . .	. . .	David Colwell	Eddie Robinson
Lavonia *	c	CM	1	(706) 356-8781	Ralph Owens	Gary Fesperman	Angela Greer	. . .	Jones Beasley	Bruce Carlisle	James Moseley
Lawrenceville	c	MC	22	(770) 963-2414	. . .	. . .	. . .	. . .	. . .	. . .	. . .
Lilburn *	c	MC	11	(770) 921-2210	Diana Preston	William Johnsa	Kathy Maner	. . .	. . .	John Davidson	. . .
Lithonia	c	MC	2	(770) 482-8136	Marcia Glenn	. . .	. . .	. . .	. . .	Manuel Norrington	. . .
Loganville	c	CM	5	(770) 466-1165	Gene Matthews	Bill Jones	Michelle Deaton	. . .	. . .	. . .	. . .
Louisville	c	CM	2	(478) 625-3166	Julian Veatch	James Rhodes	Lona Lane	. . .	Joe Cox	. . .	Tony Richbourg
Lyons	c	MC	4	(912) 526-8606	John Moore	Rick Hartley	Lynn Rowland	. . .	. . .	Rickey Newsome	Darel Corley
Macon	c	MC	97	(478) 751-7400	Clarence Ellis	Thomas Thomas	. . .	Kelly Clark	James Hartley	Rodney Monroe	Dexter White
Madison	c	CM	3	(706) 342-1251	. . .	. . .	. . .	. . .	. . .	. . .	. . .
Manchester	c	CM	3	(706) 846-3141	Dorsey Wilson	Grady McCalmon	Nancy Thompson	. . .	Fred Schmalz	Ron Jackson	Ralph Pearson
Marietta	c	CM	58	(770) 794-5562	Bill Dunaway	William Bruton	Stephanie Guy	. . .	Jackie Gibbs	Dan Flyn	. . .
Mc Donough	c	MC	8	(770) 957-3915	Richard Craig	James Lee	. . .	. . .	Don Crowell	Preston Dorsey	Gary Barham
Mc Rae	c	MC	2	(229) 868-6051	. . .	. . .	. . .	. . .	. . .	. . .	. . .
Metter	c	MC	3	(912) 685-2527	William Trapnell	Joseph Mosley	Angela Conner	. . .	Jason Douglas	William Hooper	Garland Hendrix
Milledgeville	c	MC	18	(478) 414-4092	Floyd Griffin	E. Wood	. . .	Frances Hatcher	Jerome Dietrich	Woodrow Blue	Jack Graham
Millen	c	MC	3	(478) 982-6100	. . .	James Knight	Cynthia Bragg	. . .	. . .	Dennis Simmons	Clay Boulineau
Milton *	c	CM	20	(678) 242-2500	Joseph Lockwood	. . .	J. Marchiafava	Stacey Inglis	. . .	. . .	Dan Drake
Monroe	c	MC	11	(770) 267-7536	Greg Thompson	Julian Jackson	. . .	Renee Prather	Wayne Chancey	Marvin Glass	Hugh Worley
Montezuma	c	MC	3	(478) 472-8144	. . .	. . .	. . .	. . .	. . .	. . .	. . .
Monticello	c	MC	2	(706) 468-6062	Glenn Newsome	Hugh King	Belinda Whirley	. . .	. . .	. . .	. . .
Morrow	c	CM	4	(770) 961-4002	James Millirons	John Lampl	Brenda Allen	Tom Sawyer	. . .	. . .	Jeffrey Eady
Moultrie	c	CM	14	(229) 985-1974	William McIntosh	. . .	. . .	Gary McDaniel	Kenneth Hannon	Frank Lang	Albert Ward
Nashville	c	MC	4	(229) 686-5527	Travis Harper	Mandy Luke	Johnny Hall	. . .	Buck Warren	John Clayton	. . .
Newnan *	c	CM	16	(770) 253-2682	L. Brady	Richard Bolin	Della Hill	Katrina Cline	William Whitley	Douglas Meadows	Michael Klahr
Norcross	c	MC	8	(770) 448-2122	Lillian Webb	. . .	Carol Dennen	Douglas Chastain	. . .	Richard Miller	Brad Cole
Ocilla	c	MC	3	(229) 468-5141	Donald Royal	Greg Giddens	Alicia Roberts	. . .	Mark Taibi	Billy Hancock	Roosevelt George
Palmetto	c	CM	3	(770) 463-3377	. . .	. . .	. . .	. . .	. . .	. . .	. . .
Peachtree City *	c	CM	31	(770) 487-7657	Harold Logsdon	Bernard McMullen	Betsy Tyler	Paul Salvatore	Ed Eiswerth	H. C. Clark	Tom Corbett
Pelham	c	MC	4	(229) 294-7900	Chester Shelnutt	James Davis	Letitia Smith	Ralph Williams	James Creech	Neal McCormick	Roger Barfield
Pembroke	c	MC	2	(912) 653-4413	. . .	. . .	. . .	. . .	. . .	. . .	. . .
Perry	c	CM	9	(478) 988-2700	James Worrall	R. Lee Gilmour	. . .	Brenda King	Gary Hamlin	George Potter	. . .
Pooler	c	MC	6	(912) 748-7261	Earl Carter	Dennis Baxter	Maribeth Lindler	Linda Smith	Nolan Salter	Clarence Chan	Robert Byrd
Port Wentworth	c	MC	3	(912) 964-4379	Tim Holbrook	Phillip Claxton	Janet Hendrick	Judith Harrelson	James Jackson	James Melvin	Tommy Thomas
Powder Springs *	c	CM	12	(770) 943-1666	Patricia Vaughn	Charles Nickerson	Betty Brady	Regina Auld	. . .	Larry Richardson	Rodger Swaim
Quitman	c	CM	4	(229) 263-4166	. . .	. . .	. . .	. . .	. . .	. . .	. . .
Register *	t	MC	. .	(912) 488-2424	Katie O'Grady	Mandi Pilz	. . .	. . .	. . .	Paul Motes	Allen Ryles
Richmond Hill *	c	CM	6	(912) 756-3345	. . .	Michael Melton	. . .	. . .	. . .	. . .	. . .
Rincon	c	CM	4	(912) 826-5745	Ken Lee	. . .	Wanda Hendrix	Brett Bennett	Corey Rahn	. . .	Tim Bowles
Riverdale *	c	CM	12	(770) 997-8989	Evelyn Wynn-Dixon	Iris Jessie	Stephanie Thomas	Ann Smith	DeWayne Earnest	Samuel Patterson	. . .
Rockmart	c	CM	3	(770) 684-5454	. . .	Jeffery Ellis	. . .	. . .	Larry Carter	. . .	. . .
Rome	c	CM	34	(706) 236-4400	Ronald Wallace	John Bennett	Joseph Smith	Sheree Shore	Bobbie McKenzie	Hubert Smith	W. Kirk Nulan
Rossville *	c	MC	3	(706) 866-1325	Johnny Baker	. . .	Sherry Foster	. . .	. . .	. . .	Mark Harris
Roswell *	c	MC	79	(770) 641-3727	Jere Wood	Katherine Love	Sue Creel	Julia Luke	Ricky Spencer	T. Williams	Stuart Moring
Sandersville	c	MC	6	(478) 552-2525	. . .	William Goforth	. . .	. . .	. . .	. . .	. . .
Sandy Springs	c	CM	85	(770) 730-5600	Eva Galambos	John McDonough	. . .	Steven Rapson	Jack McElfish	Eugene Wilson	Angelia Parham

Directory 1/9 continued — OFFICIALS IN U.S. MUNICIPALITIES 2,500 AND OVER IN POPULATION

Jurisdiction	Type	Form of govern-ment	2000 Popu-lation	Main telephone number	Chief elected official	Appointed administrator	Clerk of the governing board	Chief financial officer	Fire chief	Police chief	Public works director
GEORGIA continued											
Savannah *	c	CM	131	(912) 651-6484	Otis Johnson	Michael Brown	Dyanne Reese	Richard Evans	Charles Middleton	Michael Berkow	Bob Scanlon
Sky Valley *	c	CM	..	(706) 746-2204	James Martindale	Linda Smith	Mandi Cantrell	...	...	Jeff Harris	Jerry Dills
Smyrna	c	MC	40	(770) 434-6600	A. Bacon	Wayne Wright	Melinda Dameron	Claudia Edgar	...	Stanley Hook	Scott Stokes
Snellville	c	MC	15	(770) 985-3500	Brett Harrell	Russell Treadway	...	...	...	...	...
Social Circle *	c	CM	3	(770) 464-2380	James Burgess	Douglas White	...	Susan Roper	...	Jeff Johnson	...
Soperton	c	MC	2	(912) 529-6173	...	...	...	...	...	...	...
Springfield *	c	MC	1	(912) 754-6666	Barton Alderman	Brett Bennett	Linda Rineair	...	...	Paul Wynn	...
St. Marys *	c	MC	13	(912) 510-4000	Rowland Eskridge	William Shanahan	Darlene Roellig	Jennifer Brown	Robert Horton	Tim Hatch	Bobby Marr
Statesboro	c	CM	22	(912) 764-5468	William Hatcher	R. Shane Haynes	Judy McCorkle	Cindy West	Joe Beasley	Stan York	Bobby Colson
Stone Mountain *	c	CM	7	(770) 498-8984	Gary Peet	Barry Amos	Denise Hicks	...	...	Chancy Troutman	Jim Tavenner
Sugar Hill *	c	CM	11	(770) 945-6716	Gary Pirkle	Robert Hail	Jane Whittington	Kelley Canady	...	...	...
Summerville	c	MC	4	(706) 857-0900	...	...	...	...	...	...	...
Suwanee	c	MC	8	(770) 945-8996	Nick Masino	Marvin Allen	...	Amelia Sakmar	...	Michael Jones	James Miller
Swainsboro *	c	MC	6	(478) 237-7025	Charles Schwabe	Al Lawson	...	Melissa Kirby	Mike Strobridge	Johnny Shuman	Michael Connolly
Sylvania	c	CM	2	(912) 564-7411	Margaret Evans	H. Carter Crawford	Judy Hill	Stacy Mathis	Gary Weaver	Mark Tretheway	Tony Thompson
Sylvester	c	MC	5	(229) 776-8505	William Yearta	Danny Lucas	Deborah Bridges	...	Thomas Marchman	Tony Strenth	Jimmy Fowler
Tallapoosa	c	CM	2	(770) 574-2345	Micajah Bagwell	Philip Eidson	Carolyn Brown	Donna Cain	Stephen McClain	David Godfrey	...
Thomaston	c	CM	9	(706) 647-4242	Hays Arnold	Patrick Comiskey	...	Dennis Truitt	James Lifsey	Dan Greathouse	...
Thomasville	c	CM	18	(229) 228-7673	...	...	...	...	...	...	...
Thomson	c	MC	6	(706) 595-1781	Robert Knox	Donald Powers	Dianne Landers	Tammy Haire	Rick Sewell	John Hathaway	Peter Ruddick
Thunderbolt	t	MC	2	(912) 354-5533	James Petrea	...	Rose McCombs	...	Lawton Smith	Stephen Smith	Fred Corey
Tifton	c	CM	15	(229) 382-6231	Paul Johnson	Michael Vollmer	Rona Martin	Carmina Turner	James Flippo	James Smith	Cal Carpenter
Toccoa	c	CM	9	(706) 886-8451	Ferrell Morgan	William Morse	Josephine Gleason	Emory Stephens	Rodney Burdette	Jackie Whitmire	Randy Smith
Tybee Island *	c	CM	3	(912) 786-4573	Jason Buelterman	Diane Schleicher	Vivian Woods	Bonnie Kline	Clifton Sasser	James Price	Joe Wilson
Tyrone	t	CM	3	(770) 487-4038	Sheryl Lee	Barry Amos	...	...	...	Brandon Perkins	Renee Holt
Union City	c	CM	11	(770) 964-2288	Ralph Moore	Richard Bray	Barbara Steward	Theresia McDearis	Kenneth Collins	Michael Isome	Buddy Landrum
Valdosta	c	CM	43	(229) 259-3500	James Rainwater	Larry Hanson	J. Marchiafva	Richard Hamlen	James Rice	Charles Simons	...
Varnell	c	MC	1	(706) 694-8800	...	...	...	...	...	...	...
Vidalia	c	CM	10	(912) 537-7661	...	William Torrance	...	...	...	...	...
Vienna *	c	MC	2	(229) 268-4744	Emerson Lundy	Gail Bembry	...	Debra Spring	Chuck Ellis	James Reed	Nathan Jordan
Villa Rica	c	CM	4	(770) 459-7000	J. Collins	...	...	Cindy Samples	...	Michael Mansour	...
Warner Robins	c	MC	48	(478) 929-1111	Donald Walker	...	Carolyn Robbins	...	Robert Singletary	Daniel Hart	Joe Musselwhite
Washington	c	CM	4	(706) 678-3277	Willie Burns	Michael Eskew	Debbie Danner	...	Alan Poss	Michael Davis	...
Waycross	c	CM	15	(912) 287-2912	Robert Odum	Peter Pyrzenski	Jerry Grimes	Larry Gattis	Cedric Scott	Tony Tanner	Sam Ray
Waynesboro	c	CM	5	(706) 554-8000	Martin Dolin	Jerry Coalson	...	...	Ronnie Baxley	Karl Allen	...
West Point	c	MC	3	(706) 645-2226	...	George Moon	...	...	...	...	...
Winder	c	MC	10	(770) 867-3106	...	...	Jane Skelton	George Beck	Raymond Mattison	Stanley Rodgers	...
Woodbine *	c	CM	1	(912) 576-3211	W Burford Clark	Sandra Rayson	Melissa Courson	Debra Carter	...	...	Everette Sapp
Woodstock *	c	CM	10	(770) 926-8852	Donnie Henriques	Jeffrey Moon	Rhonda Pezzello	Henry Bucci	Jerry Smith	Bart Giesey	Pat Flood
Wrightsville	c	MC	2	(478) 864-3303	Phillip Boatright	...	Jewell Parker	Ralph Holmes	Stan Garnto	Steve Gresham	Lamar Lague
HAWAII											
Hilo	c	MC	45	(808) 961-8361	...	...	...	...	...	...	...
Honolulu	c	MC	836	(808) 523-4809	Mufi Hannemann	Jeff Coelho	...	Mary Waterhouse	Attilio Leonardi	Boisse Correa	Eric Takamura
IDAHO											
American Falls	c	MC	4	(208) 226-2569	...	...	...	...	...	...	...
Ammon	c	MC	6	(208) 529-4211	C. Ard	...	Aleen Jensen	...	Clarence Nelson	...	David Wadsworth
Blackfoot	c	MC	10	(208) 785-8600	Mike Virtue	...	Suzanne McNeel	...	...	R. Moore	Ron Harwell
Boise	c	MC	185	(208) 384-3850	David Bieter	...	Annette Mooney	John Faw	Renn Ross	Michael Masterson	Charles Mickelson
Bonners Ferry	c	MC	2	(208) 267-3105	Darrell Kerby	Stephen Boorman	...	...	Larry Owsley	...	...
Buhl	c	MC	3	(208) 543-5650	Barbara Gietzen	...	Sharon Sheets	...	Mark Grimes	Ronald Romero	R. Himmelberger
Burley	c	MC	9	(208) 678-2224	Jon Anderson	Mark Mitton	Melanie Haynes	...	Phil Heiner	...	Leon Bedke
Caldwell	c	MC	25	(208) 455-3000	Richard Winder	...	Betty Keller	...	Bruce Allcott	...	Gordon Law
Chubbuck	c	MC	9	(208) 237-2400	...	...	...	...	...	...	...
Coeur D'Alene	c	MC	34	(208) 769-2300	...	Wendy Hague	Susan Weathers	Troy Tymesen	Kenneth Gabriel	Thomas Cronin	...
Driggs	c	MC	1	(208) 354-2362	Louis Christensen	...	Sarah McMillon	Amy Smith	...	...	...
Eagle	c	MC	11	(208) 939-6813	Richard Yzaguirre	...	Sharon Moore	...	...	...	...
Emmett	c	MC	5	(208) 365-6050	Ronald Morgan	...	...	...	Shannon Crays	Blaine Hyde	Bruce Evans
Garden City	c	MC	10	(208) 377-1831	...	...	...	...	...	...	...
Gooding	c	MC	3	(208) 934-5669	Herb Stroud	...	Carmen Korsen	...	...	Paul Brown	Todd Bunn
Grangeville	c	MC	3	(208) 983-2851	Terry Vanderwall	...	Donna Forsman	...	Roy Powell	Wayne Sedam	Kenneth Gortsema
Hailey	t	MC	6	(208) 788-4221	...	Heather Dawson	...	...	...	...	...
Hayden	c	MC	9	(208) 772-4411	Ron McIntire	...	Vicki Rutherford	Lila Erickson	...	...	Wade Holecek
Heyburn	c	MC	2	(208) 679-8158	George Anderson	...	Linda Dayley	...	Mike Brown	George Warrell	Scott Spevak
Idaho Falls	c	MC	50	(208) 529-1248	Linda Milam	...	Rose Anderson	Robert Holm	Dean Ellis	Kent Livsey	Chad Stanger
Jerome *	c	MC	7	(208) 324-8189	Charles Correll	Benjamin Marchant	Katherine Cone	...	Craig LoSasso	Dan Hall	Walt Appell
Kellogg	c	MC	2	(208) 786-9131	Roger Mangum	...	Sandy Nearing	...	Dale Costa	John Crawford	James Sharp
Ketchum	c	MC	3	(208) 726-3841	Ed Simon	Gary Marks	Sandra Cady	...	Greg Schwab	Cory Lyman	Brian Christiansen
Kimberly	c	MC	2	(208) 423-4151	...	Polly Hulsey	...	...	...	...	...
Lewiston *	c	CM	30	(208) 746-3671	Doug Havens	John Krauss	Kari Kuchmak	Barbara Clark	Gordon Gregg	Steven Orr	Chris Davies
Mccall	c	CM	2	(208) 634-7142	Kirk Eimers	Lindley Kirkpatrick	Dan Irwin	...	...	Jerry Summers	William Keating
Meridian	c	MC	34	(208) 888-4433	Robert Corrie	...	William Berg	Stacy Kilchenmann	Kenneth Bowers	Richard Worley	Gary Smith
Montpelier	c	MC	2	(208) 847-0824	George Lane	...	Renee Bird	...	David Barnson	David Higley	Donald Toomer
Moscow *	c	MC	21	(208) 883-7000	Nancy Chaney	Gary Riedner	Stephanie Kalasz	Donald Palmer	Edward Button	Daniel Weaver	Les MacDonald
Mountain Home *	c	MC	11	(208) 587-2104	Tom Rist	...	Nina Patterson	...	Philip Gridley	John Walter	Wayne Shepherd
Nampa	c	MC	51	(208) 465-2220	R. Tom Dale	...	Diana Lambing	Todd Bunderson	Ron Anderson	Curtis Homer	...
Orofino	c	MC	3	(208) 476-4725	...	Rick Laam	Virginia Davis	...	...	Ronnie Pomerinke	Floyd Williams
Payette	c	MC	7	(208) 642-6024	Mark Heleker	John Franks	...	...	Jeff Sands	Mark Clark	...
Pocatello	c	MC	51	(208) 234-6163	Roger Chase	...	Rhonda Johnson	David Swindell	Kevin Quick	...	Greg Lanning
Post Falls *	c	MC	17	(208) 773-3511	Clay Larkin	Eric Keck	Christene Pappas	Shelly Enderud	...	Clifford Hayes	Terry Werner
Preston *	c	MC	4	(208) 852-1817	F. L. Hendrickson	...	Jerry Larsen	...	...	Val Sparrow	John Balls
Rathdrum	c	MC	4	(208) 687-0261	Brian Steele	Brett Boyer	Judy Hollenbeck	...	...	Robert Moore	Chet Anderson
Rexburg	c	MC	17	(208) 359-3020	Shawn Larsen	...	Blair Kay	Richard Horner	Spencer Larsen	Lynn Archibald	Farrell Davidson
Rigby	c	MC	2	(208) 745-8111	John Anderson	...	Anna Bidwell	...	...	Larry Anderson	Douglas Nelson
Rupert	c	MC	5	(208) 436-9600	Audrey Neiwerth	...	Linda Price	Colleen Severson	Larry Pool	Kenneth Fedders	Robert Russmann
Salmon	c	MC	3	(208) 756-3214	Stanley Davis	...	...	...	Bob Perry	Jody Seybold	Mickey Verbeck
Sandpoint *	c	MC	6	(208) 263-3310	Gretchen Hellar	...	Maree Peck	...	Robert Tyler	Mark Lockwood	Kody Van Dyk
Shelley	c	MC	3	(208) 357-3390	Eric Christensen	...	Sandy Gaydusek	...	...	Alan Dial	Rick Anderson
Soda Springs	c	MC	3	(208) 547-2600	Kirk Hansen	Lee Godfrey	Tausha Vorwaller	...	...	Joe Rice	Craig Hill
St. Anthony	c	MC	3	(208) 624-3494	Willard Beck	...	Taci Stoddard	...	Dave Fausett	James Smith	Scott Butigan
St. Maries	c	MC	2	(208) 245-2577	Robert Allen	...	...	...	...	...	...
Sun Valley	c	CM	1	(208) 622-4438	David Wilson	Sharon Hammer	Janis Wright	Michelle Fosterton	Jeffrey Carnes	Cameron Daggett	Bill Whitesell
Twin Falls	c	CM	34	(208) 735-7251	Lance Clow	Thomas Courtney	Sharon Bryan	Gary Evans	Ronald Clark	Jim Munn	Jackie Fields
Weiser	c	MC	5	(208) 549-1965	...	...	...	...	...	...	...

Directory 1/9 continued — OFFICIALS IN U.S. MUNICIPALITIES 2,500 AND OVER IN POPULATION

Jurisdiction	Type	Form of govern-ment	2000 Popu-lation	Main telephone number	Chief elected official	Appointed administrator	Clerk of the governing board	Chief financial officer	Fire chief	Police chief	Public works director
ILLINOIS											
Abingdon	c	MC	3	(309) 462-3182	Michael Brackett	. . .	B. Joanne Batson	. . .	. . .	William Robinson	Kirt Links
Addison	v	MC	35	(630) 543-4100	Lorenz Hartnig	Joseph Block	Lucille Zucchero	Roseanne Benson	. . .	Timothy Hayden	Gregory Brunst
Aledo	c	MC	3	(309) 582-7241	Lee Celske	. . .	Brenda Rick	. . .	Dennis Litwiler	Steve Struble	Jewel Bucy
Algonquin *	v	CM	23	(847) 658-2700	John Schmitt	William Ganek	Gerald Kautz	John Walde	. . .	Russell Laine	Robert Mitchard
Alsip	v	MC	19	(708) 385-6902	Patrick Kitching	. . .	Deborah Venhuizen	Greg Palumbo	Charles Geraci	Robert Troy	Vincent Cullen
Alton	c	MC	30	(618) 463-3599	Donald Sandidge	. . .	Mary Gibson	Stephanie Elliott	Timothy Spaulding	Christopher Sullivan	James Hernandez
Anna	c	MC	5	(618) 833-8528	Steve Hartline	Steven Guined	. . .	. . .	James Cross	Gordon Hopp	Russell Sullivan
Antioch	v	MC	8	(847) 395-1000	Marilyn Shineflug	Jill Velan	Candi Rowe	. . .	Dennis Volling	Charles Fagan	Bill Smith
Arcola *	c	MC	2	(217) 268-4966	Larry Ferguson	Bill Wagoner	Carol Turner	. . .	Josh Truex	Michael Phillips	Jack Logan
Arlington Heights	v	CM	76	(847) 368-5000	. . .	William Dixon	Edwina Corso	Thomas Kuehne	Glenn Ericksen	Gerald Mourning	Scott Shirley
Arthur	v	MC	2	(217) 543-2927	. . .	. . .	. . .	. . .	. . .	. . .	. . .
Auburn	c	MC	4	(217) 438-6151	. . .	. . .	. . .	. . .	. . .	. . .	. . .
Aurora	c	MC	142	(630) 892-8811	David Stover	. . .	. . .	Brian Caputo	. . .	. . .	. . .
Bannockburn *	v	MC	1	(847) 945-6080	James Barkemeyer	Maria Lasday	David Korer	Linda McCulloch	. . .	Kevin Tracz	. . .
Barrington *	v	CM	10	(847) 304-3400	Karen Darch	Denise Pieroni	Adam Frazier	Maggie Bosley	James Arie	Jeffrey Lawler	Dennis Burmeister
Barrington Hills *	v	MC	3	(847) 551-3000	Robert Abboud	Robert Kosin	. . .	. . .	. . .	Michael Murphy	. . .
Bartlett	v	CM	36	(630) 837-0800	. . .	Valerie Salmons	Linda Gallien	. . .	. . .	Daniel Palmer	Paul Kuester
Bartonville	v	MC	6	(309) 633-2053	. . .	. . .	. . .	. . .	. . .	. . .	. . .
Batavia *	c	MC	23	(630) 454-2000	Jeff Schielke	William McGrath	Maude Volk	Peggy Colby	William Darin	Gary Schira	Gary Holm
Beach Park	v	CM	10	(847) 746-1770	Milt Jensen	Kenneth Lopez	Laurie Cvengros	. . .	. . .	. . .	. . .
Beardstown *	c	MC	5	(217) 323-3110	Robert Walters	. . .	Brian Ruch	. . .	Darin Paul	Thomas Schlueter	Todd Harmeyer
Beecher	v	CM	2	(708) 946-2261	Paul Lohmann	Robert Barber	Janett Conner	. . .	David Lagesse	Jeffrey Weissgerber	Harold Cowger
Belleville	c	MC	41	(618) 233-6810	Mark Kern	. . .	Linda Fields	Nancy Boeckman	Mike Hawthorne	James Rokita	. . .
Bellwood	v	MC	20	(708) 547-3500	Donald Lemm	Roy McCampbell	Booker Brown	I. Lagen	Andre Harvey	Greg Moore	John Antonovich
Belvidere	c	CM	20	(815) 544-2612	Frederic Brereton	. . .	Shauna Arco	Pat Chamberlin	David Worrell	Jan Noble	Craig Lawler
Bensenville	v	CM	20	(630) 766-8200	John Geils	Jim Johnson	Patricia Johnson	Thomas Truty	Jack Barba	. . .	Paul Quinn
Benton	c	CO	6	(618) 439-6131	. . .	. . .	. . .	. . .	. . .	. . .	. . .
Berkeley	v	MC	5	(708) 449-8840	Michael Esposito	Lawrence DiRe	Janice McCulloch	. . .	. . .	Timothy Griffin	Robert Larem
Berwyn	c	MC	54	(708) 788-2660	Michael O'Connor	. . .	Tom Pavlik	. . .	Richard Kalivoda	Carl Dobbs	. . .
Bethalto *	v	MC	9	(618) 377-8051	Steve Bryant	. . .	Sue Lowrance	. . .	Chester Schilling	Alan Winslow	Joseph Ricci
Big Rock *	v	CM	. .	(630) 556-4365	. . .	. . .	. . .	. . .	. . .	. . .	. . .
Bloomingdale *	v	MC	21	(630) 893-7000	Robert Iden	Daniel Wennerholm	Susan Bartucci	Gary Szott	. . .	Timothy Goergen	Mike Marchi
Bloomington	c	CM	64	(309) 434-2509	Stephen Stockton	Thomas Hamilton	Tracey Covert	Brian Barnes	Keith Ranney	Roger Aikin	. . .
Blue Island	c	MC	23	(708) 396-7065	. . .	Michael Anastasia	Pamela Frasor	Linda Martin	David Haywood	Joseph Kosman	Arthur Dertz
Bolingbrook	v	CM	56	(630) 226-8400	Roger Claar	James Boan	Carol Penning	. . .	Charles Peterson	Kenneth Each	Michael Drey
Bourbonnais *	v	CM	15	(815) 937-3570	Paul Schore	Gregg Spathis	Brian Simeur	Michael Wolf	. . .	Joseph Beard	Mike Chamness
Bradley *	v	MC	12	(815) 932-2125	Gael Kent	Kimberly Dickens	Michael LaGesse	. . .	James Baird	Don Kufner	James Travis
Braidwood	c	CO	5	(815) 458-2333	Wayne Saltzman	. . .	James Hubbard	Lisa Heglund	. . .	Robert Andreina	Aubrey Glisson
Breese	c	MC	4	(618) 526-7731	Donald Maue	Robert Venhaus	. . .	. . .	. . .	James Hummert	Matthew Johnson
Bridgeview	v	MC	15	(708) 594-2525	John Oremus	Frank Bilich	Anne Cusack	Claudette Struzik	Terrence Lipinski	Vladimir Ivkovich	William Green
Broadview	v	MC	8	(708) 681-3600	Henry Vicenik	. . .	Patricia Williams	Lester Swintek	John Tierney	Raymond Pelletier	Anthony Sacco
Brookfield	v	CM	19	(708) 485-7344	Thomas Sequens	Riccardo Ginex	Kelly Mesich	. . .	Charles La Greco	. . .	. . .
Buffalo Grove *	v	CM	42	(847) 459-2500	Elliot Hartstein	William Brimm	Janet Sirabian	Scott Anderson	Terry Vavra	Steven Balinski	Gregory Boysen
Burbank	c	MC	27	(708) 599-5500	. . .	. . .	. . .	. . .	. . .	. . .	. . .
Burnham	v	MC	4	(708) 862-9150	. . .	. . .	. . .	. . .	. . .	. . .	. . .
Burr Ridge	v	CM	10	(630) 654-8181	Jo Irmen	Steven Stricker	. . .	Jerry Sapp	. . .	Herbert Timm	Howard Heil
Bushnell	c	MC	3	(309) 772-2521	Jack Promisson	. . .	. . .	. . .	. . .	Merv Hilliard	Dan Cortelyou
Cahokia	v	MC	16	(618) 337-9500	Frank Bergman	. . .	Norma Jones	Betty Sharp	David Nulsen	Richard Watson	John Torry
Cairo	c	MC	3	(618) 734-4127	James Wilson	. . .	Brenda Miller	. . .	Michael Brey	James Wright	Ronnie Harris
Calumet City	c	MC	39	(708) 891-8100	. . .	. . .	. . .	. . .	. . .	. . .	. . .
Calumet Park *	v	MC	8	(708) 389-0850	Joseph DuPar	. . .	Geraldine Galvin	. . .	Thomas Battistella	Mark Davis	Robert Talaski
Cambridge *	v	MC	2	(309) 937-2570	Jim Crouch	D. Van Meenen	. . .	. . .	. . .	. . .	Ed Dole
Canton	c	MC	15	(309) 647-0020	Jerry Bohler	. . .	Nancy Whites	. . .	John Stanko	Donald Edwards	Clifford O'Brien
Carbon Cliff *	v	MC	1	(309) 792-8235	Kenneth Williams	Dawn Tubbs	Karen Hopkins	. . .	. . .	. . .	. . .
Carbondale	c	CM	20	(618) 549-5302	Brad Cole	Allen Gill	Janet Vaught	Ernest Tessone	Jeffery Anderson	Robert Finney	Edward Reeder
Carlinville	c	MC	5	(217) 854-4076	Robert Schwab	. . .	Judy Decker	. . .	Bill Healy	David Haley	MaryBeth Bellm
Carlyle	c	MC	3	(618) 594-2468	Van Johnson	Bill Gruen	Janine Ehlers	. . .	. . .	Kent Newkirk	. . .
Carmi	c	MC	5	(618) 382-8118	. . .	. . .	. . .	. . .	. . .	. . .	. . .
Carol Stream	v	CM	40	(630) 665-7050	Ross Ferraro	Joseph Breinig	. . .	Stan Helgerson	. . .	Rick Willing	John Turner
Carpentersville	v	CM	30	(847) 426-3439	Bill Sarto	Craig Anderson	Terri Wilde	Lisa Happ	John Schuldt	David Neumann	Robert Cole
Carriers Mills	v	MC	1	(618) 994-2035	Louis Shaw	. . .	Kim Martin	. . .	Jeff Parks	William Duncan	. . .
Carrollton	c	MC	2	(217) 942-5517	Francis Baker	. . .	Denise Snyder	Patricia Seely	David Steinacher	Mike Kiger	Mike Snyder
Carterville	c	MC	4	(618) 985-2252	Charles Mausey	. . .	Joyce Carney	. . .	William Talley	Monty Jeralds	. . .
Cary	v	CM	15	(847) 639-0003	Steve Lamal	Cameron Davis	. . .	Kevin Dahlstrand	. . .	Ronald Delelio	Bradley Fleck
Casey	c	MC	2	(217) 932-2700	. . .	. . .	. . .	. . .	. . .	. . .	. . .
Caseyville	v	MC	4	(618) 344-1234	George Chance	. . .	Jack Piesbergen	. . .	. . .	. . .	Gerard Scott
Centralia	c	CM	14	(618) 533-7625	Robert Demijan	Grant Kleinhenz	. . .	William Agee	Richard Page	Robert Arnony	Donald Copple
Centreville *	c	MC	5	(618) 332-1021	Marius Jackson	. . .	DeMario Helm	. . .	. . .	Larry Wynn	Charles Rattler
Champaign *	c	CM	67	(217) 403-8700	Gerald Schweighart	Steven Carter	Marilyn Banks	Richard Schnuer	Dave Penicook	R. T. Finney	Dennis Schmidt
Channahon	v	CM	7	(815) 467-6644	Joseph Cook	James Bowden	Eileen Clark	Robert Guess	. . .	Steve Admonis	Edward Dolezal
Charleston *	c	CO	21	(217) 345-5650	John Inyart	R. Smith	Deborah Muller	Heather Kuykendall	Kris Phipps	Mark Jenkins	Curtis Buescher
Chatham	v	MC	8	(217) 483-2451	Thomas Gray	. . .	Patrick Schad	Sherry Dierking	. . .	Roy Barnett	Meredith Branham
Cherry Valley	v	MC	2	(815) 332-3441	. . .	David Nord	. . .	. . .	. . .	. . .	. . .
Chester *	c	MC	5	(618) 826-2326	Marty Bert	. . .	Nancy Eggemeyer	. . .	Michael Lochhead	Ryan Coffey	. . .
Chicago	c	MC	2896	(312) 744-0308	Richard Daley	. . .	. . .	Steve Lux	. . .	. . .	. . .
Chicago Heights	c	CO	32	(708) 756-5305	Angelo Clambrone	Rick Doggett	. . .	. . .	Ted Brown	Karla Osentowski	Albert Marconi
Chicago Ridge	v	MC	14	(708) 425-7700	Eugene Siegel	. . .	Charles Tokar	. . .	Randall Grossi	T. Baldermann	John Lind
Chillicothe *	c	MC	5	(309) 274-5056	Gary Fyke	. . .	Sharon Crabel	. . .	John Myers	Steve Maurer	Clyde Crabel
Christopher	c	MC	2	(618) 724-7648	Gary Bartolotti	. . .	Jacquelyn Murry	. . .	Charles Lutes	. . .	Dennis Gunter
Cicero	t	MC	85	(708) 656-3600	Betty Maltese	. . .	Marylin Colpo	Donald Schultz	James Smetana	Thomas Rowan	Sam Jelic
Clarendon Hills *	v	CM	7	(630) 286-5400	Thomas Karaba	Robert Bahan	Dawn Tandle	Margaret Hartnett	Brian Leahy	L. Patrick Anderson	John Hays
Clinton	c	CO	7	(217) 935-9438	Roger Cyrulik	. . .	R. Wickenhauser	. . .	Jeff Pearl	Mike Reidy	Steve Lobb
Coal City *	v	MC	4	(815) 634-8608	Neal Nelson	Matthew Fritz	Pamela Noffsinger	. . .	Harold Holsinger	Keith Hefner	Darrell Olson
Coal Valley	v	MC	3	(309) 799-3604	Stanley Engstrom	. . .	Deanna Burnett	. . .	John Diamond	Larry Buechler	Ross Hall
Collinsville	c	CM	24	(618) 346-5200	Stan Schaeffer	Robert Knabel	Louis Jackstadt	Tamara Ammann	Peter Stehman	Scott Williams	. . .
Colona *	c	MC	5	(309) 792-0571	Danny McDaniel	. . .	Lories Graham	Mary Carlson	. . .	Timothy Krebs	Rick Crew
Columbia	c	MC	7	(618) 281-7144	Lester Schneider	. . .	Wesley Hoeffken	Eugene Schorb	Michael Roediger	Joseph Edwards	. . .
Country Club Hills	c	CM	16	(708) 798-2616	Dwight Welch	Dorothy Steward	Deborah McIlvain	Alison Brothen	Garrick Kasper	William Brown	Edward Meinheit
Countryside *	c	MC	5	(708) 354-7270	Robert Conrad	Edward Bailey	Sharon Sweeney	Gail Paul	. . .	Timothy Swanson	Robert Fullar
Crest Hill *	c	MC	13	(815) 741-5100	Nicholas Churnovic	John Tomasoski	Christine Vershay	. . .	. . .	Dwayne Wilkerson	. . .
Crestwood	v	MC	11	(708) 371-4800	Chester Stranczek	Frank Gassmere	Nancy Benedetto	. . .	William Boman	John Hefley	Frank Scaccia
Crete *	v	MC	7	(708) 672-5431	Michael Einhorn	Thomas Durkin	Kathleen Wantuch	. . .	Lyle Bachert	James Paoletti	Philip Hameister
Creve Coeur	v	MC	5	(309) 699-6714	Eugene Talbot	. . .	. . .	Richard Gilliatt	Fred Lang	Michael Button	. . .
Crystal Lake *	c	CM	38	(815) 459-2020	Aaron Shepley	Gary Mayerhofer	Roger Dreher	Mark Nannini	James Moore	David Linder	Eric Lecuyer
Danville	c	MC	33	(217) 431-2200	Robert Jones	. . .	Janet Myers	Ron Neufeld	Thomas Lane	Robert Dietzen	Don Cheesman
Darien *	c	MC	22	(630) 852-5000	. . .	Bryon Vana	Joanne Coleman	. . .	. . .	Robert Pavelchik	Daniel Gombac

Directory 1/9 continued

OFFICIALS IN U.S. MUNICIPALITIES 2,500 AND OVER IN POPULATION

Jurisdiction		Type	Form of govern-ment	2000 Popu-lation	Main telephone number	Chief elected official	Appointed administrator	Clerk of the governing board	Chief financial officer	Fire chief	Police chief	Public works director
ILLINOIS continued												
De Kalb		c	CM	39	(815) 748-2000	Greg Sparrow	Mark Biernacki	Donna Johnson	Douglas Haywood	Pete Polarek	William Feithen	Richard Monas
Decatur		c	CM	81	(217) 428-2805	Paul Osborne	Ryan McCrady	Celeste Harris	Beth Couter	Leslie Albert	Mark Barthelemy	Stephen Swanson
Deer Park		v	CM	3	(847) 726-1648	Richard Karl	James Connors	Sandra Smith	...	...	...	...
Deerfield		v	CM	18	(847) 945-5000	Steven Harris	Kent Street	...	Robert Fialkowski	...	John Sliozis	Barbara Little
Des Plaines	*	c	CM	58	(847) 391-5300	Anthony Arredia	Jason Bajor	Donna McAllister	Dorothy Wisniewski	Randy Jaeger	James Prandini	Matthew Duskett
Dixmoor		v	MC	3	(708) 389-6121	...	...	...	...	...	...	...
Dixon		c	MC	15	(815) 288-1485	Donald Sheets	Rita Crundwell	Kathe Swanson	...	Mike Wilcox	Robert Short	Mike Stichter
Dolton		v	CM	25	(708) 201-3268	...	...	Judith Evans	...	Robert Kapusta	...	Robert Myers
Downers Grove		v	CM	48	(630) 434-5500	Brian Krajewski	David Fieldman	April Holden	Rita Trainor	Philip Ruscetti	Robert Porter	David Barber
Du Quoin		c	CO	6	(618) 542-3841	John Rednour	...	...	Cha Hill	Buddy Crain	James Booker	Raymond Spencer
Dupo		v	MC	3	(618) 286-3280	Ronnie Dell	...	Bruce Feltmeyer	...	Kerrey Foster	...	Randy Hamilton
Dwight	*	v	MC	4	(815) 584-3077	James Mixen	Kevin McNamara	Patricia Drechsel	...	Darrin Schull	Timothy Henson	David Bozarth
East Alton		v	MC	6	(618) 259-7714	Fred Bright	...	Lori Palmer	...	Larry Ringering	Richard Brown	Denny Weber
East Dubuque	*	c	CM	1	(815) 747-3416	Geoffrey Barklow	Al Griffiths	Nancy Roepke	...	Joe Heim	Steven O'Connell	Mark Fluhr
East Dundee		v	MC	2	(847) 426-2822	Daniel O'Leary	Frank Koehler	Sue Norton	...	...	Terry Mee	T. J. Moore
East Hazel Crest		v	CM	1	(708) 798-0213	Thomas Brown	Patricia Lazuka	...	...	William Vallow	Ray Robertson	Rory Maltrotto
East Moline	*	c	MC	20	(309) 752-1584	John Thodos	Richard Keehner	Arletta Holmes	James Hughes	Robert DeFrance	Victor Moreno	Dave Lambrecht
East Peoria		c	CO	22	(309) 698-4750	Charles Dobbelaire	James Brimberry	Veona Dinkins	...	Roger Aylward	Edward Papis	Rick Jeremiah
East St. Louis		c	CM	31	(618) 482-6811	...	Robert Betts	...	...	...	...	...
Edwardsville		c	MC	21	(618) 962-7530	Gary Niebur	Bennett Dickmann	Patty Theide	...	J. Brian Wilson	David Bopp	Timothy Harr
Effingham		c	CO	12	(217) 342-5301	Robert Utz	...	Rick Goeckner	...	Nicholas Althoff	John Lange	...
El Paso	*	c	MC	2	(309) 527-4005	Herb Arbuckle	Joel Laws	David Fever	...	...	Jeffrey Price	Chuck Arbuckle
Elburn		v	MC	2	(630) 365-5060	James Willey	...	Susan Schoo	Barbara Carlson	Marty Strausberger	Edward Kelley	Michael Anderson
Eldorado	*	c	CO	4	(618) 273-6566	Rocky James	...	Pat Mahoney	...	Michael McKinnies	Shannon Deuel	...
Elgin	*	c	CM	94	(847) 931-6100	Edward Schock	Olufemi Folarin	Diane Robertson	James Nowicki	John Henrici	Lisa Womack	John Loete
Elk Grove Village	*	v	CM	34	(847) 357-4019	Craig Johnson	Raymond Rummel	Ann Walsh	Christine Tromp	David Miller	Stephen Schmidt	Thomas Cech
Elmhurst		c	CM	42	(630) 530-3000	Thomas Marcucci	Thomas Borchert	Janet Edgley	Marilyn Gaston	Michael Kopp	Steven Neibauer	Michael Hughes
Elmwood Park	*	v	CM	25	(708) 452-7300	Peter Silvestri	John Dalicandro	Elsie Sutter	John Lannefeld	Michael Marino	Frederick Braglia	Peter Terzo
Elwood	*	v	MC	1	(815) 423-5011	...	Aimee Ingalls	Patricia Buchenau	...	...	...	...
Eureka		c	MC	4	(309) 467-2113	Scott Punke	Anne Sandvik	Marilyn Walter	...	Craig Neal	Alan Misener	James Lehman
Evanston		c	CM	74	(847) 328-2100	Lorraine Morton	Rolanda Russell	Mary Morris	...	Alan Berkowsky	Frank Kaminski	David Jennings
Evergreen Park		v	MC	20	(708) 422-1551	James Sexton	...	Catherine Aparo	...	Edward Clohessy	Michael Saunders	William Lorenzs
Fairbury		c	MC	3	(815) 692-2743	Robert Walter	Leroy McPherson	Brenda Defries	...	...	Jack Wiser	...
Fairfield		c	MC	5	(618) 842-3871	Wayne Borah	Kennett Foley	Tina Hutchcraft	...	Michael Pottorff	William Winter	...
Fairview Heights		c	MC	15	(618) 489-2000	Gail Mitchell	Drew Awsumb	Harvey Noubarian	...	...	Ed Delmore	Robert Hotz
Farmer City		c	MC	2	(309) 928-3412	...	...	...	...	...	...	...
Farmington		c	MC	2	(309) 245-2011	Cyril Stobaugh	Roger Woodcock	...	...	...	William Lally	Brad Dilts
Flora		c	CO	5	(618) 662-8313	Lewis Wolfe	...	Becky Wiley	Debra Zimmerman	Bruce Dickey	Ed McCormick	David Thompson
Flossmoor	*	v	CM	9	(708) 798-2300	Roger Molski	Bridget Wachtel	Pam Hudson	Scott Bordui	Daniel Hornback	William Miller	Greg Buenzow
Ford Heights		v	MC	3	(708) 758-3131	Saul Beck	...	Audrey Coulter	Angelia Smith	Gregory Dillard	Percy Coleman	Rufus Fisher
Forest Park	*	v	CO	15	(708) 366-2323	Anthony Calderone	...	Vanessa Moritz	Judy Kovacs	Stephen Glinke	James Ryan	Robert Kutak
Forsyth	*	v	CM	2	(217) 877-9445	Harold Gilbert	Austin Edmondson	Kathy Mizer	...	...	...	Larry Coloni
Fox Lake	*	v	MC	9	(847) 587-2151	Cindy Irwin	Nancy Schuerr	...	...	Ronald Hoehne	Edward Gerretsen	...
Fox River Grove	*	v	MC	4	(847) 639-3170	Cindy Cramer	Arthur Osten	Donna Brouder	...	Robert Kreher	Ronald Lukasik	Jon Huizinga
Frankfort		v	CM	10	(815) 469-2177	Jim Holland	Jerald Ducay	Kate Romani	Sandra Babka	...	Rob Piscia	Terry Kestel
Franklin Park		v	MC	19	(847) 671-4800	Daniel Pritchett	...	Susan Szymanski	Elliott Becker	David Traiforos	Randall Petersen	Joseph Thomas
Freeburg	*	v	CM	3	(618) 539-5545	Allen Watters	...	Mary Grau	...	...	Melvin Woodruff	Ronald Dintelmann
Freeport	*	c	MC	26	(815) 235-8200	George Gaulrapp	...	Martha Zuravel	Craig Joesten	Kevin Countryman	Jerry Whitmore	Craig Lebaron
Fulton		c	CM	3	(815) 589-2616	Paul Sikkom	...	La Vonne Huizonga	...	David Damhoff	Harvey Meade	Randy Balk
Galena	*	c	MC	3	(815) 777-1050	...	Mark Moran	Mary Beth Hyde	Cynthia Pepple	...	Gerald Westemeier	James Rigdon
Galesburg	*	c	CM	33	(309) 345-3628	Gary Smith	Dane Bragg	Anita Carlton	Gloria Osborn	John Cratty	David Christensen	Larry Cox
Galva	*	c	MC	2	(309) 932-2555	Thomas Hartman	David Dyer	Teresa Byers	...	Denny Tarleton	Jerry Clark	Myron Townsend
Geneseo	*	c	MC	6	(309) 944-6419	Patrick Eberhardt	Eric Wiederhold	Tracey Kotecki	Teresa Savage	...	Thomas Piotrowski	J. Van De Woestyne
Geneva	*	c	MC	19	(630) 232-7494	Kevin Burns	Mary McKittrick	Lynn Landberg	...	Stephen Olson	Steve Mexin	Dan Dinges
Genoa		c	MC	4	(815) 784-2327	David Rood	...	Judith Zmich	David Jepson	Ronald Anderson	Donald Smith	Richard Gentile
Georgetown		c	MC	3	(217) 662-2525	...	...	...	...	...	Michael Vice	...
Gibson City	*	c	MC	3	(217) 784-5872	Daniel Dickey	Janet Davis	Vickie Lorenzen	...	...	Steve Cushman	John Stauffer
Gilberts		v	MC	1	(847) 428-2861	Tom Wajda	Raymond Keller	Darlene Mueller	...	...	Michael Joswick	...
Gillespie		c	MC	3	(217) 839-2919	Dan Fisher	...	Jonella Rolando	...	Larry Norville	Richard Hearn	...
Glen Carbon	*	v	MC	10	(618) 288-1200	Robert Jackstadt	...	Peggy Goudy	Richard Jett	...	David Bradford	Tom Sedlacek
Glen Ellyn		v	CM	26	(630) 469-5000	Gregory Mathews	Steven Jones	Patricia O'Connor	Jon Batek	Scott Raffensparger	Philip Norton	James Foster
Glencoe		v	CM	8	(847) 835-4114	Scott Feldman	Paul Harlow	...	David Clark	...	...	David Mau
Glendale Heights		v	MC	31	(630) 260-6000	Linda Jackson	Donna Becerra	Jo Ann Borysiewicz	Benjamin Abrazaldo	...	...	Richard Dime
Glenview		v	CM	41	(847) 904-4370	Lawrence Carlson	Lawrence Hileman	...	Daniel Wiersma	Dan Bonkowski	William Fitzpatrick	William Porter
Glenwood		v	MC	9	(708) 753-2400	...	...	...	Linda Brunette	...	...	Gerald Brossmer
Godfrey		v	MC	16	(618) 466-3324	Michael Campion	...	Pamela Whisler	...	...	...	Victor Stipes
Granite City		c	MC	31	(618) 452-6235	Ronald Selph	Mike Sparks	Judith Whitaker	Mac McTaggart	Ed Hagnauer	David Ruebhausen	...
Grayslake	*	v	MC	18	(847) 223-8515	Timothy Perry	Michael Ellis	Cynthia Lee	Michael Peterson	...	Larry Herzog	William Heinz
Greenville		c	CM	6	(618) 664-1644	Alan Gaffner	David Willey	Margaret Iberg	...	...	Lou Lorton	Bill Grider
Gurnee		v	MC	28	(847) 623-7650	Donald Rudny	James Hayner	Mary Jo Kollross	Patricia Wesolowski	Fred Friedl	Robert Jones	...
Hamilton		c	MC	3	(217) 847-2936	Stephen Woodruff	...	Michelle Dorethy	...	Steve Helenthal	Walter Sellens	...
Hampshire	*	v	MC	2	(847) 683-2181	Jeffrey Magnussen	Eric Palm	Linda Vasquez	Kathyrn Michael	...	Thomas Atchison	John Bidinger
Hanover Park	*	v	CM	38	(630) 372-4200	Rodney Craig	Marc Hummel	Sherry Craig	Joan Rock	Craig Haigh	Ronald Moser	Howard Killian
Harrisburg	*	c	MC	9	(618) 253-7451	Valerie Mitchell	...	Sarah Wofford	...	Bill Summers	Bob Smith	...
Harvard		c	MC	7	(815) 943-6468	Ralph Henning	David Nelson	Andy Wells	...	...	Kenneth Mrozek	James Carbonetti
Harvey		c	CO	30	(708) 210-5300	...	...	...	...	...	...	...
Harwood Heights		v	MC	8	(708) 867-7200	Margaret Fuller	...	Dianne Larson	...	...	Martin Podosek	...
Havana		c	MC	3	(309) 543-6580	Dale Roberts	...	Ruby Miller	Harold Palmer	John Kachanuk	Kevin Noble	Don Henderson
Hawthorn Woods		v	MC	6	(847) 438-5500	Keith Hunt	James Bassett	...	...	...	Jennifer Paulus	Daniel Marcinko
Hazel Crest	*	v	CM	14	(708) 335-9600	Robert Donaldson	Robert Palmer	Florine Robinson	...	Charles Jackson	Thomas Folliard	Tim Fassnacht
Henry		c	MC	2	(309) 364-3056	...	...	Doris Goldner	...	...	Michael Surrells	Thomas Maubach
Herrin		c	MC	11	(618) 942-3175	Edward Quaglia	...	Marlene Simpson	Jody Deaton	Mike Steh	...	Joe Lapinski
Hickory Hills		c	MC	13	(708) 598-4800	Roy Faddis	...	Joann Jackson	...	...	...	Larry Boettcher
Highland	*	c	CM	8	(618) 654-9891	Joseph Michaelis	Mark Latham	Barbara Bellm	Sharon Rusteberg	Michael Kilgore	...	Joseph Gillespie
Highland Park	*	c	CM	31	(847) 432-0800	Michael Belsky	David Limardi	Shirley Fitzgerald	Elizabeth Spencer	Alan Wax	Paul Shafer	Mary Anderson
Highwood	*	c	MC	4	(847) 432-1924	Vincent Donofrio	Gregory Jackson	Susan Druktenis	...	Thomas Lovejoy	Louis Rossi	Jeff Ponsi
Hillsboro	*	c	CO	4	(217) 532-5566	William Baran	...	David Booher	Geoff Trost	Joe Lyerla	Gary Satterlee	D. McCammack
Hillside		v	MC	8	(708) 449-6450	Joseph Tamburino	Russell Wajda	Patrick O'Sullivan	...	Michael Kuryla	Frank Alonzo	Joseph Pisano
Hinsdale	*	v	CM	17	(630) 789-7000	Michael Woerner	David Cook	Barbara Grigola	Douglas Cooper	Michael Kelly	Bradley Bloom	George Franco
Hoffman Estates	*	v	CM	49	(847) 882-9100	William McLeod	James Norris	Bev Romanoff	Michael Du Charme	Robert Gorvett	Clinton Herdegen	Ken Hari
Homer Glen	*	v	MC	22	(708) 301-0632	James Daley	Paula Wallrich	Gale Skrobuton	John Sawyers	...	...	...
Hometown		c	MC	4	(708) 424-7500	Donald Roberton	...	Mary Jo Hacker	...	...	Fred Knoblauch	Joseph Madden
Homewood		v	CM	19	(708) 798-3000	Richard Hofeld	Mark Franz	Gayle Campbell	Dennis Bubenik	Al Schullo	Larry Burnson	John Schaefer
Hoopeston		c	MC	5	(217) 283-5833	Samuel Ault	...	Gail Lane	William Goodwine	Gregory Shipman	Mark Drollinger	...
Huntley		v	CM	5	(847) 669-9600	Charles Sass	...	Rita McMahon	...	...	Randall Walters	Jim Schwartz

Directory 1/9 continued OFFICIALS IN U.S. MUNICIPALITIES 2,500 AND OVER IN POPULATION

Jurisdiction	Type	Form of govern-ment	2000 Popu-lation	Main telephone number	Chief elected official	Appointed administrator	Clerk of the governing board	Chief financial officer	Fire chief	Police chief	Public works director
ILLINOIS continued											
Indian Head Park	v	CM	3	(708) 246-3080	. . .	Raymond Garritano	. . .	David Brink	. . .	. . .	Edward Santen
Inverness	v	MC	6	(847) 358-7740	John Tatooles	Curtis Carver	Patricia Ledvina	. . .	. . .	. . .	. . .
Island Lake	v	MC	8	(847) 526-8764	Charles Amrich	. . .	Kriss Becker	. . .	. . .	John Fellmann	William Kootstra
Itasca	v	MC	8	(630) 773-0835	Claudia Gruber	David Williams	Carole Schreiber	. . .	. . .	Edward Votava	Ross Hitchcock
Jacksonville	c	MC	18	(217) 479-4600	Ronald Tendick	. . .	Andy Ezard	. . .	Rick Kluge	Donald Cook	. . .
Jerseyville	c	CO	7	(618) 498-3312	Yvonne Hartmann	. . .	Catherine Ward	. . .	. . .	Bill Bridges	. . .
Johnston City	c	MC	3	(618) 983-6544	Richard Carter	. . .	Jean Hatfield	. . .	Thomas Burton	Jerald Kobler	Carl Reed
Joliet	c	CM	106	(815) 724-4020	Arthur Schultz	Thomas Thanas	Janet Traven	Robert Fraser	Richard Marose	Frederick Hayes	James Trizna
Justice	v	MC	12	(708) 458-2520	Melvin Van Allen	. . .	Kathleen Svoboda	Michelle Jones	Ronald Szarzynski	Paul Wasik	Philip Depaola
Kankakee	c	MC	27	(815) 933-0500	Donald Green	. . .	Anjanita Dumas	James Spice	Ronald Young	Michael Kinkade	Bert Dear
Kenilworth	v	CM	2	(847) 251-1666	T. Chisum	Bradly Burke	Robert Hastings	Maryann VanDyke	. . .	John Petersen	Ignazio Fiorentino
Kewanee *	c	CM	12	(309) 852-2611	Bruce Tossell	. . .	Melinda Edwards	Debra Johnson	Tom Weston	James Dison	Mike Rapczak
Kildeer	v	CM	3	(847) 438-6000	. . .	Laurel Schreiber	. . .	. . .	. . .	Jeffrey Lilly	. . .
Knoxville	c	MC	3	(309) 289-2814	Phil Myers	. . .	Margaret Bivens	. . .	. . .	Rick Pecsi	. . .
La Grange *	v	CM	15	(708) 579-2300	Elizabeth Asperger	Robert Pilipiszyn	Robert Milne	Lou Cipparrone	David Fleege	Michael Holub	Ryan Gillingham
La Grange Park	v	CM	13	(708) 354-0225	Susan Tutt-Parsons	Bohdan Proczko	Kerry Brunette	Pierre Garesche	Dean Maggos	Daniel McCollum	Julius Hansen
La Salle	c	MC	9	(815) 223-4586	Arthur Washkowiak	. . .	V. Kochanowski	Joanne Milby	William Bacidore	Thomas Kramarsic	Samuel McNeilly
Lake Barrington	v	CM	4	(847) 381-6010	. . .	Christopher Martin	. . .	. . .	. . .	. . .	. . .
Lake Bluff	v	CM	6	(847) 234-0774	Christine Letchinger	R. Irvin	Michael Klawitter	Susan Griffin	David Graf	William Gallagher	Thomas Cahill
Lake Forest *	c	CM	20	(847) 234-2600	S. Michael Rummel	Robert Kiely	. . .	Kathleen Reinertsen	W. Michael Hosking	Joseph Buerger	Thomas Naatz
Lake In The Hills *	v	MC	23	(847) 960-7400	Ed Plaza	Gerald Sagona	Denise Wasserman	Pete Stefan	. . .	. . .	Fred Mullard
Lake Zurich *	v	CM	18	(847) 438-5141	John Tolomei	Bob Vitas	Gloria Palmblad	Gerald Zochowski	T. Mastandrea	Patrick Finlon	Dave Heyden
Lakemoor	v	MC	2	(815) 385-1117	. . .	. . .	. . .	. . .	. . .	. . .	. . .
Lakewood *	v	CM	2	(815) 459-3025	Julie Richardson	Catherine Peterson	Janice Hansen	Carole Robertson	Tony Huemann	Lawrence Howell	Paul Ruscko
Lansing	v	MC	28	(708) 895-7200	. . .	. . .	. . .	. . .	. . .	. . .	. . .
Lawrenceville *	c	MC	4	(618) 943-2116	Brian Straub	. . .	Don Wagner	. . .	. . .	Mike Mefford	Roger Wimberly
Lebanon	c	MC	3	(618) 537-4976	Matthew Berberich	Tom Lenz	Pamela Koshko	. . .	Richard Rutherford	Michael Donovan	Penny Pinkstaff
Lemont *	v	MC	13	(630) 257-1590	John Piazza	Gary Holmes	Charlene Smollen	Jean Nona	. . .	Kevin Shaughnessy	Daniel Fielding
Leroy	c	MC	3	(309) 962-3031	Jane Engblom	. . .	Sue Marcum	. . .	. . .	. . .	. . .
Lewistown	c	MC	2	(309) 547-4300	Kendall Miller	. . .	Melodee Rudolph	. . .	. . .	Jeffrey Schnetzler	. . .
Libertyville	v	CM	20	(847) 362-2430	Jeffrey Harger	Kevin Bowens	Sally Kowalt	Patricia Wesolowski	Richard Carani	Patrick Carey	John Heinz
Lincoln *	c	MC	15	(217) 735-2815	Elizabeth Davis	. . .	Melanie Riggs	. . .	Kent Hulett	Stuart Erlenbush	Tracy Jackson
Lincolnshire *	v	CM	6	(847) 883-8600	Brett Blomberg	Robert Irvin	Barbara Mastandrea	Stanley Roelker	. . .	Randall Melvin	Frank Tripicchio
Lincolnwood	v	MC	12	(847) 673-1540	Peter Moy	Timothy Wiberg	Beryl Herman	Ronald Pfeiffer	Michael Hansen	Daniel Gooris	Manuel Castaneda
Lindenhurst	v	CM	12	(847) 356-8252	James Betustak	Matthew Formica	. . .	. . .	. . .	Jack McKeever	Wesley Welsh
Lisle *	v	MC	21	(630) 271-4100	Joseph Broda	Gerald Sprecher	Timothy Seeden	Kim Schiller	. . .	Michael Damico	Ray Peterson
Litchfield *	c	MC	6	(217) 324-5253	Thomas Jones	. . .	Marilyn Hartke	. . .	Matthew Weber	Bryon Wilkinson	Arthur Levoy
Lockport	c	MC	15	(815) 838-0549	Frank Mitchell	Tim Schloneger	Maria Esposito	Janice Colvin	. . .	Jim Antole	Mike Greenan
Lombard	v	CM	42	(630) 620-5700	William Mueller	David Hulseberg	. . .	Leonard Flood	George Seagraves	Raymond Byrne	Carl Goldsmith
Long Grove	v	CM	6	(847) 634-9440	Anthony Dean	David Lothspeich	Caroline Liebl	. . .	. . .	. . .	Robert Block
Loves Park *	c	MC	20	(815) 654-5030	Darryl Lindberg	. . .	Robert Burden	. . .	Philip Foley	Patrick Carrigan	Daniel Jacobson
Lynwood *	c	MC	7	(708) 758-6101	Eugene Williams	. . .	Roy Valle	. . .	. . .	David Palmer	Robert Myers
Lyons *	v	MC	10	(708) 447-8886	David Visk	Roy Witherow	Gary Benedik	Jason Hayden	Gordon Nord	Dan Babich	Alex Bojovic
Machesney Park	v	MC	20	(815) 877-5432	Linda Vaughn	Bob Mullins	Lori Mitchell	. . .	. . .	. . .	Paul Shepperd
Macomb	c	MC	18	(309) 833-2575	Mick Wisslead	Dean Torreson	Melanie Falk	. . .	Clarence John	Mike Galloway	Terry Wrestler
Madison	c	MC	4	(618) 876-6268	John Bellcoff	. . .	William Weidner	Jeanne Weidner	Charles Foley	Steven Skoklo	Robert Robbins
Mahomet *	v	CM	4	(217) 586-4456	Deb Braunig	Mell Smigielski	Cheryl Sproul	. . .	. . .	Jerry Gamble	. . .
Manhattan *	v	CM	3	(815) 418-2100	William Borgo	Marian Gibson	Mattie Becker	Kevin Sing	Dan Forsythe	William Fitzgerald	. . .
Manteno	v	CM	3	(815) 468-8224	Timothy Nugent	Craig Blanchette	Cheryl Moseley	. . .	. . .	Bernie Thompson	. . .
Marengo	c	MC	6	(815) 568-7112	Donald Lockhart	. . .	Diane Schwoch	. . .	. . .	Les Kottke	Donald Craney
Marion	c	MC	16	(618) 997-6281	Robert Butler	. . .	Diane Pritchett	. . .	Anthony Rinella	Gene Goolsby	. . .
Marissa	v	MC	2	(618) 295-2351	Steuart McClintock	. . .	Carol Smith	. . .	. . .	Michael Kerperien	William Yates
Markham	c	MC	12	(708) 331-4905	Evans Miller	. . .	Theresa Cannon	. . .	. . .	Eric Lymore	Daniel Costello
Marquette Heights	c	MC	2	(309) 382-3455	David Redfield	. . .	Ron Worrent	. . .	Ronald Smith	Roger Pentecost	Daniel Crum
Marseilles	c	CM	4	(815) 795-2133	. . .	. . .	. . .	. . .	. . .	. . .	. . .
Marshall	c	MC	3	(217) 826-2112	. . .	. . .	. . .	. . .	. . .	. . .	. . .
Maryville *	v	MC	4	(618) 345-7028	Larry Gulledge	. . .	Thelma Long	Marvin Brussatti	Kevin Flaugher	Richard Schardan	Patrick Presson
Mascoutah	c	CM	5	(618) 566-2965	Gerald Daugherty	Terry Draper	Kathleen Schuetz	Lynn Weidenbenner	Dean Juenger	. . .	Daniel Schrempp
Mason City *	c	MC	2	(217) 482-3669	David Knieriem	. . .	Karla Daubs	. . .	. . .	David Coulter	L. Dixon
Matteson	v	MC	12	(708) 283-4900	Mark Stricker	Lafayette Linear	Dorothy Grisco	Gregory Meyers	Edwin Wilkens	Norman Burnson	Vincent Laoang
Mattoon	c	CO	18	(217) 235-5654	David Carter	. . .	Susan O'Brien	. . .	Bruce Grafton	. . .	David Wortman
Maywood *	v	CM	26	(708) 450-6300	H. Yarbrough	Jason Ervin	Readith Ester	Lanya Satchell	John Cadagin	Elvia Williams	John West
Mc Cook *	v	MC	. .	(708) 447-9030	Jeffrey Tobolski	. . .	Charles Sobus	Renee Botica	Joseph Myrick	Frank Wolfe	Richard Paeth
Mc Henry	c	MC	21	(815) 363-2100	Susan Low	Douglas Maxeiner	Janice Jones	. . .	. . .	Thomas O'Meara	Jon Schmitt
Melrose Park	v	MC	23	(708) 343-4000	Ronald Serpico	. . .	Barbara Jasinski	John Gregor	James Cernauske	Vito Scavo	Ralph Tolomei
Mendota	c	MC	7	(815) 539-7459	Steve Bowne	. . .	Wendy Morris	. . .	Dennis Rutishauser	Tom Smith	Ken Arjes
Metropolis	c	MC	6	(618) 524-4016	Beth Clanahan	. . .	. . .	. . .	Michael Childers	. . .	. . .
Midlothian	v	MC	14	(708) 389-0200	Thomas Murawski	. . .	Michael Woike	Denise Borne	William Sheehy	Vincent Schavone	Richard Hansen
Milan	v	MC	5	(309) 787-8500	Duane Dawson	Steven Seiver	Barbara Lee	. . .	. . .	. . .	David Pannell
Millstadt	v	MC	2	(618) 476-1514	Alvin Mehrtens	Larry Toenses	Linda Lehr	. . .	Kurt Pellmann	Edward Wilkinson	Stan Jarvis
Minonk	c	MC	2	(309) 432-2558	Bill Koos	. . .	Jim Liner	. . .	. . .	William Butler	Charlie McGuire
Minooka	v	MC	3	(815) 467-2151	Jason Briscoe	James Grabowski	. . .	. . .	. . .	. . .	. . .
Mokena	v	CM	14	(708) 479-3900	Robert Chiszar	John Downs	Jane McGinn	Barbara Shryock	. . .	Stephen Pollak	Louis Tiberi
Moline	c	CM	43	(309) 797-0747	Donald Welvaert	Lewis Steinbrecher	Lynn Segura	Kathleen Carr	. . .	Gary Francque	Michael Waldron
Momence	c	MC	3	(815) 472-2001	. . .	. . .	. . .	. . .	. . .	. . .	. . .
Monee *	v	MC	2	(708) 534-8301	Timothy O'Donnell	. . .	Kathy Buchmeier	. . .	Carl Nieland	Russel Caruso	Ron Wolf
Monmouth	c	MC	9	(309) 734-2141	John Reitman	Eric Hanson	Susan Trevor	. . .	James Conard	Roger Johnson	. . .
Montgomery *	v	MC	5	(630) 896-8080	Marilyn Michelini	Anne Marie Gaura	Barbara Argo	Jeff Zoephel	. . .	Dennis Schmidt	Mike Pubentz
Monticello *	c	MC	5	(217) 762-2583	. . .	Floyd Allsop	. . .	. . .	Rick Dubson	John Miller	Gary Sebens
Morris	c	MC	11	(815) 942-0103	. . .	. . .	. . .	. . .	. . .	. . .	. . .
Morrison *	c	MC	4	(815) 772-7657	Roger Drey	Tim Long	Melanie Schroeder	. . .	. . .	Brian Melton	Gary Tresenriter
Morton	v	MC	15	(309) 266-5361	Norman Durflinger	David Strohl	Joseph Nohl	. . .	Joe Kelley	Nick Graff	Bob Wraight
Morton Grove	v	CM	22	(847) 965-4100	Richard Krier	Joe Wade	Carol Fritzshall	Scot Neukirch	Tom Friel	George Incledon	Andy DeMonte
Mount Carmel	c	CO	7	(618) 262-4822	George Woodcock	Merle Weems	Mark Bader	Michael Mollenhauer	Steve Partee	Jimmy Seaton	. . .
Mount Morris *	v	MC	3	(815) 734-6425	Gregory Unger	. . .	Paula Diehl	. . .	. . .	Jason White	. . .
Mount Prospect	v	CM	56	(847) 392-6000	Irvana Wilks	Michael Janonis	Lisa Angell	David Erb	Michael Figolah	John Dahlberg	Glen Andler
Mount Vernon *	c	CM	16	(618) 242-5000	Mary Chesley	Ronald Neibert	Jacqlyn Sharp	Merle Hollmann	James Brown	Chris Mendenall	Matthew Fauss
Mount Zion	v	CM	4	(217) 864-5424	Donald Robinson	Paul Ruff	Tammy Mense	. . .	. . .	Douglas Dunn	Jerry Potts
Mundelein	v	MC	30	(847) 949-3200	Marilyn Sindles	John Lobaito	Pamela Keeney	. . .	Randy Justus	Raymond Rose	Kenneth Miller
Murphysboro	c	MC	13	(618) 684-4961	Ron Williams	Gene Biby	. . .	. . .	Kevin Reeves	Jeff Bock	Dale Noble
Naperville	c	CM	128	(630) 420-6111	A. Pradel	. . .	Suzanne Gagner	Doug Krieger	John Wu	David Dial	David Van Vooren
Nashville	c	MC	3	(618) 327-3058	Raymond Kolweier	. . .	Lloyd Dinkelman	. . .	Alan Hohlt	James Shew	Thomas McFeron
New Baden *	v	MC	3	(618) 588-3813	Timothy Hoerchler	Robert Nielsen	Teri Crane	. . .	. . .	Mike Riley	Ron Renth
New Lenox	v	MC	17	(815) 485-6452	Michael Smith	Lewis Loebe	Marcia Englert	K. Auchstetter	. . .	Dan Martin	Ronald Sly
Newton	c	MC	3	(618) 783-8451	Ross McClane	. . .	Jean Ghast	. . .	. . .	Mike Swick	. . .
Niles *	v	CM	30	(847) 588-8000	Nicholas Blase	George Van Geem	Marlene Victorine	Scot Neukirch	Barry Mueller	Dean Strzelecki	Scott Jochim

Directory 1/9 continued — OFFICIALS IN U.S. MUNICIPALITIES 2,500 AND OVER IN POPULATION

Jurisdiction		Type	Form of govern-ment	2000 Popu-lation	Main telephone number	Chief elected official	Appointed administrator	Clerk of the governing board	Chief financial officer	Fire chief	Police chief	Public works director
ILLINOIS continued												
Nokomis		c	MC	2	(217) 563-2514	Joseph Gasparich	. . .	Mary Scheller	Joe Murphy	. . .	Thomas Kearns	Terry Hill
Normal	*	t	CM	45	(309) 454-2444	Christopher Koos	Mark Peterson	Wendellyn Briggs	Ronald Hill	Leland Watson	Kent Crutcher	Michael Hall
Norridge		v	MC	14	(708) 453-0800	Earl Field	. . .	J. Dunne Bernardi	. . .	. . .	Charles Ghiloni	. . .
North Aurora		v	MC	10	(630) 897-8228	Mark Ruby	Susan McLaughlin	. . .	Margaret Dolasinski	. . .	Thomas Fetzer	Michael Glock
North Chicago		c	MC	35	(847) 596-8600	Leon Rockingham	Deborah Waszak	Lori Collins	John Gantz	Theodore Wilder	Michael Newsome	. . .
North Riverside		v	MC	6	(708) 447-4211	Richard Scheck	Guy Belmonte	Charmaine Kutt	. . .	Raymond Martinek	Anthony Garvey	Tim Kutt
Northbrook		v	CM	33	(847) 272-5050	Mark Damisch	Richard Nahrstadt	Lona Lovis	Jeff Rowitz	James Reardon	. . .	James Reynolds
Northfield	*	v	CM	5	(847) 446-9200	John Birkinbine	Stacy Sigman	. . .	Steve Noble	Michael Nystrand	William Lustig	. . .
Northlake		c	CM	11	(708) 343-8700	Jeffrey Sherwin	. . .	Joanne Floistad	William Kabler	. . .	Dennis Koletsos	Dale Roberts
Oak Brook	*	v	CM	8	(630) 368-5000	John Craig	David Niemeyer	Charlotte Pruss	Darrell Langlois	James Bodony	Thomas Sheahan	Michael Hullihan
Oak Forest	*	c	MC	28	(708) 687-4050	JoAnn Kelly	John Marquart	Scott Burkhardt	Colleen Julian	Terry Lipinski	Dave DeMarco	Troy Ishler
Oak Lawn		v	CM	55	(708) 636-4400	Ernest Kolb	Larry Deetjen	Alice Powers	Gail Paul	Thomas Moran	Robert Smith	. . .
Oak Park	*	tp	CM	52	(708) 383-8005	F. Boulanger	Gavin Morgan	Gregory White	. . .	. . .	. . .	. . .
Oak Park		v	CM	52	(708) 383-6400	. . .	Thomas Barwin	Sandra Sokol	Gregory Peters	William Bell	Joseph Mendrick	John Wielebnicki
Oakbrook Terrace	*	c	CM	2	(630) 941-8300	Thomas Mazaika	Martin Bourke	Judith Leslie	. . .	. . .	Mark Collins	Craig Ward
O'Fallon	*	c	MC	21	(618) 624-4500	Gary Graham	Walter Denton	Philip Goodwin	Dean Rich	Brent Saunders	. . .	Dennis Sullivan
Oglesby		c	MC	3	(815) 883-3389	. . .	. . .	. . .	. . .	. . .	. . .	. . .
Olney	*	c	CM	8	(618) 395-7302	Tom Fehrenbacher	Randy Bukas	Belinda Henton	. . .	Norm Bissey	Rick Chaplin	. . .
Olympia Fields		v	MC	4	(708) 503-8000	Linzey Jones	David Mekarski	Jeffery Cohn	Cynthia Saenz	. . .	Jeff Chudwin	Joe Alexa
Oregon		c	CO	4	(815) 732-6321	James Barnes	. . .	Julienne Crowley	Howard Rattner	. . .	Thomas Miller	J. Dolan
Orland Hills	*	v	MC	6	(708) 349-6666	Kyle Hastings	John Daly	Mikki Burke	. . .	. . .	Thomas Scully	Micheal Worley
Orland Park	*	v	CM	51	(708) 403-6100	Daniel McLaughlin	Paul Grimes	David Maher	Annmarie Mampe	. . .	. . .	Peter Casey
Oswego		v	CM	13	(630) 554-3618	Craig Weber	Gary Adams	Jeanne Hoch	Mark Pries	. . .	Dwight Baird	Gerald Weaver
Ottawa		c	MC	18	(815) 433-0161	Robert Eschbach	. . .	Elizabeth Taylor	. . .	Richard Scott	Brian Zeilmann	. . .
Palatine	*	v	CM	65	(847) 358-7500	Rita Mullins	Reid Ottesen	Marg Duer	Paul Mehring	Norman Malcolm	John Koziol	Andrew Radetski
Palos Heights		c	MC	11	(708) 361-1800	Robert Straz	Daniel Nisavic	Mary Carik	. . .	. . .	George Yott	Gerald Martin
Palos Hills		c	MC	17	(708) 598-3400	Gerald Bennett	. . .	Rudy Mulderink	. . .	. . .	Paul Madigan	Dave Weakley
Palos Park		v	CM	4	(708) 671-3700	Carolyn Baca	Patricia Jones	Annette Mucha	. . .	. . .	Joseph Miller	Larry Miller
Pana		c	MC	5	(217) 562-3626	Larry Chaney	. . .	Terry Klein	. . .	Jerry Blackwell	Mike Harris	. . .
Paris		c	CM	9	(217) 465-7601	Craig Smith	Paul Ruff	Cathy Higgins	. . .	Herman Taylor	Ronald Humphrey	. . .
Park City		c	MC	6	(847) 623-5030	Steve Pannell	. . .	. . .	. . .	. . .	Michael Luff	. . .
Park Forest	*	v	CM	23	(708) 748-1112	John Ostenburg	Thomas Mick	Sheila McGann	Mary Dankowski	Bob Wilcox	Thomas Fleming	Kenneth Eyer
Park Ridge	*	c	CM	37	(847) 318-5200	Howard Frimark	James Hock	Betty Henneman	Diane Lembesis	Craig Gjelsten	Thomas Swoboda	Wayne Zingsheim
Pawnee		v	MC	2	(217) 625-2951	. . .	. . .	. . .	. . .	. . .	. . .	. . .
Paxton		c	MC	4	(217) 379-4022	James Kingston	. . .	Penny Stevens	Julie Burgess	Dennis Kingren	Robert Bane	Randall Haack
Pekin		c	CM	33	(309) 477-2300	Lyndell Howard	Dennis Kief	Sue McMillan	Robert Reis	John Janssen	Timothy Gillespie	. . .
Peoria		c	CM	112	(309) 494-8575	David Ransburg	Henry Holling	Mary Haynes	James Scroggins	Roy Modglin	John Stenson	S. Van Winkle
Peoria Heights		v	MC	6	(309) 686-2385	Earl Carter	Thomas Horstmann	Dyrke Maricle	. . .	Howard Gorman	Larry Hawkins	Kevin Mattlingly
Peotone		v	MC	3	(708) 258-3279	Richard Benson	George Gray	Donna Werner	. . .	John Young	Terry Budds	Thomas Blogg
Peru		c	MC	9	(815) 223-0061	Donald Baker	. . .	Judith Heuser	. . .	Russell Reed	Glenn Fredrickson	Donald Kowalczyk
Phoenix		v	MC	2	(708) 331-2636	Terry Wells	. . .	Johnnie Lane	. . .	Brandon Turner	Melvin Davis	Robert Matthews
Pinckneyville		c	CO	5	(618) 357-6916	Joseph Shirk	. . .	. . .	John Hammack	Jerry Smith	Paul Day	Fred Pabst
Pingree Grove	*	v	CM	. .	(847) 464-5533	. . .	Scott Hartman	. . .	Laura Pisarcik	. . .	. . .	. . .
Pittsfield	*	c	MC	4	(217) 285-4484	John Hayden	. . .	Cindy Prentice	. . .	Michael Braungardt	Dennis Jennings	. . .
Plainfield		v	CM	13	(815) 436-7093	Richard Rock	Christopher Minick	Susan Janick	. . .	. . .	Donald Bennett	Allen Persons
Plano		c	MC	5	(630) 552-8275	. . .	. . .	Deanna Brown	. . .	. . .	Steven Eaves	John McGinnis
Pontiac		c	CM	11	(815) 844-3396	Scott McCoy	Robert Karls	Sharon Dunham	. . .	Dennis McDugle	R. Newsome	Christopher Brock
Pontoon Beach	*	v	MC	5	(618) 931-6100	Harold Denham	. . .	Susan Daugherty	Scott Oney	Dan Kreher	Charles Luehmann	. . .
Posen		v	MC	4	(708) 385-0139	Kevin Whitney	. . .	Veronica Grabowski	George Klotz	Robert Steele	Terence Urbaniak	Patrick Griffin
Princeton		c	CO	7	(815) 875-2631	Keith Cain	Jeffrey Fiegenschuh	Clyde Wray	. . .	Terry Himes	Thomas Root	Steven Wright
Prospect Heights	*	c	CM	17	(847) 398-6070	Patrick Ludvigsen	Pamela Arrigoni	William Kearns	Barbara Barrera	. . .	Bruce Morris	Adam Boeche
Quincy	*	c	MC	40	(217) 228-4500	John Spring	Kenneth Cantrell	Virginia Hayden	Ann Scott	Scott Walker	Robert Copley	. . .
Rantoul		v	MC	12	(217) 893-1661	. . .	. . .	Jeremy Reale	Scot Brandon	Ken Waters	Paul Farber	G. Hazel
Red Bud		c	MC	3	(618) 282-2315	. . .	Pamela Kempfer	. . .	. . .	. . .	Theodore Stellhorn	David Diewald
Richmond	*	v	MC	1	(815) 678-4040	Lauri Olson	Timothy Savage	. . .	. . .	. . .	John Fryksdale	. . .
Richton Park		v	CM	12	(708) 481-8950	. . .	Motiryo Keambiroiro	. . .	Constance Hoger	Michael Spain	. . .	. . .
River Forest	*	v	CM	11	(708) 366-8500	Frank Paris	Steven Gutierrez	Catherine Adduci	Chris Soriano	James Eggert	Frank Limon	Gregory Kramer
River Grove		v	MC	10	(708) 453-8000	Marilynn May	. . .	Joseph Compell	Frank Calistro	Loren Lariviere	Rodger Loni	Brent Leder
Riverdale	*	v	MC	15	(708) 841-2200	Zenovia Evans	William Cooper	F. Richard-Bey	. . .	Gregory Knoll	Greg Baker	Donald Blacher
Riverside	*	v	CM	8	(708) 447-2700	Harold Wiaduck	Kathleen Rush	Arlene Blaha	Kevin Wachtel	Kevin Mulligan	Tom Weitzel	. . .
Riverton		v	MC	3	(217) 629-9122	Joe Rusciolelli	. . .	Connie Blissett	. . .	. . .	David Smith	Charles Stone
Riverwoods		v	MC	3	(847) 945-3990	. . .	. . .	. . .	. . .	. . .	Morris Weinstein	Russell Kraly
Robbins	*	v	CM	6	(708) 385-8940	Irene Brodie	Beverly Gavin	Pamela Bradley	. . .	Charles Lloyd	Johnnie Holmes	Charles Calhoun
Robinson		c	MC	6	(618) 544-7616	Gary Davis	Laquita Hasty	Sandrea Jared	. . .	Darrell Akers	David Marqua	William Calvert
Rochelle		c	CM	9	(815) 562-6161	Chet Olson	Ken Alberts	Bruce McKinney	Bob Withrow	Thomas McDermott	Robbie Buck	. . .
Rochester	*	v	CM	2	(217) 498-7192	. . .	Dale Laningham	Maribeth Eandi	. . .	. . .	William Marass	Wayne Beck
Rock Falls	*	c	MC	9	(815) 564-1366	David Blanton	Richard Downey	William Wescott	. . .	James Larson	Michael Kuelper	. . .
Rock Island	*	c	CM	39	(309) 732-2000	Mark Schwiebert	John Phillips	Jeanne Paggen	William Scott	Jerry Shirk	Terrence Dove	Robert Hawes
Rockford	*	c	MC	150	(815) 987-5500	Lawrence Morrissey	James Ryan	. . .	Andres Sammul	Derek Bergsten	Chet Epperson	Tim Hanson
Rolling Meadows	*	c	CM	24	(847) 394-8500	Kenneth Nelson	Sarah Phillips	Lisa Hinman	James Egeberg	Philip Burns	Steve Williams	Fred Vogt
Romeoville		v	CM	21	(815) 886-7200	John Noak	Stephen Gulden	Ray Holloway	Kirk Openchowski	Kent Adams	Andrew Barto	Dan Bromberek
Roselle	*	v	CM	23	(630) 980-2000	Gayle Smolinski	Jeffrey O'Dell	Linda McDermott	Pamela Figolah	Robert Gallas	James Kruger	Robert Burns
Rosemont		v	MC	4	(847) 825-4404	. . .	. . .	. . .	. . .	. . .	. . .	. . .
Round Lake	*	v	MC	5	(847) 546-5400	Bill Gentes	Marc Huber	Jeanne Kristan	Steve Shields	. . .	Clifton Metaxa	Davis Clark
Round Lake Beach		v	MC	25	(847) 546-2351	Richard Hill	David Kilbane	Sylvia Valadez	Julian McDonough	Paul Maplethorpe	Douglas Larsson	Curtis Cashman
Round Lake Park		v	MC	6	(847) 546-2790	. . .	. . .	Linda Lucassen	Lee Howard	Paul Maplethorpe	Bruce Johnson	George Johnson
Rushville	*	c	MC	3	(217) 322-3833	Scott Thompson	. . .	Stacey Briney	. . .	Vic Menely	Rocky Root	Drew Seal
Salem	*	c	CM	7	(618) 548-2222	Leonard Ferguson	Thomas Christie	C. Jane Marshall	Marilyn Shetley	. . .	Ron Campo	John Pruden
Sandwich		c	MC	6	(815) 786-9321	Tom Thomas	. . .	Barbara Olson	Carmen Dixon	Richard Kell	Richard Olson	. . .
Sauk Village		v	MC	10	(708) 758-3330	Roger Peckham	Richard Dieterich	Elizabeth Selvey	Beverly Sterrett	Christopher Sewell	Thomas Lacheta	Michael Wall
Savanna	*	c	MC	3	(815) 273-2251	William Lease	. . .	Walter Shrake	. . .	Shawn Picolotti	Mike Moon	John Lindeman
Savoy		v	MC	4	(217) 359-5894	Robert McCleary	Richard Helton	Billie Krueger	Clarence Well	Michael Forrest	. . .	Frank Rentchler
Schaumburg		v	CM	75	(847) 895-4500	Al Larson	Kenneth Fritz	Marilyn Karr	Douglas Ellsworth	David Schumann	Richard Casler	Steven Weinstock
Schiller Park		v	MC	11	(847) 678-2550	Anna Montana	Kevin Barr	Claudia Irsuto	Kenneth Kowitz	Thomas Deegan	Robert Radak	Ronald Sieracki
Shelbyville		c	CO	4	(217) 774-5531	. . .	. . .	. . .	. . .	. . .	. . .	. . .
Shorewood	*	v	MC	7	(815) 725-2150	Richard Chapman	Kurt Carroll	Julia Russell	Sue Berg	Robert Schwartz	Robert Puleo	Roger Barrowman
Silvis		c	MC	7	(309) 792-9181	Lyle Lohse	. . .	Barbara Fox	. . .	David Leibovitz	William Hawbaker	James Grafton
Skokie	*	v	CM	63	(847) 673-0500	George Van Dusen	Albert Rigoni	Marlene Williams	Robert Nowak	Ralph Czerwinski	Barry Silverberg	Max Slankard
South Beloit		c	CO	5	(815) 389-3023	Randy Kirichkow	. . .	. . .	. . .	Kenneth Morse	Larry Schultz	. . .
South Chicago Heights		v	MC	3	(708) 755-1880	David Owen	Paul Peterson	Melinda Villarreal	. . .	Angelo Petrarca	Ronald Diederich	Tony Renzetti
South Elgin		v	CM	16	(847) 742-5780	Jim Hansen	Larry Jones	Margaret Gray	Arthur Skibley	. . .	Christopher Merritt	Chuck Behm
South Holland		v	MC	22	(708) 210-2900	Don DeGraff	J. Wynsma	. . .	. . .	James Wiley	Warren Millsaps	Chris Niehof
South Jacksonville		v	MC	3	(217) 245-4803	Gordon Jumper	Katherine Simpson	Linda Douglass	. . .	David Hickox	Richard Evans	John Green
Sparta		c	CO	4	(618) 443-2917	W. Baue	. . .	Shirley Reimer	. . .	Bruce Dahlem	Alan Young	. . .
Spring Valley		c	MC	5	(815) 664-4221	James Narczewski	. . .	Rebecca Hansen	. . .	Gene Scheri	Michael Miroux	John Schultz
Springfield		c	MC	111	(217) 789-2000	Timothy Davlin	. . .	Cecilia Langford	Thomas Langford	Ronald Hasara	Donald Kliment	Richard Berning

Directory 1/9 continued **OFFICIALS IN U.S. MUNICIPALITIES 2,500 AND OVER IN POPULATION**

Jurisdiction	Type	Form of govern-ment	2000 Popu-lation	Main telephone number	Chief elected official	Appointed administrator	Clerk of the governing board	Chief financial officer	Fire chief	Police chief	Public works director
ILLINOIS continued											
St. Charles *	c	MC	27	(630) 377-4400	Donald Dewitte	Brian Townsend	Nancy Garrison	Christopher Minick	Patrick Mullen	James Lamkin	Mark Koenen
Staunton *	c	MC	5	(618) 635-2233	Fred Stein	. . .	Marilyn Herbeck	. . .	Rick Haase	Robert Mertz	Hank Fey
Steger	v	CM	9	(708) 754-3395	Louis Sherman	Conrad Kiebles	Carmen Recupito	. . .	Elmer Joyce	Richard Stultz	John Gilkison
Sterling *	c	CM	15	(815) 632-6621	Amy Viering	Scott Shumard	Marie Rombouts	Cindy Wilson	Arlyn Oetting	Ronald Potthoff	Vernon Gottel
Stickney	v	MC	6	(708) 749-4400	. . .	. . .	. . .	. . .	. . .	. . .	. . .
Stone Park	v	MC	5	(708) 345-5550	. . .	Guiseppe Capece	Maria Castrejon	. . .	Brian Lewis	. . .	Jim Chillemi
Streamwood	v	CM	36	(630) 837-0200	Billie Roth	Gary O'Rourke	Kittie Kopitke	David Richardson	John Nixon	Alan Popp	John White
Streator	c	CM	14	(815) 672-2517	Raymond Schmitt	Paul Nicholson	Pamela Leonard	. . .	William Wissen	Jeffery Anderson	Ralph Hermann
Sugar Grove *	v	CM	3	(630) 466-4507	Sean Michels	Brent Eichelberger	Cynthia Welsch	Justin VanVooren	. . .	Bradley Sauer	Anthony Speciale
Sullivan *	c	CO	4	(217) 728-4383	Leon Lane	. . .	G. Sides	. . .	Mike Piper	John Love	. . .
Summit	v	MC	10	(708) 563-4800	Joseph Strzelczyk	. . .	Andrew Zambrycki	. . .	John Nemeth	Chuck Wasko	Dan Trapp
Swansea *	v	MC	10	(618) 234-0044	Charles Gray	John Openlander	Lauren O'Neill	. . .	John McGuire	Michael Arnold	John Budde
Sycamore	c	MC	12	(815) 895-0786	Ken Mundy	F. Nicklas	Candace Smith	. . .	William Riddle	Donald Thomas	Fred Busse
Taylorville	c	MC	11	(217) 287-7946	J. Montgomery	. . .	Pam Peabody	Nancy France	Charles Doherty	Gregory Brotherton	Denny Macke
Thornton	v	MC	2	(708) 877-4456	Jack Swan	Jason Wicha	Cheryl Bult	. . .	Brian Kolosh	Norbert Schlesser	Ronald Bannon
Thornton *	tp	MC	180	(708) 596-6040	Frank Zuccarelli	Deborah Kopec	J. Davis-Rivera	. . .	. . .	. . .	. . .
Tinley Park *	v	MC	48	(708) 444-5000	Edward Zabrocki	Scott Niehaus	Frank German	. . .	Kenneth Dunn	Michael O'Connell	Dale Schepers
Trenton *	c	MC	2	(618) 224-7323	Robert Koentz	. . .	Carol Gajewski	Karen Buzzard	. . .	Michael Jones	Roger Maue
Troy	c	MC	8	(618) 667-9924	Thomas Caraker	R. Klaustermeier	Mary Chasteen	. . .	. . .	. . .	Alan Secrest
Tuscola	c	MC	4	(217) 253-2112	Daniel Kleiss	James Hoel	Beth Leamon	. . .	Steve Hettinger	Craig Hastings	Denny Cruzman
University Park	v	CM	6	(708) 534-6451	Alvin McCowan	. . .	Dorothy Jones	David Sevier	. . .	Melvin Easley	Ben Adcock
Urbana	c	MC	36	(217) 384-2458	Tod Satterthwaite	. . .	Phyllis Clark	Ronald Eldridge	Rex Mundt	Eddie Adair	William Gray
Vandalia *	c	MC	6	(618) 283-1196	Ricky Gottman	Jimmy Morani	Peggy Bowen	. . .	Merle Adermann	Robert McCart	John Moyer
Venice	c	MC	2	(618) 877-2412	Tyrone Echols	. . .	Wilbert Glasper	Jacob Young	Thomas Brent	James Newsome	Anthony Matthews
Vernon Hills	v	CM	20	(847) 367-3700	Roger Byrne	Michael Allison	. . .	Larry Nafrin	. . .	Mark Fleischhauer	E. Laudenslager
Villa Grove	c	MC	2	(217) 832-4721	Ronald Hunt	. . .	Brandy Hopkins	. . .	Ross Elston	Dennis Gire	Steven Duke
Villa Park	v	CM	22	(630) 834-8500	. . .	Robert Niemann	. . .	Eric Dubrowski	Robert Wilson	Ronald Ohlson	Vydas Juskelis
Virden	c	MC	3	(217) 965-5805	. . .	. . .	. . .	. . .	. . .	. . .	. . .
Wadsworth *	v	MC	3	(847) 336-7771	Glenn Ryback	Moses Amidei	Evelyn Hoselton	. . .	. . .	. . .	. . .
Warrenville	c	CM	13	(630) 393-9427	Vivian Lund	John Coakley	Emily Larson	. . .	. . .	Robert La Deur	. . .
Washington	c	MC	10	(309) 444-3196	Gary Manier	Robert Morris	Carol Moss	Joan Baxter	. . .	William Witmer	. . .
Washington Park	v	MC	5	(618) 874-2040	Robert Moore	L. Cannon-Connor	C. Hollingsworth	Sherman Sorrell	James Brown	Johnnie Matt	Lee McNatt
Waterloo	c	MC	7	(618) 939-8600	Thomas Smith	. . .	Barbara Pace	Shawn Kennedy	. . .	James Trantham	Timothy Birk
Watseka	c	MC	5	(815) 432-2711	. . .	. . .	. . .	. . .	. . .	. . .	. . .
Wauconda *	v	MC	9	(847) 526-9600	S. Saccomanno	Daniel Quick	Mary Taylor	Zaida Torres	David Dato	. . .	David Geary
Waukegan	c	MC	87	(847) 599-2500	Richard Hyde	Raymond Vukovich	Wayne Motley	Lyndon Bruessel	Patrick Gallagher	William Biang	William Johnston
West Chicago	c	CM	23	(630) 293-2200	Michael Fortner	Michael Guttman	Nancy Smith	Linda Martin	. . .	Gerald Mourning	Robert Flatter
West Dundee	v	CM	5	(847) 551-3800	Larry Keller	Joseph Cavallaro	Barbara Haines	David Danielson	Larry McManaman	Edward Dennis	Richard Monas
West Frankfort	c	MC	8	(618) 932-3262	Marion Presley	. . .	Janice Biggs	Christopher McPhail	Wes Taylor	Michael Dinn	. . .
West Peoria	c	MC	4	(309) 674-1993	James Dillon	John Carlson	Carole Stephens	Diana Jarbo	. . .	. . .	Henry Strube
Westchester *	v	CM	16	(708) 345-0020	Paul Gattuso	. . .	Kathryn Hayes	. . .	Richard Belmonte	Matt Evans	Russell Gross
Western Springs	v	CM	12	(708) 246-1800	John Lynch	Patrick Higgins	Jeanine Jasica	. . .	Frank Benak	William Rypkema	. . .
Westmont *	v	CM	24	(630) 981-6200	William Rahn	Ronald Searl	Virginia Szymski	Lisa Van Bogget	Frank Trout	James Ramey	Steve May
Westville	v	MC	3	(217) 267-2507	. . .	. . .	. . .	. . .	. . .	Jeff Keeling	. . .
Wheaton	c	CM	55	(630) 260-2000	C. James Carr	Donald Rose	Emily Consolazio	Mark Horton	Greg Berk	Mark Field	Joseph Knippen
Wheeling *	v	CM	34	(847) 459-2600	Dean Argiris	J. Rooney	Elaine Simpson	M. Mondschain	Keith MacIsaac	John Stone	Anthony Stavros
White Hall	c	MC	2	(217) 374-2345	Harold Brimm	. . .	Sue Reno	. . .	Garry Sheppard	Robert McMillen	Jay Howard
Willow Springs	v	MC	5	(708) 467-3700	Alan Nowaczyk	Bruce Trego	Sue Fredrickson	. . .	Larry Moran	Roger Alexander	James Chevalier
Willowbrook *	v	MC	8	(630) 323-8215	Robert Napoli	Philip Modaff	Leroy Hansen	Sue Stanish	. . .	Edward Konstanty	Tim Halik
Wilmette *	v	CM	27	(847) 251-2700	Christopher Canning	Timothy Frenzer	Terrence Porter	Robert Amoruso	James Dominik	George Carpenter	Donna Jakubowski
Wilmington	c	MC	5	(815) 476-2175	Roy Strong	Sheryl Puracchio	. . .	Robin Theobald	. . .	Wally Evans	Gary Van Duyne
Winfield	v	CM	8	(630) 933-7100	John Kirschbaum	. . .	. . .	. . .	. . .	Douglas Riner	Tye Loomis
Winnetka	v	CM	12	(847) 501-6000	Michael Duhl	Douglas Williams	. . .	Edward McKee	Scott Smith	Joseph DeLopez	Steven Saunders
Winthrop Harbor	v	MC	6	(847) 872-3846	Robert Loy	. . .	Jana Lee	. . .	Michael Stried	Joel Brumlik	John Hogan
Wood Dale	c	CM	13	(630) 766-4900	Kenneth Johnson	F. Douthwaite	Shirley Siebert	Robert Broznowski	. . .	. . .	Craig Wright
Wood River	c	CM	11	(618) 251-3100	David Ayres	. . .	Janet Sneed	Nancy Schneider	Steve Alexander	Jim Schneider	Steve Palen
Woodridge *	v	MC	30	(630) 852-7000	William Murphy	John Perry	Eileene Nystrom	Deborah Freischlag	. . .	Steven Herron	Christopher Bethel
Woodstock	c	CM	20	(815) 338-4300	Brian Sager	Timothy Clifton	Meghan Haak	Roscoe Stelford	. . .	Robert Lowen	John Isbell
Worth	v	MC	11	(708) 448-1181	Edward Guzdziol	. . .	Bonnie Price	. . .	Donald Stefaniak	Patrick O'Connor	W. Demonbreun
Yorkville	c	MC	6	(630) 553-4350	Arthur Prochaska	B. McLaughlin	Jackie Milschewski	Traci Pleckham	. . .	Harold Martin	Eric Dhuse
Zion	c	CO	22	(847) 746-4000	Lane Harrison	. . .	Judy Mackey	. . .	David Labelle	Larry Booth	Ron Colangelo
INDIANA											
Albany *	t	MC	2	(765) 789-6112	Phil Evans	. . .	Marcie Schlosser	. . .	Phil Bebout	Shannon Henry	. . .
Alexandria	c	MC	6	(765) 724-2541	Steve Skaggs	. . .	. . .	Janet Lynch	Mike Hensley	Jack Malston	. . .
Anderson	c	MC	59	(765) 646-9685	J. Lawler	. . .	Marie Riggs	Morris Long	Jerry Quire	Ronald Rheam	Wilbur Miller
Angola	c	MC	7	(260) 665-2514	Richard Hickman	. . .	Debra Twitchell	. . .	Raymond Meek	Jon Parrish	. . .
Attica	c	MC	3	(765) 762-2467	Harold Long	. . .	Tracy Smith	. . .	Jack O'Farrell	Timothy Quinn	Robert Smith
Auburn	c	MC	12	(260) 925-6450	Norman Yoder	. . .	Rebecca Fuller	. . .	Jerry Bauermeister	Martin McCoy	. . .
Aurora	c	MC	3	(812) 926-1777	Richard Ullrich	. . .	Richard Eaglin	. . .	. . .	Noel Houze	. . .
Austin	t	MC	4	(812) 794-2877	. . .	. . .	. . .	. . .	. . .	. . .	. . .
Avon	t	MC	6	(317) 272-0948	. . .	Thomas Klein	. . .	. . .	. . .	Jeff Ritorto	Ryan Canion
Batesville *	c	MC	6	(812) 933-6100	Rick Fledderman	. . .	Michele Balser	. . .	Todd Schutte	Stan Holt	. . .
Bedford	c	MC	13	(812) 279-6555	John Williams	. . .	Donna Brumbaugh	. . .	Carl Beauchamp	Dave Jarrard	John Dalton
Beech Grove	c	MC	14	(317) 788-4975	J. Wiley	. . .	. . .	Richard Brown	Dennis Buckley	Michael Johnson	Philip Gurganus
Berne	c	MC	4	(260) 589-8526	Blaine Fulton	. . .	Gwendolyn Maller	. . .	Armando Velasco	Richard Crider	. . .
Bicknell	c	MC	3	(812) 735-4636	Gordon Stinebaugh	. . .	Cindi Parkhill	. . .	Wayne Bement	Jeff Chambers	. . .
Bloomington	c	MC	69	(812) 339-2261	John Fernandez	James McNamara	Regina Moore	Thomas Guevara	Jeffrey Barlow	Michael Hostetler	John Freeman
Bluffton *	c	MC	9	(260) 824-0612	Ted Ellis	. . .	. . .	Tamara Runyon	David Brinneman	Tamera Schaffer	. . .
Boonville	c	MC	6	(812) 897-1230	Pamela Henrickson	. . .	. . .	. . .	Steven Byers	Roy Harmon	. . .
Brazil	c	MC	8	(812) 443-2221	Kenneth Crabb	. . .	Ruth Mohr	Carolyn Latham	Robert Bennett	Terry Harrison	James Sheese
Bremen *	t	MC	4	(574) 546-2471	Thomas Keller	. . .	Janet Anglemyer	. . .	Jerry Lanning	Matthew Hassel	. . .
Brookville	t	CO	2	(765) 647-3322	Michael Biltz	. . .	. . .	. . .	. . .	Bruce Baker	. . .
Brownsburg	t	CM	14	(317) 852-1120	Mike Green	Mark White	Jeanette Brickler	. . .	William Rosemeyer	David Galloway	. . .
Brownstown	t	MC	2	(812) 358-5500	Leroy Warren	. . .	Rebecka Stovall	. . .	. . .	Paul Starr	. . .
Butler *	c	MC	2	(260) 868-5200	Floyd Coburn	William Miller	. . .	. . .	Brian Moore	James Nichols	Ron Walter
Carmel	c	MC	37	(317) 571-2400	James Brainard	. . .	. . .	. . .	Douglas Callahan	Michael Fogarty	John Duffy
Cedar Lake *	t	CM	9	(219) 374-7000	Dennis Wilkening	Ian Nicolini	Amy Sund	. . .	Todd Wilkening	Roger Patz	Edward Robinson
Chandler *	t	CM	3	(812) 925-6882	Donald Wilkey	. . .	. . .	. . .	. . .	Marlin Weisheit	Robert Coghill
Charlestown	c	MC	5	(812) 256-7126	George Hall	James Knoebel	. . .	. . .	. . .	Ernest Crumpton	. . .
Chesterfield	t	RT	2	(765) 378-3331	Don Carpenter	Chris Parrish	. . .	. . .	Gary Hutton	Moses Beeman	. . .
Chesterton	t	RT	10	(219) 926-1641	. . .	. . .	. . .	. . .	. . .	. . .	. . .
Cicero	t	MC	4	(317) 984-4900	Michael Mauro	. . .	Janice Unger	. . .	Steven Peachey	Garry Cook	Jerry Cook
Clarksville	t	CO	21	(812) 283-1504	John Minta	. . .	. . .	. . .	. . .	. . .	. . .
Clinton	c	MC	5	(765) 832-9880	Ronald Shepard	. . .	. . .	. . .	Tim Cottrell	Paul Curry	. . .

Directory 1/9 continued — OFFICIALS IN U.S. MUNICIPALITIES 2,500 AND OVER IN POPULATION

Jurisdiction	Type	Form of govern-ment	2000 Popu-lation	Main telephone number	Chief elected official	Appointed administrator	Clerk of the governing board	Chief financial officer	Fire chief	Police chief	Public works director
INDIANA continued											
Cloverdale	t	MC	2	(765) 795-6033	. . .	. . .	. . .	. . .	. . .	. . .	. . .
Columbia City	c	MC	7	(260) 244-5141	. . .	. . .	. . .	. . .	. . .	. . .	. . .
Columbus	c	MC	39	(812) 376-2570	Fred Armstrong	. . .	John Baughn	. . .	Gary Henderson	Matthew McCord	James Norris
Connersville	c	MC	15	(765) 825-4211	Max Ellison	. . .	. . .	. . .	James Bennett	Jim Holbrook	. . .
Corydon *	t	MC	2	(812) 738-3958	Fred Cammack	. . .	. . .	Janet Frederick	Tony Ross	Richard Yetter	. . .
Covington	c	MC	2	(765) 793-3423	Bradley Crain	Richard Rennick	Debby Gurley	. . .	Richard Talbert	Tony Knecht	. . .
Crawfordsville	c	MC	15	(765) 364-5150	John Zumer	. . .	Nellie Thompson	. . .	Todd Barton	Kurt Knecht	. . .
Crown Point	c	MC	19	(219) 662-3235	Daniel Klein	. . .	Patti Olson	. . .	Gary Huys	Keith Hefner	Jay Olson
Cumberland	t	MC	5	(317) 894-3580	Sandra Cottey	D. Sheridan	Linda Jeter	. . .	. . .	Michael Crooke	Arthur Gale
Danville	t	CM	6	(317) 745-3001	Myron Anderson	Gary Eakin	Paula Frye	. . .	Mark Morgan	Garry Edwards	Rob Roberts
De Motte	t	MC	3	(219) 987-3831	. . .	John Dyke	. . .	. . .	. . .	William Arnold	Dick Higgins
Decatur	c	MC	9	(260) 724-7171	. . .	. . .	. . .	. . .	. . .	. . .	. . .
Dunkirk	c	MC	2	(765) 768-6565	Thomas Johnson	. . .	. . .	Jane Kesler	Steve Fields	Arnold Clevenger	. . .
Dyer *	t	MC	13	(219) 865-6108	Dennis Hawrot	Joseph Neeb	. . .	Tom Hoffman	Jeff Zendzian	Donald Horvat	Jay Steinmetz
East Chicago *	c	MC	32	(219) 391-8200	George Pabey	. . .	Mary Leonard	Charles Pacurar	Valentin Gomez	Angelo Machuca	. . .
Edinburg	t	CM	4	(812) 526-3512	Bill Davis	. . .	Jackie Smith	. . .	Allen Smith	Patrick Pankey	John Drybread
Elkhart	c	MC	51	(574) 294-5471	David Miller	. . .	Sue Beadle	Clara Mishler	William Johnson	Pamela Westlake	Eric Horvath
Ellettsville *	t	RT	5	(812) 876-3860	Dan Swafford	. . .	. . .	Sandra Hash	Jim Davis	Tony Bowlen	Mike Farmer
Elwood	c	MC	9	(765) 552-5076	Jerry Werline	. . .	. . .	. . .	Milt Gough	Tom Elder	. . .
Evansville	c	MC	121	(812) 436-4934	. . .	. . .	. . .	. . .	. . .	. . .	. . .
Fairmount	t	TM	2	(765) 948-4632	Melba Root	. . .	. . .	. . .	Rick Clevenger	Brian Reneau	. . .
Ferdinand	t	MC	2	(812) 367-2280	. . .	Marc Steczyk	. . .	. . .	. . .	. . .	. . .
Fishers *	t	CM	37	(317) 595-3111	Scott Faultless	Gary Huff	. . .	Linda Cordell	Kenneth Lay	George Kehl	. . .
Fort Branch	t	CM	2	(812) 753-3824	. . .	. . .	. . .	. . .	. . .	. . .	. . .
Fort Wayne	c	MC	205	(260) 427-1111	Graham Richard	Greg Purcell	Sandra Kennedy	Alvin Moll	Timothy Davie	Russell York	Gregory Meszaros
Fortville *	t	CM	3	(317) 485-4044	Sean Simmons	. . .	Boyd Mitchell	. . .	. . .	Ben Kiphart	Tony Shaw
Frankfort	c	MC	16	(765) 654-5715	Roy Scott	. . .	. . .	Marilyn Chittick	Charles Toney	William Moudy	. . .
Franklin	c	MC	19	(317) 736-3609	Norman Blankenship	Norma Brewer	Janet Alexander	. . .	Michael Herron	John Borges	Rick Littleton
Garrett	c	MC	5	(260) 357-3836	. . .	. . .	. . .	. . .	. . .	. . .	. . .
Gary	c	MC	102	(219) 881-1300	Scott King	Geraldine Tousant	Suzette Raggs	Husain Mahmoud	Robert Walker	Garnett Watson	. . .
Gas City	c	MC	5	(765) 677-3080	Eugene Linn	. . .	. . .	. . .	David Linn	James Cassidy	. . .
Goshen	c	MC	29	(574) 533-8621	Allan Kauffman	Jolinda Fradenburg	. . .	Nancy Hoke	John Alheim	Michael Kettlebar	. . .
Greencastle	c	MC	9	(765) 653-9211	Nancy Michael	. . .	. . .	Pamela Jones	Bill Newgent	Tom Sutherlin	. . .
Greendale	c	CM	4	(812) 537-2125	Douglas Hedrick	Steven Lampert	Mary Lynch	. . .	Edwin Noel	DeWayne Uhlman	. . .
Greenfield	c	MC	14	(317) 477-4310	Patricia Elmore	. . .	Larry Breese	. . .	Lewis McQueen	Rick Hoy	. . .
Greensburg	c	MC	10	(812) 663-8582	Frank Manus	. . .	. . .	L. June Ryle	Scott Chasteen	Bill Meyerose	. . .
Greenwood *	c	MC	36	(317) 887-5604	Charles Henderson	. . .	Jeannine Myers	. . .	Steven Dhondt	Joseph Pitcher	. . .
Griffith	t	MC	17	(219) 924-7500	Stan Dobosz	. . .	Ronald Szafarczyk	. . .	. . .	Ronald Kottka	Rick Konopasek
Hammond	c	MC	83	(219) 853-6300	Thomas McDermott	. . .	Gerald Bobos	Tony Bonaventura	Louis Covelli	John Cory	Thomas Golfis
Hanover	t	MC	2	(812) 866-2131	Debbie Kroger	. . .	Lucy Anderson	. . .	. . .	Marshal Lovins	. . .
Hartford City	c	MC	6	(765) 348-0412	. . .	. . .	. . .	. . .	. . .	. . .	. . .
Hebron	t	MC	3	(219) 996-4641	Peter Breuckman	. . .	. . .	. . .	David Wilson	Steven Sibbrell	Steven Martin
Highland	t	MC	23	(219) 838-1080	Daniel Dernulc	. . .	. . .	. . .	William Timmer	Peter Hojnicki	John Bach
Hobart	c	MC	25	(219) 942-1940	Linda Buzinec	. . .	. . .	. . .	William McCorkle	Robert Paulson	Tony Boren
Huntingburg	c	MC	5	(812) 683-2211	Gail Kemp	. . .	. . .	Thomas Ellsworth	Glen Kissling	Ron Bowling	. . .
Huntington	c	MC	17	(260) 356-1400	. . .	. . .	. . .	. . .	. . .	. . .	. . .
Indianapolis–Marion County	c	MC	731	(317) 327-5200	Bart Peterson	. . .	Jean Milharcic	Robert Clifford	Louis Dezelan	Michael Spears	Kumar Menon
Jasper	c	MC	12	(812) 482-4255	. . .	. . .	. . .	. . .	. . .	. . .	. . .
Jeffersonville	c	MC	27	(812) 285-6405	Thomas Galligan	. . .	Peggy Wilder	. . .	Charles Smith	Michael Pavey	. . .
Kendallville	c	MC	9	(260) 347-2452	Suzanne Handshoe	. . .	Marsha Kiersey	. . .	Michael Riehm	Kevin Jones	. . .
Knox	c	MC	3	(574) 772-4553	. . .	. . .	. . .	. . .	. . .	. . .	. . .
Kokomo *	c	MC	46	(765) 456-7470	Matt McKillip	Randy Morris	Brenda Ott	Phillip Williams	Patrick Donoghue	Thomas Dinardo	Joseph Ewing
La Porte	c	MC	21	(219) 362-8220	. . .	. . .	. . .	Teresa Ludlow	Andy Snyder	David Gariepy	. . .
Lafayette	c	MC	56	(765) 807-1000	Tony Roswarski	. . .	Cindy Murray	Michael Jones	James Morrow	James Roush	Jennifer Bonner
Lake Station *	c	MC	13	(219) 962-3111	Keith Soderquist	. . .	Brenda Samuels	. . .	Alan Janes	Michael Stills	Rueben Mendez
Lawrence	c	MC	38	(317) 549-4803	Thomas Schneider	. . .	. . .	Annetta Sweat	Mark Delong	Joseph Carter	Billy Gann
Lawrenceburg	c	MC	4	(812) 532-3553	W. Cunningham	Thomas Steidel	Jackie Stutz	. . .	Randy Abner	Bernard Hunefeld	Charles Davis
Lebanon *	c	MC	14	(765) 482-1201	John Lasley	. . .	Debra Ottinger	. . .	Ted Caldwell	Tom Garoffolo	. . .
Ligonier	c	MC	4	(574) 894-4113	Charles Musselman	. . .	Helen Gerke	. . .	Paul Pfenning	John Durham	. . .
Linton	c	MC	5	(812) 847-7754	Tommy Jones	. . .	. . .	. . .	Lonnie Eberhardt	Troy Jerrell	. . .
Logansport	c	MC	19	(574) 753-4745	Richard Hettinger	Richard Farrer	. . .	Ruth Helms	Ronald Holcomb	Patrick Shively	Klaus Hemberger
Loogootee	c	MC	2	(812) 295-3200	Brian Ader	. . .	. . .	Bettye Norris	. . .	Kelly Rayhill	. . .
Lowell	t	CM	7	(219) 696-7794	Ray Raszewski	Rick Dal Corobbo	Judith Walters	Marcia Carlson	Jack Eskridge	David Wilson	Michael Lush
Madison *	c	MC	12	(812) 265-8300	Albert Huntington	. . .	. . .	. . .	Steve Horton	Robert Wolf	. . .
Marion	c	MC	31	(765) 662-9931	William Henry	. . .	Kathi Kiley	Karen Browder	. . .	. . .	William McHaney
Markle *	t	MC	1	(260) 758-3193	Tamra Boucher	. . .	Carolyn Hamilton	. . .	Duane Brumbaugh	John Markley	Rick Asher
Martinsville	c	MC	11	(765) 342-6012	Shannon Buskirk	Roger Laymon	. . .	. . .	Timothy Fraker	Frans Hollanders	. . .
Mccordsville *	t	CM	1	(317) 335-3151	Barry Wood	Tonya Galbraith	. . .	. . .	. . .	Harold Rodgers	Ron Crider
Merrillville	t	CM	30	(219) 769-5711	Richard Hardaway	Timothy Brown	R. Ann Antich-Carr	. . .	Edward Yerga	Nicholas Bravos	Bruce Spires
Michigan City	c	MC	32	(219) 873-1400	Charles Oberlie	. . .	Thomas Fedder	John Schaefer	David Lamb	Bernhard Neitzel	Anthony Metzcus
Middletown	t	CM	2	(765) 354-2268	. . .	. . .	. . .	. . .	. . .	. . .	. . .
Mishawaka	c	MC	46	(574) 258-1600	. . .	. . .	Debbie Block	Edwina Kintner	Dale Freeman	Anthony Hazen	Philip Miller
Mitchell	c	MC	4	(812) 849-3831	Jerry Hancock	. . .	Mark Kern	. . .	Larry Caudell	Morris Chastain	. . .
Monticello	c	MC	5	(574) 583-5712	Mary Walters	. . .	. . .	. . .	Michael Keever	Kevin Harris	. . .
Mooresville	t	MC	9	(317) 831-1608	. . .	. . .	. . .	Sandra Perry	Leslie Farmer	Timothy Viles	Joe Beikman
Mount Vernon	c	MC	7	(812) 838-3317	Jackson Higgins	. . .	Cristi Wolfe	. . .	Roger Waters	Glenn Boyster	E. Stucki
Muncie	c	MC	67	(765) 747-4846	Daniel Canan	. . .	Ruth Dorer	M. Ann Kratochuil	Gary Lucas	Joseph Winkle	Michael Winkle
Munster *	t	CM	21	(219) 836-6900	Mike Mellon	Thomas DeGiulio	. . .	David Shafer	. . .	Nikola Panich	James Knesek
Nappanee	c	MC	6	(574) 773-2112	Larry Thompson	. . .	Kimberly Ingle	. . .	Donald Abel	Raymond Carich	. . .
New Albany *	c	MC	37	(812) 948-5333	Douglas England	Cheryl Cotner	Marcey Wisman	Kathlyn Garry	Matthew Juliot	Greg Crabtree	Matthew Denison
New Castle	c	MC	17	(765) 521-6803	. . .	. . .	. . .	. . .	. . .	. . .	. . .
New Chicago *	t	MC	2	(219) 962-1157	Roger Pelfrey	. . .	Lori Reno	. . .	Evin Eakins	Danny Sebben	. . .
New Haven	c	MC	12	(260) 748-7050	Terry McDonald	. . .	Paula Staak	Brenda Adams	John Bennett	Michael Sweet	David Jones
New Whiteland *	t	CM	4	(317) 535-9487	John Perrin	. . .	. . .	Maribeth Alspach	Brian Hedrick	Ed Stephenson	James Lasiter
Newburgh	t	CM	3	(812) 853-3578	. . .	Cynthia Burger	. . .	. . .	. . .	. . .	. . .
Noblesville	c	MC	28	(317) 776-6328	John Ditslear	Rusty Bodenhorn	. . .	. . .	Kenneth Gilliam	Richard Russell	. . .
North Manchester	t	MC	6	(260) 982-9800	Don Rinearson	Dan Hannaford	Miriah Tobias	. . .	Dan Renz	David Young	John Mugford
North Vernon	c	MC	6	(812) 346-5907	John Hall	. . .	Roger Short	. . .	Richard McGill	Jack Hatton	. . .
Oakland City *	c	MC	2	(812) 749-3222	Lee Ayers	. . .	Brena Willis	. . .	James Deffendall	Alec Hensley	. . .
Paoli	t	MC	3	(812) 723-2739	Johnny Henderson	. . .	Carolyn Clements	. . .	James Hickman	Ronald Shrout	. . .
Peru	c	MC	12	(765) 472-2344	Richard Blair	. . .	Jackquan Gray	. . .	Danny Sparks	William Raber	William Giornto
Petersburg	c	MC	2	(812) 354-8511	Jon Craig	. . .	Tammy Selby	. . .	Philip Taylor	Joe Hill	. . .
Plainfield *	t	MC	18	(317) 839-2561	Robin Brandgard	Richard Carlucci	Wes Bennett	. . .	Byron Anderson	Jeff Mitny	Jason Castetter
Plymouth	c	MC	9	(574) 936-2124	Jack Greenlee	. . .	Toni Hutchings	. . .	Wayne Smith	T. Chamberlin	. . .
Portage *	c	MC	33	(219) 762-7784	Olga Velazquez	. . .	. . .	Donna Pappas	William Lundy	Mark Becker	. . .

Directory 1/9 continued **OFFICIALS IN U.S. MUNICIPALITIES 2,500 AND OVER IN POPULATION**

Jurisdiction	Type	Form of govern-ment	2000 Popu-lation	Main telephone number	Chief elected official	Appointed administrator	Clerk of the governing board	Chief financial officer	Fire chief	Police chief	Public works director
INDIANA continued											
Porter	t	CM	4	(219) 926-2771	. . .	. . .	. . .	. . .	Lewis Craig	James Spanier	Karl Bauer
Portland	c	MC	6	(260) 726-9395	James Hedges	. . .	Barbara Blackford	. . .	Michael Thomas	Bart Darby	. . .
Princeton	c	MC	8	(812) 385-4428	George Taylor	. . .	Shirley Robb	. . .	Robert Embree	Nick Michas	. . .
Rensselaer *	c	MC	5	(219) 866-5212	Herbert Arihood	Donna Cochran	Frieda Bretzinger	. . .	Le Moyne Koehler	Jeff Phillips	. . .
Richmond *	c	MC	39	(765) 983-7200	Sally Hutton	. . .	Karen Chasteen	Tammy Glenn	Michael Crawley	Kris Wolski	Greg Stiens
Roanoke	t	MC	1	(260) 672-8116	. . .	. . .	. . .	. . .	. . .	. . .	. . .
Rochester *	c	MC	6	(574) 223-2510	Mark Smiley	. . .	. . .	Carla Smith	Thomas Butler	Jodi Miller	. . .
Rockville *	t	CM	2	(765) 569-6253	Norman Camerer	. . .	Lisa Wilcox	. . .	John Malone	L. Wirth	. . .
Rushville	c	MC	5	(765) 932-2672	. . .	. . .	. . .	. . .	. . .	. . .	. . .
Salem *	c	MC	6	(812) 883-4264	David Bower	. . .	Patricia Persinger	. . .	Roger Pennington	Brian Ratts	. . .
Santa Claus	t	MC	2	(812) 937-2551	Ronald Smith	. . .	. . .	Kim Christensen	Edward Hagedorn	Henry Brown	Russ Luthy
Schererville *	t	CM	24	(219) 322-2211	Perry Ferrini	Robert Volkmann	. . .	Janice Malinowski	Joseph Kruzan	Daniel Smith	Jeffrey Huet
Scottsburg	c	MC	6	(812) 752-4343	William Graham	Sue Barnett	. . .	. . .	Richard Kern	Delbert Meeks	Dennis Nicholas
Seelyville *	t	MC	1	(812) 877-2665	Jerry Jones	Brent Spier	Tamara Caton	. . .	. . .	. . .	. . .
Sellersburg	t	MC	6	(812) 246-3821	. . .	. . .	. . .	. . .	. . .	. . .	. . .
Seymour	c	MC	18	(812) 522-4020	John Burkhart	Martha McIntire	. . .	Fred Lewis	. . .	. . .	Dave Stark
Shelbyville	c	MC	17	(317) 398-6624	Frank Zerr	. . .	. . .	Rodney Meyerholtz	Kurt Lockridge	Kehrt Etherton	. . .
South Bend	c	MC	107	(574) 235-9216	Stephen Luecke	. . .	Loretta Duda	Frederick Ollett	Luther Taylor	Thomas Fautz	Gary Gilot
Speedway	t	MC	12	(317) 241-2566	. . .	. . .	. . .	. . .	. . .	. . .	. . .
Spencer	t	MC	2	(812) 829-3213	Dean Bruce	. . .	. . .	Linda Simmerman	Pete Hodge	Larry Smith	Shelley Edwards
St. John *	t	MC	8	(219) 365-6043	Michel Fryzel	Stephen Kil	Sherry Sury	. . .	Fred Willman	Fred Frego	Robert Pharazyn
Sullivan	c	MC	4	(812) 268-6077	Timothy Boles	. . .	Sue Pitts	. . .	Shawn McKinney	David Story	. . .
Syracuse	t	CM	3	(574) 457-3348	Brian Woody	. . .	Julie Kline	. . .	Mickey Scott	Tony Ciriello	Clint Houseworth
Tell City	c	MC	7	(812) 472-2349	P. Goffinet	. . .	. . .	. . .	Dennis Kessans	David Faulkenberg	. . .
Terre Haute	c	MC	59	(812) 244-2320	Judy Anderson	Luke Anderson	Charles Hanley	Margaret Lemont	John Brighton	James Horrall	Robin Drummy
Tipton	c	MC	5	(765) 675-7561	. . .	. . .	. . .	. . .	. . .	. . .	. . .
Trail Creek	t	MC	2	(219) 872-2422	Daniel Tompkins	. . .	Anne Dobbs	. . .	. . .	Eugene Pierce	. . .
Union City	c	MC	3	(765) 964-6534	Phillip DeHaven	. . .	Brenda Campbell	. . .	Timothy Troxell	Monte Poling	. . .
Upland	t	MC	3	(765) 998-7439	. . .	. . .	. . .	. . .	. . .	. . .	. . .
Valparaiso	c	MC	27	(219) 462-1161	Jon Costas	William Hanna	S. Emerson-Swihart	. . .	David Nondorf	Michael Brickner	William Oeding
Vincennes	c	MC	18	(812) 882-7285	Terry Mooney	Jane Rode	. . .	Beverly Marsh	Joe Yochum	Robert Dunham	Kirk Bouchie
Wabash	c	MC	11	(260) 563-4171	. . .	. . .	. . .	. . .	. . .	. . .	. . .
Warsaw	c	MC	12	(574) 372-9545	Ernest Wiggins	. . .	. . .	. . .	Matthew Warren	Steven Foster	Lacy Francis
Washington	c	MC	11	(812) 254-5575	David Abel	. . .	Elaine Wellman	. . .	David Chapman	Michael Healy	. . .
West Lafayette *	c	MC	28	(765) 775-5100	John Dennis	. . .	Judith Rhodes	. . .	Philip Drew	Jason Dombkowski	David Downey
Westfield *	t	MC	9	(317) 896-5570	Andrew Cook	Jerry Rosenberger	. . .	. . .	Todd Burtron	Kevin Jowitt	Kurt Wanninger
Whiting *	c	MC	5	(219) 659-3100	Robert Bercik	. . .	Margaret Drewniak	. . .	Michael Mantich	David Tobias	. . .
Winchester *	c	MC	5	(765) 584-6845	Steven Croyle	. . .	Vicki Haney	. . .	Bill Yost	Michael Burk	. . .
Winona Lake *	t	CM	3	(574) 267-7581	Joy Lohse	Craig Allebach	. . .	. . .	Mitch Titus	R. Schmitt	Pete O'Connell
Yorktown *	t	CM	4	(765) 759-4003	Steve Lowry	Tim Kelty	. . .	M. Sidey	David Coffin	Richard St. John	. . .
Zionsville	t	MC	8	(317) 873-5410	Richard Crane	Edward Mitro	John Yeo	. . .	James VanGorder	Richard Dowden	. . .
IOWA											
Adel *	c	CM	3	(515) 993-4525	James Peters	Chad Bird	Mary Hibbs	. . .	Matt Ireland	Jim McNeill	Kip Overton
Albia	c	MC	3	(641) 932-2129	Nancy Spaur	. . .	. . .	. . .	Bill Murphy	Kenneth Powers	Thomas Murphy
Algona *	c	MC	5	(515) 295-2411	Jeff Gilmore	Cole O'Donnell	Rexann McEnroe	. . .	Chuck Bell	Kevin Bangert	Heather Roberts
Alton	c	MC	1	(712) 756-4314	Norman Beltman	. . .	Stacie Dykstra	. . .	Bill Schnee	Jim Schwieson	. . .
Altoona *	c	MC	10	(515) 967-5136	Timothy Burget	Jeffery Mark	Randy Pierce	. . .	Jerry Whetstone	John Gray	Vern Willey
Ames	c	CM	50	(515) 239-5101	. . .	Steven Schainker	Diane Voss	Duane Pitcher	Clinton Petersen	Loras Jaeger	John Joiner
Anamosa	c	MC	5	(319) 462-6055	Carl Chalstrom	Patrick Callahan	Suzanne Marek	. . .	Mike Schaffer	Richard Stivers	Gary Kula
Ankeny *	c	CM	27	(515) 965-6400	Steve Van Oort	Carl Metzger	Pamela De Mouth	Jennifer Sease	Rex Mundt	. . .	Paul Moritz
Atlantic *	c	CM	7	(712) 243-4810	John Krogman	Ronald Crisp	Deb Field	. . .	Mark McNees	Steve Green	. . .
Audubon	c	MC	2	(712) 563-3269	. . .	. . .	. . .	. . .	. . .	. . .	. . .
Bancroft	c	MC	. .	(515) 885-2382	. . .	. . .	. . .	. . .	. . .	. . .	. . .
Belle Plaine	c	MC	2	(319) 444-2200	James Daily	Bill Daily	Kaye Buch	. . .	Russ Spading	Mike Smith	. . .
Belmond *	c	CM	2	(641) 444-3386	Rex Peterson	Lee Waltzing	. . .	. . .	Wayne Bruggeman	Frank Beminio	Mark Dirks
Bettendorf *	c	CM	31	(563) 344-4000	Michael Freemire	Decker Ploehn	. . .	Carol Barnes	Gerald Voelliger	Phillip Redington	Wallace Mook
Bloomfield	c	MC	2	(641) 664-2260	Hazel Nardini-Cral	. . .	Marilyn McElderry	. . .	Robert Hongland	. . .	Richard Wilcox
Bondurant	c	MC	1	(515) 967-2418	. . .	Mark Arentsen	. . .	. . .	. . .	. . .	. . .
Boone	c	CM	12	(515) 432-4211	John Slight	. . .	. . .	Ondrea Elmquist	Ed Knight	William Skare	Larry Green
Buffalo	c	MC	1	(563) 381-2226	Jack Carson	William Bowers	. . .	. . .	Terry Adams	Gage Adams	Dwain Bollman
Burlington *	c	CM	26	(319) 753-8124	Timothy Scott	Douglas Worden	K. Salisbury	Dennis Bockenstedt	Thomas Clements	Daniel Luttenegger	Ronald Knoke
Camanche *	c	MC	4	(563) 259-8342	James Robertson	. . .	Sheryl Jindrich	. . .	David Schutte	Robert Houzenga	Dave Rickertson
Carlisle	t	MC	3	(515) 989-3224	Dennis Woodruff	Neil Ruddy	. . .	. . .	Larry Dennis	. . .	Steve O'Braza
Carroll *	c	CM	10	(712) 792-1000	Jim Pedelty	Gerald Clausen	. . .	Laura Schaefer	Greg Schreck	Jeff Cayler	Randall Krauel
Carter Lake	c	MC	3	(712) 347-6320	Emil Hausner	. . .	Doreen Mowery	. . .	Douglas Brown	Shawn Kannedy	Ronald Rothmeyer
Cascade	c	MC	1	(563) 852-3114	Tim Stecklein	Randy Lansing	Shelley Annis	. . .	Rick Kremer	Fred Heim	Paul McDermott
Cedar Falls	c	MC	36	(319) 273-8600	Jon Crews	. . .	Gary Hesse	J. Rodenbeck	Steve Mitchell	Richard Ahlstrom	Bruce Sorensen
Cedar Rapids *	c	CM	120	(319) 286-5555	Kay Halloran	James Prosser	Ann Ollinger	Casey Drew	Stephen Havlik	Greg Graham	David Elgin
Centerville	c	MC	5	(641) 437-4339	John Williams	. . .	Kristen May	. . .	Robert Bozwell	Dan Howington	. . .
Chariton *	c	CM	4	(641) 774-5991	John Braida	Nels Christensen	Ruth Ryun	. . .	John Laing	Jeff Johnson	Kevin Tanner
Charles City *	c	CM	7	(641) 257-6300	James Erb	Thomas Brownlow	Trudy O'Donnell	. . .	Roy Schwickerath	Mike Wendel	. . .
Cherokee	c	MC	5	(712) 225-5749	Dennis Henrich	Donald Eikmeier	Debra Taylor	. . .	Jack Olson	Steve Schuck	. . .
Clarinda	c	CM	5	(712) 542-2136	Gordon Kokenge	Gary McClarnon	. . .	. . .	Roger Williams	Keith Brothers	Kelly Parrott
Clarion	c	CM	2	(515) 532-2847	John Ofstethun	Vicky Boyington	. . .	. . .	Ron Piotrowski	Steve Henigar	James Redemske
Clear Lake	c	MC	8	(641) 357-5267	Kirk Kraft	Scott Flory	Gail Robinson	Linda Nelson	. . .	Daniel Jackson	Joseph Weigel
Clinton	c	CM	27	(563) 242-2144	. . .	Gary Boden	. . .	Deborah Neels	Mark Regenwether	Brian Guy	. . .
Clive	c	CM	12	(515) 223-6220	Les Aasheim	Dennis Henderson	Pamela Shannon	. . .	Rickey Roe	. . .	Bartley Weller
Colfax	c	MC	2	(515) 674-4096	Jeff Jones	. . .	Kathy Mathews	. . .	Mike Noftsger	Jon Huggins	. . .
Coralville	c	CM	15	(319) 248-1700	. . .	Kelly Hayworth	Nancy Beuter	. . .	David Stannard	Barry Bedford	. . .
Council Bluffs	c	MC	58	(712) 328-4601	Thomas Hanafan	. . .	Olga Ramirez	Terry Mauer	Alan Byers	James Wilkinson	Michael Wallner
Cresco	c	MC	3	(563) 547-3101	Ronda Hughes	John Lloyd	. . .	. . .	Neal Stapelkamp	Mark Kissinger	Dennis Cauwels
Creston *	c	MC	7	(641) 782-2000	Larry Wynn	Michael Taylor	Mary Moore	. . .	Todd Jackson	Paul Ver Meer	Kevin Kruse
Davenport	c	CM	98	(563) 326-7711	Charles Brooke	Craig Malin	Jackie Ragsdale	Alan Guard	Mark Frese	Michael Bladel	. . .
De Witt *	c	MC	5	(563) 659-3811	Donald Thiltgen	Steven Lindner	Catherine Benthin	Deanna Rodriguez	John Burken	Gene Ellis	Larry Kloth
Decorah	c	MC	8	(563) 382-3651	Victor Fye	Jerry Freund	Wanda Hemesath	. . .	. . .	Tom Courtney	. . .
Denison	c	MC	7	(712) 263-3143	Ken Livingston	Gregory Seefeldt	Marcia Bretey	. . .	Mike McKinnon	Rod Bradley	. . .
Denver	c	CM	1	(319) 984-5642	Gene Leonhart	Larry Farley	. . .	. . .	Ron Milius	Terry Dehmlow	John Foust
Des Moines	c	CM	198	(515) 283-4141	T. M. F. Cownie	Richard Clark	Diane Rauh	Allen McKinley	Phillip Vorlander	William McCarthy	William Stowe
Dubuque *	c	CM	57	(563) 589-4110	Roy Buol	M. Van Milligen	Jeanne Schneider	Kenneth TeKippe	E. Brown	Kim Wadding	Donald Vogt
Durant	c	CM	1	(563) 785-4451	. . .	Greg LaFond	. . .	. . .	. . .	. . .	. . .
Dyersville	c	MC	4	(563) 875-7724	James Heavens	Mick Michel	Tricia Maiers	. . .	Merlin Clemen	Martin Botts	David Vorwald
Eagle Grove *	c	CM	3	(515) 448-4343	Ray Kellogg	Jordan Fuller	. . .	Susan Maier	. . .	Tom Anderson	Robert Lunda
Eldora	c	CM	3	(641) 939-2393	Timothy Hoy	Patrick Rigg	Eric Weinkoetz	Joyce Lawler	Bruce Harvey	Dave Twedt	Dale Seaton
Eldridge	c	MC	4	(563) 285-4841	John Strazewski	John Dowd	Denise Benson	. . .	David Ploessl	Martin Stolmeier	Brian Wessel

Directory 1/9 continued OFFICIALS IN U.S. MUNICIPALITIES 2,500 AND OVER IN POPULATION

Jurisdiction		Type	Form of govern- ment	2000 Popu- lation	Main telephone number	Chief elected official	Appointed administrator	Clerk of the governing board	Chief financial officer	Fire chief	Police chief	Public works director
IOWA continued												
Elkader		c	MC	1	(563) 245-2098	Bob Garms	Jennifer Cowsert	...	...	Mike Anderson	Marvin Duff	Jerry Gamm
Emmetsburg		c	MC	3	(712) 852-4030	Myrna Heddinger	John Bird	Jill Kliegl	...	...	Eric Hanson	William Dickey
Estherville		c	CM	6	(712) 362-7771	Lyle Hevern	...	Vaughn Brua	...	David Knox	Paul Farber	...
Evansdale		c	MC	4	(319) 232-6683	John Mardis	...	Jane Walters	...	Kent Smock	Michael Burke	...
Everly	*	c	MC	..	(712) 834-2691	Bud Meyer	...	Cheryl Hoye	Janice Thompson	Brian Kahl	...	Bruce Harden
Fairfield	*	c	MC	9	(641) 472-6193	Edward Malloy	John Brown	Joy Messer	...	Ralph Hickenbottom	Randy Cooksey	Darrel Bisgard
Forest City	*	c	MC	4	(641) 585-4597	George Wilson	...	Paul Boock	...	Mark Johnson	Daniel Davis	...
Fort Dodge		c	MC	25	(515) 576-4551	William Patterson	David Fierke	Penny Clayton	...	John Webster	Thomas Francis	Al Dorothy
Fort Madison		c	CM	10	(319) 372-7700	Steven Ireland	Byron Smith	Suellen Mead	...	Joey Herren	...	Steven Hayes
Garner		c	MC	2	(641) 923-2588	Kenton Mick	Brent Hinson	Daisy Huffman	...	Terry Jass	Thomas Kozisek	...
Gilbert		c	MC	..	(515) 233-2670	...	...	...	...	...	...	...
Glenwood	*	c	MC	5	(712) 527-4717	Dyle Downing	Mary Smith	Judith Groves	...	...	John O'Connor	Perry Cook
Glidden	*	c	MC	1	(712) 659-3010	Roger Hartwigsen	Loren Lodge	Suzanne Danner	...	Thomas Weber	...	Robert Bock
Graettinger		c	MC	..	(712) 859-3359	Brian Bonstead	...	Sandra Henderson	...	Wayne Anderson	Kevin Olson	...
Grimes		c	MC	5	(515) 986-3036	...	...	...	...	...	...	...
Grinnell		c	CM	9	(641) 236-2600	Gordon Canfield	Russell Behrens	Pamela Rupe	...	Jerry Barns	Jody Matherly	Glenn Baker
Grundy Center		c	MC	2	(319) 824-6118	Jack Stomberg	...	...	...	Gerald Hoffman	Terry Oltman	James Copeman
Guttenberg	*	c	CM	1	(563) 252-1161	James Solomon	Barry Dykhuizen	...	...	Fred Schaub	George Morteo	Dan Walke
Hampton		c	CM	4	(641) 456-4853	Pat Sackville	Ron Dunt	Robbi Stevens	...	...	Michael Gillette	...
Harlan	*	c	MC	5	(712) 755-5137	Gary Christiansen	Terry Cox	Susan Lambert	...	Roger Bissen	Frank Clark	...
Hawarden	*	c	MC	2	(712) 551-2565	Ricard Porter	...	...	Sharole Rens	Jon Strong	Michael DeBruin	Thomas Kane
Hiawatha	*	c	CM	6	(319) 393-1515	Thomas Theis	David Van Dee	Kimberly Downs	Cindy Kudrna	Michael Nesslage	Dennis Marks	Rodney Jasa
Holstein		c	MC	1	(712) 368-4898	Mary Gross	Mark Baker	...	...	Dan Ehler	...	...
Humboldt	*	c	CM	4	(515) 332-3435	Steven Samuels	Lorie Bennett	Gloria Christensen	...	Tony Hosford	Jon Reed	...
Huxley		c	MC	2	(515) 597-2561	Nels Nord	John Haldeman	Lee Ruddick	...	Kevin Deaton	Mark Pote	Jeff Peterson
Ida Grove		c	MC	2	(712) 364-2428	Dennis Ernst	...	Cindy Murray	...	Matt Wunschel	...	...
Independence	*	c	MC	6	(319) 334-2780	Frank Brimmer	Alan Johnson	Debra Lynn	...	Doug Cook	Douglas Rasmussen	...
Indianola		c	CM	12	(515) 961-9410	Jerry Kelley	Tim Zisoff	...	...	Brian Seymour	Steve Bonnett	...
Iowa City		c	CM	62	(319) 356-5000	Arthur Wilburn	Michael Lombardo	Marian Karr	Kevin O'Malley	Andrew Rocca	Samuel Hargadine	Richard Fosse
Iowa Falls	*	c	CM	5	(641) 648-2527	Jerry Welden	Brian Weuve	Jon Kies	...	Rick Gustin	Ron Kuhfus	Bruce Jeffries
Jefferson		c	CM	4	(515) 386-3111	...	Michael Palmer	Diane Kennedy	...	...	...	...
Johnston		c	MC	8	(515) 278-2344	Brian Laurenzo	James Sanders	Stephanie Reynolds	Teresa Rotschafer	Jim Krohse	Doug Nichols	Dave Cubit
Kalona	*	c	CM	1	(319) 656-2310	Jean Gustafson	Douglas Morgan	Karen Christner	...	Steve Yotty	...	Mike Bowlin
Keokuk	*	c	MC	11	(319) 524-2050	David Gudgel	...	Donna Eilers	John Russell	Mark Wessel	Thomas Crew	Gerald Moughler
Knoxville		c	CM	7	(641) 828-0550	Jon Lenger	Richard Schrad	Jody Meyer	...	Barry Reynolds	Dan Losada	Jeffrey May
Lake View		c	MC	1	(712) 657-2634	Robert Schmidt	Scott Peterson	...	...	LeRoy Olerich	Ted Helmich	Jack De Bourgh
Lamoni	*	c	MC	2	(641) 784-6311	James Hammer	Kirk Bjorland	Deanna Ballantyne	...	Travis Jeanes	Dale Killpack	Emil Segebart
Laurens		c	MC	1	(712) 841-4526	...	...	Eloise Enger	...	Clarence Siepker	Rodney Watkins	Larry Barley
Le Claire		c	CM	2	(563) 289-5441	...	Ed Choate	...	...	...	...	...
Le Mars		c	CM	9	(712) 546-7018	Virgil Van Beek	Scott Langel	Beverly Langel	Bill Cole	Wayne Schipper	Stuart Dekkenga	Charlie Eufers
Lisbon		c	MC	1	(319) 455-2459	Michael Williams	Sandra Deahl	...	...	Michael Svatosch	Ricky Scott	Tom Hoke
Madrid		c	MC	2	(515) 795-3930	Pat Regan	Todd Kilzer	Joni Drake	...	...	Tim Brown	...
Manchester		c	CM	5	(563) 927-3636	...	Timothy Vick	...	...	...	...	...
Manning		c	MC	1	(712) 655-2176	Ron Colling	...	...	...	Robert Ehlers	Larry Lesle	Tom Wittrock
Mapleton		c	MC	1	(712) 881-1351	Ray Friedrichsen	...	Mavis Skow	...	Jerry Bumstead	John Holton	Mike Hahn
Maquoketa	*	c	CM	6	(563) 652-2484	Tom Messerli	Brian Wagner	Judith Carr	...	Mark Beck	Brad Koranda	Dave Popp
Marengo		c	CM	2	(319) 642-3232	Joe Seye	Carl Schumacher	...	Barbara Barrick	Steven Meier	Galen Moser	Stuart Stukey
Marion	*	c	CM	26	(319) 377-1581	Victor Klopfenstein	Lon Pluckhahn	...	Wesley Nelson	Terry Jackson	Harry Daugherty	Tom Newbanks
Marquette	*	c	MC	..	(563) 873-3735	John Ries	Dean Hilgerson	Maryanne Trudo	...	...	Randy Grady	Jason Sullivan
Marshalltown		c	CM	26	(641) 754-5704	Gene Beach	Richard Hierstein	Shari Coughenour	...	Larry Squiers	David Walker	Lynn Couch
Mason City		c	CM	29	(641) 421-3600	Roger Bang	Brent Trout	...	Kevin Jacobson	Bob Platts	David Ellingson	William Stangler
Missouri Valley		c	MC	2	(712) 642-3502	Randy McHugh	Craig Borlin	Rita Miller	...	Keith Holtz	Ed Murray	Bob Reisland
Mitchellville		c	CM	1	(515) 967-2935	Michael Kendall	Warren Hall	Andrew Lent	...	Dwayne Heckman	Charles Sickels	Daniel Miers
Monroe		c	MC	1	(641) 259-2319	...	Carol Diekema	...	...	...	...	...
Monticello		c	MC	3	(319) 465-6435	Gerald Wilbricht	Douglas Herman	Sally Hinrichsen	...	Mark Stoneking	Ryan Evans	Dana Edwards
Mount Pleasant	*	c	MC	8	(319) 385-1470	John Freeland	Brent Schleisman	Florence Olomon	...	...	Terry Sammons	Christopher Bittle
Mount Vernon	*	c	MC	3	(319) 895-8742	Paul Tuerler	Michael Beimer	...	...	Mike Buser	Mark Winder	...
Muscatine		c	CM	22	(563) 264-1550	Richard O'Brien	A. J. Johnson	...	...	Steven Dalbey	Gary Coderoni	Randall Hill
Nevada	*	c	CM	6	(515) 382-5466	Gearold Gull	Elizabeth Hansen	T. Peterson-Smith	...	Dana Wipperman	Mike Tupper	...
New Hampton		c	MC	3	(641) 394-5906	...	...	Suellen Kolbet	...	...	Michael Anderson	...
Newton		c	CM	15	(641) 792-2787	Charles Allen	...	Candice Brown	...	Ed Clements	Thomas Wardlow	David Stewart
Nora Springs	*	c	CM	1	(641) 749-5315	...	Deborah Gaul	...	...	...	Adam Nerlien	Daniel Grauerholz
North Liberty		c	CM	5	(319) 626-5700	Thomas Salm	Ryan Heiar	...	...	Eric Vandewater	James Warkentin	Donald Colony
Norwalk		c	MC	6	(515) 981-0228	Jerry Starkweather	Mark Miller	Jennifer Sease	...	Thomas Fleming	Ed Kuhl	Dean Yordi
Oelwein	*	c	CM	6	(319) 283-5440	Larry Murphy	Steven Kendall	...	...	Wallace Rundle	Jeremy Logan	...
Onawa		c	MC	3	(712) 433-1181	Neil Leapley	Larry Burks	Chris Hogan	...	...	Gary Addy	Jeffery Sander
Orange City	*	c	CM	5	(712) 707-4885	Daryl Beltman	Duane Feekes	Janet Brown	Kent Anderson	Dennis Vander Wel	Dann DeVries	Ted Loucks
Osage		c	MC	3	(641) 732-3709	Steven Cooper	...	Cathy Penney	...	Kurt Angell	Russell Stocker	Jerry Dunlay
Osceola		c	CM	4	(641) 342-2377	Fred Diehl	William Kelly	Nancy Carmichael	...	Donald McCuddin	Martin Duffus	...
Oskaloosa	*	c	CM	10	(641) 673-9431	David Dixon	Brian James	Marilyn Miller	...	Mark Neff	John McGee	David Neubert
Ottumwa	*	c	MC	24	(641) 683-0625	Dale Uehling	J. Helfenberger	P. Ann Cullinan	Michael Heffernan	Steven O'Connor	James Clark	Larry Seals
Panora		c	CM	1	(641) 755-2164	Steven Baker	...	...	Joyce Calmer	Matt Harmon	Marty Arganbright	Jerry Buttler
Pella		c	MC	9	(641) 628-4173	Darrell Dobernecker	Michael Nardini	Ronda Brown	...	Doug Van Gorkum	M. Marcinkowski	Denny Buyert
Perry	*	c	MC	7	(515) 465-2481	Viivi Shirley	Butch Niebuhr	Jeanette Peddicord	Susie Moorhead	Chris Hinds	Daniel Brickner	Jack Butler
Pleasant Hill	*	c	MC	5	(515) 262-9368	Phil Hildebrand	Donald Sandor	Joni Haag	...	Reylon Meeks	Tim Sittig	Gary Patterson
Pocahontas	*	c	MC	1	(712) 335-4841	Brian Blomker	Robert Donahoo	Joan De Wall	...	Jeff Shearer	Byron Essing	...
Polk City	*	c	MC	2	(515) 984-6233	Mary Burton	Gary Mahannah	Sharon Nickles	Colin Adams	Jason Morse	Mark Bowersox	Mike Schulte
Prairie City	*	c	MC	1	(515) 994-2649	...	Andrew Elbert	...	...	...	...	...
Red Oak		c	MC	6	(712) 623-6510	James Johnson	Brad Wright	Mary Bolton	...	Rick Askey	Drue Powers	...
Reinbeck	*	c	MC	1	(319) 788-6404	Lon Larsen	Quentin Mayberry	...	...	...	...	...
Rock Rapids		c	MC	2	(712) 472-2553	Keith Benson	Jordan Kordahl	...	...	Chris Bixenman	Blythe Bloemendaal	Bret Huisman
Rock Valley		c	MC	2	(712) 476-5707	Kent Eknes	Tom Van Maanen	Judy Vant Hul	...	...	Monte Warburton	Myron Van Ginkel
Rolfe	*	c	MC	..	(712) 848-3124	Gloria Gunderson	...	Angela Schneider	...	Glenn Munson	Michael Morris	Dave Sandvig
Sac City		c	CM	2	(712) 662-7593	Glen Duncan	...	...	...	John Phillips	John Zimmerman	...
Sanborn		c	MC	1	(712) 729-3842	...	...	...	...	...	...	...
Sergeant Bluff		c	MC	3	(712) 943-4244	...	James Ferneau	Candice Litras	...	Michael Thompson	Dave McFarland	Roger Groves
Sheldon	*	c	CM	4	(712) 324-4651	Kurt Tatsumi	Scott Wynja	Arlene Budden	...	Jerry Meyers	Lyle Balkema	Todd Uhl
Shenandoah		c	CM	5	(712) 246-4411	Gregg Connell	Byron Harris	...	...	Ron Fox	Kevin Hughes	...
Sibley	*	c	CM	2	(712) 754-2541	Jerry Johnson	...	Kristen Vipond	...	Ken Huls	...	Wayne Poss
Sioux Center	*	c	CM	6	(712) 722-0761	Dennis Walstra	Paul Clousing	...	B. Van Schouwen	David Holland	Paul Adkins	Murray Hulstein
Sioux City		c	CM	85	(712) 279-6200	K. Van De Steeg	Paul Eckert	...	...	...	Joseph Frisbie	Dave Dorsett
Solon		c	MC	1	(319) 624-3755	Rick Jedlicka	...	Connie Evans	...	...	...	Scott Kleppe
Spencer		c	MC	11	(712) 580-7200	Reynold Peterson	...	Donna Fisher	...	Douglas Duncan	Mark Lawson	Mark White
Spirit Lake		c	CM	4	(712) 336-1871	Eric Nielsen	Mark Stevens	...	...	Dave Kollasch	Jeff Hanson	Todd Dolphin
Storm Lake		c	CM	10	(712) 732-8000	Jon Kruse	Patti Moore	...	Paul Hoye	Mike Jones	...	Patrick Kelly
Story City		c	MC	3	(515) 733-2121	Harold Holm	Mark Jackson	Pat Twedt	...	Scott Nibe	Brian Haffner	Bruce Henrichs

Directory 1/9 continued — OFFICIALS IN U.S. MUNICIPALITIES 2,500 AND OVER IN POPULATION

Jurisdiction	Type	Form of govern-ment	2000 Popu-lation	Main telephone number	Chief elected official	Appointed administrator	Clerk of the governing board	Chief financial officer	Fire chief	Police chief	Public works director
IOWA continued											
Stratford *	c	CM	..	(515) 838-2311	Michael Nepereny	Rachel Cahill	...	...	...	...	Larry Runyan
Strawberry Point *	c	CM	1	(563) 933-4482	Dale Fox	Deanna Dement	...	...	...	Robert Pope	Jeff Robinson
Tama	c	MC	2	(641) 484-3822	Richard Gibson	...	...	...	Rod Anderson	...	Stuart Eisentrager
Tipton	c	MC	3	(563) 886-6187	Donald Young	Dick Schrad	John Foley	Lorna Fletcher	John Miller	Roger Hakeman	Doug Boldt
University Heights	c	MC	..	(319) 337-6900	...	...	...	...	...	...	...
Urbandale *	c	CM	29	(515) 278-3900	Robert Andeweg	...	Debra Mains	Nicci Lamb	Jerry Holt	David Hamlin	David McKay
Vinton	c	MC	5	(319) 472-4707	John Watson	Andrew Lent	Cindy Michael	...	Scott Geissinger	Jeff Tilson	...
Washington	c	MC	7	(319) 653-6584	Edward Brown	David Plyman	Jeff Rosien	...	William Hartsock	...	...
Waterloo *	c	MC	68	(319) 291-4522	Timothy Hurley	...	Nancy Eckert	Michelle Weidner	Doug Carter	Tom Jennings	...
Waukee	c	CM	5	(515) 987-4522	William Peard	Jeffrey Kooistra	...	...	...	Larry Phillips	John Gibson
Waukon	c	MC	4	(563) 568-3492	Dwight Jones	...	Diane Sweeney	...	...	Loren Fiet	...
Waverly	c	CM	8	(319) 352-4252	Ivan Ackerman	Richard Crayne	JoEllen Raap	Jack Bachhuber	Daniel McKenzie	Richard Pursell	Michael Cherry
Webster City	c	CM	8	(515) 832-9151	Eugene Gray	Ed Sadler	Patricia Nokes	Kasie Doering	Mike Lund	Michael McConnell	...
Wellman	c	CM	1	(319) 646-2154	Ryan Miller	David Ross	Donna Wade	...	James Seward	...	...
West Bend	c	MC	..	(515) 887-2181	Laura Montag	...	Lisa Sewell	...	...	Richard Jergens	Thomas Hartman
West Branch *	c	MC	1	(319) 643-5888	...	Kyle Soukup	Debra Fiderlein	...	Kevin Stoolman	...	Brian Brennan
West Burlington	c	CM	3	(319) 752-5451	Hans Trousil	Dan Gifford	Terrie Simonson	...	...	Alex Oblein	Randy Fry
West Des Moines	c	CM	46	(515) 222-3600	Eugene Meyer	Jeffrey Pomeranz	Fern Stewart	...	Donald Cox	Jack O'Donnell	Larry Read
West Liberty *	c	CM	3	(319) 627-2418	Clifford McFerren	Chris Ward	...	...	Curt Newcomb	Paul Brewer	Russell Garner
West Point	c	MC	..	(319) 837-6313	Paul Walker	Claron White	Mary Winnike	...	...	...	Fred Boeding
West Union	c	MC	2	(563) 422-3320	...	...	...	...	...	...	...
Wilton *	c	MC	2	(563) 732-2115	Dick Summy	Mark Anderson	Lori Brown	...	Darrell Janssen	Steve Mallinger	Bryan Devore
Windsor Heights *	c	MC	4	(515) 279-3662	David Sullivan	Marketa Oliver	...	...	Christopher Cross	Gary Walters	John Wiedman
Winterset	c	MC	4	(515) 462-1422	James Olson	Mark Nitchals	...	...	R. Truckenbrod	Ken Burk	...
KANSAS											
Abilene *	c	CM	6	(785) 263-2550	Kenneth Peterson	Allen Dinkel	Penny Soukup	Eddie Balluch	Bob Sims	Bryan Dunlap	Lon Schraeder
Andover *	c	MC	6	(316) 733-1303	Benjamin Lawrence	...	Susan Renner	Elizabeth Boast	Jimmy Shaver	Michael Keller	Leslie Mangus
Anthony	c	CO	2	(620) 842-5434	John Schott	Donald Heidrick	...	...	Kenny Hudson	John Blevins	Grant Sechler
Arkansas City *	c	CM	11	(620) 441-4400	Mel Kuhn	Steven Archer	Lesley Shook	...	Randy Leach	Sean Wallace	Clay Randel
Atchison	c	CM	10	(913) 367-5500	Daniel Garrity	Justin Der	Phyllis Walton	Sheldon Hamilton	Michael McDermed	Michael Wilson	Roger Denton
Augusta *	c	CM	8	(316) 775-4510	Kristey Williams	William Keefer	Erica Jones	...	Raymond Marbut	...	...
Baldwin City	c	CM	3	(785) 594-6427	Gary Walbridge	Jeffrey Dingman	Peggy Nichols	...	Allan Craig	Michael McKenna	Bill Winegar
Basehor *	c	MC	2	(913) 724-1370	Chris Garcia	Carl Slaugh	Mary Ann Mogle	...	...	Lloyd Martley	Milton Myracle
Baxter Springs	c	MC	4	(620) 856-2114	...	...	Donna Wixon	...	William Ellsworth	David Edmondson	Robert Kirby
Bel Aire *	c	MC	5	(316) 744-2451	Brian Withrow	Arthur Lasher	Vicki Bradford	Erica Stock	...	John Daily	Terry Dreiling
Belleville	c	CM	2	(785) 527-2288	Bradley Chatfield	Allen Bachelor	Karen Dreesen	...	Duffy Strnad	Gary Frint	...
Beloit *	c	MC	4	(785) 738-3551	Rebecca Koster	Douglas Gerber	Kerry Benson	...	Steve Rugg	Frank Gent	Lloyd Littrell
Bonner Springs *	c	CM	6	(913) 422-1020	Clausie Smith	John Helin	Rita Hoag	Matilda La Plante	Clinton Long	John Haley	Kevin Bruemmer
Burlingame	c	MC	1	(785) 654-2414	Brenda Dorr	...	Christina Lewis	...	Jim Strohm	Jon Shaffer	Josh Welch
Burlington	c	MC	2	(620) 364-5334	Rick Raymer	...	Daniel Allen	...	...	Doug Jones	...
Caney	c	MC	2	(620) 879-9800	...	Donald Whitman	...	...	...	Rick Pell	...
Cedar Vale	c	MC	..	(620) 758-2244	...	...	Barbara Denney	...	...	...	John Hodgden
Chanute *	c	CM	9	(620) 431-5200	Leroy Chard	J. D. Lester	Joan Howard	James McEwen	...	...	...
Cheney *	c	CM	1	(316) 542-3622	Linda Ball	Randall Oliver	Jimmie Diskin	...	Brad Ewy	Howard Bishop	...
Cherryvale *	c	CM	2	(620) 336-2776	John Wright	John Cocking	Rebecca Swain	...	Ron Davis	Matt Dennis	Wade Webber
Clay Center *	c	MC	4	(785) 632-5454	Sharon Brown	...	Calvin Wohler	...	Jon Siemers	Bill Robinson	Billy Callaway
Clearwater *	c	MC	2	(620) 584-2311	Michael Justice	Kent Brown	Cheryl Wright	...	Marvin Schauf	Kim Demars	Ernie Misak
Coffeyville	c	CM	11	(620) 252-6121	...	Jeffrey Morris	Donna Schoonover	...	Gregory Allen	Joe Humble	Don Males
Colby	c	CM	5	(785) 460-4400	Ken Bieber	Carolyn Armstrong	Deanna Pabst	...	Robert McLemore	...	Chris Bieker
Columbus	c	CM	3	(620) 429-2159	John Brassart	Evan Capron	Janice Blancett	...	Don Kirk	Charles Sharp	Henry Burton
Concordia	c	CM	5	(785) 243-2670	Joe Jindra	Mark Skiles	Cheryl Lanoue	...	Larry Eubanks	Danny Parker	Ron Copple
Council Grove	c	CM	2	(620) 767-5417	...	...	...	...	...	...	...
De Soto *	c	MC	4	(913) 583-1182	David Anderson	Patrick Guilfoyle	Lana McPherson	Bonnie Bennett	Kevin Ritter	...	...
Derby	c	CM	17	(316) 788-1519	Dion Avello	Kathleen Sexton	...	Jean Epperson	Brad Smith	Jay Reyes	Robert Mendoza
Dodge City *	c	CM	25	(620) 225-8100	Kent Smoll	Ken Strobel	...	Nannette Pogue	Dan Williamson	John Ball	Joseph Finley
Douglass *	c	MC	1	(316) 747-2109	Mark Roberts	KaLyn Nethercot	...	...	...	...	Bill Akers
Edgerton *	c	MC	1	(913) 893-6231	Frankie Cross	David Dillner	Rita Moore	...	Max Sielert	Larry Shoop	Mike Mabrey
Edwardsville *	c	MC	4	(913) 441-3707	Heinz Rodgers	Michael Webb	Phyllis Freeman	...	Clifton Lane	Mark Mathies	...
El Dorado	c	CM	12	(316) 321-9100	Tom McKibban	Herbert Llewellyn	Kendra Waite	Dee Anne Grunder	Ken Nakaten	Tom Boren	Brad Meyer
Elkhart	c	MC	2	(620) 697-2171	...	...	Carolea Wellen	...	...	Loren Youngers	Leo Davis
Ellinwood	c	MC	2	(620) 564-3161	Frank Koelsch	...	Kim Schartz	...	Chris Komarek	Kevin PeKarek	Daryle Nielsen
Ellsworth	c	MC	2	(785) 472-5566	Robert Homolka	Jonathan Mitchell	Margaret Shepherd	...	Bob Kepka	David Smith	...
Emporia	c	CM	26	(620) 342-5105	Tom Meyers	M. Zimmerman	Susan Mendoza	Larry Bucklinger	Jack Taylor	...	Ron Childers
Eudora *	c	MC	4	(785) 542-4111	Thomas Pyle	Cheryl Beatty	Donna Oleson	...	Randy Ates	Greg Dahlem	Delbert Breithaupt
Eureka	c	CO	2	(620) 583-6511	James Bobey	...	Rebecca Schaffer	...	Doug Williams	Lowell Parker	Larry Fritts
Fairway *	c	MC	3	(913) 262-0350	John St. Clair	Katherine Smith	...	...	...	John Simmons	Bill Stogsdill
Fort Scott	c	CM	8	(620) 223-0550	Garold Billionis	Joseph Turner	Diane Clay	Susan Brown	...	...	Eric Bailey
Fredonia *	c	CO	2	(620) 378-2231	Max Payne	Steven Hutfles	...	...	Rick Brown	Melvin Richey	Junior Hufford
Frontenac	c	CM	2	(620) 231-9210	James Kennedy	Paul Bruneiti	Richard Cicero	...	Mike Hagerty	Carl Flora	...
Galena	c	MC	3	(620) 783-5265	...	...	Deborah Kitch	...	Bill Hall	Cameron Arthur	Leroy Webster
Garden City	c	CM	28	(620) 276-1160	Gary Fuller	Matthew Allen	Stacey Frizzell	Melinda Hitz	Allen Shelton	James Hawkins	Sam Curran
Gardner	c	MC	9	(913) 856-7535	...	Stewart Fairburn	Teresa Anderson	Laura Gourley	...	...	David Greene
Garnett	c	CM	3	(785) 448-5496	Michael Norman	...	...	Joyce Martin	Harold Miller	James Bond	...
Girard	c	CO	2	(620) 724-8918	Maurice Harley	Michael West	...	Coralie Bennett	Ronald Scales	Danny Fields	David Crumpacker
Goddard *	c	MC	2	(316) 794-2441	Marcey Gregory	Brian Silcott	Karen Bailey	...	...	Samuel Houston	Randy Brooks
Goodland	c	CM	4	(785) 899-4500	Richard Billinger	Kenneth Hill	Mary Volk	...	Dean Jensen	Raymond Smee	Chuck Lutters
Great Bend	c	MC	15	(620) 793-4111	Mike Allison	Howard Partington	Wayne Henneke	...	Mike Napolitano	Dean Akings	Don Craig
Greensburg	c	MC	1	(620) 723-2751	...	Steve Hewitt	...	...	...	...	Michael Hayes
Halstead	c	CM	1	(316) 835-2286	...	J. Hatfield	Dianne Mueller	...	Jim VanSchaick	Austin Hamilton	Pat Adams
Hays *	c	CM	20	(785) 628-7320	Kent Steward	Toby Dougherty	...	Kim Rupp	Gary Brown	James Braun	Brenda Herrman
Haysville	c	MC	8	(316) 529-5900	Bruce Armstrong	Carol Neugent	Carol McBeath	Beverly Rodgers	...	Michael McElroy	Randal Dorner
Herington *	c	CM	2	(785) 258-2271	Gary Schrader	Lloyd Matthes	Debbie Wendt	...	Kenneth Staatz	Gordon Schroeder	...
Hesston	c	MC	3	(620) 327-4412	John Waltner	John Carder	...	...	Lelyn Peters	Kurt Ford	Kirk Matz
Hiawatha	c	MC	3	(785) 742-7417	Crosby Gernon	Elizabeth Ladner	Vivian Constable	...	Gary Shear	Evans Woehlecke	Rick Koenig
Hill City	c	MC	1	(782) 421-2264	...	Brett McMacken	Debbie Budig	...	...	...	...
Hillsboro *	c	MC	2	(620) 947-3162	Delores Dalke	Lawrence Paine	Jan Meisinger	...	Ben Steketee	Dan Kinning	Dale Dalke
Hoisington	c	CM	2	(620) 653-4125	Clayton Williamson	...	Donita Crutcher	...	James Sekavec	Kenton Doze	Paul Zecha
Holton	c	CM	3	(785) 364-2721	Janet Zwonitzer	Glenn Rodden	Pat McClintock	...	Tony Raaf	David Lanning	...
Horton *	c	CM	1	(785) 486-2681	Tim Lentz	James Whisenant	Candice Schmitt	...	Gary Behrnes	Richard Luzier	Rex West
Hugoton *	c	MC	3	(620) 544-8531	Jack Rowden	Thomas Hicks	...	...	...	Courtney Leslie	Alton Banker
Humboldt *	c	MC	1	(620) 473-3232	Robert Sharp	Larry Tucker	Jean Flores	...	Kent Barfoot	Daniel Onnen	Craig Mintz
Hutchinson	c	CM	40	(620) 694-2620	...	John Deardoff	...	Carl Myers	Robert Forbes	James Heitschmidt	Dennis Clennan
Independence *	c	CM	9	(620) 332-2500	Derrill Unruh	Paul Sasse	Anthony Royse	...	Russell Baker	Ken Parker	Michael Passauer
Iola	c	CM	6	(620) 365-4900	Billy Maness	Judith Brigham	...	...	Donald Leapheart	James Kilby	...

Directory 1/9 continued — OFFICIALS IN U.S. MUNICIPALITIES 2,500 AND OVER IN POPULATION

Jurisdiction	Type	Form of govern-ment	2000 Popu-lation	Main telephone number	Chief elected official	Appointed administrator	Clerk of the governing board	Chief financial officer	Fire chief	Police chief	Public works director
KANSAS continued											
Junction City *	c	CM	18	(785) 238-3103	...	Rodney Barnes	...	...	Michael Steinfort	Robert Story	...
Kechi *	c	MC	1	(316) 744-9287	Ed Parker	Mac Manning	Laura Hill	...	...	Jason Doll	Larry Kallenberger
Kingman	c	MC	3	(620) 532-3111	Brad Frisbie	...	Cindy Conrardy	...	S. Drosselmeyer	John Braden	R. Robinson
Kinsley *	c	CM	1	(620) 659-3611	Rod Craft	Jay Dill	Karen Myers	...	Larry Myers	...	John Baker
La Crosse	c	CM	1	(785) 222-2511	Gerald Washburn	Duane Moeder	Sherri Stevens	...	...	...	...
Lake Quivira	c	MC	..	(913) 631-5300	Patrick McAnany	...	...	...	...	Maurice McCarthy	...
Lansing *	c	MC	9	(913) 727-3233	Kenneth Bernard	Michael Smith	...	William Lundberg	...	Steve Wayman	John Young
Larned *	c	CM	4	(620) 285-8500	Robert Pivonka	Donald Gaeddert	Pam Corby	...	Bill Clapham	Charles Orth	...
Lawrence	c	CM	80	(785) 832-3000	David Dunfield	David Corliss	Frank Reeb	Ed Mullins	James McSwain	William Olin	Charles Soules
Leavenworth *	c	CM	35	(913) 680-2604	Larry Dedeke	J. Miller	Karen Logan	Daniel Williamson	Steve Moody	Patrick Kitchens	Michael McDonald
Leawood *	c	MC	27	(913) 339-6700	Peggy Dunn	Scott Lambers	Debra Harper	Kathleen Rogers	Ben Florance	John Meier	Joseph Johnson
Lenexa *	c	MC	40	(913) 477-7500	Michael Boehm	J. Wade	Anna Ancil	Doug Robinson	Charles Rhodus	Ellen Hanson	Ronald Norris
Liberal	c	CM	19	(620) 626-0102	...	...	Debra Giskie	Toby Miller	...	Vernon Jordan	Jim Coffey
Lindsborg *	c	MC	3	(785) 227-3355	Judy Neuschafer	Gregory Du Mars	J. Lovett-Sperling	Larry Lindgren	Willard Keding	...	Timothy Dunn
Louisburg	c	MC	2	(913) 837-5371	...	...	...	...	...	...	...
Lyons	c	MC	3	(620) 257-2320	Clarence Moses	John Sweet	Jodi Oakley	...	Greg Moss	Chris Detmer	David Kendrick
Madison	c	CO	..	(620) 437-2556	Samuel Wine	...	Beth Dains	...	...	...	Dale Haney
Maize	c	MC	1	(316) 722-7561	Clair Donnelly	...	Jean Silvestri	...	...	Matthew Jensby	Ron Smothers
Manhattan *	c	CM	44	(785) 587-2489	Mark Hatesohl	Ron Fehr	Gary Fees	Bernie Hayen	Jerry Snyder	...	Dale Houdeshell
Marysville	c	MC	3	(785) 562-5331	...	Rick Shain	Paula Holle	...	...	Todd Ackerman	Gerald Gellinger
Mc Cracken	c	CM	..	(785) 394-2229	...	...	...	...	...	...	...
Mc Pherson	c	CO	13	(620) 245-2535	William Goering	Gary Meagher	...	Richard Janousek	Dennis Thrower	Michael Alkire	Stephen Schmidt
Meade *	c	MC	1	(620) 873-2091	Bud Doerflinger	Dean Cordes	Tiffany Neel	...	...	...	...
Medicine Lodge	c	CM	2	(620) 886-3908	Steven Etheridge	...	W. Kimball	...	Dennis Lunsford	Brian Miller	Gary Uhler
Merriam	c	MC	11	(913) 322-5500	...	Phillip Lammers	...	Maureen Rogers	Gerald Montgomery	Kenneth Sissom	Randall Carroll
Minneapolis	c	MC	2	(785) 392-2176	Virginia Hoover	Lowell Parrish	...	...	Michael Smith	Lanny Zadina	...
Mission *	c	MC	9	(913) 676-8350	Laura McConwell	Michael Scanlon	Martha Sumrall	...	...	Randall Wilson	Stephen Weeks
Mission Hills *	c	MC	3	(913) 362-9620	David Fromm	C. Christensen	Jill Clifton	...	...	...	...
Mulvane	c	MC	5	(316) 777-1143	James Ford	Kent Hixson	Patty Gerwick	...	Judi Patterson	David Williams	Gary Rambo
Neodesha	c	CM	2	(620) 325-2828	Casey Lair	J. D. Cox	E. Boecker	...	Charles Reynolds	Danny Thayer	Gerald Lour
Newton	c	CM	17	(316) 284-6003	Willis Heck	Randall Riggs	...	Ronald Ahsmuhs	Gary Denny	James Daily	Suzanne Loomis
Norton	c	MC	3	(785) 877-5000	...	Rob Lawson	Darla Ellis	...	...	Lynn Menagh	Dan Bainter
Oakley *	c	CM	2	(785) 672-3611	Frank Munk	Brandon Buchanan	Rose Wessel	...	Timothy Martin	Danny Shanks	James Glassman
Oberlin	c	MC	1	(785) 475-2217	...	...	...	...	...	...	...
Olathe *	c	CM	92	(913) 971-8600	Michael Copeland	John Wilkes	Debra Gragg	Ben Hart	George Bentley	Janet Thiessen	Rick Biery
Osage City	c	CM	3	(785) 528-3714	Steve Haller	N. Hernandez	Linda Jones	...	...	Fred Nech	Mike Gilliland
Osawatomie *	c	CM	4	(913) 755-2146	Philip Dudley	Bret Glendening	Ann Elmquist	...	DuWayne Tewes	...	Stephen Coffelt
Oswego *	c	MC	2	(620) 795-4433	Murl Bringle	...	Cheri Peine	...	Donnie Allison	George Elliott	Kevin Frogley
Ottawa *	c	CM	11	(785) 229-3600	...	Richard Nienstedt	Carolyn Snethen	Scott Bird	Jeff Carner	Dennis Butler	Donald Haney
Overland Park *	c	CM	149	(913) 895-6000	Carl Gerlach	John Nachbar	Marian Cook	Dave Scott	Bryan Dehner	John Douglass	Robert Lowry
Paola *	c	CM	5	(913) 259-3600	Artie Stuteville	John Wieland	Dan Droste	...	Andy Martin	David Smail	Gerry Bieker
Park City	c	MC	5	(316) 744-2026	Dee Stuart	Jack Whitson	Carol Jones	...	...	...	Rick Norman
Parsons	c	CM	11	(620) 421-7000	...	...	Deborah Lamb	...	Tim Hay	Gary Baldwin	Darrell Moyer
Phillipsburg	c	MC	2	(785) 543-5234	...	...	...	...	...	...	...
Pittsburg	c	CM	19	(620) 231-4100	Bill Rushton	...	Tammy Nagle	Jon Garrison	Donald Elmer	Mendy Hulvey	William Beasley
Plainville *	c	MC	2	(785) 434-2841	Shirley Hendrex	...	James Dryden	...	Tracy Post	Gary Knight	Gerald Hageman
Pleasanton	c	CM	1	(913) 352-8257	...	...	...	...	...	...	...
Prairie Village *	c	MC	22	(913) 381-6464	Ronald Shaffer	Quinn Bennion	Joyce Mundy	Karen Kindle	...	Wesley Jordan	Robert Pryzby
Pratt	c	CM	6	(620) 672-5571	Jeff Taylor	E. Howard	LuAnn Kramer	Betsy Koontz	David Kramer	Lonnie McCollum	Larry Koontz
Roeland Park *	c	MC	6	(913) 722-2600	Steve Petrehn	John Carter	Debra Mootz	...	...	Rex Taylor	Patrick Mundis
Rose Hill	c	MC	3	(316) 776-2712	Daniel Woydziak	Joel Pile	Kathy Dinkel	...	...	Robert Sage	Robert Edwards
Russell *	c	CM	4	(785) 483-6311	Carol Dawson	Ralph Wise	Karen Gates	...	Samuel Schmidt	Larry Vaughan	Arlyn Unrein
Sabetha	c	CO	2	(785) 284-2158	Norman Schmitt	Douglas Allen	Linda Lehman	...	Benjamin Johnson	Michael Hill	...
Salina *	c	CM	45	(785) 309-5710	John Vanier	Jason Gage	LieuAnn Elsey	Rodney Franz	J. Larry Mullikin	James Hill	Michael Fraser
Scott City	c	MC	3	(620) 872-5322	Henry Strecker	...	Brenda Davis	...	Kenneth Hoover	...	Mike Todd
Sedgwick *	c	MC	1	(316) 772-5151	Donald DeHaven	Jaclyn Reimer	Janise Enterkin	...	Richard Ludowese	Ray Huff	Tony Somers
Seneca	c	CM	2	(785) 336-2747	...	...	Jane Strathman	...	...	...	Brian Rusche
Shawnee *	c	CM	47	(913) 631-2500	Jeff Meyers	Carol Gonzales	...	Bryan Kidney	Jeff Hudson	James Morgan	Ronald Freyermuth
Spring Hill	c	CM	2	(913) 592-3664	Mark Squire	Jonathan Roberts	Beverly Hayden	Pamela Jackson	...	Paul Kalmar	Rory Hale
St. Marys	c	CM	1	(785) 437-2311	Mary Denton	...	Katherine De Mars	...	James Keating	Jimmy Hostetler	Jerry Eichem
Sterling *	c	CM	2	(620) 278-3423	Kim Witt	Rod Willis	Sandra Fankhauser	...	Richard Jones	Eddy Truelove	Andy Prebble
Stockton	c	CO	1	(785) 425-6703	...	...	Sandra Rogers	...	Alec Hrabe	Donald Jenkins	...
Tonganoxie	c	CM	2	(913) 845-2620	David Taylor	Michael Yanez	...	...	David Bennett	Kenneth Carpenter	Butch Rodgers
Topeka	c	CM	122	(785) 368-3867	William Bunten	Norton Bonaparte	Brenda Younger	Jim Langford	Howard Giles	Ronald Miller	Mike Teply
Tribune	c	MC	..	(620) 376-4278	...	...	Meredith Johnson	...	...	...	...
Ulysses	c	MC	5	(620) 356-4600	Ed Wiltse	Daron Hall	Mary Smith	...	...	Alan Olson	Ruben Flores
Valley Center	c	MC	4	(316) 755-7310	Michael McNown	...	Kristine Polian	...	Lonnie Tormey	Kelly Parks	Richard Dunn
Wamego	c	CM	4	(785) 456-9119	Errol Carley	...	Elizabeth Kern	...	Phillip Stultz	Michael Baker	Claude Asbury
Wellington	c	CM	8	(620) 326-3631	Stanley Gilliland	Adam Collins	Rose Miller	...	John Lloyd	Michael Keller	Rodney Conwell
Westwood	c	MC	1	(913) 362-1550	Karen Johnson	...	Kathleen McMahon	...	...	Carlos Wells	John Sullivan
Wichita	c	CM	344	(316) 268-4531	Carlos Mayans	Robert Layton	Patricia Graves	Kelly Carpenter	Lawrence Garcia	Norman Williams	Stephen Lackey
Winfield	c	CM	12	(620) 221-5500	Phil Jarvis	Warren Porter	...	Diane Rosecrans	Curtis Wilson	Jerry DeVore	Russ Tomevi
KENTUCKY											
Alexandria	c	MC	8	(859) 635-4125	Daniel McGinley	...	Karen Barto	...	Jeffrey Pohlman	Michael Ward	Sam Trapp
Anchorage	c	MC	2	(502) 245-4654	Peyton Hoge	...	Christine Franklin	...	Joe Frith	James Edington	Arthur Gullett
Ashland *	c	CM	21	(606) 327-2000	Tom Kelley	Kevin Gunderson	Deborah Musser	Tony Grubb	Mark Osborne	Robert Ratliff	Steve Corbitt
Barbourville	c	MC	3	(606) 546-6197	W. Hauser	James Tye	...	...	...	...	James Baker
Bardstown	c	MC	10	(502) 348-5947	Henry Spalding	...	Lonnie Parrott	...	Phillip Parrott	John Johnson	William Burba
Bardwell	c	MC	..	(270) 628-5415	...	...	...	...	...	...	...
Beaver Dam	c	CO	3	(270) 274-7106	David Taylor	Larry Carter	Brenda Dockery	...	Jerrel Shephard	...	Roscoe Simpson
Bellevue *	c	MC	6	(859) 431-8866	John Meyer	Keith Spoelker	...	Mary Scott	John Daly	William Cole	Chris Warneford
Benton *	c	MC	4	(270) 527-8677	Steve Cary	...	Michele Edwards	...	Harry Green	Gary West	...
Berea	c	MC	9	(859) 986-8528	Steven Connelly	Randall Stone	...	...	Randy Rigsby	Buford Brumley	Timothy Taylor
Bowling Green	c	CM	49	(270) 393-3000	Elaine Walker	Kevin DeFebbo	...	Jeff Meisel	...	Doug Hawkins	Emmett Wood
Calvert City	c	MC	2	(270) 395-7138	Lynn Jones	John Ward	Troy Truitt	...	Fred Ross	John Nelson	Ron Sutter
Campbellsville	c	MC	10	(270) 465-7011	Brenda Allen	...	...	...	Allen Johnson	William Cassell	...
Carrollton	c	MC	3	(502) 732-7060	Ann Deatherage	...	Becky Pyles	...	Randall Tharp	Michael Willhoite	Ronald Knight
Catlettsburg	c	MC	1	(606) 739-4533	Roger Hensley	...	Pauline Hunt	Charles Hedrick	Linzy Runyon	Mark Plummer	Roger West
Central City	c	CM	5	(270) 754-5097	Hugh Sweatt	David Rhoades	Joely Berg	...	Jerrold Moore	Steven Osteen	Wendell Shadowen
Columbia	c	MC	4	(270) 384-2501	Patrick Bell	...	Carolyn Edwards	...	Michael Glasgow	Mark Harris	...
Corbin	c	CM	7	(606) 528-0669	James Williamson	Bill Cannon	Erin Blount	...	Gary Disney	John Mullins	James Foley
Covington	c	CM	43	(859) 292-2133	Denny Bowman	John Fossett	Carol Little	Gregory Engelman	Joseph Heringhaus	Albert Bosse	Geoffrey Warneford
Crestview Hills	c	MC	2	(859) 341-7373	Paul Meier	...	...	C. Monhollen	...	Paul Herbst	James Connelly
Cumberland	c	MC	2	(606) 589-2106	...	...	...	...	...	...	...

Directory 1/9 continued — OFFICIALS IN U.S. MUNICIPALITIES 2,500 AND OVER IN POPULATION

Jurisdiction		Type	Form of govern-ment	2000 Popu-lation	Main telephone number	Chief elected official	Appointed administrator	Clerk of the governing board	Chief financial officer	Fire chief	Police chief	Public works director
KENTUCKY continued												
Cynthiana		c	CO	6	(859) 234-7150	James Brown	...	Charleen McIlvan	...	Greg Lemons	David McGuffin	Leroy Conner
Danville		c	CM	15	(859) 238-1200	John Bowling	Paul Stansbury	Donna Peek	Spencer Rodgers	Mike Thomas	...	Tony Griffin
Dawson Springs		c	MC	2	(270) 797-2781	Stacia Peyton	...	Denise Ridley	...	Terry Warren	Bill Crider	John McChesney
Dayton		c	MC	5	(859) 491-1600	Kenneth Rankle	Dennis Redmond	Donna Leger	...	Denny Lynn	Mark Brown	Donald Riley
Douglass Hills		c	MC	5	(502) 245-3600	Sherl Fetter	...	Henrietta Barker	...	...	...	...
Edgewood		c	MC	9	(859) 331-5910	John Link	Roger Rolfes	Jeanette Kemper	...	...	Anthony Kramer	Stanley Goetz
Elizabethtown		c	MC	22	(270) 765-6121	David Willmoth	Charles Bryant	Mary Chaudoin	Stephen Park	Michael Hulsey	Ruben Gardner	William Owen
Elsmere		c	MC	8	(859) 342-7911	...	...	Melissa Andress	...	...	Timothy Greene	Charles Turner
Erlanger		c	MC	16	(859) 727-2525	Thomas Rouse	...	Linda Carter	Greg Engleman	Tim Koenig	Marc Fields	Rick Bogard
Flatwoods		c	MC	7	(606) 836-9661	...	...	Sarah Armstrong	...	...	Noel Gallion	Fred Dean
Flemingsburg	*	c	MC	3	(606) 845-5951	Louie Flanery	...	Joy Roark	...	Jerry McCloud	Randy Sergent	...
Florence		c	MC	23	(859) 371-5491	Diane Whalen	Patricia Wingo	Joseph Christofield	Linda Chapman	Marc Muench	Thomas Kathman	Robert Townsend
Fort Mitchell		c	CM	8	(859) 331-1212	...	...	...	...	...	...	...
Fort Thomas	*	c	MC	16	(859) 441-1055	Mary Brown	Donald Martin	Melissa Kelly	Fred Ewald	Mark Bailey	Michael Daly	Ronald Dill
Fort Wright		c	MC	5	(606) 311-1700	Cindy Pinto	...	Jody Anderson	...	Ron Becker	Mark Brow	Tim Maloney
Frankfort		c	CM	27	(502) 875-8500	William May	Anthony Massey	...	James Rogers	Wallace Possich	Ted Evans	Dennis Minks
Franklin	*	c	CM	7	(270) 586-4497	Jim Brown	Hal Toomey	Kathy Stradtner	Cendy Dodd	...	James Powell	Clifton Beecher
Fulton		c	CM	2	(502) 472-1320	Eddie Crittendon	...	Helen Lee	Lisa Owens	Shawn Bixler	Terry Powell	Richard Tidwell
Georgetown		c	MC	18	(502) 863-9800	Everette Varney	...	Sue Lewis	Michele Pogrotsky	Robert Bruin	Greg Reeves	R. C. Linton
Glasgow		c	MC	13	(270) 651-5131	Charles Honeycutt	Leslie Settle	...	...	James Wingfield	...	Jack Chadwell
Grayson		c	CO	3	(606) 474-6651	Leda Dean	...	Martha Lemaster	...	Gregory Felty	Willard Hill	...
Greenville		c	MC	4	(502) 338-3966	...	...	...	...	...	...	...
Harlan		c	MC	2	(606) 573-2912	Daniel Howard	...	Bobbie Stark	...	William Simms	Roy Hatfield	Kenneth Hicks
Harrodsburg		c	MC	8	(859) 734-2383	...	...	...	...	M. Hockersmith	...	...
Hartford		c	MC	2	(502) 298-3612	...	...	...	...	...	...	...
Hazard		c	CM	4	(606) 436-3171	...	...	...	...	...	...	...
Henderson		c	CM	27	(270) 831-1200	Henry Lackey	...	Carolyn Williams	Robert Gunter	Terrence Lewis	Mack Brady	X. R. Royster
Hickman	*	c	CM	2	(270) 236-2535	Charles Murphy	Larry Myatt	Donna Haney	...	Jackie Duncan	Tony Grogan	...
Highland Heights		c	MC	6	(859) 441-8575	Charles Roettger	...	...	...	...	Carl Mullen	Albert Harris
Hillview	*	c	MC	7	(502) 957-5280	James Eadens	...	Betty Bradbury	...	...	Aaron Yates	Jim Bohannon
Hodgenville	*	c	MC	2	(270) 358-3832	Terry Cruse	...	MaDonna Hornback	...	Terry Ovesen	Johnny Cottrill	Tommy DeSpain
Hopkinsville		c	MC	30	(270) 890-0265	Richard Liebe	Glenn Abee	Christine Upton	Robert Martin	Fagan Pace	Kermit Yeager	Rick Deason
Hurstbourne		c	CO	3	(502) 426-4808	W. Bardenwerper	Ronald Howard	Katherine Petricek	...	...	...	...
Independence		c	MC	14	(859) 356-5302	Thomas Kriege	Daniel Groth	Patricia Taney	Amy Guenther	...	Ed Porter	Jeffrey Smith
Irvine		c	MC	2	(606) 723-2554	C. Williams	...	...	...	Anthony Murphy	James Crowe	...
Jackson		c	MC	2	(606) 666-7069	Michael Miller	...	Angela Combs	...	Roger Friley	Clyde Caudill	Ralph Cundiff
Jeffersontown		c	MC	26	(502) 267-8333	Clay Foreman	...	Frank Greenwell	...	...	Richard Sanders	...
Jenkins		c	MC	2	(606) 832-2141	Robert Shubert	...	Sandra Puckett	...	Richard Corbett	Bill Tackett	...
La Grange	*	c	MC	5	(502) 222-1433	Elsie Carter	...	Stephanie Cooper	...	...	Kevin Collett	Keith Crowder
Lakeside Park		c	MC	2	(859) 341-6670	Frank Smith	...	...	...	...	...	Robert Haglage
Lancaster		c	MC	3	(859) 792-2241	...	...	...	...	...	...	...
Lawrenceburg		c	MC	9	(502) 839-5372	Bobby Sparrow	...	...	...	Robert Hume	Harold Burris	Larry Hazlett
Lebanon		c	MC	5	(270) 692-6272	Gary Crenshaw	...	Joyce Ford	...	Richard Mattingly	Eugene Young	Robert Thompson
Leitchfield	*	c	MC	6	(270) 259-4034	William Thomason	...	Erin Embry	...	Carl Smith	Bart Glenn	Darrell Harrell
Lexington–Fayette Urban County		c	MC	225	(859) 258-3000	...	...	Liz Damrell	James Deaton	Robert Hendricks	Anthany Beatty	...
London		c	MC	5	(606) 864-4169	Kenneth Smith	...	Connie McKnight	...	Ernest Clark	Elijah Hollon	Steven Edge
Louisville–Jefferson County		c	MC	256	(502) 574-2003	Jerry Abramson	...	Bobbi Holsclaw	Jane Driskell	Gregory Frederick	Robert White	Jim Adkins
Ludlow		c	MC	4	(859) 491-1233	Ed Schroeder	...	...	...	Terry Bandy	Ray Murphy	...
Madisonville		c	MC	19	(270) 824-2100	Karen Cunningham	Lloyd Merrell	Gina Munger	Steven Ramsey	Tommy Williams	Ronald Hunt	Dennis Farris
Marion		c	MC	3	(270) 965-2266	...	...	...	...	...	...	...
Mayfield	*	c	MC	10	(270) 247-1981	Arthur Byrn	...	Tamie Johnson	...	Mike Jones	Dale Murphey	Russ Brower
Maysville		c	CM	8	(606) 564-9411	David Cartmell	...	Sharon Swisher	Romie Griffey	John Gantley	Van Ingram	...
Middlesborough		c	MC	10	(606) 248-5670	Ben Hickman	James Pursifull	Teresa Massengill	...	Tim Wilder	Jeff Sharpe	Leeman Moyers
Monticello	*	c	MC	5	(606) 348-0167	Kenneth Catron	...	Gregory Latham	...	Jerry Ferrell	Ralph Miniard	Gene Jones
Morehead		c	MC	5	(606) 784-8505	Bradley Collins	...	Diana Lindsey	...	Charles Walker	Gary Gardner	Dwain Wilson
Morganfield		c	MC	3	(270) 389-2525	Jerry Freer	David Presser	...	...	Earl Woods	Tom Carmon	...
Mount Sterling		c	MC	5	(859) 498-8725	Gary Williamson	...	...	...	...	Michael Schnell	Steve Lane
Mount Washington		c	MC	8	(502) 538-4216	...	...	Christi Franklin	...	...	Leo Oliver	...
Murray		c	MC	14	(502) 762-0309	...	...	...	...	...	...	...
Newport		c	CM	17	(859) 292-3682	Thomas Guidugli	Thomas Fromme	...	...	Larry Atwell	...	Christopher Novak
Nicholasville		c	CO	19	(859) 885-1121	Sam Corman	...	Roberta Warren	James Hood	...	Barry Waldrop	Thomas Calkins
Olive Hill		c	MC	1	(606) 286-5532	James Short	...	Don Everman	...	Rod Stephens	Daniel Tackett	Virgil Jordan
Owensboro	*	c	CM	54	(270) 687-8545	Ron Payne	William Parrish	Carol Blake	James Fulkerson	Ron Heep	John Kazlauskas	...
Paducah		c	CM	26	(270) 444-8504	William Paxton	James Zumwalt	...	Jonathan Perkins	Redell Benton	Randy Bratton	...
Paintsville		c	MC	4	(606) 789-2600	Robin Cooper	...	Virgie Castle	Robert Conley	Bob Dixon	Doug Wallen	Larry Herald
Paris	*	c	CM	9	(859) 987-2110	Donald Kiser	Russell Brunner	Cheryl Marsh	...	James Fomas	Tim Gray	Gary Barbee
Park Hills		c	MC	2	(859) 431-6252	Michael Hellmann	...	...	...	Regis Huth	Ricardo Smith	Dennis Finke
Pikeville		c	CM	6	(606) 437-5100	Steven Combs	Donovan Blackburn	Karen Harris	...	...	...	Greg May
Pineville		c	MC	2	(606) 337-2958	...	...	...	...	...	...	...
Prestonsburg		c	MC	3	(606) 886-2335	Jerry Fannin	...	Peggy Bailey	...	Chester Davis	Stanley Farler	William Harris
Princeton		c	MC	6	(270) 365-9575	...	...	...	...	...	...	...
Prospect		c	MC	4	(502) 228-1121	Lonnie Falk	Ann Simms	...	...	...	Marvin Wilson	...
Providence		c	MC	3	(270) 667-5463	Jerry Fritz	...	Sara Stevens	...	Jimmy Oakley	Archie Benton	Ralph Alexander
Radcliff	*	c	MC	21	(270) 351-4714	...	...	...	...	...	...	...
Richmond		c	CM	27	(859) 623-1000	Ann Durham	David Evans	Betty Houghton	Janet Herbst	Fred Brandenburg	David Harkleroad	Hershell Sparks
Russell		c	MC	3	(606) 836-9666	Donald Fraley	...	Joyce Conley	...	Harry Thomas	Phillip Caskey	...
Russellville		c	MC	7	(270) 726-5000	Shirley Yassmy	...	...	Jennifer Knight	John Williamson	James Pendergraff	...
Scottsville		c	MC	4	(502) 237-3238	...	...	...	...	...	...	...
Shelbyville		c	MC	10	(502) 633-8000	David Eaton	...	Inez Harris	...	...	John Kubran	Albert Minnis
Shepherdsville		c	MC	8	(502) 543-2923	Sherman Tinnell	...	Tammy Owen	...	Brad Whittaker	Doug Puckett	Jesse Walls
Shively		c	MC	15	(502) 449-5000	Sherry Conner	...	Mitzi Kasitz	...	Wendell Vincent	Ralph Miller	John Haywood
Somerset		c	MC	11	(606) 679-6366	J. P. Wiles	...	David Godsey	James Hogg	James Latham	David Biggerstaff	James Fisher
Southgate		c	MC	3	(859) 441-0075	Charles Melville	...	Rose Welscher	...	...	Michael Hall	R.Sanzenbacker
Springfield		c	MC	2	(859) 336-5440	Mike Haydon	Laurie Smith	...	...	Troy Logsdon	Fred Armstrong	Glenn Mattingly
St. Matthews		c	MC	15	(502) 895-9444	Arthur Draut	...	Gretchen Kaiser	...	...	Norman Mayer	Bill Kaiser
Stanford		c	MC	3	(606) 365-4500	Eddie Carter	...	Sandra Gooch	...	Leroy Lunsford	Keith Middleton	John Lasure
Stanton		c	MC	3	(606) 663-4459	...	...	...	...	...	...	...
Taylor Mill		c	MC	6	(859) 581-3234	Mark Kreimborg	Jill Bailey	Karen Griffith	...	Dennis Halpin	Steve Knauf	Marc Roden
Tompkinsville		c	MC	2	(502) 487-6776	...	...	Clarnell Emberton	...	...	Johnny Graves	Tom Baker
Union	*	0	MC	2	(859) 384-1511	Don Kirby	Warren Moore	Kathy Porter	...	...	...	...
Versailles		c	MC	7	(859) 873-5436	...	...	Allison White	...	Frankie Shuck	William Love	Bartley Miller
Villa Hills		c	MC	7	(859) 341-1515	Dennis Stein	...	Sue Kramer	...	George Bruns	Michael Brown	Derick Yelton
Vine Grove		c	MC	4	(270) 877-2422	Donovan Smith	...	Cary Broussard	...	Steve New	Steven Manning	Burlin Martin
Williamsburg		c	MC	5	(606) 549-6033	Roger Harrison	...	...	Teresa Black	James Privett	Denny Shelley	Truman Prewitt

Directory 1/9 continued **OFFICIALS IN U.S. MUNICIPALITIES 2,500 AND OVER IN POPULATION**

Jurisdiction	Type	Form of govern-ment	2000 Popu-lation	Main telephone number	Chief elected official	Appointed administrator	Clerk of the governing board	Chief financial officer	Fire chief	Police chief	Public works director
KENTUCKY continued											
Williamstown *	c	MC	3	(859) 824-3633	Glenn Caldwell	Douglas Beckham	Vivian Link	. . .	Les Whalen	Bobby Webb	. . .
Wilmore	c	MC	5	(859) 858-4411	Harold Rainwater	. . .	C. Brandenburg	. . .	Jeffrey Anderson	Stephen Boven	David Carlstodt
Winchester	c	CM	16	(859) 744-7017	Dodd Dixon	Kenneth Kerns	Marilyn Rowe	. . .	Daniel Castle	William Jackson	Norman Howard
LOUISIANA											
Abbeville	t	MC	11	(337) 893-8550	Mark Piazza	. . .	Kathleen Faulk	. . .	Elvin Michaud	Rick Coleman	Clay Menard
Alexandria	c	MC	46	(318) 449-5020	Edward Randolph	Delores Brewer	Nancy Thiels	David Crutchfield	Paul Smith	Darren Coutee	. . .
Amite City	t	MC	4	(985) 748-9850	. . .	. . .	. . .	. . .	. . .	. . .	. . .
Arcadia	t	MC	3	(318) 263-8456	Jesse Smith	. . .	. . .	. . .	Randy Wright	Victor Rogers	. . .
Baker	c	MC	13	(985) 778-0300	. . .	J. E. Carroll	Jean Byers	Julie Pittman	. . .	Sid Gautreaux	Glynn Cavin
Baldwin	t	MC	2	(337) 923-7523	Wayne Breaux	. . .	Sonya Charles	. . .	Gene St. Germain	Gerald Minor	. . .
Ball	t	MC	3	(318) 640-9605	Roy Hebron	. . .	Willie Bishop	. . .	. . .	Spencer Williams	. . .
Basile	t	MC	1	(337) 432-6692	Berline Sonnier	. . .	Vickie Briscoe	. . .	Mike Arnold	Allen Ivory	. . .
Bastrop	c	MC	12	(318) 283-0250	. . .	. . .	. . .	. . .	. . .	. . .	. . .
Baton Rouge–East Baton Rouge	c	MC	227	(225) 389-3129	Melvin Holden	Walter Monsour	. . .	David Medlin	Edwin Smith	Pat Englade	Fred Raiford
Berwick	t	MC	4	(985) 384-8858	. . .	. . .	. . .	. . .	. . .	. . .	. . .
Bogalusa	c	MC	13	(985) 732-6211	Mervin Taylor	Gerald Bailey	. . .	. . .	. . .	. . .	Billy Daniels
Bossier City	c	MC	56	(318) 741-8500	Lorenz Walker	Allen Austin	Dorothy Thornton	William Buffington	Samuel Halphen	Ken Halphen	Gary Neathery
Breaux Bridge	c	MC	7	(337) 332-1840	Jack Delhomme	. . .	Pattie Du Puis	. . .	. . .	. . .	Frank Leblanc
Broussard	c	MC	5	(337) 837-6681	Charles Langlinais	. . .	Tina Denais	. . .	Danny Denais	Brannon Decou	Larry Champagne
Bunkie	t	MC	4	(318) 346-7663	Gerard Moreau	. . .	. . .	. . .	Joseph Frank	Mary Fanara	Louis Redmon
Carencro	t	MC	6	(337) 896-8481	. . .	. . .	. . .	. . .	. . .	. . .	. . .
Church Point	t	MC	4	(337) 684-5693	Roger Boudreaux	. . .	. . .	. . .	. . .	Albert Venable	James Landry
Covington	c	MC	8	(985) 892-1811	Candace Watkins	. . .	Lynne Moore	. . .	Richard Badon	Jerome Di Franco	Thomas Mayronne
Crowley	c	MC	14	(337) 788-4100	. . .	Margaret Young	Judy Istre	. . .	. . .	Kendall Gibson	Albert John
De Quincy	t	MC	3	(337) 786-8241	. . .	. . .	Tammy Pinder	. . .	. . .	Michael Suchanek	Bobby Dahlquist
De Ridder	c	MC	9	(337) 462-8900	Gerald Johnson	. . .	Penelope Simmons	Ginny Brand	Marvin Whiddon	Ricky Johnson	Hershell Nutt
Delhi	t	MC	3	(318) 878-3792	. . .	. . .	. . .	. . .	. . .	. . .	. . .
Denham Springs	c	MC	8	(225) 665-8121	James De Laune	Ellis Chavers	Lerline Barnett	. . .	Robert Wascom	Jeffrey Wesley	Willie Rheams
Donaldsonville	c	CM	7	(504) 473-4247	Leroy Sullivan	Charles Oatis	Bernard Francis	Sandra Cost	Kirk Landry	. . .	Gerard Joesph
Eunice	c	MC	11	(337) 457-7389	E. Lynn Lejeune	. . .	Doug Cart	. . .	Gerald Le Jeune	James Fontenot	. . .
Farmerville	t	MC	3	(318) 368-9242	. . .	. . .	. . .	. . .	. . .	. . .	. . .
Ferriday	t	MC	3	(318) 757-3411	. . .	. . .	. . .	. . .	. . .	. . .	. . .
Franklin	c	MC	8	(337) 828-6316	Sam Jones	Lecia Verrette	. . .	Bianca Phillips	Boykin Bourgeois	Sabria McGuire	Jeremy Smith
Franklinton	t	MC	3	(985) 839-3569	Earle Brown	. . .	Faye Boyd	. . .	. . .	Lynn Armand	Cockern Linwood
Gonzales	c	MC	8	(985) 647-2841	. . .	. . .	. . .	. . .	. . .	. . .	. . .
Grambling	v	MC	4	(318) 247-6120	. . .	. . .	. . .	. . .	. . .	. . .	. . .
Gramercy	t	MC	3	(225) 869-4403	Eugene Louque	. . .	. . .	. . .	Andy Detillier	David Dufresne	. . .
Gretna	c	MC	17	(504) 363-1700	Beauregard Miller	Arthur Lawson	. . .	. . .	. . .	. . .	. . .
Hammond	c	MC	17	(985) 542-3400	Mayson Foster	Martis Jones	Lanita Johnson	Larry Francis	Paul Collura	Roddy Devall	. . .
Harahan	c	MC	9	(504) 737-6383	Paul Johnston	Margaret Broussard	Rena Sanders	. . .	Todd St. Cyr	Peter Dale	Leslie Lauricella
Haynesville	t	MC	2	(318) 624-0911	Tom Crocker	. . .	Marilyn Bush	. . .	Mark Furlow	. . .	Alvin Moss
Homer *	t	MC	3	(318) 927-3555	David Newell	B. J. Lowe	. . .	James Colvin	Dennis Butcher	Albert Mills	Lee Wells
Jackson	t	MC	4	(985) 634-7777	. . .	. . .	. . .	. . .	. . .	. . .	. . .
Jeanerette	t	MC	5	(318) 256-4587	. . .	. . .	. . .	. . .	. . .	. . .	. . .
Jena	t	MC	2	(318) 992-2148	Murphy McMillin	. . .	Cory Floyd	. . .	Don Smith	M. Smith	Don Jones
Jennings	c	MC	10	(337) 821-5500	Gregory Marcantel	. . .	Norman Cain	. . .	Tommy Deshotel	Dalton Joseph	Cyril Charles
Jonesboro	t	MC	3	(318) 259-2385	Don Essmeier	. . .	Beatrice Rice	. . .	Tim Wyatt	G. Horton	Donald Davis
Jonesville	t	MC	2	(318) 339-8596	William Edwards	. . .	Robert Swayze	. . .	Ben Adams	Clyde Walker	Sim Nichols
Kaplan	c	MC	5	(337) 643-8602	Levi Schexnider	. . .	Darlene Labry	. . .	Donald Meaux	Stephen Perry	. . .
Kenner	c	MC	70	(504) 468-7207	Louis Congemi	Joseph Nicolosi	Michelle Sheeren	Duke McConnell	Michael Zito	Nick Congemi	Michael Scardino
Kentwood *	t	MC	2	(985) 229-3451	Harold Smith	. . .	Michelle Anthony	. . .	Tommy Simmons	James Rimes	David Sellers
Kinder	t	MC	2	(337) 738-2620	. . .	. . .	. . .	. . .	. . .	. . .	. . .
Lafayette Consolidated Government	c	MC	110	(337) 291-8300	Joey Durel	Dee Stanley	Norma Dugas	Rebecca Lalumia	Robert Benoit	Jim Craft	Tom Carrol
Lake Arthur	t	MC	3	(337) 774-2211	Edley Giles	. . .	Cynthia Mallett	. . .	. . .	Cheryl Vincent	Conrad Whitman
Lake Charles	c	MC	71	(337) 491-1200	Willie Mount	. . .	Elizabeth Eastman	Ronald Kemerly	Emerson Peet	Samuel Ivey	. . .
Lake Providence	t	MC	5	(318) 559-2288	Isaac Fields	. . .	Barbara McDaniel	Leland Jong	Jimmy Coleman	Renee Jones	Frank Powell
Leesville	t	CM	6	(337) 239-2444	. . .	Delain Prewitt	. . .	. . .	Donny McKee	Bobby Hickman	Sunny Martin
Lutcher	t	MC	3	(225) 869-5823	Troas Poche	. . .	Patricia Lemoine	. . .	. . .	Corey Pittman	Nolan Scott
Mamou	t	MC	3	(337) 468-3272	. . .	. . .	Guy Pucheu	. . .	. . .	Adam Fruge	Spencer Long
Mandeville *	c	MC	10	(985) 626-3144	Edward Price	. . .	Elizabeth Gereighty	Milton Stiebing	. . .	Thomas Buell	David deGeneres
Mansfield *	c	MC	5	(318) 872-0406	Curtis McCoy	. . .	Marvin Jackson	. . .	Lee Shaver	Don English	James Ruffin
Many	t	MC	2	(318) 256-3651	. . .	. . .	. . .	. . .	. . .	. . .	. . .
Marksville	c	MC	5	(318) 253-9500	Richard Michel	. . .	Myron Gagnard	. . .	Ned Bordelon	N. Greenhouse	Jerry Ducey
Minden	c	MC	13	(318) 377-2144	Bill Robertson	Robert Green	. . .	. . .	. . .	T. Bloxom	George Rolfe
Monroe	c	MC	53	(318) 329-2284	James Mayo	David Barnes	Carolus Riley	Stacey Haynie	Jimmy Bryant	Ronald Schleuter	C. Janway
Morgan City	c	MC	12	(985) 385-1770	Tim Tregle	Michael Loupe	. . .	Lorrie Braus	Richard Anderson	Claude Christy	Vincent Matherne
Natchitoches	c	MC	17	(318) 357-3826	Joseph Sampite	. . .	Maryann Nunley	Patrick Jones	Robert Hebert	Keith Thompson	Clyde Lacaze
New Iberia	c	MC	32	(337) 369-2300	Hilda Curry	Amie Varnado	Elmire Brennan	. . .	Ronnie Bourque	. . .	James Russell
New Orleans	c	MC	484	(504) 565-6500	C. Ray Nagin	. . .	Peggy Crutchfield	Reginald Zeno	Warren McDaniels	Edwin Compass	. . .
New Roads *	t	MC	4	(225) 638-5360	Tommy Nelson	Lynette Nelson	. . .	Cherie Beard	. . .	Kevin McDonald	Elie Part
Oakdale *	c	MC	8	(318) 335-3629	Robert Abrusley	Melissa Schaefer	. . .	. . .	Thomas Moore	Bobby Gordon	Robert Staehle
Opelousas	c	MC	22	(337) 948-2532	Anna Simmons	Monica Semien	Frances Carron	. . .	Lee Cahanin	Larry Caillier	Ronald Turner
Patterson	t	MC	5	(985) 395-5205	. . .	. . .	. . .	. . .	. . .	. . .	. . .
Pineville	c	MC	13	(318) 449-5659	Clarence Fields	. . .	Ellen Melancon	Kimberly Portier	Gary Morrow	Jay Barber	Charles Moore
Plaquemine	t	MC	7	(225) 687-3116	Mark Gulotta	. . .	Sheila Migliacio	Laurie Berthelot	Mackie Guillot	Orian Gulotta	Louis Guidry
Ponchatoula	c	MC	5	(985) 386-6484	Julian Dufreche	. . .	. . .	E. LeSaicherre	. . .	Timothy Gideon	. . .
Port Allen	c	MC	5	(504) 348-5670	. . .	. . .	. . .	. . .	. . .	. . .	. . .
Port Barre	t	MC	2	(337) 585-7646	John Fontenot	. . .	Juanita Hardy	. . .	. . .	Huey Guillory	Donald Robin
Rayne	c	MC	8	(318) 334-3121	. . .	. . .	. . .	. . .	. . .	. . .	. . .
Rayville	t	MC	4	(318) 728-7501	. . .	. . .	. . .	. . .	. . .	. . .	. . .
Ruston	c	MC	20	(318) 251-8663	Dan Hollingsworth	George Byrnside	. . .	. . .	Donnie Watson	Randal Hermes	Thomas Love
Shreveport	c	MC	200	(318) 673-5150	Robert Williams	. . .	Arthur Thompson	E. Washington	Kelvin Cochran	Stephen Prator	. . .
Slidell *	c	MC	25	(985) 646-4377	Ben Morris	Robert Dunbar	Thomas Reeves	Sharon Howes	. . .	Freddie Drennan	Michael Noto
Springhill	c	MC	5	(318) 539-5681	Carroll Breaux	. . .	Faye Farrar	. . .	. . .	Ronnie Coleman	Mike Dunaway
St. Gabriel	t	MC	5	(225) 642-9600	George Grace	Yolonda Mattaur	Linda Jackson	Katrina Stewart	Floyd Sanchez	Patrick Nelson	W. Cushenberry
St. Martinville *	c	MC	6	(337) 394-2230	Thomas Nelson	. . .	Penny Granger	. . .	. . .	Paula Smith	Nolan Champagne
Sulphur	c	MC	20	(337) 527-4500	Ronald LeLeux	. . .	Arlene Blanchard	Paree Prejean	Danny Dupre	Kenneth Moss	Dennis Bergeron
Tallulah	c	MC	9	(318) 574-0964	Eddie Beckwith	. . .	. . .	Gerald Odom	. . .	Donnell Rose	. . .
Thibodaux	c	MC	14	(985) 448-5848	Lucien Cailloet	Theresa Larose	. . .	Deborah Daigle	. . .	Howard Robertson	Kermit Kraemer
Vidalia	t	MC	4	(318) 336-5206	. . .	. . .	. . .	. . .	. . .	. . .	. . .
Ville Platte	t	MC	8	(337) 363-2939	Phillip Lemoine	. . .	Bryan Savant	. . .	Ted Demourelle	Romeo Hargrove	Clifford Fontenot
Vinton	t	MC	3	(337) 589-7453	Claude Lemaire	. . .	Melba Landry	. . .	. . .	Dennis Drouillard	Charles Guillory

Directory 1/9 continued OFFICIALS IN U.S. MUNICIPALITIES 2,500 AND OVER IN POPULATION

Jurisdiction	Type	Form of govern-ment	2000 Popu-lation	Main telephone number	Chief elected official	Appointed administrator	Clerk of the governing board	Chief financial officer	Fire chief	Police chief	Public works director
LOUISIANA continued											
Vivian	t	MC	4	(318) 375-3856	Hayward McCormick	...	Diann House	...	...	Ronald Smith	Ronald Brown
Walker	t	MC	4	(225) 665-4356	Mike Grimmer	...	Janet Borne	Ronald Petty	...	Casey Grimes	Gary Green
Welsh *	t	MC	3	(337) 734-2231	Carolyn Louviere	...	Linda Le Blanc	...	John Hall	Tommy Chaisson	James Ewing
West Monroe	c	MC	13	(318) 396-2600	...	...	...	...	...	...	...
Westlake *	t	MC	4	(337) 433-0691	Daniel Cupit	...	Andrea Mahfouz	Marcy Wade	Jacques Picou	Jeremy Cryer	Brad Baker
Westwego	c	MC	10	(504) 341-3424	Robert Billiot	Christopher Trosclair	Bonnie Pertuit	...	Doyle Guidroz	Roy Juncker	Robert Utley
Winnfield	c	MC	5	(318) 628-3939	...	...	...	...	...	...	...
Winnsboro	t	MC	5	(318) 435-9087	...	...	...	...	...	...	...
Zachary *	c	MC	11	(225) 654-0287	Henry Martinez	...	...	Rebecca Kelley	Boyce Smith	John Herty	Chris Davezac
Zwolle	t	MC	1	(318) 645-6141	Marvin Frazier	...	Mindy Ezernack	...	...	...	...
MAINE											
Amity	t	CM	..	(207) 532-2485	...	Darrell Williams	...	...	...	...	...
Ashland	t	CM	1	(207) 435-2311	...	William Beaulier	...	...	Ned Labelle	Gary Ellis	...
Auburn *	c	CM	23	(207) 333-6600	John Jenkins	Glenn Aho	Mary Magno	...	Russell Werts	Philip Crowell	Robert Belz
Augusta	c	CM	18	(207) 626-2353	William Dowling	William Bridgeo	Barbara Wardwell	...	...	Wayne McCamish	John Charest
Baileyville	t	TM	1	(207) 427-3442	...	...	...	...	...	...	...
Bangor *	c	CM	31	(207) 992-4200	John Cashwell	Edward Barrett	Patti Dubois	Deborah Cyr	Jeffrey Cammack	Donald Winslow	Dana Wardwell
Bar Harbor	t	CM	4	(207) 288-4098	...	Dana Reed	Patricia Gray	Stanley Harmon	David Rand	Nathan Young	Charles Reeves
Bath	c	CM	9	(207) 443-8330	Bernard Wyman	William Giroux	Mary White	Abigail Yacoben	Stephen Hinds	Michael Field	Peter Owen
Belfast	c	CM	6	(207) 338-3370	...	Joseph Slocum	Roberta Fogg	...	James Richards	Jeffrey Trafton	...
Berwick	t	CM	6	(207) 698-1101	Thomas Fournier	Keith Trefethen	Judith Buckman	Janet Canney	Dennis Plante	Timothy Towne	Robert Perchy
Bethel	t	TM	2	(207) 824-2669	...	Scott Cole	Christen Mason	Nesta Littlefield	James Young	Darren Tripp	Robert Pilgrim
Biddeford	c	MC	20	(207) 284-9105	Jim Gratello	John Bubier	Clairma Matherne	Richard Lagarde	Raymond Gagne	Roger Beaupre	Mike Ostrosky
Blaine	t	TM	..	(207) 425-2611	...	...	...	...	...	...	...
Boothbay	t	TM	2	(207) 633-2051	C. Cunningham	John Anderson	Bonnie Lewis	...	Richard Spofford	...	Anthony Goode
Boothbay Harbor	t	TM	2	(207) 633-3671	Robert Jacobson	...	Patricia Wheeler	Julia Latter	Glenn Townsend	Stephen Clark	Joseph Lewis
Bowdoinham *	t	CM	2	(207) 666-5531	S. Ciembroniewicz	K. Durgin-Leighton	Pamela Ross	...	Jack Tourtelotte	...	Kevin Prout
Brewer	c	CM	8	(207) 989-7500	Gayle Kelly	Stephen Bost	Arthur Verow	Karen McVey	Richard Bronson	Steve Barker	David Cote
Bridgewater	t	CM	..	(207) 429-9856	Amanda Dow	...	...	...	John Barker	...	Ralph Kinney
Bridgton	t	TM	4	(207) 647-8786	...	Mitchell Berkowitz	Laurie Chadbourne	...	Thomas Harriman	David Lyons	James Kidder
Brownville	t	CM	1	(207) 965-2561	Dennis Green	Sophia Wilson	Kathy White	...	David Preble	Todd Lyford	Kevin Black
Brunswick	t	CM	21	(207) 725-6659	Charles Priest	...	Fran Smith	John Eldridge	Gary Howard	Jerry Hinton	John Foster
Bucksport	t	CM	4	(207) 469-7368	...	...	...	...	...	...	...
Buxton	t	TM	7	(207) 929-6171	Stephen Nichols	...	John Myers	...	Jeff Grinnell	Jody Thomas	Larry Owen
Calais	c	CM	3	(207) 454-2521	...	...	Theresa Porter	Pamela Bridges	Danny Carlow	Michael Milburn	Mark Magoon
Camden	t	CM	5	(207) 236-3353	Morton Strom	Roberta Smith	Carol Rogers	...	Steven Gibbons	...	Earl Weaver
Cape Elizabeth	t	CM	9	(207) 799-5251	...	Michael McGovern	Deborah Cabana	...	Philip McGouldrick	Neil Williams	Robert Malley
Caribou	c	CM	8	(207) 493-3324	...	Steven Buck	Judy Corrow	Wanda Ouellette	Roy Woods	Michael Gahagan	David Ouellette
Carmel	t	TM	2	(207) 848-3361	...	...	...	...	...	...	...
Carrabassett Valley	t	TM	..	(207) 235-2645	...	David Cota	Sherie McCatherin	...	Courtney Knapp	Ronald Moody	...
Casco	t	CM	3	(207) 627-4515	Calvin Nutting	David Morton	...	...	John Small	...	...
Castle Hill *	t	CM	..	(207) 764-3754	...	Martin Puckett	Trudence Buck	...	Richard Wark	...	Mike Pelletier
Chelsea	t	TM	2	(207) 582-4802	Richard Danforth	Mary Sabins	Judith Jones	...	Shawn Ramage	...	...
Cherryfield	t	TM	1	(207) 546-2376	Randy Derry	George Hanington	...	...	Charles Curtis	...	...
China	t	TM	4	(207) 445-2014	Thomas Barber	...	Becky Cunningham	...	Richard Morse	James Lane	...
Clinton *	t	TM	3	(207) 426-8511	Jeffrey Towne	James Rhodes	Pamela Violette	...	Gary Petley	Charles Runnels	...
Corinna	t	CM	2	(207) 278-4183	Galen McKenney	...	Tressa Gudroe	...	F. Clark	...	Stephen Lawson
Corinth	t	TM	2	(207) 285-3271	...	...	...	...	...	...	...
Crystal	t	TM	..	(207) 463-2770	...	Susan York	...	...	...	...	...
Cumberland	t	CM	7	(207) 829-2205	Jeffrey Porter	William Shane	Nadeen Daniels	Melody Main	Daniel Small	Joseph Charron	Adam Ogden
Danforth	t	CM	..	(207) 448-2321	...	...	...	...	...	...	...
Denmark	t	TM	1	(207) 452-2163	...	...	...	...	...	...	...
Dexter	t	CM	3	(207) 924-7351	Peter Haskell	Judith Doore	Shelly Watson	Marilyn Curtis	Melvin Wyman	Arthur Roy	Michael Delaware
Dixfield	t	CM	2	(207) 562-8151	G. Daley	...	Vickie Cross	...	Scott Blaisdell	Richard Pickett	David Orr
Dover-Foxcroft	t	TM	4	(207) 564-3318	Elwood Edgerly	Owen Pratt	...	...	Joseph Guyotte	Dennis Dyer	...
Dyer Brook *	t	TM	..	(207) 757-8302	David McLaughlin	Florence Hardy	...	...	...	...	...
Eagle Lake	t	CM	..	(207) 444-5125	...	...	...	...	...	...	...
East Millinocket *	t	TM	1	(207) 746-3376	Mark Scally	Shirley Tapley	Laura Ferguson	...	Leslie Brown	Garold Cramp	Danny Violette
Easton	t	TM	1	(207) 488-6652	Michael Corey	Jackalene Bradley	Cheryl Clark	...	Theodore White	...	...
Eastport	c	CM	1	(207) 853-2300	...	...	Helen Archer	...	Richard Clark	Matt Vinson	Rene O'Dell
Eliot	t	TM	5	(207) 439-1813	Stephen Beckert	Daniel Blanchette	Wendy Rawski	...	Richard Wood	Almon Boston	William Shapleigh
Ellsworth *	c	CM	6	(207) 667-2563	...	Michelle Beal	Heidi Grindle	...	Jonathan Marshall	John Deleo	Myron Grant
Exeter	t	CM	..	(207) 379-2191	James Crane	Tressa Gudroe	Jeanette Black	...	Alan Clark	...	...
Fairfield	t	CM	6	(207) 453-7911	Richard Spear	Paul Blanchette	Tracey Stevens	...	Duane Bickford	John Emery	Bruce Williams
Falmouth	t	CM	10	(207) 781-5253	Paul Davis	Nathan Poore	Kathleen Babeu	John McNaughton	Cameron Martin	Edward Tolan	Anthony Hayes
Farmingdale	t	TM	2	(207) 582-2225	...	Phyllis Weeks	...	...	...	...	...
Farmington	t	CM	7	(207) 778-6539	...	Richard Davis	Leanne Pinkham	...	Terry Bell	Richard Caton	Mitchell Boulette
Fort Fairfield *	t	CM	3	(207) 472-3800	...	Dan Foster	Mary Whitmore	...	Paul Durepo	Joseph Bubar	George Watson
Fort Kent	t	CM	4	(207) 834-3507	...	...	...	...	...	...	...
Freeport	t	CM	7	(207) 865-4743	...	Dale Olmstead	Beverly Curry	Gregory L'Heureux	Darrel Fournier	Jerry Schofield	James Plummer
Frenchville	t	CM	1	(207) 543-7301	...	...	...	...	...	...	...
Frye Island	t	CM	..	(207) 655-4551	...	Wayne Fournier	...	Calvin Nutting	Steve Persson	Dana Wessling	John Crosby
Fryeburg	t	TM	3	(207) 935-2805	David Knapp	Martin Krauter	Theresa Shaw	...	Richard Sheaff	Wayne Brooking	...
Gardiner *	c	CM	6	(207) 582-4200	Andrew MacLean	Jeffrey Kobrock	Deirdre Berglund	Sandy Runyon	Mark Kimball	James Toman	Chuck Applebee
Garland *	t	CM	..	(207) 924-3163	Sanford Giles	...	Tammy Beem	...	Henry Burrill	...	...
Glenburn *	t	CM	3	(207) 942-2905	...	...	Ruthena Brasslett	...	Kevin Chase	...	...
Gorham *	t	CM	14	(207) 222-1650	Matthew Robinson	David Cole	Christina Silberman	Maureen Finger	Robert Lefebvre	Ronald Shepard	Robert Burns
Gouldsboro *	t	CM	1	(207) 963-7582	...	...	...	...	Gary Grovogel	...	...
Gray	t	CM	6	(207) 657-3339	...	...	...	...	Jon Barton	...	Steve La Vallee
Greenbush	t	TM	1	(207) 826-2050	Albert Weatherbee	...	...	...	Edward Haverlock	...	...
Greene	t	CM	4	(207) 946-5146	Ron Grant	...	...	...	...	...	Kevin Doyle
Greenville	t	TM	1	(207) 695-2421	...	David Cota	Roxanne Lizotte	...	Michael Drinkwater	Duane Alexander	...
Guilford	t	TM	1	(207) 876-2202	William Thompson	Robert Littlefield	Joyce Burton	...	...	...	...
Hallowell	c	CM	2	(207) 623-4021	Barry Timson	James Rhodes	Deanna Hallett	...	Michael Grant	Eric Nason	Robert Rayot
Hampden	t	CM	6	(207) 862-3034	Ricky Briggs	Susan Lessard	Denise Hodsdon	Virgil Pratt	...	...	Greg Nash
Harpswell	t	TM	5	(207) 833-5771	Robert Webber	...	Laverne Vayo	...	William Beazley	...	Roland Berry
Hartland	t	TM	1	(207) 938-4401	...	...	...	...	...	...	...
Haynesville	t	TM	..	(207) 448-2090	...	Norma Malone	...	...	Steven Rouse	...	...
Hermon	t	CM	4	(207) 848-3485	...	Clinton Deschene	Carol Davis	...	Larry Willis	William Laughlin	...
Hodgdon	t	CM	1	(207) 532-6498	...	James Griffin	Cheryl Cameron	...	Dana Belyea	...	Roger Hutchinson
Holden	t	CM	2	(207) 843-5151	...	R. Varisco	Wanda Libbey	Deborah Given	...	Gene Worcester	Bruce Dowling
Hollis	t	TM	4	(207) 929-8552	...	...	Claire Dunne	...	H. Carpenter	...	Robert Hanson
Houlton	t	CM	6	(207) 532-7111	Dale Flewelling	Margaret Daigle	Cathy O'Leary	...	Milton Cone	Daniel Soucy	Leigh Stilwell
Island Falls	t	TM	..	(207) 463-2246	Dwayne Hartin	Albert Clukey	Sandra Lane	...	Lewis Conrad	...	Cecil Given

Directory 1/9 continued **OFFICIALS IN U.S. MUNICIPALITIES 2,500 AND OVER IN POPULATION**

Jurisdiction	Type	Form of govern-ment	2000 Popu-lation	Main telephone number	Chief elected official	Appointed administrator	Clerk of the governing board	Chief financial officer	Fire chief	Police chief	Public works director
MAINE continued											
Islesboro	t	TM	..	(207) 734-2253	...	...	...	...	...	...	...
Jackman	t	TM	..	(207) 668-2111	...	Kathleen MacKenzie	Diane St. Hilaire	...	William Jarvis	...	...
Jay	t	TM	4	(207) 897-6785	William Harlow	Ruth Marden	Jill Gingras	Linda Brundage	Scott Shink	Larry White	John Johnson
Kennebunk	t	TM	10	(207) 985-2102	Boyd Long	Barry Tibbetts	Betty Emmons	...	Stephen Nichols	Matthew Baker	Michael Claus
Kennebunkport *	t	TM	3	(207) 967-4243	Mathew Lanagan	Larry Mead	April Dufoe	...	Paul Moshimer	Joseph Bruni	John Hirst
Kittery	t	CM	9	(207) 439-0452	Glenn Shwaery	Jonathan Carter	Maryann Place	...	David O'Brien	Edward Strong	Richard Rossiter
Lebanon	t	TM	5	(207) 457-1171	...	...	...	...	...	...	...
Levant	t	MC	2	(207) 884-7660	...	...	Amy Eaton	...	...	...	...
Lewiston *	c	CM	35	(207) 513-3000	Laurent Gilbert	James Bennett	Kathleen Montejo	Richard Metivier	Paul LeClair	William Welch	Paul Boudreau
Limestone	t	TM	2	(207) 325-4704	Steve Leighton	Paul Beaulieu	Marlene Durepo	...	Paul Durepo	Ronald Sprague	Dale Brooker
Lincoln *	t	CM	5	(207) 794-3372	Roderick Carr	Lisa Goodwin	...	...	Phillip Dawson	William Flagg	David Lloyd
Lincolnville *	t	TM	2	(207) 763-3555	Rosendel Gerry	David Kinney	...	Jodi Hanson	Ben Hazen	Ron Young	...
Linneus	t	CM	..	(207) 532-6182	...	Frances Hutchinson	...	...	Stephen Bither	...	...
Lisbon	t	CM	9	(207) 353-3000	...	Stephen Eldridge	Twila Lycette	Cathy Ricker	P. Galipeau	David Brooks	Elwood Beal
Litchfield *	t	TM	3	(207) 268-4721	Elton Wade	Mike Byron	Elaine McFee	...	Stanley Labbe	...	Dale Gregor
Littleton *	t	TM	..	(207) 538-9862	...	Courtney Toby	...	...	...	...	William Dunbar
Livermore Falls	t	CM	3	(207) 897-2016	William Demaray	...	Kristal Flagg	...	Kenneth Jones	Ernest Steward	Kent Mitchell
Lubec	t	CM	1	(207) 733-2341	Harold Jackson	...	Diana Wilson	...	...	...	...
Ludlow	t	CM	..	(207) 532-7743	...	...	...	...	...	...	...
Lyman	t	TM	3	(207) 499-2925	...	...	...	...	...	...	...
Machias	t	CM	2	(207) 255-6621	...	...	Donna Dzierzynski	Meghan Dennison	Joey Dennison	Grady Dwelley	Michael Gooch
Madawaska *	t	CM	4	(207) 728-6351	Richard Dionne	Christina Therrien	...	Lisa Parent	Norman Cyr	Ron Pelletier	Yves Lizotte
Madison	t	TM	4	(207) 696-3971	...	Norman Dean	Kathy Estes	...	Roger Lightbody	Barry Moores	Glen Mantor
Manchester *	t	TM	2	(207) 622-1894	Terri Watson	...	Marilyn Palmer	...	Allan Hewey	...	...
Mapleton *	t	TM	1	(207) 764-3754	...	Martin Puckett	Trudence Buck	...	Richard Wark	...	Mike Pelletier
Mars Hill	t	CM	1	(207) 425-3731	Penny Rideout	R. Mersereau	...	...	...	...	Wallace Boyd
Masardis	t	CM	..	(207) 435-2841	Vernon Craig	Julia Mac Donald	...	...	Nelson Craig	...	Clive Bragdon
Mechanic Falls	t	CM	3	(207) 345-2871	Dan Blanchard	John Hawley	...	Lisa Prevost	Fred Sturtevant	Jeffrey Goss	Scott Penney
Merrill	t	CM	..	(207) 757-8286	...	...	...	...	...	...	...
Mexico	t	TM	2	(207) 364-7971	Barbara Laramee	John Madigan	Penny Duguay	...	Gary Wentzell	James Theriault	David Errington
Milbridge	t	TM	1	(207) 546-2422	Gary Willey	...	Brienne Fraser	...	Peter Sawyer	Lewis Pinkham	...
Milford	t	CM	2	(207) 827-2072	John Costigan	Barbara Cox	Dawn Adams	...	Christopher Matson	...	...
Millinocket	t	CM	5	(207) 723-7000	...	Eugene Conlogue	Roxanne Johnson	...	Wayne Campbell	Carlton Jones	Dennis Cox
Milo	t	CM	2	(207) 943-2202	Charles Buzzell	Jane Jones	Barbara Crider	...	...	...	Glenn Ricker
Monmouth *	t	TM	3	(207) 933-2206	Pauline McDougald	Curtis Lunt	...	...	...	...	...
Monroe	t	TM	..	(207) 525-5515	Jackie Robbins	...	Lois Aitken	...	Keith Nealley	...	...
Monson	t	TM	..	(207) 997-3641	...	Jeanne Reed	Julie Anderson	...	Robert Wilson	...	...
Monticello	t	TM	..	(207) 538-9500	Terrence Wade	...	Ginger Pryor	...	Edwin Ellis	...	Andrew Lynds
Mount Desert	t	TM	2	(207) 276-5531	Richard Savage	Michael MacDonald	Kimberly Parady	Jean Bonville	Christopher Farley	John Doyle	Anthony Smith
Naples	t	CM	3	(207) 693-6364	...	Derik Goodine	Judy Whynot	...	...	...	...
New Canada	t	CM	..	(207) 834-4004	Frank Jalbert	Rodney Pelletier	...	...	...	...	...
New Gloucester *	t	CM	4	(207) 926-4126	Steven Libby	...	...	...	Gary Sacco	...	Ted Shane
New Portland	t	TM	..	(207) 628-4441	Peter Gardner	Andrea Reichert	Mary Hutchins	...	Jethro Poulin	...	...
Newcastle	t	TM	1	(207) 563-3441	...	...	Lynn Maloney	...	Clayton Huntley	Mark Doe	Donald Hunt
Newport	t	TM	3	(207) 368-4410	Albert Worden	James Ricker	Paula Clark	...	...	Gary Morin	Jack Wilson
Norridgewock *	t	TM	3	(207) 634-2252	Ronald Frederick	Michelle Flewelling	Charlotte Gorman	...	David Jones	...	...
North Berwick	t	TM	4	(207) 676-3112	Gregg Drew	Dwayne Morin	Janet Belmain	...	James Moore	Randolph Jones	Michael Dunn
North Yarmouth	t	CM	3	(207) 829-3705	David Perkins	...	...	...	James Malorson	...	Donald Chaisson
Norway	t	TM	4	(207) 743-6651	...	David Holt	...	...	...	...	...
Oakfield	t	TM	..	(207) 757-8479	...	Dale Morris	...	...	...	...	...
Oakland	t	CM	5	(207) 465-7357	...	Steve Dyer	Janice Porter	Douglas Mather	Charles Pullen	Michael Tracy	Robert Laplante
Ogunquit	t	CM	..	(207) 646-5139	John Miller	...	Judy Shaw-Kagiliery	...	Edward Smith	Patricia Arnaudin	Jonathan Webber
Old Orchard Beach *	t	CM	8	(207) 934-5714	...	Stephen Gunty	Kim McLaughlin	Jill Eastman	John Glass	Dana Kelley	Mary Ann Conroy
Old Town	c	CM	8	(207) 827-3965	...	John Lord	Patricia Ramsey	Joseph Schlick	Charles Bruxh	Donald O'Halloran	David Wight
Orono *	t	CM	9	(207) 866-2556	Geoffrey Gordon	Catherine Conlow	Wanda Thomas	Annie Brown	Norman Webb	Gary Duquette	Rob Yerxa
Orrington	t	CM	3	(207) 825-3340	Paul White	Dexter Johnson	Anita Demmons	...	Michael Spencer	Jon Carson	John Hodgins
Oxford	t	CM	3	(207) 539-4431	David Ivey	...	Elle Morrison	...	Ernest Knightly	Ronald Kugell	...
Paris	t	TM	4	(207) 743-2501	...	Sharon Jackson	Elizabeth Larson	...	Bradley Frost	David Verrier	Frank Danforth
Patten	t	TM	1	(207) 528-2215	Carolyn Ryan	Paul Caruso	Lora Sleeper	...	...	...	...
Phillips	t	TM	..	(207) 639-3561	...	Laura Toothaker	...	...	...	...	Stephen Haines
Pittsfield	t	CM	4	(207) 487-3136	...	Kathryn Ruth	...	...	...	...	...
Plantation Of Reed *	pl	CM	..	(207) 456-7546	Ellen Mitchell	Mitch Lansky	Nyoka Irish	...	Blaine Irish	...	...
Poland	t	TM	4	(207) 998-4601	...	...	Judith Akers	Debbie Taber	...	...	Jeffrey Chappell
Portage Lake	t	CM	..	(207) 435-4361	Patrick Raymond	Rita Sinclair	Katherine Gagnon	...	David Bolsiridge	...	Vaughn Devoe
Portland	c	CM	64	(207) 874-8624	...	Joseph Gray	Linda Cohen	Duane Kline	F. Lamontagne	Michael Chitwood	Michael Bobinsky
Presque Isle	c	CM	9	(207) 764-2522	Donald Gardner	Thomas Stevens	Nancy Gervais	...	Darrell White	Naldo Gagnon	Gerry James
Rangeley	t	TM	1	(207) 864-3326	...	Perry Ellsworth	Kim Dolbier	...	Rudolph Davis	Phil Weymouth	Everett Quimby
Raymond	t	CM	4	(207) 655-4742	...	Donald Willard	Louise Lester	Elizabeth Cummings	Denis Morse	...	Nathan White
Readfield *	t	CM	2	(207) 685-4939	Henry Clauson	Stefan Pakulski	Robin Lint	Teresa Shaw	Matthew Dunn	...	...
Richmond *	t	CM	3	(207) 737-4305	Seth Goodall	Thomas Fortier	Judy Savage	Laurie Boucher	Andrew Pierce	Richard Heald	Richard Lachance
Rockland	c	CM	7	(207) 594-8431	Edward Mazurek	...	Stuart Sylvester	Robert Armelin	Raymond Wooster	Alfred Ockenfels	Greg Blackwell
Rockport *	t	TM	3	(207) 236-0806	Robert Peabody	...	Linda Greenlaw	Virginia Lindsey	Bruce Woodward	Mark Kelley	Steve Beveridge
Rumford *	t	CM	6	(207) 364-4576	J. Boivin	...	Jane Gaisson	Debbie Laurinaitus	Gary Wentzell	Stacy Carter	Eric Russell
Sabattus	t	MC	4	(207) 375-4331	William Henshaw	Gregory Gill	Suzanne Adams	...	Robert Scott	Thomas Fales	John Hyde
Saco *	c	CM	16	(207) 282-4191	Roland Michaud	Richard Michaud	Lucette Pellerin	Lisa Parker	Alden Murphy	Bradley Paul	Michael Bolduc
Sanford	t	RT	20	(207) 324-9100	Herbert Stone	Mark Green	Claire Morrison	Ronni Champlin	Raymond Parent	Thomas Jones	Richard Wilkins
Sangerville	t	TM	1	(207) 876-2814	Richard Pellerin	...	Alice Moulton	...	Jerry Rush	...	Ron Hall
Scarborough	t	CM	16	(207) 730-4031	Jeffery Messer	Thomas Hall	Yolanda Norton	Ruth Porter	B. Michael Thurlow	Robert Moulton	Michael Shaw
Searsport	t	CM	2	(207) 548-6372	Bruce Mills	James Gillway	Marie Dakin	...	Derek Dunbar	...	Robert Seekins
Sebago *	t	CM	1	(207) 787-2457	Ruth Douglas	...	Michele Bukoveckas	...	Ken Littlefield	...	Theodore Shane
Sherman	t	TM	..	(207) 365-4260	Robert Gould	Debra O'Roak	...	...	Harold Lane	...	...
Skowhegan	t	TM	8	(207) 474-6900	Lynda Quinn	Philip Tarr	...	...	Stephen Miller	Butch Asselin	Gregory Dore
Smyrna	t	CM	..	(207) 757-8286	...	...	...	...	...	...	...
South Berwick	t	CM	6	(207) 384-3300	David Webster	Jeffrey Grossman	Barbara Bennett	Fern Houliares	George Gorman	Dana Lajoie	Terry Oliver
South Portland *	c	CM	23	(207) 767-3201	...	James Gailey	Susan Mooney	Robert Coombs	Kevin Guimond	Edward Googins	...
Southwest Harbor	t	TM	1	(207) 244-5404	Trudy Bickford	Robin Bennett	Beatrice Grinnell	...	Sam Chisolm	David Chapais	Doug Monson
St. Agatha	t	TM	..	(207) 543-7305	Dan LaBrie	Ryan Pelletier	Joan Ouellette	...	...	...	R. Chamberlain
St. Albans *	t	CM	1	(207) 938-4568	Marian Spalding	Rhonda Stark	Stacey Desrosiers	...	David Crocker	...	Ronnie Finson
Stacyville *	t	TM	..	(207) 365-4195	...	...	Carey Splan	...	Joseph Charette	...	...
Standish *	t	CM	9	(207) 642-3461	...	Gordon Billington	Mary Chapman	Scott Gesualdi	Brent Libby	...	Roger Mosley
Stockholm *	t	TM	..	(207) 896-5659	Gregory Landeen	...	...	...	Jeffrey Page	...	...
Stockton Springs	t	TM	1	(207) 567-3404	...	...	...	...	...	...	...
Stonington	t	CM	1	(207) 367-2351	James Bray	...	Lisa Gray	...	Adelbert Gross	...	Darran Eaton
Surry *	t	TM	1	(207) 667-5912	Eleanor Carlisle	...	Angela Smith	...	Jeff Grantham	...	...
Thomaston	t	CM	3	(207) 354-6107	Lee Upham	Valmore Blastow	Joan Linscott	...	Malcolm Hyler	James Hosford	David Taylor
Topsham	t	TM	9	(207) 725-5821	Donald Russell	...	Ruth Lyons	Debra Fischer	Ken Brillant	Tim Young	Welsey Thames

Directory 1/9 continued **OFFICIALS IN U.S. MUNICIPALITIES 2,500 AND OVER IN POPULATION**

Jurisdiction	Type	Form of govern-ment	2000 Popu-lation	Main telephone number	Chief elected official	Appointed administrator	Clerk of the governing board	Chief financial officer	Fire chief	Police chief	Public works director
MAINE continued											
Tremont	t	CM	1	(207) 244-7204	Scott Grierson	...	McKenzie Clough	...	Brad Reed	William Clark	Jimmy Schlaefer
Turner *	t	TM	4	(207) 225-3414	...	Eva Leavitt	...	...	Michael Arsenault	...	...
Van Buren	t	CM	2	(207) 868-2886	Donald Dumond	Larry Cote	Kathleen Cyr	...	Ken Dumond	Jean Michaud	Robert Learnard
Vassalboro *	t	TM	4	(207) 872-2826	...	Mary Sabins	Catherine St. Pierre	...	Eric Rowe	Richard Phippen	Eugene Field
Veazie	t	CM	1	(207) 947-2781	Joseph Friedman	William Reed	Beckie Woods	...	...	Mark Leonard	George Free
Vinalhaven	t	CM	1	(207) 863-4471	...	Marjorie Stratton	...	...	...	...	...
Waldoboro *	t	TM	4	(207) 832-5369	Clinton Collamore	William Post	Linda Perry	Eileen Dondlinger	Ernest Vannah	William Labombarde	John Daigle
Warren	t	CM	3	(207) 273-2421	Edmund La Flamme	Grant Wathough	Marsha Soule	...	Edward Grinnell	...	Marvin Lewis
Washburn *	t	CM	1	(207) 455-8485	Rick Corey	Andrea Powers	Elizabeth Carter	...	Arnie Devoe	Douglas Conroy	Harold Easley
Waterboro *	t	TM	6	(207) 247-6166	Dennis Abbott	Nancy Brandt	Kerry Thorne	...	Matthew Bors	...	Fred Fay
Waterville *	c	MC	15	(207) 680-4200	Paul Lepage	Michael Roy	Arlene Strahan	Robert Boschen	David LaFountain	Joseph Massey	Mark Turner
Wells *	t	TM	9	(207) 646-5113	Joan Mooney	Jane Duncan	Jessica Keyes	...	Daniel Moore	Jo-Ann Putnam	...
West Bath *	t	CM	1	(207) 443-4342	Stephen Gardner	Pamela Hile	Robert Morris	...	Michael Demers	...	James Whorff
Westbrook *	c	MC	16	(207) 854-9105	Bruce Chuluda	Jerre Bryant	Lynda Adams	Susan Rossignol	Daniel Brock	William Baker	Tom Eldridge
Wilton	t	CM	4	(207) 645-4961	Rodney Hall	Peter Nielsen	Linda Jellison	...	Frederick Hyde	James Parker	Kenneth Vining
Windham *	t	CM	14	(207) 892-1907	Carol Waig	Anthony Plante	Linda Morrell	Brian Wolcott	Charles Hammond	Richard Lewsen	Douglas Fortier
Winslow	t	CM	7	(207) 872-2776	Howard Mette	Michael Heavener	Pamela Smiley	...	William Page	Richard Grindall	John Girioux
Winter Harbor *	t	TM	..	(207) 963-2235	...	Roger Barto	Marianne Ray	...	Robert Webber	Warren Ahrens	...
Winterport	t	CM	3	(207) 223-5055	...	Phillip Pitula	Kathy Selfridge	...	...	...	...
Winthrop	t	CM	6	(207) 377-7200	Patrice Putman	Cornell Knight	Lisa Gilliam	Jan Tewksbury	Dan Brooks	Joseph Young	Matt Burnham
Wiscasset	t	TM	3	(207) 882-8200	Duane Goud	Arthur Faucher	Sandra Johnson	...	Tim Merry	John Allen	Robert Blagden
Yarmouth	t	CM	8	(207) 846-9036	...	Nathaniel Tupper	Jennifer Doten	Maura Haliotis	Byron Fairbanks	Michael Morrill	Erik Street
York	t	CM	12	(207) 363-1000	David Marshall	Robert Yandow	M. A. Szenlawski	Elizabeth McCann	C. Balentine	Douglas Bracy	William Bray
MARYLAND											
Aberdeen	t	CM	13	(410) 272-1600	S. Simmons	Douglas Miller	...	Opiribo Jack	...	Randall Rudy	Matt Lapinsky
Accident	t	MC	..	(301) 746-6346	...	Ruth Ann Hahn	...	...	...	...	...
Annapolis	c	MC	35	(410) 263-7998	Ellen Moyer	Robert Agee	Regina Eldridge	Timothy Elliott	Jerome Smith	Michael Pristoop	...
Baltimore	c	MC	651	(410) 396-3100	Martin O'Malley	...	...	Edward Gallagher	Herman Williams	Robert Smith	...
Bel Air	t	CM	10	(410) 638-4550	David Carey	Christopher Schlehr	...	...	...	Leo Matrangola	...
Berlin	t	MC	3	(410) 641-2770	Thomas Cardinale	Anthony Carson	...	Joseph Davis	...	Arnold Downing	...
Berwyn Heights	t	MC	2	(301) 474-5000	Cheye Calvo	Edward Murphy	Kerstin Harper	...	...	Patrick Murphy	Joseph Coleman
Bladensburg	t	MC	7	(301) 927-7048	David Harrington	Doris Sarumi	...	...	...	Robert Zidek	Larry Goff
Bowie	c	CM	50	(301) 262-6200	George Robinson	David Deutsch	Pamela Fleming	Robert Patrick	...	...	Richard Henrikson
Brentwood	t	MC	2	(301) 927-3344	George Denny	Peter Jones	Linda Grigsby	...	...	...	...
Brunswick *	t	MC	4	(301) 834-7500	Carroll Jones	David Dunn	...	...	...	John Smith	Kevin Brawner
Cambridge	c	MC	10	(410) 228-4020	Cleveland Rippons	...	Edwin Kinnamon	...	Jeff Hurley	Kenneth Malik	Steven Johnson
Capitol Heights	t	CM	4	(301) 336-0626	Vivian Dodson	James Booth	...	...	...	William Harrison	...
Cecilton	t	MC	..	(410) 275-2692	...	Shelley McDonald	Brenda Cochran	...	...	...	...
Centreville	t	CM	1	(410) 758-1180	Mary McCarthy	Robert McGrory	...	...	...	Dino Pignataro	...
Chesapeake City	t	MC	..	(410) 885-2598	...	...	...	...	...	...	...
Chestertown	t	MC	4	(410) 778-0500	Margo Bailey	W. Ingersoll	...	...	...	Walter Coryell	Medford Capel
Cheverly	t	CM	6	(301) 773-8360	Julia Mosley	David Warrington	Christy Clark	...	...	Harry Robshaw	Juan Torres
Chevy Chase *	t	CM	2	(301) 654-7144	...	Todd Hoffman	Andrea Silverstone	...	...	...	...
Chevy Chase	v	CM	2	(301) 654-7300	George Kinter	Geoffrey Biddle	...	Jacqueline Parker	...	Roy Gordon	Jerry Lesesne
College Park *	c	CM	24	(301) 864-8666	Stephen Brayman	Joseph Nagro	Janeen Miller	Stephen Groh	...	...	Robert Stumpff
Crisfield	c	MC	2	(410) 968-1333	Donald Gerald	...	...	...	...	...	...
Cumberland	c	CM	21	(301) 722-2000	Lee Fiedler	Jeffrey Repp	...	Joseph Urban	William Herbaugh	Charles Hinnant	Kevin Hagerich
Delmar	t	CM	1	(410) 896-2777	Paul Niblett	Sara Bynum-King	Jessica Barnes	Wendy Brady	...	Harold Saylor	Robert Handy
Denton	t	MC	2	(410) 479-2050	...	Terry Fearins	...	...	...	Rodney Cox	Scott Getchell
District Heights	t	MC	5	(301) 336-1402	Jack Sims	...	...	...	...	Herbert Keeney	Brian Edwards
Easton	t	MC	11	(410) 822-2525	C. Butler	...	Robert Karge	...	...	Walter Chase	John Larrimore
Edmonston	t	MC	..	(301) 699-8806	...	Guy Tiberio	...	...	...	...	...
Elkton *	t	CM	11	(410) 398-0970	Joseph Fisona	Lewis George	Michelle Henson	Steve Repole	...	William Ryan	Mark Turnbull
Emmitsburg	t	CM	2	(301) 447-2313	James Hoover	David Haller	Donna DesPres	...	...	...	...
Fairmount Heights	t	MC	1	(301) 925-8585	L. Thompson-Martin	Jose Gonzalez	Alva Fields	...	...	David Rice	Carlton Whittingham
Forest Heights	t	MC	2	(301) 839-1030	Paula Noble	Cynthia Farrar	Bonita Anderson	...	...	Bernard Sewell	William Clarke
Frederick	c	MC	52	(301) 694-1440	...	Janel Flora	...	Gerald Kolbfleisch	...	Regis Raffensberger	Fred Eisenhart
Friendship Heights	v	MC	8	(301) 650-2797	Alfred Muller	Julian Mansfield	...	...	...	...	...
Frostburg	c	CO	7	(301) 689-6000	James Cotton	...	...	Candace Sandvick	...	William Evans	C. Hovatter
Fruitland *	c	CM	3	(410) 548-2800	Valerie Mann	John McDonnell	Diane Nelson	Amy Caton	Robin Townsend	Paul Jackson	P. Townsend
Gaithersburg *	c	CM	52	(301) 258-6310	Sidney Katz	Angel Jones	...	Harold Belton	...	John King	James Arnoult
Galena	t	MC	..	(410) 648-5151	...	Thomas Bass	...	...	...	...	...
Garrett Park	t	MC	..	(301) 933-7488	...	Edwin Pratt	...	...	...	...	...
Glenarden	t	CM	6	(301) 773-2100	Donjuan Williams	Kimberly O'Neil	Brenda Leake	...	...	William Reese	Darvin Arnold
Greenbelt	c	CM	21	(301) 474-8000	Judith Davis	Michael McLaughlin	Kathleen Gallagher	...	...	...	Kenneth Hall
Greensboro	t	CM	1	(410) 482-6222	...	David Kibler	Jeannette DeLude	...	...	...	...
Hagerstown	c	CM	36	(301) 790-3200	William Breichner	Bruce Zimmerman	Donna Spickler	Alfred Martin	Gary Hawbaker	Arthur Smith	Eric Deike
Hampstead *	t	MC	5	(410) 239-7408	Haven Shoemaker	Kenneth Decker	...	...	...	R. Meekins	Roger Steger
Havre De Grace *	c	MC	11	(410) 939-1800	Wayne Dougherty	Carol Mathis	...	George DeHority	...	Randall Holt	Larry Parks
Highland Beach	t	CO	..	(410) 268-2956	Raymond Langston	Crystal Chissell	Patricia Butler	Craig Herndon	...	...	Geneza Hudson
Hyattsville	c	MC	14	(301) 985-5000	William Gardiner	Elaine Murphy	Douglas Barber	...	...	...	Margaret Mallino
Indian Head	t	CM	3	(301) 743-5511	Warren Bowie	Ryan Hicks	...	Dorothy Smith	...	...	James Chase
Kensington	t	MC	1	(301) 949-2424	...	Sanford Daily	...	...	...	...	...
Kitzmiller *	t	MC	..	(301) 453-3449	James Browning	...	Diane Paugh	...	...	...	...
La Plata *	t	CM	6	(301) 934-8421	Gene Ambrogio	Daniel Mears	Judith Frazier	Joseph Norris	...	Cassin Gittins	Steve Murphy
Landover Hills	t	MC	1	(301) 773-6401	Lee Walker	Kathleen Tavel	Juanita Hood	...	...	Henry Norris	...
Laurel *	c	MC	19	(301) 725-5300	Craig Moe	Kristie Mills	Kimberley Rau	Sandra Saylor	...	David Craeford	Paul McCullagh
Laytonsville	t	MC	..	(301) 869-0042	Willard Oland	Dan Prats	Cathern Buit	...	...	...	...
Leonardtown	t	MC	1	(301) 475-9791	J. Norris	Laschelle Miller	Teri Dimsey	...	...	...	John Johnson
Manchester	t	MC	3	(410) 239-3200	...	Steve Miller	...	...	...	...	...
Middletown	t	CM	2	(301) 371-6171	...	Andrew Bowden	...	...	...	...	...
Mount Airy *	t	MC	6	(301) 831-5768	James Holt	Monika Weierbach	Barbara Jean Dixon	Frank Johnson	Ivan Browning	Palmer Grotte	...
Mount Rainier	c	MC	8	(301) 985-6585	Bryan Knedler	Jeannelle Wallace	...	...	...	Michael Scott	Edward Gabay
Mountain Lake Park	t	MC	2	(301) 334-2250	Britten Martin	...	Judy Paugh	...	...	...	...
New Carrollton *	c	MC	12	(301) 459-6100	Andrew Hanko	John Downes	Regina Robinson	Sharia Abraham	...	David Rice	Richard Robbins
New Windsor *	t	MC	1	(410) 635-6575	Sam Pierce	Wally Brown	Donna Alburn	...	...	...	Steve Strawsburg
North Chevy Chase *	v	CM	..	(301) 654-7084	Adrian Andreassi	Robert Weesner	...	...	...	...	...
North East *	t	MC	2	(410) 287-5801	Robert McKnight	M. Cook-Mackenzie	Anne Barker	...	...	Darrell Hamilton	Phillip Meekins
Ocean City *	t	CM	7	(410) 289-8778	Richard Meehan	Dennis Dare	Carol Jacobs	Martha Bennett	Samuel Villani	Bernadette DiPino	Hal Adkins
Perryville	t	MC	3	(410) 642-6066	James Eberhardt	Thomas Morsicato	Jackie Sample	...	Lloyd Beard	Chris Daly	Michael Caldwell
Pocomoke City *	c	CM	4	(410) 957-1333	Michael McDermott	Russell Blake	Carol Justice	...	...	Jeurgen Ervin	...
Poolesville	t	CO	5	(301) 428-8927	...	D. Yost	...	...	...	...	...
Port Deposit	t	MC	..	(410) 378-2121	Charles Flayhart	Sharon Weygand	...	...	Greg Miller	Marc Tomlin	Robert Rouselle
Princess Anne	t	CM	2	(410) 651-1818	...	John O'Meara	...	Brenda Benton	...	Russell Pecoraro	...

Directory 1/9 continued **OFFICIALS IN U.S. MUNICIPALITIES 2,500 AND OVER IN POPULATION**

Jurisdiction		Type	Form of government	2000 Population	Main telephone number	Chief elected official	Appointed administrator	Clerk of the governing board	Chief financial officer	Fire chief	Police chief	Public works director
MARYLAND continued												
Ridgely		t	CO	1	(410) 634-2177	L. Epperly-Glover	Joseph Mangini	...	...	...	Merlin Evans	Robin Eaton
Rising Sun		t	CO	1	(410) 658-5353	Judith Cox	...	Sandra Didra	...	...	Al Michael	...
Riverdale Park		t	MC	6	(301) 927-6381	...	Patrick Prangley	...	...	...	...	...
Rock Hall		t	CM	1	(410) 639-7611	...	Ronald Fifhian	...	...	...	...	...
Rockville		c	CM	47	(240) 314-8470	Larry Giammo	Scott Ullery	Claire Funkhouser	Donna Boxer	...	Terrance Treschuk	Eugene Cranor
Salisbury	*	c	MC	23	(410) 548-3100	Barrie Tilghman	John Pick	Brenda Colegrove	Pamela Oland	David See	Allan Webster	James Caldwell
Seat Pleasant		c	CM	4	(301) 336-2600	Eugene Kennedy	...	Sandra Yates	...	David McGill	Elliott Taylor	...
Sharpsburg		t	MC	..	(301) 432-4428	Sidney Gale	...	...	...	...	...	...
Snow Hill	*	t	CM	2	(410) 632-2080	Stephen Mathews	Albert Cohen	Georgiann Karnis	Erin Morton	...	Kirk Daughtery	Charles Dorman
St. Michaels		t	MC	1	(410) 745-9535	A. Dinkel	Cheril Thomas	...	...	...	...	...
Sudlersville		t	MC	..	(410) 438-3465	William Faust	...	...	...	...	...	...
Sykesville		t	CM	4	(410) 795-8959	...	Matthew Candland	...	...	...	...	...
Takoma Park		c	CM	17	(301) 891-7100	Kathy Porter	Barbara Matthews	Jessie Carpenter	...	...	Edward Coursey	Daryl Braithwaite
Taneytown		c	CM	5	(410) 751-1100	Henry Heine	James Schumacher	...	...	...	Gregory Woelfel	Gary Hardman
Thurmont		t	MC	5	(301) 271-7313	Martin Burns	William Blakeslee	...	Richard May	...	...	...
University Park		t	MC	2	(301) 927-4262	...	...	Amy Headley	...	...	Michael Wynnyk	L. Bloomfield
Upper Marlboro	*	t	MC	..	(301) 627-6905	Steven Sonnett	...	M. David Williams	...	...	Michael Gonnella	Lewis Carroll
Walkersville		t	CM	5	(301) 845-4500	...	Gloria Rollins	...	...	...	...	Dennis Miller
Westernport	*	t	MC	2	(301) 359-3932	Amel Morris	...	Renee Morris	...	Timothy Dayton	...	...
Westminster	*	c	MC	16	(410) 848-9000	Thomas Ferguson	Marge Wolf	Laurell Taylor	Roland Unger	...	Jeff Spaulding	Jeff Glass
MASSACHUSETTS												
Abington		t	TM	14	(781) 982-2112	John Henderson	...	Patricia McKenna	Patricia Majenski	Malcolm Whiting	Richard Franey	Richard Burns
Acton		t	TM	20	(978) 264-9603	Walter Foster	Steven Ledoux	Edward Ellis	Stephen Barrett	Robert Craig	Francis Widmayer	...
Acushnet		t	TM	10	(508) 998-0200	...	Alan Coutinho	Richard Threlfall	Cathy Doane	Paul Cote	Michael Poitras	Richard Settele
Adams		t	RT	8	(413) 743-8300	...	William Ketcham	Paul Hutchinson	Mary Beverly	...	Donald Poirot	Thomas Satko
Agawam		t	CM	28	(413) 786-0400	Richard Cohen	...	Richard Theroux	Carol Taylor	David Pisano	Robert Campbell	John Stone
Amesbury		t	RT	16	(978) 388-8100	David Hildt	...	Bonnie Kitchin	Michael Basque	William Shute	Michael Cronin	Brian Gilbert
Amherst	*	t	RT	34	(413) 259-3002	Gerald Weiss	Laurence Shaffer	Sandra Burgess	John Musante	Keith Hoyle	Charles Scherpa	Guilford Mooring
Andover	*	t	CM	31	(978) 623-8200	Ted Teichert	R. Stapczynski	Randall Hansen	Anthony Torrisi	Michael Mansfield	Brian Pattullo	John Petkus
Arlington		t	CM	42	(781) 316-3121	John Hurd	Brian Sullivan	Corinne Rainville	...	Allan McEwen	Frederick Ryan	John Bean
Ashburnham	*	t	TM	5	(978) 827-4104	Christopher Gagnon	Kevin Paicos	Linda Ramsdell	...	Paul Zbikowski	Loring Barrett	Donale Ouellette
Ashland	*	t	CM	14	(508) 881-0100	Richard Desmarais	John Petrin	...	...	William Kee	Scott Rohmer	James Lefter
Athol	*	t	RT	11	(978) 249-2368	Alan Dodge	David Ames	Nancy Burnham	...	James Wright	Timothy Anderson	Doug Walsh
Attleboro		c	MC	42	(508) 223-2222	...	...	...	...	...	...	...
Auburn		t	RT	15	(508) 832-7721	David Briggs	...	Elizabeth Prouty	Edward Kazanovicz	Roger Belhumeur	Ronald Miller	Glenn Mitchell
Avon		t	TM	4	(508) 588-0414	Deborah Jencunas	...	...	Debra Morin	...	Warren Phillips	...
Ayer		t	TM	7	(978) 772-8216	...	...	Ann Callahan	Lisa Gabree	Paul Fillebrown	Richard Rizzo	Michael Madign
Barnstable	*	t	CM	47	(508) 862-4610	Janet Joakim	John Klimm	Linda Hutchenrider	Mark Milne	...	Paul MacDonald	Mark Ells
Barre		t	TM	5	(978) 355-2504	Richard Stevens	Lorraine Leno	Ellen Glidden	Daniel Haynes	Joseph Rogowski	James Thompson	Stephen Mansfield
Bedford	*	t	TM	12	(781) 275-1111	Catherine Cordes	Richard Reed	Doreen Tremblay	Peter Naum	Kevin MacCaffrie	James Hicks	Richard Warrington
Belchertown		t	TM	12	(413) 323-0403	David Fredenburgh	Gary Brougham	...	...	Edward Bock	Robert Knight	...
Bellingham		t	TM	15	(508) 966-0040	...	Denis Fraine	...	...	...	...	...
Belmont	*	t	RT	24	(617) 993-2600	Angelo Firenze	Thomas Younger	Delores Keefe	Barbara Hagg	David Frizzell	Richard McLaughlin	Peter Castanino
Berkley	*	t	TM	5	(508) 822-3348	Mark Pettey	Paul Modlowski	Carolyn Awalt	...	John Franco	Scott Labonte	...
Beverly		c	MC	39	(978) 921-6000	William Scanlon	...	Frances MacDonald	John Dunn	Richard Pierce	Mark Ray	Michael Colllins
Billerica		t	RT	38	(978) 671-0942	James O'Donnell	William Williams	Shirley Schult	Paul Watson	Anthony Capaldo	Daniel Rosa	...
Blackstone		t	TM	8	(508) 883-1500	...	Ken Bianchi	Marianne Staples	...	Michael Sweeney	Ross Atstupenas	Thomas Devlin
Bolton	*	t	TM	4	(978) 779-2297	...	...	...	...	...	...	...
Boston		c	MC	589	(617) 635-3370	Thomas Menino	Dennis DiMarzio	Rosaria Salerno	...	Paul Christian	Paul Evans	Joseph Casazza
Bourne	*	t	TM	18	(508) 759-0600	Linda Zuern	Thomas Guerino	Barry Johnson	Linda Marzelli	David Kingsbury	Earl Baldwin	Rickie Tellier
Boxborough		t	TM	4	(978) 263-1116	Simon Bunyard	Selina Shaw	Virginia Richardson	...	Kevin Lyons	Richard Vance	Kenneth March
Boxford		t	TM	7	(978) 352-8021	Barbara Jessel	Alan Benson	Patricia Shields	...	Peter Perkins	Gordon Russell	David Durkee
Boylston		t	TM	4	(508) 869-2234	Frank Reale	Suzanne Olsen	Sandra Bourassa	Daniel Haynes	Roger Wentzell	Anthony Sahagian	Donald Parker
Braintree		t	RT	33	(781) 848-1870	...	...	Saran Gillies	...	Richard Hull	Paul Frazier	Robert Brangiforte
Brewster		t	TM	10	(508) 896-3701	John Mitchell	Charles Sumner	Joanna Krauss	Lisa Souve	Roy Jones	James Ehrhart	Allan Tkaczyk
Bridgewater		t	TM	25	(508) 697-0926	Allan Chiocca	David Canepa	Ronald Adams	...	Roderick Walsh	George Gurley	Joseph Souto
Brimfield		t	TM	3	(413) 245-4100	...	...	...	...	...	...	...
Brockton		c	MC	94	(508) 580-7123	...	...	...	...	...	...	...
Brookline		t	CM	57	(617) 730-2000	Joseph Geller	Richard Kelliher	Patrick Ward	Harvey Beth	John Spillane	Daniel O'Leary	A. De Maio
Buckland		t	CM	1	(413) 625-6330	James Budrewicz	Robert Dean	Janice Purington	...	...	...	Steven Daby
Burlington	*	t	RT	22	(781) 270-1600	Sonia Rollins	Robert Mercier	Jane Chew	Paul Sagarino	Lee Callahan	Francis Hart	John Sanchez
Cambridge	*	c	CM	101	(617) 349-4000	Denise Simmons	Robert Healy	Margaret Drury	...	Gerald Reardon	Rober Haas	Lisa Peterson
Canton		t	TM	20	(781) 821-5000	...	William Friel	...	James Murgia	Thomas Ronayne	Peter Bright	Michael Trott
Carlisle		t	TM	4	(978) 369-6155	John Ballantine	Madonna McKenzie	Charlene Hinton	...	David Flannery	David Galvin	Gary Davis
Carver		t	TM	11	(508) 866-3400	John Angley	Richard LaFond	Jean McGillicuddy	...	Craig Weston	Arthur Parker	William Halunen
Charlton	*	t	TM	11	(508) 248-2200	Frederick Swensen	...	Susan Nichols	Joan Walker	Charles Cloutier	James Pervier	Gerry Foskett
Chatham		t	TM	6	(508) 945-5100	Reginald Nickerson	William Hinchey	Joanne Holdgate	Donald Poyant	W. Schwerdtfeger	Kevin Fitzgibbons	Gilbert Borthwick
Chelmsford		t	CM	33	(978) 250-5201	Michael McCall	...	Elizabeth Delaney	...	John Parow	Raymond McCusker	James Pearson
Chelsea		c	CM	35	(617) 889-8294	...	Jay Ash	Robert Bishop	...	Louis Addonizio	Rafael Hernandez	Ted Sobolewski
Cheshire	*	t	TM	3	(413) 743-2826	Daniel Delorey	Thomas Webb	...	...	...	...	...
Chicopee		c	MC	54	(413) 594-1510	Richard Kos	Erwin Hurley	Nancy Mulvey	Sharyn Riley	Stephen Burkott	John Ferraro	Stanley Kulig
Clinton	*	t	TM	13	(978) 365-4120	Kevin Haley	Michael Ward	Philip Boyce	Diane Magliozzi	Richard Hart	Mark Laverdure	C. McGowan
Cohasset		t	TM	7	(781) 383-4105	Roseanne McMorris	William Griffin	Marion Douglas	John Buckley	Roger Lincoln	Robert Jackson	Carl Sestito
Concord	*	t	TM	16	(978) 318-3025	Gregory Howes	Christopher Whelan	Anita Tekle	Anthony Logalbo	Kenneth Willette	Leonard Wetherbee	Richard Reine
Dalton		t	CM	6	(413) 684-6100	Timothy Kirby	Kenneth Walto	Barbara Suriner	Richard Charon	...	Daniel Filiault	James Galliher
Danvers		t	RT	25	(978) 777-0001	...	Wayne Marquis	...	...	James Tutko	Stuart Chase	Don Dehart
Dartmouth		t	RT	30	(508) 910-1883	...	Michael Gagne	Eleanor White	Edward Iacaponi	...	Mark Pacheco	Manuel Branco
Dedham		t	RT	23	(781) 751-9100	Marie Louise Kehoe	William Keegan	Geraldine Pacheco	Mariellen Murphy	James Driscoll	Dennis Teehan	Paul Keane
Deerfield		t	RT	4	(413) 665-2130	John Paciorek	Bernard Kubiak	...	...	...	M. Wozniakewicz	Harold Eaton
Dennis		t	TM	15	(508) 394-8300	Cleon Turner	Robert Canevazzi	...	Janet Gibson	Paul Tucker	Michael Whalen	Dennis Hanson
Dighton	*	t	TM	6	(508) 669-6431	Thomas Pires	...	Susana Medeiros	Edward Swartz	Anthony Roderick	Robert MacDonald	Thomas Ferry
Douglas		t	TM	7	(508) 476-4000	Shirley Mosczynski	Michael Guzinski	Christine Furno	Richard Mathieu	Donald Gonynor	Patrick Foley	...
Dover		t	TM	5	(508) 785-0032	Tobe Deutschmann	David Ramsay	Barrie Clough	...	John Hughes	Joseph Griffin	Craig Hughes
Dracut		t	TM	28	(978) 452-1227	John Zimini	Dennis Piendak	Kathleen Graham	...	Leo Gaudette	Kevin Richardson	Michael Buxton
Dudley	*	t	TM	10	(508) 949-8000	Paul Joseph	Peter Jankowski	Ora Finn	...	Jeffrey Phelps	Steven Wojnar	...
Duxbury		t	CM	14	(781) 934-1100	...	Richard MacDonald	Nancy Oates	...	Kevin Nord	Mark De Luca	Tom Daley
East Bridgewater		t	TM	12	(508) 378-1600	Eric Greene	George Samia	Marcia Weidenfeller	Frank Savino	Ryon Pratt	John Silva	...
East Longmeadow	*	t	TM	14	(413) 525-5400	James Driscoll	Nick Breault	Thomas Florence	Thomas Caliento	Richard Brady	Douglas Mellis	David Gromaski
Eastham		t	TM	5	(508) 240-5900	Linda Burt	Sheila Vanderhoef	Lillian Lamperti	Jane Wall	Glenn Olson	Richard Hedlund	Stephen Douglas
Easthampton	*	t	RT	15	(413) 529-1466	Michael Tautznik	...	Barbara LaBombard	...	Kevin Croake	Bruce McMahon	Joseph Pipczynski
Easton	*	t	TM	22	(508) 230-0500	Colleen Corona	David Colton	Jeremy Gillis	Wendy Nightingale	Thomas Stone	Thomas Kominsky	Wayne Southworth
Essex		t	TM	3	(978) 768-6531	Rolf Madsen	Brendhan Zubricki	Sally Soucy	Brian Dagle	Richard Carter	David Harrell	Bruce Julian
Everett		c	MC	38	(617) 389-2100	David Raqucci	...	John Hanlon	Donald Andrew	David Butler	James Rogers	David Ravanesi
Fairhaven		t	RT	16	(508) 979-4026	Jeffrey Osuch	...	Eilleen Lowney	...	Timothy Francis	Gary Souza	Robert Carey

Directory 1/9 continued **OFFICIALS IN U.S. MUNICIPALITIES 2,500 AND OVER IN POPULATION**

Jurisdiction	Type	Form of govern-ment	2000 Popu-lation	Main telephone number	Chief elected official	Appointed administrator	Clerk of the governing board	Chief financial officer	Fire chief	Police chief	Public works director
MASSACHUSETTS continued											
Fall River	c	MC	91	(508) 324-2000	Edward Lambert	. . .	Carol Valcourt	Douglas Fiore	Edward Dawson	John Souza	Terrance Sullivan
Falmouth	t	RT	32	(508) 495-7332	Kevin Murphy	Robert Whritenour	Michael Palmer	. . .	Paul Brodeur	David Cusolito	. . .
Fitchburg	c	MC	39	(978) 345-9556	Dan Mylott	Robert Pontbraind	Anna Farrell	Richard Sarasin	Kevin Roy	Edward Cronin	Denis Meunier
Foxborough	t	TM	16	(508) 543-1200	Anthony LaChapelle	Andrew Gala	Arlene Crimmins	Randy Scollins	Robert Gaulin	Edward O'Leary	Robert Swanson
Framingham *	t	RT	66	(508) 532-5400	Jason Smith	Julian Suso	Valerie Mulvey	Mary Ellen Kelley	. . .	Steven Carl	Peter Sellers
Franklin *	c	CM	29	(508) 553-4810	. . .	Jeffrey Nutting	Deborah Pellegri	Susan Gagner	Gary McCarraher	Stephen Williams	Robert Cantoreggi
Freetown	t	TM	8	(508) 644-2204	John Ashley	Linda Remedis	Jacqueline Brown	. . .	Wayne Haskins	Carlton Abbott	Joseph Simmons
Gardner	c	MC	20	(978) 632-1900	Gerald St. Hilaire	. . .	Kathleen Lesneski	Calvin Brooks	Ronald Therrien	Neil Erickson	Dane Arnold
Georgetown *	t	TM	7	(978) 352-5755	Matthew Vincent	Stephen Delaney	Janice McGrane	. . .	Albert Beardsley	James Mulligan	Peter Durkee
Gloucester	c	MC	30	(978) 281-9700	John Bell	James McKenna	Robert Whynott	. . .	Barry McKay	James Marr	Joseph Parisi
Grafton	t	TM	14	(508) 839-5335	Craig Dauphinais	. . .	Maureen Clark	. . .	Michael Gauthier	Normand Crepeau	Roger Hammond
Granby	t	TM	6	(413) 467-7177	Patrick Curran	Christopher Martin	K. Kelly-Regan	. . .	Russell Anderson	. . .	David Desrosiers
Great Barrington	t	MC	7	(413) 528-1619	Edward Morehouse	Kevin O'Donnell	Maryellen Siok	. . .	Michael Ordyna	William Walsh	Donald Chester
Greenfield	t	RT	18	(413) 772-1577	Christine Forgey	. . .	Maureen Winsick	Michael Kociela	Mark Cogswell	David Guilbault	. . .
Groton	t	TM	9	(978) 448-9818	. . .	Mark Haddad	. . .	. . .	. . .	. . .	. . .
Groveland	t	TM	6	(978) 374-0470	William Dorke	Nancy Lewandowski	Richard Sciacca	Thomas Moses	John Clement	William Sargent	Robert Arakelian
Hadley	t	TM	4	(413) 586-0221	. . .	David Nixon	Joanna Devine	. . .	. . .	. . .	. . .
Halifax *	t	TM	7	(781) 294-1316	Margaret Fitzgerald	Charles Seelig	Marcia Cole	Laurel Rigo	Lance Benjamino	Michael Manoogian	Robert Badore
Hamilton	t	TM	8	(978) 468-5572	. . .	Candace Wheeler	Jane Wetson	. . .	Philip Stevens	Walter Cullen	Steven Kenney
Hampden *	t	TM	5	(413) 566-2151	Richard Green	Pamela Courtney	Eva Wiseman	Clifford Bombard	Peter Hatch	Jeff Farnsworth	Dana Pixley
Hanover	t	TM	13	(781) 826-2261	Viola Ryerson	Stephen Rollins	William Flynn	George Martin	Stephen Tucker	Paul Hayes	Frank Cheverie
Hanson	t	TM	9	(781) 293-2131	. . .	Earl Davis	Sandra Harris	Barbara Gomez	Allan Hoyt	Edward Savage	Richard Harris
Harvard	t	TM	5	(978) 456-4100	Richard Maiune	Timothy Bragan	Janet Vellente	. . .	. . .	. . .	James Smith
Harwich	t	TM	12	(508) 430-7513	Cyd Zeigler	. . .	Anita Doucette	M. Gallagher	Robert Peterson	William Mason	Alice Norgeot
Hatfield	t	TM	3	(413) 247-0481	Patrick Gaughan	William Szych	. . .	. . .	William Belden	David Hurley	James Reidy
Haverhill *	c	MC	58	(978) 374-2357	James Fiorentini	Andrew Herlihy	. . .	Charles Benevento	. . .	. . .	. . .
Hingham	t	TM	19	(781) 741-1400	Mathew MacIver	. . .	Eileen McCracken	Ted Alexiades	Mark Duff	Steven Carlson	Joseph Stigliani
Holbrook *	t	RT	10	(781) 767-4316	Paul Stigas	Michael Yuinits	M. Shirley Austin	. . .	Edward O'Brien	Jonathan Cordaro	Thomas Cummings
Holden	t	CM	15	(508) 829-0225	Joseph Sullivan	Brian Bullock	Kathleen Peterson	. . .	Edward Stark	George Sherrill	L. Galkowski
Holliston	t	TM	13	(508) 429-0608	. . .	. . .	. . .	. . .	. . .	. . .	. . .
Holyoke	c	MC	39	(413) 534-2176	Michael Sullivan	. . .	Susan Egan	Brian Smith	David Lafond	Anthony Scott	William Fuqua
Hopedale	t	TM	5	(508) 634-2203	Alan Ryan	Eugene Phillips	Janet Jacaruso	Linda Catanzariti	Scott Garland	Eugene Costanza	Robert DePonte
Hopkinton	t	TM	13	(508) 497-9700	. . .	. . .	. . .	. . .	Gary Daugherty	Thomas Irvin	J. T. Gaucher
Hudson	t	TM	18	(978) 562-9963	Jo Forance	Paul Blazar	Deborah Boudreau	Christopher Pile	Thomas Garrity	. . .	Anthony Marques
Hull	t	TM	11	(781) 925-2000	. . .	. . .	. . .	. . .	. . .	. . .	. . .
Ipswich *	t	CM	12	(978) 356-6600	Patrick McNally	Robert Markel	P. Carakatsane	Rita Negri	Arthur Howe	Gavin Keenan	Robert Gravino
Kingston	t	CM	11	(781) 585-0500	Olavo DeMacedo	Kevin Donovan	Mary Lou Murzyn	Joan Paquette	David McKee	Gordon Fogg	. . .
Lakeville *	t	TM	9	(508) 946-8800	Charles Evirs	Rita Garbitt	Janet Tracy	Cynthia McRae	Daniel Hopkins	Mark Sorel	Christopher Peck
Lancaster *	t	TM	7	(978) 365-3326	Stephen Kerrigan	Orlando Pacheco	D. Susan Thompson	Bonnie Holston	John Fleck	Kevin Lamb	John Foster
Lanesborough	t	TM	2	(413) 442-1167	Peter Gallant	Paul Boudreau	Judith Gallant	Phillip Abraham	Charles Durfee	Stanley Misiuk	William Decelles
Lawrence	c	MC	72	(978) 794-5858	Mary Kennedy	Jack McCarthy	P. Marchand	. . .	Richard Shafer	Robert Hayden	Raymond Difiore
Lee	t	CM	5	(413) 243-5500	Patricia Carlino	Robert Nason	Suzanne Scarpa	. . .	Ronald Driscoll	Ronald Glidden	Christopher Pompi
Leicester	t	TM	10	(508) 892-7000	Douglas Belanger	Robert Reed	Patricia Hartnett	Sandra Buxton	Robert Wilson	James Hurley	James Coughlin
Lenox	t	TM	5	(413) 637-5506	Robert Akroyd	Gregory Federspiel	Marie Colvin	. . .	Daniel Clifford	Timothy Face	Jeffrey Vincent
Leominster *	c	MC	41	(978) 534-7500	Dean Mazzarella	Elizabeth Irvine	Lynn Bouchard	. . .	Ronald Pierce	Peter Roddy	Patrick LaPointe
Lexington *	t	CM	30	(781) 862-0500	Jeanne Krieger	Carl Valente	Donna Hooper	Robert Addelson	William Middlemiss	Christopher Casey	William Hadley
Lincoln Center *	t	TM	8	(781) 259-2600	Sara Mattes	Timothy Higgins	Susan Brooks	Colleen Wilkins	Arthur Cotoni	Kevin Mooney	Chris Bibbo
Littleton	t	TM	8	(978) 952-2311	Paul Glavey	Keith Bergman	Mary Crory	Carol Wideman	Alexander McCurdy	. . .	Eric Durcing
Longmeadow	t	TM	15	(413) 565-4110	Hal Haberman	Roberta Crosbie	. . .	Paul Pasterczyk	Eric Madison	Richard Marchese	Douglas Barron
Lowell	c	CM	105	(978) 970-4000	Eileen Donoghue	Bernard Lynch	Richard Johnson	James Kennedy	William Desrosiers	Edward Davis	Edward Walsh
Ludlow	t	RT	21	(413) 583-5600	. . .	. . .	. . .	. . .	. . .	. . .	. . .
Lunenburg	t	TM	9	(978) 582-4130	Robert Bowen	Kerry Speidel	Linda Douglas	Karen Brochu	Scott Glenny	Daniel Bourgeois	John Rodriquenz
Lynn	c	MC	89	(781) 598-4000	Edward Clancy	. . .	. . .	John Pace	Curtis Numberg	John Suslak	Michael Donovan
Lynnfield	t	CM	11	(781) 334-3180	. . .	. . .	. . .	. . .	. . .	. . .	. . .
Malden	c	MC	56	(781) 397-7000	Richard Howard	. . .	Karen Anderson	Domenic Fermano	Joseph Mahoney	Kenneth Coye	Jeffery Manship
Manchester-By-The-Sea	t	CM	5	(978) 526-2000	Susan Thorne	Wayne Melville	Gretchen Wood	Charles Lane	Andrew Paskalis	Ronald Ramos	Robert Moroney
Mansfield *	t	CM	22	(508) 261-7370	Sandra Levine	John D'Agostino	Helen Christian	. . .	Neal Boldrighini	Arthur O'Neill	Ilidio Azinheira
Marblehead	t	TM	20	(781) 631-0528	Bill Conly	Anthony Sasso	Betty Brown	George Snow	Charles Maurais	John Palmer	William McLaughlin
Marion	t	CM	5	(508) 748-3550	Jonathan Dickerson	. . .	. . .	Karen Gomez	C. Davis	Lincoln Miller	Robert Zora
Marlborough	c	MC	36	(508) 460-3775	Nancy Stevens	. . .	. . .	. . .	. . .	. . .	Ron LaFreniere
Marshfield	t	TM	24	(781) 834-5563	James Fitzgerald	Rocco Longo	Sheila Sullivan	. . .	. . .	. . .	Makram Megalli
Mashpee	t	MC	12	(508) 539-1400	. . .	Joyce Mason	Deborah Dami	. . .	George Baker	Maurice Cooper	R. Taylor
Mattapoisett	t	TM	6	(508) 758-4100	Paul Lambalot	Carol Adams	Lois Ennis	Judith Mooney	Ronald Scott	James Moran	Wesley Bowman
Maynard	t	TM	10	(978) 897-1001	Anne Desmarais	Michael Gianotis	Judith Peterson	Harry Gannon	Ronald Cassidy	James Corcoran	Walter Sokolowski
Medfield	t	TM	12	(508) 359-8505	Ann Thompson	Michael Sullivan	Carol Mayer	. . .	William Kingsbury	Robert Meaney	Kenneth Feeney
Medford	c	CM	55	(781) 396-5500	Michael McGlynn	. . .	Edward Finn	. . .	. . .	. . .	. . .
Medway	t	TM	12	(508) 533-3264	Douglas Downing	Suzanne Kennedy	Maryjane White	Margery Sanford	Wayne Vinton	W. Lambirth	Lee Henry
Melrose	c	MC	27	(781) 979-4500	Robert Dolan	. . .	Mary Rita O'Shea	John Dunn	Kevin Walsh	Richard Smith	Robert Beshara
Mendon	t	TM	5	(508) 473-2312	Sharon Culter	Michael McCue	M. Bonderenko	. . .	. . .	Ernest Horn	. . .
Merrimac	t	TM	6	(978) 346-8862	. . .	. . .	. . .	. . .	. . .	. . .	. . .
Methuen	c	CM	43	(978) 794-3237	Sharon Pollard	Kathleen Healy	Tina Touma Conway	Thomas Kelly	Kenneth Bourassa	Joseph Solomon	Ray DiFiore
Middleborough *	t	TM	19	(508) 947-0928	Adam Bond	Charles Cristello	Eileen Gates	. . .	. . .	Gary Russell	Donald Boucher
Middleton	t	TM	7	(978) 777-3617	Nancy Jones	Ira Singer	Sarah George	Robert Murphy	David Leary	Paul Armitage	Robert LaBossiere
Milford *	t	RT	26	(508) 634-2303	Dino Debartolomeis	Louis Celozzi	Amy Neves	John Pyne	John Touhey	Thomas O'Loughlin	Scott Crisafulli
Millbury *	t	TM	12	(508) 865-4710	E. Bernard Plante	Robert Spain	Deborah Plante	Brian Turbitt	Matthew Belsito	Richard Handfield	John McGarry
Millis *	t	TM	7	(508) 376-7040	Andrea Wagner	Charles Aspinwall	George Ford	Kathleen LaPlant	Warren Champagne	Peter McGowan	. . .
Millville	t	MC	2	(508) 883-8433	Diane McCutcheon	Helen Coffin	Susan McNamara	Marilyn Mathieu	John Mullaly	Ronald Landry	John Dean
Milton *	t	RT	26	(617) 898-4845	Kathryn Fagan	Kevin Mearn	James Mullen	David Grab	Malcolm Larson	Richard Wells	Walter Heller
Monson	t	TM	8	(413) 267-4100	Raymond Blanchette	Gretchen Neggers	Nancy Morrell	Debi Mahar	Elmer Harris	Joseph Rebello	. . .
Montague	t	RT	8	(413) 863-3200	Patricia Pruitt	Frank Abbondanzio	Debra Bourbeau	Carolyn Olsen	Raymond Godin	Raymond Zukowski	Thomas Bergeron
Nahant	t	TM	3	(781) 581-0088	Jim Walsh	Mark Cullinan	Susan Behen	Deborah Cormier	Lee Fox	Joseph Manley	Robert Ward
Nantucket	t	TM	9	(508) 228-7255	. . .	C. Gibson	Catherine Stover	Constance Voges	Bruce Watts	William Pittman	Jeffrey Willett
Natick	t	RT	32	(508) 651-7230	Edward Dlott	Frederick Conley	Jane Hladick	Robert Palmer	Richard Fredette	Dennis Mannix	. . .
Needham *	t	RT	28	(781) 455-7500	James Healy	Kate Fitzpatrick	Theodora Eaton	. . .	Paul Buckley	Tom Leary	Richard Merson
New Bedford	c	MC	93	(508) 979-1444	Frederick Kalisz	Stephen Furtado	Michelle Ouellette	Daniel Patten	Paul Leger	Carl Moniz	Lawrence Worden
Newbury	t	TM	6	(978) 465-9241	Richard Joy	. . .	Donna Stefanile	. . .	. . .	Roger Merry	Timothy Leonard
Newburyport	c	MC	17	(978) 465-4413	. . .	. . .	. . .	. . .	John Cutter	John Connors	Dan Lynch
Newton	c	MC	83	(617) 796-1260	David Cohen	. . .	Edward English	David Wilkinson	Edward Murphy	Jose Cordero	Robert Rooney
Norfolk *	t	TM	10	(508) 528-1408	Ramesh Advani	John Hathaway	Gail Bernardo	. . .	Coleman Bushnell	Charles Stone	Remo Vito
North Adams	c	MC	14	(413) 662-3000	John Barrett	. . .	Maryann Abuisi	Beverly Cooper	Craig Rougeau	Ernest Morocco	Leo Senecal
North Andover *	t	TM	27	(978) 688-9510	Rosemary Smedile	Mark Rees	Joyce Bradshaw	Lyne Savage	William Martineau	Richard Stanley	Bruce Thibodeau
North Attleborough	t	RT	27	(508) 699-0100	Donald Hart	. . .	William Moffitt	. . .	Robert Coleman	Michael Gould	Michael Stankovich
North Brookfield	t	TM	4	(508) 867-0200	Richard Chabot	Melanie Jenkins	Sheila Buzzell	Scott Usher	. . .	. . .	Raymond Blake
North Reading	t	CM	13	(978) 664-6010	Marcia Bailey	Greg Balukonis	Barbara Stats	Thomas Tracy	Edward O'Brien	Henry Purnell	David Hanlon
Northampton	c	MC	28	(413) 587-1258	Mary Higgins	. . .	. . .	John Musante	Brian Duggan	Russell Sienkiewicz	George Andrikidis

Directory 1/9 continued — OFFICIALS IN U.S. MUNICIPALITIES 2,500 AND OVER IN POPULATION

Jurisdiction	Type	Form of govern-ment	2000 Popu-lation	Main telephone number	Chief elected official	Appointed administrator	Clerk of the governing board	Chief financial officer	Fire chief	Police chief	Public works director
MASSACHUSETTS continued											
Northborough *	t	TM	14	(508) 393-5040	Dawn Rand	John Coderre	Andrew Dowd	...	David Durgin	Mark Leahy	Kara Buzanoski
Northbridge	t	CM	13	(508) 234-2095	C. Ampagoomian	Theodore Kozak	Muriel Barry	...	Gary Nestor	Walter Warchol	Richard Sasseville
Norton	t	TM	18	(508) 285-0200	...	James Purcell	Diane Casagni	...	...	Bruce Finch	Keith Silver
Norwell	t	TM	9	(781) 659-8000	John Mariano	James Boudreau	Janice Lawson	Donna Mangan	Paul Rosebach	Theodore Ross	Paul Foulsham
Norwood	t	CM	28	(781) 762-1240	Domenic Fruci	John Carroll	Robert Thornton	...	William Sullivan	Bartley King	Joseph Welch
Oak Bluffs *	t	TM	3	(508) 693-3554	...	Michael Dutton	Deborah Ratcliff	Paul Manzi	Gilbert Forend	Erik Blake	Richard Combra
Orange *	t	TM	7	(978) 544-1100	Robert Andrews	Richard Kwiatkowski	Nancy Blackmer	Lori Blanchard	Dennis Annear	Brian Spear	...
Orleans	t	TM	6	(508) 240-3700	Jon Fuller	John Kelly	Cynthia May	David Withrow	Steven Edwards	Jeff Roy	...
Oxford	t	TM	13	(508) 987-6030	Henry LaMountain	Joseph Zeneski	...	Donald Kaminski	Jeffrey Wilson	Charles Noyes	John Phillips
Palmer	t	CM	12	(413) 283-2603	...	...	Patricia Donovan	...	Alan Roy	Robert Frydryk	...
Paxton	t	TM	4	(508) 754-7638	Michael Quinlivan	Charles Blanchard	Deirdre Malone	...	Jay Conte	Robert Desrosiers	Michael Putnam
Peabody	c	MC	48	(978) 532-3000	Peter Torigian	...	...	Patricia Schaffer	Joseph Mendonca	Robert Champayne	Richard Carnevale
Pembroke	t	TM	16	(781) 293-3844	Robert Demarco	Edwin Thorne	Donna Pratt	...	James Neenan	Gregory Wright	Michael Valenti
Pepperell	t	TM	11	(978) 433-0333	Scott Butcher	...	Lois Libby	Theresa Walsh	Wes Whittier	Alan Davis	Kim Spaulding
Pittsfield	c	MC	45	(413) 499-9340	Sara Hathaway	David Battistoni	Jody Phillips	Susan Carmel	Stephen Duffy	Anthony Riello	Bruce Collingwood
Plainville	t	TM	7	(508) 695-3142	Charles Smith	Joseph Fernandes	Kathleen Sandland	...	Edwin Harrop	Edward Merrick	Calvin Hall
Plymouth *	t	RT	51	(508) 747-1620	Richard Quintal	Mark Sylvia	Laurence Pizer	Lynne Barrett	Edward Bradley	Michael Boteiri	Roger Hammond
Provincetown *	t	CM	3	(508) 487-7000	Michele Couture	Sharon Lynn	Douglas Johnstone	Alexandra Hielala	Michael Trovato	Jeff Jaran	David Guertin
Quincy	c	MC	88	(617) 376-1000	James Sheets	John Keenan	Joseph Shea	Michael McFarland	Thomas Gorman	Thomas Frane	...
Randolph	t	RT	30	(617) 961-0900	...	...	...	...	...	...	...
Raynham	t	TM	11	(508) 824-2707	Donald McKinnon	Randall Buckner	Helen Lounsbury	Belcher Stanley	George Andrews	Peter King	Roger Stolte
Reading	t	CM	23	(781) 942-9001	James Bonazoli	P. Hechenbleikner	Cheryl Johnson	...	Gregory Burns	James Cormier	Edward McIntire
Rehoboth	t	TM	10	(508) 252-3758	Arthur Tobin	David Marciello	Kathleen Conti	...	Robert Pray	Gary Fiedler	Daniel Kelley
Revere	c	MC	47	(781) 286-8202	Thomas Ambrosino	...	John Henry	...	Eugene Doherty	Terrance Reardon	Donald Goodwin
Rochester	t	TM	4	(508) 763-3871	Richard Cutler	James Huntoon	Naida Parker	Claudette Coutu	Scott Ashworth	Walter Denham	Jeffrey Eldridge
Rockland	t	TM	17	(781) 871-1874	Keven Pratt	...	Mary Pat Kaszanek	Eric Hart	J. Michael Sammon	John Llewellyn	...
Rockport	t	TM	7	(978) 546-6894	Nicola Barletta	...	Frederick Frithsen	Dean Anderson	Russell Anderson	John McCarthy	John Tomasz
Rowley	t	TM	5	(978) 948-2705	Robert Morse	...	Jeanne Grover	Sue Bailey	...	Kevin Barry	Scott Leavitt
Rutland	t	TM	6	(508) 886-4104	James Leger	...	...	...	Thomas Ruchala	Joseph Baril	Carl Christianson
Salem	c	MC	40	(978) 745-9595	Stanley Usovicz	...	Deborah Burkinshaw	Bruce Guy	Robert Turner	Robert St. Pierre	Bruce Thibodeau
Salisbury	t	CM	7	(978) 465-2310	Henry Richenburg	Neil Harrington	Wilma McDonald	Andrew Gould	Richard Souliotis	Richard Simmons	Donald Levesque
Sandwich	t	CM	20	(508) 888-5144	Pamela Terry	George Dunham	Barbara Walling	Doreen Guild	Dennis Newman	...	Peter Tancredi
Saugus	t	CM	26	(781) 231-4126	...	...	...	...	...	...	...
Scituate	t	TM	17	(781) 545-8741	Shawn Harris	Richard Agnew	Barbara Maffucci	Mary Gallagher	Edward Hurley	Thomas Neilen	Anthony Antoniello
Seekonk	t	RT	13	(508) 336-2910	Dana Beal	...	Janet Parker	Robin Tavares	David Viera	Vito Scotti	James Tusino
Sharon	t	TM	17	(781) 784-1515	...	Benjamin Puritz	Marlene Chused	...	Dennis Mann	Joseph Bernstein	Eric Hooper
Sheffield	t	CM	3	(413) 229-2335	Janet Stanton	...	Natalie Funk	...	John Ullrich	...	Ronald Bassett
Sherborn	t	TM	4	(508) 651-7850	Paul DeRensis	Kristine Irving	Carole Marple	Ruth Hohenschau	Neil McPherson	Gary Hendron	Gary Kellaher
Shirley	t	TM	6	(978) 425-2600	Leonardo Guercio	Kyle Keady	Sylvia Shipton	Karen Kucala	Dennis Levesque	Paul Thibodeau	Albert Chevrette
Shrewsbury	t	CM	31	(508) 842-7471	Laurie Lindberg	Daniel Morgado	Ann Dagle	Mary Thompson	...	...	...
Somerset	t	TM	18	(508) 646-2800	Steven Moniz	John McAuliffe	Patricia Hart	Joseph Bolton	Stephen Rivard	Joseph Ferreira	Thomas Fitzgerald
Somerville	c	MC	77	(617) 625-6600	Michael Capuano	...	Arthur McCue	...	Kevin Kelleher	Donald Caliguri	Robert Trahan
South Hadley	t	RT	17	(413) 538-5017	Barbara Eckman	...	Lisa Napiorkowski	...	...	David LaBrie	...
Southampton	t	TM	5	(413) 529-0106	Thomas Cross	Marlene Michonski	Eileen Couture	K. Archambeault	William Barcomb	Eugene Lemoine	Edward Cauley
Southborough	t	TM	8	(508) 485-0710	Bonnie Phaneuf	Jean Kitchen	Paul Berry	...	John Mauro	William Webber	John Boland
Southbridge *	t	CM	17	(508) 764-5405	Catherine Nikolla	Christopher Clark	Madaline Daoust	Karen Harnois	Leonard Laporte	Daniel Charette	Kenneth Kalinowski
Southwick	t	TM	8	(413) 569-5995	David St. Pierre	Karl Stinehart	Paul Mormino	Linda Carr	Don Morris	Henry Labombard	Arthur Chevalier
Spencer	t	TM	11	(508) 885-7500	...	Paul Guida	Jean Mulhall	Alaine Boucher	Robert Parsons	David Darrin	Warren Ramsey
Springfield	c	MC	152	(413) 787-6068	Michael Albano	Nigel Spencer	William Metzger	Timothy Plante	Gary Cassannelli	Paula Meara	Allan Chawlek
Sterling *	t	TM	7	(978) 422-8111	Donlin Murray	Terri Ackerman	Melanie Clark	...	David Hurlbut	Gary Chamberland	William Tuttle
Stoneham	t	TM	22	(781) 279-2600	Robert Sweeney	Ronald Florino	John Hanright	Ronald Castignetti	Lawrence Lamey	Eugene Passaro	Robert Grover
Stoughton	t	CM	27	(781) 341-1300	Joseph Mokrisky	Mark Stankiewicz	...	Paul Leaver	William Stipp	Philip Dineen	Lawrence Barrett
Stow	t	TM	5	(978) 897-4514	...	William Wrigley	Linda Smart	...	David Soar	John Scichilone	Michael Clayton
Sturbridge *	t	TM	7	(508) 347-2500	Arnold Wilson	James Malloy	Lorraine Murawski	...	Leonard Senecal	Thomas Button	Gregory Morse
Sudbury	t	TM	16	(978) 443-8891	Lawrence O'Brien	Maureen Valente	...	Suzanne Petersen	Kenneth MacLean	Peter Fadgen	William Place
Sunderland	t	TM	3	(413) 665-1441	Scott Bergeron	Margaret Nartowicz	Wendy Houle	Herb Sanderson	Robert Ahearn	Jeffrey Gilbert	...
Sutton *	t	CM	8	(508) 865-8720	Michael Chizy	James Smith	Laura Rodgers	...	Paul Maynard	Dennis Towle	Mark Brigham
Swampscott	t	RT	14	(781) 596-8850	...	Andrew Maylor	Jack Paster	...	Laurence Galante	Ronald Madigan	Silvio Baruzzi
Swansea	t	TM	15	(508) 678-2981	...	...	...	...	...	...	...
Taunton *	c	MC	55	(508) 821-1000	Charles Crowley	Gill Enos	R. Marie Blackwell	...	Leman Padelford	Raymond O'Berg	Frederic Cornaglia
Templeton	t	TM	6	(978) 939-8801	Gerald Skelton	Carol Skelton	Carol Harris	Scott Sawyer	Thomas Smith	David Whitaker	Francis Chase
Tewksbury	t	TM	28	(978) 640-4300	Charles Coppola	David Cressman	Elizabeth Carey	Donna Walsh	Thomas Ryan	John Mackey	William Burris
Tisbury	t	TM	3	(508) 696-4200	Edmond Coogan	John Bugbee	Marion Mudge	Timothy McLean	Richard Clark	...	Frederick Lapiana
Topsfield	t	TM	6	(978) 887-8571	...	...	...	...	...	...	...
Townsend	t	CM	9	(978) 597-1700	Robert Rebholz	Gregory Barnes	Daniel Murphy	Richard Choate	Donald Hurme	...	Edward Kukkula
Truro	t	CM	1	(508) 349-7004	Alfred Gaechter	Pamela Nolan	...	Gertrude Brazil	E. Thomas Prada	John Thomas	Paul Morris
Tyngsborough	t	TM	11	(978) 649-2300	J. Schnackerts	...	Joanne Shifres	Leon Cote	Timothy Madden	John Miceli	Frederick Flanagan
Upton	t	TM	5	(508) 529-6901	James Bate	...	Martha Williams	...	Richard Henderson	Tom Stockwell	Bob Gilchrist
Uxbridge *	t	TM	11	(508) 278-8600	Julie Woods	Jill Myers	Holly Gallerani	...	Peter Ostroskey	Scott Freitas	Larry Bombara
Wakefield	t	TM	24	(781) 246-6390	...	Thomas Butler	Virginia Zingarelli	Kevin Gill	David Parr	Stephen Doherty	Richard Stinson
Walpole *	t	RT	22	(508) 660-7294	Kathy Winston	Michael Boynton	Ronald Fucile	Mark Good	Timothy Bailey	Richard Stillman	Robert O'Brien
Waltham	c	MC	59	(781) 893-4040	Jeannette McCarthy	...	Rosario Malone	Dennis Quinn	Thomas Keough	Edward Drew	John Bradley
Ware	t	TM	9	(413) 967-9648	John Desmond	...	Nancy Talbot	John Hirbour	Thomas Coulombe	Dennis Healey	Gilbert Sorel
Wareham	t	CM	20	(508) 291-3100	Patrick Tropeano	...	MaryAnn Silva	Robert Bliss	...	Thomas Joyce	Mark Gifford
Warren	t	TM	4	(413) 436-5701	David Delanski	Jean McCaughey	Nancy Lowell	William Schlosstein	James Dolan	Ronald Syriac	...
Warwick	t	TM	..	(978) 544-6315	...	John Columbus	...	...	...	...	...
Watertown *	t	CM	32	(617) 972-6465	Clyde Younger	Michael Driscoll	John Flynn	...	Mario Orangio	Edward Deveau	Gerald Mee
Wayland	t	CM	13	(508) 358-7755	Betsy Connolly	Frederic Turkington	Judith St. Croix	Robert Hilliard	Robert Loomer	Robert Irving	...
Webster *	t	TM	16	(508) 949-3800	...	...	Robert Craver	Pamela Regis	Gordon Forrester	Timothy Bent	Michael Suprenant
Wellesley *	t	RT	26	(781) 431-1019	...	Hans Larsen	Kathleen Nagle	Sheryl Strother	Kevin Rooney	T. Cunningham	Michael Pakstis
Wellfleet	t	TM	2	(508) 349-0300	Dale Donavon	Paul Sieloff	Dawn Rickman	Patricia Eagar	Alan Hight	Richard Rosenthal	Jameson Bell
Wenham *	t	TM	4	(978) 468-5520	John Clemenzi	Jeffrey Chelgren	Frances Hart Young	...	Robert Blanchard	Kenneth Walsh	William Tyack
West Boylston *	t	CM	7	(508) 835-3490	Allen Phillips	Leon Gaumond	Kim Hopewell	...	Richard Pauley	Dennis Minnich	John Westerling
West Bridgewater	t	TM	6	(508) 894-1200	...	Elizabeth Faricy	Nancy Morrison	Marilyn Gordon	Leonard Hurt	Robert Kominsky	Thomas Green
West Brookfield *	t	TM	3	(508) 867-1421	Barry Nadon	Johanna Barry	Sarah Allen	...	Tim Batchelor	C. O'Donnell	Jason Benoit
West Newbury *	t	TM	4	(978) 363-1100	Richard Cushing	...	Larry Murphy	Tracy Blais	Raymond Dower	Lisa Holmes	Gary Bill
West Springfield	t	RT	27	(413) 263-3232	Edward Gibson	...	Diane Foley	...	David Barkman	Thomas Burke	John Dowd
Westborough	t	TM	17	(508) 366-3030	Kristina Allen	Henry Danis	Nancy Yendriga	Leah Talbot	Walter Perron	Glenn Parker	John Walden
Westfield	c	MC	40	(413) 572-6200	...	...	...	...	...	...	...
Westford	t	CM	20	(978) 692-5500	...	Jodi Ross	Kari Tari	Suzanne Marchald	Richard Rochon	Bob Welch	...
Westminster *	t	TM	6	(978) 874-7400	Thomas O'Toole	Karen Murphy	Denise MacAloney	Donna Allard	Brenton MacAloney	Salvatore Albert	Joshua Hall
Weston *	t	TM	11	(781) 893-7320	Douglas Gillespie	Donna VanderClock	M. Nolan	...	David Soar	Steven Shaw	Robert Hoffman
Westport	t	TM	14	(508) 636-1003	Steven Tripp	John Dolan	Marlene Samson	Katherine Benoit	William Tripp	Michael Healy	Paul Pereira
Westwood *	t	TM	14	(781) 320-1028	Patrick Ahearn	Michael Jaillet	Dottie Powers	Pamela Dukeman	William Scoble	William Chase	J. Walsh
Weymouth	t	RT	53	(617) 335-2000	William Ryan	...	Franklin Fryer	Arthur Gallagher	David Madden	Thomas Higgins	Joseph Mazzotta

Directory 1/9 continued OFFICIALS IN U.S. MUNICIPALITIES 2,500 AND OVER IN POPULATION

Jurisdiction	Type	Form of govern-ment	2000 Popu-lation	Main telephone number	Chief elected official	Appointed administrator	Clerk of the governing board	Chief financial officer	Fire chief	Police chief	Public works director
MASSACHUSETTS continued											
Whatley *	t	CM	1	(413) 665-4400	Alan Sanderson	Lynn Sibley	...	Joyce Muka	John Hannum	James Sevigne	Keith Bardwell
Whitman	t	TM	13	(781) 447-7600	Daniel Holbrook	Francis Lynam	Pamela Martin	...	Timothy Travers	John Schnyer	John Pettinelli
Wilbraham	t	TM	13	(413) 596-8111	David Barry	Robert Weitz	Beverly Litchfield	Joanne Degray	Francis Nothe	Allen Stratton	Edmond Miga
Williamstown	t	CM	8	(413) 458-3500	John Madden	Peter Fohlin	Mary Kennedy	Charles St. John	Craig Pedercini	Arthur Parker	Timothy Kaiser
Wilmington *	t	CM	21	(978) 658-3311	Michael Newhouse	Michael Caira	Sharon George	Michael Morris	Edward Bradbury	Michael Begonis	Donald Onusseit
Winchendon *	t	TM	9	(978) 297-0085	...	James Kreidler	Linda Daigle	Charlotte Noponen	Allen Lafrennie	Scott Livingston	Michael Murphy
Winchester	t	RT	20	(781) 721-7133	Stephen Powes	Melvin Kleckner	Carolyn Ward	Joseph Bonner	John Nash	Joseph Perritano	Anthony Celli
Winthrop	t	RT	18	(617) 846-1077	Tom Reily	Richard White	Claire Sheltry	Michael Bertino	J. Powers	David Goldstein	David Hickey
Woburn	c	MC	37	(781) 932-4400	Thomas McLaughlin	...	William Campbell	Gerald Surette	Paul Tortolano	Philip Mahoney	Frederick Russell
Worcester	c	CM	172	(508) 799-1031	Raymond Mariano	...	David Rushford	John Pranckevicius	Gerard Dio	James Gallagher	Robert Moylan
Wrentham *	t	TM	10	(508) 384-5400	Mary Dunn	John McFeeley	Carol Mollica	Karen Jelloe	Mark Pare	James Anderson	Irving Priest
Yarmouth *	t	TM	24	(508) 398-2231	Suzanne McAuliffe	Robert Lawton	Jane Hastings	Susan Milne	Michael Walker	Michael Almonte	George Allaire
MICHIGAN											
Adrian *	c	CM	21	(517) 264-4883	Sam Rye	Dane Nelson	Pat Baker	Jeffrey Pardee	Paul Trinka	Terrence Collins	...
Albion *	c	CM	9	(517) 629-5535	William Wheaton	Michael Herman	Kerry Helmick	...	...	...	Kevin Markovich
Algonac *	c	CM	4	(810) 794-9361	James Wisdom	Patrick Burelle	Joseph Sobota	...	S. John Stier	Richard Torongeau	Paul Jarmolowicz
Allegan	c	CM	4	(616) 673-5511	Craig Van Melle	Robert Hillard	...	...	Joel Merchant	...	Victor Rose
Allen Park	c	MC	29	(313) 928-1400	Richard Huebler	Rocco Minghine	John Weise	Kristine Barann	Gregory Murphy	Dennis Gallow	David Boomer
Alma	c	CM	9	(989) 463-8336	Melvin Nyman	Phillip Moore	Barbara Gager	Paul Borle	Richard Pratt	...	Ronald Turner
Almont *	v	CM	2	(810) 798-8528	Steven Schneider	Gerald Oakes	Sally McCrea	...	...	Patrick Nael	Russell Kelley
Alpena *	c	CM	11	(989) 354-1700	Carol Shafto	Thad Taylor	Karen Hebert	...	Ken Hubbard	Kim Miller	...
Alpine	tp	MC	13	(616) 784-1262	Marta Brechting	...	Jean Wahlfield	...	Ron Christians	...	...
Ann Arbor	c	CM	114	(734) 994-2803	John Hieftje	Roger Fraser	Jacqueline Beaudry	Tom Crawford	...	Daniel Oates	Sue McCormick
Au Gres	c	MC	1	(989) 876-8811	...	...	...	...	...	...	...
Auburn	c	MC	2	(989) 662-6761	...	Jo Ella Krantz	Lucille Wiesenauer	...	...	James Klann	Ronald Perry
Auburn Hills *	c	CM	19	(248) 370-9440	Jim McDonald	Peter Auger	Linda Shannon	Gary Barnes	John Burmeister	Doreen Olko	Ronald Melchert
Bad Axe *	c	CM	3	(989) 269-7681	William Cleland	John Nugent	Kay Goebel	...	David Peruski	John Bodis	Scott Boshart
Bangor *	c	CM	1	(269) 427-5831	Richard Sutherby	Michael Selden	Linda Vaught	...	Derrick Babcock	Gary Baker	C. Thompson
Baraga	v	MC	1	(906) 353-6237	Wendell Dompier	...	Dorothy Mayo	...	...	Harold Miron	William Marlor
Bath	tp	CM	7	(517) 641-6728	Valerie Shirey	...	Kathleen McQueen	...	Art Hosford	Jack Phillips	...
Battle Creek	c	CM	53	(616) 966-3300	...	...	Deborah Owens	...	Larry Hausman	David Headings	...
Bay City	c	CM	36	(989) 894-8246	Michael Buda	Robert Belleman	Connie Deford	Gary Fields	Gary Mueller	Linda Collier	...
Bear Creek	tp	MC	5	(231) 347-0592	Dennis Keiser	...	...	...	Norman Conklin	...	...
Belding *	c	CM	5	(616) 794-1900	...	Randall DeBruine	Kareen Thomas	Samuel Andres	Gregg Moore	Dale Nelson	Ernest Thomas
Bellaire	v	MC	1	(231) 533-8213	...	Janet Person	...	...	...	...	...
Belleville *	c	CM	3	(734) 697-9323	Richard Smith	...	Lisa Long	...	Darwin Loyer	Gene Taylor	Keith Boc
Benton Harbor	c	CM	11	(269) 927-8401	...	Richard Marsh	Joyce Taylor	Jacqueline Bell	...	Samuel Harris	Michael Dancer
Berkley *	c	CM	15	(248) 658-3330	Marilyn Stephan	Jane Bais DiSessa	Mary Hughes	David Sabuda	...	...	Bruce Jerome
Bessemer	c	CM	2	(906) 663-4311	Peter Matonich	Joseph Erickson	Bruce Carlson	...	...	...	Daniel Johnson
Beverly Hills	v	CM	10	(248) 646-6404	Todd Stearn	Chris Wilson	...	Robert Wiszowaty	...	...	Tom Meszler
Big Rapids	c	CM	10	(231) 592-4000	Edward Burch	Stephen Sobers	Roberta Cline	...	...	...	Timothy Vogel
Birch Run *	v	MC	1	(989) 624-5711	Marianne Nelson	Paul Moore	Alyssa Barto	...	...	Al Swearengin	Terry Engelhardt
Birmingham	c	CM	19	(248) 644-1800	Donald Carney	Thomas Markus	Nancy Weiss	B. Ostin	Timothy Wangler	Richard Patterson	Robert Fox
Blissfield	v	CM	3	(517) 486-4347	Jae Guetschow	James Wonacott	Laura Neuman	...	...	Jane Kelley	Mark Strahan
Bloomfield Hills *	c	CM	3	(248) 644-1520	Michael Zambricki	Jay Cravens	Amy Burton	...	...	...	...
Boyne City	c	CM	3	(231) 582-6597	Eleanor Stackus	Michael Cain	Sue Hobbs	...	Dennis Amesbury	Randall Howard	Michael Wiesner
Brandon *	tp	MC	14	(248) 627-4918	Kathy Thurman	...	B. McCreery	...	David Kwapis	...	...
Breitung *	tp	MC	5	(906) 779-2050	Dennis Olson	Perry Franzoi	Samantha Coron	...	...	...	Guy Forstrom
Bridgman	c	MC	2	(616) 465-5144	...	Aaron Anthony	Elaine Thomas	...	Skip Munson	Harry Lenandson	Rich Knuth
Brighton *	c	CM	6	(810) 227-1911	Kate Lawrence	Dana Foster	Tammy Allen	David Gajda	...	Tom Wightman	M. Schindewolf
Brighton *	tp	CM	17	(810) 229-0550	H. E. Prine	...	Ann Bollin	...	...	...	...
Bronson	c	CM	2	(517) 369-7334	Thomas Rissman	David O'Rourke	Karen Smith	...	Brent Wilber	Richard Stout	Carl Ransbottom
Brooklyn *	v	CM	1	(517) 592-2591	Robert Sieghart	Victor Cardenas	Craig Douglas	...	...	...	Keith Kotsch
Brown City *	c	CM	1	(810) 346-2325	Laura Carpenter	Clinton Holmes	Kelly Pavel	...	James Groat	Ronald Smith	Philip Bartle
Buchanan *	c	CM	4	(616) 695-3844	Patrica Moore	Margaret Mullendore	Gladys Bybee	...	Tim Gowen	William Marx	Willie Brown
Buena Vista	tp	CM	10	(989) 754-6536	Dwayne Parker	Martin Williams	B. Montgomery	Alan Bailey	John Parrott	Brian Booker	Victor Killingbeck
Burton	c	MC	30	(810) 743-1500	Charles Smiley	Charles Abbey	Gayle Webster	Bradley Becker	Douglas Halstead	Bruce Whitman	Jeffrey Major
Cadillac *	c	CM	10	(231) 775-0181	William Barnett	Peter Stalker	Janice Nelson	Owen Roberts	...	...	Robert Johnson
Canton	tp	CM	76	(734) 394-5260	Thomas Yack	...	Terry Bennett	Anthony Minghine	Michael Rorabacher	...	Joseph Teramino
Capac	v	MC	1	(810) 395-4355	Mark Klug	...	Candy Franckowiak	...	...	Raymond Hawks	Donald Standel
Carleton	v	MC	2	(734) 654-6255	Glenn Goodnight	...	Lori Dahl	...	...	Larry Buckingham	...
Caro	v	CM	4	(989) 673-2226	Thomas Striffler	Donald Beavers	Karen Snider	...	David Mattlin	Benson Page	Charles Sundblad
Cascade Charter *	tp	CM	15	(616) 949-1500	Robert Beahan	William Cousins	Ron Goodyke	...	John Sigg	...	...
Caseville	v	CM	..	(989) 856-2102	...	...	Nancy Moss	Forrest Williams	...	Jamie Learman	David Quinn
Caspian	c	CM	..	(906) 265-2514	Mark Stauber	Richard Frighetto	...	...	Jerry Anderson	Curt Soderbloom	Mark Ghiggia
Cass City *	v	CM	2	(989) 872-2911	Carl Palmateer	Peter Cristiano	Nanette Walsh	...	...	Craig Haynes	Gary Barnes
Cassopolis	v	CM	1	(616) 445-8648	Julia Bell	...	Paula Beauchamp	...	William Fitzgerald	Frank Williams	Daniel Bates
Cedar Springs *	c	CM	3	(616) 696-1330	Linda Hunt	Christine Burns	Linda Branyan	Linda Lehman	Jerry Gross	Roger Parent	Gerald Hall
Center Line *	c	CM	8	(586) 757-6800	Mary Ann Zielinski	Nancy Bourgeois	...	...	...	...	Scott Baker
Charlevoix	c	CM	2	(231) 547-3270	Norman Carlson	Robert Straebel	Carol Ochs	...	Paul Ivan	Gerard Doan	Patrick Elliott
Charlotte *	c	CM	8	(517) 543-2750	Deb Shaugnessy	Gregg Guetschow	Michelle King	Christine Mossner	Kevin Fullerton	William Callahan	Amy Schoonover
Charter Township of Port Huron *	tp	CM	8	(810) 987-6600	R. Lewandowski	Michael Uskiewicz	Benita Davis	...	Craig Miller	...	Steve Peterson
Charter Township of West Bloom	tp	MC	64	(248) 451-4800	...	...	...	...	...	...	...
Cheboygan *	c	CM	5	(231) 627-9931	Leslie Tebo	Scott McNeil	K. Kwiatkowski	...	Thomas Bancroft	Kurt Jones	Michael LaLonde
Chelsea	c	CM	4	(734) 475-1771	Ann Feeney	...	Teresa Burtch	...	...	...	...
Chesaning	v	CM	2	(989) 845-3800	Douglas Corwin	...	Denise Ebenhoeh	...	...	...	Joe Pacek
Clare *	c	CM	3	(989) 386-7541	Pat Humphrey	Ken Hibl	Kay Haven	Steven Kingsbury	Doug Randle	D. Miedzianowski	Robert Bonham
Clawson	c	CM	12	(248) 435-4500	Lisa Dwyer	Richard Haberman	G. Machele Kukuk	Mark Pollock	Douglas Ballard	Bruce Henderlight	Harry Drinkwine
Clinton	tp	MC	95	(586) 286-8000	Robert Cannon	...	Dennis Tomlinson	Norman Troppens	John Murphy	Al Ernst	George Westerman
Clio *	c	CM	2	(810) 686-5850	Robert Smith	Jack Abernathy	Teresa Karsney	...	Gary Domerese	James McLellan	David Green
Coldwater *	c	CM	12	(517) 279-9501	Eugene Wallace	William Stewart	Ruth Ann Volkmer	Jeffrey Budd	...	...	David Sattler
Constantine	v	CM	2	(269) 435-2085	...	Mark Honeysett	...	Jody Boulette	...	Jeffrey Blough	J. Hamminga
Coopersville *	c	CM	3	(616) 997-9731	Kenneth Bush	Steven Patrick	Stephanie Pelkey	...	Lee Waldie	...	Ken Orquist
Corunna	c	MC	3	(989) 743-3650	Stephen Corey	Joseph Sawyer	...	...	Scott Johnson	Kim Williams	Timothy Crawford
Croswell	c	CM	2	(810) 679-2299	...	...	Suzanne Dobson	...	...	Dave Hall	Tom Dickensheets
Crystal Falls	c	CM	1	(906) 875-3212	Jeffrey Cram	Charles Nordeman	...	...	John Ahola	Jack Bicigo	Dennis Fabbri
Davison *	c	CM	5	(810) 653-2191	Fred Fortner	Dale Martin	Andrea Schroeder	...	Michael Wright	William Brandon	Brian Klaassen
De Witt *	c	CM	4	(517) 669-2441	...	Brian Vick	Denice Smith	...	Robin Ballard	Larry Jerue	Rich Miller
Dearborn	c	MC	97	(313) 943-2320	Michael Guido	Mark Guido	Kathleen Buda	James O'Connor	Michael Birrell	Timothy Strutz	Kurt Giberson
Dearborn Heights	c	MC	58	(313) 791-3420	Daniel Paletko	...	Judy Dudzinski	Donald Barrow	Andy Gurka	Michael Gust	Jack Franzil
Decatur	v	CM	1	(616) 426-6114	Carl Wickett	Martin Super	Lou Ann Conklin	...	...	David McLeese	Dale Avery
Delhi	tp	CM	22	(517) 694-2137	Stuart Goodrich	John Elsinga	Evan Hope	...	Richard Royston	...	...

Directory 1/9 continued

OFFICIALS IN U.S. MUNICIPALITIES 2,500 AND OVER IN POPULATION

Jurisdiction	Type	Form of govern-ment	2000 Popu-lation	Main telephone number	Chief elected official	Appointed administrator	Clerk of the governing board	Chief financial officer	Fire chief	Police chief	Public works director
MICHIGAN continued											
Delta	tp	CM	29	(517) 323-8500	Joseph Drolett	Richard Watkins	Janice Vedder	Jeffrey Anderson	Victor Hilbert	. . .	Stanley Wegrzyn
Detroit	c	MC	951	(313) 224-3400	Dennis Archer	Nettie Seabrooks	Jackie Currie	Valerie Johnson	Harold Watkins	Isaiah McKinnon	Clyde Dowell
Dewitt	tp	CM	12	(517) 668-0270	Rick Galardi	Rodney Taylor	Diane Mosier	. . .	Fred Koos	Brian Russell	. . .
Dexter *	v	CM	2	(734) 426-8308	Jim Seta	Donna Dettling	Carol Jones	. . .	. . .	. . .	Ed Lobdell
Dowagiac *	c	CM	6	(616) 782-2195	Donald Lyons	Kevin Anderson	James Snow	David Pilot	Harold Munson	Thomas Atkinson	Donald Hallowell
Dundee	v	CM	3	(734) 529-3430	Ted Norris	Patrick Burtch	Deborah Westbrook	Robin Moon	. . .	. . .	. . .
Durand	c	CM	3	(989) 288-3113	James Schuyler	. . .	Amy Roddy	. . .	. . .	Michael Tanner	Steven Mince
East Grand Rapids *	c	CM	10	(616) 949-2110	Cindy Bartman	Brian Donovan	Karen Brower	Laura Vanderwall	. . .	. . .	Ken Feldt
East Jordan *	c	CM	2	(231) 536-3381	. . .	David White	Cheltzi Wilson	. . .	Glen Thorman	Daniel Reece	William Breakey
East Lansing *	c	CM	46	(517) 337-1731	Victor Loomis	Theodore Staton	Nicole Evans	Mary Haskell	Randall Talifarro	Thomas Wibert	Todd Sneathen
East Tawas	c	CM	2	(989) 362-6161	Bruce Bolen	Ronald Leslie	Blinda Baker	. . .	William Deckett	Dennis Frank	Thomas Lixey
Eastpointe *	c	CM	34	(586) 445-5016	Suzanne Pixley	Darwin Parks	. . .	Susan Mancani	Danny Hagen	Michael Lauretti	Gregory Brown
Eaton Rapids	c	CM	5	(517) 663-8118	Donald Colestock	William Lefevere	Kristy Reinecke	. . .	Roger McNutt	Carl Watkins	Howard Hillard
Ecorse	c	MC	11	(313) 386-2344	James Tassis	. . .	Phyllis Cook	William Barnett	Charles Lafferty	James Hunt	. . .
Edmore	v	CM	1	(989) 427-5641	. . .	. . .	Shirley Drain	. . .	. . .	Timber Irwin	Charles Burr
Elk Rapids	v	CM	1	(231) 264-9274	Joseph Yuchasz	Robert Peterson	Barbara Manley	. . .	. . .	Michael Miles	Ronald Ridge
Emmett	tp	MC	11	(269) 968-0241	. . .	. . .	. . .	. . .	. . .	. . .	. . .
Escanaba	c	CM	13	(906) 786-9402	Judith Schwalbach	. . .	Robert Richards	Michael Dewar	. . .	. . .	Bill Farrell
Essexville *	c	CM	3	(989) 893-0772	Russell Tanner	Dale Majerczyk	Cynthia Fournier	. . .	. . .	. . .	Daniel Hansford
Evart	c	CM	1	(231) 734-2181	. . .	Roger Elkins	Martha Pattee	. . .	Shane Helmer	Kirt Vink	James Ward
Farmington	c	CM	10	(248) 474-5500	James Mitchell	Vincent Pastue	. . .	Patsy Cantrell	. . .	. . .	Kevin Gushman
Farmington Hills	c	CM	82	(248) 474-6115	Nancy Bates	Steven Brock	Kathryn Dornan	Robert Spaman	Richard Marinucci	William Dwyer	Thomas Biasell
Fenton	c	CM	10	(810) 629-2261	Sue Osborn	Lynn Markland	Melinda Carrier	. . .	. . .	. . .	Leslie Bland
Ferndale *	c	CM	22	(248) 546-2360	Craig Covey	Robert Bruner	J. Cherilynn Tallman	Jaynmarie Hubanks	Roger Schmidt	Michael Kitchen	Byron Photiades
Ferrysburg *	c	CM	3	(616) 842-5803	Jeffrey Stille	Craig Bessinger	Debbie Wierenga	. . .	Mike Olthof	Roger DeYoung	George Dunning
Flat Rock *	c	MC	8	(734) 782-2455	. . .	. . .	Lorene Butski	Richard Jones	William Vack	Neal Rossow	Bruce Hammond
Flint	c	MC	124	(810) 766-7280	Woodrow Stanley	Peggy Cook	Inez Brown	Marc Pockett	Theron Wiggins	Trevor Hampton	J. Jones
Flushing	c	CM	8	(810) 659-3130	Janice Gensel	Dennis Bow	. . .	. . .	Ronald Downing	Mark Hoornstra	Bryan Sutton
Fowlerville *	v	CM	2	(517) 223-3771	Wayne Copeland	Joseph Merucci	Kathryn Arledge	. . .	John Wright	Thomas Couling	Erin Daksiewciz
Frankenmuth *	c	CM	4	(989) 652-9901	Gary Rupprecht	Charles Graham	Phillip Kerns	. . .	. . .	Donald Mawer	Randy Braeutigam
Franklin	v	MC	2	(248) 626-9666	James Pikulas	Jon Stoppels	Eileen Pulker	. . .	Anthony Averbuch	Edward Glomb	. . .
Fraser	c	CM	15	(586) 293-3102	Marilyn Lane	Jeffrey Bremer	. . .	Patricia Jamison	. . .	. . .	B. Van Fleteren
Fremont	c	CM	4	(231) 924-2101	James Rynberg	Bryan Gruesbeck	Todd Blake	. . .	Rusty Boeskool	Philip Deur	Brian Hettinger
Garden City	c	CM	30	(734) 525-8800	. . .	David Harvey	Allyson Bettis	. . .	Michael Todd	. . .	Jack Barnes
Gaylord	c	CM	3	(989) 732-4060	Gladys Solokis	Joseph Duff	Rebecca Curtis	. . .	Tim Warren	Joseph Fitzgerald	Keith Roberts
Genoa	tp	MC	15	(810) 227-5225	Gary McCririe	Michael Archinal	Paulette Skolarus	. . .	. . .	. . .	. . .
Gibraltar	c	MC	4	(734) 676-3900	James Beaubien	Mark Kibby	Cynthia Ward	Barbara Meyer	Arthur Beauman	. . .	. . .
Gladstone	c	CM	5	(906) 428-2311	Thomas Simaeve	Brant Kucera	Linda Gray	. . .	. . .	. . .	Robert Johnson
Gladwin	c	MC	3	(989) 426-9231	Thomas Winarski	Robert Moffit	Shannon Greaves	. . .	George Alward	Charles Jones	. . .
Grand Blanc	c	MC	8	(810) 694-1118	Michael Matheny	Randall Byrne	. . .	Richard Saathoff	James Harmes	Mark Heidel	Matthew Wurtz
Grand Blanc	tp	MC	29	(810) 424-2600	. . .	. . .	. . .	. . .	. . .	. . .	. . .
Grand Haven	c	CM	11	(616) 842-3210	. . .	Patrick McGinnis	Leah Spinner	James Bonamy	. . .	. . .	Dan Czarnecki
Grand Haven	tp	CM	13	(616) 842-5988	Joanne Marcetti	William Cargo	Sue Buitenhuis	Gary Schreiber	Thomas Gerencer	. . .	Mark VerBerkmoes
Grand Ledge	c	CM	7	(517) 627-2149	Thomas Peek	Jon Bayless	Gregory Newman	. . .	John Cagle	Martin Underhill	James Eimer
Grand Rapids	tp	MC	14	(616) 361-7391	Michael DeVries	. . .	Janice Hulbert	. . .	. . .	. . .	. . .
Grand Rapids	c	CM	197	(616) 456-3166	George Heartwell	. . .	Mary Hegarty	Scott Buhrer	Robert VanSolkema	Harry Dolan	Patrick Bush
Grandville *	c	CM	16	(616) 531-3030	James Buck	Kenneth Krombeen	Mary Meines	. . .	Harvey Veldhouse	Dennis Santo	Ron Carr
Grant	c	CM	. .	(231) 834-7904	. . .	Douglas La Fave	. . .	. . .	. . .	. . .	. . .
Grayling	c	CM	1	(989) 348-2131	. . .	Allen Lowe	Michele Moshier	. . .	. . .	Karl Schriener	Douglas Duby
Green Oak	tp	MC	15	(810) 231-1333	Jan Plas	. . .	. . .	. . .	. . .	. . .	. . .
Greenville	c	CM	7	(616) 754-5645	Lloyd Walker	George Bosanic	. . .	. . .	. . .	. . .	Thomas Ledger
Grosse Ile	tp	CM	10	(734) 676-4422	Douglas Jones	. . .	Ute O'Connor	Brian Kuchik	Duncan Murdock	William Barron	Tim Taylor
Grosse Pointe	c	CM	5	(313) 885-5800	Dale Scrace	Peter Dame	Julie Arthurs	Glenn Mach	. . .	. . .	Paul Weitzel
Grosse Pointe Farms *	c	CM	9	(313) 885-6600	Ronald Kneiser	Shane Reeside	. . .	John Modzinski	. . .	Robert Ferber	Terry Brennan
Grosse Pointe Park	c	CM	12	(313) 822-6200	Palmer Heenan	Dale Krajniak	Jane Blahut	. . .	. . .	. . .	Christon Reimel
Grosse Pointe Shores	v	CM	2	(313) 881-6565	James Cooper	Michael Kenyon	Victoria Boyce	Rhonda Ricketts	. . .	. . .	Brett Smith
Grosse Pointe Woods	c	CM	17	(313) 343-2440	Robert Novitke	Mark Wollenweber	Lisa Hathaway	Clifford Maison	. . .	. . .	Joseph Ahee
Gun Plain	tp	CM	5	(616) 685-9471	Shelly Edgerton	Sherry Mason	Martha Meert	. . .	. . .	. . .	. . .
Hamtramck *	c	CM	22	(313) 876-7700	Karen Majewski	William Cooper	Edwin Norris	Nevrus Nazarko	. . .	James Doyle	Martin Ladd
Hancock	c	CM	4	(906) 482-2720	. . .	Glenn Anderson	Karen Haischer	. . .	. . .	Michael Beaudoin	Doug Hoyrynen
Harbor Beach *	c	MC	1	(989) 479-3363	Tom Wood	. . .	. . .	. . .	J. P. Lermont	. . .	Gary Shedd
Harbor Springs	c	CM	1	(231) 526-2104	. . .	Frederick Geuder	Ronald McRae	. . .	. . .	Daniel Branson	Fredrick Ward
Harper Woods *	c	CM	14	(313) 343-2500	Kenneth Poynter	James Leidlein	Mickey Todd	Laura Stowell	Sean Gunnery	R. Skotarczyk	William Snyder
Hart *	c	CM	1	(231) 873-2488	Clarence Aerts	Stanley Rickard	. . .	. . .	. . .	Daniel Leimback	. . .
Hartford	c	CM	2	(616) 621-2477	Theodore Johnson	Yemi Akinwale	Roxann Isbrecht	. . .	Ed Riley	Ramon Beltran	Daniel Staunton
Hartland	tp	MC	10	(810) 632-7498	. . .	James Wickman	. . .	. . .	. . .	. . .	. . .
Hastings	c	CM	7	(616) 945-2468	Franklin Campbell	Jeffrey Mansfield	Everil Manshum	. . .	Roger Caris	Jerry Sarver	Timothy Girrbach
Hazel Park	c	CM	18	(248) 546-4064	Jack Lloyd	Edward Klobucher	Sharon Pinch	. . .	. . .	David Niedermeier	Michael Mazzuckelli
Highland Park *	c	MC	16	(313) 252-0022	Hubert Yopp	. . .	Mattie Carter	Earnestine Williams	David Peek	Theodore Cadwell	Katreah Bey
Hillsdale *	c	CM	8	(517) 437-6441	Michael Sessions	Michael Mitchell	Parke Hayes	Bonnie Tew	. . .	. . .	Rick Rose
Holland *	c	CM	35	(616) 355-1300	Albert McGeehan	Soren Wolff	. . .	Tim Vagle	Danny Henderson	John Kruithoff	Loren Howard
Holly	v	CM	6	(248) 634-9571	Peter Clemens	. . .	Marsha Powers	. . .	Jack Hollands	Rollie Gackstetter	Marvin Swanson
Homer *	v	CM	1	(517) 568-4321	Christopher Miller	Gerald Stonebraker	Lea Nowlin	. . .	Kurt Swope	Steven Fisher	Donald Drumm
Houghton	c	CM	7	(906) 482-1700	Thomas Merz	Robert Macinnes	Kurt Kuure	. . .	James Lightfoot	Ralph Raffaelli	Mark Zenner
Howard City	v	MC	1	(231) 937-4311	. . .	Mark Rambo	. . .	. . .	. . .	. . .	. . .
Howell	c	CM	9	(517) 546-3500	. . .	Reid Charles	Rebecca Ruttan	. . .	. . .	Roger Goralski	Terry Wilson
Hudson	c	CM	2	(517) 448-8983	Lee Daugherty	Frank Goodroe	Kimberly Murphy	. . .	Terry Camp	Charles Weir	Philip Goodlock
Hudsonville	c	CM	7	(616) 669-0200	D. Van Doeselaar	Pauline Luben	Jan Wiersum	D. Van de Roovaart	Richard Mohr	Michael Wieringa	John Gorney
Huntington Woods *	c	CM	6	(248) 541-4300	Ronald Gillham	Alex Allie	Ruth Franzoni	Richard Lehmann	. . .	. . .	Larry Harworth
Huron	tp	CM	13	(734) 753-4466	. . .	. . .	. . .	. . .	. . .	. . .	. . .
Imlay City *	c	CM	3	(810) 724-2135	J. Rodney Warner	Amy Planck	. . .	. . .	Kip Reaves	. . .	Larry Lloyd
Independence *	tp	MC	32	(248) 625-5111	Dave Wagner	. . .	S. VanderVeen	Susan Hendricks	Steve Ronk	. . .	Linda Richardson
Inkster	c	CM	30	(313) 563-4232	Hilliard Hampton	. . .	V. Gutierrez-Smith	Charles Stanhouse	Mark Hubanks	Gregory Gaskin	Archer Collins
Ionia	c	MC	10	(616) 527-4170	Daniel Balice	Jason Eppler	Karen Confer	Catherine Pearce	. . .	. . .	Gary Cunningham
Iron Mountain *	c	CM	8	(906) 774-8530	Jeff VanLaanen	. . .	Jordan Stanchina	Carol Bartolameolli	Daniel Johnson	Peter Flaminio	Bob Becotte
Iron River	c	CM	1	(906) 265-4719	C. Soderbloom	. . .	Peggy Shamion	. . .	. . .	Michael Goriesky	Richard Anderson
Ironwood	c	CM	6	(906) 932-5050	Thomas Yelich	Keith Johnson	Anita Zak	Julie Frederickson	. . .	Joseph Cayer	James Davis
Ishpeming *	c	CM	6	(906) 485-1091	Gary Nelson	Alan Bakalaski	Jenifer Holli	. . .	Edward Anderson	James Bjorne	James Bertucci
Ithaca *	c	CM	3	(989) 875-3200	George Bailey	Bradley Heffner	Gayla Foster	. . .	David Nelson	David Thompson	Robert Studt
Jackson	c	CM	36	(517) 788-4046	Jerry Ludwig	William Ross	Lynn Fessel	Philip Hones	Larry Bosell	. . .	Glenn Chinavare
Jonesville *	v	MC	2	(517) 849-2104	David Steel	Adam Smith	Betsy Brooks	. . .	Dean Adair	Robert Corbett	Claude Russell
Kalamazoo	c	CM	77	(269) 337-8052	Robert Jones	Kenneth Collard	Stephen French	Angie Bennett	. . .	. . .	. . .
Kalkaska	v	CM	2	(231) 258-9191	Jeffery Fitch	Bill Cousins	. . .	Leslie Belcher	. . .	Melvin Hill	Allen Smith
Keego Harbor *	c	CM	2	(248) 682-1930	Sidney Rubin	Dale Stuart	Linda Voll	. . .	. . .	. . .	Tony Hale
Kentwood	c	MC	45	(616) 554-0732	Richard Root	. . .	Dan Kasunic	Thomas Chase	James Carr	Richard Mattice	Ron Woods
Kingsford	c	CM	5	(906) 774-3526	. . .	Darryl Wickman	. . .	. . .	. . .	. . .	Anthony Edlebeck

Directory 1/9 continued **OFFICIALS IN U.S. MUNICIPALITIES 2,500 AND OVER IN POPULATION**

Jurisdiction		Type	Form of govern-ment	2000 Popu-lation	Main telephone number	Chief elected official	Appointed administrator	Clerk of the governing board	Chief financial officer	Fire chief	Police chief	Public works director
MICHIGAN continued												
Lake Isabella		v	CM	1	(989) 644-8654	George Dunn	Timothy Wolff	Jeffrey Grey	. . .	. . .	. . .	. . .
Lake Orion		v	CM	2	(248) 693-8391	William Siver	Jo Ann Van Tassel	Arlene Nichols	Janet Adams	. . .	Jerry Narsh	Scott Baker
Lakeview		v	MC	1	(989) 352-6233	. . .	James Freed	. . .	. . .	. . .	. . .	. . .
L'Anse	*	v	MC	2	(906) 524-6116	Cheryl Dingeldey	Robert LaFave	Kathleen Goodreau	Janet Supanich	Mike Bianco	Mike LaBerge	John Falk
Lansing		c	MC	119	(517) 483-4004	. . .	. . .	Chris Swope	Douglas Rubley	Greg Martin	Mark Alley	David Berridge
Lapeer		c	CM	9	(810) 664-5231	William Sprague	Dale Kerbyson	Donna Cronce	Paul Boucher	Terrence Kluge	Todd Alexander	John Lyons
Lathrup Village	*	c	CM	4	(248) 557-2600	. . .	Jeffrey Mueller	Gloria Harris-Ford	. . .	. . .	Robert Jones	. . .
Laurium		v	CM	2	(906) 337-1600	Leonard Miller	Edward Vertin	Amber Small	. . .	Joseph Shaltz	James Lemler	. . .
Leslie	*	c	CM	2	(517) 589-8236	Ron Schmit	. . .	Denae Davenport	Cheryl Neu	Mike Fancher	Robert Delamarter	Martha Owen
Lexington		v	CM	1	(810) 359-8631	Daniel Maliniak	. . .	Karolyn McEntee	. . .	Mike Sharon	Kirk Sasinowski	Gary Flannigan
Lincoln Park	*	c	MC	40	(313) 386-1800	Frank Vaslo	Steve Duchane	Donna Breeding	Lisa Santos	Kenneth Elmore	Thomas Karnes	Robert Bartok
Linden		c	CM	2	(810) 735-7980	James McIntyre	Christopher Wren	Martha Donnelly	. . .	Brian Will	Peter Van Driessche	James Letts
Litchfield		c	CM	1	(517) 542-2921	Edwin Smith	Douglas Terry	Roger Sprague	. . .	Dan Pitts	Steve Marson	. . .
Livonia	*	c	MC	100	(734) 466-2530	Jack Kirksey	. . .	Linda Grimsby	Michael Slater	Shadd Whitehead	Robert Stevenson	. . .
Lowell		c	CM	4	(616) 897-8457	C. Jeanne Shores	David Pasquale	Betty Morlock	. . .	Frank Martin	James Valentine	Daniel DesJarden
Ludington	*	c	CM	8	(231) 845-6237	John Henderson	John Shay	Deborah Luskin	. . .	Jerry Funk	Mark Barnett	Shawn McDonald
Mackinaw City	*	v	CM	. .	(231) 436-5351	Ron Wallin	Jeffrey Lawson	Elizabeth Clemens	. . .	Frederick Thompson	Patrick Wyman	James Tamlyn
Madison Heights	*	c	CM	31	(248) 583-0829	Edward Swanson	Jon Austin	Marilyn Haley	. . .	Kevin Scheid	Kevin Sagan	. . .
Manistee	*	c	CM	6	(231) 398-2801	Cyndy Fuller	Mitchell Deisch	Michelle Wright	Edward Bradford	Sid Scrimger	David Bachman	John Garber
Manistique		c	CM	3	(906) 341-2290	John Hoag	Sheila Aldrich	Deborah Dougovito	. . .	. . .	. . .	Nicholas Bosanic
Marine City	*	c	CM	4	(810) 765-8847	Robert Lepley	John Gabor	Diana Kade	. . .	Richard Tucker	Donald Tillery	Richard Ames
Marlette		c	CM	2	(989) 635-7448	Kenneth Babich	. . .	. . .	. . .	. . .	. . .	Robert Foster
Marquette	*	c	CM	19	(906) 228-0480	John Kivela	Judy Akkala	David Bleau	Gary Simpson	Thomas Belt	Leonard Angeli	Scott Cambensy
Marquette	*	tp	CM	19	(906) 228-6220	Ray Adamini	Randell Girard	Patricia Mayer	. . .	Robert Sims	. . .	Kirk Page
Marshall		c	CM	7	(269) 781-5183	Bruce Smith	Christopher Olson	Donna Kolodica	Gail Bradstreet	. . .	Brett Pehrson	Timothy Eggleston
Marysville	*	c	CM	9	(810) 364-6613	Gary Orr	Jack Schumacher	Tina Weglarz	. . .	Tom Konik	Mark Thorner	Steven Kerr
Mason	*	c	CM	6	(517) 676-9155	. . .	Martin Colburn	. . .	Kathy Revels	Kerry Minshall	John Stressman	Rolly Olney
Mattawan	*	v	CM	2	(269) 668-2128	Terri McLean	. . .	Ruth Goheen	. . .	. . .	Donald Verhage	Tom Anthony
Mayville		v	CM	. .		. . .	. . .	. . .	. . .	. . .	. . .	. . .
Melvindale	*	c	MC	10	(313) 429-1040	James Kinard	. . .	Kelly Blevins	Paul LaManes	Daniel Wilhelm	Rickey Cadez	Eric Witte
Menominee	*	c	CM	9	(906) 863-2656	George Krah	Eric Strahl	Thomas Denike	. . .	. . .	. . .	. . .
Meridian	*	tp	CM	39	(517) 853-4200	Susan McGillicuddy	Gerald Richards	Mary Helmbrecht	Diana Hasse	Fred Cowper	David Hall	Raymond Severy
Middleville	*	v	CM	2	(616) 795-3385	. . .	George Strand	. . .	. . .	. . .	. . .	. . .
Midland		c	CM	41	(989) 837-3300	Bruce Johnson	Jon Lynch	Selina Tisdale	David Keenan	Leonardo Garcia	James St. Louis	Martin McGuire
Milan	*	c	CM	4	(734) 439-1501	Kym Muckler	Ben Swayze	. . .	. . .	. . .	Jeffery Lewis	. . .
Milford		v	CM	6	(248) 684-1515	Tom Nader	Arthur Shufflebarger	Ann Collins	Becky Jacques	. . .	Wayne Walli	Robert Calley
Monroe		c	MC	22	(734) 243-0700	C. Cappuccilli	George Brown	Charles Evans	Michael O'Connel	William Bert	John Michrina	Scott Davidson
Montague		c	CM	2	(231) 893-1155	. . .	John French	Melinda O'Connell	. . .	. . .	Robert Rought	Thomas Kroll
Montrose	*	c	CM	1	(810) 639-6168	Clinton Diffin	Frank Crosby	Christina Rush	. . .	. . .	Darrell Ellis	Everett Persall
Mount Clemens	*	c	CM	17	(586) 469-6818	Barb Dempsey	Douglas Anderson	Lynne Kennedy	Marilyn Dluge	. . .	. . .	Jeffrey Wood
Mount Morris	*	c	CM	3	(810) 686-2160	Robert Slattery	Allen LaFurgey	Lisa Baryo	. . .	Todd Rockwell	Keith Becker	Jeffrey Roth
Mount Pleasant		c	CM	25	(989) 779-5321	C. Bradley Kilmer	Kathie Grinzinger	Robert Flynn	Nancy Ridley	Greg Walterhouse	. . .	Duane Ellis
Munising		c	CM	2	(906) 387-2095	Rod DesJardins	Douglas Bovin	Sue Roberts	. . .	Dan Malone	Steven Swanberg	. . .
Muskegon		c	CM	40	(231) 724-6716	Steve Warmington	Bryon Mazade	Gail Kundinger	Timothy Paul	Mark Kincaid	. . .	Robert Kuhn
Muskegon Heights	*	c	CM	12	(231) 733-8870	Darrell Paige	Natasha Henderson	Sharon Gibbs	Lori Doody	David Alves	Clifton Johnson	Gauntrial Morris
Negaunee		c	CM	4	(906) 475-7700	Ray Rappazini	Thomas Manninen	. . .	Joan Du Shane	Tom Gardyko	Paul Waters	Dave Palmer
New Baltimore	*	c	MC	7	(586) 725-2151	T. Goldenbogen	Marc Levise	Marcella Shinksa	. . .	Ken Lawfield	John Bolgar	Thomas Gunst
New Buffalo		c	CM	2	(269) 469-1500	Raymond Wojdula	Charles Dobbins	Joan Jones	. . .	Billy Taylor	Thomas Harken	Donald Krause
Newaygo	*	c	CM	1	(231) 652-1657	Ron Armstrong	Rich Blachford	Jon Schneider	. . .	Jim Uthe	Pat Hedlund	Ron Wight
Niles	*	c	CM	12	(269) 683-4700	Michael McCauslin	Terry Eull	Ruth Harte	Sandra Naugle	Larry Lamb	Richard Huff	Neil Coulston
North Muskegon		c	CM	4	(231) 744-1621	Chris Witham	Dennis Stepke	Ann Becker	. . .	James Kersman	Thomas Korabik	Bruce Moore
Northville		c	CM	6	(248) 349-1300	Christopher Johnson	Patrick Sullivan	Dianne Massa	Nicolette Bateson	James Allen	Gary Goss	James Gallogly
Northville		tp	CM	21	(248) 449-5087	. . .	Marvin Snider	. . .	. . .	. . .	. . .	. . .
Norton Shores		c	MC	22	(231) 798-4391	Nancy Crandall	Mark Meyers	Lynne Fuller	. . .	David Purchase	Dan Shaw	Gerald Bartoszek
Norway		c	CM	2	(906) 563-9961	Edward Coates	Ray Anderson	Trisha Plante	. . .	David Bal	John Jarecki	. . .
Novi		c	CM	47	(248) 347-0460	David Landry	Clay Pearson	Maryanne Cornelius	Kathy Roy	Frank Smith	Doug Shaeffer	William McCusker
Oak Park	*	c	CM	29	(248) 691-7410	Gerald Naftaly	. . .	Sandy Gadd	James Ghedotte	. . .	. . .	Kevin Yee
Oakland Charter	*	tp	CM	13	(248) 651-4440	. . .	James Creech	. . .	. . .	. . .	. . .	. . .
Ontonagon		v	CM	1	(906) 884-2305	Scott Frazer	. . .	Joan Nygard	. . .	. . .	. . .	Jerry Roehm
Ortonville	*	v	CM	1	(248) 627-4976	Ken Quisenberry	. . .	Julie Alexander	. . .	. . .	. . .	. . .
Oscoda		tp	CM	7	(989) 739-8299	. . .	Robert Stalker	. . .	. . .	. . .	. . .	. . .
Otisville		v	CM	. .	(810) 631-4680	Tom Bess	David Tatrow	Andrea Barden	. . .	. . .	Leo Johnsen	. . .
Otsego	*	c	CM	3	(269) 692-3391	. . .	Thad Beard	Angela Cronen	Matthew Storbeck	Vincent Pagano	Gordon Konkle	David Dutton
Owosso		c	CM	15	(989) 725-0568	Linda Robertson	Joseph Fivas	Amy Kohagen	Richard Williams	Michael Bradley	Michael Rau	. . .
Oxford		v	CM	3	(248) 628-2543	George Del Vigna	Kervin Young	. . .	. . .	Jack LeRoy	M. Neymanowski	Donald Brantley
Oxford	*	tp	MC	14	(248) 628-9787	William Dunn	Deanna Burns	Curtis Wright	Renee Wilson	. . .	Lori Collier	Tracy Deveroux
Parchment		c	CM	1	(269) 349-3785	Daniel DeGraw	Dennis Durham	Curtis Flowers	. . .	Timothy Bourgeois	William Bongers	Thomas LeRoy
Park		tp	MC	17	(616) 399-4520	Amanda Price	Stuart Visser	Skip Keeter	. . .	. . .	. . .	. . .
Paw Paw	*	v	CM	3	(269) 657-3148	Roman Plaszczak	Larry Nielsen	Christopher Tapper	Ann Knafle	Joe LeMahieu	Patrick Alspaugh	John Small
Petoskey		c	CM	6	(231) 347-2500	. . .	George Korthauer	. . .	Alan Terry	. . .	Michael Vargo	Walter Goodwin
Pinconning		c	CM	1	(989) 879-2360	Michael Duranczyk	Richard Byrne	Terri Hribek	. . .	David Ramsay	Thomas Tober	Timothy Stalker
Pittsfield Charter Township	*	tp	MC	30	(734) 822-3101	Mandy Grewal	. . .	Alan Israel	. . .	Alan D'Agostino	. . .	. . .
Plainfield	*	tp	CM	30	(616) 364-8466	George Meek	Robert Homan	K. Harvey	Warren Smith	David Peterson	. . .	. . .
Plainwell	*	c	CM	3	(269) 685-6821	Richard Brooks	Erik Wilson	Noreen Farmer	. . .	. . .	. . .	Rick Updike
Pleasant Ridge		c	CM	2	(248) 541-2900	Ralph Castelli	Sherry Ball	Amy Porcs	. . .	. . .	Karl Swieczkowski	. . .
Plymouth	*	c	CM	9	(734) 453-1234	Phil Purcell	Paul Sincock	Linda Langmesser	Mark Christiansen	. . .	. . .	Chris Porman
Plymouth		tp	MC	27	(734) 453-3840	Richard Reaume	. . .	Marilyn Massengill	. . .	Randy Maycock	Thomas Tiderington	James Anulewicz
Pontiac		c	MC	66	(248) 758-3000	Willie Payne	Leon Jukowski	Vivian Spann	J. Edward Hannan	Wilburt McAdams	Rollie Gackstetter	Claudia Filler
Port Huron	*	c	CM	32	(810) 984-9723	Alan Cutcher	. . .	Pauline Repp	John Ogden	Robert Eick	William Corbett	Robert Clegg
Portage		c	CM	44	(269) 329-4412	James Graham	Maurice Evans	James Hudson	Daniel Foecking	Randolph Lawton	Richard White	Jack Hartman
Portland		c	CM	3	(517) 647-7531	Peter Weeks	. . .	Yvonne Bailey	Brenda Schrauben	. . .	David Brown	Jon Hyland
Potterville		c	CM	2	(517) 645-7641	Brian Grosnickle	. . .	R. Cwiertniewicz	. . .	Jack Fox	Van Johnson	Bradley Boyce
Reading		c	CM	1	(517) 283-2604	Michael Redenius	. . .	. . .	. . .	Michael McCauit	George Turchan	T. Stephenson
Redford		tp	MC	54	(313) 387-2700	Kevin Kelley	. . .	Garth Christie	J. Cubba	Edwin Leonard	John Buck	Leo Snage
Reed City	*	c	CM	2	(231) 832-2245	D. Fuller-Talaske	George Freeman	Jane Wekenman	. . .	Jim Decker	Charles Davis	Kevin Rambadt
Richland		tp	MC	. .	(989) 642-2097	Joel Wardin	Renee Herhold	Kevin Kreger	. . .	Gary Wade	Robert Dalton	Timothy Rohn
Richmond	*	c	CM	4	(586) 727-7571	Tim Rix	Jon Moore	Karen Stagl	. . .	Jack Smith	Dennis Privette	Paul Fejedelem
River Rouge		c	MC	9	(313) 842-0801	Greg Joseph	. . .	Charles Manley	. . .	David Chirillo	John Birrbach	Cornelius Cooper
Riverview		c	CM	13	(734) 281-4201	Tim Durand	. . .	Judy Bratcher	Doug Daysdale	Robert Hale	Dean Workman	Gerald Perry
Rochester		c	CM	10	(248) 651-9061	David Katulic	Jaymes Vettraino	Lee Ann O'Connor	. . .	Daniel Jacobson	Theodore Glynn	David Kowaleski
Rochester Hills		c	MC	68	(248) 656-4600	Patricia Somerville	. . .	Beverly Vasinski	Julie Jenuwine	G. Walterhouse	. . .	Roger Rousse
Rockford		c	CM	4	(616) 866-1537	. . .	Michael Young	Christine Bedford	Jeff Dood	Michael Reus	John Porter	Richard Johnston
Rockwood		c	MC	3	(734) 379-9496	Philip Smalley	. . .	Patricia Roxberry	. . .	Daniel Mercure	R. VanWassehnova	Adam Grabetz
Rogers City	*	c	CM	3	(989) 734-2191	Beach Hall	Mark Slown	Theresa Heinzel	. . .	Timothy Luebke	Matthew Quaine	William Robin
Romeo		v	MC	3	(586) 752-3565	Paul Reiz	. . .	Marian McLaughlin	. . .	. . .	James Vanderlinder	Rory Trowsse

Directory 1/9 continued

OFFICIALS IN U.S. MUNICIPALITIES 2,500 AND OVER IN POPULATION

Jurisdiction		Type	Form of govern-ment	2000 Popu-lation	Main telephone number	Chief elected official	Appointed administrator	Clerk of the governing board	Chief financial officer	Fire chief	Police chief	Public works director
MICHIGAN continued												
Romulus		c	MC	22	(734) 942-7512	Alan Lambert	Besey Krampitz	Linda Choate	Debra Hoffman	David Allison	Charles Kirby	Richard Suiter
Roosevelt Park	*	c	CM	3	(231) 755-3721	Robert Young	William Boehm	Tammera Haarmsen	. . .	. . .	. . .	Matt Farrar
Roscommon	*	v	CM	1	(989) 275-5743	Jesse Carlson	Thomas Gromek	Kathryn Muphy	. . .	. . .	. . .	Dave Hodges
Roseville	*	c	CM	48	(586) 445-5410	Harold Haugh	Stephen Truman	Richard Steenland	Peter Provenzano	Benjamin Foronato	Michael Pachla	Gary Bierl
Royal Oak	*	c	CM	60	(248) 246-3000	James Ellison	Thomas Hoover	Melanie Halas	Donald Johnson	Wil White	T. Quisenberry	Greg Rassel
Saginaw		tp	CM	39	(989) 791-9800	Timothy Braun	Ronald Lee	Shirley Wazny	Michele Gadd	Jim Peterson	Donald Pussehl	Herbert Grunwell
Saginaw		c	CM	61	(989) 759-1480	. . .	Darnell Earley	Yolanda Olgine	. . .	Joe Dziuban	Gerald Cliff	Thomas Darnell
Saline		c	MC	8	(734) 429-4907	Gretchen Driskell	Todd Campbell	Dianne Hill	Lee Bourgoin	Craig Hoeft	Paul Bunten	George Danneffel
Sandusky	*	c	CM	2	(810) 648-4444	. . .	. . .	Laurie Thompson	Polly Frost	. . .	. . .	Phillip Klaus
Saugatuck		c	CM	1	(616) 857-4243	. . .	Kirk Harrier	. . .	. . .	. . .	. . .	. . .
Sault Ste. Marie		c	CM	16	(906) 632-5705	Anthony Bosbous	Spencer Nebel	Lori Clarke	John Boger	Kenneth Eagle	Louis Murray	James Atkins
Schoolcraft		v	CM	1	(269) 679-4304	. . .	Cheri Lutz	. . .	. . .	. . .	. . .	. . .
Scio	*	tp	CM	15	(734) 665-2123	Spaulding Clark	Darrell Fecho	Nancy Hedberg	Sandy Egeler	Carl Ferch	. . .	Scott Martin
Scottville		c	CM	1	(231) 757-4729	Leon Begue	Amy Hansen	Deborah Howe	. . .	Rick Gleason	Larry Nichols	James Kriesel
South Haven		c	CM	5	(269) 637-0700	Dale Lewis	Kevin Anderson	Amanda Sleigh	. . .	Randy VanWynen	Rod Somerlott	Robert Stickland
South Lyon		c	CM	10	(248) 437-1735	John Doyle	David Murphy	Julie Zemke	. . .	. . .	Lloyd Collins	Steve Renwick
Southfield	*	c	CM	78	(248) 796-5000	Brenda Lawrence	James Scharret	Nancy Banks	. . .	Peter Healy	Joseph Thomas	Gary Mekjian
Southgate		c	MC	30	(734) 246-1305	Norma Wurmlinger	. . .	Tom Alexander	David Angileri	Randy Layton	. . .	Denny Gendron
Sparta		v	MC	4	(616) 887-8251	Leonard Meyer	. . .	Greta Heugel	Sharon DeLange	Jerold Bolen	Andrew Milanowski	. . .
Spring Lake	*	v	CM	2	(616) 842-1393	William Filber	Ryan Cotton	Maribeth Lawrence	. . .	. . .	Roger DeYoung	. . .
Springfield		c	CM	5	(269) 965-2354	Susan Anderson	Franklin Peterson	Kristen Vogel	Jeannine Turner	. . .	. . .	Tom Matson
St. Charles		v	CM	2	(989) 865-8287	Ray Cornford	Hal Mead	Deanna Koehler	. . .	. . .	Kevin McInerney	. . .
St. Clair		c	CM	5	(810) 329-7121	William Cedar	Scott Adkins	Janice Winn	Michael Booth	. . .	Donald Barnum	Jeff Westrick
St. Clair Shores	*	c	CM	63	(586) 445-5200	. . .	Kenneth Podolski	Mary Kotowski	Timothy Haney	Matthew Kovalcik	Charles Burnett	Curt Dumas
St. Ignace		c	CM	2	(906) 643-9671	. . .	Gary Heckman	Renee Vonderwerth	. . .	John Robinson	Timothy Matelski	Les Therrian
St. Johns		c	CM	7	(989) 224-8944	Dana Beaman	Dennis LaForest	Mindy Seavey	. . .	Richard Cornwell	. . .	Jeffrey Stephens
St. Joseph		c	CM	8	(269) 983-5541	Mary Goff	Frank Walsh	Peggy Block	. . .	Kevin Luhrs	Mark Clapp	Roy Dost
St. Louis	*	c	CM	4	(989) 681-2137	George Kubin	Robert McConkie	Nancy Roehrs	. . .	. . .	Patrick Herblet	Mark Abbott
Standish		c	CM	1	(989) 846-9588	Ray Koroliski	Tori Kelly	Becky Lakin	. . .	. . .	. . .	Greg Norgan
Sterling Heights	*	c	CM	124	(586) 446-2489	Richard Notte	Mark Vanderpool	Walter Blessed	Brian Baker	John Childs	David Vinson	Guy Kebbe
Stevensville		v	MC	1	(616) 429-1802	Michele Getz	Bret Witkowski	Deb Warragen	. . .	. . .	. . .	. . .
Stockbridge	*	v	CM	1	(517) 851-7435	Russell Mackinder	Daniel Dancer	Linda Dancer	. . .	. . .	Michael King	. . .
Sturgis		c	CM	11	(269) 651-2321	C. Sunday-Horstman	Michael Hughes	Kenneth Rhodes	Michael Vance	Michael Houck	Eugene Alli	Rick Miller
Swartz Creek		c	CM	5	(810) 635-4464	Richard Abrams	Paul Bueche	Juanita Aguilar	Mary Jo Clark	Brent Cole	Rick Clolinger	Thomas Svrcek
Sylvan Lake	*	c	CM	1	(248) 682-1440	. . .	John Martin	Dennise Clippert	. . .	. . .	Mark Silver	. . .
Tawas City		c	CM	2	(989) 362-8688	Edward Nagy	. . .	Kay Whitney	. . .	Steve Masiett	Dennis Frank	. . .
Taylor		c	MC	65	(734) 374-1491	Gregory Pitoniak	James Riddle	Dorothy West	Dean Philo	Kenneth Costella	Thomas Bonner	James Katona
Tecumseh		c	CM	8	(517) 423-2107	. . .	Kevin Welch	Laura Caterina	. . .	Joseph Tuckey	Mack Haun	Steven Johnston
Tekonsha		v	MC	. .	(517) 767-4204	Lisa Long	. . .	Howard Rigg	. . .	. . .	. . .	. . .
The Village Of Douglas	*	c	MC	2	(269) 857-1438	Matt Balmer	David Kowal	Jean Neve	Robert Drexler	John Blok	Ken Giles	Max Rodgers
Thomas		tp	CM	11	(989) 781-0150	. . .	Russell Taylor	. . .	. . .	. . .	. . .	. . .
Three Oaks		v	MC	1	(269) 756-9221	Philip Smith	. . .	Mary Nallenweg	. . .	. . .	Frank Nekvasil	Todd Noble
Three Oaks		tp	MC	2	(269) 756-9801	Charles Sittig	. . .	Elizabeth Cummings	. . .	David Flick	. . .	. . .
Three Rivers	*	c	CM	7	(269) 273-1075	Thomas Lowry	Joseph Bippus	Lindsay Howes	Cathy Lawson	Danny Tomlinson	Thomas Bringman	James Rozeboom
Tittabawassee		tp	CM	7	(989) 695-9512	. . .	Brian Kischnick	. . .	Brian Hofmeister	. . .	Robert Harken	. . .
Traverse City	*	c	CM	14	(231) 922-4440	Margaret Dodd	Robert Bifoss	Debbra Curtiss	William Twietmeyer	Edward Fisher	Michael Warren	Robert Cole
Trenton		c	MC	19	(734) 675-6500	Patricia Hartig	Robert Cady	Kyle Stack	David Flaten	Joseph Grutza	James Menna	Lawrence Dusincki
Troy	*	c	CM	80	(248) 524-3300	Louise Schilling	Phillip Nelson	Tonni Bartholomew	John Lamerato	William Nelson	Charles Craft	Timothy Richnak
Union		tp	CM	3	(989) 772-4600	James Collin	Gwen Plowman	Susan Gilpin	. . .	. . .	. . .	Kimberly Smith
Union City		v	CM	1	(517) 741-8591	Gene Tassie	Keith Baker	Diane Smith	. . .	David Hughes	Tom Case	David Johnson
Utica	*	c	MC	4	(586) 739-1600	Jacqueline Noonan	. . .	M. McGrail	Philip Paternoster	Kevin Wilseck	Michael Reaves	William Lang
Vassar		c	CM	2	(989) 823-8517	Evart Stewart	Kevin Mackey	Tina Bacon	. . .	Gary Millerov	David Manier	. . .
Vicksburg		v	CM	2	(616) 649-1919	Daniel Pryson	Matthew Crawford	. . .	. . .	. . .	M. Descheneau	Kenneth Schippers
Wakefield		c	CM	2	(906) 229-5132	. . .	. . .	. . .	. . .	. . .	. . .	. . .
Walker	*	c	CM	21	(616) 453-6311	Robert VerHeulen	C. VanderMeulen	Sarah Bydelak	Cindy Mielke	William Schmidt	C. Garcia-Lindstrom	Mark Koning
Walled Lake		c	CM	6	(248) 624-4847	. . .	Jerry Walker	Catherine Metevia	Cathrene Behrens	K. VanSparrentak	John Woychowski	Loyd Cureton
Warren		c	MC	138	(586) 574-4520	Mark Steenbergh	Michael Griner	. . .	Richard Fox	Henry Gesing	John Baird	Robert Slavko
Waterford		tp	CM	73	(248) 674-3111	Katherine Innes	. . .	Betty Fortino	. . .	Dennis Storrs	Paul Vallad	Terry Biederman
Watervliet	*	c	CM	1	(269) 463-6769	Roger Prince	Michael Hart	Cara Goodrich	. . .	Scott Richcreek	Donald Divis	Charles Thomas
Wayland	*	c	CM	3	(269) 792-2265	Burrell Stein	Deborah Nier	Sharon Baumgard	. . .	Joe Miller	Daniel Miller	Pierre Brazeau
Wayne		c	CM	19	(734) 722-2000	. . .	John Zech	Mary Carney	Thomas Norwood	Robert Dahlman	Michael Sumeracki	Gary Clark
West Branch	*	c	CM	1	(989) 345-0500	Todd Thompson	Tom Youatt	Jane Tennant	. . .	Brent Banning	Rodger Williams	Richard Dack
Westland		c	MC	86	(734) 467-3225	Sandra Cicirelli	. . .	Nancy Bonaparte	. . .	Michael Reddy	Dan Pfannes	Thomas Wilson
White Cloud	*	c	CM	1	(231) 689-1194	Donald Barnhard	Robert Sullivan	Lora Yarrington	. . .	Duane Cruzan	Robert Mendham	Gary Zatalokin
Whitehall		c	CM	2	(231) 894-4048	Emery Hatch	Scott Huebler	Karen Helmlinger	Laurie Audo	. . .	Donald Hulbert	Brian Armstrong
Williamston		c	CM	3	(517) 655-2774	. . .	Lisa Hitchcock	. . .	. . .	. . .	Mark Hetfield	Gary Haney
Wixom	*	c	CM	13	(248) 624-0894	Michael McDonald	J. Dornan	Linda Kirby	. . .	George Spencer	. . .	Michael Howell
Wolverine Lake		v	CM	4	(248) 624-1710	. . .	Sharon Miller	Rita Irwin	. . .	. . .	Joseph George	Andrew Stone
Woodhaven		c	MC	12	(734) 675-4900	Richard Truskowski	David Flaten	Sheryl McGlynn	. . .	Jan Sikes	Roy Rook	Michael Kruse
Wyandotte		c	MC	28	(734) 324-4500	Leonard Sabuda	. . .	William Griggs	Todd Drysdale	. . .	William Lilienthal	. . .
Wyoming		c	CM	69	(616) 530-7241	Douglas Hoekstra	Curtis Holt	Heidi Isakson	Timothy Smith	Gerald Ball	Edward Edwardson	William Dooley
Ypsilanti		c	CM	22	(734) 483-1100	Cheryl Farmer	Edward Koryzno	Cherry Lawson	Marilou Uy	James Roberts	George Basar	Harry Hutchison
Ypsilanti		tp	MC	49	(734) 481-0617	Ruth Ann Jamnick	. . .	Brenda Stumbo	M. Olshelfske	Larry Morabito	Michael Radzik	. . .
Zeeland		c	MC	5	(616) 772-6400	Lester Hoogland	Timothy Klunder	Nancy Tuls	Audrey Brodzinski	William Gruppen	William Olney	David Walters
Zilwaukee		c	CM	1	(989) 755-0931	Eugene Jolin	Patricia Hascall	Richard DeLong	. . .	Michael Bauer	Bruce King	Warren Davis
MINNESOTA												
Ada		c	MC	1	(218) 784-4536	. . .	. . .	. . .	. . .	. . .	. . .	. . .
Afton		c	CM	2	(651) 436-5090	Dave Engstrom	James Norman	. . .	. . .	. . .	. . .	. . .
Albert Lea		c	CM	18	(507) 377-4300	. . .	Victoria Simonsen	Sandi Behrens	Rhonda Krcil	Paul Stieler	Thomas Menning	Steve Jahnke
Albertville	*	c	MC	3	(763) 497-3384	. . .	Larry Kruse	Bridget Miller	Tina Lannes	. . .	. . .	. . .
Alexandria		c	MC	8	(320) 763-6678	H. Dan Ness	. . .	. . .	. . .	Michael Donnay	Chuck Nettestad	Truman Hanson
Andover	*	c	CM	26	(763) 755-5100	Michael Gamache	James Dickinson	. . .	. . .	Daniel Winkel	. . .	David Berkowitz
Annandale		c	CM	2	(320) 274-3055	Marian Harmoning	. . .	Sylvia Onstad	. . .	Brian Haag	Myron Morris	William McNellis
Anoka	*	c	CM	18	(763) 576-2700	Bjorn Skogquist	Timothy Cruikshank	Amy Oehlers	Lori Yager	Charles Thompson	Phil Johanson	Greg Lee
Apple Valley	*	c	CM	45	(952) 953-2500	M. Hamann-Roland	M. Lawell	Pamela Gackstetter	George Ballenger	Nealon Thompson	Scott Johnson	Todd Blomstrom
Arden Hills		c	MC	9	(651) 792-7800	Stan Harpstead	Ronald Moorse	. . .	Sue Iverson	. . .	. . .	Gregory Hoag
Aurora	*	v	MC	1	(218) 229-2614	Mary Hess	. . .	. . .	Linda Cazin	Kent Dickinson	William Lesar	C. Vreeland
Austin	*	c	MC	23	(507) 437-9940	Tom Stiehm	James Hurm	Lucy Johnson	. . .	Daniel Wilson	Paul Philipp	Jon Erichson
Barnesville	*	c	MC	2	(218) 354-2292	Ken Bauer	Michael Brethorst	. . .	Laurie Schell	. . .	Dean Ernst	Dave Riddering
Baxter	*	c	MC	5	(218) 454-5100	Darrel Olson	. . .	Beva Olson	Jeremy Vacinek	. . .	James Exsted	Trevor Walter
Bayport	*	c	MC	3	(651) 275-4404	Jon Nowaczek	. . .	. . .	Wanda Madsen	Mike Bell	Laura Eastman	Milan Horak
Becker	*	c	CM	2	(763) 261-4302	David Graning	Greg Pruszinske	Nancy Fiereck	Brenda Weller	Chad Stephens	Brent Baloun	Karla Eggink
Belle Plaine		c	MC	3	(612) 873-5553	Maynard Harms	Luayn Murphy	. . .	Dawn Meyer	Christopher Meyer	Steven Rost	Alan Fahey
Bemidji	*	c	CM	11	(218) 759-3560	Richard Lehmann	John Chattin	Kay Murphy	Ron Eischens	Dick Sather	Jerry Johnson	Andy Mack

Directory 1/9 continued **OFFICIALS IN U.S. MUNICIPALITIES 2,500 AND OVER IN POPULATION**

Jurisdiction	Type	Form of govern-ment	2000 Popu-lation	Main telephone number	Chief elected official	Appointed administrator	Clerk of the governing board	Chief financial officer	Fire chief	Police chief	Public works director
MINNESOTA continued											
Benson	c	CM	3	(320) 843-4775	Paul Kittelson	Robert Wolfington	. . .	Glen Pederson	Gregory Lee	James Crace	Robert Flaws
Big Lake	c	CM	6	(763) 263-2107	Donald Orrock	. . .	Gina Wolbeck	Corey Boyer	. . .	Sean Rifenberick	Michael Goebel
Biwabik *	c	CM	. .	(218) 865-4183	Jim Weikum	Jeffery Jacobson	Pam Berts	. . .	Dan Berg	. . .	Blake Bertram
Blaine	c	CM	44	(763) 784-6700	. . .	Clark Arneson	Jane Hall	. . .	. . .	. . .	Mike Ulrich
Bloomington	c	CM	85	(952) 563-8700	Eugene Winstead	Mark Bernhardson	Thomas Ferber	L. Economy-Scholler	Ulysses Seal	John Laux	Charles Honchell
Blue Earth	c	CM	3	(507) 526-7336	Robert Hammond	. . .	. . .	Nancy Thompson	. . .	Dean Vereide	Richard LaMont
Brainerd	c	CM	13	(218) 828-2307	James Wallin	Daniel Vogt	. . .	Theresa Goble	Fred Underhill	John Bolduc	. . .
Breckenridge	c	MC	3	(218) 643-1431	. . .	. . .	Blaine Hill	. . .	. . .	Dennis Milbrandt	Paul Stollenwerk
Breezy Point	c	MC	. .	(218) 562-4441	JoAnn Weaver	Bradley Scott	Kathy Millard	. . .	. . .	Steve Rudek	Tim Polipnick
Brooklyn Center	c	CM	29	(763) 569-3300	Myrna Kauth	Cornelius Boganey	Sharon Knutson	Daniel Jordet	Ronald Boman	Scott Bechthold	Todd Blomstrom
Brooklyn Park *	c	CM	67	(763) 424-8000	Steven Lampi	James Verbrugge	Devin Montero	Cory Kampf	Kenneth Prillaman	Michael Davis	Jon Thiel
Buffalo	c	CM	10	(763) 682-1181	Fred Naaktgeboren	Merton Auger	. . .	Mary Stubstad	Robin Barfknecht	Mitch Weinzetl	. . .
Buhl *	c	CM	. .	(218) 258-3226	Craig Pulford	. . .	Michael Buchanan	Mary Markas	Michael Lopac	. . .	John Markas
Burnsville *	c	CM	60	(952) 895-4400	Elizabeth Kautz	Craig Ebeling	Susan Olesen	Tammy Omdal	Steven Harklerode	Robert Hawkins	Henry Osmundson
Caledonia *	c	MC	2	(507) 725-3450	Robert Burns	Robert Nelson	. . .	Stephanie Mann	Charles Gavin	Randy Shefelbine	. . .
Cambridge	c	CM	5	(763) 689-3211	. . .	Stoney Hiljus	. . .	Jessie Hart	. . .	Michael Johnson	Steven Wegwerth
Cannon Falls *	c	MC	3	(507) 263-9300	Robby Robinson	Aaron Reeves	. . .	. . .	John Miller	Jeffrey McCormick	. . .
Carver	c	CM	1	(952) 448-5353	Jim Weygand	James Elmquist	Patricia Plekkenpol	. . .	Jerry Dauwalter	. . .	Paul Schultz
Centerville	c	MC	3	(651) 429-3232	Terry Sweeney	K. Moore-Sykes	Teresa Bender	Ellen Paulseth	Milo Bennett	. . .	Paul Palzar
Champlin	c	CM	22	(763) 421-8100	Steve Boynton	Bret Heitkamp	Jo Anne Brown	June Johnston	. . .	Alan Garber	. . .
Chanhassen	c	CM	20	(952) 227-1100	Thomas Furlong	Todd Gerhardt	. . .	Bruce DeJong	John Wolff	. . .	. . .
Chaska	c	CM	17	(952) 448-2851	Gary VanEyll	David Pokorney	Margo Steffel	. . .	Bruce Schueing	Scott Knight	Timothy Wiebe
Chisago City	c	CM	2	(651) 257-4162	Christopher DuBose	John Pechman	Paula Oehme	Gail Wilson	Bruce Peterson	W. Schlumbohm	Catherine Rude
Chisholm *	c	MC	4	(218) 254-7900	Michael Jugovich	Garrison Hale	. . .	Gary Krampotich	Robert Brown	Scott Erickson	. . .
Circle Pines	c	CM	4	(763) 784-5898	Keith Perlich	James Keinath	. . .	Peggy Bauman	Milo Bennett	. . .	Richard Lavell
Clara City	c	MC	1	(320) 847-2142	Orville Meints	. . .	. . .	. . .	David Lieser	Ralph Bradley	Roger Knapper
Cloquet	c	MC	11	(218) 879-3347	. . .	Brian Fritsinger	Robert Norrgard	. . .	J. Langenbrunner	. . .	James Prusak
Cohasset	c	MC	2	(218) 328-6225	. . .	. . .	Debra Sakrison	. . .	. . .	. . .	. . .
Cokato	c	MC	2	(320) 286-5505	Bruce Johnson	Donald Levens	Peggy Carlson	. . .	Dennis Johnson	. . .	Kenneth Bakke
Cologne	c	MC	1	(952) 466-2064	. . .	John Douville	Laurel Jones	. . .	. . .	. . .	. . .
Columbia Heights	c	CM	18	(763) 706-3600	Gary Peterson	Walter Fehst	. . .	William Elrite	Gary Gorman	Thomas Johnson	Kevin Hansen
Coon Rapids *	c	CM	61	(763) 755-2880	Tim Howe	Matthew Fulton	Joan Anderson	Sharon Legg	John Piper	Steve Wells	Steven Gatlin
Corcoran *	c	MC	5	(763) 420-2288	Kenneth Guenthner	Todd Bodem	Kimberly Bachmeier	. . .	. . .	Patrick Gormely	Patrick Meister
Cottage Grove *	c	CM	30	(651) 458-2800	Sandy Shiely	Ryan Schroeder	Caron Stransky	Ronald Hedberg	Robert Byerly	. . .	Les Burshten
Cottonwood	c	CM	1	(507) 423-6488	Ellen Lenz	Gregory Isaackson	. . .	. . .	. . .	. . .	. . .
Crookston	c	MC	8	(218) 281-1232	Don Osborne	Aaron Parrish	Al Chesley	. . .	Dick Rock	Paul Monteen	Patrick Kelly
Crosby	c	MC	2	(218) 546-5021	. . .	Joel Peck	. . .	. . .	. . .	. . .	. . .
Crystal *	c	CM	22	(763) 531-1000	ReNae Bowman	Anne Norris	Janet Lewis	Charles Hansen	Scott Crandall	John Banick	Thomas Mathisen
Dassel	c	CM	1	(320) 275-2454	Ava Flachmeyer	Myles Mc Grath	. . .	. . .	Dale Grochow	. . .	David Scepaniak
Dawson	c	CM	1	(320) 769-2154	Al Schacherer	David Bovee	Melva Larson	. . .	Jeff Olson	William Stock	Brent Powers
Dayton	c	CM	4	(763) 427-4589	James Jadwin	Samantha Orduno	Sandra Borders	. . .	. . .	Richard Pietrzak	Richard Hass
Deephaven	c	CM	3	(952) 474-4755	. . .	. . .	Sandra Langley	. . .	. . .	Harlan Johnson	Gerald Hudlow
Delano	c	MC	3	(763) 972-0550	John Jaunich	Philip Kern	Marlene Kittock	. . .	Bob Van Lith	. . .	Dan Alger
Detroit Lakes	c	CM	7	(218) 847-5658	Larry Buboltz	Robert Louiseau	. . .	Louis Guzek	Jeffrey Swanson	Kelvin Keena	. . .
Dilworth	c	MC	3	(218) 287-2313	Paul Marquart	Ken Parke	. . .	Gwynn Misialek	Dave Lamb	Michael Jacklovich	Donald Vogel
Dodge Center	c	CM	2	(507) 374-2575	Bill Ketchum	Lee Mattson	Julene Ellefson	. . .	. . .	. . .	Lee Fitzgerald
Duluth *	c	MC	86	(218) 723-3291	Don Ness	Lisa Potswald	Jeffrey Cox	. . .	John Strongitharm	Gordon Ramsay	James Benning
Eagan *	c	CM	63	(651) 675-5000	Mike Maguire	Thomas Hedges	Maria Petersen	Thomas Pepper	Michael Scott	James McDonald	Tom Colbert
Eagle Lake	c	MC	1	(507) 257-3218	Tim Auringer	Sack Thongvanh	Kerry Rausch	. . .	. . .	Phil Wills	Richard Reinbold
East Bethel *	c	MC	10	(763) 434-9569	Greg Hunter	Douglas Sell	Wendy Warren	Rita Pierce	Mark DuCharme	. . .	Jack Davis
East Grand Forks *	c	MC	7	(218) 773-2483	Lynn Stauss	Scott Huizenga	. . .	Gerald Lucke	Randy Gust	Michael Hedlund	John Wachter
Eden Prairie	c	CM	54	(952) 949-8300	Phil Young	. . .	Kitty Porta	Sue Kotchevar	George Esbensen	Rob Reynolds	Eugene Dietz
Edina *	c	CM	47	(952) 927-8861	James Hovland	Gordon Hughes	Debra Mangen	John Wallen	Martin Scheerer	Michael Siitari	. . .
Elk River	c	MC	16	(763) 635-1000	Stephanie Klinzing	Lori Johnson	Joan Schmidt	. . .	Bruce West	Jeffrey Beahen	. . .
Elko New Market *	c	MC	2	(952) 461-2777	. . .	Thomas Terry	. . .	. . .	. . .	. . .	. . .
Ely	c	CM	3	(218) 365-3224	Lolita Schnitzius	Lee Tessier	. . .	Bob Hedloff	Gary Klun	John Manning	Ken Hegman
Eveleth	c	MC	3	(218) 744-2501	Calvin Cassalter	J. Monahan-Junek	Sharon Stimac	. . .	. . .	Brian Lillis	Michael Wiskow
Excelsior *	c	CM	2	(952) 474-5233	Nick Ruehl	Kristin Luger	Cheri Johnson	. . .	Scott Gerber	Bryan Litsey	Dave Wisdorf
Eyota *	c	MC	1	(507) 545-2135	Wesley Bussell	. . .	Marlis Knowlton	Mike Bubany	Jerry Pike	. . .	Brad Boice
Fairmont *	c	CM	10	(507) 238-9461	Randy Quiring	James Zarling	Susan Olson	Paul Hoye	Dan Swanson	Greg Brolsma	Troy Nemmers
Falcon Heights *	c	MC	5	(651) 792-7600	Peter Lindstrom	Justin Miller	Stacey Kreuser	Roland Olson	Clem Kurhajetz	John Ohl	Tim Pittman
Faribault *	c	CM	20	(507) 334-2222	John Jasinski	Timothy Madigan	. . .	Terry Berg	Michael Monge	Daniel Collins	Mark Knoff
Farmington *	c	CM	12	(651) 280-6800	Todd Larson	Peter Herlofsky	. . .	Robin Roland	Tim Pietsch	Brian Lindquist	Todd Reiten
Fergus Falls *	c	MC	13	(218) 332-5440	Russell Anderson	Mark Sievert	. . .	William Sonmor	Mark Hovland	Timothy Brennan	Clifton Allen
Forest Lake *	c	MC	6	(651) 464-3550	Stev Stegner	Charles Robinson	Chantal Doriott	Ellen Paulseth	Gary Sigfrinius	Clark Quiring	Mike Tate
Fosston	c	MC	1	(218) 435-1959	. . .	Charles Lucken	. . .	. . .	. . .	. . .	. . .
Franklin	c	MC	. .	(507) 557-2259	Ronald Degner	. . .	Wendy Pederson	. . .	. . .	. . .	Kevin Kokesch
Fridley	c	CM	27	(763) 572-3507	Scott Lund	William Burns	Debra Skogen	Richard Pribyl	Charles McKusick	David Sallman	Jon Haukaas
Gilbert	c	MC	1	(218) 748-2232	Michael Skenzich	Gary Mackley	. . .	. . .	Richard Kohler	Mark Skelton	David Ochis
Glencoe	c	CM	5	(320) 864-5586	. . .	Mark Larson	Ruth Lange	Karla Kullman	Gary Vogt	Larry Aldape	Leroy Brelge
Glenwood	c	CM	2	(320) 634-5433	. . .	David Iverson	. . .	. . .	. . .	David Thompson	David Perryman
Golden Valley *	c	CM	20	(763) 593-8000	Linda Loomis	Thomas Burt	. . .	Sue Virnig	Mark Kuhnly	. . .	Jeannine Clancy
Goodview *	c	CM	3	(507) 452-1630	Jack Weimerskirch	. . .	Daniel Matejka	. . .	Rick Bambenek	Kent Russell	Greg Volkart
Grand Marais *	c	MC	1	(218) 387-1848	Sue Hakes	Michael Roth	. . .	Annette Dunsmoor	. . .	. . .	. . .
Grand Rapids *	c	MC	7	(218) 326-7600	Dale Adams	Shawn Gillen	. . .	Shirley Miller	Steven Flaherty	Leigh Serfling	Jeff Davies
Granite Falls *	c	CM	3	(320) 564-3011	David Smiglewski	William Lavin	Joan Taylor	Darcy Mulvihill	David Beasley	Russell Blue	Paul Krogstad
Ham Lake	c	MC	12	(763) 434-9555	. . .	. . .	. . .	. . .	. . .	. . .	. . .
Hanover	c	CM	1	(763) 497-3777	Joyce Paullin	Daniel Buchholtz	. . .	Melissa Barker	Tracey Franke	. . .	. . .
Harmony	c	CM	1	(507) 886-8122	. . .	. . .	. . .	. . .	. . .	. . .	. . .
Hastings	c	MC	18	(651) 480-2350	Michael Werner	David Osberg	. . .	Lori Webster	Mark Holmes	Michael McMenomy	T. Montgomery
Hector *	c	MC	1	(320) 848-2122	Jeff Heerdt	Barbara Hoyhtya	Barbara Johnson	. . .	Charlie Mathiowetz	Kurt Kozel	Harold Carstens
Hermantown	c	CM	7	(218) 729-6331	Dan Urshan	Lynn Lander	Nancy Sirois	. . .	Ronald Minter	Terrance Ulshafer	James Olson
Hibbing	c	CM	17	(218) 262-3486	Rick Wolff	Brian Redshaw	Patrick Garrity	Sherri Lindstrom	Tony Pogorels	Barbara Mitchel	John Fairchild
Hopkins	c	CM	17	(952) 935-8474	Eugene Maxwell	Richard Getschow	Terry Obermaier	Christine Harkess	. . .	Craig Reid	Steven Stadler
Howard Lake	c	CM	1	(320) 543-3670	. . .	. . .	. . .	. . .	Joe Drusch	. . .	. . .
Hoyt Lakes *	c	RT	2	(218) 225-2344	Marlene Pospeck	Richard Bradford	. . .	. . .	. . .	Steve Stoks	Mark Novosel
Hugo *	c	CM	6	(651) 762-6300	Francis Miron	Michael Ericson	Michele Lindau	Ronald Otkin	James Compton	. . .	Christopher Petree
Hutchinson *	c	CM	13	(320) 587-5151	Steve Cook	Gary Plotz	. . .	Kenneth Merrill	Bradley Emans	Daniel Hatten	. . .
Independence	c	MC	3	(763) 479-0527	Marvin Johnson	Toni Hirsch	. . .	. . .	. . .	. . .	. . .
International Falls	c	MC	6	(218) 283-9484	Shawn Mason	Rodney Otterness	. . .	Mike Stanich	Jerry Jensen	Chris Raboin	. . .
Inver Grove Heights	c	CM	29	(651) 450-2500	George Tourville	Joseph Lynch	Cathy Iago	Ann Lanone	William McLean	. . .	Gary Johnson
Isanti *	c	MC	2	(763) 444-5512	George Wimmer	Donald Lorsung	Irene Bauer	Kristi Smith	. . .	Ronald Sager	Patrick Meyer
Jackson *	c	MC	3	(507) 847-4410	James Jasper	Dean Albrecht	. . .	Deb Mitchell	Larry Olson	Anthony Legnani	. . .
Janesville *	c	MC	2	(507) 234-5110	. . .	Clinton Rogers	. . .	. . .	. . .	David Ulmen	David Wheelock
Jordan	c	CM	3	(952) 492-2535	. . .	Edward Shukle	. . .	Tom Nikunen	Steve Kochlin	Bob Malz	Dave Bendzick
Kasson *	c	MC	4	(507) 634-7071	Tim Tjosaas	Randy Lenth	Linda Rappe	Nancy Richardson	Bruce Musolf	Kenneth Schuck	Burton Fjerstad

Directory 1/9 continued **OFFICIALS IN U.S. MUNICIPALITIES 2,500 AND OVER IN POPULATION**

Jurisdiction	Type	Form of govern-ment	2000 Popu-lation	Main telephone number	Chief elected official	Appointed administrator	Clerk of the governing board	Chief financial officer	Fire chief	Police chief	Public works director
MINNESOTA continued											
Kenyon *	c	MC	1	(507) 789-6415	Diane Barrett	C. Heineman	. . .	Sue Dodds	Doug Noah	Lee Sjolander	Thomas Bergeson
La Crescent	c	MC	4	(507) 895-2595	Mike Poellinger	Harris Waller	Phyllis Feiock	. . .	Bernie Buehler	Todd Nelson	. . .
Lake City *	c	MC	4	(651) 345-5383	Jerry Dunbar	Ronald Johnson	Cindy Gosse	Barbara Pratt	Todd Hubbard	Lyle Schumann	Tyler Johnson
Lake Elmo	c	MC	6	(651) 777-5510	Wyn John	. . .	Sharon Lumby	Marilyn Banister	Richard Sachs	. . .	Dan Olinger
Lakefield	c	MC	1	(507) 662-5457	. . .	. . .	Kelly Rasche	Cheryl Ulferts	. . .	Jared Praska	Jim Koep
Lakeville *	c	CM	43	(952) 985-4400	Robert Johnson	Steven Mielke	Charlene Friedges	Dennis Feller	Scott Nelson	Thomas Vonhof	Christopher Petree
Lamberton	c	MC	. .	(507) 752-7601	Craig Wetter	. . .	Steven Flaig	. . .	. . .	James Clark	Wade Wellner
Lauderdale *	c	CM	2	(651) 792-7650	Jeffrey Dains	. . .	. . .	. . .	. . .	. . .	. . .
Le Sueur	c	CM	3	(507) 665-6401	Edward Rasmusen	Richard Almich	Laurie Swenson	Deborah Mediger	Le Roy Swenson	Bruce Kelly	Dean Kunze
Lexington *	c	MC	2	(763) 784-2792	Donald Valenta	Dot Heifort	. . .	. . .	Paul Pechan	Robert Makela	. . .
Lino Lakes	c	MC	16	(651) 982-2400	. . .	Gordon Heitke	. . .	Al Rolek	. . .	David Pecchia	Rick De Gardner
Litchfield	c	CM	6	(320) 693-7201	Vernon Madson	Bruce Miller	Joyce Spreiter	. . .	Gale Smith	Bruce Dicke	. . .
Little Canada	c	CM	9	(651) 484-2177	William Blesener	Joel Hanson	. . .	Michele Ruechkert	. . .	. . .	Bill Dircks
Little Falls *	c	CM	7	(320) 616-5500	. . .	. . .	. . .	. . .	Michael Nieman	Michael Pender	Gerald Lochner
Long Lake	c	CM	1	(952) 473-6961	Randy Gilbert	Steven Stahmer	Jeanette Moeller	Terry Post	. . .	. . .	Marvin Wurzer
Long Prairie	c	CM	3	(320) 732-2167	. . .	. . .	. . .	. . .	. . .	. . .	. . .
Luverne	c	CM	4	(507) 449-2388	Glen Gust	John Call	Marianne Perkins	Barbara Berghorst	Donald Deutsch	. . .	Kenneth Vos
Madison *	c	CM	1	(320) 598-7373	Greg Thole	Garrison Hale	Kathleen Weber	Deloris Churness	Ken Fernholz	Stanley Ross	Harold Hodge
Madison Lake *	c	MC	. .	(507) 243-3011	Kenneth Reichel	Kelly Steele	. . .	. . .	Debb Pongratz	Daniel Bunde	Chris Roemhildt
Mahnomen	c	MC	1	(218) 935-2573	. . .	Mitchell Berg	. . .	. . .	. . .	. . .	. . .
Mahtomedi	c	CM	7	(651) 426-3344	. . .	Scott Neilson	. . .	Marlin Amundson	Todd Rogers	. . .	Keith Arboleda
Mankato	c	CM	32	(507) 387-8600	Jeffrey Kagermeier	Patrick Hentges	Cheryl Lindquist	. . .	Allen Ratzloff	James Franklin	George Rosati
Maple Grove *	c	CM	50	(763) 494-6000	Mark Steffenson	Alan Madsen	. . .	Jim Knutson	Scott Anderson	Ramona Dohman	Gerald Butcher
Maple Plain *	c	MC	2	(763) 479-0515	John Sweeney	Jason Ziemer	. . .	. . .	Nate Jerde	Ray McCoy	. . .
Maplewood	c	CM	34	(651) 249-2000	Robert Cardinal	. . .	Karen Guilfoile	Daniel Faust	Steven Lukin	David Thomalla	R. Ahl
Marshall	c	MC	12	(507) 537-6763	Robert Byrnes	Benjamin Martig	T. Meulebroeck	. . .	Marc Klaith	. . .	Glenn Olson
Medina	c	CM	4	(763) 473-4643	Thomas Crosby	Chad Adams	. . .	Jeanne Day	. . .	Ed Belland	. . .
Melrose	c	MC	3	(320) 256-4278	Eric Senager	Brian Beeman	Patti Haase	. . .	Jeremy Kraemer	John Jensen	John Harren
Mendota Heights	c	CM	11	(651) 452-1850	John Huber	James Danielson	Kathleen Swanson	Kristen Schabacker	John Maczko	Mike Aschenbrener	. . .
Milaca	c	CM	2	(320) 983-3141	. . .	Greg Lerud	. . .	. . .	. . .	Mike Mott	Steve Burklund
Minneapolis	c	MC	382	(612) 673-3344	. . .	. . .	Merry Keefe	Patrick Born	Bonnie Bleskachek	William McManus	. . .
Minnetonka *	c	CM	51	(952) 939-8200	Jan Callison	John Gunyou	David Maeda	Merrill King	Joe Wallin	. . .	Brian Wagstrom
Minnetonka Beach Village	c	MC	. .	(952) 471-8878	Jim Gaash	Jill Teetzel	. . .	. . .	. . .	. . .	. . .
Minnetrista *	c	MC	4	(952) 446-1660	Cheryl Fischer	Michael Funk	Terri Haarstad	Brian Grimm	. . .	. . .	Robin Bowman
Montevideo	c	CM	5	(320) 269-6575	Jim Curtiss	Steven Jones	La Vonne Sundlee	Jan Flaherty	. . .	Bruce Kann	Greg Schwaegerl
Monticello *	c	CM	7	(763) 295-2711	Clint Herbst	Jeffrey O'Neill	Dawn Grossinger	Tom Kelly	Steve Joerg	. . .	Robert Paschke
Moorhead *	c	CM	32	(218) 299-5166	Mark Voxland	Michael Redlinger	Kaye Buchholz	Harlyn Ault	Joel Hewitt	David Ebinger	. . .
Mora *	c	CM	3	(320) 679-1511	Gregory Ardner	Joel Dhein	Mason Hjelle	. . .	Gene Anderson	Chris Olson	. . .
Morris	c	CM	5	(320) 589-3141	Carol Wilcox	Edward Larson	. . .	Gene Krosschell	Doug Storck	Jim Beauregard	Jim Dittbenner
Mound *	c	CM	9	(952) 472-0609	Mark Hanus	Kandis Hanson	Bonnie Ritter	Gino Businaro	Greg Pederson	Jim Kurtz	Carlton Moore
Mounds View	c	MC	12	(763) 717-4000	Robert Marty	. . .	. . .	Mark Beers	Nyle Zickmund	. . .	. . .
Mountain Iron *	c	MC	2	(218) 748-7570	Gary Skalko	Craig Wainio	. . .	. . .	Thomas Cvar	John Bachman	D. Kleinschmidt
New Brighton *	c	CM	22	(651) 638-2100	Steve Larson	Dean Lotter	. . .	Daniel Maiers	. . .	. . .	Grant Wyffels
New Hope	c	CM	20	(763) 531-5100	Martin Opem	Kirk McDonald	Valerie Leone	Julie Linnehan	. . .	Gary Link	Guy Johnson
New London	c	MC	1	(320) 354-2444	John Mack	. . .	Trudie Dubord	. . .	. . .	. . .	Loren Beck
New Prague	c	CM	4	(952) 758-4401	Craig Sindelar	Michael Johnson	. . .	. . .	Jim Becker	Dennis Rohloff	Dennis Seurer
New Ulm *	c	CM	13	(507) 359-8233	Joel Albrecht	Brian Gramentz	. . .	Reginald Vorwerk	Paul Macho	Ervin Weinkauf	Thomas Patterson
Newport	c	MC	3	(651) 459-5677	Kevin Chapdelaine	Lawrence Bodahl	Wanda Swarthout	. . .	Mark Mailand	Veidols Muiznieks	Bruce Hanson
North Branch	c	MC	8	(651) 674-8113	Gloria Karsky	Bridgitte Konrad	Ry-Chel Gaustad	David Stutelberg	Donald Brown	Jules Zimmer	Gary Schaefer
North Mankato *	c	CM	11	(507) 625-4141	Gary Zellmer	Wendell Sande	Nancy Gehrke	Steven Mork	Tim Pohlman	Christopher Boyer	Richard Peterson
North Oaks *	c	MC	3	(651) 792-7750	. . .	. . .	. . .	. . .	. . .	. . .	. . .
North St. Paul	c	CM	11	(651) 747-2400	William Sandberg	Walter Wysopal	. . .	Al Mahlum	Scott Duddeck	Tom Lauth	Mark Bartholomew
Northfield *	c	MC	17	(507) 645-8833	Mary Rossing	. . .	Deb Little	Kathleen McBride	Gerry Franek	Mark Taylor	. . .
Norwood Young America *	c	MC	3	(952) 467-1800	John Fahey	Tom Simmons	Diane Frauendienst	. . .	. . .	. . .	Brent Aretz
Oak Grove *	c	MC	5	(763) 404-7000	James Iund	Chantell Knauss	Sheryl Fiskewold	. . .	Milo Bennett	. . .	Timothy Smith
Oak Park Heights	c	CM	3	(651) 439-4439	David Beaudet	Eric Johnson	Julie Johnson	Judy Holst	. . .	Lindy Swanson	Jay Johnson
Oakdale *	c	CM	26	(651) 739-5086	Carmen Sarrack	Craig Waldron	Susan Barry	Suzanne Warren	Jeff Anderson	William Sullivan	Brian Bachmeier
Olivia *	c	MC	2	(320) 523-2361	Bill Miller	Daniel Hoffman	Mary Halliday	Kathy Herndina	. . .	Donald Davern	Kim Harrier
Orono *	c	MC	7	(952) 249-4600	James White	William Wells	Linda Vee	Ronald Olson	. . .	Correy Farniok	. . .
Ortonville	c	MC	2	(320) 839-3428	David Ellingson	. . .	Roman Taffe	. . .	Dallas Hanson	Gary Dinnel	Roger Anderson
Osseo	c	MC	2	(763) 425-2624	John Hall	Gregory Withers	LeAnn Larson	Gary Braaten	Gary Current	Michael Haller	Donald Peterson
Ostego *	c	CM	6	(763) 441-4414	Jessica Stockamp	Michael Robertson	Judy Hudson	Gary Groen	. . .	. . .	Brad Belair
Owatonna	c	MC	22	(507) 444-4300	Tom Kuntz	Kris Busse	. . .	Brad Svenby	Michael Johnson	Shaun LaDue	Jeffrey Johnson
Park Rapids *	c	MC	3	(218) 732-3163	Nancy Carroll	William Smith	Margie Vik	. . .	Don Hoffman	Terry Eilers	Scott Burlingame
Perham	c	CM	2	(218) 346-4455	Kevin Keil	. . .	Fern Nundahl	Karla McCall	Tracy Schmidt	Brian Nelson	Merle Meece
Pierz	c	MC	1	(320) 468-6471	. . .	. . .	. . .	. . .	. . .	. . .	. . .
Pine City	c	MC	3	(320) 629-2575	Jane Robbins	Donald Howard	. . .	. . .	. . .	. . .	Vern Smetana
Pine Island *	c	MC	2	(507) 356-4591	Paul Perry	Abraham Algadi	Cindy Oelkers	. . .	. . .	. . .	Mark Swarthout
Pipestone	c	MC	4	(507) 825-3324	. . .	. . .	. . .	. . .	. . .	. . .	. . .
Plainview *	c	CM	3	(507) 534-2229	Richard Sawyer	Steven Robertson	. . .	Nancy Richardson	Rich Klees	Randy Doughty	Michael Burgdorf
Plymouth *	c	CM	65	(763) 509-5000	Kelli Slavik	Laurie Ahrens	Sandra Paulson	. . .	Richard Kline	Michael Goldstein	Doran Cote
Princeton	c	CM	3	(763) 389-2040	Brian Humphrey	Mark Karnowski	. . .	Steven Jackson	. . .	David Warneke	Thomas Mismash
Prior Lake *	c	CM	15	(952) 447-9800	Jack Haugen	Francis Boyles	. . .	Jerilyn Erickson	Doug Hartman	Bill O'Rourke	Steve Albrecht
Proctor	c	MC	2	(218) 624-3641	Richard Kieren	John Foschi	. . .	. . .	John Benson	Walter Wubig	. . .
Ramsey *	c	MC	18	(763) 427-1410	Thomas Gamec	Kurtis Ulrich	Jo Thieline	Diana Lund	Dean Kapler	James Way	Brian Olson
Red Lake Falls *	c	CM	1	(218) 253-2684	Vaughn Thorfinnson	. . .	Marion Martell	. . .	Chad Schmitz	Mitch Bernstein	Scott Larson
Red Wing	c	CM	16	(651) 385-3600	V. Steffenhagen	Kay Kuhlmann	Kathy Johnson	Marshall Hallock	. . .	. . .	Dennis Tebbe
Redwood Falls	c	MC	5	(507) 637-5755	Sara Triplett	Keith Muetzel	Elaine Jenniges	. . .	Tom Stough	Mark Dressen	. . .
Renville	c	CM	1	(320) 329-8366	Loyal Fisher	Paul McLaughlin	LouAnn Ahrens	. . .	Brad Varpness	Ben Dehmlow	Peter Peterson
Richfield *	c	CM	34	(612) 861-9700	Debbie Goettel	Steven Devich	Nancy Gibbs	. . .	Brad Sveum	. . .	Michael Eastling
Robbinsdale *	c	CM	14	(763) 537-4534	Michael Holtz	Marcia Glick	. . .	Larry Jacobson	Mark Fairchild	Steve Smith	Richard McCoy
Rochester	c	MC	85	(507) 285-8082	Ardell Brede	Stevan Kvenvold	Judy Scherr	Dale Martinson	David Kapler	Roger Peterson	Richard Freese
Rockford	c	CM	3	(763) 477-6565	Michael Beyer	Nancy Evers	. . .	. . .	. . .	. . .	. . .
Rosemount *	c	CM	14	(651) 423-4411	. . .	Dwight Johnson	Amy Domeier	Jeff May	. . .	Gary Kalstabakken	. . .
Roseville *	c	CM	33	(651) 792-7000	Craig Klausing	William Malinen	Margaret Driscoll	Chris Miller	Richard Gasaway	Carol Sletner	Duane Schwartz
Rush City	c	CM	2	(320) 358-4743	Michael Skalsky	Daniel Hoffman	Susan Hochstatter	. . .	Robert Carlson	Scott Sellman	Raymond Benolken
Rushford	c	MC	1	(507) 864-2444	Les Ladewig	Winthro Block	Kathy Zacher	. . .	Mike Ebner	Sam Stensgard	Jeff Copley
Saint Michael *	c	MC	9	(763) 497-2041	. . .	Robert Derus	Diana Berning	. . .	. . .	. . .	. . .
Sandstone	c	MC	1	(320) 245-5241	Douglas McGhee	Samuel Griffith	Jane Grundmeier	Wendy Nelson	Joe Drilling	. . .	Dennis Carlson
Sartell	c	MC	9	(320) 253-2171	. . .	Patti Gartland	Peggy Schupp	. . .	. . .	Robert Ringstrom	Brad Borders
Sauk Centre	c	MC	3	(320) 352-2203	Dennis Rykken	Vicki Willer	. . .	. . .	Joe Deters	James Metcalf	Harold Wessel
Sauk Rapids	c	MC	10	(320) 258-5300	Harold Jesh	Ross Olson	. . .	Jack Kahlhamer	. . .	Curtis Gullickson	Roger Schotl
Savage *	c	CM	21	(952) 882-2660	. . .	Barry Stock	Ellen Classen	Shelly Kolling	Joel McColl	Rodney Seurer	John Powell
Scandia *	c	MC	3	(651) 433-2274	Dennis Seefeldt	Anne Hurlburt	Brenda Eklund	. . .	Steve Spence	. . .	John Morrison

Directory 1/9 continued **OFFICIALS IN U.S. MUNICIPALITIES 2,500 AND OVER IN POPULATION**

Jurisdiction	Type	Form of govern-ment	2000 Popu-lation	Main telephone number	Chief elected official	Appointed administrator	Clerk of the governing board	Chief financial officer	Fire chief	Police chief	Public works director
MINNESOTA continued											
Shakopee	c	MC	20	(952) 233-3800	William Mars	Mark McNeill	Judith Cox	Gregg Voxland	...	Daniel Hughes	Bruce Loney
Sherburn	c	CM	1	(507) 764-4491	Gerald Jenkinson	...	...	...	...	...	...
Shoreview	c	CM	25	(651) 490-4600	Sandra Martin	Terry Schwerm	...	Jeanne Haapala	Tim Boehlke	George Altendorfer	Mark Maloney
Shorewood *	c	MC	7	(952) 474-3236	Chris Lizee	Brian Heck	Jean Panchyshyn	Bonnie Burton	...	...	Lawrence Brown
Silver Bay	c	MC	2	(218) 226-4408	...	...	...	...	...	Wayne Billings	Douglas Peusetto
Sleepy Eye *	c	MC	3	(507) 794-3731	James Broich	Mark Kober	Jeanne Tauer	...	...	John Schueller	Bob Elston
South St. Paul *	c	MC	20	(651) 554-3200	...	Stephen King	Christy Wilcox	Josh Feldman	...	Daniel Vujovich	...
Spring Lake Park	v	MC	6	(763) 784-6491	Robert Nelson	Barbara Nelson	...	...	Nyle Zikmund	Dave Toth	Terry Randall
Spring Park *	c	MC	1	(952) 471-9051	Sarah Reinhardt	Jim Brimeyer	Wendy Lewin	...	...	...	David Goman
Spring Valley	v	MC	2	(507) 346-7367	Jim Struzyk	Michael Bubany	Deb Zimmer	...	Nevin Stender	...	Stu Smith
Springfield *	c	CM	2	(507) 723-3500	Mark Brown	Malcolm Tilberg	Amy Vogel	...	Charles Baumann	John Nicholson	...
St. Anthony *	c	CM	8	(612) 782-3301	Jerome Faust	Michael Mornson	Barbara Suciu	Roger Larson	John Malenick	John Ohl	Jay Hartman
St. Augusta	c	MC	3	(320) 654-0387	Ollie Mondloch	Aaron Anderson	...	...	...	...	...
St. Charles *	c	MC	3	(507) 932-3020	...	...	Janell Dahl	...	Lyle Peterson	William Eckles	Kyle Karger
St. Cloud	c	MC	59	(320) 255-7200	John Ellenbecker	Michael Williams	Gregg Engdahl	...	William Mund	Dennis Ballantine	Stephen Gaetz
St. Francis	c	MC	4	(763) 753-2630	Randy Dressen	Matthew Hylen	Barb Held	...	Ken Pace	Byron Froh	...
St. James *	c	CM	4	(507) 375-3241	Gary Sturm	Joseph McCabe	LeeAnn Nibbe	...	Jason Monnens	Mark Carvatt	...
St. Joseph	c	MC	4	(320) 363-7201	Richard Carlbom	...	Judy Weyrens	...	...	Pete Jansky	Richard Taufen
St. Louis Park *	c	CM	44	(952) 924-2500	Jeff Jacobs	Thomas Harmening	Nancy Stroth	Bruce DeJong	Luke Stemmer	John Luse	Michael Rardin
St. Paul	c	MC	287	(651) 266-6500	C. Coleman	...	Fred Owusu	Matt Smith	Timothy Fuller	William Finney	...
St. Paul Park *	c	CM	5	(651) 459-9785	John Hunziker	Kevin Walsh	Sharon Ornquist	Kim Sommerland	Kurk Lee	Michael Monahan	Lee Flandrich
St. Peter	c	CM	9	(507) 931-0663	Jerry Hawbaker	Todd Prafke	...	Paula O'Connell	Windy Block	Matthew Peters	Lewis Gesking
Staples	c	MC	3	(218) 894-2550	...	...	...	...	...	...	...
Stewartville	c	MC	5	(507) 533-4745	Chris Gray	William Schimmel	Cheryl Roeder	...	...	...	Ron Robb
Stillwater *	c	MC	15	(651) 430-8800	Ken Harycki	Larry Hansen	Diane Ward	Sharon Harrison	Stuart Glaser	John Gannaway	Shawn Sanders
Thief River Falls *	c	MC	8	(218) 681-2943	Steve Nordhagen	Jodie Torkelson	...	Lisa Johnson	Jerry Stenseth	Kim Murphy	Ron Lindberg
Thomson *	tp	MC	1	(218) 879-9719	Terry Hill	...	Rhonda Peleski	...	Jeffrey Juntunen	Thomas Foldesi	David Black
Tonka Bay	c	CM	1	(952) 474-7994	...	Jessica Loftus	...	...	Scott Gerber	Bryan Litsey	Gregory Kluver
Tracy	c	MC	2	(507) 629-5528	Stephen Ferrazzano	...	Audrey Koopman	...	Dennis Vandeputte	Bryan Hillger	Richard Robinson
Two Harbors	c	CM	3	(218) 834-5631	...	Lee Klein	...	Jill Anderson	...	Richard Hogenson	Scott Johnson
Tyler	c	CM	1	(507) 247-5556	Douglas Hess	Kristi Luger	...	...	Allan Rensvold	...	Darwin Lu Herman
Vadnais Heights	c	MC	13	(651) 204-6000	Susan Banovetz	Gerald Urban	...	Jeanne Vogt	Dave Hertog	...	...
Victoria *	c	CM	4	(952) 443-4210	...	Donald Uram	Jennifer Kretsch	Jylan Johnson	Tim Walsh	Erick Boder	Bruce Osborn
Virginia	c	CM	9	(218) 748-7500	Carolyn Gentilini	John Tourville	Lois Roskoski	Ronald Lackner	...	...	...
Wabasha	c	CM	2	(651) 565-4568	...	David Schmidt	Darlene Wallerich	...	...	...	Ted Stearns
Waconia	c	MC	6	(952) 442-2184	Don Johnson	Susan Arntz	Mary Johnson	...	...	...	Randall Sorensen
Wadena	c	MC	4	(218) 631-7707	Wayne Wolden	Bradley Swenson	...	Lloyd Lanz	Ray Beyer	Lane Waldahl	Ron Bucholz
Waite Park	c	MC	6	(320) 252-6822	Carla Schaefer	Shaunna Johnson	Jill Bauer	Keith Lindberg	Gary Curtis	James McDermott	William Schluenz
Warroad	c	CM	1	(216) 386-1454	...	...	...	...	...	...	...
Waseca *	c	CM	8	(507) 835-9700	...	J. Prentice	...	Teresa Walters	Gary Conrath	Keith Hiller	...
Watertown	c	CM	3	(952) 955-2681	Stephen Sarvi	David Mandt	...	Steven Wallner	Ned Schroeder	...	K. Gulbrandson
Waterville	c	CM	1	(507) 362-8300	...	...	...	Teresa Hill	...	Max Venero	...
Wayzata	c	CM	4	(952) 404-5300	Barry Petit	Allan Orsen	Joan Smith	David Frischmon	Paul Klapprich	Kevin Kelleher	David Dudinsky
Wells *	c	MC	2	(507) 553-6371	David Jacobson	Jeremy Germann	...	...	Mike Pyzick	Rick Herman	...
West St. Paul *	c	CM	19	(651) 552-4100	John Zanmiller	John Remkus	...	Sandy Christensen	John Ehret	Maila Shaver	Matt Saam
White Bear Lake	c	CM	24	(651) 429-8526	Paul Auger	Mark Sather	...	Don Rambow	Timothy Vadnais	Todd Miller	Mark Burch
Willmar	c	CM	18	(320) 235-4913	...	Michael Schmit	...	Steven Okins	Marvin Calvin	...	Melvin Odens
Windom *	c	CM	4	(507) 831-6129	Kirby Kruse	Steven Nasby	...	...	Dan Fossing	Jeff Shirkey	Mike Haugen
Winnebago	c	CM	1	(507) 893-3217	Scott Owen	Nathan Mathews	Susan Lynch	...	Todd Enger	Robert Toland	Darold Nienhaus
Winona	c	CM	27	(507) 457-8234	Jerry Miller	Eric Sorensen	Monica Mohan	Mary Burrichter	Ed Krall	Frank Pomeroy	...
Winsted	c	MC	2	(320) 485-2366	...	Brent Mareck	Deborah Boelter	...	...	...	...
Woodbury	c	CM	46	(651) 714-3500	...	Clinton Gridley	...	Timothy Johnson	Mike Richardson	...	David Jessup
Worthington *	c	MC	11	(507) 372-8600	Alan Oberloh	Craig Clark	Janice Oberloh	Brian Kolander	...	...	James Laffrencen
Wyoming *	c	MC	3	(651) 462-0575	Sheldon Anderson	Craig Mattson	...	...	Dennis Berry	Scott Dexter	Bill Eisenmenger
Zumbrota	c	MC	2	(507) 732-7318	Richard Bauer	Neil Jensen	...	...	Ron Horsman	Gary Selness	Rick Lohmann
MISSISSIPPI											
Aberdeen *	c	MC	6	(662) 369-8588	William Tisdale	...	Susan Honeycutt	Glen Howell	Frank Gladney	Henry Randle	...
Amory	c	MC	6	(662) 256-5721	Howard Boozer	...	Suzanne Mobley	...	Jimmy Bost	Ronnie Bowen	Bobby Cox
Baldwyn	t	MC	3	(601) 365-2383	...	...	...	...	...	...	...
Batesville	c	MC	7	(662) 563-4576	Jerry Autrey	...	Laura Herron	...	Timothy Taylor	Gerald Legge	...
Bay St. Louis	c	MC	8	(228) 467-9092	Edward Favre	Robert Parker	...	...	Robert Gavagnie	Frank McNeil	Ronald Vanney
Belzoni	c	MC	2	(601) 247-1343	T. N. Turner	...	Laura Anne Byars	...	Henry Outlaw	Richard McMillian	...
Biloxi	c	MC	50	(228) 435-6259	Andrew Holloway	...	Brenda Johnston	William Lanham	David Roberts	Tommy Moffett	Jerry Morgan
Booneville	t	MC	8	(662) 728-6810	...	...	...	...	...	...	...
Brandon	c	MC	16	(601) 825-5021	Carlo Martella	Mike Farrar	Angela Bean	...	James Rutland	Kenneth McBroom	Cathy Goolsby
Brookhaven	c	MC	9	(601) 833-2362	Robert Massengill	...	Micahel Jinks	...	Bob Watts	Arlustra Henderson	Steve Moreton
Canton	c	MC	12	(601) 859-4331	...	...	...	...	...	...	...
Carthage *	t	MC	4	(601) 267-8322	James Wallace	...	Jan Wilcher	...	Joey Jones	Kenny Moore	William Pigg
Charleston	c	MC	2	(662) 647-5841	Robert Rowe	...	Diane Stanford	...	Phil Shook	Jerry Williams	Dizzy Prine
Clarksdale	c	CO	20	(662) 621-8100	Richard Webster	...	Sylvia Burton	...	S. Washington	Glenn Coker	James Butler
Cleveland	c	MC	13	(662) 846-1471	...	...	...	...	...	...	...
Clinton	c	MC	23	(601) 924-5474	Rosemary Aultman	...	...	Russell Wall	Jonathan Burnside	Don Byington	...
Columbia *	c	MC	6	(601) 736-8201	Harold Bryant	Donna McKenzie	...	...	Larry Ratliff	Joe Van Parkman	Rusty Rowell
Columbus	c	MC	25	(662) 328-7021	Jeffrey Rupp	...	...	...	Kenneth Moore	J. Sanders	Dan Mattick
Corinth	c	MC	14	(662) 286-6644	Jerry Latch	...	Vickie Roach	...	Gerald Horner	William Cregeen	Billy Glover
Crystal Springs	c	MC	5	(601) 892-1210	Walter Rielley	...	Linda Caston	...	Abra Hines	Richard Anderson	Robert Sims
D'Iberville	c	MC	7	(228) 392-7966	...	Richard Rose	Mary Lee Williams	Sharron Perkins	Gerald Smith	Wendy Swetman	Al Gombos
Drew	c	MC	2	(662) 745-8556	James Pettigrew	...	Bettie Dickey	...	...	...	Melvin Matthews
Durant	c	MC	2	(662) 653-3221	Johnny Pritchard	Rosie Hill	Linda McDonald	...	Houston Kyzer	Jerry Bankhead	Bernard Wright
Ellisville	c	MC	3	(601) 477-3323	Tim Waldrup	...	Margaret Brewer	...	Ronnie McGilberry	Robert Russell	Stan Ishee
Forest	c	MC	5	(601) 469-2921	Nancy Chambers	...	Melissa Barnes	...	Clint Craig	Mike Lee	Randall George
Fulton	t	MC	3	(662) 862-4929	Charlie McCarthy	...	Lisa Russell	...	Charles Grimes	Ray Barrett	Dan Pate
Gautier	c	CM	11	(228) 497-8000	Ken Taylor	Sidney Runnels	Pearl Mercer	Linda Green	Michael Gray	Ed Williams	...
Greenville	c	MC	41	(601) 378-1551	Paul Artman	...	Ella Johnson	...	John Richardson	Lon Pepper	Brad Jones
Greenwood *	c	MC	18	(662) 453-2246	Sheriel Perkins	Alecia Reed-Owens	...	Cinderella Morris	Larry Griggs	Henry Purnell	Benny Herring
Grenada	c	CM	14	(601) 226-8820	John Hyneman	James Cummins	Douglas Ashmore	Valleria Blaylock	Eugene Doss	Curtis Liles	...
Gulfport	c	MC	71	(228) 868-5831	...	...	...	...	...	...	...
Hattiesburg	c	MC	44	(601) 545-4501	J. Morgan	...	Edgar Myers	Joseph Townsend	George Herrington	Charles Sims	Bennie Sellers
Hazlehurst	c	MC	4	(601) 894-3131	Randy Kimble	...	Sue Brown	...	James Harper	Ellis Stuart	...
Hernando	c	MC	6	(601) 429-9092	...	...	...	...	...	...	...
Hollandale	c	MC	3	(662) 827-2241	Willie Burnside	...	Helen Johnson	...	Mitchell Baugh	Jimmy Taylor	Lee Edwards
Holly Springs	c	MC	7	(662) 252-4280	Andre Deberry	...	Belinda McDonald	...	Kenneth Holbrook	Robert Pearson	D. Hollingsworth
Horn Lake *	c	MC	14	(662) 393-6178	Nat Baker	Andrea Freeze	Tara Warren	...	David Linville	Darryl Whaley	Spencer Shields
Houston *	c	MC	4	(662) 456-2328	Stacey Parker	...	Bobby Sanderson	...	Curtis Jernigan	Billy Voyles	Richard Nichols

Directory 1/9 continued **OFFICIALS IN U.S. MUNICIPALITIES 2,500 AND OVER IN POPULATION**

Jurisdiction	Type	Form of govern-ment	2000 Popu-lation	Main telephone number	Chief elected official	Appointed administrator	Clerk of the governing board	Chief financial officer	Fire chief	Police chief	Public works director
MISSISSIPPI continued											
Indianola *	c	MC	12	(662) 887-3101	Arthur Marble	. . .	Jane Hetzler	. . .	Rufus Powell	Charles Smith	Jimmie Strong
Itta Bena	t	MC	2	(601) 254-7231	Thelma Collins	. . .	. . .	. . .	Curtis Purnell	J. Hudson	Jimmy Pittman
Iuka	c	MC	3	(601) 423-3781	. . .	. . .	. . .	. . .	. . .	. . .	. . .
Jackson	c	MC	184	(601) 960-1084	Harvey Johnson	Otha Burton	Eddie Carr	Cynthia Melvin	Raymond McNulty	Robert Moore	Ben Wolfe
Kosciusko	c	MC	7	(662) 289-1226	Jimmy Cockroft	. . .	Janet Baird	. . .	Duane Bardine	Ronnie Adams	Wallace Simmons
Laurel	c	CO	18	(601) 428-6423	Susan Vincent	Gary Suddith	. . .	Mary Hess	James Russell	John Waterson	Kenny Hogan
Leland	c	MC	5	(662) 686-4136	Kenny Thomas	Mickey Fratesi	. . .	. . .	Robert Johnson	Wade Burns	Fred Jones
Lexington	c	MC	2	(662) 834-1261	. . .	. . .	Pamela Williams	. . .	Jim Hughes	Jessie Joiner	Keith James
Long Beach	c	MC	17	(228) 863-1556	William Skellie	Rebecca Schruff	. . .	. . .	George Bass	Wayne McDowell	Derrell Wilson
Louisville *	c	MC	7	(662) 773-9201	Daniel Yarbrough	. . .	Babs Fulton	. . .	Mike Stevenson	L. Claiborne	Kenny Morris
Magee	c	MC	4	(601) 849-3344	. . .	. . .	. . .	. . .	. . .	. . .	. . .
Mc Comb	c	CM	13	(601) 684-4000	Thomas Walman	Sam Mims	Russell Wall	. . .	Vernell Felder	Billie Hughes	. . .
Mendenhall	t	MC	2	(601) 847-1212	Randall Neely	Tim Gray	Judi May	. . .	. . .	Jimbo Sullivan	. . .
Meridian	c	MC	39	(601) 485-1927	John Smith	Kenneth Storms	Lawrence Skipper	. . .	Henry Partridge	Benny Dubose	David Jackson
Moorhead	t	CM	2	(662) 246-5461	. . .	. . .	. . .	. . .	. . .	. . .	. . .
Morton *	c	MC	3	(601) 732-8609	Greg Butler	. . .	Dorothy Redeemer	. . .	. . .	Jimmy Rogers	Terrell Harvey
Moss Point	c	MC	15	(228) 475-0300	Frank Lynn	Adlean Liddell	. . .	Shavay Gaines	Jimmy Harris	Michael Ricks	Robert Armstrong
Mound Bayou	c	MC	2	(662) 741-2193	. . .	. . .	. . .	. . .	. . .	. . .	. . .
Natchez	c	MC	18	(601) 445-7515	Phillip West	. . .	Donnie Holloway	. . .	Paul Johnson	Michael Mullins	Eric Smith
New Albany	c	MC	7	(662) 534-1010	Tim Kent	. . .	Anne Neal	. . .	Richard Hamric	David Grisham	. . .
Newton	c	MC	3	(601) 683-6181	Michael Pickens	. . .	Janice Bridges	. . .	. . .	Harvey Curry	Jerry Bounds
Ocean Springs *	c	MC	17	(228) 875-4236	Seren Ainsworth	. . .	Adrienne Howell	. . .	Mark Hare	Kerry Belk	Andre Kaufman
Okolona	c	MC	3	(662) 447-5461	Sherman Carouthers	. . .	Anna Stovall	. . .	Edward Chapman	Tommie Ivy	Robert May
Oxford *	c	MC	11	(662) 236-1310	Richard Howorth	. . .	Lisa Carwyle	. . .	Michael Hill	Michael Martin	David Bennett
Pascagoula	c	CM	26	(228) 762-1020	Matthew Avara	Kay Johnson Kell	Brenda Reed	Lloyd Marshall	Robert O'Sullivan	Eddie Stewart	Brian Nelson
Pass Christian	c	MC	6	(228) 452-3310	William McDonald	. . .	Vicki Goff	Janet Dudding	Richard Marvil	John Dubuisson	Michael Pavlisick
Pearl	c	MC	21	(601) 932-2262	Jimmy Foster	. . .	Kay Lang	Ron Morgan	Robert Williams	Bill Slade	Bud Overby
Petal	c	MC	7	(601) 545-1776	Carl Scott	. . .	Jean Ishee	. . .	Richard Bryant	Lee Shelbourn	. . .
Philadelphia	c	MC	7	(601) 656-3612	. . .	. . .	. . .	. . .	. . .	. . .	. . .
Picayune	c	CM	10	(601) 798-9770	Gregory Mitchell	James Burns	. . .	. . .	Keith Brown	James Luke	Reginald Oliver
Pontotoc	c	MC	5	(662) 489-4321	Bill Rutledge	. . .	Patricia Clayton	. . .	Jerry Russell	Larry Poole	Tim Roberts
Poplarville	c	MC	2	(601) 795-8161	Billy Spiers	Francis Stuart	Linda DuPont	Jackie Davis	Chris Carr	Charles Fazende	Sam Hale
Quitman	t	MC	2	(601) 776-3728	. . .	. . .	. . .	. . .	. . .	. . .	. . .
Richland	c	MC	6	(601) 932-3000	Mark Scarborough	. . .	Donna Diffrient	. . .	Jim McClendon	Bruce Breland	Wade Overby
Ridgeland	c	MC	20	(601) 856-7113	. . .	. . .	Ina Byrd	M. McPhearson	Elmer Waits	. . .	. . .
Ripley *	c	MC	5	(662) 837-0130	. . .	. . .	. . .	. . .	. . .	. . .	. . .
Rolling Fork	c	MC	2	(662) 873-2814	Gary Henderson	. . .	Dorothy Pearson	. . .	Robert McClendon	Eugene Bell	Billy Johnson
Ruleville	c	MC	3	(662) 756-2791	Shirley Edwards	. . .	Jane Ward	. . .	. . .	Larry Mitchell	John Downs
Senatobia	c	MC	6	(662) 562-4474	Alan Callicott	. . .	Kay Minton	. . .	Gary Copeland	Sammy Webb	Robert Morris
Shelby	c	MC	2	(601) 398-5156	. . .	. . .	. . .	. . .	. . .	. . .	. . .
Southaven *	c	MC	28	(662) 280-2489	Gregory Davis	Christopher Wilson	Glenda Smallwood	. . .	John Brackin	Thomas Long	Ray Tarrance
Starkville	c	CM	21	(662) 324-4011	Mack Rutlege	. . .	Vivian Collier	Debbie Clark	William Grantham	David Lindley	. . .
Tupelo	c	MC	34	(662) 841-6487	Larry Otis	Darrell Smith	. . .	Daphne Holcombe	Michael Burns	Harold Chaffin	Thomas Rankin
Vicksburg	c	CO	26	(601) 634-4553	Laurence Leyens	. . .	Walter Osborne	Elvin Parker	Keith Rogers	Tommy Moffett	James Rainer
Water Valley	c	MC	3	(662) 473-2431	. . .	. . .	. . .	. . .	. . .	. . .	. . .
Waveland *	c	MC	6	(228) 467-4134	John Longo	Robyn Gavagnie	. . .	. . .	David Garcia	James Varnell	. . .
Waynesboro *	t	MC	5	(601) 735-4874	Bobby Taylor	. . .	Sytrecia Hull	. . .	Willard Crocker	Leonard Frost	Harvey Hull
West Point	c	MC	12	(601) 494-2573	. . .	. . .	. . .	. . .	. . .	. . .	. . .
Wiggins	c	MC	3	(601) 928-7221	Ferris O'Neal	. . .	Teresa Ladner	. . .	Richard Tice	Reid Lowe	Jimmy Smith
Winona	c	MC	5	(601) 283-1232	H. W. Simmons	. . .	Bonita Smith	. . .	Booker Clay	Johnny Hargrove	Bain Hughes
Yazoo City	c	MC	14	(662) 746-1401	. . .	. . .	. . .	. . .	. . .	. . .	. . .
MISSOURI											
Albany *	c	MC	1	(660) 726-3935	Steven Findley	Derek Brown	Jill Cottrill	. . .	. . .	. . .	. . .
Arnold	c	MC	19	(636) 296-2100	Ronald Voss	Matthew Unrein	Rita Thompson	Jo Anne Tietjens	. . .	Dale Fredeking	Robert Eade
Ashland	c	MC	1	(573) 657-2091	Mike Asmus	Chris Heard	Darla Sapp	. . .	. . .	Scott Robbins	John Fraga
Aurora	c	CM	7	(417) 678-5121	Noelle Naillon	. . .	Kathie Needham	. . .	Robert Ward	Richard Batson	Steve Woods
Ava	c	MC	3	(417) 683-5516	Leon Harris	. . .	Marilyn Alms	. . .	. . .	Larry Smith	. . .
Ballwin	c	CM	31	(636) 227-8580	Robert Jones	Robert Kuntz	. . .	Glenda Loehr	. . .	James Biederman	Gary Kramer
Bellefontaine Neighbors	c	MC	11	(314) 867-0076	Martin Rudloff	. . .	Deni Donovan	. . .	. . .	Robert Pruett	Mike Welz
Bel-Ridge	v	MC	3	(314) 429-2878	. . .	. . .	. . .	. . .	. . .	. . .	. . .
Belton	c	CM	21	(816) 331-4331	Robert Gregory	Ronald Trivitt	Patti Ledford	Michael Wade	Steve Holle	James Person	Cliff Fain
Berkeley *	c	CM	10	(314) 524-3313	Kenneth McClendon	De'Carlon Seewood	Octavia Pittman	Mark Miles	Henry Williams	Frank McCall	Richard Faulkner
Bethany	c	MC	3	(660) 425-3511	Richard Graner	Tony Stonecypher	Marilyn Smith	. . .	John Gannan	Brian Groom	. . .
Black Jack	c	MC	6	(314) 355-0400	Norman McCourt	. . .	Monica Van Stratten	John Engelmeyer	Robert Coffman	. . .	Melvin Kosanchick
Blue Springs	c	CM	48	(816) 228-0110	Steven Steiner	Eric Johnson	Kathy Richardson	Christine Cates	. . .	Wayne McCoy	Oliver De Grate
Bolivar	c	MC	9	(417) 326-2489	Charles Ealy	. . .	Dale Newcomb	. . .	Patricia Head	Michael Seibert	. . .
Bonne Terre *	c	CM	4	(573) 358-2254	Frederick Gower	Ron Thomure	Melinda Watson	. . .	. . .	Douglas Calvert	Kevin Penberthy
Boonville	c	CM	8	(660) 882-2332	Danielle Blanck	. . .	Kimberly Justus	. . .	Tim Carmichael	Jim Gholson	M. Cauthon
Bowling Green	c	MC	3	(573) 324-5451	Dana Portwood	John Kehrman	Barb Allison	. . .	Mel Meyer	Steve Kruse	Patrick Stinnett
Branson *	c	MC	6	(417) 334-3345	Raeanne Presley	Dean Kruithof	Lisa Westfall	Lori Helle	Carl Sparks	Caroll McCullough	Larry Van Gilder
Breckenridge Hills	c	MC	4	(314) 427-6868	Archie Ledbetter	. . .	Pamela Price	. . .	. . .	Donald Kaley	. . .
Brentwood	c	MC	7	(314) 962-4800	Charles Kelly	C. Seemayer	. . .	Susan Zimmer	Robert Niemeyer	Frederick Knight	Gerald Wolf
Bridgeton *	c	MC	15	(314) 739-7500	Conrad Bowers	Thomas Haun	Carole Stahlhut	. . .	. . .	Walter Mutert	Richard Houchin
Brookfield	c	CM	4	(660) 258-3377	Richard Techau	Darrell Williams	. . .	. . .	Jerry Wine	David Hane	Robert Stufflebean
Buckner	c	MC	2	(816) 650-3191	James Parcel	. . .	. . .	. . .	Greg Pottberg	Charles Loring	Wilson Jones
Butler	c	MC	4	(660) 679-4182	Jerry Cook	Mark Arbuthnot	Janet Kirtley	. . .	James Henry	James Garnett	. . .
Cabool	c	MC	2	(417) 962-3136	Donald Wells	H. Swanson	Olive Wood	. . .	Jerry Miller	Lynn Jones	Joseph Engleman
California *	c	MC	4	(573) 796-2500	Norris Gerhart	. . .	Brian Scrivner	. . .	Allen Smith	Fred Kirchoff	Gary Wells
Camdenton *	c	MC	2	(573) 346-3600	Kerry Shannon	Steven Craig	Brenda Colter	Renee Kingston	Scott Frandsen	Laura Webster	William Jeffries
Cameron	c	CM	8	(816) 632-2177	Larry McCord	David Watson	Barbara O'Connor	. . .	Michael O'Donnell	Corey Sloan	Drew Bontrager
Cape Girardeau	c	CM	35	(573) 334-1212	Jay Knudtson	Douglas Leslie	Gayle Conrad	John Richbourg	Richard Ennis	Stephen Strong	Tim Gramling
Carl Junction	c	MC	5	(417) 649-7237	Mike Moss	James Whisenant	Maribeth Matney	. . .	. . .	Delmar Haase	Jimmy Chaligo
Carrollton *	c	MC	4	(660) 542-1414	Sharon Metz	Mary McGinness	. . .	. . .	Curtis Shields	Donald King	. . .
Carthage *	c	MC	12	(417) 237-7000	Kenneth Johnson	Thomas Short	Lynn Campbell	. . .	John Cooper	Dennis Veach	Chad Wampler
Caruthersville *	c	CM	6	(573) 333-2142	Diane Sayre	. . .	Melinda Scifres	. . .	Charles Jones	Kenneth Chastain	. . .
Centralia *	c	MC	3	(573) 682-2139	Shelley Benker	Lynn Behrns	. . .	Kathy Colvin	Marvin Rodgers	Larry Dudgeon	. . .
Chaffee	c	MC	3	(573) 887-3558	William Cannon	Ron Eskew	Diane Eftink	. . .	Mike Lee	. . .	Eric Hicks
Charleston	c	CM	4	(573) 683-3325	Brett Matthews	David Brewer	Marsha Hart	. . .	Michael Maness	Richard Couch	David Teeters
Chesterfield	c	CM	46	(636) 537-4000	John Nations	Michael Herring	Marty Demay	Jeremy Craig	. . .	Ray Johnson	Michael Geisel
Chillicothe *	c	MC	8	(660) 646-2424	Charles Haney	Dean Brookshier	Rozanne Frampton	Theresa Kelly	Joseph Rinehart	Richard Knouse	Steve Svec
Clayton *	c	CM	12	(314) 290-8449	Linda Goldstein	Craig Owens	June Waters	Donald Yucuis	George Thorp	Thomas Byrne	. . .
Clinton *	c	MC	9	(660) 885-6121	Gus Wetzel	Christy Maggi	Kelly Harrelson	. . .	Russell Ritchey	Kevin Miller	Gary Mount
Columbia *	c	CM	84	(573) 874-7235	Darwin Hindman	H. Watkins	Sheela Amin	Lori Fleming	William Markgraf	. . .	John Glascock
Crestwood *	c	CM	11	(314) 729-4700	Roy Robinson	James Eckrich	Tina Flowers	Douglas Brewer	Karl Kestler	Michael Paillou	D. Mruckovski

Directory 1/9 continued OFFICIALS IN U.S. MUNICIPALITIES 2,500 AND OVER IN POPULATION

Jurisdiction	Type	Form of govern-ment	2000 Popu-lation	Main telephone number	Chief elected official	Appointed administrator	Clerk of the governing board	Chief financial officer	Fire chief	Police chief	Public works director
MISSOURI continued											
Creve Coeur	c	CM	16	(314) 432-6000	Harold Dielmann	Mark Perkins	La Verne Collins	Daniel Smith	...	John Beardslee	Robert Gunn
Crystal City	c	MC	4	(636) 937-4614	Grant Johnston	Debbie Johns	...	...	Tony Picarella	...	Karry Friedmeyer
Dardenne Prairie *	c	MC	4	(636) 561-1718	...	...	Kimberlie Clark	...	...	...	...
De Soto	c	CM	6	(636) 586-3326	...	David Dews	Arlene Burt	...	...	Donald Kraher	...
Dellwood	c	MC	5	(314) 521-4339	...	...	...	...	...	...	...
Des Peres *	c	MC	8	(314) 835-6110	Richard Lahr	Douglas Harms	Linda Schulte	Laura Beeler	Sean Quinn	Charles Milano	Denis Knock
Desloge	c	MC	4	(573) 431-3700	...	Gregory Camp	Linda Moore	...	...	James Bullock	Gary Momot
Dexter *	c	MC	7	(573) 624-5959	Joe Weber	J Mark Stidham	Joann Steinbrueck	...	Alphonse Banken	Paul Haubold	Thomas Espey
East Prairie	c	CM	3	(573) 649-3057	Gene Ditto	Kathie Simpkins	Lori Lemons	...	John Gifford	Danny Lafferty	Joe Garner
Edmundson	c	CM	..	(314) 428-7125	...	...	...	...	...	Ron Hawkins	...
El Dorado Springs	c	CM	3	(417) 876-2521	Gene Floyd	Bruce Rogers	Lisa Janes	Vi Clevenger	Eugene Elliott	Jimmy Luster	Eric McPeak
Eldon	c	CM	4	(573) 392-2291	Ron Bly	Gary Marriott	Charlotte Dolby	Deborah Guthrie	Randy Vernon	Robert Hurtubise	...
Ellisville	c	CM	9	(636) 227-9660	Matt Pirrello	Kevin Bookout	Catherine Demeter	Lori Helle	...	Tom Felgate	Bill Schwer
Eureka	c	MC	7	(636) 938-5233	Kevin Coffey	Craig Sabo	Ralph Lindsey	Karen Crayne	Gregory Brown	Michael Wiegand	Michael Schlereth
Excelsior Springs *	c	CM	10	(816) 630-0750	Carolyn Schutte	David Haugland	...	Steven Marriott	Kent Cantrell	John McGovern	Chad Birdsong
Farmington	c	CM	13	(573) 756-1701	...	Gregory Beavers	Phyllis Hartrup	Gregory Stover	Phillip Johnson	Rick Baker	Jeffrey Blue
Fayette	c	MC	2	(660) 248-5246	Michael Hirsch	Gerard Bender	Robin Overstreet	...	James Hudson	Bryan Kunze	...
Fenton *	c	MC	4	(636) 343-2080	Dennis Hancock	Mark Sartors	Diane Monteleone	Arthur DeWitt	...	...	Dale Oberhaus
Ferguson *	c	CM	22	(314) 521-7721	Brian Fletcher	John Shaw	Debbie Matthies	Jeffrey Blume	...	...	Terry O'Neil
Festus	c	MC	9	(636) 937-4694	Walter Doyle	...	Charlene Byers	...	Charles Cayce	Timothy Lewis	William Gray
Florissant	c	MC	50	(314) 921-5700	...	...	...	Randal McDaniel	...	William Karabas	Louis Jearls
Foristell	c	MC	..	(636) 463-2123	Wanda Donnelly	Sandra Stokes	...	...	...	Douglas Johnson	...
Forsyth	c	CM	1	(417) 546-4763	...	...	...	...	James Single	...	...
Fredericktown	c	MC	3	(573) 783-3683	Philip Wulfert	C. Morgan	Caryn Sullivan	...	Darryl Asher	G. De Spain	...
Frontenac	c	MC	3	(314) 994-3200	Saundra Sobelman	...	Leesa Ross	Christine Harms	John Trout	Benjamin Branch	...
Fulton	c	CM	12	(573) 592-3111	Charles Latham	William Johnson	Carolyn Laswell	Kathleen Holschlag	Dean Buffington	Steve Myers	Darrell Dunlap
Gallatin	c	CM	1	(660) 663-2011	...	...	...	...	...	...	...
Gladstone	c	CM	26	(816) 436-2200	...	Kirk Davis	Cathy Swenson	Deborah Daily	...	...	Charles Williams
Glendale *	c	MC	5	(314) 965-3600	John Schuster	Frank Myers	Melissa Mackenberg	Daniel Lawrence	Larry Zeitzmann	Richard Black	Carl Politte
Grain Valley	c	CM	5	(816) 847-6200	Matthew Farlin	Gary Bradley	Carol Branson	Jill Shatto	...	Aaron Ambrose	Gary Hanson
Grandview	c	CM	24	(816) 316-4800	Harry Wilson	Cory Smith	Phoebe Cameron	Shirley Moses	Chuck Thacker	Larry Dickey	Lawrence Creek
Greenwood	c	MC	3		Richard DeCourcy	...	Tamara Woolford	...	...	Gary Bonine	Ryan Hunt
Hannibal	c	MC	17	(573) 221-0111	Roy Hark	Jeffrey Lagarce	Mary Baudendistel	...	John Hymers	Joey Runyon	James Burns
Harrisonville *	c	CM	8	(816) 380-8900	Kevin Wood	Keith Moody	Debbie Grant	...	Larry Francis	John Hofer	Robert Surber
Hayti	c	MC	3	(573) 359-0632	Richard Ashbaugh	...	...	...	Milford Chism	Paul Sheckell	Leonard Plunkett
Hazelwood	c	CM	26	(314) 839-3700	David Farquharson	Edwin Carlstrom	Colleen Klos	...	James Matthies	...	Thomas Manning
Herculaneum	c	MC	2	(636) 475-4447	Gina Vinyard	Jim Kasten	Stephanie Noce	...	...	...	...
Hermann	c	MC	2	(573) 486-5400	Norbert Englert	JD Lester	D. Grannemann	...	...	Frank Tennant	...
Higginsville *	c	CM	4	(660) 584-2106	Bill Kolas	Lee Barker	Richard Reyna	...	...	Shawn Smith	...
Holts Summit	c	MC	2	(573) 896-5600	Dan Cox	...	Cheryl Fletcher	...	Scott Brooks	Victor Pitman	...
Houston *	c	MC	1	(417) 967-3348	...	Larry Sutton	Tonya Foster	...	...	Carloss Kirkman	...
Independence *	c	CM	113	(816) 325-7000	Don Reimal	Robert Heacock	Jane Sharon	James Harlow	Sandra Schiess	Thomas Dailey	Howard Penrod
Jackson	c	MC	11	(573) 243-3568	Paul Sander	Stephen Wilson	Mary Waller	...	Bradley Golden	Marvin Sides	Jim Roach
Jefferson City	c	CM	39	(573) 634-6310	John Landwehr	S. Rasmussen	Phyllis Powell	Stephen Schlueter	Robert Rennick	Roger Schroeder	Patrick Sullivan
Jennings	c	MC	15	(314) 388-1164	Benjamin Sutphin	Cheryl Balke	...	Beverly Roche	James Sutphin	John Judd	...
Joplin	c	CM	45	(417) 624-0820	Phil Stinnett	R. Rohr	Barbara Hogelin	Leslie Jones	Gary Trulson	Kevin Lindsey	David Hertzberg
Kansas City	c	CM	441	(816) 513-1408	Kay Barnes	Wayne Cauthen	Millie Crossland	Jeffrey Yates	Richard Dyer	James Corwin	Stanley Harris
Kearney	c	CM	5	(816) 628-4142	Billy Dane	James Eldridge	Joan Updike	...	...	Thomas Carey	Richard Ritter
Kennett *	c	CM	11	(573) 888-9001	Roger Wheeler	Ken Goslee	Brenda Privett	...	John Mallott	Barry Tate	Larry Jones
Kimberling City	c	MC	2	(417) 739-4903	George Quest	...	Elaine Kahler	...	...	Paul Howerton	Travis Tucker
Kinloch	c	MC	..	(314) 521-3335	...	...	...	...	Lewis Miller	...	...
Kirksville *	c	CM	16	(660) 627-1225	Martha Rowe	Mari Macomber	Vickie Brumbaugh	Laura Guy-Rice	Randy Behrens	James Hughes	Mark Gaugh
Kirkwood *	c	CM	27	(314) 822-5802	Art McDonnell	Michael Brown	Elizabeth Montano	John Adams	Thomas Openlander	Jack Plummer	Todd Rehg
Knob Noster	c	CM	2	(660) 563-2595	Stanley Hall	Douglas Kermick	Robert Niffen	...	Rick Johnson	Brian Kniskern	Steven Smith
La Grange *	c	MC	1	(573) 655-4301	Timothy Rossiter	Mark Campbell	Patty Spindler	...	Henry Gunsauls	Larry Penn	Edward Ensor
La Plata	c	MC	1	(660) 332-7166	Gerald Lovingier	Ray Ivy	Betty Wheeler	...	Jerry Thomas	Kendrick Daniels	...
Ladue	c	MC	8	(314) 993-3439	Jean Quenon	...	John Williams	George Pelt	Robert Leroy	Don Wickenhauser	Dennis Bible
Lake Ozark	c	MC	..	(573) 365-5378	...	...	Rachel Kelley	...	...	David Fair	Rick Sturgeon
Lake St. Louis *	c	CM	10	(636) 625-1200	Michael Potter	Paul Markworth	Donna Daniel	Renee Roettger	...	Michael Force	Derek Koestel
Lake Tapawingo	c	CM	..	(816) 229-3722	Reed Alberg	Carl Scarborough	Ty Saigh	...	...	...	...
Lamar	c	MC	4	(417) 682-5554	Keith Divine	Lynn Calton	Carolyn Taffner	Herbert Jett	Bill Rawlings	Ronald Hager	...
Lathrop	c	MC	2	(816) 740-4251	Rodney Greer	Donald Moore	Susie Freece	...	David Eads	Raymond Sprague	Dwight Adkison
Lawson *	c	CM	1	(816) 580-3217	David Burgess	Dawn Probasco	Merry Marler	...	...	Brian LaFavor	Douglas Kessler
Lebanon	c	MC	12	(417) 532-2156	Stanley Allen	...	James Wilson	...	Samuel Schneider	Samuel Mustard	Scott Shumate
Lee'S Summit	c	CM	70	(916) 969-7300	Karen Messeri	Stephen Arbo	Denise Chisum	Conrad Lamb	Thomas Solberg	Kenneth Conlee	Chuck Owsley
Lexington	c	CM	4	(660) 259-4633	Tom Hayes	...	...	...	Kirk Smith	Don Rector	Jim Knott
Liberty	c	CM	26	(816) 792-6000	Stephen Hawkins	Curtis Wenson	...	...	Richard Lehmann	Arthur Chevalier	Steven Hansen
Louisiana	c	MC	3	(573) 754-4132	James Yokem	Kelly Henderson	Sharon Kakouris	...	Mike Lesley	James Graham	...
Macon	c	MC	5	(660) 385-2632	...	...	Gerald Maloney	...	...	...	...
Malden	c	MC	4	(573) 276-4502	Ray Santie	Rick Murray	Marilyn Fiddler	...	Winford German	Jarrett Bullock	Ted Bellers
Manchester	c	CM	19	(636) 227-1385	Larry Miles	Edwin Blattner	...	Marsha Knudtson	...	John Quinn	...
Maplewood *	c	CM	9	(314) 645-3600	Mark Langston	Martin Corcoran	Karen Scheidt	...	Terry Merrell	Mark Griffin	Anthony Traxler
Marceline	c	CM	2	(660) 376-3528	Charles Dowell	...	Elizabeth Capp	...	Larry Ervie	Tom Bendure	Kirk Lockwood
Marshall	c	MC	12	(660) 886-2225	Mitchel Geisler	Charles Tryban	Janet French	Debbie Trimble	John Rieves	James Simmerman	Paul Jensen
Marshfield	c	MC	5	(417) 468-2310	...	...	...	...	...	...	...
Maryland Heights *	c	CM	25	(314) 291-6550	Michael Moeller	Mark Levin	Marsha Jones	David Watson	...	Thomas O'Connor	Bryan Pearl
Maryville *	c	CM	10	(660) 562-8001	Chad Jackson	Matthew LeCerf	Sheila Smail	...	...	...	Greg Decker
Mexico *	c	CM	11	(573) 581-2100	Virginia Robertson	Todd Thompson	Donna Barnes	...	...	...	Kensey Russell
Milan *	c	MC	1	(660) 265-4420	G. Maulsby	Brian Wilson	Lisa Hurt	...	Gary Tipton	Maurice May	...
Moberly	c	CM	11	(660) 263-4420	Don Burton	Andrew Morris	Diane Galloway	Greg Hodge	Kenny Brandow	Dennis Cupp	Doug Henry
Moline Acres	c	MC	2	(314) 868-2433	...	...	Nina Walker	Tina Minor	...	...	Dennis DeShay
Monett	c	CO	7	(417) 235-3763	Jerry Fulp	Rex Lane	Janie Knight	Lisa Crawford	Tom Jones	David Tatum	Pete Rauch
Monroe City *	c	MC	2	(573) 735-4585	Neal Minor	James Burns	Gary Osbourne	...	Gary McElroy	Rick Stone	...
Montgomery City	c	MC	2	(573) 564-3160	Jeffrey Porter	Steven Deves	...	...	...	Michael Frye	Dorsey Stotler
Mount Vernon *	c	MC	4	(417) 466-2122	Robert Walster	John Rice	Mary Walker	...	Melvin Owens	W. Turk	Gene Stanton
Mountain Grove	c	CM	4	(417) 926-4162	Jake Slayton	Rick Outersky	Sandra Crisp	...	Paul Bushong	Tommy Gaddis	Michael Williams
Neosho *	c	CM	10	(417) 451-8050	Howard Birdsong	Jan Blase	Audrey Covey	Robert Blackwood	Greg Hickman	David McCracken	Mike Hightower
Nevada *	c	CM	8	(417) 448-2700	Michael Hutchens	Harlan Moore	Julie Stumpff	...	Robert Benn	...	Joseph Charles
New Madrid	c	CM	3	(573) 748-2866	...	Furgison Hunter	Shelby Desmore	...	...	Claude McFerren	...
Nixa	c	CM	12	(417) 725-3788	Sharon Whitehill	Brian Bingle	...	Coralee Patrick	...	...	...
Normandy	c	MC	5	(314) 385-3300	James Murphy	Brent Bury	Pam Rogers	Kay Kulage	...	John Connolly	Rodney Jarrett
North Kansas City	c	MC	4	(816) 274-6000	Gene Bruns	Pamela Windsor	Marsha Wilson	Shirley Land	H. David Williams	Glenn Ladd	Patrick Hawver
Northwoods	c	MC	4	(314) 385-8000	Errol Bush	...	Marvalda Howard	Renee Mayweather	...	Sylvester Jones	Lumis Kitchen
Oak Grove	c	CM	5	(816) 690-3773	Mark Fulks	...	Cathy Smith	...	...	...	Joe Bobadilla
Odessa	c	MC	4	(816) 230-5577	Tom Murry	Steven Sanders	Margaret Howerton	...	...	Robert Kinder	Donald Elder
O'Fallon	c	CM	46	(636) 240-2000	Paul Renaud	Robert Lowery	Sandra Stokes	Vicki Boschert	...	Steve Talbott	Ken Morgan

Directory 1/9 continued — OFFICIALS IN U.S. MUNICIPALITIES 2,500 AND OVER IN POPULATION

Jurisdiction		Type	Form of govern-ment	2000 Popu-lation	Main telephone number	Chief elected official	Appointed administrator	Clerk of the governing board	Chief financial officer	Fire chief	Police chief	Public works director
MISSOURI continued												
Olivette	*	c	CM	7	(314) 993-0444	Jean Antoine	T. McDowell	Myra Bennett	Jeffrey Steiner	John Bailot	Richard Knox	Mike Gartenberg
Osage Beach		c	MC	3	(573) 302-2000	Penny Lyons	Nancy Viselli	Diann Warner	Karri Badolato	. . .	. . .	Rick King
Osceola		c	MC	. .	(417) 646-8421	Jerry Osborn	. . .	Lila Foster	. . .	. . .	Richard Gardner	. . .
Overland		c	MC	16	(314) 428-4321	Robert Dody	Jason McConachie	. . .	Lisa Ridolfi	. . .	James Herron	. . .
Owensville		c	MC	2	(573) 437-2812	. . .	John Tracy	. . .	. . .	. . .	. . .	. . .
Ozark		c	MC	9	(417) 581-2407	Donna McQuay	Stephen Childers	Lana Calley	. . .	. . .	Lyle Hodges	. . .
Pacific		c	MC	5	(636) 271-0500	Jeffrey Titter	Harold Selby	Joann Hoehne	. . .	. . .	Ronald Reed	Edward Gass
Pagedale	*	c	MC	3	(314) 726-1200	Mary Carter	Fran Stevens	. . .	Barbara Frierson	. . .	G. Walker	. . .
Palmyra	*	c	MC	3	(573) 769-2223	Loren Graham	. . .	Rhonda Dodd	. . .	Gary Crane	Eddie Bogue	Raymond Houston
Park Hills	*	c	MC	7	(573) 431-3577	John Clark	John Kennedy	Carla Johnson	. . .	Rick Whaley	William Holloway	Don Akers
Parkville		c	MC	4	(816) 741-7676	Charles Kutz	Shannon Thompson	Barbara Lance	Justin Kuder	. . .	William Hudson	Daniel Koch
Peculiar		c	MC	2	(816) 779-5212	George Lewis	Brad Ratliff	Nora Dodge	Karen Parrot	James Toone	Dean Kelly	Charlie Mohr
Perryville		c	CM	7	(573) 547-2594	Robert Miget	William Lewis	Marilyn Dobbelare	. . .	. . .	Keith Tarrillion	Charles La Rose
Pevely	*	c	MC	3	(636) 475-4452	John Knobloch	Happy Welch	Elizabeth Stackley	. . .	. . .	Ronnie Wicks	. . .
Pine Lawn		c	MC	4	(314) 261-5500	Adrian Wright	. . .	Charlotte Graham	. . .	. . .	Donald Hardy	George Prophete
Platte City		c	CM	3	(816) 858-3046	Dave Brooks	Jason Metten	Tanya Bates	Julie Pennington	. . .	. . .	Leonard Hendricks
Plattsburgh	*	c	CM	2	(816) 539-2148	James Kennedy	Dennis Gehrt	Mickey Streeter	. . .	. . .	Zephrey Bingham	Dennis Hudson
Pleasant Hill		c	CM	5	(816) 987-3135	Clarence Hall	Mark Randall	. . .	Sandra Beatty	Jeffrey Johnson	Robert Driscoll	Bob Kee
Poplar Bluff	*	c	CM	16	(573) 785-7474	Susan Williams	Doug Bagby	Pamela Kearbey	Mark Massingham	Ralph Stucker	Danny Whiteley	. . .
Portageville		c	MC	3	(573) 379-5789	. . .	. . .	. . .	. . .	. . .	. . .	. . .
Potosi		c	MC	2	(573) 438-2767	Wayne Malugen	. . .	Doris Eye	Roger Bilderback	Richard Knight	Don Cooksey	. . .
Raymore	*	c	MC	11	(816) 331-0488	Juan Alonzo	Eric Berlin	Jean Woerner	. . .	. . .	Kris Turnbow	Michael Krass
Raytown		c	MC	30	(816) 737-6000	Jack Nesbitt	Mahesh Sharma	Karlan Curtis	. . .	Rick Mawhirter	. . .	. . .
Republic		c	MC	8	(417) 732-6065	Keith Miller	James Krischke	Beth West	. . .	Don Murray	Mark Lowe	David Brock
Richland		c	MC	2	(573) 765-4421	Lucy Henson	. . .	Tana Mitschele	. . .	. . .	. . .	Claude Hill
Richmond	*	c	MC	6	(816) 776-5304	J. Green	Rick Childers	Robin Milligan	Melanie Allwood	Lonnie Quick	Theresa Williams	C. E. Goodall
Richmond Heights		c	CM	9	(314) 645-0404	Betty Humphrey	Amy Hamilton	Patricia Villmer	Sara Fox	Charles Drexler	Rick Vilcek	Bruce Murray
Riverside	*	c	MC	2	(816) 741-3993	Kathy Rose	David Blackburn	Louise Rusick	Donna Resz	Gordon Fowlston	. . .	Jeffry Rupp
Riverview		v	CM	3	(314) 868-0700	Elizabeth Morris	. . .	Madonna Forrest	Jana Warmann	. . .	Roy Midkiff	Susan Kenkel
Rock Hill	*	c	CM	4	(314) 968-1410	Robert Salamone	George Liyeos	. . .	. . .	John Kriska	Terry Good	Ron Meyer
Rogersville		c	MC	1	(417) 753-2884	Jack Cole	Nancy Edson	Glenda Stegner	. . .	Richard Stirts	Leland McMasters	Scott Dorrell
Rolla	*	c	CM	16	(573) 426-6948	William Jenks	John Butz	Carol Daniels	Steffanie Rogers	Robert Williams	Mark Kearse	Steve Hargis
Salem		c	CM	4	(573) 729-4811	Gary Brown	. . .	Mary Happel	. . .	. . .	Clifford Jadwin	. . .
Savannah	*	c	CM	4	(816) 324-3315	Billy Kretzer	Michael Fisher	Beth Kar	. . .	Steve Oliver	Dave Vincent	Kenny Lance
Scott City		c	MC	4	(573) 264-2157	Jim Parch	Ron Eskew	Nona Walls	. . .	James Cassout	Don Cobb	Jack Rasnic
Sedalia	*	c	MC	20	(660) 827-3000	Bob Wasson	Keith Riesberg	Arlene Silvey	Pamela Burlingame	Michael Ditzfeld	John DeGonia	Bill Beck
Shrewsbury		c	MC	6	(314) 647-5795	Bert Gates	Barry Alexander	. . .	Kathryn Wehner	William Fox	Jeffrey Keller	Tony Wagner
Sikeston	*	c	CM	16	(573) 471-2512	Michael Marshall	Kevin Friend	Carroll Couch	. . .	. . .	. . .	. . .
Slater		c	MC	2	(660) 529-2271	. . .	. . .	. . .	. . .	. . .	. . .	. . .
Smithville	*	c	CM	5	(816) 532-3897	Charles Hitchborn	Gerry Vernon	Judy Clough	. . .	. . .	Ken Wilson	. . .
Springfield		c	CM	151	(417) 864-1000	Thomas Carlson	Gregory Burris	Brenda Cirtin	M. Mannix-Decker	Dan Whisler	Lynn Rowe	Marc Thornsberry
St. Ann		c	MC	13	(314) 427-8009	Carrie Cafazza	Matthew Conley	Christina Santel	. . .	. . .	Robert Schrader	Kevin McCarthy
St. Charles		c	MC	60	(636) 949-3265	Patricia York	Michael Spurgeon	Marilyn McCoy	Karen McDermott	Ernest Rhodes	James Gooch	. . .
St. Clair		c	MC	4	(636) 629-0333	Ron Blum	James Arndt	Chris Fawe	. . .	Tim Wideman	Bill Hammack	James Terry
St. James	*	c	MC	3	(573) 265-7011	Dennis Wilson	. . .	Marilyn Woolsey	Paulette Craft	Bruce Parton	Kevin Friend	Mike Licklider
St. John		c	CM	6	(314) 427-8700	Lee Taylor	Terry Milam	Donna Davis	Marilyn Betkis	. . .	. . .	James Phillips
St. Joseph		c	CM	73	(816) 271-4674	Ken Shearin	Vincent Capell	Paula Heyde	Carolyn Harrison	Jack Brown	C. Connally	J. Woody
St. Louis		c	MC	348	(314) 622-3562	Francis Slay	Jeff Rainford	Parrie May	Darlene Green	Sherman George	Joseph Mokwa	David Visintainer
St. Peters		c	MC	51	(636) 477-6600	Shawn Brown	William Charnisky	Rhonda Shaw	. . .	. . .	. . .	Russell Batzel
Ste. Genevieve		c	CM	4	(573) 883-5400	. . .	. . .	Betty Seibel	. . .	. . .	Brian Clubb	Gene Thurman
Stockton		c	MC	1	(417) 276-5210	. . .	Kendel Goslee	. . .	. . .	. . .	. . .	. . .
Sugar Creek		c	MC	3	(816) 252-4400	Stanley Salva	Ronald Martinovich	Jana Dickerson	. . .	. . .	. . .	Edward Layton
Sullivan		c	CM	6	(573) 468-4612	James Schatz	Mark Falloon	Janice Nolie	. . .	. . .	George Counts	. . .
Sunset Hills	*	c	MC	8	(314) 849-3400	Mike Svoboda	. . .	Laura Rider	. . .	. . .	William Lagrand	Anne Lamitola
Town & Country		c	MC	10	(314) 432-6606	Jonathan Dalton	John Copeland	Pamela Burdt	Betty Cotner	. . .	. . .	Douglas Hopkins
Trenton		c	CM	6	(660) 359-4310	Cathie Smith	Kerry Sampson	Cindy Simpson	. . .	Tony Ralston	Robert Lewis	. . .
Troy	*	c	MC	6	(636) 528-4712	Charles Kemper	. . .	Karen Hotfelder	. . .	. . .	Jeff Taylor	. . .
Union		c	MC	7	(636) 583-3600	Michael Livengood	. . .	Jonita Copeland	. . .	. . .	Norman Brune	Harold Lampkin
University City		c	CM	37	(314) 862-6767	. . .	Julie Feier	Joyce Pumm	. . .	Steve Olshwanger	Charles Adams	E. Shields-Benford
Valley Park		c	MC	6	(314) 225-5171	Daniel Michel	. . .	Marguerite Wilburn	. . .	. . .	. . .	James McMullen
Vandalia		c	CM	2	(573) 594-6186	Ramon Barnes	Alan Winders	Karen Schutz	Sharon Myers	. . .	Raymond Laird	Aaron Rentfro
Warrensburg	*	c	CM	16	(660) 747-9131	Donna Defrain	J. Hancock	Cynthia Gabel	. . .	Phil Johnston	Bruce Howey	Robert Crumb
Warrenton	*	c	MC	5	(636) 456-3535	Greg Costello	Terri Thorn	Chris McCormick	. . .	. . .	Davis Bernard	Rob Hamlin
Warsaw		c	CM	2	(660) 438-5522	Lou Breshars	Randy Pogue	Betty Brumbaugh	. . .	. . .	James Hanik	. . .
Washington	*	c	MC	13	(636) 390-1000	Richard Stratman	James Briggs	Brenda Mitchell	Janet Braun	Willard Halmich	Kenneth Hahn	Kevin Quaethem
Waynesville		c	MC	3	(573) 774-6171	Cliff Hammock	Bruce Harrill	Barbara Stinson	. . .	. . .	Donald McCulloch	. . .
Webb City		c	MC	9	(417) 673-4651	Glenn Dolence	Steven Garrett	Lorinda Southard	. . .	Ernie Goad	Donald Richardson	James Wallace
Webster Groves		c	CM	23	(314) 963-5300	Gerry Welch	Steven Wylie	Katie Nakazono	. . .	Michael Capriglione	Dale Curtis	Dennis Wells
Weldon Springs		c	MC	5	(636) 441-2110	Donald Licklider	. . .	M. Kwiatkowski	. . .	. . .	. . .	. . .
Wellston		c	MC	2	(314) 385-1015	James Harvey	Michael Evans	Diane Irvin	. . .	. . .	Robert Lewis	Eldright White
Wentzville	*	c	MC	6	(636) 327-5101	Paul Lambi	Dianna Wright	Vitula Skillman	Dennis Walsh	. . .	Robert Noonan	William Bensing
West Plains	*	c	CO	10	(417) 256-7176	Joe Evans	Charles Fugate	Mallory Prewett	Dixie Williams	James Bean	Charles Brotherton	Jim Davidson
Wildwood	*	c	CM	32	(636) 458-0440	Tim Woerther	Daniel Dubruiel	L. Greene-Beldner	Dawn Kaiser	. . .	. . .	Ryan Thomas
Willow Springs		c	CM	2	(417) 469-2107	David Wehmer	Ron Mersch	Darla Langford	. . .	Larry Foster	Danny Dunn	Paul Collins
Winchester	*	c	CM	1	(636) 391-0600	Gail Winham	Barbara Beckett	. . .	. . .	. . .	. . .	. . .
Windsor		c	MC	3	(660) 647-3512	. . .	. . .	. . .	. . .	. . .	. . .	. . .
Woodson Terrace		c	MC	4	(314) 427-2600	William Ratchford	Lawrence Besmer	Margaret Wilson	. . .	. . .	Robert Dowling	Micah Jacquemin
MONTANA												
Anaconda–Deer Lodge		c	CM	9	(406) 563-4000	. . .	Gene Vuckovich	Susan McNeil	. . .	William Converse	John Sullivan	. . .
Belgrade		c	CM	5	(406) 388-4994	Lee Stevens	Joseph Menicucci	Marilyn Foltz	. . .	. . .	Gregory Waldon	Henry Hathaway
Billings		c	CM	89	(406) 657-8265	Charles Tooley	Christina Volek	Marita Herold	. . .	Marvin Jochems	Jerry Archer	David Mumford
Bozeman		c	CM	27	(406) 582-2300	Steven Kirchhoff	Chris Kukulski	Robin Sullivan	Miral Gamradt	. . .	. . .	Debra Arkell
Butte-Silver Bow		c	CO	33	(406) 497-6200	Judith Jacobson	. . .	Dinah McLeod	John Shea	Robert Armstrong	John Walsh	James Johnston
Columbia Falls		c	CM	3	(406) 892-4391	Susan Nicosia	William Shaw	. . .	Sybil Noss	Robert Webber	Dave Perry	Gary Stempin
Conrad		c	MC	2	(406) 271-3623	John Shevlin	. . .	. . .	Agnes Fowler	Kevin Moritz	Gary Dent	Richard Anderson
Cut Bank		c	MC	3	(406) 873-5526	William McCauley	. . .	Mary Embleton	. . .	. . .	. . .	Lorin Lowry
Deer Lodge	*	c	MC	3	(406) 846-3649	. . .	Mary Fraley	. . .	. . .	Sanford Porter	. . .	Galen Horswill
Dillon		c	MC	3	(406) 683-4245	Martin Malesich	. . .	Faye Jones	. . .	. . .	. . .	. . .
Forsyth		c	MC	1	(406) 356-2521	Dennis Kopitzke	. . .	Doris Pinkerton	. . .	Neil Donner	Tim Fulton	Richard Thompson
Glasgow		c	MC	3	(406) 228-2476	Wilmer Zeller	. . .	Kay Jackson	. . .	Neil Chouinard	Lyndon Erickson	Jon Bengochea
Glendive		c	MC	4	(406) 365-3318	. . .	. . .	. . .	. . .	. . .	. . .	. . .
Great Falls	*	c	CM	56	(406) 771-1180	Dona Stebbins	Gregory Doyon	Peggy Bourne	Coleen Balzarini	Randall McCamley	Robert Jones	Jim Rearden
Hamilton		c	MC	3	(406) 363-2101	Jessica Randazzo	Steve Green	Rose Allen	Cody Geddes	. . .	Ryan Oster	. . .
Hardin		c	MC	3	(406) 665-9293	Ronald Adams	. . .	Theresa Hert	Lori Dorn	. . .	. . .	Larry Vandersloot

Directory 1/9 continued **OFFICIALS IN U.S. MUNICIPALITIES 2,500 AND OVER IN POPULATION**

Jurisdiction	Type	Form of govern-ment	2000 Popu-lation	Main telephone number	Chief elected official	Appointed administrator	Clerk of the governing board	Chief financial officer	Fire chief	Police chief	Public works director
MONTANA continued											
Havre *	c	MC	9	(406) 265-6719	Robert Rice	. . .	. . .	Lowell Swenson	Dave Sheppard	Jerry Nystrom	David Peterson
Helena *	c	CM	25	(406) 447-8404	James Smith	Timothy Burton	Debbie Havens	. . .	Stephen Larson	Troy McGee	John Rundquist
Kalispell	c	CM	14	(406) 758-7757	Pamela Kennedy	. . .	Theresa White	Amy Robertson	Randy Brodehl	Frank Garner	James Hansz
Laurel	c	MC	6	(406) 628-7431	Kenneth Olson	. . .	Mary Embleton	. . .	Scott Wilm	Richard Musson	Steve Klotz
Lewistown	c	MC	5	(406) 538-2302	. . .	. . .	Kathy Wallingboro	. . .	Steve Cunningham	Kevin Mynre	Bill Bandel
Libby	c	MC	2	(406) 293-2731	Anthony Berget	. . .	. . .	. . .	Tom Wood	Clayton Coker	Daniel Thede
Livingston *	c	CM	6	(406) 823-6003	Steve Caldwell	Edwin Meece	. . .	. . .	Alan Davis	Darren Raney	Clint Tinsley
Miles City *	c	MC	8	(406) 234-3462	Joe Whalen	. . .	Kori Pray	. . .	Derrick Rodgers	Kevin Krausz	Bruce Larson
Missoula	c	MC	57	(406) 552-6130	John Engen	Bruce Bender	Martha Rehbein	Brent Ramharter	Thomas Steenberg	Roy Wickman	R. King
Polson *	c	MC	4	(406) 883-8202	. . .	. . .	Aggi Loeser	. . .	John Fairchild	Douglas Chase	Tony Porrazzo
Red Lodge	c	MC	2	(406) 446-1606	. . .	. . .	. . .	. . .	. . .	. . .	. . .
Shelby	c	MC	3	(406) 434-5222	Larry Bonderud	. . .	. . .	Teri Ruff	. . .	. . .	Bill Moritz
Sidney	c	MC	4	(406) 433-2809	Bret Smelser	. . .	Brenda Thogersen	. . .	Ken Volk	Frank Di Fonzo	Terry Meldahl
Whitefish	c	CM	5	(406) 863-2400	. . .	Dennis Taylor	Necile Lorang	Michael Eve	David Sipe	William Dial	John Wilson
Wolf Point	c	MC	2	(406) 653-1852	Matt Golik	. . .	. . .	. . .	Steve Harada	Jeff Harada	Richard Isle
NEBRASKA											
Ainsworth	c	MC	1	(402) 387-2494	. . .	Kristi Thornburg	. . .	. . .	. . .	. . .	. . .
Albion	c	MC	1	(402) 395-2428	James Tishammer	Andrew Devine	. . .	. . .	Brent Lipker	James Vibsky	. . .
Alliance	c	CM	8	(308) 762-5400	Dan Kusek	Pamela Caskie	Linda Jines	. . .	David McCarty	John Kiss	. . .
Ashland *	c	CM	2	(402) 944-3387	Paul Lienke	Jessica Preister	Kathleen Sliva	. . .	Brian Whitehead	Mark Powell	. . .
Auburn	c	MC	3	(402) 274-3420	Robert Engles	. . .	Sherry Heskett	. . .	Randy Bennett	Dan White	David Hunter
Aurora	c	CM	4	(402) 694-6992	Kenneth Harter	Michael Bair	Erma Luth	. . .	Gary Gerdes	Charles Headley	William Vandeman
Beatrice *	c	MC	12	(402) 228-5200	. . .	Neal Niedfeldt	Linda Koch	. . .	Brian Daake	. . .	. . .
Bellevue	c	MC	44	(402) 293-3000	Jerry Ryan	Gary Troutman	Kay Dammast	. . .	Dale Tedder	John Stacey	Jerry Hare
Blair	c	MC	7	(402) 426-4191	James Realph	Rodney Storm	Brenda Wheeler	. . .	Lonnie Penry	Joseph Lager	Allen Schoemacker
Bloomfield *	c	MC	1	(402) 373-4396	Jim Cripe	Lyndsy Jenness	Marilyn True	. . .	Rodger Freeman	Bryan Ruhr	Dave Stark
Bridgeport	c	MC	1	(308) 262-1623	. . .	William Boyer	. . .	. . .	. . .	. . .	. . .
Broken Bow	c	MC	3	(308) 872-5831	Jim Franssen	Steve Waring	Elaine Bayer	. . .	Kent Mallette	Steve Scott	Mike Lucas
Central City	c	MC	2	(308) 946-3806	Clayton Erickson	C. Anderson	David Rish	. . .	Tim Bolling	Dennis Wagner	. . .
Chadron *	c	CM	5	(308) 432-0505	Donnie Grantham	Sandra Powell	Donna Rust	Melany Hughes	Patrick Gould	Gerald Crews	Milo Rust
Chappell	c	MC	. .	(308) 874-2401	. . .	Joan Hansen	Kim Johnson	. . .	Jim Riechman	Jeff Ortgies	. . .
Columbus	c	MC	20	(402) 564-8584	. . .	Joseph Mangiamelli	. . .	Anne Kinnison	. . .	William Gumm	. . .
Cozad	c	MC	4	(308) 784-3907	Greg Tetley	Carl York	Susan Kloepping	. . .	Dave Cullers	Mark Montgomery	. . .
Crete *	c	MC	6	(402) 826-4313	Tom Crisman	. . .	Jerry Wilcox	. . .	Mahlon Kohl	Steve Hensel	Tom Ourada
Dakota City	c	MC	1	(402) 987-3448	Charmaine Cantrell	Robert Peters	. . .	. . .	Jerry Yacevich	. . .	Danny Fager
David City	c	MC	2	(402) 367-3135	H. Smith	Joseph Johnson	Joan Kovar	. . .	Michael Hiatt	Stephen Sunday	Jim McDonald
Fairbury *	c	MC	4	(402) 729-2476	Homer Ward	. . .	Sharyl Preston	. . .	Eric Voss	Brooks Bryan	Mick Hynek
Falls City	c	CM	4	(402) 245-2707	. . .	. . .	. . .	. . .	. . .	. . .	. . .
Fremont *	c	MC	25	(402) 727-2630	Donald Edwards	Robert Hartwig	Kimberly Volk	. . .	Gary German	Timothy Mullen	Clark Boschult
Fullerton	c	MC	1	(308) 536-2428	Gretchen Treadway	Jim Kramer	. . .	. . .	. . .	. . .	Jerry Collins
Geneva	c	MC	2	(402) 759-3109	Rodney Norrie	Robert Higel	Barbara Whitley	. . .	Larry Waiss	Travis Cunningham	. . .
Gering	c	MC	7	(308) 436-5096	Starr Lehl	Lane Danielzuk	. . .	. . .	James Templar	Melvin Griggs	. . .
Gibbon	c	MC	1	(308) 468-6118	Monte Standage	Christopher Rector	Vicki Power	. . .	Gene Smith	. . .	Jerry Jergensen
Gordon	c	CM	1	(308) 282-0837	Nancy Russell	Fred Hlava	Toni Siders	. . .	Gary Paul	Loren Tesch	Michael Winter
Gothenburg *	c	MC	3	(308) 537-3677	Larry Franzen	Bruce Clymer	Connie Dalrymple	. . .	Mark Ballmer	Randy Olson	. . .
Grand Island	c	MC	42	(308) 385-5444	Ken Gnadt	Jeffrey Pederson	Cindy Johnson	Chuck Haase	. . .	Kyle Hetrick	Steven Riehle
Grant *	c	MC	1	(308) 352-2100	Mike Wyatt	Tyson McGreer	Jessie Faber	. . .	. . .	. . .	Gary Beckler
Hastings *	c	MC	24	(402) 461-2309	Matthew Rossen	Joe Patterson	Connie Hartman	. . .	Kent Gilbert	Larry Thoren	David Wacker
Hickman *	c	MC	1	(402) 792-2212	Jim Hrouda	B. Baker	Brett Baker	Kelly Oelke	Stanley Draper	Terry Wagner	Bob Lovorn
Holdrege *	c	CM	5	(308) 995-8681	Mark Rona	Robert Rager	Sheryl Nelson	. . .	. . .	Dennis DaMounde	Mark Schultz
Kearney	c	CM	27	(308) 233-3215	Bruce Blankenship	Michael Morgan	Michaelle Trembly	Wendell Wessels	. . .	Daniel Lynch	Rodney Wiederspan
Kimball	c	CM	2	(308) 235-3639	Gregory Dinges	Harold Farrar	Pamela Richter	. . .	Rick Wynne	Douglas Provance	. . .
La Vista *	c	MC	11	(402) 331-4343	Douglas Kindig	Brenda Gunn	Pamela Buethe	Sheila Lindberg	Rich Uhl	Robert Lausten	Joseph Soucie
Lexington *	c	CM	10	(308) 324-2341	John Fagot	Joseph Pepplitsch	. . .	. . .	Bo Berry	Charles Clark	Glenn Hawks
Lincoln	c	MC	225	(402) 441-7888	Don Wesely	. . .	Joan Ross	Don Herz	Michael Spadt	Tom Casady	Allan Abbott
Madison	c	CM	2	(402) 454-2675	Darrel Lyon	. . .	. . .	. . .	. . .	Roddy Waterbury	Jim Lewis
Mc Cook *	c	CM	7	(308) 345-2022	Dennis Berry	Kurt Fritsch	Lea Doak	. . .	Marc Harpham	Isaac Brown	Kyle Potthoff
Minden	c	MC	2	(308) 832-1820	Roger Jones	Brenton Lewis	. . .	. . .	Craig Space	James Huff	Gregg Hinrichsen
Nebraska City *	c	CO	7	(402) 873-5515	Jack Hobbie	. . .	Arnold Ehlers	. . .	Alan Viox	David Lacy	. . .
Norfolk *	c	MC	23	(402) 844-2010	Gordon Adams	Albert Roder	Beth Deck	Randy Gates	Shane Weidner	William Mizner	Dennis Smith
North Platte	c	MC	23	(308) 535-6724	G. Keith Richardson	James Hawks	. . .	. . .	Richard Pedersen	M. Gutschenritter	Wesley Meyer
Ogallala	c	CM	4	(308) 284-6001	Paul Foy	Harold Stewart	Jane Skinner	. . .	Bill Fortune	David Kling	. . .
Omaha	c	MC	390	(402) 444-5300	Michael Fahey	. . .	Buster Brown	Carol Ebdon	Robert Dahlquist	Thomas Warren	Norman Jackman
O'Neill	c	MC	3	(402) 336-3640	William Price	. . .	Nikki Johnston	. . .	Rodney Ludemann	Benjamin Matchett	. . .
Ord	c	MC	2	(308) 728-5791	Roger Goldfish	. . .	Sandy Kruml	. . .	Charles Green	. . .	. . .
Papillion	c	MC	16	(402) 597-2000	James Blinn	Daniel Hoins	Jennifer Niemier	Nancy Purscell	Bill Bowes	Leonard Houloose	Marty Leming
Pierce	c	MC	1	(402) 329-4535	. . .	Chad Anderson	. . .	. . .	. . .	. . .	. . .
Plainview *	c	CM	1	(402) 582-4928	Gayle Retzlaff	Michael Holton	Lori Wragge	. . .	. . .	Bruce Yosten	. . .
Plattsmouth *	c	MC	6	(402) 296-2522	R. Paul Lambert	Ervin Portis	Sandra Meyer	. . .	Mike Wilson	Brian Paulsen	Gary Hellwig
Ralston	c	MC	6	(402) 331-6677	Donald Groesser	. . .	Dolores Costanzo	. . .	Kyle Ienn	Bill White	Daniel Freshman
Ravenna *	c	MC	1	(308) 452-3273	Gerald Reimers	. . .	Kellie Crowell	. . .	Tim Lammers	Wendell Miska	Bob Absalon
Red Cloud	c	MC	1	(402) 746-2215	. . .	. . .	. . .	. . .	. . .	. . .	. . .
Scottsbluff	c	CM	14	(308) 630-4136	Randy Meininger	Rick Kuckkahn	Cindy Dickinson	Renae Griffiths	Dana Miller	Alex Moreno	Mark Bohl
Seward	c	MC	6	(402) 643-2928	Roger Glawatz	Daniel Berlowitz	. . .	Debra Schaefer	. . .	Alan Baldwin	Calvin Nordmeyer
Sidney *	c	CM	6	(308) 254-5300	Dave Weiderspon	Gary Person	G. Anthony	. . .	Keith Stone	Larry Cox	Otto Hehnke
South Sioux City *	c	MC	11	(402) 494-7500	Sandra Ehrich	Lance Hedquist	Sue Murray	. . .	Denis Campbell	Scot Ford	Paul Nolan
Springfield *	c	MC	1	(402) 253-2204	Dorothy Richards	. . .	Kathleen Fauver	. . .	Jason Lutz	. . .	Allen Post
Stanton	c	CM	1	(402) 439-2119	Harold Krumwiede	. . .	Nancy Morfeld	. . .	Richard Locke	. . .	. . .
Superior *	c	MC	2	(402) 879-4713	Billy Maxey	. . .	Jan Diehl	Sam Clark	Todd Kroeger	Perry Freeman	Larry Brittenham
Sutton	c	MC	1	(402) 773-4225	John Hull	Virg Ulmer	. . .	. . .	Pat Merrick	. . .	Kevin Finnegan
Valentine	c	CM	2	(402) 376-2323	Wassace Balliet	. . .	John Hanzlicek	. . .	Terry Engles	Robert McLean	Scott Egelhoff
Wahoo *	c	MC	3	(402) 443-3222	Daryl Reitmajer	. . .	Melissa Harrell	. . .	Corey Wagner	Kenneth Jackson	James Gibney
Wakefield *	c	MC	1	(402) 287-2080	Tom Henderson	Jim Litchfield	Kathy Skinner	. . .	Dean Ulrich	. . .	. . .
Waverly *	c	CM	2	(402) 786-2312	Mike Werner	Douglas Rix	. . .	. . .	Aaron Hummel	. . .	Tracey Whyman
Wayne	c	CM	5	(402) 375-1733	Sheryl Lindau	Lowell Johnson	. . .	. . .	Robert Woehler	Lance Webster	. . .
West Point *	c	MC	3	(402) 372-2466	Marlene Johnson	Thomas Goulette	Mary Kempf	. . .	Lyle Hansen	Michael Fisher	. . .
York *	c	MC	8	(402) 363-2600	Greg Adams	Jack Vavra	C. Thiele	Susan Tonniges	Kevin Stuhr	Donald Klug	Orville Davidson
NEVADA											
Boulder City	c	CM	14	(702) 293-9202	Robert Ferraro	Vicki Mayes	Pamella Malmstrom	Robert Kenney	Dean Molburg	Thomas Finn	Scott Hansen
Carlin	c	MC	2	(775) 754-6354	Linda Bingaman	Lorry Lipparelli	LaDawn Lawson	. . .	Will Johnston	William Bauer	Peter Aiazzi
Carson City	c	CM	52	(775) 887-2103	. . .	. . .	Alan Glover	Thomas Minton	Robert Giomi	Kenneth Furlong	Andrew Burnham
Elko	c	CM	16	(775) 777-7110	Michael Franzoia	. . .	Loralee Lynch	Dawn Stout	Alan Kightlinger	Clair Morris	. . .
Ely	c	MC	4	(775) 289-2430	. . .	Brent Hutchings	. . .	. . .	. . .	. . .	. . .

Directory 1/9 continued — OFFICIALS IN U.S. MUNICIPALITIES 2,500 AND OVER IN POPULATION

Jurisdiction	Type	Form of govern-ment	2000 Popu-lation	Main telephone number	Chief elected official	Appointed administrator	Clerk of the governing board	Chief financial officer	Fire chief	Police chief	Public works director
NEVADA continued											
Fallon	c	MC	7	(775) 423-5104	Kenneth Tedford	...	Gary Cordes	...	...	Russell Brooks	Jerry Mayfield
Fernley *	c	CM	9	(775) 784-9859	Todd Cutler	...	Lena Shumway	Bonnie Duke	...	...	Lowell Patton
Gardnerville	t	CM	3	(775) 782-7134	...	James Park	...	...	...	...	...
Henderson	c	CM	175	(702) 267-2323	James Gibson	Mary Kay Peck	Monica Simmons	...	James Cavalieri	Richard Perkins	Robert Murnane
Las Vegas	c	CM	535	(702) 229-6011	Oscar Goodman	...	Barbara Ronemus	Mark Vincent	David Washington	Michael Sheldon	Richard Goecke
Laughlin	t	CM	4	(702) 298-0828	...	Jacquelyn Brady	...	...	...	...	...
Mesquite	c	CM	9	(702) 346-5295	Bill Nicholes	Timothy Hacker	Carol Woods	David Empey	Derek Hughes	Douglas Law	Bill Tanner
North Las Vegas	c	CM	115	(702) 633-1000	Michael Montandon	Gregory Rose	Karen Storms	Philip Stoeckinger	Al Gillespie	Mark Paresi	...
Pahrump	t	CM	7	(775) 727-5107	Tim Leavitt	William Kohbarger	...	...	Barry Jennings	...	Gordon Scott
Reno	c	CM	180	(775) 334-2099	Robert Cashell	Charles McNeely	Lynette Jones	Andrew Green	Paul Wagner	Michael Poehlman	Neil Mann
Sparks	c	CM	66	(775) 353-2345	...	Shaun Carey	Deborine Dolan	Terri Thomas	...	John Dotson	Wayne Seidel
Wells	c	CM	1	(775) 752-3355	Rusty Tybo	Jolene Supp	Catherine Smith	Mary Ray	Randy Dedman	La Don Murray	David Linge
West Wendover	c	MC	4	(775) 664-3081	...	Chris Melville	Anna Bartlome	Leon Flinders	Jeffrey Knudtson	Ron Supp	Thomas Stratton
Winnemucca *	c	CM	7	(775) 623-6333	Di An Putnam	Stephen West	Eddy Davis	...	Walt Johnstone	Robert Davidson	Roger Sutton
Yerington	c	MC	2	(775) 463-3511	Doug Homestead	Dan Newell	Colleen Castello	...	...	Rod Pellegrini	Roy McDonald
NEW HAMPSHIRE											
Allenstown	t	TM	4	(603) 485-4276	Sandra McKenney	David Jodoin	Edward Cyr	...	Everett Chaput	James McGonigle	James Boisvert
Alton	t	MC	4	(603) 875-2161	James Washburn	Russell Bailey	Lisa Waterman	Paulette Wentworth	Alan Johnson	Kevin Iwans	Kenneth Roberts
Amherst	t	TM	10	(603) 673-6041	Jay Dinkel	...	Nancy Demers	Merri Howe	John DeSilva	Gary MacGuire	Bruce Berry
Andover *	t	TM	2	(603) 735-5332	Dennis Fenton	Dana Hadley	Marjorie Roy	...	...	...	...
Antrim *	t	CM	2	(603) 588-6785	Robert Flanders	Neal Cass	Donna Hanson	...	Mike Beauchamp	Scott Lester	Jim Cruthers
Ashland	t	CM	1	(603) 968-4432	Glenn Dion	Timothy Cullenen	Patricia Tucker	...	Thomas Stewart	Joseph Chivell	Mark Ober
Atkinson	t	TM	6	(603) 362-5266	...	...	Linda Jetty	Sandra La Velle	Michael Murphy	Philip Consentino	Edward Stewart
Auburn	t	TM	4	(603) 483-5052	Harland Eaton	William Herman	Joanne Linxweiler	Adele Brown	Bruce Phillips	Edward Picard	Michael Dross
Barrington	t	TM	7	(603) 664-9007	George Bailey	Carol Reilly	Sheila Marquette	...	Richard Walker	Richard Conway	Peter Cook
Bedford *	t	CM	18	(603) 472-5242	Paul Roy	Russell Marcoux	Wanda Jenkins	Crystal Dionne	Scott Wiggin	David Bailey	James Stanford
Belmont	t	TM	6	(603) 267-8300	...	...	...	...	...	...	...
Berlin	c	CM	10	(603) 752-7532	Robert Danderson	Patrick Macqueen	Debra Patrick	Blandine Shallow	Randall Trull	Peter Morency	...
Boscawen	t	RT	3	(603) 753-9188	Rhoda Hardy	Sherlene Fisher	...	...	Ray Fisher	David Croft	Richard Hollins
Bow	t	TM	7	(603) 228-1187	Leon Kenison	James Pitts	Jill Hadaway	...	Dana Abbott	Jeff Jaran	Leighton Cleverly
Bristol	t	MC	3	(603) 744-3354	...	R. Weston	Raymah Simpson	Peggy Petraszewski	Norman Skantze	John Clark	Mark Bucklin
Canaan *	t	TM	3	(603) 523-4501	Robert Reagan	Michael Capone	Vicky McAlister	Gloria Koch	William Bellion	Samuel Frank	...
Candia	t	TM	3	(603) 483-8101	Gary York	...	Christine Dupere	...	Rudolph Cartier	Michael McGillen	...
Charlestown	t	RT	4	(603) 826-4400	Brenda Ferland	David Edkins	Debra Clark	Patricia Royce	Gary Stoddard	Edward Smith	...
Chesterfield	t	TM	3	(603) 363-4624	Timothy Butterworth	Ricky Carrier	Shirley Philbrick	...	...	Earl Nelson	Stephen Bevis
Claremont *	c	CM	13	(603) 542-7002	Deborah Cutts	Guy Santagate	Gwendolyn Melcher	Mary Walter	Peter Chase	Alex Scott	Bruce Temple
Colebrook	t	CM	2	(603) 237-4070	Greg Placy	Donna Caron	Sheila Beauchemin	Camilla Stewart	Philip Ducret	Steve Cass	Kevin McKinnon
Concord	c	CM	40	(603) 225-8535	Michael Donovan	Thomas Aspell	Janice Bonenfant	James Howard	Christopher Pope	Jerome Madden	Earle Chesley
Conway	t	TM	8	(603) 447-3811	Gary Webster	Earl Sires	Rhoda Quint	...	...	Jeffrey Dicey	Paul Degliangeli
Derry *	t	CM	34	(603) 432-6100	Richard Metts	Richard Stenhouse	Denise Neale	Frank Childs	George Klauber	Edward Garone	Michael Fowler
Dover	c	CM	26	(603) 516-6000	...	J. Joyal	Judy Gaouette	Jeffrey Harrington	Perry Plummer	William Fenniman	Douglas Steele
Durham	t	CM	12	(603) 868-5571	Malcom Sandberg	Todd Selig	Lorrie Pitt	Paul Beaudon	Ronald O'Keefe	David Kurz	Michael Lynch
Enfield	t	TM	4	(603) 632-5026	...	Steven Schneider	Ilene Reed	...	David Crate	Richard Crate	Timothy Jennings
Epping	t	TM	5	(603) 679-5441	Susan McGeough	...	Linda Foley	...	Henry Letourneau	Gregory Dodge	...
Epsom *	t	TM	4	(603) 736-9002	Robert Blodgett	...	Dawn Blackwell	Nancy Wheeler	R. Yeaton	Wayne Preve	...
Exeter	t	TM	14	(603) 778-0591	Paul Binette	Russell Dean	L. H.-Macomber	Jack Sheehy	Brian Comeau	Richard Kane	Keith Noyes
Farmington	t	TM	5	(603) 755-2208	Gerald McCarthy	Anthony Minscu	Kathy Seaver	...	Richard Fowler	Scott Roberge	Joel Moulton
Franklin	c	CM	8	(603) 934-3900	Anthony Giunta	Elizabeth Corrow	Gayle Cook	Dawn Ouellette	Scott Clarenbach	Brad Haas	Brian Sullivan
Gilford	t	RT	6	(603) 527-4700	Alice Boucher	...	Denise Morrissette	...	Michael Mooney	...	Sheldon Morgan
Goffstown	t	MC	16	(603) 497-8990	Henry Boyle	S. Desruisseaux	...	Janice O'Connell	Paul Nault	Michael French	Carl Quiram
Gorham *	t	TM	2	(603) 466-3322	...	William Jackson	Grace La Pierre	Denise Vallee	George Eichler	Paul Cyr	Austin Holmes
Grantham *	t	MC	2	(603) 863-6021	Harold Haddock	Tina Stearns	Rita Eigenbrode	...	Michael Benoit	Walter Madore	Joseph Newcomb
Greenland	t	RT	3	(603) 431-711	...	Karen Anderson	...	...	...	...	...
Hampstead	t	TM	8	(603) 329-4100	Richard Hartung	Laura Buono	Tina Harrington	...	Walter Hastings	Joseph Beaudoin	Jon Worthen
Hampton *	t	TM	14	(603) 926-6766	James Workman	Frederick Welch	Jane Cypher	Michael Schwotzer	Christopher Silver	James Sullivan	John Price
Hampton Falls	t	TM	1	(603) 926-4618	...	Eric Small	Holly Knowles	...	...	...	...
Hanover *	t	TM	10	(603) 643-0742	Brian Walsh	Julia Griffin	...	...	Roger Bradley	Nicholas Giaccone	Peter Kulbacki
Haverhill *	t	TM	4	(603) 787-6800	Roderick Ladd	Glenn English	Bette Pollock	Jo Lacaillade	...	Jeffrey Williams	...
Henniker	t	RT	4	(603) 428-3221	J. Damour	Kelly Clark	K. Johnson	...	Ben Ayer	T. Russell	T. Woodley
Hillsborough	t	TM	4	(603) 464-3877	Robert Buker	John Stetser	Deborah McDonald	...	David Holmes	David Roarick	...
Hinsdale *	t	RT	4	(603) 336-5710	John Smith	Jill Collins	Tammy-Jean Akeley	...	Robert Johnson	Wayne Gallagher	Frank Podlenski
Hollis	t	RT	7	(603) 465-2780	...	Catharine Hallsworth	Nancy Jambard	Paul Calabria	Richard Towne	Russell Ux	Arthur Leblanc
Hooksett *	t	CM	11	(603) 485-8472	David Dickson	...	Leslie Nepveu	Christine Soucie	Michael Williams	Stephen Agrafiotis	...
Hopkinton	t	TM	5	(603) 746-3170	Barbara Unger	...	Sue Strickford	...	Peter Russell	Ira Midgal	David Story
Hudson	t	CO	22	(603) 886-6024	E. Madison	...	Cecile Nichols	Stephen Malizia	Francis Carpentino	Richard Gendron	Kevin Burns
Jaffrey	t	CM	5	(603) 532-7445	Franklin Sterling	Michael Hartman	Maria Chamberlain	Pamela Bernier	Francis McConnell	Martin Dunn	Randall Heglin
Keene *	c	CM	22	(603) 357-9804	Dale Pregent	John MacLean	Patricia Little	Martha Landry	Gary Lamoureux	Arthur Walker	Kurt Blomquist
Kingston	t	TM	5	(603) 642-3342	Mark Heitz	...	Ann Sullivan	Cindy Kenerson	Bill Seaman	Donald Briggs	Richard St. Hilaire
Laconia	c	CM	16	(603) 524-3877	...	Eileen Cabanel	Ann Kaligian	Pamela Reynolds	Ken Erickson	Tom Oetinger	Frank Tilton
Lancaster	t	TM	3	(603) 788-2114	...	...	...	...	...	...	...
Lebanon	c	CM	12	(603) 448-4220	...	G. Mandsager	Sandi Allard	Leonard Jarvi	Chris Christopoulos	M. James Alexander	Michael Lavalla
Lincoln	t	CM	1	(603) 745-2757	...	Peter Joseph	...	...	...	...	...
Litchfield	t	TM	7	(603) 424-4046	...	...	...	...	...	...	...
Littleton *	t	TM	5	(603) 444-3996	Burton Ingerson	Charles Connell	Judy White	Karen Noyes	Joseph Mercieri	Paul Smith	George Chartier
Londonderry *	t	TM	23	(603) 432-1100	Martin Bove	David Caron	Marguerite Seymour	Susan Hickey	Kevin MacCaffrie	Joseph Ryan	Janusz Czyzowski
Manchester	c	MC	107	(603) 624-6543	Robert Baines	...	Leo Bernier	Kevin Clougherty	Joseph Kane	John Jaskolka	Frank Thomas
Meredith	t	CM	5	(603) 279-4538	...	...	...	...	Charles Palm	John Curran	Michael Faller
Merrimack	t	TM	25	(603) 424-2331	Richard Hinch	Keith Hickey	Diane Pollock	Paul Micali	Michael Currier	Michael Milligan	Edward Chase
Milford	t	TM	13	(603) 673-2257	Noreen O'Connell	Guy Scaife	Margaret Langell	Rosemarie Evans	Francis Fraitzl	Frederick Douglas	William Ruoff
Milton	t	MC	3	(603) 652-4501	Tom Gray	...	Carol Martin	...	Andy Lucier	Mark McGowan	Patrick Smith
Moultonborough	t	CM	4	(603) 476-2347	Ernest Davis	...	Barbara Wakefield	...	Richard Plaisted	Scott Kinmond	Wayne Richardson
Nashua *	c	MC	86	(603) 589-3230	Bernard Streeter	...	Paul Bergeron	Carol Anderson	Roger Hatfield	Donald Gross	...
New Boston	t	CM	4	(603) 487-5504	Harold Strong	...	Margit Hooper	...	James Dodge	James McLaughlin	Lee Murray
New Durham	t	MC	2	(603) 859-2091	Paul Gelinas	...	Carole Ingham	...	...	Douglas Scruton	Mark Fuller
New Ipswich *	t	TM	5	(603) 878-2772	James Coffey	Marie Knowlton	Cynthia Lussier	...	David Leel	W. G. Chamberlain	Peter Goewey
New London	t	TM	4	(603) 526-4821	Ruth Clough	Jessie Levine	Linda Hardy	Carolyn Fraley	Jason Lyon	David Seastrand	Richard Lee
Newbury	t	MC	1	(603) 763-4940	...	Dennis Pavlicek	...	...	...	...	...
Newmarket *	t	CM	8	(603) 659-3617	...	Edward Wojnowski	Becky Benvenuti	Donald Parnell	...	Kevin Cyr	Richard Malasky
Newport	t	TM	6	(603) 863-1360	Gary Nichols	Daniel O'Neill	Karlene Stoddard	Paul Brown	John Marcotte	...	Larry Wiggins
Newton	t	TM	4	(603) 382-4405	John Ulcickas	Nancy Wrigley	Mary Jo McCullough	...	William Ingalls	Lawrence Streeter	Frank Gibbs
North Hampton	t	TM	4	(603) 964-8087	Donald Gould	Stephen Fournier	Susan Uchanan	...	Thomas Lambert	Brian Page	Robert Strout
Northfield	t	TM	4	(603) 286-7039	...	Joyce Fulweiler	...	...	...	...	...
Northumberland	t	CM	2	(603) 636-1450	John Normand	...	Melinda Kennett	...	Terrance Bedell	Lloyd Tippitt	Gregory Kenison
Pelham	t	RT	10	(603) 635-8233	...	...	Dorothy Marsden	Robert Blanchette	David Fisher	Evan Haglund	Donald Foss

Directory 1/9 continued **OFFICIALS IN U.S. MUNICIPALITIES 2,500 AND OVER IN POPULATION**

Jurisdiction		Type	Form of govern-ment	2000 Popu-lation	Main telephone number	Chief elected official	Appointed administrator	Clerk of the governing board	Chief financial officer	Fire chief	Police chief	Public works director
NEW HAMPSHIRE continued												
Pembroke		t	TM	6	(603) 485-4747	Larry Preston	Troy Brown	James Goff	...	Harold Paulsen	Scott Lane	James Boisvert
Peterborough		t	TM	5	(603) 924-8000	Lawrence Ross	Pamela Brenner	Robert Lambert	Nancie Vaihinger	William Naugle	Scott Guinard	Edwin Betz
Pittsfield		t	TM	3	(603) 435-6773	Arthur Morse	Jeremiah Lamson	Elizabeth Hast	...	Gary Johnson	Robert Wharem	George Bachelder
Plaistow		t	CM	7	(603) 382-8469	Barbara Hobbs	...	Barbara Tavitian	Susan Drew	Donald Petzold	Stephen Savage	Daniel Garlington
Plymouth		t	RT	5	(603) 536-1731	Timothy Naro	...	Kathleen Latuch	Karen Freitas	Brian Thibeault	Anthony Raymond	Michael Heath
Portsmouth	*	c	CM	20	(603) 431-2000	Thomas Ferrini	John Bohenko	Kelli Barnaby	Judith Belanger	Christopher LeClaire	Michael Magnant	Steven Parkinson
Raymond		t	TM	9	(603) 895-4735	Franklin Bishop	Christopher Rose	Doris Gagnon	Grace Collette	Kevin Pratt	David Salois	Dennis McCarthy
Rindge		t	TM	5	(603) 899-5181	David Collum	Edgar Gadbois	Nancy Martin	Julie Labonte	Richard Donovan	Michael Sebor	Peter Goewey
Rochester	*	c	CM	28	(603) 332-1167	John Larochelle	John Scruton	Joseph Gray	...	Norman Sanborn	David Dubois	Melodie Esterberg
Rye		t	TM	5	(603) 964-5523	Joseph Mills	...	Jane Ireland	Cynthis Gillespie	Richard O'Brien	Alan Gould	Everett Jordan
Salem		t	CM	28	(603) 890-2000	...	Henry LaBranche	Barbara Lessard	Linda Casey	Arthur Barnes	Paul Donovan	Rodney Bartlett
Sanbornton	*	0	MC	2	(603) 286-8303	Andrew Livernois	Bruce Kneuer	Jane Goss	Curt McGee	Jerry Busby	Mark Barton	John Thayer
Seabrook	*	t	CM	7	(603) 474-3311	Robert Moore	Barry Brenner	Bonnie Fowler	Debra Knowles	Jeffrey Brown	Patrick Manthorn	John Starkey
Somersworth	*	c	CM	11	(603) 692-9503	James McLin	Robert Belmore	Diane Dubois	Scott Smith	Donald Messier	Dean Crombie	John Jackman
Stratham	*	t	TM	6	(603) 772-7391	Martin Wool	Paul Deschaine	Shirley Daley	...	Robert Law	Michael Daley	Fred Hutton
Sugar Hill	*	t	TM	..	(603) 823-8468	Harry Reid	Jennifer Gaudette	Lissa Boissonneault	...	Allan Clark	David Wentworth	Douglas Glover
Sunapee	*	t	CM	3	(603) 763-2212	Richard Leone	Donna Nashawaty	Betty Ramspott	...	Daniel Ruggles	David Cahill	Anthony Bergeron
Sutton		t	CM	1	(603) 927-4416	Thomas Brooks	Elten Phillips	Janet Haines	...	Darrel Palmer	Patrick Tighe	...
Swanzey	*	t	RT	6	(603) 352-7411	Nancy Carlson	Elizabeth Fox	Deirdre Geer	...	Norman Skantze	Richard Busick	Lee Dunham
Temple		t	TM	1	(603) 878-2536	...	Debra Harling	Kathleen Nolte	...	...	...	...
Tilton		t	TM	3	(603) 286-4521	...	...	...	...	Harold Harbour	...	...
Wakefield		t	CM	4	(603) 522-6205	Paul Morrill	Robin Frost	Cynthia Bickford	Kathleen Estabrook	Todd Nason	Tim Merrill	Dan Davis
Walpole		t	TM	3	(603) 756-3672	Sheldon Sawyer	...	Sandra Smith	Teresa Fernette	Richard Hurlburt	David Hewes	James Terell
Weare		t	TM	7	(603) 529-7525	...	...	Evelyn Connor	...	Robert Richards	Gregory Begin	Carl Knapp
Wilton	*	t	TM	3	(603) 654-9451	Jane Farrell	...	...	Gary Crooker	Ray Dick	Brent Hautanen	Stephen Elliott
Winchester		t	RT	4	(603) 239-4951	Gustave Ruth	...	...	...	Barry Kellom	Gary Phillips	Dale Gray
Windham		t	RT	10	(603) 432-7732	...	David Sullivan	...	Dana Call	Steven Fruchtman	...	...
Wolfeboro	*	t	TM	6	(603) 569-8161	Shirley Ganem	David Owen	Patricia Waterman	Peter Chamberlin	Phillip Morrill	Stuart Chase	David Ford
NEW JERSEY												
Aberdeen	*	tp	CM	17	(732) 583-4200	David Sobel	Joseph Criscuolo	Karen Ventura	Angela Morin	...	John Powers	James Lauro
Absecon		c	MC	7	(609) 641-0663	Peter Elco	Terry Dolan	Carie Crone	Jessica Thompson	Stan Kolbe	Charles Smith	Lloyd Jones
Allendale		b	MC	6	(201) 818-4400	Vincent Barra	...	Gwen Gabbert	Paula Favata	Greg Andersen	Robert Herndon	George Higbie
Alpha		b	MC	2	(908) 454-0088	Thomas Fey	...	Bess Embardino	Peter Kowalick	Edward Hanics	John Haidu	Leo Pursell
Andover	*	tp	CM	6	(973) 383-4280	Gail Phoebus	Jayme Alfano	Vita Thompson	Tim Day	...	Phillip Coleman	Darren Dickinson
Asbury Park		c	CM	16	(732) 775-2100	Kenneth Saunders	Terence Reidy	Stephen Kay	Ricardo Diaz	Joseph Mirarchi	Richard Lucherini	Garrett Giberson
Atlantic City		c	MC	40	(609) 347-5300	James Whelan	...	Benjamin Fitzgerald	Joanne Shepherd	Benjamin Brenner	Benn Polk	Richard Norwood
Atlantic Highlands		b	MC	4	(732) 291-1444	Michael Harmon	Adam Hubeny	David Palamara	Catherine Campbell	Russell Mount	Gerard Vasto	...
Audubon		b	CO	9	(856) 547-0711	...	...	...	...	...	...	...
Avalon		b	MC	2	(609) 967-8200	Martin Pagliughi	Andrew Bednarek	Amy Kleuskens	James Craft	...	Stephen Sykes	Harry DeButts
Barnegat		tp	MC	15	(609) 698-0080	...	...	...	...	...	...	...
Barrington		b	MC	7	(856) 547-0706	...	...	Terry Shannon	Denise Moules	Wayne Robenolt	...	...
Bayonne		c	MC	61	(201) 858-6010	Len Kiczek	Harold Demellier	Robert Sloan	Terrance Malloy	William Kosakowski	Francis Pawlowski	Robert Kaminski
Beach Haven		b	MC	1	(609) 492-0111	Deborah Whitcraft	Richard Crane	Judith Howard	Diane Marshall	...	Stanley Markoski	Kim England
Beachwood		b	MC	10	(732) 286-6000	Harold Morris	...	...	...	...	...	...
Bedminster		tp	CM	8	(908) 234-0333	...	Susan Stanbury	Dorothy Wilkie	June Enos	...	William Stephens	Jon Mantz
Belleville	*	tp	CM	34	(973) 450-3300	Gerald DiGori	Victor Canning	Kelley Nash	...	Robert Caruso	Joseph Rotonda	James Messina
Bellmawr		b	MC	11	(609) 933-1313	...	...	...	...	...	...	...
Belmar		b	MC	6	(732) 681-3700	Kenneth Pringle	...	Margaret Plummer	Robbin Kirk	...	Richard Lynch	Anders Meuerle
Bergenfield		b	CM	26	(201) 387-4055	Kevin Clancy	Joseph Hess	...	John Mosca	Charles Hartung	Richard Baroch	Robert Bartley
Berkeley Heights		tp	MC	11	(908) 464-2700	David Cohen	Angela Devanney	Patricia Rapach	Tracy Tedesco	Anthony Padovano	David Zager	...
Berlin		b	MC	6	(856) 767-7777	...	...	...	...	...	...	...
Bernards		tp	CM	24	(908) 766-2510	William Homes	...	Denise Szabo	Dorothy Stikna	...	Thomas Kelly	Michael Beale
Bernardsville		b	MC	7	(908) 766-3000	Hugh Fenwick	Ralph Maresca	...	...	Randy Steinkopf	Thomas Sciaretta	John Mac Dowall
Beverly		c	MC	2	(609) 387-1881	Robert Lowden	...	Barbara Sheipe	...	Cornell Hawkins	...	Daniel Schoen
Bloomfield	*	tp	MC	45	(973) 680-4000	Raymond McCarthy	...	Louise Palagano	Robert Renna	Joseph Intile	Michael Sisco	Gerald MacIntyre
Bloomingdale		b	MC	7	(973) 838-0778	...	...	Jane Febbi	Dave Hollberg	Duane Muldoon	William Alexander	Joe Luke
Bogota		b	MC	8	(201) 342-1736	Steven Lonegan	...	Frances Garlicki	...	David Hanley	Gary Kohles	Robert Stauffer
Boonton		t	MC	8	(973) 402-9410	Edward Bolcar	...	Cynthia Oravits	Jeffery Theriault	John Steinhauser	...	Michael Petonak
Bordentown		c	CO	3	(609) 298-0604	Zigmont Targonski	...	...	...	Steve McGowan	Philip Castagna	Robert Erickson
Bound Brook		b	MC	10	(732) 356-0833	Frank Gilly	Thomas Brodbeck	...	Kathryn Kinney	R. Colombaroni	Kenneth Henderson	Mark Cassebaum
Bradley Beach		b	CO	4	(732) 776-2999	Stephen Schueler	Phyllis Quixley	Mary Ann Solinski	Joyce Wilkins	John Zech	Robert Denardo	Richard Bianchi
Branchburg	*	tp	CM	14	(908) 526-1300	...	Gregory Bonin	Sharon Brienza	Diane Salek	James McAleer	Brian Fitzgerald	Bruce Kosensky
Brick	*	tp	MC	76	(732) 262-1052	Stephen Acropolis	Scott Pezarras	Virginia Lampman	...	...	Ronald Dougard	John Nydam
Bridgeton	*	c	MC	22	(856) 455-3230	James Begley	Arthur Liston	Darlene Richmond	Teresa Delp	David Schoch	Mark Ott	Roy Burlew
Bridgewater	*	tp	MC	42	(908) 725-6300	Patricia Flannery	James Naples	Linda Doyle	Natasha Turchin	...	Richard Borden	John Langel
Brielle	*	b	MC	4	(732) 528-6600	Thomas Nicol	Thomas Nolan	...	Stephen Mayer	Timothy Shaak	Michael Palmer	William Burkhardt
Brigantine	*	c	CM	12	(609) 266-7600	Philip Guenther	...	Lynn Sweeney	Christian Johansen	John Frugoli	James Frugoli	Ernie Purdy
Buena		b	MC	3	(856) 697-9393	...	...	...	...	...	...	...
Burlington	*	c	MC	9	(609) 386-0200	James Fazzone	Eric Berry	Cindy Crivaro	Kenneth MacMillan	Ron Devlin	John Lazzarotti	Vincent Calisti
Butler		b	MC	7	(973) 838-7200	Ronald Assante	James Lampmann	Carol Ashley	James Kozimor	Daniel Canty	Dennis Passenti	Edward Becker
Byram		tp	CM	8	(973) 347-2500	Eskil Danielson	...	Doris Flynn	Theresa Vervaet	Paul Conklin	Ray Rafferty	Adolf Steyh
Caldwell	*	tp	MC	7	(973) 226-6100	Paul Jemas	Maureen Ruane	...	...	...	Kurt Dombrowski	Mario Bifalco
Camden		c	MC	79	(856) 757-7000	Gwendolyn Faison	Christine Tucker	Luis Pastoriza	Richard Wright	Joseph Marini	Edwin Figueroa	Patrick Keating
Cape May		c	CM	4	(609) 884-9525	...	...	Virginia Petersen	Jack Jansen	Bruce Bieber	Robert Boyd	Robert Smith
Carlstadt		b	MC	5	(201) 939-2850	William Roseman	Jane Fontana	Claire Foy	D. Griancaspro	Chris Assenheimer	John Occhiuzzo	Paul Ritchie
Carteret		b	MC	20	(732) 541-3800	...	...	Kathleen Barney	Patrick Deblasio	Brian O'Connor	John Pieczyski	Ted Surick
Cedar Grove		tp	CM	12	(973) 239-1410	...	...	...	...	...	...	...
Chatham		b	MC	8	(973) 635-0674	...	Tom Ciccarone	Susan Caljean	Dorothy Klein	Peter Glogloida	John Drake	Robert Venezia
Cherry Hill		tp	MC	69	(856) 488-7800	...	...	...	...	...	...	...
Chester	*	b	MC	1	(908) 879-5361	Dennis Verbaro	Valerie Egan	...	Vidya Nayak	Steven Feller	Andre Kedrowitsch	Paul Kapral
Cinnaminson		tp	MC	14	(856) 829-6000	Sandra Iaquinto	John Ostrowski	Grace Campbell	...	...	Michael Wallace	Carl Letterie
Clark		tp	MC	14	(732) 388-3600	Sal Bonaccorso	John Laezza	Kathleen Leonard	Robert Stanley	Andrew Beach	Anton Danco	Frances Brattole
Clayton		b	CM	7	(856) 881-2882	Patricia Gannon	...	Christine Newcomb	Donna Nestore	Harry Simpson	N. Winters	Edward Bell
Clementon		b	MC	4	(609) 783-0284	Frederick Busch	...	Patricia Porter	Stephen Considine	Randall Freiling	Robert Getz	Mark Williams
Cliffside Park		b	MC	23	(201) 945-3456	...	...	...	...	...	...	...
Clifton	*	c	CM	78	(973) 470-5800	James Anzaldi	Albert Greco	Barbara Nagy	Jonathan Capp	Jeffrey Adams	Robert Ferreri	Vincent Cahill
Clinton		t	MC	2	(908) 735-8616	...	...	...	...	...	...	...
Clinton		tp	MC	12	(908) 735-8800	Nick Corcodilos	Marvin Joss	...	Ulrich Steinberg	Marc Strauss	...	...
Closter		b	MC	8	(201) 784-0600	Fred Pitofsky	Erik Lenander	Loretta Castano	Joseph Luppino	Thomas Reineke	David Berrian	Rob Stauffer
Collingswood		b	CO	14	(856) 854-0720	M. Maley	Jean Di Gennaro	Alice Marks	Patrick Abusi	Michael Hall	Thomas Garrity	Brad Stokes
Colts Neck		t	MC	12	(732) 462-5470	Albert Yodakis	...	...	John Antonides	Michael Piotrowski	Kevin Sauter	Charles Buck
Commercial		tp	MC	5	(856) 785-3100	...	...	...	Judson Moore	...	...	...
Cranbury		tp	MC	3	(609) 395-0544	...	Christine Smeltzer	K. Cunningham	Kathleen Kovach	...	...	Thomas Witt
Cranford	*	tp	CM	22	(908) 709-7200	George Jorn	Marlena Schmid	Tara Rowley	...	Leonard Dolan	Eric Mason	...

Directory 1/9 continued OFFICIALS IN U.S. MUNICIPALITIES 2,500 AND OVER IN POPULATION

Jurisdiction	Type	Form of govern- ment	2000 Popu- lation	Main telephone number	Chief elected official	Appointed administrator	Clerk of the governing board	Chief financial officer	Fire chief	Police chief	Public works director
NEW JERSEY continued											
Cresskill *	b	MC	7	(201) 569-5400	Benedict Romeo	. . .	Barbara Nasuto	Harold Laufeld	C. Ulshoefer	Steve Lillis	Kevin Terhune
Delanco	tp	MC	3	(856) 461-0561	Kate Fitzpatrick	Steven Corcoran	Janice Lohr	Robert Hundell	Keith Mohrmann	Ed Parsons	. . .
Delran	tp	MC	15	(856) 461-7734	Joseph Stellwag	Jeffrey Hatcher	Bernadette McPhee	. . .	Joseph Bennett	Arthur Saul	. . .
Demarest	b	MC	4	(201) 768-0167	. . .	. . .	. . .	. . .	. . .	. . .	. . .
Dennis	tp	CM	6	(609) 861-9700	Ruth Blessing	J. Alessandrine	Jacqueline Justice	Glenn Clarke	. . .	. . .	Clarence Ryan
Denville	tp	MC	15	(973) 625-8300	. . .	. . .	Donna Costello	Bernard Re	Tracey Egbert	Steven Boepple	Joseph Lowell
Deptford *	tp	CM	26	(609) 845-5300	Paul Medany	Denise Rose	Dina Zawadski	Joanne Strange	. . .	John Marolt	Michael Storms
Dover	t	MC	18	(973) 366-2200	James Dodd	Bibi Garvin	Marge Verga	Kelly Toohey	Edward Ridner	Harold Valentine	Louis Acevedo
Dover	tp	MC	89	(732) 341-1000	Paul Brush	Fred Ebenau	J. Mutter	Christine Manolio	. . .	Michael Mastronardy	Robert Tully
Dumont	b	MC	17	(201) 387-5022	. . .	. . .	John Eckel	. . .	James Yelland	. . .	John Cook
Dunellen *	b	MC	6	(732) 968-3033	Robert Seader	William Robins	. . .	Scott Olsen	Jonathan Scott	Gerard Cappella	Jerry Schaffer
East Brunswick	tp	MC	46	(732) 390-6810	William Neary	James White	Elizabeth Kiss	Louis Neely	. . .	. . .	. . .
East Hanover	tp	MC	9	(973) 428-3000	Lawrence Colasurdo	C. Paduch	Marilyn Snow	Smruti Amin	George Busold	Stanley Hansen	Ray Grossmann
East Orange	c	MC	69	(973) 266-5100	Robert Bowser	Joseph Jenkins	Cynthia Brown	Linda Munro	Leonard McDaniel	Richard Wright	. . .
East Rutherford	b	MC	8	(201) 933-3444	James Cassella	. . .	Darlene Sawicki	Anthony Bianchi	Peter Hodge	. . .	Thomas Miller
East Windsor *	tp	CM	24	(609) 443-4000	Janice Mironov	Alan Fisher	Cindy Dye	Margaret Gorman	James McCann	William Spain	William Askenstedt
Eastampton	tp	CM	6	(609) 267-5723	. . .	Thomas Czerniecki	. . .	. . .	. . .	. . .	. . .
Eatontown	b	MC	14	(732) 389-7621	Gerry Tarantolo	. . .	Karen Naughton	Lesley Connolly	Bill Mego	George Jackson	Nathan Albert
Edgewater *	b	MC	7	(201) 943-1700	Nancy Merse	Gregory Franz	Barbara Rae	Joseph Iannaconi	Joseph Chevalier	Donald Martin	Thomas Quinton
Edison	tp	MC	97	(732) 248-7299	George Spadoro	Anthony Cancro	Reina Murphy	G. Bobal	G. Campbell	Edward Costello	Robert Heck
Egg Harbor	tp	MC	30	(609) 926-4000	James McCullough	Peter Miller	Patricia Indrieri	Charlene Canale	. . .	John Coyle	Lloyd Simerson
Egg Harbor City	c	MC	4	(609) 965-0081	. . .	Joseph Harney	Lillian Debow	Betty Wenzel	. . .	. . .	. . .
Elizabeth	c	MC	120	(908) 820-4000	J. C. Bollwage	Lorraine Dumke	Anthony Pillo	Anthony Zengaro	Edward Sisk	John Simon	John Papetti
Elmwood Park	b	MC	18	(201) 796-1457	Richard Mola	. . .	Dolores Camlet	. . .	Joseph Miklovic	G. Morgan	Joseph Mulligan
Emerson	b	MC	7	(201) 262-6099	Robert Menditto	Joseph Scarpa	Sandra Joaquin	Nancy Burns	Michael Cimino	Peter Mazzeo	Joseph Solimando
Englewood	c	CM	26	(201) 871-6660	Michael Wildes	Daniel Fitzpatrick	Lenore Schiavelli	. . .	Robert Moran	John Banta	Clyde Sweatt
Englewood Cliffs	b	MC	5	(201) 569-5252	Joseph Parisi	Joseph Favaro	. . .	Joseph Iannaconi	George Drimones	T. Bauernschmidt	Rodney Bialko
Essex Fells	b	MC	2	(973) 226-3400	. . .	Amey Upchurch	Francine Paserchia	Kerry Geisler	. . .	Daniel Tapper	Roger Kerr
Evesham	tp	CM	42	(856) 983-2900	Augustus Tamburro	Edward Sasdelli	Carmela Bonfrisco	Paul Thomas	Thaddeus Lowden	Joseph Cornely	Paul Tomasetti
Ewing *	tp	MC	35	(609) 883-2900	Wendell Pribila	David Thompson	Stephen Elliott	John Barrett	. . .	Robert Coulton	. . .
Fair Haven *	b	MC	5	(732) 747-0241	Michael Halfacre	Mary Howell	A. Cinquegrana	Denise Jawidzik	Larry Hartman	. . .	. . .
Fair Lawn *	b	CM	31	(201) 796-1700	Steven Weinstein	J. Kwasniewski	. . .	Barry Eccleston	Thomas Carney	Erik Rose	Ron Conte
Fairfield	tp	MC	7	(973) 882-2700	Rocco Palmieri	Joseph Catenaro	Patricia Fahy	. . .	. . .	Carolyn Centonze	M. deMontaigne
Fairview	b	MC	13	(201) 943-3300	Vincent Bellucci	Diane Testa	. . .	Joseph Rutch	David Masso	John Pinzone	. . .
Fanwood	b	MC	7	(908) 322-8236	. . .	. . .	. . .	. . .	. . .	. . .	. . .
Flemington	b	MC	4	(908) 782-8840	Austin Kutscher	. . .	Robert Hauck	Raymond Krov	Stephen Borucki	Peter Tirpok	Terry Pickering
Florence	tp	MC	10	(609) 499-2525	Michael Muchowski	Richard Brook	Joy Weiler	Sandra Blacker	Edward Kensler	Gordon Dawson	John Purakovics
Florham Park	b	MC	8	(973) 410-5300	Frank Tinari	. . .	Judith Beecher	Donna Mollineaux	Alban Kellogg	Raymond Smith	Carl Ganger
Fort Lee *	b	MC	35	(201) 592-3500	Mark Sokolich	Peggy Thomas	Neil Grant	Joseph Iannaconi	Jeff Bernard	Thomas Ripoli	Anthony Lione
Franklin *	b	MC	5	(973) 827-9280	Paul Crowley	Richard Wolak	Patricia Leasure	Grant Rome	James Nidelko	Joseph Kistle	Mike Gunderman
Franklin	tp	MC	15	(856) 694-1234	David Ferrucci	. . .	Carol Coulbourn	Frances Carder	. . .	Michael DiGiorgio	William Nese
Franklin (Somerset) *	tp	CM	50	(732) 873-2500	Brian Levine	Kenneth Daly	Ann McCarthy	Vandana Khurana	. . .	Craig Novick	. . .
Franklin Lakes	b	MC	10	(201) 891-0048	G. Thomas Donch	. . .	. . .	. . .	. . .	. . .	Brian Peterson
Freehold	b	MC	10	(732) 462-1410	Michael Wilson	Joseph Bellina	Dolores Gibson	Nancy Forman	Forrest Woolford	William Burlew	. . .
Freehold	tp	CM	31	(732) 294-2000	Raymond Kershaw	Thomas Antus	Romeo Cascaes	Debrah Defeo	. . .	Ernest Schriefer	Richard Warren
Galloway	tp	CM	31	(609) 652-3700	Charles Endicott	Thomas Henshaw	Karen Bacon	Jill Gougher	. . .	Keith Spencer	Steve Bonanni
Garfield	c	CM	29	(201) 340-2001	Louis Aloia	Anthony Librizzi	Andrew Pavlica	Soe Myint	Joseph Dymarczyk	. . .	Munzio Santora
Garwood	b	MC	4	(908) 789-0710	Dennis McCarthy	. . .	Christina Ariemma	Sue Wright	Thomas Spera	Dennis Lesak	Jeffrey Atkinson
Gibbsboro	b	MC	2	(609) 783-6655	. . .	. . .	. . .	. . .	. . .	. . .	. . .
Glassboro *	b	MC	19	(856) 881-9230	Leo McCabe	Joseph Brigandi	Patricia Frontino	Josephine Myers	Ralph Johnson	Alex Fanfarillo	Russell Clark
Glen Ridge	tp	MC	7	(973) 748-8400	Thomas Lincoln	Michael Rohal	. . .	. . .	. . .	Robert Wohlgemuth	Jay Weisenbach
Glen Rock	b	MC	11	(201) 670-3956	Richard Hahn	Lenora Benjamin	Jacqueline Scalia	. . .	. . .	Steven Cherry	Richard Van Heest
Gloucester	tp	MC	64	(856) 228-4000	Sandra Love	Thomas Cardis	Rosemary DiJosie	Candace Prince	. . .	John Stollsteimer	Gabriel Busa
Gloucester City	c	MC	11	(856) 456-0205	Robert Gorman	John Lipsett	Paul Kain	Frank Robertson	William Glassman	Theodore Howarth	James Johnson
Green Brook	tp	CM	5	(732) 968-1023	Patricia Walsh	. . .	. . .	David Dickinson	Allen Sprague	Martin Rasmussen	. . .
Guttenberg	t	MC	10	(201) 868-2315	David DelleDonna	. . .	Linda Martin	Patrick De Blasio	. . .	. . .	Michael Ronchi
Hackensack *	c	CM	42	(201) 646-3980	Michael Melfi	. . .	Debra D'Auria	. . .	Thomas Freeman	Charles Zisa	Jesse D'Amore
Hackettstown	t	MC	10	(908) 852-3130	John Di Maio	. . .	William Kuster	Jeffrey Theriault	Edward Howell	Leonard Kunz	Thomas Kitchen
Haddon	tp	CO	14	(856) 854-1176	William Park	. . .	Denise White	James Clark	. . .	Joseph Gallager	. . .
Haddon Heights	b	MC	7	(856) 547-7164	Susan Griffith	. . .	Joan Moreland	Ernest Merlino	Steve Kinky	Ronald Shute	Donald Witzig
Haddonfield *	b	CM	11	(856) 429-4700	Letitia Colombi	Sharon McCullough	Deanna Speck	Terry Henry	Joseph Riggs	Richard Tsonis	Howard Frazier
Hainesport	tp	MC	4	(609) 267-2730	Ronald Corn	Paul Tuliano	Rita Schuster	Douglas Ayrer	William Wiley	. . .	Jay Jones
Haledon	b	MC	8	(973) 595-7766	James Van Sickle	. . .	Allan Susen	Janet Wolons	. . .	. . .	Angelo Passafaro
Hamilton *	tp	MC	20	(609) 625-1511	Nelson Gaskill	Edward Sasdelli	Joan Anderson	Richard Tuthill	. . .	Jay McKeen	Robert Morley
Hamilton	tp	MC	87	(609) 890-3500	Glen Gilmore	. . .	Christina Wilder	Richard Serini	. . .	James Collins	Jeffrey Moyer
Hammonton	t	MC	12	(609) 567-4300	. . .	. . .	. . .	. . .	. . .	. . .	. . .
Harding *	tp	MC	3	(973) 267-8000	. . .	Gail McKane	Amanda Gildersleeve	Himanshu Shah	. . .	K. Gaffney	Tracy Toribio
Hardyston	tp	CM	6	(973) 823-7020	Leslie Hamilton	Marianne Smith	Jane Bakalarczyk	Grant Rome	. . .	Keith Armstrong	Robert Schulz
Harrington Park *	b	MC	4	(201) 768-1700	Paul Hoelscher	. . .	Susan Nelson	Anne Murphy	. . .	David Moppert	Mark Kiernan
Harrison	t	MC	14	(973) 268-2425	. . .	. . .	. . .	. . .	. . .	. . .	. . .
Hasbrouck Heights	b	MC	11	(201) 288-0195	William Torre	Michael Kronyak	Rose Marie Sees	Paul Garbarini	Robert Thomasey	Michael Colaneri	Robert Heck
Haworth	b	MC	3	(201) 384-4785	John De Rienzo	Ann Fay	. . .	Rebecca Overgaard	. . .	. . .	Martin Mahon
Hawthorne	b	MC	18	(973) 427-5555	Fred Criscinelli	. . .	P. Mele	MaryJeanne Hewitt	Joseph Speranza	Martin Boyd	. . .
Hazlet *	tp	MC	21	(732) 264-1700	Kevin Lavan	Michael Muscillo	Evelyn Grandi	Catherine Campbell	Frank Olivia	James Broderick	David Rooke
High Bridge	b	MC	3	(908) 638-6455	Alfred Schweikert	William Wahl	. . .	Bonnie Fleming	Craig Van Natta	Edward Spinks	Mark Banks
Highland Park	b	MC	13	(732) 572-3400	Meryl Frank	Karen Waldron	Janet Potenza	Nick Trasente	Jay Littman	. . .	Lloyd Young
Highlands	b	MC	5	(732) 872-1515	. . .	. . .	. . .	. . .	. . .	. . .	. . .
Hightstown *	b	MC	5	(609) 490-5100	Robert Patten	. . .	Candace Gallagher	George Lang	John Archer	James Eufemia	Larry Blake
Hillsdale	b	MC	10	(201) 666-4800	Timothy O'Reilly	Harold Karns	Robert Sandt	Colleen Ennis	Kimberly Saul	Frank Mikulski	Keith Durie
Hillside	tp	MC	21	(973) 926-3000	Karen McCoy Oliver	. . .	Janet Vlaisavljevic	. . .	Joe Behnke	Robert Quinlan	Scott Anderson
Hoboken	c	MC	38	(201) 420-2059	. . .	. . .	. . .	. . .	. . .	. . .	. . .
Ho-Ho-Kus	b	MC	4	(201) 652-4400	Rusty Thompson	C. Henderson	Judith Odo	. . .	. . .	Gregory Kallenberg	Michael Frank
Holmdel	tp	MC	15	(732) 946-2820	Larry Fink	. . .	Maureen Shepherd	Joseph Annecharcio	Ronald Pontrelli	Robert Phillips	Jeffrey Smith
Hopatcong *	b	MC	15	(973) 770-1200	Sylvia Petillo	Joseph Moskovitz	Lorraine Stark	Kelleyann McGann	C. Steinmetz	John Swanson	Ronald Jobeless
Hopewell	tp	MC	16	(609) 737-0605	Francesca Bartlett	. . .	Annette Bielawski	Elaine Borges	. . .	Michael Chipowsky	. . .
Howell *	tp	CM	48	(732) 938-4500	Joseph DiBella	Helene Schlegel	Bruce Davis	Jeff Filiatreault	. . .	Ronald Carter	Jeffrey Cramer
Irvington	tp	MC	61	(973) 399-8111	Wayne Smith	. . .	Harold Wiener	D. Timothy Roberts	Donald Huber	Michael Damiano	Wayne Bradley
Jackson	tp	CO	42	(732) 928-1281	Michael Broderick	. . .	Ann Eden	Lily Farley	. . .	. . .	Sergio Panunizo
Jamesburg	b	MC	6	(732) 521-2222	Joseph Dipierro	. . .	Gretchen Schauer	Jo Ann Olenik	John Miller	. . .	Wallace Fisher
Jefferson	tp	MC	19	(973) 697-1500	Russell Felter	James Leach	Lydia Magnotti	William Eagen	. . .	John Palko	David Hansen
Jersey City	c	MC	240	(201) 547-5000	Glenn Cunningham	Brian O'Reilly	Robert Byrne	Paul Soyka	Frederick Eggers	Robert Troy	John Yurchak
Keansburg	b	CM	10	(732) 787-0215	. . .	. . .	. . .	. . .	Andrew Murray	. . .	. . .
Kearny	t	MC	40	(201) 955-7400	Alberto Santos	Joseph D'Arco	Jill Waller	Shuaib Firozvi	Steven Dyl	John Dowie	Gerald Kerr
Kenilworth	b	MC	7	(908) 276-9090	Michael Tripodi	. . .	Hedy Lipke	Dianne Marus	Lou Giordino	Don Tisch	Dan Ryan
Keyport	b	MC	7	(732) 739-3900	. . .	Lorene Wright	Judith Poling	Thomas Fallon	. . .	Theodore Gajewski	George Sappah

Directory 1/9 continued — OFFICIALS IN U.S. MUNICIPALITIES 2,500 AND OVER IN POPULATION

Jurisdiction	Type	Form of govern-ment	2000 Popu-lation	Main telephone number	Chief elected official	Appointed administrator	Clerk of the governing board	Chief financial officer	Fire chief	Police chief	Public works director
NEW JERSEY continued											
Kinnelon	b	MC	9	(973) 838-5401	Glenn Sisco	. . .	Mary Ricker	. . .	. . .	John Finkle	Jeffrey LaPooh
Lakehurst	b	CM	2	(732) 657-4141	. . .	. . .	. . .	. . .	. . .	. . .	. . .
Lakewood	tp	CM	60	(732) 364-2500	Marta Harrison	Frank Edwards	B. Standowski	William Rieker	. . .	. . .	John Franklin
Lambertville	c	MC	3	(609) 397-0110	David Del Vecchio	. . .	Mary Sheppard	Linda Monteverde	Robert Hayes	Bruce Cocuzza	Paul Cronce
Lawnside	b	MC	2	(856) 573-6202	. . .	Jessie Harris	Sylvia Van Nockay	. . .	. . .	. . .	Alex Barr
Lawrence	tp	CM	29	(609) 844-7000	Gregory Puliti	Richard Krawczun	Kathleen Norcia	. . .	. . .	Daniel Posluszny	Gregory Whitehead
Leonia	b	MC	8	(201) 592-5743	. . .	. . .	. . .	. . .	. . .	. . .	. . .
Lincoln Park	b	MC	10	(973) 694-6100	David Baker	Joseph Maielle	Annette Smith	Dennis Gerber	Dan Moeller	Kenneth West	Tom Piorkowski
Linden	c	MC	39	(908) 474-8479	John Gregorio	. . .	Val Imbriaco	. . .	William Konecny	John Miliano	John Mesler
Lindenwold	b	MC	17	(609) 783-2121	Frank Delucca	. . .	Jane Barber	Helen Gielda	. . .	Frank McHenry	Robert Lodovici
Linwood	c	MC	7	(609) 927-4108	R. DePamphilis	Kenneth Mosca	Leigh Ann Napoli	Bonnie Tiemann	. . .	Charles Desch	Walter Jones
Little Egg Harbor	tp	MC	15	(609) 296-7241	. . .	. . .	. . .	. . .	. . .	. . .	. . .
Little Falls	tp	MC	11	(973) 256-0170	Janice Sandri	. . .	Joan Skal	Kathy Albanese	Edmond Pomponio	. . .	Phillip Simone
Little Ferry	b	MC	10	(201) 641-9234	. . .	C. Navarro-Steinel	Barbara Maldonado	. . .	. . .	. . .	John Bladek
Little Silver	b	TM	6	(732) 842-2400	. . .	. . .	. . .	. . .	. . .	. . .	. . .
Livingston	tp	CM	26	(973) 992-5000	David Katz	Michele Meade	Renee Green	. . .	Craig Dufford	Donald Jones	Michael Anello
Lodi	b	MC	23	(201) 365-4005	. . .	. . .	. . .	. . .	. . .	. . .	. . .
Long Branch	c	MC	31	(732) 222-7000	. . .	Howard Woolley	Irene Joline	Ronald Mehlhorn	. . .	. . .	Fred Migliaccio
Long Hill *	tp	MC	8	(908) 647-8000	George Vitureira	Richard Sheola	Christine Gatti	. . .	. . .	Daniel Hedded	. . .
Lower	tp	CM	22	(609) 886-2005	Larry Starner	. . .	Claudia Kammer	Lauren Read	. . .	John Maher	Gary Douglass
Lyndhurst	tp	CO	18	(201) 804-2457	Richard DiLascio	. . .	Helen Polito	Deborah Ferrato	Keith Carroll	James O'Connor	Brian Haggerty
Madison *	b	MC	16	(973) 593-3042	. . .	Raymond Codey	Marilyn Schaefer	Robert Kalafut	Douglas Atchison	Vincent Chirico	David Maines
Magnolia	b	MC	4	(609) 783-1520	B. Cowling-Carson	. . .	P. Joyce Harrum	Dorothea Jones	. . .	Robert Doyle	Steven Pacella
Mahwah	tp	MC	24	(201) 529-5757	Richard Martel	Brian Campion	Doris Perez	Kenneth Sesholtz	Elmore Wilson	. . .	Stanley Spiech
Manalapan	tp	MC	33	(732) 446-3200	Mary Cozzolino	. . .	Rose Ann Weeden	. . .	. . .	John McCormack	John Lewis
Manasquan	b	MC	6	(908) 223-0544	. . .	John Trengrove	Colleen Scimeca	Joanne Madden	. . .	Daniel Scimeca	James Coder
Manchester	tp	MC	38	(732) 657-8121	. . .	. . .	. . .	. . .	. . .	. . .	. . .
Manville *	b	MC	10	(908) 725-9478	Lillian Zuza	Kathryn Kinney	. . .	Lori Majeski	Thomas Collins	Mark Peltack	Philip Petrone
Maple Shade	tp	CM	19	(856) 779-9610	Gerald Mornell	George Haeuber	Patricia Berger	Donna Gallagher	. . .	Edmund Vernier	Arthur Dees
Maplewood *	tp	CM	23	(973) 762-8120	Fred Profeta	Joseph Manning	Elizabeth Fritzen	Peter Fresulone	Dennis Carragher	Robert Cimino	Gary Lenci
Margate City *	c	CO	8	(609) 822-2605	Michael Becker	Thomas Hiltner	. . .	Lisa McLaughlin	John Kelley	David Wolfson	Daniel Campbell
Marlboro	tp	MC	36	(732) 526-0200	. . .	. . .	. . .	. . .	. . .	. . .	. . .
Matawan *	b	MC	8	(732) 290-2000	Bea Duffy	. . .	Jean Montfort	Monica Antista	James Bishop	Robert McGowan	Anthony Bucco
Maywood	b	MC	9	(201) 845-2900	Thomas Murphy	Jack Terhune	Mary Rampolla	. . .	John Gargagliano	Patrick Reynolds	. . .
Medford	tp	CM	22	(609) 654-2608	Lisa Post	Michael Achey	Joyce Frenia	Katherine Burger	. . .	James Kehoe	George Snyder
Medford Lakes *	b	CM	4	(609) 654-8898	Paul Weiss	Geoffrey Urbanik	. . .	Donna Condo	. . .	Frank Martine	Patrick McCorriston
Mendham	b	CM	5	(973) 543-7152	Richard Kraft	Ralph Blakeslee	Maureen Massey	Susan Giordano	Joseph Eible	Patricia Cameron	Thomas Miller
Mendham	tp	CM	5	(973) 543-4555	. . .	Stephen Mountain	Penny Newell	Heather Webster	. . .	Thomas Costanza	David Read
Merchantville	b	MC	3	(609) 662-2474	. . .	. . .	. . .	. . .	. . .	. . .	. . .
Metuchen	b	CM	12	(732) 632-8540	Edmund O'Brien	William Boerth	Bozena Lacina	Lori Majeski	Robert Donnan	. . .	Kenneth O'Brien
Middlesex	b	MC	13	(732) 356-7400	. . .	. . .	Kathleen Anello	. . .	Edward Winters	James Benson	Jerry Schaefer
Middletown	tp	CM	66	(732) 615-2000	Joan Smith	A. Mercantante	Heidi Abs	Robert Roth	William Hibell	John Pollinger	Lawrence Werger
Midland Park *	b	MC	6	(201) 445-5720	Ester Vierheilig	Michelle Dugan	Adeline Hanna	. . .	Peter Hook	John Cassone	Rudolph Gnehm
Millburn *	tp	CM	19	(973) 564-7075	Thomas McDermott	Timothy Gordon	Joanne Monargue	Jason Gabloff	Michael Roberts	P. Boegershausen	Peter Gallitelli
Milltown	b	MC	7	(732) 828-2100	. . .	. . .	. . .	. . .	. . .	. . .	. . .
Millville	c	CO	26	(856) 825-7000	James Quinn	Lewis Thompson	. . .	R. Charlesworth	. . .	. . .	Vicki Marshall
Monmouth Beach	b	CO	3	(732) 229-2204	. . .	. . .	. . .	. . .	. . .	. . .	. . .
Monroe	tp	MC	27	(732) 521-4400	. . .	Wayne Hamilton	Sharon Doerfler	George Lang	. . .	. . .	. . .
Montclair *	tp	CM	37	(973) 509-4939	Gerald Fried	Joseph Hartnett	Linda Wanat	Gordon Stelter	Kevin Allen	David Sabagh	Steven Wood
Montgomery *	tp	CM	17	(908) 359-8211	Cecilia Birge	Donato Nieman	Donna Kukla	Walter Shepard	. . .	Robert Palmer	Arthur Villano
Montvale	b	CM	7	(201) 391-5700	George Zeller	John Doyle	Maureen Alwan	. . .	. . .	Joseph Marigliani	Robert Culvert
Montville	tp	CM	20	(973) 331-3300	Marie Cetrulo	. . .	Gertrude Atkinson	Frances Vanderhoof	. . .	Richard Cook	. . .
Moonachie	b	MC	2	(201) 641-1813	Frederick Dresser	Paul Hansen	Jean Finch	. . .	Richard Behrens	Michael McGahn	Henry Van Saders
Moorestown *	tp	CM	19	(856) 235-0912	Kevin Aberant	Christopher Schultz	Patricia Hunt	Thomas Merchel	. . .	Harry Johnson	Kenneth Ewers
Morris Plains	b	MC	5	(973) 538-2224	. . .	. . .	June Uhrin	David Banks	. . .	Douglas Scherzer	Joseph Signorelli
Morristown	t	MC	18	(973) 292-6626	John Delaney	. . .	William Chambers	Robert Calise	David Barter	Carol Williams	Jeffrey Hartke
Mount Arlington	b	MC	4	(973) 398-6832	Arthur Ondish	Joanne Sendler	Linda DeSantis	Allan Dickinson	. . .	Richard Peterson	John Tappen
Mount Ephraim	b	CO	4	(856) 931-1546	. . .	. . .	Mildred Salamone	Dorothea Jones	Mario Scullan	Christopher Ferrari	Anthony Chambers
Mount Holly	tp	CM	10	(609) 267-0170	Brooke Tidswell	Kathleen Hoffman	. . .	Christina Chambers	David Gsell	. . .	Ronald Crain
Mount Laurel	tp	CM	40	(856) 234-0001	Mark Sanchirico	Patricia Halbe	. . .	Linda Lewis	. . .	David Haas	Everett Johnson
Mount Olive	tp	MC	24	(973) 691-0900	David Scapicchio	Bill Sohl	Lisa Lashway	Sherry Jenkins	. . .	Mark Spitzer	Tim Quinn
Mountain Lakes	b	CM	4	(973) 334-3131	Jud Breslin	Gary Webb	Christina Whitaker	Dona Mooney	. . .	Robert Tovo	Mark Prusina
Mountainside	b	MC	6	(908) 232-2400	. . .	. . .	Judith Osty	Jill Goode	. . .	James Debbie	Robert Farley
National Park	b	MC	3	(609) 845-3891	. . .	. . .	. . .	. . .	. . .	. . .	. . .
Neptune	tp	CM	27	(732) 988-5200	James Manning	Philip Huhn	Richard Cottrell	Michael Bascom	. . .	James Ward	Richard Bormann
Neptune City	b	MC	5	(732) 776-7224	Robert Deeves	Joel Popkin	. . .	William Folk	Mark Balzarano	William Geschke	Gerrit Devos
Netcong	b	MC	2	(973) 347-0252	Nicholas Pompilio	Marvin Joss	D. Dalessandro	Jason Gabloff	. . .	. . .	Robert Olivo
New Brunswick	c	MC	48	(732) 745-5008	Jim Cahill	Thomas Loughlin	Daniel Torrisi	Douglas Petix	. . .	. . .	. . .
New Hanover	tp	CO	9	(609) 758-7149	. . .	. . .	. . .	. . .	. . .	. . .	. . .
New Milford *	b	MC	16	(201) 967-5044	Frank Debari	Christine Demiris	Colleen Naumov	. . .	John Stormer	Frank Papapietro	Michael Calamari
New Providence	b	MC	11	(908) 665-1400	Harold Weideli	Douglas Marvin	. . .	James Testa	Kevin Kennedy	James Venezia	John Meyer
Newark	c	MC	273	(973) 733-6400	Cory Booker	Michelle Thomas	Robert Marasco	Linda Dunn-Landofi	Lowell Jones	Anthony Ambrose	. . .
Newton	t	CM	8	(973) 383-3521	Philip Diglio	. . .	Lorraine Read	Eileen Kithcart	Christopher Blakely	John Tomasula	Christopher Bond
North Arlington	b	MC	15	(201) 991-6060	Russell Pitman	Terence Wall	Martin Gobbo	Timothy Roberts	Mark Cunningham	Louis Ghione	James McCabe
North Bergen	tp	CO	58	(201) 392-2000	Nicholas Sacco	Christopher Pianese	Carol Fontana	Robert Pittfield	. . .	. . .	Timothy Grossi
North Brunswick	tp	MC	36	(732) 247-0922	Francis Womack	Robert Lombard	Lisa Gerhartz	Ronald Amorino	Craig Snediker	Joseph Battaglia	Glenn Sandor
North Caldwell	tp	MC	7	(973) 228-6410	Melvine Levine	John Kosko	. . .	Richard Modelli	. . .	Joseph Clark	Frank Zichelli
North Haledon	b	MC	7	(973) 427-7793	Randy George	. . .	Lucille Debiak	. . .	. . .	Joseph Ferrante	. . .
North Plainfield *	b	MC	21	(908) 769-2902	Michael Giordano	David Hollod	. . .	Patrick DeBlasio	William Eaton	William Parenti	James Rodino
North Wildwood	c	MC	4	(609) 522-2030	Aldo Palombo	. . .	Jane Parson	Helen Gielda	Thomas McGarry	Gary Sloan	Timothy O'Leary
Northfield	c	MC	7	(609) 641-2832	Frank Perri	. . .	Carol Raph	Marilyn Dolcy	. . .	Kenneth Adams	James Clark
Northvale	b	MC	4	(201) 767-3330	. . .	. . .	. . .	. . .	. . .	. . .	. . .
Norwood	b	MC	5	(201) 767-7200	Gus D'Ercole	. . .	Lorraine McMackin	Maureen Neville	Scott Roberts	Frank D'Ercole	Camilo DiRese
Nutley	tp	CO	27	(973) 284-4951	Joanne Cocchiola	. . .	E. Rosario-Garcia	Rosemary Costa	Thomas Peters	John Holland	Peter Scarpelli
Oakland	b	CM	12	(201) 337-8111	J. Kendall	Charles Smiley	Lenore Tully	. . .	David Jeltes	James O'Connor	. . .
Oaklyn	b	MC	4	(609) 858-2457	Michael Lamaina	. . .	Marie Hawkins	. . .	Fred Garbrecht	Christopher Ferrari	Enrico Storino
Ocean	tp	CM	26	(732) 531-5000	William Larkin	Andrew Brannen	Deborah Smith	Stephen Gallagher	. . .	Antonio Amodio	Lawrence Iverson
Ocean City	c	MC	15	(609) 399-6111	Henry Knight	James Rutala	Angela Pileggi	John Hansen	Joe Foglio	Robert Blevin	George Savastano
Oceanport	b	MC	5	(732) 222-8221	. . .	. . .	. . .	. . .	. . .	. . .	. . .
Ogdensburg	b	MC	2	(973) 827-3444	J. Pietrodangelo	. . .	Phyllis Drouin	Michelle LaStarza	Michael Franek	George Lott	Kenneth Smith
Old Bridge *	tp	CM	60	(732) 721-5600	James Phillips	Michael Jacobs	R. Marie Saracino	. . .	. . .	Thomas Collow	Rocco Donatelli
Old Tappan *	b	MC	5	(201) 664-1849	Victor Polce	Patrick O'Brien	Jean Quinn	Rebecca Overgaard	Nicola LePore	Joseph Fasulo	Arthur Lake
Oradell	b	MC	8	(201) 261-8200	Frederick LaMonica	Wolfgang Albrecht	Laura Graham	Roy Rossow	David Gangemi	Rhynie Emanuel	Robert Stauffer
Orange Township	c	MC	29	(973) 266-4245	Mims Hackett	. . .	Dwight Mitchell	John Kelly	. . .	Edward Lucas	Robert Corrado
Palisades Park	b	MC	17	(201) 585-4100	Sandy Farber	. . .	Martin Gobbo	Roy Riggitano	George Beck	John Genovese	James Burns

Directory 1/9 continued — OFFICIALS IN U.S. MUNICIPALITIES 2,500 AND OVER IN POPULATION

Jurisdiction	Type	Form of govern-ment	2000 Popu-lation	Main telephone number	Chief elected official	Appointed administrator	Clerk of the governing board	Chief financial officer	Fire chief	Police chief	Public works director
NEW JERSEY continued											
Palmyra	b	MC	7	(856) 829-6100	Robert Leather	Marianne Hulme	Grace Carr	...	Richard Derby	Robert Fow	Brian McCleary
Paramus	b	MC	25	(201) 265-2100	...	...	Ian Shore	Joseph Citro	...	Fred Corrubia	Brian Koenig
Park Ridge	b	MC	8	(201) 573-1800	Donald Ruschman	Gregory Franz	...	Ann Kilmartin	...	R. Oppenheimer	William Beattie
Parsippany-Troy Hills	tp	MC	50	(973) 263-4294	Michael Luther	Jasmine Lim	Judith Silver	Ruby Malcolm	...	Michael Peckerman	Robert Schneider
Passaic	c	MC	67	(973) 365-5500	Samuel Rivera	Gregory Hill	W. S.-Shabaka	...	Louis Imparato	Stanley Jarensky	Theodore Evans
Paterson	c	MC	149	(973) 321-1310	Jose Torres	Eli Burgos	J. Williams Warren	Margaret Cherone	James Pasquariello	Lawrence Spagnola	Manuel Ojeda
Paulsboro	b	MC	6	(856) 423-1500	John Burzichelli	...	Kathy Van Scoy	John Salvatore	Gary Stevenson	Kenneth Ridinger	...
Pemberton	tp	MC	28	(609) 894-8201	Robert McCullough	David Thompson	Mary Young	John Schoenberg	...	Stephen Emery	Frank Chapman
Pennington	b	MC	2	(609) 737-0276	...	...	...	...	...	...	...
Penns Grove	b	MC	4	(856) 299-0098	Paul Morris	...	Sharon Williams	Stephen Labb	Joseph Grasso	Gary Doubledee	Santiago Rosario
Pennsauken	tp	CM	35	(609) 665-1000	Jack Killion	Bob Cummings	Patrica Gudis	Ronald Crane	Gene Sheppard	John Coffey	John Figueroa
Pequannock	tp	CM	12	(973) 835-5700	Lawrence Blomberg	Kevin Boyle	Elizabeth Eley	David Hollberg	Bryan Daley	William Montono	Charles McKearnin
Perth Amboy	c	MC	47	(732) 826-0290	Joseph Vas	Donald Perlee	Elaine Kiczula	Jill Goldy	Lawrence Cattano	Michael Kohut	Kenneth Schwartz
Phillipsburg	t	MC	15	(908) 454-5500	Thomas Corcoran	Frank Tolotta	Michele Broubalow	Joseph Hriczak	...	James Mac Aulay	...
Pine Hill	b	MC	10	(609) 783-7400	Curtis Noe	...	Joan Schneebele	...	...	Judd Booker	Robert McGlinchey
Piscataway	tp	MC	47	(732) 562-2308	Brian Wahler	...	Ann Nolan	Victoria Miragliotta	...	Kevin Harris	Joseph Scranton
Pitman	b	MC	9	(609) 589-3522	Bruce Ware	...	...	Earl Kelly	Ray Kelley	Scott Campbell	Edward Lewis
Plainfield	c	CM	47	(908) 753-3219	Albert McWilliams	Marc Dashield	Laddie Wyatt	Peter Sepelya	Cecil Allen	Edward Santiago	Priscilla Castles
Plainsboro *	tp	MC	20	(609) 799-0909	Peter Cantu	Robert Sheehan	Carol Torres	Wendy Wulstein	...	Richard Furda	Neil Blitz
Pleasantville *	c	MC	19	(609) 484-3600	Ralph Peterson	Marvin Hopkins	Gloria Griffin	Ted Freedman	Leroy Borden	Duane Comeaux	Robert Oglesby
Point Pleasant	b	CM	19	(732) 892-3434	Martin Konkus	David Maffei	...	Judith Block	Daniel Mulligan	Raymond Hilling	Dennis Sears
Point Pleasant Beach	b	MC	5	(732) 892-1118	Thomas Vogel	...	MaryAnn Ellsworth	Christine Riehl	...	Daniel DePolo	Robert Meany
Pompton Lakes	b	MC	10	(973) 835-0144	John Murrin	Lawrence Pollex	Carol Kehoe	...	Albert Evangelista	Albert Ekkers	Ben Steltzer
Princeton	b	MC	14	(609) 924-3118	Marvin Reed	Robert Bruschi	Andrea Quinty	Decimus Marsh	...	Charles Davall	Wayne Carr
Princeton	tp	CM	16	(609) 924-5176	Phyllis Marchand	James Pascale	Linda McDermott	John Clawson	...	Anthony Gaylord	...
Prospect Park	b	MC	5	(973) 790-7902	William Kubofcik	B. Varcadipone	Yancy Wazirmas	Stephen Sanzari	Douglas Struyk	Frank Franco	Kenneth Valt
Rahway	c	MC	26	(732) 827-2000	James Kennedy	Bob Gorman	Jean Kuc	Frank Ruggiero	Edward Fritz	Kevin White	John Ross
Ramsey	b	MC	14	(201) 825-3400	John Scerbo	Nicholas Saros	Nancy Ecke	Richard Mathieson	George Sutherland	Joseph Delaney	William Horton
Randolph	tp	CM	24	(973) 989-7100	Jon Huston	John Lovell	Frances Bertrand	Michael Soccio	James Reynolds	James McLagan	...
Raritan	b	MC	6	(908) 231-1300	Anthony Hudak	Daniel Jaxel	Pamela Heufner	Carolyn Gara	Carl Memoli	Michael Sniscak	A. DiGiuseppantonio
Raritan *	tp	CM	19	(908) 806-6100	John King	Allan Pietrefesa	Dorothy Gooditis	...	Michael Mangin	Glenn Tabasko	Dirk Streuning
Red Bank	b	MC	11	(732) 530-2740	...	Stanley Sickels	Carol Vivona	Bruce Loversidge	...	James Clayton	J. Buonacquista
Ridgefield	b	MC	10	(201) 943-5215	Anthony Suarez	Roberta Stern	Stewart Veale	...	John Hoffman	John Bogovich	N. Gambardella
Ridgefield Park	v	CO	12	(201) 641-4950	...	...	...	...	...	...	...
Ridgewood *	v	CM	24	(201) 670-5500	David Pfund	James Ten Hoeve	Heather Mailander	Dorothy Stikna	James Bombace	William Corcoran	...
Ringwood	b	CM	12	(973) 962-7037	Theodore Taukus	...	...	...	...	Armando Dimuzio	Edward Haack
River Edge	b	MC	10	(201) 599-6300	James Kirk	...	Grace Gutekunst	...	George O'Connell	Ronald Starace	John Pusterla
River Vale	tp	MC	9	(201) 664-2346	George Paschalis	Robert Galeone	Roy Blumenthal	Roy Rossow	...	Aaron Back	Peter Wayne
Riverdale	b	MC	2	(973) 835-4060	...	...	...	...	...	...	...
Riverside	tp	CO	7	(856) 461-0284	James Ott	...	Patricia Collinsworth	Deborah Crowe	...	...	Eric March
Riverton	b	MC	2	(856) 829-0120	Robert Martin	...	Mary Longbottom	Marianne Hulme	Scott Reed	Robert Norcross	...
Rochelle Park	tp	CO	5	(201) 587-7730	...	...	Virginia De Maria	Joseph Manzella	Sal Antista	Richard Zavinsky	John Tanucilli
Rockaway	b	MC	6	(973) 627-2000	...	...	...	...	...	...	...
Rockaway *	tp	MC	22	(973) 627-7200	Louis Sceusi	Gregory Poff	Mary Cilurso	Lisa Palmieri	Robert Jenkins	Walter Ardin	Edward Hollenbeck
Roseland	b	MC	5	(973) 403-6030	...	Thomas Kaczynski	...	Maureen Chumacas	Kent Yates	Richard McDonough	Gary Schall
Roselle	b	MC	21	(908) 245-5600	Garrett Smith	Cheryl Fuller	Rhona Bluestein	Kenneth Blum	Robert Hill	Peter DeRose	Carl Bowles
Roselle Park	b	MC	13	(908) 245-6222	Joseph Delorio	...	Arlene Triano	Gregory Mayers	Joseph Signorello	Warren Wielgus	Frank Wirzbicki
Roxbury	tp	CM	23	(973) 448-2007	Fred Hall	Christopher Raths	Betty De Croce	Lisa Spring	Michael Piccitto	Mark Noll	...
Rumson	b	MC	7	(732) 842-3300	...	...	...	...	...	...	...
Runnemede	b	MC	8	(856) 939-5161	...	...	...	...	...	...	...
Rutherford	b	MC	18	(201) 460-3000	B. McPherson	Leslie Shenkler	Mary Kriston	Edward Cortright	Donald Tomko	Edward Caughey	Douglas Adamo
Saddle Brook *	tp	MC	13	(201) 843-7100	Raymond Santalucia	Robert Elia	Peter LoDico	Durene Ayers	Charles Cerone	Robert Kugler	Charles Cerone
Saddle River	b	MC	3	(201) 327-2609	Conrad Caruso	Charles Cuccia	Marie Macari	...	Brian Yates	Tim McWilliams	Bruce Mautz
Salem	c	MC	5	(856) 935-0372	...	...	Barbara Wright	David Crescenzi	John Ayars	Ronald Sorrell	Fred Mucci
Sayreville	b	MC	40	(732) 390-7000	Kennedy O'Brien	Jeffrey Bertrand	Theresa Farbaniec	Wayne Kronowski	Robert Lasko	John Garbowski	Bernard Bailey
Scotch Plains	tp	CM	22	(908) 322-6700	...	Michael Capabianco	Barbara Riepe	Lori Majeski	Jonathon Ellis	Marshall Nelson	Walter Di Nizo
Sea Girt	b	MC	2	(732) 449-9433	Edward Ahern	...	...	...	...	Edward Sidely	Kevin Thompson
Sea Isle City	c	CO	2	(609) 263-4461	Leonard Desiderio	...	Theresa Tighe	...	...	H. Muller	...
Secaucus	t	MC	15	(201) 330-2000	Anthony Just	...	Geraldine Morgan	Margaret Barkala	Charles Oplach	Dennis Corcoran	Michael Gonnelli
Shrewsbury	b	MC	3	(732) 741-4200	Emilia Siciliano	...	Lynn Neil	Lesley Connolly	...	John Wilson	Robert Wentway
Somerdale	b	MC	5	(609) 783-6320	...	...	...	...	...	...	...
Somers Point	c	MC	11	(609) 927-9088	Tony Martin	William Swain	Carol Degrassi	John Hansen	Frank Denan	Orville Mathis	Richard Gray
Somerville *	b	MC	12	(908) 725-2300	David Hollod	Ralph Sternadori	...	Janet Kelk	Bruce Kessler	Dennis Manning	Peter Hendershot
South Amboy	c	MC	7	(732) 727-4600	...	...	...	...	...	...	...
South Bound Brook	b	MC	4	(732) 356-0258	Jo Anne Schubert	...	Donald Kazar	Randy Bahr	Michael Tomaro	Robert Verry	Ken Pine
South Brunswick	tp	CO	37	(732) 329-4000	Frank Gambatese	Matthew Watkins	Barbara Gut	Ralph Palmieri	Robert Davidson	Michael Paquette	Raymond Olsen
South Orange Village *	tp	CO	16	(973) 378-7715	Douglas Newman	John Gross	Lynn Cucciniello	...	Jeffrey Markey	James Chelel	Mario Luciani
South Plainfield	b	MC	21	(732) 754-9000	Daniel Gallagher	...	James Eckert	Ronald Zilinski	John Mocharski	...	Joseph Glowacki
South River *	b	MC	15	(732) 257-1999	Raymond Eppinger	Andrew Salerno	Pat O'Connor	K. Sivananthan	Peter Swecanski	Wesley Bomba	George Lyons
South Toms River	b	MC	3	(732) 349-0403	...	...	...	...	...	...	...
Southampton	tp	MC	10	(609) 859-2676	James Young	...	...	Nancy Gower	...	...	Charles Oatman
Sparta *	tp	CM	18	(973) 729-4493	Brian Brady	Henry Underhill	Miriam Tower	Mike Ganrino	...	Ernie Reigstadt	Jim Zepp
Spotswood	b	MC	7	(732) 251-0700	Barry Zagnit	Ron Fasanello	Patricia De Stefano	Barbara Petren	Jason Michels	Karl Martin	Patrick Pacyna
Spring Lake	b	MC	3	(732) 449-0800	Thomas Byrne	...	Mary Anne Coogan	Susan Schreck	...	Robert Dawson	Robert Winemiller
Spring Lake Heights	b	MC	5	(732) 449-3500	...	...	Claire Barrett	...	...	...	Arthur Herner
Springfield	tp	RT	13	(973) 912-2200	Sy Mullman	...	Kathleen Wisniewski	Marie Sedlak	William Gras	William Chisholm	Kenneth Homlish
Stafford	tp	CM	22	(609) 597-1000	Carl Block	Paul Shives	Bernadette Park	Suzanne Babcock	...	Larry Parker	Ronald Cop
Stanhope	b	MC	3	(973) 347-0159	Diana Kuncken	Richard Stewart	Antoinette Battaglia	...	Jeff Jozowski	Steven Pittigher	William Storms
Stratford	b	MC	7	(856) 783-0600	Thomas Angelucci	John Keenan	...	John Fabritiis	Stephen Gagliardi	John Brown	Frank Gagliardi
Summit	c	MC	21	(908) 522-3600	Jordan Glatt	Christopher Cotter	David Hughes	Ronald Angelo	James Connelly	Robert Lucid	Paul Cascais
Teaneck *	tp	CM	37	(201) 837-4807	...	...	L. A.-Hernandez	Anthony Bianchi	Robert Montgomery	Robert Wilson	...
Tenafly	b	CM	13	(201) 568-6100	Peter Rustin	Joseph Di Giacomo	Nancy Hatten	Karen Palermo	Richard Philpott	Michael Bruno	J. Robert Beutel
Tinton Falls	b	MC	15	(732) 542-3400	Peter Maclearie	William Dempsey	Karen Mount-Taylor	Stephen Pfeffer	...	Gerald Turning	John Bucciero
Totowa	b	MC	9	(973) 956-1000	...	...	...	...	...	...	...
Trenton	c	MC	85	(609) 989-3000	Douglas Palmer	Renee Haynes	...	Ronald Zilinski	Richard Laird	Joseph Santiago	Eric Jackson
Union	tp	MC	50	(908) 688-2800	Joseph Florio	Frank Bradley	Eileen Birch	Debbie Cyburt	Frederic Fretz	Thomas Kraemer	...
Union Beach	b	MC	6	(732) 264-2277	...	...	...	...	...	...	...
Union City	c	CO	67	(201) 348-5754	Raul Garcia	...	Michael Licameli	Jorge Carmona	Thomas Tormey	Paul Hanak	Sergio Panunzio
Upper Saddle River	b	MC	7	(201) 327-2196	Nicholas Rotonda	Michael Mariniello	Rose Vido	...	...	Theodore Preusch	Craig Rossiter
Ventnor City *	c	CO	12	(609) 823-7900	Timothy Kreischer	Andrew McCrosson	Sandra Biagi	Barry Ludy	Bertram Sabo	Wayne Arnold	David Smith
Vernon	tp	CM	24	(973) 764-4055	...	Melinda Carlton	Patricia Lycosky	Monica Goscicki	...	Roy Wherry	David Pullis
Verona *	tp	MC	13	(973) 239-3220	Robert Detore	Joseph Martin	Evelyn Hill	Dorothy Trimmer	Pat McEvoy	Douglas Huber	...
Vineland	c	MC	56	(856) 794-4000	Perry Barse	Paul Trivellini	Keith Petrosky	Mary Chalow	Peter Finley	Mario Brunetta	Joseph Bond
Waldwick	b	MC	9	(201) 652-5300	Rick VanderWende	Gary Kratz	Paula Jaegge	Mary Viviani	Joseph Alvarez	Mark Messner	Joseph Agugliaro
Wall	tp	MC	25	(732) 449-8444	Edward Thompson	Joseph Verruni	Lorraine Kobacz	Stephen Mayer	...	Roy Hall	Kenneth Critchlow
Wallington	b	MC	11	(973) 777-0318	Walter Wargacki	Witold Baginski	...	Charles Cuccia	Ken Friedman	Anthony Benevento	...

Directory 1/9 continued — **OFFICIALS IN U.S. MUNICIPALITIES 2,500 AND OVER IN POPULATION**

Jurisdiction	Type	Form of govern-ment	2000 Popu-lation	Main telephone number	Chief elected official	Appointed administrator	Clerk of the governing board	Chief financial officer	Fire chief	Police chief	Public works director
NEW JERSEY continued											
Wanaque	b	MC	10	(973) 839-3000	Warren Hagstrom	Thomas Carroll	Katherine Falone	Maryann Brindisi	Scott Montegari	John Reno	. . .
Wantage	tp	MC	10	(973) 875-7192	Paul Grau	James Doherty	. . .	Michelle Lastarza	Parker Space	. . .	Bob Wagner
Warren	tp	RT	14	(908) 753-8000	Victor Sordillo	Mark Krane	Patricia DiRocco	S. Boswell	. . .	William Stahl	Ewald Friedrich
Washington	b	CM	6	(908) 689-3600	M. VanDeursen	John Corica	Linda Hendershot	Kay Stasyshan	Joseph Fox	George Cortellesi	John Burd
Washington (Bergen)	tp	MC	9	(201) 664-4404	Rudolph Wenzel	. . .	. . .	. . .	. . .	. . .	. . .
Washington (Glcstr)	tp	MC	47	(856) 589-0520	Randy Davidson	. . .	Leticia Lamonica	Mary Breslin	Everett Hoffman	Frances Burke	Kenneth Patrone
Washington (Morris) *	tp	MC	17	(908) 876-3315	Kennethson Short	Dianne Gallets	. . .	Kevin Lifer	Michael Cuccaro	Ted Ehrenburg	Scott Frech
Washington (Warren)	tp	MC	6	(908) 689-7200	John Horensky	. . .	Mary O'Neil	C. Gangaware	James Vergos	James McDonald	Peter De Boer
Watchung	b	MC	5	(908) 756-0080	Albert Ellis	Laureen Fellin	. . .	William Hance	Steve Peterson	John Frosoni	Charles Gunther
Wayne	tp	MC	47	(973) 694-1800	David Waks	Neal Bellet	Katherine Pusterla	Robert Miller	. . .	Raymond Riga	. . .
Weehawken	tp	CO	12	(201) 319-6005	Richard Turner	James Marchetti	Theresa Ulrich	Laurie Cotter	Edward Flood	Jeffrey Welz	Orlando Giusto
West Caldwell	tp	MC	10	(973) 226-2300	Joseph Tempesta	Benedict Martorana	. . .	Russell Jarger	Charles Holden	Charles Tubbs	William Frint
West Deptford	tp	CM	19	(856) 845-4004	Anna Docimo	. . .	Raymond Sherman	Richard Giuliani	. . .	Craig Mangano	Edward Phelps
West Long Branch *	b	MC	8	(732) 229-1756	Janet Tucci	. . .	Lori Cole	Gail Watkins	Michael Ciaglia	Arthur Cosentino	Earl Reed
West Milford *	tp	CM	25	(973) 728-7000	. . .	. . .	Antoinette Battaglia	Arthur Magnotti	. . .	Paul Costello	Gerald Storms
West New York	t	CO	45	(201) 295-5100	Albio Sires	Richard Turner	Carmela Riccie	Darren Maloney	. . .	Silverio Vega	Lawrence Riccardi
West Orange	tp	MC	39	(973) 325-4050	John McKeon	John Sayers	Nancy O'Hara	Edward Coleman	. . .	James Abbott	Leonard Lepore
West Paterson	b	MC	10	(973) 345-8100	Pat Lepore	. . .	. . .	Joseph McCluskey	Joseph Macones	Joseph Renne	George Galbraith
West Windsor	tp	MC	21	(609) 799-2400	Shing-Fu Hsueh	Christopher Marion	Sharon Young	Joanne Louth	. . .	Joseph Pica	George Spille
Westfield	t	MC	29	(908) 789-4040	. . .	James Gildea	. . .	. . .	. . .	. . .	. . .
Westville	b	MC	4	(856) 456-0030	William Packer	William Bittner	Richard Burr	. . .	. . .	Frederick Lederer	. . .
Westwood *	b	MC	10	(201) 664-7100	John Birkner	Robert Hoffmann	Karen Hughes	Raymond Herr	Robert Saul	Frank Regino	Richard Woods
Wharton	b	MC	6	(973) 361-8444	Leo Finnegan	Jon Rheinhardt	G. Voight-Cherna	. . .	Kyle Door	Anthony Fernandez	Walter VanKirk
Wildwood	c	MC	5	(609) 522-2444	Bernie Troiano	. . .	Patricia Rhodes	Jeanette Powers	Conrad Johnson	Joseph Fisher	. . .
Wildwood Crest	b	CO	3	(609) 522-3843	John Pantalone	Kevin Yecco	. . .	Stephen Ritchie	Jack Holland	Thomas Sinsheimer	Joyce Gould
Willingboro	tp	CM	36	(609) 877-2200	Eddie Campbell	Joanne Diggs	Marie Annese	. . .	Anthony Burnett	Donna Dimitri	Richard Brevogel
Woodbine	b	MC	2	(609) 861-2153	William Pikolycky	. . .	Frances Pettit	Sharon McCullough	Douglas Watkins	. . .	Clarence Ryan
Woodbridge	tp	MC	97	(732) 634-4500	Frank Pelzman	Robert Landolfi	John Mitch	Margaret Gorman	. . .	William Trenery	Gerald MacIntyre
Woodbury	c	MC	10	(609) 845-1300	. . .	. . .	. . .	. . .	. . .	. . .	. . .
Woodbury Heights	b	MC	2	(856) 848-2832	. . .	. . .	. . .	. . .	. . .	. . .	. . .
Woodcliff Lake	b	MC	5	(201) 391-4977	. . .	. . .	Darlene Schnure	Gene Vinci	. . .	. . .	Edward Barboni
Woodlynne *	b	MC	2	(856) 962-8300	J. Coyle	. . .	Veronica Gitto	Joanne Mitcho	Kenneth Steward	John Ragan	Robert Kenny
Wood-Ridge *	b	MC	7	(201) 939-0202	Paul Calocino	. . .	Diane Thornley	Doris Marek	Anthony Gentile	Joseph Rutigliano	John Sabia
Woodstown	b	MC	3	(856) 769-2200	Richard Pfeffer	. . .	Jeanette Gerlack	James Hackett	Carl Castagliuolo	George Lacy	Frank Mitchell
Woolwich	tp	MC	3	(856) 467-2666	. . .	. . .	. . .	. . .	. . .	. . .	. . .
Wrightstown	b	MC	. .	(609) 723-4450	Jozsef Farago	. . .	Donna Snyder	Barbara Petren	. . .	. . .	. . .
Wyckoff	tp	CM	16	(201) 891-7000	Joseph Fiorenzo	Robert Shannon	Joyce Santimauro	Diana Lindner	Rick Alnor	John Ydo	Scott Fisher
NEW MEXICO											
Alamogordo *	c	CM	35	(505) 439-4399	Donald Carroll	Matt McNeile	Renee Cantin	Lee Ann Nichols	. . .	. . .	Brian Cesar
Albuquerque	c	MC	448	(505) 768-3700	Martin Chavez	Bruce Perlman	Millie Santillanes	Anna Lamberson	Robert Ortega	Ray Schultz	Leonard Garcia
Angel Fire	v	MC	1	(505) 377-3232	Alvin Clanton	Melissa Vossmer	Elizabeth Sanchez	. . .	Orlando Sandoval	William Kitts	Marvin Sheriff
Artesia	c	MC	10	(505) 746-2122	Daniel Reyes	. . .	Barbara Kilough	. . .	. . .	. . .	. . .
Aztec *	c	CM	6	(505) 334-7600	Mike Arnold	David Velasquez	Rebecca Howard	John Gallegos	Burt Bennett	Michael Heal	Steve Christensen
Bayard	v	MC	2	(505) 537-3327	Rudolfo Martinez	. . .	Kristina Ortiz	. . .	. . .	Ascencion Manzano	Eddie Sedillos
Belen	t	CM	6	(505) 864-8221	Ronnie Torres	Sally Garley	. . .	Mildred Garley	Lenor Pena	Lawrence Romero	John Duran
Bernalillo *	t	CM	6	(505) 867-3311	Patricia Chavez	Stephen Jerge	Ida Fierro	Santiago Chavez	John Estrada	Fred Radosevich	. . .
Bloomfield	c	MC	6	(505) 632-6300	. . .	Keith Johnson	Carol Miller	Kevin Rodolph	George Duncan	Andrew Standley	Curtis Lynch
Bosque Farms	v	MC	3	(505) 869-2358	Wayne Ake	. . .	. . .	. . .	Spencer Wood	Joe Stidham	Dominic Romero
Carlsbad	c	CM	25	(505) 887-1191	Gary Perkowski	Arthur Burgess	. . .	Pearlene Bradshaw	Thomas Duffin	James Koch	. . .
Clayton	t	CM	2	(505) 374-8331	Garth Boyce	Harry Staven	Theresa Gard	. . .	Fred Sinclair	Scott Julian	Judson Davis
Cloudcroft	v	MC	. .	(505) 682-2411	David Venalbe	Michael Nivison	Patricia Taylor	. . .	. . .	Gene Green	. . .
Clovis	c	CM	32	(505) 769-7828	David Lansford	Joe Thomas	. . .	Leigh Melancon	Sam McCallie	Bill Carey	Harry Wang
Corrales *	v	MC	7	(505) 897-0502	Philip Gasteyer	Nora Scherzinger	. . .	Renee Ward	Anthony Martinez	Ray Vigil	Tony Tafoya
Deming *	c	MC	14	(575) 546-8848	. . .	Richard McInturff	. . .	Stephen Duran	David Kinman	Michael Carillo	Louis Jenkins
Elephant Butte	c	MC	1	(575) 744-4892	. . .	Alan Briley	. . .	. . .	. . .	. . .	. . .
Espanola *	c	CM	9	(505) 747-6100	Joseph Maestas	Veronica Albin	Lucas Gautier	. . .	John Kitchen	. . .	Leroy Archuleta
Eunice	c	MC	2	(505) 394-2576	James Brown	. . .	Dawn Money	. . .	Jerry Harper	Kevin Burnam	Larry Haase
Farmington	c	CM	37	(505) 599-1132	William Standley	Robert Mayes	Gina Morris	Herman Mason	Robert Martin	Mike Burridge	Joseph Schmitz
Gallup	c	CM	20	(505) 863-1221	Robert Rosebrough	. . .	Ruth Ruiz	. . .	Louis Chavez	Daniel Kneale	Stanley Henderson
Grants *	c	CM	8	(505) 287-7927	. . .	. . .	. . .	. . .	. . .	. . .	. . .
Hobbs	c	CM	28	(505) 397-9229	Monty Newman	Eric Honeyfield	Kristi Parker	Roger Hines	Brady Graham	Tony Knott	Scott Bussell
Jal	c	MC	1	(505) 395-3340	Mary Claiborne	. . .	Skeet Posey	. . .	Ronnie Walls	Larry Burns	Frederick Seifts
Las Cruces	c	CM	74	(505) 528-3401	William Mattiace	Terrence Moore	Shirley Clark	Mark Sutter	Adolf Zubia	Harry Romero	Michael Johnson
Las Vegas	c	CM	14	(505) 454-1401	Tony Martinez	. . .	Ronald Maestas	Ann Gallegos	Robert Gonzales	Albert Mares	Benny Romero
Lordsburg	c	CM	3	(505) 542-3421	Arthur Smith	. . .	Irene Galvan	. . .	. . .	John McDonald	. . .
Los Lunas	v	MC	10	(505) 865-9689	Louis Huning	Phillip Jaramillo	. . .	Monica Clarke	Atilano Chavez	Nick Balido	Betty Behrend
Los Ranchos De Albuquerque	v	MC	5	(505) 344-6582	Harry Stowers	Juan Vigil	Annabelle Martinez	Sylvia Pesce	. . .	. . .	Dale Addison
Lovington *	c	CM	9	(505) 396-2884	Dixie Drummond	Mike Leighton	Rhonda Jones	. . .	James Williams	Chan Kim	. . .
Milan	v	MC	1	(505) 285-6694	Thomas Ortega	Carlos Montoya	. . .	. . .	Keith Austin	Jerry Stephens	Ben Chavez
Portales *	c	CM	11	(575) 356-6662	Orlando Ortega	Debi Lee	Joan Terry	. . .	John Bridges	Jeffrey Gill	Thomas Howell
Questa	v	CM	1	(505) 586-0694	Malaquias Rael	Brent Jaramillo	. . .	. . .	Max Ortega	Frank Gallegos	Joey Vigil
Raton	c	CM	7	(505) 445-9551	Joe Apache	. . .	Michael Lannon	. . .	Dave Pasquale	Vincent Mares	Pete Mileta
Rio Rancho	c	MC	51	(505) 891-5000	James Owen	James Jimenez	Christina Gonzales	Richard Kristof	. . .	. . .	Kenneth Curtis
Roswell *	c	CM	45	(575) 624-6700	Sam LaGrone	John Capps	David Kunko	Larry Fry	James Salas	Robert Smith	John Miscavage
Ruidoso *	v	CM	7	(505) 258-4343	L. Nunley	Dan Higgins	Irma Nava	Michael Steininger	Thomas Gavin	Wolfgang Born	Randall Camp
Ruidoso Downs	c	MC	1	(505) 378-4422	Bob Miller	. . .	. . .	. . .	. . .	. . .	Dan Gens
Santa Fe	c	CM	62	(505) 955-6601	Larry Delgado	Galen Buller	Yolanda Vigil	Kathryn Raveling	Chris Rivera	Beverly Lennen	. . .
Santa Rosa	c	MC	2	(505) 472-3404	Joseph Campos	Timothy Dodge	Carol Tapia	Yolanda Garcia	. . .	James Moncayo	. . .
Silver City	t	CM	10	(505) 538-3731	Terry Fortenberry	. . .	Jane Toumajanian	Alex Brown	Rudy Bencomo	John Calender	Peter Pena
Socorro	c	MC	8	(505) 835-0240	. . .	. . .	Pat Salome	. . .	Robert Brunson	Johnnie Trujillo	. . .
Sunland Park	c	MC	13	(505) 589-7565	. . .	Malcolm Wilson	Juan Fuentes	. . .	Robert Monsivaiz	Ricardo Perez	. . .
Taos	t	MC	4	(505) 751-2000	Bobby Duran	Daniel Miera	Renee Lucero	Marietta Fambro	Eric Montoya	Eddie Lucero	Francisco Espinoza
Taos Ski Valley	v	CM	. .	(505) 776-8220	. . .	Susan Steele	. . .	. . .	. . .	. . .	. . .
Truth Or Consequences	c	CM	7	(575) 894-6673	. . .	. . .	. . .	. . .	. . .	. . .	. . .
Tucumcari *	c	CM	5	(505) 461-3451	Antonio Apodaca	. . .	J. Maddaford	John Garcia	Michael Cherry	Roger Hatcher	. . .
Tularosa	v	MC	2	(505) 585-2771	Demetrio Montoya	. . .	Dianna Brusuelas	Louanne Garcia	Robert Chavez	Frank Sackman	Trinidad Guilez
NEW YORK											
Airmont *	v	MC	7	(845) 357-8111	Dennis Kay	. . .	Irene Murphy	. . .	. . .	. . .	. . .
Akron	v	MC	3	(716) 542-9636	Ray Perkins	Daniel Borchert	. . .	. . .	. . .	Richard Lauricella	Robert Kowalik
Albany	c	MC	95	(518) 434-5075	Gerald Jennings	Philip Calderone	John Marsolais	Christopher Hearley	James Larson	James Turley	. . .
Albion *	v	MC	7	(585) 589-9176	. . .	. . .	Linda Babcock	. . .	Eric Bradsahw	Dean London	Dale Brooks
Alfred *	v	MC	3	(607) 587-9188	Craig Clark	. . .	. . .	Kathryn Koegel	. . .	Timothy O'Grady	James McNulty

Directory 1/9 continued

OFFICIALS IN U.S. MUNICIPALITIES 2,500 AND OVER IN POPULATION

Jurisdiction		Type	Form of govern-ment	2000 Popu-lation	Main telephone number	Chief elected official	Appointed administrator	Clerk of the governing board	Chief financial officer	Fire chief	Police chief	Public works director
NEW YORK continued												
Amherst		t	MC	116	(716) 631-7000	Satish Mohan	...	Susan Jaros	Frank Belliotti	...	John Askey	...
Amityville		v	MC	9	(631) 264-6000	Peter Imbert	Diane Sheridan	...	Donna Barnett	Arthur Smith	Woodrow Cromarty	Bruce Hopper
Amsterdam		c	MC	18	(518) 841-4300	John Duchessi	...	Jane Di Caprio	Kim Brumley	Richard Liberti	Thomas Brownell	Raymond Halgas
Ardsley	*	v	CM	4	(914) 693-1550	Jay Leon	George Calvi	Barbara Berardi	...	Richard Thompson	Emil Califano	Louis Pascone
Attica		v	MC	2	(585) 591-0898	...	...	...	...	...	...	...
Auburn	*	c	CM	28	(315) 255-4146	Timothy Lattimore	Mark Palesh	Debra McCormick	Lisa Green	Michael Hammon	Gary Giannotta	Gerald Del Favero
Avon	*	v	MC	2	(585) 226-8118	Thomas Freeman	...	Patricia Baker	...	Jeremy Batzel	James Carney	John Barrett
Babylon		v	MC	12	(631) 669-1500	E. Conroy	...	Patricia Carley	...	James Anderson	...	Charles Gardner
Babylon		t	MC	211	(631) 957-3000	...	...	...	...	...	...	...
Baldwinsville		v	MC	7	(315) 635-3521	...	...	...	...	...	...	...
Ballston Spa		v	MC	5	(518) 885-5711	...	...	Patricia Bowers	Mary Munday	...	Charles Koenig	Joseph Thompson
Batavia		t	MC	5	(585) 343-1729	...	...	Teressa Morasco	Gregory Post	...	...	...
Batavia		c	CM	16	(585) 345-6300	...	Jason Molino	...	...	...	...	B. Walker
Bath		v	MC	5	(607) 776-3811	...	...	Florence Mulcahy	...	...	David Rouse	Matthew Benesh
Bayville		v	MC	7	(516) 628-1439	...	...	...	...	...	...	...
Beacon		c	MC	13	(845) 838-5000	Clara Gould	Meredith Robson	Carla Eylers	Toni Tracy	Dennis Lahey	Richard Sassi	Robert Riley
Bedford		t	MC	18	(914) 864-0045	Lee Roberts	...	Lisbeth Fumagalli	Patricia Ploss	...	Chris Menzel	...
Bellport		v	MC	2	(631) 286-0327	Frank Trotta	...	...	...	...	...	...
Binghamton		c	MC	47	(607) 772-7000	Matthew Ryan	...	Eric Denk	Beverly Palmer	Clifford Colgan	...	Lou Kelly
Blasdell		v	CM	2	(716) 822-1921	...	Ernest Jewett	Sandra Corcoran	...	...	...	Robert Bushen
Briarcliff Manor		v	CM	7	(914) 944-2782	Peter Chatzky	...	Christine Dennett	...	William Ventura	Ronald Trainham	Robert Ferreira
Brighton	*	t	MC	35	(585) 784-5250	Sandra Frankel	...	Susan Kramarsky	Paula Parker	...	Thomas Voelkl	Thomas Low
Brightwaters	*	v	MC	3	(631) 665-1280	...	...	...	...	...	...	...
Brockport	*	v	MC	8	(585) 637-5300	Morton Wexler	...	Leslie Morelli	...	Christian McCullough	Daniel Varrenti	Harry Donahue
Bronxville		v	CM	6	(914) 337-6500	Mary Marvin	Harold Porr	...	...	...	Brian Downey	Rocco Circosta
Brookville		v	MC	2	(516) 626-1792	Richard Goodwin	Nancy Graikoski	...	...	...	...	...
Buffalo		c	MC	292	(716) 851-4841	Anthony Masiello	...	...	...	Kevin Comerford	...	...
Camden		v	MC	2	(315) 245-0560	Cristen Harlander	...	Tamara Bonomo	...	...	Richard Paul	Jerry Williamson
Camillus	*	t	MC	23	(315) 488-1335	Mary Ann Coogan	...	M. D.-McMahon	...	...	Tom Winn	...
Canandaigua	*	c	CM	11	(585) 396-5000	Ellen Pomimeni	Kay James	...	...	Matthew Snyder	Jonathan Welch	Louis Loy
Canastota		v	MC	4	(315) 697-7559	Mark Lavonas	Bernadette Andaloro	Sena Clarke	...	Douglas Chandler	Guy Blazier	Ronald Bennett
Canisteo		v	MC	2	(607) 698-2711	...	...	...	...	...	...	...
Canton	*	v	MC	5	(315) 386-2871	Charlotte Ramsay	...	...	...	...	...	Brien Hallahan
Carthage		v	CO	3	(315) 493-1060	G. McIlroy	...	Linda Weir	...	William Blunden	Reevie Rockhill	Daniel Trembley
Catskill		v	MC	4	(518) 943-3830	...	...	Carolyn Pardy	...	...	Roger Masse	Lewis O'Connor
Cayuga Heights	*	v	MC	3	(607) 257-1238	James Gilmore	...	Norma Manning	...	George Tamborelle	Thomas Boyce	Brent Cross
Cazenovia	*	v	MC	2	(315) 655-3041	Thomas Dougherty	...	Katherine Burns	...	Samuel Usborne	David Amico	William Carr
Cedarhurst		v	MC	6	(516) 295-5770	...	...	...	...	...	...	...
Chestnut Ridge		v	MC	7	(914) 425-2805	Jerome Kobre	Florence Mandel	...	...	Walter Morris	...	...
Chittenango		v	MC	4	(315) 687-3936	Robert Freunscht	...	Jill Doss	...	...	Jeffrey Paul	Raymond Snyder
Cobleskill		v	MC	4	(518) 234-3891	William Gilmore	...	Sheila Hay-Gillespie	...	Douglas Angle	Michael O'Brien	Thomas Fissell
Cohoes		c	MC	15	(518) 237-7641	John McDonald	...	Lori Yando	Michael Durocher	Joseph Fahd	Bill Heslin	Kenneth Radliff
Colonie		v	MC	7	(518) 869-7562	...	...	...	...	...	...	...
Colonie		t	MC	79	(518) 783-2734	...	...	...	...	...	...	...
Corinth		v	MC	2	(518) 654-2012	...	...	...	...	...	...	...
Corning		c	CM	10	(607) 962-8148	Alan Lewis	Mark Ryckman	Rose Blackwell	Margaret Horn	William Cummings	Richard Faulisi	Richard Biggio
Cornwall-On-Hudson		v	MC	3	(845) 534-4200	Joseph Gross	...	Jeanne Mahoney	...	Jeffrey Armitage	Charles Williams	...
Cortland		c	MC	18	(607) 756-7312	Mary Leonard	...	William Wood	William Damiano	Dennis Baron	James Nichols	C. Bistocchi
Cortlandt		t	MC	38	(914) 734-1000	Linda Puglisi	...	Joann Dyckman	Glenn Cestaro	...	...	Richard McIntyre
Coxsackie		v	MC	2	(518) 731-2718	Henry Rausch	...	Angela Wilsey	...	Robert Frank	...	John Halsted
Croton-On-Hudson		v	CM	7	(914) 271-4848	Gregory Schmidt	Abraham Zambrano	Pauline DiSanto	...	Gary Diggs	Dennis Coxen	Kenneth Kraft
Dannemora		v	MC	4	(518) 492-7000	Michael Bennett	...	Donna Taylor	...	Richard Akey	...	Thomas Tripp
Dansville	*	v	MC	4	(585) 335-5330	William Dixon	Keith Petti	Donna Clark	...	...	...	...
Delhi		v	MC	2	(607) 746-2258	David Truscott	...	Margaret Reinman	...	Gerard Garofollow	Robert Walsh	David Curley
Depew		v	MC	16	(716) 683-1400	Robert Kucewicz	...	Joan Priebe	Elizabeth Melock	Michael Pelleterri	James Brennan	John Wojcik
Dobbs Ferry		v	MC	10	(914) 693-2203	Brian Monahan	...	Elizabeth Dreaper	...	Dennis Roth	George Longworth	James Dunn
Dolgeville		v	MC	2	(315) 429-3112	...	...	Tammy Chmielewski	...	...	Howard Lanphier	...
Dunkirk	*	c	MC	13	(716) 366-0452	Richard Frey	...	William Tuggle	...	Keith Ahlstrom	David Ortolano	Anthony Gugino
East Aurora		v	CM	6	(716) 652-6000	David DiPierto	Kimberly LaMarche	...	...	Roger LeBlanc	Ronald Krowka	Matthew Hoeh
East Hills		v	MC	6	(516) 621-5600	Michael Koblenz	Donna Gooch	...	...	...	Barry Lamb	Carmine Ceriello
East Rochester		v	CM	6	(585) 586-3553	...	...	...	...	...	...	...
East Rockaway	*	v	MC	10	(516) 887-6300	Edward Sieban	John Mirando	...	...	Robert Klose	...	John Keating
East Syracuse		v	MC	3	(315) 437-3541	Lorene Dadey	...	Patricia Derby	...	...	Douglas Robertson	Ronald Russell
East Williston		v	MC	2	(516) 746-0782	Nancy Zolezzi	Jeanne Lyons	...	...	John McWhirk	...	Daniel Creighton
Ellenville		v	CM	4	(845) 647-7080	Jeffrey Kaplan	Elliott Auerbach	Ann Bowler	Linda Polkoski	...	Phil Mattracion	...
Elmira		c	CM	30	(607) 737-5644	Stephen Hughes	John Burin	Angela Williams	Joy Bates	Donald Harrison	James Waters	Ronald Hawley
Elmira Heights		v	MC	4	(607) 734-7156	Arthur Caparula	...	...	...	...	Robert Hauptman	Jean Cazorla
Elmsford		v	MC	4	(914) 592-6555	...	...	...	...	...	...	...
Endicott	*	v	MC	13	(607) 757-2421	Joan Pulse	...	Jacquelyn Ingraham	Thomas Johnson	Stephen Hrustich	Michael Cox	Richard Miller
Fairport		v	MC	5	(585) 223-0313	Clark King	Kenneth Moore	...	...	...	...	Douglas Waite
Falconer		v	MC	2	(716) 665-4400	David Krieg	...	Gloria Anderson	...	Wayne Oste	...	Samuel Ognibene
Fallsburg		t	CM	12	(845) 434-8810	Steven Levine	...	Patricia Haaf	Linda Kinney	...	Brent Lawrence	William Illing
Farmingdale		v	MC	8	(516) 249-0093	George Graf	David Smollett	...	...	...	...	Fred Zamparelle
Fayetteville		v	MC	4	(315) 637-9864	Mark Olson	...	Lorie Corsette	...	Paul Hildreth	...	James Craw
Floral Park		v	MC	15	(516) 326-6300	Steven Corbett	Nancy McCloughlin	...	...	V. Brooks	Michael Reid	Louis Di Sunno
Flower Hill		v	MC	4	(516) 627-2253	...	...	...	...	...	...	...
Fort Edward		v	MC	3	(518) 747-4023	Edward Ryan	...	...	Daniel Smatko	Matthew Altizio	Mitchell Suprenant	Robert Dickinson
Fort Plain		v	MC	2	(518) 993-4271	Guy Barton	...	Susanne Mahn	...	Bud Wainer	Robert Thomas	...
Frankfort		v	MC	2	(315) 895-7651	Frank Moracco	...	Sharon Carlesimo	...	Charles Conigliaro	Steven Conley	Ronald Vivacqua
Fredonia		v	MC	10	(716) 679-2302	Frank Pagano	James Sedota	...	...	Perry Mitchell	Daniel Johnson	Richard Lascola
Freeport		v	MC	43	(516) 377-2200	William Glacken	...	Anna Knoeller	Thomas Preston	Arthur Burdette	Michael Woodward	Louis Digrazia
Fulton		c	MC	11	(315) 592-7330	Daryl Hayden	...	Joseph Tetro	James Laboda	Anthony Gorea	Mark Spawn	Daniel O'Brien
Garden City		v	MC	21	(516) 465-4000	Harold Hecken	Robert Schoelle	Joan Gallaer	...	Richard Chiarello	Ernest Cipullo	Robert Mangan
Gates		t	TM	29	(585) 247-6100	Ralph Esposito	...	Richard Warner	...	...	Thomas Roche	John Lathrop
Geneseo		v	MC	7	(585) 243-1177	Richard Hatheway	...	...	Marsha Merrick	Frank Manzo	Eric Osganian	Douglas Welch
Geneva	*	c	CM	13	(315) 789-4369	Stu Einstein	Mathew Horn	Lori Guinan	Tara Clark	Bruce Moore	Frank Pane	Gordon Eddington
Glen Cove		c	MC	26	(516) 676-2000	...	...	Carolyn Willson	John Macari	Joseph Solomito	Timothy Edwards	Gerald Gardruits
Glens Falls		c	MC	14	(518) 761-3800	Robert Regan	...	Robert Curtis	Bruce Crouser	Ronald Cote	Richard Carey	Robert Schiavoni
Gloversville		c	MC	15	(518) 773-4500	...	...	...	...	...	...	...
Goshen	*	v	MC	5	(845) 294-6750	Robert Weinberger	...	Margaret Strobl	...	...	James Watt	Michael Nuzzolese
Goshen		t	MC	12	(845) 294-6250	...	...	...	...	...	...	...
Gouverneur		v	MC	4	(315) 287-1720	Alfred Netto	Karen Lancto	Sheryl Simmons	...	Vinnie Ferry	David Whitton	Glenn McCollum
Gowanda		v	MC	2	(716) 532-3353	Richard Klancer	...	Kathleen Mohawk	...	Steve Raiport	Joseph Alessi	Michael Hutchinson
Granville		v	MC	2	(518) 642-2640	Jay Niles	...	...	Richard Roberts	Russel Bronson	Ernest Bassett	George Johnson
Great Neck		v	MC	9	(516) 482-0019	Ralph Kreitzman	John Dominsky	...	...	...	...	Louis Massaro

Directory 1/9 continued — OFFICIALS IN U.S. MUNICIPALITIES 2,500 AND OVER IN POPULATION

Jurisdiction	Type	Form of govern-ment	2000 Popu-lation	Main telephone number	Chief elected official	Appointed administrator	Clerk of the governing board	Chief financial officer	Fire chief	Police chief	Public works director
NEW YORK continued											
Great Neck Estates	v	MC	2	(516) 482-8283	Lawrence Nadel	...	Kathleen Santelli	...	...	John McNulty	Sandor Schweiger
Great Neck Plaza	v	MC	6	(516) 482-4500	...	...	...	...	...	...	...
Green Island	v	MC	2	(518) 273-2201	Ellen McNulty-Ryan	Sean Ward	Anne Strizzi	...	David Carl	John Nardone	Ronald Rootes
Greenburgh	t	MC	86	(914) 993-1540	Paul Feiner	...	Alfreda Williams	Norah McAvoy	...	John Kapica	Al Regula
Greenwood Lake	v	MC	3	(914) 477-9215	Roger Jacobsen	Robert Langan	Doris Hawkins	...	...	E. Baldesweiler	Michael Batz
Hamburg *	v	MC	10	(716) 649-0200	Thomas Moses	Donald Witkowski	...	...	Brian Horwood	Dennis Gleason	...
Hamilton	v	CM	3	(315) 824-1111	Sue McVaugh	Paul Kogut	Ronda Winn	...	Bob Holcomb	James Tilbe	Sean Graham
Harrison	v	MC	24	(914) 835-2000	Ronald Bianchi	...	Joan Walsh	Maureen MacKenzie	...	David Hall	Robert Wasp
Hastings-On-Hudson	v	CM	7	(914) 478-3400	William Lee Kinnally	Francis Frobel	...	...	Leslie Jenkins	Joseph Marsic	Michael Gunther
Haverstraw	v	MC	10	(914) 429-0300	...	...	Emma Velez	...	Carl Gitlan	John Reilly	Andrew Connors
Hempstead	v	MC	56	(516) 489-3400	...	...	...	...	...	...	...
Hempstead	t	MC	755	(516) 489-5000	Richard Guardino	...	Kate Murray	...	...	...	...
Herkimer	v	MC	7	(315) 866-3303	Mark Ainsworth	...	Bonnie Yatarola	...	Alfonso Varlaro	Joseph Malone	James Franco
Highland Falls *	v	MC	3	(845) 446-3400	Joseph D'Onofrio	...	Regina Taylor	...	William Lee	Peter Miller	Gary Boyce
Hilton	v	MC	5	(585) 392-4144	William Carter	...	...	...	...	...	Thomas Tilebein
Homer *	v	MC	3	(607) 749-3322	Michael McDermott	...	Louanne Randall	...	Phil Hess	Daniel Mack	Michael Galeotti
Hoosick Falls	v	MC	3	(518) 686-7072	Donald Bogardus	...	Denise McMahon	Judy Vandemar	Paul Daverdonis	Royal Howard	Timothy Stratton
Hornell	c	MC	9	(607) 324-7421	Shawn Hogan	...	Bernard McAneney	Thelma Pelych	Vincent Kelly	...	David Oakes
Horseheads	v	CM	6	(607) 739-5691	Patricia Gross	...	S. Cunningham	...	Richard Sullivan	David Kole	Christopher Lawrick
Hudson	c	MC	7	(518) 828-1030	Kenneth Cranna	...	Bonita Colwell	Kevin Walsh	Patrick Colwell	Ellis Richardson	Charles Butterworth
Hudson Falls *	v	MC	6	(518) 747-5426	John Barton	...	Kathryn Fitzpatrick	...	Paul Dietrich	Randy Diamond	Michael Fiorillo
Huntington	t	MC	195	(631) 351-3014	...	...	...	...	...	...	...
Ilion	v	MC	8	(315) 895-7449	Charles Haggerty	Mark Cushman	...	Gale Hatch	Karl Tripple	Anthony Licari	...
Irondequoit	t	MC	52	(585) 467-8840	David Schantz	...	Lydia Dzus	John Bovenzi	...	Robert Longdue	Timothy Oakes
Irvington	v	MC	6	(914) 591-7070	Erin Malloy	Lawrence Schopher	Edward Ritter	...	James Ruffler	Louis Grieco	Gregory Nilsson
Island Park	v	MC	4	(516) 431-0600	...	...	...	...	...	...	...
Islandia	v	MC	3	(516) 348-1133	...	...	...	...	...	...	...
Islip	t	MC	322	(631) 244-5500	Pete McGowan	...	Joan Johnson	...	...	...	...
Ithaca	c	MC	29	(607) 274-6539	Alan Cohen	...	Julie Holcomb	Steven Thayer	Brian Wilbur	Victor Loo	William Gray
Jamestown	c	MC	31	(716) 483-7600	Samuel Teresi	...	Shirley Sanfilipo	James Olson	Lance Hedlund	...	Jeffrey Lehman
Johnson City	v	MC	15	(607) 798-7861	...	...	...	...	...	...	...
Johnstown	c	MC	8	(518) 736-4011	William Pollak	...	Marilyn Muzzi	Michael Gifford	Steven Hart	Gregory Horning	Christopher Foss
Kenmore	v	MC	16	(716) 873-5700	John Beaumont	Kathleen Johnson	...	...	Jeffrey Tamsen	Samuel Cammilleri	Charles Sottile
Kings Point	v	MC	5	(516) 482-7872	...	...	...	...	...	...	...
Kingston	c	MC	23	(845) 331-0080	James Sottile	...	Kathy Janeczek	Penny Radel	Richard Salzmann	Gerald Keller	Steven Gorsline
Lackawanna	c	MC	19	(716) 827-6464	Norman Polanski	...	Joseph Carnevale	Robert Marciniak	Reynold Jennetti	Dennis O'Hara	Leo Murphy
Lake Grove	v	MC	10	(516) 585-2000	...	Leroy Heoffner	Carmela Constant	...	...	...	Douglas Colino
Lake Success	v	CM	2	(516) 482-4411	Roberta Chavis	...	...	...	...	William Roberts	Richard Faraci
Lakewood	v	MC	3	(716) 763-8557	...	...	...	...	...	...	...
Lancaster *	v	MC	11	(716) 683-2105	William Carsdale	...	Michael Stegmeier	...	John Burke	...	Mark Gee
Lansing	v	MC	3	(607) 257-0424	Donald Hartill	...	...	...	...	...	John Courtney
Larchmont	v	MC	6	(914) 834-6230	Kenneth Bialo	...	Eileen Finn	...	Brian Payne	Stephen Rubeo	Joseph Bedard
Lawrence	v	MC	6	(516) 239-4600	...	...	...	...	...	...	...
Le Roy	v	CM	4	(585) 768-2527	William Horgan	...	...	...	...	Samuel Steffenilla	Robert Walters
Lewiston	v	MC	2	(716) 754-8271	Richard Soluri	...	...	...	William Fyfe	...	David Jacobs
Liberty	v	CM	3	(845) 292-2250	William Smith	...	Judy Zurawski	...	...	Michael DeFrank	Peter Parks
Lindenhurst	v	MC	27	(516) 957-7500	Lynda Distler	Shawn Cullinane	...	...	Henry Batz	...	...
Little Falls	c	MC	5	(315) 823-2400	...	...	...	...	James Staffo	...	...
Liverpool	v	MC	2	(315) 457-3441	Marlene Ward	...	Mary Ellen Sims	David Murray	...	Donald Morris	William Asmus
Lloyd Harbor	v	MC	3	(631) 549-8893	Leland Hairr	...	Kristi King	...	...	Bernard Welsh	George McCabe
Lockport	c	MC	22	(716) 439-6665	Michael Tucker	...	Richard Mullaney	...	Thomas Passoite	Neil Merritt	...
Long Beach	c	CM	35	(516) 431-1000	Michael Zapson	Glen Spiritis	Marcia Markowitz	Michael Barlotta	...	Thomas Browne	Robert Raab
Lowville	v	MC	3	(315) 376-2834	Robert King	Eric Virkler	...	...	...	Eric Fredenburg	Mark Tabolt
Lynbrook	v	MC	19	(516) 599-8300	...	...	...	...	...	...	...
Lyons	v	MC	3	(315) 946-4531	John Cinelli	...	Diana Marro	...	Charles Witt	Michael Donalty	...
Malone	v	MC	6	(518) 483-4570	Joyce Tavernier	...	Elizabeth Bessette	...	...	Gerald Moll	Frank Riley
Malverne	v	MC	8	(516) 599-1200	Anthony Panzarella	Teresa Emmel	...	...	...	Glen Jacobson	Paul Jessup
Mamaroneck	v	CM	18	(914) 777-7703	Philip Trifiletti	...	...	Agostino Fusco	Barry Casterella	Edward Flynn	Anthony Iacovelli
Mamaroneck	t	CM	28	(914) 381-7810	...	Stephen Altieri	Patricia DiCioccio	...	...	Richard Rivera	Marco Gennarelli
Manlius	v	MC	4	(315) 682-9171	...	Cheryl Haskins	...	...	...	...	John Maher
Manorhaven	v	MC	6	(516) 883-7000	...	...	...	...	...	...	...
Massapequa Park	v	MC	17	(516) 798-0244	James Altadonna	Peggy Caltabiano	...	...	...	...	John LaMarca
Massena	v	MC	11	(315) 769-8625	Kenneth MacDonnell	...	Patricia Dumas	...	R. Gray	Timmy Currier	Hassan Fayad
Mechanicville	c	CO	5	(518) 664-8331	Thomas Higgins	...	Paul Guilianelle	Nicholas Forte	Charlie Wheeler	Peter Clements	Daniel Robens
Medina	v	MC	6	(716) 798-0710	Herbert Brant	...	E. Crowley	...	Gregory Barhite	Jose Avila	E. Houseknecht
Menands	v	MC	3	(518) 434-2922	John Bishop	...	William Smith	...	Donald Handerhan	Michael O'Brien	Timothy Boyd
Middletown	c	MC	25	(845) 346-4150	Joseph Destefano	Russell Russo	Charles Mitchell	...	...	Louis Ogden	Alfred Fusco
Mineola *	v	MC	19	(516) 746-0750	Jack Martins	...	Joseph Scalero	...	Scott Holliday	...	Thomas Rini
Minoa	v	MC	3	(315) 656-3100	John Regan	...	Karen Curulla	...	...	...	Thomas Petterelli
Mohawk	v	MC	2	(315) 866-4312	Irene Dibble	...	Judy Bray	...	Leo Kinville	Joseph Malone	Kevin Wheelock
Monroe	v	MC	7	(845) 782-8341	Joseph Mancuso	...	Virginia Carey	...	...	Dominic Giudice	Anthony Vaccaro
Montebello	v	MC	3	(914) 368-2211	Kathryn Ellsworth	...	Debra Mastroeni	...	...	...	...
Monticello	v	CM	6	(845) 794-6130	Gary Sommers	...	Edith Schop	...	Carl Houman	Michael Brennan	Steve Kozachuk
Morrisville	v	MC	2	(315) 684-7007	Michelle Forward	...	Amy Will	...	Richard Gorton	...	Raymond Heh
Mount Kisco	v	CM	9	(914) 241-0500	Mark Farrell	James Palmer	...	...	Jack Marshall	Robert Dagostino	George Brown
Mount Morris	v	MC	3	(585) 658-4160	James Murray	...	Donald Scalia	...	...	Sherman Yates	Patsy Zingaru
Mount Vernon	c	MC	68	(914) 665-2300	Ernest Davis	...	Lisa Copeland	Maureen Walker	Al Everett	...	James Finch
Munsey Park	v	MC	2	(516) 365-7790	Harry Nicolaides	Helen Averso	...	...	...	...	...
Muttontown	v	MC	3	(516) 364-2240	...	...	...	...	...	...	...
New Castle *	t	CM	17	(914) 234-4771	Janet Wells	Gennaro Faiella	Jill Shapiro	...	...	James Baynes	Anthony Vaccaro
New Hempstead	v	MC	4	(845) 354-8100	Lawrence Dessau	...	Carole Vazquez	...	...	...	...
New Hyde Park	v	MC	9	(516) 354-0022	...	...	...	...	...	...	...
New Paltz *	v	MC	6	(845) 255-0130	Terry Dungan	...	Kelly Stengel	...	David Weeks	Raymond Zappone	G. Bleu Terwilliger
New Rochelle *	c	CM	72	(914) 654-2000	Noam Bramson	Charles Strome	Dorothy Allen	Howard Rattner	Raymond Kiernan	Patrick Carroll	Jeffrey Coleman
New York	c	MC	8008	(212) 669-8090	Michael Bloomberg	...	...	...	Nicholas Scoppetta	Raymond Kelly	...
New York Mills	v	MC	3	(315) 736-9212	Michael Dubiel	...	Sharon Guca	...	Ron Roman	Stephen Verminski	Joseph Cotrupe
Newark	v	MC	9	(315) 331-4770	...	...	John Trickey	...	...	Richard Bogan	James Bridgeman
Newburgh	c	CM	28	(845) 569-7320	Andrew Marino	...	Lorene Vitek	Marie Gida	James Morrill	William Bloom	George Garrison
Niagara Falls	c	CM	55	(716) 286-4300	...	William Bradberry	Cynthia Baxter	Maria Brown	William Correa	Christopher Carlin	Paul Colangelo
North Hempstead	t	MC	222	(516) 627-0590	May Newburger	...	Michele Schimmel	...	...	...	Gil Anderson
North Syracuse *	v	MC	6	(315) 458-0900	John Heindorf	...	Nancy Fortin	...	Mark Hogan	Thomas Connelly	Gary Wilmer
North Tonawanda	c	MC	33	(716) 695-8555	Mary Kabasakalian	...	Michael Cox	...	David Rogge	Carl Stiles	Gary Franklin
Northport	v	MC	7	(631) 261-7502	Peter Nolan	...	D. Smith	Dorothy Dugan	Anthony Graziano	...	Joseph Correia
Norwich	c	MC	7	(607) 334-1200	...	...	...	Brian Molinaro	John Tighe	Joseph Angelino	Carl Ivarson
Nyack	v	MC	6	(845) 358-0548	Terry Hekker	...	Berta Campbell	...	...	...	Joe Stach
Oakfield *	v	CM	1	(585) 948-5862	Richard Pastecki	...	Joyce Grazioplene	...	...	...	David Laney

Directory 1/9 continued — OFFICIALS IN U.S. MUNICIPALITIES 2,500 AND OVER IN POPULATION

Jurisdiction	Type	Form of govern-ment	2000 Popu-lation	Main telephone number	Chief elected official	Appointed administrator	Clerk of the governing board	Chief financial officer	Fire chief	Police chief	Public works director
NEW YORK continued											
Ocean Beach	v	MC	..	(631) 583-5940	Joseph Loeffler	Anne Minerva	...	...	Franklin Silsdorf	Edward Paradiso	Kevin Schelling
Ogdensburg *	c	CM	12	(315) 393-6100	William Nelson	Arthur Sciorra	Kathleen Bouchard	Philip Cosmo	Steven Badlam	Richard Polniak	Kit Smith
Old Westbury	v	MC	4	(516) 626-0800	...	...	Kenneth Callahan	...	...	William Doerrie	John Ingram
Olean	c	MC	15	(716) 376-5615	John Ash	...	David John	Theodore Luty	John Gibbons	Patrick Brandow	Peter Marcus
Oneida *	c	MC	10	(315) 363-4800	Leo Matzke	...	Jane Mariani	Joan Cukierski	Donald Hudson	David Meeker	...
Oneonta *	c	MC	13	(607) 432-0670	John Nader	...	James Koury	David Martindale	Robert Barnes	Joseph Redmond	...
Orangetown	t	MC	47	(845) 359-5100	...	...	...	...	...	...	...
Orchard Park *	v	MC	3	(716) 662-9327	John Wilson	...	...	...	...	...	Andrew Slotman
Ossining	v	CM	24	(914) 941-3554	Miguel Hernandez	Linda Cooper	Mary Ann Roberts	...	...	Joseph Burton	...
Ossining	t	MC	36	(914) 762-6000	John Chervokas	...	...	...	...	Kenneth Donato	...
Oswego	c	MC	17	(315) 342-8159	Randolph Bateman	...	Barbara Sugar	Deborah Coad	Edward Geers	Michael Dehm	Richard Bateman
Owego *	v	MC	3	(607) 687-3555	Edward Arrington	...	...	Lynne Mieczkowski	Thomas Taft	Edward McCulskey	Jeff Soules
Palmyra	v	MC	3	(315) 597-4849	Victoria Daly	...	...	...	...	David Dalton	...
Patchogue	v	MC	11	(631) 475-4300	Stephen Keegan	...	Mary Pontieri	...	John Parris	Jeffrey Kracht	Daniel Wirshup
Peekskill	c	CM	22	(914) 737-3400	John Testa	...	Pamela Beach	...	...	Eugene Tumolo	David Greener
Pelham *	v	MC	6	(914) 738-2015	Edward Hotchkiss	Richard Slingerland	Terri Rouke	...	Curtis Taylor	Joseph Benefico	Harry Pallett
Pelham Manor *	v	CM	5	(914) 738-8820	Thomas Lavin	John Pierpont	...	...	Joseph Ruggerio	Alfred Mosiello	...
Penfield	t	MC	34	(585) 340-8600	Channing Philbrick	...	Cassie Williams	Robert Beedon	...	...	Jim Fletcher
Penn Yan	v	MC	5	(315) 536-3015	Douglas Marchionda	...	Linda Banach	...	Kevin Pallar	Stephen Hill	Edward Balsley
Perry	v	MC	3	(585) 237-2216	Dennis Vergason	...	...	...	Arnold Wilson	...	Ryan Dure
Plattsburgh	c	MC	18	(518) 561-7701	Daniel Stewart	...	Keith Herkalo	James Buran	James Squires	Desmond Racicot	Kevin Murphy
Pleasantville	v	CM	7	(914) 769-1900	Bernard Gordon	Patricia Dwyer	Judith Weintraub	...	...	Anthony Chiarlitti	Stephen Johnson
Port Chester *	v	CM	27	(914) 939-2200	Dennis Pilla	Christopher Russo	...	...	Joseph Publiese	Joseph Krzeminski	James Cole
Port Jefferson	v	MC	7	(516) 473-4724	...	...	...	...	...	...	...
Port Jervis	c	MC	8	(845) 858-4014	R. Worden	...	...	James Hinkley	Joseph Kowal	William Wagner	Vincent Lopez
Port Washington North	v	MC	2	(516) 883-5900	Thomas Pellegrino	...	Palma Torrisi	...	...	...	Edward Ratkoski
Potsdam	v	CM	9	(315) 265-7480	Ruth Garner	Michael Weil	Lori Queor	...	...	John Kaplan	Bruce Henderson
Poughkeepsie *	c	MC	29	(845) 451-4035	John Tkazyik	Michael Long	Deanne Flynn	Camilo Bunyi	Kenneth Boyd	Ronald Knapp	Stephen Miko
Queensbury	t	MC	25	(518) 761-8201	Dennis Brower	William Lavery	Darleen Dougher	Henry Hess	Steve Smith	...	Perley Rice
Ramapo	t	MC	108	(845) 357-5100	C. St. Lawrence	...	Christian Sampson	Ilan Schoenberger	...	Peter Brower	Ted Dzurinko
Ravena	v	MC	3	(518) 756-8233	...	...	Nancy Warner	...	Joel Trombley	...	Bernard Persico
Rensselaer *	c	MC	7	(518) 462-6424	Daniel Dwyer	...	Maureen Nardacci	...	Phil Foust	Fredrick Fusco	Thomas Capuanno
Rhinebeck *	v	MC	3	(845) 876-7015	Richard Cunningham	Gail Haskins	...	...	Doug Eighmy	Peter Dunn	George Wyant
Rochester	c	MC	219	(585) 428-7115	William Johnson	Jeffrey Carlson	Carolee Conklin	Vincent Carfagna	Floyd Madison	Robert Duffy	Edward Doherty
Rockville Centre	v	MC	24	(516) 678-9300	...	...	...	...	...	John McKeon	Harold Weed
Rome *	c	MC	34	(315) 336-6000	James Brown	Tammy Burkhart	Louise Glasso	...	Roger Sabia	Kevin Beach	Frank Tallarino
Rye *	c	CM	14	(914) 967-4603	Steve Otis	O. Paul Shew	Dawn Nodarse	...	George Hogben	...	...
Rye Brook *	c	CM	8	(914) 939-1121	Joan Feinstein	C. Bradbury	...	...	...	Greg Austin	...
Sag Harbor	v	MC	2	(631) 725-0222	Gregory Ferraris	Sandra Schroeder	...	...	Philip Garypie	Thomas Fabiano	James Early
Salamanca	c	MC	6	(716) 945-3890	C. Vecchiarella	...	April Vecchiarella	Linda Rychcik	Barney Lee	Edward Gimbrone	Raymond Wilson
Sands Point	v	MC	2	(516) 883-3044	Leonard Wurzel	Randy Bond	...	Lynn Najman	...	Owen Kirby	Brian Gunderson
Saranac Lake *	v	CM	5	(518) 891-4150	Thomas Michael	Martin Murphy	Kareen Tyler	...	Ed Woodard	Donald Perryman	Robert Martin
Saratoga Springs	c	CO	26	(518) 587-3550	J. O'Connell	...	Edward Valentine	Michael Lenz	Robert Cogan	Kenneth King	Joseph O'Neill
Saugerties	v	MC	4	(845) 246-2321	Robert Yerick	...	Mary Frank	Barbara Griffis	Brian Martin	William Kimble	Kevin Kiefer
Scarsdale	v	CM	17	(914) 722-1110	Beverly Sved	Alfred Gatta	Donna Conkling	James Heslop	Walter Felice	John Brogan	Benedict Salanitro
Schenectady	c	MC	61	(518) 382-5000	Albert Jurczynski	...	Carolyn Friello	Michael Strenka	Robert Farstad	Michael Geraci	Milton Mitchell
Scotia	v	MC	7	(518) 374-1071	...	...	...	...	...	...	...
Sea Cliff	v	MC	5	(516) 671-0080	Eileen Kriieb	Daniel Maddock	Peter Hesse	...	...	...	Tom Bellingham
Seneca Falls	v	CM	6	(315) 568-8107	Diana Smith	Constance Sowards	...	...	...	Frederick Capozzi	William Gladis
Sherrill	c	CM	3	(315) 363-2440	Joseph Shay	David Barker	...	Michael Holmes	...	James Hastings	Gary Onyan
Sidney	v	MC	4	(607) 561-2324	James Warren	...	...	...	John Gilmore	Craig Whitten	David Stevens
Silver Creek	v	MC	2	(716) 934-3240	...	Thomas Postle	...	...	...	Louis Pelletter	Robert Groat
Skaneateles	v	MC	2	(315) 685-0730	James Rhinehart	...	Sally Sheehan	...	David Card	Jack McNeil	Robert Green
Sleepy Hollow	v	CM	9	(914) 631-1440	Sean Treacy	Anthony Giaccio	Angela Everett	Sanjay Shah	Lenny Rutigliano	...	Joe Defeo
Sloan *	v	MC	3	(716) 897-1560	Leonard Szymanski	...	Debra Smith	...	Phillip Spider	...	Sean McGee
Sloatsburg	v	MC	3	(845) 753-2727	Carl Wright	...	Thomas Bollatto	...	...	...	Michael Demartino
Smithtown	t	MC	115	(631) 360-7512	Patrick Vecchio	...	Vincent Puleo	Anthony Minerva	...	...	...
Solvay	v	MC	6	(315) 468-1651	...	...	Cheryl Libertone	...	...	Richard Cox	David Pettitt
Somers	t	MC	18	(914) 277-3323	Mary Beth Murphy	...	Kathleen Pacella	...	...	Michael Driscoll	Thomas Chiaverini
South Glens Falls	v	MC	3	(518) 793-1455	Robert Phinney	...	Karin Blood	...	Jake Losaw	Kevin Judd	John Dixon
South Nyack	v	MC	3	(845) 358-0287	Richard Helmke	...	Sara Seiler	...	...	Alan Colsey	James Johnson
Southampton	v	MC	3	(631) 283-0247	Mark Epley	J. Van Nostrand	...	...	Brian Cooke	Lars King	Gary Aldrich
Spencerport	v	MC	3	(585) 352-6775	Theodore Walker	Alan Scheg	P. Cunningham	Linda Harissis	...	...	Thomas West
Spring Valley	v	MC	25	(845) 352-1100	George Darden	Barry Harris	Sherry Scott	...	Fred Thibault	Anthony Furco	John Ackerson
Springville	v	MC	4	(716) 592-4936	Gary Eppolito	...	Deborah Murphy	...	Dennis Dains	...	Karl Lux
Suffern	v	MC	11	(845) 357-2600	James Giannettino	...	Virginia Menschner	...	Donald Schreck	Frank Finch	Joseph Hornick
Syracuse	c	MC	147	(315) 448-8780	Matthew Driscoll	Kenneth Mokrzycki	John Copanas	Brian Roulin	John Cowin	Dennis Duval	James Collins
Tarrytown *	v	CM	11	(914) 631-1885	Eileen Pilla	Michael Blau	Louise Camilliere	...	Patrick Derivan	Scott Brown	...
Thomaston *	v	MC	2	(516) 482-3110	Robert Stern	Barbara Daniels	...	...	...	...	W. Mazurkiewicz
Ticonderoga	v	MC	2	(518) 585-6265	Robert Dedrick	...	Paula Buckman	...	...	Jeffrey Cook	Phillip Huestis
Tonawanda	c	MC	16	(716) 695-8645	Alice Roth	...	Janice Bodie	...	Thomas Miller	Mark Winters	Neal Myers
Troy *	c	MC	49	(518) 270-4401	Harry Tutunjian	Daniel Crawley	William McInerney	Deborah Witkowski	Thomas Garrett	Nicholas Kaiser	Bob Mirch
Tuckahoe *	v	MC	6	(914) 961-3100	John Fitzpatrick	...	Susan Ciamarra	...	...	John Costanzo	Frank DiMarco
Tupper Lake *	v	MC	3	(518) 359-3341	Michael Desmarais	Mary Casagrain	Michelle Moeller	...	...	Thomas Fee	Michael Sparks
Union	t	MC	56	(607) 786-2915	John Cheevers	...	Gail Springer	Gary Leighton	...	...	Kenneth Del Bianco
Utica	c	MC	60	(315) 792-0300	...	...	...	...	...	...	...
Valley Stream	v	MC	36	(516) 825-4200	Edward Cahill	Vincent Ang	...	John Mastromarino	...	...	...
Voorheesville	v	MC	2	(518) 765-2692	Robert Conway	...	Linda Pasquali	...	Frank Papa	...	William Smith
Walden *	v	CM	6	(845) 778-2177	Rebecca Pearson	James Politi	Nancy Mitchell	...	...	Jeffrey Holmes	Anthony Lamendola
Walton *	v	MC	3	(607) 865-4358	Edward Snow	...	Virginia O'Dell	...	...	David Halaquist	Joseph Cetta
Wappingers Falls	v	MC	4	(845) 297-8773	...	...	...	...	...	...	...
Warsaw	v	MC	3	(585) 786-2120	Daniel Moran	...	Linda Hoffmeister	...	...	William Blythe	Gilbert Stearns
Warwick	v	MC	6	(845) 986-2031	Michael Newhard	...	Jacqueline Mongelli	...	...	...	Steven Sisco
Waterloo	v	MC	5	(315) 539-9131	...	...	...	...	...	...	...
Watertown	c	CM	26	(315) 785-7730	Jeffrey Graham	Mary Corriveau	Donna Dutton	James Mills	Daniel Gaumont	Joseph Goss	Eugene Hayes
Watervliet	c	CM	10	(518) 270-3800	Robert Carlson	Paul Murphy	Bruce Hidley	Robert Fahr	...	Gerald Beston	...
Waverly *	v	MC	4	(607) 565-8106	Kyle McDuffee	...	...	...	...	Grady Updyke	Douglas Kinsley
Webster	v	MC	5	(585) 265-3770	...	...	...	...	...	...	...
Wellsville	v	MC	5	(585) 593-1121	Susan Goetschius	...	Janice Givens	...	David Sweet	James Cicirello	William Whitfield
Wesley Hills	v	MC	4	(845) 354-0400	Robert Frankl	Helen Schiela	...	Marvin Nyman	...	...	...
West Haverstraw	v	MC	10	(845) 947-2800	Edward Zugibe	...	O. Miller	...	...	...	David Barbera
West Seneca	t	MC	45	(716) 674-5600	...	...	...	...	...	...	...
Westbury	v	MC	14	(516) 334-1700	Ernest Strada	Thomas Savino	...	...	...	...	Dennis Maher
Westfield *	v	MC	3	(716) 326-4961	Ronald Catalano	Vincent Luce	...	...	...	Ken Machemer	...
White Plains	c	MC	53	(914) 422-1200	Joseph Delfino	Paul Wood	Janice Minieri	G. Cuneo-Harwood	Richard Lyman	James Bradley	Joseph Nicoletti
Whitehall	v	MC	2	(518) 499-0871	Patricia Norton	...	...	Joan Douglas	...	Richard Rizzo	Donald Williams

Directory 1/9 continued — OFFICIALS IN U.S. MUNICIPALITIES 2,500 AND OVER IN POPULATION

Jurisdiction		Type	Form of govern- ment	2000 Popu- lation	Main telephone number	Chief elected official	Appointed administrator	Clerk of the governing board	Chief financial officer	Fire chief	Police chief	Public works director
NEW YORK continued												
Whitesboro		v	MC	3	(315) 736-1613	Richard Pugh	. . .	Susan Goding	. . .	. . .	Dominick Hiffa	Charles Tritten
Williamsville		v	CM	5	(716) 632-4120	F. Hazlett	. . .	. . .	. . .	James Zymanek	. . .	Anthony Grisanti
Williston Park		v	MC	7	(516) 746-2193	. . .	. . .	. . .	. . .	. . .	. . .	. . .
Woodridge		v	CM	. .	(845) 434-7447	Ivan Katz	. . .	Diane Garritt	. . .	Eric Akerley	John Calvello	Carl Garritt
Yonkers		c	MC	196	(914) 377-6180	John Spencer	Philip Amicone	Joan Deierlein	James La Perche	Anthony Pagano	Charles Cola	John Liszewski
Yorktown		t	MC	36	(914) 962-5722	. . .	. . .	Alice Roker	Joan Goldberg	. . .	Daniel McMahon	. . .
Yorkville		v	MC	2	(315) 736-9391	Michael Mahoney	. . .	Helen Petruccione	. . .	George Farley	Kirk Lanahan	Conrad Chaya
NORTH CAROLINA												
Aberdeen	*	t	CM	3	(910) 944-1115	Elizabeth Mofield	William Zell	Nancy Matthews	Beth Wentland	Phillip Richardson	Michael Connor	Rickie Monroe
Ahoskie	*	t	CM	4	(252) 332-5146	Linda Blackburn	Charles Hammond	Evelyn Howard	. . .	Kenneth Dilday	Troy Fitzhugh	Kirk Rogers
Albemarle		c	CM	15	(704) 984-9400	Roger Snyder	Raymond Allen	. . .	Colleen Jones	George McDaniel	Gerald Michael	James Coble
Angier		t	CM	3	(919) 639-2071	Wanda Gregory	Coley Price	Tina Westy	Jason Forelines	. . .	Anthony Poppler	Henry Cook
Apex		t	CM	20	(919) 249-3400	Keith Weatherly	Bruce Radford	Georgia Evangelist	Richard Smiley	Mark Haraway	Jack Lewis	Timothy Donnelly
Archdale	*	c	CM	9	(336) 431-9141	Bertha Stone	Jerry Yarborough	Patsy Doughtery	Lori Nurse	. . .	Gary Lewallen	Michael Shuler
Asheboro		c	CM	21	(336) 629-2037	David Jarrell	John Ogburn	Holly Hartman	Deborah Juberg	James Smith	Gary Mason	Robert Kivett
Asheville		c	CM	68	(828) 259-5695	Charles Worley	Gary Jackson	Magdalen Burleson	Benjamin Durant	Gregory Grayson	William Hogan	Franklin Combs
Atlantic Beach	*	t	CM	1	(252) 726-2121	A. B. Cooper	Pete Allen	Kelly Nash	. . .	Adam Snyder	Allen Smith	Marc Schulze
Ayden		t	CM	4	(252) 746-7030	Stephen Tripp	Adam Mitchell	Dorothy Bridges	Christopher Tucker	Barry Wood	Charles Crudup	Henry Hardison
Badin		t	CM	1	(704) 422-3470	James Harrsion	. . .	Lorraine Tucker	. . .	. . .	Bryan Lambert	Floyd Carter
Bald Head Island	*	v	CM	. .	(910) 457-9700	Larry Lammert	Calvin Peck	Amy Candler	Shelia Boyd	Jerome Munna	Richard Herring	Wendell Liddle
Beaufort		t	CM	3	(252) 728-2141	Ann Carter	Terri Parker-Eakes	Della Knight	Betsy Gilchrist	James Lynch	Steve Lewis	John Young
Beech Mountain		t	CM	. .	(828) 387-4236	Richard Owen	. . .	Reba Greene	Sally Rominger	. . .	Marvin Hefner	William Hatch
Belhaven	*	t	CM	1	(252) 943-3055	Adam O'Neal	Guinn Leverett	Marie Adams	Andrew Harris	Derrick Meyers	Fred Clingenpeel	Paul Woods
Belmont		c	CM	8	(704) 825-5586	Richard Boyce	Barry Webb	Mozelle Lingafeldt	. . .	George Attice	David James	David Isenhour
Belville		t	CM	1	(910) 371-2456	. . .	Tracie Davis	. . .	. . .	. . .	. . .	. . .
Benson		t	CM	2	(919) 894-3553	. . .	Keith Langdon	Connie Sorrell	. . .	. . .	Kenneth Edwards	Billy Addison
Bermuda Run		t	CM	1	(336) 998-0906	John Ferguson	Ron Bell	. . .	. . .	. . .	. . .	. . .
Bessemer City	*	c	CM	5	(704) 629-5542	William Hovis	. . .	. . .	Donna Lumsden	. . .	. . .	James Ramsey
Beulaville		t	CM	1	(910) 298-4647	Joseph Edwards	Scotty Summerlin	Lori Williams	. . .	. . .	Hal Williams	Earl Sanderson
Biltmore Forest	*	t	CM	1	(828) 274-0824	George Goosmann	Nelson Smith	. . .	. . .	. . .	J. Eric Tinsley	Terry Crouch
Biscoe		t	CM	1	(910) 428-4112	James Blake	Allen Lockhart	Lisa Cagle	. . .	Kelly Kellem	James Myrick	David Asbill
Black Mountain	*	t	CM	7	(828) 669-9102	Carl Bartlett	Marcia Onieal	Shirley Raines	. . .	Steve Jones	Kevin Pressley	Robert Watts
Bladenboro		t	CM	1	(910) 863-3655	. . .	Delane Jackson	. . .	. . .	. . .	. . .	. . .
Blowing Rock		t	CM	1	(828) 295-5200	James Lawrence	Scott Hildebran	Barbara Beach	. . .	Marcus Hickman	James Tolbert	Johnny Lentz
Boiling Spring Lakes		c	CM	2	(910) 845-2614	Joan Kinney	David Lewis	. . .	. . .	. . .	Richard White	Larry Modlin
Boiling Springs		t	CM	3	(704) 434-2357	Max Hamrick	Zach Trogdon	Kim Greene	Rhonda Allen	Neal McSwain	James Clary	Joey Gantt
Boone	*	t	CM	13	(828) 268-6200	Loretta Clawson	Gregory Young	Freida Van Allen	Amy Davis	Reginald Hassler	William Post	J. Brown
Brevard		c	CM	6	(828) 884-4123	James Harris	Joseph Albright	Glenda Sansosti	Terrell Scruggs	. . .	Dennis Wilde	Donald Owen
Bryson City	*	0	CM	1	(828) 488-3335	Brad Walker	Larry Callicutt	. . .	. . .	. . .	. . .	. . .
Burgaw	*	t	CM	3	(910) 259-2151	Kenneth Cowan	Martin Beach	Sylvia Raynor	Cynthia Jones	William George	Wilbert King	Douglas Riseden
Burlington	*	c	CM	44	(336) 222-5000	Ronnie Wall	Harold Owen	Jondeen Terry	Linda Hollifield	Jay Smith	Michael Williams	Robert Patterson
Cajah's Mountain		t	CM	2	(828) 728-5053	. . .	. . .	. . .	. . .	. . .	. . .	. . .
Calabash		t	CM	. .	(910) 579-6747	. . .	Vincent Long	. . .	. . .	. . .	. . .	. . .
Canton	*	t	CM	4	(828) 648-2363	Patrick Smathers	Albert Matthews	. . .	. . .	James Smathers	William Guillet	. . .
Carolina Beach	*	t	CM	4	(910) 458-2999	Joel Macon	Timothy Owens	Lynn Prusa	Dawn Johnson	Jonathan Rorie	William Younginer	Brian Stanberry
Carrboro		t	CM	16	(919) 942-8541	Mark Chilton	Steven Stewart	Sarah Williamson	. . .	Travis Crabtree	Carolyn Hutchison	George Seiz
Carthage	*	t	CM	1	(910) 947-2331	Ronnie Fields	Carol Cleetwood	Melissa Adams	Linda Phillips	Christopher Tyner	C. McKenzie	Rocky Davis
Cary		t	CM	94	(919) 469-4070	Glen Lang	Benjamin Shivar	Sue Rowland	Karen Mills	Raymond Cain	Windy Hunter	Michael Bajorek
Caswell Beach		t	CM	. .	(910) 278-5471	. . .	Jim Carter	Linda Bethune	Judy Williamson	. . .	. . .	. . .
Catawba		t	CM	. .	(828) 241-2215	Thomas Jones	Jonathan Kanipe	Kathy Johnson	. . .	Donald Robinson	Cecil Cook	Cary Broadwell
Cedar Point		0	CM	. .	(252) 393-7898	Harry Redfearn	Christopher Seaberg	Jackie Paylor	. . .	. . .	. . .	Donald Redfearn
Chadbourn		t	CM	2	(910) 654-4148	Leo Mercer	Dottie Thomas	. . .	. . .	Randy Guyton	Timothy Stoker	Michael Foss
Chapel Hill		t	CM	48	(919) 968-2700	Kevin Foy	Roger Stancil	Sabrina Oliver	Kay Johnson	Daniel Jones	Gregg Jarvies	William Letteri
Charlotte		c	CM	540	(704) 336-2285	Patrick McCrory	Curt Walton	Brenda Freeze	Greg Gaskins	Luther Fincher	. . .	. . .
Cherryville	*	c	CM	5	(704) 435-1709	Robert Austell	David Hodgkins	Kelly Sellers	Bonny Alexander	Jeff Cash	Woodrow Burgess	Brandon Abernathy
China Grove		t	CM	3	(704) 857-2466	Donald Bringle	. . .	Gail Carter	Mary Jo Bopp	. . .	. . .	. . .
Claremont		c	CM	1	(828) 459-7009	Glenn Morrison	Doris Bumgarner	. . .	Stephanie Corn	Gary Sigmon	Gerald Tolbert	Thomas Winkler
Clayton		t	CM	6	(919) 553-5002	Douglas McCormac	R. Biggs	Jessica Coutu	Marc Jones	Lee Barbee	. . .	. . .
Clemmons		v	CM	13	(336) 766-7511	Edward Brewer	Gary Looper	Marsha Sucharski	K. Stroud	. . .	. . .	Larry Kirby
Clinton		c	CM	8	(910) 299-4907	Luther Starling	John Connet	Elizabeth Fortner	Betty Brewer	Phillip Miller	Michael Brim	Chris Doherty
Columbus		t	CM	. .	(828) 894-8236	Kathleen McMillian	Tim Holloman	Donna Butler	Kathy Gregory	. . .	Butch Kennedy	Wendell Pace
Concord		c	CM	55	(704) 920-5200	Jeffrey Padgett	W. Hiatt	Vickie Weant	Joyce Allman	Terry Holloway	Merlyn Hamilton	. . .
Conover	*	c	CM	6	(828) 464-1191	Bruce Eckard	Donald Duncan	Cara Reed	Vickie Schlichting	James Hincon	Gary Lafone	Jimmy Clark
Cornelius		t	CM	11	(704) 892-6031	Gary Knox	Anthony Roberts	Carolyn Sigmon	Jackie Huffman	Jim Barbee	Ronald McKinney	Ricky Overcash
Cramerton		t	CM	2	(704) 824-4337	Cathy Biles	Michael Peoples	LuAnn Ellis	. . .	. . .	David Young	. . .
Creedmoor	*	c	CM	2	(919) 528-3332	Darryl Moss	. . .	Sandra Harper	Lenessa Hawkins	. . .	Timothy Benware	. . .
Dallas		t	MC	3	(704) 922-3176	Rick Coleman	Steven Miller	Maria Stroupe	. . .	David Callahan	Gary Buckner	John Ferguson
Davidson	*	t	MC	7	(704) 892-7591	John Woods	Leamon Brice	. . .	Peggy Smith	Jeff Almond	. . .	Doug Wright
Dobson		t	CM	1	(336) 386-8962	. . .	J. Atkins	. . .	. . .	. . .	. . .	. . .
Drexel		t	CM	1	(828) 437-7421	Richard Propst	Matthew Settlemyer	Sherry Carswell	. . .	James Richards	Michael Swink	Johnny Rowe
Duck	*	t	CM	. .	(252) 255-1234	Donald Morrison	Christopher Layton	Lori Kopec	. . .	Donna Black	Phillip Ferguson	. . .
Dunn	*	c	CM	9	(910) 230-3500	William Elmore	Ronald Autry	Joyce Valley	Renee Daughtry	Austin Tew	Bernard Jones	Billy Addison
Durham		c	CM	187	(919) 560-4214	William Bell	Thomas Bonfield	Dorothy Gray	Kenneth Pennoyer	Otis Cooper	Jose Lopez	Kathryn Kalb
Eden		c	CM	15	(336) 623-2110	John Grogan	Stephen Corcoran	Kim Scott	Tammie McMichael	Doug Cline	Gary Benthin	Dennis Asbury
Edenton		t	CM	5	(252) 482-7352	Roland Vaughan	A.-Marie Knighton	. . .	Janet Hines	Charlie Westbrook	Gregory Bonner	Jimmy Patterson
Elizabeth City		c	CM	17	(252) 337-6677	Charles Foster	Richard Olson	Dianne Pierce	Sarah Blanchard	William Pritchard	Charles Crudup	Paul Fredette
Elizabethtown	*	t	MC	3	(910) 862-2066	Sylvia Campbell	Eddie Madden	Juanita Hester	Jan Lennon	Ennis Graham	Robert Kinlaw	Pat Devane
Elkin		t	CM	4	(336) 835-9800	Thomas Gwyn	Lloyd Payne	Catherine Tilley	John Holcomb	Thomas Wheeler	Carmel Wagoner	Robert Fuller
Elon College		t	CM	6	(336) 584-3601	Roxie Schmidt	Michael Dula	Sabrina Oliver	. . .	Walter King	Dan Ingle	Donald Wagoner
Emerald Isle		t	CM	3	(252) 354-3424	Arthur Schools	Frank Rush	Rhonda Ferebee	Georgia Overman	William Walker	William Hargett	John Dunn
Enfield		t	CM	2	(252) 445-3146	Edward Jones	. . .	Jannie Burnette	Bobby Davis	. . .	. . .	Clyde Spence
Erwin	*	t	CM	4	(910) 897-5140	Patsy Carson	Bryan Thompson	Cynthia Patterson	. . .	. . .	. . .	Mark Byrd
Fairmont	*	t	CM	2	(910) 628-9766	Charles Kemp	H. Proctor	Jennifer Larson	Linda Vause	James Thompson	. . .	Ronnie Seals
Farmville		t	CM	4	(252) 753-5774	Robert Evans	Richard Hicks	Amy Bryan	. . .	. . .	Robert Smith	David Shackleford
Fayetteville	*	c	CM	121	(910) 433-1635	Anthony Chavonne	Dale Iman	Candice White	Lisa Smith	B. Nichols	Tom Bergamine	Steve Blanchard
Fletcher		t	CM	4	(828) 687-3985	Robert Parrish	Mark Biberdorf	Janice Sherlock	Carol Plack	. . .	John Moss	Ronnie Frady
Forest City		t	CM	7	(828) 245-0148	Grover Bradley	Charles Summey	Sandra Mayse	F. Walden	L. McCurry	Randy Chapman	Scott Hoyle
Franklin		t	MC	3	(828) 524-2516	. . .	Mike Decker	. . .	Janet Anderson	Howard Haithcock	Terry Bradley	Harry Gibson
Franklinton		t	CM	1	(919) 494-2520	J. Kearney	Sharon Garner	Kim Worley	. . .	Darrell Chalk	Ray Gilliam	. . .
Fremont		t	CM	1	(919) 242-6234	. . .	Kerry McDuffie	. . .	. . .	. . .	. . .	. . .
Fuquay-Varina	*	t	CM	7	(919) 552-3191	John Byrne	Andy Hedrick	Rose John	. . .	Anthony Mauldin	Larry Smith	Arthur Mouberry
Gamewell		c	MC	3	(828) 754-1991	Jack Roberts	Mary Carter	. . .	. . .	. . .	. . .	. . .
Garner	*	t	CM	17	(919) 772-4688	Ronnie Williams	F. Watkins	Judy Bass	Linwood Jones	. . .	Thomas Moss	Paul Cox
Gastonia	*	c	CM	66	(704) 866-6719	Jennifer Stultz	James Palenick	Virginia Creighton	Cindy Fortune	. . .	Tim Adams	H. Bernhardt

Directory 1/9 continued

OFFICIALS IN U.S. MUNICIPALITIES 2,500 AND OVER IN POPULATION

Jurisdiction	Type	Form of govern- ment	2000 Popu- lation	Main telephone number	Chief elected official	Appointed administrator	Clerk of the governing board	Chief financial officer	Fire chief	Police chief	Public works director
NORTH CAROLINA continued											
Gibsonville	t	CM	4	(336) 449-4144	Leonard Williams	Robert Baxley	Laurie Yarbrough	Connie Woody	Clarence Owen	Anthony Cole	Coy May
Goldsboro *	c	CM	39	(919) 580-4357	Alfonzo King	Joseph Huffman	Melissa Brewer	Kaye Scott	Gary Whaley	Timothy Bell	Karen Brashear
Graham	c	CM	12	(336) 570-6700	Bill Cooke	Chris Rollins	Eydie May	Sandra King	John Andrews	Milford Miller	Donnell Braxton
Granite Falls	t	CM	4	(828) 396-3131	Barry Hayes	Linda Story	Judy Mackie	Brenda Poe	Thomas Laws	Richard Bolick	William Hamilton
Green Level	t	CM	2	(336) 578-3443	...	...	...	...	...	...	...
Greensboro	c	CM	223	(336) 373-2065	Keith Holiday	Mitchell Johnson	Juanita Cooper	Richard Lusk	Johnny Teeters	...	...
Greenville	c	CM	60	(252) 329-2489	Robert Parrott	Wayne Bowers	Wanda Elks	Bernita Demery	Mike Burton	William Anderson	Thomas Tysinger
Grifton	t	CM	2	(252) 524-5168	Timothy Bright	Shawn Condin	Patricia Bryan	...	Ed Meeks	Warren Morrisette	Robert Williams
Hamlet	c	CM	6	(910) 582-2651	William Garner	Marchell David	Tammy Kirkley	Michael Deese	David Knight	Robert Bristow	...
Harrisburg	t	MC	4	(704) 455-5614	...	Joel Davis	...	...	...	...	...
Havelock *	c	CM	22	(919) 444-6402	Jimmy Sanders	James Freeman	Cindy Morgan	Lee Tillman	Rick Zaccardelli	Wayne Cyrus	John Quill
Haw River	t	CM	1	(336) 578-0784	Buddy Boggs	Jeffrey Earp	Misty Hagood	...	Ronnie Wade	Phillip Felts	Charles Allen
Henderson	c	CM	16	(252) 431-6000	Donald Seifert	A. Griffin	Dianne White	...	Daniel Wilkerson	Glen Allen	James Morgan
Hendersonville *	c	CM	10	(828) 697-3000	Greg Newman	William Ferguson	Tammie Drake	James Rudisill	Beau Lovelace	Herbert Blake	Tom Wooten
Hickory	c	CM	37	(828) 323-7412	G. Wright	Mick Berry	Pamela Tallent	Deanna Rios	Thomas Alexander	Thomas Adkins	Charles Hansen
High Point *	c	CM	85	(336) 883-3259	Rebecca Smothers	Stribling Boynton	Lisa Vierling	Jeffrey Moore	David Taylor	James Fealy	Chris Thompson
Hillsborough	t	CM	5	(919) 732-2104	Tom Stevens	Eric Peterson	Donna Armbrister	Greg Siler	...	Clarence Birkhead	...
Holden Beach	t	CM	..	(910) 842-6488	...	David Hewett	Joyce Shore	Kate White	...	Wallace Layne	J. Hickman
Holly Springs	t	CM	9	(919) 552-6221	Dick Sears	Carl Dean	Joni Powell	Drew Holland	...	...	Luncie McNeil
Hope Mills	t	CM	11	(910) 424-4555	...	Randy Beeman	Phyllis Register	David Stafford	Lee Sudia	John Hodges	James McLaurin
Hudson *	t	CM	3	(828) 728-8272	Billy Beane	Rebecca Bentley	Tamra Swanson	...	...	David Greene	David Davenport
Huntersville *	t	CM	24	(704) 875-6541	Jill Swain	Gregory Ferguson	Janet Pierson	Janet Stoner	...	Philip Potter	Max Buchanan
Indian Trail	t	CM	11	(704) 821-8114	Sandy Moore	Edward Humphries	...	Janice Chandler	...	...	...
Jacksonville	c	CM	66	(910) 938-5227	Jan Slagle	Kristoff Bauer	Carmen Miracle	...	Rick McIntyre	Michael Yaniero	Grant Sparks
Jamestown *	t	CM	..	(336) 454-1138	Keith Volz	Kathryn Billings	Martha Wolfe	Judy Gallman	...	...	Chuck Smith
Jonesville	t	CM	1	(336) 835-3426	Delos Martin	Ron Niland	...	Debbie Welborn	Keith Macy	Tim Gwyn	Roger Martin
Kannapolis *	c	CM	36	(704) 920-4300	Robert Misenheimer	Michael Legg	Bridgette Bell	Michael Shinn	Cyde Hiers	James Chavis	Wilmer Melton
Kenly	t	CM	1	(919) 284-2116	Herbert Hales	Elvin Shelton	Sharon Evans	...	Paul Whitehurst	Josh Gibson	Kenneth Thompson
Kernersville	t	CM	17	(336) 996-3121	Curtis Swisher	Roger Bryant	Dale Martin	...	Jimmy Barrow	Grady Stocktown	Timothy Shields
Kill Devil Hills *	t	CM	5	(252) 449-5300	Raymond Sturza	Debora Diaz	Mary Quidley	Beverly Gist	Thomas Penland	Gary Britt	...
King *	c	CM	5	(336) 983-8265	Jack Warren	John Cater	Tamara Hatley	Christine Whicker	Randy Williams	Tim Ledford	Ricky Lewis
Kings Mountain	c	CM	9	(704) 734-0333	Edgar Murphrey	Marilyn Sellers	...	Lori Hall	Frank Burns	Melvin Proctor	Jackie Barnette
Kinston	c	CM	23	(252) 939-3120	Orice Ritch	Scott Stevens	Carol Barwick	Keith Fiaschetti	Bill Johnson	Annette Boyd	Rhonda Barwick
Kitty Hawk *	t	CM	2	(252) 261-3552	Clifton Perry	John Stockton	Lynn Morris	Mike Eubank	James Spivey	David Ward	Willie Midgett
Knightdale *	t	CM	5	(919) 217-2220	Jeanne Bonds	Gary McConkey	...	Ren Wiles	Timothy Guffey	...	Tracy Pedigo
La Grange	t	MC	2	(252) 566-3186	Woodard Gurley	John Craft	Phyllis Harrison	...	David Holmes	John Sullivan	Aubrey Rouse
Lake Lure	t	CM	1	(828) 625-9983	James Proctor	...	Mary Flack	Sam Karr	Ron Morgan	Charles Hester	Tony Hennessee
Lake Waccamaw	t	CM	1	(910) 646-3700	Bolling McNeil	Darren Currie	...	...	...	Timothy Barrett	Mike Prostinak
Laurel Park *	t	CM	1	(828) 693-4840	Henry Johnson	James Ball	Kimberly Hensley	Dona Mennella	...	Donald Fisher	Marc Landreth
Laurinburg *	c	CM	15	(910) 276-8257	Ann Slaughter	Craig Honeycutt	Dee Hammond	Cynthia Carpenter	...	John Evans	...
Leland *	t	CM	1	(910) 371-0148	Walter Futch	Bill Farris	Carol Ann Floyd	Donna Strickland	...	Timothy Jayne	Jimmy Strickland
Lenoir *	c	CM	16	(828) 757-2200	David Barlow	W. Bailey	Shirley Cannon	Danny Gilbert	Kenneth Briscoe	Joseph Reynolds	Charles Beck
Lewisville	t	CM	8	(336) 945-5558	Robert Stebbins	Cecil Wood	Joyce Walker	...	...	...	George Hauser
Lexington *	c	CM	19	(336) 243-2489	John Walser	John Gray	Sara Lanier	Terra Greene	Thad Dickerson	John Lollis	Rick Comer
Liberty	t	CM	2	(336) 622-4276	John Stanley	...	Sandra Dixon	Nancy Granger	J. R. Beard	Jerry Brown	Roby Woods
Lillington *	t	CM	2	(910) 893-2654	Glenn McFadden	Tommy Burns	Vickie Wilder	Cherie Turner	John Bethune	Frank Powers	Tim Smith
Lincolnton	c	CM	9	(704) 736-8980	Bobby Huitt	Jeff Emory	Donna Flowers	Georgetta Williams	Robert Gates	Harold Abernathy	Stephen Peeler
Locust *	c	CM	2	(704) 888-5260	Harold Greene	James Inman	Lora Flieger	Michael Rupp	Dennis White	Ted Haigler	Tim Flieger
Long View	t	CM	4	(828) 322-3921	Norman Cook	David Epley	Denise Danielson	Peggy Willis	Eric Shepherd	Buck Rogers	Gary Workman
Louisburg	t	CM	3	(919) 496-3406	...	...	Carolyn Patterson	Denise Harris	Timmy Smith	Tommy Leonard	Gary Cottrell
Lowell	c	MC	2	(704) 824-3518	...	Ben Blackburn	...	...	...	...	...
Lucama	t	CM	..	(252) 239-0560	...	...	...	...	...	...	...
Lumberton	c	CM	20	(910) 671-3832	Ray Pennington	Thomas Horne	Laney Sapp	Rebecca Maynor	James Cox	Robert Grice	Henry Ivey
Madison	t	CM	2	(336) 427-0221	Kenneth Hawkins	Robert Scott	Lannette Johnson	...	Fred Butts	Perry Webster	Keith Tucker
Maggie Valley *	t	CM	..	(828) 926-0866	Roger McElroy	Timothy Barth	Vickie Best	Shayne Wheeler	...	Scott Sutton	Michael McHaffey
Maiden *	t	CM	3	(828) 428-5000	Robert Smyre	William Herms	Wendy Vanover	...	Burl Shieum	Troy Church	Billy Price
Manteo	t	CO	1	(252) 473-2133	...	Kermit Skinner	Rebecca Breiholz	Sally Defosse	...	...	James McClease
Marion *	c	CM	4	(828) 652-3551	A. Clark	J. Boyette	...	Harriett Thomas	James Neal	Mika Elliott	E. Hollifield
Marshville	t	CM	2	(704) 624-2515	Franklin Deese	Carl Webber	Shelley Maness	...	...	Mike Gaddy	Bivens Steele
Matthews	t	CM	22	(704) 847-4411	Royce Myers	Harley Blodgett	Jill Pleimann	...	...	Robin Hunter	Ralph Messera
Maxton *	t	MC	2	(910) 844-5231	Gladys Dean	Katrina Tatum	...	Myra Tyndall	...	Paul McDowell	Leonard Green
Mayodan	t	CM	2	(336) 427-0241	Billy Smith	Debra Cardwell	Melessa Hopper	Marcia Pulliam	Bryant Garner	Lawrence Shelton	David Baker
Mebane	t	CM	7	(919) 563-5901	Glendel Stephenson	Robert Wilson	Elaine Hicks	...	Bob Louis	Gary Bumgarner	Jimmy Jobe
Mills River	t	CM	6	(828) 890-2901	Roger Snyder	Jaime Adrignola	Susan Powell	...	...	...	...
Mint Hill	t	MC	14	(704) 545-9726	...	Brian Welch	Beth Hamrick	...	...	Brian Barnhardt	Dwayne Dorton
Mocksville	t	CM	4	(336) 751-2259	Francis Slate	Christine Sanders	...	...	Phil Crowe	Jack Keller	Danny Smith
Monroe *	c	CM	26	(704) 282-4500	Bobby Kilgore	F. Meadows	Jeanne Deese	...	Ronald Fowler	Debra Duncan	...
Montreat *	t	MC	..	(828) 669-8002	Letta Jean Taylor	Ron Nalley	Misty Gedlinske	Stefan Stackhouse	...	William McClintock	Charles Caldwell
Mooresville *	t	CM	18	(704) 663-3800	William Thunburg	Steven Husemann	Janet Pope	Maia Setzer	Wesley Greene	...	John Finan
Morehead City *	t	CM	7	(252) 726-6848	...	Robert Martin	Jeanne Giblin	Ellen Sewell	Wes Lail	Wrenn Johnson	David McCabe
Morganton	c	CM	17	(828) 437-8863	...	Sally Sandy	Debbie Ogle	Karen Duncan	...	...	Joseph Lookadoo
Morrisville	t	CM	5	(919) 463-6200	...	John Whitson	Diana Davis	Julia Ketchum	Todd Wright	Ira Jones	Maurice Gunn
Mount Airy	c	CM	8	(336) 786-3501	Jack Loftis	Donald Brookshire	...	John Overton	Benny Brannock	Ronald Hill	Jeffery Boyles
Mount Gilead	t	CM	1	(910) 439-5111	Earl Poplin	Lee Capps	...	Mary Lucas	Tommy Gaddy	Ronnie Jarman	Curtis Speakman
Mount Holly	c	CM	9	(704) 827-3931	Robert Black	Eric Davis	...	...	John Calder	C. Benson	Donald Price
Mount Olive	t	CM	4	(919) 658-9537	Buster Huggins	Charles Brown	Arlene Talton	...	Steve Martin	Emmett Ballree	Ervin Holland
Mount Pleasant *	t	CM	1	(704) 436-9803	Troy Barnhardt	Adrian Cox	Cathy Whittington	...	...	...	Al Slover
Murfreesboro *	t	MC	2	(252) 398-5904	Lynn Johnson	Cathy Davison	Joleatha Chestnutt	...	Bryant Cook	...	Gene Byrd
Nags Head	t	CM	2	(252) 441-5508	Robert Muller	...	Carolyn Morris	...	...	...	David Clark
Nashville *	t	CM	4	(252) 459-4511	Donald Street	Preston Mitchell	Cynthia Brake	Barbara Woodall	Timothy Pope	William Creech	Larry Williams
New Bern	c	CM	23	(252) 636-4000	Thomas Bayliss	Walter Hartman	Vickie Johnson	Mary Muraglia	Robert Aster	Frank Palombo	Danny Meadows
Newport	t	CM	3	(252) 223-4749	Derryl Garner	Richard Casey	Penny Weiss	Gay Cox	Rob Holt	Jeffrey Clark	Marty Mensch
Newton *	c	CM	12	(828) 695-4260	Robert Mullinax	Everette Clark	Beunice Roberts	...	Kevin Yoder	Donald Brown	Martin Wilson
North Topsail Beach *	c	CM	..	(910) 328-1349	Donald Martin	Lara Burleson	Carin Faulkner	Lydia King	...	Casey Fillinger	Thomas Best
North Wilkesboro	t	CM	4	(336) 667-7129	George Church	William Perkins	V. Kay Minton	Patsy Billings	Niki Hamby	Randy Rhodes	Robert Bauguess
Norwood	t	CM	2	(704) 463-5423	Darrell Almond	Dwight Smith	Pam Lisenby	...	...	...	...
Oak Island	t	CM	6	(910) 278-5011	Helen Cashwell	Jerry Walters	...	Cathy Harvell	Alan Essey	Thomas Johnson	Gene Kudgus
Oak Ridge	t	CM	3	(336) 644-7009	Ray Combs	Bruce Oakley	Larry Harville	Sam Anders	...	...	...
Ocean Isle Beach	t	CM	..	(910) 579-2166	...	Daisy Ivey	...	...	...	...	...
Oriental	t	CM	..	(252) 249-0555	...	Wyatt Cutler	...	...	...	...	...
Oxford	c	CM	8	(919) 603-1100	Alvin Woodlief	Mark Donham	Barbara Rote	Kelway Howard	Lanny Dillehay	John Wolford	...
Pembroke	t	CM	2	(910) 521-9758	...	McDuffie Cummings	...	...	...	...	...
Pilot Mountain	t	CM	1	(336) 368-2248	...	Blair Knox	...	...	...	...	...
Pinehurst	v	CM	9	(910) 295-1900	...	Andrew Wilkison	Linda Brown	...	Jimmy McCaskill	Ernest Hooker	Walter Morgan
Pinetops *	t	CM	1	(252) 827-4435	J. Cobb	Gregory Bethea	...	...	...	...	Phil Webb

Directory 1/9 continued **OFFICIALS IN U.S. MUNICIPALITIES 2,500 AND OVER IN POPULATION**

Jurisdiction	Type	Form of govern-ment	2000 Popu-lation	Main telephone number	Chief elected official	Appointed administrator	Clerk of the governing board	Chief financial officer	Fire chief	Police chief	Public works director
NORTH CAROLINA continued											
Pineville	t	CM	3	(704) 889-2291	George Fowler	Michael Rose	Sara Rodriguez	Ann Wilson	Billy Griffin	Robert Merchant	Bobby Howington
Pittsboro *	t	CM	2	(919) 542-4621	Randolph Voller	William Terry	Alice Lloyd	Scott Borror	. . .	David Collins	John Poteat
Plymouth	t	CM	4	(252) 793-9101	Jarahnee Bailey	James Tripp	. . .	. . .	Jack Barnes	Steve O'Neil	William Ehrenbeck
Princeville	t	CM	. .	(252) 823-1057	P. Everette-Oates	Samuel Knight	Diana Draughn	Pamela Barlow	. . .	Gary Foxx	. . .
Raeford *	c	CM	3	(910) 875-8161	John McNeill	. . .	. . .	Raymond Teal	Dickie Lippard	Kevin Locklear	Johnny Melton
Raleigh *	c	CM	276	(919) 890-3315	Charles Meeker	J. Allen	Gail Smith	Perry James	John McGrath	Harry Dolan	Carl Dawson
Randleman	c	CM	3	(336) 495-7500	. . .	Tony Sears	. . .	Nicole Belgarde	Martin Leonard	Steve Leonard	. . .
Red Springs *	t	CM	3	(910) 843-5241	George Paris	Billy Farmer	Barbara Bounds	Regenia Humphrey	Marvin McDonald	Troy McDuffie	George Hall
Reidsville *	c	CM	14	(336) 349-1058	. . .	Dennis Almond	Angela Stadler	Christopher Phillips	David Bracken	William Hunt	. . .
Rhodhiss *	t	CM	. .	(828) 396-8400	. . .	Barbara Harmon	. . .	. . .	Larry Yount	Timothy Anthony	Will Dennis
Richlands	t	CM	. .	(910) 324-3301	Marvin Trott	Gregg Whitehead	Eva Brown	. . .	. . .	Thomas Bennett	Jimmy Powell
River Bend *	t	CM	2	(252) 638-3870	John Kirkland	Andrew Havens	Ann Katsuyoshi	Margaret Boggs	. . .	Earl Pratt	C. Massengill
Roanoke Rapids	c	CM	16	(252) 533-2800	Drewery Beale	. . .	Lisa Vincent	Phyllis Lee	Kenneth Carawan	James Lawson	James Parnell
Rockingham	c	CM	9	(910) 997-5546	Eugene McLaurin	Monty Crump	Johnsye Lunsford	Hazel Tew	Curtis Bennett	Robert Voorhees	Richard Haugen
Rocky Mount *	c	CM	55	(252) 972-1111	David Combs	Stephen Raper	Jean Bailey	Amy Staton	Keith Harris	John Manley	Jonathan Boone
Rolesville	t	CM	. .	(919) 556-3506	Nancy Kelly	Matthew Livingston	Lynn House	. . .	. . .	Jimmy Green	. . .
Rose Hill	t	MC	1	(910) 289-3159	Clarence Brown	Thomas Drum	Jeannette Cloud	. . .	. . .	Michael O'Connell	Jerry James
Roxboro *	c	CM	8	(336) 599-3116	Thomas Brown	Jonathan Barlow	Trevie Adams	James Overton	Kenneth Torain	Jeffrey Insley	Andrew Oakley
Rutherfordton	t	MC	4	(828) 287-3520	Sally Lesher	Karen Andrews	Jennifer Armstrong	Rus Scherer	Charles Blanton	Kevin Lovelace	Keith Ward
Saint Pauls *	t	CM	2	(910) 865-5164	Gordon Westbrook	Stuart Turille	Annie Espey	. . .	Evans Jackson	Tommy Hagens	Wayne McDuffie
Salisbury	c	CM	26	(704) 638-5270	Susan Kluttz	David Treme	Myra Heard	John Sofley	Samuel Brady	Lester Wilhelm	Vernon Sherrill
Sanford *	c	CM	23	(919) 775-8348	Cornelia Olive	Phillip Hegwer	Bonnie White	Melissa Miller	Teddy Barber	Ronald Yarborough	Larry Thomas
Sawmills *	t	CM	4	(828) 396-7903	Bobby Austin	. . .	Susan Noll	Karen Clontz	. . .	. . .	Arnold Arrowood
Scotland Neck	t	MC	2	(252) 826-3152	Robert Partin	Russell Tutor	Nancy Jackson	. . .	Bruce Josey	Doug Pilgreen	Doug Braddy
Selma	t	CM	5	(919) 965-9841	Charles Hester	Richard Douglas	Fran Davis	Erica Walters	Joe Price	Charles Bowen	Terry Keen
Seven Devils *	t	CM	. .	(828) 963-5343	Bob Dodson	Robert Lambert	Karen Daniels	Debbie Powers	Bobby Powell	Chuck Davis	Kevin Aldridge
Shallotte	t	MC	1	(910) 754-4032	. . .	Paul Sabiston	. . .	Maria Gaither	. . .	Rodney Gause	Albert Hughes
Sharpsburg	t	CM	2	(252) 446-9441	. . .	Sonya Meeks	. . .	. . .	. . .	. . .	. . .
Shelby	c	CM	19	(704) 484-6471	W. Ted Alexander	James Howell	Bernadette Parduski	Ted Phillips	William Hunt	Tandy Carter	Brad Cornwell
Siler City	t	CM	6	(919) 742-4731	Charles Turner	Joel Brower	Karen Alman	Wanda Ingold	Mitch Vann	Lewis Phillips	Arthur Green
Smithfield	t	CM	11	(919) 934-2116	William Jordan	Peter Connet	Debra Holmes	Robert Plowman	Patrick Harris	Steven Gillikin	Marty Anderson
Southern Pines *	t	CM	10	(910) 692-7021	Mike Haney	Reagan Parsons	. . .	Crystal Gabric	Hampton Williams	John Letteney	. . .
Southern Shores	t	CM	2	(252) 261-2394	Paul Sutherland	Webb Fuller	Carrie Gordin	. . .	. . .	Thaddeous Pledger	Glenn Alexander
Southport	c	CM	2	(910) 457-7929	Norman Holden	. . .	Regina Alexander	Patty Miller	Gregory Cumbee	Jerry Dove	Robert Grant
Spencer *	t	CM	3	(704) 633-2231	Jody Everhart	Larry Smith	Lisa Perdue	. . .	Joel Baker	Robert Bennett	Barry Pruett
Spindale	t	CM	4	(828) 286-3466	. . .	John Lewis	Teresa Curtis	Kathleen Swafford	Harton Turner	Charles Deviney	Benny Brooks
Spring Hope	t	CM	1	(252) 478-5186	James Gwaltney	John Holpe	. . .	. . .	. . .	Timothy Denton	George Meeks
Spring Lake	t	CM	8	(910) 436-0241	Ethel Clark	Edward Faison	Cora Nunes	Allen Coats	Robert Doberstein	Alvin Brown	Daniel Gerald
Spruce Pine *	t	CM	2	(828) 765-3000	Ralph Hise	Richard Canipe	Darlene Johnson	David Lindsey	. . .	Coy Hollifield	Elbert Stamey
Stallings *	t	CM	3	(704) 821-8557	Lynda Paxton	Brian Matthews	Erinn Nichols	. . .	. . .	David Plyler	. . .
Stanley	t	CM	3	(704) 263-4779	Judith Johnson	Robert Greback	Evyonne Smith	Reva Braswell	. . .	Heath Jenkins	Hildreth Miller
Stantonsburg	0	CM	. .	(252) 238-3608	. . .	Gary Davis	. . .	. . .	. . .	. . .	. . .
Statesville	c	CM	23	(704) 878-3550	Constantine Kutteh	Robert Hites	Mary Craddock	Lisa Salmon	. . .	Stephen Hampton	. . .
Stoneville	t	MC	1	(336) 573-9393	Sammy Tuggle	Robert Wyatt	Marilyn Smith	Amy Winn	Hugh Belton	Gary Walker	Jerry Whitt
Sugar Mountain	v	MC	. .	(828) 898-9292	David Nixon	David Lane	Amy Keller	Kay Sudderth	. . .	David Henson	David Webb
Sunset Beach	t	CM	1	(910) 579-6297	Ronald Klein	Linda Fluegel	Kimberly Cochran	James Jones	Chris Barbee	Lisa Massey	John Hancock
Surf City *	t	CM	1	(910) 328-4131	A. D. Guy	J. Moore	Patricia Arnold	Jane Kirk	Joey Rivenbark	Michael Halstrad	Dean Wise
Swansboro *	t	CM	1	(910) 326-4428	Scott Chadwick	Patrick Thomas	Paula Webb	Marina Williams	Bob Penrod	Edward Parrish	Steve Edwards
Tabor City	t	CM	2	(910) 653-3458	. . .	Al Leonard	. . .	. . .	. . .	. . .	. . .
Tarboro	t	CM	11	(252) 641-4200	Donald Morris	Samuel Noble	Pamela Pate	Janet Lewis	William Whitaker	Robert Cherry	David Cashwell
Taylorsville	t	CM	1	(828) 632-2218	Guy Barriger	David Odom	Yolanda Prince	. . .	. . .	Anthony Jones	David Robinette
Thomasville	c	CM	19	(336) 475-4210	Joe Bennett	. . .	Betty Almond	Tony Jarrett	Martin Dailey	Larry Murdock	. . .
Tobaccoville	v	CM	1	(336) 983-0029	Keith Snow	Leo Corder	Robin Key	. . .	. . .	. . .	Dale Hauser
Topsail Beach	t	CM	. .	(910) 328-5841	Edward Parrish	Steven Foster	Stephanie Rivenbark	. . .	Andy Cavender	Rickey Smith	Charles Derrick
Trent Woods	t	MC	4	(252) 637-9810	J. Day	. . .	Tina Woolard	Glenda Bynum	. . .	Michael Register	Michael Haber
Trinity	c	CM	6	(336) 431-2841	. . .	Ann Bailie	Debbie Hinson	. . .	. . .	. . .	. . .
Troutman	t	CM	1	(704) 528-7600	Elbert Richardson	David Saleeby	Kim Davis	Steve Shealy	. . .	. . .	. . .
Troy	t	CM	3	(910) 572-3661	Roy Maness	Karl Zephir	. . .	Cathy Maness	Joe Huntley	E. Phillips	Gray Walls
Tryon *	t	CM	1	(828) 859-6654	J. Peoples	. . .	Susan Bell	. . .	Joey Davis	Jeff Arrowood	Joel Burrell
Valdese *	t	CM	4	(828) 879-2120	James Hatley	Jeffrey Morse	Thelda Rhoney	Jerry LaMaster	Charles Watts	John Suttle	Bryan Duckworth
Wadesboro	t	CM	3	(704) 694-5171	Lynn Horton	John Witherspoon	Nancy Huntley	. . .	Eddie Pope	. . .	Ben Barber
Wake Forest	t	CM	12	(919) 554-6100	Vivian Jones	Mark Williams	Joyce Wilson	Aileen Staples	. . .	. . .	Michael Barton
Walkertown	t	CM	4	(336) 595-4212	Kenneth Davis	Scott Snow	Carol McKinnie	. . .	. . .	. . .	. . .
Wallace	t	CM	3	(910) 285-4136	Charles Farrior	Roger Cornatzer	. . .	Anna Leary	Thomas Townsend	Bobby Maready	. . .
Walnut Cove *	t	CM	1	(336) 591-4809	John Hodgkin	Homer Dearmin	Leslie Falstreau	. . .	Tommy Ball	James Hill	Kevin Webb
Warrenton	t	CM	. .	(252) 257-3315	. . .	Larry Carver	. . .	. . .	. . .	Freddie Robinson	Paul Brown
Warsaw	t	MC	3	(910) 293-7814	Win Batten	Jason Burrell	. . .	Myra Mays	John Blackmore	Raymond Wood	Gerald Lanier
Washington *	c	CM	9	(252) 975-9319	Lee Rumley	James Smith	Rita Thompson	. . .	Jimmy Davis	Joseph Stringer	Raymond Lewis
Waxhaw	0	CM	2	(704) 843-2195	. . .	Francis McLaurin	. . .	. . .	. . .	. . .	. . .
Waynesville *	t	CM	9	(828) 452-2491	Gavin Brown	A. Galloway	Phyllis McClure	Eddie Caldwell	Joey Webb	William Hollingsed	Fred Baker
Weaverville	t	CM	2	(828) 645-7116	Mary Stroud	Michael Morgan	Shelby Shields	Brenda Ayers	Fred Sims	Gregory Stephens	Lawrence Sprinkle
Weddington *	t	CM	6	(704) 846-2709	Nancy Anderson	. . .	Amy McCollum	Leslie Gaylord	. . .	. . .	. . .
Wendell	t	CM	4	(919) 365-4444	Lucius Jones	David Bone	. . .	Barbara Raper	. . .	Joseph Privette	Donnie Ayscue
West Jefferson	t	CM	1	(336) 246-3551	Dale Baldwin	Steven McGinnis	. . .	Katherine Howell	Calvin Green	James Williams	David Hamilton
Whiteville	c	CM	5	(910) 642-8046	Anne Jones	Joshua Ray	. . .	Douglas Palmer	Bill Poe	Robert Memory	. . .
Wilkesboro	t	CM	3	(336) 838-3951	Norman Call	Kenneth Noland	Josephine Cass	. . .	Mike Testerman	Robert Bowlin	Jim Wyatt
Williamston *	t	MC	5	(252) 792-5142	Tommy Roberson	Donald Christopher	Glinda Fox	Ronnie Wilson	James Peele	Mark Smith	Kerry Spivey
Wilmington	c	CM	75	(910) 341-7800	Harper Peterson	Sterling Cheatham	A. Spicer-Sidbury	William McAbee	Samuel Hill	John Cease	. . .
Wilson *	c	CM	44	(252) 399-2300	Calvin Rose	Grant Goings	Rebecca Rose	Gordon Baker	Donald Oliver	Harris Tyson	. . .
Windsor	t	CM	2	(252) 794-2331	. . .	Allen Castelloe	. . .	. . .	. . .	. . .	. . .
Wingate *	t	MC	2	(704) 233-4411	Bill Braswell	Greyson Blanchard	Karen Wingo	. . .	. . .	Barry Glass	Mike Brower
Winston-Salem *	c	CM	185	(336) 747-6800	Allen Joines	Lee Garrity	Renee Henderson	Denise Bell	Antony Farmer	Scott Cunningham	. . .
Winterville	t	CM	4	(252) 756-2221	Douglas Jackson	William Whisnant	Tangi Leary	Anthony Bowers	. . .	Billy Wilkes	Bobby Crawford
Woodfin	t	MC	3	(828) 253-4887	Alvin Honeycott	Jason Young	Cheryl Mears	. . .	. . .	William Krause	Dewey Wills
Wrightsville Beach	t	CM	2	(910) 256-7900	James Roberts	Robert Simpson	Sylvia Holleman	Peggy Jones	. . .	John Carey	Michael Vukelich
Yadkinville	t	CM	2	(336) 679-8732	Hubert Gregory	Kenneth Larking	Nancy Hollar	. . .	. . .	William Parks	Perry Williams
Yanceyville *	t	CM	2	(336) 694-5431	Dan Printz	David Parrish	. . .	Carolyn Hall	. . .	. . .	Mark Guthrie
Youngsville *	t	CM	. .	(919) 556-5073	Samuel Hardwick	Brenda Robbins	Emily Hurd	. . .	. . .	Phillip Pritchett	. . .
Zebulon	t	CM	4	(919) 269-7455	Robert Matheny	Richard Hardin	Lisa Markland	Emily Thomas	Sidney Perry	Timothy Hayworth	Kenneth Waldroup
NORTH DAKOTA											
Beulah	c	MC	3	(701) 873-4637	. . .	. . .	. . .	. . .	. . .	. . .	. . .
Bismarck *	c	CO	55	(701) 222-6471	John Warford	William Wocken	. . .	Sheila Hillman	Joel Boespflug	Keith Witt	. . .
Bottineau	c	MC	2	(701) 228-3232	. . .	. . .	. . .	. . .	. . .	. . .	. . .
Carrington	c	MC	2	(701) 652-2911	Donald Frye	Vicky Triplett	. . .	. . .	. . .	Randy Munkeby	Doug Schroeder

Directory 1/9 continued **OFFICIALS IN U.S. MUNICIPALITIES 2,500 AND OVER IN POPULATION**

Jurisdiction	Type	Form of govern-ment	2000 Popu-lation	Main telephone number	Chief elected official	Appointed administrator	Clerk of the governing board	Chief financial officer	Fire chief	Police chief	Public works director
NORTH DAKOTA continued											
Cavalier	c	MC	1	(701) 265-8800	Ronald Storie	Thomas Trenbeath	Christal Schlecht	Katie Werner	...	David Peterson	Barry Walton
Devils Lake	c	CO	7	(701) 662-7600	Fred Bott	Terry Johnston	Carol Donnelly	...	James Moe	Bruce Kemmet	...
Dickinson *	c	CO	16	(701) 456-7744	Dennis Johnson	...	Cindy Selinger	Tina Fisher	Robert Sivak	Chuck Rummel	Roger Rapp
Fargo *	c	MC	90	(701) 241-1334	Dennis Walaker	Patrick Zavoral	...	Kent Costin	Bruce Hoover	Keith Ternes	...
Grafton	c	MC	4	(701) 352-1561	...	...	...	...	...	...	...
Grand Forks *	c	MC	49	(701) 746-2665	Michael Brown	Richard Duquette	...	John Schmisek	Peter O'Neill	John Packett	Todd Feland
Harvey	c	MC	1	(701) 324-2000	Wes Arnold	Kim Moen	...	...	Gary Troftgruben	Larry Hoffer	Robert Weninger
Jamestown	c	MC	15	(701) 252-5900	...	...	...	...	...	...	...
Mandan	c	CO	16	(701) 667-3210	Robert Dykshoorn	Kevin Christ	...	...	Pete Gartner	...	Pete Snider
Minot *	c	CM	36	(701) 857-4756	Curt Zimbelman	David Waind	...	Cindy Hemphill	C. J. Craven	Jeffrey Balentine	Alan Walter
Rugby	c	MC	2	(701) 776-6181	Dale Niewoehner	Howard Burns	Phyllis Johnson	...	William Hartl	Robert Walls	Jerome Voeller
Valley City	c	CO	6	(701) 845-1700	...	...	...	...	...	...	...
Wahpeton	c	MC	8	(701) 642-8448	Duane Schmitz	Shawn Kessel	...	Darcie Huwe	Don Klovstad	Scott Throsteinson	Randall Nelson
Watford City	c	MC	1	(701) 444-2533	...	Lowell Cutshaw	...	...	...	...	...
West Fargo *	c	CO	14	(701) 433-5300	Richard Mattern	Jim Brownlee	Verna Mangin	Sharon Schacher	Roy Schatschneider	Arland Rasmussen	Barry Johnson
Williston	c	CO	12	(701) 572-8161	...	...	...	...	...	...	...
OHIO											
Ada	v	MC	5	(419) 634-4045	...	...	...	...	...	Ray Mumma	...
Akron	c	MC	217	(330) 375-2726	Donald Plusquellic	Jerry Holland	...	Diane Miller-Dawson	Charles Gladman	Max Rothal	Paul Barnett
Alliance	c	MC	23	(330) 821-3110	Toni Middleton	John Blaser	...	Alexander Zumbar	James Reese	Lawrence Dordea	...
Amberley *	v	CM	3	(513) 531-8675	Charles Kamine	Bernard Boraten	Patricia Eisenmann	Margaret Crowley	...	John Monahan	Stephen Rasfeld
Amherst	c	MC	11	(440) 988-4380	John Higgins	...	Olga Sivinski	Diane Eswine	Ralph Zilch	Lonnie Dillon	...
Anderson Township	tp	MC	43	(513) 688-8400	Russell Jackson	Henry Dolive	Kenneth Dietz	...	Mark Ober	...	Richard Shelley
Anna	v	MC	1	(937) 394-3751	...	Jon Hulsmeyer	Kathleen Eshleman	...	...	Charles Shepherd	Daniel Patterson
Arcanum	v	MC	2	(937) 692-8500	Larry Foureman	Philip Courtright	...	Lori Huffman	Ken Williams	Dan Light	...
Archbold	v	MC	4	(419) 445-4726	James Wyse	Dennis Howell	Laurie Storrer	Joan Lovejoy	...	Martin Schmidt	...
Ashland	c	MC	21	(419) 289-3426	William Strine	...	...	Nancy Boyd	...	...	...
Ashtabula	c	MC	20	(440) 992-7103	Robert Beacom	August Pugliese	La Vette Hennigan	Michael Zullo	Ron Pristera	...	Dominic Iarocci
Ashville	v	CM	3	(740) 983-6367	Chuck Wise	Frank Christman	...	Nelson Embrey	...	Jerry Pennington	...
Athens *	c	MC	21	(740) 592-3338	Paul Wiehl	Paula Moseley	Debra Walker	Kathy Hecht	Robert Troxel	Richard Mayer	Andrew Stone
Aurora	c	MC	13	(330) 995-9100	Lynn McGill	...	Tracy Humbert	Robert Paul	David Barnes	Seth Riewaldt	John Trew
Avon	c	MC	11	(440) 937-7800	James Smith	...	Ellen Young	Robert Hamilton	Frank Root	John Vilagi	...
Avon Lake *	c	MC	18	(440) 933-6141	Karl Zuber	...	...	Tom DiLellio	William Morris	David Owad	John Kniepper
Baltimore	v	MC	2	(740) 862-4491	Robert Kalish	Terry McGrath	...	Florence Welker	...	Bret Rogers	...
Barberton	c	MC	27	(330) 753-6611	...	...	...	...	...	...	...
Barnesville	v	CM	4	(740) 425-3444	Thomas Michelli	Roger Deal	...	Amy Jackson	Robert Smith	David Norris	...
Bay Village	c	MC	16	(440) 871-2200	Deborah Sutherland	...	Joan Kemper	Steven Presley	Gregory Jackson	David Wright	James Sears
Beachwood	c	MC	12	(216) 464-1070	Merle Gorden	...	Carol Vinyard	David Pfaff	Patrick Kearns	Mark Sechrist	Dale Pekarek
Beavercreek *	c	CM	37	(937) 427-5500	Julie Van	Michael Cornell	Christine Bucheit	Bill Kucera	...	John Turner	Ronald Huff
Bedford	c	CM	14	(440) 232-1600	Daniel Pocek	Robert Reid	Kathleen Lynch	Frank Gambosi	David Nagy	Gregory Duber	Clinton Bellar
Bedford Heights *	c	MC	11	(440) 786-3200	...	...	Patricia Stahl	Mark Cegelka	Ken Ledford	Tim Kalavsky	Nick Baucco
Bellaire	c	MC	4	(740) 676-6538	...	...	...	...	...	...	...
Bellbrook *	c	CM	7	(937) 848-4666	...	...	...	...	...	...	...
Bellefontaine	c	MC	13	(937) 592-4376	Robert Lentz	Garon Carmean	...	Tim Decker	James Holycross	Bradley Kunze	...
Bellevue	c	MC	8	(419) 484-8400	George Branco	Gary Haynes	Vickie Dauch	Linda Cooper-Smith	Sherrard Barr	Richard Englund	...
Belpre	c	MC	6	(740) 423-7592	Richard Thomas	Willis Neff	...	Patrick Hines	Wesley Walker	Ira Walker	Michael Betz
Berea	c	MC	18	(440) 826-5800	Joseph Biddlecombe	...	...	Dana Kavander	Theodore Novak	Harry Bernhardt	R. Brown
Bethel *	v	CM	2	(513) 734-2243	John Swarthout	...	...	...	...	...	...
Bethel	tp	CM	4	(937) 845-8472	...	...	Deborah Watson	...	F. Reittinger	...	...
Bexley	c	MC	13	(614) 235-8694	David Madison	...	...	Beecher Hale	...	John Carruthers	Dorothy Pritchard
Blanchester	v	MC	4	(937) 783-4702	Harry Brumbaugh	...	James Walker	...	...	Robert Gable	Myers James
Blue Ash *	c	CM	12	(513) 745-8500	Jack Buckman	David Waltz	Susan Bennett	Sherry Poppe	Rick Brown	Chris Wallace	Michael Duncan
Bluffton	v	MC	3	(419) 358-2066	...	James Mehaffie	...	...	...	...	...
Botkins *	v	MC	1	(937) 693-3856	Steve Woodruff	Michael Van Brocklin	Ed Brown	...	Steve Steinke	Wayne Glass	Robert Drees
Bowling Green	c	MC	29	(419) 353-6200	John Quinn	John Fawcett	Kay Scherreik	Brian Bushong	Stephen Meredith	...	Brian Craft
Brecksville *	c	MC	13	(440) 526-4351	Jerry Hruby	...	Mary Scullin	Virginia Price	Edwin Egut	Dennis Kancler	Robert Pech
Bridgeport	v	MC	2	(740) 635-9998	John Callarik	...	Betty Riley	...	Mark Subasic	William Frasher	...
Broadview Heights *	c	MC	15	(440) 526-4357	Glenn Goodwin	...	Annette Phelps	Linda Pertz	Lee Ippolito	Robert Lipton	Raymond Mack
Brook Park	c	MC	21	(216) 433-1300	Thomas Coyne	...	Roseann Armstrong	Gregory Cingle	Neal Donnelly	Thomas Dease	...
Brooklyn	c	MC	11	(216) 351-2133	John Coyne	...	Nathan Felker	...	Daniel Smetana	James Maloney	T. Morgan
Brooklyn Heights	v	MC	1	(216) 749-4300	Michael Procuk	...	...	...	Michael Lasky	Joseph Kocab	...
Brookville	c	CM	5	(937) 833-2135	...	John Wright	...	Sonja Keaton	James Nickel	Edgar Preston	...
Brunswick	c	CM	33	(330) 225-9144	...	Robert Zienkowski	Barb Ortiz	Bill White	Mark Schrade	Carl DeForest	Sam Scaffide
Bryan	c	MC	8	(419) 636-4232	Douglas Johnson	...	...	John Seele	Jerry Manon	Gregory Brillhart	Stephen Casebere
Buckeye Lake	v	MC	3	(740) 928-7100	Frank Foster	...	Tim Matheny	...	Pete Leindecker	Ronald Small	...
Bucyrus	c	MC	13	(419) 562-6767	Douglas Wilson	Jack Binnix	Regina Zornes	Carol Wagner	Daniel Ross	Michael Corwin	...
Byesville	v	MC	2	(740) 685-5901	Donald Gadd	Richard Rausch	Tracey Cain	...	Brian Sills	John Hornak	Thomas McVicker
Cadiz *	v	MC	3	(740) 942-8844	Ken Zitko	...	...	...	Ryan Keesey	Bryan Dowdle	Thomas Carter
Cambridge *	c	MC	11	(740) 439-1240	Charles Schaub	Robert Ley	Sharon Cassler	Sue Ellen Johnson	William Minter	Brian Neff	Jerry Williams
Campbell *	c	MC	9	(330) 755-1451	John Dill	Charles Terek	Judith Clement	Dennis Stephens	David Horvath	Nicholas Phillips	Robert Davis
Canal Fulton *	c	MC	5	(330) 854-2225	John Grogan	Mark Cozy	Tammy Marthey	Scott Svab	Ray Green	David Frisone	Daniel Mayberry
Canal Winchester *	v	MC	4	(614) 837-7493	Michael Ebert	...	...	Nanisa Osborn	...	...	Matthew Peoples
Canfield *	c	CM	7	(330) 533-1101	William Kay	Charles Tieche	Patricia Matevich	Sandra Mayberry	...	David Blystone	...
Canton	c	MC	80	(330) 489-3000	Richard Watkins	Michael Miller	Debra Vanckunas	Kim Perez	James Scott	Dean McKim	Kevin Monroe
Cardington *	v	MC	1	(419) 864-7607	Vicki Wise	Daniel Ralley	Athena Abraham	Kathy Belcher	...	...	...
Carey	v	MC	3	(419) 396-7681	Dallas Risner	Roy Johnson	Antonia Ahlberg	...	Chad Snyder	Dennis Yingling	Todd Spurlock
Carlisle *	v	CM	5	(937) 746-0555	Tim Humphries	Sherry Callahan	Flo Cracraft	Julie Duffy	Gregory Wallace	Timothy Boggess	Dan Casson
Carrollton *	v	MC	3	(330) 627-2411	Stan Bright	Robert Fowler	...	Judi Noble	...	Ronald Yeager	Michael Leslie
Cedarville	v	MC	3	(937) 766-2061	James Phipps	Paul Terrell	...	...	...	Keith Stigers	...
Celina	c	MC	10	(419) 586-6464	Craig Klopfleisch	Thomas Schwartz	Barbara Belknap	Patrick Smith	Douglas Kuhn	David Slusser	Dennis Zahn
Centerville *	c	CM	23	(937) 433-7151	Mark Kingseed	Gregory Horn	Debbie James	...	William Gaul	Stephen Walker	Robert James
Chagrin Falls	v	MC	4	(440) 247-5050	Thomas Brick	Benjamin Himes	...	David Bloom	James Leffler	James Brosius	...
Chardon *	c	CM	5	(440) 286-2600	Karen Simpson	David Lelko	Amy Day	Jeffrey Smock	Larry Gaspar	Tim McKenna	Gayland Moore
Cheviot	c	MC	9	(513) 661-2700	J. Laumann	Steven Neal	...	Debra Gooch	...	...	Thomas Braun
Chillicothe	c	MC	21	(740) 774-1185	Margaret Planton	...	...	William Morrissey	Bruce Vaughan	...	Richard Johnson
Cincinnati	c	CM	331	(513) 352-2400	Mark Mallory	Milton Dohoney	Melissa Autry	Joe Gray	Robert Wright	Thomas Streicher	Andrew Glenn
Circleville *	c	MC	13	(740) 477-2551	...	...	Linda Chancey	Gayle Spangler	Tim Tener	...	Terry Elliott
Clayton	c	MC	13	(937) 836-3500	Joyce Deitering	David Rowlands	Wilbur Sussman	Kevin Schweitzer	...	...	...
Cleveland	c	MC	478	(216) 664-2000	Frank Jackson	Darnell Brown	...	Sharon Dumas	...	...	...
Cleveland Heights *	c	CM	49	(216) 291-4444	...	Robert Downey	...	Thomas Malone	Kevin Mohr	Martin Lentz	Alex Mannarino
Clyde	c	CM	6	(419) 547-6898	...	Daniel Weaver	Tami Steinbauer	Christine May	James Andrews	Bruce Gower	...
Coal Grove	v	MC	2	(740) 533-0102	Bernard McKnight	Mark Dean	Juanita Markel	...	...	John Goldcamp	...
Coldwater	v	MC	4	(419) 678-4881	Vern Stammen	...	Clyde Bellinger	...	...	Gery Thobe	John Moorman
Colerain Township *	tp	MC	60	(513) 385-7500	Keith Corman	David Foglesong	...	Heather Harlow	G. Smith	Steven Sarver	Bruce McClain

Directory 1/9 continued — OFFICIALS IN U.S. MUNICIPALITIES 2,500 AND OVER IN POPULATION

Jurisdiction	Type	Form of govern- ment	2000 Popu- lation	Main telephone number	Chief elected official	Appointed administrator	Clerk of the governing board	Chief financial officer	Fire chief	Police chief	Public works director
OHIO continued											
Columbiana *	v	CM	5	(330) 482-2173	Lowell Schloneger	Keith Chamberlin	Deann Davis	Mary Dicken	Charles Flohr	John Krawchyk	Jay Groner
Columbus	c	MC	711	(614) 645-8100	Michael Coleman	...	Timothy McSweeney	Joel Taylor	Ned Pettus	James Jackson	Linda Page
Conneaut *	c	CM	12	(440) 593-7401	James Jones	Robert Schaumleffel	Pamela Harper	John Williams	Bim Orrenmaa	John Arcaro	Bob Howland
Copley *	tp	MC	13	(330) 666-1853	Helen Humphrys	Peggy Spraggins	...	Janice Marhall	Michael Benson	Michael Mier	...
Cortland	v	MC	6	(330) 637-3916	Curt Moll	...	Donna Lyden	Fran Moyer	William Novakovich	Gary Mink	Don Wittman
Coshocton	c	MC	11	(740) 622-1465	Timothy Turner	Jerry Stenner	...	Lois Murphy	Mike Layton	...	...
Covington	v	MC	2	(937) 473-2102	Lowell Yingst	...	...	Kay McKinney	C. Westfall	Rick Wright	Michael Manson
Crestline	c	MC	5	(419) 683-3800	Peter Dzugan	Eugene Toy	Annette Johnston	Jody Wagoner	David Bauer	Edward Wilhite	...
Crooksville	v	MC	2	(740) 982-2656	Douglas Cannon	Thomas Collins	Kathy Campbell	...	Kenneth Alexander	Robin Zinn	...
Cuyahoga Falls *	c	MC	49	(330) 971-8000	Don Robart	...	...	Joseph Brodzinsky	Paul Moledor	John Conley	Valerie Wax Carr
Dayton	c	CM	166	(937) 333-4047	Rhine McLin	Rashad Young	Leonard Roberts	Cheryl Garrett	Larry Collins	Julian Davis	Frederick Stovall
Deer Park *	c	MC	5	(513) 794-8860	David Collins	Michael Berens	...	John Applegate	...	Michael Schlie	...
Deerfield *	tp	MC	25	(513) 701-6958	...	Daniel Evers	John Wahle	...	Robert Eisele	Brian Tinch	Larry Weis
Defiance *	c	MC	16	(419) 782-3199	Bob Armstrong	Jeff Leonard	...	John Seele	Mark Marentette	Timothy Tobias	...
Delaware *	c	CM	25	(740) 203-1000	Windell Wheeler	R. Homan	Christine Shaw	Dean Stelzer	John Donahue	Russell Martin	Tim Browning
Delhi *	tp	MC	30	(513) 922-3111	Jerome Luebbers	Gerard Schroeder	Kenneth Ryan	...	William Zoz	James Howarth	Robert Bass
Delphos	c	MC	6	(419) 695-4010	Gerald Neumeier	Gregory Berquist	...	Tom Jettinghoff	David McNeal	David Wagner	...
Delta *	v	CM	2	(419) 822-4500	Dan Miller	Derek Allen	Valerie Edwards	...	...	Garry Chamberlin	...
Dennison	v	MC	2	(740) 922-4072	...	...	...	...	Charles Pulley	...	...
Dover *	c	MC	12	(330) 343-6395	R. Homrighausen	...	...	Mary Fox	Russell Volkert	Ronald Johnson	...
Dublin	c	CM	31	(614) 410-4400	Thomas McCash	...	Anne Clarke	Marsha Grigsby	...	...	...
East Cleveland	c	MC	27	(216) 681-5020	Eric Brewer	...	...	...	Bobby Jenkins	Mitchell Guyton	R. Kenniebrew
East Liverpool	c	MC	13	(330) 385-3381	Dolores Satow	Paul Wise	...	Kim Woomer	Gerald Barcus	Michael McVay	Robert Disch
East Palestine	c	CM	4	(330) 426-4367	Raymond Hull	Gary Clark	Cindy Clark	Constance Robinson	Brett Todd	Clyde Hoffmeister	John Jurjaucic
Eastlake	c	MC	20	(440) 951-1416	Dan Dilberto	...	Deborah Cendvoski	John Masterson	Richard Sabo	John Ruth	William Philipp
Eaton	c	CM	8	(937) 456-4125	Robert Ball	Martin Gabbard	...	Leslie Renner	Richard Crowe	Jeff Fuller	John Hornbrook
Elmwood Place	v	MC	2	(513) 242-2578	Richard Ellison	...	Ronald Hamm	...	Terry Zimmerman	Douglas Herberger	...
Elyria	c	MC	55	(440) 326-1404	William Grace	...	...	Thaddeus Pileski	John Zielinski	Michael Medders	Thomas Brand
Englewood *	c	CM	12	(937) 836-5106	Patricia Burnside	Eric Smith	...	Janine Cooper	Elmer Bergman	Mark Brownfield	...
Enon *	v	MC	2	(937) 864-7870	Jerry Crane	Timothy Howard	Stephen Trout	...	...	Paul Wilmer	...
Euclid	c	MC	52	(440) 289-2700	...	...	...	...	...	...	...
Evendale *	v	MC	3	(513) 563-2244	Don Apking	...	Michelle Ficke	George Snyder	John Vail	Gary Foust	Jim Bothe
Fairborn *	c	CM	32	(937) 754-3020	Gary Woodward	Deborah McDonnell	Julie Taylor	Randall Groves	Michael Riley	Terry Barlow	Robert Sowers
Fairfield	tp	MC	15	(513) 887-4400	Joe McAbee	Kate Earley	Chris Fontaine	...	Dave Downie	D. Kirsch	...
Fairfield	c	CM	42	(513) 867-5300	Ronald D'Epifanio	Arthur Pizzano	Dena Morsch	Mary Hopton	Donald Bennett	Michael Dickey	David Bock
Fairlawn	c	MC	7	(330) 668-9500	William Roth	...	Tonja Caldwell	Jerry Apple	Glenn Goodrich	Kenneth Walsh	John Sellars
Fairport Harbor	v	MC	3	(440) 352-3620	Frank Sarosy	Thomas Hilston	...	...	Jeffrey Hogya	Mark Kish	...
Fairview Park *	c	MC	17	(440) 356-4400	Eileen Patton	...	Traci Waldron	Ted Kowalski	David Simon	Patrick Nealon	...
Fayette	v	CM	1	(419) 237-2116	Anita VanZile	Thomas Spiess	...	Lisa Zuver	Tom Franks	Rick Kline	...
Findlay	c	MC	38	(419) 424-7137	John Stozich	Robert Ruse	Sally Cassidy	Janet Wobser	Roy De Vore	Tom Renninger	...
Forest Park	c	CM	19	(513) 595-5200	...	Ray Hodges	Kathy Lives	...	Patricia Brooks	Kenneth Hughes	Dave Buesking
Fort Shawnee	v	MC	3	(419) 991-2015	Dennis Shaffer	...	...	Twyla Overman	...	Benjamin Kehres	...
Fostoria	c	MC	13	(419) 435-8282	John Davoli	Ronald Reinhard	Paul Allison	...	Russell Rite	Phil Hobbs	...
Franklin *	c	CM	11	(937) 746-9921	Scott Lipps	James Lukas	Jane McGee	Mike Robinette	J. Westendorf	Gordon Ellis	Howard Lewis
Fremont	c	MC	17	(419) 334-2687	Terry Overmyer	...	...	...	Daniel De Vanna	Monte Huss	Kenneth Myers
Gahanna	c	MC	32	(614) 342-4000	R. Stinchcomb	...	Connie McGlish	W. Isler	Dennis Murphy	...	Roland Hall
Galion *	c	CM	11	(419) 468-1680	...	David Oles	...	James Graff	Michael Christini	Brian Saterfield	...
Gallipolis	c	CM	4	(740) 446-1789	Dow Saunders	R. Jenkins	...	Annette Landers	W. Poling	Roger Brandeberry	...
Garfield Heights	c	MC	30	(216) 475-1100	Thomas Longo	...	...	Richard Obert	Anthony Collova	Thomas Murphy	Timothy McLaughlin
Geneva	c	CM	6	(440) 466-4675	Dennis Brown	James Pearson	Laurie Donatone	Juanita Stuetzer	Doug Starkey	Daniel Dudik	Gary Hydinger
Georgetown	v	CM	3	(937) 378-6395	John Jandes	Kelly Jones	Vickie Bradley	...	...	Forrest Coburn	...
Germantown	c	CM	4	(937) 855-7255	Theodore Landis	...	Anna Casto	Rebecca Jamison	Scott Anding	Roy McGill	...
Girard	c	MC	10	(330) 545-3879	...	...	...	...	...	...	...
Glenwillow	v	MC	..	(440) 232-8788	...	...	...	...	...	...	...
Golf Manor	v	MC	3	(513) 531-7491	Donna Faulk	Stephen Tilley	Gregory Doening	...	Gregory Bollmon	...	...
Grandview Heights	c	MC	6	(614) 488-3159	N. Sexton	Patrik Bowman	...	James Nicholson	Henry Kauffman	Rollin Kiser	Sam Troiano
Granville *	v	CM	3	(740) 587-0707	Melissa Hartfield	Donald Holycross	Beverly Adzic	Molly Roberts	...	Jim Mason	Terry Hopkins
Green	c	MC	22	(330) 896-6602	Daniel Croghan	...	Molly Kapeluck	Laurence Rush	Robert Calderone	...	...
Green	tp	MC	55	(513) 574-4848	William Seitz	Kevin Celarek	Stephen Grote	...	...	...	Adam Goetzman
Greenfield	c	MC	4	(937) 981-3048	Betty Jackman	Charles Bowman	...	Jaclyn Emerick	Steven Campbell	Robin Roche	...
Greenhills *	v	CM	4	(513) 825-2100	Oscar Hoffmann	Jane Berry	...	Kathryn Brokaw	Anthony Spaeth	Thomas Doyle	John Hester
Greenville *	c	MC	13	(937) 548-1482	Michael Bowers	...	...	Nancy Myers	Mark Wolf	Dennis Butts	...
Grove City	c	MC	27	(614) 277-3000	Cheryl Grossman	...	Tami Kelly	Robert Behlen	...	James McKean	James Blackburn
Groveport	v	MC	3	(614) 836-5301	Lance Westcamp	J. Morris	Julie Fisher	Kenneth Salak	...	Bary Murphy	Dennis Moore
Hamilton	c	CM	60	(513) 785-7030	Donald Ryan	Michael Samoviski	Ina Allen	William Moller	Joseph Schutte	Neil Ferdelman	R. Reigelsperger
Hanover	tp	MC	7	(513) 896-9059	...	Bruce Henry	...	...	...	...	...
Harrison	c	MC	7	(513) 367-2111	Daniel Gieringer	...	...	James Satger	Alan Kinnett	...	James Lauver
Harrison Township	tp	MC	2	(937) 890-5611	George Curry	Marlyn Flee	Linda Pickard	...	Ronald Casey	...	Randy Brooks
Heath	c	MC	8	(740) 522-1420	Daniel Dupps	...	Lynn Hunt	Carolyn Broyles	Rick Taylor	Gordon Ellis	...
Hebron	v	MC	2	(740) 928-2261	Clifford Mason	Michael Mcfarland	Vicky Fulk	...	Randy Weekly	Mike Carney	...
Hicksville	v	MC	3	(419) 542-6138	Janis Meyer	Kent Miller	Diane Collins	...	...	Laurie Szabo	...
Highland Heights	c	MC	8	(440) 461-2440	Scott Coleman	...	...	Anthony Ianiro	Edward Berrcin	James Cook	Thomas Evans
Hilliard *	c	MC	24	(614) 876-7361	Donald Schonhardt	...	Tara Maine	M. Kelly-Underwood	David Long	Rodney Garnett	Clyde Seidle
Hillsboro	c	MC	6	(937) 393-5219	Dick Zink	Ralph Holt	Beverly Brown	Rosemary Ryan	Gerald Powell	Nicholas Thompson	...
Hubbard	c	MC	8	(330) 534-3090	George Praznik	William Colletta	Linda Green	Michael Villano	...	Raymond Moffitt	...
Huber Heights *	c	CM	38	(937) 233-1423	...	E. Wilson Benson	Anthony Rodgers	Donnie Jones	Robert Maimone	Robert Schommer	Alexander Hynds
Hudson *	c	CM	22	(330) 650-1799	William Currin	Anthony Bales	Mary Ann George	Jeffrey Knoblauch	Robert Carter	David Robbins	Priscilla Blanchard
Huron	c	CM	7	(419) 433-5000	...	Andrew White	...	Catherine Ramey	Paul Berlin	Randy Glovinsky	...
Independence	c	MC	7	(216) 524-4131	Fred Ramos	...	Angela Zeleznik	John Veres	Peter Nelson	Michael Dugan	David Snyderburn
Indian Hill *	v	CM	5	(513) 561-6500	Eppa Rixey	Michael Burns	Paul Riordan	Nadine Weber	...	Charles Schlie	John Davis
Ironton	c	MC	11	(740) 532-3833	John Elam	...	Janet Hieronimus	Cynthia Anderson	Thomas Runyon	James Carey	John McCabe
Jackson *	c	MC	6	(740) 286-3224	Randy Heath	William Sheward	Tera Brown	Carl Barnett	Doug Reed	Carl Eisnaugle	...
Jackson	tp	MC	32	(614) 875-2742	...	Michael Lilly	...	...	...	...	...
Jefferson	v	MC	3	(440) 576-3941	Judy Maloney	Terry Finger	...	...	John Wayman	Steve Febel	...
Johnstown *	v	MC	3	(740) 967-3177	Karl VanDeest	...	Regina Hunt	Sandra Berry	...	Donald Corbin	Jack Liggett
Kent *	c	CM	27	(330) 676-7500	John Fender	David Ruller	Linda Copley	Barbara Rissland	James Williams	James Peach	Gene Roberts
Kenton	c	MC	8	(419) 674-4850	Gary Ritzler	Ronald Shaffer	Brenda Keckler	Cynthia Layman	Russell Blue	John Vermillion	Burl Helton
Kettering	c	CM	57	(937) 296-2400	Marilou Smith	Mark Schwieterman	Connie Gaw	Nancy Gregory	Robert Zickler	James O'Dell	...
Kirtland	c	MC	6	(440) 256-3332	Edward Podojil	...	Valerie Beres	Keith Martinet	Anthony Hutton	Wayne Baumgart	Carmelo Catania
Lake	tp	MC	25	(330) 877-9479	Don Myers	Carolyn Casey	Ben Sommers	...	...	Don Hensley	...
Lakemore	v	MC	2	(330) 733-6125	Richard Humm	William Bookman	Sandra Stafford	...	Clarence Bittner	Rodney Sands	...
Lakewood	c	MC	56	(216) 521-7580	Madeline Cain	...	Mary Hagan	Glenda Blasko	Lawrence Mroz	Timothy Malley	William Boag
Lancaster	c	MC	35	(740) 687-6676	Arthur Wallace	Earl Strawn	...	Mary Green	Steven Sells	Randall Lutz	...
Lebanon	c	CM	16	(513) 932-3060	Amy Brewer	George Clements	...	Sharee Dick	Michael Hannigan	Kenneth Burns	...
Leipsic *	v	CM	2	(419) 943-2009	Kevin Benton	James Russell	R. Schortgen	...	David Goodwin	Chad Schmersal	Kevin Lammon

Directory 1/9 continued **OFFICIALS IN U.S. MUNICIPALITIES 2,500 AND OVER IN POPULATION**

Jurisdiction		Type	Form of govern-ment	2000 Popu-lation	Main telephone number	Chief elected official	Appointed administrator	Clerk of the governing board	Chief financial officer	Fire chief	Police chief	Public works director
OHIO continued												
Lewisburg	*	v	CM	1	(937) 962-4377	David Scott	Patrick Bravo	...	R. Schlotterbeck	Robert Sewert	Randall Creech	...
Lexington	*	v	MC	4	(419) 884-0765	Eugene Parkison	Randy Pore	Brenda Wilson	James Banks	Rich Compton	Brett Pauley	...
Liberty	*	tp	MC	15	(740) 938-2000	Curt Sybert	David Anderson	...	Mark Gerber	John Bernans	...	John Wlakup
Liberty		tp	MC	22	(513) 759-7500	...	Dina Minneci	...	Roger Reynolds	Paul Stumpf	...	...
Lima		c	MC	40	(419) 221-5125	David Berger	Catherine Garlock	Sally Clemans	Eugene Reaman	Ted Brookman	Joseph Garlock	J. Elstro
Lincoln Heights		v	CM	4	(513) 733-5900	Lovey Andrews	...	Elizabeth Smith	Carnell Mathews	...	Earnest McCowen	Alan Blackwell
Lisbon		v	MC	2	(330) 424-5503	Michael Lewis	...	...	...	David Lewton	John Higgins	Mike Ours
Lockland		v	MC	3	(513) 761-1124	...	...	Wayne Poe	Charlene Case	Gary Wehmeyer	Kenneth Johnson	...
Lodi		v	MC	3	(330) 948-2040	Tom Longsdorf	...	...	...	...	Steve Sivard	Donald Eaken
Logan		c	MC	6	(740) 385-4060	Paula Tucker	...	Bridget Brandon	Kim Miller	Brian Robertson	Aaron Miller	...
London		c	MC	8	(740) 852-3243	David Eades	...	...	Kathy McClelland	Matthew Noble	Michael Creamer	...
Lorain		c	MC	68	(440) 204-2005	Joseph Koziura	George Koury	Steve Bansek	Ronald Mantini	Phillip Dore	Cel Rivera	Robert De Santis
Lordstown		v	MC	3	(330) 824-2507	Arno Hill	...	Judith Hall	...	James Wishart	Brent Milhoan	Lee Davis
Loudonville		v	MC	2	(419) 994-3214	John Burkhart	...	Jane Hollinger	Sandra Lavengood	...	Scott Shoudt	Keith Edgington
Louisville		c	CM	8	(330) 875-3321	Cynthia Kerchner	Edmund Ault	...	William Rouse	Dennis Myers	James Miller	James McBeath
Loveland		c	CM	11	(513) 683-0150	Brad Greenberg	Thomas Carroll	...	William Taphorn	...	...	Larry Moreland
Lyndhurst		c	MC	15	(440) 442-5777	Joseph Cicero	...	...	Mary Kovalchik	Gerald Telzrow	Anthony Adinolfi	Frederick Glady
Macedonia		c	MC	9	(330) 468-8300	Barbara Kornuc	...	...	Joseph Mirtel	Timothy Black	Jon Golden	...
Madeira		c	CM	8	(513) 561-7228	...	Thomas Moeller	...	...	...	...	...
Mansfield		c	MC	49	(419) 755-9695	Lydia Reid	...	...	Sandra Converse	Michael Hartson	Philip Messer	Francis Fisher
Maple Heights		c	MC	26	(216) 587-9008	...	...	Linda Sigado	Keith Schuster	James Castelucci	Richard Maracz	...
Mariemont		v	MC	3	(513) 271-3246	Charles Lemon	...	Stanley Bahler	...	James Fordyce	Richard Pope	J. Schreckenhofer
Marietta		c	MC	14	(740) 373-1387	Joe Matthews	Robert Boersma	Susan Joyce	Sharon Adams	Ted Baker	Brett McKitrick	...
Marion	*	c	MC	35	(740) 387-2020	Scott Schertzer	...	...	Kelly Carr	Allen Gruber	Tom Bell	...
Martins Ferry	*	c	MC	7	(740) 633-2876	Phil Wallace	John Davies	Joanne Regis	...	Ed Duke	...	...
Marysville		c	MC	15	(937) 642-6015	Steven Lowe	...	Connie Patterson	John Morehart	Gary Johnson	Eugene Mayer	...
Mason		c	CM	22	(513) 229-8510	Peter Beck	Eric Hansen	Terry Schulte	...	Rich Fletcher	Ronald Ferrell	David Riggs
Massillon		c	MC	31	(330) 830-1700	Francis Cicchinelli	Alan Climer	Sharon Howell	...	Tommy Matthews	Mark Weldon	...
Maumee		c	MC	15	(419) 897-7115	Timothy Wagener	John Jezak	...	David Hazard	Richard Monto	Robert Zink	Larry Gamble
Mayfield		v	MC	3	(440) 461-2210	Bruce Rinker	...	Mary Betsa	Philip Brett	David Mohr	Patrick Dearden	Douglas Metzung
Mayfield Heights	*	c	MC	19	(440) 442-2626	M. Egensperger	...	...	Robert Tribby	Michael Forte	Joseph Donnelly	Andrew Fornaro
Mc Donald		v	MC	3	(330) 530-5472	Thomas Hannon	...	Barbara Urban	...	Michael Badila	Jimmy Tyree	Edward Dometrovich
Medina		c	MC	25	(330) 725-8861	Jane Leaver	...	Catherine Horn	Keith Dirham	William Herthneck	Dennis Hanwell	Serafino Piccoli
Mentor		c	CM	50	(440) 255-1100	Ray Kirchner	John Konrad	Elizabeth Limestahl	David Malinowski	Richard Harvey	Daniel Llewellyn	Matthew Schweikert
Mentor-On-The-Lake		c	MC	8	(440) 257-7216	John Rogers	Kip Molenaar	...	...	Robert Mahoney	James Lyons	Dwayne Bailey
Miami		tp	CM	36	(513) 248-3725	Joseph Uecker	David Duckworth	Eric Ferry	...	James Whitworth	Steven Bailey	Walter Fischer
Miami		tp	CM	45	(937) 433-9969	David Coffey	Gregory Hanahan	...	Robert Fowler	David Fulmer	John Krug	James Woolf
Miamisburg		c	CM	19	(937) 866-3303	Richard Church	William Nelson	Judith Barney	George Perrine	Robert Bobbitt	Thomas Schenck	Stephen Morrison
Middleburg Heights		c	MC	15	(440) 234-8811	Gary Starr	Jeffrey Minch	Mary Meola	Timothy Pope	Bernard Benedict	John Maddox	Frank Castelli
Middleport		v	MC	2	(740) 992-2705	Sandy Iannarelli	...	...	Susan Baker	David Hoffman	Bruce Swift	Bradford Anderson
Middletown	*	c	CM	51	(513) 425-7766	Lawrence Mulligan	Judith Gilleland	Betsy Parr	Russell Carolus	Steven Botts	Gregory Schwarber	David Duritsch
Milan		v	MC	1	(419) 499-2944	Michael Bagnato	Gene Rospert	...	Mary Bruno	...	James Ward	...
Milan		tp	CO	3	(419) 499-2354	...	...	James Verbridge	...	Larry Doerner	...	...
Milford	*	c	CM	6	(513) 831-4192	Lou Bishop	Loretta Rokey	Joanne Trilety	Harry Steger	John Cooper	Mark Machan	Michael Haight
Millersburg		v	CM	3	(330) 674-1886	...	Andrew Jones	...	Karen Shaffer	...	S. Vaughn	...
Minerva		v	CM	3	(330) 868-7705	...	David Harp	Gail Bender	...	Richard McClellan	Robert First	Steve Jackson
Mingo Junction		v	MC	3	(740) 535-1616	...	Keith Murtland	...	...	John Brettell	Michael Maguschak	...
Minster	*	v	MC	2	(419) 628-3497	Dennis Kitzmiller	Donald Harrod	...	John Stechschulte	Dale Dues	Randy Houseworth	Carl Wuebker
Mogadore		v	MC	3	(330) 628-4896	Fred Farina	...	Juliann McCulley	...	Don Adams	David Quillen	...
Monroe	*	c	CM	7	(513) 539-7374	Robert Routson	William Brock	...	Kacey Waggaman	Mark Neu	Gregory Homer	Bradley Collins
Monroeville		v	MC	1	(419) 465-4443	Sharon Miller	...	Bonnie Beck	...	...	...	...
Montgomery	*	c	CM	10	(513) 891-2424	Gerri Harbison	Cheryl Hilvert	Susan Hamm	James Hanson	Paul Wright	Don Simpson	L. Nikula
Montpelier		v	CM	4	(419) 485-5543	William Shatzer	Pamela Lucas	...	Kelly Hephner	Dail Fritsch	Bill Noethen	...
Moraine	*	c	CM	6	(937) 535-1000	Jean Matheny	David Hicks	Steve French	Jim Kimmel	Anthony Trick	Thomas Schenck	...
Moreland Hills		v	MC	3	(440) 248-1188	Alvin Croucher	...	Claudette Pesti	Thomas Zammikiel	...	Frank Swanek	James Borsi
Mount Gilead	*	v	MC	3	(419) 946-1931	Thomas Whiston	Neil Rogers	Sue Mermann	...	Donald Staiger	Brian Zerman	...
Mount Healthy		c	MC	7	(513) 931-8840	Terry Todd	...	Becky Ramey	James Roy	Tom Harris	Albert Schaefer	...
Mount Vernon		c	MC	14	(740) 393-9521	Richard Mavis	...	Janet Brown	Terry Scott	...	...	David Carpenter
Munroe Falls		v	MC	5	(330) 688-7491	Brad Sisak	...	Amy Locy	Theodore Gordon	James Bowery	Steve Stahl	...
Napoleon		c	CM	9	(419) 599-1235	J. Small	Jon Bisher	...	Gregory Heath	Lynn Hancock	Robert Weitzel	...
Nelsonville		c	CM	5	(740) 753-1314	Clinton Stanley	Fred Holmes	Susan Harmony	Aileen Lehman	...	David Heineking	...
New Albany		v	CM	3	(614) 855-3913	Nancy Ferguson	Joseph Stefanov	...	James Nicholson	...	Mark Chaney	Mark Nemec
New Boston		c	MC	2	(740) 456-4103	James Warren	...	Kathy Kammerer	...	Chris Bender	Darrold Clark	...
New Bremen		v	MC	2	(419) 629-2447	Jeffrey Pape	...	Diane Gast	...	Robert Kuck	Douglas Harrod	...
New Lebanon	*	v	CM	4	(937) 687-1341	Craig Roberts	George Markus	...	Brenda Etter	...	Rickey Daulton	...
New Lexington		c	MC	4	(740) 342-0401	Janine Conrad	John McCort	Jennifer Dennis	Teri Moore	Mike Bringardner	Jeff Newlon	Chuck Hicks
New Miami		v	MC	2	(513) 896-7337	Kenneth Cheek	...	...	Joseph Ebbing	Gerald Cook	Gary Vaughn	Jamie Cook
New Philadelphia	*	c	MC	17	(330) 364-4491	Ronald Brodzinski	...	Diane Roudebush	Elizabeth Gundy	James Parrish	Jeffrey Urban	James Zucal
New Richmond	*	v	MC	2	(513) 553-4146	Terry Durette	David Kennedy	...	Lynn Baird	Mark Baird	...	Leo Hurst
Newark	*	c	MC	46	(740) 670-7543	Bob Diebold	...	Diana Hufford	Stephen Johnson	Jack Stickradt	Steven Sarver	Kathleen Barch
Newburgh Heights		v	MC	2	(216) 641-4650	Paul Ruggles	...	Debra Malinowski	...	Richard Pugsley	Michael McKeon	...
Newcomerstown		v	MC	4	(740) 498-5881	Jimmie Carr	...	...	...	...	Brian Hursey	...
Newton Falls		c	CM	5	(330) 872-0806	Thomas Moorehead	Jack Haney	Kathleen King	Marcia Cunningham	Richard Bauman	Robert Carlson	Harry Shaver
Niles		c	MC	20	(330) 544-9000	Ralph Infante	...	...	Neil Buccino	Charles Semple	Bruce Simeone	Samuel Natoli
North Baltimore		v	MC	3	(419) 257-2394	Ned Sponsler	...	Richard Van Mooy	Chasity McCartney	Donald Baltz	Gerald Perry	...
North Canton	*	c	MC	16	(330) 499-8223	David Held	Earle Wise	...	Alexander Zumbar	John Bacon	Michael Grimes	...
North College Hill		c	MC	10	(513) 521-7413	Daniel Brooks	...	Collen Bens	Carol Wullkotte	Michael Lotz	John Fulmer	John Knuf
North Kingsville		v	MC	2	(440) 224-0091	Ronald McVoy	...	...	...	Brian Lehtonen	Robert Houser	...
North Olmsted	*	c	MC	34	(440) 777-8000	Thomas O'Grady	...	Barbara Seman	Carrie Copfer	Thomas Klecan	Wayne Wozniak	Duane Limpert
North Ridgeville		c	MC	22	(440) 353-0819	Deanna Hill	Thomas Sweeney	Beverly Gillock	Chris Costin	Rick Miller	Ronald Bauer	...
North Royalton	*	c	MC	28	(440) 237-5686	Cathy Luks	...	Laura Haller	Karen Fegan	Michael Fabish	Paul Bican	William Mayer
Northfield		v	MC	3	(330) 467-7139	Victor Milani	...	Cheryl Kennon	Robert Riedel	...	Mark Wentz	Anthony Fiorilli
Northwood	*	c	MC	5	(419) 693-9327	Mark Stoner	Patricia Bacon	Lynn Goertz	Toby Schroyer	Tim Romstadt	...	Craig Meier
Norton	*	c	MC	11	(330) 825-7815	David Koontz	Rick Ryland	Karla Richards	John Moss	Mike Schultz	Thad Hete	...
Norwalk		c	MC	16	(419) 663-6700	Brooks Hartmann	James Koch	Kascie Horrigan	Diane Eschen	Robert Bores	Kevin Cashen	Ralph Seward
Norwood		c	MC	21	(513) 396-8150	Joseph Hochbein	Jeff Miller	...	Donnie Jones	...	Tim Brown	Larry Moreland
Oak Harbor	*	v	MC	2	(419) 898-5561	Fred Conley	John Liske	...	Jenny Busche	...	Steve Weirich	Randall Genzman
Oakwood		v	MC	3	(440) 232-9988	Gary Gottschalk	...	...	...	...	Robert Semik	Thomas Haba
Oakwood		c	CM	9	(937) 298-0600	Dorothy Cook	Norbert Klopsch	Cathy Blum	Brad Beachdell	...	...	Kevin Weaver
Oberlin	*	c	CM	8	(440) 775-7206	David Sonner	Eric Norenberg	Belinda Anderson	Salvatore Talarico	Dennis Kirin	Thomas Miller	Jeffrey Baumann
Obetz		v	MC	3	(614) 491-1080	Louise Crabtree	...	D. Hubner Smith	...	...	Richard Minerd	...
Olmsted Falls		c	MC	7	(440) 235-5550	...	...	...	...	...	...	...
Ontario		v	MC	5	(419) 529-3818	D. Kreisher	Calvin Miller	...	Shirley Bowman	...	Timothy McClaran	...
Oregon		c	MC	19	(419) 698-7095	James Haley	Kenneth Filipiak	Mary Finger	Sandra Bihn	Raymond Walendzak	Thomas Gulch	Michael White
Orrville		c	MC	8	(330) 684-5000	Dennis Steiner	Becky Jewell	...	James Leggett	Robert Ballentine	Joseph Routh	Dan Preising
Ottawa		v	MC	4	(419) 523-5020	Kenneth Maag	John Williams	Barbara Doepker	...	John Love	Richard Knowlton	Karen Kovolo

Directory 1/9 continued — OFFICIALS IN U.S. MUNICIPALITIES 2,500 AND OVER IN POPULATION

Jurisdiction		Type	Form of govern-ment	2000 Popu-lation	Main telephone number	Chief elected official	Appointed administrator	Clerk of the governing board	Chief financial officer	Fire chief	Police chief	Public works director
OHIO continued												
Ottawa Hills		v	CM	4	(419) 536-1111	Jean Youngen	Marc Thompson	Gay Macarthur	Karen Urbanik	Donald Farley	Ronald Jand	. . .
Oxford	*	c	CM	21	(513) 524-5200	Prudence Dana	Douglas Elliott	. . .	Joseph Newlin	John Detherage	Stephan Schwein	Michael Dreisbach
Painesville		c	CM	17	(440) 392-5786	William Horvath	Rita McMahon	Jennifer Bell	Timothy Petric	Mark Mlachak	Gary Smith	Kevin Lynch
Parma		c	MC	85	(440) 885-8000	Dean DePiero	. . .	Michael Hughes	Dennis Kish	John French	Daniel Hoffman	Brian Higgins
Parma Heights	*	c	MC	21	(440) 884-9600	Martin Zanotti	. . .	. . .	Terrence Hickey	Bryan Sloan	Daniel Teel	Joseph Tal
Pataskala		c	CM	10	(740) 927-2021	. . .	Timothy Boland	. . .	. . .	. . .	. . .	. . .
Paulding		v	MC	3	(419) 399-4011	Greg White	Harry Wiebe	. . .	Melissa Tope	Todd Weidenhamer	Randy Crawford	. . .
Pepper Pike	*	c	MC	6	(216) 831-8500	Bruce Akers	. . .	S. Brett-O'Connor	Prashant Shah	Thomas Hartman	Jack Crivel	Robert Girardi
Perrysburg		c	MC	16	(419) 872-8010	Timothy McCarthy	John Alexander	. . .	David Creps	Ronn Thompson	Nelson Evans	Jon Eckel
Pickerington		c	CO	9	(614) 837-3974	Mitch O'Brien	Timothy Hansley	Lynda Yartin	Linda Fersch	. . .	Michael Taylor	Edward Drobina
Pierce		tp	MC	12	(513) 752-6262	Bonnie Batchler	Dave Elmer	. . .	Karen Register	Aaron Boggs	James Smith	Daryl Berry
Pioneer		v	MC	1	(419) 737-2614	David Thompson	. . .	. . .	. . .	Dennis Fackler	Judith Lineberger	William Rains
Piqua	*	c	CM	20	(937) 778-2053	Robert DeBrosse	Fredrick Enderle	Rebecca Cool	Cynthia Holtzapple	Gary Connell	. . .	. . .
Plain		tp	MC	51	(330) 492-4689	Pamela Bossart	. . .	Claude Shriver	Jo Reikowski	John Sabo	. . .	. . .
Plain City		v	MC	2	(614) 873-5040	. . .	. . .	. . .	. . .	. . .	. . .	. . .
Poland		v	MC	2	(330) 757-2112	. . .	. . .	. . .	. . .	. . .	. . .	. . .
Pomeroy		v	MC	1	(740) 992-2246	. . .	John Anderson	Kathy Hysell	. . .	. . .	Mark Proffitt	. . .
Port Clinton		c	MC	6	(419) 734-5522	Thomas Brown	Richard Babcock	. . .	Nancy O'Neal	John Morton	Thomas Blohm	. . .
Portsmouth	*	c	CM	20	(740) 354-8807	James Kalb	Crystal Wyghorst	Jo Aeh	M. Trent Williams	Mike Raison	Charles Horner	Christopher Murphy
Powell		v	CM	6	(614) 885-5380	Dan Wiencek	Stephen Lutz	Dawn Nauman	Nanette Metz	. . .	Gary Vest	. . .
Ravenna	*	c	MC	11	(330) 296-2152	Kevin Poland	. . .	Kathryn Halay	Kimble Cecora	Geoffrey Cleveland	Randall McCoy	Donald Kainrad
Reading		c	MC	11	(513) 733-3725	Robert Bemmes	Albert Elmlinger	Miriam Lapple	Douglas Sand	Kevin Kaiser	Gregory Hilling	Darrell Courtney
Reynoldsburg		c	MC	32	(614) 322-6808	Robert McPherson	. . .	Nancy Frazier	Richard Harris	. . .	David Suciu	. . .
Richfield		v	MC	3	(330) 659-9201	Michael Lyons	. . .	Joyce Remec	Eleanor Lukovics	Joseph Stopak	Dale Canter	. . .
Richmond Heights		c	MC	10	(216) 486-2474	Daniel Ursu	. . .	Betsy Traben	Lynda Rossiter	Michael Cek	Gene Rowe	Donald Lazar
Rittman		c	CM	6	(330) 925-2045	William Robertson	Larry Boggs	Barbara Brooks	Cindy Mann	Don Sweigert	. . .	David Simpson
Riverside		c	CM	23	(937) 233-1801	Kenneth Curp	Bryan Chodkowski	MaryAnn Brane	Robert Gillian	Dan Alig	George Brown	Terrence Nealy
Rocky River		c	MC	20	(440) 331-0600	William Knoble	. . .	. . .	. . .	Christopher Flynn	Donald Wagner	. . .
Rossford	*	c	MC	6	(419) 666-0210	William Verbosky	Edward Ciecka	Robert Watrol	Karen Freeman	James Verbosky	Robert Vespi	David Jones
Sabina		v	MC	2	(937) 584-2123	. . .	Karma Henson	. . .	. . .	. . .	Tim Tyree	Rob Dean
Salem	*	c	MC	12	(330) 332-4241	Jerry Wolford	. . .	. . .	James Armeni	Jeffrey Hughes	Robert Floor	Donald Weingart
Sandusky	*	c	CM	27	(419) 627-5844	Craig Stahl	Matthew Kline	Joyce Brown	Edward Widman	Mike Meinzer	Kim Nuesse	Randy Whitman
Sebring		v	CM	4	(330) 938-9340	John Smith	Douglas Burchard	Malea Sanor	. . .	James Cannell	Ray Heverly	Bill Sanor
Seven Hills		c	MC	12	(216) 524-4421	Gerald Trafis	. . .	. . .	Albert Lippucci	Anthony Hosta	John Fechko	John Miller
Shadyside		c	MC	3	(740) 676-5972	. . .	Richard Melanko	. . .	. . .	Mark Badia	Russell Patt	Howard Heslop
Shaker Heights	*	c	MC	29	(216) 491-1427	Earl Leiken	Jeri Chaikin	. . .	. . .	Donald Barnes	D. Scott Lee	William Boag
Sharonville	*	c	MC	13	(513) 563-1144	Virgil Lovitt	. . .	Martha Funk	Amy Moore	Ralph Hammonds	Michael Schappa	Tom Losekamp
Sheffield Lake		c	MC	9	(440) 949-7141	John Piskura	. . .	Dorothy Fantauzzi	Tammy Smith	Mike Conrad	Larry Shepherd	William Gardner
Shelby	*	c	MC	9	(419) 347-5131	William Freytag	Brad Harvey	. . .	Robert Lafferty	Scott Hartman	Charles Roub	. . .
Sidney		c	CM	20	(937) 498-2335	Frank Mariano	Steven Stilwell	Jocele Fahnestock	. . .	Stan Crosley	Steven Wearly	S. Gosciewski
Silver Lake		v	MC	3	(330) 923-5233	Bernie Hovey	. . .	Teresa Spohn	. . .	. . .	Gary DeMoss	Richard Fenwick
Silverton	*	c	MC	5	(513) 936-6240	John Smith	Mark Wendling	Meredith George	Thomas Peterson	Donald Newman	Michael Daudistel	. . .
Solon		c	MC	21	(440) 248-1155	Kevin Patton	. . .	Carol McConoughey	Duane Weber	William Shaw	Wayne Godzich	Jim Stanek
South Charleston		v	CM	1	(937) 462-7167	Marilyn Jarvis	Sarah Wildman	. . .	Bonnie White	. . .	Beryl McCloud	Ralph Cook
South Euclid		c	MC	23	(216) 381-0400	Georgine Welo	. . .	. . .	Joseph Filippo	Thomas Cannell	Matthew Capadona	Ed Gallagher
South Lebanon		v	MC	2	(513) 494-2296	James Smith	John Louallen	. . .	Debra Humston	. . .	Derrick Hollon	Larry Easterly
South Point		v	MC	3	(740) 377-4838	William Gaskin	Patrick Leighty	. . .	Scott Thomas	Richard Stevens	Carl Vance	. . .
South Russell		v	MC	4	(440) 338-7843	William Young	. . .	Nancy Gallagher	. . .	. . .	. . .	. . .
Springboro	*	c	CM	12	(937) 748-4343	John Agenbroad	Christine Thompson	Lori Martin	Robyn Brown	. . .	Jeffrey Kruithoff	Barry Conway
Springdale		c	MC	10	(513) 346-5700	Doyle Webster	Cecil Osborn	Edward Knox	Jeff Williams	Dan Shroyer	Mike Laage	David Butsch
Springfield		tp	CM	13	(513) 522-1410	Tom Bryan	M. Hinnenkamp	John Waksmundski	. . .	Robert Leininger	David Heimpold	John Musselman
Springfield	*	c	CM	65	(937) 324-7700	Warren Copeland	. . .	Connie Chappell	Mark Beckdahl	J. Beers	Stephen Moody	James Mann
St. Bernard		c	MC	4	(513) 242-7770	Barbara Siegel	. . .	Carol Ungruhe	C. Vonder Meulen	James Dwertman	Allen Rusche	Herb Siegel
St. Clairsville		c	MC	5	(740) 695-1324	Robert Vincenzo	. . .	Kathy Kaluger	Jill Lucidi	. . .	Martin Kendzora	Dennis Bigler
St. Marys	*	c	MC	8	(419) 394-3303	Gregory Freewalt	Thomas Hitchcock	. . .	Douglas Riesen	Kenneth Cline	Greg Foxhoven	. . .
Steubenville	*	c	CM	19	(740) 283-6133	Domenick Mucci	Bruce Williams	Pamela Orlando	Michael Marshall	Terri Kovach	William McCafferty	. . .
Stow		c	MC	32	(330) 689-2700	Lee Schaffer	. . .	Bonnie Emahiser	John Baranek	Steven Groves	Louis Dirker	Dano Koehler
Streetsboro		c	MC	12	(330) 626-4942	Sally Henzel	. . .	Pamela Hejduk	D. Weber	Gerald Vicha	Ronald Schmid	Robert Langham
Strongsville		c	MC	43	(440) 580-3151	Thomas Perciak	. . .	Leslie Seefried	Donald Batke	Robert Moody	Charles Goss	Joseph Walker
Struthers	*	c	MC	11	(330) 755-2181	Terry Stocker	Ed Wildes	Megan Shorthouse	Tina Morell	Harold Milligan	Robert Norris	John Sveda
Sugarcreek		tp	MC	6	(937) 848-8426	. . .	Barry Tiffany	. . .	. . .	. . .	. . .	. . .
Sunbury	*	v	MC	2	(740) 965-2684	Leonard Weatherby	Dave Martin	. . .	. . .	. . .	. . .	. . .
Swanton		v	CM	3	(419) 826-9515	Tandy Grubbs	John Syx	Mary Lou Perrin	Barbara Guess	James Guy	Homer Chapa	. . .
Sycamore		tp	CM	19	(513) 791-8447	Richard Kent	Lori Thompson	Robert Porter	. . .	. . .	. . .	. . .
Sylvania		c	MC	18	(419) 885-8998	Craig Stough	. . .	Margaret Rauch	John Plock	Christopher Maurer	Gerald Sobb	Jeffrey Ballmer
Sylvania	*	tp	CM	44	(419) 882-0031	Pam Hanley	Hugh Thomas	David Simko	Jim Beck	Fred Welsh	Robert Metzger	Greg Huffman
Tallmadge		c	MC	16	(330) 633-0145	Christopher Grimm	. . .	Susan Wilson	Jill Stritch	Dennis Crossen	Mike Duvall	David Kline
Thornville	*	v	MC	. .	(740) 246-6020	Beth Patrick	Ronald Koehler	Anna Cox	Melissa Tremblay	. . .	Nicholas Garver	. . .
Tiffin		c	MC	18	(419) 448-5401	Bernard Hohman	Wayne Stephens	. . .	Debora Pine	William Ennis	David Lagrange	Susan Kuhn
Tipp City	*	c	CM	9	(937) 667-8425	Patrick Hale	Jon Crusey	Misty Cox	Richard Drennen	Steve Kessler	Thomas Davidson	Milton Eichman
Toledo		c	CO	313	(419) 245-1500	Carleton Finkbeiner	Robert Reinbolt	Gerald Dendinger	John Sherburne	Michael Bell	Michael Navarre	Robert Williams
Toronto	*	c	MC	5	(740) 537-3743	John Geddis	Susan Kulstad	Linda Burkey	Robert Owen	David Solomon	Danny Mosti	John Skrabak
Trenton		c	CM	8	(513) 988-6304	Roy Wilham	Robert Leichman	Julie Muterspaw	Michael Engel	Thomas Puckett	Rodney Hale	. . .
Trotwood		c	CM	27	(937) 837-7771	Donald McLaurin	Michael Lucking	Lois Singleton	Jon Stoops	Paul Hutsonpillar	Michael Etter	Thomas Odenigbo
Troy	*	c	MC	21	(937) 335-1725	Michael Beamish	Patrick Titterington	Sue Knight	Richard Cultice	C. Boehringer	Charles Phelps	. . .
Twinsburg	*	tp	MC	2	(330) 425-4497	Carol Gasper	Robert Kagler	. . .	Tania Lardell	. . .	. . .	Jeffrey Johnson
Twinsburg		c	MC	17	(330) 425-7161	Katherine Procop	. . .	Cynthia Kaderle	Jo Anne Terry	Richard Racine	Richard Deal	Chris Campbell
Uhrichsville		c	MC	5	(740) 922-1242	. . .	. . .	. . .	. . .	. . .	. . .	. . .
Union	*	c	CM	5	(937) 836-8624	. . .	John Applegate	. . .	Denise Winemiller	. . .	Michael Blackwell	. . .
Union		tp	CM	42	(513) 752-1741	. . .	Doug Walker	. . .	. . .	Stanley Deimling	Terry Zinser	. . .
Union City		v	MC	1	(937) 968-4305	Scott Stahl	. . .	. . .	Judy Henry	. . .	Harold Schafer	Mike Grimes
University Heights	*	c	MC	14	(216) 932-7800	Beryl Rothschild	. . .	Nancy English	Arman Ochoa	John Pitchler	Gary Stehlik	. . .
Upper Arlington	*	c	CM	33	(614) 583-5040	Donald Leach	Virginia Barney	Beverly Clevenger	Catherine Armstrong	Mitchell Ross	Brian Quinn	Larry Helscel
Upper Sandusky		c	MC	6	(419) 294-3862	Kenneth Richardson	. . .	. . .	Jean Hollanshead	Tom Fox	Robert Hollis	. . .
Urbana	*	c	MC	11	(937) 652-4300	Ruth Zerkle	Bruce Evilsizor	. . .	. . .	James McIntosh	Pat Wagner	. . .
Van Wert		c	MC	10	(419) 238-1237	Stephen Gelves	Jay Fleming	. . .	Martha Balyeat	James Steele	Joel Hammond	. . .
Vandalia		c	CM	14	(937) 898-5891	William Loy	Jeffrey Hoagland	. . .	James Bell	John Sands	Douglas Knight	. . .
Vermilion	*	c	MC	10	(440) 204-2400	Jean Anderson	. . .	Gwen Fisher	Michelle Bowens	Chris Stempowski	Robert Kish	Dan Squires
Versailles		v	CM	2	(937) 526-3294	. . .	. . .	. . .	. . .	. . .	. . .	. . .
Wadsworth		c	MC	18	(330) 335-1521	Caesar Carrino	William Lyren	. . .	John Moss	Ralph Copley	David Singleton	. . .
Walbridge		v	MC	2	(419) 666-1830	Daniel Wilczynski	Steve Smith	. . .	Patricia Crawford	. . .	Richard Solether	. . .
Walton Hills	*	v	MC	2	(440) 232-7800	Marlene Anielski	. . .	. . .	Vic Nogalo	Jim Schade	Gary Rhines	Dan Stucky
Wapakoneta		c	MC	9	(419) 738-3011	Donald Wittwer	Rex Katterheinrich	Carlene Koch	Gail Walter	Christopher Agnew	David Harrison	Meril Simpson
Warren		c	MC	46	(330) 841-2610	Michael O'Brien	William Franklin	Darla Neugebauer	David Griffing	Kenneth Nussle	John Mandopoulos	Robert Davis
Warrensville Heights		c	MC	15	(216) 587-6500	Marcia Fudge	. . .	Yvonne McMillion	Rubin Moultrie	. . .	. . .	. . .
Washington		tp	CM	7	(937) 433-0152	. . .	Jesse Lightle	Thomas Zobrist	Michael Barlow	Kenneth Parks	. . .	. . .

Directory 1/9 continued **OFFICIALS IN U.S. MUNICIPALITIES 2,500 AND OVER IN POPULATION**

Jurisdiction	Type	Form of govern-ment	2000 Popu-lation	Main telephone number	Chief elected official	Appointed administrator	Clerk of the governing board	Chief financial officer	Fire chief	Police chief	Public works director
OHIO continued											
Washington	c	CM	13	(740) 636-2340	. . .	. . .	. . .	Tom Riley	Dan Fowler	Larry Mongold	Joe Burbage
Waterville *	v	CM	4	(419) 878-8100	Derek Merrin	James Bagdonas	Jennifer Carter	Dale Knepper	Steven Parons	Robert Selders	Kenneth Blair
Wauseon	c	MC	7	(419) 335-9022	Jerry Dehnbostel	. . .	Margaret Murphy	Jon Schamp	Marvin Wheeler	Keith Torbett	Dennis Richardson
Waverly *	c	MC	4	(740) 947-5162	Dale Reed	. . .	Tammy Miller	Harvey Whaley	R. Armbruster	Larry Roe	. . .
Waynesville *	v	CM	2	(513) 897-8015	Ernie Lawson	Bruce Snell	. . .	Linda Jones	. . .	Kenny McCloud	. . .
Wellington	v	MC	4	(440) 647-4626	. . .	Robert Dupee	Karen Webb	. . .	. . .	Richard Rollins	Robert Box
Wellston	c	MC	6	(740) 384-2720	Edgar Hayburn	. . .	Mary Jarvis	J. Glass	Dan Gill	Mark Jacobs	Larry Walburn
Wellsville	c	MC	4	(330) 532-2510	. . .	. . .	. . .	. . .	. . .	. . .	. . .
West Carrollton *	c	CM	14	(937) 859-5183	Jeffery Sanner	Bradley Townsend	Nancy Trimble	Thomas Reilly	John Keister	Richard Barnhart	Richard Norton
West Chester	tp	CM	54	(513) 777-5900	George Lang	Judith Boyko	Patricia Williams	. . .	James Detherage	John Bruce	. . .
West Jefferson	v	MC	4	(614) 879-7363	. . .	. . .	Jack Herrel	. . .	. . .	Frank Cox	Robert Carter
West Milton *	v	CM	4	(937) 698-1500	. . .	Martin Gabbard	. . .	Jill Grise	Dennis Frantz	Tracey Hendricks	. . .
West Salem *	v	MC	1	(419) 853-4400	Janet Kenyon	Richard Witucki	. . .	Patricia Foradori	. . .	Don Sims	. . .
West Union	v	MC	2	(937) 544-5326	Harold Dryden	Richard Potter	Ruth Young	. . .	John Bradford	Harry Baldwin	. . .
Westerville	c	CM	35	(614) 901-6400	Damian Wetterauer	David Collinsworth	Mary Johnston	John Winkel	Bernard Ingles	Joseph Morbitzer	Frank Wiseman
Westlake	c	MC	31	(440) 871-3300	Dennis Clough	. . .	. . .	Anne Fritz	Richard Pietrick	Richard Walling	Donald Glauner
Whitehall	c	MC	19	(614) 237-9803	John Wolfe	Kathy Crandall	Dawn Williams	Kim Maggard	Timothy Tilton	James Stacy	. . .
Whitehouse *	v	MC	2	(419) 877-5383	Angela Kuhn	Dennis Recker	Susan Miller	Jordan Daugherty	Daryl McNutt	Edward Kaplan	Steve Pilcher
Wickliffe	c	MC	13	(440) 943-7100	Thomas Ruffner	. . .	C. Theophylactos	Martin Germ	Daniel Helsel	James Fox	Daniel Paschke
Willard	c	CM	6	(419) 933-2591	Michael Elmlinger	Brian Humphress	Jo Ann Jones	Jody Wagoner	Richard Myers	Thomas King	. . .
Williamsburg	v	MC	2	(513) 724-6107	Mary Ann Lefker	Patti Bates	. . .	Denise Wehrum	. . .	Michael Gregory	Jeremy Fite
Willoughby	c	MC	22	(440) 951-2800	David Anderson	. . .	Loretta Radebaugh	Raymond Rogowski	Al Zwegat	Conrad Straube	Angelo Tomaselli
Willoughby Hills	c	MC	8	(440) 946-1234	Mort O'Ryan	Jim Teknipp	Terri Poppy	. . .	Rich Harmon	George Malec	. . .
Willowick *	c	MC	14	(440) 585-3700	Richard Bonde	. . .	. . .	Cheryl Killen	Robert Posipanka	Michael Lazor	Joseph Dominick
Wilmington	c	MC	11	(937) 382-5458	David Raizk	Lawrence Reinsmith	. . .	. . .	Fred Shutts	Michael Hatten	. . .
Windham	v	MC	2	(330) 326-2622	Jess Starkey	Kevin Knight	. . .	Shelley Craine	Clair Simpson	Jacob DeSalvo	William Szymanski
Wintersville	v	MC	4	(740) 266-3175	. . .	. . .	. . .	. . .	. . .	Edward Laman	Perry Poole
Woodlawn	v	CM	2	(513) 771-6130	. . .	Evonne Kovach	Brenda Love	R. Hardy	Richard Mynatt	Walter Obermeyer	Terry Meadows
Woodsfield	v	MC	2	(740) 472-0418	Lester Bolon	. . .	Patricia Templeton	. . .	Michael Young	Manifred Keylor	. . .
Wooster	c	MC	24	(330) 263-5200	James Howey	Michael Sigg	Sheila Stanley	Andrei Dordea	Stanley Brown	Steven Thornton	Michael Hunter
Worthington	c	CM	14	(614) 436-3100	. . .	Matthew Greeson	D. Kay Thress	Steven Gandee	Scott Highley	Michael Mauger	David Groth
Wyoming *	c	CM	8	(513) 821-7600	Barry Porter	Robert Harrison	. . .	Jennifer Chavarria	Robert Rielage	Gary Baldauf	Terrance Huxel
Xenia	c	CM	24	(937) 376-7232	John Saraga	James Percival	. . .	Mark Bazelak	Jeffrey Leaming	Donald Person	. . .
Yellow Springs	v	CM	3	(937) 767-7202	Karen Wintrow	Mark Cundiff	Deborah Benning	. . .	. . .	John Grote	. . .
Youngstown	c	MC	82	(330) 742-8995	. . .	Richard Groucutt	. . .	. . .	. . .	. . .	. . .
Zanesville	c	MC	25	(740) 455-0603	Howard Zwelling	. . .	Joan Ziemer	Dale Raines	Dave Lacy	Eric Lambes	Michael Sims
OKLAHOMA											
Ada *	c	CM	15	(580) 436-6300	Barbara Young	David Hathcoat	Sally Pool	Donna Doolen	Marion Harris	Michael Miller	. . .
Altus	c	MC	21	(580) 481-2200	T. Gramling	Michael Nettles	La June White	Shirley Norton	Kenneth Ward	Mike Patterson	Robert Stephenson
Alva *	c	MC	5	(580) 327-1340	Lynn Chaffee	Steven Tomberlin	Wayne Lane	. . .	Allen Schwerdtfeger	Arlo Darr	Randy Rhodes
Anadarko *	c	CM	6	(405) 247-2481	Marilyn Shannon	. . .	Karen Thomsen	Robert Brooks	Dennis Wilkerson	Keith Tillis	Bill Rowton
Antlers	c	CM	2	(580) 298-3756	Brent Franks	Mike Winningham	Athelta Gay	Robin Byrum	Randy Janoe	Dwayne Morgan	Craig Wilson
Ardmore	c	CM	23	(580) 226-2100	. . .	Dan Parrott	. . .	Penny Long	. . .	. . .	Robert Whitaker
Atoka	c	CM	2	(580) 889-3341	Bill Miller	Martha Allen	Donna Guinn	Joann Duckworth	Donnie Allen	John Smithart	Stephen Smith
Bartlesville	c	CM	34	(918) 338-4200	. . .	. . .	. . .	. . .	Robert Hasbrook	Leo Willey	Edgar Gordon
Bethany *	c	CM	20	(405) 789-2146	Bryan Taylor	John Shugart	. . .	Sandra Kimerer	David Beck	Neal Troutman	Jim McGill
Bixby	c	CM	13	(918) 366-4430	Joe Williams	Micky Webb	Cheryl Sasser	. . .	Steve Abel	Anthony Stephens	Bea Aamodt
Blackwell	c	CM	7	(580) 363-7250	Eugene Braly	Sara Norris	Teresa Moses	. . .	Tommy Beliel	Lauren Johnson	. . .
Blanchard	c	CM	2	(405) 485-9392	Tom Sacchieri	Bill Edwards	Camille Dowers	. . .	. . .	Henry Weber	Monte Ketcham
Boise City	c	CM	1	(580) 544-2271	. . .	Rodney Avery	. . .	. . .	. . .	. . .	. . .
Bristow	c	MC	4	(918) 367-2237	Leon Pinson	. . .	Sabrina Mounce	. . .	Bob Grant	Perry Low	Fred Wesley
Broken Arrow	c	CM	74	(918) 259-2400	Richard Carter	James Twombly	Linda Fagundes	Thomas Caldwell	Dennis McIntire	Todd Wuestewald	. . .
Broken Bow	c	CM	4	(580) 584-2885	Jerry Smith	Mark Guthrie	Vickie Pieratt	. . .	Roger Ross	Hurschel Thomas	Gary Swift
Catoosa	c	MC	5	(918) 266-2505	Curtis Conley	. . .	Judy Scullawl	. . .	. . .	Raymond Rodgers	. . .
Chandler	c	CM	2	(405) 258-3200	Tom Knight	James Melson	Kay Pentecost	. . .	Bobby Johnson	Kevin Towler	David Nickell
Checotah	c	MC	3	(918) 473-5411	James Hayes	. . .	Shirley Fox	Bette Sanders	Raymon Webster	Terry Cossey	Wayne Williams
Cherokee	c	CM	1	(580) 596-3052	Rosemary Whittet	Brandon Wright	Roberta Berry	. . .	Kevin Lingemann	Paul Michael	. . .
Chickasha *	c	CM	15	(405) 222-6020	. . .	Larry Shelton	. . .	Gina Snedeker	Greg Gibson	Lynn Williams	Larry Fuchs
Choctaw	c	CM	9	(405) 390-8198	Bobbie Freeman	Robert Floyd	Linda Bomgren	. . .	Loren Bumgarner	William Carter	Bernie Nauheimer
Claremore	c	CM	15	(918) 341-2365	. . .	Troy Powell	Carlene Webber	. . .	Bradd Clark	Michael Perry	Charles Andrle
Cleveland	c	CM	3	(918) 358-3506	Dale Norrid	Elizie Smith	Viriginia Masters	. . .	Jo Burger	Marvin Howard	Les Taber
Clinton *	c	CM	8	(580) 323-0261	Allen Bryson	Grayson Bottom	Lisa Anders	. . .	Price Anders	David Crabtree	Arnold Adams
Coalgate *	c	CM	2	(580) 927-3914	Michael Elkins	Roger Cosper	Sherlyn Walker	. . .	David Holt	Kenny Pebworth	Walter Roebuck
Collinsville *	c	MC	4	(918) 371-1010	Stan Sallee	Pamela Polk	Kelly Young	. . .	Russell Young	Charlie Annis	. . .
Comanche	c	CM	1	(580) 439-8832	. . .	Rodney Love	Janice Willis	. . .	David Coder	Jack Shutts	. . .
Commerce	c	MC	2	(918) 675-4373	Jim Mullen	. . .	Vicki Turner	. . .	. . .	. . .	David Creason
Cordell	c	MC	2	(580) 832-3825	K. Damon	R. McClanathan	. . .	. . .	Tom Merrill	Gary Coburn	. . .
Coweta	c	CM	7	(918) 486-2189	Robert Morton	Steven Whitlock	. . .	. . .	Craig Hinton	Derrick Palmer	Frank Dailey
Crescent	c	CM	1	(405) 969-2538	. . .	. . .	Tiffany Tillman	. . .	. . .	Kris Kelley	Frank De Fuentes
Cushing	c	CM	8	(918) 225-0277	Rodger Floyd	Andrew Katz	Cindy Vickers	. . .	John Henckel	William Myers	. . .
Davis	c	CM	2	(580) 369-3333	. . .	Donald Brittin	Paula Pollard	. . .	. . .	Darryl McCurtain	Ralph Thomasson
Del City *	c	CM	22	(405) 671-3015	Brian Linley	Mark Edwards	. . .	Carol Noble	Jim Hock	James Taylor	William Graham
Dewey	c	CM	3	(918) 534-2272	Joe Franco	Nicholas Brown	Annette Breshears	. . .	Earl James	Bill Breshears	Chester Williams
Drumright *	c	CM	2	(918) 352-2631	Ed Fitzgerald	George Jones	Susan White	. . .	Loren Andrews	Rocky Pinson	Rick Dillard
Duncan *	c	CM	22	(580) 252-0250	Gene Brown	Clyde Shaw	. . .	Gerald Morris	Larry Sullins	Jeff Johnson	R. Vaughn
Durant	c	CM	13	(580) 924-7205	Jerry Tomlinson	. . .	Leta McNatt	. . .	Steve Dow	Gary Rudick	Jerry Yandell
Edmond *	c	CM	68	(405) 348-8830	S. Gragg-Naifeh	Larry Stevens	Nancy Nichols	Ross VanderHamm	Gilbert Harryman	Bob Ricks	. . .
El Reno *	c	CM	16	(405) 262-4070	Matt White	Antonio Rivera	. . .	Guy Love	Kent Lagaly	Ken Brown	Jim Luckett
Elk City	c	CM	10	(580) 225-3230	Teresa Mullican	Guy Hylton	Cheryl Sipes	. . .	Rick Shelton	William Putman	. . .
Enid	c	CM	47	(580) 234-0400	Irv Honigsburg	William Gamble	Linda Parks	Joan Riley	Philip Clover	Rick West	William Beck
Eufaula	c	MC	2	(918) 689-2534	Dean Smith	. . .	Donna Hysell	. . .	Thomas Foresee	Anthony Garrett	Vernon Hysell
Fairview	c	CM	2	(580) 227-4416	Kenneth Carmack	Dale Sides	Anita Gifford	. . .	Greg Harmon	Hank Weber	Curt Martin
Fort Gibson	t	CM	4	(918) 478-3551	Bob Peebles	Kathryn Carson	Deborah Daniels	. . .	Larry Cooper	Richard Slader	. . .
Frederick *	c	CM	4	(580) 335-7551	Eddie Whitworth	Robert Johnston	Maria Arumugan	Fabian Reyes	Melvin Newman	Ricky Guill	. . .
Glenpool	c	CM	8	(918) 322-5409	. . .	H. Tinker	. . .	. . .	. . .	. . .	. . .
Grandfield	c	CM	1	(580) 479-5215	. . .	. . .	. . .	. . .	. . .	. . .	. . .
Grove	c	CM	5	(918) 786-6107	Carolyn Nuckolls	Bruce Johnson	F. Ivonne Buzzard	. . .	D. Lee Dollarhide	James Wall	Ken Crowder
Guthrie *	c	CM	9	(405) 282-0493	Chuck Burtcher	Melody Kellogg	Wanda Calvert	. . .	Lester Branch	Damon Devereaux	Maxine Pruitt
Guymon *	c	CM	10	(580) 338-0137	Peggy Keenan	Tedd Graham	Melissa Bond	. . .	Chris Purdy	Eddie Adamson	Ivan Clark
Harrah	c	CM	4	(405) 454-2951	Davee Davis	Earl Burson	Alice Davis	Michele Cogdill	Murrel Coleman	Eddie Holland	Joe Morgan
Healdton	c	CM	2	(580) 229-1283	David Smith	Dale Milam	Vivian Glenn	. . .	. . .	. . .	Ray Glenn
Heavener	c	CM	3	(918) 653-2217	Mark Morris	Mike Kennerson	Sharon Loar	. . .	Max Roberts	Don Richards	Carroll Smallwood
Henryetta	c	CM	6	(918) 652-3348	. . .	. . .	Donna White	. . .	Raymond Eldridge	Audie Cole	Richard Kramer
Hobart	c	CM	3	(580) 726-3100	Tom Talley	Willard Brown	Nancy Ledford	. . .	Jerry Lankford	Dale Uptergrove	Jerry Gather

Directory 1/9 continued OFFICIALS IN U.S. MUNICIPALITIES 2,500 AND OVER IN POPULATION

Jurisdiction	Type	Form of govern- ment	2000 Popu- lation	Main telephone number	Chief elected official	Appointed administrator	Clerk of the governing board	Chief financial officer	Fire chief	Police chief	Public works director
OKLAHOMA continued											
Holdenville	c	MC	4	(405) 379-3397	. . .	. . .	. . .	. . .	Dwight Barnett	. . .	. . .
Hollis	c	CM	2	(580) 688-2167	. . .	. . .	. . .	. . .	. . .	. . .	. . .
Hominy	c	CM	2	(918) 885-2164	R. Tex Bayouth	Patricia Wikel	Melissa Cupp	. . .	Steven Pitts	. . .	. . .
Hugo	c	CM	5	(580) 326-7755	Bill Cavner	. . .	. . .	. . .	Tom Pence	Layton Cox	Gary Lippard
Idabel *	c	MC	6	(580) 286-7608	Jerry Shinn	. . .	Tina Foshee	. . .	Proctor Young	Jim Coffman	Steve Surratt
Jenks	c	CM	9	(918) 299-5883	Vic Vreeland	. . .	. . .	Kenda Rice	Bob Douglas	Don Selle	. . .
Kingfisher	c	CM	4	(405) 375-3705	Roger Phillips	Reuben Pulis	Jack Graham	. . .	Kenneth Bengs	Tom Jones	. . .
Konawa	c	CM	1	(580) 925-3775	. . .	B. Dye	Wanda Lowry	. . .	. . .	. . .	. . .
Lawton	c	CM	92	(580) 581-3392	. . .	Larry Mitchell	. . .	Richard Endicott	Barton Hadley	Harold Thorne	Gerald Ihler
Lindsay	c	CM	2	(405) 756-2019	. . .	. . .	. . .	. . .	. . .	. . .	. . .
Lone Grove	c	CM	4	(580) 657-3111	Dickie Welch	Harrell Kennedy	Terri Downs	. . .	Billy Christian	Robert Oldham	Charles Gilbert
Madill *	c	CM	3	(580) 795-5586	Kevin Eppler	Robert Watts	Carol Painter	. . .	J. Keith Pruitt	James Fullingim	Bobby Kaney
Mangum *	c	CM	2	(580) 782-2250	Robert Zinn	. . .	Staci Goode	. . .	Steven Slaton	Dale Rogers	Terry Warren
Mannford	c	MC	2	(918) 865-4314	. . .	Mike Nunneley	Joyce Martin	Cecilia Ward	Bob Evans	Virgil Reed	John Anson
Marlow	c	CM	4	(580) 658-5401	Gary Vining	Janice Cain	Michael Bullard	Donald Green	. . .	Robert Hill	. . .
Mc Alester	c	CM	17	(918) 423-9300	Dale Covington	Mark Roath	Bobbie Lanz	. . .	Joe Benson	Dale Nave	. . .
Mc Loud *	t	MC	3	(405) 964-5264	Jon Barrett	Larry Dillon	Kay Heinz	. . .	Mike Bickel	Gary Rowe	Billie Sneed
Medford *	c	CM	1	(580) 395-2823	Don Bowman	Dea Kretchmar	Barbara Bush	. . .	. . .	Roger Christman	Dennis Brittain
Miami *	c	MC	13	(918) 542-6685	Brent Brassfield	Huey Long	. . .	Charles Tomlin	Kevin Trease	Gary Anderson	. . .
Midwest City	c	CM	54	(405) 739-1232	Russell Smith	John Henson	Rhonda Atkins	Judy Redman	Randall Olsen	Robert Clabes	. . .
Moore	c	CM	41	(405) 793-5000	Lewis Glenn	Stephen Eddy	. . .	Jim Corbett	Charles Stephens	Ted Williams	Richard Sandefur
Muldrow	t	MC	3	(918) 427-3226	Carl Fugett	David Taylor	. . .	Dorothy Chandler	Jim Mabray	Tony Lewis	Joe Shamblin
Muskogee *	c	CM	38	(918) 682-6602	John Hammons	James Buckley	Pamala Bush	. . .	Derek Tatum	Rex Eskridge	Michael Stewart
Mustang	c	CM	13	(405) 376-4521	Chad McDowell	David Cockrell	Patricia Winham	Brenda Wright	Alvin McClung	Monte James	. . .
Newcastle	c	CM	5	(405) 387-4427	James Wilson	Nick Nazar	Shirley Guffey	. . .	Steven Bowers	Larry Hodges	Bill Canary
Newkirk	c	CM	2	(580) 362-2117	Michael Gibson	Harold Harris	Jane Thomas	. . .	Jerry Evans	John Hobbs	Jack Bagg
Nichols Hills	c	CM	4	(405) 843-6637	Kathy Walker	David Poole	. . .	Cathy Keller	Keith Bryan	Richard Mask	Charles Hooper
Nicoma Park	t	MC	2	(405) 769-5673	William Green	. . .	Beverly McManus	. . .	James Shonts	Eric Crews	. . .
Noble	t	CM	5	(405) 872-9251	Dee Downer	Harry Hill	Sarita Scott	. . .	James Stufflebean	Paul Boyd	Elza Harris
Norman *	c	CM	95	(405) 366-5491	Cindy Rosenthal	Steven Lewis	Brenda Hall	Anthony Francisco	James Fullingim	Phil Cotten	Shawn O'Leary
Nowata	c	CM	3	(918) 273-3538	John Carroll	Dave Neely	Tracy Mitchell	. . .	Randy Lawson	Bill Tate	Donald Lewis
Okeene	t	CM	1	(580) 822-3035	Angela Ohman	Mary Jac Rauh	. . .	. . .	. . .	Robert Cancemi	Keith Richardson
Okemah	c	CM	3	(918) 623-1050	Luna Burnett	Robert Baxter	Roberta Rutland	. . .	. . .	Edward Smith	Jerry Turner
Oklahoma City *	c	CM	506	(405) 297-2530	Mick Cornett	James Couch	Frances Kersey	Laura Johnson	Keith Bryant	William Citty	Dennis Clowers
Okmulgee *	c	CM	13	(918) 756-4060	Brian Priegel	Robert Baxter	Ronnia Andrews	. . .	Richard Mitchell	Joe Prentice	Charles Miller
Owasso *	c	CM	18	(918) 376-1500	Craig Theondel	Rodney Ray	. . .	Angela Hess	Bradd Clark	Dan Yancey	Roger Stevens
Pauls Valley	c	CM	6	(405) 238-3308	Tim Gamble	. . .	Barbara Plummer	. . .	Joe Eddy	James Frizell	. . .
Pawhuska	c	CM	3	(918) 287-3040	. . .	. . .	Virginia Kelderman	. . .	Laban Miles	Kevin St. Peter	Mark Chamberlain
Perkins	c	CM	2	(405) 547-2445	. . .	Peter Seikel	. . .	. . .	. . .	. . .	. . .
Perry	c	MC	5	(580) 336-4241	Charles Hall	Jim Davis	. . .	Randolph Meachan	Paul Hinchey	Michael Thomas	. . .
Piedmont	c	CM	3	(405) 373-2621	Mike Drea	Michael Vaughn	Amanda Percival	. . .	Mike Southard	. . .	Bud Stuber
Pocola	t	MC	3	(918) 436-2388	John Farris	. . .	Glenda Harris	. . .	Joe Pendleton	Russell Nichols	. . .
Ponca City	c	CM	25	(580) 767-0323	Richard Stone	Craig Stephenson	. . .	Marc La Bossiere	. . .	Clayton Johnson	. . .
Poteau	c	MC	7	(918) 647-4191	Jeff Shockley	. . .	Cindy Pollard	. . .	Jon Pickel	Billy Smith	Mark Collins
Prague	c	CM	2	(405) 567-2270	J. McBride	Louis Devereaux	Christi Riddle	. . .	Starland Davis	Jim Bartlett	. . .
Pryor	c	MC	8	(918) 825-0888	Jimmy Tramel	. . .	Eva Smith	. . .	David Harrison	Dennis Nichols	. . .
Purcell	c	CM	5	(405) 527-6561	Albert Hudson	B. Darlene Duncan	Tina Allison	. . .	Michael Clifton	David Tompkins	. . .
Sallisaw	c	CM	7	(918) 775-6241	Shannon Vann	Bill Baker	Robert Park	. . .	Michael Tubbs	Gary Philpot	. . .
Sand Springs *	c	CM	17	(918) 246-2500	Robert Walker	Douglas Enevoldsen	Bruce Ford	. . .	Mark Joslin	Daniel Bradley	Derek Campbell
Sapulpa *	c	CM	19	(918) 224-3040	Douglas Haught	Thomas DeArman	Shirley Burzio	Pamela Vann	. . .	James Wall	. . .
Sayre	c	MC	4	(580) 928-2260	Jack Ivester	Jack McKennon	Elaine Barker	. . .	Sammy Green	Jeff Lambert	. . .
Seminole	c	CM	6	(405) 382-4330	Vicki Spears	Steven Saxon	Diane Johnson	. . .	Roy Lemmings	Christopher Mills	Michael Grant
Shawnee	c	CM	28	(405) 878-1669	. . .	. . .	. . .	Neva Treiber	. . .	William Mathis	Jim Bierd
Skiatook	t	CM	5	(918) 396-2797	Don Branscum	R. McClanathan	. . .	Shirley Lett	Jeff Perry	Richard Davis	. . .
Spencer	c	CM	3	(405) 771-3226	Earl Syth	Nicole Mukes	Evrett White	. . .	Ron Kelley	Olan Boydstun	Larry Mathews
Stigler *	c	CM	2	(918) 967-2164	Larry Godfrey	Jim Smith	Cheryl Monks	. . .	Jim Pearson	Richard Dickson	Roger Edwards
Stillwater *	c	CM	39	(405) 372-0025	Roger McMillian	Dan Galloway	Clara Welch	Marcy Alexander	Marion Blackwell	Norman McNickle	Ralph Kinder
Stroud *	c	CM	2	(918) 968-2890	Joseph Hankins	Steve Gilbert	Gayle Thornton	. . .	Roger Mcelyea	Brett Gipson	Jimmy Lewis
Sulphur	c	MC	4	(580) 622-5096	Mitch Hull	William Holley	Shannon Couch	. . .	Dayton Burnside	David Shores	Keith Woodell
Tahlequah	c	MC	14	(918) 456-0651	Jenny Cook	Kevin Smith	Deb Corn	. . .	Mike Swim	Norman Fisher	. . .
Tecumseh	c	CM	6	(405) 598-2188	Greg Wilson	David Johnson	Joanne Medley	. . .	Jimmy Stokes	Gary Crosby	. . .
The Village	c	CM	10	(405) 751-8861	Stanley Alexander	Bruce Stone	. . .	. . .	Dewayne Price	Michael Robinson	Larry Walton
Tishomingo	c	CM	3	(580) 371-2369	Rex Morrell	Jack Yates	Geneva Carr	. . .	Tom Winkler	Wayne Solomon	Wayne Taylor
Tonkawa	c	CM	3	(580) 628-2508	. . .	John Ramey	Deborah Miner	. . .	Kirk Henderson	Bill Jordan	Darrell Steelmon
Tulsa	c	MC	393	(918) 596-7440	Kathy Taylor	. . .	. . .	Michael Kier	Alan LaCroix	David Been	Charles Hardt
Tuttle *	c	CM	4	(405) 381-2335	Henry Biddy	Timothy Young	Cheryl LaFerney	Becky Wright	Gerald Cook	Donald Cluck	Tommy Chester
Vinita	c	MC	6	(918) 256-8552	Jesse Johnson	Charles Enyart	Linda Scott	. . .	Jimmie Butcher	George Hicks	. . .
Wagoner *	c	MC	7	(918) 485-4586	Joshua Hughes	Larry Morgan	Linda Gaylor	. . .	Kelly Grooms	Terry Hornbuckle	Kenneth Peters
Walters	c	CM	2	(580) 875-3337	. . .	John Sheppard	Dollie Glenn	. . .	Richard Lewallen	Mike Carter	. . .
Warr Acres	c	MC	9	(405) 789-2892	Tommy Pike	. . .	Nancy Jones	. . .	Bob Cunningham	David Smith	Gerald Wright
Watonga *	c	MC	4	(580) 623-4669	. . .	. . .	. . .	. . .	. . .	. . .	. . .
Waurika	c	CM	1	(580) 222-2713	Dana Eck	Kenneth Ferreira	Donna Brown	. . .	Harold Winton	James Jones	. . .
Waynoka	c	MC	. .	(580) 824-2261	Charlene Bixler	. . .	. . .	Sharlotte Bolar	Larry Milledge	Kermit Criswell	. . .
Weatherford	c	MC	9	(580) 772-7451	Gary Rader	Tony Davenport	. . .	. . .	Dean Brown	Byron Cox	Arnold Miller
Wetumka	c	CM	1	(405) 452-3251	Bob Fansher	Don Kardokus	J. Smith	Pat Griggs	Robert Spradlin	. . .	. . .
Wewoka	c	CM	3	(405) 257-2413	. . .	David Fuqua	. . .	. . .	. . .	. . .	. . .
Wilburton	c	MC	2	(918) 465-5361	Danny Baldwin	. . .	Denise Brunk	. . .	. . .	. . .	. . .
Woodward *	c	CM	11	(580) 256-2280	Bill Fanning	D. Riffel	Catherine Coleman	. . .	Steve Day	Harvey Rutherford	Thomas Goff
Wynnewood	c	CM	2	(405) 665-2307	John Warren	. . .	Beverly Collier	. . .	Jeff Green	Troy Bishop	Don Harmon
Yale	c	CM	1	(918) 387-2405	James Matlock	Joe Johnson	Sharon Crisjohn	. . .	Jeff Morphew	Rick Gibson	Wes Thurman
Yukon *	c	CM	21	(405) 354-1895	John Alberts	James Crosby	Patricia Hargis	. . .	Jeff Lara	Gary Wieczorek	Jerry Reed
OREGON											
Adair Village *	c	MC	. .	(541) 745-5507	William Currier	Drew Foster	. . .	. . .	. . .	. . .	. . .
Albany *	c	CM	40	(541) 917-7500	Dan Bedore	Roland Hare	Betty Langwell	Stewart Taylor	John Bradner	Edward Boyd	D. Taniguchi-Dennis
Amity	c	CM	1	(503) 835-3711	. . .	. . .	Heidi Blaine	. . .	. . .	. . .	. . .
Ashland *	c	MC	19	(541) 488-6002	John Stromberg	Martha Bennett	. . .	Lee Tuneberg	Keith Woodley	Terry Holderness	Mike Faught
Astoria *	c	CM	9	(503) 325-5824	Willis VanDusen	Paul Benoit	. . .	John Snyder	Lenard Hansen	Peter Curzon	Ken Cook
Aumsville *	c	CM	3	(503) 749-2030	Harold White	Maryann Hills	Colleen Rogers	Dianne Pursell	. . .	Michael Andall	Steve Oslie
Baker City	c	CM	9	(541) 523-6541	Karen Yeakley	Stephen Brocato	. . .	Roger Dexter	. . .	Jim Tomlinson	Dick Fleming
Bandon	c	MC	2	(541) 347-2437	Mary Schamehorn	Matt Winkel	Marie Ducharme	Carolyn Stephens	. . .	Bob Webb	Richard Anderson
Banks *	c	MC	1	(503) 324-5112	Mike Lyda	James Hough	Jolynn Becker	. . .	. . .	. . .	. . .
Beaverton	c	MC	76	(503) 526-2201	Rob Drake	. . .	. . .	Patrick O'Claire	. . .	David Bishop	. . .
Bend	c	CM	52	(541) 388-5502	Oran Teater	Eric King	Patricia Stell	M. Escheveste	Larry Langston	Andrew Jordan	Michael Elmore
Boardman	c	CM	2	(541) 481-9252	. . .	. . .	Lila Killingbeck	Kenneth Fleck	. . .	Mark Calbick	Jeffrey Hayzlett

Directory 1/9 continued

OFFICIALS IN U.S. MUNICIPALITIES 2,500 AND OVER IN POPULATION

Jurisdiction	Type	Form of govern-ment	2000 Popu-lation	Main telephone number	Chief elected official	Appointed administrator	Clerk of the governing board	Chief financial officer	Fire chief	Police chief	Public works director
OREGON continued											
Brookings *	c	CM	5	(541) 469-2163	Larry Anderson	Gary Milliman	Joyce Heffington	. . .	William Sharp	Christopher Wallace	John Cowan
Brownsville *	c	CM	1	(541) 466-5666	C. Shipley-Kalupa	Scott McDowell	. . .	. . .	. . .	. . .	Kurt Riemer
Burns	c	CM	3	(541) 573-5255	Laura Van Cleave	. . .	Dauna Wensenk	. . .	Bill Guindon	Rob Nou	David Cullens
Canby	c	CM	12	(503) 266-4021	Melody Thompson	Mark Adcock	Kim Scheafer	. . .	. . .	Ken Pagano	Roy Hester
Cannon Beach *	c	CM	1	(503) 436-8050	Mike Morgan	Richard Mays	. . .	. . .	. . .	Gene Halliburton	Mark See
Canyonville *	c	MC	1	(541) 839-4258	Charles Spindel	Cheryl Masotto	Joan Beckman	. . .	. . .	. . .	Tony Lakey
Carlton *	c	MC	1	(503) 852-7575	Kathie Oriet	Steven Weaver	Apryl Denman	. . .	Terry Lucich	Frank Butler	Bryan Burnham
Cascade Locks	c	CM	1	(541) 374-8484	Ralph Hesgard	Bernard Seeger	. . .	Katherine Mast	. . .	. . .	Richard McCulley
Central Point *	c	CM	12	(541) 664-3321	Henry Williams	Phillip Messina	Deanna Casey	Bev Adams	. . .	Jon Zeliff	Robert Pierce
Clatskanie	c	CM	1	(503) 728-2622	Chip Waisanier	Preston Polasek	Tina Hendricks	Arlene Long	. . .	Marvin Hoover	. . .
Coburg	c	MC	. .	(541) 682-7850	. . .	William Hudson	. . .	. . .	. . .	. . .	. . .
Condon	c	MC	. .	(541) 384-2711	N. Dale Thompson	Kathryn Greiner	. . .	. . .	. . .	William Gubser	Larry Durfrey
Coos Bay	c	CM	15	(541) 269-1181	Joe Benetti	Charles Freeman	. . .	Janell Howard	Stan Gibson	Eura Washburn	Jim Hossley
Coquille	c	CM	4	(541) 396-2115	. . .	Terence O'Connor	. . .	. . .	Dave Waddington	Michael Reaves	John Higgins
Cornelius *	c	CM	9	(503) 357-9112	William Bash	David Waffle	Debby Roth	. . .	Chris Asanovic	Paul Rubenstein	Mark Crowell
Corvallis	c	CM	52	(541) 766-6902	Helen Berg	Jon Nelson	Sue Mariner	Nancy Brewer	Dan Campbell	Gary Boldizsar	Steve Rogers
Cottage Grove	c	CM	8	(541) 942-5501	Gary Williams	Richard Meyers	Joan Hoehn	Roberta McClintock	. . .	Michael Grover	Robert Sisson
Creswell *	c	MC	3	(541) 895-2531	Robert Hooker	Mark Shrives	Roberta Tharp	Layli Nichols	Paul Furrer	. . .	Roy Sprout
Dallas *	c	CM	12	(503) 831-3502	Jim Fairchild	Jerry Wyatt	. . .	. . .	Bill Hahn	Tom Simpson	Fred Braun
Damascus *	c	CM	9	(503) 658-8545	Jim Wright	James Bennett	. . .	Dan O'Dell	. . .	Paul Steigleder	Steve Gaschler
Dayton	c	MC	2	(503) 864-2221	. . .	Sue Hollis	. . .	. . .	. . .	. . .	. . .
Dundee *	c	CM	2	(503) 538-3922	Don Sundeen	Rob Daykin	Debra Manning	Sheryl Hartman	John Stock	. . .	. . .
Durham	c	CM	1	(503) 639-6851	Gery Schirado	Roland Signett	. . .	. . .	. . .	. . .	. . .
Eagle Point *	c	MC	4	(541) 826-4212	Leon Sherman	David Hussell	Dena Roberts	Melissa Owens	. . .	David Strand	Robert Miller
Enterprise	c	MC	1	(541) 426-4196	. . .	Michele Young	. . .	. . .	. . .	. . .	. . .
Estacada	c	CM	2	(503) 630-8270	Robert Austin	Randy Ealy	Denise Carey	. . .	. . .	. . .	William Strawn
Eugene	c	CM	137	(541) 682-5061	James Torrey	Jon Ruiz	. . .	Cindi Hamm	Thomas Tallon	Thad Buchanan	Kurt Corey
Fairview *	c	MC	9	(503) 665-7929	Mike Weatherby	Joseph Gall	. . .	Samantha Landau	. . .	Ken Johnson	Bob Cochran
Florence *	c	CM	7	(541) 997-3436	Phil Brubaker	Robert Willoughby	Barbara Miller	David Armstrong	. . .	Lynn Lamm	Mike Miller
Forest Grove	c	CM	17	(503) 359-3200	. . .	Michael Sykes	Catherine Jansen	Paul Downey	Robert Davis	Thomas Lowther	Robert Foster
Gearhart	c	MC	. .	(503) 738-5501	. . .	Dennis McNally	. . .	. . .	William Eddy	. . .	. . .
Gervais	c	CM	2	(503) 792-4222	Shanti Platt	Sam Sasaki	. . .	. . .	. . .	. . .	David Miller
Gladstone	c	CM	11	(503) 656-5225	Wade Byers	Ron Partch	. . .	. . .	Charles Ames	Frank Grace	. . .
Gold Beach *	c	CM	1	(541) 247-7029	James Wernicke	Don Flynn	Heather Wainscott	Jodi Hatfield	Bruce Floyd	Russ Merkley	Jeff Denney
Granite *	c	MC	. .	(541) 755-5100	Steven Smith	. . .	Dolores Schnitzer	. . .	. . .	. . .	Mitchell Fielding
Grants Pass	c	CM	30	(541) 474-6360	Len Holzinger	David Frasher	. . .	. . .	. . .	. . .	Dave Wright
Gresham	c	CM	90	(503) 661-3000	Charles Becker	Erik Kvarsten	Debbie Jermann	Terrance McCall	Scott Lewis	Carla Piluso	David Rouse
Happy Valley	c	CM	4	(503) 760-3325	Rob Wheeler	Catherin Daw	. . .	Barbara Muller	. . .	. . .	. . .
Harrisburg	c	CM	2	(541) 995-6655	. . .	Bruce Cleeton	. . .	. . .	. . .	. . .	. . .
Heppner *	c	CM	1	(541) 676-9618	Les Paustain	Dave DeMayo	. . .	. . .	. . .	. . .	Brian Harmon
Hermiston *	c	CM	13	(541) 567-5521	Bob Severson	Edward Brookshier	. . .	Bob Irby	. . .	Daniel Coulombe	. . .
Hillsboro *	c	CM	70	(503) 681-6100	Jerry Willey	Sarah Jo Chaplen	Amber Ames	Margaret Echeveste	Gary Seidel	Lila Ashenbrenner	Roy Gibson
Hood River	c	CM	5	(541) 386-1488	Paul Cummings	Robert Francis	Anita Smith	Steven Everroad	Gary Willis	Richard Younkins	. . .
Hubbard	c	MC	2	(503) 981-9633	. . .	. . .	. . .	. . .	. . .	. . .	. . .
Independence	c	CM	6	(503) 838-1212	Larry Dalton	Greg Ellis	Charlotte Townsend	David Gephart	. . .	Vernon Wells	Kenneth Perkins
Jacksonville	c	CM	2	(541) 899-8910	James Lewis	Paul Wyntergreen	Kathy Hall	. . .	Tracy Shaw	David Towe	Jeff Alvis
Jefferson	c	MC	2	(541) 327-2768	Michael Myers	. . .	Janet Powell	. . .	. . .	. . .	Steve Human
Joseph	c	MC	1	(541) 432-3832	Peggy Kite-Martin	. . .	. . .	Noma McDaniel	Herman Ortmann	. . .	James Lewis
Junction City	c	MC	4	(541) 998-2153	Jon Edwards	David Clyne	. . .	Barbara Scott	. . .	Laddie Hancock	David Renshaw
Keizer *	c	CM	32	(503) 390-3700	Lore Christopher	Christopher Eppley	. . .	Susan Gahlsdorf	. . .	Marc Adams	Rob Kissler
King City	c	CM	1	(503) 639-4082	. . .	David Wells	. . .	Bhavana Nesargi	. . .	Charles Fessler	. . .
Klamath Falls *	c	CM	19	(541) 883-5317	Todd Kellstrom	Jeffrey Ball	. . .	Phyllis Shidler	. . .	Jim Hunter	Mike Kuenzi
La Grande *	c	CM	12	(541) 962-1302	Colleen Johnson	Robert Strope	Alexandra Lund	Eldon Slippy	Bruce Weimer	Derick Reddington	Norman Paullus
Lafayette *	0	MC	2	(503) 864-2451	Chris Heisler	Diane Rinks	Jamie Rhodes	. . .	Terry Lucich	. . .	. . .
Lake Oswego	c	CM	35	(503) 635-0215	Judie Hammerstad	Alexander McIntyre	Robyn Christie	Richard Seals	Ed Wilson	Dan Duncan	E. Papadopoulos
Lakeview	t	MC	2	(541) 947-2029	. . .	Raymond Simms	. . .	Marlisa Jameson	Kenneth Chartier	David King	Ronald Wilkie
Lebanon	c	CM	12	(541) 451-7476	Kenneth Tombs	John Hitt	. . .	Casey Cole	. . .	Michael Healy	James Ruef
Lincoln City	c	CM	7	(541) 996-2152	Lori Hollingsworth	David Hawker	Oneita McCalman	Ron Tierney	. . .	Mike Holden	Lance Burke
Lowell	c	CM	. .	(541) 937-2157	. . .	Charles Spies	. . .	. . .	. . .	. . .	. . .
Madras	c	CM	5	(541) 475-2344	Richard Allen	Mike Morgan	Karen Coleman	Brenda Black	. . .	Tommy Adams	Gus Burril
Manzanita	c	CM	. .	(503) 368-5343	Joyce Raker	Jerald Taylor	Judith New	. . .	. . .	. . .	Bret Siler
Mc Minnville	c	CM	26	(503) 434-7301	Edward Gormley	Kent Taylor	. . .	Carole Benedict	Jay Lilly	Ron Noble	Mike Bisset
Medford *	c	CM	63	(541) 774-2000	Gary Wheeler	Michael Dyal	. . .	Alison Chan	Dave Bierweiler	Randy Schoen	Cory Crebbin
Mill City	c	CM	1	(503) 897-2302	Tim Kirsch	Deborah Hogan	Stacie Cook	Renee Short	. . .	. . .	John Dickinson
Milton-Freewater	c	CM	6	(541) 938-5531	Lewis Key	Delphine Palmer	. . .	Dave Richmond	Shane Garner	Mike Gallaher	Howard Moss
Milwaukie	c	CM	20	(503) 786-7555	Carolyn Tomei	Michael Swanson	Pat Duval	Steve Smith	. . .	Brent Collier	James Brink
Molalla *	c	CM	5	(503) 829-6855	Mike Clarke	John Atkins	Sadie Cramer	Peggy Johnson	. . .	Jerry Giger	Malcolm Bowie
Monmouth *	c	CM	7	(503) 838-0722	John Oberst	Scott McClure	Phyllis Bolman	Mark Dunmire	Jason Cane	Darrell Tallan	Craig Johns
Monroe	c	MC	. .	(541) 847-5175	. . .	Aaron Palmquist	. . .	. . .	. . .	. . .	James Hickey
Mount Angel *	c	CM	3	(503) 845-9291	Rick Schiedler	James Hunt	. . .	Tracy Grambusch	Don Fleck	Brent Earhart	Daniel Bernt
Myrtle Creek	c	CM	3	(541) 863-3171	Jerry Pothier	Aaron Cubic	Charity Hays	Jeanne Babcock	Bill Leming	Cecil Earp	Steven Johnson
Myrtle Point *	c	CM	2	(541) 572-2626	Michael Johnson	Randall Whobrey	B. Kirkpatrick	Amy McCall	Dan Gardner	Rock Rakossi	. . .
Nehalem	c	CM	. .	(503) 368-5627	Shirley Kalkhoven	Michael Nitzsche	Dee Anne Stockton	. . .	Steve Van Dyke	. . .	Don Davidson
Newberg *	c	CM	18	(503) 537-1240	Robert Andrews	Daniel Danicic	Norma Alley	Elizabeth Comfort	Al Blodgett	Brian Casey	Howard Hamilton
Newport	c	CM	9	(541) 574-0603	William Bain	. . .	Margaret Hawker	Janice Riessbeck	Richard Crook	Mark Miranda	Lee Ritzman
North Bend	c	CM	9	(541) 756-8500	Rick Wetherell	Jan Willis	Angie Kellar	Juana Bell	Scott Graham	Steve Scibelli	. . .
Nyssa	c	CM	3	(541) 372-2264	Bob Fehlman	Roberta Donovan	Hilda Contreras	Helen Holtz	Pedro Vasquez	Dennis Francis	Myra Harley
Oakridge *	c	CM	3	(541) 782-2258	Don Hampton	Gordon Zimmerman	. . .	Pam Hart	Tim Demers	Louis Gomez	Kevin Urban
Ontario *	c	CM	10	(541) 889-7684	Joe Dominick	Henry Lawrence	Tori Ankrum	Rachel Hopper	Allan Higinbotham	Mike Kee	Charles Mickelson
Oregon City *	c	CM	25	(503) 657-0891	Alice Norris	Larry Patterson	Nancy Ide	David Wimmer	. . .	. . .	Nancy Kraushaar
Pendleton	c	CM	16	(541) 966-0201	Phillip Houk	Lawrence Lehman	. . .	Linda Carter	John Fowler	Stuart Roberts	Robert Patterson
Philomath	c	CM	3	(541) 929-6148	. . .	Randy Kugler	Ruth Post	. . .	. . .	Ken Eluer	Beau Vencill
Phoenix *	c	MC	4	(541) 535-1955	Carlos DeBritto	Jane Turner	. . .	. . .	. . .	Derek Bowker	Bob Lewis
Pilot Rock	c	CM	1	(541) 443-2811	. . .	Jackie Carey	Amanda Howard	. . .	. . .	Ronnie Layton	Steve Draper
Port Orford	c	CM	1	(541) 332-3681	. . .	. . .	Patricia Clark	Robert Ewalt	. . .	William Rush	David Pace
Portland	c	CO	529	(503) 823-3572	Vera Katz	. . .	Karla Moore-Love	. . .	. . .	Charles Moose	Felicia Trader
Prineville *	c	CM	7	(541) 447-5627	Mike Wendel	. . .	Lisa Morgan	Liz Schutte	. . .	Eric Bush	. . .
Rainier	c	CM	1	(503) 556-7301	Jerry Cole	Lars Gare	. . .	. . .	. . .	. . .	. . .
Redmond *	c	CM	13	(541) 923-7739	Alan Unger	Michael Patterson	Patricia Leymaster	Bryce DuPere	Tim Moor	Ronnie Roberts	Chris Doty
Reedsport	c	CM	4	(541) 271-3603	Keith Tymchuk	Scott Somers	. . .	Vera Koch	Tom Anderson	Shawn Essex	Floyd Dollar
Roseburg *	c	CM	20	(541) 672-7701	Larry Rich	P. Swanson	Sheila Cox	Cheryl Guyett	Jack Cooley	Mark Nickel	Nicole Messenger
Salem	c	CM	136	(503) 588-6162	Janet Taylor	Linda Norris	. . .	Glen Merritt	Marcus Knode	Walter Myers	Timothy Gerling
Sandy *	c	CM	5	(503) 668-5533	Linda Malone	Scott Lazenby	Karen Evatt	. . .	. . .	Harold Skelton	Mike Walker
Scappoose	c	CM	4	(503) 543-7146	Glenn Dorschler	Jon Hanken	Susan Pentecost	Jill Herr	. . .	Douglas Greisen	Terry Andrews
Seaside *	c	CM	5	(503) 738-5511	Donald Larson	Mark Winstanley	. . .	Al Peinhardt	Joseph Dotson	Robert Gross	Neal Wallace
Shady Cove	c	MC	2	(541) 878-2225	Ruth Keith	Elise Smurzynski	Margaret Borgen	. . .	. . .	Richard Mendenhall	George Bostic

Directory 1/9 continued OFFICIALS IN U.S. MUNICIPALITIES 2,500 AND OVER IN POPULATION

Jurisdiction	Type	Form of govern-ment	2000 Popu-lation	Main telephone number	Chief elected official	Appointed administrator	Clerk of the governing board	Chief financial officer	Fire chief	Police chief	Public works director
OREGON continued											
Sheridan *	c	CM	3	(503) 843-2347	Veldon Adamson	Francis Sheridan	Patricia Henderson	Joel Wade	. . .	. . .	Lonnie Hinchcliff
Sherwood	c	CM	11	(503) 625-5522	Keith Mays	. . .	Sylvia Murphy	Christina Robuck	. . .	William Middleton	Craig Sheldon
Silverton *	c	CM	7	(503) 873-5321	Stu Rasmussen	Bryan Cosgrove	. . .	Kathleen Zaragoza	. . .	Richard Lewis	Richard Barstad
Sisters *	c	MC	. .	(541) 549-6022	M. David Elliot	Eileen Stein	. . .	Lisa Young	. . .	. . .	Brad Grimm
Springfield *	c	CM	52	(541) 726-3700	Sidney Leiken	Gino Grimaldi	Amy Sowa	Robert Duey	Dennis Murphy	Jerry Smith	Susan Smith
St. Helens	c	MC	10	(503) 397-6272	Randy Peterson	Chad Olsen	. . .	Marilyn Peterson	. . .	Steve Salle	Timothy Homann
Stayton *	c	CM	6	(503) 769-3425	Gerry Aboud	Christopher Childs	. . .	Christine Shaffer	Jack Carriger	Rich Sebens	Dave Kinney
Sutherlin *	c	CM	6	(541) 459-2856	Lee Sparks	. . .	. . .	David Harker	Joel King	Thomas Boggs	Michael Gray
Sweet Home *	c	CM	8	(541) 367-8969	Craig Fentiman	Craig Martin	. . .	Patricia Gray	. . .	Robert Burford	Michael Adams
Talent	c	CM	5	(541) 535-1566	Marian Telerski	Jay Henry	. . .	Holly Haviland	. . .	Robert Rector	Lester Naught
The Dalles	c	CM	12	(541) 296-5481	David Beckley	Nolan Young	Julie Krueger	Robert Moody	. . .	Jay Waterbury	Brian Stahl
Tigard	c	CM	41	(503) 639-4171	. . .	Craig Prosser	Catherine Wheatley	. . .	. . .	William Dickinson	Edward Wegner
Tillamook	c	CM	4	(503) 842-2472	Robert McPheeters	Mark Gervasi	Susan Huntsman	B. Sorensen	. . .	Terrence Wright	Michael Mahoney
Toledo	c	CM	3	(541) 336-2247	. . .	Michelle Amberg	Renee Ballinger	. . .	William Ewing	Donald Denison	Herbert Jennings
Troutdale	c	CM	13	(503) 665-5175	Paul Thalhofer	. . .	Debbie Stickney	Kathy Leader	. . .	David Nelson	James Galloway
Tualatin	c	CM	22	(503) 692-2000	Lou Ogden	Sherilyn Lombos	Maureen Smith	. . .	. . .	Kent Barker	Daniel Boss
Turner *	c	CM	1	(503) 743-2155	Carly Strauss	David Sawyer	Suzanne Studer	. . .	. . .	Gary Will	Terry Rust
Umatilla *	c	CM	4	(541) 922-3226	David Trott	Larry Clucas	Linda Gettmann	. . .	. . .	Darla Huxel	Roger Frances
Veneta	c	MC	2	(541) 935-2191	Tim Brooker	Ric Ingham	. . .	. . .	. . .	. . .	. . .
Vernonia *	c	MC	2	(503) 429-5291	Sally Harrison	. . .	Kate Conley	Cindy Naillon	Paul Epler	Mathew Workman	Jeff Burch
Waldport	c	CM	2	(541) 563-3561	Scott Beckstead	Nancy Leonard	Reda Quinlan	. . .	. . .	. . .	Rick McClung
Warrenton	c	CM	4	(503) 861-2233	Paul Rodriguez	Robert Maxfield	Linda Engbretson	Laurie Sawrey	Frank Ames	. . .	. . .
West Linn *	c	CM	22	(503) 657-0331	David Dodds	Christopher Jordan	Nancy Davis	Elizabeth Carlson	. . .	John Ellison	Ronald Hudson
Wilsonville	c	CM	13	(503) 682-1011	. . .	Arlene Loble	Sandy King	Gary Wallis	. . .	. . .	Jeff Bauman
Winston *	c	CM	4	(541) 679-6739	Rex Stevens	David Van Dermark	. . .	Ann Munson	. . .	Scott Gugel	Jennifer Sikes
Wood Village *	c	CM	2	(503) 667-6211	David Fuller	Sheila Ritz	. . .	Peggy Jo Minter	Scott Lewis	Robert Skipper	Randall Jones
Woodburn *	c	CM	20	(503) 982-5228	Kathryn Figley	Scott Derickson	Mary Tennant	David Gillespie	. . .	Scott Russell	Dan Brown
PENNSYLVANIA											
Abington *	tp	MC	1	(570) 586-0111	Jeff Thurston	William White	Jacqueline Bisch	. . .	. . .	Daniel Mooney	Thomas James
Abington	tp	MC	56	(267) 536-1000	Barbara Ferrara	Burton Conway	. . .	Susan Matiza	Kenneth Clark	William Kelly	Ed Micciolo
Akron	b	MC	4	(717) 859-1600	John McBeth	Reed Imhoff	. . .	. . .	Larry Hanke	. . .	Kenneth Gestewitz
Aldan	b	MC	4	(610) 626-3553	. . .	. . .	. . .	. . .	. . .	. . .	. . .
Aleppo *	tp	MC	1	(412) 741-6555	Frank Bialek	Gwen Patterson	. . .	. . .	William Davis	Norbert Micklos	Mark Kerr
Aliquippa	b	CO	11	(724) 375-5188	James Mansueti	. . .	. . .	Dennis Panagitsas	Darryl Jones	Ralph Pallante	Bernie Hall
Allegheny	tp	MC	8	(724) 842-4641	Kathy Starr	David Soboslay	Susan Teagarden	Carol Waronsky	. . .	Timothy Solla	Steven Kanas
Allentown *	c	MC	106	(610) 437-7523	Ed Pawlowski	Kenneth Bennington	Michael Hanlon	Lawrence Hilliard	Robert Scheirer	Roger MacLean	Richard Young
Altoona	c	CM	49	(814) 949-2410	Thomas Martin	Joseph Weakland	Linda Rickens	Omar Strohm	Reynold Santone	. . .	David Diedrich
Ambler	b	CM	6	(215) 646-1000	Bud Wahl	Rocco Wack	. . .	. . .	Charles Baily	. . .	James Wack
Ambridge	b	CM	7	(724) 266-4070	. . .	Kristen Denne	Joanne Trella	. . .	David Drewnowski	David Sabol	. . .
Amity	tp	CM	8	(610) 689-6000	Leslie Sacks	Charles Lyon	Linda McCue	. . .	. . .	Noel Roy	. . .
Antis *	tp	CM	6	(814) 742-7361	. . .	Jeffrey Ziegler	. . .	. . .	. . .	. . .	. . .
Archbald *	b	MC	6	(570) 876-1800	Ed Fairbrother	Michael Narcavage	Colleen Smith	Bill Durkin	Robert Harvey	Timothy Trently	Michael Zielinski
Arnold	c	MC	5	(412) 337-4441	. . .	. . .	. . .	. . .	. . .	. . .	. . .
Ashland	b	MC	3	(570) 875-2411	Rosemarie Noon	Edward Wallace	. . .	. . .	Thomas Towers	Adam Bernodin	. . .
Ashley	b	MC	2	(570) 824-1364	George Oravic	Kathleen Krofchok	. . .	. . .	Joseph McGlynn	David Cerski	Robert Hess
Aspinwall	b	MC	2	(412) 781-0213	. . .	Edward Warchol	Georgene Veltri	. . .	. . .	Charles Clouse	Lee Albacker
Aston	tp	CM	16	(610) 494-2915	James McGinn	Richard Lehr	. . .	. . .	Thomas Morgan	Albert Fasano	Russell Palmore
Athens	b	MC	3	(570) 888-2120	. . .	. . .	. . .	. . .	. . .	C. Hutchinson	. . .
Avalon *	b	CM	5	(412) 761-5820	Edward Kildare	Harry Dilmore	. . .	Thomas Michalow	William Carney	Robert Howie	Keith Lorey
Avoca	b	MC	2	(570) 457-4947	Joseph Satkowski	Ann Backlasky	Stephen Yokimishyn	. . .	. . .	Edward Lukowich	Keith Patterson
Baden	b	MC	4	(724) 869-3700	Carol Sambol	Susan Blum	Michael Miketa	Michael Stuban	David Trzcianka	. . .	John Peoples
Baldwin	b	MC	19	(412) 882-9600	Alexander Bennett	Timothy Little	Judy Assad	. . .	. . .	. . .	Mark Stephenson
Bally *	b	MC	1	(610) 845-2351	. . .	. . .	. . .	. . .	. . .	. . .	. . .
Bangor	b	MC	5	(610) 588-2216	Bonnie La Bar	Lynn Martocci	Linda Paynter	Cynthia Weiss	Robert Owens	Henry Schollhammer	. . .
Barnesboro	b	MC	2	(814) 948-8230	Eva Wargo	Fred Nastasi	. . .	. . .	Dave Hassen	Kevin Stanek	Dave Suchar
Beaver	b	MC	4	(724) 773-6700	. . .	. . .	. . .	. . .	. . .	. . .	. . .
Beaver Falls	c	CO	9	(724) 847-2800	Karl Boak	. . .	Paula Burdine	Leonard Chiappetta	Mark Stowe	Gary Minnitte	Ted Krzemienski
Beavertown	b	MC	. .	(570) 658-2505	David Hassinger	Chris Weller	. . .	. . .	William Mattern	. . .	. . .
Bedford	b	MC	3	(814) 623-8192	William Leibfreid	John Montgomery	Beverly Fisher	. . .	Rocky Fetter	Charwin Reicheldorfer	. . .
Bedminster *	tp	MC	4	(215) 795-2190	Eric Schaffhausen	John Terry	Jean Herstine	. . .	. . .	Mark Offner	Jeff Heacock
Bellefonte	b	CM	6	(814) 355-1501	Joseph Heidt	Ralph Stewart	Suzanne Egli	. . .	. . .	Duane Dixon	William Comly
Bellevue	b	CM	8	(412) 766-6164	Paul Cusick	David Golebiewski	Marsha Smith	Lori Forbes	Charles Amrhein	Michael Bookser	Murl Thompson
Bensalem	tp	CM	58	(215) 633-3600	Joseph Digirolamo	William Cmorey	. . .	John McGinley	Joseph Scanlon	. . .	James Ryan
Bentleyville	b	MC	2	(724) 239-2112	Lena Greenfield	. . .	Sheryl Hreha	. . .	Ronald Sicchitano	. . .	Arthur Blackburn
Benzinger	tp	MC	8	(814) 781-1274	. . .	. . .	. . .	. . .	. . .	. . .	. . .
Berwick	b	CM	10	(570) 752-2723	Gary Pinterich	Shane Pepe	. . .	. . .	Bill Coolbaugh	Frank Brennan	Robert Markle
Bethlehem	tp	CM	21	(610) 814-6400	Allan Robertson	Jon Hammer	Judy Todaro	Andrew Freda	. . .	Daniel Pancoast	Richard Grube
Bethlehem *	c	MC	71	(610) 865-7000	John Callahan	. . .	Cynthia Biedenkopf	Dennis Reichard	George Barkanic	Randall Miller	Michael Alkhal
Big Beaver *	b	MC	2	(724) 827-2416	. . .	. . .	. . .	. . .	. . .	. . .	. . .
Birdsboro	b	CM	5	(610) 582-6030	Robert Myers	Randall Miller	Michelle Cramer	. . .	. . .	Theodore Roth	. . .
Blairsville	b	CM	3	(412) 459-9100	Raymond Baker	Edward Smith	Mary Brown	. . .	Daniel Duralli	. . .	Joseph Spiaggi
Blakely *	b	MC	7	(570) 383-3340	J. Acciare-Mariani	. . .	. . .	Edward Alco	Walter Yankovitch	Guy Salerno	. . .
Bloomsburg	t	MC	12	(570) 784-7703	Charles Coffman	Carol Mas	. . .	. . .	Hugh Gross	Leo Sokoloski	John Barton
Blossburg	b	MC	1	(570) 638-2452	John Backman	George Lloyd	Sally Ward	. . .	. . .	. . .	. . .
Boyertown	b	CM	3	(610) 367-2688	. . .	. . .	. . .	. . .	. . .	. . .	. . .
Brackenridge	b	CM	3	(724) 224-0800	. . .	. . .	Carol Jones	. . .	. . .	Jamie Bock	Joseph Chifulini
Braddock	b	CM	2	(412) 271-1018	Pauline Abdullah	. . .	Clara Jones	. . .	Thomas Petrovic	William Moore	. . .
Braddock Hills	b	CM	1	(412) 241-5080	. . .	. . .	. . .	. . .	Robert Henkel	Frank Gardone	Thomas McQuade
Bradford	c	CM	9	(814) 362-3884	Michele Corignani	John Peterson	. . .	Katherine Graff	William McCormack	Roger Sager	Gary Alcock
Brentwood *	b	MC	10	(412) 884-1500	. . .	George Zboyovsky	. . .	. . .	. . .	. . .	. . .
Bridgeport	b	MC	4	(610) 272-1811	. . .	. . .	. . .	. . .	Steven Wanczyk	. . .	. . .
Bridgeville	b	CM	5	(412) 221-6012	. . .	. . .	. . .	. . .	. . .	. . .	. . .
Brighton	tp	CM	8	(724) 774-4803	Jack Erath	Bryan Dehart	. . .	. . .	. . .	Stanley Guza	. . .
Bristol	b	MC	9	(215) 788-3828	. . .	. . .	. . .	. . .	. . .	. . .	. . .
Bristol *	tp	CM	55	(215) 785-0500	Samuel Fenton	Jeff Bartlett	. . .	Gail Gordon	. . .	James McAndrew	Jason Lawson
Brookhaven	b	MC	7	(610) 874-2557	. . .	. . .	. . .	. . .	. . .	. . .	. . .
Brookville	b	MC	4	(814) 849-5321	Chip Wonderling	. . .	Stephen Rowan	. . .	Denny Allgiver	Kenneth Dworek	. . .
Brownsville	b	MC	2	(724) 785-5761	. . .	. . .	. . .	. . .	. . .	. . .	. . .
Buckingham *	tp	CM	16	(215) 794-8834	Maggie Rash	Dana Cozza	. . .	Jill Pistory	. . .	Steven Daniels	Michael Taylor
Butler	tp	MC	7	(570) 788-3547	Ramson Young	Steven Hahn	. . .	Erin Braddock	. . .	. . .	. . .
Butler *	c	CO	15	(724) 285-4124	Margaret Stock	. . .	Mindy Gall	George Kelly	George Ban	Timothy Fennell	Joseph Bratkovich
Butler	tp	MC	17	(724) 283-3430	. . .	Gerald Patterson	. . .	. . .	. . .	. . .	. . .
California	b	MC	5	(724) 938-8878	John Greenlief	. . .	Diane Pagac	Edwin Glab	Thomas Hartley	Joseph Dochinez	John Mariscotti
Callimont	b	MC	. .	(814) 634-0010	Arlene Feeney	. . .	. . .	. . .	. . .	. . .	. . .

Directory 1/9 continued — OFFICIALS IN U.S. MUNICIPALITIES 2,500 AND OVER IN POPULATION

Jurisdiction	Type	Form of government	2000 Population	Main telephone number	Chief elected official	Appointed administrator	Clerk of the governing board	Chief financial officer	Fire chief	Police chief	Public works director
PENNSYLVANIA continued											
Caln *	tp	MC	11	(610) 384-0600	Jill Hammond	Gregory Prowant	...	Barry Luber	David Aberts	Brian Byerly	...
Cambridge Springs	b	CM	2	(814) 398-2311	Joseph Tuminello	Peggy Lewis	Sandra Pude	...	Richard Massung	Eugene Woznicki	Kenneth Dine
Camp Hill	b	CM	7	(717) 737-3456	Philip Murren	Edward Knittel	...	Natalie Lee	Rob Kozicki	Gregory Ammons	Tim Maro
Canonsburg	b	CM	8	(724) 745-1800	Anthony Colaizzo	Terry Hazlett	...	...	Harold Coleman	R. T. Bell	Chester Osiecki
Canton	tp	CM	8	(724) 225-8990	...	...	Lori Castle	...	...	...	...
Carbondale	c	MC	9	(570) 282-4110	...	Fred Moase	Michele Bannon	...	...	...	...
Carlisle *	b	CM	17	(717) 249-4422	Kirk Wilson	Stephen Hietsch	Stacey Hamilton	John O'Neill	Robert Kennedy	Stephen Margeson	Michael Keiser
Carnegie *	b	CM	8	(412) 276-1414	...	Stephen Vincenti	...	...	John Kandracs	...	Leonard Mitkoski
Carroll Valley	b	MC	3	(717) 642-8269	Grady Edwards	David Hazlett	Barbara Hertz	...	...	Richard Hileman	...
Castle Shannon	b	CM	8	(412) 885-9200	Regis Zezulewicz	Thomas Hartswick	Linda Karlovich	...	William Reffner	Harold Lane	...
Catasauqua	b	CM	6	(610) 264-0571	Barbara Schlegel	Eugene Goldfeder	...	...	Samuel Burrows	Douglas Kish	Jeffrey MacHose
Center	tp	MC	11	(724) 774-0271	Tony Amadio	...	...	Rachael Del Tondo	Dennis Morrison	Barry Kramer	...
Centerville *	b	MC	3	(724) 785-9206	Patsy Ricciuti	...	...	...	...	David Simon	...
Chalfont	b	MC	3	(215) 822-7295	Robert Cleland	Melissa Shafer	Barbara Qualteria	...	Randy Teschner	Frank Campbell	J. Michael Bishop
Chambersburg	b	CM	17	(717) 264-5151	William McLaughlin	Eric Oyer	Tanya Mickey	Casimir Rzomp	...	Michael Defrank	Robert Wagner
Chanceford *	tp	CM	5	(717) 927-6401	David Gemmill	Brenda Gohn	...	...	Ronald Witmer	...	...
Charleroi *	b	MC	4	(724) 483-6011	Frank Paterra	Robert Hodgson	Carl Minkovich	...	Robert Whiten	Michael Matyas	Thomas Santoro
Chartiers *	tp	CM	7	(724) 745-3415	Harlan Shober	Alice Derian	Wendy Williams	...	...	James Horvath	Edward Jeffries
Cheltenham	tp	CM	36	(215) 887-6200	Jeffrey Mauldower	David Kraynik	...	Rosemary Poppert	Michael Moonblatt	John Scholly	Richard Young
Chester	c	MC	36	(610) 447-7700	...	...	Sara Bingnear	Monir Ahmed	Joseph Cliffe	...	Patricia West
Chippewa	tp	CM	7	(724) 843-8177	...	...	...	...	...	Robert Berchtold	...
Churchill	b	MC	3	(412) 241-7113	Richard Farrell	Craig Robinson	...	...	...	Allen Park	Ralph Zatlin
Clairton	c	CM	8	(412) 233-8113	Dominic Serapiglia	Ralph Imbrogno	Frances Jones	Scott Andrejchak	John Lattanzi	...	Perry Ohm
Clarion	b	CM	6	(814) 226-7707	Ronald Wilshire	Nancy Freenock	...	...	...	Mark Hall	Bradley Stutzman
Clarks Summit	b	CM	5	(570) 586-9316	Harold Kelly	Barbara Grabfelder	...	...	...	...	...
Clearfield	b	CM	6	(814) 765-7817	Patty Gilliland	...	...	Pamela Peters	Brett Owens	Jeffrey Rhone	William Beveridge
Clifton Heights	b	MC	6	(610) 623-1000	Mike Galantino	...	Shannon Ostien	...	Jim Kneass	Walter Senkow	John Grace
Coaldale *	b	RT	2	(570) 645-6310	Claire Remington	...	...	...	Richard Marek	Timothy Delaney	Kenneth Hankey
Coatesville	c	CM	10	(610) 384-0300	Stephon Hines	...	...	Elizabeth McQuiston	Glen Davis	Dominic Bellizzi	Donald Wilkinson
Colebrookdale	tp	MC	5	(610) 369-1362	Todd Gamler	Cindy Conrad	...	...	...	Christopher Schott	Bruce Sands
College *	tp	CM	8	(814) 231-3021	...	Adam Brumbaugh	...	Robert Long	...	...	Garry Williams
Collegeville	b	MC	8	(610) 489-9208	Dennis Parker	Geoffrey Thompson	Donna Artiuch	...	Jeffrey Wentworth	Barton Bucher	Joseph Hastings
Collingdale	b	CM	8	(610) 586-0500	...	...	...	...	...	...	...
Columbia	b	CM	10	(717) 684-2467	...	...	...	Georgianna Schreck	Chuck Anderson	Joseph Greenya	Ron Miller
Colwyn	b	CM	2	(610) 461-2000	James McAnamy	Daniel McEnhill	Kelly Winter	Earl Reed	Rahn Monreal	Bryan Hills	Martha Van Auken
Concord	tp	CM	9	(610) 459-8911	Dominic Pileggi	Robert Willert	...	...	Frederick Field	...	Harry Shire
Connellsville	c	MC	9	(724) 628-2020	...	...	...	...	...	...	...
Conshohocken *	b	MC	7	(610) 828-1092	Sandra Caterbone	Francis Marabella	...	...	Robert Phipps	James Dougherty	C. Buek
Conway *	b	MC	2	(724) 869-5550	Gregory Ritorto	Diane McKay	...	...	Robert Charlovich	Anthony Blum	Brian Giles
Coopersburg	b	MC	2	(610) 282-3307	Joseph Volk	Dawn Sadimas	Carol Anderson	...	Thomas Reinhard	Daniel Trexler	Dennis Nace
Coplay *	b	MC	3	(610) 262-6088	John Milander	...	Veronica Caciolo	...	David Buskaritz	Vincent Genovese	Daniel Pavelko
Coraopolis	b	MC	6	(412) 264-3002	Mary Sike	Thomas Cellante	...	...	Larry Byrge	Alan DeRusso	...
Cornwall	b	MC	3	(717) 274-3436	...	...	...	...	...	...	...
Corry	c	CO	6	(814) 663-7041	...	...	...	...	...	...	...
Coudersport	b	MC	2	(814) 274-9776	George Hults	Marlin Moore	Gwendolyn Bretz	...	Brian Wilson	Lee Gross	...
Crafton	b	MC	6	(412) 921-0752	Charles Wooster	...	...	...	William Finlay	Harold Rost	Joseph Pitnaro
Cranberry *	tp	CM	23	(724) 776-4806	John Milius	Jerry Andree	...	Vanessa Gleason	Mark Nanna	...	Jason Dailey
Cranberry Township	tp	CM	7	(814) 676-8812	Patrick Andres	Frank Pankratz	Margaret Allaman	...	...	...	Mike Erwin
Crescent	tp	CM	2	(724) 457-8100	David Hays	Patrica Moser	...	...	...	Todd Miller	...
Cross Roads	b	CM	..	(717) 993-6669	...	...	...	...	...	...	...
Cumberland	tp	CM	5	(717) 334-6485	...	Florence McLeish	...	...	...	...	...
Cumru	tp	CO	13	(610) 777-1343	Ray Henry	James Sigworth	Jeanne Johnston	Peggy Carpenter	G. Kellenberger	Brian Hiester	Robert McNichols
Curwensville	b	MC	2	(814) 236-1840	...	...	...	...	...	...	...
Dallas	b	CM	2	(570) 675-1389	John Oliver	Joseph Moskovitz	...	...	Harry Vivian	James Drury	John Cybulski
Dallastown	b	MC	4	(717) 244-6626	Beverly Scott	Connie Stokes	Melody Hess	...	Dennis List	...	Brett Patterson
Danville	b	MC	4	(570) 275-3091	Ed Coleman	Thomas Graham	Kathleen Creasy	Shannon Berkey	Brian Witmer	Rae Leighow	Robert Haas
Darby	tp	CO	10	(610) 586-1514	Lawrence Patterson	John Ryan	...	...	...	Robert Thompson	Charles Joyner
Darby	b	MC	10	(610) 586-1102	Angela Maskart	Joseph Possenti	Rita Tucker	...	Edward Gannon	Robert Smythe	Aaron Ockimey
Delta	b	CM	..	(717) 456-6248	Jenalyn Williams	...	...	...	...	...	William Ailes
Denver *	b	CM	3	(717) 336-2831	Danny Rabold	Michael Hession	Joan High	...	Matt Martzall	George Beever	George Whetsel
Derry	b	MC	2	(724) 694-2030	Ronald Bolen	...	...	...	William Woods	Charles Dyche	...
Derry	tp	CM	21	(717) 533-2057	Frank O'Connell	James Negley	...	...	...	William Smith	Thomas Clark
Dickson City	b	MC	6	(717) 489-4758	Bob Wilitshire	Ken Novack	Kathy Simone	...	Tony Zalewski	Bill Stadnitski	...
Dillsburg	b	CM	2	(717) 432-9969	...	...	...	...	...	...	...
Donora	b	MC	5	(412) 379-6600	...	...	...	...	...	...	...
Dormont	b	MC	9	(412) 561-8900	Thomas Lloyd	...	Vickie McGurk	Sherri Pruce	Dennis Davis	Russell McKibben	Anthony Kobistek
Dover	tp	CM	18	(717) 292-3634	...	Michael Morris	...	...	...	...	...
Downingtown	b	CM	7	(610) 269-0344	Michael Menna	Anthony Gambale	...	...	Gregg Nelms	James McGowan	Steve Sullins
Doylestown	b	CM	8	(215) 345-4140	Tom Jarret	John Davis	...	Caroline Leiter	Michael Wood	James Donnelly	Daniel Lightcap
Doylestown *	tp	CM	17	(215) 348-9915	Barbara Lyons	Stephanie Mason	...	William Wightman	Robert Lanetti	Stephen White	Richard John
Dravosburg	b	MC	2	(412) 466-5200	...	...	Brenda Honick	...	...	Ken Holland	Ron Vezzani
Du Bois *	c	CM	8	(814) 371-2000	John Suplizio	...	...	DeLean Wagner	Joe Bigar	Steve Davis	Steve Swope
Dublin	b	CM	2	(215) 249-3310	Kent Moore	Eleanor Sadorf	Marybeth Cody	...	...	Brian Lehman	Stefan Green
Duncannon	b	CM	1	(717) 834-4311	...	Dan Rapp	...	...	...	...	...
Dunmore	b	CM	14	(570) 344-4590	Patrick Loughney	Richard Carr	...	Mary Rice	Vincent Arnone	Mecca Salvatore	Maglio Salvatore
Dupont	b	MC	2	(570) 666-6216	Ann Marie O'Malley	William Riccetti	...	...	Charles Tetlak	Anthony De Mark	Paul Houdyshell
Duquesne	c	MC	7	(412) 469-3770	...	...	...	...	...	...	...
Duryea	b	MC	4	(570) 655-2829	...	...	...	...	...	...	...
East Caln *	tp	CM	2	(610) 269-1989	Donald Mahue	Barbara Kelly	Melba Forcine	Bonnie Lucy	...	Brian Gallagher	...
East Conventry	tp	CM	4	(610) 495-5443	David Leinbach	...	...	...	Joel McMillan	John Theobald	Ray Kolb
East Goshen	tp	CM	16	(610) 692-7171	...	Louis Smith	Marie Clevenger	...	...	C. Mac Intyre	Mark Miller
East Hempfield *	tp	CM	21	(717) 898-3100	Susan Bernhardt	Robert Krimmel	...	Gary Kline	...	Douglas Bagnoli	Perry Madonna
East Hopewell	tp	CM	2	(717) 993-6529	...	...	...	...	...	...	...
East Lampeter	tp	CM	13	(717) 393-1567	Glenn Eberly	Ralph Hutchison	...	Jeanne Glick	...	John Bowman	Charles Thomas
East Lansdowne	b	CM	2	(610) 623-7131	James France	George Bobnak	Julie McDevitt	Lindsay Crosby	Larry Mellon	Thomas Pearlingi	Robert Kleinberg
East Mc Keesport	b	MC	2	(412) 824-2531	Robert Howard	Connie Rosenbayger	...	William Daugherty	Paul Marcoz	Richard Michaels	...
East Nantmeal	tp	TM	1	(610) 458-5780	Virginia Devaney	...	...	...	...	...	Raymond Nestorick
East Norriton	tp	CM	13	(610) 275-2800	Donald Gracia	Helmuth Baerwald	...	William Scurry	George Myers	John McGowan	Joseph Sorgini
East Pennsboro	tp	CO	18	(717) 732-0711	George DeMartyn	Robert Gill	...	...	...	Dennis McMaster	...
East Petersburg	b	CM	4	(717) 569-9282	Cathleen Panus	James Williams	...	...	...	...	Herbert Mattern
East Rockhill	tp	MC	5	(215) 257-9156	...	Anne Klepfer	...	...	...	...	...
East Stroudsburg *	b	CM	9	(570) 421-8300	Roger Delarco	James Phillips	...	Berrill Dennis	John Fahl	John Baujan	...
East Vincent *	tp	CM	5	(610) 993-4424	John Funk	Mary Flagg	Edward Miller	Sheila Mauger	...	William Demski	Darwin Schafer
East Whiteland *	tp	CM	9	(610) 648-0600	Virginia McMichael	Terry Woodman	...	George Lokken	Ken Hurley	Eugene Dooley	William Steele
Easton	c	MC	26	(610) 250-6600	Thomas Goldsmith	W. Steckman	Thomas Hess	Pat Vulcano	Francis Chisesi	Lawrence Palmer	Kristie Miers
Easttown	tp	CM	10	(610) 644-9000	...	...	...	...	...	...	...

Directory 1/9 continued **OFFICIALS IN U.S. MUNICIPALITIES 2,500 AND OVER IN POPULATION**

Jurisdiction	Type	Form of govern-ment	2000 Popu-lation	Main telephone number	Chief elected official	Appointed administrator	Clerk of the governing board	Chief financial officer	Fire chief	Police chief	Public works director
PENNSYLVANIA continued											
Ebensburg	b	CM	3	(814) 472-7166	Charles Moyer	Daniel Penatzer	Theresa Chaffin	Sharon Burkett	...	George Brady	Charles Voyda
Economy	b	MC	9	(724) 869-4779	Kenneth Campbell	Randy Kunkle	...	Marie Hagg	John Thomas	Tom Harrington	Earl Fitzgerald
Eddystone	b	MC	2	(610) 874-1100	Charles Rowles	Patricia Rodden	...	...	...	Raymond Rodden	Tom Belton
Edgewood	b	CM	3	(412) 242-4824	Joseph Young	Kurt Ferguson	Michael Bowen	David Amatangelo	Edward Bechtold	...	Richard Christenson
Edgeworth	b	CM	1	(412) 741-2866	Robert McGinnis	Martin McDaniel	...	...	...	...	Fred Gregorich
Edinboro *	b	CM	6	(814) 734-1812	Mary Horne	Taras Jemetz	...	...	Matthew Seagren	Jeffrey Craft	Butch Shafer
Edwardsville	b	MC	4	(570) 288-6484	Bernard Pubaskas	Charles Szalkowski	...	...	Ray King	David Souchick	Michael Wozniak
Elizabeth	tp	MC	13	(412) 751-2880	Joanne Beckowitz	Malisa Migliori	...	...	...	Robert Wallace	Keith Shaffer
Elizabethtown *	b	CM	11	(717) 367-1700	Douglas Pfautz	Peter Whipple	...	...	...	Dennis Landvater	Wayne Devan
Ellwood City *	b	CM	8	(724) 758-7777	Anthony Court	Dom Viccari	Mary Ann Viccari	...	Connie Mac Donald	...	Randy Gatto
Emmaus	b	CM	11	(610) 965-9292	...	Craig Neely	Johanna Green	Alan France	Robert Reiss	David Faust	Daniel Delong
Emporium	b	CM	2	(814) 486-0768	James Slusarick	Robert Aversa	Joyce Beichner	...	Raymond Housler	Allen Neyman	Timothy Leydig
Emsworth	b	MC	2	(412) 761-1161	Keith Johnston	David Venturella	Cathy Jones	...	Robert Bennett	...	Steven Ference
Ephrata	b	CM	13	(717) 738-9232	Fred Thomas	Gary Nace	...	Gail Bare	...	Steven Annibali	Robert Thompson
Erie	c	MC	103	(814) 870-1234	Joyce Savocchio	...	James Klemm	Charles Herron	Gregory Martin	Paul De Dionisio	John Barzano
Etna	b	CM	3	(412) 781-0569	Peter Ramage	Mary Ellen Ramage	Patricia Ruby	...	Gregory Porter	William Grover	Keith Olash
Exeter	b	MC	5	(570) 654-6816	Richard Murawski	...	...	John Petrucci	Donald Skursky	John McNeil	...
Exeter *	tp	CM	21	(610) 779-5660	Dona Starr	Troy Bingaman	Nancy Jack	Carol Leinbach	Robert Jordan	Christopher Neidert	Clarence Hamm
Fairview Township *	tp	CM	14	(717) 901-5200	Perry Albert	Paula Tezik	...	...	William Carlisle	Bernard Dugan	Michael Fleming
Falls	tp	CM	34	(215) 949-9000	Allen Wilson	Wayne Bergman	...	Peter Gray	Edward Copper	Arnold Conoline	Walter Almond
Farrell	c	CM	6	(724) 983-2703	Eugene Pacsi	Lavon Saternow	Nadine Shimshock	...	Joseph Santell	...	Gerald Multari
Felton *	b	CM	..	(717) 246-6493	Anna O'Berry	Joy Flinchbaugh	...	...	Scott Gingrich	...	...
Ferguson *	tp	CM	14	(814) 238-4651	Richard Mascolo	Mark Kunkle	...	Eric Endersen	Stan Clouser	Diane Conrad	David Modricker
Findlay *	tp	CM	5	(724) 695-0500	Thomas Gallant	Gary Klingman	...	...	Robert Lambert	Jesse Lesko	John O'Neal
Fleetwood	b	MC	4	(610) 944-8220	Alexander Szoke	...	Lois Geist	...	Steve Bleiler	Ray Nester	Robert Weidner
Folcroft	b	MC	6	(610) 522-1305	Kathleen Kelly	...	Judith Serratore	...	Frank Foglio	Edward Christie	Daniel Falcone
Ford City *	b	MC	3	(724) 763-3081	Marc Mantini	...	Lisa Bittner	...	Ron Wojcik	Ron Kligensmith	Peter Milito
Forest Hills *	b	CM	6	(412) 351-7330	Michael Belmonte	Steven Morus	Roberta McGreevy	...	Ray Heller	William Fabrizi	Jim Theilacker
Forks	tp	CM	8	(610) 252-0785	Dave Hoff	Richard Schnaedter	Barbara Bartek	James Farley	Bryan Weis	Gregory Dorney	Mark Roberts
Forty Fort	b	MC	4	(717) 287-8586	Andy Tuzinski	...	Paula Lucas	Denise Syms	James Shedlarski	Eric Morgantini	Robert Barnard
Foster	tp	CO	4	(814) 362-4656	Robert Slike	...	Donna Griesbaum	...	Scott Hannahs	Jeffrey Wolbert	Joseph Sweet
Fountain Hill	b	MC	4	(610) 867-0301	...	...	...	...	...	...	...
Fox Chapel	b	CM	5	(412) 963-1100	Nathan Parker	Gary Koehler	Dana Abate	Joy Hardt	...	David Laux	Albert Biernesser
Frackville	b	MC	4	(570) 874-3860	...	...	...	...	...	...	...
Franconia *	tp	CM	11	(215) 723-1137	Steven Barndt	Kevin Baver	...	David Bernhauser	Paul Stoudt	Joseph Kozeniewski	Paul Nice
Franklin	c	CM	7	(814) 437-1485	Robert Heller	E. Gabrys	...	Cheryl Carson	James Wetzel	Jeff Storm	...
Franklin Park *	b	CM	11	(412) 364-4115	L. Shupe	Ambrose Rocca	...	...	...	Donald Dorsch	Ronald Merriman
Freeland *	b	CM	3	(570) 636-0111	Paul Thomas	...	...	...	Joseph Stepansky	...	...
Geistown *	b	MC	2	(814) 266-8313	Donna Locher	Sandra Porada	Karen Giebfried	...	Douglas Ream	James McGrath	Dennis Ryan
Gettysburg	b	CM	7	(717) 334-1160	John Eline	...	Sara Stull	...	Larry Weikery	Frederick Gantz	John Lawver
Girard	b	CM	3	(814) 774-9683	Alfred Noble	Richard Higley	...	...	Robert Orr	Daniel Bucho	Guy McDonald
Glassport	b	MC	4	(412) 672-7400	Anthony Pepe	Nancy Piazza	Andrea Foster	...	...	Bernard Dworek	Dan Kunf
Glenolden *	b	MC	7	(610) 583-3221	Thomas Danzi	Brian Hoover	Donna Williams	...	Joseph Locke	Michael Donohue	...
Green Tree *	b	CM	4	(412) 921-1110	Mark Sampogna	W Montz	...	...	Daniel Walsh	...	Kary Rahner
Greencastle *	b	CM	3	(717) 597-7143	Charles Eckstine	Kenneth Womack	...	...	...	John Phillippy	...
Greensburg *	c	MC	15	(724) 838-4324	Karl Eisaman	Susan Trout	...	Mary Perez	John Hutchinson	Walter Lyons	Rick Hoyle
Greenville *	b	CM	6	(724) 588-4193	Pete Longiotti	Ryan Eggleston	Nancy Little	...	Stephen Thompson	Dennis Stephens	Paul Boyer
Grove City	b	CM	8	(724) 458-7060	George Pokrant	...	...	...	Jeffrey Badger	Dean Osborne	Barry Spiker
Halfmoon Township	tp	CM	2	(814) 692-9800	D. C. Bracken-Piper	Karen Brown	Gregory Love	...	...	...	Scott Brown
Hamburg	b	CM	4	(610) 562-7821	...	Lynda Albright	...	...	...	...	Richard Pickel
Hampden *	tp	CM	24	(717) 761-0119	Melvyn Finkelstein	Michael Gossert	...	Janice Jensen	Richard Flinn	Michael Andreoli	Steven Campbell
Hampton	tp	CM	15	(412) 486-0400	...	W. Lochner	Susan Bernet	Albert Presto	...	...	Alex Zarenko
Hanover	tp	CM	1	(610) 264-1069	Bruce Paulus	Sandra Pudliner	Vicky Roth	...	Robin Yoder	...	Bruce Pudliner
Hanover *	b	CM	14	(717) 637-3877	John Gerken	Bruce Rebert	Dorothy Miller	...	James Roth	Gary Brown	Randal Baugher
Harmony	tp	CO	3	(724) 266-1910	...	...	...	...	...	...	...
Harris	tp	CM	4	(814) 466-6228	Dennis Hameister	Amy Farkas	Suzanne Shirvani	Walter Cheatle	...	...	Allen Klinger
Harrisburg	c	MC	48	(717) 255-6475	Stephen Reed	Linda Lingle	Vicki Williams	Robert Kroboth	Donald Konkle	Charles Kellar	James Close
Harrison	tp	CO	11	(724) 226-1393	George Conroy	Faith Payne	...	...	...	Michael Klein	Robert Hines
Hatboro	b	CM	7	(215) 443-9100	Thomas McMackin	...	...	...	Steve Plum	Frank Campbell	W. Stauch
Hatfield	b	CM	2	(215) 855-0781	John Weierman	...	Scott Smith	...	Robert Kahler	Mark Toomey	Gerald Heffner
Hatfield	tp	CM	16	(215) 855-0900	John Norman	Stephanie Teoli	...	John Hall	Steve Walt	...	Nick DeMeno
Haverford	tp	CM	48	(610) 446-1000	...	Michael English	...	George Rementer	James Marino	Gary Hoover	...
Hazleton *	c	MC	23	(717) 459-4961	Louis Barletta	Mary Ellen Lieb	Lisa Shema	...	Donald Leshko	Robert Ferdinand	Robert Dougherty
Heidelberg *	tp	MC	3	(610) 767-9297	David Fink	Daniel Stonehouse	...	...	...	...	...
Hellertown *	b	CM	5	(610) 838-7041	Gail Nolf	Charles Luthar	Janice Unangst	T.-L. Krasnansky	Rickey Delmore	Robert Balum	Thomas Henshaw
Hempfield *	tp	CO	40	(724) 834-7232	John Silvis	...	...	...	...	...	Michael Volpe
Hermitage *	c	CM	16	(724) 981-0800	Duane Piccirilli	Gary Hinkson	...	Jami Kirila	Robert Goeltz	Patrick McElhinney	...
Highspire	b	CM	2	(717) 939-3303	Wayne Shank	John McHale	...	...	Justin Varnicle	Mark Stonbraker	John Ingiosi
Hilltown	tp	CM	12	(215) 453-6000	John McIlhinney	C. Christman	Lynda Seimes	...	...	C. Engelhart	Thomas Buzby
Hollidaysburg	b	CM	5	(814) 695-7543	James Shoemaker	...	Ann Andrews	Robert Kuntz	Brian Seiler	David Shiffler	David Zeek
Homer City	b	CM	1	(724) 479-8005	Arlene Barker	Stanley Buggey	Karen Valyo	...	Carl Filler	John Griffith	Butch Hiner
Homestead	b	CM	3	(412) 461-1340	Lloyd Cunningham	Richard Sharkey	Jacquelyne Tomko	...	William Purfory	Mark Zeger	Daniel Kelly
Honesdale	b	MC	4	(717) 253-0731	H. Richard Osborne	...	...	...	...	Frank Rosler	William Corcoran
Honey Brook	tp	CM	6	(610) 273-3970	...	Michael Brown	...	...	...	...	...
Hopewell *	tp	CM	5	(717) 933-2027	David Wisnom	Patricia Schaub	...	...	...	...	...
Hopewell	tp	CO	13	(412) 378-1460	Tim Force	...	Pat Owens	Andy Brunette	Steve Seaman	Eugene Ungarean	Chas Srafin
Horsham *	tp	CM	24	(215) 643-3131	Joanna Furia	Michael McGee	...	Richard Sabol	...	Robert Ruxton	William Pietzsch
Hughesville	b	CM	2	(717) 584-5272	D. Davis	...	...	...	...	...	...
Hummelstown	b	MC	4	(717) 566-2555	...	Michael O'Keefe	Donna Spittle	...	Charles Cogan	Charles Dowell	Rich Engle
Huntingdon	b	CM	6	(814) 643-3966	Foster Ulrich	Daniel Varner	...	...	...	...	...
Indian Lake	b	CM	..	(814) 754-8161	...	...	...	...	...	...	...
Indiana	tp	CM	6	(412) 767-5333	...	Daniel Anderson	...	...	...	Robert Wilson	John Carson
Indiana	b	MC	14	(724) 465-6691	...	...	...	...	...	...	...
Industry *	b	MC	1	(724) 643-4360	...	...	Jeannie Caffro	...	Charles Ward	Garold Miller	...
Ingram	b	CM	3	(412) 921-3625	Frank Petrell	Cindy Dzadovsky	Chrissy Testa	...	George Beerhalter	George Jak	Tom Dzadovsky
Irwin	b	CM	4	(724) 864-3100	Daniel Rose	...	Connie Serman	...	...	John Karasek	Randy Altman
Jackson	tp	CM	3	(724) 452-5581	Ralph DeLuigi	Richard Crown	Sarah Richards	...	Tim Sapienza	Len Keller	Robert Russell
Jackson	tp	CM	6	(717) 225-5661	...	William Conn	...	...	...	...	...
Jeannette	c	MC	10	(724) 527-4000	...	Ronald Dinsmore	...	...	...	...	...
Jefferson Hills	b	CM	9	(412) 655-7735	Kevin McFarland	Douglas Arndt	Saundra Mortle	...	...	John Maple	William McVicker
Jenkintown	b	CM	4	(215) 885-0700	Vincent McCabe	Edwin Geissler	Tricia Anderson	...	Gary Bachman	Albert Divalentino	Mike Micciolo
Jersey Shore	b	CM	4	(570) 398-0104	Cheryl Brungard	...	...	Martha Gottschall	...	Martin Jeirles	Randy Stover
Jessup	b	MC	4	(717) 489-0411	...	...	...	...	...	...	...
Jim Thorpe	b	MC	4	(717) 325-3025	Michael Sofranko	...	Louise McClafferty	...	Patrick McGinley	Barry Andrews	...
Johnsonburg	b	CM	3	(814) 965-5682	Hudnell Caldwell	Mary Polaski	...	...	Jack Fowler	...	Louis Cherry
Johnstown *	c	CM	23	(814) 533-2001	Thomas Trigona	Curtis Davis	...	Mary Johnston	Anthony Kovacic	Craig Foust	Darby Sprincz

Directory 1/9 continued

OFFICIALS IN U.S. MUNICIPALITIES 2,500 AND OVER IN POPULATION

Jurisdiction	Type	Form of government	2000 Population	Main telephone number	Chief elected official	Appointed administrator	Clerk of the governing board	Chief financial officer	Fire chief	Police chief	Public works director
PENNSYLVANIA continued											
Kane	b	CM	4	(814) 837-9240	Edgar James	Michael Holtz	...	...	David Silvis	William Osmer	...
Kenhorst	b	CM	2	(610) 777-7327	...	...	...	...	...	...	...
Kennett Square	b	CM	5	(610) 444-6020	...	...	...	Kathy Holliday	...	Albert McCarthy	Joseph Scalise
Kingston	tp	CM	7	(570) 696-3809	...	Kelly Cook	Kathleen Sebastian	...	...	James Balavage	Donald Fritzges
Kingston	c	MC	13	(570) 288-4576	...	Paul Keating	...	Carol Urban	Robert Cannon	Daniel Beky	Russel Kratz
Kittanning	b	MC	4	(412) 543-2091	...	...	...	...	...	...	...
Kulpmont	b	MC	2	(570) 373-1521	Robert Slaby	Frank Chesney	...	Ann Martino	Matthew Siko	Edward Grego	George Malakoski
Kutztown	b	CM	5	(610) 683-6131	Carl Mantz	...	...	Eric Ely	Robert Hauck	Theodore Cole	...
Lancaster	tp	CM	13	(717) 291-1213	...	David Clouser	...	Diana Hess	...	...	J. Eckenrode
Lancaster	c	MC	56	(717) 291-4711	Charles Smithgall	Carol Roland	Janet Spleen	...	Jeffrey Pierce	William Heim	C. Katzenmoyer
Lansdale	b	CM	16	(215) 368-1691	Benjamin Gross	F. Mangan	...	Brian Shapiro	Jay Daveler	Joseph McGuriman	Jacob Ziegler
Lansdowne	b	CM	11	(610) 623-7300	Anthony Campuzano	Craig Totaro	...	...	Tom Young	Daniel Kortan	William Johnson
Lansford	b	MC	4	(570) 645-3900	Robert Gaughan	...	...	...	Joe Cannon	James Strauss	...
Larksville	b	MC	4	(570) 714-9846	Robert Wallace	...	...	...	Andrew Kachmark	Tony Kopko	Paul Kachinko
Latrobe	c	MC	8	(724) 539-8548	Tom Marflak	Richard Stadler	...	Barbara Buck	John Brasille	Charles Huska	Joseph Bush
Laureldale	b	MC	3	(610) 929-8700	...	...	...	...	...	...	...
Lebanon	c	CO	24	(717) 273-6711	Robert Anspach	Trish Ward	Cheryl Gibson	Gerald Weise	Barry Fisher	William Harvey	Jonathan Beers
Leechburg	b	MC	2	(724) 842-8511	...	...	...	...	...	...	...
Lehighton	b	CM	5	(610) 377-4002	Wilbur Bauchspies	John Hanosek	Carol Clay	...	John Kuller	Dennis Wentz	Alton Steigerwalt
Lemoyne	b	CM	3	(717) 737-6843	James Yates	Howard Dougherty	...	Jan Boyer	Ronald Frank	...	John Paden
Lewisburg	b	CM	5	(570) 523-3614	Peter Bergonia	Chad Smith	Debra Depew	...	...	Paul Yost	George Stump
Lewistown	b	CM	8	(717) 248-1361	Fred Saxton	David Frey	...	...	Robert McCaa	...	Frank Hernandez
Liberty	b	MC	2	(717) 324-3461	Darrie Mase	Beverly Mase	...	...	Tony Baker	...	John Zeafla
Limerick	tp	CM	13	(610) 495-6432	Thomas DiBello	Daniel Kerr	Karen Willman	...	Dennis Rumler	W. Weaver	William Bradford
Lititz	b	CM	9	(717) 626-2044	Timothy Snyder	Sue Barry	...	...	...	Douglas Shertzer	Gary Rynier
Littlestown	b	MC	3	(717) 359-5101	Rick Adams	Linda Hess	Sandy Conrad	...	William Sheely	Donald Baker	Tim Topper
Lock Haven	c	CM	9	(570) 893-5900	Richard Vilello	...	...	...	Robert Neff	Elwood Hocker	...
Logan	tp	MC	11	(814) 944-5349	Frank Meloy	Bonnie Lewis	...	Tiffany Noonan	...	Ronald Heller	David Lynch
London Grove	tp	CM	5	(610) 345-0100	...	Steven Brown	...	...	...	...	...
Londonderry	tp	CM	5	(717) 944-1803	...	Steve Letavic	...	...	...	...	...
Lower Allen	tp	CM	17	(717) 975-7575	John Titzel	Thomas Vernau	...	Nancy Dietel	...	...	Gary Frazer
Lower Burrell	c	MC	12	(724) 335-9875	Donald Kinosz	...	...	Brian Eshbaugh	...	Tracy Lindo	Richard Kotecki
Lower Chanceford	tp	CM	2	(717) 862-3589	J. Taylor	...	...	...	...	...	...
Lower Frederick	tp	CM	4	(610) 287-8857	Bill McGovern	Tamara Twardowski	...	...	...	...	...
Lower Gwynedd	tp	CM	10	(215) 646-5302	Edward Brandt	Larry Comunale	Carole Culberth	Karen Yeutter	...	Gerrard Gray	Robert Pierson
Lower Macungie	tp	MC	19	(610) 966-4343	...	...	...	...	...	...	...
Lower Makefield	tp	CM	32	(215) 493-3646	...	Terry Fedorchak	...	Brian McCloskey	...	Kenneth Coluzzi	James Coyne
Lower Merion	tp	CM	59	(610) 645-6102	Bruce Reed	Douglas Cleland	Eileen Trainer	Dean Dortone	Charles McGarvey	Joseph Daly	Donald Cannon
Lower Moreland	tp	MC	11	(215) 947-3100	Kurt Mayer	Richard Mellor	...	Marion Marucci	...	Peter Hasson	H. Lawrence
Lower Nazareth	tp	CM	5	(610) 759-7434	...	Timm Tenges	...	...	...	...	...
Lower Paxton	tp	CM	44	(717) 657-5600	William Hawk	George Wolfe	...	Donna Speakman	...	...	Joseph Sutor
Lower Pottsgrove	tp	MC	11	(610) 323-0436	Bruce Foltz	Rodney Hawthorne	...	...	Dennis Miller	Raymond Bechtel	Richard Yoder
Lower Providence	tp	CM	22	(610) 539-8020	Craig Dininny	...	...	...	Bryan McFarland	Francis Carroll	David Shafter
Lower Salford Township	tp	CM	12	(215) 256-8087	...	J. Plank	...	...	...	...	...
Lower Saucon	tp	CM	9	(610) 865-3291	...	Jack Cahalan	...	Martha Chase	...	Guy Lesser	Roger Rasich
Lower Southampton	tp	CO	19	(215) 357-7300	Michael Connelly	Theodore Taylor	Janet Hude	Ken Wallace	William Raymond	William Wiegman	Randy Behmke
Lower Swatara	tp	CM	8	(215) 939-9377	...	...	...	...	...	...	...
Lower Windsor	tp	CM	7	(717) 244-6813	Kelly Skiptunas	Kelly Kelch	Tricia Smeltzer	...	...	David Sterner	Kim Miller
Luzerne	b	MC	2	(570) 287-7633	Rosemary Sigmond	Bonnie Arnone	...	...	David White	...	Howard Fox
Mahanoy City	b	CM	4	(570) 773-2150	Michael Di Baggio	...	Sonia Hiney	...	Frank Bedisky	Mark Wiekrykas	John Wilner
Malvern	b	CM	3	(610) 644-2602	Henry Briggs	Sandra Kelley	Lois Thorpe	...	Gerald Vaughn	Michael McMahon	Ira Dutter
Manchester	b	MC	2	(717) 266-1022	...	...	...	...	...	...	...
Manchester	tp	CM	12	(717) 764-4646	John D'Ottavio	David Raver	...	...	Richard Shank	Carl Segatti	Kenneth Goodyear
Manheim	b	CM	4	(717) 665-2461	Thomas Showers	Robert Stoner	...	...	Rick Houser	Barry Weidman	Barry Bracken
Manheim	tp	CM	33	(717) 569-6408	...	Michael Rimer	...	Valerie Calhoun	Rick Kane	Paul Rager	Carl Neff
Mansfield	b	CM	3	(570) 662-2315	...	...	...	...	...	...	...
Marcus Hook	b	MC	2	(610) 485-1341	...	Bruce Dorbian	...	...	...	...	...
Marietta	b	MC	2	(717) 426-4143	Oliver Overlander	Jody Shaffner	...	...	Paul Armold	...	...
Marple	tp	MC	23	(610) 356-4040	Martin Nash	Joseph Flicker	...	...	...	...	...
Marysville	b	CM	2	(717) 957-3110	Joseph Raisner	Marita Kelley	...	...	Kenneth Seitz	Jacob Stoss	George Sponsler
Masontown	b	MC	3	(412) 583-7731	...	...	...	...	...	...	...
Mc Adoo	b	MC	2	(570) 929-1182	Gregory Kurtz	...	Margie Rodgers	Joseph Jevitt	...	Joseph Litchko	Ed Wanyo
Mc Candless	t	CM	28	(412) 364-0616	Robert Powers	Tobias Cordek	...	...	...	Gary Anderson	Mark Sabina
Mc Donald	b	MC	2	(724) 926-8711	Marilou Ritchie	...	Gloria Stroop	...	...	Mark Dorsey	...
Mc Kees Rocks	b	MC	6	(412) 331-2498	Richard Keenan	William Beck	Charlotte Myers	...	Nicholas Radoycis	Robert Martineau	Richard Naughton
Mc Keesport	c	MC	24	(412) 675-5050	...	...	...	...	...	...	...
Mc Sherrystown	b	MC	2	(717) 637-1838	...	...	...	...	...	...	...
Meadville	c	CM	13	(814) 724-6000	Richard Friedberg	Joseph Chriest	Ronald Rushton	Timothy Groves	Larndo Hedrick	David Acker	...
Mechanicsburg	b	CM	9	(717) 691-3310	Brian Rider	Patrick Dennis	...	...	Larry Seagrist	David Spotts	...
Media	b	MC	5	(610) 566-5210	Joan Hagan	Jeffrey Smith	Marianne States	Jordan Blane	James Jeffery	Martin Wusinich	Ralph De Rosa
Mercer	b	MC	2	(724) 662-3980	Ted Isoldi	Debbie Scruci	...	...	William Finnley	David Fockler	Dennis Heasley
Mercersburg	b	CM	1	(717) 328-3116	Robert Brindle	James Leventry	Thelma Corrales	...	...	Larry Thomas	Lee Beck
Meyersdale	b	CM	2	(814) 634-5110	Paul Fuller	...	Patricia Ackerman	...	David Lauver	Vernon Bowman	...
Middlesex	tp	CM	5	(724) 898-3571	George Phillips	Scot Fodi	...	...	Dave Vanatta	Randy Ruediger	Jim Benninger
Middletown	b	CM	9	(717) 948-3000	Dale Sinniger	Jeffrey Stonehill	...	Karen Casciotti	Kenton Whitebread	Keith Reismiller	Solomon Swartz
Middletown	tp	CM	16	(610) 565-2700	...	W. Clark	...	Timothy Sander	...	...	...
Middletown (Levittown)	tp	CM	44	(215) 750-3800	Robert McMonagle	...	...	Jean Reukauf	...	Frank McKenna	Kenneth Banks
Midland	b	CM	3	(724) 643-4170	Angela Adkins	Diane Kemp	Erma Di Renzo	...	James Ulizio	Joseph D'Itri	Michael Miller
Mifflinburg	b	CM	3	(570) 966-1013	Donald Bitner	Margaret Metzger	...	...	...	...	Steven Benner
Millcreek	tp	MC	46	(814) 833-1111	...	...	...	...	...	...	...
Millersburg	b	MC	2	(717) 692-2389	...	...	...	...	...	...	...
Millersville	b	MC	7	(717) 872-4645	Richard Moriarty	Edward Arnold	...	...	Keith Eshleman	John Rochat	Andrew Boxleitner
Millvale	b	MC	4	(412) 821-2777	Jim Burn	Virginia Heller	...	Don Gillespie	Gary Witkowski	...	...
Milton	b	CM	6	(717) 742-8759	Scott Jones	Lawrence Wilver	Wanda Walls	...	Fred Kurtz	Michael Warns	Charles Beck
Minersville	b	MC	4	(570) 544-2149	...	...	...	...	...	...	...
Monaca	b	CM	6	(724) 775-9600	Thomas Ely	Stephen Vincenti	Georgina Wilson	...	...	Frank Primo	Dan Colville
Monessen	c	MC	8	(412) 684-9712	Robert Leone	John De Luca	...	Ernest Wisyanski	Tim Billick	John Bachinski	Ed Burdock
Monongahela	c	MC	4	(412) 258-5500	Kenneth Cole	...	Carole Foglia	Thomas Caudill	Frank Hnatik	Dennis Mendicino	Robert Kepics
Monroeville	b	CM	29	(412) 856-1000	Sean Logan	Marshall Bond	...	Susan Werksman	...	George Polnar	Eugene Mezeutch
Montgomery	b	CM	1	(570) 547-1671	...	John Lynch	...	...	...	...	...
Montgomery	tp	CM	22	(215) 393-6900	Warren Greenberg	John Nagel	...	...	David Vasconez	Richard Brady	Kevin Costello
Montoursville	b	CM	4	(570) 368-2486	...	...	...	...	...	...	...
Moon	tp	CM	22	(412) 262-1700	Tim McLaughlin	Gregory Smith	Janet Sieracki	Lisa Lapaglia	Charles Belgie	Leo McCarthy	...
Moosic	b	MC	5	(717) 457-5480	...	Jane Sterling	...	...	...	...	...
Morrisville	b	CM	10	(215) 295-8181	...	Victoria Keller	...	...	...	...	...
Mount Carmel	b	CM	6	(570) 339-4486	John Jones	Joseph Bass	...	...	Jack Williams	Brian Shurock	...

Directory 1/9 continued OFFICIALS IN U.S. MUNICIPALITIES 2,500 AND OVER IN POPULATION

Jurisdiction		Type	Form of govern-ment	2000 Popu-lation	Main telephone number	Chief elected official	Appointed administrator	Clerk of the governing board	Chief financial officer	Fire chief	Police chief	Public works director
PENNSYLVANIA continued												
Mount Joy		b	CM	6	(717) 653-2300	. . .	Terry Kauffman	. . .	. . .	. . .	John Sweigart	Scott Hershey
Mount Joy		tp	CM	7	(717) 367-8917	Robert Miller	Charles Kraus	. . .	. . .	. . .	. . .	David Hummer
Mount Lebanon	*	c	CM	33	(412) 343-3400	John Daley	Stephen Feller	. . .	William McKain	Nicolas Sohyda	C. McDonough	Tom Kelley
Mount Oliver		b	MC	3	(412) 431-8107	Martin Palma	Joanne Malloy	. . .	. . .	. . .	Frank Mosesso	. . .
Mount Penn		b	MC	3	(610) 799-5151	Josh Nowotarski	Ann Ftorski	. . .	. . .	Timothy Waldman	. . .	. . .
Mount Pleasant		b	MC	4	(724) 547-6745	Steven Fontanazza	Margene Wilczynski	. . .	. . .	Gerald Lucia	Gregory Smolka	. . .
Mount Union		b	MC	2	(814) 542-4051	Herbert Kidd	Eric Powell	. . .	. . .	Michael Goodman	Douglas Gummo	Robert Himes
Muncy		b	MC	2	(570) 546-3952	Michael Fornwalt	Edward Coup	. . .	. . .	. . .	Richard Sutton	Dave Alexander
Munhall		b	MC	12	(412) 464-7310	. . .	. . .	. . .	. . .	. . .	. . .	. . .
Municipality of Bethel Park	*	c	CM	33	(412) 831-6800	Clifford Morton	William Spagnol	. . .	Mark Romito	Dante Bongiorni	John Mackey	Robert Cygrymus
Murrysville	*	c	MC	18	(724) 327-2100	Joyce Somers	John Barrett	. . .	Diane Heming	. . .	Thomas Seefeld	Richard Connors
Myerstown		b	MC	3	(717) 866-5038	Ellsworth Troutman	Robin Hemperly	Denise Krall	Lee Smith	Mitch Hemperly	Phillip Stark	Randall Brown
Nanticoke		c	MC	10	(717) 735-2200	Wasil Kobela	Kenneth Johnson	Michael Yurkowski	Donna Wall	William Ives	Chester Zaremba	Joseph Mikilonis
Nanty-Glo		b	MC	3	(814) 749-0331	T. Cunningham	. . .	Melissa Weekes	. . .	Joseph Lamantia	Richard Miller	. . .
Narberth		b	CM	4	(610) 664-2840	Dennis Sharkey	William Martin	. . .	. . .	John Thomas	Art Pauoni	. . .
Nazareth		b	CM	6	(610) 264-1069	. . .	Sandra Pudliner	Pina Romano	. . .	. . .	. . .	Bruce Pudliner
Nesquehoning	*	b	MC	3	(570) 669-9588	Donato DeMarco	RoniSue Ahner	Shawn Coniglio	. . .	John McArdle	Sean Smith	. . .
Nether Providence		tp	CO	13	(610) 566-4516	. . .	Gary Cummings	. . .	April Reeser	. . .	Richard Slifer	John Ellis
New Brighton		b	CM	6	(724) 846-1870	Paul Spickerman	Larry Morley	Marleen Ionta	. . .	Jeff Bolland	Dale Nicholson	William Caplinger
New Britain		t	CM	3	(215) 348-4586	. . .	Robin Trymbiski	. . .	. . .	. . .	David Sempowski	. . .
New Britain	*	tp	CM	10	(215) 822-1391	James Scanzillo	Eileen Bradley	. . .	. . .	Randal Teschner	Robert Scafidi	Wayne Fultz
New Castle		c	MC	26	(412) 656-3500	. . .	. . .	. . .	. . .	. . .	. . .	. . .
New Cumberland		b	CM	7	(717) 774-0404	John Murray	S. Sultzaberger	. . .	. . .	Michael Kann	Oren Kauffman	. . .
New Eagle		b	MC	2	(412) 258-4477	. . .	. . .	. . .	. . .	. . .	. . .	. . .
New Hanover		tp	CM	7	(610) 323-1008	Martin Dyas	. . .	Maryann Brennan	Janice Reid	. . .	Michael Dykie	R. Batchelder
New Holland		b	CM	5	(717) 354-4567	. . .	James Fulcher	. . .	. . .	. . .	. . .	. . .
New Hope	*	b	CM	2	(215) 862-3347	Sharyn Keiser	John Burke	Joann Connell	. . .	Craig Forbes	Rick Pasqualini	Tom Carroll
New Kensington		c	CO	14	(412) 337-4523	. . .	. . .	. . .	. . .	. . .	. . .	. . .
New Stanton	*	b	MC	1	(724) 925-9700	Joseph Kazan	. . .	Anita Hoffman	. . .	Bob Liberty	. . .	Melvin Steele
New Wilmington		b	MC	2	(412) 946-8167	. . .	. . .	. . .	. . .	. . .	. . .	. . .
Newtown		b	MC	2	(215) 968-2109	. . .	. . .	. . .	. . .	. . .	. . .	. . .
Newtown		tp	CM	11	(610) 356-0200	Peter DeLiberty	James Sheldrake	. . .	. . .	Doug Everlof	Leon Hunter	Charles Steinmetz
Newtown Township		tp	CM	18	(215) 968-2800	Scott Harp	Joseph Czajkowski	Judy Setar	Elaine Gibbs	Donald Harris	Martin Duffy	. . .
Newville		b	CM	1	(717) 776-7633	Jerry Gilbert	Fred Potzer	. . .	. . .	. . .	. . .	. . .
Norristown	*	b	MC	31	(610) 272-8080	Theodore LeBlanc	David Forrest	Sandra Felice-Grubb	Monica DeCaro	Thomas O'Donnell	. . .	Joseph Picard
North Braddock		b	CM	6	(412) 271-1306	. . .	. . .	. . .	. . .	. . .	. . .	. . .
North Catasauqua		b	MC	2	(610) 264-1504	William McGinley	Francis Roberts	Helen Hutt	. . .	Francis Hadik	Kim Moyer	Gregory Loch
North Codorus		tp	CM	7	(717) 225-4812	John Rebert	. . .	Mary Aikens	. . .	Larry Wildasin	. . .	Laverne Oversmith
North Cornwall		tp	CM	4	(717) 273-9200	Randy Hoffman	John Primus	Stacey Kindt	. . .	. . .	Thomas Gates	Thomas Long
North Coventry		tp	CM	7	(610) 323-1694	William Deegan	. . .	. . .	. . .	Randall Richter	Michael Benyo	Joseph Wood
North East		b	MC	4	(814) 725-8611	. . .	Benjamin Breniman	. . .	. . .	. . .	. . .	. . .
North Fayette	*	tp	CM	12	(724) 693-9601	A. Morosetti	Robert Grimm	Carol Stenzel	. . .	. . .	Jeffrey Falconer	Victor Rogale
North Huntingdon		tp	CM	29	(724) 863-3806	Thomas Kerber	Kelly Wolfe	. . .	. . .	. . .	Michael Daugherty	Richard Albert
North Londonderry	*	tp	MC	6	(717) 838-1373	Ronald Fouche	Gordon Watts	Judy Miller	Lisa Daubert	. . .	Kevin Snyder	. . .
North Middleton		tp	MC	10	(717) 243-8550	William Myers	Deborah Ealer	Dana Dunkle	. . .	Dave Dick	Jeffrey Rudolph	Lester Brickner
North Strabane		tp	CM	10	(724) 745-8880	Brian Spicer	Frank Siffrinn	. . .	Jamie Schaller	Gary Zimak	Dan Strimel	Harry Hayman
North Versailles		tp	MC	12	(412) 823-6602	. . .	. . .	. . .	. . .	. . .	. . .	. . .
North Wales		b	CM	3	(215) 699-4424	Jocelyn Tenney	Susan Patton	Sandra Rhoads	. . .	William Goltz	Barry Hackert	Thomas Costella
Northampton		b	MC	9	(610) 262-2576	Thomas Reenock	Gene Zarayko	Barbara Matuczinski	. . .	Robert Siegfried	Laird Brownmiller	Stephen Gerny
Northampton	*	tp	CM	39	(215) 357-6800	Peter Palestina	Robert Pellegrino	. . .	. . .	Robert Sutherland	M. Pilla	Pasquale Giradi
Northumberland	*	b	MC	3	(570) 473-3414	Bryan Wolfe	Janice Bowman	J. Sanders-Ressler	. . .	James Troup	Timothy Fink	Thomas Slodysko
Norwood		b	MC	5	(610) 586-5800	. . .	. . .	. . .	. . .	. . .	. . .	. . .
Oakmont	*	b	CM	6	(412) 828-3232	Michael Federici	Daniel Mator	. . .	. . .	William Peoples	David DiSanti	. . .
O'Hara	*	tp	CM	9	(412) 782-1400	Robert Smith	Julie Jakubec	. . .	. . .	. . .	James Farringer	Loren Kephart
Ohio		tp	CO	3	(412) 364-6321	Herbert Hartle	John Sullivan	Eleanor Owens	. . .	. . .	Norbert Micklos	Danny Weigle
Ohioville		b	MC	3	(724) 643-1920	Linda Wells	Diane Kemp	Debra Doughty	. . .	Clarence Dawson	Ronald Lutton	Bruce Thorne
Oil City	*	c	CM	11	(814) 678-3012	Sonja Hawkins	Thomas Rockovich	. . .	Michelle Hoovler	Steve Hinds	Robert Wenner	Miles Truitt
Old Forge		b	MC	8	(717) 457-8852	. . .	. . .	. . .	. . .	. . .	. . .	. . .
Olyphant		b	MC	4	(570) 489-2135	Michael Wargo	Stephen Klem	Patricia Angradi	Frank Campbell	Dave Kurkovitz	James Foley	Peter Kolcharno
Orwigsburg		b	MC	3	(570) 366-3103	. . .	. . .	. . .	. . .	. . .	. . .	. . .
Oxford	*	b	MC	4	(610) 932-2500	John Ware	Betsy Brantner	Virginia Holt	. . .	San Terrt	John Slauch	Thomas Hindman
Palmer	*	tp	CM	16	(610) 253-7191	David Colver	Robert Anckaitis	. . .	Sheri Young	Delmar Grube	Bruce Fretz	Thomas Adams
Palmerton		b	CM	5	(610) 826-2505	John Neff	Rodger Danielson	Anita Harry	. . .	Christopher Kegel	George Taptich	Joseph Kercsmar
Palmyra		b	CM	7	(717) 838-6361	Richard Mazzocca	Sherry Capello	. . .	. . .	. . .	Stanley Jasinski	Craig Campbell
Parkesburg		b	MC	3	(610) 857-2616	K. Knickerbocker	Lester Thomas	Wendy Keegan	David Jones	Richard Klingler	Brian Sheller	. . .
Patton	*	tp	CM	11	(814) 234-0271	Elliot Abrams	Douglas Erickson	. . .	Kim Wyatt	. . .	John Petrick	Brent Brubaker
Peach Bottom		tp	CM	4	(717) 456-5083	. . .	. . .	. . .	. . .	. . .	. . .	. . .
Pen Argyl		b	MC	3	(610) 863-4119	Judith Piper	Robin Zmoda	. . .	. . .	Dean Parson	Philip Viglione	Steven Bender
Penbrook		b	MC	3	(717) 232-3733	Richard Stottlemyer	. . .	Linda Losh	Michael Goodman	Joe Nickle	David Hiester	Frederick Pace
Penn	*	tp	CM	1	(724) 586-1165	. . .	Gregory Primm	Linda Furka	. . .	. . .	Cheryl Cranmer	Douglas Roth
Penn	*	tp	CM	14	(717) 632-7366	Michael Johnson	Jeffrey Garvick	. . .	. . .	Jan Cromer	Russell Rhodes	Kevin Mahan
Penn Hills		c	CM	46	(412) 798-2100	Anthony DeLuca	. . .	Diane Fitzhenry	E. Schrecengost	John Mason	Howard Burton	Mohammed Rayan
Penndel		b	MC	2	(215) 757-5153	Arlene Harms	Barbara Vasquez	Michelle Nigra	. . .	. . .	Stephen Burke	. . .
Perkasie		b	CM	8	(215) 257-5065	Eadie Burke	Daniel Olpere	. . .	. . .	. . .	Paul Dickinson	Phil Ivins
Peters	*	tp	CM	17	(724) 941-4180	Fran Arcuri	Michael Silvestri	. . .	. . .	Daniel Coyle	Harry Fruecht	Peter Overcashier
Philadelphia		c	MC	1517	(215) 686-2331	John Street	Camille Barnett	Patricia Rafferty	Vincent Jannetti	Lloyd Ayers	Lynne Abraham	Richard Tustin
Philipsburg		b	MC	3	(814) 342-3440	Sandra Martin	John Knowles	Barbara Godissart	. . .	. . .	William Stouffer	. . .
Phoenixville		b	CM	14	(610) 933-8801	Louis Amici	Ernest Krack	Susan Dinato	Steven Nease	James Gable	John Kalavik	Brian Watson
Pine	*	tp	CM	7	(724) 625-1591	Michael Dennehy	Cheryl Fischer	. . .	. . .	Kenneth Young	T. Amann	Jack Fasick
Pitcairn		b	MC	3	(412) 372-6500	Orelio Vecchio	. . .	Judy Shipley	Josephine Higgins	. . .	David McIntyre	Rocco Trunzo
Pittsburgh		c	MC	334	(412) 255-2519	Luke Ravenstahl	. . .	Linda Wasler	Ellen McLean	Peter Michali	Robert McNeilly	Guy Costa
Pittston		c	CO	8	(570) 654-0513	Michael Lombardo	. . .	Ronald Mortimer	Chris Latona	James Rooney	Jeffrey Tayoun	George Renfer
Pleasant		tp	MC	2	(814) 723-5240	Marshall Gern	. . .	. . .	. . .	. . .	. . .	. . .
Pleasant Hills		b	MC	8	(412) 655-3300	. . .	. . .	. . .	. . .	. . .	. . .	. . .
Plum		b	CM	26	(412) 795-6800	. . .	. . .	. . .	. . .	. . .	Terry Focareta	William Berchick
Plumstead		tp	CM	11	(215) 766-8914	Frank Froio	Carolyn McCreary	. . .	. . .	. . .	Duane Hasenauer	Alan Bleam
Plymouth		b	MC	6	(717) 779-1011	Frank Coughlin	Joseph Mazur	Dorothy Woodruff	. . .	Jason Ravert	Myles Collins	James Hunlock
Plymouth	*	tp	CM	16	(610) 277-4100	Joseph Prestia	Karen Weiss	. . .	Timothy Creelman	. . .	Joseph Lawrence	C. Loschiavo
Port Allegany		b	CM	2	(814) 642-2526	Joseph Demott	John Gaydeski	Barbara Fink	. . .	Tom Johnson	. . .	. . .
Port Carbon	*	b	MC	2	(570) 622-2255	Thomas Pavlick	. . .	Margaret McBreen	Ray Steranko	Michael Welsh	Jon Bowman	. . .
Port Vue		b	MC	4	(412) 664-9323	. . .	. . .	. . .	. . .	. . .	. . .	. . .
Portage		b	CM	2	(814) 736-4330	Joyce French	. . .	. . .	. . .	. . .	Donald Kehn	Donald Squillario
Pottstown	*	b	CM	21	(610) 970-6510	David Garner	Raymond Lopez	. . .	. . .	Richard Lengel	Mark Flanders	Douglass Yerger
Pottsville		c	CM	15	(570) 622-1234	John Reiley	Thomas Palamar	Julie Rescorla	Michael Halcovage	Todd March	Joseph Murton	James Muldowney
Prospect Park		b	MC	6	(610) 532-1007	Donald Cook	. . .	Deborah Luty	Peter Subers	James Simmonds	John Saddic	Glen Schwenke

Directory 1/9 continued OFFICIALS IN U.S. MUNICIPALITIES 2,500 AND OVER IN POPULATION

Jurisdiction	Type	Form of govern-ment	2000 Popu-lation	Main telephone number	Chief elected official	Appointed administrator	Clerk of the governing board	Chief financial officer	Fire chief	Police chief	Public works director
PENNSYLVANIA continued											
Punxsutawney	b	CM	6	(814) 938-4480	Susan Glessner	Benjamin White	Jill Carey	...	Donald Bosak	Thomas Fedigan	Joseph DeFelice
Quakertown	b	CM	8	(215) 536-5001	Raymond Fulmer	Scott McElree	...	...	...	James McFadden	Joseph Murgia
Radnor *	tp	CM	30	(610) 688-5600	Harry Mahoney	David Bashore	Concetta Clayton	Aimee Cuthhbertson	...	John Rutty	John Stauffer
Rankin	b	MC	2	(412) 271-1027	...	...	...	...	...	...	...
Reading	c	MC	81	(610) 655-6012	Paul Angstadt	...	Linda Kelleher	Tammie Kipp	William Rehr	Keith Mooney	D. Mucha
Red Lion	b	CM	6	(717) 244-3475	...	...	...	...	...	...	...
Reynoldsville	b	MC	2	(814) 653-2110	...	...	...	...	...	...	...
Richland	tp	CM	9	(215) 536-4066	Craig Staats	Stephen Sechriest	Tracey Virnelson	...	...	Lawrence Cerami	Thomas Roeder
Richland	tp	CM	12	(814) 266-2922	...	...	...	...	...	...	...
Richland (Allegheny)	tp	MC	9	(412) 443-5921	...	Dean Bastianini	...	...	...	...	Lee Geortz
Ridgway	b	CM	4	(814) 776-1125	...	Martin Schuller	...	...	John Wygant	Ralph Tettis	...
Ridley *	tp	CM	30	(610) 534-4800	Robert Willert	Anne Howanski	...	Chris Betlzer	...	Charles Howley	Jack De Pietro
Ridley Park	b	MC	7	(610) 532-2100	Henry Eberle	Robert Poole	Charlotte Heimbacher	...	...	Robert Marks	Richard Miles
Roaring Spring	b	MC	2	(814) 224-4814	...	...	...	...	...	...	...
Robinson	tp	CM	12	(412) 788-8120	...	Richard Charnovich	Mildred Cvengros	...	...	Dale Vietmeier	Paul Kashmer
Rochester	b	CM	4	(724) 775-1200	...	...	...	...	...	...	...
Rockledge *	b	MC	2	(215) 379-8572	Joseph Denelsbeck	Grace Metzinger	Joyce Hines	...	Russell Hellyer	James Leary	Clint Snyder
Ross	tp	CM	32	(412) 931-7055	...	...	...	Virginia Finnegan	Frank Stright	Gregory Tenos	James Stack
Rostraver	tp	MC	11	(724) 929-8877	Nick Lorenzo	...	Pamela Beard	...	...	Greg Resetar	Thomas Backstrom
Royersford	b	CM	4	(610) 948-3737	...	...	...	...	...	...	...
Salisbury *	tp	CM	13	(610) 797-4000	Larry Unger	Randy Soriano	...	Cathy Bonaskiewich	...	Allen Stiles	John Andreas
Sandy	tp	CM	11	(814) 371-4220	...	M. Stojek	Barbara Hopkins	...	...	...	...
Saxonburg *	b	MC	1	(724) 352-1400	William Gillespie	Mary Papik	Linda Kovacik	...	Gary Cooper	Erik Bergstrom	Thomas Grech
Sayre	b	CM	5	(570) 888-7739	Henry Farley	David Jarrett	...	...	...	Kevin Guinane	Blane Lathrop
Schuylkill Haven	b	CM	5	(570) 385-2841	John Dudley	...	...	...	...	Robert Schaeffer	...
Scott	tp	CM	17	(412) 276-5300	Donald Diebold	Denise Fitzgerald	...	Sandy Novelli	...	Stanley Butkus	Randy Lubin
Scottdale	b	CM	4	(724) 887-8220	Eugene Beran	Barry Whoric	...	...	Scott Rollinson	Tony Martin	...
Scranton	c	MC	76	(570) 348-4100	Christopher Doherty	Leonard Kresefski	James Wintermantel	R. Novembrino	Harvey Appelgate	James Klee	Rocco Damiano
Selinsgrove	b	CM	5	(570) 374-2311	...	John Bickhart	...	...	...	Thomas Garlock	Gary Klingler
Sellersville	b	CM	4	(215) 257-5075	...	...	...	...	...	...	...
Seven Fields	b	CM	1	(724) 776-3090	...	Thomas Smith	...	...	...	...	Bret Cole
Sewickley	b	CM	3	(412) 741-4015	John Wise	Kevin Flannery	Fran Frynkewicz	...	Jeff Neff	John Mook	...
Sewickley Heights	b	CM	..	(412) 741-5119	S. Phil Hundley	William Rohe	Julienne Giuliani	...	Bill Davis	Herbert Ford	Jeff Marek
Shaler *	tp	CM	29	(412) 486-9700	Thomas McElhane	Timothy Rogers	...	Judith Kording	...	Jeffrey Gally	James Henderson
Shamokin	c	MC	8	(570) 644-0876	James Yurick	William Strausser	...	Ed O'Donnell	Richard Jilinski	Richard Nichols	Ronald Bradley
Sharon	c	MC	16	(724) 983-3220	Robert Lucas	...	Sharronda Faber	Michael Gasparich	Terence Whalen	Thomas Burke	...
Sharon Hill	b	MC	5	(610) 586-8200	Joseph Botta	William Scott	Connie Hamond	...	William Benecke	Joseph Kelly	...
Sharpsburg *	b	MC	3	(412) 781-0546	Joseph Panza	Ronald Borczyk	Barbara Ruhle	...	Lawrence Trozzo	Leo Rudzki	...
Sharpsville	b	CM	4	(412) 962-7896	Kenneth Robertson	...	...	...	Andrew Totin	Willard Thompson	Dale Bulcher
Shenandoah	b	MC	5	(717) 462-1918	...	...	...	...	...	...	...
Shillington	b	CM	5	(610) 777-1338	C. Yetter	Michael Mountz	Jan Boyd	...	Bruce Squibb	Andrew Hivner	Earl Bare
Shippensburg	b	CM	5	(717) 532-2147	Mark Buterbaugh	William Wolfe	...	...	Jamie White	...	W. Del Grande
Shrewsbury	b	MC	3	(717) 235-4371	...	...	...	...	...	...	...
Silver Spring	tp	MC	10	(717) 766-0178	Wayne Pecht	William Cook	Karen Dunlevy	...	...	James Sadler	...
Sinking Spring	b	MC	2	(610) 678-4903	...	...	...	...	...	...	...
Skippack Township	tp	CM	6	(610) 454-0909	...	Theodore Locker	Peggy White	...	Ronald Wilkie	...	William Parkins
Slatington *	b	CM	4	(610) 767-2131	Walter Niedermeyer	Herb Pfeiffer	Sue Guedes	...	Keith Weaver	Dave Rachman	John Bolton
Slippery Rock *	b	MC	3	(724) 794-6391	David Miller	...	...	...	Dave Taggert	Frederick Emigh	Paul Dickey
Solebury	tp	CM	7	(215) 297-5656	...	...	...	...	...	...	...
Somerset *	b	CM	6	(814) 443-2661	Mary Ann Smith	Benedict Vinzani	...	Brett Peters	Gary Thomas	Randolph Cox	George Svirsko
Souderton	b	CM	6	(215) 723-4371	...	P. Coll	...	...	...	...	...
South Fayette	tp	CM	12	(412) 221-8700	...	Michael Hoy	...	...	...	...	...
South Greensburg	b	MC	2	(724) 837-8858	...	...	...	...	...	...	...
South Hanover	tp	MC	4	(717) 566-0224	...	Brian Engle	Kay Stare	...	...	...	Scott Plouse
South Lebanon	tp	CM	8	(717) 274-0481	...	...	...	...	...	...	...
South Park *	tp	CM	14	(412) 831-7000	George Smith	Mark Schroyer	Vivian Cecere	Deborah Petrovich	...	Joseph Ferrelli	Bruce Beaver
South Strabane	tp	CM	7	(724) 225-9055	...	John Stickle	...	...	Scott Reese	Donald Zofchak	D. Mankey
South Whitehall	tp	CO	18	(610) 398-0401	Gary Search	Gerald Gasda	...	Linda Perry	...	Thomas Toth	James Weber
South Williamsport	b	CM	6	(570) 322-0158	...	...	...	...	...	...	...
Southmont	b	MC	2	(814) 255-3104	Kevin Pile	...	Mary Magistro	Loretta Spak	Chet Borosky	Andy Havas	Jan Bosley
Southwest Greensburg	b	MC	2	(724) 834-0360	Shaun Teacher	...	...	...	Edward Milliron	James Santmyer	John Warren
Spring *	tp	MC	21	(610) 678-5393	Alan Kreider	Leon Mazurie	Sheryl Kressler	John Groller	John Schach	Michael Messner	Jay Vaughan
Spring City *	b	CM	3	(610) 948-3660	...	Dennis Rittenhouse	...	...	...	...	...
Spring Garden	tp	CM	11	(717) 848-2858	David Meckley	Gregory Maust	Wendy Stermer	Mary Yonker	Barry Emig	George Swartz	Edward Salabsky
Springdale *	b	MC	3	(724) 274-6800	Jason Fry	April Winklmann	...	...	Kevin Wilhelm	Joseph Naviglia	Bill Cadamore
Springettsbury *	tp	CM	23	(717) 757-3521	William Schenck	John Holman	...	Jack Hadge	Robert McCoy	David Eshbach	Charles Lauer
Springfield *	tp	CM	4	(610) 346-6700	James Brownlow	Richard Schilling	Debbie Godshall	...	Willard Helm	Mark Laudenslager	...
Springfield	tp	CM	19	(215) 836-7600	Kenneth Bradley	Donald Berger	Carol Holcomb	...	...	Randall Hummel	John Connor
Springfield	tp	CM	24	(215) 544-1300	E. Lehman	Michael Lefevre	...	...	...	...	...
St. Clair	b	MC	3	(527) 429-0640	Michael McCord	Roland Price	...	...	...	Michael Carey	Don Hosler
St. Marys	c	CM	14	(814) 781-1718	David Meier	David Greene	Tammy Lang	Carol Yost	Mike Kraus	Todd Caltagarone	...
State College *	b	CM	38	(814) 234-7100	William Welch	Thomas Fountaine	Cynthia Hanscom	Michael Groff	...	Thomas King	Mark Whitfield
Steelton	b	MC	5	(717) 939-9842	Michael Rozman	Michael Musser	...	...	Eugene Vance	Kenneth Lenker	Joseph Conjar
Stewartstown	b	CM	1	(717) 993-2963	...	...	...	...	...	...	...
Stowe	tp	CO	6	(412) 331-4050	Frank Carpellotti	...	Marie Incorvati	...	Martin Jacobs	Stephen Homer	Nick Pegorelli
Strasburg	b	CM	2	(717) 687-7732	...	...	...	...	...	...	...
Stroudsburg	b	CM	5	(570) 421-5444	Kim Diddio	Barbara Quarantello	...	...	Clement Kochanski	John Baujan	Jack Lesoine
Sugar Creek	b	CM	5	(814) 432-4717	Tom Sloss	Bonnie Beightol	...	...	Stephen McElhaney	...	Richard Phillips
Sugarcreek	tp	MC	1	(724) 526-3261	...	...	...	...	...	...	...
Summit Hill	b	MC	2	(570) 645-2305	...	...	...	...	...	...	...
Sunbury	c	CO	10	(717) 286-7820	David Persing	...	Theresa Nichols	William Mackey	Richard Neff	Charles McAndrew	...
Susquehanna	tp	MC	21	(717) 545-4751	Graffus Johnston	...	...	...	...	...	...
Swarthmore	b	CM	6	(610) 543-4599	Elisabeth Aaron	Jane Billings	Cathy Van Sant	...	Cris Hansen	Brian Craig	Charles Rowles
Swatara *	tp	CM	22	(717) 564-2551	Timothy Berard	Paul Cornell	...	John Guerrisi	Darrin Robinson	David Bogdanovic	Curtis Wilbern
Swissvale	b	MC	9	(412) 271-7101	Charles Martoni	Thomas Esposito	Elizabeth Deluca	...	Ken Johnston	Henry Ohrman	Michael Viglietta
Swoyersville	b	MC	5	(717) 288-6581	Fred Romanowski	Gene Breznay	Shirley Gavlick	...	...	John Shemo	Edward Volack
Tamaqua	b	CM	7	(570) 668-0300	Kenneth Smulligan	Kevin Steigerwalt	Georgia Depos	...	Thomas Schlorf	George Woodward	...
Tarentum	b	CM	4	(724) 224-1818	Tim Cornuet	C. Turner	Ann Conroy	...	...	David Sieber	David Hilliard
Taylor	b	MC	6	(570) 562-1400	...	...	...	...	...	...	...
Telford *	b	CM	4	(215) 723-5000	Jay Stover	Mark Fournier	...	Daphne Hollowbush	Raymond Fegley	Douglas Bickel	Donald Beck
Thornbury	tp	MC	2	(610) 399-1425	...	Cary Vargo	...	...	...	...	...
Throop *	b	MC	4	(570) 489-8311	Thomas Lukasewicz	...	Elaine Morrell	...	Ed Bocan	Keith Jones	Robert Kalinoski
Titusville	c	CM	6	(814) 827-5300	Brian Sanford	Mary Nau	...	Julie Clowes	John Crotty	Michael Simmons	Randall Nebel
Tobyhanna	tp	CM	6	(570) 646-1212	John Kerrick	...	...	...	Troy Counterman	John Lamberton	...
Towamencin	tp	CM	17	(215) 368-7602	H. Charles Wilson	...	James Sinz	Maureen Doyle	James Geslak	Joseph Kirschner	Dennis Carney
Towanda	b	CM	3	(717) 265-2696	Richard Snell	Thomas Fairchild	Mary Harris	...	Arthur Johnson	Dale Cole	Fred Johnson

Directory 1/9 continued — OFFICIALS IN U.S. MUNICIPALITIES 2,500 AND OVER IN POPULATION

Jurisdiction	Type	Form of govern-ment	2000 Popu-lation	Main telephone number	Chief elected official	Appointed administrator	Clerk of the governing board	Chief financial officer	Fire chief	Police chief	Public works director
PENNSYLVANIA continued											
Trafford	b	CM	3	(412) 372-7652	Thomas Babes	Lisa Mallik	Diane Bonifati	...	...	Ronald Troy	...
Tredyffrin	tp	CM	29	(610) 644-1400	Judy DiFilippo	Marie Gleason	...	David Brill	...	Richard Harkness	William Bryant
Troy	b	CM	1	(570) 297-2966	Jerry May	Alan Roloson	Debra Hulslander	...	Roy Vargson	Greg Hostettler	...
Turtle Creek *	b	MC	6	(412) 824-2500	...	Dolores Porter	...	...	John Osman	Dale Kraeer	Nick Laurito
Tyrone *	b	CM	5	(814) 684-1330	James Kilmartin	Sharon Dannaway	...	Phyllis Garhart	...	Joseph Beachem	...
Union	tp	MC	3	(717) 935-2890	I. Esh	...	...	...	...	...	...
Union *	tp	MC	3	(610) 582-3769	Donald Basile	Carol Lewis	...	...	...	...	Ken Geiger
Union City	b	CM	3	(814) 438-2331	Brian Tufts	Cheryl Capela	...	...	Robert Seitz	Marvin Tubbs	Raymond Rhodes
Uniontown	c	MC	12	(724) 430-2900	James Sileo	...	Grace Giachetti	Robert Lloyd	James Wood	Kyle Sneddon	Donald Miller
Upland	b	MC	2	(610) 874-7317	...	...	...	...	...	...	...
Upper Allen	tp	CM	15	(717) 766-0756	...	Richard Laskey	...	Laurel Yohe	...	...	Donald Worden
Upper Chichester	tp	MC	16	(610) 855-5881	...	...	...	...	...	...	...
Upper Darby	tp	MC	81	(610) 734-7622	F. Raymond Shay	Thomas Judge	Richard Nolan	James Smith	Edward Cubler	Michael Chitwood	Joseph Vasturia
Upper Dublin	tp	CM	25	(215) 643-1600	Robert Pesavento	Paul Leonard	...	...	C. Samtmann	Terrence Thompson	Charles Oyler
Upper Gwynedd	tp	MC	14	(215) 699-7777	James Santi	Leonard Perrone	...	Michael Sultanik	Jeffrey Mullaly	Robert Freed	Willard Troxel
Upper Hanover	tp	CM	4	(215) 679-4401	...	Stanley Seitzinger	...	...	...	...	...
Upper Leacock	tp	CM	8	(717) 656-9755	Richard Heilig	Michael Morris	...	...	...	...	Denny Millhouse
Upper Makefield *	tp	CM	7	(215) 968-3340	Daniel Rattigan	Stephanie Teoli	...	Sandra Wenitsky	...	Mark Schmidt	Robert Johnson
Upper Merion *	tp	CM	26	(610) 265-2600	Ralph Volpe	Ronald Wagenmann	...	Nickolas Hiriak	...	Ronald Fonock	Robert Norman
Upper Moreland	tp	CM	24	(215) 659-3100	Richard Booth	David Dodies	...	...	...	William Moffett	Jack Snyder
Upper Pottsgrove *	tp	CM	4	(610) 323-8675	Elwood Taylor	Jack Layne	...	Cynthia Saylor	Tom Mattingly	Bryan Ross	Frank Quinter
Upper Providence	tp	CM	9	(610) 565-4944	William O'Donnell	Anthony Hamaday	...	Joanne Moore	Donald Wilkins	Thomas Davis	David Pyser
Upper Providence	tp	CM	15	(610) 933-9179	Robert Fieo	George Waterman	Kathleen Stuehler	...	Donald Stiteler	Donald Sherid	Thomas Broadbelt
Upper Saucon	tp	CM	11	(610) 282-1171	Stephen Wagner	Thomas Beil	...	Robert Kassel	Charles Castetter	Robert Coyle	Donald Eck
Upper Southampton	tp	MC	15	(215) 322-9700	John Held	...	...	Anoop Tolani	Mark Showmaker	David Schultz	Wayne Crompton
Upper St. Clair	tp	CM	19	(412) 831-9000	...	Matthew Serakowski	...	August Stache	...	Ronald Pardini	F. Robinson
Upper Uwchlan	tp	CM	6	(610) 458-9400	...	John Roughan	Elaine Benson	...	...	John DeMarco	Michael Heckman
Upper Yoder	tp	CM	5	(814) 255-5243	...	...	...	...	...	...	...
Uwchlan *	tp	CM	16	(610) 363-9450	Fred Gaines	Douglass Hanley	Katie Churchill	...	Richard Ruth	Joseph Pontarelli	James Peterson
Vandergrift	b	CM	5	(724) 567-7818	Jack Jewart	Stephen Delledonne	Melissa Holmes	...	Thomas Holmes	Louis Purificato	...
Vernon	tp	MC	5	(814) 337-8126	...	David Stone	...	...	...	...	...
Verona	b	MC	3	(412) 828-8080	...	...	Annette Bracken	...	Thomas Tihey	Guy Truby	Robert Gaggie
Warminster *	tp	MC	31	(215) 443-5414	Frank Feinberg	Robert Tate	...	Ginnie Gehring	James Krueger	Michael Murphy	George Mullen
Warren *	c	CM	11	(814) 723-6300	Mark Phillips	James Nelles	...	Donna Risinger	Sam Pascuzzi	Raymond Zydonik	Brent Ordiway
Warrington	tp	CM	17	(215) 343-9350	Glenn McKay	Timothy Tieperman	...	Vivian Bell	Christopher Harvey	James Miller	Carl Sames
Warwick	tp	CM	11	(215) 343-6100	...	Gail Weniger	...	Rosemarie Christie	...	Joseph Costello	Robert Benninghoff
Warwick	tp	CM	15	(717) 626-8900	...	Daniel Zimmerman	...	...	...	...	Dean Saylor
Washington	c	MC	15	(724) 223-4200	Kenneth Westcott	Samuel Stockton	Cathy Voytek	Matt Staniszewski	Linn Brookman	John Haddad	Robert Nicolella
Watsontown	b	CM	2	(570) 538-1000	Harriet Miller	Paul Kreckel	Polly Keefer	...	Mark Burrows	Dennis Derr	...
Waynesboro	b	CM	9	(717) 762-2101	...	Lloyd Hamberger	...	...	...	...	...
Waynesburg	b	CM	4	(724) 627-8111	Charles Berryhill	G. Howard	Bonnie Baily	Murray Hoy	Larry Marshall	Timothy Hawfield	Danny Scott
Weatherly	b	CM	2	(570) 427-8640	...	Harold Pudliner	Eloise Hinterleiter	...	Richard Knepper	Brian Cara	Arthur Michael
Wellsboro	b	CM	3	(717) 724-3186	R. Decamp	Susan Leedy	Florence Martino	...	Mark Cooper	John Wheeler	Mark Dieffenbach
Wesleyville	b	MC	3	(814) 899-9124	Terry St. Denny	Peter Nye	...	...	Earl Clark	George Hooker	Clayton Smith
West Bradford *	tp	CM	10	(610) 269-4174	John Haiko	Jack Hines	...	Nancy Althouse	...	...	...
West Caln	tp	CM	7	(610) 384-5643	...	...	...	...	...	...	...
West Chester	b	CM	17	(610) 692-7574	Robert Whetstone	Ernie McNeely	...	Douglas Kapp	Kevin Corcoran	John Green	Robert Wilpizeski
West Conshohocken	b	CM	1	(610) 828-9747	Patricia Barr	Michael Leonard	Terry Fox	...	Dennis Frankenfield	Joseph Clayborne	Michael McGuire
West Deer *	tp	CM	11	(724) 265-3680	...	John Shepherd	...	...	...	Jon Lape	Mike Funk
West Goshen	tp	CM	20	(610) 696-5266	Robert White	Casey LaLonde	Sandra Turley	Jeanne Denham	Andrea Testa	Michael Carroll	R. Halvorsen
West Hanover	tp	CM	6	(717) 652-4841	...	...	...	...	Brian Cassell	...	Harold Harman
West Hazleton *	b	MC	3	(570) 455-3695	Daniel Guydish	...	...	Jane Mikulca	Robert Ward	Thomas Wallace	Paul Swinesburg
West Homestead	b	MC	2	(412) 461-1844	John Dindak	...	Elsie Fekety	...	...	...	...
West Lampeter	tp	CM	13	(717) 464-3731	James Kalenich	Raymond D'Agostino	...	...	Sean Alexander	James Walsh	James Kreider
West Manchester *	tp	CM	17	(717) 792-3505	...	Jan Dell	...	Jennifer Risser	David Nichols	Arthur Smith	R. Haifley
West Mifflin	b	CM	22	(412) 466-8170	William Welsh	Howard Bednar	...	...	...	Frank Diener	James Hess
West Newton	b	MC	3	(724) 872-6860	...	...	...	...	...	...	...
West Norriton *	tp	CO	15	(610) 631-0450	...	Joseph Hein	...	...	...	Robert Adams	Thomas Cinaglia
West Pikeland	tp	MC	3	(610) 827-7660	...	...	...	...	...	...	...
West Pittston	b	MC	5	(570) 655-7782	Carl Rosencrance	Rick Melvin	Ellen Riddle	...	John Janczewski	Ralph Zezza	Robert Dovin
West Pottsgrove *	tp	MC	3	(610) 323-7717	...	Edward Whetstone	...	...	...	...	...
West Reading	b	CM	4	(610) 374-8273	Robert Shuttlesworth	Lorri Swan	Rosalie Loeper	...	Sherry Fabriziani	Edward Fabriziani	...
West Rockhill *	tp	CM	4	(215) 257-9063	Donal Duvall	Greg Lippincott	Lora Sulahian	...	...	...	Randy Lemon
West View	b	MC	7	(412) 931-2800	...	...	...	...	...	...	...
West Whiteland *	tp	CM	16	(610) 363-9525	Diane Snyder	Michael Cotter	Patricia Launi	Cathy Kleponis	George Turner	Ralph Burton	Joseph Roscioli
West Wyoming	b	MC	2	(717) 693-1311	...	...	...	...	...	...	...
West York	b	MC	4	(717) 846-8889	...	...	...	...	...	...	...
Westmont	b	MC	5	(814) 255-3865	...	...	...	...	...	...	...
Westtown	tp	CM	10	(610) 692-1930	...	Robert Layman	Sandra Preston	...	...	...	Mark Gross
White	tp	CM	1	(724) 843-2819	Tom Bozic	Antoinette Wiley	...	...	...	Lou Adrian	Charles Currie
White *	tp	CM	14	(724) 463-8585	Robert Overdorff	Larry Garner	...	...	...	...	...
White Oak	b	CM	8	(412) 672-9727	Margaret Kadar	...	Nancy Greenland	...	...	Bruce Greenland	Ron Baldridge
Whitehall	b	MC	14	(412) 884-0505	...	James Leventry	Marilyn Moore	Beverly Weikel	Hobart Moore	J. Schmitt	David King
Whitehall	tp	MC	24	(610) 437-5524	Glenn Solt	Jack Meyers	...	Deborah Bowman	Robert Benner	Theodore Kohuth	John Rackus
Whitemarsh *	tp	CM	16	(610) 825-3535	Leslie Richards	C. van De Velde	...	Thomas Mullin	Calvin Bononborger	Eileen Behr	Jerry Breitmayer
Whitpain	tp	CM	18	(610) 277-2400	Leigh Narducci	Phyllis Lieberman	...	John Crawford	...	Joseph Stemple	Ronald Cione
Wilkes-Barre	c	MC	43	(570) 826-8222	Thomas McGroarty	John Murphy	James Ryan	John Koval	James Delaney	Anthony George	Albert Clocker
Wilkins	tp	CM	6	(412) 824-6650	Peter Wychis	Rebecca Bradley	Mae Franc	...	Leonard Hill	Keith Guthrie	Paul Vargo
Wilkinsburg *	b	CM	19	(412) 244-2900	John Thompson	Marla Marcinko	...	David Egler	Owen McAfee	Ophelia Coleman	Melanie Hall
Williamsport	c	MC	30	(717) 327-7500	Phillip Preziosi	...	Diane Ellis	Robert Fox	Harold Anthony	William Miller	George Holliday
Willistown	tp	CM	10	(610) 647-5300	David Rawson	Hugh Murray	Donna Monardo	...	...	Jay Molvie	John Di Mascio
Wilson	b	MC	7	(610) 258-6142	David Perruso	Walter Boran	Lisa Guth	...	Michael Collins	Richard Nace	Gregory Drake
Wind Gap	b	MC	2	(610) 863-7288	...	...	...	...	...	...	...
Windber	b	CM	4	(814) 467-9014	...	Richard Wargo	Christine Mulcahy	...	...	Richard Skiles	...
Windsor	tp	CM	12	(717) 244-3512	...	...	...	...	...	...	...
Woodard	tp	CM	3	(814) 378-8178	...	...	...	...	...	...	...
Wormleysburg	b	CM	2	(717) 763-4483	Thomas Kargams	Gary Berresford	...	...	...	...	...
Wrightstown	tp	MC	2	(215) 598-3313	...	Eileen Bradley	...	...	...	...	...
Wyoming	b	MC	3	(717) 693-0291	Michael Podwika	Patricia Carter	...	...	...	John Gilligan	Larry Selenski
Wyomissing	b	CM	8	(610) 376-7481	Ronald Stanko	Kevin Tobias	Rosemar Schnable	...	Bruce Longenecker	Jeffrey Biehl	James Baab
Yardley	b	MC	2	(215) 493-6832	S. Edward Johnson	Chris Harding	...	...	...	James O'Neill	...
Yeadon *	b	CM	11	(610) 284-1606	Jacqueline Mosley	...	...	Joseph Bartley	Craig Jeffries	Donald Molineux	...
York	tp	MC	23	(717) 741-3861	David Hamberger	Elizabeth Heathcote	...	Joseph Robinson	Paul Reichenbach	Thomas Gross	Mark Clark
York	c	MC	40	(717) 849-2301	John Brenner	Michael O'Rourke	Dianna Thompson	Carol Brown	John Senft	Mark Whitman	James Gross
Youngsville	b	CM	1	(814) 563-4604	Bruce Williams	Ronald Bosworth	Sherry Martin	...	Wallace Tydus	Gerald Calaldo	...
Youngwood	b	MC	4	(724) 925-3660	...	...	...	...	...	...	...
Zelienople	b	CM	4	(724) 452-6610	Charles Underwood	Donald Pepe	...	...	Andrew Mathew	Jim Miller	Mark Matscherz

Directory 1/9 continued OFFICIALS IN U.S. MUNICIPALITIES 2,500 AND OVER IN POPULATION

Jurisdiction	Type	Form of govern-ment	2000 Popu-lation	Main telephone number	Chief elected official	Appointed administrator	Clerk of the governing board	Chief financial officer	Fire chief	Police chief	Public works director
RHODE ISLAND											
Barrington *	t	CM	16	(401) 247-1900	June Speakman	Peter Deangelis	Lorraine Derois	Dean Huff	Gerald Bessette	John La Cross	Alan Corvi
Bristol	t	TM	22	(401) 253-7000	Joseph Parella	. . .	Diane Mederos	John Day	David Sylvaria	Russel Serpa	Paul Romano
Burrillville *	t	CM	15	(401) 568-4300	Nancy Binns	Michael Wood	Louise Phaneuf	John Mainville	. . .	Bernard Gannon	Richard Bernardo
Central Falls	c	MC	18	(401) 727-7400	Charles Moreau	. . .	Elizabeth Crowley	John Kuzmiski	Rene Coutu	Joseph Moran	Joseph Nield
Charlestown	t	CM	7	(401) 364-1210	. . .	. . .	Jodi LaCroix	. . .	. . .	Thomas Sharkey	Alan Arsenault
Coventry	t	CM	33	(401) 821-6400	. . .	Paul Sprague	. . .	Warren West	. . .	. . .	Sheila Patnode
Cranston	c	MC	79	(401) 461-1000	Stephen Laffey	. . .	Maria Wall	Jerome Baron	Robert Warren	Michael Chalek	Marco Schiappa
Cumberland	t	MC	31	(401) 728-2400	David Iwuc	David Fernandes	Patricia Skurka	Thomas Bruce	. . .	John Desmarais	Robert Joyal
East Greenwich *	t	CM	12	(401) 886-8665	. . .	William Sequino	Deidra Kettelle	Kathleen Raposa	John McKenna	David Desjarlais	Joseph Duarte
East Providence *	c	CM	48	(401) 435-7520	Isadore Ramos	Richard Brown	Virginia Nunes	James McDonald	Joseph Klucznik	Hubert Paquette	Stephen Coutu
Exeter *	t	RT	6	(401) 294-3891	Richard Kenyon	. . .	Cheryl Chorney	. . .	Scott Kettelle	Richard Brown	S. Mattscheck
Foster	t	CM	4	(401) 392-9200	Janet Dannecker	. . .	Anne Irons	. . .	. . .	Donald Kettelle	Bradford Gove
Glocester	t	MC	9	(401) 568-6206	Charles Poirier	. . .	Jean Fecteau	Thomas Mainville	. . .	Jamie Hainsworth	Alan Whitford
Hopkinton	t	TM	7	(401) 377-7777	Linda DiOrio	William DiLibero	Elizabeth Martin	Janice Bergeron	. . .	John Scuncio	Charles Niles
Jamestown *	t	CM	5	(401) 423-7200	Julio DiGiando	Bruce Keiser	Arlene Petit	Christina Collins	James Bryer	Thomas Tighe	Steven Goslee
Johnston	t	MC	28	(401) 553-8855	William Macera	. . .	Robin Pimental	. . .	Victor Cipriano	Richard Tamburini	Anthony Venditelli
Lincoln	t	MC	20	(401) 333-1100	Sue Sheppard	. . .	Karen Allen	Stephen Woerner	John McCaughey	Robert Kells	John MacQueen
Little Compton	t	MC	3	(401) 635-4400	Robert Mushen	. . .	Carol Wordell	. . .	Harry Hallgring	Sidney Wordell	Michael Mello
Middletown	t	CM	17	(401) 846-5781	Paul Rodrigues	Shawn Brown	Barbara Nash	. . .	Stephen Martin	Anthony Pesare	Thomas O'Loughlin
Narragansett	t	CM	16	(401) 789-1044	Anne-Marie Silveira	. . .	Carol Robbins	David Krugman	James Cotter	J. Smith	David Ousterhout
New Shoreham	t	CM	1	(401) 466-3200	Richard Kiley	. . .	Susan Shea	Mary Balser	Kirk Littlefield	William McCombe	. . .
Newport *	c	CM	26	(401) 845-5444	Stephen Waluk	Edward Lavallee	Kathleen Silvia	Laura Sitrin	Edward McCarthy	Michael McKenna	Julia Forgue
North Kingstown *	t	CM	26	(401) 294-3331	Anthony Miccolis	Michael Embury	James Marques	Patricia Sunderland	David Murray	Edward Charboneau	Philippe Bergeron
North Providence	t	MC	32	(401) 232-0900	A. Mollis	John Fleming	Maryann DeAngelus	Maria Vallee	Alfred Bertoncini	Ernest Spaziano	Glenn Corrente
North Smithfield	t	MC	10	(401) 767-2202	Robert Lowe	. . .	Debra Todd	Jill Gemma	Joel Jillson	Steven Reynolds	. . .
Pawtucket *	c	MC	72	(401) 728-0500	James Doyle	Harvey Goulet	Janice LaPorte	Ronald Wunschel	Timothy McLaughlin	George Kelley	John Carney
Portsmouth	t	MC	17	(401) 683-9118	Dennis Canario	Robert Driscoll	K. Viera Beaudoin	David Faucher	Jeffrey Lynch	Lance Hebert	David Kehew
Providence	c	MC	173	(401) 421-7740	David Cicilline	. . .	. . .	Alexander Prignano	James Rattigan	Richard Sullivan	Ferdinand Ihenacho
Richmond *	t	RT	7	(401) 539-9000	B. Reddish	. . .	Tracy Hay	. . .	. . .	Raymond Driscoll	Scott Barber
Scituate	t	MC	10	(401) 647-2822	. . .	. . .	Margaret Long	. . .	. . .	William Mack	Richard Iverson
Smithfield *	t	CM	20	(401) 233-1000	. . .	Dennis Finlay	Dianne Ady	. . .	Joseph Mollo	William McGarry	. . .
South Kingstown	t	CM	27	(401) 789-9331	Barbara Hackey	Stephen Alfred	Dale Holberton	Alan Lord	. . .	Vincent Vespia	Jon Schock
Tiverton	t	CM	15	(401) 625-6700	Donald Bollin	. . .	Hannibal Costa	. . .	Alan Jack	George Arruda	John Ratcliffe
Warren	t	CM	11	(401) 245-7554	. . .	Mike Abruzzi	Rita Galinelli	. . .	Alexander Galinelli	Thomas Gordon	John Massed
Warwick	c	MC	85	(401) 738-2000	Scott Avedisian	Barbara Caniglia	Marie Bennett	Ernest Zmyslinski	John Chartier	Stephen McCartney	Edmund Sarno
West Greenwich	t	TM	5	(401) 392-3800	Thaylen Waltonen	Kevin Breene	Janet Olsson	. . .	. . .	Gary Malikowski	David Andrews
West Warwick	t	CM	29	(401) 822-9219	J.-Marie DiMasi	James Thomas	David Clayton	Malcolm Moore	Charles Hall	Peter Brousseau	Paul Thomas
Westerly	t	CM	22	(401) 348-2500	. . .	Joseph Turo	Donna Giordano	. . .	David Sayles	J. Smith	. . .
Woonsocket	c	MC	43	(401) 762-6400	Susan Menard	Michael Annarummo	Pauline Payeur	. . .	Henry Renaud	Robert Morris	. . .
SOUTH CAROLINA											
Abbeville *	c	CM	5	(864) 459-5017	Harold McNeill	Nolan Wiggins	Kathy Wilson	Fran Strickland	George Speer	Patrick Henderson	Franklin Lewis
Aiken	c	CM	25	(803) 642-7654	F. Cavanaugh	Roger LeDuc	Sara Ridout	Anita Lilly	. . .	. . .	Larry Morris
Allendale	t	MC	4	(803) 584-4619	Chuck Cochran	DeWayne Ennis	. . .	Marilyn Leonard	. . .	James Youse	Maner Blackwood
Anderson	c	CM	25	(864) 231-2200	Richard Shirley	John Moore	. . .	Peggy Maxwell	Jack Abraham	Derrill McConnell	Tony Norris
Andrews	t	MC	3	(803) 264-8666	. . .	. . .	. . .	. . .	. . .	. . .	. . .
Atlantic Beach	t	CM	. .	(843) 272-5287	Irene Armstrong	Carolyn Montomery	Cheryl Pereira	Rolanda McDuffie	. . .	. . .	. . .
Awendaw	t	MC	1	(843) 928-3100	. . .	Dan Martin	. . .	. . .	. . .	. . .	. . .
Bamberg	c	MC	3	(803) 245-5128	. . .	. . .	. . .	. . .	. . .	. . .	. . .
Barnwell	c	MC	5	(803) 259-3266	. . .	. . .	. . .	. . .	. . .	. . .	. . .
Batesburg-Leesville	t	CM	5	(803) 532-4601	James Wiszowaty	Joan Taylor	Judy Edwards	. . .	Tommy Shealy	William Oswald	. . .
Beaufort	c	CM	12	(843) 525-7070	William Rauch	Scott Dadson	Beverly Gay	. . .	Wendell Wilburn	Jeff Dowling	Isiah Smalls
Belton	c	MC	4	(864) 338-7773	. . .	David Watson	. . .	. . .	Alan Sims	David Dockins	Derrall Foster
Bennettsville	c	CM	9	(843) 479-9001	. . .	Max Alderman	. . .	Wesley Park	Harvey Odom	Larry McNeil	Thomas Bostick
Bishopville	t	MC	3	(803) 484-9418	Thomas Alexander	William McCutchen	Hannah Tention	Suzette Robinson	. . .	Altagracia Simon	Luther Bramlett
Blackville	t	MC	2	(803) 284-2444	David Kenner	. . .	Harriett McKnight	. . .	Charles Epps	Kenneth Bamberg	Edward Rockwell
Bluffton	t	MC	1	(843) 706-4500	Henry Johnston	William Workman	Sandra Lunceford	Michael Nolte	. . .	John Brown	Harold Cooler
Calhoun Falls	t	CM	2	(864) 418-8512	Johnnie Waller	. . .	Peggy Waters	. . .	Darrell Manning	Mike Alewine	. . .
Camden	c	CM	6	(803) 432-2421	Mary Clark	G. Broom	Betty Slade	Mel Pearson	John Bowers	Joseph Floyd	Tom Couch
Cayce	c	CM	12	(803) 796-9020	. . .	John Sharpe	. . .	. . .	. . .	. . .	Frank Robinson
Central	t	MC	3	(864) 639-6381	Mac Martin	Phillip Mishoe	Sandra Brown	Jerri Martin	Ben Smith	Kerry Avery	Dean Martin
Charleston	c	MC	96	(843) 577-6970	Joseph Riley	. . .	Vanessa Maybank	Stephen Bedard	Russell Thomas	Reuben Greenberg	. . .
Cheraw *	t	MC	5	(843) 537-8401	Scott Hunter	J. Taylor	. . .	. . .	John Melton	Jay Brooks	Donna Byrd
Chester	c	CM	6	(803) 581-2123	. . .	. . .	. . .	. . .	David McAbee	Anthony Staten	Raymond Douglas
Clemson *	c	MC	11	(864) 653-2030	Larry Abernathy	Richard Cotton	Beverly Coleman	Tom Sparacino	. . .	James Dixon	David Conner
Clinton	c	CM	8	(864) 833-2790	Myra Nichols	Joshua Kay	Tammy Templeton	. . .	. . .	A. Barker	Ralph Lewis
Clover	t	MC	4	(803) 222-9495	Donnie Burris	Allison Harvey	Shannon Nix	. . .	Charlie Love	Legrand Guerry	Mark Geouge
Columbia	c	CM	116	(803) 545-3000	Bob Coble	Charles Austin	Erika Salley	Melisa Caughman	Bradley Anderson	Harold Crisp	Melissa Gentry
Conway	c	CM	11	(803) 248-1760	Gregory Martin	Bill Graham	Cyndi Gore	Michael Hardee	Darrel McDowell	Samuel Hendrick	Jerry Barnhill
Darlington	c	MC	6	(843) 398-4000	James Ward	Rodney Langley	Gloria Pridgen	. . .	James Stone	Jay Cox	Dale Freeze
Denmark	t	MC	3	(803) 793-3734	Elona Davis	Thomas Robertson	. . .	. . .	. . .	. . .	Timothy Freeman
Dillon *	c	CM	6	(843) 774-0040	J. Davis	Richard Wagner	Lynn Bowman	Janet Bethea	Keith Bailey	Joe Rogers	Hardy Jackson
Easley *	c	MC	17	(864) 855-7900	M. Christopherson	Jonathan Simons	Dianne Carter	. . .	Huey Womack	William Traber	Lamar Hunnicutt
Edgefield	t	MC	4	(803) 637-4014	Ken Durham	. . .	Charlotte Cheatham	. . .	Roger Ellis	Ronald Carter	David Coleman
Edisto Beach	t	MC	. .	(843) 869-2505	Burley Lyons	Linda Woods	. . .	. . .	William Simmons	H. Trent Canady	Robert Doud
Florence	c	CM	30	(843) 665-3158	Frank Willis	David Williams	. . .	Thomas Chandler	Joseph Robertson	Anson Shells	Andrew Griffin
Folly Beach	c	CM	2	(843) 588-2447	Vernon Knox	Toni Connor-Rooks	Marlene Estridge	Charles McManus	. . .	. . .	Steve Robinson
Forest Acres *	c	CM	10	(803) 782-9475	Frank Brunson	Mark Williams	. . .	Robert Massa	. . .	Marion Sealy	Joseph Paschal
Fort Mill	t	CM	7	(803) 547-2116	Charles Powers	David Hudspeth	April Beachum	Chantay Bouler	Kenneth Kerber	Jeffrey Helms	William Broom
Fountain Inn	t	MC	6	(864) 862-4421	Gary Long	. . .	Sandra Woods	. . .	Dale Watson	Anthony Morton	Roger Case
Gaffney *	c	MC	12	(864) 206-3303	Henry Jolly	James Taylor	Leighann Smuggs	Ginny Wallace	Nathan Ellis	John O'Donald	Michael Teague
Georgetown	c	MC	8	(843) 545-4000	Lynn Wilson	Miles Hadley	Ann Mercer	Jessica Miller	Joseph Tanner	Dan Furr	Sterling Geathers
Goose Creek	c	CM	29	(843) 797-6220	Michael Heitzler	Dennis Harmon	Kelly Lovette	Ronald Faretra	Steve Chapman	Harvey Becker	Steven Price
Great Falls	t	MC	2	(803) 482-2055	H. Starnes	. . .	Julie Blackwell	Don Camp	John Hipp	John Brown	Gary McManus
Greenville	c	CM	56	(864) 467-4530	Knox White	James Bourey	Cheryle Ratliff	Stephen Keef	William McDowell	Willie Johnson	Daniel Durig
Greenwood *	c	CM	22	(864) 942-8414	Floyd Nicholson	Steven Brown	. . .	Steffanie Dorn	Ronald Strange	Gerald Brooks	Billy Allen
Greer	c	CM	16	(864) 848-2150	Richard Danner	Edward Driggers	Lucia Polson	David Seifert	Christopher Harvey	Harold Crisp	James Johnson
Hampton	t	MC	2	(803) 943-2951	John Rhoden	. . .	Michelle Brown	. . .	Wade Freeman	Perry McAlheney	Walter Barefoot
Hanahan	c	MC	12	(843) 554-4221	William Cobb	Stephen Mason	Debra Lewis	Kathleen Armstrong	Jerry Barham	Donald Wilcox	Kenneth Prosser
Hardeeville *	c	CM	1	(843) 784-2231	Bronco Bostick	James Griffin	Lori Pomarico	Dennis Averkin	Dan Morgan	Richard Nagy	Joe Gailey
Hartsville	c	CM	7	(843) 383-3018	William Gaskins	James Pennington	. . .	Renee Douglas	William Heathman	L. Tim Kemp	Mike Welch
Hemingway	t	MC	. .	(843) 558-2824	Grady Richardson	Joseph Lee	Cindy Owens	. . .	George Sutton	Sandy Thompson	Ken Laster
Hilton Head Island *	t	CM	33	(843) 341-4600	Thomas Peeples	Stephen Riley	Betsy Mosteller	Susan Simmons	Lavarn Lucas	. . .	. . .
Hollywood *	t	MC	3	(843) 889-3222	Gerald Schuster	. . .	Wendy Ward	. . .	. . .	. . .	. . .
Honea Path	t	CM	3	(864) 369-2466	. . .	. . .	. . .	. . .	. . .	. . .	. . .
Irmo	t	CM	11	(803) 781-7050	John Gibbons	John Hanson	. . .	P. McMahon	. . .	. . .	. . .

Directory 1/9 continued **OFFICIALS IN U.S. MUNICIPALITIES 2,500 AND OVER IN POPULATION**

Jurisdiction		Type	Form of govern-ment	2000 Popu-lation	Main telephone number	Chief elected official	Appointed administrator	Clerk of the governing board	Chief financial officer	Fire chief	Police chief	Public works director
SOUTH CAROLINA continued												
Isle of Palms		c	MC	4	(843) 886-6428	F. Sottile	Linda Tucker	Janet Mauldin	. . .	Ann Marie Graham	T. Buckhannon	David Mobley
Johnston		t	MC	2	(803) 275-2488	Willie Campbell	. . .	. . .	. . .	John Clark	Chris Aston	Stuart Smith
Kershaw	*	t	MC	1	(803) 475-6065	Tommy Baker	Tony Starnes	Sandra Morgan	. . .	Tracy Caldwell	Billy Hilton	Don Rutledge
Kiawah Island	*	t	MC	1	(843) 768-9166	James Piet	Tumiko Rucker	Pat Wallis	. . .	. . .	. . .	. . .
Kingstree		t	CM	3	(843) 355-7484	James Kirby	Bradley Smith	Patricia Graham	. . .	Curtis Graham	Robert Ford	James Tisdale
Lake City		c	CM	6	(843) 374-5421	Arthur Martin	. . .	Cherline Miles	Jaunita Bradley	. . .	Lev Brown	. . .
Lancaster		c	CM	8	(803) 286-8414	. . .	. . .	Brenisha Wells	. . .	Dennis Cole	Jimmy Balkcum	. . .
Landrum		c	MC	2	(864) 457-3712	E. Brannon	James Edwards	. . .	. . .	. . .	. . .	. . .
Laurens		c	MC	9	(864) 984-0144	James Goss	A. Madden	. . .	. . .	William Hughes	Robin Morse	Oscar Tribble
Lexington	*	t	CM	9	(803) 951-4164	Randy Halfacre	James Duckett	Becky Hildebrand	Kathy Roberts	. . .	Terrence Greene	Alan Lutz
Liberty		c	MC	3	(864) 850-3505	Eddie Hughes	. . .	Dawn Lewis	. . .	Kevin McClain	Robert Griffin	Raymond Jones
Loris		c	MC	2	(843) 756-4004	David Stoudenmire	. . .	Martha Dorman	. . .	Jerry Hardee	Marshall Russell	Rodney Hardee
Manning		c	CM	4	(803) 435-8477	Kevin Johnson	Mary Adger	. . .	Charles Hemingway	Mitchell McElveen	Randy Garrett	Lowell Hardy
Marion	*	t	MC	7	(843) 423-5961	Bobby Gerald	. . .	Lakesha Shannon	. . .	Alan Ammons	Willie Smith	Mike Shall
Mauldin	*	c	MC	15	(864) 288-4910	R. Jones	Raymond Eubanks	Cindy Miller	. . .	Russell Sapp	John Davidson	Thomas Lynn
Mc Coll		t	MC	2	(843) 523-5341	. . .	. . .	Sandra Brewer	. . .	. . .	Thomas Langley	Marshall Grooms
Moncks Corner		t	MC	5	(843) 761-6650	William Peagler	. . .	Marilyn Baker	. . .	David Miller	Chad Caldwell	James Bodiford
Mount Pleasant		t	MC	47	(843) 884-8517	Harry Hallman	Robert Burdette	Carol Hunter	Jeanne Griffin	Harry Mims	Ronald Perry	Joseph Peele
Mullins		t	MC	5	(803) 464-9583	Joseph George	J. C. Richardson	Brenda Ivey	. . .	. . .	Jimmy Alford	Kenneth Johnson
Myrtle Beach	*	c	CM	22	(843) 918-1114	John Rhodes	Thomas Leath	Joan Grove	Michael Shelton	James Payne	Warren Gall	William Oliver
Newberry		c	CM	10	(803) 321-1000	. . .	Eric Budds	. . .	Marie Hickman	Joseph Palmer	Lewis Swindler	Arnold Hiller
North Augusta		c	CM	17	(803) 441-4202	Lark Jones	Charles Bennett	Donna Young	John Potter	. . .	. . .	Thomas Zeaser
North Charleston	*	c	MC	79	(843) 740-2501	R. Summey	Raymond Anderson	Ellen Clark	Edward Newton	Leonard Judge	John Zumalt	James Hutto
North Myrtle Beach		c	CM	10	(843) 280-5555	Marilyn Hatley	John Smithson	. . .	Randy Wright	Thomas Barstow	. . .	Kevin Blayton
Orangeburg		c	CM	12	(803) 533-6000	Paul Miller	John Yow	. . .	Carrie Johnson	. . .	Wendell Davis	Durwood Bowder
Pageland	*	t	MC	2	(843) 672-7292	Carroll Faile	. . .	Linda Long	. . .	Bruce Rivers	Johnny Sowell	Wesley Miles
Pendleton	*	t	MC	2	(864) 646-9409	Carol Burdette	Theresa Perry	Amber Barnes	. . .	. . .	. . .	Richard Bork
Pickens		c	MC	3	(864) 878-6421	David Owens	Christopher Eldridge	. . .	. . .	David Porter	Tommy Ellenburg	Henry Anthony
Port Royal		t	MC	3	(843) 986-2200	Samuel Murray	Milton Willis	Tanya Payne	. . .	Wendell Wilburn	James Cadien	Jeff Coppinger
Ridgeland		t	MC	2	(843) 726-7500	Ralph Tuten	Jason Taylor	Penelope Daley	. . .	John Mingledorff	Richard Zareva	James Mixson
Rock Hill	*	c	CM	49	(803) 329-7000	Doug Echols	Carey Smith	. . .	. . .	Kenneth Blackmon	John Gregory	Bobby Banks
Saluda	*	t	MC	3	(864) 445-3522	Frank Addy	Randy Cole	Claudia Cochran	. . .	Edwin Riley	Michael Clancey	Robert Langford
Seneca	*	t	MC	7	(864) 885-2700	John Fields	Gregory Dietterick	. . .	Walter Smith	. . .	. . .	Benny Burrell
Simpsonville		c	MC	14	(864) 967-9526	Dennis Waldrop	Russell Hawes	. . .	Robert Harrison	Jess Majors	Charles Reece	Joseph Carter
Spartanburg		c	CM	39	(864) 596-2000	William Barnet	Mark Scott	Connie Littlejohn	Dennis Locke	Phillip Caruso	Jennifer Kindall	. . .
Springdale		t	CM	2	(803) 794-0408	Pat Smith	Natalie McKelvey	. . .	. . .	. . .	Matthew Johnson	Terry Montgomery
Summerton	*	t	CM	1	(803) 485-2525	Jay Bruner	Bruce Behrens	. . .	. . .	. . .	. . .	. . .
Summerville	*	t	MC	27	(843) 871-6000	Berlin Myers	Dennis Pieper	. . .	Kristina Plymel	Marc Melfi	Bruce Owens	. . .
Sumter		c	CM	39	(803) 436-2583	Stephen Creech	Deron McCormick	Sherry Evans	David Brown	Douglas Mathis	Harold Johnson	Al Harris
Surfside Beach	*	t	MC	4	(843) 913-6111	Roy Hyman	Edwin Booth	Debra Herrmann	. . .	Robert Packard	. . .	Terry Grady
Tega Cay		c	MC	4	(803) 548-3512	. . .	Grant Duffield	Dora Perry	. . .	. . .	Rick Evelsizer	John Lathan
Travelers Rest		c	CM	4	(864) 834-7958	Roy Reynolds	Dianna Gracely	Gail Braziel	. . .	Richard Johnson	Timothy Christy	Francis Allen
Trenton		t	MC	. .	(803) 275-2538	. . .	W. Welborn	. . .	. . .	. . .	. . .	. . .
Union		c	MC	8	(864) 429-1702	Bruce Morgan	. . .	Gloria Rogers	Walker Gallman	Phillip Moore	. . .	Perry Harmon
Walhalla		t	MC	3	(864) 638-4343	Julian Stoudemire	. . .	Nancy Goehle	Karen Burgess	Greg Fowler	. . .	James Moore
Walterboro	*	c	CM	5	(843) 549-2548	Charles Sweat	Jeffrey Lord	Betty Hudson	William Floyd	. . .	. . .	Charlie Chewning
Ware Shoals		t	CM	2	(864) 456-7478	. . .	. . .	Sherry Busbee	. . .	. . .	. . .	. . .
West Columbia		c	CM	13	(803) 791-1880	Wyman Rish	J. Cunningham	Marta McKinnon	. . .	Ronald Scarboro	Dennis Tyndall	Joseph Owens
Westminster		t	MC	2	(864) 647-3200	Vera Duke	. . .	Donna Owen	. . .	Bobby Williams	William Strachan	Gary Cobb
Williamston	*	t	MC	3	(864) 847-7473	Carthel Crout	Phyllis Lollis	. . .	. . .	Steve Ellison	David Baker	Timothy Hood
Williston		t	MC	3	(803) 266-7015	Thomas Rivers	. . .	Patricia Fowler	. . .	. . .	Roger Kaney	John Melton
Winnsboro	*	t	CM	3	(803) 635-4943	Roger Gaddy	Don Wood	Anne Stewart	Kathy Belton	. . .	. . .	Leon Adams
Woodruff		c	CM	4	(864) 476-8154	Jerald Craig	. . .	. . .	. . .	J. Westmoreland	Michael Cromer	Gerald Bailey
York		c	CM	6	(803) 684-2341	W. Connolly	. . .	Nelle Pittman	. . .	Domenico Manera	Ronnie Roberts	Charles Helms
SOUTH DAKOTA												
Aberdeen		c	CM	24	(605) 626-7025	Tim Rich	. . .	. . .	Karl Alberts	John Stahl	. . .	Robin Bobzien
Belle Fourche		c	MC	4	(605) 892-2494	Bill Schmidt	. . .	. . .	Gloria Landphere	Ken Firnen	Larry Roberdeau	Leslie Snoozy
Beresford		c	CM	2	(605) 763-2008	Brent Palmer	Jerry Zeimetz	. . .	Kathy Moller	Tarz Mullinix	Larry Christensen	Dan Andre
Box Elder	*	c	MC	2	(605) 923-1404	Alfred Dial	. . .	Mystee Roth	Debbie Knapp	Roger Williams	John Keegan	Al Todd
Brandon		c	MC	3	(605) 582-6515	Michael Schultz	Dennis Olson	Janell Boor	Ellaine Henriksen	Larry Johnson	Phil Youngdale	Wayne Fletcher
Brookings		c	CO	18	(605) 692-6281	. . .	Jeffrey Weldon	Shari Thornes	Rita Thompson	Darrell Hartmann	Bryan Gums	. . .
Canton		c	CO	3	(605) 987-2881	Patrick Van Wyhe	Kyle Cwach	Karen Leffier	. . .	Trevor Erle	Stephan Warnock	Palmer Ericksen
Custer		c	MC	1	(605) 673-4824	. . .	. . .	. . .	. . .	. . .	. . .	. . .
Dell Rapids		c	CM	2	(605) 428-3595	Scott Fiegen	. . .	. . .	Vicky Haskell	. . .	. . .	Larry Schildhauer
Elk Point		c	MC	1	(605) 356-2141	Isabel Trobaugh	. . .	. . .	. . .	Jason Welch	Ryan Fleek	Mark Rubida
Hartford	*	c	MC	1	(605) 528-6187	. . .	Roland VanDerWerff	. . .	. . .	. . .	. . .	. . .
Hot Springs		c	MC	4	(605) 745-3135	. . .	. . .	. . .	. . .	. . .	. . .	. . .
Huron		c	CO	11	(605) 353-8502	Mary Pearson	. . .	Carol Tschetter	Paullyn Carey	John Coughlin	Douglas Schmitt	. . .
Lead		c	CO	3	(605) 584-1401	Thomas Nelson	Patrick Milos	Jeneen Mack	. . .	Ray Bubb	John Wainman	John Bunch
Lennox		c	MC	2	(605) 647-2286	. . .	Justin Weiland	. . .	. . .	. . .	. . .	. . .
Madison		c	CO	6	(605) 256-4586	. . .	. . .	. . .	Jeff Heinemeyer	Jerald Johnson	Ken Scott	Dick Birk
Milbank		c	MC	3	(605) 432-9575	Dale Aesoph	Jason Kettwig	Pat Berkner	Cynthia Schumacher	Ron Bjerke	Tim Kwasniewski	Larry Tietjen
Mitchell	*	c	MC	14	(605) 995-8420	Louis Sebert	. . .	. . .	Marilyn Wilson	Steve Willis	Lyndon Overweg	Tim McGannon
Mobridge		c	MC	3	(605) 845-3509	Taylor Oster	Steve Gasser	. . .	Lori Heil	. . .	Michael Nehls	Brad Milliken
Pierre		c	CO	13	(605) 773-7407	Dennis Eisnach	. . .	. . .	Kenneth Hericks	Tom Kurtenbach	Allen Aden	Rodney Liesinger
Rapid City		c	MC	59	(605) 394-4110	Jerome Munson	. . .	. . .	James Preston	Gary Shepherd	Craig Tieszen	. . .
Redfield		c	MC	2	(605) 472-4550	Duane Sanger	. . .	. . .	Joan Marlette	Richard Gruenwald	. . .	James Haider
Sioux Falls		c	CO	123	(605) 367-8740	Dave Munson	. . .	Dianne Metli	Eugene Rowenhorst	Donn Hill	Doug Barthel	. . .
Sisseton		c	CM	2	(605) 698-3391	. . .	. . .	. . .	. . .	. . .	. . .	. . .
Spearfish	*	c	MC	8	(605) 642-1334	Jerry Krambeck	Greg Sund	. . .	Elizabeth Benning	Pat Kellogg	Pat Rotert	Cheryl Johnson
Sturgis		c	CM	6	(605) 347-4422	. . .	. . .	. . .	. . .	Ron Koan	. . .	. . .
Vermillion	*	c	CM	9	(605) 677-7050	Dan Christopherson	John Prescott	. . .	Michael Carlson	Douglas Brunick	Art Mabry	Harold Holoch
Watertown		c	MC	20	(605) 882-6200	Brenda Barger	. . .	. . .	Tracy Turbak	Larry Anderson	Terry Lohr	Herbert Blomquist
Winner	*	c	MC	3	(605) 842-2606	Richard Lewis	. . .	. . .	Jack Day	Walter Harter	Paul Schueth	Dennis Schroeder
Yankton	*	c	CM	13	(605) 668-5222	Dan Specht	Douglas Russell	. . .	Al Viereck	Tom Kurtenbach	Duane Heeney	Kevin Kuhl
TENNESSEE												
Adams		t	CM	. .	(615) 696-2593	Omer Brooksher	. . .	. . .	. . .	Ray Brown	. . .	. . .
Alamo		t	MC	2	(731) 696-4551	. . .	. . .	Melinda East	Sharon Kail	. . .	Jimmy Irvin	Steve Hughes
Alcoa		c	CM	7	(865) 380-4700	Donald Mull	Mark Johnson	. . .	Ray Richesin	Larry Graves	Wayne Chodak	Kenneth Wiggins
Algood		c	MC	2	(931) 537-9545	. . .	Freddie Maxwell	. . .	. . .	Lloyd Norris	. . .	. . .
Ashland City	*	t	CM	3	(615) 792-4211	Gary Norwood	. . .	. . .	. . .	Chuck Walker	Marc Coulon	Thomas McCormick
Athens	*	c	CM	13	(423) 744-2703	Hal Buttram	Mitchell Moore	Leslie McKee	Brad Harris	Robert Miller	Charles Ziegler	Shawn Lindsey
Atoka		t	MC	3	(901) 837-5300	Charles Walker	Mark Johnson	Juanita Ayers	. . .	Jay Bonson	Jessie Poole	Walter Billings

Directory 1/9
continued

OFFICIALS IN U.S. MUNICIPALITIES 2,500 AND OVER IN POPULATION

Jurisdiction	Type	Form of govern-ment	2000 Popu-lation	Main telephone number	Chief elected official	Appointed administrator	Clerk of the governing board	Chief financial officer	Fire chief	Police chief	Public works director
TENNESSEE continued											
Bartlett	c	MC	40	(901) 385-6400	A. Keith McDonald	Jay Rainey	Gail Russo	Mark Brown	James Graves	Marcus Hopper	Toby Adkison
Beersheba Springs	t	CM	..	(931) 692-3314	...	...	...	...	...	...	...
Belle Meade	c	CM	2	(615) 297-6041	...	Beth Reardon	...	...	...	Jimmy Binkley	George Bartlett
Berry Hill	c	CM	..	(615) 292-5531	William Spray	Joseph Baker	Cheri Thompson	...	...	Robert Bennett	Kennith Bush
Bolivar	c	MC	5	(731) 658-2020	...	...	...	...	...	...	...
Brentwood *	c	CM	23	(615) 371-0060	Joe Reagan	Michael Walker	Debbie Hedgepath	Carson Swinford	Kenny Lane	Ricky Watson	Jeff Donegan
Bristol *	c	CM	24	(423) 989-5500	James Messimer	Jeffrey Broughton	...	Tara Musick	Bob Barnes	Blaine Wade	...
Brownsville	t	MC	10	(731) 772-1212	Webb Banks	...	...	...	Mark Foster	Gill Kendrick	Bobby Mayer
Camden	t	MC	3	(731) 584-4656	James Travis	...	Phyllis Woodard	...	Tom Bordonaro	George Smith	...
Carthage	c	MC	2	(615) 735-1881	David Bowman	...	Brenda McKinley	Joyce Rash	...	Jimmy Williams	Charles Massey
Centerville *	t	MC	3	(931) 729-4246	Ronnie Martin	...	...	Scott Powers	...	Roger Livengood	Danny Hudgins
Charleston *	t	CM	..	(423) 336-1483	Walter Goode	Caroline Geren	Janet Newport	...	Dewey Woody	John Hayden	Sheridian Johnston
Chattanooga	c	CO	155	(423) 757-5200	Ron Littlefield	Dan Johnson	Carol O'Neal	Daisy Madison	Jim Coppinger	J. Dotson	William McDonald
Church Hill	t	MC	5	(423) 357-6161	...	...	...	...	...	...	...
Clarksville	c	MC	103	(931) 645-7444	...	...	Sylvia Skinner	Wilbur Berry	Michael Roberts	Mark Smith	Dwight Luton
Cleveland	c	CO	37	(423) 559-3313	John Rowland	Joseph Cate	Janice Casteel	...	Chuck Atchley	Wesley Snyder	Tom Grant
Clifton *	c	CM	2	(931) 676-3370	Wayne Brandon	Dana Deem	Libb Nutt	...	Jerry Warren	Byron Skelton	...
Clinton	c	MC	9	(865) 457-0424	Winfred Shoopman	James Jones	Regina Ridenour	Vickie Fagan	...	Richard Scarbrough	Robert Murphy
Collegedale	c	CM	7	(423) 396-3135	John Turner	Ted Rogers	Jamie Bialeschki	Michelle Brown	...	Dennis Cramer	Rodney Keeton
Collierville *	t	MC	31	(901) 457-2200	Stanley Joyner	James Lewellen	Deborah Carmack	Mary Bevill	Jerry Crawford	Lawrence Goodwin	Wilbur Betty
Collinwood	c	CM	1	(931) 724-9107	Jasper Brewer	Ryan Tyhuis	...	...	Sherman Martin	Daniel Farris	Ricky Bratton
Columbia	c	CM	33	(931) 560-1510	William Gentner	Paul Boyer	...	Patti Baltzer	Donald Martin	Barry Crotzer	Ken Donaldson
Cookeville *	c	CM	23	(931) 526-9591	Charles Womack	Jim Shipley	Cathy McClain	Mike Davidson	John Kendrick	Bob Terry	Greg Brown
Covington *	c	MC	8	(901) 476-9613	...	...	...	...	...	...	...
Crossville	c	CM	8	(931) 484-5113	J. Graham	...	Sam Oglesby	Amanda Houston	Michael Turner	David Beaty	Richard Campbell
Dandridge	t	CM	2	(865) 397-7420	George Gantte	James Hutchins	...	Cathy Dixon	Chuck McSpadden	Carson Williams	Gregg Gann
Dayton	c	CM	6	(423) 775-1817	...	Victor Welch	...	...	Jack Arnold	Kenneth Walker	...
Dickson	t	MC	12	(615) 441-9508	Don Weiss	Tom Waychoff	Dianne Eubank	...	Eugene Tidwell	Ricky Chandler	Lee Mathis
Dover *	t	MC	1	(931) 232-5907	...	Wade Tosh	...	...	...	...	...
Dunlap	c	MC	4	(423) 949-2115	George Wagner	...	Mary Phipps	...	...	Clinton Huth	Clayton Smith
Dyersburg	c	MC	17	(731) 286-7607	...	...	...	...	...	...	...
East Ridge	t	CO	20	(423) 867-7711	Fred Pruett	David Mays	...	...	...	Steve Mize	...
Elizabethton	c	CM	13	(423) 547-6200	Pat Bowers	...	Sidney Cox	...	Michael Shouse	...	Ted Leger
Erwin	t	MC	5	(423) 743-6231	William Lewis	Randy Trivette	Jan Day	...	James Bailey	James Hicks	Carroll Mumpower
Etowah *	c	CM	3	(423) 263-2202	Joel Blair	Andrew Hyatt	...	Melissa Henderson	Daniel Ammons	Phil Robinette	Billy Ingram
Fairview	c	CM	5	(615) 799-2484	...	Shirley Forehand	...	Kathleen Daugherty	...	Terry Harris	...
Farragut *	t	CM	17	(865) 966-7057	Eddy Ford	Daniel Olson	...	...	...	...	William McKelvey
Fayetteville *	c	MC	6	(931) 433-6154	Gwen Shelton	...	...	...	Danny Travis	Doug Carver	Joe Abernathy
Forest Hills	c	CM	4	(615) 383-8447	Charles Evers	Alan Deck	...	...	...	...	...
Franklin *	t	MC	41	(615) 791-3217	Jerry Sherber	Eric Stuckey	...	Judy Kennedy	Rocky Garzarek	Jackie Moore	...
Gallatin	c	MC	23	(615) 452-5400	Don Wright	Suzan Nickerson	Connie Kittrell	Matthew Stewart	Joe Womack	Walter Tangel	Thomas Murray
Gatlinburg	c	CM	3	(865) 436-1400	Mike Werner	Cindy Ogle	...	David Beeler	Gregory Patterson	Randall Brackins	Ronald Greene
Germantown	c	MC	37	(901) 757-7200	...	Patrick Lawton	Judy Simerson	John Dluhos	Dennis Wolf	Richard Hall	Sam Beach
Goodlettsville *	c	CM	13	(615) 851-2200	John Finch	James Thomas	Ann Crawford	Julie High	Phillip Gibson	Richard Pope	Bill Brasier
Greenbrier	t	MC	4	(615) 643-4531	Billy Wilson	...	...	...	...	...	William Maitland
Greeneville	t	MC	15	(423) 639-7105	...	...	...	...	...	...	...
Halls	t	MC	2	(731) 836-9653	...	...	...	...	...	...	Alan Cherry
Harriman	c	MC	6	(865) 882-9414	Jerry Davis	Bob Tidwell	Tracey Bolden	...	Wayne Best	Randy Heidel	Darrell Langley
Hartsville–Trousdale County	c	MC	2	(615) 374-2461	Jerry Clift	...	Harold Gregory	...	...	Ray Russell	...
Henderson	c	MC	5	(731) 983-5000	Charles Patterson	Jim Garland	Darian Denton	...	Jimmy Carter	Tommy Davis	Jerry King
Hendersonville	c	MC	40	(615) 822-1000	...	...	Connie Bilbrey	Marylou Piper	Jamie Steele	...	Gerald Horton
Hohenwald	c	MC	3	(931) 796-2231	...	...	...	...	...	...	...
Humboldt	c	MC	9	(731) 784-2511	Allen Barker	...	Stacey Williamson	Howard Hadley	Chester Owens	Raymond Simmons	David Sikes
Huntingdon	t	MC	4	(731) 986-2900	Dale Kelley	Martha Taylor	...	...	Robert Brewer	Joe Parker	Jerry Nolen
Jackson	c	MC	59	(731) 425-8252	Charles Farmer	...	...	Alan Laffoon	Michael Morgan	Richard Staples	Johnny Williams
Jasper	t	MC	3	(423) 942-3180	...	...	...	...	...	...	...
Jefferson City	c	CM	7	(865) 475-9071	Darrell Helton	John Johnson	...	...	Robert Turner	William Clark	Michael Jones
Jellico	c	MC	2	(423) 784-6351	John Clifton	...	...	Linda Meadors	John Perkins	Ned Smiddy	Gene Beck
Johnson City *	c	CM	55	(423) 434-6001	Phil Roe	M. Denis Peterson	...	Janet Jennings	Paul Greene	John Lowry	Phil Pindzola
Jonesborough	t	CM	4	(423) 753-1030	Tobie Bledsoe	Robert Browning	...	Abbey Miller	Bobby Freeman	Steve Wheat	Jeff Thomas
Kingsport *	c	CM	44	(423) 229-9401	Dennis Phillips	John Campbell	Elizabeth Gilbert	James Demming	J. Craig Dye	Gale Osborne	Ryan McReynolds
Kingston *	c	CM	5	(865) 376-6584	W. Troy Beets	James Pinkerton	Eleanor Neal	Carolyn Brewer	Saul Gordon	James Washam	Tim Clark
Knoxville	c	MC	173	(865) 215-2106	...	...	...	James York	H. Hamlin	Phillip Keith	Bob Whetsel
La Follette	c	CM	7	(423) 562-4961	Clifford Jennings	David Young	Debbie Pierce	Terry Sweat	...	Jack Widner	Connie Robinson
La Vergne	c	CM	18	(615) 793-6295	...	Mark Moshea	...	...	...	Steve Lindsay	Robert Burns
Lafayette	c	MC	3	(615) 666-2194	Bill Wells	Annette Morgan	Deneshia Hesson	...	Keith Scruggs	Jerry Dallas	...
Lake City	t	CO	2	(865) 426-2838	Graydon Lovely	...	...	Jean Hayton	Ricky Ferguson	James Shetterly	James Wills
Lakeland	c	CM	6	(901) 867-2717	Scott Carmichael	Robert Wherry	Sontidra Franklin	...	...	...	...
Lakesite	c	MC	1	(423) 842-2533	...	David Edwards	...	...	...	...	...
Lakewood	c	CM	2	(615) 847-2187	Charles Gann	...	Alysia Prince	...	...	Jackie Camp	...
Lawrenceburg	c	CO	10	(931) 762-4459	Allen Chapman	Ken Hinson	...	...	Barry Kelley	Terry Shay	...
Lebanon	c	MC	20	(615) 443-2839	Don Fox	...	...	Hal Bittinger	Wayne Driver	Scott Bowen	Jeff Baines
Lenoir City	c	MC	6	(865) 986-2715	Charles Eblen	Walter Hurst	...	...	Richard Martin	Jack Fine	John Johnson
Lewisburg	c	CM	10	(931) 359-1544	Robert Phillips	Gordon Fuller	...	...	John Redd	Mike Hunter	Bill Wheat
Lexington	c	MC	7	(731) 968-6657	David Jowers	Sue Wood	...	...	Danny Barker	Roger Loftin	...
Livingston	t	MC	3	(931) 823-1269	Frank Martin	...	Phyllis Looper	...	Rocky Dial	Roger Phillips	Tim Coffee
Loudon	c	CM	4	(865) 458-2033	Bernie Swiney	Lynn Mills	Stephanie Putkonen	...	Michael Brubaker	James Webb	Billy Fagg
Madisonville *	t	MC	3	(423) 442-9416	Alfred McClendon	Ted Cagle	Connie White	V. Watson-Sisco	John Talent	Gregg Breeden	Donnie Chambers
Manchester	c	CM	8	(931) 728-4652	Johnnie Brown	...	...	Nina Moffitt	...	...	Ed Anderson
Martin	c	MC	10	(731) 587-3126	Randy Brundige	Richard Tidwell	...	...	...	...	Charles Vowell
Maryville	c	CM	23	(865) 273-3425	Joe Swann	Gregory McClain	...	Debbie Caughron	Marvin Mitchell	Tony Crisp	Angie Luckie
Maynardville	c	CM	1	(865) 992-3821	Herbert Richardson	Porter Massengill	...	Hazel Gillenwater	Darrell Whits	Gerald Simmons	...
Mc Kenzie	c	MC	5	(731) 352-2292	Walter Winchester	...	Charlie Beal	...	Brian Tucker	Harry Cooper	Tim Waldrup
Mcminnville	c	MC	12	(931) 473-1200	Royce Davenort	David Rutherford	Shirley Durham	...	Kevin Lawrence	...	William Brock
Memphis	c	MC	650	(901) 576-6569	Willie Herenton	Rick Masson	...	Charles Williamson	...	...	...
Milan *	t	MC	7	(731) 686-3301	...	...	...	...	...	...	...
Millersville	c	MC	5	(615) 859-0880	Dan Toole	Robert Mobley	...	Holly Murphy	Kirt Brinkley	Ronnie Williams	Frank Wilkerson
Millington	c	MC	10	(901) 872-4051	Terry Jones	...	Carolyn Madill	Richard Almond	Charles Carter	Richard Jewell	Jack Huffman
Monterey	t	MC	2	(931) 839-3770	John Bowden	...	Linda Sproles	...	...	Bruce Breedlove	Claude Reams
Morristown	c	CM	24	(423) 581-0100	Gary Johnson	James Crumley	Nellie Spradling	Dynise Robertson	William Honeycutt	Roger Overholt	...
Mount Carmel	t	MC	4	(423) 357-8125	...	...	Deborah Perry	...	...	Jeffery Jackson	Carl Cradic
Mount Juliet	c	CM	12	(615) 754-2552	Kevin Mack	Randy Robertson	...	Shelia Luckett	...	Charles McCrary	Hatton Wright
Mount Pleasant	c	CM	4	(931) 379-7717	Willie Baker	...	...	Debora McMullin	Tim Smith	James Wilson	James Holden
Mountain City	c	MC	2	(423) 727-0696	...	David Kitchell	...	...	...	...	...

Directory 1/9 continued — OFFICIALS IN U.S. MUNICIPALITIES 2,500 AND OVER IN POPULATION

Jurisdiction	Type	Form of govern-ment	2000 Popu-lation	Main telephone number	Chief elected official	Appointed administrator	Clerk of the governing board	Chief financial officer	Fire chief	Police chief	Public works director
TENNESSEE continued											
Murfreesboro	c	CM	68	(615) 893-5210	John Bragg	Roger Haley	...	...	David Baxter	Glenn Chrisman	...
Nashville-Davidson	c	MC	510	(615) 862-6640	William Purcell	Billy Phillips	Marilyn Swing	David Manning	Stephen Halford	Emmett Turner	...
Newbern	c	MC	2	(731) 627-3221	Thomas Parnell	Steve Anderson	...	...	Bill Berry	Harold Dunivant	K. Dennison
Newport	t	CM	7	(423) 623-7323	Connie Ball	...	Amanda White	...	Wayne Butler	Maurice Schults	Ben Hicks
Norris *	c	CM	1	(865) 494-7645	...	...	...	...	...	Danny Humphrey	Shirley Walker
Oak Hill	c	CM	4	(615) 371-8291	...	...	...	...	...	...	...
Oak Ridge	c	CM	27	(865) 425-3550	David Bradshaw	James O'Connor	Jacquelyn Bernard	Janice McGinnis	William Bailey	David Beams	...
Oliver Springs	t	CM	3	(865) 435-7722	Chris Hepler	David Bolling	Karen Campbell	Ramona Walker	Terry Phillips	Kenneth Morgan	Troy Burney
Oneida	t	MC	3	(423) 569-4295	...	...	...	...	...	...	...
Paris *	c	CM	9	(731) 641-1402	David Travis	Jack Tarkington	...	David Smith	Michael Williams	Thomas Cooper	Billy King
Pigeon Forge	c	CM	5	(865) 453-9061	Keith Whaley	Earlene Teaster	Mable Ellis	Dennis Clabo	Tony Watson	Jack Baldwin	Jerol Miller
Pittman Center	t	MC	..	(865) 436-5499	...	Sherry Spicer-Dudley	...	...	...	...	...
Portland	t	MC	8	(615) 325-6776	Jim Calloway	...	...	...	...	...	Kenneth Wilber
Pulaski *	c	MC	7	(931) 363-2516	Daniel Speer	Terry Harrison	Donna Goens	...	Jimmy Thompson	Stanley Newton	Floyd Poppenhouse
Red Bank *	c	CM	12	(423) 877-1103	Joe Glasscock	Christopher Dorsey	...	Carolyn Lewis	Mark Mathews	Larry Sneed	Wayne Hamill
Ripley	c	MC	7	(731) 635-4000	Richard Douglas	Donna Buckner	...	...	Jim Jarrett	Dennis King	Leamon Pennington
Rockwood *	c	CO	5	(865) 354-0163	Michael Miller	...	Susan Thomas	...	Robert Wertz	Billy Stinnett	Tom Pierce
Rogersville	t	MC	4	(423) 272-7497	Jim Sells	William Lyons	...	...	Hal Price	Larry Lawson	...
Samburg *	t	CM	..	(731) 538-3235	Larry Davis	...	Carrie Hogg	...	Guy Hogg	...	...
Savannah *	c	CM	6	(731) 925-3300	Phillip Lay	Garry Welch	Judy Grant	...	Jerry Shelly	Donald Derr	Virgil Morris
Selmer	t	MC	4	(731) 645-3241	Jimmy Whittington	...	Ann Henderson	...	...	R. Leonard	Floyd Hawkins
Sevierville	c	CM	11	(865) 453-5504	Bryan Atchley	...	Kimberly Graves	Lynn McClurg	Michael Rawlings	Don Myers	Bryon Fortner
Shelbyville	c	CM	16	(931) 684-2691	Geneva Smith	Edward Craig	Alicia Holliman	Gary Cantrell	John Habel	Austin Swing	Mark Clanton
Signal Mountain	t	CM	7	(423) 886-2177	James Althaus	Honna Rogers	...	...	...	Larry Eddings	Mitchell Lawson
Smithville	t	MC	3	(615) 597-4745	Cecil Burger	...	...	Robert Vandergriff	Charlie Parker	Richard Jennings	...
Smyrna	t	MC	25	(615) 459-2553	Paul Johns	Mark O'Neal	J. Woods	Jeanne Nolan	William Culbertson	Kevin Arnold	Chuck Boyett
Soddy-Daisy	c	CM	11	(423) 332-5323	Tommy Shipley	Janice Cagle	...	Sara Burris	...	Allen Branum	Bill Renfro
South Fulton *	c	CM	2	(731) 479-2151	...	Jeff Vowell	Debra Beadles	...	Tommy Smith	Andy Crocker	Hubert Maynard
South Pittsburg *	c	CM	3	(423) 837-5000	Mike Killian	Tom Landers	Carolyn Case	Mary Faye Payne	Freddie Cook	Dale Higdon	Russell McCain
Sparta *	c	MC	4	(931) 836-3248	...	Marty Carmichael	Jennifer Roberts	Tonya Tindle	Ed Kay	Jeff Guth	Ross Fann
Spring City *	t	CM	2	(423) 365-6441	Mary Garrison	Woody Evans	...	Robin Bolton	Jay Wright	Jason Yuhas	Dwight Mathis
Spring Hill	c	MC	7	(931) 486-2252	Ray Williams	...	April Goad	...	Clyde Farmer	Reggie Pope	John McCord
Springfield	c	CM	14	(615) 382-2200	Dave Fisher	Paul Nutting	Connie Watson	Bobby Lehman	David Greer	Mike Wilhoit	Allan Ellis
St. Joseph	c	CM	..	(931) 845-4141	...	Robert Cheekwood	...	...	...	...	...
Sweetwater	c	MC	5	(423) 337-6979	...	...	...	...	...	...	...
Tennessee Ridge	t	CM	1	(931) 721-3385	Kenneth Dunavant	Larry Laxton	Leslie Rucker	Woodrow Adams	Spencer Bryant	...	Jerry Bryant
Trenton	c	MC	4	(731) 855-2013	Tommy Litton	...	...	Sammy Dickey	Barry Green	William Sanders	...
Tullahoma *	c	CM	17	(931) 455-2648	Troy Bisby	Louis Baltz	...	Susan Wilson	Richard Shasteen	Paul Blackwell	Wayne Limbaugh
Tusculum	c	CM	1	(423) 638-6211	John Foster	...	Eva Sams	...	...	Danny Greene	Warren Cutshall
Union City	c	CM	10	(731) 885-1341	Terry Hailey	Don Thornton	...	...	Kelly Edmison	Joe Garner	Dean Laird
Watauga	c	CM	..	(423) 928-3490	Kenneth Ray	Hattie Skeans	Shirley Fair	...	...	...	...
Waverly	t	MC	4	(931) 296-2101	David Vaughn	W. Frazier	Kathy Camuzie	Sarah Tinnell	...	C. Frazier	Johnny Whitfield
Waynesboro	c	CM	2	(931) 722-5458	William White	Victor Lay	...	...	Douglas Gobbell	Thomas Seitz	Howard Riley
White House	c	MC	7	(615) 672-4350	Stan McAfee	Angela Carrier	Anne Love	C. Soporowski	Joe Palmer	Gerald Herman	Edward Hickman
Whitwell	c	CM	1	(423) 658-5151	Glenn Henry	Jim Trayer	Angela Cookston	Tina Seagroves	Debbie Suggs	Ryan Meeks	...
Winchester	t	MC	7	(931) 967-4771	...	Beth Rhoton	...	...	...	...	...
TEXAS											
Abernathy	c	CM	2	(806) 298-2546	Shane Cunningham	Frank Russell	Heilda Cannon	...	Kelley Vandygriff	Chris Lopez	Michael Grimsley
Abilene *	c	CM	115	(325) 676-6267	Norm Archibald	Larry Gilley	Danette Dunlap	Mindy Patterson	Ken Dozier	Melvin Martin	Paul Knippel
Addison *	t	CM	14	(972) 450-2817	Joseph Chow	Ronald Whitehead	...	Randolph Moravec	Noel Padden	Ron Davis	Nancy Cline
Alamo	c	MC	14	(956) 787-0006	...	Luciano Ozuna	...	Enrique Guzman	Rolando Espinosa	Arturo Espinosa	Jose Villescas
Alamo Heights	c	MC	7	(210) 822-3331	Louis Cooper	Rebecca Waldman	...	Cynthia Barr	Darren Smith	Giles Fortson	Jim Gray
Albany	c	MC	1		...	Bobby Russell	...	...	...	...	...
Alice *	c	CM	19	(361) 668-7210	Juan Rodriguez	Ray De Los Santos	Rene Marshall	Hector Hinojosa	Dean Van Nest	Daniel Bueno	...
Allen *	c	CM	43	(214) 509-4100	Steven Terrell	Peter Vargas	Shelley George	Kevin Hammeke	William Hawley	William Rushing	Stephen Massey
Alpine	c	CM	5	(432) 837-3301	Mickey Clouse	Jesse Garcia	Margaret Taylor	Ricky Chavez	...	...	Hector Ramirez
Alton	c	CM	4	(956) 581-2733	Salvador Vela	Jorge Arcaute	...	...	Elias Saldivar	Jose Vela	Rudy Garza
Alvarado *	c	MC	3	(817) 790-3351	Tom Durington	Don Ives	Debbie Wilkins	Kelle Whitfill	Richard Van Winkle	John Allen	Terry Hafer
Alvin *	c	CM	21	(281) 388-4295	Gary Appelt	Paul Horn	Thomas Peebles	Suzy Kou	Rex Klesel	Michael Merkel	David Kocurek
Alvord *	t	MC	1	(940) 427-5916	Frank Knittel	Richard Tow	Tammy Edwards	...	Monty Nivens	...	Earnest Dobyns
Amarillo	c	CM	173	(806) 378-3000	Trent Sisemore	Alan Taylor	Donna Deright	Dean Frigo	Steve Ross	Jerry Neal	Michael Rice
Andrews	c	CM	9	(915) 523-4820	Greg Sweeney	Len Wilson	...	Kitty Bristow	Joe Harper	Dolphus Jones	Larry Fleming
Angleton	c	CM	18	(979) 849-4364	Matt Sebesta	Greg Smith	David Emswiler	Susie Hernandez	...	David Ashburn	Robert Heinemeyer
Anna	c	CM	1	(972) 924-3325	...	Philip Sanders	...	...	...	...	...
Anson	c	CM	2	(915) 823-2411	E. Spraberry	...	Lou Wilson	...	Bill Cromeens	Bobby Evans	Freddy Elkins
Anthony	t	MC	3	(915) 886-3944	...	...	Myriam Uribe	...	...	Edward Miranda	Jesus Almaraz
Aransas Pass	c	CM	8	(361) 758-5301	Jesus Galvan	Kandi Hubert	Karen Mayer	Marie Roddell	Gilbert Ritz	Darryl Jones	Darren Gurley
Argyle *	c	MC	2	(940) 464-7273	Richard Tucker	Lyle Dresher	Codi Delcambre	Kim Collins	...	William Tackett	Troy Norton
Arlington	c	CM	332	(817) 459-6869	Robert Cluck	James Holgersson	Barbara Heptig	...	Robin Paulsgrove	Theron Bowman	Robert Lowry
Athens	c	CM	11	(903) 675-5131	Jerry King	Pam Burton	Pam Watson	David Hopkins	Dan Barnes	Dave Harris	Don Herriage
Atlanta	c	CM	5	(903) 796-2192	Keith Crow	Mike Ahrens	Janice Elliott	Jacqueline Jones	David Burden	Mike Dupree	Tom Townsend
Austin	c	CM	656	(512) 974-3215	William Wynn	Marc Ott	Shirley Brown	John Stephens	...	Stanley Knee	Peter Rieck
Azle	c	CM	9	(817) 444-2541	Russ Braudis	Craig Lemin	...	...	Thomas Scott	Stephen Myers	...
Balch Springs	c	CM	19	(972) 557-6070	Brenda Haas	...	Cindy Gross	...	Richard Woodham	Gary Moore	William McDonald
Balcones Heights	c	MC	3	(210) 735-9148	James Craven	Sean Pate	...	JoAnn Vidal	Benjamin Hoeffner	Kenneth Menn	...
Ballinger	c	CM	4	(325) 365-3511	Joe Shelby	Tommy New	...	...	Lonnie Bishop	J. C. Gore	Carl Williams
Bastrop	c	CM	5	(512) 303-7305	Tom Scott	Michael Talbot	Teresa Valdez	Lamar Ozley	Henry Perry	David Board	Lee Weatherford
Bay City	c	MC	18	(979) 245-6550	Charles Martinez	...	...	...	...	...	Jon Abshier
Baytown *	c	CM	66	(281) 422-8281	Stephen DonCarlos	Garrison Brumback	Eileen Hall	L. Daws	...	Charles Shaffer	Herbert Thomas
Beaumont	c	CM	113	(409) 880-3716	Guy Goodson	James Hayes	Rose Jones	Max Duplant	Michel Bertrand	Frank Coffin	Thomas Warner
Bedford	c	CM	47	(817) 952-2100	Richard Hurt	Beverly Queen	Rita Frick	Thomas Ross	Stephen Bass	David Flory	James Wood
Bee Cave	c	CM	..	(512) 767-6600	Caroline Murphy	Frank Salvato	Sherry Mashburn	...	...	Steven Gonzalez	...
Beeville	c	CM	13	(361) 358-4641	...	Ford Patton	Tomas Saenz	Robert Aguilar	...	Joe Salinas	John Standlea
Bellaire	c	CM	15	(713) 662-8222	Mary Ann Goode	Bernard Satterwhite	Tracy Dutton	Louise Richman	Joe Bettega	Randall Mack	...
Bellmead	c	CM	9	(254) 799-2436	...	S. Radcliffe	...	...	James Karl	Robert Harold	Michael Willis
Bellville	c	CM	3	(979) 865-3136	James Bishop	J. Johnston	Cheryl Robertson	...	Warren Klump	...	...
Belton	c	CM	14	(254) 933-5800	Jim Covington	Sam Listi	Connie Torres	Cristy Daniell	Roy Harmon	Michael Sleeth	Les Hallbuaer
Benbrook *	c	CM	20	(817) 249-3000	Jerry Dittrich	Andrew Wayman	Joanna King	David Ragsdale	Tommy Davis	James Mills	Walter Shumac
Big Lake	c	MC	2	(915) 884-2511	...	Evelyn Ammons	...	...	Alan Garner	...	Troy Kuykendall
Big Spring *	c	CM	25	(432) 264-2346	...	Gary Fuqua	...	Peggy Walker	Brian Jensen	Lonnie Smith	...
Bishop	t	CM	3	(361) 584-2567	Geraldine Rypple	Cynthia Contreras	Delma Salinas	...	...	Larry Lawrence	Albert Guajardo
Boerne *	c	CM	6	(830) 249-9511	...	Ronald Bowman	...	Sandra Mattick	Doug Meckel	Gary Miller	Michael Mann
Bonham	c	CM	9	(903) 583-7555	Roy Floyd	Corby Alexander	Janell Cain	...	William Palya	Mike Bankston	Ronald Ford
Booker	c	MC	1	(806) 658-4579	Lois Sheets	Donald Kerns	Jaque Stephens	...	Roger Almenroad	...	...

Directory 1/9 continued — OFFICIALS IN U.S. MUNICIPALITIES 2,500 AND OVER IN POPULATION

Jurisdiction		Type	Form of govern-ment	2000 Popu-lation	Main telephone number	Chief elected official	Appointed administrator	Clerk of the governing board	Chief financial officer	Fire chief	Police chief	Public works director
TEXAS continued												
Borger		c	CM	14	(806) 273-0903	Jeff Brain	Wanda Klause	. . .	Glynn Carlock	Bob Watson	Jimmy Adams	Henry Veach
Bovina		c	CM	1	(806) 251-1116	Stan Miller	. . .	. . .	. . .	. . .	Leon Saddler	Andres Garcia
Bowie	*	c	CM	5	(940) 872-1114	Larry Cox	James Cantwell	Mitzi Wallace	Renita Bishop	Doug Page	David Scruggs	. . .
Boyd		c	MC	1	(940) 433-5166	. . .	. . .	. . .	. . .	. . .	. . .	. . .
Brady	*	c	CM	5	(325) 597-2152	James Stewart	James Minor	. . .	Lisa Remini	Joe Foster	Tommy Payne	Rufus Beam
Brazoria	*	c	CM	2	(979) 798-2489	Ken Corley	Teresa Borders	Sheila Williams	. . .	Marcus Rabren	Neal Longbotham	John Jordan
Breckenridge	*	c	CM	5	(254) 559-8287	Jim McKay	Gary Ernest	. . .	. . .	Roger McMullen	Larry Mahan	Jason Pollei
Brenham	*	c	CM	13	(979) 337-7200	Milton Tate	Terry Roberts	Jeana Bellinger	Carolyn Miller	Ricky Boeker	. . .	John Baker
Bridge City		c	CM	8	(409) 735-6801	John Dubose	. . .	Terry Jordan	. . .	. . .	Stephen Faircloth	. . .
Bridgeport	*	c	MC	4	(940) 683-3400	Donald Majka	Van James	. . .	Amy Standard	Michael McComis	Randall Singleton	David Turnbow
Brownfield		c	CM	9	(806) 637-4547	Nancy Wade	Eldon Jobe	. . .	Mary Collins	Marvin Dawson	Roy Rice	Willie Herrera
Brownsville		c	CM	139	(956) 548-6000	Blanca Vela	Charles Cabler	Melissa Morales	Pete Gonzalez	Ramiro Torres	Ben Reyna	Carlos Ayala
Brownwood	*	c	CM	18	(325) 646-5775	Bert Massey	Bobby Rountree	. . .	Walter Middleton	Del Albright	Virgil Cowin	Keith Pulaski
Bryan		c	CM	65	(979) 209-5000	Jay Watson	David Watkins	Mary Stratta	Kathy Davidson	Michael Donoho	Michael Strope	. . .
Buda	*	c	CM	2	(512) 312-0084	Bobby Lane	Kenneth Williams	Toni Milam	Sarah Mangham	Clay Huckaby	Bo Kidd	Michael Beggs
Bullard		c	MC	1	(903) 894-7223	C. R. Vaughan	Larry Morgan	Deborah Jessup	. . .	. . .	. . .	. . .
Bulverde		c	MC	3	(830) 438-3612	. . .	John Hobson	. . .	. . .	. . .	. . .	. . .
Bunker Hill Village		c	MC	3	(713) 467-9762	. . .	Ruthie Sager	Valerie Cantu	. . .	Cleve Calagna	. . .	Ron Garrison
Burkburnett	*	c	CM	10	(940) 569-2263	Carl Law	Michael Slye	Patricia Holley	. . .	Rodney Ryalls	Michael Tracey	Michael Whaley
Burleson		c	CM	20	(817) 447-5400	Ken Shetter	Curtis Hawk	Mary Kayser	Charles Harris	Gary Wisdom	Thomas Cowan	Morris Stringer
Burnet		c	CM	4	(512) 756-6093	. . .	Michael Steele	Christy Fath	J. Laudenschlager	Mark Ingram	. . .	Danny Lester
Cactus		c	CM	2		. . .	Jeffrey Jenkins	. . .	. . .	. . .	. . .	. . .
Caldwell	*	c	CM	3	(979) 567-3901	Bernard Rychlik	Billy Clemons	. . .	. . .	David Pevehouse	Paul Lilly	. . .
Cameron		c	MC	5	(254) 697-6646	William Meacham	. . .	Amy Kopriva	. . .	. . .	Leonard Doskocil	. . .
Canadian		t	CM	2	(806) 323-6473	. . .	Colby Waters	. . .	. . .	. . .	. . .	. . .
Canton	*	c	CM	3	(903) 567-2826	Rusty Wilson	Andy McCuistion	. . .	. . .	Charles Bazhaw	Mike Echols	Rick Malone
Canyon	*	c	CM	12	(806) 655-5000	Quinn Alexander	Randy Criswell	Gretchen Mercer	Chris Sharp	Mike Kelley	Bobby Griffin	Dan Reese
Carrizo Springs		c	CM	5	(830) 876-2476	Ralph Salinas	Mario Martinez	P. Garcia Vargs	Nicolas Cardona	Jose Rodriguez	. . .	Ruben Garcia
Carrollton	*	c	CM	109	(972) 466-3090	. . .	Leonard Martin	Ashley Mitchell	Robert Scott	John Murphy	David James	Robert Kopp
Carthage		c	CM	6	(903) 693-3868	Carson Joines	Brenda Samford	Joyce Whitehead	Debbie Pierce	. . .	Duane Baushke	William McMillan
Castle Hills		c	CM	4	(210) 342-2341	Marcy Harper	Michael Rietz	Linda Gill	. . .	Gerald Riedel	Donald Davis	Rick Harada
Castroville		c	MC	2	(830) 931-4070	Jesse Byars	Joseph Painter	. . .	Cheryl Peery	. . .	Lee McVay	Bruce Alexander
Cedar Hill	*	c	CM	32	(972) 291-5100	Rob Franke	Alan Sims	Lyn Hill	William Browder	Stephen Pollock	Steve Rhodes	Ruth Antebi
Cedar Park		c	CM	26	(512) 401-5000	Bob Lemon	Brenda Eivens	Leann Barnes	Joyce Herring	Chris Connealy	Henry Fluck	. . .
Celina	*	c	MC	1	(972) 382-2682	Jim Lewis	Jason Gray	Vicki Faulkner	Jay Toutounchian	Jerry Duffield	Joe Williams	Joseph Johnson
Center		c	CM	5	(936) 598-2941	John Windham	Chad Nehring	Terre Noble	Robin Andrews	Vernon Byndom	Walter Shofner	John Holt
Chandler		c	MC	2	(903) 849-6853	. . .	Jim Moffeit	. . .	. . .	. . .	. . .	. . .
Childress		c	CM	6	(940) 937-3684	. . .	Jerry Cummins	. . .	Charlene Smith	Steve Jones	Reece Bowen	Gilbert Bailey
Cibolo	*	c	MC	3	(210) 658-9900	Jennifer Hartman	Todd Parton	Peggy Cimics	Lara Feagins	Roger Niemietz	Tom Curd	. . .
Cisco	*	c	CM	3	(254) 442-2111	Joe Wheatley	Jim Baker	Virginia Dill	Peggy Ledbetter	Walter Fairbanks	Larry Weikel	Cecil Boles
Clarksville		c	CM	3	(903) 427-3834	Ann Rushing	Belinda Peek	Rosalind Rosser	Lorene Beers	Allan Thompson	Weldon Warren	. . .
Clear Lake Shores		c	CM	1	(281) 334-2799	Katherine McIntyre	Karen McDaniel	Christy Stroup	. . .	Larry Steed	Paul Shelley	. . .
Cleburne	*	c	CM	26	(817) 645-0900	Ted Reynolds	Chester Nolen	Joy Doty	Thomas Wilmore	John Ishmael	Terry Powell	David Esquivel
Cleveland	*	c	CM	7	(281) 592-2667	. . .	. . .	Kelly McDonald	Kellan Shaw	Steve Wheeler	Ike Hines	Mike Ulbig
Clifton		c	MC	3	(254) 675-8337	Raymond Zuehlke	Charles McLean	. . .	Pamela Harvey	Russell Jenkins	Rex Childress	Jim Burch
Clute		c	CM	10	(979) 265-2541	Jerry Adkins	Kyle McCain	Sarah Oakes	. . .	. . .	Mark Wicker	Robert Ray
Clyde	*	t	MC	3	(325) 893-4234	Dustin Hawk	Mary Daly	C. Jean Gilmore	. . .	Billy Dezern	Jerome Chaney	. . .
Cockrell Hill		c	MC	4	(214) 330-6333	Luis Carrera	. . .	. . .	. . .	Mike Burns	C. Smith	Danny Thomas
Coleman	*	c	CM	5	(325) 625-5114	Nick Poldrack	Larry Weise	. . .	. . .	Richard Hensley	Jay Moses	Bob Ray
College Station		c	CM	67	(979) 764-3500	Ronald Silvia	Glenn Brown	Connie Hooks	Charles Cryan	R. B. Alley	Edgar Feldman	Mark Smith
Colleyville		c	CM	19	(817) 503-1000	David Kelly	. . .	Cynthia Singleton	Terrell Leake	. . .	Tommy Ingram	Keith Fisher
Colorado City		c	CM	4	(325) 728-3464	Jim Baum	Paul Catoe	Connie Baker	Connie Ponko	Rufino Martinez	Shawn Myatt	Rick Carver
Columbus		c	MC	3	(979) 732-2366	Paula Frnka	. . .	Jill Ready	. . .	Robert Walla	Robert Connor	Michael Poncik
Comanche		c	MC	4	(915) 356-2616	. . .	. . .	. . .	. . .	. . .	. . .	. . .
Commerce		c	CM	7	(903) 886-1100	Sheryl Zelhardt	Dion Miller	Marty Cunningham	. . .	Tommy Eaton	Kerry Crews	Tracy Lunceford
Conroe		c	MC	36	(936) 539-4431	Tommy Metcalf	Jerry McGuire	Marla Porter	Stephen Williams	. . .	John Lindon	L. Towery
Converse		c	CM	11	(210) 658-5356	Al Suarez	Samuel Hughes	. . .	Gerald Wilson	Richard Wendt	Richard Jamison	Lupe Perez
Coppell		c	CM	35	(972) 462-0022	. . .	Clay Phillips	Elizabeth Ball	Jennifer Miller	. . .	. . .	Kenneth Griffin
Copper Canyon		t	MC	1	(940) 241-2677	Sue Tejnl	Quentin Hix	Virginia Moore	. . .	. . .	. . .	. . .
Copperas Cove		c	CM	29	(254) 547-4221	J. Darossett	Andrea Gardner	Rose Mansfield	. . .	. . .	. . .	David Brinegar
Corinth		c	CM	11	(940) 498-3200	Victor Burgess	. . .	Kimberly Pence	Kathy DuBose	Jason Collier	Darrell Brown	Don Locke
Corpus Christi		c	CM	277	(361) 880-3315	. . .	Angel Escobar	Armando Chapa	. . .	Juan Adame	Pedro Alvarez	. . .
Corsicana	*	c	CM	24	(903) 654-4800	Clifford Brown	. . .	. . .	Cathy McMullan	Donald McMullan	G. Cox	Ron Lynch
Cotulla	*	c	MC	3	(830) 879-2367	Joe Lozano	Higinio Martinez	. . .	. . .	. . .	. . .	. . .
Crandall	*	c	CM	2	(972) 427-3771	Joe Baker	Heath Kaplan	. . .	. . .	Tim Atkins	Dean Winters	Joe Villarreal
Crane		c	MC	3	(432) 558-3563	. . .	. . .	. . .	. . .	. . .	. . .	. . .
Crockett		c	CM	7	(936) 544-5156	Wayne Mask	Ronald Duncan	Mitzi Thompson	. . .	Darrell Deckard	Jimmy Fisher	. . .
Crowley		c	CM	7	(817) 297-2201	Billy Davis	Truitt Gilbreath	Martha Najera	Cathy Coffman	Robert Loftin	Kirk Nemitz	Jim McDonald
Crystal City		c	CM	7	(830) 374-3477	. . .	Diana Palacios	. . .	Emma Flores	Delwin Hale	Luis Contreras	. . .
Cuero		c	CM	6	(361) 275-3476	W. Edge	. . .	. . .	Sandra Oehlke	William Tolbert	Glenn Mutchler	. . .
Daingerfield		c	CM	2	(903) 645-3906	Lou Slaughter	Marty Byers	Margie Hargrove	Heide Edmonson	. . .	Joseph Farino	. . .
Dalhart		c	CM	7	(806) 249-5511	. . .	Greg Duggan	. . .	. . .	. . .	. . .	. . .
Dallas	*	c	CM	1188	(214) 670-3120	Tom Leppert	Mary Suhm	Deborah Watkins	David Cook	Eddie Burns	David Kunkle	Rick Galceran
Dalworthington Gardens		c	MC	2	(817) 275-1234	. . .	Melinda Brittain	. . .	. . .	. . .	. . .	. . .
Dayton	*	t	CM	5	(936) 258-2642	Steve Stephens	David Douglas	Terry Brown	Chris Contreras	Terry Boyett	Pete Douzat	Toby Stroughter
De Soto	*	c	CM	37	(972) 230-9601	Bobby Waddle	James Baugh	Laura Hallmark	Camelia Browder	Fred Hart	William Brodnax	Thomas Johnson
Decatur		c	MC	5	(940) 627-2741	Joe Lambert	Brett Shannon	Diane Cockrell	. . .	Mike Richardson	Rex Hoskins	Earl Smith
Deer Park	*	c	CM	28	(281) 478-7245	Wayne Riddle	Ronald Crabtree	Sandra Watkins	H. Nelson	Greg Bridges	Ken Findley	Nader Naderi
Del Rio		c	CM	33	(830) 774-8616	Dora Alcala	. . .	Juanita Douglas	Frances Rodriguez	Harold Bean	Manuel Herrera	Alejandro Garcia
Denison		c	CM	22	(903) 465-2720	Wayne Cabaniss	Larry Cruise	Nina Jones	Andy Wilkins	Bill Taylor	Jimmy Lovell	Jerry White
Denton		c	CM	80	(940) 349-8200	Euline Brock	George Campbell	Jennifer Walters	L. Langley	Edward Chadwick	Charles Wiley	. . .
Denver City		t	MC	3	(806) 592-5426	David Bruton	Stan David	Beverly Prather	. . .	Carl Whittaker	Jack Miller	Perry Ham
Devine		c	MC	4	(830) 663-2804	Steve Lopez	. . .	Dora Rodriguez	. . .	. . .	Robert Flores	Ed Gentry
Diboll		c	MC	5	(936) 829-4757	Bill Brown	Dennis McDuffie	Ernestine Cavazos	Elvia Garza	Charlie Mann	Kent Havard	Doug McCoy
Dickinson	*	c	MC	17	(281) 337-2489	Julie Masters	Julie Johnston	Rena Hardage	Usha Mathew	Jasper Liggio	Ron Morales	Kellis George
Dilley		c	MC	3	(830) 965-1624	Russell Foster	Felix Arambula	Juanita Gonzalez	Irma Rodriguez	J. C. Molina	. . .	Rudy Olivarez
Dimmitt		t	MC	4	(806) 647-2155	. . .	Don Sheffy	. . .	. . .	. . .	Ray Aleman	Saul Arce
Donna		c	CM	14	(956) 464-3314	Ricardo Morales	Juan Ortiz	Martha Alvarado	Daniel Downs	David Simmons	Ruben De Leon	. . .
Dublin		c	MC	3	(254) 445-3331	Brian Boudreaux	Jerry Guillory	Rhonda Keilers	. . .	James Fritts	Lannie Lee	Jimmy Williams
Dumas		c	MC	13	(806) 935-4101	Johnnie Rhoades	Vince DiPiazza	Kim Rehkopf	Dorothy Williams	Paul Jenkins	Dale Alwan	Tommy Raper
Duncanville	*	c	CM	36	(972) 780-5000	David Green	J. Cagle	Dara Crabtree	Frank Trando	David Giordano	Robert Brown	Dennis Schwartz
Eagle Lake	*	c	CM	3	(979) 234-2640	Mike Morales	. . .	Sylvia Rucka	. . .	Howard Wilkerson	William Lattimore	Thurston Webb
Eagle Pass		c	CM	22	(830) 773-1111	Joaquin Rodriguez	Roberto Gonzalez	. . .	Manuel Contreras	Rogelio Dela Cruz	Jose Castaneda	Hector Chavez
Early		c	CM	2	(915) 643-5451	David Brooks	Kenneth Thomas	. . .	. . .	Travis Eoff	Audie Pinson	Stephen Walker
Eastland		c	CM	3	(254) 629-8321	Jerry Mathews	David Maddox	Shirley Stuart	Leslie Zander	Phillip Arther	Cecil Funderburgh	Bobby Jacoby

Directory 1/9 continued — OFFICIALS IN U.S. MUNICIPALITIES 2,500 AND OVER IN POPULATION

Jurisdiction		Type	Form of govern-ment	2000 Popu-lation	Main telephone number	Chief elected official	Appointed administrator	Clerk of the governing board	Chief financial officer	Fire chief	Police chief	Public works director
TEXAS continued												
Edcouch		t	CM	3	(956) 262-2140	...	...	...	...	...	...	...
Edgecliff Village		t	MC	2	(817) 293-4313	Ed Lucas	...	Sherrie Rundle	...	Kevin Davis	...	Bob Parker
Edinburg		c	CM	48	(956) 383-5661	Joe Ochoa	W. Smith-Sturgis	Myra Garza	Ascencion Alonzo	Shawn Snider	Quirino Munoz	Daniel Tijerina
Edna		c	CM	5	(361) 782-3122	Joe Hermes	Kenneth Pryor	...	Olga Salomon	Wendel Hamilton	Clinton Wooldridge	Brad Ryan
El Campo		c	CM	10	(979) 541-5000	Kenneth Martin	John Steelman	...	Courtney Sladek	Jimmy George	Jimmy Elliott	Brad Ramsey
El Lago		c	MC	3	(281) 326-1951	Brad Emel	...	...	...	Ray Cook	...	...
El Paso		c	CM	563	(915) 541-4509	John Cook	Joyce Wilson	Richarda Momsen	C. Arrieta-Candelaria	Roberto Rivera	...	...
Electra	*	c	CM	3	(940) 495-2146	Glen Branch	Stephen Giesbrecht	Kim Cryer	...	Greg Lynn	Johnny Morris	Carl Simon
Elgin		c	MC	5	(512) 285-5721	Eric Carlson	...	Shirley Garvell	...	Mike Carter	Steven Huckabay	Joe Marten
Elsa		c	CM	5	(956) 262-2127	Ramiro Alvarado	...	Frieda Reyes	...	Gregorio Ramirez	Gerald Senk	Severo Trevino
Ennis		c	CM	16	(972) 875-1234	Russell Thomas	Stephen Howerton	...	Shirley Trull	David Hopkins	Dale Holt	Roy Callahan
Euless		c	CM	46	(817) 685-1475	Mary Saleh	Gary McKamie	Susan Crim	Vicki Rodriquez	Lee Koontz	Mike Brown	Ron Young
Everman		c	MC	5	(817) 293-0525	James Stephenson	Donna Anderson	Judy Thompson	Scott Holoway	Donnie Hurd	Randy Sanders	Michael Box
Fair Oaks Ranch	*	c	MC	4	(210) 698-0900	Boots Gaubatz	Roy Thomas	Carole Vanzant	Kristin Hansen	...	Scott Rubin	Ronald Emmons
Fairfield		c	MC	3	(903) 389-2633	...	...	...	...	...	...	...
Fairview	*	t	MC	2	(972) 562-0522	Sim Israeloff	John Godwin	M. Lewis-Sirriani	Brenda Bowman	Dick Price	Granver Tolliver	Aron Holmgren
Falfurrias		c	CO	5	(361) 325-2420	J. Guerra	Aurora Rodriguez	Leocadia Benavides	...	...	Baldemar Rivera	Kenneth Martin
Farmers Branch		c	CM	27	(972) 247-3131	Bob Phelps	Gary Greer	Cindee Peters	Charles Cox	Kyle King	Sidney Fuller	...
Farmersville	*	c	CM	3	(972) 782-6151	Donald Smith	Alan Hein	...	Daphne Hamlin	Kim Morris	Wayne Pickett	...
Fate		c	CM	..	(972) 771-4601	...	...	...	...	...	...	...
Ferris	*	c	CM	2	(972) 544-2110	Jim Parks	David Chavez	Patricia Bradley	...	Eddie Duran	Frank Mooney	Charlie James
Flatonia	*	t	CM	1	(361) 865-3548	Jeff Hairgrove	...	Melissa Brunner	...	Gregg Robinson	Mike Noak	Jack Daulas
Floresville		c	MC	5	(830) 393-3105	Raymond Ramirez	Gary Pelech	...	Evelyn Grimes	...	Daniel Martinez	Vincent Griego
Flower Mound	*	t	CM	50	(972) 874-6000	Jody Smith	Harlan Jefferson	Paula Lawrence	Charles Springer	Eric Metzger	Kenneth Brooker	Kenneth Parr
Floydada		t	CM	3	(806) 983-2834	Bobby Gilliland	Gary Brown	Karen Lawson	...	...	Darrell Gooch	Jack Alaniz
Forest Hill	*	c	CM	12	(817) 568-3000	James Gosey	David Miller	Jacquelyn Allen	Debbie Maness	Pat Ekiss	Rex Phelps	...
Forney		c	CM	5	(972) 552-2291	...	Brian Brooks	...	...	...	...	...
Fort Stockton		c	CM	7	(432) 336-8525	Ruben Falcon	Rafael Castillo	Delma Gonzalez	Penny Smith	Melvin Thomas	Juan Castro	Brad Newton
Fort Worth		c	CM	534	(817) 871-8900	...	Dale Fisseler	Gloria Pearson	Karen Montgomery	...	Ralph Mendoza	...
Fredericksburg		t	MC	8	(830) 997-7521	Tim Crenwelge	Gary Neffendorf	Shelley Britton	Brad Kott	...	Paul Oestreich	Jerry Bain
Freeport	*	c	CM	12	(979) 233-3526	Larry McDonald	...	Delia Munoz	Bob Welch	John Stanford	Jeff Pynes	Larry Fansher
Freer	*	c	MC	3	(512) 394-6612	Arnoldo Cantu	Cynthia Lackey	Nelia Alaniz	...	James Finney	James Torres	...
Friendswood		c	CM	29	(281) 996-3200	David Smith	...	Deloris McKenzie	...	...	Robert Wieners	Kazem Hamidian
Friona	*	c	CM	3	(806) 250-2761	John Taylor	Terri Johnson	...	Patricia Phipps	Jim Taylor	Fraustino Salinaz	Kenneth Ford
Frisco		c	CM	33	(972) 335-5555	Michael Simpson	George Purefoy	Nan Parker	Nell Lange	Mack Borchardt	Todd Renshaw	Gary Hartwell
Fritch	*	c	CM	2	(806) 857-3143	Kevin Keener	Ernest Terry	Emily West	...	Calvin Nickell	Terry Cox	Alvin Clark
Gainesville		c	CM	15	(940) 668-4500	Glenn Loch	...	Rita Gray	Daniel Parker	Steven Boone	Carl Dunlap	...
Galena Park		c	MC	10	(713) 672-2556	Robert Barrett	Margaret Stevens	Janie Guerrero	Rae Moreau	Paul Grider	Robert Pruett	John Cooper
Galveston		c	CM	57	(409) 797-3500	Lyda Thomas	Steven Leblanc	Barbara Lawrence	...	...	Robert Pierce	Brandon Wade
Garland		c	CM	215	(972) 205-2000	...	William Dollar	Linda Larson	George Kauffman	Daniel Grammer	Larry Wilson	Jack May
Gatesville		c	CM	15	(254) 865-8951	David Byrom	Roger Mumby	Darleen Hodges	Brenda Kiphen	Billy Vaden	Nathan Gohlke	Doyle Barton
George West		c	CM	2	(361) 449-1556	August Caron	Terri Garza	Jacquelyn Harborth	...	Lloyd Clifton	Ray Garcia	Benjamin Tanguma
Georgetown		c	CM	28	(512) 930-3652	Gary Nelon	Paul Brandenburg	Sandra Lee	Micki Rundell	Anthony Lincoln	David Morgan	...
Giddings		c	CM	5	(979) 540-2710	James Arndt	Paul Kipp	Dianne Schneider	...	James Garner	...	Serapio Garza
Gilmer		c	CM	4	(903) 843-2552	R. Cross	Ron Stephens	Heather Steelman	Mary Bates	J. Steelman	James Grunden	Brian Rodgers
Gladewater		c	CM	6	(903) 845-2196	John Tallent	James Stokes	...	Melba Haralson	Wayne Smith	Jimmy Davis	...
Glenn Heights	*	c	CM	7	(972) 223-1690	Clark Choate	...	...	Patrick Harvey	Chris Shook	...	Drew Roberts
Goldthwaite		c	CM	1	(915) 648-3186	Danny Hammond	Robert Lindsey	Tammy Clifton	...	...	...	...
Goliad		c	MC	1	(361) 645-3454	...	C. J. Snipes	...	...	...	...	...
Gonzales		c	CM	7	(830) 672-2815	Bobby O'Neal	David Huseman	Jean Collins	Joe Cavazos	Glenn Lohse	Tim Crow	Raymie Zella
Graham		c	CM	8	(940) 549-3324	Douglas Strond	Larry Fields	...	Hugh Nanny	Terry Watkins	Jim Nance	Chester Smith
Granbury		c	CM	5	(817) 573-1114	David Southern	...	Dee Arcos	Bob Evart	H. Robertson	Randy Jaquess	Richard English
Grand Prairie		c	CM	127	(972) 237-8012	Charles England	Thomas Hart	Catherine DiMaggio	Diana Ortiz	Clifton Nelson	Glen Hill	Ron McCuller
Grand Saline		c	MC	3	(903) 962-3122	...	Stephen Ashley	...	...	Robert Coffman	Daniel Zajac	Gene Putman
Granite Shoals		c	MC	2	(830) 598-2424	Pat Crochet	...	Ronda Reichle	...	George Cambanis	J. P. Wilson	...
Grapevine		c	CM	42	(817) 410-3000	William Tate	Bruno Rumbelow	Linda Huff	Fred Werner	David Anderson	Richard Wilkins	Jerry Hodge
Greenville	*	c	CM	23	(903) 457-3100	Tom Oliver	Steven Alexander	Debra Newell	...	...	Harold Roseberry	Massoud Ebrahim
Gregory		c	MC	2	(361) 643-6562	...	Norma Garcia	...	...	...	Robert Garza	Cesario Vela
Groesbeck		c	MC	4	(254) 729-3293	Jackie Levingston	Martha Stanton	Brenda Jackson	...	Charles Bratcher	Jerri Almy	Keith Tilley
Groves		c	CM	15	(409) 962-4471	Brad Bailey	D. Sosa	Kimbra Caldwell	Jeri Rainey	Dale Jackson	Stephen Savoy	...
Groveton		c	MC	1	(936) 642-1122	...	...	Carolyn Davis	...	...	Jon Archer	...
Gun Barrel City		c	CM	5	(903) 887-1087	...	Gerry Boren	...	...	...	...	...
Hallettsville	*	c	MC	2	(361) 798-3681	Warren Grindeland	Tom Donnelly	...	...	Anthony Ludwig	Randal Schlauch	Ervin Kolacny
Haltom City	*	c	CM	39	(817) 222-7700	William Lanford	Thomas Muir	Arturo Camacho	Calvert Welch	Robert Rhodes	Kenneth Burton	David Fain
Hamilton	*	c	MC	2	(254) 386-8116	...	Bill Funderburk	Jane Dodson	...	...	...	Ronnie Harris
Hamlin		c	MC	2	(915) 576-2711	Jack Shields	...	...	...	...	Mike Middleton	...
Harker Heights		c	CM	17	(254) 953-5600	Mary Gauer	Steve Carpenter	...	Alberta Barrett	Leon Charpentier	Michael Gentry	Mark Hyde
Harlingen	*	c	CM	57	(956) 216-5020	Chris Boswell	Craig Lonon	Sylvia Trevino	Roel Gutierrez	Mike Rinaldi	Daniel Castillo	Dan Serna
Haskell		c	CM	3	(940) 864-2355	Ken Land	Brandon Anderson	Loretta Gray	...	Bill Steele	Tom Bassett	Dave Miller
Hearne		c	CM	4	(979) 279-3461	...	Ruben Gomez	Anna Florida	Leslie Ely	Marcus Hilton	Robert Parsley	Cowboy Poole
Heath	*	c	CM	4	(972) 771-6228	...	Edward Thatcher	...	...	...	...	Pedram Farahnak
Hedwig Village		c	MC	2	(713) 465-6009	Sue Speck	Beth Staton	...	...	...	David Barber	Lane Standley
Helotes		c	CM	4	(210) 695-8877	Jonathan Allan	Marie Gelles	Theresa Helbert	...	Walton Daugherty	Mort Ault	...
Hemphill		t	CM	1	(409) 787-2251	...	Donald Iles	...	...	...	...	...
Hempstead		c	MC	4	(979) 826-2486	...	...	...	...	...	...	...
Henderson		c	CM	11	(903) 657-6551	John Fullen	Randall Freeman	Kelly Poovey	Trina Freeman	Dwayne Pirtle	John Waldie	Davis Brown
Henrietta	*	c	CM	3	(940) 538-4316	...	...	Carol Loucks	...	...	...	James Scarber
Hereford		c	CM	14	(806) 363-7100	...	Rick Hanna	...	...	...	David Wagner	Paul Kilpatrick
Hewitt	*	c	CM	11	(254) 666-6171	Charles Turner	Dennis Woodard	Lydia Lopez	Lee Garcia	Glenn Arthur	James Barton	Paul Holroyd
Hico	*	c	MC	1	(254) 796-4620	...	Lambert Little	Sandra Polk	Anita Mueller	...	Gregg Bewley	Scott Perry
Hidalgo	*	c	CM	7	(956) 843-2286	...	Joe Vera	...	Xavier Moron	Juan Reyes	Vernon Rosser	Ruben Puente
Highland Park		t	CM	8	(214) 521-4161	William White	William Lindley	...	...	...	...	James Fisher
Highland Village	*	c	CM	12	(972) 899-5131	Dianne Costa	Michael Leavitt	Alicia Richardson	Kenneth Heerman	Lonnie Tatum	Edward O'Bara	Matthew Kite
Hill Country Village	*	c	MC	1	(210) 494-3671	Kirk Francis	Francisco Morales	...	...	...	...	...
Hillsboro		c	CM	8	(254) 582-3271	John Erwin	Jack Harper	Betty Harrell	...	Burney Baskett	Carl Cain	...
Hitchcock		c	MC	6	(409) 986-5591	Lee Sander	...	Rose Marie Theiler	...	Scott Fleming	Glen Manis	John Dieringer
Hollywood Park		c	MC	2	(210) 494-2023	Ellen Alkire	...	Barbara Haddock	...	Javier Garcia	Frank Ballard	Jimmy Arroyo
Hondo	*	c	CM	7	(830) 426-3380	James Danner	Robert Herrera	...	Yolanda Benitez	...	John Martinez	Timothy Fousse
Horseshoe Bay	*	c	CM	3	(830) 598-8741	Robert Lambert	Stan Farmer	Teresa Moore	...	...	Bill Lane	Jeffrey Koska
Houston		c	MC	1953	(713) 837-0311	Bill White	Anthony Hall	Anna Russell	Judy Johnson	Phil Boriskie	Harold Hurtt	Michael Marcotte
Hudson Oaks		c	MC	1	(682) 229-2400	Pat Deen	S. C.-Husband	...	...	...	Kenneth West	...
Humble		c	MC	14	(281) 446-3061	Donald McMannes	William Boeske	Stella Daniel	Dixie Kellum	Gary Outlaw	Gary Warman	Barry Brock
Hunters Creek Village		c	MC	4	(713) 465-2150	...	...	...	...	...	...	...
Huntsville		c	CM	35	(936) 291-5401	J. Turner	William Baine	Dana Welter	Winston Duke	Tom Grisham	...	Glenn Isbell
Hurst	*	c	CM	36	(817) 788-7000	Richard Ward	W. Weegar	Rita Frick	Anita Thetford	John Brown	Steve Moore	Ron Haynes
Hutchins		c	MC	2	(972) 225-6121	Mary Washington	Donna Holder	Cheryl Wesley	Joe Wallace	Stacey Hickson	Rick Hutcherson	Curley White

Directory 1/9 continued

OFFICIALS IN U.S. MUNICIPALITIES 2,500 AND OVER IN POPULATION

Jurisdiction	Type	Form of govern-ment	2000 Popu-lation	Main telephone number	Chief elected official	Appointed administrator	Clerk of the governing board	Chief financial officer	Fire chief	Police chief	Public works director
TEXAS continued											
Hutto *	c	CM	1	(512) 759-4030	Kenneth Love	Edward Broussard	Debbie Chelf	Laurie Brewer	. . .	Dwain Jones	Scot Stromsness
Idalou	t	MC	2		. . .	Jeffrey Snyder	. . .	. . .	. . .	. . .	. . .
Ingleside *	c	CM	9	(361) 776-2517	Stella Herrmann	James Gray	Kimberly Drysdale	Paul Baen	Chad Champion	Stan Bynum	Donald Paty
Iowa Park	c	CM	6	(940) 592-2131	Randy Catlin	Michael Price	Janice Newman	Tammy Persick	Danny Skinner	Steve Klempa	Kenneth Lytle
Irving	c	CM	191	(972) 721-2600	Joe Putnam	. . .	. . .	Catherine Duncan	Jack Hickey	William Cannaday	Jack Angel
Jacinto City	c	CM	10	(713) 674-8424	Mike Jackson	Jack Maner	Joyce Raines	. . .	Lon Squyres	Joe Ayala	Kyle Reed
Jacksboro	c	CM	4	(940) 567-6321	Jerry Craft	Shawna Dowell	Shirley Grantham	Eddie Peacock	Jeremy Jennings	Frank Mooney	. . .
Jacksonville	c	CM	13	(903) 586-3510	Kenneth Durrett	Mo Raissi	Betty Thompson	Jan Tomlinson	Rodney Kelley	Mark Johnson	. . .
Jamaica Beach	c	CM	1	(409) 737-1142	Victor Pierson	John Brick	. . .	. . .	. . .	Debbie Kershaw	. . .
Jasper	c	CM	8	(409) 389-4651	R. Horn	Alan Grindstaff	Betty Glenn	Judy Nash	. . .	Stanley Christopher	Joe Matthews
Jefferson	c	MC	2	(903) 665-3922	Ned Fratangelo	James Gibson	Anita Perot	. . .	. . .	. . .	. . .
Jersey Village *	c	CM	6	(713) 466-2100	Russell Hamley	Norbert Castro	Lorri Coody	Isabel Kato	Mark Bitz	Charles Wedemeyer	Danny Segundo
Jones Creek *	v	MC	2	(979) 233-2700	Howard Rape	Linda Shepard	Arevelia Ortiz	. . .	. . .	. . .	. . .
Joshua *	c	MC	4	(817) 558-7447	Merle Breitenstein	Paulette Hartman	Mary Beth Thomas	LaDonna Davis	. . .	. . .	Bruce Hewett
Jourdanton	c	CM	3	(830) 769-3589	Tammy Clark	Daniel Nick	Cindy Trevino	. . .	David Prasifka	Ronald Lawson	. . .
Junction	c	CO	2	(915) 446-2622	. . .	Kathleen Saiz	Maria Alvarado	. . .	. . .	Steven Brown	Audren Tomlinson
Karnes City	t	MC	3	(830) 780-3422	. . .	. . .	. . .	. . .	. . .	. . .	. . .
Katy	c	MC	11	(281) 391-9181	. . .	. . .	. . .	. . .	. . .	. . .	. . .
Kaufman *	c	CM	6	(972) 932-2216	William Fortner	Curtis Snow	Jo Ann Talbot	Cathy Cummins	Eddie Brown	Michael Holder	Richard Underwood
Keene *	c	MC	5	(817) 641-3336	Roy Robinson	Ismael Lopez	Barbara Fuller	William Guinn	Matt Gillin	Rocky Alberti	Mike Baze
Keller	c	CM	27	(817) 743-4000	Pat McGrail	Daniel O'Leary	Sheila Stephens	Johnny Phifer	Kelly King	Mark Hafner	Gregory Dickens
Kemp	c	CM	1	(903) 498-3191	. . .	Melinda Oliver	Jimmie Lou Webb	. . .	. . .	Richard Arnold	Joe Villareal
Kenedy *	c	MC	3	(512) 583-2230	Ruhman Franklin	Reggie Winters	. . .	. . .	Rudy Seinz	Dwight DeBose	Johnny Rodriguz
Kennedale *	c	CM	5	(817) 985-2100	Bryan Lankhorst	Bob Hart	Kathy Turner	Sakura Dedrick	Mike McMurray	Tommy Williams	Larry Ledbetter
Kermit *	c	CM	5	(915) 586-3460	Ted Westmoreland	Sam Watson	Gloria Sanez	Frankie Rolfe	Odie Marshall	Scott Williams	John Shepard
Kerrville	c	CM	20	(830) 257-8000	. . .	. . .	. . .	. . .	Raymond Holloway	. . .	. . .
Kilgore *	c	CM	11	(903) 984-5081	Joe Parker	Jeffrey Howell	Karen Custer	Lawanna Chrisman	. . .	. . .	David Hackley
Killeen	c	CM	86	(254) 501-7831	Timothy Hancock	Connie Green	. . .	Barbara Gonzales	Jerry Gardner	Dennis Reed	James Butler
Kingsville	c	CM	25	(361) 595-8017	Sam Fugate	Carlos Yerena	Edna Lopez	. . .	Alonzo Lopez	Ricardo Torres	. . .
Kirby	c	CM	8	(210) 661-3198	. . .	Zina Tedford	Alva Gardner	Timothy Bolda	Kevin Riedel	Marvin Ivy	Sidney Lankford
Kountze	c	MC	2	(409) 246-3463	Charles Bilal	James Davis	Abbe Overstreet	Dee Zimmerman	Dale Williford	Michael Parrish	Ervin Jordan
Kyle	c	CM	5	(512) 268-5341	. . .	Thomas Mattis	. . .	. . .	. . .	. . .	. . .
La Coste	c	MC	1	(830) 762-3609	. . .	C. Salzman	. . .	. . .	. . .	. . .	. . .
La Feria	c	MC	6	(956) 797-2261	. . .	Sunny Philip	Olga Oberwetter	. . .	. . .	Donato Garcia	Javier Martinez
La Grange *	c	CM	4	(979) 968-5805	Janet Moerbe	Shawn Raborn	Lisa Oltmann	Brett Wolff	. . .	Jackie Skelton	. . .
La Marque	c	CM	13	(409) 938-9200	Larry Crow	Robert Ewart	Susan Welch	Susan Lang	Todd Zacherl	Richard Price	Michael Morgan
La Porte	c	CM	31	(281) 471-5020	Alton Porter	Ronald Bottoms	Martha Gillett	. . .	Mike Boaze	Richard Reff	Steve Gillett
Lacy-Lakeview	c	MC	5	(254) 799-2458	Calvin Hodde	Michael Nicoletti	. . .	Connie Foreman	. . .	. . .	Keith Bond
Lago Vista	c	CM	4	(512) 267-1155	. . .	. . .	Joyce Stapleton	. . .	. . .	Danny Smith	Bill Angelo
Laguna Vista	t	CM	1	(956) 943-1793	. . .	. . .	. . .	. . .	Mike Meyn	Robert McGinnis	. . .
Lake Dallas *	c	MC	6	(940) 497-2226	Anthony Marino	Earl Berner	Beverly Weikum	. . .	. . .	Nick Ristagno	Johnny Webber
Lake Jackson *	c	CM	26	(979) 415-2400	Bob Sipple	William Yenne	Alice Rodgers	Pamela Eaves	Mike Harper	Paul Hromadka	Jesse Nisbett
Lake Worth	c	MC	4	(817) 237-1211	Walter Bowen	Joey Highfill	. . .	Vicki Mikel	Mark Cone	Ron Wadkins	Jamye Sexton
Lakeway *	c	CM	4	(512) 314-7500	Steve Swan	Steven Jones	Christy Fath	Nancy Klingman	. . .	Gordon Bowers	David Ferry
Lamesa	c	CM	9	(806) 872-2124	. . .	Fernando Vera	Maria Aguayo	. . .	Geno Todd	Richard Garcia	Arbie Taylor
Lampasas	c	CM	6	(512) 556-6831	Jack Calvert	Michael Stoldt	Stacy Brack	Vicki Kinsey	Terry Lindsey	Timothy Angermann	Randy Clark
Lancaster	c	CM	25	(972) 227-2111	Joe Tillotson	Rickey Childers	. . .	. . .	Richard Knopf	Daniel Shiner	James Smith
Laredo	c	CM	176	(956) 795-2192	Elizabeth Flores	Carlos Villarreal	Gustavo Guevara	Rosario Cabello	Luis Sosa	Agustin Dovalina	Jose Guerra
League City	c	CM	45	(281) 332-3431	. . .	Chris Reed	. . .	Monica Kohlenberg	. . .	Michael Jez	Chris Peifer
Leander *	c	CM	7	(512) 528-2712	John Cowman	Anthony Johnson	Debbie Haile	Robert Powers	Jerry Williams	. . .	. . .
Leon Valley	c	CM	9	(210) 684-1391	Chris Riley	Lanny Lambert	Marie Feutz	. . .	Stan Irwin	Randall Wallace	Fred Stolz
Levelland *	c	CM	12	(806) 894-0113	Hugh Bradley	Richard Osburn	Beth Walls	Sarianne Beversdorf	Marvin Brewer	Tony Cowan	Pat Riley
Lewisville *	c	CM	77	(972) 219-3400	Gene Carey	Claude King	Julie Heinze	Joe Barrett	Richard Lasky	Steve McFadden	Don Locke
Liberty	c	CM	8	(936) 336-3684	Bruce Halstead	Ronald Wood	Aneisha Nugent	Naomi Herrington	. . .	William Griffin	. . .
Lindale	c	MC	2	(903) 882-3422	. . .	Owen Scott	. . .	. . .	. . .	. . .	. . .
Little Elm	t	CM	3	(214) 975-0400	Frank Kastner	Ivan Langford	Kathy Phillips	Ryan Adams	Joe Florentino	Waylan Rhodes	Doug Peach
Littlefield	c	CM	6	(806) 385-9202	Shirley Mann	Danny Davis	Concha Aleman	. . .	Jamie Grey	Bill McMinn	Michael Williamson
Live Oak *	c	CM	9	(210) 653-9140	Joseph Painter	Matthew Smith	Deborah Goza	Leroy Kowalik	Charles Foster	Ron Echols	Mark Wagster
Livingston	c	CM	5	(936) 327-4311	Ben Ogletree	Marilyn Sutton	Irene Nicks	. . .	Corky Cochran	Dennis Clifton	William Haecker
Llano	c	MC	3	(915) 247-4158	C. Bauman	Frank deGraffenried	Martha Box	Lynda Kuder	. . .	. . .	. . .
Lockhart	c	CM	11	(512) 398-3461	Ray Sanders	. . .	Connie Ortiz	Stephanie House	Jerry Doyle	. . .	Vance Rodgers
Longview *	c	CM	73	(903) 237-1000	Jay Dean	David Willard	Lois McCaleb	Angela Coen	Michael Pruitt	J. B. McCaleb	Keith Bonds
Lorena *	c	CM	1	(254) 857-4641	Chuck Roper	John Moran	Monica Hendrix	Linda Klump	James Menefee	Thomas Dickson	. . .
Los Fresnos *	c	CM	4	(956) 233-5768	David Winstead	Mark Milum	Pam Denny	Celina Gonzales	Gene Daniels	James Harris	Carlos Salazar
Lubbock	c	CM	199	(806) 775-3000	Marc McDougal	Lee Dumbauld	Rebecca Garza	. . .	Steven Hailey	Claude Jones	Terry Ellerbrook
Lucas	c	MC	2	(972) 727-8999	. . .	Robert Patrick	. . .	. . .	. . .	. . .	. . .
Lufkin	c	CM	32	(936) 633-0228	. . .	Paul Parker	Atha Martin	Douglas Wood	Fenton Prewitt	Larry Brazil	Kenneth Williams
Luling *	c	CM	5	(830) 875-2481	Mike Hendricks	Robert Berger	Martha Velasquez	Sonny Rougeou	Thomas Harmon	John Cochran	Chris Powell
Madisonville	c	CM	4	(936) 348-2748	Scott Singletary	. . .	Joyce Shiflet	Ruth Smith	Thom Jones	George Sweetir	Vivian Sheffield
Malakoff	c	CM	2	(903) 489-0699	Patricia Isaacson	Thomas Caffall	. . .	. . .	David Files	. . .	. . .
Mansfield	c	CM	28	(817) 473-9371	David Harry	Clayton Chandler	. . .	Peter Phillis	Alexander Rodriguez	Steven Noonkester	Bud Ervin
Manvel	c	MC	3	(281) 489-0630	Delores Martin	. . .	Florence Schumann	. . .	. . .	Ralph Garcia	Fred White
Marble Falls	c	CM	4	(830) 693-3615	Nona Fox	Judy Miller	Christina Laine	Margie Cardenas	Jack Floyd	Mark Whitacre	Perry Malkemus
Marlin	c	MC	6	(254) 883-5542	Tom Black	Gordon Pierce	Dora Vaughan	. . .	Roderick Robinson	Marion Humphrey	Dewey Lee
Marshall	c	CM	23	(903) 935-4416	. . .	Frank Johnson	. . .	. . .	. . .	. . .	. . .
Mathis	c	MC	5	(361) 547-3343	Vicente Gonzalez	. . .	. . .	Kalee Webb	. . .	Oscar Maldonado	Lucio Munoz
Mc Allen	c	CM	106	(956) 972-7160	Leo Montalvo	Mike Perez	Annette Villarreal	Jerry Dale	. . .	Victor Rodriguez	Carlos Sanchez
Mc Gregor	c	CM	4	(254) 840-2806	Felix Morris	Joseph Portugal	. . .	Christine Otter	Ronnie Spradley	Jeff Straub	Jerry Lowrance
Mc Kinney	c	CM	54	(972) 547-7500	Bill Whitfield	L. Ragan	Jennifer Sproull	Jennifer Fung	Mark Wallace	Douglas Kowalski	. . .
Meadows *	c	MC	4	(806) 539-2377	Eloisa Cuellar	. . .	. . .	. . .	Roberto Campos	. . .	Roberto Camdos
Melissa	c	CM	1	(972) 838-2338	David Dorman	Jason Little	Linda Bannister	Gail Dansby	David Wright	Duane Smith	Mark Maulding
Memphis *	c	MC	2	(806) 259-3001	Robert Maddox	Nelwyn Ward	Cindy Woodard	. . .	James Edwards	Jehromie Penrod	Kirby Gardenhire
Menard	c	CM	1	(915) 396-4706	. . .	Sharon Key	Lupe McSherry	. . .	. . .	. . .	Rhome Hill
Mercedes	c	CM	13	(956) 565-3114	Joel Quintanilla	. . .	Arcelia Felix	Gilda Cordova	. . .	Omar Lucio	Jesse Villarreal
Mesquite	c	CM	124	(972) 288-7711	Mike Anderson	Ted Barron	Judy Womack	Donald Simons	Jim Stark	Gary Westphal	Tim Tumulty
Mexia	c	CM	6	(254) 562-4100	Steve Brewer	. . .	. . .	Carolyn Martin	Clayton Shivers	Richard Hawthorne	Fred Samford
Midland	c	CM	94	(432) 685-7100	Mike Canon	Courtney Sharp	Kaylah McCord	Robert McNaughton	Andrew Mehl	John Urby	Charles Swallow
Midlothian	c	CM	7	(972) 775-3481	Boyce Whatley	Ronald Stephens	Lou Jameson	Jimmie McClure	David Schrodt	William Campbell	Adam Mergener
Mineola	c	MC	4	(903) 569-6183	N. Smith	. . .	David Stevenson	. . .	. . .	Charles Bittner	. . .
Mineral Wells	c	CM	16	(940) 328-1211	Earl Medlin	Lance Howerton	Juanita Formby	Scott Blasor	Robert Spears	Jerry White	. . .
Mission	c	CM	45	(956) 580-8650	Norberto Salinas	Julio Cerda	Anna Carrillo	Janie Flores	Ricardo Saldana	Leonardo Longoria	Francisco Flores
Missouri City	c	CM	52	(281) 261-4260	. . .	. . .	. . .	. . .	Russell Sander	. . .	David Dorger
Monahans	c	CM	6	(915) 943-4343	David Cutbirth	David Mills	. . .	Shirlan Turner	Billy Riley	David Watts	. . .
Morgan'S Point	c	CM	. .	(281) 471-2171	. . .	Kenneth Bays	Jenny Redden	. . .	. . .	. . .	Robe Belgau
Morton *	c	MC	2	(806) 266-8850	Edward Akin	Brenda Shaw	. . .	. . .	Edward Amalla	. . .	Frank Enriquez
Mount Pleasant	c	CM	13	(903) 575-4000	Jerry Boatner	. . .	. . .	Brenda Reynolds	Larry McRae	. . .	Darrell Grubbs

Directory 1/9 continued — OFFICIALS IN U.S. MUNICIPALITIES 2,500 AND OVER IN POPULATION

Jurisdiction	Type	Form of govern-ment	2000 Popu-lation	Main telephone number	Chief elected official	Appointed administrator	Clerk of the governing board	Chief financial officer	Fire chief	Police chief	Public works director
TEXAS continued											
Muenster	c	CM	1	(940) 759-2236	John Pagel	Stan Endres	Micallee Matson	. . .	Herbie Knabe	Robert Stovall	. . .
Muleshoe	c	CM	4	(806) 272-4528	Victor Leal	David Brunson	LeAnn Gallman	. . .	Richard Ronek	Don Carter	Ramon Sanchez
Munday	c	MC	1	(940) 422-4331	. . .	John Weeks	. . .	. . .	. . .	. . .	. . .
Murphy *	c	MC	3	(972) 468-4006	Bret Baldwin	James Fisher	Aimee Nemer	Linda Truitt	Mark Lee	GM Cox	Johnny Boles
Nacogdoches *	c	CM	29	(936) 559-2506	Bob Dunn	James Jeffers	Lila Fuller	Jack Sparks	Keith Kiplinger	Jimmie Sevey	Wayne Shepherd
Nassau Bay	c	CM	4	(281) 333-4211	Donald Matter	John Kennedy	Patsy Jones	David Quick	. . .	Ronald Wrobleski	Phil Briscoe
Navasota	c	CM	6	(936) 825-6475	Patricia Gruner	Brad Stafford	. . .	Geraldine Binford	Jason Katkoski	. . .	Gary Johnson
Nederland *	c	CM	17	(409) 723-1500	R. A. Nugent	Christopher Duque	La Donna Floyd	. . .	Gary Collins	Darrell Bush	Steve Hamilton
New Boston	t	MC	4	(903) 628-5596	Johnny Branson	Carol Ensey	Gladys Nelson	. . .	. . .	Kerry Pinkham	R. Thomas
New Braunfels *	c	CM	36	(830) 221-4000	Bruce Boyer	Michael Morrison	Michael Resendez	Deborah Korinchock	John Robinson	Ronald Everett	Steven Ramsey
Nocona	c	MC	3	(940) 825-3282	. . .	Lynn Henley	Revell Hardison	. . .	. . .	Kent Holcomb	. . .
North Richland Hills	c	CM	55	(817) 427-6000	Tommy Brown	Larry Cunningham	Patricia Hutson	. . .	Andrew Jones	Jerry McGlasson	Gregory Dickens
Northlake *	t	MC	. .	(940) 648-3290	Peter Dewing	Drew Corn	Shirley Rogers	. . .	. . .	David Henley	Larry Roumell
Oak Leaf *	c	MC	1	(972) 617-2660	. . .	. . .	Ronda Quintana	. . .	. . .	. . .	. . .
Oak Point	c	CM	1	(972) 294-2312	Duane Olson	Richard Martin	Mary Beth Thomas	. . .	. . .	. . .	Mike Sloggett
Oak Ridge North	c	CM	2	(281) 292-4648	. . .	Paul Mendes	Su Powell	. . .	. . .	Andrew Walters	Lawrence Bienvenu
Odessa	c	CM	90	(432) 335-3200	Larry Melton	Richard Morton	Norma Aguilar	James Zentner	Richard Dietz	Chris Pipes	Matt Squyres
Olmos Park	c	CM	2	(210) 824-3281	Gerald Dubinski	Amy Buckert	. . .	. . .	Mark Medbury	Louis Alcoser	. . .
Olney	c	CM	3	(940) 564-2102	Mary Schoonover	Danny Parker	Lee Campbell	Wanda Clifton	Garry Keeter	Scott Given	Ronnie Stroud
Orange *	c	CM	18	(409) 886-3611	William Claybar	. . .	Kerry Kittrell	Susan English	David Frenzel	Sam Kittrell	James Wolf
Ovilla	c	CM	3	(972) 617-7262	William Turner	John McDonald	Tammy McCoy	. . .	Donnie Pickard	Michael Moon	Tony Bumpus
Palacios	c	MC	5	(361) 972-3605	John Connor	Charles Winfield	Patsy Gibson	. . .	Don Kopecky	Bernando Gurrerro	John Martinez
Palestine	c	CM	17	(903) 731-8400	George Foss	R. Brown	Ann Pesce	Robert Sherrill	Henry York	Charles Edge	Ron Sullivan
Pampa	c	CM	17	(806) 669-5750	Lonny Robbins	. . .	Phyllis Jeffers	. . .	Kim Powell	Trevlyn Pitner	Richard Morris
Panhandle	c	CM	2	(806) 537-3517	Les McNeill	Loren Brant	Connie McKiernan	. . .	Roy Tarpley	Jeffery Oldham	Lenro Jennings
Pantego	t	CM	2	(817) 274-1381	Dorothy Aderholt	Doug Davis	Norma Zenk	Fitzhugh Newsome	Thomas Griffith	Jon Coulter	Ronald Edwards
Paris *	c	CM	25	(903) 785-7511	Jesse Freelen	Kevin Carruth	Janice Ellis	Warren Anderson	Ronnie Grooms	Roger Louis	Shawn Napier
Parker	c	MC	1	(972) 442-6811	. . .	Dena Daniel	. . .	. . .	. . .	. . .	. . .
Pasadena	c	MC	141	(713) 477-1511	John Manlove	. . .	Linda Rorick	Wayne Long	Jerry Gardner	Mike Massey	Melvin Embry
Pearland	c	CM	37	(281) 652-1600	. . .	William Eisen	. . .	Claire Manthei	. . .	Chris Doyle	Jerry Burns
Pearsall	c	CM	7	(830) 334-3676	Roland Segovir	Jose Trevino	Amy Padilla	. . .	Steve Parsons	Ray Talamarto	Alex Hernandez
Pecos	c	CM	9	(915) 445-2421	Dot Stafford	. . .	Geneva Martinez	Steve McCormick	Doug Cox	Troy Moore	Octavio Garcia
Perryton	c	CM	7	(806) 435-4014	. . .	David Landis	. . .	. . .	. . .	. . .	. . .
Pflugerville *	c	CM	16	(512) 990-4363	Jeff Coleman	David Buesing	Karen Thompson	. . .	. . .	. . .	James Wills
Pharr	c	CO	46	(956) 702-5335	Ricardo Medina	Fred Sandoval	Dora Garza	Juan Guerra	Jaime Guzman	Jesse Medina	Frank Vecchio
Pilot Point	c	MC	3	(940) 686-2165	. . .	Vicky Varnau	. . .	. . .	. . .	. . .	. . .
Pinehurst	c	CM	2	(409) 886-2221	. . .	C. Nash	. . .	. . .	. . .	. . .	. . .
Piney Point Village *	c	MC	3	(713) 782-0271	Carol Fox	Lorena Briel	Samantha Watts	. . .	Anthony Calagna	Gary Brye	Bob Peach
Pittsburg	c	CM	4	(903) 856-3621	. . .	. . .	Margaret Jackson	. . .	. . .	Martin Pessink	Wayne Hadderton
Plainview	c	CM	22	(806) 296-1100	John Anderson	Greg Ingham	Belinda Hinojosa	Jack Keller	H. Glass	William Mull	John Berry
Plano	c	CM	222	(972) 941-7000	Pat Evans	T. Muehlenbeck	Elaine Bealke	John McGrane	Hugo Esparza	Greg Rushin	Jimmy Foster
Pleasanton *	c	CM	8	(830) 569-3867	William Carroll	Kathy Coronado	Cynthia Urrabazo	. . .	Chuck Garris	Gary Soward	Juan Martinez
Port Aransas *	c	CM	3	(361) 749-4111	Claude Brown	Michael Kovacs	. . .	Darla Honea	Scott Mack	. . .	Douglas Box
Port Arthur	c	CM	57	(409) 983-8100	Deloris Prince	Stephen Fitzgibbons	Terri Hanks	Rebecca Underhill	Larry Richard	William Blanton	John Comeaux
Port Isabel	c	CM	4	(956) 943-2682	Pat Marchan	Robert Garcia	Nancy Davalos	Pete Capistran	Hector Bennett	Joel Ochoa	Baldemar Alaniz
Port Lavaca	c	CM	12	(361) 552-9795	Allen Tharling	Gary Broz	. . .	Gerald Durocher	Raymond Tennisen	John Stewart	. . .
Port Neches *	c	CM	13	(409) 727-2182	Glenn Johnson	Andre' Wimer	Patty Faulk	Amy Guidroz	Steve Curran	Paul Lemoine	Taylor Shelton
Portland	c	CM	14	(361) 643-6501	David Krebs	Michael Tanner	Annette Rodriguez	Sandra Clarkson	James Nelson	Randy Wright	Kim Parker
Post *	c	CM	3	(806) 495-2811	Kim Mills	Richard Walton	. . .	. . .	Leslie Looney	. . .	Paul Perez
Poteet	c	MC	3	(830) 742-3574	Diana Martinez	. . .	Cathy Leal	. . .	Pete Ramirez	Frank Leal	Adolfo Rodriguez
Pottsboro *	c	CM	1	(903) 786-2281	Frank Budra	Kevin Farley	Denise Smith	. . .	Donnie Glenn	Brett Arterburn	Darren Vaden
Prairie View	c	MC	4	(936) 857-3711	Frank Jaconson	. . .	. . .	. . .	Frank Jackson	Wilbert White	Scott Spidale
Premont	c	MC	2	(361) 348-2022	Mario Rodriguez	. . .	Iris Flores	. . .	Jerry Larue	. . .	Lorenzo Cabrera
Princeton	c	MC	3	(972) 736-2416	Kathy Davis	Lee Lawrence	Thomas Wyatt	Lara Feagins	Mike Woody	Rick Cantrell	. . .
Progreso	c	MC	4	(956) 565-0241	Arturo Valdez	. . .	Ana Delgado	Ponciano Garcia	. . .	Xavier Martinez	. . .
Prosper *	t	CM	2	(972) 346-2640	Charles Niswanger	Michael Land	Matthew Denton	Matthew Garrett	Ronnie Tucker	Kirk McFarlin	Frank Jaromin
Quanah	c	CM	3	(940) 663-5536	Jess Adkins	. . .	Paula Wilson	Patricia Elliott	Ricky Burton	Guy Smith	Tony Tallant
Ralls	c	MC	2		. . .	J. R. Parker	. . .	. . .	. . .	. . .	. . .
Ranger *	c	CO	2	(254) 647-3522	John Casey	. . .	Troy Emery	Margaret Green	Louis Fox	Elton McCoy	Adam Lopez
Ransom Canyon	t	MC	1	(806) 829-2470	. . .	Melissa Verett	. . .	. . .	. . .	. . .	. . .
Raymondville	c	CM	9	(956) 689-2443	C. Crowell	Eleazar Garcia	. . .	. . .	. . .	. . .	Octavio Correa
Red Oak *	c	CM	4	(972) 617-3638	Alan Hugley	Eric Thompson	Cynthia Olguin	Miykael Reeve	. . .	Craig Rudolph	Charles Brewer
Refugio	c	MC	2	(512) 526-5361	Ray Jaso	. . .	Callie Shreckengost	. . .	Don Pullin	Chris Brock	Clifford Lynn
Richardson *	c	CM	91	(972) 744-4000	Steve Mitchell	William Keffler	Pamela Schmidt	Kenton Pfeil	Alan Palomba	David Zacharias	Jerry Ortega
Richland Hills	c	CM	8	(817) 299-1800	David Ragan	James Quin	Kim Sutter	Barbara Mann	Davis Anderson	Barbara Childress	Michael Barnes
Richmond *	t	CM	11	(281) 342-5456	Hilmar Moore	Robert Gilmore	Ramona Matak	Terri Vela	Stephen Noto	William Whitworth	Lenert Kurtz
Richwood	c	MC	3	(979) 265-2082	Sandra Boykin	. . .	Karen Schrom	. . .	Mark Guthrie	Glenn Patton	Don Malone
Rio Grande City	c	CM	11	(956) 487-0672	Kevin Hiles	Juan Zuniga	Holly Guerrero	Mary Barrera	Ricardo Reyes	Guadalupe Marquez	Fernando Guerra
River Oaks	c	MC	6	(817) 626-5421	Herman Earwood	Linda Ryan	. . .	. . .	David Hubbard	Daniel Chisholm	Marvin Gregory
Roanoke	c	CM	2	(817) 491-2411	. . .	James Stathatos	. . .	. . .	. . .	. . .	. . .
Robinson	c	MC	7	(254) 662-1415	Bryan Ferguson	Richard Fletcher	Linda Vranich	Karen Sanchez	Gerald Groppe	Rusty Smith	Dale Pattillo
Robstown	c	MC	12	(361) 387-4589	Rodrigo Ramon	Paula Wakefield	. . .	Isabel Barrientes	Richard Gonzalez	Carlos Pena	Roy Gutierrez
Rockdale	c	CM	5	(512) 446-2511	John Shoemake	Abbey Flemming	Shelli Turner	. . .	Elvis McQuinn	Thomas Harris	Eddie Zapata
Rockport	c	CM	7	(361) 729-2213	Todd Pearson	Thomas Blazek	Irma Parker	Jacky Cockerham	. . .	Tim Jayroe	Billy Dick
Rockwall	c	CM	17	(972) 771-7700	Ken Jones	Julie Couch	Belinda Page	. . .	Mark Poindexter	William Watkins	Chuck Todd
Roma	c	CM	9	(956) 849-1411	Fernando Pena	Rogeio Salinas	Josie Hinojosa	Marco Soto	Jose Garcia	Emilio Montalvo	Jorge Munoz
Rosebud	c	CM	1	(254) 583-7926	Ken Hensel	Megan Henderson	Kim Kennedy	. . .	Rick Trubee	Earl Winebrenner	Rudy Reyna
Rosenberg *	c	CM	24	(832) 595-3310	Joe Gurecky	Jack Hamlett	Linda Cernosek	Mindi Snyder	Kathleen Hutchens	Robert Gracia	Kenneth Jansky
Round Rock	c	CM	61	(512) 218-5490	Nyle Maxwell	James Nuse	Christine Martinez	Cindy Demers	Lynn Bizzell	Paul Conner	Tom Word
Rowlett	c	CM	44	(972) 412-6100	Christopher Johnson	George Harris	Janita Quinn	Brian Funderburk	Lawrence Wright	James Walling	Patrick Baugh
Royse City	c	MC	2	(972) 636-2250	Jim Mellody	Karen Philippi	Brenda Craft	. . .	Richard Bell	. . .	. . .
Rusk	c	CM	5	(903) 683-2213	. . .	Michael Murray	. . .	. . .	Wayne Morgan	Ronny Miller	Gene Kelley
Sachse	c	CM	9	(972) 495-1212	Mike Felix	Allen Barnes	Terrence Smith	Alan Dickerson	Doug Kendrick	Richard Benedict	Joey Crase
Saginaw	c	CM	12	(817) 232-4640	Gary Brinkley	Nan Stanford	Nelda Mays	. . .	Bob Harvey	Roger Macon	Terry Highfill
San Angelo	c	CM	88	(915) 657-4221	. . .	Harold Dominguez	Kathy Keane	Michael Dane	Brian Dunn	Joe Gibson	Will Wilde
San Antonio *	c	CM	1144	(210) 207-7080	Phil Hardberger	Sheryl Sculley	Leticia Vacek	Ben Gorzell	Charles Hood	William McManus	Majed Al-Ghafry
San Augustine	c	MC	2	(936) 275-2121	. . .	Duke Lyons	Cinda Garner	. . .	. . .	Ken Delaserda	. . .
San Benito	c	CM	23	(956) 361-3800	Cesar Gonzalez	Manuel Lara	Lupita Passenent	. . .	. . .	. . .	. . .
San Diego	c	MC	4	(361) 279-3341	Alfredo Cardenas	Ramon Tanguma	Isabel Trevino	Ernesto Sanchez	. . .	Abelizario Escalan	. . .
San Juan	c	CM	26	(956) 702-6400	. . .	Guillermo Seguin	. . .	Steven Austin	Tirso Garza	Juan Garza	John Avielz
San Marcos	c	CM	34	(512) 393-8000	Robert Habingreither	Rick Menchaca	Janis Womack	James Gonzales	Todd Derkacz	. . .	Richard Mendoza
Sanger *	c	MC	4	(940) 458-7930	Joe Higgs	Michael Brice	Rose Chavez	. . .	David Pennington	Curtis Amyx	Robert Woods
Sansom Park Village	c	MC	4	(817) 626-3791	Mike Wasser	Deana McMullen	. . .	. . .	. . .	. . .	. . .
Santa Fe *	c	CM	9	(409) 925-6412	Robert Cheek	Joe Dickson	Janet Davis	. . .	Tommy Anderson	. . .	Chris Beanland
Santa Rosa	c	MC	2		. . .	Jose Lopez	. . .	. . .	. . .	. . .	. . .
Schertz *	c	CM	18	(210) 619-1000	Hal Baldwin	Donald Taylor	Judy Tokar	Juan Santova	Glen Outlaw	Stephen Starr	Sam Willoughby

Directory 1/9 continued **OFFICIALS IN U.S. MUNICIPALITIES 2,500 AND OVER IN POPULATION**

Jurisdiction		Type	Form of govern-ment	2000 Popu-lation	Main telephone number	Chief elected official	Appointed administrator	Clerk of the governing board	Chief financial officer	Fire chief	Police chief	Public works director
TEXAS continued												
Seabrook		c	CM	9	(281) 474-3201	...	...	...	...	...	...	Gary Jones
Seagoville		c	CM	10	(972) 287-2050	Calvin Travers	...	Ruth Sorrells	Shirley Booth	Tommy Lemond	I. Smith	Michael Hitt
Seagraves		c	MC	2	(806) 387-2593	...	Catherine Mitchell	Jacqueline Orum	...	...	Richard Cordell	James Fischer
Sealy		c	CM	5	(979) 885-3511	Betty Reinbeck	Christopher Coffman	Krisha Langton	Steven Kutra	...	Brad Murray	Larry Mayberry
Seguin	*	c	CM	22	(830) 379-3212	Betty Matthies	Douglas Faseler	...	Susan Caddell	Scott Mycue	Kevin Kelso	Ruben Perez
Selma		c	CM	..	(210) 651-6661	Jim Parma	Kenneth Roberts	...	...	Ric Braun	Sydnor Hall	...
Seminole		c	CM	5	(915) 758-3676	Wayne Mixon	Tommy Phillips	...	...	...	...	...
Seymour		c	MC	2	(940) 889-3148	Dan Craighead	Joseph Shephard	Conchita Torrez	Mary Griffin	Randy Coltharp	Tommy Duncan	...
Shamrock		c	CM	2	(806) 256-3281	...	...	...	...	...	...	...
Shavano Park		c	CM	1	(210) 493-3478	Pete Fleischhacker	Manny Longoria	Brian Harrison	James Percival	Linc Surber	Leo Stewart	Rogelio Quiroqa
Shenandoah	*	c	MC	1	(281) 298-5522	Garry Watts	Chip Vansteenberg	Susan Hensley	...	...	John Chancellor	Brian LaBorde
Sherman	*	c	CM	35	(903) 892-7201	Bill Magers	George Olson	Linda Ashby	...	Jeffrey Jones	Tom Watt	Jeffrey Miller
Shoreacres		c	CM	1	(281) 471-2244	Nancy Edmonson	David Stall	...	...	...	Randall French	Eloy Gonzalez
Silsbee	*	c	CM	6	(409) 385-2863	Herbert Muckleroy	Charles Bartosh	...	...	Berl Slaydan	Dennis Allen	Joe Moreno
Sinton		t	CM	5	(361) 364-2381	...	Ira Knox	Betty Wood	...	...	Eugene Deleon	Beverly Agomuo
Slaton		c	CM	6	(806) 828-2000	Laura Wilson	Roger McKinney	Toni Chrestman	...	Joe Scott	Jeff Creager	Doyce Field
Smithville		c	CM	3	(512) 237-3282	Renee Blaschke	Price Middlebrook	Brenda Page	...	...	Delvin Dockery	Jack Page
Snyder	*	c	CM	10	(325) 573-4957	Francine Allen Noah	Merle Taylor	Teresa Wall	Jeanne Johnson	Perry Westmoreland	Terry Luecke	Bobby Kenner
Sonora	*	c	MC	2	(325) 387-2558	...	Dean Carrell	Patti Prather	...	Rick Cearley	...	...
Sour Lake		c	MC	1	(409) 287-3573	...	Larry Saurage	...	...	...	...	...
South Houston		c	MC	15	(713) 947-7700	Joe Soto	...	Maria Vega	...	Jesse Garcia	Herbet Gilbert	...
South Padre Island	*	t	CM	2	(956) 761-6456	Robert Pinkerton	Dewey Cashwell	Susan Hill	Lawrence Homan	Burney Baskett	Robert Rodriguez	Scott Fry
Southlake		c	CM	21	(817) 481-1653	Andy Wambsganss	Shana Yelverton	Lori Farwell	Sharon Elam	Robert Finn	Marlin Price	Pedram Farahnak
Southside Place		c	MC	1	(713) 668-2341	Richard Rothfelder	David Moss	...	...	...	...	...
Spearman		c	CM	3	(806) 659-2524	...	Edward Hansen	Cheryl Salgado	...	...	...	Danny Parker
Spring Valley		c	MC	3	(713) 465-8308	Tammy Canon	R. Rockenbaugh	Betty Lusk	...	...	John Cook	...
Stafford		t	MC	15	(281) 261-3900	Leonard Scarcella	...	...	Karen Austin	Mike Melton	Bonny Krahn	Lawrence Vaccaro
Stamford	*	c	CM	3	(325) 773-2591	Johnny Anders	Roy Rice	Susan Trotter	Kim Keith	Wyatt Oakley	Darwin Huston	Gary Bell
Stanton		c	CM	2	(432) 756-3336	...	Danny Fryar	...	...	...	...	...
Stephenville		c	CM	14	(254) 918-1220	Rusty Jergins	Mark Kaiser	Cindy Stafford	Donald Ives	Jimmy Chew	Mark Johnson	...
Sugar Land		c	CM	63	(281) 275-2700	David Wallace	Allen Bogard	G. Gundermann	Linda Symank	Dannie Smith	Steve Griffith	Tommy Haynes
Sulphur Springs		c	CM	14	(903) 885-7541	Brad Burgin	Marc Maxwell	Sharon Ricketson	Peter Karstens	Gerry Cleaver	James Bayuk	...
Sundown		c	CM	1	(806) 229-3131	Jim Winn	...	Toni Wilson	...	Doug Barry	Jerry Escobar	Barry Stephens
Sunnyvale		t	CM	2	(972) 226-7177	Jim Phaup	Hugh Campbell	...	...	...	...	...
Sunray		c	CM	1	(806) 948-4111	...	...	...	Kathy Lee	...	Tommy Bogart	K. Perry
Sunset Valley		c	MC	..	(512) 892-1383	...	...	...	...	...	...	...
Sweeny		c	CM	3	(979) 548-3321	Larry Piper	Tim Moss	Reatta Minshew	...	Billy Ward	Gary Stroud	Homer Toscano
Sweetwater	*	c	CM	11	(325) 236-6313	...	Edward Brown	...	Carolyn Lawrence	Grant Madden	James Kelley	Ray Adames
Taft		c	MC	3	(512) 528-3512	...	Florencio Sauceda	...	...	...	David Wood	Ruth Robertson
Tahoka		c	CM	2	(806) 998-4211	Mike Mensch	Jerry Webster	Cheryl Krey	...	Steve Miller	Doyle Lee	David Graves
Taylor	*	c	CM	13	(512) 352-3675	Rodney Hortenstine	Jim Dunaway	Susan Brock	Rosemarie Dennis	Bruce Watson	Jeffrey Straub	Danny Thomas
Taylor Lake Village	*	c	MC	3	(281) 326-2843	Natalie O'Neill	...	...	...	...	...	...
Teague	*	c	MC	4	(254) 739-2547	Jacquline Utsey	Don Doering	Beverly Johnson	Michelle Lyons	Tim Hedrick	Dennis Cox	Gus Ramirez
Temple	*	c	CM	54	(254) 298-5650	William Jones	David Blackburn	Clydette Entzminger	Tracie Barnard	Lonzo Wallace	Gary Smith	Bruce Butscher
Terrell		c	CM	13	(972) 551-6600	Frances Anderson	Torry Edwards	...	John Rounsavall	James Harper	Michael Shewmake	Robert Rogers
Terrell Hills	*	c	CM	5	(210) 824-7401	J. Camp	James Browne	Betty Gover	...	...	Greg Whitlock	Jimmy Phelps
Texarkana		c	CM	34	(903) 798-3915	James Bramlett	George Shackelford	Geri Haddock	Charles Bassett	Harry Simms	Danny Alexander	Philip Ball
Texas City		c	MC	41	(409) 643-5930	Matthew Doyle	...	Pamela Lawrence	Cheryl Hunter	Gerald Grimm	Robert Burby	Thomas Kessler
The Colony	*	c	CM	26	(972) 624-3135	John Dillard	Dale Cheatham	Christie Wilson	Rebecca Koo	Scott Thompson	Joseph Clark	Stephen Eubanks
Tomball	*	c	CM	9	(281) 351-5484	Gretchen Fagan	Jan Belcher	Doris Speer	...	Randall Parr	Robert Hauck	David Kauffman
Trophy Club		t	MC	6	(682) 831-4600	Scott Smith	Donna Welsh	Diane Cockrell	Roger Unger	...	...	...
Tulia		c	CM	5	(806) 995-3547	John Emmitt	Ricky Crownover	Barbara Cabe	...	Wayne Nevins	Jimmy McCaslin	Roy Campbell
Tyler	*	c	CM	83	(903) 531-1112	Joey Seeber	Robert Turner	Cassandra Brager	Daniel Crawford	Neal Franklin	Gary Swindle	Gregory Morgan
Uhland		c	MC	..	(512) 398-7399	...	Diana Woods	...	...	...	...	...
Universal City		c	CM	14	(210) 659-0333	...	Kenneth Taylor	Alene Patton	Karl McCormick	Ross Wallace	Floyd Bryant	Antonio Rivas
University Park	*	c	CM	23	(214) 363-1644	James Holmes	T. Livingston	...	Kent Austin	Randy Howell	Gary Adams	Bud Smallwood
Uvalde		c	CM	14	(830) 278-3315	Gus Neutze	John Harrell	...	Jorge Trevino	Jimmy Howard	Joel Sanchez	...
Van Alstyne		c	CM	2	(903) 482-5426	...	...	...	...	...	...	...
Van Horn		t	MC	2	(432) 283-2050	...	Rebecca Brewster	Virginia Carrasco	Jodi Corrales	...	...	Raquel Mendez
Venus	*	t	MC	..	(972) 366-3348	Carolyn Welcher	Jerry Reed	...	...	...	...	...
Vernon		c	CM	11	(940) 552-2581	R. Couch	...	...	Jerry Rogers	...	...	Ronnie Richie
Victoria		c	CM	60	(361) 485-3500	Will Armstrong	Charles Windwehen	Scarlet Swoboda	Gilbert Reyna	Vance Riley	Howard Ure	John Johnston
Vidor	*	c	MC	11	(409) 769-5473	Ray Long	Ricky Jorgensen	Rhonda Haskins	Lorrie Taylor	...	Eric Foerster	Byron Richard
Waco		c	CM	113	(254) 750-5600	Mike Morrison	Larry Groth	Patricia Ervin	Janice Andrews	Jon Fasana	Gilbert Miller	...
Wake Village		c	MC	5	(903) 838-0515	Mike Huddleston	Bob Long	Wanda Sandlin	...	Bruce Dinsmore	Tony Estes	...
Watauga	*	c	CM	21	(817) 514-5819	Harry Jeffries	Kerry Lacy	Daniela Place	Scott Neils	William Crawford	Rande Benjamine	Johnnie Reagan
Waxahachie	*	c	CM	21	(972) 937-7330	Ron Wilkinson	Paul Stevens	Lori Saunders	Charles Harris	David Hudgins	Charles Edge	Jeff Chambers
Weatherford		c	CM	19	(817) 598-4000	Joe Tison	...	Angie Winkle	Renita Bishop	George Teague	Jerry Blaisdell	...
Webster	*	c	CM	9	(281) 332-1826	Floyd Myers	Wayne Sabo	Pauline Small	Michael Rodgers	Patrick Shipp	Ray Smiley	Shannon Hicks
Weimar		c	CM	1	(979) 725-8554	...	Randal Jones	Dolores Stoever	Wade Cernosek	...	Bill Livingston	...
Wellington		c	CM	2	(806) 447-2544	...	Jon Sessions	...	...	...	...	...
Weslaco		c	CM	26	(956) 968-3181	...	Anthony Covacevich	...	James Hiebert	Arturo Avila	Juan Martinez	Juan Flores
West Columbia		c	CM	4	(979) 345-3123	David Foster	Deborah Sutherland	Kelli Kuban	Rhonda Weems	Jimmy Chafin	Don Fairrel	...
West Lake Hills		c	MC	3	(512) 327-3628	...	Robert Wood	Janet Rogers	...	...	...	...
West Orange	*	c	MC	4	(409) 883-3468	Roy McDonald	...	Theresa Van Meter	...	Randy Veitch	Michael Stelly	Ron Garrison
West Tawakoni	*	c	MC	1	(903) 447-2285	Pete Yoho	Cloy Richards	Annette Lemons	Susan Roberts	...	Jack Schultz	Ken Newville
West University Place		c	CM	14	(713) 668-4441	Richard Ballanfant	Michael Ross	Kaylynn Holloway	Walter Thomas	Terry Stevenson	...	Ronald Wicker
Westlake	*	t	CM	..	(817) 430-0941	Scott Bradley	Thomas Brymer	Kim Sutter	Debbie Piper	Don Wilson	...	Jarrod Greenwood
Westworth Village		c	MC	2	(817) 738-3673	Andy Foutenot	Gary Robinson	Shelli Branson	...	Don Day	Doug Reim	...
Wharton	*	c	CM	9	(979) 532-2491	David Samuelson	Andres Garza	...	Joyce Vasut	Bobby Barnett	Timothy Guin	Carter Miska
White Oak		c	MC	5	(903) 759-3936	Tim Vaughn	Ralph Weaver	Lisa Blount	...	Jimmy Nall	...	Kelly Mitchell
White Settlement		c	CM	14	(817) 246-4971	...	Jimmie Burnett	Lucy Polk	...	...	David Place	Mark White
Whitesboro		t	MC	3	(903) 564-3311	W. D. Welch	Michael Marter	Brenda Goldsmith	...	Kevin Walton	Scott Taylor	Donald Zielke
Wichita Falls		c	CM	104	(940) 761-7404	Lanham Lyne	Darron Leiker	Lydia Toress	James Dockery	Earl Foster	Dennis Bachman	John Taylor
Willis		c	MC	3	(936) 856-4611	Leonard Reed	James McAlister	Brenda Burns	...	...	James Nowak	Jerry Humphreys
Wills Point		c	CM	3	(903) 873-2578	Roy Caldwell	Carman Girdley	Carla Oldacre	...	Robert Tisdale	Rickey Willis	Scott Drake
Wimberley		v	MC	3	(512) 847-0025	...	Donald Ferguson	...	...	...	...	...
Windcrest		c	MC	5	(210) 655-0022	Jack Leonhardt	F. Cain	Tracy Freimarck	...	Tom Winn	Rick Pruitt	Byron Vick
Winnsboro		c	MC	3	(903) 342-3654	Carolyn Jones	Ronny Knight	Nina Browning	Wanda Renshaw	...	James Whittiker	...
Winters		c	CM	2	(915) 754-4424	Dawson McGuffin	Mir Hassan	Saffron Gibbs	...	Jack Davis	L. Balentine	Charles Grenwelge
Woodlands Township	*	tp	CM	64	(281) 363-2447	...	Donald Norrell	...	Monique Sharp	...	...	...
Woodville	*	t	MC	2	(409) 283-2234	Ben Bythewood	Charles Comte	Terri Bible	...	Tommy Shane	Scott Yosko	...
Woodway		c	CM	8	(254) 772-4480	Donald Baker	Yousry Zakhary	Jennifer Canady	William Klump	...	...	...
Wylie	*	c	CM	15	(972) 442-8100	...	Mindy Manson	Carole Ehrlich	Melissa Beard	Randy Corbin	John Duscio	Mike Sferra
Yoakum		c	CM	5	(361) 293-6321	Anita Rodriguez	Calvin Cook	Theresa Bowe	Charlotte Morrow	Phillip Baker	Arthur Rogers	...

Directory 1/9 continued — OFFICIALS IN U.S. MUNICIPALITIES 2,500 AND OVER IN POPULATION

Jurisdiction	Type	Form of govern-ment	2000 Popu-lation	Main telephone number	Chief elected official	Appointed administrator	Clerk of the governing board	Chief financial officer	Fire chief	Police chief	Public works director
UTAH											
Alpine	c	MC	7	(801) 756-6347	Don Watkins	Ted Stillman	Janis Williams	. . .	. . .	. . .	Jay Healey
Alta	t	MC	. .	(801) 742-3522	Tom Pollard	John Guldner	Katherine Black	. . .	. . .	Jerry Larson	. . .
American Fork	c	MC	21	(801) 763-3000	Ted Barratt	Carl Wanlass	Richard Colborn	. . .	Paul Peters	John Durrant	. . .
Blanding	c	CM	3	(435) 678-2791	Calvin Balch	Chris Webb	Patricia Bartlett	. . .	Gordon Hawkins	Melvin Halliday	Jeff Black
Bluffdale	c	CM	4	(801) 254-2200	. . .	. . .	. . .	. . .	. . .	. . .	. . .
Bountiful	c	CM	41	(801) 298-6118	Joe Johnson	Thomas Hardy	. . .	Kim Coleman	George Sumner	Paul Rapp	. . .
Brian Head	t	CM	. .	(435) 677-2029	H. Deutschlander	Judy Gubler	. . .	. . .	. . .	Wade Carpenter	Randy Rasmussen
Brigham City	c	MC	17	(435) 734-2001	David Kano	. . .	. . .	Dennis Sheffield	Art Petersen	James Paine	Bruce Leonard
Cedar City	c	MC	20	(435) 586-2950	Harold Shirley	Ronald Chandler	Bonnie Moritz	Jace Bunting	Paul Irons	Glen Miller	Kit Wareham
Cedar Hills	c	MC	3	(801) 785-9668	Michael McGee	Konrad Hildebrandt	Kim Holindrake	Richard Knapp	Craig Carlisle	. . .	. . .
Centerville	c	CM	14	(801) 295-3477	Michael Deamer	Steve Thacker	Marilyn Holje	Blaine Lutz	George Sumner	Neal Worsley	Randy Randall
Clearfield *	c	CM	25	(801) 525-2700	Don Wood	Christopher Hillman	Nancy Dean	. . .	. . .	Jim Schilling	Scott Hodge
Clinton	c	CM	12	(801) 774-2600	Lane Adams	. . .	. . .	. . .	Floyd Petersen	Bill Chilson	Michael Child
Cottonwood Heights	c	CM	27	(801) 545-4154	Kelvyn Cullimore	Liane Stillman	. . .	Dave Muir	. . .	Jon Fassett	Mike Allen
Draper *	c	CM	25	(801) 576-6500	Darrell Smith	Layne Long	Tracy Norr	Danyce Steck	. . .	. . .	David Decker
Eagle Mountain *	t	CM	2	(801) 789-6600	Heather Jackson	John Hendrickson	Fionnuala Kofoed	Gordon Burt	Rand Andrus	. . .	Chris Trusty
Ephraim	c	MC	4	(435) 283-4631	Clifford Birrell	Richard Anderson	Leigh Ann Warnock	Nevin Holmberg	. . .	Ronald Rasmussen	Chad Parry
Farmington	c	CM	12	(801) 451-2383	Scott Harbertson	Max Forbush	Margy Lomax	Keith Johnson	Larry Gregory	Wayne Hansen	Walt Hokanson
Fruit Heights	c	MC	4	(801) 546-0861	Richard Harvey	Richard Marchant	. . .	. . .	. . .	. . .	Jack Palmer
Grantsville	c	MC	6	(435) 884-3411	Merle Cole	Wendy Palmer	. . .	. . .	Lowell Anderson	Danny Johnson	. . .
Gunnison	c	MC	2	(435) 528-7969	. . .	. . .	. . .	. . .	. . .	. . .	. . .
Heber *	c	MC	7	(435) 654-0757	David Phillips	Mark Anderson	Paulette Thurber	. . .	. . .	Edward Rhoades	Stephen Tozier
Helper	c	MC	2	(435) 472-5391	Joseph Bonacci	Jona Skerl	. . .	. . .	Mike Zamantakis	George Zamantakis	. . .
Highland	c	MC	8	(801) 756-5751	Jesse Adamson	Damon Edwards	Winifred Jensen	Lynn Ruff	. . .	. . .	Lloyd Hansen
Hurricane	c	CM	8	(435) 635-2811	. . .	Clark Fawcett	. . .	. . .	Ed Campbell	Lynn Excell	Mac Hall
Hyrum	c	MC	6	(435) 245-6033	. . .	. . .	. . .	. . .	. . .	. . .	. . .
Ivins	t	MC	4	(435) 674-5503	. . .	. . .	. . .	. . .	. . .	. . .	. . .
Kaysville	c	CM	20	(801) 546-1235	. . .	John Thacker	. . .	. . .	. . .	. . .	. . .
La Verkin	c	MC	3	(435) 625-2581	. . .	. . .	. . .	. . .	. . .	. . .	. . .
Layton *	c	CM	58	(801) 336-3800	Jerry Stevenson	Alex Jensen	. . .	Steven Ashby	Kevin Ward	Terry Keefe	Terry Coburn
Lehi *	c	MC	19	(801) 768-7100	Howard Johnson	James Davidson	Connie Ashton	Dave Sanderson	Dale Ekins	Chad Smith	James Hewitson
Lindon *	c	CM	8	(801) 785-5043	James Dain	Ott Dameron	Debra Cullimore	Jamie Bennee	. . .	Cody Cullimore	Don Peterson
Logan	c	MC	42	(435) 716-9043	Douglas Thompson	Laurie Tanner	Lois Price	. . .	Mark Meaker	Richard Hendricks	Mark Nielsen
Manila	t	CM	. .	(435) 784-3143	Chuck Dickison	. . .	Judy Archibald	. . .	. . .	. . .	Jerry Muir
Mapleton	c	MC	5	(801) 489-5655	Dean Allan	Robert Bradshaw	Debbie Walser	. . .	. . .	Mike Roberts	M. Bird
Midvale *	c	MC	27	(801) 567-7200	JoAnn Seghini	Kane Loader	Rori Clark	. . .	Stephen Higgs	. . .	Keith Ludwig
Moab	c	CM	4	(435) 259-5121	David Sakrison	Donna Metzler	Rachel Ellison	. . .	. . .	Mike Navarre	Brent Williams
Monticello	c	CM	1	(435) 587-2271	C. Pehrson	C. Schafer	Rita Walker	. . .	. . .	Kent Adair	Nathan Langston
Murray *	c	MC	34	(801) 264-2656	Daniel Snarr	Jan Wells	Carol Heales	Donald Whetzel	Gilbert Rodriguez	Peter Fondaco	Douglas Hill
Nephi *	c	MC	4	(435) 623-0822	Mark Jones	J. McKnight	. . .	R. Painter	. . .	Chad Bowles	Edwin Park
North Ogden *	c	MC	15	(801) 782-7211	Gary Harrop	Edward Dickie	S. Annette Spendlove	Debbie Cardenas	Lynn Froerer	Polo Afuvai	Melvin Blanchard
North Salt Lake	c	MC	8	(801) 936-3877	Kay Briggs	Collin Wood	LaRae Dillingham	Brian Passey	. . .	Steve Harder	Rod Wood
Ogden City	c	MC	77	(801) 629-8730	Matthew Godfrey	John Patterson	Cindi Mansell	A. Arrington	Michael Mathieu	Jon Greiner	. . .
Orem	c	CM	84	(801) 229-7035	Jerry Washburn	James Reams	. . .	. . .	Scott Gurney	. . .	Bruce Chesnut
Panquitch	c	CM	1	(435) 676-8585	Janet Oldham	Allen Henrie	Cindy Johnson	. . .	. . .	. . .	Dave Owens
Park City *	c	MC	7	(435) 615-5242	. . .	Thomas Bakaly	. . .	Lori Collett	. . .	Wade Carpenter	Jerry Gibbs
Payson	c	CM	12	(801) 465-5200	Bernall Evans	Richard Nelson	Cheryl Hobbs	Jeanette Curtis	Scott Spencer	Franklyn Rowland	. . .
Pleasant Grove	c	MC	23	(801) 785-5045	Lloyd Ash	. . .	Charmaine Childs	K. Driggs	Mark Hales	. . .	Frank Mills
Pleasant View	c	MC	5	(801) 782-8529	. . .	. . .	. . .	. . .	. . .	. . .	. . .
Price	c	MC	8	(435) 637-5010	Joe Piccolo	. . .	Joanne Lessar	Pat Larsen	Kent Boyack	Aleck Shilaos	Gary Sonntag
Providence	c	MC	4	(435) 752-9441	Alma Leonhardt	Brent Speth	Peggy Giles	. . .	. . .	. . .	Leroy Barnes
Provo	c	MC	105	(801) 852-6000	Lewis Billings	Wayne Parker	Marilyn Perry	George Karlsven	Scott Alvord	. . .	Merril Bingham
Richfield	c	CM	6	(435) 896-6439	. . .	Renald Farnsworth	Michele Jolley	Michael Langston	. . .	. . .	. . .
Riverdale	c	MC	7	(801) 394-5541	J. Bruce Burrows	Larry Hansen	Marilyn Hansen	Lynn Fortie	Doug Illum	Dave Hansen	Lynn Moulding
Riverton *	c	MC	25	(801) 254-0704	Bill Applegarth	Lance Blackwood	Maria Cosby	Lisa Dudley	. . .	. . .	. . .
Roosevelt	c	MC	4	(435) 722-5001	Dennis Jenkins	Dallas Hancock	Carolyn Wilcken	Justin Johnson	Kenny McDonald	Rick Harrison	Roger Eschler
Roy	c	CM	32	(801) 774-1000	Joe Ritchie	Christopher Davis	. . .	. . .	Jon Ritchie	Greg Whinham	Mike Mansfield
Salem	c	MC	4	(801) 423-2770	. . .	. . .	. . .	. . .	. . .	. . .	. . .
Salina	c	MC	2	(435) 529-7304	Jim Reynolds	. . .	Sherri Westbrook	. . .	J. R. Carter	Greg Harwood	Jim Casto
Salt Lake City	c	MC	181	(801) 535-7704	Ross Anderson	. . .	. . .	Gordon Hoskins	Charles Querry	Charles Dinse	Richard Graham
Sandy City	c	MC	88	(801) 568-7100	Thomas Dolan	Byron Jorgenson	Dianne Aubrey	. . .	Donald Chase	Stephen Chapman	Rick Smith
Santa Clara	c	CM	4	(435) 673-6712	Rick Rosenberg	Matthew Brower	. . .	Wally Ritchie	. . .	. . .	Jack Taylor
Santaquin	c	MC	4	(801) 754-3211	. . .	Stefan Chatwin	. . .	. . .	. . .	. . .	. . .
Saratoga Springs	c	CM	1	(801) 766-9793	Timothy Parker	Kenneth Leetham	Lori Yates	. . .	Dave Vickers	. . .	George Leatham
Smithfield	c	MC	7	(435) 563-6226	Archy Winn	James Gass	Connie Gittins	. . .	Jay Downs	Johnny McCoy	Doug Petersen
South Jordan *	c	MC	29	(801) 254-3742	William Money	John Geilmann	Mary Ann Dean	Dean Lundell	Chris Evans	Lindsay Shepherd	Donald Bruey
South Ogden	c	CM	14	(801) 622-2700	George Garwood	J. Darrington	Dana Pollard	Steve Liebersbach	Brian Minster	. . .	Paul Tippets
South Salt Lake	c	MC	22	(801) 483-6000	Wes Losser	. . .	Dawn Deakin	Gail Carlson	Steven Foote	Theresa Garner	Kyle Kingsbury
South Weber	c	MC	4	(801) 479-3177	. . .	Matthew Dixon	. . .	. . .	. . .	. . .	. . .
Spanish Fork	c	CM	20	(801) 798-5000	Dale Barney	David Oyler	. . .	Kent Clark	Clyde Johnson	. . .	Richard Heap
Springdale *	t	CM	. .	(435) 772-3434	Pat Cluff	Richard Wixom	Fay Cope	. . .	. . .	Kurt Wright	Dale Harris
Springville *	c	MC	20	(801) 489-2700	Gene Mangum	Troy Fitzgerald	Venla Gubler	David Allen	Phil Whitney	Scott Finlayson	Brad Stapley
St. George	c	MC	49	(435) 634-5800	Dan McArthur	Gary Esplin	Gay Cragun	Phil Peterson	Robert Stoker	. . .	Larry Bulloch
Sunset	c	MC	5	(801) 825-1628	Janice Galbraith	. . .	Susan Hale	. . .	Neil Coker	Ken Eborn	Mickey Hennessee
Syracuse *	c	MC	9	(801) 825-1477	Fred Panucci	Rodger Worthen	Cassie Brown	Lamar Holt	Craig Cottrell	Brian Wallace	Michael Waite
Taylorsville *	c	MC	57	(801) 963-5400	Russ Wall	John Morgan	Cheryl Cottle	Scott Harrington	Donald Berry	Del Craig	. . .
Tooele	c	MC	22	(435) 843-0110	Patrick Dunlavy	. . .	Sharon Dawson	Glenn Caldwell	. . .	Ronald Kirby	. . .
Tremonton	c	MC	5	(435) 257-2625	Max Weese	Richard Woodworth	Darlene Hess	. . .	Blair Westergard	S. Hodges	Paul Fulgham
Vernal	c	CM	7	(435) 789-2255	William Kremin	Kenneth Bassett	. . .	Harley Hales	Dennis Paulson	Michael Hamner	. . .
Washington	c	CM	8	(435) 628-1666	. . .	Roger Carter	. . .	. . .	Charles Tandy	. . .	. . .
Washington Terrace *	c	MC	8	(801) 393-8681	. . .	Mark Christensen	Marci Heil	Shari Garrett	Kasey Bush	. . .	Steve Harris
West Bountiful	c	MC	4	(801) 292-4486	James Behunin	. . .	Beverly Haslam	Brian Passey	. . .	Randy Lloyd	Blake Anderson
West Jordan	c	CM	68	(801) 569-5000	. . .	. . .	Melanie Briggs	David Hales	Jacob Nielson	Ken McGuire	. . .
West Point *	c	CM	6	(801) 776-0970	Erik Craythorne	Gary Hill	. . .	. . .	Roger Bodily	Bud Cox	. . .
West Valley City *	c	CM	108	(801) 966-3600	Dennis Nordfelt	Wayne Pyle	Sheri McKendrick	James Welch	Vannie Summers	Thayle Nielsen	Russell Willardson
Woods Cross	c	CM	6	(801) 292-4421	Jerry Larrabee	Gary Uresk	Alan Low	. . .	. . .	Paul Howard	Scott Anderson
VERMONT											
Barre	t	CM	7	(802) 479-9331	. . .	Carl Rogers	Donna Kelty	. . .	. . .	Michael Stevens	. . .
Barre	c	CM	9	(802) 476-0240	Harry Monti	John Craig	Eugene Stratton	. . .	Peter John	Trevor Whipple	Reginald Abare
Barton	t	TM	2	(802) 525-6222	Robert Croteau	. . .	. . .	. . .	. . .	. . .	. . .
Bellows Falls	v	CM	3	(802) 463-3964	Katherine Hennesey	John Schempf	Ann Dibernardo	. . .	William Weston	Frederick Gardy	. . .
Bennington	t	CM	15	(802) 442-1037	Sharyn Brush	Stuart Hurd	Timothy Corcoran	David Essaff	Phil Frasier	Richard Gauthier	. . .
Bethel	t	CM	1	(802) 234-9340	Neal Fox	Delbert Cloud	Jean Burnham	. . .	Robert Dean	James Bennett	. . .
Brandon	t	CM	3	(802) 247-3635	Lynn Saunders	. . .	William Dick	Denise Mahoney	. . .	. . .	. . .

Directory 1/9
continued

OFFICIALS IN U.S. MUNICIPALITIES 2,500 AND OVER IN POPULATION

Jurisdiction	Type	Form of govern-ment	2000 Popu-lation	Main telephone number	Chief elected official	Appointed administrator	Clerk of the governing board	Chief financial officer	Fire chief	Police chief	Public works director
VERMONT continued											
Brattleboro	t	CM	12	(802) 254-4541	Stephen Steidle	Barbara Sondag	Annette Cappy	Barbara Vinci	David Emery	John Martin	Stephen Barrett
Bristol	v	CM	1	(802) 453-2410	...	...	...	...	...	...	...
Bristol	t	CM	3	(802) 453-2410	...	...	...	...	...	...	...
Burlington	c	MC	38	(802) 865-7145	Peter Clavelle	...	JoAnne LaMarche	...	...	Alana Ennis	Steven Goodkind
Castleton	t	CM	4	(800) 468-5319	Patrick Eagan	Beverly Davidson	Ellen La Fleche	Melanie Combs	C. Mulholland	Douglas Norton	Clarence Decker
Cavendish	t	CM	1	(802) 226-7291	Sandra Stearns	Richard Svec	...	...	...	...	...
Charlotte	t	TM	3	(802) 425-3071	Ellie Russell	Gloria Warden	Mary Mead	...	Chris Davis	...	...
Chester	t	TM	3	(802) 875-2173	...	Susan Spaulding	...	...	...	...	...
Colchester	t	CM	16	(802) 264-5500	...	Albin Voegele	Karen Richard	Joan Boehm	...	Charles Kirker	Bryan Osborne
Derby	t	TM	4	(802) 766-4906	Thomas Bailey	...	Elizabeth Lahar	...	Craig Ellam	Bruce Warner	William Duma
Dorset	* t	CM	2	(802) 362-4571	Chris Brooks	...	Sandy Pinsonault	...	...	...	Jim Hewes
Essex	t	TM	18	(802) 878-1341	...	Patrick Scheidel	Cheryl Moomey	Douglas Fisher	Howard Rice	Leo Nadeau	Dennis Lutz
Essex Junction	* v	CM	8	(802) 878-6944	...	David Crawford	Susan Hill	Lauren Morrisseau	Chris Gaboriault	...	Rick Jones
Fair Haven	t	CM	2	(802) 265-3010	John Lulck	...	Suzanne Dechame	...	Donald Howard	Raymond Viger	John Eaton
Hardwick	t	TM	3	(802) 472-6120	...	Daniel Hill	...	...	...	James Dziobek	Alan May
Hartford	* t	CM	10	(802) 295-9353	Gayle Ottmann	Hunter Rieseberg	Mary Hill	...	Steve Locke	...	Richard Menge
Hartland	t	TM	3	(802) 436-2444	Thomas White	Robert Stacey	Clyde Jenne	Carolyn Trombly	Mark Cote	Anthony Leonard	...
Hinesburg	* t	TM	4	(802) 482-2096	Jonathan Trefry	Jeanne Wilson	Melissa Ross	...	Alton Barber	Chris Morrell	...
Jericho	t	TM	5	(802) 899-4936	...	...	...	...	...	...	...
Johnson	t	TM	3	(802) 635-2611	...	...	...	...	...	...	...
Killington	* t	CM	..	(802) 422-3241	Norman Holcomb	Kathleen Ramsay	Lucrecia Wonsor	...	Steven Finer	Scott Bigelow	...
Ludlow	t	CM	2	(802) 228-2841	Keith Arlund	...	Nettie Gruber	...	...	...	David Norton
Lyndon	t	TM	5	(802) 626-5785	...	...	...	...	...	...	...
Manchester	t	CM	4	(802) 362-1313	Ivan Beattie	...	Linda Spence	Ruth Woodard	...	Manfred Wessner	...
Middlebury	t	CM	8	(802) 388-8107	John Tenny	William Finger	Ann Webster	...	Richard Cole	Thomas Hanley	Daniel Werner
Milton	t	TM	9	(802) 893-6655	Kenneth Nolan	Sanford Miller	John Cushing	...	Donald Turner	Brett Van Noordt	...
Montpelier	* c	CM	8	(802) 223-9502	Mary Hooper	William Fraser	...	Sandra Gallup	Norman Lewis	Anthony Facos	Todd Law
Morristown	t	TM	5	(802) 888-5147	Shaun Bryer	...	Mary Ann Wilson	Carol Bradley	Wallace Reeve	Richard Keith	Robert Melfy
Newport	c	CM	5	(802) 334-5136	Richard Baraw	John Ward	...	...	Robert George	Paul Duquette	Thomas Bernier
North Troy	v	CM	..	(802) 988-4700	...	...	Jim Wentworth	...	...	...	...
Northfield	t	CM	3	(802) 485-6121	Donald Wallace	Nanci Allard	Kimberly Pombar	...	...	Jeffrey Shaw	William Lyon
Norwich	t	CM	3	(802) 649-0127	Alison May	Peter Webster	Bonnie Munday	Roberta Robinson	...	...	...
Pittsford	t	CM	3	(802) 483-6500	Margaret Flory	...	Gordon Delong	...	Tom Hooker	Joseph Warfle	Shawn Erickson
Poultney	v	CM	1	(802) 287-4003	...	...	...	...	...	...	...
Poultney	t	CM	3	(802) 287-9751	...	...	...	...	...	...	...
Pownal	t	TM	3	(802) 823-7757	...	...	...	...	...	...	...
Randolph	t	CM	4	(802) 728-5433	...	Peter Butterfield	Joyce Mazzucco	...	...	James Krakowiecki	Joseph Voci
Richmond	t	TM	4	(802) 434-5170	...	Ronald Rodjenski	Velma Ploufee	...	...	William Miller	Kendall Chamberlin
Rockingham	t	CM	5	(802) 463-3964	Lamont Barnett	John Schempf	Doreen Aldrich	Deane Haskell	Denis Jeffrey	...	Everett Hammond
Rutland	t	TM	4	(802) 773-2528	...	...	Marie Hyjek	...	Joseph Denardo	Brian Abbey	...
Rutland	c	MC	17	(802) 773-1800	Jeffrey Wennberg	...	Rosemary Finley	...	Craig Shelly	Anthony Bossi	Warren Conner
Shaftsbury	* t	TM	3	(802) 442-4043	Lon McClintock	...	Judith Stratton	...	Joe Vadakin	...	Ronald Daniels
Shelburne	t	CM	6	(802) 985-5111	Chris Neme	Paul Bohne	Colleen Haag	Peter Frankenburg	Craig Wooster	James Warden	Bernie Gagnon
South Burlington	c	CM	15	(802) 846-4105	James Condos	Charles Hafter	Donna Kinville	...	Douglas Brent	Lealand Graham	Bruce Hoar
Springfield	t	CM	9	(802) 885-2104	John Follett	Robert Forquittes	Bonnie Reynolds	Jeffrey Mobus	...	Douglas Johnston	Harry Henderson
St. Albans	t	CM	5	(802) 524-2415	...	Daniel Lindley	Anna Bourdon	...	Harold Cross	...	Steve Beauregard
St. Albans	c	CM	7	(802) 524-1500	Peter Des Lauriers	Dominic Cloud	Dianna Baraby	Jacques Bergeron	...	Gary Taylor	Allen Robtoy
St. Johnsbury	* t	CM	7	(802) 748-3926	...	Michael Welch	Sandra Grenier	...	Troy Ruggles	Richard Leighton	Larry Gadapee
Stowe	t	CM	4	(802) 253-7350	Richard Marron	Charles Safford	...	Karla Spaulding	Wendall Mansfield	Ken Kaplan	...
Swanton	v	CM	2	(802) 868-3397	Neal Speer	George Lague	Christine Davis	...	Peter Prouty	Michael McCarthy	Michael Menard
Swanton	t	TM	6	(802) 868-4421	Mark Hojaboom	Richard Thompson	Doris Raleigh	...	...	...	...
Troy	t	TM	1	(802) 988-2663	...	...	...	...	...	...	...
Vergennes	c	CM	2	(802) 877-3637	Thelma Oxholm	...	Joan Devine	...	Ralph Jackman	Mike Lowe	Carroll O'Connor
Wallingford	t	TM	1	(802) 446-2336	...	Christine O'Gorman	...	...	...	...	...
Waterbury	t	CM	4	(802) 244-7033	Edward Steele	William Shepeluk	Donna Centonze	...	...	...	...
Weathersfield	* t	CM	2	(802) 674-2626	Henry Cobb	Laurence Melen	Flora Ann Dango	Christopher Adams	...	Richard Brown	Westley Hazeltine
West Rutland	t	TM	2	(802) 438-2263	Edward Gilman	...	Jayne Pratt	...	Joe Skaza	...	...
Westminster	* t	CM	3	(802) 722-4255	William Noyes	Glenn Smith	Doreen Woodward	...	...	...	...
Williamstown	* t	TM	3	(802) 433-6671	Linda Riddell	...	Deborah Palmer	...	Ed Eaton	...	Bernie Duff
Williston	t	TM	7	(802) 878-0919	Virginia Lyons	Richard McGuire	Deborah Beckett	Susan Lamb	Kenneth Morton	James Dimmick	Neil Boyden
Wilmington	t	TM	2	(802) 464-8591	Frederick Skwirut	...	Susan Manton	Laurie Boyd	Troy Johnson	Joseph Szarejko	...
Windsor	t	CM	3	(802) 674-6786	...	Stephen Cottrell	...	...	...	...	...
Winhall	* t	MC	..	(802) 297-2119	T. David Glabach	Dennis McCarthy	Elizabeth Jenks	...	Harold Coleman	Jeffery Whitesell	Randy Kimball
Winooski	c	CM	6	(802) 655-6410	Clement Bissonnette	Joshua Handverger	...	...	David Bergeron	Steve McQueen	Steve Woodworth
Woodstock	v	CM	..	(802) 457-3456	...	...	...	...	...	Byron Kelly	...
Woodstock	t	TM	3	(802) 457-3456	...	Philip Swanson	Jerome Morgan	...	...	...	Glenn Frederick
VIRGINIA											
Abingdon	* t	CM	7	(276) 628-3167	Lois Humphreys	Gregory Kelly	Cecile Rosenbaum	Mark Godbey	Joey Burke	Phillip Sullivan	John Dew
Alexandria	* c	CM	128	(703) 838-4424	William Euille	James Hartmann	J. Henderson	Laura Triggs	Adam Thiel	David Baker	Richard Baier
Altavista	* t	CM	3	(434) 369-5001	James Burgess	J. Coggsdale	...	...	...	Thomas Neal	John Tomlin
Amherst	t	CM	2	(434) 946-7885	...	Jack Hobbs	...	...	...	...	...
Appalachia	t	CM	1	(276) 565-3900	Gary Bush	Bobby Dorton	...	...	Robert Anderson	Roy Munsey	Bobby Reynolds
Appomattox	t	MC	1	(434) 352-8268	Ronald Spiggle	David Garrett	Bobbie Mullins	...	Timothy Garrett	...	Jeff Elder
Ashland	t	CM	6	(804) 798-9219	Angela LaCombe	Charles Hartgrove	Carolyn Barnett	...	...	Frederic Pleasants	Michael Davis
Bedford	* c	CM	6	(540) 587-6001	W. Tharp	Charles Kolakowski	Teresa Hatcher	Rosemarie Jordan	Brad Creasy	James Day	Jeff Weddle
Berryville	* t	CM	2	(540) 955-1099	Wilson Kirby	Keith Dalton	Celeste Heath	...	...	Neal White	Richard Boor
Big Stone Gap	* t	CM	4	(276) 523-0115	Barbara Orndorff	Patrick Murphy	Judy Hall	...	Billy Chandler	Davey Horner	Charles Burke
Blacksburg	t	CM	39	(540) 961-1100	Roger Hedgepeth	Marc Verniel	Donna Caldwell	Susan Kaiser	B. Bolte	William Brown	Kelly Mattingly
Blackstone	t	CM	3	(434) 292-7251	...	James Palmore	Joan Palmore	Charles Wells	...	Wayne Shields	John Lee
Bluefield	t	CM	5	(276) 322-4626	William King	Daryl Day	Patricia Douthat	...	James Hardy	Jack Asbury	...
Bowling Green	t	CM	..	(804) 633-6212	Frank Benser	...	Virginia Brooks	...	...	Robert Hall	Dan Curran
Bridgewater	t	CM	5	(540) 828-3390	Hallie Dinkel	Bob Holton	Carleen Loveless	Theodore Flory	...	Robert Hill	Jeffrey Riddleberger
Bristol	c	CM	17	(276) 645-7300	Paul Hurley	Paul Spangler	Steven Allen	...	Walt Ford	William Price	...
Broadway	t	CM	2	(540) 896-5152	...	Kyle O'Brien	Maria Kline	...	...	Jay Lantz	...
Brookneal	t	MC	1	(434) 376-3124	Phyllis Campbell	Joseph Williams	Beth Elder	...	Jim Hires	...	Mike Crews
Buena Vista	c	CM	6	(540) 261-8600	James Jones	...	Janie Coffey	Timothy Dudley	Tommy Keiser	Lewis Plogger	Dewey Tyree
Cape Charles	t	CM	1	(757) 331-3259	Frank Lewis	Joe Vaccaro	Jennie Moore	...	...	David Eder	Mike Thornes
Charlottesville	c	CM	45	(434) 970-3490	Virginia Daugherty	Gary O'Connell	Jeanne Cox	Aubrey Watts	Julian Taliaferro	Julian Rittenhouse	Judith Mueller
Chase City	t	CM	2	(434) 372-5136	A. Reid	Rickey Reese	Cynthia Gordon	...	Winthy Hatcher	J. Jordon	Stanley Duckworth
Chatham	t	CM	1	(434) 432-9515	L. Elton Pruitt	...	...	...	Landon Worsham	Floyd Poindexter	Robert Hanson
Chesapeake	c	CM	199	(757) 382-6151	William Ward	William Harrell	Dolores Moore	Nancy Tracy	R. Best	Richard Justice	Patricia Biegler
Chincoteague	t	CM	4	(757) 336-6519	...	Robert Ritter	...	...	...	...	...
Christiansburg	* t	CM	16	(540) 382-6128	Richard Ballengee	Robert Terpenny	Michele Stipes	...	James Epperly	Mark Sisson	Wayne Nelson
Clarksville	t	CM	1	(434) 374-8177	Benjy Burnett	Melinda Moran	...	Tara Glover	Robert Wilkerson	...	Terry Hite

Directory 1/9 continued   OFFICIALS IN U.S. MUNICIPALITIES 2,500 AND OVER IN POPULATION

Jurisdiction		Type	Form of govern-ment	2000 Popu-lation	Main telephone number	Chief elected official	Appointed administrator	Clerk of the governing board	Chief financial officer	Fire chief	Police chief	Public works director
VIRGINIA continued												
Clifton Forge	*	t	CM	4	(540) 863-2500	. . .	Tracey Shiflett	Mary McElwee	LeeAnna Tyler	Mark Nicely	Barry Balser	Oliver Campbell
Coeburn		t	CM	1	(276) 395-3323	G. Wells	Loretta Mays	. . .	. . .	Cliff Hawkins	Willie Stout	Danny Jordan
Colonial Beach		t	CM	3	(804) 224-7181	George Bone	. . .	Barbara Goff	Mary Bowen	. . .	Courtlandt Turner	Robert Murphy
Colonial Heights		c	CM	16	(804) 520-9265	J. Kollman	Richard Anzolut	Kimberly Rollinson	William Johnson	Allan Moore	Richard Schurman	Charles Loving
Covington	*	c	CM	6	(540) 965-6300	Stephanie Clark	John Doane	Edith Wood	Linda Brown	Wes Walker	J. Broughman	Jack Munsey
Crewe		t	CM	2	(434) 645-9453	Wilfred Wilson	William Walker	. . .	. . .	. . .	William Abel	Ralph Shelton
Culpeper	*	t	CM	9	(540) 829-8250	Pranas Rimeikis	Jeffrey Muzzy	Donna Foster	. . .	. . .	Daniel Boring	Robert Thornhill
Danville	*	c	CM	48	(434) 799-5240	Sherman Saunders	Matthew Lacy	Annette Crane	Barbara Dameron	David Eagle	Phillip Broadfoot	Richard Drazenovich
Dublin		t	CM	2	(540) 674-4731	Benny Skeens	William Parker	. . .	. . .	. . .	Jay Vest	Garnett Lyons
Dumfries		t	CM	4	(703) 221-3400	Fred Yohey	. . .	Donna Johnson	. . .	. . .	Calvin Johnson	Greg Tkac
Elkton		t	CM	2	(540) 298-1951	. . .	. . .	Richard Carey	. . .	. . .	Richard Pullen	Jarrod Shifflett
Emporia		c	CM	5	(434) 634-3332	Samuel Adams	Brian Thrower	Andrea Hines	Ann Magee	Warren Rawlings	Mallory Daughtry	. . .
Fairfax		c	CM	21	(703) 293-7120	Robert Lederer	Robert Sisson	. . .	. . .	. . .	Richard Rappoport	John Veneziano
Falls Church		c	CM	10	(703) 248-5000	Daniel Gardner	F. Shields	Kathleen Buschow	. . .	. . .	Robert Murray	Moe Wadda
Farmville		t	CM	6	(434) 392-5686	Sydnor Newman	Gerald Spates	Lisa Hricko	. . .	. . .	Stuart Dunnavant	Robin Atkins
Franklin	*	c	CM	8	(757) 562-8550	. . .	. . .	. . .	. . .	Vincent Holt	Phillip Hardison	Russell Pace
Fredericksburg	*	c	CM	19	(540) 372-1010	Thomas Tomzak	Phillip Rodenberg	Mary Smith	Clarence Robinson	Edwin Allen	David Nye	P. Fawcett
Front Royal	*	t	CM	13	(540) 635-8007	James Eastham	James Graham	Jennifer Berry	Kim Gilkey-Breeden	. . .	. . .	George Shadman
Galax	*	c	CM	6	(276) 236-5773	C. Mitchell	Keith Holland	. . .	Nikki Shank	David Hankley	Richard Clark	Charles Joyce
Gate City		t	CM	2	(276) 386-3831	. . .	. . .	. . .	. . .	. . .	. . .	. . .
Glasgow		t	CM	1	(540) 258-2246	Sam Blackburn	Ryan Spitzer	. . .	. . .	Richard Spangler	Damon Propst	Armond Falgoust
Gordonsville	*	t	MC	1	(540) 832-2233	Robert Coiner	Sabrina Martyn	Olga Washington	. . .	. . .	Christopher Spare	Vincent Seal
Grundy		t	CM	1	(276) 935-2551	John Fleenor	Chuck Crabtree	. . .	. . .	Donnie Compton	Barney Stiltner	. . .
Hampton		c	CM	146	(757) 727-8311	Mamie Locke	Jesse Wallace	Diana Hughes	Karl Daughtrey	. . .	Thomas Townsend	Edward Henifin
Harrisonburg		c	CM	40	(540) 432-8920	Rodney Eagle	Kurt Hodgen	Yvonne Ryan	Lester Seal	Larry Shifflett	Donald Harper	James Baker
Haymarket	*	t	CM	. .	(703) 753-2600	Pamela Stutz	Mason Swearingen	Jennifer Preli	James Naradzay	. . .	James Roop	. . .
Herndon	*	t	CM	21	(703) 787-7368	Steve DeBenedittis	Arthur Anselene	Victoria Wellershaus	Mary Tuohy	. . .	Toussaint Summers	Robert Boxer
Hillsville	*	t	CM	2	(276) 728-2128	William Tate	Larry South	Vickie Yonce	. . .	. . .	Steven Williams	Terry Cole
Hopewell		c	CM	22	(804) 541-2245	James Patterson	Edwin Daley	Ann Romano	Elesteen Hager	Steve Brown	Rex Marks	Phillip Elliott
Kilmarnock	*	t	CM	1	(804) 435-1552	. . .	. . .	Jackie Blencowe	. . .	Ben Balderson	Mike Bedell	. . .
Lebanon		t	CM	3	(276) 889-7200	. . .	. . .	. . .	. . .	. . .	. . .	. . .
Leesburg		t	CM	28	(703) 777-2420	Kristen Umstattd	. . .	Judith Ahalt	Norman Butts	. . .	Joseph Price	Thomas Mason
Lexington	*	c	CM	6	(540) 462-3700	John Knapp	T. Ellestad	Sharon Edwards	Curtis Higgins	Dave Clark	Steve Crowder	David Woody
Louisa		t	CM	1	(540) 967-1400	Charles Rosson	Brian Marks	Jessica Ellis	. . .	. . .	Stan Batten	. . .
Lovettsville		t	CM	. .	(540) 822-5788	Elaine Walker	Keith Markel	Judy Kromholz	Lance Gladstone	. . .	. . .	. . .
Luray	*	t	CM	4	(540) 743-5511	Barry Presgraves	Rick Black	. . .	. . .	. . .	Page Campbell	Lynn Mathews
Lynchburg	*	c	CM	65	(434) 455-3990	Joan Foster	L. Payne	Patricia Kost	Donna Witt	Steven Ferguson	Parks Snead	David Owen
Manassas	*	c	CM	35	(703) 257-8200	Harry Parrish	Lawrence Hughes	Kimberly Allen	Patricia Weiler	Michael Wood	John Skinner	Michael Moon
Manassas Park		c	CM	10	(703) 335-8800	Frank Jones	Mercury Payton	Lana Conner	Gary Fields	John O'Neal	John Evans	Kathleen Gammell
Marion		t	CM	6	(276) 783-4113	. . .	John Clark	Dixie Sheets	. . .	. . .	Michael Roberts	Roy Burke
Martinsville	*	c	CM	15	(276) 403-5000	Kathy Lawson	Clarence Monday	. . .	. . .	Kenneth Draper	Michael Rogers	Leon Towarnicki
Middleburg		t	CM	. .	(540) 687-5152	Betsy Davis	Jerry Schiro	. . .	. . .	. . .	Steven Webber	. . .
Narrows		t	CM	2	(540) 726-2423	. . .	. . .	. . .	. . .	. . .	Thomas Gautier	. . .
New Market		t	CM	1	(540) 740-3432	Thomas Constable	Chris Boies	Deborah Ritchie	. . .	. . .	Steven Crisman	Orville Ryman
Newport News	*	c	CM	180	(757) 926-8000	Joe Frank	Randy Hildebrandt	Mabel Washington	LaVerne Lovett	Kenneth Jones	James Fox	H. Fowler
Norfolk		c	CM	234	(757) 664-4486	Paul Fraim	Regina Williams	Robert Daughtrey	Steven DeMik	. . .	Bruce Marquis	John Keifer
Norton		c	CM	3	(276) 679-1160	B. Raines	Ernest Ward	Mary Brown	Teresa Belcher	David Mullins	Samuel Mongle	Richard Hurt
Orange	*	t	CM	4	(540) 672-5005	Henry Carter	Cole Hendrix	Wendy Chewning	Lydia Hadley	. . .	James Fenwick	Jeff Dodson
Pearisburg		t	CM	2	(540) 921-0340	Barabara Stafford	Kenneth Vittum	Judy Harrell	. . .	Richard Stump	Jackie Marlin	Rick Tawney
Petersburg	*	c	CM	33	(804) 733-2324	Annie Mickens	B. Canada	Nykesha Jackson	. . .	Thomas Hairston	John Dixon, III	Michael Briddell
Poquoson		c	CM	11	(757) 868-3000	Gordon Helsel	. . .	. . .	Lisa Dessoffy	Robert Holloway	Clifford Bowen	J. Montgomery
Portsmouth	*	c	CM	100	(757) 393-8626	James Holley	Kenneth Chandler	Debra White	. . .	. . .	Frank Kitzerow	James Spacek
Pulaski	*	t	CM	9	(540) 994-8696	Jeffery Worrell	John Hawley	Patricia Cruise	. . .	Bill Webb	Gary Roche	. . .
Purcellville		t	MC	3	(540) 338-7421	William Durhan	Robert Lohr	Richmond Coburn	. . .	. . .	. . .	Karin McKnight
Radford		c	CM	15	(540) 731-3603	Thomas Starnes	Anthony Cox	. . .	Patricia Cox	Robert Simpkins	Gary Harmon	Jimmy Dean
Richlands	*	t	CM	4	(276) 964-2566	Kenneth Wysor	Timothy Taylor	Elva Vandyke	. . .	William Vance	William Puckett	Jim Taylor
Richmond	*	c	MC	197	(804) 646-5660	Rudolph McCollum	. . .	Edna Keys-Chavis	Andrew Rountree	Robert Creecy	Andre Parker	. . .
Roanoke		c	CM	94	(540) 853-2231	Ralph Smith	Darlene Burcham	Mary Parker	Jesse Hall	. . .	Atlas Gaskins	Robert Bengtson
Rocky Mount		t	CM	4	(540) 483-7660	Mark Newbill	Clifton Ervin	Patricia Hooke	Linda Woody	. . .	R. Jenkins	Cecil Mason
Round Hill		t	MC	. .	(540) 338-7878	Francis Etro	John Barkley	. . .	. . .	. . .	. . .	Alan Wolverton
Rural Retreat		t	MC	1	(276) 686-4221	Timothy Litz	Raymond Matney	. . .	. . .	David Evans	Robert Lewis	. . .
Salem		c	CM	24	(540) 375-3060	Howard Packett	Kevin Boggess	Krystal Coleman	Frank Turk	Chester Counts	James Bryant	Melvin Doughty
Scottsville	*	t	MC	. .	(434) 286-9267	R. Phipps	Clark Draper	Amy Moyer	. . .	. . .	. . .	. . .
Shenandoah		t	CM	1	(540) 652-8164	Clinton Lucas	Larry Dovel	. . .	Cindy Breeden	. . .	Peter Monteleone	Mark Armentrout
Smithfield	*	t	CM	6	(757) 365-4200	David Hare	Peter Stephenson	Sharon Thomas	. . .	Jason Stallings	Mark Marshall	Darrel Hurst
South Boston	*	t	CM	8	(434) 575-4200	Carroll Thackston	Ted Daniel	Jane Jones	Lester Scott	Steve Phillips	James Binner	Alan Auld
South Hill		t	CM	4	(434) 447-3191	Earl Horne	. . .	Anna Cratch	Heidi Porter	Rosser Wells	Norman Hudson	Bill Wilson
Staunton	*	c	CM	23	(540) 332-3800	Lacy King	Stephen Owen	Deborah Sutton	Jeanne Colvin	Michael Myers	James Williams	Thomas Sliwoski
Strasburg		t	CM	4	(540) 465-9197	Harry Applegate	Kevin Fauber	Amy Keller	Mary Price	. . .	Marshall Robinson	John Rhodes
Suffolk	*	c	CM	63	(757) 514-4120	Curtis Milteer	Selena Cuffee-Glenn	Henry Murden	. . .	. . .	. . .	Eric Nielsen
Tappahannock		t	CM	2	(804) 443-3336	Roy Gladding	George Belfield	Patsy Bryant	. . .	. . .	James Barrett	Kenneth Gillis
Tazewell		t	CM	4	(276) 988-2501	Charles Green	Jerry Wood	. . .	. . .	A. Buchanan	Roy Brewster	Danny Whitt
Timberville	*	t	CM	1	(540) 896-7058	. . .	Austin Garber	. . .	. . .	. . .	. . .	. . .
Victoria		t	CM	1	(434) 696-2343	Carol Watson	. . .	Diane Harding	. . .	. . .	James Dayton	M Carl Ashworth
Vienna	*	t	CM	14	(703) 255-6300	M. Seeman	John Schoeberlein	Carol Orndorff	Philip Grant	. . .	Robert Carlisle	Dennis King
Vinton	*	t	CM	7	(540) 983-0607	Bradley Grose	C. Lawrence	Darleen Bailey	Barry Thompson	. . .	Herbert Cooley	Michael Kennedy
Virginia Beach		c	CM	425	(757) 427-8374	Meyera Oberndorf	James Spore	Ruth Smith	Patricia Phillips	Gregory Cade	Alfred Jacocks	. . .
Warrenton		t	CM	6	(540) 347-1101	George Fitch	Kenneth McLawhon	Evelyn Weimer	Richard Heartley	. . .	. . .	Edward Tucker
Waynesboro		c	CM	19	(540) 942-6719	Thomas Reynolds	Michael Hamp	Bonnie Hamby	Sarah Hash-Rodgers	Charles Scott	Douglas Davis	Brian McReynolds
West Point	*	t	MC	2	(804) 843-3330	Jame Hudson	Trenton Funkhouser	Karen Barrow	. . .	. . .	William Hodges	Walter Feurer
Williamsburg	*	c	CM	11	(757) 220-6100	Jeanne Zeidler	Jackson Tuttle	Donna Scott	Philip Serra	T. Weiler	James Yost	Daniel Clayton
Winchester		c	CM	23	(540) 667-1815	Elizabeth Minor	J. Godfrey	Leticia Chavez	Mary Blowe	Frank Wright	Eric Varnau	. . .
Windsor		t	CM	. .	(757) 242-4288	Wesley Garris	John Rowe	Patricia Mann	. . .	William Copeland	. . .	. . .
Wise	*	t	CM	3	(276) 328-6013	Caynor Smith	Beverly Owens	. . .	. . .	Conley Holbrook	Anthony Bates	Gregory Jefferson
Woodstock	*	t	CM	3	(540) 459-3621	William Moyers	Larry Bradford	. . .	Mandy Belyea	Warren Schennum	Jerry Miller	James Didawick
Wytheville	*	t	CM	7	(276) 223-3321	Trenton Crewe	Curtis Sutherland	Sharon Hackler	. . .	Ronnie King	Harry Ayers	Dennis Hackler
WASHINGTON												
Aberdeen		c	MC	16	(360) 533-4100	Chuck Gurrad	. . .	. . .	Fred Thurman	Steve Mitchell	. . .	Jim Robertson
Airway Heights		c	MC	4	(509) 244-5578	Dale Perry	Albert Tripp	. . .	. . .	John Schoen	Lee Bennett	. . .
Anacortes		c	MC	14	(360) 299-1970	Dean Maxwell	. . .	. . .	. . .	Richard Curtis	Michael King	Robert Hyde
Arlington		c	MC	11	(360) 403-3421	Margaret Larson	Allen Johnson	. . .	Kathy Peterson	Jim Rankin	John Gray	Len Olive
Auburn		c	MC	40	(253) 288-3000	Peter Lewis	. . .	Danielle Daskam	Shelley Coleman	Robert Johnson	James Kelly	Dennis Dowdy
Bainbridge Island		c	MC	20	(206) 842-2545	Darlene Kordonowy	Mark Dombroski	Susan Kasper	Elray Konkel	. . .	Matt Haney	Randy Witt
Battle Ground	*	c	MC	9	(360) 342-5000	Michael Ciraulo	Dennis Osborn	Claire Lider	C. Huber Nickerson	. . .	James McDaniel	Scott Sawyer

Directory 1/9 continued   **OFFICIALS IN U.S. MUNICIPALITIES 2,500 AND OVER IN POPULATION**

Jurisdiction	Type	Form of govern-ment	2000 Popu-lation	Main telephone number	Chief elected official	Appointed administrator	Clerk of the governing board	Chief financial officer	Fire chief	Police chief	Public works director
WASHINGTON continued											
Bellevue	c	CM	109	(425) 452-6800	Connie Marshall	Steven Sarkozy	Myrna Basich	...	Mario Trevino	James Montgomery	Lloyd Warren
Bellingham	c	MC	67	(360) 676-6960	Mark Asmundson	...	...	John Carter	Mike Leigh	Randall Carroll	Richard McKinley
Black Diamond	* c	MC	3	(360) 886-2560	Howard Botts	Gwendolyn Voelpel	...	Mayene Miller	Greg Smith	Jamey Kiblinger	Seth Boettcher
Blaine	* c	CM	3	(360) 332-8311	Bonnie Onyon	Gary Tomsic	Sheri Sanchez	Meredith Riley	Tom Fields	Mike Haslip	Steve Banham
Bonney Lake	c	MC	9	(253) 862-8602	Neil Johnson	Don Morrison	Harwood Edvalson	...	...	Mike Mitchell	Dan Grigsby
Bothell	c	CM	30	(425) 489-3437	Mark Lamb	Robert Stowe	Jo Anne Trudel	Tami Schackman	...	Forrest Conover	Doug Jacobson
Bremerton	c	MC	37	(360) 473-5846	Cary Bozeman	...	Paula Johnston	...	Allison Duke	Robert Forbes	Phil Williams
Brier	c	MC	6	(425) 775-5440	Gary Starks	...	...	...	...	Don Lane	...
Buckley	c	MC	4	(360) 829-1960	John Blanusa	Dave Schmidt	Alice Money	Sheila Bazzar	Alan Predmore	Art McGehee	P. Brendel
Burien	* c	CM	31	(206) 241-4647	Joan McGilton	Michael Martin	Monica Lusk	Tabatha Miller	...	...	Stephen Clark
Burlington	c	MC	6	(360) 755-0531	Roger Tjeerdsma	Jon Aarstad	Judith Sheahan	Richard Patrick	Mark Anderson	Gerald Bowers	...
Camas	c	MC	12	(360) 834-6864	Paul Dennis	Lloyd Halverson	...	Joan Durgin	Leo Leon	Donald Chaney	Monte Brachmann
Carnation	c	CM	1	(425) 333-4192	Yvonne Funderburg	Candice Bock	Mary Otness	...	...	Glenn Merryman	James Dorsey
Castle Rock	c	MC	2	(360) 274-8181	Barbara Larsen	...	Ryana Covington	...	Eric Koreis	Robert Heuer	David Vorse
Centralia	* c	CM	14	(360) 330-7670	Timothy Browning	...	Deena Bilodeau	Bradley Ford	Jim Walkowski	Robert Berg	Kahle Jennings
Chehalis	* c	CM	7	(360) 748-6664	Anthony Ketchum	Merlin MacReynold	Judy Schave	Eva Lindgren	Kelvin Johnson	Glenn Schaffer	Tim Grochowski
Chelan	c	MC	3	(509) 682-4037	W. Mitchell Atkinson	James Reinbold	Linda Allison-Liles	Heidi Kollmeyer	...	Edwin Bush	Dwane Van Epps
Cheney	c	MC	8	(509) 498-9203	Amy Sooy	Arlene Fisher	...	...	John Montague	Jeff Sale	Donald Mac Donald
Clarkston	c	CO	7	(509) 758-5541	Donna Engle	...	Vickie Storey	...	Steven Cooper	Joel Hastings	James Martin
Cle Elum	c	CM	1	(509) 674-2262	Gary Berndt	...	DeLiela Bannister	...	...	Brennen Milloy	Jim Leonhard
Clyde Hill	* c	MC	2	(425) 453-7800	George Martin	Mitchell Wasserman	Courtney Benjamin	John Gagan	...	William Archer	Allan Newbill
Colfax	c	MC	2	(509) 397-3861	Norma Becker	Emily Adams	Carol Larson	...	Carl Thompson	Barney Buckley	...
College Place	c	MC	7	(509) 529-1200	Edward Ammon	...	...	Robert Zielfelder	Patrick Shipp	Dennis Lepiane	Paul Hartwig
Colville	c	MC	4	(509) 684-5094	Duane Scott	...	Holly Pannell	...	Rick Naff	D. Meshishnek	Harlan Elsasser
Connell	c	MC	2	(509) 234-2701	Gary Walton	...	Joan Eckman	...	...	Rick Rochleau	Patrick Munyan
Covington	* c	CM	13	(253) 638-1110	Margaret Harto	Derek Matheson	Jacqueline Cronk	Rob Hendrickson	Jim Schneider	Kevin Klason	Glenn Akramoff
Davenport	* c	MC	1	(509) 725-4352	Karen Carruth	Steven Goemmel	David Leath	...	Eugene Johnson	...	Fred Bell
Dayton	c	MC	2	(509) 382-2361	William Graham	Sheila McCaw	...	...	Robert Allbee	...	Jim Costello
Des Moines	c	CM	29	(206) 878-4595	Robert Sheckler	Anthony Piasecki	Denis Staab	Paula Henderson	Al Church	Roger Baker	Grant Fredricks
Dupont	* c	MC	2	(253) 964-8121	Tamara Jenkins	William McDonald	Erin Larsen	Dawn Masko	Robert Merritt	Ron Goodpaster	Peter Zahn
East Wenatchee	* c	MC	5	(509) 884-9515	Steven Lacy	...	Dana Barnard	...	...	John Harrison	Brandon Mauseth
Edgewood	c	CM	9	(253) 952-3299	...	Ronald Wilde	...	...	...	Robert Santoro	...
Edmonds	c	MC	39	(425) 775-2525	Barbara Fahey	...	Sandra Chase	Peggy Hetzler	Tom Tomberg	Robin Hickok	Noel Miller
Ellensburg	c	CM	15	(509) 962-7204	Obie O'Brien	Theodore Barkley	Coreen Reno	Ade' Ariwoola	Richard Elliott	Dale Miller	John Akers
Elma	t	MC	3	(360) 482-2212	David Osgood	...	Diana Easton	...	Ken Evans	Jean Wilson	James Starks
Enumclaw	c	MC	11	(360) 825-3591	John Wise	Mark Bauer	Marcia Hopkins	Mark Turley	Joseph Kolisch	Bruce Weigel	Christopher Searcy
Ephrata	c	CM	6	(509) 754-4601	Chris Jacobson	James Cherf	Leslie Trachsler	...	James Burns	Joseph Varick	William Sangster
Everett	c	MC	91	(425) 257-8700	...	Jim Langus	Sharon Marks	...	Terry Ollis	James Scharf	Clair Olivers
Federal Way	* c	CM	83	(253) 835-2604	Jack Dovey	Neal Beets	Carol McNeilly	Bryant Enge	...	Brian Wilson	...
Ferndale	c	CM	8	(360) 384-4302	Gary Jensen	Gregory Young	Linda Knutson	Mark Peterson	...	Michael Knapp	Bob Ceicle
Fife	c	MC	4	(253) 922-2489	...	Steve Worthington	...	Steven Marcotte	...	Brad Blackburn	Russell Blount
Fircrest	* c	CM	5	(253) 564-8901	David Viafore	Bill Brandon	Rick Rosenbladt	Colleen Corcoran	...	John Cheesman	Bill Larkin
Forks	c	MC	3	(360) 374-5412	Nedra Reed	...	...	Daniel Leinan	...	Michael Powell	David Zellar
Gig Harbor	c	MC	6	(253) 851-8136	Charles Hunter	Robert Karlinsey	Molly Towslee	David Rodenbach	...	Mitchell Barker	...
Goldendale	c	CM	3	(509) 773-3771	Mark Sigfrinius	Larry Bellamy	...	...	Lawrence Browning	David Hill	David Griffin
Grandview	* c	MC	8	(509) 882-9200	Norm Childress	Scott Staples	Anita Palacios	...	Pat Mason	David Charvet	Castulo Arteaga
Hoquiam	c	MC	9	(360) 532-5700	Jack Durney	...	...	Michael Folkers	Ray Pumphrey	Rick Thomas	M. Parsons
Issaquah	c	MC	11	(425) 837-3020	Ava Frisinger	Leon Kos	Tina Eggers	James Blake	...	Dave Draveling	Bob Brock
Kelso	c	CM	11	(360) 423-1371	Donald Gregory	Paul Brachvogel	Veryl Anderson	...	...	Wayne Nelson	David Sypher
Kenmore	c	CM	18	(425) 398-8900	Randy Eastwood	...	Lynn Batchelor	...	...	Cliff Sether	Theodore Carlson
Kennewick	c	CM	54	(509) 585-4200	James Beaver	Robert Hammond	Valerie Loffler	Marie Mosley	Bobby Kirk	Ken Hohenberg	E. Russ Burtner
Kent	c	MC	79	(253) 856-5700	James White	John Hodgson	Brenda Jacober	...	James Schneider	Edward Crawford	Don Wickstrom
Kirkland	c	CM	45	(425) 828-1100	Lawrence Springer	David Ramsay	...	...	Jeffery Blake	Stanley Aston	James Arndt
La Conner	t	MC	..	(360) 466-3125	Wayne Everton	Shani Taha	...	Lorraine Taylor	Dan Taylor	...	Brian Lease
Lacey	* c	CM	31	(360) 491-3214	Graeme Sackrison	Greg Cuoio	Carol Litten	Blaine Martin	...	Dusty Pierpoint	Scott Egger
Lake Forest Park	c	MC	13	(206) 368-5440	David Hutchinson	David Cline	Susan Stine	...	...	...	Frank Zenk
Lake Stevens	* c	MC	6	(425) 334-1012	Vern Little	Jan Berg	Norma Scott	...	...	Randy Celori	David Ostergaard
Lakewood	c	CM	58	(253) 589-2489	Claudia Thomas	Andrew Neiditz	Alice Bush	Galen Kidd	...	Larry Saunders	Don Wickstrom
Leavenworth	c	MC	2	(509) 548-5275	William Bauer	David Torgler	Cheryl Grant	...	...	...	Mike Deason
Liberty Lake	c	MC	4	(509) 755-6702	...	...	...	...	...	...	...
Long Beach	c	MC	1	(360) 642-4421	...	Eugene Miles	...	...	...	...	...
Longview	* c	CM	34	(360) 442-5004	Kurt Anangnostou	Robert Gregory	...	Kurt Sacha	Daryl McDaniel	Alex Perez	Jeff Cameron
Lynden	c	CM	9	(360) 354-4270	Jack Louws	William Verwolf	...	Teresa Camfield	Gary Baar	Jack Foster	Duane Huskey
Lynnwood	c	MC	33	(425) 775-1971	...	...	...	John Moir	Gary Olson	Steven Jensen	William Franz
Maple Valley	* c	CM	14	(425) 413-8800	Laure Iddings	Christy Todd	Irvalene Moni	Laurence McCarthy	Timothy Lemon	...	...
Marysville	c	MC	25	(360) 363-8000	Dennis Kendall	Mary Swenson	Gerry Becker	Sandy Langdon	...	Robert Carden	Paul Roberts
Medical Lake	c	MC	3	(509) 565-5000	Delmar Harland	Curtis Kelling	...	Pamela McBroom	Gino Palomino	Anthony Harbolt	John Ross
Medina	c	CM	3	(425) 454-6400	Miles Adam	Michael Caldwell	Rachel Baker	Jan Burdue	...	Jeffrey Chen	Joe Willis
Mercer Island	c	CM	22	(206) 236-5300	Alan Merkle	Richard Conrad	Christine Eggers	Chip Corder	Walter Mauldin	Ronald Elsoe	Glenn Boettcher
Mill Creek	* c	CM	11	(425) 745-1891	Terry Ryan	Timothy Burns	Kelly Chelin	Landy Manuel	...	Robert Crannell	Tom Gathmann
Milton	t	MC	5	(253) 922-8733	John Williams	...	Kathleen Browning	Gene Bray	Steve McKeen	Stan Jack	Mark Burlingame
Monroe	* c	MC	13	(360) 794-7400	Donnetta Walser	Tim Quenzer	Eadye Martinson	Carol Grey	...	...	Gene Brazel
Montesano	* c	MC	3	(360) 249-3021	Richard Stone	...	Kristy Powell	...	Ken Walkington	Raymond Sowers	Mike Wincewicz
Moses Lake	* c	CM	14	(509) 766-9201	Ron Covey	Joseph Gavinski	...	Ronald Cone	Tom Taylor	Dean Mitchell	Gary Harer
Mount Vernon	c	MC	26	(360) 336-0630	Skye Richendrfer	...	...	Alicia Huschka	Stephen Abel	Mike Barsness	John Buckley
Mountlake Terrace	* c	CM	20	(425) 776-1161	Jerry Smith	John Caulfield	Virginia Olsen	Sonja Springer	...	Scott Smith	Lawrence Water
Mukilteo	c	MC	18	(425) 355-4141	Joe Marine	Lee Walton	Christina Boughman	Scott James	Michael Springer	Michael Murphy	Larry Waters
Newcastle	c	CM	7	(425) 649-4444	...	John Starbard	Laura Hathaway	...	...	...	James Walker
Normandy Park	* c	CM	6	(206) 248-7603	John Wiltse	Douglas Schulze	Ronald Moore	Cherie Gibson	...	Rick Kieffer	Karl Franta
North Bend	* c	MC	4	(425) 888-1211	Kenneth Hearing	Duncan Wilson	Cheryl Proffitt	Elena Montgomery	...	Joseph Hodgson	Ron Garrow
Oak Harbor	c	MC	19	(360) 679-5551	Steve Dernbach	Earl Silvers	Rosemary Morrison	Douglas Merriman	Mark Soptich	Antonio Barge	Cathy Rosen
Ocean Shores	* c	CM	3	(360) 289-2488	Terry Veitz	...	Diane Houston	...	David Cowardin	...	John Gow
Olympia	c	CM	42	(360) 753-8447	Mark Foutch	Steven Hall	Debbie Krumpols	Jane Kirkemo	Larry Dibble	Gary Michel	D Mucha
Omak	c	MC	4	(509) 826-1170	...	...	...	Trish Butler	Kevin Bowling	L. Schreckengast	Fred Sheldon
Orting	* c	MC	3	(360) 893-2219	Cheryl Temple	Mark Bethune	...	Susan Davis	Randy Shelton	...	Dean Kaelin
Othello	c	MC	5	(509) 488-5686	Shannon McKay	Ehman Sheldon	Debbie Kudrna	Michael Bailey	...	Alvia Dunnagan	Jay Van Ness
Pacific	c	MC	5	(253) 929-1100	Richard Hildreth	...	Sandy Paul-Lyle	Lynne Simons	Harold Philbin	...	John Walsh
Pasco	* c	CM	32	(509) 545-3404	Joyce Olson	Gary Crutchfield	Debra Clark	...	Robert Gear	Denis Austin	Bob Alberts
Port Angeles	* c	CM	18	(360) 457-0411	...	Kent Myers	Becky Upton	G. Ziomkowski	Daniel McKeen	Terry Gallagher	Glenn Cutler
Port Orchard	* c	MC	7	(360) 876-4407	Lary Coppola	...	Patti Kirkpatrick	...	...	Alan Townsend	...
Port Townsend	* c	MC	8	(360) 379-4404	Michelle Sandoval	David Timmons	Pamela Kolacy	Michael Legarsky	...	Connor Daily	Kenneth Clow
Poulsbo	c	MC	6	(360) 779-3901	Donna Bruce	...	Karol Jones	Nanci Lien	...	Jeff Doran	Jeff Lincoln
Prosser	* c	MC	4	(509) 786-2332	...	Charles Bush	Sherry Biggs	Cathleen Koch	Douglas Merritt	Pat McCullough	L. J. Da Corsi
Pullman	* c	MC	24	(509) 338-3207	Glenn Johnson	John Sherman	...	Troy Woo	Patrick Wilkins	William Weatherly	Mark Workman
Puyallup	c	CM	33	(253) 841-5550	Kathy Turner	Gary McLean	Barbara Price	Scott McCarty	Merle Frank	Robin James	Mark Hoppen

Directory 1/9 continued OFFICIALS IN U.S. MUNICIPALITIES 2,500 AND OVER IN POPULATION

Jurisdiction	Type	Form of govern-ment	2000 Popu-lation	Main telephone number	Chief elected official	Appointed administrator	Clerk of the governing board	Chief financial officer	Fire chief	Police chief	Public works director
WASHINGTON continued											
Quincy	c	MC	5	(509) 787-3523	Richard Zimbelman	...	...	Sue Miller	...	William Gonzales	Dan Frazier
Raymond	c	CO	2	(360) 942-4100	...	...	Janet Jarvi	...	Tom Betrozoff	William Wilson	Rebecca Chaffee
Redmond	c	MC	45	(425) 556-2900	Rosemarie Ives	...	Bonnie Mattson	Lenda Crawford	John Ryan	Steven Harris	Carol Osborne
Renton *	c	MC	50	(425) 430-7650	K. Keolker-Wheeler	Jay Covington	Bonnie Walton	Iwen Wang	Ira Daniels	Kevin Milosevich	Gregg Zimmerman
Richland	c	CM	38	(509) 942-7390	Larry Haler	Cynthia Johnson	...	...	Glenn Johnason	David Lewis	Pete Squires
Ridgefield	c	MC	2	(360) 887-3557	...	George Fox	...	Kay Kammer	...	Bruce Hall	Justin Clary
Roslyn	c	MC	1	(509) 649-3105	Jeri Porter	...	Maria Fischer	Shannon Johansen	Steve Wynn	...	...
Sammamish *	c	CM	34	(425) 295-0500	Lee Fellinge	Bunyamin Yazici	Melonie Anderson	...	Lee Soptich	Brad Thompson	John Cunningham
Seatac	c	CM	25	(206) 973-4800	Gene Fisher	Craig Ward	Kristina Gregg	Mike McCarty	Bob Meyer	Jim Graddon	Dale Schroeder
Seattle	c	MC	563	(206) 684-4000	Gregory Nickels	...	Judith Pippin	Dwight Dively	Gregory Dean	R. Kerlikowske	...
Sedro-Woolley	c	MC	8	(360) 855-1661	Sharon Dillon	...	Patsy Nelson	...	Dean Klinger	Dave Cooper	Rick Blair
Selah	c	MC	6	(509) 698-7327	Robert Jones	Frank Sweet	Dale Novobielski	...	Jerry Davis	Rick Gutierrez	Joseph Henne
Sequim *	c	CM	4	(360) 683-4139	Laura Dubois	...	Karen Kuznek	...	...	Robert Spinks	James Bay
Shelton *	c	CO	8	(360) 426-4491	John Tarrant	Michael O'Leary	...	Cathy Beierle	...	Terry Davenport	...
Shoreline	c	CM	53	(206) 546-1700	Robert Ransom	Robert Olander	Scott Passey	Debra Tarry	...	...	Paul Haines
Snohomish	c	CM	8	(360) 568-3115	...	Larry Bauman	Torchie Corey	...	...	...	Dan Takasugi
Snoqualmie	c	MC	1	(425) 888-1555	Matthew Larson	Robert Larson	Joann Warren	Harry Oestreich	Bob Rowe	James Schaffer	Kirk Holmes
Spokane	c	MC	195	(509) 625-6250	Dennis Hession	John Pilcher	Terri Pfister	Gavin Cooley	Robert Williams	Anne Kirkpatrick	Dave Mandyke
Spokane Valley *	c	CM	82	(509) 921-1000	...	David Mercier	Christine Bainbridge	Ken Thompson	...	Rick VanLeuven	Neil Kersten
Stanwood	c	MC	3	(360) 629-2181	Matthew McCune	...	Linda Jeffries	Landy Manuel	...	...	William Beckman
Steilacoom	t	MC	6	(253) 581-1912	Ron Lucas	Paul Loveless	Susan Wilson	...	...	...	Johnny Bednarczyk
Sultan	c	CM	3	(360) 793-2231	Ben Tolson	Deborah Knight	Laura Koenig	...	...	Fred Walser	Connie Dunn
Sumas *	c	MC	..	(360) 988-5711	Robert Bromley	...	...	Geri Lewis	...	Chris Haugen	Rod Fadden
Sumner *	c	MC	8	(253) 863-8300	David Enslow	John Doan	Terri Berry	Beth Anne Wroe	...	John Galle	William Pugh
Sunnyside	c	CM	13	(509) 837-3997	Edward Prilucik	Eric Swansen	Deborah Estrada	Scott James	Aaron Markham	Edwin Radder	Jim Bridges
Tacoma *	c	CM	193	(253) 591-5000	William Baarsma	Eric Anderson	Doris Sorum	Robert Biles	Ronald Stephens	Donald Ramsdell	...
Toledo *	c	MC	..	(360) 864-4564	...	...	Michelle Whitten	...	...	...	Loren Steveson
Toppenish *	c	CM	8	(509) 865-6319	Loren Belton	William Murphy	...	Linda Mead	...	...	Lance Hoyt
Tukwila *	c	MC	17	(206) 433-1831	Jim Haggerton	...	Christy O'Flaherty	Shawn Hunstock	Nick Olivas	David Haynes	James Morrow
Tumwater	c	MC	12	(360) 754-5855	Ralph Osgood	Doug Baker	...	Gayla Gjertsen	Rich Ridgeway	H. Vandiver	Jay Eaton
Union Gap	c	MC	5	(509) 248-0432	...	...	...	...	...	...	...
University Place *	c	CM	29	(253) 566-5656	Linda Bird	Robert Jean	Emelita Genetia	David Layden	Mitch Sagers	Jim Andrews	Gary Cooper
Vancouver	c	CM	143	(360) 619-1005	Royce Pollard	Patrick McDonnell	...	...	Don Bivins	Clifford Cook	Brian Carlson
Walla Walla *	c	CM	29	(509) 527-4522	Dan Johnson	Duane Cole	Kammy Hill	...	Terrence Thomas	Charles Fulton	Craig Sivley
Wapato	c	MC	4	(509) 877-2334	Jesse Farias	...	Rosie Rumsey	...	Jose Valdez	Richard Sanchez	Gary Potter
Washougal	c	MC	8	(360) 835-8501	Jeff Guard	Nabiel Shawa	...	Rebecca Hasart	Ronald Caster	Robert Garwood	...
Wenatchee	c	CO	27	(509) 664-3300	...	...	...	Mark Calhoun	...	...	...
West Richland *	c	MC	8	(509) 967-3431	Dale Jackson	David Weiser	Julie Richardson	Howard Roberts	...	Layne Erdman	Roscoe Slade
Woodinville	c	CM	9	(425) 489-2700	...	Richard Leahy	Jennifer Kuhn	Jim Katica	Steve Smith	Ken Wardstrom	Mick Monken
Woodland	c	MC	3	(360) 225-8281	Doug Monge	...	...	...	Anthony Brentin	Robert Stephenson	R. VanderZanden
Yakima	c	CM	71	(509) 575-6090	...	Richard Zais	Karen Roberts	Rita Debord	Dennis Mayo	Samuel Granato	C. Waarvick
Yelm	c	MC	3	(360) 458-3244	Ron Harding	Shelly Badger	Janine Schnepf	Tanya Robacker	...	Todd Stancil	Tim Peterson
WEST VIRGINIA											
Barboursville	v	MC	3	(304) 736-8994	Nancy Cartmill	...	...	Charles Woolcock	Paul Ritchie	Frank Simpson	Steve Parsons
Beckley	c	MC	17	(304) 256-1768	...	...	...	...	...	...	...
Bethlehem	v	MC	2	(304) 242-4180	...	...	...	...	...	...	...
Bluefield	c	CM	11	(304) 327-2401	Linda Whalen	Mark Henne	Drema Shireman	Larkin Calhoun	Tony Hodges	Joe Wilson	Dallas Fowler
Bridgeport	c	CM	7	(304) 842-8217	Leonard Timms	A. Kim Haws	Judith Lawson	Keith Boggs	John Vanlandingham	Jack Clayton	Daniel Ferrell
Buckhannon	c	MC	5	(304) 472-1651	E. Poundstone	...	...	...	Larry Mackey	Frederic Gaudet	...
Charles Town *	c	MC	2	(304) 725-2311	Peggy Smith	Gary Rawlings	Joseph Cosentini	Tara Hostler	...	Barry Subelsky	Jane Arnett
Charleston *	c	MC	53	(304) 348-8015	Daniel Jones	David Molgaard	James Rieshman	Joseph Estep	Randy Stanley	Brent Webster	Donald Carr
Chester	c	MC	2	(304) 387-2820	...	...	...	...	...	...	...
Clarksburg	c	CM	16	(304) 624-1600	Sam Lopez	Martin Howe	Annette Wright	Frank Ferrari	Joe Gonzalez	John Walker	Frank Scercelli
Dunbar	c	MC	8	(304) 766-0222	...	...	...	...	...	...	...
Elkins	c	MC	7	(304) 636-1414	...	...	Philip Graziani	...	...	Mike Taylor	...
Fairmont	c	CM	19	(304) 366-6211	Nick Fantasia	James Snider	Janet Keller	Eileen Layman	Gregg Freme	Stephen Cain	Michael DeMary
Fayetteville	t	CM	2	(304) 574-0101	James Murdock	Cecil Gibson	Paula Ballard	...	John Vernon	Paul Tygrett	...
Follansbee	c	CM	3	(304) 527-1330	Anthony Paesano	Kevin Diserio	David Kurcina	...	Larry Rea	John Schwertfeger	Steve Meca
Grafton *	c	CM	5	(304) 265-1412	Thomas Bartlett	Kevin Stead	Larry Richman	...	Craig Crimm	Robert Beltner	Gerald Weber
Hinton	c	CM	2	(304) 466-3255	Cleo Matthews	C. Meadows	Sherry Allen	...	Leon Pivont	Richard Poe	Ralph Trout
Huntington	c	MC	51	(304) 696-5580	David Felinton	Conrad Thornburgh	Barbara Nelson	Robert Wilhelm	Gregory Fuller	Arthur Baumgardner	George McClennen
Hurricane	c	MC	5	(304) 562-5896	Raymond Peak	...	...	...	...	Lawrence Foster	...
Kenova	c	MC	3	(304) 453-1571	Larry Smith	...	Sheila Wheeler	...	Steve Salyers	Ronnie Dickerson	...
Keyser	c	MC	5	(304) 788-1511	Roger Newlin	Kathy Merrill	...	...	...	Karen Shoemaker	...
Kingwood	t	MC	2	(304) 329-1225	Fred Peddicord	...	Eleanor Williams	...	...	Thomas Martin	Claude Waugerman
Lewisburg *	c	MC	3	(304) 645-2080	John Manchester	...	Shannon Ninnemann	...	Wayne Pennington	Tim Stover	Mark Carver
Logan	t	MC	1	(304) 752-4044	Claude Ellis	...	Dolores Lopes	Jeff Vallet	Vernon Beckett	David White	...
Madison	c	MC	2	(304) 369-2762	...	...	...	...	...	...	...
Mannington	t	MC	2	(304) 986-2700	Orval Price	...	Michele Fluharty	...	Joel McCann	David James	Richard Stevens
Martinsburg	c	CM	14	(304) 264-2131	George Karos	Mark Baldwin	...	Mark Spickler	Paul Bragg	Theodore Anderson	Ben Leonard
Montgomery	t	MC	2	(304) 442-5181	...	...	...	...	...	...	...
Morgantown	c	CM	26	(304) 284-7405	Ronald Justice	Dan Boroff	Linda Little	Denise White	David Fetty	Robert Lucci	Terry Hough
Moundsville	c	CM	9	(304) 845-3394	...	Allen Hendershot	Sondra Hewitt	...	Noel Clark	James Kudlak	James Richmond
Mullens	t	MC	1	(304) 294-7132	S. Brewer	...	William Mongeni	...	Rick Rice	James Miller	James Roop
New Martinsville	c	MC	5	(304) 455-9120	James Herrick	...	Bonnie Shannon	...	Kent Longwell	Timothy Cecil	Gary Lemons
Nitro	t	MC	6	(304) 755-0701	...	...	...	...	...	...	...
Oak Hill	c	CM	7	(304) 469-9541	...	...	...	...	...	...	...
Paden City	t	MC	2	(304) 337-2295	Anthony Sapp	...	Judy Lyons	Ginger Wilcox	James Richmond	Scott Dalrymple	Clifford Duke
Parkersburg	c	MC	33	(304) 424-8400	Jimmy Colombo	...	Connie Shaffer	Randall Craig	John Knapp	Robert Newell	William Slater
Philippi	c	CM	2	(304) 457-3700	Caton Hill	Karen Weaver	Tamula Stemple	Whitni Kines	John Green	...	Buddy Shreve
Point Pleasant	c	MC	4	(304) 675-2360	Charles McCann	...	Donald Whitten	...	Vernon Quintrell	James Scites	...
Princeton *	c	CM	6	(304) 487-5020	Dewey Russell	Wayne Shumate	Kenneth Clay	Kelly Davis	Shawn Vest	William Harman	Kenneth Rose
Ranson	c	MC	2	(304) 725-1010	A. Hamill	Paul Mills	Elizabeth Stroop	Stephen Hudson	...	William Roper	James Spradley
Ravenswood	c	CM	4	(304) 273-2621	Lucy Harbert	...	Kendra Liegey	...	Terry Drennen	Paul Hesson	Edwin Flinn
Richwood	c	MC	2	(304) 846-2596	Jeromy Rose	...	Emily Williams	Ronnie Bragg	John Greer	Larry Tinney	Frank White
Ripley	c	MC	3	(304) 372-3482	Ollie Harvey	...	...	...	...	Tom McCrady	Tim King
Ronceverte *	c	MC	1	(304) 647-5455	Gail White	Blaine Oborn	...	...	...	...	...
Salem	c	CM	2	(304) 782-1318	...	...	...	...	...	...	...
Shinnston	c	CM	2	(304) 592-2126	Sammy De Marco	...	Debra Herndon	...	...	Michael Secreto	...
South Charleston	c	MC	13	(304) 744-5301	Richard Robb	...	Jack Woolwine	Rodger Raybourn	Claude Sigman	David Dunlap	Franklin Mullens
Spencer	c	MC	2	(304) 927-1640	...	...	...	...	...	...	...
St. Albans	c	MC	11	(304) 722-3391	Jack Gessel	...	B. Cunningham	...	Dwight Pettry	Homer Clark	Orville Browning
St. Marys *	c	CM	2	(304) 684-2401	L. Paul Ingram	Thomas Painter	Linda Wilson	...	Lee Ogdin	William Stull	Ron Cokeley
Summersville	t	MC	3	(304) 872-1211	Stanley Adkins	...	Michael Brown	Ronald Hancock	Joe Boso	Ray Moore	Robert Hilleary

Directory 1/9 continued — OFFICIALS IN U.S. MUNICIPALITIES 2,500 AND OVER IN POPULATION

Jurisdiction	Type	Form of govern-ment	2000 Popu-lation	Main telephone number	Chief elected official	Appointed administrator	Clerk of the governing board	Chief financial officer	Fire chief	Police chief	Public works director
WEST VIRGINIA continued											
Vienna	c	MC	10	(304) 295-4541	David Nohe	. . .	Carla Starcher	. . .	Daniel Goodwin	Gary Deem	Craig Metz
Weirton	c	CM	20	(304) 797-8501	William Miller	Gary Dufour	Dolores Ostrander	Valerie Means	Kessler Cole	Lance Scott	Brae Bryant
Welch	c	CM	2	(304) 436-3113	Martha Moore	. . .	Robin Owens	. . .	Dennie Hale	Robert Bowman	Robert Lee
Wellsburg *	c	CM	2	(304) 737-2104	Wayne Campbell	. . .	Mary Blum	. . .	. . .	Stanley Kins	. . .
Weston	c	MC	4	(304) 269-6141	Jon Tucci	Frank Robinette	. . .	Rebecca Swisher	Michael Young	Roger Clem	. . .
Westover	c	MC	3	(304) 296-6860	Suzanne Kenney	Jim Rutledge	Lahomma Brock	. . .	David Clawges	James Smith	Roger Malone
Wheeling *	c	CM	31	(304) 234-3694	Andy McKenzie	Robert Herron	Janice Jones	Michael Klug	Larry Helms	Kevin Gessler	Russell Jebbia
White Sulphur Springs *	c	MC	2	(304) 536-1454	Debra Fogus	. . .	James Perrow	L. Coleman-Barker	Paul Fogus	James Hylton	. . .
Williamson	c	MC	3	(304) 235-1510	Sam Kapourales	. . .	. . .	. . .	Grover Phillips	Roby Pope	Dewey Dingess
Williamstown	c	MC	2	(304) 375-7761	Marvin Stead	. . .	Susan Wooddell	. . .	. . .	. . .	Robert Kimble
WISCONSIN											
Adams	c	MC	1	(608) 339-6516	Kenneth Romell	Robert Ellisor	Linda Ritchie	. . .	. . .	James Gold	David Mead
Algoma	c	MC	3	(920) 487-5203	Virginia Haske	Thomas Romdenne	. . .	. . .	Thomas Ackerman	Daniel Brusky	Gary Paape
Allouez	v	CM	14	(920) 448-2800	Camron McCain	Susan Foxworthy	. . .	. . .	. . .	. . .	Tom Meier
Altoona	c	CM	6	(715) 839-6092	Larry Sturz	Ronald Rusmussen	. . .	. . .	. . .	. . .	Henry Gleason
Amery *	c	MC	2	(715) 268-7486	. . .	Darcy Long	Jody Ferguson	. . .	Richard Van Blaricom	Thomas Marson	Allen McCarty
Antigo *	c	MC	8	(715) 623-3633	Samuel Hardin	. . .	Kaye Matucheski	. . .	Jon Petroskey	William Brandt	. . .
Appleton	c	MC	70	(920) 832-6400	Timothy Hanna	. . .	Cynthia Hesse	Lisa Maertz	Neil Cameron	Richard Myers	Paula Vandehey
Ashland	c	MC	8	(715) 682-7071	Fred Schnoor	. . .	Rae Buckwheat	Michael Screnock	Keith Tveit	Daniel Crawford	James Struck
Ashwaubenon	v	MC	17	(920) 492-2327	Norbert DeCleene	. . .	Dawn Collins	Greg Wenholz	Paul Hawley	. . .	Keith Watermolen
Baraboo *	c	MC	10	(608) 355-2700	Patrick Liston	Edward Geick	Cheryl Giese	. . .	Kevin Stieve	Craig Olsen	Robert Koss
Barron *	c	MC	3	(715) 537-5631	David Vruwink	. . .	Tony Slagstad	. . .	Larry Johnson	Byron Miller	David Hanson
Bayside	v	CM	4	(414) 351-8811	Samuel Dickman	Andrew Pederson	. . .	. . .	. . .	Bruce Resnick	Joel Hawkins
Beaver Dam *	c	MC	15	(920) 887-4600	. . .	. . .	. . .	. . .	. . .	. . .	. . .
Bellevue	v	CM	9	(920) 468-5225	. . .	Aaron Oppenheimer	Karen Simons	. . .	. . .	. . .	Ronald Umentum
Beloit *	t	CM	7	(608) 364-2980	Greg Groves	Robert Museus	Karry Devault	. . .	Dennis Ahrens	John Wilson	Howard Hemmer
Beloit *	c	CM	35	(608) 364-6610	. . .	Larry Arft	Carol Alexander	. . .	Bradley Liggett	Sam Lathrop	David Botts
Berlin	c	CM	5	(920) 361-5400	. . .	. . .	Jodie Olson	. . .	John Stetter	Dennis Plantz	Brian Freimark
Black River Falls	c	MC	3	(715) 284-5514	Joseph Hunter	William Arndt	. . .	. . .	Steven Schreiber	Donald Gilberg	Todd Gomer
Bloomer	c	MC	3	(715) 568-3032	Randy Summerfield	. . .	. . .	. . .	. . .	Michael Bungartz	. . .
Boscobel	c	MC	3	(608) 375-5001	Stephen Wetter	Arlie Harris	. . .	. . .	Jeff Boughton	James Reynolds	Michael Reynolds
Brillion *	c	MC	2	(920) 756-2250	Gerald Sonnabend	Lori Gosz	. . .	. . .	Richard Janke	Scott Kaphingst	. . .
Bristol	t	MC	4	(262) 857-2368	Richard Gossling	Randall Kerkman	Amy Klemko	Kathleen Gerretsen	Mike Moran	. . .	. . .
Brodhead *	c	MC	3	(608) 897-4018	Douglas Pinnow	. . .	Nancy Schoeller	. . .	Jay Bohan	Tom Moczynski	Randy Rosheisen
Brookfield	t	CM	6	(262) 796-3788	. . .	Richard Czopp	Jane Carlson	. . .	. . .	. . .	. . .
Brookfield	c	MC	38	(262) 796-6642	Jeffrey Speaker	. . .	Kris Schmidt	Robert Scott	John Dahms	Daniel Tushaus	Thomas Grisa
Brown Deer *	v	CM	12	(414) 371-3000	Carl Krueger	Russell Van Gompel	. . .	. . .	. . .	Steven Rinzel	Larry Neitzel
Buchanan *	t	MC	5	(920) 734-8599	. . .	Angela Gorall	. . .	. . .	Mike Grones	. . .	. . .
Burlington *	c	CM	9	(262) 342-1171	Robert Miller	Kevin Lahner	Beverly Gull	Bridget Lois	. . .	Scott Eisenhauer	Connie Wilson
Butler *	v	CM	1	(262) 783-2525	Walter Woloszyk	Tim Rhode	. . .	. . .	Ron Worgull	Mike Cosgrove	. . .
Caledonia	v	CM	23	(262) 835-4451	Jonathan Delagrave	Thomas Lebak	Wendy Christensen	Larry Borchert	Peter Waselchuk	Jeffrey Meier	Robert Wittke
Campbell *	t	MC	4	(608) 793-0050	Scott Johnson	Travis Parish	. . .	. . .	. . .	Ron Latva	. . .
Cedarburg	t	CM	5	(262) 377-4509	Dave Valentine	James Culotta	Karen Behrens	. . .	. . .	. . .	Thomas Marquardt
Cedarburg *	c	MC	10	(262) 375-7600	Gregory Myers	Christy Mertes	Constance McHugh	. . .	Richard Van Dinter	Thomas Frank	Thomas Wiza
Chenequa	v	CM	. .	(262) 367-2239	Bryce Styza	Robert Douglas	Bonita Zimdars	. . .	Richard Hagemann	. . .	Jeff Kante
Chilton	c	MC	3	(920) 849-2451	Bill Engler	. . .	. . .	. . .	Jim Kurtz	Dennis Plantz	Todd Schwarz
Chippewa Falls	c	MC	12	(715) 726-2719	Daniel Hedrington	Ron Singel	Frank Braswell	. . .	Edward Mishefske	Joseph Coughlin	John Allen
Clayton *	t	MC	2	(920) 836-2007	. . .	Richard Johnston	S. Nester-Huebner	. . .	. . .	. . .	. . .
Clinton *	v	MC	2	(608) 676-5304	Mary Jensen	Philip Rath	. . .	. . .	John Rindfleisch	James Korth	Roger Johnson
Clintonville	c	MC	4	(715) 823-7600	Robert Gay	Lisa Kuss	Chris Vollrath	. . .	John Krubsack	Terry Lorge	Michael McCord
Columbus	c	MC	4	(920) 623-5900	William Wendt	Boyd Kraemer	Anne Donahue	. . .	Glenn Dykstra	Gerald Sallmann	Michael Healy
Combined Locks	v	MC	2	(920) 788-2059	Ed Wulgaert	Mark Van Thiel	. . .	. . .	Rick Strick	Steve Wulgaert	Mark Ristau
Coon Valley	v	MC	. .	(608) 452-3168	Michael Johnson	. . .	Michael Borgen	. . .	. . .	Michael Raasch	John Langaard
Cottage Grove	v	MC	4	(608) 839-4704	Kenneth Dahl	. . .	Kim Manley	. . .	. . .	John Gould	James Hessling
Cudahy	c	MC	18	(414) 769-2203	Raymond Glowacki	. . .	Philip Brannon	. . .	Richard Demien	Mark Hayes	Michael Clark
De Forest *	v	CM	7	(608) 846-6751	Jeffrey Miller	JoAnn Miller	LuAnn Leggett	Steve Fahlgren	David Arnold	Robert Henze	P. Vander Sanden
De Pere	c	CM	20	(920) 339-4044	Mike Walsh	Lawrence Delo	Dave Minten	Joseph Zegers	Robert Kiser	Derek Beiderwieden	Roy Simonson
Delafield *	c	MC	6	(262) 646-6220	Ed McAleer	Timothy Schuenke	Gina Gresch	. . .	Jack Edwards	Scott Taubel	Thomas Hafner
Delavan	t	CM	4	(262) 728-3471	Marvin Herman	. . .	Colleen Endish	. . .	. . .	Andrew Mayer	James Wolfgram
Delavan *	c	MC	7	(262) 728-5585	Melvin Nieuwenhuis	Joseph Salitros	Susan Kitzman	. . .	Neil Flood	Tim O'Neill	Mark Wendorf
Denmark	v	MC	1	(920) 863-6400	. . .	Gordon Ellis	. . .	. . .	. . .	. . .	. . .
Dodgeville	c	MC	4	(608) 935-5228	. . .	. . .	. . .	. . .	. . .	. . .	. . .
East Troy *	v	CM	3	(262) 642-6255	William Loesch	. . .	. . .	. . .	Mike Barutha	Alan Boyes	Tom Rossmiller
Eau Claire	c	CM	61	(715) 839-4921	Mark Lewis	Michael Huggins	Donna Austad	Rebecca Noland	. . .	. . .	William Bittner
Edgerton *	c	MC	4	(608) 884-3341	Erik Thompson	Ramona Flanigan	Cinthia Hegglund	. . .	. . .	Thomas Klubertanz	Tom Hartzell
Elkhorn	c	MC	7	(262) 723-2219	Paul Ormson	Samuel Tapson	Nancy Jacobson	Samuel West	Dennis Hommen	John Giese	Terry Weter
Elm Grove *	v	CM	6	(262) 782-6700	Neil Palmer	David DeAngelis	Mary Stredni	Monica Hughes	William Selzer	James Gage	Michael Flaherty
Elroy	c	MC	1	(608) 462-2400	Don Baldwin	. . .	. . .	. . .	. . .	Dave Wagner	Ed Gashi
Evansville *	c	MC	4	(608) 882-2266	Sandy Decker	Dan Wietecha	Judy Walton	Eric Jepperson	. . .	Scott McElroy	David Wartenweiler
Fitchburg *	t	MC	20	(608) 270-4200	Thomas Clauder	Anthony Roach	Linda Cory	Nancy Solberg	Randall Pickering	Thomas Blatter	Paul Woodard
Fond Du Lac	c	CM	42	(920) 322-3623	Marty Ryan	Thomas Herre	Theresa Hochrein	Hal Wortman	Joe Clow	Duane Johnson	Mark Lentz
Fontana-On-Geneva Lake	v	CM	1	(262) 275-6136	. . .	Kelly Hayden-Staggs	Phyllis Smith	. . .	. . .	Steven Olson	Craig Workman
Fort Atkinson *	c	CM	11	(920) 563-7760	Loren Gray	John Wilmet	Faith Elford	. . .	Thomas Emrick	Tony Brus	Tom Kramp
Fox Lake	c	MC	1	(920) 928-2280	Richard Klomsten	William Petracek	Susan Hollnagel	. . .	William Frank	Patrick Lynch	Douglas Buchda
Fox Point *	v	CM	7	(414) 351-8900	Michael West	Susan Robertson	Tanya O'Malley	. . .	. . .	Thomas Czaja	Scott Brandmeier
Franklin *	c	MC	29	(414) 858-1100	. . .	. . .	Sandi Wesolowski	Cal Patterson	James Martins	Richard Oliva	Jerry Schaefer
Germantown	v	CM	18	(262) 250-4750	Charles Hargan	David Schornack	Jane Wilms	Kim Rath	Gary Pollpeter	Raymond Van Male	Allan Caverson
Glendale *	c	MC	13	(414) 228-1714	Jerome Tepper	Richard Maslowski	. . .	Shawn Lanser	David Berousek	Tom Czarnyszka	Dave Eastman
Grafton	v	CM	10	(262) 375-5300	James Brunnquell	Darrell Hofland	Teri Dylak	. . .	David Harvey	Charles Wenten	David Murphy
Grand Chute	t	CM	18	(920) 832-1573	Michael Marsden	. . .	Judith Christjohn	. . .	Todd Farley	Edgar Kopp	. . .
Green Bay	c	MC	102	(920) 448-3147	Jim Schmitt	. . .	Sue Badeau	Doug Daul	Jeff Stauber	James Arts	Carl Weber
Green Lake *	c	MC	1	(920) 294-6912	Charles Mirr	. . .	Barbara Dugenske	. . .	William Wagner	Stephen Huber	Glen McCarty
Greendale	v	CM	14	(414) 423-2100	Scott Leonard	Todd Michaels	. . .	. . .	Gary Fedder	Robert Dams	Carl Tisonik
Greenfield	c	MC	35	(414) 329-5208	Timothy Seider	. . .	Donna Rynders	Milton Vandermeuse	Roland Poppy	Francis Springob	Richard Sokol
Greenville	t	MC	6	(920) 757-5151	. . .	David Tebo	. . .	. . .	Glenn Kelly	. . .	. . .
Hales Corners	v	CM	7	(414) 529-6161	James Ryan	Michael Weber	. . .	. . .	David Bialk	Kent Bieganski	Michael Martin
Hartford	c	CM	10	(262) 673-8204	Scott Henke	. . .	Marjorie Savana	Gary Koppelberger	Robert Baus	Thomas Jones	. . .
Hartland	v	CM	7	(262) 367-2714	David Lamerand	Wallace Thiel	Constance Casper	Joicelyn Schwager	Allen Wilde	Robert Rosch	James Wilson
Hillsboro *	c	CM	1	(608) 489-2521	Alan Picha	Brett Klein	Sheila Schraufnagel	. . .	. . .	Thomas Richardson	. . .
Hobart *	v	MC	5	(920) 869-1011	Rich Heidel	Elaine Willman	Mary Smith	. . .	Robert Van De Hey	Randy Bani	Rick Kinney
Holman	v	CM	6	(608) 526-4336	. . .	Catherine Schmit	. . .	. . .	. . .	Mike McHugh	Phil Scholze
Horicon	c	MC	3	(920) 485-3500	James Grigg	. . .	David Pasewald	. . .	James Bandsma	Joseph Adamson	S. Bogenschneider
Hortonville *	v	CM	2	(920) 779-6011	Roger Retzlaff	J. Mitchell	Lynne Mischker	. . .	Dave Dorn	Michael Sullivan	Ronald Austreng
Howard *	v	CM	13	(920) 434-4640	Burt McIntyre	Joshua Smith	. . .	Chris Haltom	Ed Janke	. . .	Robert Bartelt

Directory 1/9 continued — OFFICIALS IN U.S. MUNICIPALITIES 2,500 AND OVER IN POPULATION

Jurisdiction	Type	Form of govern- ment	2000 Popu- lation	Main telephone number	Chief elected official	Appointed administrator	Clerk of the governing board	Chief financial officer	Fire chief	Police chief	Public works director
WISCONSIN continued											
Hudson	c	MC	8	(715) 386-4765	Jack Breault	Devin Willi	Nancy Norvold	Betty Caruso	James Frye	Richard Trende	James Eulberg
Jackson *	v	CM	4	(262) 677-9001	Scott Mittelsteadt	...	Susan Rank	...	John Skodinski	Jed Dolnick	Brian Kober
Janesville *	c	CM	59	(608) 755-3080	...	Eric Levitt	Jean Wulf	...	Larry Grorud	Burton Mahan	Jack Messer
Jefferson	c	MC	7	(920) 674-7700	Arnold Brawders	...	Tanya Stewart	...	...	...	Daniel Ludwig
Johnson Creek	v	MC	1	(920) 699-2296	...	Paul Moderacki	Joan Dykstra	...	...	...	...
Kaukauna *	c	MC	12	(920) 766-6300	Eugene Rosin	...	Susan Duda	Steve Giebel	Paul Hirte	John Manion	John Sundelius
Kenosha *	c	MC	90	(262) 653-4130	Keith Bosman	Frank Pacetti	Michael Higgins	Carol Stancato	John Thomsen	John Morrissey	Ronald Bursek
Kewaskum	v	CM	3	(262) 626-8484	...	Matt Heiser	...	...	Mark Groeschel	Richard Knoebel	Jerry Gilles
Kewaunee	c	MC	2	(920) 388-5000	Jerome Zelten	...	...	...	Greg Hlinak	David Decramer	Michael Ley
Kiel	c	MC	3	(920) 894-2909	...	...	...	...	...	...	...
Kimberly	v	CM	6	(920) 788-7500	Charles Kuen	Rick Hermus	Sandra Haas	...	...	David Peterson	D. V. Boogaard
Kronenwetter	v	CM	5	(715) 693-4200	Rick Smith	...	Krystal Bokelman	...	Roger James	Daniel Joling	Lisa Myles
La Crosse *	c	MC	51	(608) 789-7595	Mark Johnsrud	...	Teri Lehrke	...	Gregg Cleveland	Edward Kondracki	Dale Hexom
La Pointe	t	MC	..	(715) 747-6914	...	B. Cunningham	...	...	...	...	...
Ladysmith	c	MC	3	(715) 532-2600	Ronald Moore	Alan Christianson	Kathleen Stewart	Joel Dutenhoefer	Scott Bingham	Norman Rozak	William Christianson
Lake Geneva *	c	MC	7	(262) 248-3673	William Chesen	Dennis Jordan	Diana Dykstra	...	Brent Connelly	Michael Rasmussen	Daniel Winkler
Lake Mills	c	CM	4	(920) 648-2344	Danny Stevens	Steven Wilke	James Heilman	...	Richard Heinz	Kathleen Hansen	John Tremain
Lancaster *	c	CM	4	(608) 723-4246	Jerome Wehrle	Scot Simpson	David Kurihara	...	Robert Little	Dan Jacobson	Jerry Carroll
Little Chute *	v	CM	10	(920) 788-7380	Charles Fischer	Charles Kell	Vicki Karch	Dale Haug	R. Vanden Heuvel	...	Roy Van Gheem
Long Lake	t	MC	..	(715) 674-6974	Wally Cooper	...	J. Behrmann	...	...	...	...
Luck *	v	MC	1	(715) 472-2221	...	Kristina Handt	...	...	...	...	...
Madison	c	MC	208	(608) 266-4611	Dave Cieslewicz	...	Ray Fisher	Dean Brasser	Debra Amesqua	Richard Williams	...
Manitowoc *	c	MC	34	(920) 686-6950	Kevin Crawford	...	Jennifer Hudon	Brian Ruechel	Charles Herzog	Perry Kingsbury	William Handlos
Maple Bluff	v	CM	1	(608) 244-3048	John Larson	...	...	...	Eric Dahl	Timothy Krueger	Thomas Schroeder
Marinette	c	MC	11	(715) 732-5141	Douglas Oitzinger	...	James Anderson	Yuzhen Liu	Joseph Giver	Jeffery Skorik	Brian Miller
Marshfield	c	MC	18	(715) 387-6597	Michael Meyers	Michael Brehm	Debbie Hall	Keith Strey	Gregg Cleveland	Joseph Stroik	Daniel Knoek
Mauston *	c	MC	3	(608) 847-6676	Brian McGuire	Brian Yerges	Renee Hazelton	...	Kim Hale	Mark Messer	Rob Nelson
Mayville	c	MC	4	(920) 387-7900	Ronald Sternat	...	Kathie Wild	...	Roger Williams	William Linzenmeyer	Vern Hilker
Mc Farland	v	CM	6	(608) 838-3153	Erik Thoresen	...	Donald Peterson	...	Gary Garmon	Greg Leck	Dennis Dancker
Medford	c	MC	4	(715) 748-4321	Michael Wellner	John Fales	Virginia Brost	...	...	Ted Bever	...
Menasha *	t	CM	15	(920) 720-7100	Arden Tews	Jeffrey Sturgell	Karen Tweedie	Myra Piergrossi	Keith Kiesow	Rod McCants	...
Menasha	c	MC	16	(920) 967-5117	Joseph Laux	...	Joan Smogoleski	Thomas Stoffel	Patrick O'Brien	Robert Stanke	Mark Radtke
Menomonee Falls *	v	CM	32	(262) 532-4200	Richard Rechlicz	Mark Fitzgerald	Kathleen Karalewitz	Mary Datka	Robert Coon	Anna Ruzinski	Arlyn Johnson
Menomonie	c	CM	14	(715) 232-2187	Dennis Kropp	Lowell Prange	JoAnn Kadinger	...	Jack Baus	Dennis Beety	Randy Eide
Mequon *	c	MC	21	(262) 242-3100	Christine Nuernberg	Lee Szymborski	...	Thomas Watson	David Bialk	Steve Graff	Jon Garms
Merrill	c	MC	10	(715) 536-5594	Douglas Williams	Tony Chladek	William Heideman	Katherine Unertl	Norm Hanson	Neil Strobel	...
Merton	v	MC	1	(262) 538-0820	...	...	...	...	...	...	...
Middleton	t	CM	4	(608) 833-5887	Milo Breunig	David Shaw	...	...	...	...	...
Middleton	c	MC	15	(608) 827-1050	...	Michael Davis	...	Tim Studer	Mark Rauls	Larry Fass	Hank Simon
Milton *	c	MC	5	(608) 868-6900	Nathan Bruce	Todd Schmidt	Nancy Zastrow	...	Loren Lippincott	Jerry Schuetz	Howard Robinson
Milwaukee *	c	MC	596	(414) 286-3387	John Norquist	Steven Jacquart	Ronald Leonhardt	Waldemar Morics	William Wentlandt	Arthur Jones	M. Schifalacqua
Mondovi	c	MC	2	(715) 926-3866	Sharon Beauchamp	...	Daniel Lauersdorf	...	Dennis Brion	Terry Pittman	Randy Gruber
Monona *	c	CM	8	(608) 222-2525	Robb Kahl	Patrick Marsh	Joan Andrusz	Marc Houtakker	Robert Van Etten	Walter Ostrenga	...
Monroe	c	MC	10	(608) 329-2500	William Ross	Mark Vahlsing	James Myers	Kathie Lindsay	Thomas Casey	Frederick Kelley	Nathan Klassy
Mosinee	c	CM	4	(715) 693-2275	Alan Erickson	Jeff Gates	Bruce Jamroz	...	...	Kenneth Muelling	Kevin Breit
Mount Horeb	v	MC	5	(608) 437-6884	John Zimmel	Patrick Dann	Cheryl Sutter	...	Charles Himsel	Scott Sterland	Laurel Grindle
Mount Pleasant	v	CM	23	(262) 554-8750	Mark Gleason	...	Juliet Edwards	Dancy Bugni	William Bouma	James Madjoch	...
Mukwonago	v	MC	6	(262) 363-6420	James Wagner	...	Steve Braatz	...	Jeffrey Rolfe	Fred Winchowky	T. Brandemuehl
Mukwonago	t	TM	6	(262) 363-4555	David Dubey	...	...	...	...	Grant Turner	...
Muskego	c	MC	21	(262) 679-5675	Mark Slocomb	...	Jean Marenda	Dawn Gunderson	...	John Johnson	Wayne Delikat
Neenah	c	MC	24	(920) 751-4604	...	...	...	...	...	...	...
Neillsville *	c	MC	2	(715) 743-2105	Diane Murphy	...	Rex Roehl	...	Matt Meyer	Bradley Lindner	David Flynn
Nekoosa	c	MC	2	(715) 886-3811	Gordon Freeman	...	...	...	Ken Hartje	...	Terry Shymanski
New Berlin	c	MC	38	(262) 786-8610	Jack Chiovatero	...	Marilyn Gauger	Michael Holzinger	Edward Dobernig	Joseph Rieder	...
New Glarus	v	CM	2	(608) 527-2510	...	Nicholas Owen	Lynne Erb	...	...	Steven Allbaugh	Scott Jelle
New Holstein	c	MC	3	(920) 898-5766	...	...	...	...	...	...	...
New Lisbon	c	MC	1	(608) 562-5213	Lloyd Chase	...	...	...	Lynn Willard	Brent Granger	...
New London *	c	MC	7	(920) 982-8500	Gary Henke	Kent Hager	...	James Villiesse	Bart Roloff	Kevin Wilkinson	Carol Radtke
New Richmond	c	MC	6	(715) 246-4268	...	Dennis Horner	Helen Demulling	...	James Vanderwyst	Mark Samelstad	John Berends
Niagara *	c	MC	..	(715) 251-3235	Joseph Stern	Donald Novak	...	...	Fredrick Harvath	Karl Lamoreaux	Dennis Payette
North Fond Du Lac	v	MC	4	(920) 929-3765	James Moon	...	...	...	...	William Lamb	Michael Tolvstad
Oak Creek	c	MC	28	(414) 768-6500	Richard Bolender	Patrick DeGrave	Beverly Buretta	R. Ann Underberg	Brian Satula	Thomas Bauer	...
Oconomowoc	t	MC	7	(262) 567-0251	...	...	Nancy Lins	...	...	...	...
Oconomowoc	c	MC	12	(262) 569-3235	Maurice Sullivan	Diane Gard	Diane Coenen	Sarah Kitsembel	Glenn Leidel	...	Mark Frye
Oconto	c	MC	4	(920) 834-7711	Donald Nerenhausen	...	Linda Belongia	...	Michael Hoppe	Dale Carper	...
Oconto Falls	c	CM	2	(920) 846-4505	Don Osborne	Vicki Roberts	...	Eve Wallace	Tim Magnim	Mike Roberts	Gerry Lemirande
Omro	c	MC	3	(920) 685-7000	Bob Breu	Linda Kutchenriter	...	...	...	James Reed	Gary Marks
Onalaska	t	TM	5	(608) 783-4958	...	...	...	...	...	...	...
Onalaska	c	MC	14	(608) 781-9530	James Bialecki	...	Cari Burmaster	Fred Buehler	...	Randy Williams	C. Jarrod Holter
Oregon	v	MC	7	(608) 835-3118	Gerald Luebke	Michael Gracz	Georgia Johnson	Renee Hoeft	...	...	Mark Below
Osceola	v	CM	2	(715) 294-3498	Charles Jensen	Neil Soltis	...	...	Don Stark	Tim Lauridsen	James Schmidt
Oshkosh	c	CM	62	(920) 236-5000	Frank Tower	Mark Rohloff	Pamela Urbrig	Edward Nokes	Tim Franz	Scott Greuel	David Patek
Paddock Lake	v	MC	3	(262) 843-2400	David Buehn	John Burg	Emily Uhlenhake	...	...	...	...
Palmyra	v	MC	1	(262) 495-8316	Timothy Gorsegner	...	Laurie Mueller	...	Ryan Meyers	Charles Warren	Scott Halbrucker
Park Falls *	c	MC	2	(715) 762-2436	...	...	Arla Homann	...	Larry Reas	Scott Straetz	Dennis Wartgow
Peshtigo *	c	MC	3	(715) 582-3041	Thomas Strouf	...	Mary Wills	...	Steven Anderson	Thomas Hartwig	...
Pewaukee *	v	MC	8	(262) 691-5660	Charles Nichols	Scott Gosse	Susan Atherton	...	...	Edward Baumann	David White
Pewaukee *	c	CM	11	(262) 691-0770	Scott Klein	Tammy LaBorde	Kelly DeMotto	...	Matthew Pinter	Gary Bach	Jeffrey Weigel
Platteville	c	CM	9	(608) 348-9741	Ed White	David Berner	Annette Dutcher	Duane Borger	Bob Leighty	Doug McKinley	Howard Crofoot
Pleasant Prairie	v	MC	16	(262) 694-1400	John Steinbrink	Michael Pollocoff	Jane Romanowski	...	Paul Guilbert	Brian Wagner	...
Plover	v	CM	10	(715) 345-5250	Daniel Schlutter	Daniel Mahoney	Karen Swanson	...	Tim Kluck	Roger Zebro	Bill Konkol
Plymouth	c	MC	7	(920) 893-1271	William Kiley	...	Patricia Huberty	...	Ronald Nicolaus	Donn Davis	William Immich
Port Washington	c	MC	10	(262) 284-5585	Scott Huebner	Mark Grams	...	...	Marc Eernisse	Edward Rudolph	Rob VandenNoven
Portage	c	MC	9	(608) 742-2176	Jeff Grothman	Laurence Plaster	Marie Moe	...	Curtis Ray	Kenneth Manthey	...
Poynette *	v	MC	2	(608) 635-2122	Steve Tomlinson	...	Susan Finstad	...	...	Donald White	Michael Paulcheck
Prairie Du Chien	c	MC	6	(608) 326-6406	MaryJane Faas	...	...	...	Mark Hoppenjan	Michael King	...
Prairie Du Sac	v	CM	3	(608) 643-2421	Cheryl Sherman	Alan Wildman	...	...	James Hambrecht	Gerald Strunz	Patrick Drone
Prescott	c	CM	3	(715) 262-5544	Sheila Wojtowicz	Lloyd Matthes	...	...	...	James Schneider	Jeffrey Kittleson
Princeton	c	MC	1	(920) 295-6612	Matt Schneider	Joshua Schoemann	...	...	George Jachthuber	Don Metoxen	...
Pulaski	v	CO	3	(920) 822-5182	Ronald Kryger	...	Karen Ostrowski	...	...	Randal Dunford	Thomas Holewinski
Racine	c	MC	81	(262) 636-9175	James Smith	Benjamin Hughes	Karen Norton	Jerome Maller	John Hilmer	...	Richard Jones
Reedsburg *	c	MC	7	(608) 524-6404	Carl Stolte	John Dougherty	Anna Meister	...	Craig Douglas	Wilbur Abel	William Meyer
Rhinelander *	c	MC	7	(715) 365-8602	Richard Johns	William Bell	Mary Raith	Julie Ostrander	Terry Williams	Mike Steffes	Randolph Knuth
Rib Mountain	t	CM	6	(715) 842-0983	...	Gaylene Rhoden	Patricia Jahns	...	...	...	...
Rice Lake *	c	MC	8	(715) 234-7088	Daniel Fitzgerald	Curtis Snyder	Kathleen Morse	...	James Resac	John Sommerfeld	Gary Neuman
Richfield *	v	CM	..	(262) 628-2260	Diane Pedersen	Toby Cotter	Pam Spranger	...	Terry Kohl	Brian Rahn	Joe Klemm

Directory 1/9 continued — **OFFICIALS IN U.S. MUNICIPALITIES 2,500 AND OVER IN POPULATION**

Jurisdiction		Type	Form of govern-ment	2000 Popu-lation	Main telephone number	Chief elected official	Appointed administrator	Clerk of the governing board	Chief financial officer	Fire chief	Police chief	Public works director
WISCONSIN continued												
Richland Center		c	MC	5	(608) 647-3466	Larry Fowler	. . .	Jude Elliott	. . .	Robert Bindl	John Annear	Richard Wilson
Ripon		c	MC	6	(920) 748-4916	Aaron Kramer	Steven Barg	. . .	. . .	. . .	David Lukoski	. . .
River Falls		c	MC	12	(715) 425-0900	Don Richards	. . .	Lu Ann Hecht	Julie Bergstrom	Robert Schwalen	Roger Leque	. . .
River Hills		v	CM	1	(414) 352-8213	Robert Brunner	Thomas Tollaksen	Carolyn Toms-Neary	. . .	David Berousek	Tom Rischmann	Kurt Fredrickson
Rothschild	*	v	MC	4	(715) 359-3660	Neal Torney	. . .	Sheila Pudelko	. . .	Steven Fritz	William Schremp	. . .
Salem		t	MC	9	(262) 843-2313	. . .	Patrick Casey	. . .	. . .	. . .	. . .	. . .
Sauk City		v	CM	3	(608) 643-3932	. . .	Vicki Breunig	. . .	. . .	. . .	Gerald Strunz	Herman Mack
Saukville	*	v	CM	4	(262) 284-9423	Barbara Dickmann	Dawn Wagner	. . .	. . .	Gilly Schultz	William Meloy	Roy Wilhelm
Seymour	*	c	MC	3	(920) 833-2209	Kenneth Rottier	. . .	Susan Garsow	. . .	Steve Krabbe	Edwin Janz	Michael Pepin
Shawano		c	MC	8	(715) 524-4611	. . .	James Stadler	Marlene Brath	. . .	Douglas Knope	. . .	Rick Stautz
Sheboygan		c	MC	50	(920) 459-3373	James Schramm	. . .	Patricia Lohse	Richard Gebhart	Mark Zeier	David Kirk	Thomas Holtan
Sheboygan Falls		c	MC	6	(920) 467-7900	. . .	. . .	. . .	. . .	. . .	. . .	. . .
Sherwood	*	v	MC	1	(920) 989-1589	David Miller	Randall Friday	Ellen Maxymek	. . .	. . .	. . .	. . .
Shorewood		v	CM	13	(414) 847-2700	Mark Kohlenberg	M. Swartz	Kathleen Greig	. . .	. . .	David Banaszynski	James Bartnicki
Shorewood Hills		v	CM	1	(608) 267-2680	Peter Hans	Karl Frantz	Jennifer Anderson	. . .	Thomas De Meuse	Jerry Jansen	Dennis Lybeck
Sister Bay	*	v	MC	. .	(920) 854-4118	Denise Bhirdo	Robert Kufrin	Christy Sully	Juliana Neuman	Chris Hecht	. . .	Steve Jacobson
Slinger		v	MC	3	(262) 644-5265	Russell Brandt	Maureen Murphy	. . .	. . .	. . .	Dean Schmidt	. . .
South Milwaukee	*	c	MC	21	(414) 762-2222	Thomas Zepecki	Tamara Mayzik	Kathleen Lisowski	. . .	Jay Behling	Ann Wellens	Richard Davidoff
Sparta	*	c	MC	8	(608) 269-4340	John Sund	Kenneth Witt	Barb Pederson	. . .	Scott Lindemann	Mike Kass	Jordan Skiff
Spring Green		v	CM	1	(608) 588-2335	Greg Prem	. . .	Wendy Crary	. . .	Lin Gunderson	Kevin Wilkins	Greg Wipperfurth
St. Croix Falls		c	MC	2	(715) 483-3929	Brad Foss	Ed Emerson	Bonita Leggitt	. . .	Dale Anderson	Jack Rydeen	Scott Brust
St. Francis		c	MC	8	(414) 481-2300	. . .	Ralph Voltner	. . .	. . .	. . .	. . .	. . .
Stevens Point		c	MC	24	(715) 346-1569	Gary Wescott	. . .	Victoria Zdroik	John Schlice	Mark Barnes	Douglas Carpenter	. . .
Stoughton		c	MC	12	(608) 873-6677	Helen Johnson	. . .	Judy Kinning	. . .	Marty Lamers	Patrick O'Connor	Karl Manthe
Sturgeon Bay	*	c	MC	9	(920) 746-2900	Thomas Voegele	Steven McNeil	Stephanie Reinhardt	Valerie Clarizio	Timothy Herlache	Daniel Trelka	. . .
Sturtevant		v	MC	5	(262) 886-7201	Steven Jansen	. . .	Donna Deuster	. . .	. . .	. . .	. . .
Suamico		v	MC	8	(920) 434-2212	Elizabeth Sheedy	Karen Matze	Bonnie Swan	Kay Magyar	Thomas Hussin	Dennis Kocken	Timothy Krause
Sun Prairie		c	MC	20	(608) 825-1192	Joseph Chase	Patrick Cannon	D. Hermann Brown	. . .	Steve Knaus	Frank Sleeter	Larry Herman
Superior		c	MC	27	(715) 395-7210	David Ross	. . .	Margaret Ciccone	Jean Vito	Tad Matheson	Floyd Peters	Jeffrey Vito
Sussex		v	CM	8	(262) 246-5200	Patricia Bartlett	Evan Teich	. . .	. . .	Thomas Schlei	. . .	Raymond Grzys
Thiensville	*	v	CO	3	(262) 242-3720	Karl Hertz	Dianne Robertson	. . .	. . .	William Rausch	Richard Preston	Robert Gehrke
Thorp		c	MC	1	(715) 669-5371	Richard Wnek	Randall Reeg	. . .	. . .	. . .	Sharon Verges	Timothy McCredden
Tomah		c	MC	8	(608) 374-7422	Charles Ludeking	John Rusch	Jo Ann Cram	. . .	. . .	Chris Anderson	Kenneth Patterson
Tomahawk		c	MC	3	(715) 453-4040	Jonathan Rose	. . .	Paul Garner	. . .	John Peeters	Mike Smitley	Mark Dochnahl
Trempealeau		v	MC	1	(608) 534-6434	. . .	Travis Cooke	Vicki Freeman	. . .	. . .	Stanley Ridgeway	Todd Lakey
Turtle Lake		v	MC	1	(715) 986-2134	Laurie Tarman	. . .	Frances Duncanson	. . .	. . .	Al Gabe	Cory Davis
Twin Lakes		v	MC	5	(262) 877-2858	Cathleen Zamazal	David Cox	Dorothy Sandona	. . .	Bruce Haase	Robert O'Hallen	. . .
Two Rivers		c	CM	12	(920) 793-5525	. . .	Gregory Buckley	. . .	. . .	Kevin Timm	Joseph Collins	Bill Scola
Union Grove		v	CM	4	(262) 878-1818	Robert Orre	C. Rademacher	Janice Winget	. . .	. . .	. . .	L. Behling
Verona	*	c	MC	7	(608) 845-6495	Jon Hochkammer	Shawn Murphy	Judy Masarik	. . .	Jeff Stein	Bernard Coughlin	Ronald Rieder
Viroqua		c	MC	4	(608) 637-7154	Larry Fanta	Jeffrey Gohlke	. . .	. . .	Steve Skrede	Mark Rahr	Thomas Henry
Washburn	*	c	MC	2	(715) 373-6160	Ralph Brzezinski	Scott Kluver	Vickie Swanson	. . .	. . .	Ken Johnson	Mike Decur
Washington	*	t	MC	. .	(920) 847-2522	. . .	. . .	. . .	. . .	. . .	. . .	. . .
Washington		t	CM	6	(715) 834-3257	. . .	. . .	. . .	. . .	. . .	. . .	. . .
Waterford		v	MC	4	(262) 534-7912	Dave Richmond	Rebecca Ewald	Michelle Allender	. . .	Steve Denman	John Schanning	Randall Niewolny
Watertown		c	MC	21	(920) 262-4000	Frederick Smith	. . .	Michael Hoppenrath	. . .	Dick Olson	Chuck McGee	Brian Field
Waukesha		c	MC	64	(262) 524-3500	Larry Nelson	Lori Curtis Luther	. . .	Steve Neaman	Allen LaConte	Leslie Sharrock	Paul Feller
Waunakee	*	v	CM	8	(608) 850-8500	John Laubmeier	William Barlow	Julee Helt	David Ferris	Gary Acker	Kevin Plendl	. . .
Waupaca		c	MC	5	(715) 258-4411	Brian Smith	Henry Veleker	. . .	. . .	Jeff Olson	Timothy Goke	John Edlebeck
Waupun		c	MC	10	(920) 324-7900	Jodi Steger	Gary Rogers	Kyle Clark	. . .	Jeff Berry	Dale Herringa	Richard Flynn
Wausau		c	MC	38	(715) 261-6610	Linda Lawrence	. . .	K. Michaels-Sagger	Maryanne Groat	Gary Buchburger	William Brandimore	John Hess
Wauwatosa		c	MC	47	(414) 479-8915	. . .	James Archambo	Carla Ledesma	Ronald Braier	Dean Redman	. . .	William Kappel
West Allis	*	c	MC	61	(414) 302-8200	Dan Devine	Paul Ziehler	. . .	Gary Schmid	Steven Hook	Mike Jungbluth	Michael Pertmer
West Bend	*	c	MC	28	(262) 335-5114	Kristine Deiss	Dennis Melvin	Amy Reuteman	. . .	James Vest	Kenneth Meuler	Terry Kiekhaefer
West Milwaukee		v	MC	4	(414) 645-1530	Ronald Hayward	Kim Egan-Mueller	. . .	. . .	. . .	Eugene Oldenburg	James Stenzel
West Salem		v	CM	4	(608) 786-1858	. . .	Teresa Schnitzler	. . .	. . .	. . .	Dennis Abbott	Wade Peterson
Weston		v	CM	12	(715) 359-6114	Vilas Machmueller	Dean Zuleger	Sherry Weinkauf	John Jacobs	Loren White	Daniel Vergin	Keith Donner
Weyauwega		c	MC	1	(920) 867-2635	. . .	Sheryl Scheuermann	. . .	. . .	. . .	. . .	. . .
Whitefish Bay		v	CM	14	(414) 962-6690	Kathleen Pritchard	James Grassman	. . .	. . .	. . .	Gary Mikulec	. . .
Whitewater	*	c	CM	13	(262) 473-0500	. . .	Kevin Brunner	Michele Smith	Doug Saubert	Howard Higgins	James Coan	Dean Fischer
Winneconne	*	v	CM	2	(920) 582-4381	John Rogers	Steve Volkert	Jacquin Jensen	. . .	Ryan Krings	Peter Running	Patrick Geisendorfer
Winsdor		t	MC	5	(608) 846-3854	. . .	. . .	. . .	. . .	. . .	. . .	. . .
Wisconsin Dells		c	MC	2	(608) 254-2012	Ben Borcher	. . .	Dale Darling	. . .	Mark Hamm	Dean Edgington	Michael Horkan
Wisconsin Rapids		c	MC	18	(715) 421-8200	Mary Jo Carson	. . .	Shane Blaser	Timothy Desory	Mitchell Waite	Kurt Keuer	. . .
Wittenberg		v	MC	1	(715) 253-6063	. . .	. . .	. . .	. . .	. . .	. . .	. . .
Wrightstown	*	v	MC	1	(920) 532-5567	Steve Johnson	. . .	Jean Brandt	. . .	Mike Schampers	Perry Kingsbury	Dan Stephany
WYOMING												
Afton		t	MC	1	(307) 885-9831	Chad Jensen	. . .	Lisa Hokunson	. . .	Allan Sessions	Tim Heggenstaller	Blake Robinson
Buffalo		t	MC	3	(307) 684-5566	Bruce Hepp	. . .	Kay Wertz	. . .	Gomer Gammon	Mike Dahmer	Leslie Hook
Casper		c	CM	49	(307) 235-8400	Barbara Peryam	Thomas Forslund	. . .	Velton McDonald	Mark Young	Thomas Pagel	Philip Stuckert
Cheyenne		c	MC	53	(307) 637-6300	Leo Pando	. . .	Carol Intlekofer	. . .	Dennis Piester	John Powell	Jackie Smith
Cody	*	c	MC	8	(307) 527-7511	Nancy Brown	McFerrin Whiteman	. . .	. . .	. . .	Perry Rockvam	Stephen Payne
Douglas		c	CM	5	(307) 358-3462	Sherri Mullinnix	Bobbe Fitzhugh	. . .	. . .	. . .	Lori Emmert	Brian Sweeney
Evanston		c	MC	11	(307) 783-6307	Mark Harris	James Davis	. . .	. . .	. . .	. . .	Brian Honey
Evansville		t	MC	2	(307) 234-6530	. . .	. . .	. . .	. . .	. . .	. . .	. . .
Gillette	*	c	CM	19	(307) 686-5200	Duane Evenson	. . .	Karlene Abelseth	Michelle Tompkins	. . .	Richard Adrieans	James Evensen
Glenrock		t	MC	2	(307) 436-9294	Steven Cielinski	. . .	Donna Geho	. . .	. . .	Michael Colling	Dave Andrews
Green River		c	MC	11	(307) 872-0500	David Gomez	Barry Cook	Jeff Nieters	. . .	George Nomis	Greg Gillen	Michael Nelson
Jackson		t	CM	8	(307) 733-3932	Mark Barron	Robert McLaurin	. . .	Kevin Watson	. . .	Dan Zivkovich	Larry Pardee
Kemmerer		c	CM	2	(307) 828-2350	Jim Carroll	John Roberts	Glenda Young	. . .	. . .	Jay Phillips	. . .
Lander		c	MC	6	(307) 332-2870	Mick Wolfe	. . .	Sharon Anderson	. . .	. . .	Richard Currah	Mickey Simmons
Laramie		c	CM	27	(307) 721-5200	Fred Homer	Janine Jordan	R. Sue Jones	. . .	Randy Vickers	. . .	Terry Haugen
Lovell		t	CM	2	(307) 548-6551	. . .	. . .	. . .	. . .	. . .	. . .	. . .
Lyman		t	MC	1	(307) 787-6595	Oliver Moretti	. . .	Lynn Arnell	. . .	. . .	Dean Iannelli	Andrew Spray
Mills		t	MC	2	(307) 234-6679	Robert Goff	. . .	Sue Regennas	. . .	Ronald Schindler	Jerry Endresen	Robert McPherson
Newcastle		c	MC	3	(307) 746-3535	Edward Wagoner	. . .	Gregory James	. . .	Donny Munger	Andrew Macke	Douglas Sankey
Powell		c	CM	5	(307) 754-5106	James Milburn	. . .	Ardyce Busboom	. . .	. . .	Timothy Feathers	. . .
Rawlins	*	c	CM	8	(307) 328-4500	Kenneth Klouda	Steven Golnar	Marla Brown	. . .	Scott Hannum	James Reed	Arthur Stolns
Riverton		c	CM	9	(307) 856-2227	John Vincent	James Napier	Gloria Leadbetter	. . .	. . .	John Snell	William Urbigkit
Rock Springs	*	c	MC	18	(307) 352-1500	Timothy Kaumo	. . .	. . .	. . .	Lyle Armstrong	Michael Lowell	Paul Kauchich
Sheridan	*	c	MC	15	(307) 674-6483	Dave Kinskey	. . .	Scott Badley	. . .	Patrick Reitz	Mike Card	Nicholas Bateson
Thermopolis		t	MC	3	(307) 864-3838	. . .	. . .	Tracey Van Huele	. . .	. . .	James Weisbeck	Earnest Slagle
Torrington		t	MC	5	(307) 532-5666	Mike Varney	. . .	Sandy Pittman	. . .	Dennis Estes	Billy Janes	Jim Foster
Wheatland		t	MC	3	(307) 322-2962	Joel Dingman	. . .	Cindy Kahler	. . .	. . .	Steve Gilmore	. . .
Worland	*	c	MC	5	(307) 347-2486	Kreg Lombard	. . .	Tracy Glanz	. . .	. . .	Greg Bankert	Gene Cliame

Directory 1/10   **OFFICIALS IN U.S. COUNTIES 2,500 AND OVER IN POPULATION**

Data collection

The names appearing in this directory were obtained from the ICMA database of local government employees. Local governments that have provided updated information are designated by an asterisk (*). For those that have not, the directories show the names of officials from the most recent update.

As noted in "Inside the *Year Book*," there are certain unorganized areas of some states that have a county designation from the Census Bureau for strictly administrative purposes and are not included in the *Year Book* databases. Along with

12 areas in Alaska, 2 areas in South Dakota, and 1 area in Montana, these comprise all 8 areas in Connecticut and all 5 areas in Rhode Island.

Form of government

CM   Council-manager
CE   Council–elected executive
C   Commission

Population

Population figures are rounded; 14,500 will appear as 15.

(. .) Less than 500 population

Other codes

. . . Data not reported or not applicable

Note: Because of the low number of responses to the *Country Form of Government* surveys, the form-of-government data presented in this table may not be the most current.

Jurisdiction	Form of govern- ment	2000 Popu- lation	Main telephone number	Chief elected official	Appointed administrator	Clerk of the governing board	Chief financial officer	Director of personnel	Chief law enforcement official
ALABAMA									
Autauga	CM	43	(334) 361-3701	Clyde Chambliss	Steven Golsan	. . .	. . .	. . .	. . .
Baldwin	CM	140	(251) 937-9561	Wayne Gruenloh	Michael Thompson	. . .	Locke Williams	Susan Lovett	Hoss Mack
Barbour *	C	29	(334) 775-3203	Kenneth Gilmore	Kristy Stell	. . .	. . .	. . .	Leroy Upshaw
Bibb	C	20	(205) 926-3114	. . .	Mark Tyner	. . .	. . .	. . .	Keith Hannah
Blount	C	51	(205) 274-9111	. . .	. . .	. . .	. . .	. . .	. . .
Bullock	CM	11	(334) 738-3883	Ronald Smith	Lillie Hall	Marion Milbry	Janne Brabham	. . .	Raymond Rodgers
Butler	CM	21	(334) 382-3612	. . .	. . .	Diane Kilpatrick	. . .	. . .	Diane Harris
Calhoun	CM	112	(256) 241-2800	. . .	Kenneth Joiner	. . .	. . .	. . .	Larry Amerson
Chambers	CM	36	(334) 864-4341	Jack Bunn	Don Hoyt	Regina Norris	. . .	. . .	Calvin Lockhart
Cherokee	C	23	(256) 927-3079	. . .	. . .	. . .	. . .	. . .	. . .
Chilton	CM	39	(205) 755-1551	. . .	Vanessa Hendrick	Edith Gentry	. . .	Cathy Martin	Billy Fulmer
Choctaw	C	15	(205) 459-2100	. . .	. . .	. . .	. . .	. . .	. . .
Clarke *	CM	27	(251) 275-3507	. . .	. . .	. . .	Annie Morris	. . .	Bobby Moore
Clay	C	14	(256) 354-7888	Ricky Burney	Lou Hanners	Jeffery Colborn	. . .	. . .	Charlie Toland
Cleburne	CM	14	(256) 463-7130	Ryan Robertson	Steven Swafford	Mary Thomas	Melissa Wood	. . .	Joe Jacks
Coffee *	CM	43	(334) 894-5556	. . .	Kathryn Lolley	Myrna Cowen	. . .	. . .	Dave Sutton
Colbert	CM	54	(256) 386-8500	. . .	. . .	. . .	. . .	. . .	. . .
Conecuh	CM	14	(251) 578-2095	. . .	. . .	. . .	. . .	Sandra Smith	Dudley Godwin
Coosa	CM	12	(205) 377-2420	. . .	Sherrie Kelley	. . .	. . .	. . .	. . .
Covington	C	37	(334) 222-3613	. . .	. . .	. . .	. . .	. . .	. . .
Crenshaw *	CM	13	(334) 335-6568	Ronnie Hudson	David Smyth	Julie Shaulis	. . .	. . .	Charles West
Cullman	C	77	(205) 739-3530	. . .	. . .	. . .	. . .	. . .	. . .
Dale	C	49	(334) 774-6262	C. Johnston	. . .	. . .	. . .	Peggy Roper	James Mixon
Dallas	C	46	(334) 877-4803	Roy Moore	. . .	. . .	. . .	Marilyn Riddle	Harris Huffman
De Kalb	CM	64	(256) 845-8500	Sidney Holcomb	Matt Sharp	. . .	. . .	. . .	. . .
Elmore	CM	65	(334) 567-1156	Joe Faulk	Lera Medders	. . .	. . .	. . .	William Franklin
Escambia	CM	38	(251) 867-0828	. . .	. . .	. . .	. . .	. . .	. . .
Etowah	CM	103	(256) 549-5393	. . .	. . .	. . .	. . .	James Naugher	James Hayes
Fayette	CM	18	(205) 932-4510	. . .	John Gordon	. . .	. . .	Bobbie Kemp	Richard White
Franklin *	C	31	(205) 332-8850	Barry Moore	. . .	. . .	. . .	. . .	. . .
Geneva	C	25	(334) 684-5600	. . .	. . .	. . .	. . .	. . .	. . .
Greene	CM	9	(205) 372-3349	Chris Beeker	. . .	. . .	. . .	. . .	Johnny Isaac
Hale	C	17	(334) 624-4257	Leland Avery	Tricia Galbreath	. . .	. . .	. . .	Kenneth Ellis
Henry	CM	16	(334) 585-3257	. . .	. . .	. . .	. . .	. . .	. . .
Houston	C	88	(334) 677-4777	Mark Culver	Roy Roberts	Karen Price	. . .	Jeff Baker	Lamar Glover
Jackson	C	53	(256) 574-9280	James Tidmore	Terry West	Valerie Harris	. . .	Shirley Morris	Terry Wells
Jefferson	C	662	(205) 325-5523	Gary White	Orville Ifill	. . .	Steve Sayler	Ben Payton	Mike Hale
Lamar	C	15	(205) 695-7333	. . .	. . .	. . .	. . .	. . .	. . .
Lauderdale	C	87	(256) 760-5750	Dewey Mitchell	. . .	. . .	. . .	. . .	Charles Townsend
Lawrence	CM	34	(256) 974-0663	. . .	. . .	. . .	. . .	Kim Oas	. . .
Lee	C	115	(334) 745-9767	Bill English	Roger Rendleman	. . .	. . .	. . .	. . .
Limestone	CE	65	(256) 233-6400	Charles Seibert	. . .	Pamela Ball	Emily Ezzell	Anita Jewell	Michael Blakely
Lowndes	CM	13	(334) 548-2331	Charlie King	Jacquelyn Thomas	Geraldine Ingram	. . .	. . .	Willie Vaughner
Macon	C	24	(334) 727-5120	Jesse Upshaw	. . .	. . .	Susan Thomas	Gertrude Benjamin	David Warren
Madison	C	276	(256) 532-3492	Mike Gillespie	Edsel Baites	. . .	Judy Teague	Gail Medley	Blake Dorning
Marengo	C	22	(334) 295-2200	. . .	. . .	. . .	. . .	John Marler	. . .
Marion	CM	31	(205) 921-3172	Bobby Burleson	. . .	Gearldean Lindsey	. . .	. . .	E. B. Purser
Marshall	CE	82	(256) 571-7701	. . .	Nancy Willson	. . .	. . .	Christy Kelley	. . .
Mobile	CE	399	(251) 574-5077	Mike Dean	John Pafenbach	. . .	Michelle Herman	. . .	Jack Tillman
Monroe	C	24	(251) 743-3782	. . .	. . .	. . .	. . .	. . .	. . .
Montgomery	CE	223	(334) 832-1259	Todd Strange	Donald Mims	. . .	Sandra Johnson	Barbara Montoya	D. T. Marshall
Morgan	C	111	(256) 351-4600	. . .	. . .	. . .	. . .	. . .	. . .
Perry	C	11	(334) 683-2200	Johnny Flowers	. . .	Walta Kennie	. . .	. . .	James Hood
Pickens	CE	20	(205) 367-2020	Tony Junkin	Cheryl Gary	Marva Gipson	. . .	. . .	David Abston
Pike *	C	29	(334) 566-6374	Robin Sullivan	Harry Sanders	. . .	Debra Gibson	McKenzie Wilson	Russell Thomas
Randolph	CM	22	(256) 357-4980	Mack Diamond	. . .	Kathy Breed	Cindy Arrington	Lisa Green	. . .
Russell	C	49	(334) 298-6426	Clifford Lee	. . .	. . .	. . .	. . .	. . .
Shelby	CM	143	(205) 669-3740	. . .	Alex Dudchock	. . .	William Burbage	Jennifer Ray	Christopher Curry
St. Clair *	CM	64	(205) 594-2100	Stanley Batemon	Kellie Long	. . .	Donna Wood	Judith Abernathy	Terry Surles
Sumter	CM	14	(205) 652-2731	. . .	. . .	. . .	. . .	. . .	. . .
Talladega	C	80	(205) 362-1357	. . .	. . .	. . .	. . .	. . .	. . .
Tallapoosa	C	41	(256) 825-4268	Johnny Allen	. . .	. . .	. . .	Deborah Dobbs	James Abbett
Tuscaloosa	C	164	(205) 349-3870	C. McCollum	. . .	Robert Johnston	William Lamb	Melvin Vines	Edmund Sexton
Walker	C	70	(205) 384-7230	Bruce Hamrick	Jill Farris	. . .	. . .	Edith Duncan	John Tirey
Washington	C	18	(251) 847-2208	John Armstrong	Mary Carpenter	. . .	. . .	. . .	William Wheat
Wilcox *	C	13	(334) 682-9112	Mark Curl	Clarissa Dear	. . .	. . .	Demetria Turk	Prince Arnold
Winston	C	24	(205) 489-5026	Roger Hayes	. . .	Joanie Wright	. . .	. . .	David Sutherland
ALASKA									
Aleutians East	CM	2	(907) 383-2699	Dick Jacobsen	. . .	Tina Anderson	Cynthia Samuelson	. . .	. . .
Bristol Bay	CM	1	(907) 246-4224	. . .	. . .	. . .	. . .	. . .	Jerry Castleberry
Denali	C	1	(907) 683-1330	David Talerico	. . .	Gail Pieknik	. . .	. . .	. . .
Fairbanks North Star	CM	82	(907) 459-1000	Rhonda Boyles	. . .	Mona Drexler	Michael Lamb	Sallie Stuvek	. . .
Haines	CE	2	(907) 766-2711	. . .	. . .	Jacqueline Lawson	. . .	Jerry Lapp	. . .
Kenai Peninsula	CE	40	(907) 262-4441	Dale Bagley	. . .	Linda Murphy	. . .	Richard Campbell	. . .

Directory 1/10 continued   **OFFICIALS IN U.S. COUNTIES 2,500 AND OVER IN POPULATION**

Jurisdiction	Form of govern-ment	2000 Popu-lation	Main telephone number	Chief elected official	Appointed administrator	Clerk of the governing board	Chief financial officer	Director of personnel	Chief law enforcement official
ALASKA continued									
Ketchikan Gateway . *	CM	14	(907) 228-6625	Dave Kiffer	Dan Bockhorst	Harriett Edwards	Mike Houts	. . .	Jerry Cegelske
Kodiak Island	CE	13	(907) 486-9301	Jerome Selby	Rick Gifford	Donna Smith	Karleton Short	Rachael Nelson	. . .
Lake And Peninsula	CM	1	(907) 246-3421	Glen Alsworth	Jeff Currier	Sheila Bergey	George Castaneda	. . .	. . .
Matanuska Susitna .	CM	59	(907) 745-4801	Curt Menard	John Duffy	Lonnie McKechnie	. . .	Patrick Julian	. . .
North Slope	CM	5	(907) 852-2611	Edward Itta	George Olemaun	. . .	John Ames	Jeri Cleveland	Don Grimes
Northwest Arctic . . .	CM	7	(907) 442-2500	Reggie Cleveland	Chuck Greene	Valarie Romane	Judith Hassinger	Linda Joule	. . .
Yakutat	CM	. .	(907) 784-3323	David Stone	. . .	Catherine Bremner	Constance Klushkan	. . .	. . .
ARIZONA									
Apache	CE	69	(928) 337-4364	Joe Shirley	Delwin Wengert	Sue Hall	Karla Rogers	. . .	C. Lee
Cochise	CM	117	(520) 432-9700	Pat Call	Jody Klein	Nadine Parkhurst	Lois Klein	Ken Wallace	Larry Dever
Coconino . . . . *	CM	116	(928) 779-6690	Deb Hill	Steven Peru	Wendi Escoffier	Sandra Schulz	Allison Eckert	Joseph Richards
Gila	CM	51	(928) 425-3231	Ron Christensen	John Nelson	. . .	Dave Patterson	Susan Mitchell	John Armer
Graham	CM	33	(928) 428-3250	. . .	. . .	Terry Cooper	Clel Flake	. . .	Frank Hughes
Greenlee . . . . *	CE	8	(928) 865-2072	Hector Ruedas	Deborah Gale	. . .	. . .	. . .	Steven Tucker
La Paz	CM	19	(928) 669-6115	Clifford Edey	. . .	Donna Hale	Ava Alcaida	. . .	Hal Collett
Maricopa . . . . *	CM	3072	(602) 506-1950	Andrew Kunasek	David Smith	Fran McCarrol	Thomas Manos	Elizabeth Yaquinto	Joseph Arpaio
Mohave	CM	155	(928) 753-0729	Tom Sockwell	Ronnie Walker	Barbara Bracken	John Timko	Geoff Riches	Thomas Sheahan
Navajo	CM	97	(928) 524-4000	Percy Deal	James Jayne	. . .	Clinton Shreeve	Gilbert Gonzales	Gary Butler
Pima	CM	843	(520) 740-8672	. . .	Chuck Huckelberry	Lori Godoshian	Thomas Burke	Gwendolyn Hatcher	Clarence Dupnik
Pinal	CM	179	(520) 866-6228	Lionel Ruiz	Terry Doolittle	. . .	Victoria Prins	Michael Arnold	Chris Vasquez
Santa Cruz	CM	38	(520) 761-7800	Manuel Ruiz	Gregory Lucero	Melinda Meek	Jennifer St. John	Carlos Rivera	Marco Estrada
Yavapai	CE	167	(928) 771-3252	. . .	Julie Ayers	. . .	John Zander	Alan Vigneron	. . .
Yuma	CM	160	(928) 373-1013	Lenore Stuart	Robert Pickels	. . .	Douglas Allen	Alonzo Strange	Ralph Ogden
ARKANSAS									
Arkansas	C	20	(870) 673-3181	. . .	. . .	. . .	. . .	. . .	. . .
Ashley	C	24	(870) 853-2000	Larry Kinnaird	. . .	Genie Kersten	. . .	. . .	James Robinson
Baxter	C	38	(870) 425-2755	Joe Bodenhamer	. . .	Rhonda Porter	. . .	. . .	. . .
Benton	C	153	(479) 271-1000	Gary Black	Travis Harp	Mary Slinkard	Richard McComas	Janie Robinson	Andrew Lee
Boone	C	33	(870) 741-9724	Mike Moore	. . .	Kristie Blevins	Linda Brown	. . .	Dan Hickman
Bradley	CE	12	(870) 226-3464	Noel Rice	. . .	Janet Kimbrell	. . .	. . .	William Belin
Calhoun	C	5	(870) 798-4818	Arthur Jones	. . .	Alma Davis	. . .	. . .	John Ables
Carroll	CE	25	(870) 423-2967	. . .	. . .	. . .	. . .	. . .	. . .
Chicot	CE	14	(870) 265-8015	Fred Zieman	. . .	Pam Donaldson	. . .	. . .	Floyd White
Clark	C	23	(870) 246-5847	Ron Daniell	. . .	Rhonda Williams	. . .	. . .	Troy Tucker
Clay	C	17	(870) 598-2667	. . .	Gary Howell	Sharon Williams	. . .	. . .	Ronnie Cole
Cleburne	CE	24	(501) 362-8141	Claude Dill	Patsy McNeese	Dana Guffey	. . .	. . .	Marty Moss
Cleveland	C	8	(870) 325-6521	Vernon Dollar	. . .	Sharon Gray	. . .	. . .	Joe King
Columbia	CE	25	(870) 234-2542	. . .	. . .	. . .	. . .	. . .	. . .
Conway	CE	20	(501) 354-9640	Jimmy Hart	Rebecca Spires	Debra Hartman	. . .	. . .	Mark Flowers
Craighead	C	82	(870) 933-4500	. . .	. . .	. . .	. . .	. . .	. . .
Crawford	C	53	(479) 474-1312	Harold Loyd	. . .	Patti Hill	. . .	. . .	James Ballard
Crittenden	C	50	(870) 739-4434	Melton Holt	. . .	Ruth Trent	. . .	. . .	Richard Busby
Cross	C	19	(870) 238-3373	. . .	. . .	. . .	. . .	. . .	. . .
Dallas	CE	9	(870) 352-3317	Jimmy Jones	. . .	Janice Mc Daniel	. . .	. . .	Donny Ford
Desha	C	15	(870) 877-2426	. . .	. . .	. . .	. . .	. . .	. . .
Drew	CE	18	(870) 460-6200	Damon Lampkin	. . .	Lyna Gulledge	. . .	. . .	. . .
Faulkner	C	86	(501) 450-4900	. . .	. . .	. . .	. . .	. . .	. . .
Franklin	CE	17	(479) 667-4726	Joe Powell	Kathy McDonald	Sharon Needham	Donna Vaughn	. . .	Reed Hayes
Fulton	C	11	(870) 895-3341	Curren Everett	. . .	Gene Maguffee	. . .	. . .	. . .
Garland	CE	88	(501) 622-3600	Larry Williams	. . .	Vicki Rima	. . .	Valerie Dodge	. . .
Grant	C	16	(870) 942-2551	Dan Nall	. . .	Carol Ewing	. . .	. . .	Sammy Pruitt
Greene	C	37	(870) 239-6300	. . .	. . .	. . .	. . .	. . .	. . .
Hempstead	C	23	(870) 777-2241	Charles Martin	. . .	Jackie Ridling	. . .	. . .	Jerry Crane
Hot Spring	C	30	(501) 332-2261	. . .	. . .	. . .	. . .	. . .	. . .
Howard	C	14	(870) 845-7500	Max Tackett	. . .	Shirley Dildy	. . .	. . .	Butch Morris
Independence	CE	34	(870) 793-8800	David Wyatt	Rita Potts	Margaret Boothby	. . .	. . .	Ron Webb
Izard . . . . *	C	13	(870) 368-4328	Eddie Cooper	. . .	Rhonda Halbrook	Marilyn Downing	. . .	Joe Martz
Jackson	CE	18	(870) 523-7400	Jerry Carlew	. . .	Pamela Graham	Dottie Calhoun	. . .	David Lucas
Jefferson	C	84	(870) 541-5360	Jack Jones	Winnie Eastman	Pamela Ratliff	. . .	. . .	W. Brassell
Johnson	C	22	(479) 754-3967	. . .	. . .	. . .	. . .	. . .	. . .
Lafayette	C	8	(870) 921-4858	Frank Scroggins	. . .	Diane Fletcher	. . .	. . .	Danny Ormond
Lawrence	C	17	(870) 886-1110	Alex Latham	. . .	Tina Stowers	. . .	. . .	Dan Ellison
Lee	CE	12	(870) 295-2339	. . .	. . .	. . .	. . .	. . .	. . .
Lincoln	C	14	(870) 628-4147	. . .	. . .	. . .	. . .	. . .	. . .
Little River	C	13	(870) 898-7202	Carolyn Coleman	. . .	Linda Coleman	Deanna Bishop	. . .	Danny Russell
Logan	C	22	(479) 963-3601	. . .	. . .	. . .	. . .	. . .	. . .
Lonoke	C	52	(501) 676-6403	Don Bevis	. . .	Myrtle Finch	. . .	. . .	J. Isaac
Madison	C	14	(479) 738-6721	. . .	. . .	. . .	. . .	. . .	. . .
Marion	C	16	(870) 449-6231	. . .	. . .	. . .	. . .	. . .	. . .
Miller	CE	40	(870) 774-1501	Hubert Easley	. . .	Ann Nicholas	. . .	. . .	H. Phillips
Mississippi	CE	51	(870) 763-3212	. . .	. . .	. . .	. . .	. . .	. . .
Monroe	C	10	(870) 747-3632	Tom Catlett	. . .	Janet Tweedle	. . .	. . .	Larry Morris
Montgomery	C	9	(870) 867-3521	Ted Elder	. . .	Debbie Baxter	. . .	. . .	Barry Spivey
Nevada	C	9	(870) 887-3115	James Brown	. . .	Julie Stockton	Sydney De Charme	. . .	Steve Otwell
Newton	C	8	(870) 446-5127	Harold Smith	Carolyn McCutcheon	Hubert Robinson	. . .	. . .	Mark Rupp
Ouachita	C	28	(870) 837-2210	Mike Hesterly	. . .	Britt Williford	. . .	. . .	Paul Lucas
Perry . . . . *	C	10	(501) 889-5128	True Robinson	. . .	Barbara Lovell	. . .	. . .	Scott Montgomery
Phillips	CM	26	(870) 338-5500	. . .	. . .	. . .	. . .	. . .	. . .
Pike	CE	11	(870) 285-2743	Donald Baker	. . .	Sandy Campbell	. . .	. . .	Jerry Jones
Poinsett	C	25	(870) 578-4412	William Craft	. . .	Fonda Condra	. . .	. . .	Larry Mills
Polk	C	20	(479) 394-8100	Ray Stanley	. . .	Terri Harrison	. . .	. . .	Mike Oglesby
Pope	C	54	(479) 968-6064	. . .	. . .	. . .	. . .	. . .	. . .
Prairie	C	9	(870) 256-3741	Butch Calhoun	. . .	Karan Tate	. . .	. . .	Randy Raper
Pulaski	CE	361	(501) 340-6110	Floyd Villines	. . .	. . .	Ron Quillin	Temperlene Smith	Randy Johnson
Randolph	CE	18	(870) 892-5264	Michael Davis	. . .	Janis Mock	. . .	. . .	Rob Samons
Saline	C	83	(501) 303-5600	Lanny Fite	. . .	Freddy Burton	. . .	. . .	Judy Pridgen
Scott	CE	10	(479) 637-2155	Charlie Vaughan	Edna Piles	James Owens	. . .	. . .	Buck Byford
Searcy	C	8	(870) 448-3807	Paul Lee	. . .	Wesley Smith	. . .	. . .	George Sutterfield
Sebastian	CE	115	(479) 783-6139	David Hudson	Tom Minton	Nancy Brewer	Virginia Reed	. . .	Paul Atkinson
Sevier	CE	15	(870) 642-2425	Dick Tallman	. . .	Sandra Dunn	. . .	. . .	John Partain
Sharp	C	17	(870) 994-7338	Joe Stidman	. . .	Tommy Estes	. . .	. . .	Dale Weaver
St. Francis	CE	29	(870) 261-1700	Carl Cisco	. . .	. . .	. . .	. . .	Dave Partman
Stone	C	11	(870) 269-3351	. . .	. . .	Donna Wilson	. . .	. . .	. . .
Union	C	45	(870) 864-1910	. . .	. . .	. . .	. . .	. . .	. . .
Van Buren	C	16	(479) 745-2443	Robert Bramlett	Pam Baugus	Ester Bass	. . .	Bobbye Bennett	Dennis Bradley
Washington	C	157	(479) 444-1728	Jerry Hunton	John Gibson	Marilyn Edwards	. . .	Naomi Mitchell	Steve Whitmill
White	CE	67	(501) 279-6233	. . .	. . .	. . .	. . .	. . .	. . .
Woodruff	CM	8	(870) 347-5206	William Simmons	Erlene Sawyer	Becky Hicks	. . .	. . .	Jack Caperton
Yell	C	21	(479) 495-4860	Jimmy Witt	. . .	Carolyn Morris	. . .	. . .	Bill Gilkey

Directory 1/10 continued OFFICIALS IN U.S. COUNTIES 2,500 AND OVER IN POPULATION

Jurisdiction		Form of govern-ment	2000 Popu-lation	Main telephone number	Chief elected official	Appointed administrator	Clerk of the governing board	Chief financial officer	Director of personnel	Chief law enforcement official
CALIFORNIA										
Alameda		CM	1443	(510) 272-6471	...	Susan Muranishi	Crystal Hishida	Patrick O'Connell	Denise Eaton-May	Charles Plummer
Alpine		CE	1	(530) 694-2287	Herman Zellmer	...	Barbara Jones	Marilyn McKenzie	...	Henry Veatch
Amador		C	35	(209) 223-6456	Louis Boitano	Theresa Daly	Sheldon Johnson	Joe Lowe	...	Martin Ryan
Butte		CM	203	(530) 538-7651	...	...	Candace Grubbs	David Houser	Jeanne Gravette	Perry Reniff
Calaveras		CE	40	(209) 754-6303	...	Robert Lawton	Karen Varni	...	...	Dennis Downum
Colusa		CE	18	(530) 458-0420	Christy Scofield	...	Kathleen Moran	Peggy Scroggins	...	Scott Marshall
Contra Costa		CM	948	(925) 335-1080	John Gioia	David Twa	Stephen Weir	...	Lori Gentles	Warren Rupf
Del Norte		C	27	(707) 464-7214	Jack Reese	Jeannine Galatioto	Donna Walsh	Christie Babich	...	Dean Wilson
El Dorado		CM	156	(530) 621-5530	...	Gayle Erbe-Hamlin	Cindy Keck	Joe Harn	Mark Gregerson	Jeffrey Neves
Fresno		CM	799	(559) 488-3266	Bob Waterston	Bart Bohn	Victor Salazar	...	Ralph Jimenez	Margaret Mims
Glenn		C	26	(530) 934-6451	Denny Bungarz	David Shoemaker	...	Don Santoro	John Greco	Robert Shadley
Humboldt	*	CM	126	(707) 445-7266	Jill Geist	Loretta Nickolaus	Kathy Hayes	Michael Giacone	Richard Haeg	Gary Philp
Imperial		CM	142	(760) 482-4488	Gary Wyatt	...	Dolores Provencio	Douglas Newland	Nellie Lerma	...
Inyo		CM	17	(760) 878-0373	...	Kevin Carunchio	...	...	...	...
Kern		CM	661	(661) 868-3480	...	...	...	Ann Barnett	Kay Madden	Mack Wimbish
Kings		CM	129	(559) 582-3211	Jon Rachford	Larry Spikes	Catherine Venturella	Darrell Warnock	Allison Picard	Ron Calhoun
Lake	*	C	58	(707) 263-2213	Edward Robey	Kelly Cox	...	Judy Murray	Kathy Ferguson	Rodney Mitchell
Lassen	*	CM	33	(530) 251-8349	...	John Ketelsen	Julie Bustamante	M. Karen Fouch	Ronald Vossler	Steven Warren
Los Angeles		CM	9519	(213) 974-1101	Yvonne Burke	William Fujioka	Conny McCormack	J. Tyler McCauley	Michael Henry	Leroy Baca
Madera	*	CM	123	(559) 675-7705	...	Stell Manfredi	Rebecca Martinez	Robert DeWall	Kathy Taylor	John Anderson
Marin		CE	247	(415) 499-6111	...	Matthew Hymel	Diane Sauer	Richard Arrow	Laura Armor	Robert Doyle
Mariposa	*	CE	17	(209) 966-3222	Lyle Turpin	Richard Benson	...	Chris Ebie	...	Brian Muller
Mendocino		CM	86	(707) 463-4441	...	Tom Mitchell	Marsha Wharff	Dennis Huey	...	Anthony Craver
Merced		CM	210	(209) 385-7682	...	Demitrios Tatum	...	James Ball	Beverly Morse	Gary Carlson
Modoc		C	9	(530) 233-6200	...	Michael Maxwell	Stephanie Northrup	...	...	...
Mono		CM	12	(760) 932-5410	Mary Pipersky	David Wilbrecht	Renn Nolan	Lauretta Cochran	Stephanie Kentala	Dan Paranick
Monterey		CE	401	(831) 755-5115	Dave Potter	Lew Bauman	Darlene Drain	Rosie Pando	...	Mike Kanalakis
Napa		CE	124	(707) 253-4303	Brad Wagenknecht	Nancy Watt-Collins	Pamela Miller	Pamela Kindig	Dennis Morris	Gary Simpson
Nevada	*	CM	92	(530) 265-1218	Hank Weston	Richard Haffey	Cathy Thompson	Joe Christoffel	Gayle Satchwell	Keith Royal
Orange		CM	2846	(714) 834-5315	...	Thomas Mauk	Gary Granville	Gary Burton	Jan Walden	Michael Carona
Placer		CE	248	(530) 889-4060	...	Thomas Miller	Jim McCauley	Kathy Martinis	Nancy Nittler	Edward Bonner
Plumas		C	20	(530) 283-6444	Bobby Pearson	Jack Ingstad	Kathleen Williams	Michael Tedrick	Gayla Trumbo	Terry Bergstrand
Riverside		CM	1545	(909) 955-3500	...	David Parrish	Gary Orso	Charles Corser	Ronald Komers	Robert Doyle
Sacramento		CM	1223	(916) 440-7097	...	Terry Schutten	...	...	Mike DeBord	...
San Benito	*	CM	53	(831) 636-4000	...	Susan Thompson	Joe Paul Gonzalez	...	Rich Inman	...
San Bernardino		CM	1709	(909) 387-4811	Jerry Eaves	...	...	Errol Mackzum	Barbara Musselman	Gary Penrod
San Diego		CM	2813	(619) 531-5100	...	Walter Ekard	...	William Kelly	Carlos Arauz	William Kolender
San Joaquin	*	CE	563	(209) 468-3203	...	Manuel Lopez	Lois Sabyoun	Adrian Van Houten	Cynthia Clays	Steve Moore
San Luis Obispo		CM	246	(805) 781-5011	Harry Ovitt	David Edge	Julie Rodewald	Gere Sibbach	...	James Hedges
San Mateo		CM	707	(650) 363-4000	Rose Jacobs Gibson	John Maltbie	...	Tom Huening	Mary Welch	Donald Horsley
Santa Barbara		CM	399	(805) 568-3400	Joni Gray	Michael Brown	...	Robert Geis	Ann Goodrich	Jim Thomas
Santa Clara		CM	1682	(408) 299-5830	...	Peter Kutras	Brenda Davis	John Guthrie	...	Laurie Smith
Santa Cruz	*	CM	255	(831) 454-2600	Ellen Pirie	Susan Mauriello	Richard Bedal	Gary Knutson	Dania Wong	Mark Tracy
Shasta		CM	163	(530) 225-5561	Glenn Hawes	Lawrence Lees	...	Richard Graham	Harry Albright	Jim Pope
Sierra		C	3	(530) 289-3295	...	...	...	Van Maddox	...	Leland Adams
Siskiyou		CM	44	(530) 842-8017	...	Howard Moody	Colleen Baker	Leanna Dancer	...	Charles Byrd
Solano		CM	394	(707) 421-6170	William Carroll	Michael Johnson	Chuck Lomeli	William Eldridge	Yolanda Ivigon	Rick Hulse
Sonoma		CM	458	(707) 565-2331	Paul Kelley	Robert Deis	Eeve Lewis	Rodney Dole	Ray Myers	William Cogbill
Stanislaus		CM	446	(209) 525-6341	...	Richard Robinson	Lee Lundrigan	Larry Haugh	...	Mark Puthuff
Sutter	*	CE	78	(530) 822-7100	...	Larry Combs	Donna Johnston	Robert Stark	Mary Lynn Carlton	J. Paul Parker
Tehama		CM	56	(530) 527-4655	...	Williams Goodwin	Beverly Ross	LeRoy Anderson	Michelle Schafer	Clay Parker
Trinity		C	13	(530) 623-1325	Billie Millie	...	Dero Forslund	David Nelson	...	Lorrac Craig
Tulare	*	CM	368	(559) 733-6266	Phil Cox	Jean Rousseau	Gregory Hardcastle	Rita Woodward	Tim Huntley	Bill Wittman
Tuolumne	*	CE	54	(209) 533-5511	Richard Pland	Craig Pedro	Alicia Jamar	Deborah Russell	Eric Larson	James Mele
Ventura	*	CM	753	(805) 654-5129	Linda Parks	Marty Robinson	Richard Dean	Christine Cohen	John Nicoll	Bob Brooks
Yolo		CM	168	(530) 666-8055	Lynnel Pollock	Sharon Jensen	Fredericka Oakley	Howard Newens	Mindi Nunes	Ed Prieto
Yuba		CM	60	(530) 741-6281	Don Schrader	Robert Bendorf	Donna Stottlemeyer	Dean Sellers	Beverly Barnes	Virginia Black
COLORADO										
Adams		CM	363	(303) 654-6070	Elaine Valente	Terry Funderburk	Carol Snyder	Richard Lemke	Stuart Shepard	Douglas Darr
Alamosa	*	CM	14	(719) 589-4848	George Wilkinson	Barry Shioshita	Melanie Woodward	Jowanda Villyard	Constance Ricci	David Stone
Arapahoe		CE	487	(303) 795-4400	...	...	Donnetta Davidson	Charles Green	Ann Harden	Patrick Sullivan
Archuleta	*	C	9	(970) 264-8375	Eugene Crabtree	Gregory Schulte	June Madrid	Donald Warn	Kathy Wendt	William Richards
Baca		C	4	(719) 523-4521	...	Candy Briles	...	...	...	...
Bent	*	C	5	(719) 456-2223	James Coffielo	Gary Pritchard	Patricia Nickell	Phyllis Lutz	...	Gerry Oyen
Boulder		C	291	(303) 441-3131	Paul Danish	...	...	...	Peggy Jackson	Joseph Pelle
Chaffee		CM	16	(719) 539-2218	Timothy Glenn	Kathy Leinz	Joyce Reno	Dan Short	...	Timothy Walker
Cheyenne		CM	2	(719) 767-5872	Ronald Rehfeld	Lara Crowell	Kay Feyh	...	...	Virgil Drescher
Clear Creek		CM	9	(303) 679-2300	Joan Drury	Selby Myers	Pam Phipps	Carl Small	Cate Camp	Don Krueger
Conejos		C	8	(719) 376-5772	Le Roy Valasquez	Tressesa Martinez	Andrew Perea	...	...	Isaac Gallegos
Costilla		C	3	(719) 672-3372	Edward Vigil	...	Delores Burns	Julie Gallegos	...	Roger Benton
Crowley	*	CM	5	(719) 267-5225	T. E. Allumbaugh	...	Lucile Nichols	Michael Apker	...	Miles Clark
Custer		C	3	(719) 783-9067	...	Francis Ferron	...	...	...	...
Delta		CM	27	(970) 874-2100	Jim Ventrello	Susan Hansen	Lela McCracken	Margaret Davey	Wade Hall	William Blair
Dolores		C	1	(970) 677-2383	Leroy Gore	...	Earlene White	...	...	Jerry Martin
Douglas		CM	175	(303) 660-7427	...	Douglas DeBord	Jack Arrowsmith	...	Jessica McCoy	David Weaver
Eagle		CM	41	(970) 328-8600	Michael Gallagher	...	Teak Simonton	Michael Roeper	Carla Budd	Joe Hoy
El Paso		C	516	(719) 520-6426	...	Jeffrey Greene	Eileen Gilbert	...	Imad Karaki	Terry Maketa
Elbert		C	19	(303) 621-3199	John Metli	...	Amy Fordyce	...	Kathi Lancaster	...
Fremont		CM	46	(719) 276-7333	...	...	Norma Hatfield	Dana Angel	George Overstreet	...
Garfield		CM	43	(970) 945-1377	John Martin	Ed Green	Mildred Alsdorf	Patsy Hernandez	Judith Osman	Lou Vallario
Gilpin		C	4	(303) 582-5214	Jeanne Nicholson	Roger Baker	Jessica Lovingier	Clorinda Smith	Susie Allen	Bruce Hartman
Grand		CM	12	(970) 725-3347	Robert Anderson	Lurline Curran	Sara Rosene	Denise Harvey	...	Rodney Johnson
Gunnison	*	CM	13	(970) 641-0248	Hap Channell	Matthew Birnie	Stella Dominguez	Linda Nienhueser	Debbie Moore	Rick Murdie
Hinsdale		CM	..	(970) 944-2225	Flynn Mangum	Laurie Vierheller	Linda Ragle	...	...	William Denison
Huerfano		C	7	(719) 738-2370	...	...	...	...	...	...
Jackson		C	1	(970) 723-4660	Richard Wyatt	William Crowder	Charlene Geer	...	...	Rick Rizor
Jefferson		CM	527	(303) 271-6511	...	James Moore	Faye Griffin	...	...	Theodore Mink
Kiowa	*	C	1	(719) 438-5810	Rodney Brown	Debra Immer	Debra Lening	Gary Woodward	...	Forrest Frazee
Kit Carson		C	8	(719) 346-8139	Jim Whitmore	...	Della Calhoon	Carol Fritz	Erva Carpenter	Steve Goering
La Plata		CM	43	(970) 382-6200	Robert Lieb	...	Linda Daley	Wayne Bedor	Kelli Ganevsky	Sydney Schirard
Lake		C	7	(719) 486-1410	Bill Hollenback	...	...	...	...	Edward Holte
Larimer		CE	251	(970) 498-7010	Kathay Rennels	Frank Lancaster	Scott Doyle	Carol Block	Wynette Cerciello	James Alderden
Las Animas		C	15	(719) 846-2081	Robert Valdez	William Cordova	Bernard Gonzales	Leeann Fabec	Kimberly Chavez	James Casias
Lincoln		C	6	(719) 743-2810	Ted Lyons	Roxie Devers	Corinne Lengel	...	...	Tom Nestor
Logan		C	20	(970) 522-0888	Eugene Meisner	...	Roberta Perry	...	...	Robert Bollish
Mesa		CM	116	(970) 244-1856	...	Jon Peacock	Janice Ward	Marcia Arnhold	Nancie Flenard	Stanley Hilkey
Mineral		C	..	(719) 658-2331	...	Les Cahill	...	...	...	...
Moffat		CE	13	(970) 824-5517	Saed Tayyara	...	Elaine Sullivan	...	Lynnette Running	Timothy Jantz
Montezuma		C	23	(970) 565-8317	G. Story	Thomas Weaver	Evalena Ritthaler	Mary Sanders	...	Sherman Kennell

Directory 1/10 continued — OFFICIALS IN U.S. COUNTIES 2,500 AND OVER IN POPULATION

Jurisdiction	Form of government	2000 Population	Main telephone number	Chief elected official	Appointed administrator	Clerk of the governing board	Chief financial officer	Director of personnel	Chief law enforcement official
COLORADO continued									
Montrose	CM	33	(970) 249-7755	Betsey Hale	Joseph Kerby	Carol Kruse	Nita Emerson	Nancy Eloe	Warren Waterman
Morgan	C	27	(970) 542-3505	Mike Harms	...	Connie Ingmire	Michelle Covelli	David Bute	James Crone
Otero	CE	20	(719) 383-3000	Robert Bauserman	George Shioshita	Sharon Sisnroy	...	...	Christopher Johnson
Ouray	C	3	(970) 325-7320	...	Connie Hunt	Michelle Olin	...	...	Dominick Mattiui
Park	CM	14	(719) 836-4201	Leni Walker	...	Debra Green	Kathy Boyce	Cynthia Gharst	Fred Wegener
Phillips	CM	4	(970) 854-3778	Quentin Biesemeier	Randy Schafer	Beth Cumming	...	...	Rob Urbach
Pitkin	CM	14	(970) 920-5200	...	Hilary Smith	Janice Vos Caudill	Deborah Nelson	Phylis Mattice	Bob Braudis
Prowers	CM	14	(719) 336-8025	Leroy Mauch	Jo Dorenkamp	Dorothy McCaslin	...	...	James Faull
Pueblo	C	141	(719) 583-6000	Matt Peulen	...	Christella Munoz	Aimee Tihonovich	Myrna Gibson	Dan Corsentino
Rio Blanco	CE	5	(970) 878-3627	Forrest Nelson	...	Nancy Amick	Thomas Judd	Teresa Anderson	Si Woodruff
Rio Grande	CE	12	(719) 657-2744	Ralph Rominger	...	Sandra Jackson	Suzanne Benton	...	Brian Norton
Routt	* CE	19	(970) 879-0108	Diane Mitsch Bush	Thomas Sullivan	Karen Weinland	Daniel Strnad	Christine Hensen	Gary Wall
Saguache	* CM	5	(719) 655-2231	Sam Pace	...	Melinda Myers	...	April Quintana	Michael Norris
San Juan	C	..	(970) 387-5766	Ernest Kuhlman	William Norman	Dorothy Zanoni	...	...	Greg Leithauser
San Miguel	CM	6	(970) 327-3844	Art Goodtimes	Lynn Black	Doris Ruffe	Gordon Glockson	...	William Masters
Sedgwick	CE	2	(970) 474-3346	...	...	Patrice Carter	...	...	Rick Ingwersen
Summit	* CM	23	(970) 453-2951	Bob French	Gary Martinez	Cheri Brunvand	Martina Ferris	Scott Vargo	John Minor
Teller	CM	20	(719) 689-2988	James Ignatius	Sheryl Decker	Patricia Crowson	Laurie Litwin	Lindsey Chapman	Kevin Dougherty
Washington	CE	4	(970) 345-2701	Dennis Everhart	Scott Harold	Garland Wahl	Debra Cooper	...	Larry Kuntz
Weld	C	180	(970) 336-7220	David Long	...	Steve Moreno	Donald Warden	...	John Cooke
Yuma	CM	9	(970) 332-5796	Robin Wiley	Linda Briggs	Beverly Wenger	Vicky Southards	...	Sam McCoy
DELAWARE									
Kent	* C	126	(302) 744-2305	P. Brooks Banta	Michael Petit De Mange	Loretta Wootten	Susan Durham	Allan Kujala	James Higdon
New Castle	CE	500	(302) 395-5555	Christopher Coons	Jeffrey Bullock	Betsy Gardner	Michael Strine	Charlotte Crowell	David McAllister
Sussex	CM	156	(302) 855-7700	Dale Dukes	Robert Stickels	Robin Griffith	David Baker	Dennis Cordrey	...
FLORIDA									
Alachua	CM	217	(352) 374-5219	Rodney Long	Randall Reid	J. K. Irby	Walter Barry	Kim Baldry	Stephen Oelrich
Baker	* CM	22	(904) 259-3613	...	Joseph Cone	Al Fraser	Debbie Perryman	Cathy Williams	Joey Dobson
Bay	* CM	148	(850) 784-4013	Michael Ropa	Edwin Smith	Bill Kinsaul	Joseph Rogers	Christy Cook	Frank McKeithin
Bradford	C	26	(904) 964-6280	...	...	Ray Norman	James Farrell	...	Robert Millner
Brevard	CM	476	(321) 633-2000	Ron Pritchard	Peggy Busacca	...	...	Frank Abbate	...
Broward	* CM	1623	(954) 357-6001	Kristin Jacobs	...	...	Phillip Allen	James Acton	...
Calhoun	CM	13	(904) 674-4545	...	...	...	...	...	...
Charlotte	CM	141	(941) 743-1200	...	Roger Baltz	...	...	Magali Kain	...
Citrus	CM	118	(352) 527-5400	Vicki Phillips	...	Betty Strifler	Catherine Taylor	Richard Petitt	Jeffrey Dawsey
Clay	* CM	140	(904) 269-6387	...	Fritz Behring	James Jett	Donald Moore	Richard O'Connell	Scott Lancaster
Collier	CM	251	(941) 774-8460	John Norris	James Mudd	Dwight Brock	Crystal Kinzel	Jennifer Edwards	Don Hunter
Columbia	CM	56	(386) 755-4100	Ronald Williams	Dale Williams	...	P. Cason	Debi Dyal	Frank Owens
De Soto	* CM	32	(863) 993-4808	Elton Langford	...	Mitzie McGavic	...	...	William Wise
Dixie	C	13	(352) 498-1205	John Driggers	...	...	...	...	...
Escambia	CM	294	(850) 595-4900	James Dickson	Robert McLaughlin	Ernie Magaha	Wanda McBrearty	Rod Powell	Ron McNesby
Flagler	CM	49	(386) 437-7480	James Darby	Craig Coffey	Gail Wadsworth	Phil Pulliam	Joe Mayer	Don Fleming
Franklin	CE	11	(850) 653-8861	...	Alan Pierce	Marcia Johnson	...	...	Mike Mock
Gadsden	CM	45	(850) 875-8660	Bill McGill	...	Nicholas Thomas	...	Arthur Lawson	W. Woodham
Gilchrist	CM	14	(352) 463-3170	Randy Durden	Ronald McQueen	Joseph Gilliam	Samuel Ferguson	...	David Turner
Glades	CM	10	(863) 946-6000	Robert Giesler	Wendell Taylor	Joseph Flint	Jerry Beck	...	James Rider
Gulf	C	13	(850) 229-6106	Billy Traylor	Donald Butler	Becky Norris	Carla Hand	...	Joe Nugent
Hamilton	CM	13	(386) 792-1288	Lewis Vaughn	Danny Johnson	...	Greg Godwin	...	...
Hardee	CM	26	(863) 773-2161	William Lambert	Lexton Albritton	B. Bradley	Kathy Crawford	Jane Long	Loren Cogburn
Hendry	CM	36	(941) 675-5352	Janet Taylor	...	...	Christine Pratt	Ellen Strickland	...
Hernando	CM	130	(352) 754-4000	Betty Whitehouse	David Hamilton	Karen Nicolai	George Zoettlein	Barbara Dupre	Richard Nugent
Highlands	* CM	87	(863) 402-6809	...	Michael Wright	Robert Germaine	...	John Minor	...
Hillsborough	* CM	998	(813) 272-5750	Ken Hagan	Patricia Bean	Pat Frank	Eric Johnson	George Williams	David Gee
Holmes	C	18	(850) 547-1100	...	...	...	...	...	...
Indian River	CM	112	(561) 567-8000	...	Joseph Baird	...	...	Ron Baker	...
Jackson	* CM	46	(850) 482-9633	Jeremy Branch	Ted Lakey	Dale Guthrie	Lucretia Farris	Lennetta Greene	Lou Roberts
Jefferson	CE	12	(850) 342-0218	...	...	...	...	Annie Charron	...
Lafayette	C	7	(386) 294-1600	...	...	...	...	...	...
Lake	CM	210	(352) 343-9694	Welton Cadwell	...	James Watkins	Barbara Minkoff	Michael Milanowski	George Knupp
Lee	CM	440	(941) 533-2245	Bob Janes	Donald Stilwell	...	William Bergquist	...	...
Leon	CM	239	(850) 488-9962	...	Parwez Alam	...	...	Reginald Ofuani	...
Levy	CM	34	(352) 486-5100	...	...	...	...	...	...
Liberty	* C	7	(850) 643-2215	Albert Butcher	...	Robert Hill	Charla Kearce	Lisa Shuler	Donnie Conyers
Madison	CM	18	(850) 973-3179	Michael Salls	Allen Cherry	...	Tim Sanders	...	Joe Peavy
Manatee	CM	264	(941) 748-4501	Jonathan Bruce	Edwin Hunzeker	R. B. Shore	James Seuffert	Garry Dye	...
Marion	CM	258	(352) 620-3340	Parnell Townley	Patrick Howard	...	...	Andrew Adams	...
Martin	CM	126	(772) 288-5515	Michael DiTerlizzi	Duncan Ballantyne	Marsha Ewing	...	Linda Skelton	Robert Crowder
Miami-Dade	CE	2076	(305) 375-5311	...	George Burgess	Harvey Ruvin	David Morris	Donald Allen	Carlos Alvarez
Monroe	* CM	79	(305) 294-4641	...	...	...	Tina Boan	Teresa Aguiar	...
Nassau	* CM	57	(904) 321-5908	Barry Holloway	Edward Sealover	John Crawford	...	Chili Pope	Tommy Seagraves
Okaloosa	CM	170	(850) 689-5870	Sherry Campbell	James Curry	Don Howard	Gary Stanford	Kay Godwin	Charles Morris
Okeechobee	CM	35	(863) 763-6441	Clif Betts	Lyndon Bonner	Sharon Robertson	Edward Sizemore	...	O. Raulerson
Orange	CM	896	(407) 836-5661	Richard Crotty	Ajit Lalchandani	...	...	James Daye	...
Osceola	CM	172	(407) 343-2200	Paul Owen	Michael Freilinger	Paula Carpenter	Tom Klinker	Mary Cooper	Robert Hansell
Palm Beach	CM	1131	(561) 616-6888	Karen Marcus	Robert Weisman	...	Richard Roberts	Janis Brunell	...
Pasco	CM	344	(727) 847-8103	...	John Gallagher	...	Michael Nurrenbrock	Barbara De Simone	...
Pinellas	CM	921	(727) 464-3367	Kenneth Welch	Robert LaSala	Kenneth Burke	...	David Libby	Jim Coats
Polk	CE	483	(863) 534-6030	Neil Combee	Robert Herr	...	...	Percy Harden	...
Putnam	* CM	70	(386) 329-0200	...	Rick Leary	John Smith	Michael Anderson	Kenneth McClinton	Dean Kelly
Santa Rosa	CM	117	(850) 983-1863	Robert Cole	W. Walker	...	Joel Haniford	Devann Cook	...
Sarasota	CM	325	(941) 861-5000	David Mills	James Ley	Karen Rushing	Jeffrey Seward	Joanie Whitley	Geoffrey Monge
Seminole	CM	365	(407) 665-7945	Daryl McLain	Cynthia Coto	Maryanne Morse	Robert Wilson	Janet Davis	Don Eslinger
St. Johns	* CM	169	(904) 209-2530	...	Michael Wanchick	Cheryl Strickland	Michael Givens	Karen Van Volkinburg	David Shoar
St. Lucie	CM	192	(561) 462-1546	Doug Coward	Faye Outlaw	Jo Ann Holman	Marie Govin	Carl Holeva	Ken Mascara
Sumter	C	53	(352) 569-6042	Richard Hoffman	...	Gloria Hayward	John Lege	Kitty Fields	Bill Farmer
Suwannee	C	34	(386) 364-3400	Eddy Hillhouse	Edward Allen	...	W. Henderson	...	Al Williams
Taylor	C	19	(850) 838-2097	Daryll Gunter	Wayne Humphries	Annie Murphy	Tammy Taylor	Amy Cooper	...
Union	C	13	(386) 496-3711	Regina Parrish	...	...	Donna Jackson	...	Jerry Whitehead
Volusia	* CM	443	(386) 736-5951	Frank Bruno	Jarnes Dinneen	Marcy Zimmerman	Charlene Weaver	Tom Motes	Ben Johnson
Wakulla	CM	22	(850) 926-0919	Maxie Lawhon	Benjamin Pingree	Brent Thurmond	Tim Barden	...	David Harvey
Walton	C	40	(850) 892-8115	...	Ronnie Bell	Daniel Bodiford	...	Gary Mattison	Quinn McMillian
Washington	CM	20	(850) 638-6200	Hulan Carter	Peter Herbert	Linda Cook	...	Jennifer Cook	...
GEORGIA									
Appling	* C	17	(912) 367-8100	Virgil Carter	Mike Phillips	Chrissy Harris	Lee Lewis	Yvonne Sellers	Benny DeLoach
Atkinson	CE	7	(912) 422-3391	Edwin Davis	...	Joyce Taylor	...	Judith Mancil	Herman Tucker
Augusta-Richmond County	CE	199	(706) 821-2850	Bob Young	Fredrick Russell	Lena Bonner	David Persaud	Brenda Byrd-Pelaez	Ronald Strength
Bacon	CE	10	(912) 632-5214	Eugene Dyal	...	Mary Wheeler	...	...	Richard Foskey

Directory 1/10   OFFICIALS IN U.S. COUNTIES 2,500 AND OVER IN POPULATION
continued

Jurisdiction		Form of govern-ment	2000 Popu-lation	Main telephone number	Chief elected official	Appointed administrator	Clerk of the governing board	Chief financial officer	Director of personnel	Chief law enforcement official
GEORGIA continued										
Baker		C	4	(229) 734-3000	...	...	...	...	...	...
Baldwin	*	C	44	(478) 445-4791	Bubba Williams	Joan Minton	Cynthia Cunningham	Linda Zarkowsky	Patsy Dalton	William Massee
Banks		CE	14	(706) 677-6200	Gene Hart	Angela Sheppard	Regina Gailey	...	Judy Greer	Charles Chapman
Barrow		CM	46	(770) 307-3114	Walter Elder	Larry Price	Michelle Sims	Jeanne Horacek	Tammy Esco	Joel Robinson
Bartow	*	C	76	(770) 387-5020	Clarence Brown	Stephen Bradley	Kathy Gill	Jo Taylor	Sandra Southern	Clark Millsap
Ben Hill		CE	17	(229) 426-5112	Larry Davis	David McCranie	Paula Jones	...	Donna Lampkin	Bobby McLemore
Berrien		CM	16	(229) 686-5421	Delma Roberts	Elaine Shiver	Darlene Nix	...	...	Gerald Brogdon
Bibb		CE	153	(478) 621-6343	Charles Bishop	Steve Layson	Shelia Thurmond	Deborah Martin	Tommy Brown	Jerry Modena
Bleckley		CE	11	(478) 934-3200	Billy Smith	...	Sandra Higgins	...	...	Harold Lancaster
Brantley		C	14	(912) 462-5256	...	Charles Madray	...	...	...	...
Brooks		CM	16	(229) 263-5561	Wayne Carroll	Robert O'Barr	Patricia Wright	...	...	...
Bryan		CM	23	(912) 653-3839	H Warnell	Waverly Jones	Donna Waters	...	...	Clyde Smith
Bulloch		CM	55	(912) 764-6245	Garrett Nevil	Thomas Couch	Evelyn Wilson	...	Kymberly Kuebler	Arnold Akins
Burke		CE	22	(706) 554-2324	Jimmy Dixon	C. Hopper	...	...	...	Gregory Coursey
Butts		CM	19	(770) 775-8200	Gerald Kersey	Van Whaler	Margaret Holloway	Deborah Upshaw	...	Joseph Pope
Calhoun		C	6	(229) 849-4835	...	...	...	...	...	...
Camden		CM	43	(229) 576-5601	...	Steve Howard	...	Michael Fender	Penny Woodard	William Smith
Candler	*	CM	9	(912) 685-2835	H. Lanier	...	Doris Strickland	...	...	Charles Bell
Carroll		CE	87	(770) 830-5800	William Chappell	...	Susan Mabry	Don Johnson	Anne Lee	Terry Langley
Catoosa		CM	53	(706) 965-2500	William Clark	Michael Mahn	Martha Davis	Carl Henson	...	Phil Summers
Charlton		C	10	(912) 496-2549	Steve Nance	...	Jenifer Nobles	...	...	...
Chatham		CM	232	(912) 652-7878	Pete Liakakia	Russell Abolt	Sybil Tillman	Linda Cramer	Michael Kaigler	Al St. Lawrence
Chattahoochee		CM	14	(706) 929-3602	Larry Dillard	W. Elvin Hardy	Ann Sills	...	...	Glynn Cooper
Chattooga		C	25	(706) 857-0700	James Parker	...	Martha Tucker	...	...	R. Kellett
Cherokee		CM	141	(678) 493-6000	Leavitt Ahrens	Jerry Cooper	Sheila Corbin	Amy Davis	Kay Bolick	Roger Garrison
Clay	*	CM	3	(229) 768-3238	Gerald Anderson	Pamela Ward	Teresa Smith	...	...	...
Clayton		CE	236	(770) 477-3208	Eldrin Bell	...	Shelby Haywood	Angela Jackson	Renee Bright	Victor Hill
Clinch		C	6	(912) 487-2667	...	...	...	...	...	...
Cobb		CM	607	(770) 528-2600	Sam Olens	David Hankerson	Carol Granger	Brad Bowers	Tony Hagler	Lee New
Coffee	*	CM	37	(912) 384-4799	Frank Jackson	Wesley Vickers	Joann Metts	...	Princess Leggett	Jerry Pope
Colquitt		CM	42	(229) 891-7400	Maxwell Hancock	Jack Byrd	Deborah Cox	Miriam Smith	...	Charles Whittington
Columbia	*	CM	89	(706) 868-3379	Ron Cross	Steven Szablewski	Erin Hall	Leanne De Loach	Marcia Lowry	Clay Whittle
Cook		CM	15	(229) 896-2266	...	Faye Hughes	...	...	...	...
Coweta		CM	89	(770) 254-2604	Kathryn Schlumper	L. Gay	Roxie Clark	Rickey Smoot	Rick Watson	Michael Yeager
Crawford		C	12	(478) 836-3328	...	Martha Leary	...	...	...	...
Crisp		CM	21	(229) 276-2672	Ferrell Henry	Lester Crapse	...	Sherrie Leverett	...	Donnie Haralson
Dade		CE	15	(706) 657-4625	Ted Rumley	Jason Ford	Larry Cooper	...	...	Philip Street
Dawson		2	15	(706) 344-3501	Mike Berg	Kevin Tanner	Cathy Maher	Lowayne Craig	Jay Sessions	Billy Carlisle
De Kalb		CE	665	(404) 371-2000	Vernon Jones	...	...	Michael Bell	Richard Conley	Thomas Brown
Decatur		C	28	(229) 248-3030	Marvin Rentz	...	Faye Gunn	...	...	Wiley Griffin
Dodge		C	19	(478) 374-4361	Dan McCranie	Kelly Bowen	Linda Lowery	...	...	Lawton Douglas
Dooly		CM	11	(229) 268-4228	...	...	...	...	...	...
Dougherty		CM	96	(229) 431-2122	Jeff Sinyard	Richard Crowdis	Barbara Russell	Gail Kohler	Alice Jenkins	Donald Cheek
Douglas		CM	92	(770) 920-7435	Rita Rainwater	G. Linton	Aida Tullis	Robert Harshbarger	Raymond Martin	Phil Miller
Early		C	12	(229) 723-4304	...	Kathy English	...	...	...	...
Echols		CM	3	(229) 559-6538	...	...	Brenda Stalvey	...	...	Jimmy McDuffie
Effingham		CM	37	(912) 754-2153	Verna Phillips	Ed Williams	Patrice Morris	Joanna Floyd	Rushe Sero	Barry Haston
Elbert		CM	20	(706) 283-2000	...	...	Phyllis Thompson	...	...	...
Emanuel		C	21	(478) 237-3881	...	Ezra Price	...	...	...	Marvin Bradley
Evans		C	10	(912) 739-1141	...	Caughey Hearn	Liz Lynn	Bryan Rodgers	...	...
Fannin		C	19	(706) 632-2203	Richard Vollrath	...	Diane Thomas	...	Janice Bailey	George Ensley
Fayette	*	CM	91	(770) 460-5730	Jack Smith	Jack Krakeel	Carol Chandler	Mary Holland	Connie Boehnke	Wayne Hannah
Floyd	*	CM	90	(706) 291-5111	...	Kevin Poe	Kathy Arp	Gary Burkhalter	Larry Johnson	Bill Shiflett
Forsyth	*	CE	98	(770) 781-3088	Charles Laughinghouse	Douglas Derrer	Greg Allen	William Thomas	Patricia Carson	Ted Paxton
Franklin	*	CM	20	(706) 384-2483	Samuel Elrod	...	Laverne Hilley	Franklin Ginn	Elaine Evans	Steve Thomas
Fulton		CM	816	(404) 730-6710	Mike Kenn	Zachary Williams	Mark Massey	Patrick O'Connor	Robert Brandes	Jacquelyn Barrett
Gilmer		C	23	(706) 635-4361	Rayburn Smith	...	Kimberly Rogers	...	...	Carl Bernhart
Glascock		C	2	(706) 598-2671	Thomas Chalker	...	...	...	...	Bryan Bopp
Glynn		CM	67	(912) 554-7170	...	...	Vanessa Mincey	Phyllis McNicoll	Rebecca Rowell	Wayne Bennett
Gordon		CM	44	(706) 629-3795	...	Randall Dowling	Annette Berry	Brent Burdette	Garah Childers	Jerry Davis
Grady	*	CM	23	(229) 377-1512	Robert Burns	Rusty Moye	Ann Mobley	Mary Mayer	...	Harry Young
Greene		CM	14	(706) 453-7716	Vincent Duvall	Byron Lombard	Elna Hutchinson	Amanda Smith	Yalonde Reese	Chris Houston
Gwinnett		CM	588	(770) 822-7900	Wayne Hill	Jock Connell	Brenda Maddox	Lisa Johnsa	Roderick Powell	William Dean
Habersham		CM	35	(706) 754-6264	Jim Butterworth	Janeann Allison	Lisa Ritchie	...	Lynn Merritt	DeRay Fincher
Hall	*	CM	139	(770) 531-6712	Tom Oliver	Charley Nix	Heather Bates	Michaela Thompson	...	Steve Cronic
Hancock		C	10	(706) 444-5746	Samuel Duggan	...	Mamie Smith	...	...	Tomlyn Primus
Haralson		C	25	(770) 646-2002	Amos Sparks	Charles Walker	Charlene Smith	...	...	Ronnie Kimball
Harris		CM	23	(706) 628-4958	Harry Lange	Daniel Bridges	Nancy McMichael	Jennie Shelhorse	...	Robert Jolley
Hart	*	C	22	(706) 376-2024	Joey Dorsey	Jon Caime	Lawana Kahn	Felicia Adams	...	Mike Cleveland
Heard	*	C	11	(706) 675-3821	June Jackson	...	Patty Jiles	...	...	Ross Henry
Henry		CM	119	(770) 954-2400	Leland Maddox	Robert Magnaghi	Susan Craig	James Schuster	Alice Oliver	Mac Nale
Houston		CE	110	(478) 542-2115	Ned Sanders	...	Angela Thompson	Sandi Stalnaker	Harold Wilson	Cullen Talton
Irwin		C	9	(229) 468-9441	Armond Morris	...	...	...	...	Donnie Youghn
Jackson	*	C	41	(706) 367-1199	Pat Bell	Richard Hampton	Erica Johnson	John Hulsey	Melanie Thomas	Stanley Evans
Jasper		C	11	(706) 468-4900	Jerry Crow	Phil Peevy	...	...	...	...
Jeff Davis		CM	12	(912) 375-6611	Clyde McCall	James Carter	Sherri Lytle	...	...	...
Jefferson		CM	17	(478) 625-3332	Gardner Hobbs	James Rodgers	Mary Lamb	...	...	Timothy Fields
Jenkins		C	8	(478) 982-2563	James Henry	Carol Cates	Joyce Mixon	...	...	Michael Morris
Johnson		CM	8	(478) 864-3388	Billy Dudley	K. Strange	Ann Buxton	Betty Watkins	...	Robert Reece
Jones	*	CM	23	(478) 986-6405	J. Hawkins	James Washburn	Leila Land	...	...	...
Lamar	*	CM	15	(770) 358-5146	Jay Matthews	Wayne Patterson	Gretchen Ellerby	...	Lavetrece Warner	Larry Waller
Lanier	*	CM	7	(229) 482-2088	George Hamm	Albert Studstill	Donna Studstill	...	...	Charles Norton
Laurens		CM	44	(478) 272-4755	...	Bryan Rogers	...	Scott Bourassa	...	Kenneth Webb
Lee		CM	24	(229) 759-6000	Billy Mathis	Alan Ours	Christi Dockery	Darlow Maxwell	...	Harold Breeden
Liberty		C	61	(912) 876-2164	John McIver	Joseph Brown	Deanna Pflieger	Kimberly McGlothlin	...	James Martin
Lincoln		CE	8	(706) 359-4444	Tommy Drew	...	Bruce Beggs	...	...	Edwin Bentley
Long		C	10	(912) 545-2494	Randall Wilson	Lisa Long	Mary Odum	...	Crystal Knowles	...
Lowndes		CM	92	(229) 671-2400	...	Joseph Pritchard	Phyllis Waters	Stephanie Black	Mickey Tillman	Ashley Paulk
Lumpkin	*	CM	21	(706) 864-3742	...	Stanley Kelley	Ruth Bohac	Allison Martin	Fran Sullens	...
Macon		C	14	(478) 472-7021	Charles Allen	...	Roselyn Starling	...	...	...
Madison		CE	25	(706) 795-5664	Wesley Nash	C. Fortson	...	...	Connie Benge	Clayton Lowe
Marion		CM	7	(229) 649-2603	...	...	...	...	...	...
Mc Duffie		C	21	(706) 595-2100	Charlie Newton	Donald Norton	Annette Finley	Jimmy Whitaker	Ruthie Thomas	Logan Marshall
Mc Intosh	*	C	10	(912) 437-6671	...	Luther Smart	...	...	...	...
Meriwether		CM	22	(706) 672-1314	Charles Neely	Paul Penn	Beverly Thomas	...	...	Steve Whitlock
Miller		CM	6	(229) 758-4104	India Taylor	...	Debbie Cox	...	...	Herbert Glass
Mitchell		CM	23	(229) 336-2000	Benjamin Hayward	Bennett Adams	Shelia Cannon	...	...	William Bozeman
Monroe	*	C	21	(478) 994-7000	James Vaughn	...	Cindy Crowley	Barbara Baswell	Janet Abbott	John Bittick
Montgomery		C	8	(912) 583-2363	...	...	...	...	...	Robert Markley
Morgan		CM	15	(706) 342-0725	William Nabors	Michael Lamar	...	...	...	...

Directory 1/10   OFFICIALS IN U.S. COUNTIES 2,500 AND OVER IN POPULATION
continued

Jurisdiction	Form of govern-ment	2000 Popu-lation	Main telephone number	Chief elected official	Appointed administrator	Clerk of the governing board	Chief financial officer	Director of personnel	Chief law enforcement official
GEORGIA continued									
Murray	* C	36	(706) 517-1400	Jim Welch	Tom Starnes	...	Tommy Parker	Christy Capehart	Howard Ensley
Newton	CM	62	(678) 625-1210	R. Aaron Varner	John Middleton	Jackie Smith	Marsha Allen	Becky Heisten	Joseph Nichols
Oconee	* CM	26	(706) 769-3938	Melvin Davis	Alan Theriault	Gina Lindsey	Jeff Benko	Malinda Smith	Scott Berry
Oglethorpe	* C	12	(706) 743-5270	Billy Pittard	...	Shonda Peterman	...	...	Mike Smith
Paulding	CE	81	(770) 443-7514	Jerry Shearin	...	...	Pat Brannum	Lillian Norton	...
Peach	C	23	(478) 825-2535	James Khoury	...	Marcia Johnson	...	...	Terry Deese
Pickens	* C	22	(706) 253-8809	Robert Jones	...	Deborah Watson	Mechelle Champion	Debra Champion	Donnie Craig
Pierce	C	15	(912) 449-2022	James Dennison	Nicole Wood	Mollie Howard	...	Tina White	Richard King
Pike	CM	13	(770) 567-3406	Bobby Blount	Stephen Marro	Tabitha Weaver	...	...	James Thomas
Polk	CM	38	(770) 749-2100	Billy Croker	...	Dawn Turner	Muriel Dulaney	...	Bobby Sparks
Pulaski	* C	9	(478) 783-4154	C. Brooks Bailey	...	Vickie Vaughn	...	...	...
Putnam	C	18	(706) 485-5826	Howard McMichael	William Clack	Helen Carnes	...	...	Howard Sills
Quitman	C	2	(229) 334-0903	C. Redding	...	Carolyn Wilson	...	...	Lon Ming
Rabun	C	15	(706) 782-5271	...	Jimmy Bleckley	Debra Westberg	...	...	Michael Carnes
Randolph	C	7	(229) 732-6440	Charles Simmons	...	Keisha Burkes	...	...	...
Rockdale	CE	70	(770) 929-4000	...	William Sands	Jennifer Rutledge	Deb Dobbs	...	Thomas Wigington
Schley	C	3	(229) 937-2609	...	...	...	...	...	...
Screven	CM	15	(912) 564-7535	...	Rick Jordan	Frankie Kirkland	...	Dee Cail	R. Kile
Seminole	* CM	9	(229) 524-2878	Tommy Rogers	Marty Shingler	Donna Jones	...	...	Heath Elliott
Spalding	CM	58	(770) 467-4200	...	William Wilson	...	...	William Gay	James Stewart
Stephens	CM	25	(706) 886-9491	Steve Chitwood	John Rutan	Nancy Downs	Phyllis Ayers	...	Eugene Sorrells
Stewart	C	5	(229) 838-6769	John Patterson	...	...	...	...	Larry Jones
Sumter	CM	33	(229) 928-4500	William Bowen	Lynn Taylor	Rayetta Floyd	Ann Barefoot	Christopher Ryan	Pete Smith
Talbot	* C	6	(706) 665-3220	Franklin Holmes	Sandra Higginbotham	Teresa Callaway	Brenda Crawford	...	John Johnson
Taliaferro	C	2	(706) 456-2494	Charles Ware	...	Ruby Randolph	...	...	James Leslie
Tattnall	C	22	(912) 557-4335	John Parker	...	Faye Hussey	...	...	Quinton Rush
Taylor	CM	8	(478) 862-3336	Clinton Perry	Lenda Taunton	...	...	Vera Moore	Jeff Watson
Telfair	* C	11	(229) 868-5688	Wilson Bowen	...	Nancy Livingston	...	...	Jim Williamson
Terrell	CE	10	(229) 995-4476	Wilbur Gamble	...	Beth Parnacott	...	...	John Bowens
Thomas	CM	42	(229) 225-4100	Josh Herring	Michael Stephenson	Monnette Monahan	...	...	R. Carlton Powell
Tift	CM	38	(229) 386-7850	James Spurlin	...	...	...	Deborah Benson	Gary Vowell
Toombs	C	26	(912) 526-3311	Charles Rustin	...	Sara Taylor	Louie Powell	...	Alvie Light
Towns	C	9	(706) 896-2276	...	...	...	...	...	...
Treutlen	CE	6	(912) 529-3664	George McLendon	...	Sylvia Norris	...	...	Wayne Hooks
Troup	CM	58	(706) 883-1610	Richard Wolfe	Michael Dobbs	...	Stewart Mills	Lavelle Barnes	Donny Turner
Turner	CM	9	(229) 567-4313	...	...	...	...	...	...
Twiggs	CM	10	(478) 945-3629	Ray Bennett	Glenn Barton	...	...	...	Darion Mitchum
Union	C	17	(706) 439-6000	Lamar Paris	...	...	Patti Holder	...	Scott Stephens
Upson	CM	27	(706) 647-7012	Glenn Collins	...	...	...	...	Don Peacock
Walker	C	61	(706) 638-1437	Bebe Heiskell	...	Briggitt Garrett	Gregory McConnell	...	Steven Wilson
Walton	* C	60	(770) 267-1301	Kevin Little	...	Leta Talbird	Linda Hanna	Karen Fraser	Joe Chapman
Ware	CM	35	(912) 287-4300	Ralph Tyson	Gail Boyd	Pam Gibson	Harrison Tillman	JoAnn Drawdy	Ronnie McQuaig
Warren	C	6	(706) 465-2171	...	...	...	...	...	...
Washington	* C	21	(478) 552-2325	Tommy Walker	Lee Lord	...	...	...	John Carter
Wayne	CM	26	(912) 427-5900	...	Nancy Jones	Angie Parker	...	...	...
Webster	C	2	(229) 828-5775	Dave Wills	...	Margie Everett	Joyce Starrak	...	Robbie Wells
Wheeler	C	6	(912) 568-7135	...	...	...	...	...	...
White	CM	19	(706) 865-2235	Chris Nonnemaker	Alton Brown	Jean Welborn	Vickie Neikirk	...	Neal Walden
Whitfield	* CE	83	(706) 275-7500	Mike Babb	Robert McLeod	Barbara Love	Ron Hale	Jackie Palacios	Scott Chitwood
Wilcox	C	8	(229) 467-2737	Homer Conner	...	Hazel Keen	...	...	...
Wilkes	C	10	(706) 678-2511	...	David Tyler	...	...	...	...
Wilkinson	C	10	(478) 946-2236	Dennis Holder	...	...	...	...	Richard Chatman
Worth	* CM	21	(229) 776-8200	Dan Miller	Robert Zellner	Deborah Robinson	LaVerne Watkins	Buffy Walker	Freddie Tompkins
HAWAII									
Hawaii	CE	148	(808) 961-8361	Harry Kim	Dixie Kaetsu	Casey Jarmin	William Takaba	Michael Ben	Lawrence Mahuna
Kauai	CE	58	(808) 241-6595	Maryanne Kusaka	...	Peter Nakamura	Wallace Rezentes	Allan Tanigawa	George Freitas
Maui	CE	128	(808) 244-7855	Charmaine Tavares	Sheri Morrison	...	Kalbert Young	Lynn Krieg	Thomas Phillips
IDAHO									
Ada	C	300	(208) 287-6990	Judy Peavey-Derr	...	J. Navarro	...	Terry Johnson	Vaughn Killeen
Adams	C	3	(208) 253-4561	Ray Bennett	...	Michael Fisk	...	...	Rich Green
Bannock	* C	75	(208) 236-7217	Larry Ghan	...	Dale Hatch	Kristi Klauser	Bobette Wilson	Lorin Nielsen
Bear Lake	CE	6	(208) 945-2212	...	...	...	...	...	...
Benewah	* C	9	(208) 245-3212	Jack Buell	...	J. Michele Reynolds	...	...	Robert Kirts
Bingham	C	41	(208) 785-8040	...	...	Judie Hampton	...	Steven Barton	Dayle Holm
Blaine	CM	18	(208) 788-5505	C. Dennis Wright	Michael McNees	Marsha Riemann	...	...	Jerry Femling
Boise	CE	6	(208) 392-4431	...	...	Constance Swearingen	Patricia Coleman	...	Drew Bodie
Bonner	CE	36	(208) 265-1438	Dale Van Stone	...	Marie Scott	Karen Weldon	Jan Morrison	Evan Roos
Bonneville	C	82	(208) 529-1350	Roger Christensen	...	Ronald Longmore	...	Dan Byron	Byron Stommel
Boundary	C	9	(208) 267-7212	Ronald Smith	...	Diane Cartwright	...	Michael Weland	George Voyles
Butte	C	2	(208) 527-3021	Judith Bailey	...	Anna Perez	...	...	Cary Van Etter
Camas	C	..	(208) 764-2242	...	...	Rollie Bennett	...	...	D. Rast
Canyon	C	131	(208) 454-7300	...	...	...	...	...	...
Caribou	C	7	(208) 547-4324	Max Rigby	...	Edie Izatt	Linda Godfrey	...	Ray Van Vleet
Cassia	* C	21	(208) 878-7302	Dennis Crane	Kerry McMurray	Larry Mickelsen	Cara Petterson	...	James Higens
Clark	C	1	(208) 374-5304	Greg Shenton	...	Lisa Black	...	...	Craig King
Clearwater	* C	8	(208) 476-3615	Don Ebert	...	Carrie Bird	...	...	Chris Goetz
Custer	C	4	(208) 879-2360	Ted Strickler	...	Ethel Peck	...	...	Micky Rosskelley
Elmore	C	29	(208) 587-2130	Larry Rose	...	Gail Best	Merrilee Hiler	Linda Pickett	Rick Layher
Franklin	C	11	(208) 852-1090	Brad Smith	...	V. Larsen	Rae Lajohnson	...	Don Beckstead
Fremont	C	11	(208) 624-7332	Bill Forbush	...	Abbie Mace	...	...	Thomas Stegelmeier
Gem	* C	15	(208) 365-4561	Lan Smith	...	Shelly Gannon	...	...	Chuck Rolland
Gooding	CE	14	(208) 934-4841	...	...	Helen Edward	...	...	Shaun Gough
Idaho	C	15	(208) 983-2751	Patricia Holmberg	...	Rose Gehring	...	...	Lawrence Dasenbrock
Jefferson	C	19	(208) 745-7756	...	...	A. Christine Boulter	...	Marilyn Vanderbeek	Blair Olsen
Jerome	C	18	(208) 324-8811	Veronica Lienman	...	Cheryl Watts	...	...	Jim Weaver
Kootenai	C	108	(208) 446-1640	Gus Johnston	...	Daniel English	David McDowell	...	Rocky Watson
Latah	C	34	(208) 882-8580	John Nelson	...	Susan Peterson	...	...	Wayne Rausch
Lemhi	* C	7	(208) 756-2815	Richard Snyder	...	Terri Morton	...	...	Sam Slavin
Lewis	* C	3	(208) 937-2661	Charles Doty	...	Cathy Larson	...	...	Brian Brokop
Lincoln	C	4	(208) 886-7641	Jerry Nance	...	Liz Kime	...	...	Kent McBride
Madison	C	27	(208) 356-3662	...	...	Marilyn Rasmussen	...	...	Roy Klingler
Minidoka	C	20	(208) 436-9511	Daniel Stapelman	...	Duane Smith	...	...	Kevin Halverson
Nez Perce	C	37	(208) 799-3090	Ron Wittman	...	Patricia Weeks	...	...	Jim Dorion
Oneida	C	4	(208) 766-4116	Gerald Goodenough	...	Shirlee Blaisdell	...	...	Jeff Semrad
Owyhee	C	10	(208) 495-2421	...	...	Cynthia Eaton	...	...	Gary Aman

Directory 1/10   OFFICIALS IN U.S. COUNTIES 2,500 AND OVER IN POPULATION
continued

Jurisdiction	Form of govern- ment	2000 Popu- lation	Main telephone number	Chief elected official	Appointed administrator	Clerk of the governing board	Chief financial officer	Director of personnel	Chief law enforcement official
IDAHO continued									
Payette	* C	20	(208) 642-6000	Rudolph Endrikat	...	Betty Dressen	...	...	Charles Huff
Power	C	7	(208) 226-7611	Kenneth Estep	...	Christine Steinlight	...	...	Howard Sprague
Shoshone	C	13	(208) 752-3331	...	...	...	...	...	...
Teton	C	5	(208) 354-2905	...	...	...	...	...	...
Twin Falls	* C	64	(208) 736-4000	Tom Mikesell	...	Kristina Glascock	...	Elaine Molignoni	Wayne Tousley
Valley	C	7	(208) 382-7100	...	...	Leland Heinrich	...	...	Patti Bolen
Washington	C	9	(208) 414-2092	Diana Thomas	...	Sharon Widner	...	...	Marvin Williams
ILLINOIS									
Adams	C	68	(217) 223-6300	...	...	...	...	...	...
Alexander	C	9	(618) 734-7000	...	...	...	...	...	...
Bond	C	17	(618) 664-1966	...	...	Randy Reitz	...	...	Jeff Brown
Boone	CE	41	(815) 547-4770	Donald Meier	Kenneth Terrinoni	Sylvia Schroeder	...	...	...
Brown	CE	6	(217) 773-3421	Eugene Kerr	...	Judy Woodworth	...	...	Gerald Kempf
Bureau	CE	35	(815) 875-0373	James Lilley	...	Kami Hieronymus	...	...	John Thompson
Calhoun	C	5	(618) 576-2351	Vince Tepen	...	Lucille Kress	...	...	Richard Meyer
Carroll	C	16	(815) 244-0221	...	...	...	...	...	...
Cass	C	13	(217) 452-7217	...	...	...	...	...	...
Champaign	CM	179	(217) 384-3776	Barbara Wysocki	...	Mark Shelden	...	...	Daniel Walsh
Christian	CE	35	(217) 824-4011	John Curtin	...	Linda Curtin	...	...	Robert Kindermann
Clark	* C	17	(217) 826-8311	John Hammond	...	William Downey	...	...	Jerry Parsley
Clay	* C	14	(618) 665-3626	...	...	Brenda Britton	...	...	Jim Sulsberger
Clinton	C	35	(618) 594-2464	...	...	Thomas La Caze	...	...	Mike Kreke
Coles	C	53	(217) 348-0595	...	...	...	...	...	...
Cook	CE	5376	(312) 603-5500	John Stroger	Mark Kilgallon	David Orr	Barbara Sutton	...	...
Crawford	CE	20	(618) 546-1212	Joe Bliss	...	Patty Lycan	...	...	Tom Weger
Cumberland	* C	11	(217) 849-2631	...	...	Julie Gentry	...	...	Stephen Ozier
De Kalb	CM	88	(815) 895-7189	...	Ray Bockman	Sharon Holmes	Gary Hanson	...	Roger Scott
De Witt	C	16	(217) 935-5917	Duane Harris	...	Jayne Usher	...	...	Roger Massey
Douglas	C	19	(217) 253-2411	...	...	...	...	...	...
Du Page	CE	904	(630) 407-6300	...	...	Gary King	George Kouba	Cara Perrone	John Zaruba
Edgar	* C	19	(217) 466-7433	James Keller	...	Rebecca Kraemer	...	...	Tim Crippes
Edwards	C	6	(618) 445-2115	...	...	Mary Smith	...	...	Scott Meserole
Effingham	* C	34	(217) 342-4990	Carolyn Willenburg	...	Kerry Hirtzel	...	...	John Monnet
Fayette	CE	21	(618) 283-5000	Stephen Knebel	...	Terri Braun	...	...	Aaron Lay
Ford	CE	14	(217) 379-2721	Debbie Smith	...	Linda Kellerhals	...	...	Mark Doran
Franklin	* CM	39	(618) 439-3743	Randall Crocker	...	Dave Dobill	...	...	Bill Wilson
Fulton	CM	38	(309) 547-3041	...	Mark Lynch	James Nelson	Doug Manock	...	Jeff Standard
Gallatin	C	6	(618) 269-3025	Randy Drone	...	Elizabeth Wrangel	...	...	Raymond Martin
Greene	C	14	(217) 942-5443	...	...	...	...	...	Michael Fry
Grundy	* C	37	(815) 941-3400	Francis Halpin	Dan Duffy	Lana Phillips	...	Amanda Andreano	Terry Marketti
Hamilton	C	8	(618) 643-2721	James Deen	...	Lovella Craddock	Keith Botsch	...	Gregory Brenner
Hancock	CM	20	(217) 357-3911	David Walker	...	Kerry Asbridge	...	...	Karen Andrews
Hardin	* CE	4	(618) 287-2251	Wayne Eichorn	...	Mary Denton	...	...	Tom Seiner
Henderson	C	8	(309) 867-2911	Barbara Lumbeck	...	Joyce Meloan	...	...	Daryl Thompson
Henry	C	51	(309) 937-3574	Marvin Gradert	Dick Erickson	Mark Henrichs	...	...	Gilbert Cady
Iroquois	C	31	(815) 432-6963	Ronald Schroeder	...	...	...	...	Eldon Sprau
Jackson	* C	59	(618) 687-7240	John Evans	...	Larry Reinhardt	Michelle Tweedy	...	Robert Burns
Jasper	C	10	(618) 783-3124	...	...	...	...	...	...
Jefferson	CE	40	(618) 244-8000	Ted Buck	...	Connie Simmons	...	...	...
Jersey	C	21	(618) 498-5571	Howard Landon	...	Linda Crotchett	...	...	Paul Cunningham
Jo Daviess	* CM	22	(815) 777-6557	Marvin Schultz	Dan Reimer	Jean Dimke	...	...	Leo Hefel
Johnson	C	12	(618) 658-3611	Max Ray	...	Robin Whitehead	...	...	Elry Faulkner
Kane	CE	404	(630) 232-3560	...	...	...	...	...	...
Kankakee	C	103	(815) 937-3642	Karl Kruse	...	Bruce Clark	Steven McCarty	...	Timothy Bukowski
Kendall	C	54	(630) 553-4171	...	Jeffrey Wilkins	Paul Anderson	...	...	Richard Randall
Knox	CM	55	(309) 345-3840	Sally Keener	...	Scott Erickson	...	...	Jim Thompson
La Salle	* C	111	(815) 434-8242	...	...	...	...	...	...
Lake	CE	644	(847) 377-2000	Suzanne Schmidt	Barry Burton	Willard Helander	Gary Gordon	...	Gary Del Re
Lawrence	CE	15	(618) 943-2346	Charles Gillespie	...	Teresa Linton	...	...	Russell Adams
Lee	C	36	(815) 288-5676	James Seeberg	...	Nancy Nelson	...	...	Tim Bivins
Livingston	CM	39	(815) 844-6378	Bill Flott	Alina Hartley	Kristy Masching	...	Linda Daniels	Robert McCarty
Logan	CE	31	(217) 732-6400	...	...	...	...	...	Jerry Dawson
Macon	C	114	(217) 424-1470	Robert Sampson	...	Steve Bean	Amy Stockwell	...	...
Macoupin	C	49	(217) 854-3214	Andrew Manar	...	Michele Zippay	...	...	...
Madison	* CE	258	(618) 296-7040	Alan Dunstan	Joseph Parente	Mark Von Nida	Rick Faccin	Christine Sillery	Robert Hertz
Marion	C	41	(618) 548-3400	Ralph Johnnie	...	Cliff Neudecker	...	...	Gerald Benjamin
Marshall	* C	13	(309) 246-3667	Denny Bogner	...	Andrea Mahoney Platt	...	...	Robert Russell
Mason	C	16	(309) 543-6661	...	...	...	...	...	...
Massac	C	15	(618) 524-5213	Doris Vogt	...	John Taylor	Deborah Beal	Terri Johnston	Sam Dunning
Mc Donough	CE	32	(309) 837-2308	...	...	...	...	...	...
Mc Henry	* CM	260	(815) 334-4000	Kenneth Koehler	Peter Austin	Katherine Schultz	Ralph Sarbaugh	...	Keith Nygren
Mc Lean	* CM	150	(309) 888-5110	Matt Sorensen	John Zeunik	Peggy Milton	...	...	Mike Emery
Menard	* C	12	(217) 632-3201	...	...	Gene Treseler	...	...	Charles Jones
Mercer	CE	16	(309) 582-7021	Kevin Basala	...	Tom Hanson	...	...	...
Monroe	C	27	(618) 939-8681	Robert Rippelmeyer	Grace Miller	Dennis Knobloch	...	...	Daniel Kelley
Montgomery	C	30	(217) 532-9530	...	...	Sandy Leitheiser	...	...	Jim Vazzi
Morgan	C	36	(217) 245-4619	Virgil Smith	Dan Little	Barbara Gross	...	...	James Robson
Moultrie	CE	14	(217) 728-4389	...	...	Georgia England	Ron White	Earline Reed	Jeff Thomas
Ogle	* CM	51	(815) 732-3201	Ed Rice	...	Rebecca Huntley	...	...	Gregory Beitel
Peoria	CM	183	(309) 672-6947	David Williams	F. Urich	JoAnn Thomas	Erik Bush	Kate VanBeek	Michael McCoy
Perry	C	23	(618) 357-5116	Danny Wildermuth	...	Don Hirsch	...	...	Keith Kellerman
Piatt	C	16	(217) 762-7009	Robert Scheffer	...	Pat Rhoades	...	...	Robert Manint
Pike	CE	17	(217) 285-6812	Allen Seiler	...	Roger Yaeger	Melisa Borrowman	...	Mike Lord
Pope	C	4	(618) 683-4466	David Bramlet	...	Connie Gibbs	Ann Ferrell	...	John Crabb
Pulaski	C	7	(618) 748-9360	...	...	Tanna Goins	...	...	Kenneth Moore
Putnam	CM	6	(815) 925-7129	Duane Calbow	...	Daniel Kuhn	...	...	Kevin Doyle
Randolph	* C	33	(618) 826-5000	...	...	...	...	...	...
Richland	* C	16	(618) 392-3111	Leo Ledeker	...	Alice Mullinax	Greg Amerman	...	Andrew Hires
Rock Island	* C	149	(309) 558-3605	James Bohnsack	...	Richard Leibovitz	...	Meg Hoskins	Michael Huff
Saline	C	26	(618) 252-6228	Kermit Coffee	...	Willie McClusky	...	...	...
Sangamon	CM	188	(217) 753-6630	Andy Vanmeter	...	Joseph Aiello	Joseph Cavanagh	...	...
Schuyler	* CE	7	(217) 322-4734	Max McClelland	...	Linda Ward	...	...	Don Schieferdecker
Scott	C	5	(217) 742-5532	...	...	Barbara McDade	...	...	...
Shelby	C	22	(217) 774-4421	...	...	Kathy Lantz	...	...	Michael Miller
St. Clair	CE	256	(618) 277-6600	...	...	...	...	...	...
Stark	C	6	(309) 286-5901	Michael Bigger	...	Linda Pyell	...	...	Jimmie Dison

Directory 1/10   **OFFICIALS IN U.S. COUNTIES 2,500 AND OVER IN POPULATION**
continued

Jurisdiction	Form of government	2000 Population	Main telephone number	Chief elected official	Appointed administrator	Clerk of the governing board	Chief financial officer	Director of personnel	Chief law enforcement official
ILLINOIS continued									
Stephenson	* CM	48	(815) 235-8277	John Blum	Russell Mulnix	Vici Otte	...	...	David Snyders
Tazewell	CM	128	(309) 477-2272	James Unsicker	David Jones	Christie Webb	...	...	Robert Huston
Union	C	18	(618) 833-5711	...	...	...	...	...	...
Vermilion	CM	83	(217) 431-2550	Todd Lee	...	Lynn Foster	Linda Anstey	Nancy Boose	William Hartshorn
Wabash	* C	12	(618) 262-4561	Charles Sanders	...	Marie Kolb	...	...	Arnold Keeling
Warren	C	18	(309) 734-8592	William Reichow	Mike Pearson	Janet Hammond	...	...	Richard Hart
Washington	C	15	(618) 327-8314	...	...	...	...	...	...
Wayne	* C	17	(618) 842-5182	...	...	Donna Endsley	...	...	Jimmy Hinkle
White	C	15	(618) 382-7211	Ronnie Wooten	...	...	...	...	Douglas Maier
Whiteside	CM	60	(815) 772-5100	Tony Arduini	Michael Zurn	Dan Heusinkveld	...	Deborah Workman	Roger Schipper
Will	CE	502	(815) 722-5753	Joseph Mikan	...	Nancy Schultz Voots	Stephen Weber	J. Gregory Pike	Paul Kaupas
Williamson	C	61	(618) 997-1301	Rex Piper	...	Barney Boren	...	...	Tom Cundiff
Winnebago	CE	278	(815) 987-3034	...	Steven Chapman	...	...	...	...
Woodford	* C	35	(309) 467-7343	...	...	Debbie Harms	...	...	James Pierceall
INDIANA									
Adams	C	33	(260) 724-2600	Michael Ripley	...	D. O'Shaunessey	...	...	...
Allen	C	331	(260) 449-7217	Linda Bloom	...	Therese Brown	...	Brian Dumford	Kenneth Fries
Bartholomew	CE	71	(812) 379-1513	Larry Kleinhenz	...	Norma Trimpe	Nancy McKinney	...	Kenneth Whipker
Benton	C	9	(765) 884-0760	Mel Budreau	...	Janet Hasser	Joan Schluttenhofer	...	Boston Pritchett
Blackford	C	14	(765) 348-1620	Fred Walker	...	Laura Coons	Kathy Bantz	...	John Lancaster
Boone	C	46	(765) 482-2940	...	...	Penny Bogan	Gretchen Smith	...	Ken Campbell
Brown	C	14	(812) 988-5485	James Gredy	...	Benita Fox	Mari Miller	...	Robert Stogsdill
Carroll	* C	20	(765) 564-3172	Loren Hylton	...	Nancy Mattox	Beth Myers	...	Tony Burns
Cass	CE	40	(574) 753-7727	...	...	Linda Crimmins	Dawn Conner	...	Gene Isaacs
Clark	C	96	(812) 285-6400	Ralph Guthrie	...	Keith Groth	...	...	Michael Becher
Clay	C	26	(812) 448-9005	Angela Modesitt	Susan Kellum	Mary Brown	...	...	...
Clinton	C	33	(765) 659-6309	...	...	...	...	...	...
Crawford	CE	10	(812) 338-2601	Randy Gilmore	...	Peggy Bullington	Terry Stroud	...	Richard Scott
Daviess	C	29	(812) 254-1090	...	...	Rosemary Abel	...	...	...
De Kalb	CM	40	(260) 925-2362	William Ort	...	Marilyn Miller	Mary Bowman	...	Jay Oberholtzer
Dearborn	C	46	(812) 537-1040	...	...	...	...	...	...
Decatur	C	24	(812) 663-2570	Thomas Menkedick	...	Beverly Stiers	Mary Doggett	...	...
Delaware	* C	118	(765) 747-7730	Tom Bennington	...	Steven Craycraft	Judith Rust	Julie Hillgrove	George Sheridan
Dubois	* C	39	(812) 481-7000	Randall Fleck	...	Kathleen Hopf	...	...	Terry Tanner
Elkhart	C	182	(574) 535-6725	Terry Rodino	Thomas Byers	Stephanie Burgess	David Hess	Floyd Hindbaugh	Michael Books
Fayette	C	25	(765) 825-8987	...	...	Melinda Sudhoff	...	...	Frank Jackson
Floyd	C	70	(881) 294-8549	Larry Denison	...	Betty Hammond	William Jenks	William Burkhart	Leland Watson
Fountain	C	17	(765) 793-2243	...	...	Patricia Gritten	Colleen Chambers	...	Robert Bass
Franklin	C	22	(765) 647-4985	Louis Linkel	...	Marlene Flaspohler	...	...	Dale Maxie
Fulton	* C	20	(574) 223-2912	Richard Powell	...	Letty McKee	Denise Bonnell	Penny Bramble	Walker Conley
Gibson	* C	32	(812) 386-6474	...	...	Becky Woodburn	...	...	R. Allen Harmon
Grant	CM	73	(765) 668-8871	...	...	Carolyn Mowery	Judith Carmichael	...	...
Greene	C	33	(812) 384-8658	Thomas Britton	...	Thomas Franklin	David Bailey	...	William Allen
Hamilton	C	182	(317) 776-8401	...	...	Tamela Baitz	Robin Mills	Sheena Randall	Larry Cook
Hancock	C	55	(317) 477-1105	...	...	Sharon Burris	...	...	Calvin Gray
Harrison	C	34	(812) 738-8241	Terry Miller	...	Carole Gaither	Karen Engleman	...	C. Wendell Smith
Hendricks	CM	104	(317) 745-9221	...	...	Cindy Spence	...	...	...
Henry	CE	48	(765) 529-4705	...	...	Patricia French	Linda Ratcliff	...	Kim Cronk
Howard	* C	84	(765) 456-7010	David Trine	Lawrence Murrell	Mona Myers	Ann Wells	Wanda McKillip	Marshall Talbert
Huntington	* CM	38	(260) 358-4822	...	...	Vicki Stoffel	Kathy Juillerat	...	Kent Farthing
Jackson	C	41	(812) 358-6161	Gary Darlage	...	Sarah Benter	Debra Eggeman	...	...
Jasper	C	30	(219) 866-4930	Richard Maxwell	...	Arlene Castongia	Rita Steele	...	James Wallace
Jay	CE	21	(260) 726-4951	...	...	...	...	...	...
Jefferson	C	31	(812) 265-8944	Julie Berry	Joe Robinson	Kim Smith	Sandra Shelton	...	William Andrews
Jennings	C	27	(812) 352-3016	...	...	Janice Ramey	Edwin Judd	...	Earl Taggart
Johnson	CM	115	(317) 736-5000	James Rhoades	...	Jill Jackson	Deborah Shutta	...	Terry McLaughlin
Knox	C	39	(812) 885-2502	Dodi Blackburn	...	Brenda Hall	...	...	Jerry Mooney
Kosciusko	CM	74	(574) 372-2475	...	Ronald Robinson	...	...	...	Aaron Rovenstine
La Grange	C	34	(260) 499-6310	Richard Strayer	...	June Prill	Kay Myers	...	Greg Dhaene
La Porte	C	110	(574) 326-6808	Clay Turner	...	Ann Sperak	Kenneth Layton	...	Robert Blair
Lake	C	484	(219) 755-3200	Rudolph Clay	John Dull	Anna Anton	Dante Rondelli	...	John Buncich
Lawrence	* C	45	(812) 275-3111	...	...	Julie Brinegar	...	...	Samuel Craig
Madison	CE	133	(765) 642-0186	...	...	...	...	...	...
Marion	CE	860	(317) 327-4622	Philip Borst	...	Doris Sadler	Martha Womacks	...	Frank Anderson
Marshall	CE	45	(574) 935-8555	Kevin Overmyer	...	Janice Fisher	Jan Quivey	...	Robert Ruff
Martin	CM	10	(812) 247-3731	...	...	John Hunt	...	...	...
Miami	C	36	(765) 472-3901	Brenda Weaver	...	Trudy McCrae	...	...	Charles McCord
Monroe	C	120	(812) 349-2550	...	...	...	Barbara Clark	...	...
Montgomery	C	37	(765) 364-6400	Stephen Hester	G. Plunkett	Cindy Edmiston	Janet Harris	Carrie Hocking	Dennis Rice
Morgan	C	66	(765) 342-1025	...	...	Janice Wilson	Patricia Carlson	...	Donald Hartman
Newton	C	14	(219) 474-6081	Russell Collins	...	Candice Myers	Jacqueline Knafel	...	Gary Leatherman
Noble	* C	46	(260) 636-2658	J. Hal Stump	...	Constance Althoff	Connie Smith	...	Eldon Fancher
Ohio	* C	5	(812) 438-2062	Connie Brown	...	Roger Purkhiser	...	...	Richard Dixon
Orange	* C	19	(812) 723-3600	...	...	Julie Bandy	Bobby Hall	...	Stephen Cradick
Owen	C	21	(812) 829-5000	Nick Robertson	...	Vickie White	Diana Hazlett	...	Charles Bollinger
Parke	C	17	(765) 569-3422	...	...	Deborah Weatherholt	Deborah Elder	...	Jon Deer
Perry	C	18	(812) 547-2758	L. Fortwendel	Diane Gebhard	Shirley Van Meter	Teresia Leslie	...	Todd Meadors
Pike	* C	12	(812) 354-6451	Stephen Stidd	...	Pamela Mishler Fish	James Murphy	...	David Reynolds
Porter	C	146	(219) 465-3355	Larry Sheets	...	...	...	...	...
Posey	C	27	(812) 838-1306	...	...	Janet Kennedy	Thomas Shank	Christi Hoffa	Paul Grandstaff
Pulaski	C	13	(574) 946-3653	Richard Sommers	...	Opal Sutherlin	Stephanie Campbell	...	Steve Fenwick
Putnam	* CE	36	(765) 653-5513	...	...	Claudia Thornburg	David Kelly	...	Jay Harris
Randolph	* C	27	(765) 584-6700	Noel Carpenter	...	Ginger Bradford	Mary McCoy	...	William Davison
Ripley	C	26	(812) 689-6311	...	...	Deborah Richardson	...	...	Jeff Sherwood
Rush	* CE	18	(765) 932-2086	Thomas Barnes	...	Karen Roth	...	Marsha Miller-Smith	Thomas Herald
Scott	C	22	(812) 752-8408	Billy Comer	...	Carol Stohry	Amy Glackman	Michael Flynn	Michael Bowlby
Shelby	* C	43	(317) 398-5537	Robert Wade	...	Ann Jochim	...	...	Kermitt Lindsey
Spencer	C	20	(812) 649-4376	Dan Rininger	...	Rita Glenn	Mike Eby	Phyllis Emmons	Frank Canarecci
St. Joseph	* C	265	(574) 235-9547	Robert Kovach	...	Rhonda Milner	Michaelene Houston	...	Robert Sims
Starke	C	23	(574) 772-9101	Daniel Bau	...	Debra Arnett	Kim Koomler	...	Richard Lewis
Steuben	CE	33	(260) 668-1000	F Mayo Sanders	...	Rochelle Parris	...	...	John Waterman
Sullivan	C	21	(812) 268-4491	Ray McCammon	...	Ginger Peters	Rachel Bladen	...	Nathan Hughes
Switzerland	* C	9	(812) 427-3302	K. C. Banta	...	Linda Phillips	...	Shirley Mennen	Tracy Brown
Tippecanoe	CE	148	(765) 423-9215	K. Benson	...	...	...	...	...
Tipton	CE	16	(765) 675-2795	...	...	Patricia Hensley	Virginia Bostick	...	Steve Leverton
Union	C	7	(765) 458-5464	Allen Paddock	...				

Jurisdiction	Form of govern- ment	2000 Popu- lation	Main telephone number	Chief elected official	Appointed administrator	Clerk of the governing board	Chief financial officer	Director of personnel	Chief law enforcement official
INDIANA continued									
Vanderburgh	C	171	(812) 435-5241	...	...	Susan Kirk	...	...	Brad Ellsworth
Vermillion	C	16	(765) 492-3570	Timothy Wilson	...	Martha Padish	Ruth Ann Swinford	...	Kim Hawkins
Vigo	C	105	(812) 462-3000	William Bryan	...	William Mansard	Raymond Watts	...	William Harris
Wabash	CM	34	(260) 563-0661	Lester Templin	Jim Dils	Lori Draper	Bob Fuller	...	Leroy Striker
Warren	C	8	(765) 762-3275	Thomas Hetrick	...	Carolyn Weston	Michelle Hetrick	...	Russell Hart
Warrick *	CM	52	(812) 897-6120	Don Williams	Roger Emmons	Shannon Weisheit	Lawrence Lacer	...	Marvin Heilman
Washington *	C	27	(812) 883-4805	...	...	Rita Martin	Sarah Bachman	...	Claude Combs
Wayne *	C	71	(765) 973-9209	Mary Heyob	...	SueAnne Lower	...	Vickie Hill	Matt Strittmatter
Wells	C	27	(260) 824-6470	...	...	Betsy Noe	...	...	Brooks Mounsey
White	CE	25	(574) 583-5761	Mary Pool	Julie McKenzie	Bruce Lambert	...	...	John Roberts
Whitley	C	30	(260) 248-3100	James Argerbright	...	Cindy Greer	Linda Gerig	Paula Reimers	Mark Hodges
IOWA									
Adair *	CM	8	(641) 743-2546	Bill Lamb	...	Mindy Schaefer	...	...	Brad Newton
Adams *	C	4	(641) 322-3340	Karl McCarty	...	...	Nichole Tucker	...	Bill Lyddon
Allamakee *	C	14	(563) 568-3522	Lennie Burke	...	Pam Benjegerdes	...	...	Tim Heiderscheit
Appanoose	C	13	(641) 856-6191	Wayne Sheston	...	Linda Demry	...	...	...
Audubon	C	6	(712) 563-2584	LaVerne Deist	...	Kim Johnson	Lisa Frederiksen	...	Todd Johnson
Benton	C	25	(319) 472-4869	Jason Sanders	...	...	...	...	Kenneth Popenhagen
Black Hawk *	C	128	(319) 833-3009	Frank Magsamen	...	...	Grant Veedor	June Watkins	Anthony Thompson
Boone *	C	26	(515) 433-0502	Albert Sorensen	Bill Lusher	Philippe Meier	...	Sara Behn	Ronald Fehr
Bremer	CE	23	(319) 352-0340	...	...	...	Kathy Thoms	...	Duane Hildebrandt
Buchanan	C	21	(319) 334-3578	Leo Donnelly	...	Vicki Brasch	Cynthia Witt	...	Bill Wolfgram
Buena Vista *	C	20	(712) 749-2542	Paul Merten	...	Shari O'Bannon	Karen Strawn	...	Gary Launderville
Butler	C	15	(319) 267-2670	Holly Fokkena	...	...	...	...	Jason Johnson
Calhoun	CM	11	(712) 297-7741	...	...	...	Judy Howrey	...	Bill Davis
Carroll *	C	21	(712) 792-9802	...	...	...	...	...	Douglas Bass
Cass *	C	14	(712) 243-4570	Don Volk	...	Joyce Jensen	Dale Sunderman	...	Bill Sage
Cedar *	C	18	(563) 886-3168	...	...	...	Betty Ellerhoff	...	Dan Hannes
Cerro Gordo	C	46	(641) 421-3021	Jay Urdahl	...	Michelle Rush	Heather Mathre	...	Kevin Pals
Cherokee	C	13	(712) 225-6704	Ronald Wetherell	...	Dawn Coombs	Bonnie Ebel	...	Dave Scott
Chickasaw	CE	13	(641) 394-2100	Virgil Pickar	...	Cindy Messersmith	...	...	Patrick Wegman
Clarke	C	9	(641) 342-3315	Myron Manley	...	Marsha Parsons	Judy Church	...	Bill Kerns
Clay	C	17	(712) 262-1569	Kenneth Chalstrom	...	Shirley Goyette	Marjorie Pitts	...	Randy Krukow
Clayton *	C	18	(563) 245-1106	Randy Keehner	...	...	...	...	Michael Tschirgi
Clinton *	C	50	(563) 244-0575	Grant Wilke	...	...	...	...	Michael Wolf
Crawford	C	16	(712) 263-3045	Daniel Muhlbauer	...	...	Cecilia Fineran	...	Thomas Hogan
Dallas	C	40	(515) 993-5814	Mark Hanson	Connie Kinnard	...	Gene Krumm	Joni Fagen	Brian Gilbert
Davis *	CE	8	(641) 664-2101	Dale Taylor	...	Jeannie Houser	...	...	Dave Davis
Decatur *	C	8	(641) 446-4382	...	...	...	...	...	...
Delaware	C	18	(563) 927-2515	William Skinner	...	...	Sharon McCrabb	...	Ronald Wilhelm
Des Moines	CM	42	(319) 753-8232	Edgar Blow	...	Kathryn Waterhouse	Carol Copeland	...	William Johnstone
Dickinson	C	16	(712) 336-3356	...	...	...	...	...	...
Dubuque	C	89	(563) 589-4441	Donna Smith	Mary Ann Specht	...	Denise Dolan	...	Ken Runde
Emmet *	C	11	(712) 362-4261	Beverly Juhl	Ronald Smith	...	Vickie Jurrens	...	Larry Lamack
Fayette *	CE	22	(563) 422-3497	...	...	...	Lori Moellers	...	Martin Fisher
Floyd *	C	16	(641) 257-6131	Arlin Enabnit	...	Barb Fuls	...	Gloria Carr	Rick Lynch
Franklin *	C	10	(641) 456-5622	Michael Nolte	Corey Eberling	...	Michelle Giddings	...	Larry Richtsmeier
Fremont	C	8	(712) 374-2031	Chuck Larson	Earl Hendrickson	Marsha Smith	Joan Kirk	...	...
Greene *	C	10	(515) 386-5680	Guy Richardson	...	Mary Gilley	Jane Heun	...	Thomas Heater
Grundy	C	12	(319) 824-3122	Mark Schildroth	...	...	...	...	Rick Penning
Guthrie	C	11	(641) 747-3619	James Petersen	...	...	John Rutledge	...	Roger Baird
Hamilton	C	16	(515) 832-9510	Doug Bailey	...	Kim Schaa	...	...	Dennis Hagenson
Hancock	C	12	(641) 923-3163	Florence Greiman	...	...	...	...	Scott Dodd
Hardin	C	18	(641) 939-8113	Jim Johnson	...	...	Renee McClellan	...	Timothy Smith
Harrison	C	15	(712) 644-2401	Larry King	...	Dean Rodwald	...	...	Terry Baxter
Henry	C	20	(319) 385-0756	...	...	Christine Brakeville	Hettie Maschmann	...	Allen Wittmer
Howard	C	9	(563) 547-2880	Mary Jo Wilhelm	...	Cherri Caffrey	...	Craig Fencl	Mark Grinhaug
Humboldt *	C	10	(515) 332-1571	John Christianson	...	Peggy Rice	...	...	Dean Kruger
Ida	C	7	(712) 364-2626	Robert Paulstud	...	...	Lorna Steenbock	...	Wade Harriman
Iowa	C	15	(319) 642-3923	...	...	...	...	...	...
Jackson	C	20	(563) 652-3144	John Willey	...	...	...	...	Russell Kettmann
Jasper *	C	37	(641) 787-1024	Rick Tiedje	...	...	Dennis Parrott	Dennis Simon	Michael Balmer
Jefferson	C	16	(641) 472-2840	...	...	...	...	...	Frank Bell
Johnson	C	111	(319) 356-6000	Mike Lehman	...	...	...	Lora Shramek	Lonny Pulkrabek
Jones	C	20	(319) 462-2282	Joe Cruise	...	...	Janine Sulzner	...	Mark Denniston
Keokuk	C	11	(641) 622-2320	William Deitrich	...	Marilyn Wells	...	...	Ron George
Kossuth *	C	17	(515) 295-2718	Jack Plathe	...	Mary Ellen Munn	Amber Garman	...	Steve Kollasch
Lee *	C	38	(319) 372-6557	...	...	...	...	...	H. D. Jones
Linn	C	191	(319) 892-5120	Lu Barron	...	Linda Langenberg	Stephen Tucker	Thomas Flanders	Donald Zeller
Louisa *	C	12	(319) 523-3371	Frank Jamison	...	...	Sylvia Belzer	Kay Smith	Curtis Braby
Lucas	C	9	(641) 774-4512	Larry Davis	...	...	G. Patterson	...	Delbert Longley
Lyon	C	11	(712) 472-3713	Kenneth Mellema	...	...	Richard Heidloff	...	Kevin Hammer
Madison	C	14	(515) 462-3914	...	...	...	...	...	...
Mahaska	C	22	(641) 673-7148	Henry VanWeelden	...	...	Kay Swanson	...	Paul DeGeest
Marion	C	32	(641) 828-2217	William Shepherd	...	Joan Noftsger	Dody Devries	...	Marv Van Haaften
Marshall	C	39	(641) 754-6330	Gordie Johnson	...	...	...	...	Ted Kamatchus
Mills	C	14	(712) 527-4729	...	...	...	...	...	Mack Taylor
Mitchell	C	10	(641) 732-5861	...	...	...	...	...	...
Monona	C	10	(712) 433-2191	Richard Merritt	...	Karen Kahl	Benita Davis	...	Jeffrey Pratt
Monroe	C	8	(641) 932-7706	Dennis Ryan	...	C. Brothers	...	...	William Owens
Montgomery	C	11	(712) 623-5127	Glen Benskin	...	...	...	...	Tony Updegrove
Muscatine *	C	41	(563) 263-5317	Thomas Furlong	Nancy Schreiber	...	Leslie Soule	...	R. Orr
O'Brien	CE	15	(712) 757-3225	Dan Struve	...	Jeff Roos	Barb Rohwer	...	...
Osceola	CE	7	(712) 754-2241	Barbara Echter	...	Eileen Grave	...	...	Edward Harskamp
Page	C	16	(712) 542-5018	...	...	...	...	...	...
Palo Alto *	CE	10	(712) 852-2924	Ronald Graettinger	...	Gary Leonard	...	...	Dennis Goeders
Plymouth	C	24	(712) 546-6100	Jim Henrich	...	...	...	Karen Meyer	Mike Van Otterloo
Pocahontas	C	8	(712) 335-3361	...	...	Carol Williams	Margene Bunda	...	Robert Lampe
Polk	CM	374	(515) 286-3000	John Mauro	Ronald Olson	Thomas Parkins	Larry Millang	Diana Williams	...
Pottawattamie	C	87	(712) 328-5700	Melvyn Houser	...	...	Marilyn Drake	Mary Davis	Jeff Danker
Poweshiek	C	18	(641) 623-5723	...	...	...	...	...	...
Ringgold	CE	5	(641) 464-3239	Wayne Kemery	...	...	...	...	Michael Sobotka
Sac	C	11	(712) 662-7401	...	...	...	...	...	...
Scott *	CM	158	(563) 326-8611	Jim Hancock	Dee Bruemmer	...	Sarah Kautz	...	Denny Conard
Shelby	C	13	(712) 755-3831	...	...	...	Marsha Carter	...	Gene Cavenaugh
Sioux *	C	31	(712) 737-2216	...	...	...	Lois Huitink	...	Daniel Altena

Directory 1/10 continued — OFFICIALS IN U.S. COUNTIES 2,500 AND OVER IN POPULATION

Jurisdiction	Form of government	2000 Population	Main telephone number	Chief elected official	Appointed administrator	Clerk of the governing board	Chief financial officer	Director of personnel	Chief law enforcement official
IOWA continued									
Story	C	79	(515) 382-6581	Wayne Clinton	...	Mary Mosiman	...	Sherry Howard	Paul Fitzgerald
Tama	C	18	(641) 484-2740	James Ledvina	...	Ann Hendricks	...	...	Mike Richardson
Taylor	* C	6	(712) 523-2280	...	...	Lori Reed	Bonny Baker	...	Lonnie Weed
Union	C	12	(641) 782-7218	Michael King	...	...	Sandy Hysell	...	Rick Piel
Van Buren	* CM	7	(319) 293-3129	Gary Adam	...	Jon Finney	...	...	Dan Tedrow
Wapello	C	36	(641) 683-0025	Jerry Parker	...	Phyllis Dean	...	...	Donald Kirkendall
Warren	* C	40	(515) 961-1001	G. Middleswart	...	...	Traci Vandealinden	...	James Lee
Washington	C	20	(319) 653-7715	Jack Dillon	...	Julie Johnson	William Fredrick	...	Jerry Dunbar
Wayne	CE	6	(641) 872-2242	Jerry O'Dell	...	Sue Ruble	...	...	Keith Davis
Webster	C	40	(515) 573-7175	...	...	...	Carol Messerly	...	Charles Griggs
Winnebago	* C	11	(641) 585-3412	Jennifer Fjelstad	...	...	...	...	Douglas Jenson
Winneshiek	* C	21	(563) 382-5085	Dean Darling	...	Georgiann Schweinefus	...	...	Leon Bohr
Woodbury	CE	103	(712) 279-6480	Maurice Welte	...	...	Patrick Gill	John Pellersels	David Amick
Worth	* CE	7	(641) 324-2316	Jeff Creger	...	...	...	...	Jay Langenbau
Wright	* C	14	(515) 532-2771	Rodney Toftey	Betty Ellis	Janelle Bites	...	...	Paul Schultz
KANSAS									
Allen	CE	14	(620) 365-1407	Kent Thompson	...	Sherrie Riebel	...	...	Thomas Williams
Anderson	C	8	(785) 448-6841	Dean Register	...	Phyllis Gettler	...	...	Darin Dalsing
Atchison	C	16	(913) 367-1653	Susie Pick	...	Pauline Lee	...	...	...
Barber	CE	5	(620) 886-3961	Mike Thomas	...	Debbie Wesley	...	...	Tommy Tomson
Barton	CE	28	(620) 793-1800	Kirby Krier	...	Donna Zimmerman	...	...	Buck Causey
Bourbon	* C	15	(620) 223-3800	Gary Houston	...	Joanne Long	...	Kendell Mason	Ronald Gray
Brown	* C	10	(785) 742-2581	Steve Roberts	...	Debbie Parker	...	...	John Merchant
Butler	CM	59	(316) 322-4300	...	William Johnson	Ronald Roberts	...	...	Craig Murphy
Chase	C	3	(620) 273-6423	Alan Phipps	...	Nadine Buell	...	...	Gerald Ingalls
Chautauqua	CE	4	(620) 725-5800	Mike Champlin	...	Lori Martin	Peggy McAfee	...	...
Cherokee	CM	22	(620) 429-2042	...	...	Sandra Soper	...	Melody Sanderson	Steven Norman
Cheyenne	* C	3	(785) 332-8800	Tim Raile	...	Terry Miller	...	...	Eddie Dankenbring
Clark	C	2	(620) 635-2813	Betty Jo Denton	...	Rebecca Mishler	...	...	N. Brad Harris
Clay	C	8	(785) 632-2552	David Thurlow	...	Mary Brown	...	...	Charles Dunn
Cloud	* C	10	(785) 243-8110	Bill Garrison	...	Linda Bogart	...	...	Brian Marks
Coffey	CE	8	(620) 364-2191	Gene Merry	...	Vernon Birk	...	...	Randy Rogers
Comanche	C	1	(620) 582-2361	Velma Basnett	...	Alice Smith	...	...	Dave Timmons
Cowley	CE	36	(620) 221-5400	...	Leroy Alsup	Carmelita Clarkson	...	...	Robert Odell
Crawford	C	38	(620) 724-6115	Tom Moody	Bob Kmiec	Don Pyle	Heather Hurt	...	Sandy Horton
Decatur	* CE	3	(785) 475-8102	...	...	Colleen Geihsler	...	...	Ken Badsky
Dickinson	C	19	(785) 263-3774	...	...	...	...	...	...
Doniphan	C	8	(785) 985-3513	Paul Scott	...	Peggy Franken	...	...	Michael Batchelder
Douglas	* CM	99	(785) 832-5328	Bob Johnson	G. Weinaug	Jamie Shew	...	...	Ken McGovern
Edwards	C	3	(620) 659-3000	...	...	...	...	...	...
Elk	C	3	(620) 374-2490	...	...	Donna Kaminska	...	...	Doug Hanks
Ellis	* CE	27	(785) 628-9410	Perry Henman	...	Alberta Klaus	...	...	Ed Harbin
Ellsworth	C	6	(785) 472-4161	...	...	...	...	...	...
Finney	* CM	40	(785) 272-3500	Larry Jones	Peter Olson	Elsa Ulrich	...	...	Kevin Bascue
Ford	CM	32	(620) 227-4550	T. Kim Goodnight	Edward Elam	...	Victoria Wells	...	Carl Bush
Franklin	CM	24	(785) 229-3485	Roy Dunn	...	Shari Perry	...	Gayla Stofko	Craig Davis
Geary	C	27	(785) 238-4300	Florence Whitebread	...	Rebecca Bossemeyer	Therese Hoff	Lisa Eickholt	William Deppish
Gove	C	3	(785) 938-2300	Manlen Tuttle	...	Julie Hawkey	...	...	Allan Weber
Graham	C	2	(785) 421-3453	Barbara Bell	...	...	...	...	Don Scott
Grant	* CE	7	(620) 356-1335	Martin Long	...	Linda McHenry	...	...	Lance Babcock
Gray	C	5	(620) 855-3618	...	...	Bonnie Swartz	...	...	Bernard Kramer
Greeley	C	1	(620) 376-4256	Michael Thon	...	Linda Firner	...	...	Bradley Clark
Greenwood	C	7	(620) 583-8121	...	...	Debbie Wyckoff	...	...	Rory Kenneson
Hamilton	* C	2	(620) 384-5629	Jamie Cheatum	...	Marcia Ashmore	...	...	Richard Garza
Harper	CE	6	(620) 842-5555	Harold Pearl	Irvin Creech	Cheryl Adelhardt	...	...	Kirk Rogers
Harvey	CM	32	(316) 284-6806	Max Graber	...	Margaret Wright	Charles Summers	Linda Kientz	Byron Motter
Haskell	CM	4	(620) 675-2263	...	...	Sharon Hinkle	...	...	Larry Phoenix
Hodgeman	* C	2	(620) 357-6421	...	...	...	...	...	...
Jackson	C	12	(785) 364-2891	...	...	...	...	Kathy Mick	...
Jefferson	C	18	(785) 863-2272	David Christy	...	...	...	...	Roy Dunnaway
Jewell	C	3	(785) 378-4020	Frank Langer	...	Carla Waugh	...	...	John Owen
Johnson	CM	451	(913) 715-5000	Annabeth Surbaugh	Michael Press	Beverly Baker	...	...	Frank Denning
Kearny	C	4	(620) 355-6551	...	...	...	...	...	...
Kingman	C	8	(620) 532-2521	Garry Smith	...	Inge Luntsford	...	...	Randy Hill
Kiowa	C	3	(620) 723-3366	Earl Liggett	...	Evelyn Grimm	...	...	Galen Marble
Labette	CM	22	(620) 795-2138	Brian Kinzie	Jim Cook	Linda Schreppel	...	...	William Blundell
Lane	CM	2	(620) 397-5653	Thomas Bennett	...	Crysta Torson	...	...	Donald Wilson
Leavenworth	C	68	(913) 684-0400	...	...	...	...	...	...
Lincoln	CM	3	(785) 524-4757	Doug Gomel	...	Dawn Harlow	...	...	John Lamar McLeod
Linn	C	9	(913) 795-2668	Herbert Pemberton	...	David Lamb	...	...	Marvin Stites
Logan	C	3	(785) 672-4244	...	...	...	...	...	...
Lyon	C	35	(620) 342-4950	...	Marshall Miller	Karen Hartenbower	Larry Tucker	...	Gary Eichorn
Marion	* C	13	(620) 382-2185	Bob Hein	...	Carol Maggard	...	...	Lee Becker
Marshall	C	10	(785) 562-5361	Charles Loiseau	...	Gayle Landoll	...	...	Kenneth Coggins
Mcpherson	CM	29	(620) 241-8149	...	Richard Witte	Susan Meng	...	...	Larry Powell
Meade	C	4	(620) 873-8700	Max Johannsen	Harold Rickers	Dannice Meyer	...	...	Michael Cox
Miami	* CM	28	(913) 294-9500	Jim Wise	Shane Krull	Janet White	...	Brenda Carlson	Frank Kelly
Mitchell	C	6	(785) 738-3652	Terry Collins	...	Chris Treaster	...	...	Douglas Daugherty
Montgomery	C	36	(620) 330-1111	...	...	...	...	...	...
Morris	C	6	(620) 767-5518	Robert Mark	...	Michelle Garrett	Patty Carson	...	Roy Meierhoff
Morton	C	3	(620) 697-2157	...	...	Mary Gilmore	...	Julie Wares	...
Nemaha	* CE	10	(785) 336-2170	...	...	...	...	...	...
Neosho	* C	16	(620) 244-3800	Hugo Spieker	...	Randal Neely	...	...	James Keath
Ness	C	3	(785) 798-2401	Frederick Flax	...	Ramona Meis	...	...	Larry Tittel
Norton	C	5	(785) 877-5710	Lloyd Ritter	...	Dorothy Shearer	Valerie Babcock	...	...
Osage	C	17	(785) 828-4812	...	Delton Gilliland	Rhonda Beets	...	...	Kenneth Lippert
Osborne	C	4	(785) 346-2431	...	...	...	...	...	Curtis Miner
Ottawa	C	6	(785) 392-2279	Kathy Luthi	...	Mary Arganbright	...	...	Kenneth White
Pawnee	CM	7	(620) 285-3721	Arlis Atteberry	...	Ruth Searight	...	...	...
Phillips	C	6	(785) 543-6825	Rodger VanLoenen	...	Linda McDowell	...	...	Le Roy Stephen
Pottawatomie	CM	18	(785) 457-3314	Barbara Kolde	Robert Reece	Susan Figge	...	...	Greg Riat
Pratt	* C	9	(620) 672-4110	...	...	Sherry Kruse	...	...	Vernon Chinn
Rawlins	* C	2	(785) 626-3351	Wilbur Henry	...	Krystal Hutfles	...	...	William Finley
Reno	CM	64	(620) 694-2982	Frances Garcia	...	Shari Gagnebin	Tim Davies	Kristie Evans	Randy Henderson
Republic	C	5	(785) 527-7231	Linda Holl	...	Vickie Hall	...	...	Ronald Blad
Rice	C	10	(620) 257-2232	Bill Oswalt	...	Alicia Showalter	...	...	Steve Bundy

Directory 1/10 OFFICIALS IN U.S. COUNTIES 2,500 AND OVER IN POPULATION
continued

Jurisdiction	Form of govern- ment	2000 Popu- lation	Main telephone number	Chief elected official	Appointed administrator	Clerk of the governing board	Chief financial officer	Director of personnel	Chief law enforcement official
KANSAS continued									
Riley	C	62	(785) 537-6200	...	...	Rich Vargo	Johnette Horne	Cindy Volanti	...
Rooks	* CE	5	(785) 425-6391	Robert Schamel	...	Clara Strutt	...	...	Randy Axelson
Rush	C	3	(785) 222-2731	Larry Wiedeman	...	Barbara Matal	...	...	Ward Corsair
Russell	C	7	(785) 483-3418	...	Lenny Tyson	Simone Ginther	...	...	John Fletcher
Saline	* CM	53	(785) 309-5812	Randall Duncan	Rita Deister	Donald Merriman	...	Marilyn Leamer	Glen Kochanowski
Scott	C	5	(620) 872-2420	...	...	Pamela Faurot	...	...	Alan Stewart
Sedgwick	CE	452	(316) 660-7057	Ben Sciortino	William Buchanan	Don Brace	Chris Chronis	Jo Templin	Gary Steed
Seward	CM	22	(620) 626-3212	...	...	Stacia Long	...	April Warden	Bill McBryde
Shawnee	C	169	(785) 233-8200	Victor Miller	...	Cynthia Beck	Marti Leisinger	Richard Davis	Richard Barta
Sheridan	C	2	(785) 675-3361	...	...	...	...	...	...
Sherman	C	6	(785) 899-4800	...	...	...	...	...	...
Smith	C	4	(785) 282-5110	Roger Allen	...	Lela Rogers	...	...	Alvin Gaines
Stafford	C	4	(620) 549-3509	...	...	Dorothy Stites	...	...	Jeff Parr
Stanton	C	2	(620) 492-2140	Martie Floyd	...	Sharon Dimitt	...	...	Edward Bezona
Stevens	C	5	(620) 544-2541	...	...	Pamela Bensel	...	...	Ted Heaton
Sumner	C	25	(620) 326-3395	...	...	Shane Shields	...	...	Shawn DeJarnett
Thomas	C	8	(785) 462-4500	Ron Evans	...	...	...	...	Thomas Jones
Trego	CE	3	(785) 743-5773	Toby Lynd	...	Lori Augustine	...	...	Richard Schneider
Wabaunsee	C	6	(785) 765-3414	Fred Howard	...	Jennifer Savage	...	...	Craig Spomer
Wallace	CE	1	(785) 852-4282	Bruce Buck	...	Melody Fulton	...	...	Larry Townsend
Washington	C	6	(785) 325-2974	Marcia Funke	...	Louella Kern	...	...	Verni Overbeck
Wichita	CM	2	(620) 375-2731	Dan Nickelson	...	Karla Ridder	...	...	Randy Keeton
Wilson	C	10	(620) 378-4337	Fred Rinne	Kris Marple	Maurine Burns	...	...	Paul Ammann
Woodson	C	3	(620) 625-2179	...	...	...	...	...	...
Wyandotte County– Kansas City	CM	157	(913) 573-5000	Joe Reardon	Dennis Hays	Thomas Roberts	...	Patty Knoll	Ronald Miller
KENTUCKY									
Adair	C	17	(502) 384-2801	Jerry Vaughan	...	...	...	...	...
Allen	C	17	(502) 237-3631	...	...	...	...	...	...
Anderson	* C	19	(502) 839-3471	Steve Cornish	...	Jason Denny	Rick Waddle	...	Troy Young
Ballard	C	8	(502) 335-5176	Bill Graves	...	Lynn Lane	Belinda Sullivan	...	Todd Cooper
Barren	CE	38	(270) 651-3338	Davie Greer	...	Pamela Browning	...	...	Barney Jones
Bath	C	11	(606) 674-6346	Ray Bailey	Sandra Crouch	Glen Thomas	...	...	Randall Armitage
Bell	C	30	(606) 337-3076	...	...	...	...	...	...
Boone	C	85	(606) 334-2100	Larry Burcham	Jeffrey Earlywine	Jerry Rouse	Lisa Buerkley	Marilyn Rouse	Edward Ammann
Bourbon	C	19	(859) 987-2135	Charles Hinkle	...	Richard Eads	...	...	...
Boyd	C	49	(606) 739-4134	Billy Ross	Jesse Ross	Debbie Jones	Linda Cassity	...	...
Boyle	C	27	(606) 238-1118	Anthony Wilder	...	Denise Curtsinger	Mary Lynn	...	Karl Luttrell
Bracken	C	8	(606) 735-2300	Lovell Jett	Tina Cummins	...	...	...	Michael Nelson
Breathitt	CE	16	(606) 666-3810	...	...	...	...	...	...
Breckinridge	C	18	(270) 756-2269	Tom Moorman	...	Jill Irwin	Lisa Hoskins	...	Todd Pate
Bullitt	C	61	(502) 543-2262	Kenneth Rigdon	...	Nora McCawley	...	...	Paul Parsley
Butler	CE	13	(270) 526-3433	...	David Fields	...	...	...	...
Caldwell	* CE	13	(502) 365-6660	Gerald Knight	...	Toni Watson	Betty Holt	...	Stan Hudson
Calloway	C	34	(502) 753-2920	...	...	...	...	...	...
Campbell	CE	88	(859) 292-3838	Steve Pendery	Robert Horine	Susan Prather	Jim Seibert	Naguanda Deaton	Keith Hill
Carlisle	C	5	(270) 628-5451	...	...	...	...	...	...
Carroll	CE	10	(502) 732-7000	Gene McMurry	Traci Courtney	Marketta Brock	...	...	...
Carter	C	26	(606) 474-5366	Charles Wallace	...	Hugh McDavid	...	...	Kevin McDavid
Casey	C	15	(606) 787-8311	...	Ronald Wright	Eva Miller	...	...	...
Christian	CE	72	(270) 887-4100	Steve Tribble	...	Michael Kem	...	...	William Gloyd
Clark	CE	33	(859) 745-0200	John Myers	Liz Elswick	Anita Jones	...	...	Ray Caudill
Clay	* C	24	(606) 598-2071	Carl Sizemore	Tommy Harmon	Freddy Thompson	Diana Roberts	...	...
Clinton	CE	9	(606) 387-5234	...	...	Jim Elmore	...	...	...
Crittenden	* C	9	(270) 965-5251	Fred Brown	...	Carolyn Byford	Daphenia Downs	...	Wayne Agent
Cumberland	C	7	(270) 864-3444	Tim Hicks	...	...	Eugenia Ferguson	...	James Pruitt
Daviess	C	91	(270) 685-8424	Louis Haire	Anthony Sook	...	Larry Carroll	Marsha Hardesty	...
Edmondson	C	11	(270) 597-2819	N. E. Reed	...	Larry Carroll	...	...	Billy Joe Honeycutt
Elliott	C	6	(606) 738-5821	D. Blair	...	Kyle Faulkner	...	...	Elwood Flannery
Estill	* C	15	(606) 723-7524	Wallace Taylor	Teresa Sparks	Sherry Fox	Christine Brandenburg	...	Gary Freeman
Fleming	C	13	(606) 845-8801	...	...	...	...	...	...
Floyd	CE	42	(606) 886-9193	Paul Thompson	...	Carla Boyd	Turner Campbell	...	John Blackburn
Franklin	CE	47	(502) 875-8751	Robert Roach	...	Shirley Brown	Susan Laurenson	...	Ted Collin
Fulton	C	7	(270) 236-2594	...	...	Leslie LaRue	...	...	...
Gallatin	C	7	(859) 567-5691	George Zubaty	...	Tracy Miles	Elaine Lillard	...	...
Garrard	C	14	(859) 792-3531	Ray Hammonds	...	Shelton Moss	...	Rita Hinds	...
Grant	* CE	22	(859) 823-7561	Darrell Link	...	Judith Fortner	Patricia Conrad	Connie McClure	Randall Middleton
Graves	C	37	(502) 247-3626	Tony Smith	...	Glen Bruce	...	...	Robert Morgan
Grayson	CE	24	(270) 259-3024	...	...	...	...	...	Joe Hudson
Green	C	11	(270) 932-4024	Mary Baron	...	Alice Clark	...	...	...
Greenup	C	36	(606) 932-6564	...	...	...	...	...	...
Hancock	C	8	(270) 927-8137	...	...	...	...	...	...
Hardin	* C	94	(270) 765-4491	Harry Berry	...	Kenneth Tabb	...	Vonetta Grey	Charles Williams
Harlan	C	33	(606) 573-4771	Joseph Grieshop	...	Wanda Clem	...	...	Stephen Duff
Harrison	CE	17	(859) 234-7136	Dean Peak	Wanda Jones	Linda Fucnish	Judy Cunningham	...	Bruce Hampton
Hart	C	17	(270) 524-5219	...	...	...	...	...	...
Henderson	C	44	(270) 826-3971	Sandy Watkins	...	Renny Matthews	Rebecca Carroll	...	Dennis Clary
Henry	CE	15	(502) 845-5707	Thomas Bryant	Peggy Bryant	Rhonda Carpenter	...	...	Ray Powell
Hickman	C	5	(270) 653-6195	Gregory Pruitt	Carol Malugin	Sophia Barclay	Nancy Pruitt	Scott Smith	J. Moran
Hopkins	* C	46	(270) 821-8294	Donald Carroll	...	Kim Blue	...	...	S. Frank Latham
Jackson	C	13	(606) 287-8562	...	...	...	...	...	...
Jessamine	C	39	(859) 885-4500	...	...	...	...	...	...
Johnson	C	23	(606) 789-2550	...	...	...	...	...	...
Kenton	C	151	(859) 491-2800	Richard Murgatroyd	R. Kimmich	William Aylor	...	Joseph Shriver	William Dorsey
Knott	C	17	(606) 785-5592	...	...	...	...	...	...
Knox	C	31	(606) 546-6192	Raymond Smith	Bruce Murphy	Mike Corey	Tammy Mays	...	John Pickard
Larue	C	13	(270) 358-4400	Tommy Turner	Brenda Miller	...	Janet Propes	...	Merle Edlin
Laurel	C	52	(606) 864-5158	Lawrence Kuhl	...	Dean Johnson	...	...	...
Lawrence	CE	15	(606) 638-4102	Phillip Carter	...	...	...	...	...
Lee	CM	7	(606) 464-4100	...	...	...	...	...	...
Leslie	C	12	(606) 672-3200	...	...	...	...	...	...
Letcher	C	25	(606) 633-2129	Carroll Smith	...	Winston Meade	...	...	Stephen Banks
Lewis	C	14	(606) 796-2722	...	...	Shirley Hinton	Robert Blaine	...	William Lewis
Lincoln	C	23	(606) 365-2534	...	...	...	...	...	...
Livingston	C	9	(502) 928-2105	Joe Ward	...	James Jones	Nerva Richards	...	...
Logan	C	26	(270) 726-3116	...	...	...	...	...	...
Lyon	CE	8	(502) 388-7311	...	...	...	...	...	...

Directory 1/10 OFFICIALS IN U.S. COUNTIES 2,500 AND OVER IN POPULATION
continued

Jurisdiction	Form of government	2000 Population	Main telephone number	Chief elected official	Appointed administrator	Clerk of the governing board	Chief financial officer	Director of personnel	Chief law enforcement official
KENTUCKY continued									
Madison	C	70	(859) 624-4702	Kent Clark	Linda Ginter	Mary Ginter	Shirl Cross	...	Cecil Cochron
Magoffin	C	13	(606) 349-2313	Paul Salyer	Marcella Salyer	Haden Arnett	...	Tammy Mullins	Pat Montgomery
Marion	C	18	(270) 692-3451	John Mattingly	...	Karen Spalding	...	...	Carroll Kirkland
Marshall	C	30	(270) 527-4740	...	...	...	...	...	...
Martin	C	12	(606) 298-2800	...	...	...	...	...	...
Mason	C	16	(606) 564-6706	James Gallenstein	...	Frances Cotterill	...	...	Tony Wenz
Mc Cracken	C	65	(270) 444-4707	Danny Orazine	Steve Doolittle	Randy Otey	Angie Brown	...	Frank Augustus
Mc Creary	C	17	(660) 376-2413	Jimmie Green	Bruce Murphy	Jo Kidd	Sue Kidd	...	Regal Bruner
Mc Lean	C	9	(270) 273-3213	Larry Whitaker	...	Linda Johnson	Betty Ray	...	Lester Stratton
Meade	CE	26	(270) 422-3967	William Haynes	...	...	...	...	Clifford Wise
Menifee	CE	6	(606) 768-3482	Hershell Sexton	...	Joann Spencer	...	...	Rodney Coffey
Mercer	C	20	(859) 734-5135	...	...	...	...	...	...
Metcalfe	C	10	(270) 432-3181	Don Butler	...	Carol England	Lorrie Boston	...	Rondal Shirley
Monroe	C	11	(502) 487-5505	Wilbur Graves	...	...	...	...	Jerry Gee
Montgomery	* C	22	(859) 498-8707	B. Wilson	Casey Jones	Judy Witt	...	...	Fred Shortridge
Morgan	CE	13	(606) 743-3898	...	...	...	...	...	...
Muhlenberg	C	31	(270) 338-2520	Rodney Kirtley	...	Gaylan Spurlin	...	...	Jerry Mayhugh
Nelson	C	37	(502) 348-1801	...	...	...	...	...	...
Nicholas	C	6	(859) 289-2404	...	...	...	...	...	...
Ohio	* C	22	(270) 298-4400	David Jones	Bob Cox	Bess Ralph	Janice Embry	...	Elvis Doolin
Oldham	CE	46	(502) 222-9357	Mary Ellen Kinser	James Morse	Ann Brown	Shawn Boyle	...	Michael Griffin
Owen	C	10	(502) 484-3405	William O'Banion	Cindy Ellis	Eugene Young	Pam Miller	...	Zemer Hammond
Owsley	* C	4	(606) 593-6202	Cale Turner	...	Sid Gabbard	Barbara Whittaker	...	Kelly Shouse
Pendleton	C	14	(859) 654-4321	Henry Bertram	...	...	Vicky King	...	...
Perry	C	29	(606) 436-4513	Denny Noble	...	Haven King	Kay Spicer	...	Les Borgett
Pike	* C	68	(606) 432-6247	Wayne Rutherford	John Hays	Rose Farley	Rhonda James	...	...
Powell	C	13	(606) 663-2834	Bobby Drake	...	Rhonda Barnett	...	...	Joe Martin
Pulaski	CM	56	(606) 678-4856	Louie Floyd	Dale Weddle	Willard Hansford	Ethel Vanhook	Joan Muse	...
Robertson	C	2	(606) 724-5615	Gordon Buckler	Tara McCord	Stephanie Hendricks	...	...	Randy Insko
Rockcastle	C	16	(606) 256-2856	Buzz Carloftis	...	Norma Houk	Joseph Clontz	...	Shirley Smith
Rowan	CE	22	(606) 784-5151	Clyde Thomas	Timothy Gibbs	Jean Bailey	Maryann Stevens	Becky Banks	Jack Carter
Russell	C	16	(270) 343-2112	Charles Smith	...	Brigette Popplewell	...	...	...
Scott	C	33	(502) 863-7850	George Lusby	Michael Wright	Donna Perry	...	...	...
Shelby	C	33	(502) 633-1220	Bobby Stratton	Robert Rothenburger	Sue Perry	Karen Blake	Gail Renfro	Mike Armstrong
Simpson	C	16	(270) 586-7184	...	...	Bobby Phillps	...	...	...
Spencer	C	11	(502) 477-3211	David Jenkins	Karen Curtsinger	Robin Waldridge	Judy Puckett	...	Steve Coulter
Taylor	C	22	(270) 465-7729	Eddie Rogers	...	Randall Phillips	Alice Lee	...	John Shipp
Todd	* CE	11	(270) 265-9966	Arthur Green	...	Misty Glover	Amanda Petrie	...	Billy Stokes
Trigg	CE	12	(270) 522-8459	Berlin Moore	...	Wanda Thomas	...	...	Randy Clark
Trimble	C	8	(502) 255-7196	...	...	Jerry Powell	...	...	Dennis Long
Union	C	15	(270) 389-1081	Larry Jenkins	...	...	Vicki O'Nan	...	James Girten
Warren	CE	92	(270) 843-4146	Michael Buchanon	Sue Greathouse	Dorothy Owens	Vicki Duckett	...	Jerry Gaines
Washington	C	10	(859) 336-5410	John Settles	William Logsdon	A. H. Robertson	Carla Hardin	...	Tommy Bartley
Wayne	* C	19	(606) 348-4241	Greg Rankin	Peggy Baker	...	...	Sue Thompson	Charles Boston
Webster	C	14	(270) 639-5042	James Townsend	...	Valerie Franklin	Janice Marks	...	Frankie Springfield
Whitley	C	35	(606) 549-6000	Leroy Gilbert	...	...	Tracy Davis	...	...
Wolfe	CE	7	(606) 668-3040	Raymond Hurst	...	...	Barbara Phillips	...	...
Woodford	C	23	(859) 873-4139	...	...	...	...	...	...
LOUISIANA									
Acadia	CE	58	(337) 788-8800	Cecelia Broussard	Katry Martin	...	...	...	Kenneth Goss
Allen	C	25	(337) 639-4328	Kenneth Hebert	...	Sandria Goodman	...	...	...
Ascension	CE	76	(225) 621-5700	...	Cedric Grant	Suzanne Patterson	Gwen LeBlanc	C. W. McCord	...
Assumption	CM	23	(985) 369-7435	Martin Triche	Bettie Monson	Lawrence Bergeron	...	Calvin James	Thomas Mabile
Avoyelles	C	41	(318) 253-9208	Kirby Roy	Allison Laborde	...	...	...	...
Beauregard	C	32	(337) 463-7019	Jerry Kern	...	Pauline Marshall	...	...	...
Bienville	C	15	(318) 263-2019	...	...	...	...	...	...
Bossier	* CM	98	(318) 965-2329	Edwin Shell	William Altimus	...	...	...	Larry Deen
Caddo	CM	252	(318) 226-6906	...	William Hanna	Jerry Spears	Erica Bryant	Maria Eades	...
Calcasieu	CM	183	(337) 437-3500	...	S. McMurry	...	Jerry Milner	Cheryl Heisser	...
Caldwell	C	10	(318) 649-2681	...	Monty Adams	...	...	...	...
Cameron	C	9	(337) 775-5718	Charles Sandifer	Earnestine Horn	Carl Broussard	Darrell Williams	...	James Savoie
Catahoula	CE	10	(318) 744-5435	...	...	...	...	...	...
Claiborne	C	16	(318) 927-9601	...	...	...	...	...	...
Concordia	CE	20	(318) 336-5953	Rodney Smith	Russell Wagoner	Clyde Webber	...	...	Randy Maxwell
De Soto	CM	25	(318) 872-0738	Marlin Caston	Don Edington	Shirley Wheless	Betty Woods	S. Mayweather	Hugh Bennett
East Carroll	C	9	(318) 559-2256	Joseph Jackson	Major Watson	...	...	...	...
East Feliciana	C	21	(225) 683-8577	James Hunt	Clarence Payne	...	Judith Kelly	...	T. Maglone
Evangeline	C	35	(337) 363-5651	William Guidry	...	...	...	...	...
Franklin	CE	21	(318) 435-9429	Carey Stevens	Emmett Book	Jenny Curtis	Sherri Wiltshire	...	...
Grant	C	18	(318) 627-3246	...	...	...	...	...	...
Iberia	C	73	(337) 365-8246	...	...	...	...	...	...
Iberville	CM	33	(985) 687-5190	...	...	...	...	...	...
Jackson	C	15	(318) 259-5680	...	...	...	...	...	...
Jefferson	C	455	(504) 736-6400	Timothy Coulon	Tim Whitmer	Terrie Rodrigue	Nancy Cassagne	Martin Schwegmann	Harry Lee
Jefferson Davis	C	31	(337) 824-4792	...	...	...	...	...	...
La Salle	C	14	(318) 992-2101	...	...	...	...	...	...
Lafourche	CM	89	(985) 446-8427	Gerald Breaux	...	Joel Pierce	Veronica Gonzales	Kristy Chiasson	...
Lincoln	CM	42	(318) 513-6200	Joyce Huntington	Richard Durrett	...	...	Annie Hamlin	...
Livingston	CE	91	(985) 686-2266	Dewey Ratcliff	...	Mary Kistler	Tracie Eisworth	...	...
Madison	C	13	(318) 574-3451	Thomas Williams	Margarett Smith	Rhonda Brooks	...	...	Earl Pinkney
Morehouse	C	31	(318) 281-4132	...	...	...	...	...	...
Natchitoches	C	39	(318) 352-2714	...	Bobby Dean	...	...	...	...
Ouachita	CE	147	(318) 327-1340	Daryll Berry	Tom Janway	...	...	La Quita Danna	...
Plaquemines	CE	26	(504) 682-0081	...	...	...	...	...	...
Pointe Coupee	C	22	(225) 638-9556	Owen Bello	David Cifreo	Gerrie Patin	...	Bertell Dixon	Paul Smith
Rapides	C	126	(318) 473-6660	Jerry Wood	...	Angie Richmond	Bruce Kelly	...	William Hilton
Red River	* C	9	(318) 932-5719	Jessie Davis	...	...	...	...	Johnny Norman
Richland	C	20	(318) 728-2061	Ronnie Gilley	...	...	...	...	...
Sabine	CE	23	(318) 256-5637	...	...	...	...	...	...
St. Bernard	CE	67	(504) 278-4200	Charles Ponstein	Danny Menesses	...	Barbara Bench	Kevin Clark	...
St. Charles	* CE	48	(985) 783-5000	Vernon St. Pierre	Timothy Vial	...	Grant Dussom	Sandra Zimmer	...
St. Helena	CM	10	(225) 222-4549	Jule Wascom	Deborah Strickland	...	...	...	Ronald Ficklin
St. James	CE	21	(225) 562-2387	Dale Hymel	John Lubrano	Gerard Schexnayder	Arile Laiche	Sidney Oubre	...
St. John The Baptist	CE	43	(985) 652-9569	Bill Hubbard	Pat McTopy	...	...	Stacey Cador	...
St. Landry	CE	87	(337) 948-3688	...	...	...	...	...	...
St. Martin	CE	48	(337) 394-2200	Guy Cormier	Gerard Durand	...	Claire Lastrapes	...	...

Directory 1/10 continued — OFFICIALS IN U.S. COUNTIES 2,500 AND OVER IN POPULATION

Jurisdiction		Form of govern-ment	2000 Popu-lation	Main telephone number	Chief elected official	Appointed administrator	Clerk of the governing board	Chief financial officer	Director of personnel	Chief law enforcement official
LOUISIANA continued										
St. Mary		CE	53	(337) 828-4100	William Cefalu	Henry La Grange	Kimberly Pusateri	...	...	...
St. Tammany		CM	191	(985) 898-2362	Kevin Davis	William Oiler	Diane Hueschen	Leslie Long	Sherri Mederos	Rodney Strain
Tangipahoa		CE	100	(985) 748-3211	Gordon Burgess	Jeffery McKneely	Margie Allen	Melissa Cowart	Virginia Baker	...
Tensas		C	6	(318) 766-3542	...	...	...	...	...	...
Terrebonne Parish Consolidated		CE	104	(985) 873-6474	Robert Bergeron	Al Levron	Paul Labat	...	William Torres	Pat Boudreaux
Union		CE	22	(318) 368-8687	...	Dennis Reeves	Peggy Tate	...	...	...
Vermilion	*	C	53	(337) 898-4300	Gerald Butaud	...	...	...	...	Michael Couvillion
Vernon		C	52	(337) 238-1384	...	...	...	...	...	...
Washington		CM	43	(985) 839-7825	M. Taylor	...	Sylvia Forbes	Carole McMillan	...	...
Webster		C	41	(318) 377-7564	Charles Walker	Ronda Carnahan	...	...	...	...
West Baton Rouge		CE	21	(225) 383-4755	Riley Berthelot	Joseph Delapasse	Sharon Zito	...	...	...
West Carroll		CM	12	(318) 428-3390	Richard Strong	Martha Stephens	...	...	...	...
West Feliciana		C	15	(985) 635-3794	...	...	...	...	...	...
Winn		C	16	(318) 628-5824	Lamar Tarver	Thelma Jarnagin	...	...	...	James Jordan
MAINE										
Androscoggin		C	103	(207) 786-8390	...	...	...	...	...	...
Aroostook		CM	73	(207) 493-3318	Paul Adams	Douglas Beaulieu	...	...	...	James Madore
Cumberland		CM	265	(207) 775-6809	Esther Clenott	Peter Crichton	Barbara Buckley	Victor LaBrecque	Wanda Pettersen	Mark Dion
Franklin		CM	29	(207) 778-6614	...	...	...	...	...	...
Hancock		C	51	(207) 667-9542	Dennis Damon	Ray Bickford	...	...	...	William Clark
Kennebec		CM	117	(207) 622-0971	George Jabar	Robert Devlin	...	...	...	Everett Flannery
Knox	*	CM	39	(207) 594-0420	...	Andrew Hart	...	...	...	Donna Dennison
Lincoln	*	CM	33	(207) 882-6311	Sheridan Bond	James McMahon	...	...	...	Todd Brackett
Oxford		C	54	(207) 743-6359	...	...	...	...	...	...
Penobscot		CM	144	(207) 942-8535	...	William Collins	...	...	...	Glenn Ross
Piscataquis		C	17	(207) 564-2161	W. Bartley	Michael Henderson	...	...	...	John Goggin
Sagadahoc		CM	35	(207) 443-8200	Alan Houston	Pamela Corrigan	...	Sheila Leavitt	...	Mark Westrum
Somerset		C	50	(207) 474-9861	Dorothy Canelli	...	...	...	...	Barry De Long
Waldo		C	36	(207) 338-3282	John Hyk	...	Barbara Arseneau	...	Michelle Adams	Scott Story
Washington	*	CM	33	(207) 255-3127	Christopher Gardner	Linda Pagels-Wentworth	...	...	...	Donald Smith
York		C	186	(207) 324-1572	William Layman	David Adjutant	Rachel Sherman	...	April Powell	Philip Cote
MARYLAND										
Allegany	*	CM	74	(301) 777-2190	James Stakem	Vance Ishler	Carol Gaffney	Jerry Frantz	Brian Westfall	David Goad
Anne Arundel		CE	489	(410) 222-1831	Janet Owens	...	...	John Hammond	Randall Schultz	Larry Tolliver
Baltimore		CE	754	(410) 887-2004	James Smith	Anthony Marchione	...	Fred Homan	Theresa Hill	Terrence Sheridan
Calvert		CM	74	(410) 535-1600	Wilson Parran	A. Douglas Parran	Corinne Cook	Terry Shannon	Gail Bourdon	Edward Evans
Caroline	*	CE	29	(410) 479-0660	John Cole	Richard Barton	...	Barbara Spicher	...	Philip Brown
Carroll	*	CE	150	(410) 386-2400	Julia Gouge	Steven Powell	Kathryn Rauschenberg	Robert Burk	Carole Hammen	Kenneth Tregoning
Cecil		CM	85	(410) 996-5250	...	Alfred Wein	...	...	Donna Nichols	Rodney Kennedy
Charles		CE	120	(301) 645-0585	Murray Levy	Paul Comfort	Linda Rollins	Richard Winkler	Ann Pokora	...
Dorchester		C	30	(410) 228-1700	Glenn Bramble	Jane Baynard	...	Michael Spears	Becky Dennis	James Phillips
Frederick	*	CM	195	(301) 600-9000	Jan Gardner	Ronald Hart	...	John Kroll	Mitchell Hose	Charles Jenkins
Garrett	*	CM	29	(301) 334-8970	Dennie Glotfelty	R. Pagenhardt	...	Wendy Yoder	...	Gary Berkebile
Harford		CE	218	(410) 638-3201	James Harkins	John O'Neill	...	...	James Richardson	Howard Walter
Howard		CE	247	(410) 313-2300	James Robey	Raquel Sanudo	...	Dale Neubert	Jimmie Saylor	Wayne Livesay
Kent	*	CM	19	(410) 778-4595	Roy Crow	Susanne Hayman	Janice Fletcher	Patricia Merritt	Marty Hale	John Price
Montgomery		CE	873	(240) 777-1000	...	Timothy Firestine	...	...	Joseph Adler	...
Prince George'S		CE	801	(301) 883-6330	Jack Johnson	John Kines	Redis Floyd	Gail Francis	...	Gerald Wilson
Queen Annes		CM	40	(410) 758-4098	Ted Moeller	Paul Comfort	Lynda Palmatary	Joseph Zimmerman	Richard Mayer	Charles Crossley
Somerset		CE	24	(410) 651-0320	Charles Boston	Charles Massey	...	Charles Muir	Deborah Mahan	Robert Jones
St. Marys		CM	86	(301) 475-4200	Francis Russell	John Savich	...	Elaine Kramer	Susan Sabo	Timothy Cameron
Talbot	*	CM	33	(410) 770-8010	Thomas Duncan	Andrew Hollis	Susan Moran	John Lehner	...	Dallas Pope
Washington		CM	131	(240) 313-2216	Gregory Snook	Gregory Murray	Joni Bitner	Debra Murray	Dave Hankinson	Charles Mades
Wicomico		CE	84	(410) 334-3105	...	Theodore Shea	...	Patricia Petersen	Edward Cox	Hunter Nelms
Worcester		CM	46	(410) 632-1194	...	Gerald Mason	...	Harold Higgins	Deirdre Rouse	Charles Martin
MASSACHUSETTS										
Barnstable		CM	222	(508) 362-2511	Robert O'Leary	...	...	...	...	...
Bristol		C	534	(508) 824-9681	Maria Lopes	...	Marc Santos	P. Harrington	...	Thomas Hodgson
Dukes		C	14	(508) 696-3840	Paul Strauss	E. Winn Davis	Joseph Sollitto	...	...	Michael McCormack
Norfolk		C	650	(781) 461-6105	...	Henry Ainslie	Nicholas Barbadoro	Robert Hall	Ann Brown	Michael Bellotti
Plymouth		C	472	(508) 830-9100	John Riordan	Rosalie Rodick	Francis Powers	...	...	Joseph McDonough
MICHIGAN										
Alcona		CM	11	(989) 724-6807	Kevin Boyat	...	Gayle Simmons	...	...	Douglas Ellinger
Alger		C	9	(906) 387-2076	...	...	Mary Ann Froberg	...	...	David Cromell
Allegan	*	CM	105	(269) 673-0205	Steven McNeal	Robert Sarro	Joyce Watts	David Van de Roovaart	Debbie Daniels	Frederick Anderson
Alpena		CE	31	(989) 354-9500	Mark Hall	Jeff Thornton	Bonnie Friedrichs	...	Cam Habermehl	Steven Kieliszewski
Antrim		CM	23	(616) 533-8607	...	...	Laura Sexton	...	...	Dale Roggenbeck
Arenac		CM	17	(989) 846-4626	Raymond Daniels	...	Rickey Rockwell	...	...	Ronald Bouldin
Baraga		C	8	(906) 524-6183	Michael Koskinen	...	Nelda Bishop	...	...	Bob Teddy
Barry		CM	56	(269) 945-1400	Clare Tripp	...	Debbie Smith	Michael Brown	...	Darrin Leaf
Bay		CE	110	(989) 895-4098	Brian Elder	Thomas Hickner	Cynthia Luczak	Michael Regulski	Kenneth Petersen	John Miller
Benzie		CM	15	(616) 882-9671	...	Charles Clarke	Dawn Olney	Linda Wilson	...	Robert Blank
Berrien		CM	162	(269) 983-7111	...	William Wolf	M. Stine	...	...	James Cherry
Branch		C	45	(517) 279-8411	Charlene Burch	Daniel Kaepp	Judy Elliott	Sandy Thatcher	John Dean	Ted Gordon
Calhoun		CE	137	(269) 781-0980	...	...	Anne Norlander	...	Alexander Lamm	Allen Byam
Cass	*	CM	51	(269) 445-4420	Robert Wagel	Terry Proctor	Barb Wilson	Becky Moore	...	Victor Fitz
Charlevoix		CM	26	(231) 547-7200	...	...	Jane Brannon	...	...	George Lasater
Cheboygan		CM	26	(231) 627-8855	Linda Socha	Michael Overton	Mary Ellen Tryban	Kari Kortz	Timothy Garey	Dale Clarmont
Chippewa		CM	38	(906) 635-6300	...	...	...	...	...	...
Clare		C	31	(989) 539-2510	Karen Lipovsky	...	Carol McAulay	...	...	Jeffery Goyt
Clinton		CM	64	(989) 224-5120	John Arehart	Ryan Wood	Diane Zuker	Craig Longnecker	...	Chuck Sherman
Crawford		CM	14	(989) 348-2841	Lynette Corlew	Paul Compo	Sandra Moore	...	...	Kirk Wakefield
Delta		C	38	(906) 789-5100	...	...	...	...	...	...
Dickinson		C	27	(906) 774-2573	Frank Smith	Kathryn Pascoe	Dolly Cook	...	...	Donald Charlevoix
Eaton		CM	103	(517) 543-7500	Leonard Peters	James Stewart	Fran Fuller	John Fuentes	...	Rick Jones
Emmet		C	31	(231) 348-1702	Jim Tamlyn	...	Irene Granger	Cynthia Van Allen	...	Peter Wallin
Genesee		C	436	(810) 257-3034	...	...	Michael Carr	George Martini	Steven Stratton	Robert Pickell
Gladwin	*	C	26	(989) 426-7351	Terry Whittington	...	Laura Brandon	...	...	Michael Shea
Gogebic		CM	17	(906) 667-0411	...	Juliane Giackino	Gerald Pelissero	...	...	Larry Sanders
Grand Traverse		CM	77	(231) 922-4599	Wayne Schmidt	Dennis Aloia	Linda Coburn	Dean Bott	Brenda Ransom	Scott Fewins
Gratiot	*	CM	42	(989) 875-5282	...	Brian Smith	Carol Vernon	...	...	...

Directory 1/10 **OFFICIALS IN U.S. COUNTIES 2,500 AND OVER IN POPULATION**
continued

Jurisdiction		Form of government	2000 Population	Main telephone number	Chief elected official	Appointed administrator	Clerk of the governing board	Chief financial officer	Director of personnel	Chief law enforcement official
MICHIGAN continued										
Hillsdale	*	C	46	(517) 437-3391	...	...	Marney Kast	...	...	Stanley Buchardt
Houghton		C	36	(906) 482-8307	Jackie Niemi	John Kelly	Mary Schoos	...	...	...
Huron		CM	36	(989) 269-8242	...	...	...	...	...	...
Ingham		CM	279	(517) 887-4327	Mark Grebner	...	Michael Bryanton	Giamcomo Restuccia	...	Gene Wriggelsworth
Ionia		C	61	(616) 527-5300	...	Mark Howe	...	...	...	...
Iosco		CM	27	(989) 362-4212	Larry Erickson	...	Michael Welsch	Elite Shellenbarger	...	Craig Herriman
Iron		CM	13	(906) 875-3301	Patti Peretto	Jan Huizing	Joan Luhtanen	Thomas Lesandrini	...	Robert Remondini
Isabella	*	CM	63	(989) 772-0911	David Ling	Timothy Dolehanty	Joyce Swan	...	...	Larry Burdick
Jackson		CM	158	(517) 788-4000	James Shotwell	Randall Treacher	Amanda Riska	Gerard Cyrocki	Joni Johnson	Henry Zavislak
Kalamazoo		CM	238	(269) 384-8087	David Buskirk	Peter Battani	Timothy Snow	William Dundon	Jo Woods	...
Kalkaska		C	16	(231) 258-3304	Michael Cox	...	Patricia Rodgers	Frank Wright	...	Jerry Cannon
Kent	*	CM	574	(616) 632-7570	Roger Morgan	Daryl Delabbio	Mary Hollinrake	Robert White	Don Clack	Lawrence Stelma
Keweenaw	*	C	2	(906) 337-2229	Donald Keith	...	Marilyn Winquist	...	...	Ronald Lahti
Lake	*	C	11	(231) 745-2725	James Clark	...	Shelly Myers	...	Lori DeWolf	Robert Hilts
Lapeer		CM	87	(810) 667-0366	David Taylor	John Biscoe	Marlene Bruns	Craig Horton	...	Byron Konschuh
Leelanau		CM	21	(616) 256-9711	...	David Gill	...	...	...	...
Lenawee		CM	98	(517) 264-4508	Larry Gould	Cheryl Whipple	Roxann Holloway	Kathleen Bernardo	Beverly Kampmueller	Larry Richardson
Livingston		C	156	(517) 546-1010	David Domas	Robert Block	Margaret Dunleavy	Belinda Peters	Barbara Brooks	Donald Homan
Luce		C	7	(906) 293-5521	Beth Gibson	...	Kathy Mahar	Deborah Johnson	...	Kevin Erickson
Mackinac		CM	11	(906) 643-7300	...	...	Mary Tamlyn	...	...	Scott Strait
Macomb		CM	788	(586) 469-5100	...	...	Carmella Sabaugh	David Diegel	Ted Cwiek	Mark Hackel
Manistee	*	CM	24	(231) 398-3500	Allan O'Shea	Thomas Kaminski	Marilyn Kliber	...	Karen Molby	Dale Kowalkowski
Marquette		CM	64	(906) 225-8151	Gerald Corkin	Steven Powers	Connie Branam	Susan Vercoe	John Greenberg	Gary Walker
Mason		C	28	(231) 843-7999	Thomas Posma	...	Jim Riffle	...	...	Laude Hartrum
Mecosta		CM	40	(616) 796-2505	Ray Steinke	Paul Bullock	Marcee Purcell	Mindy Saxton	...	John Sonntag
Menominee	*	CM	25	(906) 863-7779	...	Brian Neumeier	Mike Jasper	...	...	Kenny Marks
Midland		CE	82	(989) 832-6775	Otis Wilson	David Benda	Karen Holcomb	...	Richard Busch	John Reder
Missaukee	*	C	14	(231) 839-4967	Susan Rogers	...	Carolyn Flore	...	...	James Bosscher
Monroe		CM	145	(734) 240-7295	V. Roe	...	Geraldine Allen	Charles Londo	...	Tilman Crutchfield
Montcalm		CM	61	(989) 831-7300	Patrick Carr	...	Kristen Millard	Chris Hyzer	Brenda Taeter	William Barnwell
Montmorency	*	CM	10	(989) 785-8000	...	Candace Fox	Cheryl Neilsen	...	...	Donald Edwards
Muskegon		CM	170	(231) 724-6442	James Derezinski	James Borushko	Karen Buie	...	...	George Jurkas
Newaygo		CM	47	(231) 689-7200	Adam Wright	Tobi Lake	Laurel Breuker	Donna Kipp	Jodie McGarry	Michael Mercer
Oakland		CE	1194	(248) 858-0535	L. Patterson	Douglas Williams	Ruth Johnson	Jeffrey Pardee	Judith Eaton	Michael Bouchard
Oceana		CM	26	(231) 873-4835	Larry VanSickle	Paul Inglis	Rebecca Griffin	...	...	Terry Shaw
Ogemaw		C	21	(989) 345-0215	...	...	Gary Klacking	...	...	Howard Hanft
Ontonagon		C	7	(906) 884-4255	...	...	Judith Roehm	...	...	John Gravier
Osceola		C	23	(231) 832-6196	...	Susan Vander Pol	Karen Bluhm	...	...	James Crawford
Oscoda		C	9	(989) 826-1109	...	...	Jeri Winton	...	...	Michael Larrison
Otsego	*	CM	23	(989) 731-7520	Kenneth Glasser	John Burt	Susan DeFeyter	Rachel Frisch	Trisha Adam	James McBride
Ottawa		CM	238	(616) 738-4800	Dennis Swartout	Alan Vanderberg	Daniel Krueger	Rosemary Zink	Rich Schurkamp	Gary Rosema
Presque Isle		C	14	(989) 734-3288	...	...	Susan Rhode	...	Gary Wozniak	Terry Flewelling
Roscommon		C	25	(989) 275-7861	Larry Mead	...	Ann Bonk	Cheryl Mollard	Abby Roth	Fran Staley
Saginaw		CM	210	(989) 790-5210	Robert Fish	...	Susan Kaltenbach	Nathan Baldermann	Larry Polk	Charles Brown
Sanilac	*	CM	44	(810) 648-2933	John Merriman	John Males	Linda Kozfkay	...	...	James Young
Schoolcraft		CM	8	(906) 341-3618	Ernest Hoholik	...	Sigrid Hedberg	...	...	Gary Maddox
Shiawassee	*	C	71	(989) 743-2222	...	Margaret McAvoy	...	...	...	Dean Porter
St. Clair		CM	164	(810) 989-6910	...	Shaun Groden	Marilyn Dunn	Robert Kempf	Terry Pettee	Edward Lane
St. Joseph	*	CM	62	(269) 467-5500	...	Judy West-Wing	Pattie Bender	Daniel Carey	Elishia Arver	Brad Balk
Tuscola		CE	58	(989) 672-3700	...	Michael Hoagland	Margie White-Cormier	...	Carrie Krampits	Thomas Kern
Van Buren		C	76	(269) 657-8200	...	...	Shirley Jackson	...	...	Dale Gribler
Washtenaw		CE	322	(734) 222-6800	Leah Gunn	Robert Guenzel	Peggy Haines	Peter Ballios	...	Daniel Minzey
Wayne		CE	2061	(313) 224-5901	...	Robert Ficano	Kathy Garrett	Carla Sledge	Mark Ulicny	...
Wexford		C	30	(231) 779-9453	Leslie Housler	...	Elaine Richardson	...	...	Gary Finstrom
MINNESOTA										
Aitkin		CM	15	(218) 927-7276	...	Patrick Wussow	...	Kirk Peysar	Cindi Hills	Scott Turner
Anoka	*	CM	298	(763) 421-4760	Dennis Berg	Terry Johnson	...	Cevin Petersen	Melanie Ault	Bruce Andersohn
Becker		CM	30	(218) 846-7309	Roger Winter	Brian Berg	Sonia Johnson	...	Nancy Grabanski	Tim Gordon
Beltrami	*	CM	39	(218) 333-4155	Jim Lucachick	Anthony Murphy	...	Kay Mack	Linda Tran	Phil Hodapp
Benton		CM	34	(320) 968-5000	Duane Grandy	Rick Speak	...	Dona Pederson	...	Jim McMahon
Big Stone		CM	5	(320) 839-2525	Doug Tomschin	...	...	Michelle Knutson	Sue Schultz	John Haukos
Blue Earth		CM	55	(507) 389-8100	...	Dennis McCoy	...	...	...	...
Brown		CM	26	(507) 233-6603	Charles Guggisberg	Charles Enter	...	Marlin Helget	Leah Crabtree	Timothy Brennan
Carlton		C	31	(218) 384-4281	...	...	...	Paul Gassert	R. Stafford	Kelly Lake
Carver		CM	70	(952) 361-1500	...	David Hemze	...	David Frischmon	Doris Krogman	Byron Olson
Cass		CM	27	(218) 547-3300	Bob Stranne	Robert Yochum	Norma Geinert	Larry Wolfe	Jack Paul	Jim Dowson
Chippewa		C	13	(320) 269-7447	Gene VanBinsbergen	...	...	...	...	Stacy Tufto
Chisago	*	CM	41	(651) 213-1300	Bennett Montzka	John Moosey	Deanna Lilientham	Dennis Freed	Renee Kirchner	Todd Rivard
Clay		CM	51	(218) 299-5002	John Evert	Vijay Sethi	...	Lori Johnson	Terry Jacobson	William Bergquist
Clearwater		C	8	(218) 694-6130	...	...	...	Daniel Stenseng	...	Dennis Trandem
Cook		C	5	(218) 387-2282	Wesley Hedstrom	...	...	Carol Greszczyk	Janet Simonen	...
Cottonwood		CE	12	(507) 831-1905	John Oeltjenbruns	...	...	J. Johnson	...	Jason Purrington
Crow Wing		CM	55	(218) 824-1067	Dewayne Tautges	Timothy Houle	...	Michael Carlson	Tami Laska	Todd Dahl
Dakota		CM	355	(651) 437-3191	Michael Tuner	Brandt Richardson	Mary Scheide	Richard Neumann	Will Volk	Donald Gudmundson
Dodge		CM	17	(507) 635-6239	Klaus Alberts	David McKnight	...	Thomas Olney	Lisa Hager	Guy Thompson
Douglas		C	32	(320) 762-2381	Harvey Tewes	...	...	...	William Schalow	William Ingebrigtsen
Faribault		C	16	(507) 526-6211	...	...	...	...	...	...
Fillmore		CM	21	(507) 765-4566	Randy Dahl	Karen Brown	...	...	...	Daryl Jensen
Freeborn		CM	32	(507) 377-5241	Glen Mathiason	John Kluever	...	William Helfritz	Susan Phillips	Mark Harig
Goodhue		CM	44	(651) 385-3001	...	Scott Arneson	...	Brad Johnson	Melissa Cushing	Dean Albers
Grant		C	6	(218) 685-4502	...	...	...	...	Zelda Avery	Dwight Walvatne
Hennepin		CM	1116	(612) 348-3000	...	Richard Johnson	Kay Mitchell	...	Rafael Viscasillas	Patrick McGowan
Houston	*	C	19	(507) 725-5822	Ann Thompson	Char Meiners	...	Casey Bradley	Timothy Comstock	Doug Ely
Hubbard		C	18	(218) 732-9023	...	Jack Paul	Luann Boltan	Pam Heeren	...	Gary Mills
Isanti		CM	31	(763) 689-3859	George Laison	Jerry Tvedt	...	T. Treichel	...	L. Southerland
Itasca		C	43	(218) 327-2847	...	Irene Koski	...	Jeff Walker	Louise Koglin Fideldy	Patrick Medure
Jackson		CM	11	(507) 847-4182	Robert Ferguson	Janice Fransen	...	Ben Pribyl	...	Roger Hawkinson
Kanabec		C	14	(320) 679-5367	...	Alan Peterson	...	...	...	Steve Schulz
Kandiyohi	*	CM	41	(320) 231-6215	Richard Larson	Wayne Thompson	...	Sam Modderman	Jeffrey McMahan	Dan Hartog
Kittson		C	5	(218) 843-2655	Marilyn Gustafson	...	...	...	...	Ray Hunt
Koochiching		C	14	(218) 283-1152	Charles Lepper	Teresa Jaksa	...	Robert Peterson	...	Brian Youso
Lac Qui Parle		CM	8	(218) 598-7444	...	...	...	Stanton Bjorgan	...	Graylen Carlson
Lake		CE	11	(218) 834-8300	Larry Larson	...	Wilma Rahn	Steven McMahon	Julie Svir-Peters	Carey Johnson
Lake Of The Woods		CM	4	(218) 634-2430	...	Alan Christensen	...	John Hoscheid	...	Dallas Block
Le Sueur	*	C	25	(507) 357-2251	Joseph Doherty	Peggy Donovan	...	...	Cindy Westerhouse	Dave Gliszinski
Lincoln		C	6	(507) 694-1529	...	...	...	Kathy Schreurs	...	Jack Vizecky
Lyon		CM	25	(507) 537-6980	Philip Nelson	Loren Stomberg	...	...	...	Joel Dahl

Directory 1/10   OFFICIALS IN U.S. COUNTIES 2,500 AND OVER IN POPULATION
continued

Jurisdiction	Form of govern-ment	2000 Popu-lation	Main telephone number	Chief elected official	Appointed administrator	Clerk of the governing board	Chief financial officer	Director of personnel	Chief law enforcement official
MINNESOTA continued									
Mahnomen	C	5	(218) 935-5669	Franklin Thompson	...	...	...	...	Richard Rooney
Marshall	C	10	(218) 745-4851	...	...	...	...	...	...
Martin	CM	21	(507) 238-3126	Steve Pierce	Scott Higgins	...	...	...	Robert Meschke
Mcleod	C	34	(320) 864-5551	Ray Bayerl	...	...	Cindy Schultz	Mary Jo Wieseler	Wayne Vinkemeier
Meeker	CM	22	(320) 693-5200	Stephanie Beckman	Paul Virnig	...	...	...	Mike Hirman
Mille Lacs	CM	22	(320) 983-8218	...	Roxy Traxler	...	Philip Thompson	Lisa Herges	Brent Lindgren
Morrison	CM	31	(320) 632-2941	Bill Block	...	...	Russ Nygren	...	Paul Tschida
Mower	CM	38	(507) 437-9549	Richard Cummings	Craig Oscarson	Susan Davis	Sherwood Vereide	Allan Cordes	Barry Simonson
Murray	CE	9	(507) 836-6148	William Sauer	...	...	Gary Spaeth	Robert Klingle	Steve Telkamp
* Nicollet	CM	29	(507) 931-6800	...	Robert Podhradsky	Margo Brown	Bridgette Kennedy	Chris Wersal	David Lange
Nobles	CM	20	(507) 372-8241	...	Melvin Ruppert	...	...	...	Kent Wilkening
Norman	C	7	(218) 784-5471	Lee Ann Hall	...	Kari Aanenson	...	...	Myron Thronson
Olmsted	CM	124	(507) 285-8115	Kenneth Brown	Richard Devlin	...	Robert Bendzick	David Mueller	Steven Borchardt
Otter Tail	C	57	(218) 998-8000	...	Larry Krohn	...	...	...	...
* Pennington	CM	13	(218) 683-7000	...	...	...	Kenneth Olson	...	Michael Hruby
Pine	CM	26	(320) 629-6781	Alan Hancock	John Stieben	...	Kaye Jorgensen	...	Mark Mansavage
Pipestone	C	9	(507) 825-6760	...	Sharon Hanson	...	...	Judy Oldemeyer	Dan Delaney
Polk	CE	31	(218) 281-5408	Lyle Eisert	John Schmalenberg	...	...	...	Douglas Qualley
Pope	CM	11	(320) 634-5029	Dean Paulson	Riaz Aziz	...	Donna Quandt	...	Thomas Larson
* Ramsey	CM	511	(651) 266-8000	...	Julianne Kleinschmidt	Bonnie Jackelen	...	Gail Blackstone	Robert Fletcher
Red Lake	CE	4	(218) 253-2598	Robert Schmitz	...	...	...	...	Mitch Bernstein
* Redwood	CM	16	(507) 637-4016	John Schueller	...	...	Jean Price	Vicki Knoblach	Richard Morris
Renville	CE	17	(320) 523-3710	...	Sara Folsted	...	...	...	...
Rice	CM	56	(507) 332-6100	...	Gary Weiers	...	...	...	Richard Cook
Rock	C	9	(507) 283-4173	...	...	...	...	...	...
Roseau	C	16	(218) 463-2541	...	...	...	...	...	...
Scott	CM	89	(952) 445-7750	Robert Vogel	David Unmacht	Tracy Cervenka	Kevin Ellsworth	Jack Kemme	Dave Menden
* Sherburne	CM	64	(763) 241-2700	Rachel Leonard	Brian Bensen	...	Diane Arnold	Roxanne Chmielewski	Bruce Anderson
Sibley	CE	15	(507) 237-4070	Leo Bauer	...	...	Lisa Pfarr	Roseann Nagel	Bruce Ponath
St. Louis	CM	200	(218) 726-2422	Stephen Raukar	...	Paul Tynjala	...	Anthony Bruno	Ross Litman
* Stearns	CM	133	(320) 656-3600	Vince Schaefer	George Rindelaub	...	Randy Schreifels	Jennifer Thorsten	John Sanner
Steele	CM	33	(507) 444-7400	Bruce Kubicek	Dave Severson	...	...	...	Gary Ringhofer
Stevens	CM	10	(320) 589-7417	Paul Watzke	James Thoreen	...	Neil Wiese	...	Randal Willis
Swift	CE	11	(320) 843-4069	Douglas Anderson	...	...	Byron Giese	...	Scott Mattison
Todd	C	24	(320) 732-2467	Anthony Haasser	Nathan Burkett	...	Kathy Gresser	...	David Kircher
Traverse	CM	4	(320) 563-4652	David Naatz	...	...	John Muellenbach	...	Donald Montonye
* Wabasha	CM	21	(651) 565-3001	Pete Riester	David Johnson	...	Patrick Moga	...	Rodney Bartsh
Wadena	C	13	(218) 631-7650	Charleen West	...	...	...	...	Michael Carr
Waseca	CM	19	(507) 835-0630	Wendell Armstrong	Bruce Boyce	...	Joan Manthe	...	Timothy Dann
Washington	CM	201	(651) 430-6081	Dennis Hegberg	James Schug	Patricia Raddatz	Edison Vizuete	Kay McAloney	James Frank
Watonwan	CM	11	(507) 375-1298	Lester Reckow	...	Lisa Schumann	Donald Kuhlman	...	Gary Menssen
Wilkin	CM	7	(218) 643-7165	...	...	Wayne Bezenek	...	...	Tom Matejka
* Winona	CM	49	(507) 457-6353	Dwayne Voegeli	Robert Reinert	...	Patrick Moga	Maureen Holte	David Brand
* Wright	CM	89	(763) 682-3900	...	...	Richard Norman	...	...	Gary Miller
* Yellow Medicine	C	11	(320) 564-5841	...	Ryan Krosch	...	Lois Bonde	...	Bill Flaten
MISSISSIPPI									
Adams	C	34	(601) 446-6684	...	...	...	...	...	...
Alcorn	C	34	(601) 286-7702	...	...	...	...	...	...
Amite	C	13	(601) 657-8022	...	...	...	...	...	...
Attala	C	19	(601) 289-2921	Sam Lewis	...	Gerry Taylor	...	...	Troy Steed
Benton	C	8	(601) 224-6305	...	...	...	...	...	...
Bolivar	CE	40	(662) 846-5877	...	...	...	...	...	...
Calhoun	CM	15	(601) 412-3117	...	...	...	...	...	...
Carroll	C	10	(601) 237-9274	...	...	...	...	...	...
Chickasaw	CM	19	(601) 456-2513	...	...	...	...	...	...
Choctaw	C	9	(601) 285-6329	...	...	...	...	...	...
Claiborne	CM	11	(601) 437-4992	...	...	...	Gloria Dotson	...	Frank Davis
Clarke	C	17	(601) 776-2126	...	...	...	...	...	...
Clay	C	21	(601) 494-3124	...	...	...	...	...	...
Coahoma	C	30	(662) 624-3000	Eddie Smith	Hugh Stubbs	...	Linda Humber	...	Andrew Thompson
Copiah	C	28	(601) 894-1858	...	...	...	...	...	...
Covington	C	19	(601) 765-4242	...	...	...	...	...	...
De Soto	C	107	(601) 429-5011	Jessie Medlin	Michael Garriga	...	Dale Thompson	Ginger Allison	James Riley
Forrest	C	72	(601) 545-6000	Lynn Cartlidge	Betty Carlisle	Jimmy Havard	Penny Steed	...	Billy McGie
Franklin	CE	8	(601) 384-2670	...	...	...	...	...	...
George	C	19	(601) 947-7506	...	...	...	...	...	...
* Greene	C	13	(601) 394-2394	...	...	Cheryl McLeod	...	...	Kevin Fortinberry
* Grenada	C	23	(601) 226-1821	...	...	...	...	Angela Mullen	Alton Strider
Hancock	C	42	(228) 467-0712	Timothy Kellar	...	...	Patty Greer	...	Ronnie Peterson
Harrison	CM	189	(228) 865-4207	Larry Benefield	Pamela Ulrich	John McAdams	Jenel Tompkins	Gene Evans	Joe Price
Hinds	C	250	(601) 968-6501	...	Anthony Brister	...	...	...	...
Holmes	C	21	(662) 834-2508	...	...	...	...	...	...
Humphreys	C	11	(601) 247-1740	...	...	...	...	...	...
Issaquena	CE	2	(662) 873-2761	...	...	...	...	...	...
Itawamba	C	22	(662) 862-3421	Danny Holley	Gary Franks	...	Jim Witt	...	Leon Hayes
Jackson	C	131	(228) 769-3000	...	...	...	...	...	...
Jasper	C	18	(601) 764-3368	...	...	...	...	...	...
Jefferson	C	9	(601) 786-3021	...	...	...	...	...	...
Jefferson Davis	C	13	(601) 792-4204	Bennie Polk	...	Jack Berry	...	Faye Bedwell	Henry McCullan
Jones	C	64	(601) 428-3139	...	...	...	...	...	...
Kemper	C	10	(601) 743-4477	...	...	...	...	...	...
Lafayette	C	38	(601) 234-2131	...	...	...	...	...	...
Lamar	CM	39	(601) 794-8504	Fred Hatten	George Fries	Sandra Morris	Cary Hartfield	...	Danny Rigel
Lauderdale	CE	78	(601) 482-9701	...	Rex Hiatt	...	...	...	...
Lawrence	C	13	(601) 587-7351	Calvin Fortenberry	Kelly Miller	Shelia Smithie	...	...	Joel Thames
Leake	CM	20	(601) 267-7371	...	...	...	...	Margaret Smith	...
Lee	CM	75	(662) 841-9100	...	Ronald Bell	...	...	...	...
Leflore	C	37	(601) 453-6203	...	...	...	...	...	...
Lincoln	C	33	(601) 835-3412	...	...	...	...	...	...
Lowndes	C	61	(601) 329-5800	...	...	...	...	...	...
Madison	CM	74	(601) 855-5500	...	Donnie Caughman	Arthur Johnston	...	...	...
Marion	C	25	(601) 736-2691	...	...	...	...	...	...
Marshall	C	34	(601) 252-7903	...	...	...	...	...	...
Monroe	C	38	(601) 369-8143	...	...	...	...	...	...
Montgomery	C	12	(601) 283-2333	Ron Wood	...	...	...	...	...
Neshoba	CM	28	(601) 656-3581	...	...	...	...	...	...
* Newton	CM	21	(601) 635-4150	Kenneth Harris	Steve Seale	George Hayes	Debra Jackson	Pam Upton	Jackie Knight
Noxubee	CE	12	(662) 726-4243	...	...	...	...	...	...

Directory 1/10   **OFFICIALS IN U.S. COUNTIES 2,500 AND OVER IN POPULATION**
continued

Jurisdiction	Form of govern-ment	2000 Popu-lation	Main telephone number	Chief elected official	Appointed administrator	Clerk of the governing board	Chief financial officer	Director of personnel	Chief law enforcement official
MISSISSIPPI continued									
Oktibbeha	C	42	(601) 323-5834	...		...	...		...
Panola	C	34	(662) 563-6200	Robert Avant	David Chandler	Sally Fisher	...	...	David Bryan
Pearl River	C	48	(601) 798-8013	...	Adrian Lumpkin	...	...	...	...
Perry	C	12	(601) 964-8370	...		...	...		...
Pike	CM	38	(601) 783-5289	Aubrey Matthews	Chuck Lambert	Joel Barr	...	Dorothy Parker	...
Pontotoc	C	26	(662) 489-3900	Billy Simmons	...	Reggie Collums	...	...	...
Prentiss	C	25	(662) 728-8151	...		...	...		...
Quitman	C	10	(662) 326-2661	...	T. H. Scipper	...	...		...
Rankin	CM	115	(601) 825-2217	...	Norman McLeod	Leonard Adkins	...	...	...
Scott	C	28	(601) 469-1926	...	...	...	...	...	...
Sharkey	C	6	(662) 873-2755	...	...	...	...	...	...
Simpson	C	27	(601) 847-1418	...	...	...	...	...	...
Smith	C	16	(601) 782-4000	...	...	...	...	...	...
Stone	C	13	(601) 928-5266	...	...	...	...	...	...
Sunflower	CM	34	(662) 887-4703	...	...	...	...	...	...
Tallahatchie	C	14	(662) 647-5551	...	...	...	...	...	...
Tate	C	25	(662) 562-5661	...	...	...	...	...	...
Tippah	CE	20	(662) 837-7374	...	...	Daniel Shackelford	...		C. L. Crum
Tishomingo	C	19	(601) 423-7032	...	...	...	...	...	...
Tunica	CM	9	(662) 363-1465	Cedric Burnett	Kenneth Murphree	Susie White	Clifton Johnson		Calvin Hamp
Union	C	25	(662) 534-1900	...	...	...	...	...	...
Walthall	C	15	(601) 876-3553	...		...	...	...	...
Warren	C	49	(601) 634-8073	Michael Mayfield	Rick Polk	Beth Britt	...		William Pace
Washington	C	62	(601) 332-8355	...	...	...	...	...	...
Wayne	C	21	(601) 735-3414	Fred Andrews	...	Brenda Ainsworth	Sylvia Chancellor	...	...
Webster	C	10	(662) 258-4131	Larry Crowley	...	Lady Doolittle	...	Charla Griffin	Robert Cooksey
Wilkinson	C	10	(601) 888-4381	...	...	...	...	...	...
Winston	C	20	(662) 773-3631	...	...	...	...	...	...
Yalobusha	C	13	(601) 473-2091	...	...	...	...	...	...
Yazoo	C	28	(662) 746-2661	...	...	...	...	...	...
MISSOURI									
Adair	* C	24	(660) 665-3350	Gary Jones	...	Sandy Collop	...	...	Robert Hardwick
Andrew	C	16	(816) 324-3624	Larry Atkins	...	Daniel Hegeman	...	...	N. Howard
Atchison	C	6	(660) 744-6214	...	...	Susette Taylor	...	...	Dennis Martin
Audrain	C	25	(573) 473-5822	...	...	...	...	...	Donald Bolli
Barry	C	34	(417) 847-2561	...	...	...	...		...
Barton	CE	12	(417) 682-3529	Mike Davis	...	Kristina Crockett	...	...	Shannon Higgins
Bates	C	16	(660) 679-3371	...	...	...	...	...	...
Benton	CE	17	(660) 438-7326	...	...	...	...	...	...
Bollinger	C	12	(573) 238-1900	Wayne Johnson	...	Diane Holzum	...	...	Terry Wiseman
Boone	C	135	(573) 886-4395	Keith Schnarre	...	Wendy Noren	June Pitchford	Betty Dickneite	Dwayne Carey
Buchanan	C	85	(816) 271-1503	Thomas Mann	...	Pat Conway	William Bennett	Kendra Ezzell	...
Butler	C	40	(573) 686-8050	Joseph Humphrey	...	John Dunivan	...	...	...
Caldwell	C	8	(816) 586-2571	Raymond Hartley	...	Shari Lee	...	...	Kirby Brelsford
Callaway	C	40	(573) 642-0730	Emil Fritz	...	Linda Love	...	Serena Morgan	Harry Lee
Camden	C	37	(573) 346-4440	...	...	...	...	...	...
Cape Girardeau	C	68	(573) 243-3547	Gerald Jones	...	Kara Clark	David Ludwig	...	...
Carroll	C	10	(660) 542-0615	Nelson Heil	...	Peggy McGaugh	...	...	Joseph Arnold
Carter	C	5	(573) 323-4527	Gene Oakley	...	Rebecca Gibbs	...	...	Greg Melton
Cass	C	82	(816) 380-8102	Gary Mallory	...	Janet Burlingame	Julie Cooper	...	Dwight Diehl
Cedar	CE	13	(417) 276-6700	Kenneth Whitesell	...	Sheryl Swopes	...	...	Aaron Spillman
Chariton	C	8	(660) 288-3273	Tony McCollum	...	Susan Littleton	...	...	Christopher Hughes
Christian	* CM	54	(417) 581-6369	John Grubaugh	...	Kay Brown	Susan Yarnell	...	Joey Kyle
Clark	C	7	(660) 727-3283	Paul Allen	John Heinze	Leih Hayden	...	...	Roy Gilbert
Clay	C	184	(816) 407-3600	Ed Quick	Alexa Barton	Tom Brandom	Vic Hulbert	Lisa Farr	Paul Vescovo
Clinton	C	18	(816) 539-3713	...	...	...	...	...	...
Cole	C	71	(573) 634-9100	Robert Jones	...	William Deeken	James LePage	L. Steinkuehler	John Hemeyer
Cooper	C	16	(660) 882-2114	...	...	...	...	...	...
Crawford	C	22	(573) 775-2376	...	...	Connie Smith	...	...	...
Dade	C	7	(417) 637-2724	Rex Wilkinson	...	Larry McGuire	...	...	Wayne Spain
Dallas	C	15	(417) 345-2632	...	...	...	...	...	...
Daviess	C	8	(660) 663-2641	...	...	...	...	...	...
De Kalb	C	11	(816) 449-5402	David Lippold	...	Mary Berry	...	Joan Pearl	...
Dent	C	14	(573) 729-3044	...	...	Janet Inman	...	...	...
Douglas	CM	13	(417) 683-4714	Donald Potter	...	Karry Davis	...	...	Gary Koop
Dunklin	CE	33	(573) 888-2796	...	...	...	...	...	...
Franklin	C	93	(636) 583-6355	Gene Scott	...	Tom Herbst	Ralph Sudholt	...	...
Gasconade	C	15	(573) 486-5427	Charles Schlottach	...	Roger Prior	...	...	Glenn Ebker
Gentry	C	6	(660) 726-3525	...	...	...	...	...	...
Greene	CM	240	(417) 868-4116	David Coonrod	...	Richard Struckhoff	...	Hillary Murray	Jack Merritt
Grundy	* C	10	(660) 359-4040	Rick Hull	...	Kristi Urich	...	...	Rodney Herring
Harrison	C	8	(660) 425-6424	Steve Francis	Mick Parkhurst	Barbara Gates	...	...	Richard Stratton
Henry	C	21	(660) 885-6963	...	...	...	...	...	...
Hickory	C	8	(417) 745-6450	Kent Parson	...	Jeanne Lindsey	...	...	Ray Tipton
Holt	C	5	(660) 446-3303	...	...	...	...	...	...
Howard	CE	10	(660) 248-2193	William Eaton	...	William Hiu	Kathryne Harper	...	Charles Polson
Howell	C	37	(417) 256-2591	...	...	...	...	...	...
Iron	C	10	(573) 546-2912	Terry Nichols	...	Norma Owens	...	...	Allen Mathes
Jackson	* CE	654	(816) 881-3135	Michael Saunders	Fred Siems	...	Q. Troy Thomas	Joanne Mossie	Thomas Phillips
Jasper	CE	104	(417) 358-0421	...	...	...	...	...	...
Jefferson	C	198	(636) 797-5381	Samuel Rauls	Mark Abel	Wes Wagner	Dorothy Stafford	Joan Masters	Oliver Boyer
Johnson	C	48	(660) 747-2633	William Brenner	...	Gilbert Powers	Cheryl Dolan	Lisa Shore	Charles Heiss
Knox	* C	4	(660) 397-2184	L. P. Mayfield	...	Debbie Mccurren	...	...	Mike Kite
Laclede	C	32	(417) 532-5471	...	...	...	...	...	...
Lafayette	C	32	(660) 259-4315	...	...	Linda Niendick	Cherie Mason	...	Kerrick Alumbaugh
Lawrence	* C	35	(417) 466-2638	...	...	Gary Emerson	...	...	Brad DeLay
Lewis	* C	10	(573) 767-5205	Nancy Goehl	...	Sharon Schlager	...	...	David Parrish
Lincoln	C	38	(636) 528-6300	...	...	...	...	...	...
Linn	C	13	(660) 895-5417	Rick Solomon	Randy Wade	...	...	...	Tom Parks
Livingston	C	14	(660) 646-2200	...	...	...	...	...	...
Macon	* C	15	(660) 385-2913	Roger Kohl	...	Pat Clarke	...	...	...
Madison	C	11	(573) 783-2176	Robert Mooney	...	Joan Whitener	Danny Thompson	...	David Lewis
Maries	C	8	(573) 422-3388	...	...	...	...	...	...
Marion	CE	28	(573) 769-2549	Lyndon Bode	...	Robert Ravenscraft	...	Valerie Dornberger	John Waldschlager
Mc Donald	* C	21	(417) 223-2938	Larry Jones	...	Barbara Williams	...	...	Robert Evenson
Mercer	C	3	(660) 748-3425	Russell Hobbs	...	Carolyn Kost	Ray Woodward	...	...
Miller	C	23	(573) 369-2317	...	...	...	...	...	...
Mississippi	C	13	(573) 683-2146	Jim Blumenberg	...	Hubert De Lay	...	...	Larry Turley
Moniteau	C	14	(660) 796-2213	Robert Hogge	...	...	...	...	Kenneth Jones
Monroe	CE	9	(660) 327-5106	Donald Simpson	...	Sandra Carter	...	...	Gary Tawney

Directory 1/10   **OFFICIALS IN U.S. COUNTIES 2,500 AND OVER IN POPULATION**
continued

Jurisdiction	Form of government	2000 Population	Main telephone number	Chief elected official	Appointed administrator	Clerk of the governing board	Chief financial officer	Director of personnel	Chief law enforcement official
MISSOURI continued									
Montgomery	C	12	(573) 564-3357	...	...	...	...	...	...
Morgan	C	19	(573) 378-4643	Rodney Schad	...	Cathy Daniels	...	...	James Petty
New Madrid	C	19	(573) 748-2524	...	...	...	...	...	...
Newton	C	52	(417) 451-8220	Glenn Wilson	...	Kay Baum	...	...	Ron Doerge
Nodaway	C	21	(660) 582-2251	Lester Keith	...	John Zimmerman	...	...	Ben Espey
Oregon	C	10	(417) 778-7475	...	...	...	...	...	...
Osage	C	13	(573) 897-2139	...	...	...	...	...	...
Ozark	C	9	(417) 679-3516	...	...	...	...	...	...
Pemiscot	C	20	(573) 333-4203	...	...	...	...	...	...
Perry	C	18	(573) 547-4242	Thomas Sutterer	...	Randy Taylor	...	...	Gary Schaaf
Pettis	C	39	(660) 826-5395	Todd Smith	Larry Wilson	Pam Doane	...	...	Gary Starke
Phelps	C	39	(573) 458-6000	Randy Verkamp	...	Carol Bennett	...	...	Don Blankenship
Pike	C	18	(573) 324-2412	Clark Pointer	...	Jim Ford	...	...	Jim Wells
Platte	C	73	(816) 858-2232	Betty Knight	...	Sandra Krohne	Sandra Thomas	Rita Rubick	Richard Anderson
Polk	C	26	(417) 326-4031	Roy Harms	...	Sue Entlicher	...	...	Steve Bruce
Pulaski	* C	41	(573) 774-4701	Bill Ransdall	...	Diana Linnenbringer	...	...	James King
Putnam	C	5	(660) 947-2674	...	...	...	...	...	...
Ralls	CM	9	(573) 985-7111	George Lane	...	Ernest Duckworth	...	...	Bernard Berghager
Randolph	C	24	(660) 277-4717	...	...	...	...	...	...
Ray	C	23	(816) 776-4502	Jeff Adams	...	Paul Rogers	...	...	Sam Clemens
Reynolds	C	6	(573) 648-2494	Paul Wood	...	Mike Harper	...	...	Gary Barton
Ripley	C	13	(573) 996-3215	...	...	...	...	...	...
Saline	C	23	(660) 886-9050	Becky Plattner	...	Ken Bryant	...	...	Wally George
Schuyler	C	4	(660) 457-3842	...	...	...	...	...	...
Scotland	C	4	(660) 465-7027	Mike Stephenson	...	Betty Lodewegen	...	...	Wayne Winn
Scott	C	40	(573) 545-3549	...	...	...	...	...	...
Shannon	* C	8	(573) 226-3414	Charles Orchard	...	Shelly McAfee	...	...	Steven Blunkall
Shelby	C	6	(573) 633-2181	Glennon Eagan	...	Tracy Smith	...	...	Daniel Parshall
St. Charles	C	283	(636) 949-7320	Joseph Ortwerth	...	...	Rebecca Craig	William Kauffman	Timothy Swope
St. Clair	C	9	(417) 646-2315	Jay Knight	...	Donna Houston	...	...	Ronald Snodgrass
St. Francois	C	55	(573) 756-3623	...	...	...	...	...	...
St. Louis	CE	1016	(314) 615-5000	George Westfall	James Baker	Suzanne Richeda-Pratl	Glenn Pearl	Kirk McCarley	Ronald Battelle
Ste. Genevieve	CE	16	(573) 883-5589	Albert Fults	...	Kay Basler	...	...	Gary Stolzer
Stoddard	C	29	(573) 568-3339	...	...	...	...	...	...
Stone	C	28	(417) 357-6127	...	...	...	...	...	...
Sullivan	C	7	(660) 265-3786	...	...	...	...	...	...
Taney	CM	39	(417) 546-7201	Chuck Pennel	Tressa Luttrell	Donna Neeley	Rick Findley	...	Jimmie Russell
Texas	C	23	(417) 967-2112	Don Shelhammer	...	Don Troutman	...	...	Carl Watson
Vernon	* C	20	(417) 448-2500	C. David Darnold	...	Tammi Beach	...	...	Ron Peckman
Warren	C	24	(636) 456-3331	Fred Vahle	...	Barbara Daly	...	...	Kevin Harrison
Washington	C	23	(573) 438-4901	Robert Reed	...	Janet Adams	...	...	...
Wayne	C	13	(573) 224-3011	Brian Polk	...	Alan Lutes	...	...	Phillip Burton
Webster	C	31	(417) 468-2223	...	...	...	...	...	...
Worth	C	2	(660) 564-2219	Billy Mozingo	...	Lisa Hargrave	...	...	...
Wright	CE	17	(417) 741-6661	Rex Epperly	...	Tony Dugger	...	...	Garrell Mitchell
MONTANA									
Beaverhead	C	9	(406) 683-5245	...	...	...	...	...	...
Big Horn	C	12	(406) 665-3520	...	...	...	...	...	...
Blaine	C	7	(406) 357-3250	...	...	Sandra Boardman	...	...	Theron Paulsen
Broadwater	* C	4	(406) 266-3443	James Hohn	...	Elaine Graveley	Natalie Tomeo	...	Rich Thompson
Carbon	C	9	(406) 446-1595	...	...	...	...	...	...
Carter	C	1	(406) 775-8749	Milton Markuson	...	Pamela Castleberry	...	...	Rusty Jardee
Cascade	C	80	(406) 454-6810	...	...	Rita Hudak	Tom Meech	Richard Letang	John Shandell
Chouteau	C	5	(406) 622-3631	...	...	...	...	...	...
Custer	C	11	(406) 233-3343	Duane Mathison	...	Beth Milligan	...	...	Tony Harbaugh
Daniels	C	2	(406) 487-5561	Lalon Trang	...	Kristy Jones	...	...	Myron Baldry
Dawson	* C	9	(406) 365-3058	Adam Gartner	...	...	...	...	Craig Anderson
Fallon	C	2	(406) 778-7107	Roddy Rost	...	Brenda Wood	...	...	Timothy Barkley
Fergus	C	11	(406) 538-5119	Kathie Bailey	...	Kathy Fleharty	...	...	Ronald Rowton
Flathead	CM	74	(406) 758-5522	Robert Watne	...	Paula Robinson	...	RaeAnn Campbell	...
Gallatin	CM	67	(406) 582-3045	William Murdock	Earl Mathers	Shelley Vance	Ed Blackman	Randy Kuyath	Jim Cashell
Garfield	C	1	(406) 557-2760	...	...	...	Janet Sherer	...	Kelly Pierson
Glacier	C	13	(406) 873-5063	...	...	...	...	...	...
Golden Valley	* C	1	(406) 568-2231	...	...	Mary Lu Ringler	...	...	...
Granite	CM	2	(406) 859-3771	Clifford Nelson	...	Blanche McLure	...	...	Stephen Immenschuh
Hill	C	16	(406) 265-5481	Kathleen Bessette	...	Diane Mellem	...	Cyndee Peterson	Gregory Szudera
Jefferson	C	10	(406) 225-4000	Leonard Wortman	...	Bonnie Ramey	Sue Miller	Chuck Notbohm	Thomas Dawson
Judith Basin	C	2	(406) 566-2277	Richard Cervenka	Henry Vaskey	Amanda Kelly	...	...	John Shilling
Lake	CE	26	(406) 883-7211	Paddy Trusler	...	Ruth Hodges	Sandra Weaver	...	...
Lewis & Clark	CM	55	(406) 447-8304	Ed Tinsley	Ronald Alles	...	Nancy Everson	...	Cheryl Liedle
Liberty	C	2	(406) 759-5365	Paul Johnson	...	Maureen Cicon	...	...	Richard Burrows
Lincoln	C	18	(406) 293-7781	Gerald Criner	Bill Bischoff	...	Coral Cummings	...	...
Madison	* C	6	(406) 843-4277	David Schulz	...	Peggy Kaatz	Vicki Tilstra	...	Dave Schenk
Mc Cone	C	1	(406) 485-3505	...	...	Kae Fritz	...	...	Dave Harris
Meagher	C	1	(406) 547-3612	...	...	...	...	...	...
Mineral	C	3	(406) 822-3520	...	...	...	...	...	...
Missoula	C	95	(406) 721-5700	...	...	...	Dale Bickell	Steve Johnson	Doug Chase
Musselshell	* C	4	(406) 323-1104	Larry Lekse	...	Jane Mang	...	...	Woodrow Weitzeil
Park	C	15	(406) 222-4100	Dan Gutebier	...	Denise Nelson	Joe Morse	...	Clark Carpenter
Petroleum	CM	..	(406) 429-5551	Lloyd Rowton	Stephanie Downs	Mary Brindley	...	...	William Troutwine
Phillips	* C	4	(406) 654-2423	Richard Dunbar	...	...	Lauren Hines	...	Thomas Miller
Pondera	CE	6	(406) 278-4000	...	...	...	...	...	...
Powder River	* C	1	(406) 436-2361	Ray Traub	...	Karen Amende	Valli Gaskill	...	John Blain
Powell	C	7	(406) 846-3680	Ralph Mannix	...	Diane Grey	...	...	Scott Howard
Prairie	C	1	(406) 637-5575	...	...	...	...	...	...
Ravalli	CM	36	(406) 375-6500	Greg Chilcott	...	Nedra Taylor	...	...	Christopher Hoffman
Richland	C	9	(406) 482-1706	Mark Rehbein	...	Penni Lewis	...	...	Brad Baisch
Roosevelt	C	10	(406) 653-1590	...	...	...	...	...	...
Rosebud	* C	9	(406) 346-2251	Daniel Sioux	...	Geraldine Custer	...	...	Randy Allies
Sanders	CE	10	(406) 827-6942	...	...	Jennine Robbins	...	...	Gene Arnold
Sheridan	C	4	(406) 765-2310	Gordon Kampen	Robert Nikolaisen	Milton Hovland	...	...	Mike Overland
Stillwater	* C	8	(406) 322-8010	Maureen Davey	...	Pauline Mishler	Joseph Morse	...	Clifford Brophy
Sweet Grass	C	3	(406) 932-5152	...	...	Shery Bjorndal	Victoria Uehling	...	Daniel Tronrud
Teton	C	6	(406) 466-2693	Robert Krause	...	Shirley Jensen	Diane Ameline	...	...
Toole	C	5	(406) 424-8300	Ben Ober	...	Mary Ann Harwood	...	Jewel Moritz	Michael Lamey
Treasure	C	..	(406) 342-5547	Norris Cole	...	Ruth Baker	...	...	Wayne Robison
Valley	CE	7	(406) 228-8221	Eleanor Pratt	...	Lynne Nyquist	...	...	Richard Wessler
Wheatland	C	2	(406) 632-4891	Richard Moe	...	Carol Clark	...	...	Steve Riveland
Wibaux	CE	1	(406) 796-2481	Thomas Nelson	...	...	Patricia Zinda	...	George Zorzakis
Yellowstone	CM	129	(406) 256-2705	James Reno	...	...	Scott Turner	Dwight Vigness	Chuck Maxwell

Directory 1/10   OFFICIALS IN U.S. COUNTIES 2,500 AND OVER IN POPULATION
continued

Jurisdiction	Form of govern-ment	2000 Popu-lation	Main telephone number	Chief elected official	Appointed administrator	Clerk of the governing board	Chief financial officer	Director of personnel	Chief law enforcement official
NEBRASKA									
Adams	C	31	(402) 461-7107	Larry Woodman	...	Chrisella Lewis	...	...	Gregg Magee
Antelope	CM	7	(402) 887-4410	...	...	...	...	...	...
Arthur	C	..	(308) 764-2203	...	...	...	...	...	...
Banner	CE	..	(308) 436-5265	George Van Pelt	...	Sharon Sandberg	...	...	Kenneth Mooney
Blaine	CM	..	(308) 547-2222	...	...	April Wescott	...	...	Timothy Sierks
Boone	C	6	(402) 395-2055	...	...	...	...	...	...
Box Butte	C	12	(308) 762-6565	...	...	...	...	...	...
Boyd	C	2	(402) 775-2391	Kenneth Boettcher	...	Phyllis Black	Joseph Hostert	...	...
Brown	CE	3	(402) 387-2705	...	...	...	...	...	...
Buffalo	C	42	(308) 236-1226	...	...	Judy Jobman	...	...	Neil Miller
Burt	C	7	(402) 374-1955	...	...	...	...	...	...
Butler *	C	8	(402) 367-7430	David Mach	...	...	...	...	Mark Hecker
Cass	C	24	(402) 296-9300	Richard Stone	...	Alan Wohlfarth	Richard Wassinger	...	William Brueggemann
Cedar	C	9	(402) 254-7411	Richard Donner	...	David Dowling	...	...	Larry Koranda
Chase	C	4	(308) 882-7500	Don Weiss	...	Debra Clark	...	...	Tim Sutherland
Cherry	C	6	(402) 376-2420	...	...	...	...	...	...
Cheyenne	C	9	(308) 254-2141	...	...	...	...	...	...
Clay	CE	7	(402) 762-3463	Kendall Ham	...	Janet Hajny	...	...	Jeffrey Franklin
Colfax	C	10	(402) 352-8504	Earl Wendt	...	Sharon Bohaboj	...	...	Lynn Blum
Cuming *	C	10	(402) 372-6002	...	...	Bonnie Vogltance	...	...	Bradley Boyum
Custer	C	11	(308) 872-5701	...	...	Constance Gracey	...	...	...
Dakota	CE	20	(402) 987-2125	...	...	Theodore Piepho	...	...	James Wagner
Dawes	C	9	(308) 432-0102	...	...	...	...	...	...
Dawson	CM	24	(308) 324-2127	...	...	...	...	...	...
Deuel	C	2	(308) 874-3308	...	...	...	...	...	...
Dixon	C	6	(402) 755-2208	Russell Fleury	...	Diane Mohr	...	...	Dean Chase
Dodge *	C	36	(402) 727-2767	Bob Missel	...	Fred Mytty	...	...	Dan Weddle
Douglas	CM	463	(402) 444-7000	Carole Woods-Harris	Kathleen Kelley	Thomas Cavanaugh	Steve Walker	John Taylor	Timothy Dunning
Dundy	C	2	(308) 423-2058	Boyd Blair	...	Tony Lutz	...	...	...
Fillmore *	C	6	(402) 759-4931	Steven Yates	...	Amy Nelson	...	...	William Burgess
Franklin	C	3	(308) 425-6202	...	...	...	...	...	...
Frontier	C	3	(308) 367-8641	...	...	...	...	...	...
Furnas	C	5	(308) 268-4145	...	...	...	...	...	...
Gage	C	22	(402) 223-1300	Harvey Spilker	...	Sandra Eltiste	...	...	Jerry Dewitt
Garden	C	2	(308) 772-3924	Ron Klemke	William Campbell	Lorie Koester	...	...	Jim Winn
Garfield	C	1	(308) 346-4161	Martin Robbins	Daniel Hruza	...	...	...	Larry Donner
Gosper	C	2	(308) 785-2611	...	...	Cynthia Evans	...	...	David Schutz
Grant	C	..	(308) 458-2488	Frances Davis	...	Tonchita Ring	Sharon Applegarth	...	Mark Crouse
Greeley	C	2	(308) 428-2965	Thomas Smith	...	Catherine Sweeney	...	...	David Weeks
Hall	C	53	(308) 385-5080	Irene Abernethy	...	Marla Conley	...	...	Jerome Watson
Hamilton	CE	9	(402) 694-3443	Steven Jacobsen	...	Donita Friesen	...	...	Kirk Handrup
Harlan	C	3	(308) 928-2173	Douglas Horwart	...	Shirley Bailey	...	...	Chris Becker
Hayes	C	1	(308) 286-3413	Cletis Walker	...	Joan Lauenroth	...	...	Donald Miller
Hitchcock	CM	3	(308) 334-5646	...	...	Margaret Pollmann	...	...	D. Leggott
Holt	C	11	(402) 336-1762	...	...	...	...	...	...
Hooker	C	..	(308) 546-2244	...	...	...	...	...	...
Howard	CM	6	(308) 754-4343	...	...	Marge Palmberg	...	...	Harold Schenck
Jefferson	CE	8	(402) 729-2323	Tony Likens	...	Sandra Stelling	...	...	Nels Sorensen
Johnson *	C	4	(402) 335-6300	Terry Keebler	...	Kathleen Nieveen	...	...	James Wenzl
Kearney	C	6	(308) 832-2723	...	...	...	...	...	...
Keith	CE	8	(308) 284-4726	...	...	...	...	...	...
Keya Paha	C	..	(402) 497-3791	Dewey Peterson	Ted Eichenberger	Karen Hallock	...	...	Wayne Crome
Kimball	C	4	(308) 235-2241	...	...	...	...	...	...
Knox	C	9	(402) 288-4282	...	...	...	...	...	...
Lancaster	C	250	(402) 441-7447	Ray Stevens	Kerry Eagan	Bruce Medcalf	David Kroeker	Don Taute	Terry Wagner
Lincoln	C	34	(308) 534-4350	Joe Hewgley	...	Rebecca Rossell	...	...	Jerome Kramer
Logan	C	..	(308) 636-2311	...	...	Pat Harvey	...	...	Dan Kramer
Loup	C	..	(308) 942-3135	...	...	...	...	...	...
Madison *	C	35	(402) 454-3311	Jerry McCallum	...	Nancy Scheer	...	...	Vern Hjorth
Mc Pherson	C	..	(308) 587-2363	...	...	...	...	...	...
Merrick *	C	8	(308) 946-2881	...	...	Marcia Wichmann	...	...	Anthony McPhillips
Morrill	C	5	(308) 262-1760	...	...	...	...	...	...
Nance *	C	4	(308) 536-2331	Dennis Jarecke	...	Danette Zarek	...	...	...
Nemaha	C	7	(402) 274-4213	...	...	...	...	...	...
Nuckolls	C	5	(402) 225-4361	...	...	Jackie Kassebaum	...	...	James Marr
Otoe	CM	15	(402) 873-9500	Joy Schroder	...	Janene Bennett	...	...	James Gress
Pawnee	C	3	(402) 852-2380	...	...	Carol Young	...	...	Arthur Baldridge
Perkins *	C	3	(308) 352-4643	...	...	Rita Long	...	...	James Brueggeman
Phelps	C	9	(308) 995-4469	Eldon Steinbrink	...	Sally Fox	...	...	Thomas Nutt
Pierce	C	7	(402) 329-4225	Marvin Elwood	...	Carol Peters	...	...	...
Platte	C	31	(402) 563-4904	Ronald Pfeifer	...	Diane Pinger	...	...	Jon Zavadil
Polk	C	5	(402) 747-5431	Michael Simonsen	...	Debra Girard	...	...	Jim Davis
Red Willow *	C	11	(308) 345-1552	Earl McNutt	...	Pauletta Gerver	...	...	Gene Mahon
Richardson	C	9	(402) 245-2911	...	...	...	...	...	...
Rock	C	1	(402) 684-3933	...	...	...	...	...	...
Saline	C	13	(402) 821-2374	Willis Luedke	...	Linda Kastanek	...	...	Alan Moore
Sarpy	C	122	(402) 593-4486	Tim Gay	Mark Wayne	Debra Houghtaling	Brian Hanson	Renee Lansman	Patrick Thomas
Saunders	C	19	(402) 443-8101	...	...	...	...	...	...
Scotts Bluff *	CM	36	(308) 436-6718	Mark Masterton	...	Vera Dulaney	Gwen Greely	Jerry Crable	Jim Lawson
Seward	C	16	(402) 643-2883	Leslie Nelson	...	Sherry Schweitzer	Bob Dahms	...	Roger Anderson
Sheridan	C	6	(308) 327-2633	...	...	...	...	...	...
Sherman *	C	3	(308) 745-1513	Eldon Kieborz	...	Marcy Sekutera	...	...	Michael Janulewicz
Sioux	C	1	(308) 668-2443	Harold Keener	...	Wendi McCormick	...	...	...
Stanton	C	6	(402) 439-2222	Glen Steffensmeier	...	Rita Roenfeldt	...	...	Mike Unger
Thayer	C	6	(402) 768-6126	Lawarence Traudt	...	Marie Rauner	...	...	Davie Lee
Thomas	C	..	(308) 645-2261	Stan Pettit	...	Wendy Rinestine	...	...	Randy Barnes
Thurston	C	7	(402) 385-2343	Teri Lamplot	...	Tammy Moore	...	...	Charles Obermeyer
Valley *	C	4	(308) 728-3700	...	...	Jenette Lindsey	...	...	Casey Hurlburt
Washington *	CE	18	(402) 426-6822	...	...	Merry Truhlsen	...	...	Michael Robinson
Wayne	C	9	(402) 375-2288	...	...	Debra Finn	...	...	LeRoy Janssen
Webster	C	4	(402) 746-2716	...	...	...	...	...	...
Wheeler	C	..	(308) 654-3235	...	...	...	...	...	...
York	C	14	(402) 362-7759	Bob Wolfe	...	Patricia Bredenkamp	...	...	Dale Radcliff
NEVADA									
Churchill	CM	23	(775) 428-1311	Gwen Washburn	Brad Goetsch	Gloria Venturacci	Alan Kalt	Geof Stark	Richard Ingram
Clark	CM	1375	(702) 455-3530	Bruce Woodbury	Virginia Valentine	Shirley Parraguirre	George Stevens	Raymond Visconti	Jerry Keller
Douglas	CM	41	(775) 782-9821	Stephen Weissinger	T. Brown	Barbara Reed	Claudette Springmeyer	Sheila Dugan	Ronald Pierini

Directory 1/10 OFFICIALS IN U.S. COUNTIES 2,500 AND OVER IN POPULATION
continued

Jurisdiction	Form of government	2000 Population	Main telephone number	Chief elected official	Appointed administrator	Clerk of the governing board	Chief financial officer	Director of personnel	Chief law enforcement official
NEVADA continued									
Elko	CM	45	(775) 738-4375	...	Robert Stokes	Winifred Smith	Cash Minor	...	Arthur Harris
Esmeralda	CE	..	(775) 485-3406	R. J. Gillum	...	LaCinda Elgan	Karen Scott	...	Ken Elgan
Eureka	C	1	(775) 237-5263	Peter Goicoechea	...	Joan Shangle	Michael Rebaleati	...	Kenneth Jones
Humboldt	CM	16	(775) 623-6300	John Milton	William Deist	Tami Spero	Bruce Brooks	...	Gene Hill
Lander	CM	5	(775) 635-2885	Jimmie Fouts	...	Gladys Burris	Raye Fagg	...	Kenny Moore
Lincoln	C	4	(775) 962-5495	Timothy Perkins	...	Alice Hogan	Leslie Boucher	...	Dahl Bradfield
Lyon *	CM	34	(775) 463-6531	Don Tibbals	Dennis Stark	Nikki Bryan	Joshua Foli	Steve Englert	Allen Veil
Mineral *	C	5	(775) 945-3676	...	...	...	...	Christine Hoferer	Edward Smith
Nye *	CM	32	(775) 482-8191	...	Richard Osborne	Sandra Merlino	Tammy Otero	Danelle Shamrell	Anthony Demeo
Pershing	C	6	(775) 273-2208	Dave Ayoob	...	Donna Giles	Darlene Moura	...	Ron Skinner
Storey	C	3	(775) 847-0968	Henry Bland	Marilou Walling	Doreen Bacus	...	...	Robert Del Carlo
Washoe *	CM	339	(775) 328-2081	Robert Larkin	Katy Simon	Amy Harvey	John Sherman	Katey Fox	Mike Haley
White Pine	C	9	(775) 289-8841	...	...	Donna Bath	...	...	Bernie Romero
NEW HAMPSHIRE									
Belknap	CM	56	(603) 527-5400	Mark Thurston	Debra Shackett	...	...	...	Dan Collis
Carroll	C	43	(603) 539-2428	Brenda Presby	Marjorie Webster	...	...	...	Scott Carr
Cheshire	C	73	(603) 352-8215	...	John Wozmak	...	Sheryl Trombly	...	Richard Foote
Coos	C	33	(603) 246-3321	...	...	...	...	...	...
Grafton	CM	81	(603) 787-6941	...	Julie Clough	Raymond Burton	...	Karen Clough	...
Hillsborough	C	380	(603) 627-5600	...	Gregory Wenger	...	...	Virginia Chandler	...
Merrimack	CE	136	(603) 228-0331	...	...	...	...	Sara Lewko	...
Rockingham	C	277	(603) 679-5335	Maureen Barrows	...	...	Theresa Young	Martha Roy	Daniel Linehan
Strafford	CM	112	(603) 742-1458	...	...	...	...	...	...
Sullivan	C	40	(603) 863-2560	...	Ed DeRubio	...	...	...	...
NEW JERSEY									
Atlantic	CE	252	(609) 345-6700	Dennis Levinson	Helen Walsh	Michael Garvin	...	Donna Lee	Jeffrey Blitz
Bergen	CE	884	(201) 336-6200	William Schuber	Timothy Dacey	...	...	...	Jack Schmidig
Burlington	C	423	(609) 265-5020	James Wujcik	Frederick Galdo	Philip Haines	Kurt Brock	Daniel Hornickel	Jean Stanfield
Camden	CE	508	(856) 225-5000	Jeffrey Nash	Mark Lonetto	Lee Sasse	David McPeak	Richard Dodson	Michael McLaughlin
Cape May	C	102	(609) 465-1060	Daniel Beyel	...	Angela Pulvino	Edmund Grant	Eileen Ballinghoff	James Plousis
Cumberland	CE	146	(856) 453-2125	Douglas Fisher	David Gray	Clair Miller	Gerald Seneski	Ralph Brownlee	...
Essex	C	793	(973) 621-4977	James Treffinger	Ronald Manzella	Patrick McNally	Anthony Abbaleo	Lucille Davino	Armando Fontoura
Gloucester	CM	254	(856) 853-3264	Stephen Sweeney	...	James Hogan	Gary Schwarz	...	Andrew Yurick
Hudson	CE	608	(201) 795-6255	Robert Janiszewski	Abraham Antun	Janet Haynes	Wade Frazee	Larry Henderson	Joseph Cassidy
Hunterdon	CE	121	(908) 788-1102	...	Cynthia Yard	Denise Doolan	...	Cheryl Wieder	J. Patrick Barnes
Mercer	CE	350	(609) 989-6676	Robert Prunetti	Andrew Mair	Catherine Dicostanzo	David Miller	Harris Kline	Daniel Giaquinto
Middlesex	CM	750	(732) 745-3090	David Crabiel	John Pulomena	Margaret Pemberton	Albert Kuchinskas	J. Cross	...
Monmouth	CM	615	(732) 431-7300	Harry Larrison	Robert Czech	M. French	Mark Acker	Fredrica Brown	Joseph Oxley
Morris	CE	470	(973) 285-6000	Douglas Cabana	James Rosenberg	Ilene St. John	Glenn Roe	Herman Hoopes	John Dangler
Ocean	CM	510	(732) 244-2121	John Bartlett	Steven Pollock	M. Haines	Julie Tarrant	Keith Goetting	William Polhemus
Passaic	CE	489	(973) 881-4402	...	...	Gilda Gill	Joanne Bell	Robin Weinstein	John Cooksey
Salem	C	64	(856) 935-7510	C. Sparks	Earl Gage	Barbara Lucas	Brian Newman	Susan Dobrinsky	Wayne Forrest
Somerset	CE	297	(908) 231-7000	Peter Palmer	Richard Williams	Elaine Morgan	Bernard Re	Ron Tappan	Robert Untig
Sussex *	CM	144	(973) 579-0350	Harold Wirths	John Eskilson	Joanne Rajoppi	Lawrence Caroselli	Gregory Hardoby	Daniel Vaniska
Union	CM	522	(908) 527-4100	Deborah Scanlon	George Devanney	...	Charles Houck	Jerry Coyle	Don Kelley
Warren	CM	102	(908) 475-6500	Susan Dickey	Steve Marvin				
NEW MEXICO									
Bernalillo	CM	556	(505) 768-4000	...	...	Mary Herrera	Daniel Mayfield	Renetta Torres	Darren White
Catron	CM	3	(505) 533-6423	Ed Wehrheim	William Aymar	Sharon Armijo	...	...	Ian Fletcher
Chaves	CM	61	(505) 624-6600	...	...	Rhoda Coakley	Mary Chacon	Sheila Nunez	...
Cibola	C	25	(505) 287-9431	Isaac Padilla	David Ulibarri	Eileen Martinez	John Alexander	Syble Valles	Manuel Lujan
Colfax	CM	14	(505) 445-9661	Whitney Hite	...	Rayetta Trujillo	...	...	Patrick Casias
Curry *	CM	45	(575) 763-6016	Frank Blackburn	Richard Smith	Coni Jo Lyman	Mark Lansford	Lance Pyle	Matthew Murray
De Baca	C	2	(505) 355-2601	...	...	Nancy Sparks	...	...	Brent Sena
Dona Ana *	CE	174	(505) 647-7200	Leticia Benavidez	Brian Haines	Lynn Ellins	...	Kathe Stark	Todd Garrison
Eddy	CE	51	(505) 887-9511	Lucky Briggs	Stephen Massey	V. Blenden	Debbie Penaluna	Susan Collins	D. Waller
Grant	CM	31	(505) 574-0000	Henry Torres	Jon Saari	Jeff Carbajal	Erlinda Vasquez	...	...
Guadalupe	CM	4	(505) 472-3306	...	...	...	...	...	...
Harding	CM	..	(505) 673-2301	Michael Lewis	Arlene Aragon	Elizabeth Martinez	Lucille Quintana	...	Freddie Gift
Hidalgo	CM	5	(505) 542-9428	Louise Peterson	Roger Ellis	Carmen Acosta	Connie Corbell	...	Robert Hall
Lea *	CM	55	(505) 396-8605	Gary Schubert	Michael Beverly	Pat Chappelle	Rick Bruce	Anne Behl	Roderick Coffman
Lincoln	CM	19	(505) 648-2385	Rex Wilson	Thomas Stewart	Tammie Maddox	Glenna Robbins	...	Thomas Sullivan
Los Alamos *	CM	18	(505) 663-1750	James Hall	Max Baker	Mary Kraemer	Steven Lynne	Sharyl Hofer	Wayne Torpy
Luna	CM	25	(505) 546-0494	Dennis Armijo	Scott Vinson	Natalie Pacheco	...	Danny Gonzales	Gary Ciccotelli
Mc Kinley	CE	74	(505) 722-3868	Earnest Becenti	Irvin Harrison	Carol Sloan	Judie Karuklis	...	Frank Gonzales
Mora	C	5	(505) 387-5279	Juan Espinoza	Phillip Cantu	Charlotte Duran	Doris Casados	Geraldine Martinez	John Sanchez
Otero	CM	62	(505) 437-7427	...	Timothy Smith	Robyn Holmes	Donna Brandon	...	John Blansett
Quay	CM	10	(505) 461-2112	Glenn Briscoe	Bob Lamm	...	Nadine Angel	Donna Dominguez	Jack Huntley
Rio Arriba	CE	41	(505) 588-7254	...	Lorenzo Valdez	Fred Vigil	Charlene Sanchez	Jessica Madrid	Joe Mascarenas
Roosevelt	CM	18	(505) 356-5307	Gene Creighton	Charlene Hardin	Janet Collins	Tammy Lee	...	Thomas Gossett
San Juan	CM	113	(505) 334-4502	...	Keith Johns	Fran Hanhardt	Robert Wasson	Charlene Scott	Bob Melton
San Miguel	C	30	(505) 425-9333	...	Les Montoya	Paul Maez	Melinda Gonzalez	...	Chris Najar
Sandoval	C	89	(505) 867-7500	...	Debbie Hays	Victoria Dunlap	Leroy Arquero	Tammie Gerrard	Ray Rivera
Santa Fe	CM	129	(505) 986-6369	...	Roman Abeyta	Valerie Espinoza	Katherine Miller	Helen Quintana	Raymond Sisneros
Sierra	C	13	(505) 894-6215	Russell Peterson	Janet Carrejo	Janice Sanchez	...	Janette Monsibaiz	Ronald Brown
Socorro	CE	18	(505) 835-0589	...	Matejka Ray-Olguin	Carmen Gallegos	...	...	...
Taos	CM	29	(505) 737-6300	Gabriel Romero	...	Elaine Montano	Edwin Fernandez	Renee Gutierrez	Charlie Martinez
Torrance	CM	16	(505) 246-4752	James Frost	Jon Ansley	Linda Kayser	Tracy Sedillo	...	Pete Golden
Union	CM	4	(505) 374-8896	Thomas Gonzales	Della Wetsel	Freida Birdwell	...	...	Albert Johnston
Valencia	CE	66	(505) 866-2004	...	...	...	...	...	...
NEW YORK									
Albany	CE	294	(518) 447-7040	Charles Houghtaling	Michael Breslin	Thomas Clingan	Michael Conners	Joyce Timmons	James Campbell
Allegany	C	49	(585) 268-9217	...	John Margeson	...	...	...	...
Broome	CE	200	(607) 778-2109	...	...	...	...	...	...
Cattaraugus	CE	83	(716) 938-9111	Gerard Fitzpatrick	John Searles	James Griffith	Joseph Keller	Howard Peterson	Ernest Dustman
Cayuga	CM	81	(315) 253-1273	Herbert Marshall	...	Susan Dwyer	...	Joseph Porpiglia	C. Outhouse
Chautauqua	CE	139	(716) 753-4000	Mark Thomas	...	John Dillenburg	Robert Beckman	Joycelyn Bermingham	Joseph Gerace
Chemung	CE	91	(607) 737-2918	G. Tranter	...	Katherine Hughes	Steven Hoover	Bonnie Carrier	Christopher Moss
Chenango	CE	51	(607) 337-1770	Richard Decker	...	Thomas Whittaker	William Evans	...	Thomas Loughren
Clinton	CE	79	(518) 565-4600	Donald Garrant	William Bingel	John Zurlo	Greg Bell	Alan Gibson	...
Columbia	C	63	(518) 828-1527	Gerald Simons	...	Gladys Goesch	...	Barbara Haywood	James Bertram
Cortland	C	48	(607) 753-5048	Scott Steve	Scott Schrader	Carletta Edwards	...	...	Duane Whiteman
Delaware	C	48	(607) 746-2603	...	...	...	...	...	...
Dutchess	CE	280	(845) 486-2169	William Steinhaus	...	William Paroli	Rita Brannen	Douglas McHoul	Fred Scoralick
Erie	CE	950	(716) 858-8500	...	...	...	...	...	...
Essex	CM	38	(518) 873-3360	Teresa Sayward	Clifford Donaldson	Deborah Weber	...	Ruth McDonough	Henry Hommes

Directory 1/10 continued — OFFICIALS IN U.S. COUNTIES 2,500 AND OVER IN POPULATION

Jurisdiction	Form of govern-ment	2000 Popu-lation	Main telephone number	Chief elected official	Appointed administrator	Clerk of the governing board	Chief financial officer	Director of personnel	Chief law enforcement official
NEW YORK continued									
Franklin	CM	51	(518) 481-1675	Earl Lavoie	James Feeley	Wanda Murtagh	...	Donna Barnes	Jack Pelkey
Fulton	C	55	(518) 736-5540	Peter Stone	Jon Stead	William Eschler	...	Edith Pashley	Thomas Lorey
Genesee *	CM	60	(585) 344-2550	Mary Pat Hancock	Jay Gsell	Carolyn Pratt	...	Karen Marchese	Gary Maha
Greene	CE	48	(518) 943-3080	Frank Stabile	...	Donald Olson	...	Audrey Adrezin	Richard Hussey
Hamilton	C	5	(518) 548-6651	...	William Farber	Laura Abrams	...	Kimberly Parslow	Douglas Parker
Herkimer	CM	64	(315) 867-1002	Leonard Hendrix	James Wallace	Sylvia Rowan	Bernard Decker	Jeffrey Whittemore	Christopher Farber
Jefferson	CM	111	(315) 785-3147	Kent Burto	Robert Hagemann	Jo Ann Wilder	...	Stephen Miller	John Burns
Lewis	CM	26	(315) 376-5356	...	Sharon Cihocki	Teresa Kenealy	...	Mary Van Brocklin	Louis Tabolt
Livingston	CM	64	(585) 243-7000	Dennis House	Dominic Mazza	James Culbertson	Arlene Johnston	Tish Lynn	...
Madison	C	69	(315) 366-2011	...	...	...	...	...	...
Monroe	CE	735	(585) 753-1000	Maggie Brooks	James Smith	Cheryl Dinolfo	Steve Gleason	Brayton Connard	Patrick O'Flynn
Montgomery	C	49	(518) 853-3431	...	...	...	...	...	...
Nassau	CE	1334	(516) 535-3131	...	Thomas Suozzi	Karen Murphy	Arthur Gianelli	Jo-Ann Goldson	...
Niagara	CM	219	(716) 439-7177	Bradley Erck	Gregory Lewis	Paul Oates	Sharon Sacco	Bruce Fenwick	Thomas Beilein
Oneida	CE	235	(315) 798-5725	Ralph Eannace	...	Richard Allen	Anthony Carvelli	Mary Berie	Daniel Middaugh
Onondaga	CE	458	(315) 435-3537	Nicholas Pirro	Edward Kochian	Cynthia Miano	...	Elaine Walter	Kevin Walsh
Ontario	CE	100	(585) 396-4465	Carmen Orlando	Geoffrey Astles	Karen DeMay	Catherine Bentzoni	John Garvey	Philip Povero
Orange	CE	341	(845) 294-5151	Joseph Rampe	Chris Dunleavy	Donna Benson	Joel Kleiman	J. Dan Bloomer	Francis Phillips
Orleans	CE	44	(585) 589-7053	Marcia Tuohey	Stanley Dudek	Kathleen Ahlberg	...	Sandra Bower	Scott Hess
Oswego	CE	122	(315) 349-8367	...	John Tierney	George Williams	...	Maurice Hurd	Reuel Todd
Otsego	C	61	(607) 547-4200	...	...	...	...	...	...
Putnam	CE	95	(845) 225-0860	Robert Bondi	John Tully	Dennis Sant	William Carlin	Paul Eldridge	Donald Smith
Rensselaer	CE	152	(518) 270-2700	...	...	Doreen Connolly	Thomas Mannix	Susan Martin	...
Rockland	CE	286	(845) 638-5000	C. Vanderhoef	...	Edward Gorman	George Rene	Patricia Prendergast	James Kralic
Saratoga	CM	200	(518) 885-2225	Robert Stokes	David Wickerham	...	...	William Baker	James Bowen
Schenectady *	CM	146	(518) 388-4233	Susan Savage	Kathleen Rooney	John Woodward	George Davidson	Kathleen Heap	Harry Buffardi
Schoharie	C	31	(518) 295-8347	James Brown	...	David Hallock	William Cherry	Lorrie Gordon	John Bates
Schuyler	CM	19	(607) 535-8179	Thomas Gifford	Timothy O'Hearn	Linda Compton	...	Gail Hughey	Michael Maloney
Seneca	CM	33	(315) 539-5655	Robert Favreau	...	Christina Lotz	Nicholas Sciotti	...	Thomas Fox
St. Lawrence	CE	111	(315) 379-2210	Alex MacKinnon	Karen St. Hilaire	Patricia Ritchie	...	Natalie Aldrich	Gary Jarvis
Steuben	CM	98	(607) 776-9631	DeWitt Baker	Mark Alger	Christine Kane	...	Robert Biehl	Richard Tweddell
Suffolk	CE	1419	(631) 853-4000	Robert Gaffney	Eric Kopp	Edward Romaine	Joseph Sawicki	Alan Schneider	John Gallagher
Sullivan	CE	73	(845) 794-3000	Leni Binder	David Fanslau	...	Richard La Condre	Pamela Rourke	Daniel Hogue
Tioga *	CM	51	(607) 687-8203	...	...	...	Jane Bradley	Bethany O'Rourke	Gary Howard
Tompkins	CM	96	(607) 274-5526	Tim Joseph	Stephen Whicher	Catherine Covert	David Squires	Anita Fitzpatrick	Peter Meskill
Ulster	CE	177	(845) 340-3800	David Donaldson	Michael Hein	Nina Postupack	...	Brenda Bartholomew	J. Richard Bockel-mann
Warren	CM	63	(518) 761-6535	...	...	...	...	...	...
Washington	C	61	(518) 746-2250	JoAnn Trinkle	Kevin Hayes	Debra Prehoda	Kenneth Talkington	Barbara Winchell	Roger Le Claire
Wayne *	C	93	(315) 946-7483	James Hoffman	James Marquette	...	...	Peter Stirpe	Richard Pisciotti
Westchester	CE	923	(914) 995-2114	Andrew Spano	...	Leonard Spano	Peter Pucillo	Paula Zeman	Louis D'Aliso
Wyoming	CM	43	(585) 786-8830	...	...	Jean Krotz	...	Sally Wing	Allen Capwell
Yates *	CM	24	(315) 536-5112	Robert Multer	Sarah Purdy	Connie Hayes	...	Wendy Gibson	Ronald Spike
NORTH CAROLINA									
Alamance *	CM	130	(336) 228-1312	...	David Smith	Patricia Jones	Amy Weaver	Sherry Hook	Terry Johnson
Alexander	CM	33	(828) 632-9332	...	Richard French	Jamie Starnes	Jennifer Herman	Sandra Gregory	Hayden Bentley
Alleghany	CM	10	(336) 372-4179	Robert Edwards	J. Adams	Karen Evans	Joy Hines	...	Mike Caudill
Anson	CM	25	(704) 694-3342	Bill Thacker	...	Bonnie Huntley	Dorothy Tyson	...	James Sellers
Ashe	CM	24	(336) 219-2501	Larry Rhodes	Daniel McMillan	Ann Clark	Sandra Long	...	Jim Hartley
Avery *	CE	17	(828) 733-8201	Kenny Poteat	Robert Wiseman	Cindy Turbyfill	Timothy Greene	Nancy Johnson	Kevin Frye
Beaufort	CM	44	(252) 946-0079	...	Paul Spruill	Sharon Singleton	Angela Andrew	...	Alan Jordan
Bertie *	CE	19	(252) 794-5300	Norman Cherry	Zee Lamb	Misty Edwards	Lydia Hoggard	Carolyn Fornes	Charles Atkins
Bladen	CM	32	(910) 862-6700	Gregory Taylor	Gregory Martin	Kathy Britt	Lisa Coleman	Stephanie Moultrie	Stephen Bunn
Brunswick *	CM	73	(910) 253-2000	William Sue	Marty Lawing	Deborah Gore	Ann Hardy	Margaret Grissett	John Ingram
Buncombe	CM	206	(828) 250-4166	Nathan Ramsey	Wanda Greene	Kathy Hughes	Donna Clark	Robert Thornberry	Bobby Medford
Burke *	CM	89	(828) 439-4356	Ruth Ann Suttle	Ronald Lewis	Vicki Craigo	...	Kelley Dickens	John McDevitt
Cabarrus	CM	131	(704) 920-2200	Carolyn Carpenter	John Day	Susie Bonds	...	Donald Cummings	David Riley
Caldwell	CM	77	(828) 757-1300	Herb Greene	William White	Kathy Myers	Laurie Faw	David Hill	Gary Clark
Camden *	CM	6	(252) 338-1919	Philip Faison	Randell Woodruff	Ava Gurganus	Clarann Mansfield	Stephanie Jackson	Tony Perry
Carteret *	CM	59	(252) 728-8450	Douglas Harris	John Langdon	Jeanette Deese	...	Myles McLoughlin	Asa Buck
Caswell	CM	23	(336) 694-4193	George Ward	Kevin Howard	Wanda Smith	Gwendolyn Vaughn	Nichole McLaughlin	Michael Welch
Catawba *	CM	141	(828) 465-8200	Katherine Barnes	Tom Lundy	Barbara Morris	Rodney Miller	...	L. Huffman
Chatham	CM	49	(919) 542-8200	Margaret Pollard	Charles Horne	Sandra Lee	Vicki McConnell	Kim Bush	Donald Whitt
Cherokee	CM	24	(828) 837-5527	Barbara Vicknair	David Badger	R. Lindsay	William Block	...	Kevin Lovin
Chowan	CM	14	(252) 482-8431	Ralph Cole	J. Rascoe	Susanne Stallings	Lisa Jones	Carrie Byrum	Dwayne Goodwin
Clay	CE	8	(704) 389-0089	...	...	...	...	...	...
Cleveland *	CM	96	(704) 484-4833	Mary Accor	David Dear	Kerri Melton	Chris Crepps	R. Pearson	Raymond Hamrick
Columbus *	CM	54	(910) 640-6600	James Prevatte	...	June Hall	Bobbie Faircloth	Virginia Taylor	Christopher Batten
Craven	CM	91	(252) 636-6602	George Brown	Harold Blizzard	Gwendolyn Bryan	Richard Hemphill	...	Jerry Monette
Cumberland	CE	302	(910) 678-7653	Talmadge Baggett	James Martin	Marsha Fogle	...	James Lawson	Earl Butler
Currituck	CM	18	(252) 232-2075	Paul O'Neal	Daniel Scanlon	Gwendolyn Tatem	Sandra Hill	Derinda Leary	Susan Johnson
Dare *	CM	29	(252) 475-5821	Warren Judge	Terry Wheeler	Frances Harris	John Clawson	Thomas O'Neal	Rodney Midgett
Davidson	CM	147	(336) 242-2000	Fred Sink	Robert Hyatt	...	Jane Kiker	Keli Greer	Gerald Hege
Davie *	CM	34	(336) 753-6001	Thomas Fleming	Beth Dirks	Brenda Hunter	Robin West	...	Andy Stokes
Duplin	CE	49	(910) 296-2100	Larry Howard	...	...	Teresa Lanier	...	Blake Wallace
Durham	CM	223	(919) 560-0000	Ellen Reckhow	Michael Ruffin	Garry Umstead	George Quick	Marqueta Welton	Worth Hill
Edgecombe *	CM	55	(252) 641-7834	Charlie Harrell	Lorenzo Carmon	Carolyn Hedgepeth	JoAnne Harrell	...	James Knight
Forsyth	CM	306	(336) 703-2400	Gloria Whisenhunt	J. Watts	Jane Cole	Paul Fulton	Carol Gearhart	William Schatzman
Franklin	CM	47	(919) 496-5994	Harry Foy	...	...	Charles Murray	Ursula Hairston	Jerry Jones
Gaston	CM	190	(704) 866-3100	...	Jan Winters	Martha Jordan	Ronald Courtney	Charles Vinson	Leroy Russell
Gates	CE	10	(252) 357-1240	William Harrell	Melinda Hoggard	Timothy Russell	...	...	Edward Webb
Graham *	CM	7	(828) 479-7961	Bruce Snyder	...	Kim Crisp	Machelle Crisp	...	Russell Moody
Granville *	CM	48	(919) 693-4761	James Lumpkins	Brian Alligood	Bobbie Wilson	Michael Felts	Justin Ayscue	David Smith
Greene *	CM	18	(252) 747-3446	Bennie Heath	Donald Davenport	...	Shawna Wooten	...	Ernest Smith
Guilford	CM	421	(336) 641-3383	Robert Landreth	...	Efthemia Varitimidis	Brenda Jones	Sharisse Fuller	B. Barnes
Halifax	CE	57	(252) 583-1688	Carolyn Johnson	Tony Brown	Lynne Simeon	Linda Taylor	...	Jeff Frazier
Harnett	CM	91	(910) 893-7555	Teddy Byrd	...	Kay Blanchard	Vanessa Young	Charles Hill	Larry Rollins
Haywood	CE	54	(828) 452-6625	Mark Swanger	David Cotton	...	Julia Davis	La Neah Parton	Richard Alexander
Henderson	CE	89	(828) 697-4669	...	Steven Wyatt	Elizabeth Corn	James McLelland	Janice Prichard	Rick Davis
Hertford	CM	22	(252) 358-7805	Johnnie Farmer	Loria Williams	...	Robbin Stephenson	...	Juan Vaughan
Hoke	CM	33	(910) 875-8751	Robert Wright	Timothy Johnson	Linda Revels	Leo Hunt	Edward Crutchfield	Hubert Peterkin
Hyde	CM	5	(252) 926-4178	Beatrice Emmert	Carl Classon	...	Emily Thomas	...	L. Johnson
Iredell *	CM	122	(704) 878-3000	Marvin Norman	Joel Mashburn	Jean Moore	Susan Blumenstein	Carolyn Harris	Phillip Redmond
Jackson	CE	33	(828) 586-4055	K. Buchanan	Kenneth Westmoreland	Evelyn Baker	Darlene Fox	...	James Ashe
Johnston *	CE	121	(919) 989-5100	Wade Stewart	Rick Hester	Paula Woodard	James McLamb	Joseph LaCarter	Roger Bizzell
Jones *	CM	10	(252) 448-7571	Joseph Wiggins	Franky Howard	Jennifer Gray	Melissa Moore-Freeman	...	John Hall
Lee *	CM	49	(919) 718-4615	Richard Hayes	John Crumpton	Gaynell Lee	Lisa Minter	Joyce McGehee	Tracy Carter
Lenoir	CM	59	(252) 559-6450	George Graham	Mike Jarman	Lashanda Aytch	Tommy Hollowell	...	William Smith
Lincoln	CE	63	(704) 736-8471	Jerry Cochrane	...	Amy Long	Leon Harmon	Audrey Setzer	Barbara Pickens

Directory 1/10 **OFFICIALS IN U.S. COUNTIES 2,500 AND OVER IN POPULATION**
continued

Jurisdiction	Form of govern-ment	2000 Popu-lation	Main telephone number	Chief elected official	Appointed administrator	Clerk of the governing board	Chief financial officer	Director of personnel	Chief law enforcement official
NORTH CAROLINA continued									
Macon	CM	29	(828) 349-2000	Allan Bryson	C. Horton	...	Evelyn Southard	Charles Nicholson	Robert Holland
Madison	CE	19	(828) 649-2521	Anthony Willis	...	Bruce Briggs	Beverly Wyatt	Karen Ensley	James Brown
Martin *	CM	25	(252) 789-4300	Ronnie Smith	Russell Overman	Linda Hardison	Cindy Ange	...	Dan Gibbs
Mc Dowell	CM	42	(828) 652-7121	Andrew Webb	Charles Abernathy	Carrie Padgett	Alison Morgan	Lesa Silver	Jackie Turner
Mecklenburg	CM	695	(704) 336-7600	Tom Cox	Harry Jones	Janice Paige	J. Weatherly	Susan Hutchins	James Pendergraph
Mitchell *	CM	15	(828) 688-2139	Marvin Miller	Charles Vines	Kathy Young	Mavis Parsley	...	Ken Fox
Montgomery	CM	26	(910) 576-4221	Billy Maness	Lance Metzler	...	Janice Shaw	...	Jeff Jordan
Moore *	CE	74	(910) 947-6362	Tim Lea	Thomas McSwain	Megan Owrey	Lisa Hughes	Teri Alesch	Lane Carter
Nash	CE	87	(252) 459-9800	J. Mayo	Robert Murphy	...	Lynne Anderson	Sheila Freeman	Jimmy Grimes
New Hanover *	CM	160	(910) 798-7178	Robert Greer	Bruce Shell	Sheila Schult	Avril Pinder	Cathy Morgan	Sidney Causey
Northampton	CM	22	(252) 574-0236	Virginia Spruill	Wayne Jenkins	Kay Flythe	Dorothy Vick	Marcenda Rogers	Wardie Vincent
Onslow	CM	150	(910) 347-4717	Delma Collins	...	Beth Purcell	Alvin Barrett	Wayne Morris	Edward Brown
Orange	CM	118	(919) 732-8181	Margaret Brown	Laura Blackmon	Donna Baker	Kenneth Chavious	...	Lindy Pendergrass
Pamlico	CM	12	(252) 745-3133	...	Timothy Buck	Kathy Cayton	...	Sherry Watts	Danny Pugh
Pasquotank	CM	34	(252) 337-6648	William Trueblood	Randy Keaton	Karen Jennings	Sheri Bulman	Margaret Jones	Randy Cartwright
Pender *	CE	41	(910) 259-1200	Stephen Holland	Rick Benton	...	David McCole	...	Carson Smith
Perquimans	CM	11	(252) 426-8484	Mack Nixon	Bobby Darden	Mary Hunnicutt	Sharon Ward	...	Eric Tilley
Person	CM	35	(336) 597-1720	S. Knott	Heidi York	Faye Fuller	...	...	Dennis Oakley
Pitt *	CM	133	(252) 902-3050	Melvin McLawhorn	Donald Elliott	Patricia Staton	...	Florida Hardy	Mac Manning
Polk	CM	18	(828) 894-3301	Timothy McCormack	...	Pamela Thomas	Sandra Hughes	...	David Satterfield
Randolph	CM	130	(336) 318-6600	Harold Holmes	Richard Wells	Cheryl Ivey	William Massie	Kim Newsom	Maynard Reid
Richmond	CM	46	(910) 997-8211	Kenneth Robinette	James Haynes	Marian Savage	Mac Steagall	...	Dale Furr
Robeson	CM	123	(910) 671-3016	Johnny Hunt	Kenneth Windley	Tamala Freeman	Kellie Blue	...	Kenneth Sealey
Rockingham	CM	91	(336) 342-8100	Harold Hoover	Thomas Robinson	Pamela Robertson	Michael Apple	...	Samuel Page
Rowan	CE	130	(704) 216-8100	Arnold Chamberlain	Gary Page	Carolyn Athey	Leslie Heidrick	Darlene Boling	George Wilhelm
Rutherford	CM	62	(828) 287-6145	Charles Hill	John Condrey	Hazel Haynes	Robert Bole	Judith Toney	Daniel Good
Sampson	CE	60	(910) 592-6308	Norman Naylor	Scott Sauer	...	Sylvia Blinson	...	O. L. McCullen
Scotland	CM	35	(910) 277-2406	J. D. Willis	...	Ann Kurtzman	Kevin Patterson	Susan Butler	James Blalock
Stanly *	CM	58	(704) 986-3600	Tony Dennis	Andrew Lucas	Tyler Brummitt	Toby Hinson	Emily Valentine	Rick Burris
Stokes	CE	44	(336) 593-2811	...	Rick Morris	...	...	...	Graham Atkinson
Surry *	CM	71	(336) 401-8201	Craig Hunter	Dennis Thompson	Conchita Atkins	Betty Taylor	Sandra Snow	Curtis Cochran
Swain	CE	12	(828) 488-9273	Glenn Jones	Linda Cable	Cindi Woodard	Vida Cody	Elise Bryson	Robert Orr
Transylvania	CE	29	(828) 884-3100	Raymond Miller	Arthur Wilson	Kimberly Conover	Gay Poor	Sheila Cozart	Harry Hemilright
Tyrrell	C	4	(252) 796-1371	Thomas Spruill	James Brickhouse	Connie Hopkins	...	...	...
Union	CM	123	(704) 283-3500	...	Alfred Greene	...	...	William Watson	R. Breedlove
Vance	CM	42	(252) 738-2001	J. Pegram	Jerry Ayscue	Kelly Grissom	Jerry Tucker	Argretta Reid	John Baker
Wake	CM	627	(919) 856-6090	Linda Coleman	David Cooke	Gwendolyn Reynolds	David Frazier	John Kuhls	Johnny Williams
Warren *	CM	19	(252) 257-3115	Clinton Alston	Linda Worth	Angelena Dunlap	Barry Mayo	Elgin Lane	Janice Spruill
Washington *	CM	13	(252) 793-5823	Billy Corey	David Peoples	Lois Askew	Gayle Critcher	...	Mark Shook
Watauga	CE	42	(828) 265-8000	Jim Deal	Robert Nelson	Anita Fogle	Doris Isaacs	...	Carey Winders
Wayne	CM	113	(919) 731-1435	...	William Smith	Marcia Wilson	E. Norman Ricks	Harriett Guy	Dane Mastin
Wilkes	CM	65	(336) 651-7300	Charles Sink	Gary Page	Alene Faw	Jerry Shepherd	...	Wayne Gay
Wilson	CM	73	(252) 399-2803	...	Ellis Williford	...	Phyllis Vick	...	Mike Cain
Yadkin	CM	36	(336) 679-4200	D. C. Swaim	Stan Kiser	Melinda Vestal	Sheron Church	...	...
Yancey	CE	17	(828) 682-3971	David McIntosh	Michele Lawhern	Todd Bailey	Jean Buchanan	Brandi Adkins	Kermit Banks
NORTH DAKOTA									
Adams	C	2	(701) 567-4363	Ramon Barnes	...	Ginger Dangerud	...	...	Eugene Molbert
Barnes	C	11	(701) 845-8500	Palmer Paulson	...	...	Edward McGough	Linda Anderson	Randy McClaflin
Benson	C	6	(701) 473-5458	Curtis Hvinden	...	...	...	...	Steve Rohrer
Billings *	C	..	(701) 623-4377	...	...	Donna Adams	Joan Jurgens	...	David Jurgens
Bottineau	C	7	(701) 228-2225	Ronald Block	...	...	Mae Streich	...	...
Bowman	CM	3	(701) 523-3130	...	...	Annetta Anderson	...	...	...
Burke	CM	2	(701) 377-2861	Terry Nelson	...	...	Teri Baumann	...	Barry Jager
Burleigh	C	69	(701) 222-6669	Kevin Glatt	...	...	Clyde Thompson	Renae Gall	Patrick Heinert
Cass *	CM	123	(701) 241-5720	Ken Pawluk	Bonnie Johnson	Dorothy Howard	Mike Montplaisir	...	Paul Laney
Cavalier	C	4	(701) 256-2229	Jerome Dosmann	...	...	...	...	David Zeis
Dickey	C	5	(701) 349-3249	Jerry Walsh	...	...	Lawrence Hoffman	...	Jim Bohannon
Divide *	C	2	(701) 965-6351	Gerald Brady	...	Penny Hagen	Gayle Jastrzebski	...	Lauren Throntveit
Dunn *	C	3	(701) 573-4448	Cliff Ferebee	...	Chris Larsen	Reinhard Hauck	...	Larry Boepple
Eddy	C	2	(701) 947-2434	...	...	...	Wanda Kurtz	...	Lawrence Schagunn
Emmons	C	4	(701) 254-4807	Harvey Reamann	...	Anna Dockter	...	...	Rueben Richter
Foster	C	3	(701) 652-2441	...	...	...	Roger Schlotman	...	John Statema
Golden Valley *	C	1	(701) 872-4331	...	...	...	Cecilia Stedman	...	Scott Steele
Grand Forks	C	66	(701) 780-8415	Greg Malm	Edward Nierode	...	Doris Bring	...	Dan Hill
Grant	C	2	(701) 622-3275	Daniel Stewart	...	Joyce Stern	...	...	Steve Bay
Griggs *	C	2	(701) 797-3117	...	...	...	Cynthia Anton	Janet Tenneson	Robert Hook
Hettinger	C	2	(701) 824-2073	...	...	...	...	...	...
Kidder *	C	2	(701) 475-2632	...	...	...	...	...	...
La Moure	C	4	(701) 883-5301	Richard Aberle	...	...	Michial Johnson	...	Gary Jensen
Logan	C	2	(701) 754-2425	Mike Vetter	...	...	Blanche Schumacher	...	Steve Engelhardt
Mc Henry	CM	5	(701) 537-5724	...	...	...	Darlene Carpenter	...	Marvin Sola
Mc Intosh	CE	3	(701) 288-3347	Gina Ketterling	...	...	Lanette Blumhardt	...	Paul Peters
Mc Kenzie	C	5	(701) 444-3616	Richard Cayko	...	Ann Johnsrud	Frances Olson	...	Ron Rankin
Mc Lean	CE	9	(701) 462-8541	...	...	Mary Ann Anderson	Marlan Hvinden	...	Don Charging
Mercer *	C	8	(701) 745-3292	Monte Erhardt	Wayne Enze	...	...	...	Dean Danzeisen
Morton	C	25	(701) 667-3414	...	...	...	Paul Trauger	Paula Graner	Robert Erhardt
Mountrail	C	6	(701) 628-2145	Robert Wheeling	...	Karen Eliason	...	...	Kenneth Halvorson
Nelson	CE	3	(701) 247-2463	...	...	Ruth Stevens	W. Davidson	...	Dale Quam
Oliver	C	2	(701) 794-8721	Barbara Fleming	...	Kim Wilkens	...	...	David Hilliard
Pembina	C	8	(701) 265-4231	Dorothy Robinson	...	Nancy Johnson	...	...	Joe Martindale
Pierce *	C	4	(701) 776-5225	Karin Fursather	...	Carla Marks	...	...	Robert Graber
Ramsey *	C	12	(701) 662-7009	Pam Brekke	...	...	Elizabeth Fischer	...	Steve Nelson
Ransom	C	5	(701) 683-5823	Connie Gilbert	Kathy Schultz	Valorie Lukes	...	...	Conrad Steinhaus
Renville	C	2	(701) 756-6301	...	...	...	Susan Ritter	...	Brent Johnson
Richland	C	17	(701) 642-7700	Perry Miller	...	...	Harris Bailey	...	Larry Leshovsky
Rolette	C	13	(701) 477-5665	Robert Leonard	...	...	Judith Boppre	...	Tony Sims
Sargent	C	4	(701) 724-6241	...	...	...	...	...	...
Sheridan	CE	1	(701) 363-2205	Shirley Murray	...	...	...	...	Lawrence Gessner
Sioux	C	4	(701) 854-3481	Larry Silbernagel	...	...	Barbara Hettich	...	Frank Landeis
Slope *	C	..	(701) 879-6276	Michael Teske	...	...	Lorrie Buzalsky	...	Pat Lorge
Stark *	C	22	(701) 456-7630	Duane Wolf	...	RaeDeen Weinberger	...	...	Clarence Tuhy
Steele	C	2	(701) 524-2110	David Washburn	...	...	Ruth Gullicks	...	Wayne Beckman
Stutsman *	C	21	(701) 252-9035	Mark Klose	...	Karen Samek	Noel Johnson	...	David Orr
Towner	C	2	(701) 968-4340	David Lagein	...	...	Kent Haugen	...	Vaughn Klier
Traill	C	8	(701) 636-4458	...	...	...	Rebecca Braaten	...	Michael Crocker
Walsh	C	12	(701) 352-2851	...	...	...	...	...	...
Ward	C	58	(701) 857-6420	Darlene Watne	...	...	Devra Smesatd	Colleen Houmann	Vern Erck
Wells	C	5	(701) 547-3521	...	...	...	...	...	...
Williams	C	19	(701) 577-4500	Daniel Kalil	...	...	Beth Innis	...	Scott Busching

Directory 1/10 — OFFICIALS IN U.S. COUNTIES 2,500 AND OVER IN POPULATION
continued

Jurisdiction	Form of govern-ment	2000 Popu-lation	Main telephone number	Chief elected official	Appointed administrator	Clerk of the governing board	Chief financial officer	Director of personnel	Chief law enforcement official
OHIO									
Adams	C	27	(937) 544-3286	Paul Rothwell	...	Linda Mendenhall	Carroll Newman	...	...
Allen	CE	108	(419) 228-3700	Gregory Sneary	Rebecca Saine	Kelli Singhaus	Ben Diepenbrock	Crystal Balo	Daniel Beck
Ashland *	C	52	(419) 289-0000	Kim Edwards	...	Gail Crossen	Philip Leibolt	...	Estel Risner
Ashtabula	CE	102	(440) 576-9090	...	Joseph Pedro	...	...	...	...
Athens	C	62	(740) 592-3224	Bill Theisen	...	Crystal Mitchell	David Lovett	...	...
Auglaize *	C	46	(419) 739-6710	John Bergman	Joseph Lenhart	Sue Ellen Kohler	Janet Schuler	...	Allen Solomon
Belmont	CE	70	(614) 425-1118	...	...	Jayne Long	...	...	...
Brown	C	42	(937) 378-3956	...	Timothy Williams	Beverly Gallimore	Doug Green	...	Dwayne Wenninger
Butler	CM	332	(513) 887-3000	Michael Fox	...	Flora Butler	...	Douglas Duckett	Don Gabbard
Carroll *	C	28	(330) 627-5122	...	...	Sonja Leggett	E. Leroy Van Horne	...	Dale Williams
Champaign	C	38	(937) 772-7001	...	Andrea Millice	...	...	...	Joseph Lynch
Clark	CE	144	(937) 328-2405	Roger Tackett	W. Howard	Michelle Noble	George Sodders	Cathy Balas	Gene Kelly
Clermont	CM	177	(513) 732-7300	Mary Walker	David Spinney	Judith Kocica	Susanne Scheetz	Robert Sander	Albert Rodenberg
Clinton	C	40	(937) 382-2054	...	Mark Brooker	...	...	...	...
Columbiana	C	112	(330) 424-9511	...	...	...	...	...	...
Coshocton	C	36	(740) 622-1753	Alice Moore	...	Mary Beck	Richard Tompkins	...	...
Crawford	C	46	(419) 562-4602	Barbara Blackford	Mary Jo Allan	Glory Chaney	Donald Long	...	Ronald Shawber
Cuyahoga	CM	1393	(216) 443-7190	Tim McCormack	Dennis Madden	Maragret Hile	Robin Blinn	Janice Anderson	Toby Spencer
Darke	C	53	(937) 547-7312	...	...	...	...	...	David Westrick
Defiance	C	39	(419) 782-4761	Richard Cromwell	Rebecca Wagner	Alison Grimes	...	...	...
Delaware	CM	109	(740) 833-2100	Roy Jackson	David Cannon	...	Jon Peterson	Myra Williamson	...
Erie *	CM	79	(419) 627-7672	Nancy McKeen	Michael Bixler	Carolyn Hauenstein	Tom Paul	Margaret Rudolph	Terry Lyons
Fairfield	CM	122	(740) 687-7190	...	...	Carri Brown	Jon Slater	Aundrea Cordle	Gary Demastry
Fayette	C	28	(740) 335-0720	Bob Peterson	...	Judy Rambo	Penny Johnson	...	Vernon Stanforth
Franklin	CM	1068	(614) 462-6224	Jack Graf	Don Brown	Debra Willaman	Kenneth Wilson	Margaret Snow	Jim Karnes
Fulton	C	42	(419) 337-9255	Jack Graf	Vond Hall	Mary Gype	John Trudel	...	Darrell Merillat
Gallia	C	31	(614) 446-4612	Harold Montgomery	Karen Sprague	Connie Johnson	Ronald Canaday	...	James Taylor
Geauga	CE	90	(440) 285-2222	William Repke	David Lair	...	Tracy Jemison	...	George Simmons
Greene	CM	147	(937) 562-5004	Reed Madden	Howard Poston	Judy Minton	L. Delaney	Marsha Jordan-Smart	Gene Fischer
Guernsey	C	40	(740) 432-9200	...	...	Cheryl Edwards	...	...	...
Hamilton *	CM	845	(513) 946-4700	Todd Portune	Patrick Thompson	Jacqueline Panioto	...	Gary Berger	Simon Leis
Hancock	C	71	(419) 424-7044	...	...	...	...	...	...
Hardin *	C	31	(419) 674-2240	Gerald Potter	...	...	Michael Bacon	...	Craig Leeth
Harrison	C	15	(740) 942-8861	...	...	Barbara Yoho	Patrick Moore	...	Mark Miller
Henry	C	29	(419) 592-4876	Richard Bennett	Anita Smith	Vicki Glick	Kevin Nye	...	John Nye
Highland	C	40	(937) 393-1911	...	...	...	...	...	...
Hocking	C	28	(740) 385-2127	Gary Starner	Roger Hinerman	...	Kenneth Wilson	...	Lanny North
Holmes	C	38	(330) 674-4901	...	...	Susan Haun	...	...	...
Huron	CE	59	(419) 668-3092	Karen Wilhelm	Mary Cain	Ann Winters	...	...	Richard Sutherland
Jackson	C	32	(740) 286-3301	Ponney Cisco	...	Angela Cemini	Edward Jarvis	...	Gregg Kiefer
Jefferson	C	73	(740) 283-8500	...	...	...	...	...	...
Knox	C	54	(740) 393-6703	Robert Durbin	...	Rochelle Shackle	Margaret Ruhl	...	...
Lake	CE	227	(440) 350-2524	Mildred Teuscher	Kenneth Gauntner	Lynn Mazeika	Dale Langbehn	...	Daniel Dunlap
Lawrence *	C	62	(740) 533-4300	Jason Stephens	Tammy Meade	...	Ray Dutey	...	Jeff Lawless
Licking	C	145	(740) 349-6117	Albert Ashbrook	Michael Smith	...	George Buchanan	...	...
Logan	C	46	(937) 599-7823	...	...	Kacy Kirby	...	...	...
Lorain	CM	284	(440) 329-5000	David Moore	James Cordes	Theresa Upton	John Rokasy	Jeff Fogt	Martin Mahony
Lucas	CM	455	(419) 213-4500	Sandy Isenburg	Michael Beazley	Nancy Poskar	Larry Kaczala	Gwen Moore	James Telb
Madison *	CE	40	(740) 852-2972	David Dhume	...	Regina Bogenrife	Jim Williamson	...	Jim Sabin
Mahoning	C	257	(330) 740-2130	...	George Tablack	...	...	J. Sellards	...
Marion	CE	66	(740) 223-4001	Andy Appelfeller	Lenora Mayes	Sylvia Almendinger	Joseph Campbell	...	John Butterworth
Medina	C	151	(330) 723-3641	Sharon Ray	John Stricker	Pamela Terrill	Michael Kovak	Patricia Larsen	Neil Hassinger
Meigs	C	23	(740) 992-2698	...	Kim Everman	...	Mark Giesige	...	Jeff Gray
Mercer	C	40	(419) 586-3178	...	...	...	Chris Peeples	Teresa Clegg	Charles Cox
Miami	C	98	(937) 440-5910	John Evans	...	...	...	...	Glen Schwaben
Monroe	C	15	(740) 472-0873	Gary Hudson	...	Kitty Kahrig	...	...	...
Montgomery	CM	559	(937) 225-4000	Vickie Pegg	Deborah Feldman	Juanita Hunn	Tom Black	Leon Walker	...
Morgan	C	14	(740) 962-4752	...	...	...	...	...	...
Morrow	C	31	(419) 946-4085	Donald Weaver	...	Shirley Fissel	Mary Holtrey	...	...
Muskingum *	CE	84	(740) 455-7100	...	...	Susan Culbertson	Anita Adams	Michelle Campbell	Matthew Lutz
Noble	C	14	(740) 732-2969	...	...	...	...	...	...
Ottawa	C	40	(419) 734-6700	...	Jere Witt	...	...	...	...
Paulding	C	20	(419) 399-8215	Tony Burkley	Stanley Searing	Joanne Goerlitz	Bill Bolenbaugh	...	David Harrow
Perry *	CM	34	(740) 342-2074	John Altier	...	Timothy Wollenberg	Teresa Stevenson	...	William Barker
Pickaway	C	52	(740) 474-6093	...	Daniel Bradhurst	...	...	...	...
Pike *	C	27	(740) 947-4817	...	...	...	...	...	...
Portage	C	152	(330) 297-3600	Charles Keiper	...	Deborah Mazanec	Eric Sponseller	Lynn Leslie	Duane Kaley
Preble	C	42	(937) 456-8143	...	Kenneth Moreland	Connie Crowell	...	...	...
Putnam	C	34	(419) 523-3656	...	...	Mary Wiener	Marlene Lahey	...	Ronald Diemer
Richland	C	128	(419) 755-5500	...	...	...	...	...	...
Ross	C	73	(740) 702-3085	James Caldwell	Kelly Shelton	...	Stephen Neal	...	Ronald Nichols
Sandusky	CE	61	(419) 332-2657	...	...	...	...	Tim Grabenstetter	...
Scioto	C	79	(740) 355-8356	Thomas Reiser	...	Inez Bloomfield	David Green	...	Marty Donini
Seneca	C	58	(419) 447-4550	Kenneth Estep	Stacy Wilson	Kathy McClenathan	Larry Beidelschies	...	Tom Steyer
Shelby *	C	47	(937) 498-7226	Dale Deloye	...	Judy Snodgrass	...	...	...
Stark	CE	378	(330) 451-7371	...	...	...	...	...	...
Summit	CE	542	(330) 643-2500	Nick Kostandaras	Russell Pry	John Thomas	Linda Phelps	Leonard Foster	Drew Alexander
Trumbull	CM	225	(330) 675-2589	Joseph Angelo	...	Paulette Godfrey	David Hines	James Keating	Thomas Altiere
Tuscarawas	C	90	(330) 364-8811	William Ress	...	Jane Clay	J. Matt Judy	...	Walter Wilson
Union	C	40	(937) 645-3012	...	...	Carol Speelman	Nancy Dixon	Jane Harris	Stan Owens
Van Wert	C	29	(419) 238-0843	Gary Adams	...	...	Cindy Owings	...	David Hickey
Vinton	C	12	(740) 596-4571	Michael Bledsoe	Brande Minton	...	Tina Davis	Susan Spencer	William Arris
Warren *	C	158	(513) 695-1250	C. Michael Kilburn	David Gully	...	Tiffany Ferrell-Sauer	...	Robert Schlicher
Washington	C	63	(740) 373-6623	Sandra Matthews	Patrick Herron	Judy Van Dyk	Janet Seaman	...	...
Wayne	C	111	(330) 287-5400	...	...	...	...	...	...
Williams	C	39	(419) 636-2059	...	...	...	...	...	...
Wood	CE	121	(419) 354-9000	James Carter	Andrew Kalmar	Kristy Muir	Michael Sibbersen	...	Mark Wasylyshyn
Wyandot	CM	22	(419) 294-3836	...	Martha Shrider	...	...	...	...
OKLAHOMA									
Adair	C	21	(918) 696-7198	...	...	...	...	...	...
Alfalfa	C	6	(580) 596-2392	...	...	...	...	...	...
Atoka	C	13	(580) 889-5157	...	...	...	...	...	...
Beaver *	C	5	(580) 625-3418	Brad Raven	...	Karen Schell	...	...	Reuben Parker
Beckham	C	19	(580) 928-2457	Carl Simon	...	Clydene Manning	...	...	Scott Jay
Blaine	C	11	(580) 623-5890	Farrol Boyd	...	Sharon Gates	...	...	Ricky Ainsworth
Bryan	C	36	(580) 924-2201	Tony Simmons	Quinton Jones	Patricia Brady	...	...	Bill Sturch
Caddo	CE	30	(405) 247-3105	Carlos Squires	Craig Gibson	Patrice Dolch	...	...	Gene Cain
Canadian	C	87	(405) 262-1070	...	...	...	...	...	...
Carter	C	45	(580) 223-8162	...	...	...	...	...	...
Cherokee	C	42	(918) 456-3171	...	...	Marshel Benett	...	...	...
Choctaw	C	15	(580) 326-3778	Danny Antwine	...	Emily Vanworth	...	...	Lewis Collins

Jurisdiction	Form of govern-ment	2000 Popu-lation	Main telephone number	Chief elected official	Appointed administrator	Clerk of the governing board	Chief financial officer	Director of personnel	Chief law enforcement official
OKLAHOMA continued									
Cimarron	C	3	(580) 544-3420	Kenneth Maness	...	Dwilene Holbert	...	...	Ken Miller
Cleveland	* C	208	(405) 366-0200	...	...	Tammy Howard	...	...	Dewayne Beggs
Coal	C	6	(580) 927-3122	John Ward	...	Marie Depasse	...	Alvin Rebworth	Tony Taylor
Comanche	C	114	(580) 353-3717	...	...	...	...	...	...
Cotton	C	6	(580) 875-3026	Elmer Beisch	...	Linda Thompson	...	...	Paul Jeffrey
Craig	C	14	(918) 256-2507	James Smith	...	Tammy Malone	...	...	Jimmie Sooter
Creek	C	67	(918) 224-0278	Dana Hudgins	Johnny Burke	Betty Rentz	...	...	Steve Toliver
Custer	C	26	(580) 323-4420	...	...	...	...	...	...
Delaware	C	37	(918) 253-4520	...	...	Carol Fortner	...	...	...
Dewey	* C	4	(580) 328-5361	Everett Carman	...	Sandra Clendenny	...	...	Carl Freeman
Ellis	C	4	(580) 885-7301	Terry Fagala	...	Lynn Smith	...	...	DeWayne Miller
Garfield	C	57	(580) 237-0225	Wendell Vencl	...	Kathy Hughes	...	...	Bill Winchester
Garvin	C	27	(580) 268-2685	Rex Carlton	...	Gina Cottrell	...	Evelyn Bradley	Bobby Davis
Grady	CE	45	(405) 224-7388	Sharon Porter	...	Sharon Shoemake	...	...	Kieran McMullen
Grant	C	5	(580) 395-2214	Max Hess	John Futhey	Debbie Kretchmar	...	...	Roland Hula
Greer	C	6	(580) 782-2329	...	...	...	...	...	...
Harmon	C	3	(580) 688-3658	...	...	...	...	...	...
Harper	C	3	(580) 735-2870	...	...	...	...	...	...
Haskell	C	11	(918) 967-4352	...	...	...	...	...	...
Hughes	C	14	(405) 379-5487	Jerry Martin	...	Joquita Walton	...	...	Houston Yeager
Jackson	C	28	(580) 482-4420	...	...	...	...	...	...
Jefferson	* C	6	(580) 228-2029	Billy Kidd	...	Gloria England	...	...	Michael Bryant
Johnston	C	10	(580) 371-3184	...	...	Delores Muse	...	...	...
Kay	* C	48	(580) 362-2537	Steve Austin	...	Tammy Reese	...	...	Everette Van Hoesen
Kingfisher	C	13	(405) 375-3887	Judge Pritchett	...	Jane Hightower	Albert Post	...	...
Kiowa	C	10	(580) 726-5286	Robert Boelte	...	Geanea Watson	...	...	Buck Jones
Latimer	C	10	(918) 465-3543	John Medders	...	Shirley Brinkley	...	...	Melvin Holly
Le Flore	C	48	(918) 647-2527	...	...	...	...	...	A. Brixey
Lincoln	C	32	(405) 258-1264	Ted O'Donnell	...	Debbie Greenfield	...	...	Randy Richardson
Logan	C	33	(405) 282-0266	Kevin Leach	Mark Sharpton	Mary Lou Orndorff	...	...	Joe Russell
Love	C	8	(580) 276-3059	Don Reed	...	Dora Jackson	...	...	Tom Shaffer
Major	C	7	(580) 227-4732	Kelly Wahl	...	...	...	...	Robert Wilder
Marshall	* C	13	(580) 795-3165	Royce Bartee	...	Ann Hartin	...	...	Frank Cantey
Mayes	C	38	(918) 825-0639	Jim Montgomery	...	Lori Parsons	...	...	Don Hewett
Mc Clain	* CE	27	(405) 527-3360	Charles Foster	...	Lois Hawkins	...	...	Richard McPeak
Mc Curtain	C	34	(580) 286-7428	Aubrey Thompson	Eugene Burke	Karen Conaway	Tom Porton	...	Bobby Gray
Mc Intosh	C	19	(918) 689-3375	Glen Coleman	...	Diana Curtis	...	...	...
Murray	C	12	(580) 622-2854	...	...	...	...	...	Charles Pearson
Muskogee	C	69	(918) 682-9601	Gene Wallace	...	Karen Anderson	...	...	Jerry Cook
Noble	C	11	(580) 336-2141	...	...	Ronita Coldiron	...	...	James Hallett
Nowata	C	10	(918) 273-2480	Dale Epperson	...	Teresa Jackson	...	...	Jack Choate
Okfuskee	C	11	(918) 623-1724	...	...	Dianne Flanders	...	...	John Whetsel
Oklahoma	C	660	(405) 278-1500	Stuart Earnest	Blair Schoeb	Carolynn Caudill	John Rahhal	...	...
Okmulgee	C	39	(918) 756-3836	...	...	...	...	...	Russell Cottle
Osage	C	44	(918) 287-3136	Clarence Brantley	Scott Hilton	Toby Bighorse	Sharon Casebolt	...	Jack Harkins
Ottawa	C	33	(918) 542-9408	James Leake	...	Carol Randall	...	...	Dwight Woodrell
Pawnee	C	16	(918) 762-2732	Royce Brien	...	Marcelee Welch	...	...	Carl Hiner
Payne	C	68	(405) 624-9300	Carl Moreland	...	Sherri Schieffer	...	...	Jerome Amaranto
Pittsburg	C	43	(918) 423-6865	Randy Crone	...	Debbie Burch	...	...	...
Pontotoc	C	35	(580) 332-1425	...	...	...	...	...	Weldon Cantrell
Pottawatomie	C	65	(405) 273-4305	Bob Guinn	...	Nancy Bryce	Steve Sanders	...	Elvin Flood
Pushmataha	CE	11	(580) 298-2512	Eddy McIntosh	...	Albert Brown	...	...	...
Roger Mills	C	3	(580) 497-3365	...	...	...	...	...	...
Rogers	C	70	(918) 341-0585	...	...	...	...	...	Joe Craig
Seminole	* C	24	(405) 257-2501	Fred Combs	...	Tahasha Wilcots	...	...	...
Sequoyah	C	38	(918) 775-5539	...	...	...	...	...	...
Stephens	C	43	(580) 255-8460	...	...	...	...	...	...
Texas	C	20	(580) 338-3233	Gary Winters	...	...	...	...	Billy Hanes
Tillman	C	9	(580) 335-2156	Joe Don Dickey	...	Jerri Boyd	...	...	...
Tulsa	C	563	(918) 596-5000	...	...	...	...	Terry Tallent	Johnny Cannon
Wagoner	C	57	(918) 485-7780	Jim Hargrove	...	Carolyn Kusler	...	...	...
Washington	C	48	(918) 337-2820	...	...	...	...	...	...
Washita	C	11	(580) 832-5016	...	...	...	...	...	...
Woods	CE	9	(580) 327-0998	...	...	...	...	...	...
Woodward	C	18	(580) 256-8097	...	...	...	...	...	...
OREGON									
Baker	CM	16	(541) 523-8200	...	...	James Morales	Mary Otley	Libet Hatch	Diana Simpson
Benton	* CM	78	(541) 766-6081	Jay Dixon	...	Mary Raethke	Marc Gonzales	Nancy Drury	Craig Roberts
Clackamas	CE	338	(503) 655-8459	...	Jonathan Mantay	Lori Davidson	Michael Robison	Robin Young	John Raichl
Clatsop	CE	35	(503) 325-1000	Joe Bakkensen	Scott Derickson	Elizabeth Huser	Paul Downey	Jean Ripa	Phil Derby
Columbia	C	43	(888) 397-7210	Tony Hyde	...	Terri Turi	...	Janis Falcon	Andy Jackson
Coos	C	62	(541) 396-3121	Beverly Owen	...	Dee Berman	...	...	...
Crook	CE	19	(541) 447-6555	Fred Rodgers	...	Renee Kolen	Mary Johnson	...	Lyle Owens
Curry	C	21	(541) 247-7011	Marlyn Schafer	...	Nancy Blankenship	Geoffrey Buchheim	Julie Swift	Larry Blanton
Deschutes	* CM	115	(541) 388-6570	...	David Kanner	Barbara Nielsen	Marty Wynne	Debbie Legg	Chris Brown
Douglas	C	100	(541) 440-4405	Doug Robertson	...	Rena Kennedy	Sandee Correll	Jim Bruce	Paul Barnett
Gilliam	C	1	(541) 384-2311	Laura Pryor	...	Kathy McKinnon	...	...	...
Grant	CE	7	(541) 575-0059	Dennis Reynolds	William Gibbs	Maria Turriaga	Kathy Smith	La Dene Hurd	David Glerup
Harney	* CE	7	(541) 573-6356	Steven Grasty	...	Sandra Berry	...	Denise Ford	Joe Wampler
Hood River	CM	20	(541) 386-3970	Chuck Thomsen	David Meriwether	Kathy Beckett	Sandra Borowy	...	Michael Winters
Jackson	CM	181	(541) 774-6036	Jack Walker	Danny Jordan	Kathy Marston	Gary Cadle	...	Jack Jones
Jefferson	* CM	19	(541) 475-2449	Mike Ahern	Jeffrey Rasmussen	Georgette Brown	Kathie Rohde	Kent Granat	David Daniel
Josephine	C	75	(541) 474-5217	Jim Brock	...	Linda Smith	...	E. Johnson	Tim Evinger
Klamath	* C	63	(541) 883-4296	John Elliott	...	Stacie Geaney	DeEtta Vincent	...	Phillip McDonald
Lake	C	7	(541) 947-6006	...	...	Annette Newingham	Kaylene Blackburn	Greta Utecht	Russel Burger
Lane	CM	322	(541) 682-3665	C. Sorenson	Jeff Spartz	Dana Jenkins	James Weider	...	Dennis Dotson
Lincoln	C	44	(541) 265-4157	Jean Cowan	...	Steven Druckenmiller	...	...	Tim Mueller
Linn	* CM	103	(541) 967-3825	Roger Nyquist	Ralph Wyatt	Deborah Delong	...	...	Andrew Bentz
Malheur	CM	31	(541) 473-5183	Russell Hursh	Nancy Moore	Alan Davidson	...	...	Raul Rameriz
Marion	CM	284	(503) 589-3295	...	John Lattimer	Bobbi Childers	Fred Carlson	Theresa Van Dusen	Ken Matlack
Morrow	CE	10	(541) 676-5620	Terry Tallman	...	Debora Boystad	Dave Boyer	Karen Wolff	Bernie Guisto
Multnomah	C	660	(503) 248-3100	Dianne Lynn	Tony Mounts	Val Unger	...	Gail Parnell	Robert Wolfe
Polk	* C	62	(503) 623-8173	Mike Propes	Gregory Hansen	Linda Cornie	...	...	Brad Lohrey
Sherman	C	1	(541) 565-3416	Gary Thompson	...	Josephine Veltri	...	...	Tom Dye
Tillamook	C	24	(503) 842-3403	Gina Firman	...	Jean Hemphill	Dan Leighty	Craig Schwinck	John Trumbo
Umatilla	C	70	(541) 276-7111	Emile Holeman	Marcia Wells	Robin Church	...	James Barrow	Boyd Rasmussen
Union	* C	24	(541) 963-1001	Steve McClure	Shelley Burgess	Charlotte McIver	...	...	Fred Steen
Wallowa	C	7	(541) 426-4543	Mike Hayward	Gail Tally	...	...	...	...
Wasco	C	23	(541) 296-2276	...	...	Barbara Sitton	...	...	Robert Gordon
Washington	CM	445	(503) 846-8685	Tom Brian	Robert Davis	Jan Coleman	...	...	Robert Hudspeth
Wheeler	* C	1	(541) 763-2400	Jeanne Burch	...	...	...	...	Jack Crabtree
Yamhill	CM	84	(503) 472-9371	Mary Stern	John Krawczyk			Steven Mikami	

Directory 1/10 continued   OFFICIALS IN U.S. COUNTIES 2,500 AND OVER IN POPULATION

Jurisdiction	Form of govern- ment	2000 Popu- lation	Main telephone number	Chief elected official	Appointed administrator	Clerk of the governing board	Chief financial officer	Director of personnel	Chief law enforcement official
PENNSYLVANIA									
Adams	C	91	(717) 334-6781	Harry Stokes	Brenda Constable	...	Kathy Fissel	David Zobel	Bernard Miller
Allegheny	CE	1281	(412) 350-5300	Jim Roddey	Robert Webb	...	Carmen Torockio	Allison Lee-Mann	Kenneth Fulton
Armstrong	C	72	(724) 543-2500	...	...	...	...	...	...
Beaver	C	181	(724) 728-5700	Beatrice Schulte	Robert Cyphert	...	Connie Javens	S. Richard Darbut	Felix Deluca
Bedford	C	49	(814) 623-4807	...	...	...	...	...	...
Berks *	C	373	(610) 478-6118	Mark Scott	William Dennis	Terry Styer	...	Jennifer Biehn	Eric Weaknecht
Blair	C	129	(814) 695-5541	...	...	...	...	...	...
Bradford	CM	62	(717) 265-1727	...	...	...	...	...	...
Bucks	CM	597	(215) 348-6100	Michael Fitzpatrick	David Steinbach	...	Stanley Allen	Jerry Fuqua	Lawrence Michaels
Butler	CE	174	(724) 285-4731	...	...	...	...	Lori Altman	...
Cambria	C	152	(814) 472-1606	Fred Soisson	...	Edward Sholtis	Michael Gelles	...	Robert Kolar
Cameron	C	5	(814) 486-2315	...	...	...	...	...	...
Carbon *	CM	58	(570) 325-3611	Wayne Nothstein	Randall Smith	...	Robert Crampsie	Dawn Bowman	Dwight Nothstein
Centre	CM	135	(814) 355-6748	Vicki Wedler	...	...	Denise Elbell	Francis Bogert	Dennis Nau
Chester	C	433	(610) 344-6280	Colin Hanna	Karen Martynick	Edward Schmid	Caroline Cassels	Thomas Czulewicz	Anthony Sarcione
Clarion *	C	41	(814) 226-4000	Donna Oberlander	...	Sharon Roxbury	Donna Reinsel	Kristin Clark	William Peck
Clearfield	C	83	(814) 765-2641	Michael Lytle	...	Lisa McFadden	Claudia Read	Mary Mood	Chester Hawkins
Clinton	C	37	(570) 893-4000	Daniel Vilello	Kathy Conrad	...	...	Gloria Stinson	Charles Ankney
Columbia	CM	64	(717) 389-5600	Leroy Diehl	Gail Kipp	...	Norma Beyers	Janet Weeks	Harry Roadarmel
Crawford	C	90	(814) 333-7400	Morris Waid	Marlene Robertson	...	Robyn Sye	...	Francis Schultz
Cumberland	CM	213	(717) 240-6100	Nancy Besch	...	John Connolly	Gay McGeary	Dan Hartnett	Thomas Kline
Dauphin	C	251	(717) 780-6230	Jeffrey Haste	Robert Burns	...	...	Faye Fisher	Edward Marsico
Delaware	CM	550	(610) 891-4852	...	...	...	...	...	...
Elk	CM	35	(814) 776-1161	June Sorg	Peggy Aharrah	...	...	...	...
Erie	CE	280	(814) 451-6000	Rick Schenker	...	...	Tom Lyons	Peter Callan	Robert Merski
Fayette	CE	148	(724) 430-1202	Vincent Vicites	Warren Hughes	Judith Bodkin	Mark Roberts	...	Gary Brownfield
Forest	C	4	(814) 755-3537	Basil Huffman	Virginia Call	...	...	...	Robert Wolfgang
Franklin	C	129	(717) 261-3154	...	...	...	...	...	...
Fulton	C	14	(717) 485-3691	...	...	...	...	...	...
Greene	C	40	(724) 852-5210	Dave Coder	Gene Lee	...	John Stets	Tracy Zivkovich	Richard Ketchem
Huntingdon	C	45	(814) 643-3091	R. Dean Fluke	Cinnamon Bair	...	Sherri Rogers	...	William Walters
Indiana	C	89	(724) 465-3805	Bernie Smith	Helen Hill	...	...	Margaret Karp	Donald Beckwith
Jefferson	C	45	(814) 849-1653	Ira Sunderland	...	Julie Coleman	...	Debbie Rodriguez	Thomas Demko
Juniata	C	22	(717) 436-8991	...	...	...	...	...	...
Lackawanna	C	213	(925) 963-6771	Joseph Corcoran	William Jenkins	...	Vince Wiercinski	Anthony Bernardi	Michael Barrasse
Lancaster	CE	470	(717) 299-8000	Paul Thibault	Mark Esterbrook	...	Benjamin Hess	J. Myers	Philip Bomberger
Lawrence	C	94	(412) 656-2164	Daniel Vogler	James Gagliano	...	Maryann Reiter	Susan Quimby	...
Lebanon	C	120	(717) 274-2801	William Carpenter	Jamie Wolgemuth	...	Robert Mettley	Gary Robson	Deirdre Eshleman
Lehigh *	CE	312	(610) 782-3130	Donald Cunningham	Frank Kane	Stephen Samuelson	Brian Kahler	...	...
Luzerne	C	319	(570) 825-1500	...	...	Samuel Guesto	...	...	...
Lycoming *	CE	120	(570) 327-2200	Rebecca Burke	...	William Burd	Robert Noll	Ann Gehret	Eric Linhardt
Mc Kean *	CM	45	(814) 887-5571	Joseph DeMott	...	Audrey Irons	Dustin Laurie	...	John Pavlock
Mercer	CM	120	(724) 662-3800	Cloyd Brenneman	Kenneth Ammann	...	Tresa Templeton	...	James Epstein
Mifflin	C	46	(717) 248-6733	Susan McCartney	...	Peggy Finkenbiner	...	...	Joseph Bradley
Monroe	C	138	(570) 420-3434	Mario Scavello	Robert Gress	...	Kenneth Sztukowski	Daniel Hite	Todd Martin
Montgomery	C	750	(610) 278-3052	Michael Marino	Robert Graf	...	Jon Ganser	Peter Leis	Bruce Caster
Montour	C	18	(717) 271-3000	...	...	...	...	...	...
Northampton	CE	267	(610) 559-3000	...	John Conklin	Frank Flisser	...	Peter Regina	Alfred Diomedo
Northumberland	C	94	(570) 988-4100	Allen Cwalina	William Stesney	...	Edward Zack	Walter Kalinoski	Anthony Rosini
Perry	C	43	(717) 582-2131	Mark Keller	...	Sharon Charles	Kathleen Penn	...	Carl Nace
Pike	CM	46	(717) 296-7613	Karl Wagner	...	Gary Orben	...	...	Phil Bueki
Potter *	CE	18	(814) 274-8290	Douglas Morley	...	...	...	...	Kenneth Sauley
Schuylkill	C	150	(570) 622-5570	Frank Staudenmeier	Darlene Dolzani	Jean Heffner	Gary Hornberger	S. Thomas White	Francis McAndrew
Snyder	C	37	(570) 837-0691	...	...	...	...	...	...
Somerset	C	80	(814) 443-1434	Robert Will	...	...	...	...	Carl Brown
Sullivan	CM	6	(570) 946-5201	Betty Reibson	Lynne Strabryla	Naomi English	Kathy Robbins	...	Burton Adams
Susquehanna	C	42	(570) 278-4600	Roberta Kelly	Suzanne Brainard	Mary Evans	...	Sylvia Beamer	Lance Benedict
Tioga	CM	41	(570) 723-8191	Mark Hamilton	Derek Williams	...	...	Brian Morral	John Perry
Union	C	41	(570) 524-8631	William Haas	Diana Robinson	...	...	...	John Schrawder
Venango	CM	57	(814) 432-9500	Robert Murray	Denise Jones	...	Tamara Varsek	Connie Hazelton	E. Price
Warren	C	43	(814) 723-7550	...	...	...	...	...	...
Washington	C	202	(724) 228-6738	John Bevec	...	Cathi Kresh	Roger Metcalfe	Michelle Miller-Kotula	Larry Maggi
Wayne	C	47	(717) 253-5970	...	...	...	...	...	...
Westmoreland	CE	369	(724) 830-3780	Richard Vidmer	...	Lana August	Dennis Adams	Betsy Griffin	John Peck
Wyoming	C	28	(570) 836-3200	Tony Litwin	William Gaylord	...	...	...	...
York	C	381	(717) 771-9214	...	Charles Noll	Vickie Glatfelter	...	Sharon Luker	William Hose
SOUTH CAROLINA									
Abbeville	CM	26	(864) 366-6690	Ernest Gunnells	Timothy Moulder	Lynn Sopolosky	Barry Devore	...	Charles Goodwin
Aiken	CM	142	(803) 642-2012	Ronnie Young	J. Killian	...	Terry Bodiford	Dorothy Powell	...
Allendale	C	11	(803) 584-3438	J. Wall	Arthur Williams	Sue Welch	...	...	Frances Coath
Anderson	CM	165	(864) 260-4031	...	Joey Preston	Cathy Phillips	Rita Davis	Kathy Fullbright	Gordon Taylor
Bamberg	CM	16	(803) 245-5191	John Williamson	Lawrence Clark	Rose Shepherd	Booker Patrick	Ruthie Brown	J. Darnell
Barnwell *	CM	23	(803) 541-1000	Lowell Jowers	Pickens Williams	Verger Ashley	Hugh Quattlebaum	Lisa Boland	Marvin Carroll
Beaufort *	CM	120	(843) 470-2650	William Newton	Gary Kubic	Suzanne Rainey	Thomas Henrikson	Suzanne Gregory	Phennis Tanner
Berkeley *	C	142	(843) 719-4234	Daniel Davis	...	Barbara Austin	Kace Smith	Leonitta Turner	...
Calhoun	CM	15	(803) 874-2435	...	...	...	...	...	...
Charleston	CM	309	(843) 723-6716	Barrett Lawrimore	Michael O'Neal	Beverly Craven	Keith Bustraan	Barbara Demarco	James Cannon
Cherokee	CE	52	(864) 487-2560	Lemuel Parris	...	Katie Baines	Michael Vassey	Betty Vernon	Billy Blanton
Chester	CE	34	(803) 385-5133	...	...	...	...	...	...
Chesterfield	CE	42	(843) 623-2535	Bruce Rivers	William Frick	Elizabeth Eddins	...	Peggy Smith	Kenny Welch
Clarendon *	CM	32	(803) 435-9654	Dwight Stewart	William Houser	Betty Pritchard	Lynden Anthony	Linda Lemon	Randy Garrett
Colleton	C	38	(803) 549-5221	Steven Murdaugh	Douglas Burns	Ruth Mayer	...	...	George Malone
Darlington	CE	67	(843) 398-4104	...	...	Jessie Bishop	Phyllis Griffitts	...	Walter Campbell
Dillon *	CM	30	(843) 774-1400	Clarence McRae	William Young	Lisa Gray	...	...	Harold Grice
Dorchester	CM	96	(843) 563-0242	Randy Scott	Jason Ward	Sandy Lawley	Tommi Garrick	Anne Ayer	...
Edgefield	CE	24	(803) 637-4000	Charles Kneece	...	Barbara Stark	Teresa Strom	Lee Anderson	Adell Dobey
Fairfield	CM	23	(803) 635-1415	David Brown	Philip Hinely	Shryll Brown	Annie McDaniel	Callie Bell	Herman Young
Florence *	CM	125	(843) 665-3044	...	Richard Starks	Connie Haselden	Kevin Yokim	Bonita Andrews	William Boone
Georgetown	CE	55	(843) 546-4189	Johnny Morant	Henry Hemingway	Karen Scott	David Parks	...	A. Cribb
Greenville	CM	379	(864) 467-7150	Phyllis Henderson	Joseph Kernell	Theresa Kizer	...	Vivian Anthony	Stephen Loftis
Greenwood	CM	66	(864) 942-8501	...	Victor Carpenter	...	...	...	...
Hampton *	CE	21	(803) 914-2100	Hugh Gray	Sabrena Graham	Aline Newton	Mike Meyer	...	T. C. Smalls
Horry	CM	196	(843) 915-5230	Chandler Prosser	Danny Knight	Patricia Hartley	Beth Fryar	Patrick Owens	...
Jasper	CM	20	(843) 726-7702	Avery Cleland	Andrew Fulghum	Judith Frank	Ronald Malphrus	Edith Drayton	Benjamin Riley
Kershaw	CM	52	(803) 425-1500	Steve Kelly	Robert Boland	Mamie Jones	Steve Bratton	...	Stephen McCaskill
Lancaster *	CM	61	(803) 285-1565	Rudy Carter	Steve Willis	Irene Plyler	Veronica Thompson	Lisa Robinson	Barry Faile
Laurens	CM	69	(864) 984-5484	...	Ernest Segars	Betty Walsh	...	Columbus Stephens	James Moore
Lee	CE	20	(803) 484-5341	...	...	...	...	...	...
Lexington *	CM	216	(803) 359-8000	William Derrick	William Brooks	Diana Burnett	Larry Porth	Lori Adler	James Metts

Directory 1/10 **OFFICIALS IN U.S. COUNTIES 2,500 AND OVER IN POPULATION**
continued

Jurisdiction	Form of govern- ment	2000 Popu- lation	Main telephone number	Chief elected official	Appointed administrator	Clerk of the governing board	Chief financial officer	Director of personnel	Chief law enforcement official
SOUTH CAROLINA continued									
Marion	CE	35	(843) 423-8201	...	...	Susan Rivers	Samuel Sparkman	Grover McQueen	Fred Knight
Marlboro	* CM	28	(843) 479-5600	...	Robert Kimrey	Sheree Bowick	Peggy Trammel	...	George Reid
Mccormick	* CM	9	(864) 852-2231	Alonzo Harrison	Bruce Cooley	Jackie Bowers	Debbie Cromer	Tommy Shields	James Foster
Newberry	CE	36	(803) 321-2100	Mike Hawkins	...	Elizabeth Hulse	Phyllis Lombard	Kay Olbon	James Singleton
Oconee	C	66	(864) 638-4252	...	Dale Surrett	Jacqueline Turner	Gloria Breland	Marion Boyd	Larry Williams
Orangeburg	CM	91	(803) 533-6151	Harry Wimberly	Joseph Clark	Donna Owen	Ralph Guarino	Jennifer Graham	David Stone
Pickens	CE	110	(864) 898-5900	Jennifer Willis	...	Barbara Scott	Daniel Driggers	T. Hanna	Leon Lott
Richland	* CM	320	(803) 576-2050	Joseph McEachern	J. Milton Pope	Karen Whittle	...	Miriam McCoy	Jason Booth
Saluda	* C	19	(864) 445-4500	Thomas Horne	Sandra Padget	Deborah Ziegler	Alfred Rickett	Tony Bell	Chuck Wright
Spartanburg	CE	253	(864) 596-2525	Jeff Horton	Darryl Breed	Mary Blanding	Pam Craven	Lorraine Dennis	Anthony Dennis
Sumter	CE	104	(803) 773-1581	Vivian Fleming-McGhaney	William Noonan	Lisha Graham	Liz Brown	Jacquelyn Hailes	Kelvin Washington
Union	CM	29	(864) 429-1600	...	Richard Treme	Tonya Huell	Elizabeth Latham	Lisa Davidson	Bruce Bryant
Williamsburg	C	37	(843) 354-9321	...					
York	* CM	164	(803) 684-8511	Houston Motz	James Baker				
SOUTH DAKOTA									
Aurora	C	3	(605) 942-7752	...	...	...	...	...	...
Beadle	C	17	(605) 353-8400	Roger Chase	...	...	Connie Muth	...	Tom Beerman
Bennett	C	3	(605) 685-6931	...	...	...	...	...	...
Bon Homme	C	7	(605) 589-4212	Allen Sternhagen	...	Katherine Horacek	...	...	Marty Stanwick
Brookings	CM	28	(605) 696-8205	...	...	Janet Willmott	...	Stephanie Vogel	Mark Milbrandt
Brown	C	35	(605) 626-7110	Tom Fischbach	...	...	...	...	Darrell Miller
Brule	* CE	5	(605) 234-4430	Brad Carson	...	Judy Busack	Pamela Petrak	...	Wayne Willman
Buffalo	C	2	(605) 293-3217	Lloyd Lutter	...	...	...	Elaine Wulff	Richard Davis
Butte	C	9	(605) 892-4485	Donald Kivimaki	...	...	Sally Pflaumer	Lisa Schaefbauer	Lacey Perman
Campbell	C	1	(605) 955-3366	Arlene Odde	...	...	...	...	Ray Westendorf
Charles Mix	C	9	(605) 487-7131	...	...	Monica Walder	Norman Cihak	...	Rob McGraw
Clark	C	4	(605) 532-5921	Francis Hass	...	Nancy Worth	Kay Mahlen	...	Andrew Howe
Clay	* CE	13	(605) 677-7120	Leo Powell	...	Ruth Bremer	Kathryn Heles	Carrie Crum	Keith Olson
Codington	CM	25	(605) 882-6297	Ed Spevak	...	Cindy Brugman	Carol Maloney	...	Keith Gall
Corson	C	4	(605) 273-4229	Dorothy Schuh	...	Jessie VanLishout	...	...	David Miles
Custer	CE	7	(605) 673-8173	Joe McFarland	...	...	Chris Schutt	...	Douglas Nelson
Davison	C	18	(605) 995-8608	...	...	...	Kathy Goetsch	...	Lynn Pederson
Day	C	6	(605) 345-9500	...	...	...	...	...	Jim Fisher
Deuel	C	4	(605) 874-2330	Darold Hunt	...	...	Pam Lynde	...	...
Dewey	C	5	(605) 865-3672	Adele Enright	...	Jean Tehle	...	...	...
Douglas	CE	3	(605) 724-2423	...	...	...	...	...	...
Edmunds	C	4	(605) 426-6762	...	...	...	...	...	Jeffrey Tarrell
Fall River	C	7	(605) 745-5130	Glen Reaser	...	...	Sue Ganje	...	...
Faulk	C	2	(605) 598-6224	...	...	...	...	...	Michael McKernan
Grant	C	7	(605) 432-6711	Richard Berens	...	Karen Hooth	Karen Layher	...	Charles Wolf
Gregory	* CM	4	(605) 775-2664	...	...	...	James Waterbury	...	Larry Hanes
Haakon	* CM	2	(605) 859-2800	...	Rita O'Connell	Carol Schofield	Patricia Freeman	...	...
Hamlin	C	5	(605) 783-3201	...	...	...	...	...	Kurt Hall
Hand	C	3	(605) 853-2182	Larry Hurd	...	...	Betty Morford	...	...
Hanson	C	3	(605) 239-4714	...	...	...	...	...	...
Harding	C	1	(605) 375-3313	...	...	...	...	...	Mike Leidholt
Hughes	* CM	16	(605) 773-7451	...	Kevin Hipple	...	Shellie Baker	...	Jack Holden
Hutchinson	C	8	(605) 387-4212	Gillas Stern	...	Jerome Hoff	...	...	Mike Volek
Hyde	C	1	(605) 852-2519	...	...	Duane Johnson	Connie Conrad	...	Arlo Madsen
Jackson	C	2	(605) 837-2422	...	...	Harvey Byrd	Vicki Wilson	...	...
Jerauld	C	2	(605) 539-1202	...	...	...	...	...	...
Jones	C	1	(605) 669-2242	...	...	...	...	...	Charles Smith
Kingsbury	C	5	(605) 854-3832	Diane Schultz	...	...	...	...	Roger Hartman
Lake	C	11	(605) 256-7600	George Vanhove	...	...	Kay Schmidt	...	...
Lawrence	C	21	(605) 578-1941	...	...	...	...	...	Dennis Johnson
Lincoln	* C	24	(605) 764-2581	Otto Hagedorn	...	...	Paula Feucht	...	Donald Manger
Lyman	C	3	(605) 869-2247	Pam Michalek	...	Tracy Brakke	...	...	Dale Elsen
Marshall	C	4	(605) 448-2401	...	...	Julie Hagen	...	...	Eugene Taylor
Mc Cook	C	5	(605) 425-2791	...	...	...	Geralyn Sherman	...	David Ackerman
Mc Pherson	CE	2	(605) 439-3314	Steven Serr	...	...	...	...	Ron Merwin
Meade	* C	24	(605) 720-1625	Robert Mallow	...	...	Lisa Schieffer	Joell Romick	Tate Mallory
Mellette	CE	2	(605) 259-3291	Alvin Huber	...	...	Julie Dimond	...	Lanny Klinkhammer
Miner	C	2	(605) 772-4671	Rollin Schulz	...	...	Cindy Callies	...	Mike Milstead
Minnehaha	CM	148	(605) 367-4206	...	Ken McFarland	Sue Roust	...	Nora Buckman	Jerry Hoffman
Moody	CM	6	(605) 997-3161	...	...	...	Jean Larson	...	Don Holloway
Pennington	C	88	(605) 394-2153	Ken Davis	Ron Buskerud	...	Julie Pearson	...	Kelly Serr
Perkins	CM	3	(605) 244-5624	Mike Schweitzer	...	...	Fern Brockel	...	...
Potter	C	2	(605) 765-9408	...	...	...	...	...	Neil Long
Roberts	C	10	(605) 698-7336	Wayne Johnson	...	...	...	...	Thomas Fridley
Sanborn	C	2	(605) 796-4513	Diane Larson	...	...	...	...	Jeff Not Help Him
Shannon	C	12	(605) 745-3996	Connie Whirlwind Horse	...	...	...	...	Leslie Helm
Spink	C	7	(605) 472-4580	Gerald Zerbel	...	...	Barbara Lenling	...	Brad Rathbun
Stanley	C	2	(605) 223-7780	Donald Jacobson	...	Beverly Stoeser	Lola Scott	...	...
Sully	C	1	(605) 258-2541	...	...	...	...	...	Patrick Swallow
Todd	C	9	(605) 842-3727	Gregg Grimshaw	...	Louise Flisram	Kathleen Flakus	...	Clifford Schroeder
Tripp	C	6	(605) 842-3727	Ray Petersek	...	...	...	...	Byron Nogelmeier
Turner	CM	8	(605) 297-3153	...	...	Sheila Hagemann	...	...	Dan Limoges
Union	C	12	(605) 356-2101	...	...	...	Carol Klumper	...	Duane Mohr
Walworth	* C	5	(605) 649-7878	Jerry Frailing	...	Susan Eisemann	Gwenn Ackerman	...	Dave Hunhoff
Yankton	* C	21	(605) 260-4400	Bruce Jensen	...	...	Paula Jones	...	Robert Menzel
Ziebach	* C	2	(605) 365-5157	Clinton Farlee	...	...	Cindy Longbrake	...	
TENNESSEE									
Anderson	CE	71	(865) 457-5400	Rex Lynch	...	Jeff Cole	Gail Cook	...	Bill White
Bedford	CE	37	(931) 684-7944	Jimmy Woodson	...	...	Angie Petty	...	R. Parker
Benton	C	16	(731) 584-6011	Jimmy Wiseman	...	Wanda Malin	...	...	Tony King
Bledsoe	C	12	(423) 447-6855	Bill Wheeler	Sheri Pendergrass	...	...	...	Bob Swafford
Blount	CE	105	(865) 982-1302	...	...	Donna Simpson	...	...	Daniel Gilley
Bradley	C	87	(423) 476-0502	D. Davis	...	Sue Nance	Jeff Marlow	Michael Willis	Gary Perkins
Campbell	* CE	39	(423) 562-2526	Jeff Hall	J. H. Willoughby	...	...	...	Kenneth Wetzell
Cannon	CE	12	(615) 563-2320	Robert Gannon	...	...	...	...	Bendall Bartholomew
Carroll	C	29	(731) 986-1936	Kenny McBride	...	Mary Gouge	Jason Cody	...	John Henson
Carter	CE	56	(423) 542-1801	Raymond Fair	...	William Hall	Franklin Luppe	Clyde White	John Holder
Cheatham	CE	35	(615) 792-4316	William Orange	...	Johnny Garner	Lance Beshires	...	Paul Hodges
Chester	C	15	(731) 989-5672	Troy Kilzer	...	...	...	...	...
Claiborne	C	29	(423) 626-5236	...	...	Patricia Hix	...	...	Cecil Anderson
Clay	CE	7	(931) 243-2161	Frank Halsell	...	Janice Butler	Anne Williams	...	David Ramsey
Cocke	C	33	(423) 623-8791	Charles Moore	Bettye Carver	...	Marianna Edinger	...	Stephen Graves
Coffee	C	48	(931) 723-5100	David Pennington	...	...			

Directory 1/10   OFFICIALS IN U.S. COUNTIES 2,500 AND OVER IN POPULATION
continued

Jurisdiction	Form of govern-ment	2000 Popu-lation	Main telephone number	Chief elected official	Appointed administrator	Clerk of the governing board	Chief financial officer	Director of personnel	Chief law enforcement official
TENNESSEE continued									
Crockett	CE	14	(731) 696-5460	E. Dove	...	...	Gary Spraggins	...	Troy Klyce
Cumberland	C	46	(931) 484-6165	Brock Hill	...	Pete Stubbs	Nathan Brock	...	Butch Burgess
De Kalb	C	17	(615) 597-5175	...	Larry Webb	John Thweatt	...	...	Kenneth Pack
Decatur	C	11	(731) 852-2131	Kenneth Broadway	...	Randy Pope	...	...	Ronald Kenner
Dickson	C	43	(615) 789-7003	Linda Frazier	...	Phillip Simons	...	...	Tom Wall
Dyer	C	37	(731) 286-7800	...	...	...	...	...	...
Fayette *	CE	28	(901) 465-5202	Rhea Taylor	...	Sue Culver	...	...	Bobby Riles
Fentress	C	16	(931) 879-7713	...	...	...	...	...	...
Franklin	C	39	(931) 967-2905	Montgomery Adams	...	Nina Tucker	Joyce Miller	...	Mike Foster
Gibson	C	48	(731) 855-7613	Ronnie Riley	...	...	...	...	Joe Shepard
Giles	CE	29	(931) 363-5300	William Wakefield	...	Carol Wade	Judy Roberts	...	Eddie Bass
Grainger	C	20	(865) 828-3513	Michael Hammer	...	Barbara Jackson	...	...	Richard McElhaney
Greene	C	62	(423) 798-1775	...	...	...	...	...	...
Grundy	C	14	(931) 692-3718	Michael Partin	...	Jimmy Rogers	Beverly Myers	...	Robert Meeks
Hamblen	C	58	(423) 586-1931	David Purkey	...	Linda Wilder	...	Sonia Miller	Otto Purkey
Hamilton *	C	307	(423) 209-6180	Claude Ramsey	Jeannine Alday	William Knowles	Louis Wright	Rebecca Hunter	James Hammond
Hancock	C	6	(423) 733-4341	...	...	...	...	...	...
Hardeman	CE	28	(731) 658-3266	...	...	...	...	...	...
Hardin	C	25	(731) 925-9078	Kevin Davis	...	Connie Stephens	...	...	Sammy Davidson
Hawkins *	C	53	(423) 272-7359	Crockett Lee	...	Carroll Jenkins	...	...	Roger Christain
Haywood	C	19	(731) 772-1432	John Sharpe	...	Ann Medford	William Howse	...	Melvin Bond
Henderson	C	25	(731) 968-0122	...	...	...	...	...	...
Henry	C	31	(731) 642-5212	Brent Greer	Faye Scott	Jerry Bomar	...	...	David Bumpus
Hickman	C	22	(931) 729-2492	...	...	...	...	...	...
Houston	C	8	(931) 289-3633	George Clark	Ann Lewis	Robert Brown	Annette Baggett	...	Kenneth Barnes
Humphreys	C	17	(931) 296-7795	...	...	...	...	...	...
Jackson	C	10	(931) 268-9888	...	...	...	...	...	...
Jefferson	C	44	(865) 397-3800	Gary Holiway	Doug Moody	Rick Farrar	...	...	David Davenport
Johnson	C	17	(423) 727-9696	Dick Grayson	...	...	Peggy Doine	...	...
Knox	C	382	(865) 215-2321	Michael Ragsdale	William Arms	...	John Werner	Frances Fogerson	Timothy Hutchison
Lake	C	7	(731) 253-7382	Macie Roberson	...	Jo Ann Mills	...	...	Paul Jones
Lauderdale	C	27	(731) 635-3500	...	...	...	...	...	...
Lawrence	C	39	(931) 762-7700	Ametra Bailey	...	Chuck Kizer	Teresa Purcell	...	William Dorning
Lewis	CE	11	(931) 796-3378	Kenneth Turnbow	Johnny Clayton	Sandra Clayton	...	...	Dwayne Kilpatrick
Lincoln	C	31	(931) 433-2454	...	...	...	...	...	...
Loudon	C	39	(865) 458-4664	...	...	Riley Wampler	...	...	...
Macon *	C	20	(615) 666-2363	Shelvy Linville	Tammy Russell	...	Anita Hesson	Kristy Robert	Mark Gammons
Madison	C	91	(865) 397-3800	James Leech	Regetta Nelson	Freddie Pruitt	Gary Ligon	Tony White	David Woolfork
Marion	C	27	(423) 942-2552	Howell Moss	...	Patsy Hudson	...	...	Jim Webb
Marshall	CE	26	(931) 359-1279	...	...	...	...	...	...
Maury	C	69	(931) 375-2400	James Bailey	...	Nancy Thompson	Malinda Stanford	Shirley Harmon	Enoch George
Mc Minn *	CE	49	(423) 745-7634	Ronald Banks	...	Rhonda Cooley	Jason Luallen	...	Steve Frisbie
Mc Nairy	C	24	(731) 645-3472	Mike Smith	Fairy Hunter	Ronnie Price	Billy Wolfe	...	Paul Ervin
Meigs	C	11	(423) 334-5850	Ken Jones	...	Janie Rowland	...	...	Walter Hickman
Monroe	CE	38	(423) 442-3981	Allan Watson	Jean Samples	LouAnn Carmley	Brian Tallent	...	Doug Watson
Montgomery	CE	134	(931) 648-5715	Douglas Weiland	...	...	Rachel Reddick	Michael Moore	Norman Lewis
Moore	C	5	(931) 759-7076	...	...	...	...	...	...
Morgan	CE	19	(423) 346-6288	Larry Kilby	...	...	Brian Leopper	...	...
Obion	C	32	(731) 885-9611	...	...	...	...	...	...
Overton *	CE	20	(931) 823-5639	...	...	...	...	...	...
Perry	C	7	(931) 589-2216	...	...	...	...	...	...
Pickett *	CE	4	(931) 864-3798	Stephen Bilbrey	...	...	...	...	...
Polk	C	16	(423) 338-2841	...	...	...	...	...	...
Putnam	C	62	(931) 526-2161	...	...	...	...	...	...
Rhea	C	28	(423) 775-7803	Billy Patton	Lorraine Phillips	Linda Shaver	...	...	Mike Neah
Roane	C	51	(865) 376-5578	Kenneth Yager	...	Dorothy Marshall	...	...	David Haggard
Robertson	C	54	(615) 384-0202	Howard Bradley	...	Susan Atchley	...	...	Gene Bollinger
Rutherford	C	182	(615) 898-7795	Nancy Allen	Paul Long	Georgia Lynch	...	...	Truman Jones
Scott	C	21	(423) 663-2355	...	...	...	...	...	...
Sequatchie	CE	11	(423) 949-3479	David Barker	...	Charlotte Cagle	...	...	Ronnie Hitchcock
Sevier	C	71	(865) 453-6136	...	...	...	...	...	...
Shelby	CE	897	(901) 545-4342	A. C. Wharton	John Fowlkes	Jayne Creson	James Huntzicker	Paul Boyd	Mark Luttrell
Smith	C	17	(615) 735-2294	Michael Nesbitt	...	James Norris	...	Connie Gentry	Ronnie Lankford
Stewart	C	12	(931) 232-3100	Rickie Joiner	...	Jimmy Fitzhugh	...	...	John Vinson
Sullivan	C	153	(423) 323-6417	Steve Godsey	...	Jean Gammon	Larry Bailey	Gayvern Moore	J Wayne Anderson
Sumner *	C	130	(615) 442-1132	Anthony Holt	...	Bill Kemp	Rachel Nichols	Ann Whiteside	Bob Barker
Tipton	C	51	(901) 476-0219	...	...	...	...	...	...
Unicoi	C	17	(423) 743-9391	Larry Rose	...	...	...	...	David Harris
Union	CE	17	(865) 992-3061	...	...	...	...	...	...
Van Buren	CE	5	(931) 946-2314	...	...	...	...	...	...
Warren	C	38	(931) 473-2505	...	...	...	...	...	...
Washington	C	107	(423) 753-1666	...	...	...	...	...	...
Wayne	C	16	(931) 722-3653	Gilda Collie	...	Joey Horton	...	...	Carl Skelton
Weakley	CM	34	(731) 364-5413	...	...	...	...	...	...
White	C	23	(931) 836-3216	Herd Sullivan	...	Connie Jolley	Keith Ryder	...	James O'Conner
Williamson *	C	126	(615) 790-5700	Rogers Anderson	...	...	David Coleman	Michael Weber	Ricky Headley
Wilson	C	88	(615) 443-2630	...	...	...	...	...	...
TEXAS									
Anderson	C	55	(903) 723-7402	...	...	Wanda Burke	...	...	...
Andrews *	C	13	(915) 524-1401	Richard Dolgener	...	Kenda Heckler	Rod Noble	...	Sam Jones
Angelina	C	80	(936) 634-5413	Joe Berry	...	JoAn Chastain	Jesse Austin	...	David Henson
Aransas	CE	22	(361) 790-0124	Glenn Guillory	...	Peggy Friebele	...	...	Mark Gilliam
Archer *	C	8	(940) 574-4811	Gary Beesinger	...	Karren Winter	...	...	Staci Beesinger
Armstrong	C	2	(806) 226-3221	Edwin Reed	...	Joe Reck	Ronald Patterson	...	Carmella Jones
Atascosa	C	38	(830) 769-3093	Diana Bautista	...	Diane Gonzales	Staci Jones	...	Tommy Williams
Austin *	CE	23	(979) 865-5911	Carolyn Bilski	...	Carrie Gregor	Betty Jez	...	R. Burger
Bailey	C	6	(806) 272-3077	Marilyn Cox	...	Sherri Harrison	...	...	Richard Wills
Bandera	C	17	(830) 796-3781	Richard Evans	...	Bernice Bates	...	...	James MacMillan
Bastrop	C	57	(512) 332-7201	Ronnie McDonald	...	Shirley Wilhelm	Jim Wither	Robert Pena	Richard Hernandez
Baylor	CE	4	(940) 888-3553	James Coltharp	...	Clara Coker	...	...	Bob Elliott
Bee	CE	32	(361) 362-3260	David Silva	...	Mirella Davis	Susana Moron	...	Carlos Carrizales
Bell	C	237	(254) 933-5118	Jon Burrows	...	Vada Sutton	Donna Eakin	...	Dan Smith
Bexar	C	1392	(210) 335-2545	Nelson Wolff	...	Margaret Montemayor	David Smith	Veronica Sauceda	Ralph Lopez
Blanco	C	8	(830) 868-4266	George Byars	...	Dorothy Uecker	Doris Cage	...	William Elsbury
Borden	CM	..	(806) 756-4391	...	...	...	...	...	...
Bosque	C	17	(254) 435-2382	Cole Word	Jane Murphey	Betty Outlaw	...	...	Charles Jones
Bowie	C	89	(903) 628-6700	James Carlow	...	...	...	...	James Prince
Brazoria	C	241	(979) 849-5711	...	...	...	...	...	...
Brazos	C	152	(979) 775-7400	Alvin Jones	...	...	John Reynolds	Jennifer Salazar	Christopher Kirk

Directory 1/10   OFFICIALS IN U.S. COUNTIES 2,500 AND OVER IN POPULATION
continued

Jurisdiction	Form of govern- ment	2000 Popu- lation	Main telephone number	Chief elected official	Appointed administrator	Clerk of the governing board	Chief financial officer	Director of personnel	Chief law enforcement official
TEXAS continued									
Brewster	C	8	(915) 837-2412	...	...	...	...	...	Jeff Fuston
Briscoe	C	1	(806) 823-2131	Loyd Nance	...	Bena Hester	...	...	...
Brooks *	C	7	(361) 325-5604	Raul Ramirez	Mary Ann Pulido	Frutoso Garza	Corina Molina	...	Reynaldo Rodriguez
Brown	C	37	(915) 643-3254	...	...	...	...	...	...
Burleson	C	16	(979) 567-2305	...	...	...	...	...	...
Burnet	C	34	(512) 756-5420	Martin McLean	...	Janet Parker	...	...	Joe Pollock
Caldwell	C	32	(512) 398-1828	H. T. Wright	...	Nina Sells	...	...	Daniel Law
Calhoun	C	20	(361) 553-4610	Arlene Marshall	...	Janice Paul	Ben Comiskey	...	Burnard Browning
Callahan	CM	12	(915) 854-1399	Roger Corn	...	Jeanie Bohannon	...	...	Eddie Curtis
Cameron	CM	335	(956) 544-0827	Gilberto Hinojosa	...	...	Xavier Villarreal	Manuel Villarreal	...
Camp	C	11	(903) 856-3845	Preston Combest	...	Elaine Young	...	...	Charles Elonger
Carson	C	6	(806) 537-3622	...	...	...	...	...	...
Cass	C	30	(903) 756-5181	Charles McMichael	...	Jannis Mitchell	Carol Cox	...	Paul Boone
Castro *	C	8	(806) 647-3338	William Sava	...	Joyce Thomas	Celeste Jones	...	Sal Rivera
Chambers	C	26	(409) 267-8295	Frank Sylvia	Robert Sparks	Norma Rowland	Bonita McMurrey	...	Monroe Kreuzer
Cherokee	CM	46	(903) 683-2350	...	...	...	...	...	...
Childress	C	7	(940) 937-2221	...	...	...	...	...	...
Clay	C	11	(940) 538-5911	Kenneth Liggett	...	Kay Hutchison	...	...	Paul Benning
Cochran	C	3	(806) 266-5508	Robert Yeary	...	Rita Tyson	Danny Wiseley	...	Wallace Stalcup
Coke	C	3	(915) 453-2641	...	Stover Taylor	Mary Grim	...	...	Rick Styles
Coleman	C	9	(915) 625-4218	...	...	...	...	...	...
Collin	CM	491	(972) 548-4606	Ronald Harris	Bill Bilyeu	...	...	Cynthia Jacobson	Terry Box
Collingsworth	C	3	(806) 447-2408	...	...	Jackie Johnson	...	...	Russell Lee
Colorado	C	20	(979) 732-2604	Al Jamison	Raymie Kana	Darlene Hayek	...	...	Reinhard Wied
Comal *	CE	78	(830) 643-5859	Danny Scheel	...	Joy Streater	David Renken	Bob Grazioli	Bob Holder
Comanche	C	14	(915) 356-2466	...	...	...	...	...	...
Concho *	C	3	(915) 732-4321	Allen Amos	...	Barbara Hoffman	...	...	Richard Doane
Cooke	C	36	(940) 668-5433	...	...	...	...	...	...
Coryell	C	74	(254) 865-5911	...	...	...	...	...	...
Cottle	CE	1	(806) 492-3613	...	...	Jan Irons	...	...	Kenneth Burns
Crane	C	3	(432) 558-1100	John Farmer	...	Judy Crawford	Mindy Edmiston	...	Danny Simmons
Crockett	C	4	(915) 392-2965	...	...	...	...	...	...
Crosby *	CE	7	(806) 675-2241	Davey Abell	...	Linda Jones	Catherine Wall	...	David Barker
Culberson	C	2	(915) 283-2059	...	John Conoly	Linda McDonald	Francisco Gomez	...	Glenn Humphries
Dallam *	C	6	(806) 244-2450	David Field	...	Terri Banks	...	...	Bruce Scott
Dallas	C	2218	(214) 653-6067	Margaret Keliher	Jon Clemson	Paula Stephens	Ryan Brown	Mattye Taylor	James Bowles
Dawson	CE	14	(806) 872-7544	Sam Saleh	Don Stephens	Gloria Vera	Gene Defee	...	John Garcia
De Witt	C	20	(361) 275-2116	Ben Prause	...	Elva Petersen	Barbara Martin	...	Gary Edwards
Deaf Smith *	CE	18	(806) 363-7000	...	...	...	...	...	...
Delta	C	5	(903) 395-3030	Hugh Whitney	Clarica Burns	Patsy Barton	...	...	Benny Fisher
Denton	C	432	(940) 349-3080	Mary Horn	Patricia Larson	Cynthia Mitchell	James Wells	Amy Phillips	Weldon Lucas
Dickens	C	2	(806) 623-5532	...	...	...	...	...	...
Dimmit	CE	10	(830) 876-3569	...	...	...	...	...	...
Donley *	C	3	(806) 874-2328	Jack Hall	...	Fay Vargas	...	...	Charles Blackburn
Duval	C	13	(361) 279-3322	...	...	...	...	...	...
Eastland	C	18	(254) 629-1263	...	...	Cathy Jentho	Loretta Key	...	...
Ector	CE	121	(915) 498-4025	James Jordan	...	Barbara Bedford	David Austin	Patricia Mac Allister	Reginald Yearwood
Edwards	C	2	(830) 683-2235	...	...	...	...	...	...
El Paso *	CE	679	(915) 546-2218	Anthony Cobos	Jaime Perez	Delia Briones	Edward Dion	Betsy Keller	Richard Wiles
Ellis	C	111	(972) 825-5126	Chad Adams	...	...	Michael Navarro	...	...
Erath	C	33	(254) 965-1452	Tab Thompson	James Young	Nelda Crockett	...	...	Tommy Bryant
Falls	CM	18	(254) 883-1426	Thomas Sehon	...	Frances Braswell	...	...	Benell Kirk
Fannin *	C	31	(903) 583-7451	Butch Henderson	...	Tammy Rich	...	...	Kenneth Moore
Fayette	C	21	(979) 968-6469	Edward Janecka	...	Carolyn Roberts	Dan Von Rosenberg	...	Keith Korenek
Fisher	CE	4	(325) 776-3257	Marshal Bennett	Betty Vaught	Patricia Thomson	...	...	Mickey Counts
Floyd	C	7	(806) 983-4900	William Hardin	...	Marilyn Holcomb	...	...	Billy Gilmore
Foard	C	1	(940) 684-1365	Charlie Bell	...	Pat Aydelott	...	...	...
Fort Bend	C	354	(281) 341-8619	...	...	...	...	...	...
Franklin	C	9	(903) 537-2342	Gerald Hubbell	...	Betty Crane	...	...	...
Freestone	C	17	(903) 389-2635	...	...	...	...	...	...
Frio	C	16	(830) 334-2154	Carlos Garcia	...	Gloria Cubriel	...	...	...
Gaines	C	14	(432) 758-5411	Tom Keyes	...	...	...	...	Jon Key
Galveston	C	250	(409) 762-8621	...	...	...	...	Rosa Franco	...
Garza *	C	4	(000) 000-0000	Lee Norman	...	James Plummer	...	...	Cliff Laws
Gillespie	C	20	(830) 997-7502	Mark Stroeher	...	Mary Lynn Rusche	Nathan Craddock	...	Milton Jung
Glasscock	C	1	(915) 354-2415	...	...	...	...	...	...
Goliad	C	6	(512) 645-3337	...	...	...	...	...	Glen Sachtleben
Gonzales	C	18	(830) 672-6397	David Bird	...	Lee Riedel	...	...	Don Copeland
Gray	C	22	(806) 669-8001	Richard Peet	Elaine Morris	Wanda Carter	...	...	...
Grayson *	C	110	(903) 813-4091	Drue Bynum	...	...	James Rivers	Lee Salinas	J. Keith Gary
Gregg	C	111	(903) 758-6181	...	...	...	...	...	...
Grimes	C	23	(936) 873-2111	...	...	David Pasket	Joy Dymke	Phillis Allen	Donald Sowell
Guadalupe	CE	89	(830) 303-4188	Mike Wiggins	...	Teresa Kiel	Kristen Klein	...	...
Hale	C	36	(806) 291-5210	...	...	Deborah Williams	...	...	David Mull
Hall *	C	3	(806) 259-2511	Ray Powell	...	Raye Bailey	...	...	Tim Wiginton
Hamilton	C	8	(254) 386-3518	...	...	...	...	...	...
Hansford	C	5	(806) 659-4100	Benny Wilson	Cindy Scribner	Kim Vera	...	...	Gary Evans
Hardeman	C	4	(940) 663-2911	Kenneth McNabb	...	Linda Walker	...	...	Randy Akers
Hardin	C	48	(409) 246-5130	Billy Caraway	...	Glenda Alston	Freddie Barclay	...	Ed Cain
Harris	C	3400	(713) 755-8140	Robert Eckels	...	Beverly Kaufman	Barbara Schott	Joyce Cambric	Tommy Thomas
Harrison	C	62	(903) 923-4018	Wayne McWhorter	Marc Palmer	Patricia Cox	...	Velma McGlothin	William McCool
Hartley	CE	5	(806) 235-3572	Ronnie Gordon	...	Diane Thompson	...	...	Johnny Williams
Haskell	C	6	(940) 864-2851	David Davis	...	Rhonda Moeller	...	...	...
Hays	C	97	(512) 393-2215	...	...	...	...	...	...
Hemphill	C	3	(806) 323-6521	Bob Gober	...	Davene Hendershot	...	...	Billy Bowen
Henderson	C	73	(903) 675-6119	David Holstein	Wesley Johnston	Gwen Moffeit	Karen Smith	...	Ronny Brownlow
Hidalgo	C	569	(956) 318-2660	...	...	...	...	...	...
Hill	C	32	(254) 582-4060	Kenneth Davis	Susan Swilling	Ruth Pelham	...	...	Brent Button
Hockley	C	22	(806) 894-6070	Larry Sprowls	Gene Rush	Donna Stanley	...	...	Donald Caddell
Hood	C	41	(817) 579-3208	Don Cleveland	...	Lynn Dewberry	Lawrence Levine	...	William Hardin
Hopkins	CE	31	(903) 885-1178	...	...	...	...	...	Darrel Bobbitt
Houston	C	23	(936) 544-3255	R. Von Doenhoff	Louis Cook	Bridgett Lamb	...	...	Stan Parker
Howard *	CE	33	(432) 264-2218	Mark Barr	...	...	Jackie Olson	...	Jerry Kresta
Hudspeth	C	3	(915) 369-3511	Billy Love	...	Patricia Bramblett	James Peace	...	...
Hunt *	C	76	(903) 408-4100	...	...	Linda Brooks	...	...	Guy Rowh
Hutchinson	C	23	(806) 878-4010	Jack Worsham	...	Beverly Turner	...	...	Jimmy Mortin
Irion	C	1	(915) 835-4361	...	...	Riba Criner	...	...	...
Jack	C	8	(940) 567-2241	...	...	...	...	...	Andy Louderback
Jackson *	C	14	(361) 782-3402	Albert Stafford	Carole Darilek	Kenneth McElveen	...	...	Ronald McBride
Jasper	C	35	(409) 384-2461	Joe Folk	Druscilla Miller	Judith Wright	...	Donna Kelley	

Directory 1/10   OFFICIALS IN U.S. COUNTIES 2,500 AND OVER IN POPULATION
continued

Jurisdiction	Form of govern-ment	2000 Popu-lation	Main telephone number	Chief elected official	Appointed administrator	Clerk of the governing board	Chief financial officer	Director of personnel	Chief law enforcement official
TEXAS continued									
Jeff Davis	C	2	(915) 426-3968	Peggy Robertson	...	Sue Blackley	...	...	Steve Bailey
Jefferson	C	252	(409) 835-8400	Carl Griffith	...	Sandra Walker	James Swain	Cary Erickson	George Woods
Jim Hogg	C	5	(512) 527-3015	...	...	...	...	...	...
Jim Wells	C	39	(361) 668-5706	...	...	...	...	...	...
Johnson	C	126	(817) 556-6305	...	...	...	...	...	...
Jones	C	20	(915) 823-3741	...	...	...	...	...	...
Karnes	C	15	(830) 780-3938	Alfred Pawelek	...	Elizabeth Swize	Arline Matthews	...	...
Kaufman	CE	71	(972) 932-4331	...	...	...	...	...	...
Kendall	C	23	(830) 249-9343	James Gooden	...	Darlene Herrin	...	...	Henry Hodge
Kenedy	C	..	(512) 294-5224	...	...	...	...	...	...
Kent	CE	..	(806) 237-3381	...	...	...	...	...	...
Kerr *	C	43	(830) 792-2211	...	...	Jannett Pieper	...	...	William Hierholzer
Kimble *	C	4	(915) 446-2724	Delbert Roberts	...	Haydee Torres	...	...	...
King	C	..	(806) 596-4411	Royce McLaury	...	Linda Lewis	...	...	Terry Lambeth
Kinney	C	3	(830) 563-2401	Herbert Senne	...	Dora Sandoval	Sandra Fitzpatrick	...	Leland Burgess
Kleberg	C	31	(361) 595-8585	Pete De La Garza	...	Sam Deanda	...	...	Winston Kelly
Knox	C	4	(940) 454-2191	...	...	...	...	...	...
La Salle	C	5	(830) 879-2117	...	...	...	...	...	...
Lamar	C	48	(903) 737-2410	M. Superville	...	Kathy Marlowe	Kevin Parsons	...	B. McCoy
Lamb	C	14	(806) 385-4222	Wayne Whiteaker	...	Bill Johnson	...	...	Jerry Collins
Lampasas	C	17	(512) 556-8271	...	Wayne Boultinghouse	Connie Hartmann	...	...	Gordon Morris
Lavaca	C	19	(512) 798-2301	...	...	...	...	...	...
Lee	C	15	(979) 542-3178	Evan Gonzales	...	Carol Dismukes	...	...	Joe Goodson
Leon	C	15	(903) 536-2331	Byron Ryder	...	Carla McEachern	Donald Doucet	...	Larry Watson
Liberty	C	70	(936) 336-8071	...	...	...	...	...	...
Limestone *	C	22	(254) 729-5504	Daniel Burkeen	...	Peggy Beck	Deborah Watson	...	Dennis Wilson
Lipscomb	C	3	(806) 862-3821	Willis Smith	...	Kimberly Blau	...	...	James Robertson
Live Oak	C	12	(361) 449-2733	James Huff	Traginia Smith	Mildred James	Violet Person	...	Larry Busby
Llano *	C	17	(325) 247-7730	R. G. Floyd	...	Bette Hoy	...	...	Nathan Garrett
Loving	C	..	(915) 377-2362	Donald Creager	Janie Parker	Beverly Hanson	...	...	Richard Putnam
Lubbock	C	242	(806) 775-1097	Thomas Head	...	Anna Davidson	...	...	Charles Bartley
Lynn	C	6	(806) 561-4222	John Brandon	...	Susan Tipton	...	...	Charles Smith
Madison	C	12	(936) 348-2670	Cecil Neely	Melissa Mosley	...	...	...	Daniel Douget
Marion	CM	10	(903) 665-3261	Gene Terry	...	Betty Smith	Shanna Fuquay	...	William McCay
Martin	C	4	(915) 756-3631	Charles Blocker	...	Susan Hull	H. Howard	...	C. Welling
Mason	CE	3	(325) 347-5556	Jerry Bearden	...	Beatrice Langehennig	...	...	Clint Low
Matagorda	CE	37	(979) 244-7680	...	...	...	...	...	...
Maverick	C	47	(830) 773-3824	Rogelio Escobedo	...	Sara Montemayor	Carlos Pereda	...	Salvador Rios
Mc Culloch	C	8	(915) 597-0733	Randy Young	...	Tina Smith	...	...	Clyde Howell
Mc Lennan	C	213	(254) 757-5158	James Lewis	...	...	Steve Moore	Terrence Powers	Jack Harwell
Mc Mullen	C	..	(512) 274-3341	...	...	Nell Hodgin	...	Elaine Franklin	W. Potts
Medina	C	39	(830) 741-6000	David Montgomery	Jennifer Adlong	Elva Miranda	...	...	Gilberto Rodriguez
Menard	C	2	(915) 396-4789	Charles Childers	...	Elsie Maserang	...	...	Clay Wagner
Midland	CE	116	(432) 688-4310	William Morrow	...	Shauna Brown	...	...	Gary Painter
Milam	C	24	(254) 697-6596	Frank Summers	...	La Verne Soefje	Jeanie Hrozek	...	Charles West
Mills	C	5	(325) 648-2222	...	...	Carolyn Foster	...	...	Douglas Storey
Mitchell	C	9	(325) 728-8356	Ray Mayo	...	Debby Carlock	Susan Buckalew	...	Patrick Toombs
Montague	C	19	(940) 894-2401	James Kittrell	...	Gayle Edwards	Brenda Milligan	...	Chris Hamilton
Montgomery	C	293	(936) 756-0561	Alan Sadler	...	Mark Turnbull	Linda Breazeale	Diane Bass	Tommy Gage
Moore	C	20	(806) 935-5588	Kari Campbell	...	Brenda McKanna	...	...	J. DeArmond
Morris	C	13	(903) 645-3691	J. Jennings	...	Vicki Camp	...	...	...
Motley *	C	1	(806) 347-2334	Ed Smith	...	Kate Hurt	...	...	Michael Crutchley
Nacogdoches	C	59	(936) 560-7755	Susan Kennedy	Clara Flores	Carol Wilson	...	...	Thomas Kerss
Navarro	C	45	(903) 654-3090	...	...	...	...	...	...
Newton	C	15	(409) 379-5691	Truman Dougharty	...	Mary Cobb	...	...	Wayne Powell
Nolan *	C	15	(915) 235-2263	Tim Fambrough	...	Pat McGowan	Judy Kasper	...	Jim Kelly
Nueces	C	313	(361) 888-0111	Richard Borchard	Edward Castoria	Ernest Briones	Margaret Hayes	Elsa Saenz	Larry Olivares
Ochiltree	C	9	(806) 435-8075	...	...	...	...	...	...
Oldham	C	2	(806) 267-2607	Don Allred	...	Rebecca Groneman	...	...	David Medlin
Orange	C	84	(409) 883-7740	Carl Thibodeaux	...	...	...	...	Michael White
Palo Pinto	C	27	(940) 659-1253	Mickey West	...	...	Sharon Allen	...	Larry Watson
Panola	C	22	(903) 693-3091	John Cordray	...	Mickey Dorman	Sidney Burns	...	Paul Ellett
Parker	C	88	(817) 599-6591	Mark Riley	...	Alice Brunson	...	Jim Thorp	Leonard Brown
Parmer	C	10	(806) 481-3383	...	...	...	...	...	...
Pecos	C	16	(432) 336-3461	Joe Shuster	Kay Hardwick	Judy Deerfield	...	...	Clifton Harris
Polk *	C	41	(936) 327-6802	John Thompson	...	Barbara Middleton	Ray Stelly	Jeanette Montgomery	Kenneth Hammack
Potter	C	113	(806) 349-4835	Arthur Ware	...	Sue Daniel	Kerry Hood	Janie Brown	Michael Shumate
Presidio	C	7	(915) 729-4452	...	...	...	...	...	...
Rains	CM	9	(903) 474-9999	Joe Dougherty	...	Linda Wallace	...	...	Richard Wilson
Randall	C	104	(806) 468-5500	Ernie Houdashell	...	Sue Bartolino	Bob Raef	...	Joel Richardson
Reagan	C	3	(915) 884-2233	Mike Elkins	Jane Gay	Terri Pullig	...	...	Efrain Gonzales
Real	C	3	(830) 232-5304	W. Sansom	...	Bella Rubio	...	...	James Brice
Red River	C	14	(903) 427-2401	...	...	...	...	...	...
Reeves	C	13	(915) 445-4503	Jimmy Galindo	...	Dianne Florez	Lynn Owens	Belinda Salcido	Arnulfo Gomez
Refugio	C	7	(361) 526-4223	Roger Fagan	...	Ruby Garcia	Diana Moss	...	James Hodges
Roberts *	C	..	(806) 868-3721	Vernon Cook	...	Donna Goodman	DeAnn Williams	...	Dana Miller
Robertson	C	16	(979) 828-3542	...	...	...	...	...	...
Rockwall	C	43	(972) 882-0200	Bill Bell	...	Lisa Constant	John Blackwood	...	Harold Eavenson
Runnels	C	11	(325) 365-2633	Marilyn Egan	...	Elesa Ocker	Darlene Smith	...	William Baird
Rusk *	C	47	(903) 657-0302	Sandra Hodges	Carolyn Walters	Joyce Lewis	Ronald Moody	...	Danny Pirtle
Sabine	CE	10	(409) 787-3543	...	...	...	...	...	...
San Augustine	C	8	(936) 275-2762	...	...	...	...	...	...
San Jacinto	CM	22	(936) 653-4331	Fritz Faulkner	...	Charlene Vann	...	...	...
San Patricio	C	67	(361) 364-6272	...	...	...	...	Norma Rivera	...
San Saba	C	6	(915) 372-3635	Harlen Barker	...	Kim Wells	...	...	John Wells
Schleicher	C	2	(915) 853-2766	Johnny Griffin	...	Peggy Williams	...	...	David Doran
Scurry	C	16	(915) 573-5332	...	...	...	...	...	...
Shackelford	C	3	(915) 762-2232	Ross Montgomery	...	Cheri Hawkins	...	...	Larry Bonner
Shelby	C	25	(936) 598-3535	Floyd Watson	...	Allison Harbison	Tracey Strong	...	Newton Johnson
Sherman	C	3	(806) 396-2021	...	...	...	...	...	...
Smith	C	174	(903) 590-2600	Larry Raig	...	Judy Carnes	Nancy Braswell	Denise Rebolini	...
Somervell	C	6	(254) 897-2322	...	...	...	...	...	...
Starr	CE	53	(956) 487-5223	Jose Martinez	Bernardo Garcia	Maria Gutierrez	Mario Lopez	Elisa Beas	Rene Fuentes
Stephens	C	9	(254) 559-2190	...	...	...	...	...	...
Sterling	C	1	(915) 378-8511	Robert Browne	...	Diane Haar	...	...	Charlie Howard
Stonewall	C	1	(254) 989-3393	...	...	...	...	...	...
Sutton	CE	4	(915) 387-2711	Carla Garner	...	Bobbie Smith	Charles Graves	...	Bill Webster
Swisher	C	8	(806) 995-3504	Harold Keeter	...	Brenda Hudson	...	...	Larry Stewart
Tarrant	CM	1446	(817) 884-1111	Tom Vandergriff	G. Maenius	Suzanne Henderson	S. Tidwell	Gerald Wright	Dee Anderson
Taylor	CE	126	(915) 674-1380	...	...	Janice Lyons	B. McDowell	...	...

Directory 1/10   OFFICIALS IN U.S. COUNTIES 2,500 AND OVER IN POPULATION
continued

Jurisdiction	Form of govern- ment	2000 Popu- lation	Main telephone number	Chief elected official	Appointed administrator	Clerk of the governing board	Chief financial officer	Director of personnel	Chief law enforcement official
TEXAS continued									
Terrell	C	1	(432) 345-2391	...	...	...	...	...	...
Terry	C	12	(806) 637-6421	Douglas Ryburn	Alan Bayer	Ann Willis	...	...	...
Throckmorton	CE	1	(940) 849-3081	...	...	...	...	...	...
Titus	CM	28	(903) 572-8101	Danny Crooks	...	Sherry Mars	Carl Johnson	...	Arvel Shepard
Tom Green	C	104	(915) 659-5202	Michael Brown	...	Elizabeth McGill	Ed Sturivant	Milly Wilson	Dan Gray
Travis	C	812	(512) 854-9020	Samuel Biscoe	...	Dana DeBeauvoir	Christian Smith	Linda Moore Smith	Margo Frasier
Trinity	C	13	(936) 642-1443	...	...	...	...	...	...
Tyler	C	20	(409) 283-3054	Jacques Blanchette	...	Donece Gregory	...	...	Jessie Wolf
Upshur	C	35	(903) 843-3083	...	...	Monetta Sides	Elizabeth Craig	...	Dan Brown
Upton	* C	3	(432) 693-2321	Vikki Bradley	...	Lucille Hutcherson	Alice Chapman	Lydia Steele	Beaumont Watkins
Uvalde	C	25	(830) 278-3216	William Mitchell	Valerie Ramos	Elena Cardenas	Frank Lowe	Gloria Villarreal	D' Wayne Jernigan
Val Verde	C	44	(830) 774-7543	Mike Fernandez	...	Elizabeth Everitt	...	...	R. Burnett
Van Zandt	C	48	(903) 567-2551	Jeffrey Fisher	...	Val Havar	Judy McAdams	Joyce Dean	Michael Ratcliff
Victoria	CE	84	(361) 578-0752	Helen Walker	...	James Patton	Dan Clower	...	Victor Graham
Walker	C	61	(936) 436-4910	Sherri Pegoda	...	...	...	...	...
Waller	C	32	(979) 826-3357	...	...	...	...	...	...
Ward	C	10	(915) 943-3209	...	...	...	...	...	...
Washington	CM	30	(979) 277-6200	...	...	...	...	...	...
Webb	C	193	(956) 721-2500	...	...	...	...	...	...
Wharton	C	41	(979) 532-4612	Lawrence Naiser	...	Sandra Sanders	Donna Thorton	...	Jess Howell
Wheeler	C	5	(806) 826-5544	...	...	...	...	...	...
Wichita	C	131	(940) 766-8100	Woodrow Gossom	...	Lloyd Lueck	Deborah Stevens	Michele Arseneau	Thomas Callahan
Wilbarger	C	14	(940) 553-2300	Gary Streit	...	Fran McGee	...	...	David Quisenberry
Willacy	C	20	(956) 689-2710	...	...	...	...	...	...
Williamson	C	249	(512) 930-4300	John Doerfler	...	...	...	...	James Wilson
Wilson	C	32	(830) 393-3126	...	...	Eva Martinez	...	...	...
Winkler	C	7	(915) 586-2526	Bonnie Leck	Kay Warren	Sonja Fullen	...	...	Robert Roberts
Wise	CE	48	(940) 627-5743	Dick Chase	...	Sherry Parker-Lemmon	Ann McCuiston	...	David Walker
Wood	C	36	(903) 763-4186	William Alexander	Becky Burford	Brenda Taylor	...	...	Billy Skinner
Yoakum	C	7	(806) 456-8794	Dallas Brewer	Hazel Lowrey	Deborah Rushing	...	...	Don Corzine
Young	* C	17	(940) 362-4301	Stephen Crawford	...	Carolyn Collins	Cheryl Roberts	...	Bryan Walls
Zapata	C	12	(956) 765-9920	Norma Ramirez	Maria Villarreal	Consuelo Villarreal	Alejandro Ramirez	Sylvia Mendoza	Sigifredo Gonzalez
Zavala	C	11	(830) 374-2442	Joe Luna	...	Oralia Trevino	Carlos Pereda	...	...
UTAH									
Beaver	C	6	(801) 438-6463	...	...	...	...	...	...
Box Elder	C	42	(435) 734-3347	Clark Davis	...	LuAnn Adams	Tom Bennett	Peggy Madsen	J. Yeates
Cache	C	91	(435) 755-1850	M. Lemon	...	Jill Zollinger	Tamra Stones	James Smith	G. Nelson
Carbon	C	20	(435) 637-4700	...	...	...	Keri Pallesen	...	Richard Esslworth
Daggett	* C	..	(435) 784-3210	Stewart Leith	...	...	...	Mel Miles	Bud Cox
Davis	* C	238	(801) 451-3415	Bret Millburn	...	...	Steve Rawlings	Carrie Mascaro	Mervin Gustin
Duchesne	C	14	(435) 738-1144	Larry Ross	...	Diane Freston	...	...	...
Emery	C	10	(801) 381-2119	...	...	...	...	...	...
Garfield	C	4	(435) 676-8826	...	...	...	...	...	Jim Nyland
Grand	CM	8	(435) 259-1321	...	Judy Bane	Fran Townsend	Joseph Gubler	Claire Dalton	David Benson
Iron	C	33	(435) 477-8332	Dennis Stowell	...	David Yardley	...	...	Alden Orme
Juab	C	8	(435) 623-3410	William Howarth	Michael Seely	Patricia Ingram	...	...	Lamont Smith
Kane	C	6	(435) 644-2458	Norman Carroll	...	...	...	...	...
Millard	C	12	(801) 743-6223	...	...	...	Stacy Lafitte	Eileen Nelson	Gene Ercanbrack
Morgan	C	7	(801) 845-4018	Reed Wilde	...	...	...	...	...
Piute	C	1	(435) 577-2840	...	...	...	Pamela Shaul	...	Dale Stacey
Rich	C	1	(435) 793-2415	Norman Weston	...	...	Craig Sorensen	Felix McGowan	...
Salt Lake	C	898	(801) 468-3000	Nancy Workman	Doug Willmore	Sherrie Swensen	John Fellmeth	...	Mike Lacy
San Juan	CM	14	(435) 587-3225	J. Lewis	Richard Bailey	Norman Johnson	Ilene Frischknecht	...	Kevin Holman
Sanpete	C	22	(435) 835-2142	Claudia Jarrett	...	Sandy Neill	...	Patricia Langston	Neldon Torgerson
Sevier	* C	18	(435) 893-0400	Gary Mason	...	Steven Wall	Blake Frazier	...	David Edmunds
Summit	C	29	(435) 336-3247	Sally Elliot	Brian Bellamy	Kent Jones	Michael Jensen	Pamela Ayala	Frank Park
Tooele	C	40	(435) 843-3100	Dennis Rockwell	...	Dennis Ewing	...	...	...
Uintah	C	25	(435) 781-0770	...	...	...	Danene Jackson	Lana Jensen	James Tracy
Utah	C	368	(801) 851-8158	Jerry Grover	...	Kim Jackson	...	...	Michael Spanos
Wasatch	C	15	(435) 654-3211	...	...	Brent Titcomb	...	Alis Ritz	Glenwood Humphries
Washington	C	90	(801) 634-5700	Gayle Aldred	...	Calvin Robison	...	...	...
Wayne	* C	2	(435) 836-2765	Thomas Jeffery	...	Ryan Torgerson	...	Brad Dee	Brad Slater
Weber	C	196	(801) 399-8408	Glen Burton	...	Linda Lunceford	...	...	...
VERMONT									
Addison	C	35	(802) 388-7741	...	...	...	...	...	...
Bennington	CE	36	(802) 442-8528	...	...	...	...	...	...
Caledonia	C	29	(802) 748-6600	Roy Vance	...	Kathleen Pearl	Edward Senecal	...	Michael Bergeron
Chittenden	C	146	(802) 863-3467	...	...	Diane Lavallee	...	...	...
Essex	C	6	(802) 676-3910	...	...	...	...	...	...
Franklin	C	45	(802) 524-3863	...	...	...	...	...	...
Grand Isle	C	6	(802) 372-8350	...	...	...	...	...	...
Lamoille	C	23	(802) 888-2207	...	...	...	...	...	...
Orange	CM	28	(802) 685-4610	Patricia Davis	Donald Hisey	Rodney Ackerman	...	...	Dennis McClure
Orleans	C	26	(802) 334-5136	Karin Zisselsberger	Kenneth Magoon	Charles Blake	...	...	David Winslow
Rutland	C	63	(802) 775-4394	...	...	...	...	...	...
Washington	C	58	(802) 828-2091	...	...	...	...	...	...
Windham	C	44	(802) 365-7979	...	...	...	...	...	...
Windsor	C	57	(802) 457-2121	...	...	...	...	...	...
VIRGINIA									
Accomack	CE	38	(757) 787-5700	Gregory Duncan	Steven Miner	Samuel Cooper	Reed Ennis	Linda Warner	Robert Crockett
Albemarle	CM	79	(434) 296-5841	Charlotte Humphris	Robert Tucker	Ella Carey	Melvin Breeden	J. Jennings	John Miller
Alleghany	* CM	12	(540) 863-6600	Cletus Nicely	John Strutner	Melissa Landis	Susan Myers	...	Kevin Helms
Amelia	CM	11	(804) 561-3039	...	Thomas Harris	...	...	...	...
Amherst	CE	31	(434) 946-9400	Leon Parrish	...	Roy Mayo	...	...	L. J. Ayers
Appomattox	* C	13	(434) 352-2637	William Craft	Aileen Ferguson	Barbara Williams	...	...	Oscar Staples
Arlington	CM	189	(703) 228-3000	Paul Ferguson	Ron Carlee	Antoinette Copeland	Jeffrey Bergin	Marcia Foster	Michael Scott
Augusta	CM	65	(540) 245-5600	...	Patrick Coffield	John Davis	Joseph Davis	Faith Souder	Randall Fisher
Bath	CM	5	(540) 839-7221	Percy Nowlin	...	...	...	...	Charles Black
Bedford	* CE	60	(540) 586-7601	...	Kathleen Guzi	...	Susan Crawford	Cheryl Dean	Michael Brown
Bland	* C	6	(276) 688-4622	Jason Ramsey	Jonathan Sweet	...	Teresa Tolbert	Carol Hall	Jerry Thompson
Botetourt	* CM	30	(540) 473-8220	Don Assaid	Gerald Burgess	...	Anthony Zerrilla	Mary Blackburn	Ronald Sprinkle
Brunswick	CM	18	(434) 848-3107	Bernard Jones	Charlotte Woolridge	Tammy Newcomb	Marilyn Brammer	Correna Roark	James Woodley
Buchanan	CE	26	(276) 935-6500	...	...	James Berins	Vonda Slone	...	Paul Crouse
Buckingham	CM	15	(434) 969-4242	Joe Chambers	Rebecca Carter	...	Karl Carter	...	Danny Williams
Campbell	CM	51	(434) 332-9525	J. D. Puckett	R. Laurrell	Deborah Hughes	Alan Lane	Shameka Wright	Terry Gaddy
Caroline	CM	22	(804) 633-5380	Calvin Taylor	Percy Ashcraft	Ray Campbell	John Sieg	...	Homer Johnson
Carroll	CE	29	(276) 728-3331	...	...	Ronald Newman	...	...	...

Directory 1/10   OFFICIALS IN U.S. COUNTIES 2,500 AND OVER IN POPULATION
continued

Jurisdiction		Form of govern-ment	2000 Popu-lation	Main telephone number	Chief elected official	Appointed administrator	Clerk of the governing board	Chief financial officer	Director of personnel	Chief law enforcement official
VIRGINIA continued										
Charles City		CM	6	(804) 829-2401	Michael Holmes	...	...	...	...	Beverley Washington
Charlotte	*	CM	12	(434) 542-5117	...	Russell Clark	Stuart Fallen	Norma Tuck	...	Thomas Jones
Chesterfield		CE	259	(804) 748-1551	Arthur Warren	James Stegmaier	Lisa Elko	Barry Condrey	Kristin Brown	Thierry Dupuis
Clarke		CM	12	(540) 955-5100	A. Dunning	David Ash	James Wood	Thomas Judge	...	...
Craig	*	CM	5	(540) 864-5010	Helen Looney	Richard Flora	...	...	...	Clifford Davidson
Culpeper		CM	34	(540) 727-3427	John Coates	Frank Bossio	...	Valerie Lamb	Susanne Taylor	Harlan Hart
Cumberland	*	CM	9	(804) 492-3625	William Osl	Judy Ownby	...	...	...	Darrell Hodges
Dickenson	*	CE	16	(276) 926-1676	Donnie Rife	Mark Vanover	Richard Edwards	Ronald Triplett	Betty Hill	Bobby Hammons
Dinwiddie		CE	24	(804) 469-4500	Harrison Moody	...	Alma Russell	Glenice Townsend	...	Samuel Shands
Essex		CE	9	(804) 443-4331	Margaret Davis	David Whitlow	...	...	...	Stanley Clarke
Fairfax		CM	969	(703) 324-2000	...	Anthony Griffin	Nancy Vehrs	...	Peter Schroth	John Manger
Fauquier	*	CM	55	(540) 347-8600	Henry Atherton	Paul McCulla	...	Janice Bourne	Francine Bouldin	Charlie Fox
Floyd	*	CM	13	(540) 745-9300	David Ingram	Daniel Campbell	...	...	...	Shannon Zeman
Fluvanna		CE	20	(434) 591-1910	Andrew Sheridan	...	Alice Jones	Brenda Browning	...	Ryant Washington
Franklin	*	CM	47	(540) 483-3033	W. Angell	Richard Huff	Alice Hall	Vincent Copenhaver	Phyllis Scott	E. Hunt
Frederick		CM	59	(540) 665-5600	Richard Shickle	John Riley	Rebecca Hogan	Cheryl Shiffler	Paula Nofsinger	Robert Williamson
Giles		CE	16	(540) 921-2525	Howard Morris	John Talbott	Scarlet Ratcliffe	...	...	Larry Falls
Gloucester	*	CM	34	(804) 693-4042	Teresa Altemus	Brenda Garton	Dawn Hobgood	Nickie Champion	Patricia Michura	Steve Gentry
Goochland		CM	16	(804) 556-5300	Andrew Pryor	Gregory Wolfrey	...	...	Cynthia Clements	James Agnew
Grayson		CM	17	(276) 773-2471	...	Donald Young	Charles Sturgill	...	...	Jerry Wilson
Greene		CE	15	(434) 985-5201	Steve Catalano	...	Marie Durer	Tracy Morris	...	Scott Haas
Greensville		CM	11	(434) 348-4205	Peggy Wiley	Kenneth Whittington	...	Brenda Parson	Alice Whitby	Wyatt Lee
Halifax	*	CM	37	(434) 476-3300	William Fitzgerald	Jerry Gwaltney	...	Stephanie Jackson	...	Stanley Noblin
Hanover		CM	86	(804) 537-6000	John Gordon	Cecil Harris	...	Terry Stone	Nan Eddleton	V. Cook
Henrico	*	CM	262	(804) 501-4386	David Kaechele	Virgil Hazelett	Barry Lawrence	John Vithoulkas	George Cauble	Henry Stanley
Henry		CE	57	(276) 634-4601	...	Ralph Summerlin	...	Jimmie Wright	...	Frank Cassell
Highland		C	2	(540) 468-2447	...	...	...	...	...	...
Isle Of Wight	*	CM	29	(757) 357-3191	Stan Clark	W. Caskey	Carey Storm	Liesl DeVary	Emily Haywood	Charles Phelps
James City	*	CM	48	(757) 253-6728	Jay Harrison	Sanford Wanner	...	John McDonald	Carol Luckam	Emmett Harmon
King & Queen		CM	6	(804) 785-5975	...	...	...	...	...	Earnest Walton
King George	*	CE	16	(540) 775-9181	James Howard	Travis Quesenberry	...	...	...	C. Dobson
King William		CM	13	(804) 769-4926	C. Thomas Redd	Frank Pleva	Marian White	...	...	Jeffrey Walton
Lancaster		CM	11	(804) 462-5129	Patrick Frere	William Pennell	Constance Kennedy	...	...	Ronald Crockett
Lee		CM	23	(276) 346-7714	James Sutphin	David Poe	Beverly Anderson	...	...	Gary Parsons
Loudoun		CM	211	(703) 777-0213	Scott York	Kirby Bowers	Gary Clemens	Mark Adams	Susan Hack	Stephen Simpson
Louisa		CM	25	(540) 967-0401	Fitzgerald Barnes	C. Lintecum	Susan Hopkins	...	Sherry Vena	Ashland Fortune
Lunenburg		C	13	(434) 696-2142	...	Catherine Giorgetti	...	...	...	Wesley Adams
Madison		C	12	(540) 948-6700	...	Stephen Utz	...	Teresa Jones	...	Robert Russell
Mathews		CE	9	(804) 725-7172	Geneva Putt	Stephen Whiteway	Eugene Callis	...	...	Danny Howlett
Mecklenburg		CM	32	(434) 738-6191	...	Polly Johnson	...	...	...	...
Middlesex		CE	9	(804) 758-4330	...	...	...	...	...	...
Montgomery	*	CM	83	(540) 382-5700	Annette Perkins	B. Goodman	Vickie Swinney	Angela Hill	Karen Edmonds	James Whitt
Nelson		CM	14	(434) 263-7000	Thomas Harvey	Stephen Carter	Judith Smythers	Debra McCann	...	Gary Brantley
New Kent	*	CM	13	(804) 966-9861	...	John Budesky	...	Mary Altemus	Darla Stanley	Farrar Howard
Northampton	*	CM	13	(757) 678-0440	Jeffrey Walker	Katherine Nunez	Traci Johnson	Glenda Miller	...	John Robbins
Northumberland		CE	12	(804) 580-7666	Daniel Pritchard	Kenneth Eads	J. Steve Thomas	...	...	L. Middleton
Nottoway		CE	15	(434) 645-8696	...	Ronald Roark	James King	...	...	Larry Parrish
Orange		CE	25	(540) 672-3313	Roderic Slayton	William Rolfe	Linda Timmon	Valerie Lamb	...	Charles Feldman
Page		CM	23	(540) 743-4142	Tommy LaFrance	Mark Belton	...	...	...	Daniel Presgraves
Patrick		CE	19	(276) 694-6094	David Young	...	Susan Gasterini	...	...	...
Pittsylvania		CE	61	(434) 432-7700	Michael Irby	William Sleeper	...	Kimberly Vanderhyde	...	Grover Plaster
Powhatan		CM	22	(804) 598-5610	Robert Cosby	Carolyn Cios	...	...	Stephanie Davis	Lynn Woodcock
Prince Edward		CM	19	(434) 392-8837	William Fore	Mildred Hampton	Machelle Eppes	...	...	Travis Harris
Prince George	*	CM	33	(804) 722-8600	Henry Parker	John Kines	Teresa Knott	Saa'dia Talbert	Rose Ford	Edward Frankenstein
Prince William		CM	280	(703) 792-6640	Sean Connaughton	Craig Gerhart	...	Christopher Martino	Cleil Fitzwater	Charlie Deane
Pulaski	*	CE	35	(540) 980-7705	Joseph Sheffey	Peter Huber	Gena Hanks	Diane Newby	...	James Davis
Rappahannock	*	C	6	(540) 675-5330	Robert Anderson	John McCarthy	L. Bruce	...	...	Larry Sherertz
Richmond		CM	8	(804) 333-3415	C. Gray	William Duncanson	...	...	...	Gene Sydnor
Roanoke		CM	85	(540) 772-2006	...	...	Mary Allen	Diane Hyatt	Joe Sgroi	John Cease
Rockbridge		CM	20	(540) 463-4361	W. Edwards	Claire Collins	D. Patterson	R. E. Claytor	...	Robert Day
Rockingham	*	CM	67	(540) 564-3000	...	Joseph Paxton	...	James Allmendinger	Stephen Riddlebarger	Donald Farley
Russell		CE	30	(276) 889-8000	Frank Horton	James Gillespie	Joseph Gilmer	...	...	Trigg Fields
Scott		CM	23	(276) 386-6521	...	...	...	...	...	Jerry Broadwater
Shenandoah	*	CE	35	(540) 459-6165	Beverley Fleming	Vincent Poling	...	Garland Miller	...	Larry Green
Smyth		CM	33	(540) 783-3298	Joseph Staley	Edwin Whitmore	...	...	...	R. Bradley
Southampton		CM	17	(757) 653-3015	Dallas Jones	Michael Johnson	...	Julia Williams	...	Vernie Francis
Spotsylvania	*	CM	90	(540) 507-7010	Jerry Logan	Charles Barnes	Aimee Mann	Tammy Petrie	...	Howard Smith
Stafford		CM	92	(540) 658-8603	...	Anthony Romanello	Marsha Beard	...	...	Charles Jett
Surry		CM	6	(757) 294-5271	Reginald Harrison	Tyrone Franklin	...	Melissa Motton	...	Harold Brown
Sussex		CE	12	(434) 246-5511	Rufus Tyler	Mary Jones	Gary Williams	...	...	E. Kitchen
Tazewell		CE	44	(276) 988-1200	Donnie Lowe	James Spencer	...	Arlene Matney	...	Henry Caudill
Warren		CM	31	(540) 636-4600	Joe Derting	Douglas Stanley	Mark Reeter	Carolyn Stimmel	Anita Mabie	Daniel McEathron
Washington		CM	51	(276) 676-6204	...	...	...	...	...	Fred Newman
Westmoreland	*	CM	16	(804) 493-0130	Darryl Fisher	Norman Risavi	Gwynne Chatham	Victor Nash	...	C. Balderson
Wise		CM	40	(276) 328-2321	Robert Adkins	...	...	...	Jeffery Gilliam	Ronald Oakes
Wythe	*	CE	27	(276) 223-6020	Wythe Sharitz	R. Dalton	...	...	...	Doug King
York		CM	56	(757) 890-3320	James Burgett	James McReynolds	Mary Simmons	MaryCarol White	Laurie Blanton	Joseph Diggs
WASHINGTON										
Adams		C	16	(509) 659-0090	...	...	Paulette Gibler	...	...	Douglas Barger
Asotin		CM	20	(509) 243-4160	...	...	...	...	...	...
Benton		CM	142	(509) 737-2777	...	...	...	...	...	...
Chelan		C	66	(509) 664-5216	...	...	...	...	...	...
Clallam	*	CM	64	(360) 417-2242	Michael Chapman	James Jones	Trish Holden	Stanton Creasey	Marjorie Upham	William Benedict
Clark	*	CE	345	(360) 397-2456	Betty Sue Morris	Glyn Barron	Sherry Parker	John Ingram	Francine Reis	Garry Lucas
Columbia		C	4	(509) 382-4541	Richard Jones	...	D. Lynne Leseman	...	...	Michael Berglund
Cowlitz		C	92	(360) 577-3065	...	...	Teri Nielsen	Claire Hauge	...	Bill Mahoney
Douglas		CM	32	(509) 884-9444	Dane Keane	...	Marilyn Northrop	Karen Goodwin	...	Daniel Laroche
Ferry		C	7	(509) 775-5200	Michael Blankenship	...	Jean Booher	Joyce Schertenleib	...	Pete Werner
Franklin		CM	49	(509) 545-3535	Robert Koch	Fred Bowen	Michael Killian	Thomas Westerman	...	Richard Lathim
Garfield		CM	2	(509) 843-1411	Dean Burton	...	Donna Deal	...	...	Larry Bowles
Grant	*	C	74	(509) 754-2011	Le Roy Allison	...	Kimberly Allen	David Firebaugh	Tammie Hechler	Frank DeTrolio
Grays Harbor		C	67	(360) 249-3731	...	...	Cheryl Brown	...	...	...
Island		C	71	(360) 679-7372	William McDowell	...	Sharon Franzen	...	Richard Toft	Michael Hawley
Jefferson	*	CM	25	(360) 385-9100	Phil Johnson	Philip Morley	Ruth Gordan	...	Lorna Delaney	Mike Brasfield
King		CE	1737	(206) 296-1737	Ron Sims	James Buck	Anne Noris	Steve Call	Anita Whitfield	Sue Rahr
Kitsap		CM	231	(360) 337-7185	...	Nancy Buonanno Grennan	David Peterson	Karen Flynn	Penny Starkey	Stephen Boyer
Kittitas		C	33	(509) 962-7508	Perry Huston	...	...	...	Kirk Eslinger	...
Klickitat		C	19	(509) 773-7171	Donald Struck	...	Saundra Olson	...	Lori Walford	Chris Mace

Directory 1/10   **OFFICIALS IN U.S. COUNTIES 2,500 AND OVER IN POPULATION**
continued

Jurisdiction	Form of govern- ment	2000 Popu- lation	Main telephone number	Chief elected official	Appointed administrator	Clerk of the governing board	Chief financial officer	Director of personnel	Chief law enforcement official
WASHINGTON continued									
Lewis	C	68	(360) 748-9121	Richard Graham	Connie Robins	Nettie Jungers	Larry Grove	. . .	John McCroskey
Lincoln	C	10	(509) 725-4971	Mason Hopkins	. . .	Peggy Semprimoznik	. . .	. . .	John Coley
Mason	* CM	49	(360) 427-9670	. . .	. . .	Rebecca Rogers	. . .	T. J. Martin	Casey Salisbury
Okanogan	C	39	(509) 422-7100	Mary Lou Peterson	. . .	Jackie Bradley	. . .	Nanette Kallunki	Frank Rogers
Pacific	C	20	(360) 875-9337	Jon Kaino	Vyrle Hill	Virginia Leach	Ida Taylor	. . .	John Didion
Pend Oreille	CE	11	(509) 447-4119	Mike Hanson	. . .	Fawneil Opp	. . .	. . .	Gerald Weeks
Pierce	C	700	(253) 798-7272	. . .	. . .	Kevin Stock	Patrick Kenney	Betsy Sawyers	Paul Pastor
San Juan	* CM	14	(360) 378-2898	. . .	Donald Rose	Joan White	F. Henley	Pamela Morais	William Cumming
Skagit	* CM	102	(360) 336-9433	. . .	Tim Holloran	. . .	. . .	Kathy Brown	. . .
Skamania	CM	9	(509) 427-9447	Robert Talent	. . .	Rena Hollis	. . .	. . .	Dave Brown
Snohomish	CE	606	(425) 388-3411	Kirke Sievers	Aaron Reardon	. . .	Roger Neumaier	Bridget Clawson	Rick Bart
Spokane	* CE	417	(509) 477-5750	. . .	Marshall Farnell	Tom Fallquist	. . .	Cathy Malzahn	Ozzie Knezovich
Stevens	C	40	(509) 684-3751	Malcolm Friedman	. . .	Patty Chester	Tim Gray	. . .	Craig Thayer
Thurston	CE	207	(360) 754-3800	Bob MacLeod	Donald Krupp	Betty Gould	John Bartz	Bill Kenny	Gary Edwards
Wahkiakum	C	3	(360) 795-3219	Daniel Cothren	. . .	Barbara Blix	. . .	. . .	Daniel Bardsley
Walla Walla	C	55	(509) 527-3200	David Carey	. . .	Connie Vinti	Gordon Heimbigner	Jay Winter	Mike Humphreys
Whatcom	* CE	166	(360) 676-6802	Pete Kremen	. . .	N. F. Jackson	Brad Bennett	Karen Doens	William Elfo
Whitman	C	40	(509) 397-6205	. . .	Sharron Cunningham	. . .	. . .	. . .	. . .
Yakima	CM	222	(509) 574-2210	Ron Gamache	. . .	Kim Eaton	Craig Warner	Linda Dixon	Kenneth Irwin
WEST VIRGINIA									
Barbour	C	15	(304) 457-2232	. . .	. . .	John Small	. . .	. . .	. . .
Berkeley	CM	75	(304) 267-3000	Steven Teufel	. . .	. . .	. . .	. . .	William Randy Smith
Boone	CM	25	(304) 369-7301	. . .	. . .	John Jordan	. . .	. . .	. . .
Braxton	C	14	(304) 765-2833	Roy Huffman	. . .	. . .	. . .	. . .	. . .
Brooke	C	25	(304) 737-3661	. . .	. . .	. . .	. . .	. . .	. . .
Cabell	C	96	(304) 526-8634	. . .	. . .	. . .	. . .	. . .	. . .
Calhoun	C	7	(304) 354-6725	. . .	. . .	. . .	. . .	. . .	. . .
Clay	C	10	(304) 587-4259	R. Sizemore	. . .	Judy Moore	. . .	. . .	. . .
Doddridge	C	7	(304) 873-2631	. . .	. . .	. . .	. . .	. . .	. . .
Fayette	CM	47	(304) 574-1200	John Witt	Charlotte Holly	Kelvin Holliday	. . .	. . .	William Laird
Gilmer	C	7	(304) 462-7641	Charles Hess	. . .	Beverly Marks	. . .	. . .	Mickey Metz
Grant	C	11	(304) 257-4550	. . .	. . .	. . .	. . .	. . .	. . .
Greenbrier	C	34	(304) 647-6603	Betty Crookshanks	. . .	W. J. Livesay	Joyce Moody	. . .	Roger Sheppard
Hampshire	C	20	(304) 822-5112	O. Bradfield	. . .	Nancy Feller	. . .	. . .	. . .
Hancock	C	32	(304) 564-3311	David Cline	Sharon Ulbright	Eleanor Straight	Cindy Jones	Carol Kaser	. . .
Hardy	C	12	(304) 538-2929	. . .	Robert Andre	Susan Thomas	. . .	. . .	James Jack
Harrison	C	68	(304) 624-8500	Conrad Diaz	. . .	. . .	. . .	. . .	. . .
Jackson	C	28	(304) 372-2011	. . .	. . .	. . .	. . .	. . .	. . .
Jefferson	CM	42	(304) 725-9761	James Knode	Leslie Smith	Jennifer Maghan	. . .	. . .	. . .
Kanawha	* C	200	(304) 357-0100	Kent Carper	Brent Pauley	. . .	David Fontalbert	. . .	Joseph Wagoner
Lewis	C	16	(304) 269-8200	Samuel Hicks	Phyllis Corathers	Mary Myers	. . .	Debra Hull	James Scites
Lincoln	C	22	(304) 824-3336	. . .	. . .	Greg Stowers	. . .	. . .	Wavle Hunter
Logan	C	37	(304) 792-8600	Arthur Kirkendall	. . .	. . .	N. Wooten	. . .	Junior Slaughter
Marion	C	56	(304) 367-5400	James Sago	Sharon Shaffer	Barbara Core	Janice Cosco	. . .	. . .
Marshall	C	35	(304) 845-1220	. . .	. . .	. . .	. . .	. . .	. . .
Mason	CM	25	(304) 675-1110	. . .	. . .	. . .	. . .	. . .	. . .
Mc Dowell	C	27	(304) 436-8344	. . .	. . .	. . .	. . .	. . .	. . .
Mercer	CE	62	(304) 487-8306	Joe Coburn	. . .	Rudolph Jennings	. . .	. . .	Darrell Bailey
Mineral	C	27	(304) 788-3924	Jack Bowers	Michael Bland	Carl Thomas	. . .	Debra Weasenforth	Paul Sabin
Mingo	C	28	(304) 235-0348	. . .	. . .	. . .	. . .	. . .	. . .
Monongalia	CM	81	(304) 291-7257	Robert Bell	Diane Demedici	Michael Oliverio	Joseph Bartolo	. . .	. . .
Monroe	C	14	(304) 772-3096	. . .	. . .	. . .	. . .	. . .	. . .
Morgan	C	14	(304) 258-8547	Glen Stotler	William Clark	Debra Kesecker	Cathy Payne	. . .	. . .
Nicholas	C	26	(304) 872-3630	. . .	. . .	. . .	. . .	. . .	. . .
Ohio	C	47	(304) 234-3628	David Sims	Gregory Stewart	Chester Kloss	. . .	. . .	. . .
Pendleton	C	8	(304) 358-2505	. . .	. . .	. . .	. . .	. . .	. . .
Pleasants	C	7	(304) 684-3542	Joe Reckard	Tina Oldfield	Sue Morgan	Julie Richard	. . .	Ted Maston
Pocahontas	C	9	(304) 799-4549	. . .	. . .	. . .	. . .	. . .	. . .
Preston	C	29	(304) 329-1805	. . .	. . .	. . .	. . .	. . .	. . .
Putnam	C	51	(304) 586-0202	. . .	. . .	. . .	. . .	. . .	. . .
Raleigh	C	79	(304) 255-9146	. . .	. . .	. . .	. . .	. . .	. . .
Randolph	C	28	(304) 636-2057	. . .	. . .	. . .	. . .	. . .	. . .
Ritchie	C	10	(304) 643-2164	Samuel Rogers	. . .	Susan Scott	. . .	. . .	. . .
Roane	C	15	(304) 927-2860	. . .	. . .	. . .	. . .	. . .	. . .
Summers	C	12	(304) 466-7100	Lonnie Mullins	. . .	Mary Merritt	. . .	. . .	Garry Wheeler
Taylor	C	16	(304) 265-1401	. . .	. . .	Linda Cale	. . .	. . .	. . .
Tucker	CM	7	(304) 478-2866	Jerome Di Bacco	C. Tuesing	Lora Thomas	. . .	. . .	. . .
Tyler	C	9	(304) 758-2103	Arthur Mason	. . .	Debbie Wilfong	. . .	. . .	Sherman Baxa
Upshur	CM	23	(304) 472-0535	Kenneth Davidson	William Parker	Robert Pasley	. . .	. . .	. . .
Wayne	CM	42	(304) 272-6369	William Wellman	. . .	Terry Payne	. . .	. . .	Dwayne Vandeven- der
Webster	C	9	(304) 847-5780	William Armentrout	. . .	. . .	. . .	. . .	. . .
Wetzel	CE	17	(304) 455-8224	Donald Mason	. . .	Carol Haught	. . .	. . .	Thomas Shepherd
Wirt	C	5	(304) 275-4271	. . .	. . .	. . .	. . .	. . .	. . .
Wood	* CE	87	(304) 424-1984	Rick Modesitt	Marty Seufer	Jamie Six	. . .	. . .	Jeff Sandy
Wyoming	C	25	(304) 732-8000	. . .	. . .	. . .	. . .	. . .	. . .
WISCONSIN									
Adams	CE	18	(608) 339-4267	. . .	. . .	Beverly Ward	. . .	Nicholas Funkhouser	Larry Warren
Ashland	CE	16	(715) 682-7000	Kenneth Lindquist	Thomas Kieweg	Patricia Somppi	. . .	. . .	John Kovach
Barron	* CM	44	(715) 537-6200	Jess Miller	Duane Hebert	DeeAnn Cook	Jeffrey French	Rachael Richie	Chris Fitzgerald
Bayfield	* CM	15	(715) 373-6181	William Kacvinsky	Mark Abeles-Allison	Scott Fibert	. . .	. . .	Robert Follis
Brown	CE	226	(920) 448-4065	Carol Kelso	Roger De Groot	Darlene Marcelle	. . .	. . .	Dennis Kocken
Buffalo	CM	13	(608) 685-6234	David Ernst	Del Twidt	Roxann Halverson	. . .	. . .	Michael Schmidtknecht
Burnett	CM	15	(715) 349-2181	. . .	Candace Fitzgerald	Helen Steffen	. . .	. . .	Timothy Curtin
Calumet	* CM	40	(920) 849-2361	. . .	Jay Shambeau	Beth Hauser	Daniel DeBonis	Patrick Glynn	Gerald Pagel
Chippewa	CM	55	(715) 726-7969	. . .	William Reynolds	Kathleen Bernier	George McDowell	. . .	James Kowalczyk
Clark	C	33	(715) 743-5148	Wayne Hendrickson	. . .	Christina Jensen	Terri Domaszek	Wendy Bautch	Louis Rosandich
Columbia	C	52	(608) 742-9668	Susan Martin	. . .	Jean Miller	Lois Schepp	. . .	Steven Rowe
Crawford	C	17	(608) 326-0201	Robert Dillman	. . .	Janet Geisler	. . .	. . .	Robert Ostrander
Dane	CE	426	(608) 266-4125	Kathleen Falk	. . .	Joseph Parisi	Chuck Hicklin	. . .	Gary Hamblin
Dodge	* C	85	(920) 386-3600	Russell Kottke	Jim Mielke	Karen Gibson	G. Gorst	Joseph Rains	Todd Nehls
Door	* CM	27	(920) 746-5511	Leo Zipperer	Michael Serpe	Jill Lau	Shirley Scalish	Kelly Hendee	Terry Vogel
Douglas	CM	43	(715) 395-1429	Douglas Finn	Steve Koszarek	Susan Sandvick	Ann Doucette	. . .	Charlie Law
Dunn	* CM	39	(715) 232-2429	Jane Hoyt	Eugene Smith	Lorraine Hartung	Mary Behling	Joann Olson	Dennis Smith
Eau Claire	CM	93	(715) 839-5106	. . .	J. McCarty	Janet Loomis	Scott Rasmussen	Heather Baker	Ronald Cramer
Florence	C	5	(715) 528-3201	Edwin Kelley	. . .	. . .	. . .	Robert Anderson	Jeffrey Rickaby
Fond Du Lac	CE	97	(920) 929-3000	Allen Buechel	. . .	Joyce Buechel	Karen Kuehl	Richard Brzozowski	Gary Pucker

Directory 1/10 OFFICIALS IN U.S. COUNTIES 2,500 AND OVER IN POPULATION
continued

Jurisdiction	Form of govern-ment	2000 Popu-lation	Main telephone number	Chief elected official	Appointed administrator	Clerk of the governing board	Chief financial officer	Director of personnel	Chief law enforcement official
WISCONSIN continued									
Forest	C	10	(715) 478-2422	...	...	...	...	...	...
Grant	CE	49	(608) 723-2711	Eugene Bartels	...	Chris Carl	...	Joyce Roling	Keith Govier
Green	C	33	(608) 328-9430	Robert Hoesly	...	Michael Doyle	Rhonda Hunter	...	...
Green Lake *	CM	19	(920) 294-4005	Orrin Helmer	...	Margaret Bostelmann	...	...	Mark Podoll
Iowa *	CM	22	(608) 935-0374	Mark Masters	Randolph Terronez	Greg Klusendorf	Roxanne Hamilton	Bud Trader	Steven Michek
Iron	CM	6	(715) 561-3375	...	...	...	...	...	...
Jackson *	CM	19	(715) 284-0216	Dennis Eberhardt	...	Kyle Deno	...	Tam Burgau	Duane Waldera
Jefferson	CE	74	(920) 674-7101	Sharon Schmeling	Gary Petre	Donna Oleson	...	Terri Palm-Kostroski	Paul Milbrath
Juneau	C	24	(608) 847-9344	...	...	Edna Highland	...	Barbara Hoile	...
Kenosha	CE	149	(262) 653-6422	...	Jim Kreuser	Edna Highland	David Geertsen	Robert Riedl	...
Kewaunee	CM	20	(920) 388-7164	Gerald Novickis	Edward Dorner	Linda Teske	...	...	John Cmeyla
La Crosse *	CM	107	(608) 785-9640	Steven Doyle	Steven O'Malley	Marion Naegle	Gary Ingvalson	Robert Taunt	Steven Helgeson
Lafayette	C	16	(608) 776-4850	Wilson Wayne	...	...	Joy Galle	...	Scott Pedley
Langlade	C	20	(715) 627-6200	Alfred Schultz	...	Kathryn Jacob	Jeff Mundinger	...	Dave Stegar
Lincoln *	CM	29	(715) 539-1011	Robert Lussow	John Mulder	Robert Kunkel	Dan Leydet	...	Jeff Jaeger
Manitowoc	CE	82	(920) 683-4060	...	...	Daniel Fischer	Todd Reckelberg	Sharon Cornils	Thomas Kocourek
Marathon	CM	125	(715) 261-1451	Keith Langenhahn	Mort McBain	Nanette Kottke	Kristi Kordus	Frank Matel	Randall Hoenisch
Marinette	C	43	(715) 732-7406	...	Steven Corbeille	Katherine Brandt	...	...	Michael Kessler
Marquette	C	15	(608) 297-9173	...	...	James Thalacyer	...	Brent Miller	Rick Fullmer
Menominee	CE	4	(715) 799-3024	...	Ron Corn	Carol Latender	...	...	Bryan Lepscier
Milwaukee	CE	940	(414) 278-4143	Scott Walker	Linda Seemeyer	Mark Ryan	Scott Manske	Charles McDowell	David Clarke
Monroe *	CM	40	(608) 269-8719	Dennis Hubbard	...	...	...	Ken Kittleson	Dennis Pedersen
Oconto	CM	35	(920) 834-6800	Leland Rymer	Kevin Hamann	Judy Ferris	Terry Hinds	...	Michael Jansen
Oneida	C	36	(715) 369-6154	...	...	...	...	...	...
Outagamie	CE	160	(920) 832-1672	James Schuette	...	James Hensel	Edward Czaja	Robert Sunstrom	Bradley Gehring
Ozaukee	CM	82	(262) 284-8321	Leroy Biey	Thomas Meaux	Harold Dobberpuhl	...	Michael Puksich	Maurice Straub
Pepin	CM	7	(715) 672-8704	Peggy Schlosser	Lawrence Kromar	Marcia Bauer	...	Darlene Brunner	John Andrews
Pierce *	CM	36	(715) 273-3531	Richard Wilhelm	...	Jamie Feuerhelm	Julie Brickner	Sandra Langer	Nancy Hove
Polk	C	41	(715) 485-9270	Robert Blake	...	Cathy Albrecht	...	Rodney Beyer	Ann Hrayduck
Portage	CE	67	(715) 346-1327	Clarence Hintz	...	Roger Wrycza	Daryl De Deker	...	Stanley Potocki
Price	C	15	(715) 339-3325	...	...	Clarence Cvengros	...	Lori Blair-Hill	Wallace Krenzke
Racine	CE	188	(262) 636-3118	William McReynolds	...	Joan Rennet	Douglas Stansil	Karen Galbraith	Robert Carlson
Richland	C	17	(608) 647-2197	...	...	...	...	...	...
Rock *	CM	152	(608) 757-5520	J. Podzilni	Craig Knutson	Lori Stottler	Jeffrey Smith	John Becker	Robert Spoden
Rusk	CM	15	(715) 532-2100	...	...	Denise Nelson	Rosemary Schmit	Dave Willingham	Dean Meyer
Sauk	CM	55	(608) 355-3286	Marty Krueger	Kathryn Schauf	Beverly Mielke	Kerry Beghin	Michelle Koehler	Randy Stammen
Sawyer	C	16	(715) 634-4866	...	...	Kris Mayberry	...	Carol Larson	James Meier
Shawano	CM	40	(715) 526-9135	Marshal Giese	Frank Pascarella	Rosemary Bohm	Diane Rusch	Judith Rank	Robert Schmidt
Sheboygan	CM	112	(920) 459-3003	Daniel LeMahieu	Adam Payne	Julie Glancey	Timothy Finch	Louella Conway	Alonna Koenig
St. Croix *	CM	63	(715) 386-4600	...	Charles Whiting	Cindy Campbell	Michelle Pietrick	Tammy Funk	Dennis Hillstead
Taylor	CM	19	(715) 748-1400	Herbert Bergmann	...	Roger Emmerich	...	Charles Rude	William Breneman
Trempealeau	C	27	(715) 538-2311	Barbara Semb	...	Paul Syverson	...	Beverly Monahan	Randall Niederkorn
Vernon *	CE	28	(608) 637-5303	Tom Spenner	...	Ronald Hoff	...	Linda Kica	Gene Cary
Vilas	C	21	(715) 479-3600	...	...	...	...	...	...
Walworth *	CM	93	(262) 741-7950	Nancy Russell	David Bretl	Kimberly Bushey	Nicole Andersen	...	David Graves
Washburn	CM	16	(715) 468-4624	Michael Bobin	...	John Brown	Michael Keefe	...	Terrence Dryden
Washington	C	117	(262) 335-4489	Herbert Tennies	Douglas Johnson	Brenda Jaszewski	Susan Haag	Peter German	Dale Schmidt
Waukesha	CE	360	(262) 548-7902	James Dwyer	Daniel Vrakas	Kathy Nickolaus	...	Susan Zastrow	Daniel Trawicki
Waupaca	CM	51	(715) 258-6210	Duane Brown	...	...	James Bernhagen	Amanda Welch	Steven Liebe
Waushara *	CM	23	(920) 787-0431	Norman Weiss	Debra Behringer	John Benz	...	...	David Peterson
Winnebago	CE	156	(920) 236-4800	Jane Vandehey	...	Susan Ertmer	Charles Orenstein	Frederick Bau	Michael Brooks
Wood	C	75	(715) 421-8457	Charles Gurtler	...	Cynthia Meyers	Michael Martin	Edward Reed	Thomas Reichert
WYOMING									
Albany	CE	32	(307) 721-5535	Tim Chesnut	...	Jackie Gonzales	...	...	James Pond
Big Horn	C	11	(307) 568-2357	...	...	...	...	...	...
Campbell	C	33	(307) 682-7283	Craig Mader	Robert Palmer	Susan Saunders	...	Charlotte Terry	...
Carbon	C	15	(307) 328-2668	...	...	William Harshman	...	...	Jerry Colson
Converse	CE	12	(307) 358-2244	James Willox	Ed Werner	Lucile Taylor	...	...	Clint Becker
Crook	C	5	(307) 283-1323	Floyd Canfield	...	...	...	...	Steve Stahla
Fremont	CE	35	(307) 332-1063	Lanny Applegate	...	Julia Freese	...	...	Skip Hornecker
Goshen	C	12	(307) 532-4051	...	...	...	...	...	...
Hot Springs	C	4	(307) 864-3515	...	...	...	...	...	...
Johnson	C	7	(307) 684-7555	...	...	...	...	...	...
Laramie	C	81	(307) 633-4355	...	...	...	...	...	...
Lincoln	C	14	(307) 877-9056	Kathy Davison	...	Jeanne Wagner	...	...	Lee Gardner
Natrona	C	66	(307) 235-9206	...	...	Mary Collins	...	...	Mark Benton
Niobrara	C	2	(307) 334-2211	Tom Wasserburger	...	Becky Freeman	...	...	Rick Zerbe
Park	C	25	(307) 527-8600	Timothy Morrison	...	Karen Carter	...	...	David Doyle
Platte	C	8	(307) 322-2315	Alden Prosser	...	Jean Dixon	...	...	Steve Keigley
Sheridan	C	26	(307) 674-2900	Lawrence Durante	Maria Kennah	Audrey Koltiska	...	...	Dave Hoefmeier
Sublette	C	5	(307) 367-4372	Betty Fear	...	Mary Lankford	...	...	Bardy Bardin
Sweetwater	C	37	(307) 872-6400	John Pallesen	Robert Gordon	Loretta Bailiff	...	Garry McLean	David Gray
Teton *	CM	18	(307) 733-8094	Andy Schwartz	Janice Friedlund	S. Daigle	...	Jalene Utzinger	Bob Zimmer
Uinta	C	19	(307) 783-1700	Craig Welling	Brent Morris	Lynne Fox	...	...	Forrest Bright
Washakie	CE	8	(307) 347-6491	Alice Lass	...	Mary Strauch	...	...	...
Weston	C	6	(307) 746-4744	...	...	...	...	...	...

D2

Professional, Special Assistance, and Educational Organizations Serving Local and State Governments

This article briefly describes 81 organizations that provide services of particular importance to cities, counties, and other local and state governments. Most of the organizations are membership groups for school administrators, health officers, city planners, city managers, public works directors, city attorneys, and other administrators who are appointed rather than elected. Several are general service and representational organizations for states, cities, counties, and administrators and citizens. Some organizations provide distinctive research, technological, consulting, and educational programs on a cost-of-service basis and have been established to meet specific needs of state and local governments. The others support educational activities and conduct research in urban affairs or government administration, thereby indirectly strengthening professionalism in government administration.

The assistance available through the secretariats of these national organizations provides an excellent method of obtaining expert advice and actual information on specific problems. The information secured in this way enables local and state officials to improve administrative practices, organization, and methods and thus improve the quality of services rendered. Many of these organizations also are active in raising the professional standards of their members through in-service training, special conferences and seminars, and other kinds of professional development.

Research on current problems is a continuing activity of many of these groups, and all issue a variety of publications ranging from newsletters and occasional bulletins to diversified books, monographs, research papers, conference proceedings, and regular and special reports.

These organizations provide many of the services that in other countries would be the responsibility of the national government. They arrange annual conferences, answer inquiries, provide in-service training and other kinds of professional development, provide placement services for members, and develop service and cost standards for various activities. Most of the organizations listed have individual memberships, and several also have agency or institutional memberships. Some of these organizations have service mem-

berships that may be based on the population of the jurisdiction, the annual revenue of the jurisdiction or agency, or other criteria that roughly measure the costs of providing service. In addition to these kinds of membership fees, some of the organizations provide specialized consulting, training, and information services both by annual subscription and by charges for specific projects.

LISTING OF ORGANIZATIONS

Academy for State and Local Government
444 North Capitol Street, N.W., Suite 345
Washington, D.C. 20001-1512
(202) 434-4850
Principal: Dawn Hatzer
Publication list available on request

Purpose: To coordinate cooperative efforts among federal, state, and local governments; the private sector; and the country's research community in addressing key issues facing state and local governments. Also serves as a policy center for joint projects and programs of ICMA and the Council of State Governments, National Association of Counties, National Conference of State Legislatures, National Governors Association, National League of Cities, and U.S. Conference of Mayors. The State and Local Legal Center, an arm of the academy, is devoted to the interests of state and local governments in the Supreme Court. Established 1971.

Airports Council International–North America (ACI-NA)
1775 K Street, N.W., Suite 500
Washington, D.C. 20006
(202) 293-8500; fax (202) 331-1362
Web site: aci-na.org
President: Greg Principato
Major publications: *Airport Highlights,* studies, surveys, reports

Purpose: To promote sound policies dealing with the financing, construction, management, operations, and development of airports; to provide reference and resource facilities and information for airport operators; and to act as the "voice" of airports to governmental agencies, officials, and the public on problems and solutions concerning airport operations. Established 1948.

American Association of Airport Executives (AAAE)
601 Madison Street, Suite 400
Alexandria, Virginia 22314
(703) 824-0500; fax (703) 820-1395
Web site: aaae.org
President: Charles M. Barclay
Major publications: *Airport Report; Airport Magazine*

Purpose: To assist airport managers in performing their complex and diverse responsibilities through an airport management reference library; a consulting service; publications containing technical, administrative, legal, and operational information; an electronic bulletin board system; a professional accreditation program for airport executives; and Aviation News and Training Network, a private satellite broadcast network for airport employee training and news. Established 1928.

American Association of Port Authorities (AAPA)
1010 Duke Street
Alexandria, Virginia 22314-3589
(703) 684-5700; fax (703) 684-6321
E-mail: info@aapa-ports.org
Web site: aapa-ports.org
President: Kurt J. Nagle

Purpose: To promote the common interests of the port community and provide leadership on trade, transportation, environmental, and other issues related to port development and

operations. As the alliance of ports of the Western Hemisphere, AAPA furthers public understanding of the essential role fulfilled by ports within the global transportation system. It also serves as a resource to help members accomplish their professional responsibilities. Established 1912.

American Association of School Administrators (AASA)

801 North Quincy Street, Suite 700
Arlington, Virginia 22203
(703) 528-0700; fax (703) 841-1543
Web site: aasa.org
Executive Director: Daniel A. Domenech
Major publications: *The School Administrator, Leadership News,* Critical Issues Series

Purpose: To develop qualified educational leaders and support excellence in educational administration; to initiate and support laws, policies, research, and practices that will improve education; to promote programs and activities that focus on leadership for learning and excellence in education; and to cultivate a climate in which quality education can thrive. Established 1865.

American College of Healthcare Executives (ACHE)

One North Franklin Street, Suite 1700
Chicago, Illinois 60606-3491
(312) 424-2800; fax (312) 424-0023
Web site: ache.org
President/CEO: Thomas C. Dolan, PhD, FACHE, CAE
Major publications: *Journal of Healthcare Management; Healthcare Executive; Frontiers of Health Services Management;* miscellaneous studies and task force, committee, and seminar reports

Purpose: To be the professional membership society for health care executives; to meet its members' professional, educational, and leadership needs; to promote high ethical standards and conduct; and to advance health care leadership and management excellence. Established 1933.

American Institute of Architects (AIA)

1735 New York Avenue, N.W.
Washington, D.C. 20006
(202) 626-7300; fax (202) 626-7547
(800) 242-3837
Web site: aia.org
Executive Vice President/CEO:
    Christine McEntee
Major publication: *AIArchitect*

Purpose: To organize and unite in fellowship the members of the architectural profession; to promote the aesthetic, scientific, and practical efficiency of the profession; to advance the science and art of planning and building by advancing the standards of architectural education, training, and practice; to coordinate the efforts of the building industry and the profession of architecture to ensure the advancement of living standards for people through improved environment; and to make the profession of architecture one of ever-increasing service to society. Established 1857.

American Library Association (ALA)

50 East Huron Street
Chicago, Illinois 60611
(312) 280-1392; fax (312) 944-3897
(800) 545-2433
Also at 1615 New Hampshire Avenue, N.W.
Washington, D.C. 20009-2520
(202) 628-8410; fax (202) 628-8419
Web site: www.ala.org
Executive Director: Keith Michael Fiels
Major publications: *American Libraries, Booklist, Book Links*

Purpose: To assist libraries and librarians in promoting and improving library service and librarianship. Established 1876.

American Planning Association (APA), and its professional institute, the American Institute of Certified Planners (AICP)

1776 Massachusetts Avenue, N.W.
Washington, D.C. 20036-1904
(202) 872-0611; fax (202) 872-0643
Also at 122 South Michigan Avenue, Suite 1600
Chicago, Illinois 60603
(312) 431-9100; fax (312) 431-9985
Web site: planning.org
Executive Director/CEO: Paul Farmer, FAICP
Major publications: *Journal of the APA, Planning, Planning and Environmental Law, Zoning Practice, The Commissioner, Practicing Planner, Interact, APA Advocate,* Planning Advisory Service (PAS) Reports

Purpose: To encourage planning that will meet the needs of people and society more effectively. APA is a nonprofit public interest and research organization that represents 43,000 practicing planners, officials, and citizens who are involved with urban and rural planning issues. Sixty-five percent of its members work for state and local government agencies and are involved, on a day-to-day basis, in formulating planning policies and preparing land use regulations. AICP is APA's professional institute, providing recognized leadership nationwide in the certification of professional planners, ethics, professional development, planning education, and the standards of planning practice. APA resulted from the consolidation of the American Institute of Planners, founded in 1917, and the American Society of Planning Officials, established in 1934.

American Public Gas Association (APGA)

201 Massachusetts Avenue, N.E., Suite C-4
Washington, D.C. 20002
(202) 464-2742; fax (202) 464-0246
E-mail: bkalisch@apga.org
Web site: apga.org
President: Bert Kalisch
Major publications: *Public Gas News* (biweekly newsletter), *Publicly Owned Natural Gas System Directory* (annual), *The Source* (quarterly magazine)

Purpose: To be an advocate for publicly owned natural gas distribution systems, and to effectively educate and communicate with members to promote safety, awareness, performance, and competitiveness. Established 1961.

American Public Health Association (APHA)

800 I Street, N.W.
Washington, D.C. 20001-3710
(202) 777-2742; fax (202) 777-2534
Web site: apha.org
Executive Director: Georges C. Benjamin, MD
Major publications: *American Journal of Public Health, The Nation's Health*

Purpose: To protect the health of the public through the maintenance of standards for scientific procedures, legislative education, and the practical application of innovative health programs. Established 1872.

American Public Human Services Association (APHSA)

810 First Street, N.E., Suite 500
Washington, D.C. 20002
(202) 682-0100; fax (202) 289-6555
Web site: aphsa.org
Executive Director: Jerry W. Friedman
Major publications: *Policy and Practice* magazine, *Public Human Services Directory, This Week in Health, This Week in Washington, W-Memo, Working for Tomorrow*

Purpose: To develop and promote policies and practices that improve the health and well-being of families, children, and adults. Established 1930.

American Public Power Association (APPA)

1875 Connecticut Avenue, N.W.
Washington, D.C. 20009
(202) 467-2900; fax (202) 467-2910
Web site: appanet.org
President and CEO: Mark Crisson
Major publications: *Public Power* (bimonthly magazine), *Public Power Weekly* (newsletter), *Public Power Daily*

Purpose: To promote the efficiency and benefits of publicly owned electric systems; to achieve cooperation among public systems; to protect the interests of publicly owned utilities; and to provide service in the fields of management and operation, energy conservation, consumer services, public relations, engineering, design, construction, research,

and accounting practice. APPA represents more than 2,000 community-owned electric utilities and provides services in the areas of government relations, engineering and operations, accounting and finance, energy research and development, management, customer relations, and public communications. The association represents public power interests before Congress, federal agencies, and the courts; provides educational programs and energy planning services in technical and management areas; and collects, analyzes, and disseminates information on public power and the electric utility industry. APPA publishes a weekly newsletter, bimonthly magazine, and many specialized publications; funds energy research and development projects; recognizes utilities and individuals for excellence in management and operations; and serves as a resource for federal, state, and local policy makers and officials, news reporters, public interest and other organizations, and the general public on public power and energy issues. Established 1940.

American Public Transportation Association (APTA)

1666 K Street, N.W., Suite 1100
Washington, D.C. 20006
(202) 496-4800; fax (202) 496-4321
Web site: apta.com
President: William W. Millar
Major publications: *Passenger Transport, Public Transportation Fact Book*

Purpose: To represent the operators of and suppliers to public transit; to provide a medium for discussion, exchange of experiences, and comparative study of industry affairs; and to research and investigate methods to improve public transit. The association also assists public transit entities with special issues, and collects and makes available public transit–related data and information. Established 1882.

American Public Works Association (APWA)

2345 Grand Boulevard, Suite 700
Kansas City, Missouri 64108-2641
(816) 472-6100; fax (816) 472-1610
Also at 1401 K Street, N.W., 11th Floor
Washington, D.C. 20005
(202) 408-9541; fax (202) 408-9542
Web site: apwa.net
Executive Director: Peter B. King
Major publications: *APWA Reporter* (12 issues), research reports, technical publications and manuals

Purpose: To serve its members by promoting professional excellence and public awareness through education, advocacy, and the exchange of knowledge. Established 1894.

American Society for Public Administration (ASPA)

1301 Pennsylvania Avenue, N.W., Suite 840
Washington, D.C. 20004
(202) 393-7878; fax (202) 638-4952
Web site: aspanet.org
Executive Director: Antoinette A. Samuel, CAE
Major publications: *Public Administration Review, PA Times*

Purpose: To improve the management of public service at all levels of government; to advocate on behalf of public service; to advance the science, processes, and art of public administration; and to disseminate information and facilitate the exchange of knowledge among persons interested in the practice or teaching of public administration. Established 1939.

American Water Works Association (AWWA)

6666 West Quincy Avenue
Denver, Colorado 80235
(303) 794-7711; fax (303) 795-1440
Also at 1300 I Street, N.W., Suite 701 West
Washington, D.C. 20005
(202) 628-8303
Web site: awwa.org
Executive Director: Gary Zimmerman
Major publications: *Total Water Management: Practices for a Sustainable Future; AWWA Journal, MainStream, OpFlow, WaterWeek*

Purpose: To promote public health and welfare in the provision of drinking water of unquestionable and sufficient quality. Established 1881.

Association of Public-Safety Communications Officials— International, Inc.

351 North Williamson Boulevard
Daytona Beach, Florida 32114-1112
(386) 322-2500; fax (386) 322-2501
Also at 1725 DeSales Street, N.W., Suite 808
Washington, D.C. 20036
(202) 833-2700; fax (202) 833-5700
Web site: aapa-ports.org/
Executive Director: George S. Rice Jr.
Major publications: *APCO BULLETIN, The Journal of Public Safety Communications, Public Safety Operating Procedures Manual,* APCO training courses

Purpose: To promote the development and progress of public safety telecommunications through research, planning, and training; to promote cooperation among public safety agencies; to perform frequency coordination for radio services administered by the Federal Communications Commission; and to act as a liaison with federal regulatory bodies. Established 1935.

Association of Public Treasurers of the United States and Canada (APT US&C)

962 Wayne Avenue, Suite 910
Silver Spring, Maryland 20910
(301) 495-5560; fax (301) 495-5561
Web site: aptusc.org
Executive Director: Lindsey Dively
Major publications: *Technical Topics, Treasury Notes; Spotlights* (newsletter)

Purpose: To enhance local treasury management by providing educational training, technical assistance, legislative services, and a forum for treasurers to exchange ideas and develop policy papers and positions. Established 1965.

Canadian Association of Municipal Administrators (CAMA)

P.O. Box 128, Station A
Fredericton, New Brunswick E3B 4Y2
(866) 771-2262; fax (506) 460-2134
Web site: camacam.ca
Executive Secretary: Jennifer Goodine
Major publication: *Insights and Innovations* (newsletter)

Purpose: To achieve greater communication and cooperation among municipal managers across Canada, and to focus the talents of its members on the preservation and advancement of municipal government by enhancing the quality of municipal management in Canada. Established 1972.

Center for State and Local Government Excellence (SLGE)

777 North Capitol Street, N.E., Suite 500
Washington, D.C. 20002-4201
(202) 682-6100; fax (202) 962-3604
Web site: slge.org
Executive Director: Elizabeth Kellar
Major publications: Issue briefs, including "The Miracle of State and Local Pension Funding," "The Crisis in State and Local Government Retiree Health Plans: Myths and Realities," "Security: What Americans Want from a Job"; and a number of other research studies and reports on public sector pensions, retiree health plans, public opinion surveys, and workforce demographics.

Purpose: To help state and local governments become knowledgeable and competitive employers so they can attract and retain talented, committed, and well-prepared individuals to public service. Research areas are workforce analysis and implications of changing demographics; competitive employment practices; compensation analysis; state and local government retirement plans; post-employment and retiree health care benefits; and financial wellness and retirement planning. Established 2006

Council of State Community Development Agencies (COSCDA)

1825 K Street, Suite 515
Washington, D.C. 20006
(202) 293-5820; fax (202) 293-2820
Web site: coscda.org
Executive Director: Dianne Taylor
Major publication: *The National Line*

Purpose: To help state agencies keep abreast of state and federal initiatives in community and economic development, housing, public facilities, and local assistance, and to improve state programs through interstate coordination. Established 1974.

Council of State Governments (CSG)

2760 Research Park Drive
P.O. Box 11910
Lexington, Kentucky 40578-1910
(859) 244-8000; fax (859) 244-8001
Web site: csg.org
Executive Director/CEO: Daniel M. Sprague
Major publications: *Book of the States, State Government News* magazine, *CSG State Directories*

Purpose: To prepare states for the future by interpreting changing national and international trends and conditions; to promote the sovereignty of the states and their role in the American federal system; to advocate multi-state problem solving and partnerships; and to build leadership skills to improve decision making. CSG is a multibranch and regionally focused association of the states, U.S. territories, and commonwealths. Established 1933.

Federation of Canadian Municipalities (FCM)

24 Clarence Street
Ottawa, Ontario K1N 5P3
(613) 241-5221; fax (613) 241-7440
E-mail: federation@fcm.ca
Web site: fcm.ca
Chief Executive Officer: Brock Carlton
Major publications: *Forum* (national magazine), *Crossroads: The Newsletter for the International Centre for Municipal Development*

Purpose: To represent the interests of all municipalities on policy and program matters within federal jurisdictions. Policy and program priorities are determined by FCM's board of directors, standing committees, and task forces. Issues include payments in lieu of taxes, goods and service taxes, economic development, municipal infrastructure, environment, transportation, community safety and crime prevention, quality-of-life social indicators, housing, race relations, and international trade and aid. FCM members include Canada's largest cities, small urban and rural communities, and the 18 major provincial and territorial municipal associations; together these members represent more than 20 million Canadians. Established 1937.

Government Finance Officers Association (GFOA)

203 North LaSalle Street, Suite 2700
Chicago, Illinois 60601-1210
(312) 977-9700; fax (312) 977-4806
Also at 1301 Pennsylvania Avenue, N.W., Suite 309
Washington, D.C. 20004
(202) 393-8020; fax (202) 393-0780
Web site: gfoa.org
Executive Director/CEO: Jeffrey L. Esser
Major publications: GFOA *Newsletter; Government Finance Review Magazine; Public Investor; GAAFR Review; Pension & Benefits Update; Governmental Accounting, Auditing, and Financial Reporting; Investing Public Funds; Elected Official's Series; Local Government Finance: Concepts and Practices*

Purpose: To enhance and promote the professional management of governmental financial resources by identifying, developing, and advancing fiscal strategies, policies, and practices for the public benefit. Established 1906.

Government Management Information Sciences Users Group (GMIS)

P.O. Box 27923
Austin, Texas 78755
(512) 220-1497; fax (512) 857-7711
Web site: gmis.org
GMIS Listserv: Headquarters@GMIS.org
Executive Director: Bruce Miller

Purpose: To provide a forum for the exchange of ideas, information, and techniques; and to foster enhancements in hardware, software, and communication developments as they relate to government activities. State and local government agencies are members represented by their top computer or information technology professionals. The GMIS Annual Educational Conference promotes sharing of ideas and the latest technology. GMIS sponsors an annual "Professional of the Year" program, publishes a newsletter, and provides organizational support to 19 state chapters. State chapters enable member agencies within a geographical area to develop close relationships and to foster the spirit and intent of GMIS through cooperation, assistance, and mutual support. GMIS is affiliated with KommITS, a sister organization of local governments in Sweden; SOC-ITM in the United Kingdom; ALGIM in New Zealand; VIAG in The Netherlands; MISA/ASIM in Ontario, Canada; LOLA-International (Linked Organisation of Local Authority ICT Societies); and V-ICT-OR in Belgium. Established 1971.

Governmental Accounting Standards Board (GASB)

401 Merritt 7
P.O. Box 5116
Norwalk, Connecticut 06856-5116
(203) 847-0700; fax (203) 849-9714
Web site: gasb.org
Chairman: Robert Attmore
Major publications: Governmental Accounting Standards Series; Codification of Standards; implementation guides; exposure drafts; Preliminary Views documents; *The GASB Report* (monthly newsletter); plain-language user guides

Purpose: To establish standards of financial accounting and reporting for state and local governmental entities. GASB standards guide the preparation of those entities' external financial reports so that users of the reports can obtain the state and local government financial information needed to make economic, social, and political decisions. Interested parties are encouraged to read and comment on discussion documents of proposed standards, which can be downloaded free of charge from the GASB Web site. Final standards, guides to implementing standards and using government financial reports, and subscriptions to the GASB's publications can be ordered through the Web site as well. GASB's Web site also provides up-to-date information about current projects, forms for submitting technical questions and signing up for e-mail news alerts, a section devoted to financial report users, and a link to its Performance Measurement for Government Web site. The GASB is overseen by the Financial Accounting Foundation's Board of Trustees. Established 1984.

Governmental Research Association (GRA)

P.O. Box 292300
Samford University
Birmingham, Alabama 35229
(205) 726-2482; fax (205) 726-2900
Web site: graonline.org
President: Ran Coble
Major publications: *Directory of Organizations and Individuals Professionally Engaged in Governmental Research and Related Activities* (annual); *GRA Reporter* (quarterly)

Purpose: To promote and coordinate the activities of governmental research agencies; to encourage the development of effective organization and methods for the administration and operation of government; to encourage the development of common standards for the appraisal of results; to facilitate the

exchange of ideas and experiences; and to serve as a clearinghouse. Established 1914.

ICMA

777 North Capitol Street, N.E., Suite 500
Washington, D.C. 20002-4201
(202) 289-4262; fax (202) 962-3500
Web site: icma.org
Executive Director: Robert J. O'Neill
Major publications: *Effective Supervisory Practices, The Ethics Edge, Managing Local Government Services, Budgeting: A Guide for Local Governments, A Revenue Guide for Local Government, How Effective Are Your Community Services?,* "Green" Books, *The Municipal Year Book, Public Management (PM)* magazine, *IQ Reports, ICMA Newsletter;* self-study courses, training packages

Purpose: To create excellence in local governance by developing and advocating professional management of local government worldwide. ICMA provides member support; publications, data, and information; peer and results-oriented assistance; and training and professional development to more than 9,000 city, town, and county experts and other individuals throughout the world. The management decisions made by ICMA's members affect 185 million individuals living in thousands of communities, from small villages and towns to large metropolitan areas. Established 1914.

ICMA Retirement Corporation (ICMA-RC)

777 North Capitol Street, N.E.
Washington, D.C. 20002
(202) 962-4600; fax (202) 962-4601
(800) 669-7400
Web site: icmarc.org
President/CEO: Joan McCallen

Purpose: To promote and facilitate portable retirement savings by state and local government employees. An independent, not-for-profit corporation focused on providing retirement plans and related services for more than 800,000 public employees in over 8,000 retirement plans, ICMA-RC's emphasis is on providing the best services, investment options, tools, and educational materials to help public employees build retirement security. Consistent with that mission, the corporation provides administrative, investment, and education services, as well as other retirement-related products, exclusively to state and local government employees. Established 1972.

Institute of Internal Auditors, Inc. (The IIA)

247 Maitland Avenue
Altamonte Springs, Florida 32701-4201
(407) 937-1100; fax (407) 937-1101
Web site: theiia.org
President: David A. Richards, CIA
Major publications: *Internal Auditor, Tone at the Top* (quarterly corporate governance newsletter)

Purpose: To provide comprehensive professional development and standards for the practice of internal auditing; and to research, disseminate, and promote education in internal auditing and internal control. The IIA offers the Certified Government Auditing Professional (CGAP) to distinguish leaders in public sector auditing. In addition to providing quality assessment services, the IIA performs custom on-site seminars for government auditors and offers educational products that address issues pertaining to government auditing. An international professional association with global headquarters in Altamonte Springs, Florida, the IIA has more than 140,000 members in internal auditing, governance, internal control, information technology audit, education, and security. With representation from more than 165 countries, the IIA is the internal audit profession's global voice, recognized authority, acknowledged leader, chief advocate, and principal educator worldwide. Established 1941.

Institute of Public Administration (IPA)

180 Graham Hall
University of Delaware
Newark, Delaware 19716-7380
(302) 831-8971; fax (302) 831-3488
Web site: ipa.udel.ed
President: Jerome R. Lewis
Major publications: IPA *Report* (semiannual), newsletter, conference proceedings

Purpose: To provide research, training, education, consulting, and advisory services in the United States and abroad in areas of public policy, government structure, public authorities, public enterprises, government procurement, personnel management and training, public/private sector improvements, economic development, charter revision, local government legislative bodies, planning and management, intergovernmental program responsibilities and relationships, and public ethics. Established 1906.

Institute of Transportation Engineers (ITE)

1099 14th Street, N.W., Suite 300 West
Washington, D.C. 20005-3438
(202) 289-0222; fax (202) 289-7722
Web site: ite.org
Executive Director: Thomas W. Brahms
Major publications: *Trip Generation, Parking Generation; Innovative Bicycle Treatments; Transportation and Land Use Development; Transportation Engineering Hand-book; Transportation Planning Handbook; Parking Handbook for Small Communities; Manual of Transportation Engineering Studies; Traffic Safety Toolbox, A Primer on Traffic Safety; Manual of Uniform Traffic Control Devices, 2003; Traffic Control Devices Handbook; ITE Journal*

Purpose: To promote professional development in the field through education, research, development of public awareness, and exchange of information. Established 1930.

International Association of Assembly Managers (IAAM)

635 Fritz Drive, Suite 100
Coppell, Texas 75019-4442
(972) 906-7441; fax (972) 906-7418
Web site: iaam.org
Executive Director: Dexter King, CFE
Major publications: *Facility Manager, IAAM Guide to Members and Services, IAAM E-News, Venue Safety & Security* magazine

Purpose: To educate, advocate for, and inspire public assembly venue professionals worldwide. Established 1925.

International Association of Assessing Officers (IAAO)

314 West 10th Street
Kansas City, Missouri 64105
(816) 701-8100; fax (816) 701-8149
Web site: iaao.org
Executive Director: Lisa J. Daniels
Major publications: *Journal of Property Tax Assessment and Administration; Property Appraisal and Assessment Administration; Property Assessment Valuation,* 2nd ed. (1996); *Mass Appraisal of Real Property* (1999); *GIS Guidelines for Assessors,* 2nd ed. (with URISA) (1999); assessment standards

Purpose: To provide leadership in accurate property valuation, property tax administration, and property tax policy throughout the world. Established 1934.

International Association of Chiefs of Police (IACP)

515 North Washington Street
Alexandria, Virginia 22314-2357
(703) 836-6767; fax (703) 836-4543
(800) THE IACP
Web site: theiacp.org
Executive Director: Daniel N. Rosenblatt
Major publications: *Police Chief, Training Keys*

Purpose: To advance the art of police science through the development and dissemination of improved administrative, technical, and operational practices, and to promote the use of such practices in police work. IACP fosters police cooperation through the exchange of information among police administrators, and encourages all police officers to adhere to high standards of performance and conduct. Established 1893.

International Association of Fire Chiefs (IAFC)

4025 Fair Ridge Drive, Suite 300
Fairfax, Virginia 22033-2868
(703) 273-0911; fax (703) 273-9363
Web site: iafc.org
Executive Director Mark Light, CAE
Major publication: *On Scene* (twice-monthly newsletter)

Purpose: To enhance the professionalism and capabilities of career and volunteer fire chiefs, chief fire officers, and managers of emergency service organizations throughout the international community through vision, services, information, education, and representation. Established 1873.

International Code Council

500 New Jersey Avenue, N.W., 6th Floor
Washington, D.C. 20001-2070
(888) 422-7233; fax (202) 783-2348
Web site: iccsafe.org
Chief Executive Officer: Richard P. Weiland
Major publication: *The International Codes*

Purpose: To promote building safety and fire prevention by developing the codes used to construct residential and commercial buildings, including homes and schools. Most U.S. cities, counties, and states that adopt codes choose the international codes developed by the ICC, a membership organization. Established 1994.

International Economic Development Council (IEDC)

734 15th Street, N.W., Suite 900
Washington, D.C. 20005
(202) 223-7800; fax (202) 223-4745
Web site: iedconline.org
President/CEO: Jeffrey A. Finkle
Major publications: *Economic Development Journal, Economic Development Now, Federal Directory, Federal Review, Budget Overview*

Purpose: To help economic development professionals improve the quality of life in their communities. With more than 4,000 members, IEDC represents all levels of government, academia, and private industry, providing a broad range of member services that includes research, advisory services, conferences, professional certification, professional development, publications, and legislative tracking. Established 2001.

International Institute of Municipal Clerks (IIMC)

8331 Utica Avenue, Suite 200
Rancho Cucamonga, California 91730
(909) 944-4162; fax (909) 944-8545
(800) 251-1639
Web site: iimc.com

Executive Director: Chris Shalby
Major publications: *IIMC News Digest; The Language of Local Government; Meeting Administration Handbook; Parliamentary Procedures in Local Government; Role Call: Strategy for a Professional Clerk;* "Partners in Democracy" video, case study packets, technical bulletins

Purpose: To improve the administration of state, provincial, county, and local governments by maintaining central facilities for study and research devoted to the improvement of methods and procedures relating to the municipal clerk's, secretary's, or recorder's duties; and by sponsoring professional career development institutes in 46 universities. IIMC also sponsors an annual conference, distance learning programs, a monthly magazine, and a resource center; offers a self-study course in supervision and records and information management; and administers a professional certification program. Established 1947.

International Municipal Lawyers Association (IMLA)

7910 Woodmont Avenue, Suite 1440
Bethesda, Maryland 20814
(202) 466-5424; fax (202) 785-0152
E-mail: info@imla.org
Web site: imla.org
General Counsel/Executive Director: Chuck Thompson
Major publications: *The IMLA Model Ordinance Service, Municipal Lawyer*

Purpose: To provide continuing legal education events, publications, research, legal advocacy assistance, and excellent networking opportunities for the local government legal community. IMLA is a membership organization of U.S. and Canadian city and county attorneys. Established 1935.

International Public Management Association for Human Resources (IPMA-HR)

1617 Duke Street
Alexandria, Virginia 22314
(703) 549-7100; fax (703) 684-0948
Web site: ipma-hr.org
Executive Director: Neil E. Reichenberg
Major publications: *Public Personnel Management, HR Bulletin, IPMA-HR News*

Purpose: To improve service to the public by promoting quality human resource management in the public sector. Established 1973.

League of Women Voters of the United States (LWVUS)

1730 M Street, N.W., Suite 1000
Washington, D.C. 20036-4508
(202) 429-1965; fax (202) 429-0854

Web site: lwv.org
Executive Director: Nancy Tate
Major publications: *Choosing the President 2008: A Citizen's Guide to the Electoral Process; Observing Your Government in Action: Protecting Your Right to Know; Citizens Building Communities: ABC's of Public Dialogue; For the Public Record: A Documentary History of the League of Women Voters; Local Voices: Citizen Conversations on Civil Liberties and Secure Communities; Looking for Sunshine: Protecting Your Right to Know; The National Voter* magazine

Purpose: To encourage informed and active participation in government and to influence public policy through education and advocacy. The league's current advocacy priorities are civil liberties and homeland security, the D.C. Voting Rights Education Project, democracy agenda, global democracy, a fair judiciary, immigration, openness in government, public advocacy for voter protection, redistricting reform, voter information, campaign finance, lobbying, and election reform. The League of Women Voters Education Fund, a separate but complementary organization, provides research and public education services to the public to encourage and enable citizen participation in government. Current public education programs include voter outreach and education, the Vote 411.org Web site, election reform, judicial independence, and international forms and exchange activities. The league is a nonpartisan political organization. Established 1920.

Maritime Municipal Training and Development Board (MMTDB)

Don Smeltzer Training and Management Consultants
3-644 Portland Street, Suite 516
Dartmouth, Nova Scotia B2W 2M3
(902) 439-8092; fax: (902) 484-6113
E-mail: Don@munisource.org
Web site for municipal government information: munisource.org
Executive Director: A. Donald Smeltzer

Purpose: To provide quality management, education, and training services to the municipal public sector and volunteer organizations. Professional contacts are maintained with associates throughout North America and elsewhere, enabling the company to respond to many management and organizational needs. Established 1974.

National Animal Control Association (NACA)

P.O. Box 480851
Kansas City, Missouri 64148-0851
(913) 768-1319; fax (913) 768-1378

Web site: nacanet.org
President: Mark Kumpf
Major publications: *The NACA News* newsletter, *The NACA Training Guide*

Purpose: To provide training for animal control personnel; consultation and guidance for local governments on animal control ordinances, animal shelter design, budget and program planning, and staff training; and public education. Established 1978.

National Association of Counties (NACo)

25 Massachusetts Avenue, N.W., 5th Floor
Washington, D.C. 20001-1431
(202) 393-6226; fax (202) 393-2630
Web site: naco.org
Executive Director: Larry Naake
Major publication: *County News, NACo e-News*

Purpose: To serve as the voice of America's counties. As the only national organization that represents county governments in the United States, NACo provides essential services to the nation's 1,066 counties. The association advances issues with a unified voice before the federal government, improves the public's understanding of county government, assists counties in finding and sharing innovative solutions through education and research, and provides value-added services to save counties and taxpayers money. Established 1935.

National Association of County and City Health Officials (NACCHO)

1100 17th Street, 2nd Floor
Washington, D.C. 20036
(202) 783-5550; fax (202) 783-1583
Web site: naccho.org
Executive Director: Robert M. (Bobby) Pestronk
Major publications: *Who's Who in Local Public Health* (annual), *Public Health Dispatch* (newsletter), *NACCHO Exchange* (quarterly), research briefs and videos

Purpose: To support efforts that protect and improve the health of all people and all communities by promoting national policy, developing resources and programs, seeking health equity, and supporting effective local public health practice and systems. Established 1993.

National Association for County Community and Economic Development (NACCED)

2025 M Street, N.W., Suite 800
Washington, D.C. 20036-3309
(202) 367-1149; fax (202) 367-2149
Web site: nacced.org
Executive Director: John Murphy

Purpose: To help develop the technical capacity of county agencies in administering community development, economic development, and affordable housing programs. Created as an affiliate of the National Association of Counties (NACo), NACCED is a nonprofit national organization that also serves as a voice within NACo to articulate the needs, concerns, and interests of county agencies. Established 1978.

National Association of Development Organizations (NADO)

400 North Capitol Street, N.W., Suite 390
Washington, D.C. 20001
(202) 624-7806; fax (202) 624-8813
Web site: nado.org
Executive Director: Matthew Chase
Major publications: *Regional Development Digest, EDFS Reporter, NADO News*

Purpose: To provide training, information, and representation for regional development organizations serving small metropolitan and rural America. Building on nearly four decades of experience, the association offers its members exclusive access to a variety of services and benefits—all of which are crafted to enhance the activities, programs, and prospects of regional development organizations. Established 1967.

National Association of Housing and Redevelopment Officials (NAHRO)

630 Eye Street, N.W.
Washington, D.C. 20001
(202) 289-3500; fax (202) 289-8181
(877) 866-2476
Web site: nahro.org
Executive Director: Saul N. Ramirez
Major publications: *Journal of Housing and Community Development, NAHRO Monitor, Directory of Local Agencies, Commissioners Dictionary, The NAHRO Public Relations Handbook, Commissioners Handbook*

Purpose: To serve as a professional membership organization representing local housing authorities; community development agencies; and professionals in the housing, community development, and redevelopment fields. Divided into eight regions and 43 chapters, NAHRO works to provide safe, decent, and affordable housing for low- and moderate-income persons. NAHRO provides its 20,000 members with information on federal policy, legislation, regulations, and funding. It also provides professional development and training programs in all phases of agency operations, including management, maintenance, and procurement. In addition, NAHRO sponsors a legislative conference, a summer conference, and a national conference and exhibition every year. Established 1933.

National Association of Regional Councils (NARC)

1666 Connecticut Avenue, N.W., Suite 300
Washington, D.C. 20009-1038
(202) 986-1032; fax (202) 986-1038
Web site: narc.org
Executive Director: Fred Abousleman

Purpose: To promote regional approaches and collaboration in addressing diverse development challenges. A nonprofit membership organization and public interest group, NARC has represented the interests of its members and has advanced regional cooperation through effective interaction and advocacy with Congress, federal officials, and other related agencies and interest groups for more than 40 years. Its member organizations are composed of multiple local government units that work together to serve American communities, large and small, urban and rural. Among the issues it addresses are transportation, homeland security and regional preparedness, economic and community development, the environment, and a variety of community issues of interest to member organizations. NARC provides its members with valuable information and research on key national policy issues, federal policy developments, and best practices; in addition, it conducts enriching training sessions, conferences workshops, and satellite telecasts. Established 1967.

National Association of Schools of Public Affairs and Administration (NASPAA)

1029 Vermont Avenue, N.W., Suite 1100
Washington, D.C. 20005
(202) 628-8965; fax (202) 626-4978
E-mail: naspaa@naspaa.org
Web site: naspaa.org
Executive Director: Laurel McFarland
Major publications: *Journal of Public Affairs Education (J-PAE), Newsletter, MPA Accreditation Standards, MPA/MPP Brochure,* peer review and accreditation documents

Purpose: To serve as a national and international center for information about programs and developments in the area of public affairs and administration; to foster goals and standards of educational excellence; to represent members' concerns and interests in the formulation and support of national, state, and local policies for public affairs education and research; and to serve as a specialized accrediting agency for MPA/MPP degrees. Established 1970.

National Association of State Chief Information Officers (NASCIO)

c/o AMR Management Services
201 East Main Street, Suite 1405
Lexington, Kentucky 40507

(859) 514-9156; fax (859) 514-9166

Web site: nascio.org

Executive Director: Douglas Robinson

Major publications: *NASCIO Exchange* (newsletter), *Issues Focus Report*

Purpose: To represent state chief information officers and be the leading forum for addressing the opportunities for, and implications and challenges of, improving the business of government through the application of information technology. Established 1969.

National Association of Towns and Townships (NATaT)

1130 Connecticut Avenue, N.W., Suite 300

Washington, D.C. 20036

(202) 331-8500; fax (202) 331-1598

Web site: natat.org

Federal Director: Jennifer Imo

Major publication: *Washington Report*

Purpose: To strengthen the effectiveness of town and township government by educating lawmakers and public policy officials about how small-town governments operate and by advocating policies on their behalf in Washington, D.C. Established 1976.

National Career Development Association (NCDA)

522 21st Street, N.W., #120

Washington, D.C. 20006

(202) 293-7587; fax (202) 887-5546

Web site: ncdaonline.org

Executive Director: Deneen Pennington

Major publications: *Adult Career Development; The Career Counseling Casebook; A Counselor's Guide to Career Assessment Resources; Experiential Activities for Teaching Career Development Courses and Facilitating Work Groups; The Internet: A Tool for Career Planning*

Purpose: To promote the career development of all people over the life span. To achieve this mission, NCDA provides services to the public and to professionals involved with or interested in career development; these services include professional development activities, publications, research, public information, professional standards, advocacy, and recognition for achievement and service. Established 1913.

National Civic League (NCL)

1640 Logan Street

Denver, Colorado 80203

(303) 571-4343; fax (303) 571-4404

E-mail: kristins@ncl.org

Web site: ncl.org

President: Gloria Rubio-Cortés

Major publications: *The Community Visioning and Strategic Planning Handbook, Model County Charter, National Civic Review, 8th Edition of the Model City Charter, New Civic Index*

Purpose: To strengthen democracy by increasing the capacity of our nation's people to fully participate in and build healthy and prosperous communities across America. NCL facilitates community-wide strategic planning in transportation-oriented development, parks and recreation, and other issues. We are good at the science of local government, the art of public engagement, and the celebration of the progress that can be achieved when people work together. NCL is the home of the All-America City Awards and the MetLife Foundation Ambassadors in Education Awards. Established 1894.

National Community Development Association (NCDA)

522 21st Street, N.W., #120

Washington, D.C. 20006

(202) 293-7587; fax (202) 887-5546

Web site: ncdaonline.org

Executive Director: Cardell Cooper

Purpose: To help local governments develop high-quality, locally responsive programs for making communities better places in which to live, particularly for low- and moderate-income people. A national nonprofit association, NCDA represents cities and counties nationwide that administer U.S. Department of Housing and Urban Development funding; the Community Development Block Grant program, and the HOME Investment Partnerships program. Established 1968.

National Conference of State Legislatures (NCSL)

7700 East First Place

Denver, Colorado 80230

(303) 364-7700; fax (303) 364-7800

Also at 444 North Capitol Street, N.W., Suite 515

Washington, D.C. 20001-1201

(202) 624-5400; fax (202) 737-1069

Web site: ncsl.org

Executive Director: William T. Pound

Major publications: *Capitol to Capitol, Federal Update, State Legislatures*

Purpose: To improve the quality and effectiveness of state legislatures; to ensure that states have a strong, cohesive voice in the federal decision-making process; and to foster interstate communication and cooperation. Established 1975.

National Environmental Health Association (NEHA)

720 South Colorado Boulevard, Suite 1000-N

Denver, Colorado 80246-1925

(303) 756-9090; fax (303) 691-9490

E-mail: staff@neha.org

Web site: neha.org

Executive Director: Nelson E. Fabian

Major publications: *Journal of Environmental Health* and more than 200 other publications

Purpose: To advance the professional in the environmental field through education, professional meetings, and the dissemination of information. The association also publishes information relating to environmental health and protection and promotes professionalism in the field. Established 1937.

National Fire Protection Association (NFPA)

One Batterymarch Park

Quincy, Massachusetts 02169-7471

(617) 770-3000; fax (617) 770-0700

Web site: nfpa.org

President/CEO: James M. Shannon

Major publications: *Fire Protection Handbook, Fire Technology, NFPA Journal, National Electrical Code®, National Fire Codes®, Life Safety Code®, Risk Watch™, Learn Not to Burn® Curriculum,* textbooks, manuals, training packages, detailed analyses of important fires, fire officers guides, and more

Purpose: To reduce the worldwide burden of fire and other hazards on the quality of life by providing and advocating scientifically based consensus codes and standards, research, training, and education. Established 1896.

National Governors Association (NGA)

Hall of the States

444 North Capitol Street, Suite 267

Washington, D.C. 20001-1512

(202) 624-5300; fax (202) 624-5313

Web site: nga.org

Executive Director: Raymond C. Scheppach

Major publications: *The Fiscal Survey of States, Policy Positions,* reports on a wide range of state issues

Purpose: To act as a liaison between the states and the federal government, and to serve as a clearinghouse for information and ideas on state and national issues. Established 1908.

National Housing Conference (NHC)

1801 K Street, N.W., Suite M-100

Washington, D.C. 20006-1301

(202) 466-2121; fax (202) 466-2122

Web site: nhc.org

President/CEO: Conrad Egan

Major publications: *New Century Housing, NHC at Work, NHC Affordable Housing Policy Review, Washington Wire*

Purpose: To promote better communities and affordable housing for Americans through education and advocacy. Established 1931.

National Institute of Governmental Purchasing (NIGP)

151 Spring Street

Herndon, Virginia 20170-5223

(703) 736-8900; fax (703) 736-2818
(800) FOR NIGP (367-6447)
Web site: nigp.org
Chief Executive Officer: Rick Grimm, CPPO, CPPB
Industry-specific publications: *GoPro: Government Procurement* magazine, a bi-monthly publication distributed to NIGP members and procurement professionals; *NIGP Buy-Weekly,* an e-newsletter for public procurement professionals; *NIGP Dictionary of Purchasing Terms*

Purpose: To develop, support, and promote the public procurement profession through premier educational and research programs, professional support, and advocacy initiatives that benefit members and constituents. As a vibrant international association, NIGP seeks to create a world in which public procurement practitioners are highly regarded members of a respected professional order. NIGP offers resources and seminars that address current industry issues and trends affecting the way governments do business. The Learning and Education to Advance Procurement (LEAP) curriculum is the basis for all educational offerings. NIGP also offers procurement management auditing and consulting services; the Government Contractor Certificate program, a training/certificate program to enhance partnerships with industry and ensure quality proposals in the government contracting process; online libraries of specifications, research projects, and reports; the NIGP Commodity/Service Coding System, a universal language identifying commodities and services; an accreditation program; formal award recognition in public purchasing based on standards to enhance purchasing operations and credibility; and E-Net, an electronic network for members. Additionally, NIGP supports the Universal Public Purchasing Certification Council (UPPCC) and its two-level certification program for public purchasing personnel: CPPB (Certified Professional Public Buyer) and CPPO (Certified Public Purchasing Officer). Established 1944.

National League of Cities (NLC)

1301 Pennsylvania Avenue, N.W., Suite 550
Washington, D.C. 20004-1763
(202) 626-3000; fax (202) 626-3043
Web site: nlc.org
Executive Director: Donald J. Borut
President: Council member Cynthia Mccollum
Major publications: *Nation's Cities Weekly,* guide books, directories, and research reports

Purpose: To strengthen and promote cities as centers of opportunity, leadership, and governance; to serve as an advocate for its members in Washington in the legislative, administrative, and judicial processes that affect them; and to develop and pursue a national urban policy that meets the present and future needs of the nation's urban communities and the people who live in them. The league also offers training, technical assistance, and information to local government and state league officials to help them improve the quality of local government, and it researches and analyzes policy issues of importance to urban America. Established 1924.

National Public Employer Labor Relations Association (NPELRA)

1012 South Coast Highway, Suite M
Oceanside, California 92054
(760) 433-1686; fax (760) 433-1687
E-mail: info@npelra.org
Web site: npelra.org
Executive Director: Michael T. Kolb

Purpose: To provide its members with high-quality, progressive labor relations advice that balances the needs of management, employees, and the public; to promote the interests of public sector management in the judicial and legislative arenas; and to provide opportunities for networking among members by establishing state and regional organizations throughout the country. The premier organization for public sector labor relations and human resource professionals, NPELRA is a network of state and regional affiliates whose more than 3,000 members around the country represent public employers in a wide range of areas, from employee-management contract negotiations to arbitration under grievance and arbitration procedures. The governmental agencies represented in NPELRA employ more than 4 million workers in federal, state, and local government. Established 1971.

National Recreation and Park Association (NRPA)

22377 Belmont Ridge Road
Ashburn, Virginia 20148
(703) 858-0784; fax (703) 858-0794
Web site: nrpa.org
Chief Executive Officer: Barbara Tulipane
Major publications: *Parks & Recreation Magazine; Journal of Leisure Research; Therapeutic Recreation Journal; Park, Recreation and Leisure Facilities Site Planning Guidelines; The Proximate Principle: The Impact of Parks, Open Space, and Water Features on Residential Property Values and the Property Tax Base*

Purpose: To advance parks, recreation, and environmental conservation efforts that enhance the quality of life for all people. Established 1965.

National School Boards Association (NSBA)

1680 Duke Street
Alexandria, Virginia 22314-3493
(703) 838-6722; fax (703) 683-7590
Web site: nsba.org
Executive Director: Anne L. Bryant
Major publications: *American School Board Journal, Inquiry and Analysis, Leadership Insider, School Board News, Technology Leadership New*

Purpose: To work with and through all of its federation members to foster excellence and equity in public education through school board leadership. Established 1940.

Police Executive Research Forum (PERF)

1120 Connecticut Avenue, N.W., Suite 930
Washington, D.C. 20036
(202) 466-7820; fax (202) 466-7826
Web site: policeforum.org
Executive Director: Chuck Wexler
Major publications: *Subject to Debate* (monthly newsletter)

Purpose: To improve policing and advance professionalism through research and involvement in public policy debate. Incorporated in 1977, PERF is a national membership organization of progressive police executives from the largest city, county, and state law enforcement agencies. Its primary sources of operating revenues are government grants and contracts, and partnerships with private foundations and other organizations. Established 1976.

Police Foundation

1201 Connecticut Avenue, N.W.
Washington, D.C. 20036-2636
(202) 833-1460; fax (202) 659-9149
E-mail: pfinfo@policefoundation.org
Web site: policefoundation.org
President: Hubert Williams
Major publications: *Ideas in American Policing* series, *Crime Mapping News,* and research and technical assistance reports on a wide range of law enforcement and public safety issues; a publications list and many foundation publications are available online

Purpose: To improve American policing through research, evaluation, training, field experimentation, technical assistance, technology, and information. Objective, nonpartisan, and nonprofit, the foundation assists federal, state, and local governments in such areas as community policing, strategic planning, crime mapping, civil disorder preparedness and response, police use of force, police misconduct, ethics, operational and administrative review, program evaluation, police-community relations, and police chief selection. The foundation's Crime Mapping

and Problem Analysis Laboratory works to advance the understanding and pioneer new applications of computer mapping, and it provides training and technical assistance to police agencies. Established 1970.

Public Entity Risk Institute (PERI)

11350 Random Hills Road, Suite 210
Fairfax, Virginia 22030
(703) 352-1846; fax (703) 352-6339
E-mail: ghoetmer@riskinstitute.org
Web site: riskinstitute.org
Executive Director: Gerard J. Hoetmer
Major publications: *Emergency Management in Higher Education: Current Practices and Conversations; Emergency Management: The American Experience 1900–2005; Risk Management Resource Guide; Risk Identification and Analysis: A Guide for Small Public Entities; Community Leadership in a Risky World; Limiting Small Town Liability: A Risk Management Primer; Characteristics of Effective Emergency Management Structures; Are You Ready? What Lawyers Need to Know about Emergency Preparedness and Disaster Recovery; Holistic Disaster Recovery: Ideas for Building Local Sustainability after a Natural Disaster; Surviving Extreme Events: A Guide to Help Small Businesses and Not-for-Profit Organizations Prepare for and Recover from Extreme Events; PERIScope Newsletter*

Purpose: To provide risk management education and training resources for local governments and school districts, small businesses, and nonprofits. PERI is a nonprofit, non-membership organization. Its Web site serves as a resource center and clearinghouse with information on a wide range of topics, including disaster management and hazard mitigation, risk financing and insurance, safety and health, workers' compensation, and technology risks. PERI also operates a national benchmarking database, known as the PERI Data Exchange, which allows local governments to compare their liability and workers' compensation losses with those of their peers, and to identify strategies to reduce losses and control costs. Local governments that submit data to the database receive prime benchmarking reports at no cost. Established 1996.

Public Risk Management Association (PRIMA)

500 Montgomery Street, Suite 750
Alexandria, Virginia 22314-1516
(703) 528-7701; fax (703) 739-0200
E-mail: info@primacentral.org
Web site: primacentral.org
Executive Director: Lisa Lopinsky
Major publications: *Public Risk Magazine, Public Sector Risk Management Manual;* special reports: *Cost of Risk Evaluation in State and Local Government, 1998 Tort*

Liability Today: A Guide for State and Local Governments; videos: *Shaping a Secure Future*

Purpose: To promote effective risk management in the public interest as an essential component of administration. Established 1978.

Public Technology Institute (PTI)

1301 Pennsylvania Avenue, N.W., Suite 830
Washington, D.C. 20004
(202) 626-2400; fax (202) 626-2498
E-mail: press@pti.nw.dc.us
Web site: pti.org
Executive Director: Alan R. Shark
Major publications: *Winning Solutions* (annual); *Online* magazine (prismonline.org); *Slow Down, You're Going Too Fast: A Local Official's Guide to Traffic Calming; Roads Less Traveled: Intelligent Transportation Systems for Sustainable Communities; Sustainable Building Technical Manual; Smart Moves: A Decision Maker's Guide to the Intelligent Transportation Infrastructure; gis://the next management tool; Mission Possible: Strong Governance Structures for the Integration of Justice Information Systems; E-Government: Factors Affecting ROI; E-Government: A Strategic Planning Guide for Local Officials; Why Not Do It Ourselves? A Resource Guide for Local Government Officials and Citizens Regarding Public Ownership of Utility Systems; Greening the Fleet: A Local Government Guide to Alternative Fuels and Vehicles;* numerous case studies on energy and environmental technology development and sustainable management

Purpose: To identify and test technologies and management approaches that help all local governments provide the best possible services to citizens and business communities. With ICMA, NLC, and NACo, PTI works with progressive member cities and counties to (1) make communities "well-connected" by advancing communication capabilities; (2) develop tools and processes for wise decision making; and (3) promote sustainable approaches that ensure a balance between economic development and a clean, quality environment. PTI's member program engages cities and counties as laboratories for research, development, and public enterprise to advance technology applications in telecommunications, energy, the environment, transportation, and public safety. To disseminate member research, PTI provides print and electronic resources, and peer consultation and networking. Through partnerships with private vendors, PTI offers several technology products and services that help local governments save money by bypassing rigorist RFP requirements as they are competitively bid and chosen for superior quality

and competitive pricing. PTI's research and development division continues to examine information and Internet technology, public safety, geographic information systems (GIS), energy-conserving technologies, sustainable management, and intelligent transportation systems. Established 1971.

Sister Cities International (SCI)

1301 Pennsylvania Avenue, N.W., Suite 850
Washington, D.C. 20004
(202) 347-8630; fax (202) 393-6524
E-mail: info@sister-cities.org
Web site: sister-cities.org
Executive Director: Patrick Madden
Major publications: Sister Cities International Membership Directory, *Sister Cities News, Report to the Membership* (bimonthly)

Purpose: To promote sustainable development, youth involvement, cultural understanding, and humanitarian assistance, and to increase global cooperation at the local level by creating and strengthening partnerships among U.S. and international communities. With its international headquarters in Washington, D.C., SCI is a nonprofit, citizen diplomacy network that officially certifies, represents, and supports partnerships between U.S. cities, counties, states, and similar jurisdictions in other countries to ensure their continued commitment and success. The SCI network represents nearly 700 U.S. communities and over 1,800 international communities, making up more than 2,500 partnerships in 126 countries around the world. Established 1967.

Solid Waste Association of North America (SWANA)

P.O. Box 7219
Silver Spring, Maryland 20907-7219
(301) 585-2898; fax (301) 589-7068
(800) 467-9262
E-mail: info@swana.org
Web site: swana.org
Executive Director: John H. Skinner, PhD
Purpose: To advance the practice of environmentally and economically sound municipal solid waste management in North America. Established 1961.

Special Libraries Association (SLA)

331 South Patrick Street
Alexandria, Virginia 22314-3501
(703) 647-4900; fax (703) 647-4901
E-mail: sla@sla.org
Web site: sla.org
Chief Executive Officer: Janice R. Lachance
Major publications: *Information Outlook*
Purpose: To further the professional growth and success of its membership. Headquartered in Alexandria, Virginia, SLA is the international association representing the

interests of thousands of information professionals in 84 countries. The association offers a variety of programs and services designed to help its members serve their customers more effectively and succeed in an increasingly challenging global information arena. Established 1909.

Universal Public Purchasing Certification Council (UPPCC)

151 Spring Street
Herndon, Virginia 20170
(800) 367-6447 Fax: (703) 796-9611
E-mail: certification@uppcc.org
Web site: uppcc.org
Program Administrator: Ann Peshoff

Purpose: To more effectively promote and ensure professionalism in public sector procurement, the UPPCC is charged with identifying and establishing a standard of competency for the public procurement profession; establishing and monitoring eligibility requirements of those interested in achieving certification; and furthering the cause of certification in the public sector. Jointly established as an independent, not-for-profit entity in 1978 by the National Institute of Governmental Purchasing (NIGP) and the National Association of State Procurement Officials (NASPO), the UPPCC administers two certification programs: the Certified Public Purchasing Officer (CPPO) program, which applies to individuals who have demonstrated prescribed levels of professional competency as buyers in governmental purchasing, and the Certified Professional Public Buyer (CPPB) program, which applies to similar individuals who also assume managerial functions within their jurisdictions or agencies. These programs have been established to meet the requirements of all public purchasing personnel in federal, state, and local governments. Certification, which reflects established standards and competencies for those engaged in governmental purchasing and attests to the purchaser's ability to obtain maximum value for the taxpayer's dollar, is applicable to all public and governmental organizations, regardless of size. As the trend in governmental purchasing is for mandatory certification of procurement professionals, these credentials communicate to the taxpayer that the public employee who

manages tax dollars has reached a level of education and practical experience within government purchasing to be recognized by the UPPCC. Established 1978.

Urban Affairs Association (UAA)

298 Graham Hall
University of Delaware
Newark, Delaware 19716
(302) 831-1681; fax (302) 831-4225
Web site: udel.edu/uaa
Executive Director: Dr. Margaret Wilder
Major publications: *Journal of Urban Affairs, Urban Affairs* (a newsletter)

Purpose: To encourage the dissemination of information and research findings about urbanism and urbanization; to support the development of university education, research, and service programs in urban affairs; and to foster the development of urban affairs as a professional and academic field. Established 1969.

Urban Institute (UI)

2100 M Street, N.W.
Washington, D.C. 20037
(202) 833-7200
Web site: urban.org
President: Robert D. Reischauer
Publications: Research papers, policy briefs, events, podcasts, web modules, and books on social and economic issues, including health care, welfare reform, immigration policy, tax reform, prisoner reentry, housing policy, retirement, charitable giving, school accountability, economic development, and community revitalization; all publications available online except books.

Purpose: To respond to needs for objective analyses and basic information on the social and economic challenges confronting the nation and for nonpartisan evaluation of the government policies and programs designed to alleviate such problems. Established 1968.

Urban and Regional Information Systems Association (URISA)

1460 Renaissance Drive, Suite 305
Park Ridge, Illinois 60068
(847) 824-6300; fax (847) 824-6363
Web site: urisa.org
Executive Director: Wendy Nelson
Major publications: *URISA Journal, URISA News,* Quick Studies, books and com-

pendiums, salary surveys, conference proceedings, videos

Purpose: To promote the effective and ethical use of spatial information and information technologies for the understanding and management of urban and regional systems. URISA is a nonprofit, professional, educational, and multidisciplinary association where professionals from all parts of the spatial data community can come together and share concerns and ideas. It is the professional home of choice for public sector GIS and information technology executives throughout the United States, Canada, and other countries worldwide. Established 1963.

U.S. Conference of Mayors (USCM)

1620 Eye Street, N.W.
Washington, D.C. 20006
(202) 293-7330; fax (202) 293-2352
E-mail: info@usmayors.org
Web site: usmayors.org
CEO & Executive Director: Tom Cochran
Major publications: *U.S. Mayor, Mayors of America's Principal Cities*

Purpose: To act as the official nonpartisan organization of cities with populations of 30,000 or more; to aid the development of effective national urban policy; to ensure that federal policy meets urban needs; and to provide mayors with leadership and management tools. Each city is represented in the conference by its mayor. Established 1932.

Water Environment Federation (WEF)

601 Wythe Street
Alexandria, Virginia 22314-1994
(703) 684-2552; fax (703) 684-2492
(800) 666-0206
Web sites: wef.org and weftec.org
Executive Director: William Bertera
Major publications: *Water Environment Research, Water Practice, Water Environment and Technology, Operations Forum, Water Environment Regulation Watch, Biosolids Technical Bulletin, Utility Executive Technical Bulletin,* series of Manuals of Practice

Purpose: To develop and disseminate technical information concerning the preservation and enhancement of the global water environment. As an integral component of its mandate, the federation has pledged to act as a source of education to the general public as well as to individuals engaged in the water environment field. Established 1928.

Authors and Contributors

Chyleen A. Arbon is assistant professor of public management at Brigham Young University's Romney Institute of Public Management. Prior to this, she worked for the Utah legislature as a policy analyst. Her research interests include equity in public policy and public management decision making, criminal justice policy, and alternative work schedules. She received her doctorate in political science from the University of Utah.

David R. Berman is a senior research fellow at the Morrison Institute for Public Policy and a professor emeritus of political science at Arizona State University. His research has been supported by numerous grants and contracts. Along with being a regular contributor to the *Municipal Year Book,* he has produced eight books and more than 60 published papers, book chapters, or referred articles dealing with state and local government, politics, and public policy; among his works are *Local Government and the States: Autonomy, Politics, and Policy* (2003) and, most recently, *Radicalism in the Mountain West* (2007). Before coming to Arizona State, Professor Berman was a research associate with the National League of Cities. He has served as a consultant for the U.S. Advisory Commission on Intergovernmental Relations, and has been on the executive committees of the American Political Science Association's Federalism and Intergovernmental Section, and of the American Society for Public Administration's Section on Intergovernmental Administration and Management. He holds a bachelor's degree from Rockford College in Rockford, Illinois, and both a master's degree and a doctorate from the American University in Washington, D.C.

Lydia Bjornlund is a private consultant and freelance writer, working primarily on training materials and topics related to local government, land conservation, and the environment. She has also written several books for children, mostly on American history and government. Before beginning Bjornlund Communications of Oakton, Virginia, in 1996, she was senior curriculum specialist at ICMA. She holds a bachelor of arts degree from Williams College and a master's degree in education from Harvard University.

Shea Riggsbee Denning, a specialist in motor vehicle law, is assistant professor of public law and government at the School of Government of the University of North Carolina (UNC) at Chapel Hill. She earned an AB in journalism and mass communication, and a JD with high honors from UNC–Chapel Hill, where she was also Order of the Coif and an articles editor of the *North Carolina Law Review.*

Gregory J. Dyson, senior vice president, chief operations and marketing officer, joined ICMA Retirement Corporation (ICMA-RC) in 2002 and is a member of the senior management team. An experienced marketing and financial services professional who provides an innovative approach to management, marketing, and client services, Mr. Dyson is responsible for ICMA-RC's product management and development, corporate branding/positioning, public affairs, client and corporate communications, and support for new business development. He also oversees the strategic direction of all client services, including plan sponsor and investor services' communications, financial planning services, and participant account operations. Mr. Dyson is on the board of directors of the Center for State and Local Government Excellence. He is also an officer of the Vantagepoint Public Employee Memorial Scholarship Fund, a member of the ICMA Corporate Partner Council, a member of the National Forum of Black Public Administrators, and a past co-chair of the National League of Cities (NLC) Corporate Partnership Advisory Council. He is on NLC's National Black Caucus of Local Elected Officials Foundation Board. Mr. Dyson holds an undergraduate degree in journalism and government from Ohio Wesleyan University and an MBA from the Darden School at the University of Virginia.

Rex L. Facer II is assistant professor of public finance and management and the Warren Jones Fellow at Brigham Young University's Romney Institute of Public Management. He has been a visiting fellow at the Lincoln Institute of Land Policy and previously worked at the University of Georgia's Carl Vinson Institute of Government. He lectures internationally on local government and local tax policy, and he has been involved in several applied public finance and management projects for local governments and state agencies. His recent research focuses on infrastructure finance, budgetary decision making, and alternative work schedules.

Siegrun Fox Freyss is professor of political science and director of the Master of Science in Public Administration program at the California State University, Los Angeles. Her research interests are in local politics, urban policies, and municipal management. She is the editor of *Human Resource Management in Local Government: An Essential Guide,* published by ICMA, and the author of numerous articles published in academic journals and as book chapters. She holds a doctorate in government from the Claremont Graduate University and received her bachelor's as well as her master's degrees in urban planning from the Technical University in Munich, Germany.

Kathy Harm, CFP®, is a consultant to ICMA-RC. From 1983 to 2006, she held a variety of customer service, relationship management, and marketing positions at ICMA-RC before retiring as director of retiree health programs. Prior to joining ICMA-RC, she served in several local government jurisdictions in planning, personnel, and management positions. She authored *A Public Employee's Guide to Retirement Planning* for the Government Finance Officers Association, and she has written numerous articles on retirement and retiree health for such publications as *PM* magazine, ICMA's MIS series, *American City and County,* and *Government Finance Review.* In addition, she has been a frequent speaker on retirement and retiree health issues at national and state public sector conferences. Ms. Harm holds the Certified Financial Planner (CFP®) designation as well as FINRA Series 6, 63, and 26 registrations. She earned her bachelor's degree from Syracuse University.

Amir Hefetz is a lecturer in the Department of Town and Regional Planning at the Technion Institute in Haifa, Israel. He has done extensive research on privatization among local governments in the United States. His research gives special emphasis to the dynamics of privatization and uneven spatial effects of government restructuring.

Robert P. Joyce, a specialist in the law of education, the law of elections, and the law of employment, is professor of public law and government at the School of Government of the University of North Carolina (UNC) at Chapel Hill. He has practiced law in New York City and in North Carolina. His undergraduate degree is from UNC, and his law degree is from Harvard.

James M. Markham, a specialist in criminal law and procedure with a focus on the law of sentencing, corrections, and the conditions of confinement, is assistant professor of public law and government at the School of Government of the University of North Carolina at Chapel Hill. He earned a bachelor's degree with honors from Harvard College and a law degree with high honors, Order of the Coif, from Duke University, where he was editor-in-chief of the *Duke Law Journal.* Prior to attending law school, Professor Markham served five years in the U.S. Air Force as an intelligence officer and foreign area officer.

Christopher B. McLaughlin, a specialist in the law of local taxation, is assistant professor of public law and government at the School of Government of the University of North Carolina at Chapel Hill. He practiced law in Boston and Maine, and served as adjunct professor and assistant dean for student affairs at Duke University Law School. Professor McLaughlin is a magna cum laude graduate of the University of Pennsylvania's Wharton School of Business and of Duke University Law School, where he was also Order of the Coif.

Evelina R. Moulder, director of ICMA's survey research, is responsible for the development of survey instruments, design of the sample, design of logic checks, quality control, and analysis of survey results. Among the surveys conducted by ICMA under her supervision are economic development, e-government, financing infrastructure, homeland security, labor-management relations, parks and recreation, police and fire personnel and expenditures, service delivery, technology, and SARA Title III. She has also directed several survey projects funded by other organizations. With more than 20 years of experience in local government survey research, Ms. Moulder has collaborated extensively with government agencies, professors, the private sector, and other researchers in survey development, and she has played a key role in ICMA's homeland security and emergency response initiatives, including concept and proposal development.

Joyce C. Powell serves as a senior consultant in compensation systems with the Waters Consulting Group in Dallas, Texas, helping clients develop custom compensation programs to meet their corporate philosophy and overall compensation strategy. A certified compensation professional with more than 18 years of hands-on experience, she

has served as an independent consultant working for major corporations in a myriad of industries, including energy and oil, health care, and information services. She also served as the supervisor of compensation and human resources for a subsidiary of a Fortune 500 company.

Edgar E. Ramirez de la Cruz is assistant professor in the School of Public Affairs at Arizona State University. His primary interest is urban governance; other interests include growth management, land use regulations, public management, and networks. His research has appeared in *Urban Affairs Review,* the *International Review of Public Administration,* and various edited books. He earned his MPA from El Centro de Investigación y Docencia Económicas (CIDE) in Mexico, and his PhD in public administration from the Askew School of Public Administration and Policy at Florida State University.

Craig Small is a vice president with ICMA-RC, where he manages retiree health care products and services for state and local governments. Prior to joining ICMA-RC, Mr. Small was associate treasurer of the District of Columbia, where his responsibilities included management of the District's 401(a) and 457 retirement plans, retiree health care trust fund, and 529 college savings plan. He previously structured bond issues for municipalities while serving in the public finance group of a major investment bank. Mr. Small received his BA from Penn State University and his MBA from Harvard University.

James H. Svara is a professor of public affairs at Arizona State University and the director of the Center for Urban Innovation. He specializes in local government leadership, management, and ethics. He is a fellow of the National Academy of Public Administration, a member of the board of the Alliance for Innovation, and an honorary member of ICMA, and he has served on the ICMA Strategic Planning Committee. His book *The Facilitative Leader in City Hall: Reexamining the Scope and Contributions* was recently published by CRC Press in the American Society of Public Administration's Book Series in Public Administration and Public Policy.

Karen Thoreson is the chief operating officer/deputy director for the Alliance for Innovation. Prior to working for the Alliance, she was economic development director for the city of Glendale, Arizona. She also served as assistant city manager of Tucson, overseeing downtown revitalization, and as director of the community services department, which managed the city's affordable housing programs, human services, and neighborhood revitalization. Ms. Thoreson began her career in local government in Boulder, Colorado. She has been a trainer and a speaker on public-private partnerships, community revitalization, innovation, and strategic planning; served as national president for the National Association of Housing and Redevelopment Organization from 1999 to 2001; and she is currently active in local, state, and national groups. She has a bachelor's degree from the University of Minnesota and a master's degree in public administration from the University of Northern Colorado.

Gordon Tiffany, CFP®, CFS, is director of financial and retirement education for ICMA-RC. For the two decades prior to joining ICMA-RC in 1991 he was a city manager and county administrator. A Certified Financial Planner (CFP®) and a Certified Fund Specialist (CFS), Mr. Tiffany is the author of ICMA-RC's retirement planning workbook series, *Charting Your Course: A Retirement Planning Guide for Public Sector Employees,* as well as of numerous articles on public employee financial and retirement planning. He is a frequent speaker on public employee financial and retirement planning matters at national and state public sector conferences and employee groups, and he has been a guest on the CNNfn (financial news) program, *Your Money.* He holds FINRA Series NASD 6, 63, 65 and 26 registrations. He has a BA and an MPA degree.

Lori L. Wadsworth is assistant professor of public management at Brigham Young University's Romney Institute of Public Management, where she teaches human resource management and ethics. Her research interests include work-family interaction, use of flexible benefits, social support, and ethics. She received her PhD in human resource management and organizational behavior from the University of Utah.

Mildred E. Warner is a professor in the City and Regional Planning Department at Cornell University, where her work is concentrated primarily on the role of local government in community development. Her research focuses on devolution, privatization, and their implications for local government service delivery. She also studies economic development and the role of local services. She publishes widely in the public administration, planning, and economic development literature. She also directs the graduate program in City and Regional Planning.

Rollie O. Waters is president and founder of the Waters Consulting Group, Inc., in Dallas, Texas. Since 1976, he has been a management consultant to private and public sector clients, both national and international, and has given various lectures and seminars for organizations in the areas of compensation design and performance management. Known nationwide as one of the foremost authorities in compensation and performance management system design for the public sector, he has spoken before such organizations as the American Management Association, Southern Methodist University, the University of Maryland, the California Institute of Technology, the Texas Municipal League, and the International Personnel Management Association, as well as before several international companies based in Great Britain.

Jeffrey B. Welty, a specialist in criminal law and procedure, is assistant professor of public law and government at the School of Government of the University of North Carolina at Chapel Hill. He previously practiced criminal defense law in Durham, North Carolina. Professor Welty earned a bachelor's degree from the University of California at Berkeley, and a master's degree in economics and a JD with highest honors from Duke University, where he was executive editor of *Duke Law Journal.*

Cumulative Index, 2005–2009

Cumulative Index, 2005–2009

The cumulative index comprises the years 2005 through 2009 of *The Municipal Year Book*. Entries prior to 2005 are found in earlier editions.

How to Use This Index. Entries run in chronological order, starting with 2005. The **year** is in **boldface** numerals, followed by a colon (e.g., **05:**); the relevant page numbers follow. Years are separated by semicolons.

Mortgage Bankers Association, **09:** 38
Motor vehicles
 cell phone parking program, **08:** 39
 emission standards, **05:** 72–73
 municipal, **07:** 42
Municipal administration. *See also* Canada;
 City managers; Local government;
 Salaries
 international municipal management associations directory, **05:** 179–180; **06:**
  187–188; **07:** 181–182; **08:** 176–177;
  09: 182–184
 municipal officials directory, **05:** 184–271;
  06: 191–282; **07:** 187–278; **08:** 181–
  274; **09:** 188–277
 salaries, **05:** 79–99; **06:** 83–105; **07:** 75–98;
  08: 73–94; **09:** 81–102
Municipal Automated Vehicle-Sharing Program
 (Philadelphia), **07:** 42
Municipal government. *See also* Council-
 manager (administrator) government
 chief appointed official, **08:** 9–15, 27–28
 chief elected official, **08:** 30–32
 committees and citizen boards, **08:** 33
 council member elections, **08:** 32
 council member terms, **08:** 33
 forms of, **08:** 9–15, 27, 30
 initiative, referenda, and recall provisions,
  08: 28–30
 survey, **08:** 27–33
Municipalities. *See* Directories; Finances; Local
 government; Municipal administration;
 Municipal government; Individual city
 data
Music, children and youth programs, **06:** 28

National Academy of Sciences, **07:** 15
National Animal Control Association, **05:** 312;
 06: 323–324; **07:** 318; **08:** 315; **09:**
 315–316
National Association of Area Agencies on
 Aging, **07:** 3, 03
National Association of Counties (NACo), **05:**
 12–13, 312; **06:** 324; **07:** 3, 319; **08:**
 21–26, 59, 315–316; **09:** 68, 70, 316
 Joint Center for Sustainable Communities,
  05: 9, 12–13
National Association of County and City Health
 Officials, **05:** 312; **06:** 324; **07:** 318–
 319; **09:** 316
National Association for County Community
 and Economic Development, **05:** 312;
 06: 324; **07:** 321; **08:** 316; **09:** 316
National Association of Development Organizations, **05:** 312; **06:** 324; **07:** 319; **08:**
 316; **09:** 316
National Association of Housing and Redevelopment Officials, **05:** 312; **06:** 324; **07:**
 319; **08:** 316; **09:** 316
National Association of Regional Councils,
 05: 312; **06:** 324; **07:** 319; **08:** 316;
 09: 316
National Association of Schools of Public
 Affairs and Administration, **05:** 312; **06:**
 324; **07:** 319; **08:** 316; **09:** 316
National Association of State Chief Information
 Officers, **05:** 313; **06:** 324; **07:** 319; **08:**
 316; **09:** 316–317

National Association of State Retirement
 Administrators, **09:** 36
National Association of Towns and Townships,
 05: 313; **06:** 324–325; **07:** 319–320; **08:**
 316–317; **09:** 317
National Bureau of Economic Research, **09:**
 34, 35
National Career Development Association, **05:**
 313; **06:** 325; **07:** 320; **08:** 317; **09:** 317
National Caregiver Support Program, **07:** 64
National Center for Atmospheric Research, **07:**
 15
National Center for Small Communities, **05:**
 313; **06:** 325
National Center on Education Disability and
 Juvenile Justice (EDJJ), **08:** 36
National Civic League, **05:** 313; **06:** 325; **07:**
 320; **08:** 317; **09:** 317
National Climate Assessment (U.S.), **07:** 15–16,
 19
National Community Development Association,
 05: 313; **06:** 325; **07:** 320; **08:** 317; **09:**
 317
National Conference of State Legislatures,
 05: 313; **06:** 325; **07:** 320; **08:** 317;
 09: 317
National Congress for Community Economic
 Development, **05:** 313; **06:** 325
National Counterterrorism Center, **05:** 64
National Environmental Health Association,
 05: 313–314; **06:** 325; **07:** 320; **08:** 317;
 09: 317
National Fire Protection Association, **05:** 314;
 06: 325; **07:** 320; **08:** 317; **09:** 317
National Governors Association, **05:** 314; **06:**
 325–326; **07:** 320; **08:** 317; **09:** 317
National Governors Conference. *See* National
 Governors Association
National Housing Conference, **05:** 314; **06:** 326;
 07: 320; **08:** 317; **09:** 317
National Institute of Governmental Purchas-
 ing, **05:** 314; **06:** 326; **07:** 321–322; **08:**
 317–318; **09:** 317–318
National Institute of Science and Technology,
 08: 59
National League of Cities, **05:** 314; **06:** 326; **07:**
 3, 321; **08:** 318; **09:** 9, 318
National Municipal League. *See* National Civic
 League
National Public Employer Labor Relations
 Association, **05:** 314; **06:** 326; **07:** 321;
 08: 318; **09:** 318
National Recreation and Park Association,
 05: 314; **06:** 326; **07:** 321; **08:** 318;
 09: 318
National Recreation Foundation, **06:** 27
National Rifle Association
 lawsuits against gun manufacturers, **05:** 50
 local gun control ordinances, **05:** 50; **06:** 47;
  07: 50; **08:** 48; **09:** 56–57
 relations with states, **06:** 41
National School Boards Association, **05:**
 314–315; **06:** 326; **07:** 321; **08:** 318;
 09: 318
National security. *See* Antiterrorism measures;
 Department of Homeland Security
 (DHS)
National security letters, **07:** 60
Native Americans, **06:** 51

Natural disasters. *See* Department of Homeland
 Security (DHS); Emergency preparedness; Federal Emergency Management
 Agency (FEMA); Homeland security;
 Hurricane Katrina
Nebraska
 agency for community affairs, **05:** 173; **06:**
  181; **07:** 175; **08:** 169; **09:** 175
 association of counties, **05:** 181; **06:** 189; **07:**
  183; **08:** 178; **09:** 185
 consolidation efforts, **07:** 56
 council of governments, **07:** 185
 mandates, **05:** 48; **06:** 46
 municipal league, **05:** 170; **06:** 178; **07:** 172;
  08: 166; **09:** 172
 municipal management association, **05:** 177;
  06: 185; **07:** 179; **08:** 174; **09:** 179
 state and local spending, **07:** 55
 TABOR tax issues, **07:** 53
 telecommunications, **05:** 50; **07:** 51
Neighborhood Quality of Life Study (Chesapeake, Va.), **09:** 42–43
Neighborhood Strength Index (Arlington, Tex.),
 09: 43
Neighborhood Watch programs, **07:** 7
Nepal, municipal management association, **09:**
 183
Netherlands, municipal management associa-
 tion, **05:** 179; **06:** 187; **07:** 182; **08:** 177;
 09: 183
Network governance, as community power
 structure, **09:** 6, 8
Nevada
 agency for community affairs, **05:** 173; **06:**
  181; **07:** 175; **08:** 169; **09:** 175
 association of counties, **05:** 181; **06:** 189; **07:**
  183; **08:** 178; **09:** 185
 municipal league, **05:** 170; **06:** 178; **07:** 172;
  08: 166; **09:** 172
 municipal management association, **05:** 177;
  06: 185; **07:** 179; **08:** 174; **09:** 180
 state and local spending, **07:** 55
New Hampshire
 agency for community affairs, **05:** 173; **06:**
  181; **07:** 175; **08:** 169; **09:** 175
 anti-smoking measures, **05:** 50; **08:** 48
 association of counties, **05:** 181; **06:** 189; **07:**
  183; **08:** 178; **09:** 185
 benefits reductions, **09:** 55
 education, **06:** 53
 home rule, **05:** 48; **07:** 47, 48; **08:** 45, 46;
  09: 53
 municipal league, **05:** 171; **06:** 179; **07:** 173;
  08: 167; **09:** 173
 municipal management association, **05:** 177;
  06: 185; **07:** 179; **08:** 46, 174; **09:** 180
 open-records law, **09:** 55
 sales tax, **05:** 53; **06:** 51
 state and local spending, **07:** 55
 state support for education, **06:** 53; **07:** 55
New Jersey
 agency for community affairs, **05:** 173; **06:**
  181; **07:** 175; **08:** 169; **09:** 175
 association of counties, **05:** 181; **06:** 189; **07:**
  183; **08:** 178; **09:** 185
 benefits reductions, **09:** 55
 eminent domain, **09:** 57
 gun control, **09:** 57
 living-wage ordinances, **06:** 48; **07:** 51

The Municipal Year Book 2009
  Volume 76

Composition by
  Circle Graphics
  Columbia, Maryland

Printing and binding by
  Edwards Brothers, Inc.
  Ann Arbor, Michigan